Perspectives from the Past

PRIMARY SOURCES IN WESTERN CIVILIZATIONS

Fourth Edition

Perspectives from the Past

PRIMARY SOURCES IN WESTERN CIVILIZATIONS

Fourth Edition

VOLUME 1

From the Ancient Near East through
the Age of Absolutism

JAMES M. BROPHY · JOSHUA COLE · STEVEN EPSTEIN

JOHN ROBERTSON · THOMAS MAX SAFLEY

W · W · NORTON & COMPANY NEW YORK · LONDON

W. W. Norton & Company has been independent since its founding in 1923, when William Warder Norton and Mary D. Herter Norton first published lectures delivered at the People's Institute, the adult education division of New York City's Cooper Union. The firm soon expanded its program beyond the Institute, publishing books by celebrated academics from America and abroad. By mid-century, the two major pillars of Norton's publishing program—trade books and college texts—were firmly established. In the 1950s, the Norton family transferred control of the company to its employees, and today—with a staff of four hundred and a comparable number of trade, college, and professional titles published each year—W. W. Norton & Company stands as the largest and oldest publishing house owned wholly by its employees.

Composition: DBS, Inc.
Manufacturing: The Courier Companies—Westford
Book design: Jack Meserole
Production manager: Christine D'Antonio

Acknowledgments and copyrights continue on page 765, which serves
as a continuation of the copyright page.

Library of Congress Cataloging-in-Publication Data

Perspectives from the past : primary sources in Western civilizations/
James M. Brophy ... [et al.]. —4th ed.
    p. cm.
Includes bibliographical references.
ISBN 978-0-393-93287-4 (pbk. : v. 1)—ISBN 978-0-393-93288-1 (pbk. : v. 2)
I. Brophy, James M.
CB245.P45 2009
909'.09821--dc22

                                                    2008049889

W. W. Norton & Company, Inc., 500 Fifth Avenue, New York, N.Y. 10110
www.wwnorton.com

W. W. Norton & Company Ltd., Castle House,
75/76 Wells Street, London W1T 3QT

5 6 7 8 9 0

ABOUT THE AUTHORS

JAMES M. BROPHY is professor of modern European history at the University of Delaware, where he has taught since 1992. He received his B.A. from Vassar College and did his graduate training at Universität Tübingen and Indiana University, where he specialized in the social and political history of nineteenth-century Europe. He is the author of *Capitalism, Politics, and Railroads in Prussia, 1830–1870* (1998), *Popular Culture and the Public Sphere in the Rhineland, 1800–1850* (2007), and numerous articles on nineteenth-century German history. He further serves on the board of editors for the journal, *Central European History*. He regularly teaches the Western civilization survey as well as courses and seminars on historiography, nationalism, modern European history, modern German history, and the Holocaust.

JOSHUA COLE is associate professor of history at the University of Michigan. He received his B.A. from Brown University and his M.A. and Ph.D. from the University of California, Berkeley. The author of *The Power of Large Numbers: Population, Politics, and Gender in Nineteenth-Century France* (2000), he has also published articles on French and German social and cultural history in the modern period. His current research is on the legacy of colonial violence in France, Algeria, and Madagascar, with a focus on the problems created by this history of violence in the postcolonial world. He has enjoyed teaching European history in a global context since 1993.

STEVEN EPSTEIN teaches history at the University of Kansas. He was educated at Swarthmore College, St. John's College Cambridge, and Harvard, where he developed his interests in medieval social and economic history. He is the author of *Purity Lost: Transgressing Boundaries in the Eastern Mediterranean, 1000–1400* (2007), *Speaking of Slavery: Color, Ethnicity, and Human Bondage in Italy* (2001), *Genoa and the Genoese 958–1528* (1996), *Wage Labor and Guilds in Medieval Europe* (1991), and other works on medieval history. He has taught the first half of the Western civilization survey for over fifteen years.

JOHN ROBERTSON received both his M.A. (1976) and his Ph.D. (1981) in ancient history from the University of Pennsylvania. A specialist in the social and economic history of the ancient Near East, he has published several articles in major scholarly journals and contributed articles to such major reference works as the *Anchor Bible Dictionary, Civilizations of the Ancient Near East,* and the *Blackwell Companion to the Ancient Near East.* He has also participated in archaeological excavations in Syria and Greece as well as the American Southwest. Since 1982, he has been a member of the faculty of the department of history at Central Michigan University, where he has taught the history of Western civilization for both the department of history and the university honors program, as well as more specialized courses in the history of the ancient Near East and the Islamic and modern Middle East.

THOMAS MAX SAFLEY teaches the history of early modern Europe at the University of Pennsylvania. A specialist in economic and social history, he has particular research interests in the history of marriage and the family, of poverty and charity, and of labor and business. In addition to numerous articles and reviews, he is the author of *Let No Man Put Asunder: The Control of Marriage in the German Southwest, 1550–1620* (1984), *Charity and Economy in the Orphanages of Early Modern Augsburg* (1996), *Matheus Miller's Memoir: A Merchant's Life in the Seventeenth Century* (2000), and *The Children of the Laboring Poor: Expectation and Experience among the Orphans of Early Modern Augsburg* (2004). He is co-editor of *The Workplace before the Factory: Artisans and Proletarians, 1500–1800* (1993) and *The Reformation of Charity: The Secular and the Sacred in Early Modern Poor Relief* (2003). He also serves on the editorial board of the *Sixteenth Century Journal*. At the University of Pennsylvania, he regularly teaches the introductory survey of European history and advanced lecture courses on the early modern period. He also offers a broad array of undergraduate and graduate seminars.

CONTENTS

CHAPTER 1 ∽ THE ORIGINS OF WESTERN CIVILIZATIONS   1

CHAPTER 4 ✑ THE EXPANSION OF GREECE   168

CHAPTER 5 ✑ ROMAN CIVILIZATION   214

CHAPTER 6 ❧ CHRISTIANITY AND THE TRANSFORMATION OF THE ROMAN WORLD   264

CHAPTER 7 ❧ ROME'S THREE HEIRS: THE BYZANTINE, ISLAMIC, AND EARLY MEDIEVAL WORLDS   309

CHAPTER 8 ⌒ THE EXPANSION OF EUROPE: ECONOMY, SOCIETY, AND POLITICS IN THE HIGH MIDDLE AGES, 1000–1300   350

CHAPTER 9 ⌒ THE HIGH MIDDLE AGES: RELIGIOUS AND INTELLECTUAL DEVELOPMENTS, 1000–1300   391

CHAPTER 10 ❧ THE LATER MIDDLE AGES, 1300–1500   438

CHAPTER 11 ❧ COMMERCE, CONQUEST, AND COLONIZATION, 1300–1600   497

CHAPTER 12 ⟡ THE CIVILIZATION OF THE RENAISSANCE, c. 1350–1550   542

CHAPTER 13 ⟡ REFORMATIONS OF RELIGION   591

CHAPTER 14 ❧ RELIGIOUS WARS AND STATE BUILDING 1540–1660   654

CHAPTER 15 ❧ ABSOLUTISM AND EMPIRE, 1660–1789   709

PREFACE FOR INSTRUCTORS

The authors of this text are very pleased to have been afforded the opportunity to design and compile this reader, which is the outgrowth of approximately eighty-five years of combined experience teaching the history of Western civilization. In the course of acquiring that experience, the authors were frustrated by what we perceived as serious shortcomings in most of the available supplementary readers. Among the more notable deficiencies are a frequent overemphasis on political and intellectual history at the expense of social and economic history and on elite culture at the expense of sources relating to the experiences of people of lesser socioeconomic station and, especially, of women. There is also an underrepresentation of sources relating the experiences and perspectives of European societies east of what is today Germany and a focus on Western civilization that often has neglected to address the West's important interactions with, and development of attitudes toward, non-Western peoples and civilizations. Some texts, in a laudable attempt to be more inclusive, incorporate more selections to serve up a veritable smorgasbord of thematically unlinked snippets, many of them so abbreviated or cited so disjointedly that the student can hardly gain a proper appreciation of their context or of the nature and structure of the documents from which they are derived. For ancient and medieval sources, this problem is all too often compounded by the use of translations that are either obsolete (from the standpoint of recent advances in philology) or rendered in an antiquated idiom that is hardly conducive to engaging students' interest. Finally, many readers are compiled by only one editor, who, whatever his or her experience and scholarly credentials, may understandably be hard pressed to command adequately the range and variety of primary sources available for examining the diverse aspects of Western civilization.

We by no means have the hubris to believe that what we have assembled will satisfy all the desiderata of every instructor. Nonetheless, to address the concerns noted above, and others, we have endeavored to produce a text that incorporates, as much as possible, the following features:

- Selections that consist of complete texts or lengthy excerpts of primary-source documents, ranging from one to eight pages in length and rendered in authoritative and eloquent, yet idiomatic, translations.

- Recognition that visual artifacts are also meaningful primary sources. Each chapter of this edition contains two visual features (photographs, paintings, posters, cartoons, sculptures, etc.) intended to help students learn how to analyze and interpret visual sources.

- An appropriate balance of primary sources from the Western canon, works that are illustrative of the origins and development of Western political institutions, intellectual life, and high culture or that illustrate aspects of social and economic history as well as more mundane aspects of life in Western societies. In other words, we have strived to provide selections pertinent to the lives, roles, achievements, and contributions of elite and commoner, ruler and ruled, master and servant, man and woman.

- Selections that reflect the experiences and perspectives of women and the dynamics of gender relations, including family and household structure.

- Selections that attempt to place a focus on the western European experience within a broader, even global perspective, by including selections relating to eastern Europe, the ancient and Islamic Middle East, Africa, Asia, and the Western Hemisphere. Thus, interspersed among the works of Western authors are excerpts from ancient Egyptian and Babylonian literature and private letters, the Qur'an, and works of such figures as Ibn Khaldun, Ibn Battuta, Bernal Diaz de Castillo, Edward Morel, Mohandas Gandhi, Frantz Fanon, Chai Ling, and the Ayatollah Ruhollah Khomeini. Readings such as these are intended to help students trace the evolution of the concept of the West and its relations with the non-West—matters of immense significance as an increasingly global society stands at the beginning of the twenty-first century.

- The incorporation of several unifying questions and issues to link documents both within and among chapters in a coherent, pedagogically useful internal framework. The documents in this reader have been chosen with an overarching purpose of interweaving a number of thematic threads that compose vital elements in the colorful fabrics of Western civilization: What are the status, responsibilities, and rights of the individual within the local community and broader society, and how have they changed over time? How have people defined their own communities, and how have they viewed outsiders? Who should have power within and over the community and society, and why? How have people responded to changes in the material world around them? Who or what controls the cosmos, and how have humankind's perceptions of its appropriate role and function within the cosmos changed?

The pedagogical and critical apparatus provided in this reader has been designed to guide the student to an appreciation of the sources but without imparting too much in the way of historical interpretation. For each chapter we have supplied an introduction that provides a historical context for the readings and alerts the student to the thematic threads that link them. Each reading in turn has an introduction that supplies an even more specific context and alerts the student to issues of interpretation or biased perspective. Finally, each selection is accompanied by several questions intended to stimulate analysis and discussion. The placement of these questions after each selection is quite intentional, as it is our hope that students will engage each document without a preconceived or predetermined sense of why it may be important and will instead learn to trust their own critical capacities and discern the significance of a reading on their own.

Obviously, to organize a project as complex as a reader of this kind and to bring it to a successful and timely fruition require the skills, support, inspiration, and dedication of many people other than the authors. We wish to express our admiration and profound gratitude to the editorial and marketing staff of W. W. Norton, especially to Kate Feighery, Jason Spears, Lory Frenkel, Marian Johnson, Aaron Javsicas, and, most especially, to Jon Durbin, who assembled the team, helped us to define and refine our work, organized the project, offered useful insight and judicious criticism, and kept all of us on task and on time. The credit for this reader is surely as much theirs as ours. Karl Bakeman has taken over supervising the reader and shepherding us through the third edition and now the fourth edition, and we are grateful for his suggestions and support.

For this edition we have included the following new documents:

- From *Lamentation over the Destruction of Sumer and Urim*
- Hippocrates, from "On Airs, Waters, and Places"
- Isocrates, from "Panegyricus"
- From *Digenis Akritis*
- Muhammad, "The Cow"
- From *The Anonymous Treatise on Husbandry*
- Leo Africanus, from "The Book of Grenada"
- Martin Luther, 95 Theses
- Katharina Schütz Zell, from "Letter to Sir Caspar Schwenckfeld"
- Francis Xavier, from "Letter from India"
- The Carmelite Mission to Persia, from "Father Vincent: An Audience with 'Abbâs"

- Thomas Harrison, "Speech from the Gallows"
- Jacqueline Pascal, from "Rule For Children"

In addition, we would like to thank the following faculty for their thoughtful reviews and comments as we developed the fourth edition: Stephen Frank, University of California, Los Angeles; Christine Kooi, Louisiana State University; Allyson Dalmore, Marquette; Liesl Smith, Gordon College; Daniel Williamson, Hillyer College; C. F. Reynold, University of Western Ontario; Karl Boughan, College of Charleston; and James Munson, Longwood University.

PREFACE FOR STUDENTS

The purpose of this collection of illustrations and documents is to provide the student with the raw materials of history, the sources, in the form of the objects and written words that survive from the past. Your textbook relies on such documents, known as primary sources, as well as on the works of many past and present historians who have analyzed and interpreted these sources—the secondary literature. In some cases the historians were themselves sources, eye-witnesses to the events they recorded. Authors of textbooks select which facts and interpretations they think you should know, and so the textbook filters what you think about the human past by limiting the information available to you. Textbooks are useful because they provide a coherent historical narrative for students of history, but it is important to remember that they are only an introduction to the rich complexity of human experience over time.

A collection of historical documents and artifacts provides a vital supplement to the textbook, but it also has problems. First, the sources, mostly not intended for us to read and study, exist for the reasons that prompted some people to create them and others to preserve them. These reasons may include a measure of lies, self-deception, or ignorance about what was really happening and being recorded. So we must ask the following questions about any document or object—a treaty, contract, painting, photograph, poem, newspaper article, or sculpture: Why does it exist? What specific purpose did it serve when it was done? Who is its author? What motives prompted the creator to produce this material in this form?

The second major problem is that we, the editors of this collection, have selected, from millions of possible choices, these particular documents and objects, and not others. Even in this process, because of the limitations of space and our own personal experiences, we present a necessarily partial and highly selective view of Western civilization (also because of space limitations, it has been necessary to delete portions from some of the longer sections).* Our purpose is not to repeat what you can find in the textbook but to give you the opportunity to see and discuss how historians, now including you, make history out of documents and objects, and their understanding of why people behave the way they do.

The illustrations in this collection provide a glimpse at the millions of material objects that survive from the past. These churches, buildings, paintings, mosaics, sculptures, photographs, and other items make up an important set of sources for the historian to consider about the past. It is certainly difficult to appreciate an immense building or a small manuscript painting from a photograph. Nevertheless, the editors of this collection include illustrations in the Fourth Edition to make clear the full range of sources that historians utilize. Also, the illustrations in many cases complement the written documents and in every case provide opportunities for a broader discussion of historical questions and the variety of sources that can help answer them.

Before exploring in more detail what documents are, we should be clear about what history is. Simply put, history is what we can say about the human past, in this case about the vast area of Western civilization from its remote origins to the most recent past. We can say, or write, things about the past because people left us their words, in the form of documents, and we can, like detectives, question these sources and then try to understand what happened. Before the written word, there is no history in the strictest sense; instead there are preliterate societies and the tens of thousands of years for which we know only what the anthropologists and archaeologists can tell us from the physical remains of bodies and objects made by human hands. And yet during this time profoundly important human institutions like language, the family, and religion first appeared. History begins with writing because that is when the documentation starts. These accomplishments of our remote ancestors occurred over tens of thousands of years, broken into ages of stone, copper, and bronze. Objects and images, but no words, reveal advances in weapons, art, farming, and other activities.

Although history cannot exist without written documents, we must remember that this evidence is complex and ambiguous. In the first place, it first appears in ancient languages, and the majority of documents in this book were not originally in English. The act of translating the documents into modern English raises another barrier or filter, and we must use our imaginations to

---

We indicate omissions, no matter how brief, with three spaced asterisks (* *), running them in when the opening, middle, or closing of a paragraph has been deleted and centering them between lines when a full paragraph is dropped. Why asterisks, when ellipsis dots are the standard? Because authors use ellipsis dots, and we want to distinguish our deletions from theirs.

recreate the past worlds in which modern words like *liberty, race,* or *sin* had different meanings. One job of the historian is to understand the language of the documents in their widest possible contexts. All the authors intended their documents to communicate something, but as time passes, languages and contexts change, and so it becomes more difficult for us to figure out what a document meant then and may mean now. Language is an imperfect way to communicate, but we must make the best of what we have. If we recollect how difficult it is sometimes to understand the events we see and experience, then we can perhaps understand how careful we must be when we interpret someone else's report about an event in the past, especially when that past is far removed in space and time from our experience.

The documents give us the language, or testimony, of witnesses, observers, or people with some point to make. Some documents claim to reveal religious truths and interpreting these claims requires historians to inquire respectfully and sincerely. Historical evidence, like any other, must be examined for flaws, contradictions, lies, and what it tells us that the writer did not necessarily intend to reveal. Like a patient detective, we must question our witnesses with a full awareness of their limited and often-biased perception, piecing together our knowledge of their history with the aid of multiple testimonies and a broad context. Consider the document, whatever it is, as testimony and a piece of a bigger puzzle, many of the remaining pieces of which are missing or broken. It is useful at the beginning to be clear about the simple issues—What type of document is this evidence? Who wrote it? Where and when was it written? Why does it exist? Try to understand the context of the document by relating it to the wider world—how do words by Plato or about the Nazi Party fit with what you already know about ancient Greece or twentieth-century Germany?

When the document, or witness, has been correctly identified and placed in some context, we may then interrogate it further by asking questions about the words before us. Not all documents suggest the same questions, but there are some general questions that apply to nearly every document. One place to begin is to ask, Who or what is left out? Once you see the main point, it is interesting to ask what the documents tell us about people and subjects often left out of the records—women, children, or religious or ethnic minorities, for example. Or, if the document is about a religious minority, we can ask what it tells us about the majority. Take the document and try to turn it inside out by determining the basic assumptions or biases of its author, and then explore what has been intentionally or unintentionally left out. Look for anomalies— pieces of evidence that appear out of place or simply weird; they are often clues to understanding the distances between us and the sources. Another way to ask a fresh question of an old witness is to look beneath the surface and see what else is there. For example, if the document in question seems mainly to offer evidence on religion, ask what it tells us about the economy or contemporary eating habits or whatever else might occur to you. Documents frequently reveal excellent information on topics far from their ostensible subjects, if we remember to ask.

Every document in this collection is some kind of story, either long or short. The stories are almost all nonfiction, at least in theory, but they all have characters; a plot, or story line; and above all a point to the story, the meaning. We have suggested some possible meanings in the sample questions at the end of each document, but these questions are just there to help your thinking or get a discussion going, about the many possible meanings of the documents. You can ask what the meaning was in the document's own time, as well as what we might now see as a meaning that makes sense to us of some pieces of the past. The point of the story in a document may often concern a central issue in history, the process of change. If history is what we can say about the human past, then the most important words describe how change occurs, for example, rapidly, as in revolutions and wars, or more slowly, as in marriage customs or family life. Every document casts some light on human change, and the meaning of the story often relates to why something changed.

History is often at its dullest when a document simply describes a static situation, for example, a law or farming. However, even a good description reveals choices and emphasis. If you ask, Why this law now? Why farm in this way? How did these activities influence human behavior? you can see that the real subject of nearly all documents is human change, on some level. You will find that people can and will strongly disagree about the meaning of a story: they can and will use the same evidence from a document to draw radically different meanings. This is one of the challenges of history and what makes it fun, for some explanations and meanings make more sense than others in the broader context of what you know about an episode or period of history. Argue about meaning, and you will learn something about not only your own biases and values but also the process of sifting facts for good arguments and answers. These skills have a value well beyond the study of history.

The documents and objects in this collection, even the most general works of philosophy or social analysis, reveal the particular and contingent aspects of history. Even the most abstract of these documents and objects comes from a specific time, place, and person and sheds some light on a unique set of circumstances. When history is like the other social sciences (anthropology, economics, sociology, political science, and others), it tries to deal with typical or average people, societies, or behavior. When history is like the other humanities (literature, philosophy, religion, art, and others), it stresses individual people, their quirks and uniqueness. The documents and objects also illustrate the contingent aspect of history, which unlike the social or natural sciences but like the humanities, appears to lack rules or laws. History depends on what people did, subject to the restrictions of their natures, resources, climate, and other natural factors—people with histories of their own! Rerunning this history is not like a movie, and it would never turn out the same way twice, for it is specific and contingent to the way it turned out this time. The documents and objects do not tell a story of an orderly progression from simple to complex societies or from bad to good ones. Instead, history continues, and people cope, or not, with the issues of religious faith, family life, making a living, and creating artifacts and documents. These documents and objects collectively provide perspectives on how experiments in living succeeded or failed. We invite you to use them to learn more about the people of the past than the textbooks can say and to use your imaginations to get these witnesses to answer your questions about the process and meaning of human change.

WHERE TO BEGIN?

[handwritten annotations:]
- main contemporary issues addressed?
- relevance or object/doc in its own time?
  " " in 21st C?

This checklist is a series of questions that can be used to analyze most of the documents and objects in this reader.

[handwritten arrows pointing to first three items]

✔ What type of document or object is this evidence?

✔ Why does the document or object exist? What motives prompted the author to create the material in this form?

✔ Who created this work?

✔ Who or what is left out—women, children, minorities, members of the majority?

✔ In addition to the main subject, what other kinds of information can be obtained?

✔ How do the subjects of the document or object relate to what we know about broader society?

✔ What was the meaning of the document or object in its own time? What is its meaning for the audience?

✔ What does the document or object tell us about change or stability in society?

---

1 ⮑ THE ORIGINS OF WESTERN CIVILIZATIONS

In the history of humankind's sojourn on this planet, no development has been more momentous, or more fraught with consequence, than the emergence of civilization. Just what exactly constitutes "civilization" has been debated by scholars for years. But as evidenced by the appearance of states, cities, complex economies, and writing, among other characteristics, civilizations can be said to have arisen independently in several areas across the globe. By far the earliest of them, however, arose in that region of southwestern Asia and northern Africa that we today refer to as the Middle East.

But during the many preceding millennia of the eras that we now refer to as the Paleolithic (literally, "Old Stone Age") and Neolithic ("New Stone Age"), humankind also attained perhaps equally monumental achievements, without which cities and civilizations could never have developed. Those achievements are too numerous to catalogue here, but among the more significant are certainly the harnessing of fire, the creation of technologies for hunting wild animals and foraging for wild plants, and the domestication of those same wild-food sources in the process that resulted in agriculture and herding, the developments that made the Neolithic village life possible. With these very early developments, there also emerged an awareness of powers and forces beyond the realm of the purely "natural," powers that, though unseen, might bring abundance or disaster if not properly recognized and, if necessary, propitiated. Such powers might be inherent in the life force of the animals and plants upon which early humans depended; they might also lie in some mysterious, unknowable realm inhabited by the dead, including one's ancestors. Until relatively recently, historians had often relegated these so-called prehistoric achievements and ideas to an era of dim savagery that many believed was better left to the scrutiny of anthropologists and archaeologists. Today, however, more and more scholars are embracing the concept of "deep" or "macro" history, in the belief that even though these earliest human societies and achievements date to a preliterate (i.e., before writing) era, we have been mistaken to deny them a place in the unfolding of human "history." Indeed, by calling them "prehistoric," perhaps we have been segregating our "modern" consciousness in the shallow end of the almost immeasurably deeper pool of what constitutes humankind's shared experience on this planet. We surely can embrace such a longer view of "history" while still recognizing the stupendous, and rapid, amplifying of that human experience by the quantum leap ahead that sprang from the soil of what is now the Middle East.

By about 5000 B.C.E.,[1] in what is now eastern Iraq, a Neolithic people to whom archaeologists refer as the Samarrans began to settle in villages where rainfall alone could not support agriculture. Their pioneering efforts in the technology of canal irrigation paved the way for the emergence of cities and, with them, the civilization of ancient Sumer. The world's first cities arose in the floodplain of Lower Mesopotamia, the land between the Tigris and Euphrates rivers (modern-day southern Iraq), more than 5,000 years ago, as large population centers governed by administrators powerful enough to organize and direct the construction of large architectural complexes, quite likely temples. These efforts were fueled by agricultural production on an unprecedented scale, entailing the cultivation of thousands of acres of wheat, barley, and other foodstuffs. The floodplain's wondrous fertility could be unleashed only by the profuse application of irrigation water brought from the Euphrates and (perhaps to a lesser extent) the Tigris. Organizing the digging and maintaining of irrigation canals; the plowing, sowing, and harvesting of the fields; and the maintaining of huge flocks of livestock was a truly formidable task.

By about 3200 B.C.E., the huge size and increasingly complex administration of these great estates necessitated the creation of a new technology that itself shaped the future of civilization: writing. Primitive pictographs incised on clay tablets evolved into a system that we today refer to as cuneiform (literally, "nail-shaped") that spread throughout the ancient Near East, where it remained in use for almost 3,000 years. The scribes of ancient Mesopotamia (and Anatolia, Syria, Iran, and even Egypt) bequeathed to us a remarkably durable legacy of tens of thousands of records—mostly clay tablets, but also inscriptions on stone monuments and objects. Most of the tablets are detailed accounts of the administration of temples, palaces, and public institutions, tediously dry in themselves but, when reconstructed into coherent archives, crucial evidence of social and economic organization. The remaining records—among them, royal inscriptions, letters, poems, hymns, prayers, law "codes," contracts, and a variety of literary works—provide, at best, tantalizing samples from what was once a vast corpus. Enough has survived, nonetheless, to enable us to reconstruct a complex sequence of dynasties and political configurations in the history of Mesopotamia and the Near East. But perhaps more appealing to our common humanity, these records allow us at least limited insight into the enduring structures of life and the everyday concerns of people who seem to have felt very strongly that their fortune and existence depended utterly on ensur-

---

[1] B.C.E. means "before the common era." [Editor.]

ing the continued good favor of their gods. Those gods might bestow upon them benevolence and plenty or, just as likely, abandon them to destitution and catastrophe, the latter all too often brought by the rampages of "barbarian" invaders or the no less destructive rampages of the normally life-sustaining rivers.

By 2000 B.C.E., the solid foundations of Mesopotamian civilization had been shaken by some major tremors. Imperial dynasties established by the great conqueror Sargon of Akkad and then by the kings of the Third Dynasty of Ur had flourished then ebbed, although the idealized memory of Sargon's rule would inspire future Mesopotamian kings for the next 1,500 years. The next 400 years were ushered in by chieftains of recently arrived tribal groups known as Amorites who established themselves in small kingdoms in the urbanized regions of Sumer and Akkad. In time, one of those minor Amorite kingdoms, Babylon, was to establish itself, and its god Marduk, as supreme. With the ascent of its great king Hammurabi shortly after 1800 B.C.E., Babylon took center stage in Lower Mesopotamia (henceforth, Babylonia), not to relinquish its leading role there until the era of Alexander the Great's successors. Babylon's rise was possible, though, only because Hammurabi proved himself a master "player" in an era when (as thousands of cuneiform tablets from the palace of Mari on the Euphrates testify for us) power politics, trade and diplomacy, and competition for prized resources encompassed an arena extending from Anatolia to the Persian Gulf, and from Iran to the Mediterranean as far as Crete. His dynasty's fall, around 150 years later, would come at the hands of a relatively new "player," the Hittite rulers of the Anatolian kingdom of Hatti, whose rise ushered onto the ancient Near Eastern stage speakers and writers of a language that we can identify as Indo-European and as thereby related to the later languages of western Europe (and India). When the curtain eventually lifts again in Babylonia, another new, nonindigenous ruling group, the Kassites, will have taken charge. Yet, like the Amorites before them—and the Akkadian kings before them, the Kassites are "captured"—or, perhaps, "captivated"—by the enduring traditions and structures of an already ancient Sumerian civilization.

Civilization arose along the Nile River somewhat later than it had in the Tigris-Euphrates floodplain, but Egyptian civilization soon assumed its own distinct form and identity. According to their later traditions, the Egyptians believed that a king named Menes had been the first to unite the two rival kingdoms of Upper Egypt (the long Nile valley) and Lower Egypt (the Nile delta). From a modern vantage point, we detect scant traces of a ruler named Menes in the earliest Egyptian records, and most scholars are convinced that the unification of Egypt was much more complicated than the pulling together of two kingdoms. Nonetheless, by around 3100 B.C.E., what some have identified as the world's first unified nation-state had been created. For the next 3,000 years, the people of Egypt regarded the absolute rule of a semi-divine king (who by the mid-second millennium B.C.E. came to be known as pharaoh) as the only desirable state of affairs. Upon his shoulders fell the responsibility of preserving the stability of the cosmos (what the Egyptians called ma'at), an essential ingredient of which was securing the unity of the "Two Lands" of Upper and Lower Egypt. Only through the king's vigorous stewardship might chaos and calamity be averted. Over time, there developed around the king's person a royal court and hierarchical administration that was served by a class of professional (and mostly male) bureaucrats ("scribes") highly trained in the hieroglyphic script and its hieratic derivative. Through their efforts, the manpower and resources of the kingdom could be marshaled to ensure the king's success, both in this world and the next. It is from the records they have left us—inscribed and painted on temple and tomb walls, or written on papyrus or even flakes of stone—that we glean our hard-won knowledge of ancient Egyptian history and culture.

Neither the grandeur of Egyptian kingship nor the king's preservation of cosmic harmony would have been possible, of course, without the Nile River. As the Greek "father of history" Herodotus so succinctly put it, Egypt is "the river's gift." Until the completion of the Aswan High Dam in the early 1970s, every year, between July and October, the Nile overflowed its banks, bringing life-sustaining water and rich silt that, together with the generative power of the sun, literally resurrected the black land of the Nile Valley. It may well be that in this annual resurrection of the land was born the Egyptian concept of a resurrection and continued existence after death (though only if proper preparations were made and precautions taken). Often, modern observers tend to focus on the Egyptians' supposed morbid preoccupation with death and the hereafter. In part, that perception stems from the accidents of archaeological preservation. Millennia of floods and silt deposits, combined with continued human occupation of town and village sites, have largely obliterated the towns and villages of the ancient Egyptians. Most of what has been left to us are the remains of temples and tombs, built in the low desert where the Nile's floods did not reach; that the remaining records say so much about kings, gods, and death should hardly surprise us. As some of the documents in this chapter make clear, however, the ancient Egyptians did not while away their lives dreamily pining for death.

By 2000 B.C.E., Egypt, like Mesopotamia, had been rocked by adversity, as the disintegration of the Old Kingdom brought, for the first time, the disruption of the divinely ordained, cosmic stability of ma'at that underpinned Egypt's civilization. The reunification forged by the rulers of Thebes (whose god Amun, like Babylon's Marduk, would soon emerge supreme) with the advent of the Middle Kingdom brought renewed strength and cultural vitality, as well as the assertion of Egyptian interests and power as far away as Nubia to the south, Crete to the north, and Palestine to the east. The Middle Kingdom also saw a reassertion of royal traditions and absolutism, though punctuated by the lingering memory of the chaos that had once plagued Egypt. In time, that threat of chaos would again become real: "vile Asiatic" newcomers recently arrived from Palestine into the Nile Delta would assert political control as the Hyksos dynasties of Lower Egypt. Egypt would once again be divided, but now, for the first time, by the abomination of "barbarian" invasion. Once again, it would be a royal family from Amun's city

Thebes that would restore the unity of "The Two Lands" of Upper and Lower Egypt, this time by expelling the invaders, chasing them back into Palestine, and subsequently, perhaps as insurance against a repetition of such an abomination, conquering and ruling most of the eastern Mediterranean seaboard from the Sinai to Syria, as well as the region of Nubia into the interior of Africa.

"Prehistory": Neolithic Remains
FROM Tell as-Sultan (Jericho)

The site of Tell as-Sultan has been identified by modern archaeologists as the location of the site of ancient Jericho, famous in the Hebrew Bible as the city where the early Israelites, led by Joshua, blew their horns and caused the walls to come tumbling down. But from as early as around 8000 B.C.E., Jericho (though we have no idea what it was called then) was the site of one of the world's first major towns, the excavated remains of which have left us tantalizing, though enigmatic, clues about early religious beliefs and social and political organization, as seen in the two images provided here. The tower, which dates to around 8000 B.C.E., is about twenty-eight feet high and thirty-three feet in diameter, had interior stairs to the top, and seems to have been part of a fortification wall around the settlement. Equally intriguing is the skull, one of a number that have been found at Jericho and other

sites in the region and dating to perhaps as early as 7000 B.C.E. The skull was detached from the body. Mud plaster was applied to it; shell was inserted into the eye sockets, presumably to produce a more lifelike image of the deceased (in other specimens, complete shells were inserted, with an effect like closed eyes); and red ochre (to approximate skin color? blood?) was applied to the surface as well. Skulls such as these tend to be found not in graves but rather within houses, where they seem to have been displayed. Whatever their meaning and purpose may have been, both the tower and the skull give us reason to ponder the complexity of human social organization, ritual, and belief several millennia before the emergence of cities, civilizations, and written "historical" records.

REVIEW QUESTIONS

1. How much effort, and of how many people, might have been needed to build the tower? Would the construction have required an overseer? If so, who might have served in that capacity? From what possible sources might such an overseer's authority have been derived?

2. Can you come up with any reasons why the skull, and others like it, received this kind of special treatment? Can you identify any parallels in later times as regards this kind of treatment of human remains?

FROM *Atrahasis:* An Account of the Great Flood

The theme of a great flood appears in several works of ancient Mesopotamian literature, including the Sumerian King List, The Epic of Gilgamesh, *and the following work, the earliest known example of flood literature dates to about 1700 B.C.E. Its hero, Atrahasis (literally, "exceedingly wise"), is a figure of great antiquity who reappears under different names in later flood stories (including Ut-napishtim in* The Epic of Gilgamesh*); some scholars have traced versions of his name into later Greek, Roman, and Arabic tales. As will become apparent, however, this is much more than a flood story, for it also gives us one version of why and how, according to ancient Mesopotamian belief, humans came into being.*

From *Before the Muses: An Anthology of Akkadian Literature,* translated by Benjamin R. Foster (3rd ed.; Bethesda, Md.: CDL Press, 2005).

When gods were man,
They did forced labor, they bore drudgery.
Great indeed was the drudgery of the gods,
The forced labor was heavy, the misery too much:

The great Anunna-gods, the seven, were burdening
The Igigi-gods with forced labor.
Anu their father was king,
Their counsellor was the warrior Enlil,

Their prefect was Ninurta, . . .
Anu went up to heaven,
Enlil took the earth for his subjects,

*   *   *

They burdened the Igigi-gods with forced labor.
The gods were digging watercourses,
The waterways of the gods, the life of the land,
The Igigi-gods were digging watercourses,
The waterways of the gods, the life of the land.
The Igigi-gods dug the Tigris river,
And the Euphrates thereafter.
Springs they opened up from the depths,
Wells . . . they established. . . .
They heaped up all the mountains. . . .
They counted years of drudgery, . . .
forced labor they bore night and day.
They were complaining, denouncing,
Muttering down in the ditch,
"Let us face up to our foreman the prefect,
"He must take off this our heavy burden upon us!
"The god, counsellor of the gods, the warrior,
"Come, let us remove him from his dwelling,
"Enlil, counsellor of the gods, the warrior,
"Come, let us remove him from his dwelling!" . . .

*   *   *

"Now then, call for battle!
"Battle let us stir up, warfare!"
The gods heard his words,
They set fire to their tools,
They put fire to their spades,
And flame to their workbaskets.
Off they went, one and all,
To the gate of the warrior Enlil's abode.
It was night, half-way through the watch,
The house was surrounded, but the god did not
    know.
It was night, half-way through the watch,
Ekur was surrounded, but Enlil did not know!
Kalkal noticed it and looked out,
He touched the bolt and looked out.
Kalkal woke Nusku,
And they listened to the clamor of the Igigi-
    gods.
Nusku woke his lord,

He got him out of bed,
"My lord, your house is surrounded,
"Battle has run right up to your gate.
"Enlil, your house is surrounded,
"Battle has run right up to your gate!"
Enlil had provided weapons for his dwelling.
Enlil made ready to speak,
And said to the courier Nusku,
"Nusku, bar your gate,
Get your weapons and stand before me."
Nusku barred his gate,
Got his weapons and stood before Enlil.
Nusku made ready to speak,
And said to the warrior Enlil,
"My lord, your face is gone pale as tamarisk,
"Your own offspring! Why did you fear?
"My lord, your face is gone pale as tamarisk,
"Your own offspring! Why do you fear?
"Send that they bring Anu down here,
"And that they bring Enki before you."
He sent and they brought Anu down to him,
They brought Enki before him.
Anu, king of heaven, was present,
The king of the depths, Enki, was
With the great Anunna-gods present,
Enlil arose, the debate was underway.
Enlil made ready to speak,
And said to the great gods,
"Against me would they be trying this?
"Shall I make battle against my own offspring?
"What did I see with my very own eyes?
"Battle ran right up to my gate!"
Anu made ready to speak,
And said to the warrior Enlil,
"The reason why the Igigi-gods
"Surrounded your gate,
"Let Nusku go out, let him learn their cause,
"Let him take to your sons
"Your great command."
Enlil made ready to speak,
And said to the courier Nusku,
"Nusku, open your gate,
"Take your weapons, go out to the group.
"In the group of all the gods
"Bow down, stand up, and repeat to them our
    command:

'Anu, your father,
'Your counsellor, the warrior Enlil,
'Your prefect, Ninurta,
'And your bailiff Ennugi have sent me to
    say,
    "Who is the god who was instigator of
        battle?
    "Who is the god who was instigator of
        hostilities?
    "Who is it that stirred up war,
    "That battle has run up to the gate of
        Enlil?"'"

Nusku took the command, opened his gate,
Took his weapons and went with the command
    of Enlil.
In the group of all the gods,
He bowed down, stood up, set forth the
    command,
"Anu, your father,
"Your counsellor, the warrior Enlil,
"Your prefect, Ninurta,
"And your bailiff Ennugi have sent me to say:

    'Who is the god who was instigator of battle?
    'Who is the god who was instigator of hostili-
        ties?
    'Who is it that stirred up war,

Ea made ready to speak,
And said to the gods his brethren,
"What do we denounce them for?
"Their forced labor was heavy, their misery too
    much.
"Every day the earth was . . .
"The outcry was loud, we could hear their
    clamor.
"There is a task to be done,
"Mami, the birth-goddess, is present,
"Let the mother-goddess create a human being,
"Let man assume the drudgery of god."
They summoned and asked the birth-goddess,
The midwife of the gods, wise Mami,
"Will you be the birth-goddess, creatress of
    humankind?
"Create a human being, let him bear the yoke,
"The yoke let him bear, the task of Enlil,
"Let man assume the drudgery of god."

Nintu made ready to speak,
And said to the great gods,
"It is not for me to do it,
"This task is Enki's.
"He is the one who purifies everything,
"Let him give me the clay so I can do the
    making."
Enki made ready to speak,
And said to the great gods,
"On the first, seventh, and fifteenth days of the
    month,
"I will establish a purification, a bath.
"Let one god be slaughtered,
"Then let the gods be purified in it.
"Let Nintu mix clay with his flesh and blood,
"Let that same god and man be thoroughly mixed
    in the clay.
"Let us hear the drumbeat for the rest of time,
"From the flesh of the god let a spirit remain,
"Let it make the living know its sign,
"Lest he be forgotten, let the spirit remain."
The great Anunna-gods, who administer
    destinies,
Answered "Yes!" in the assembly.
On the first, seventh, and fifteenth days of the
    month,
He established a purification, a bath.
They slaughtered Aw-ila, who had the inspiration,
    in their assembly.
Nintu mixed the clay with his flesh and blood.
That same god and man were thoroughly mixed
    in the clay.
For the rest of time they would hear the drum-
    beat,
From the flesh of the god a spirit remained.
It would make the living know its sign,
Lest he be forgotten, the spirit remained.
After she had mixed that clay,
He summoned the Anunna, the great gods.
The Igigi, the great gods, spat upon the clay.
Mami made ready to speak,
And said to the great gods,
"You ordered me the task and I have completed it!
"You have slaughtered the god, along with his
    inspiration.
"I have done away with your heavy forced labor,
"I have imposed your drudgery on man.

"You have bestowed clamor upon humankind.
   'That battle has run up to the gate of Enlil?'"
The Igigi answered him in the group,
They were defiant, the labor gang
"Every one of us gods has declared war,
"We formed our group in the ditch.
"Excessive drudgery has killed us,
"Our forced labor was heavy, our misery too
   much!
"And so every one of us gods
"Has resolved on a battle with Enlil."
Nusku took the command,
He went, he brought back . . . .
"My lord, you sent me to the group of the gods,
"I went, I bowed down, I stood up,
"I set forth your great command,
"All the Igigi-gods, the labor gangs, were defiant
   against it,

   'Every one of us gods has declared war,
   'We have formed our group in the ditch.
   'Excessive drudgery has killed us,
   'Our forced labor was heavy, the misery too
     much!
   'Now, every one of us gods
   'Has resolved on a battle with Enlil.'"

When he heard that speech,
Enlil's tears flowed down,
Enlil became disturbed at what he said.
He said to the warrior Anu,
"Noble one, you should take authority off with
   you to heaven.
"Take the power you still have.
"With the great gods in session before you,
"Summon one god, let them make a new
   authority."
"I have released the yoke, I have made restoration."
They heard this speech of hers,
They ran, restored, and kissed her feet, saying,
"Formerly we used to call you 'Mami',
"Now let your name be 'Mistress-of-All-the Gods'
   (Belet-kala-ili)."

      *   *   *

Twelve hundred years had not gone by,
The land had grown numerous, the peoples had
   increased,

The land was bellowing like a bull.
The god was disturbed with their uproar,
Enlil heard their clamor.
He said to the great gods,
"The clamor of humankind has become burden-
   some to me,
"I am losing sleep to their uproar . . . .
"Let there be ague . . .
But he, Atrahasis, his god was Enki,
He was exceedingly wise.
He would speak with his god,
And his god would speak with him!
Atrahasis made ready to speak,
And said to his lord, . . .
"Will they impose the disease on us forever?"
Enki made ready to speak,
And said to his servant,
"Summon the elders
"At the usual time in your house.
"Command:

   'Let heralds proclaim,
   'Let them raise a loud clamor in the land:
     "Do not reverence your own gods,
     "Do not pray to your own goddesses,
     "Seek the door of Namtar,
     "Bring a baked loaf before it."'

"May the flour offering please him,
"May he be shamed by the gift and withdraw his
   hand."
Atrahasis received the command,
And assembled the elders to his gate.
Atrahasis made ready to speak,
And said to the elders,
"Elders . . .
"Command:

   'Let heralds proclaim,
   'Let them raise a loud clamor in the land:
     "Do not reverence your own gods,
     "Do not pray to your own goddesses,
     "Seek the door of Namtar,
     "Bring a baked loaf before it."'

"May the flour offering please him,
"May he be shamed by the gift and withdraw his
   hand."
Atrahasis received the command,

And assembled the elders to his gate.
Atrahasis made ready to speak,
And said to the elders,
"Elders . . .
"Command:

'Let heralds proclaim,
'Let them raise a loud clamor in the land:
    "Do not reverence your own gods,
    "Do not pray to your own goddesses,
    "Seek the door of Namtar,
    "Bring a baked loaf before it."'

"May the flour offering please him,
"May he be shamed by the gift and withdraw his
    hand."
The elders heeded his words,
They built a temple for Namtar in the city.
They commanded and the heralds proclaimed,
They raised a loud clamor in the land,
They did not reverence their own gods,
They did not pray to their own goddesses,
They sought the door of Namtar,
They brought a baked loaf before it.
The flour offering pleased him,
He was shamed by the gift and withdrew his hand.
The ague left them,
They resumed their clamor,

*   *   *

Twelve hundred years had not gone by,
The land had grown numerous, the peoples had
    increased,
The land was bellowing like a bull.
The god became disturbed by their uproar,
Enlil heard their clamor.
He said to the great gods,
"The clamor of humankind has become burden-
    some to me,
"I am losing sleep to their uproar.
"Cut off provisions for the peoples,
"Let plant life be too scanty for their hunger.
"Let Adad withdraw his rain,
"Below, let the flood not come up from the
    depths.
"Let the wind come to parch the ground,
"Let the clouds billow but discharge not a drop.
"Let the field reduce its yields,

"Let the grain-goddess close her bosom.
"Let there be no rejoicing for them, . . .

*   *   *

Enki made ready to speak,
Saying to his servant,
"Summon the elders
"At the usual time in your house.
"Command:

'Let heralds proclaim,
'Let them raise a loud clamor in the land:
    "Do not reverence your own gods,
    "Do not pray to your own goddesses,
    "Seek the door of Adad
    "Bring a baked loaf before it."'

"May the flour offering please him,
"May he be shamed by the gift and withdraw his
    hand.
"May he rain down mist in the morning,
"May he stealthily rain down dew in the night,
"That the fields just as stealthily bear ninefold."
They built a temple for Adad in the city.
They commanded and the heralds proclaimed,
They raised a loud clamor in the land,
They did not reverence their own gods,
They did not pray to their own goddesses,
They sought the door of Adad,
They brought a baked loaf before it.
The flour offering pleased him,
He was shamed by the gift and withdrew his hand.
He rained down mist in the morning,
And stealthily rained down dew in the night,
The fields just as stealthily bore ninefold.
Their handsome features returned,
Their former clamor resumed.

*   *   *

*[Enlil sends a famine. Atrahasis wants to communi-
cate with Enki, but apparently knows that the god
is now under oath not to speak directly with him.
He sleeps by the water for an indirect communication in dreams.]*

Out of the city he [Atrahasis] set his foot,
Every day he would weep,
Bringing dream offerings in the morning.

"My god would speak to me, but he is under
   oath,
"He will inform me in dreams.
"Enki would speak to me, but he is under oath,
"He will inform me in dreams." . . .
He cast the dream offering into the water,
He would sit facing the river, weeping constantly.
When the waterway was silent,
He made libation at night,
Sleep would come double fast.
He said to the waterway of the river,
"May the waterway take this, may the river bear it
   away,
"May my gift be set before Enki, my lord.
"May Enki see it and think of me,
"May he [   ],
"This night may I have a dream."
After he had sent the message by the waterway,
He sat down to weep facing the river,
From the bank [   ]
To the depths his present went down.
Enki heard his clamor,
He summoned his hairy hero-men and said,
"The man who [   ],
"Let this same one [   ],
"Go, take him my command,
"Ask him, tell me the news of his land."

                *   *   *

The flood did not rise from the depths.
The womb of earth did not bear,
Plant life did not come forth.
People were not seen about,
The black fields whitened,
The broad plain was filled up with salts.
The first year they ate old grain,
The second year they exhausted their stores.
When the third year came,
Their features were gray from hunger,
Their faces were crusted, like crusted malt,
Life was ebbing, little by little.
Tall people shriveled in body,
They walked hunched in the street.
Broad-shouldered people turned slender,
Their long stance grew short.
Messengers took the command,
They went before the sea,

They stood and told him,
Their orders to Enki the leader

                *   *   *

*[Humanity has been saved from famine, apparently
by a flood of fish.]*

Enlil was filled with anger at Enki,
"All we great Anunna-gods
"Resolved together on a rule.
"Anu and Adad watched over the upper regions,
"I watched over the lower earth.
"Where Enki went,
"He released the yoke, he made restoration.
"He let loose produce for the peoples,
"He put shade in the glare of the sun."
Enlil made ready to speak,
He said to the vizier Nusku,
"Let them bring to me the two comrades,
"Let them send them into my presence."
They brought to him the two comrades.
The warrior Enlil said to them,
"All we great Anunna-gods
"Resolved together on a rule.
"Anu and Adad watched over the upper regions,
"I watched over the lower earth.
"Where you (Enki) went
"You released the yoke, you made restoration.
"You let loose produce for the peoples,
"You put shade in the glare of the sun."

                *   *   *

"Let us be sure to bind the leader Enki,
   who manages all, by oath."
Enki made ready to speak,
And said to the gods his brethren,
"Why would you bind me by oath [   ]?
"Am I to bring my hands against my own peoples?
"The flood that you are speaking of to me,
"Who is to do it? I do not know.
"Am I to produce a flood?
"The task of that is Enlil's.
"Let him choose,
"Let Shullat and Hanish go in front,
"Let Errakal tear out the mooring poles,
"Let Ninurta go make the dikes overflow.

                *   *   *

The gods commanded annihilation,
Enlil committed the evil deed against the
  peoples.

[Atrahasis has had a dream from Enki, and wishes
to know its meaning.]

Atrahasis made ready to speak,
And said to his lord,
"Make me know the meaning of the dream,
"[   ] let me know, that I may look out for its
  consequence."
Enki made ready to speak,
And said to his servant,
"You might say, 'Am I to be looking out while in
  the bedroom?'
"Do you pay attention to the message that I speak
  for you:

  'Wall, listen to me!
  'Reed wall, pay attention to all my words!
  'Flee house, build boat,
  'Forsake possessions, and save life.
  'The boat that you build, . . .
  'Cover her with tarpaulins,
  'Roof her over like the depths,
  'So that the sun will not see inside her,
  'Let her be roofed over fore and aft.
  'The gear should be very firm,
  'The pitch should be firm, make her strong.
  'I shall shower down upon you later
  'A windfall of birds, a spate of fishes.'"

He opened the water clock and filled it,
He told it (the wall?) of the coming of the seven-
  day deluge.
Atrahasis received the command,
He assembled the elders at his gate.
Atrahasis made ready to speak,
And said to the elders,
"My god does not agree with your god,
"Enki and Enlil are constantly angry with each
  other.
"They have expelled me from the land.
"Since I have always reverenced Enki,
"He told me this. ＊ ＊ ＊
The carpenter carried his ax,
The reed-worker carried his stone.

The rich man carried the pitch,
The poor man brought the materials needed.

＊　＊　＊

Pure animals he slaughtered, cattle . . .
Fat animals he killed, sheep . . .
He chose . . . and brought on board.
The birds flying in the heavens,
The cattle and of the cattle-god,
The creatures of the steppe,
[ ] he brought on board . . .
[ ] he invited his people . . .
[ ] to a feast.
[ ] his family he brought on board.
While one was eating and another was drinking,
He went in and out; he could not sit,
  he could not take his place,
For his heart was broken, he was retching gall.
The outlook of the weather changed,
Adad began to roar in the clouds.
The god they heard, his clamor.
He brought pitch to seal his door.
By the time he had bolted his door,
Adad was roaring in the clouds.
The winds were furious as he set forth,
He cut the mooring rope, he released the boat.

＊　＊　＊

Anzu rent the sky with his talons, ＊ ＊ ＊
the flood came forth,
Its destructive power came upon the peoples like
  a battle.
One person did not see another,
They could not recognize each other in the catas-
  trophe.
The deluge bellowed like a bull,
The wind resounded like a screaming eagle.
The darkness was dense, the sun was gone,
The offspring became like flies.
The gods became afraid of the clamor of the
  deluge,
They took refuge in heaven,
They crouched outside.
Anu became afraid of the clamor of the deluge,
It was terrifying the gods.
Enki was beside himself,
That his sons were carried off before him.

Nintu, the great lady,
Gnawed her lips in agony.
The Anunna, the great gods,
Were sitting in thirst and hunger.
The goddess saw it, weeping,
The midwife of the gods, the wise Mami,
"Let the day grow dark,
"Let it turn back to gloom!
"In the assembly of the gods,
"How did I agree with them on annihilation?
"Was Enlil so strong that he forced me to speak?
"Like that Tiruru, did he make my speech con-
    fused?
"Of my own accord, from myself alone,
"To my own charge have I heard my people's
    clamor!
"My offspring—with no help from me—have be-
    come like flies.
"And as for me, how to dwell in this abode of
    grief, my clamor fallen silent?
"Shall I go up to heaven,
"I would take up my dwelling in a well-lardered
    house!
"Where has Anu gone to, the chief decision-maker,
"Whose sons, the gods, heeded his command?
"He who irrationally brought about the flood,
"And relegated the peoples to catastrophe?"

*   *   *

Nintu was wailing . . .
"As dragonflies a watercourse, they have filled the
    sea.
"Like rafts they lie against the river meadow,
"Like rafts capsized they lie against the bank.
"I saw and wept over them,
"I have exhausted my lamentation for them."
She wept, giving vent to her feelings,
While Nintu wailed, her emotion was spent.
The gods wept with her for the land.
She had her fill of woe, she was thirsty for beer.
Where she sat weeping, they too sat,
Like sheep, they filled a streambed.
Their lips were agonized with thirst,
They were suffering pangs of hunger.
Seven days and seven nights
There came the deluge, the storm, the flood.

[Atrahasis offers sacrifice to the gods.]

*   *   *

The gods sniffed the savor,
They were gathered like flies around the
    offering.
After they had eaten the offering,
Nintu arose to rail against all of them,
"Where has Anu come to, the chief decision-
    maker?
"Has Enlil drawn nigh the incense?
"They who irrationally brought about the
    flood,
"And relegated the peoples to catastrophe?
"You resolved upon annihilation,
"So now the people's bright countenances are
    turned gray."
Then she drew nigh the big fly ornaments . . .
"Mine is their woe! Proclaim my destiny!
"Let him get me out of my misery, let him show
    me the way.

*   *   *

"Let these flies be jewelry around my neck,
"That I may remember it every day and
    forever."
The warrior Enlil saw the vessel,
And was filled with anger at the Igigi-gods.
"All we great Anunna-gods
"Resolved together on an oath.
"Where did life escape?
"How did a man survive the catastrophe?"
Anu made ready to speak,
And said to the warrior Enlil,
"Who could do this but Enki?
"He revealed the command."
Enki made ready to speak,
And said to the great gods,
"I did it indeed for your sakes!
"I am responsible for safeguarding life.

*   *   *

Enlil made ready to speak,
And said to Ea the leader,
"Come, summon Nintu the birth-goddess,
"Do you and she take counsel together in the
    assembly."
Enki made ready to speak,
And said to Nintu the birth-goddess,

"You, birth-goddess, creatress of destinies,
"Establish death for all peoples! * * *
"Now then, let there be a third woman among the
    people,
"Among the people are the woman who has
    borne and the woman who has not borne.
"Let there be also among the people the she-
    demon,
"Let her snatch the baby from the lap of her who
    bore it,
"Establish high priestesses and priestesses,
"Let them be taboo, and so cut down childbirth.

*   *   *

REVIEW QUESTIONS

1. According to this account of the great flood,
   why were humans created?
2. Why did the gods decide to send a flood on
   humankind?
3. What does this myth suggest about the proper
   relationship between gods and humankind and,
   by extension, about the place of humans in the
   cosmos?
4. Does Atrahasis's role parallel that of a well-
   known figure from the Hebrew Bible's Book of
   Genesis?

FROM *The Epic of Gilgamesh*

With the exception of the Hebrew Bible, The Epic of Gilgamesh *is the most celebrated literary work of the ancient Near East. Although Gilgamesh almost certainly
was an actual ruler of the Sumerian city of Uruk in the early third millennium
B.C.E., the Akkadian epic that developed around him (elements of which can be
found in even earlier Sumerian stories about him) is most prized today not as a
historical source for his era but as one of world literature's earliest and most profound statements on the human condition, and especially on the inescapability of
human mortality. And, although it is not included in the excerpt that follows, the
epic also contains by far the most detailed account of the Flood that is to be found
in Mesopotamian literature. (In fact, the discovery of a cuneiform tablet containing
this story, with its obvious parallels to the story of Noah and the Flood in the biblical Book of Genesis, helped to foster continued archaeological expeditions to Iraq
in the late nineteenth and early twentieth centuries.)*

From *The Epic of Gilgamesh: A New Translation, Analogues, Criticism,* translated by Benjamin
R. Foster (New York: Norton, 2001), pp. 3–12, 60–62, 66, 80–82.

FROM Tablet I

He who saw the wellspring, the foundations of
    the land,
Who knew [. . .], was wise in all things,
Gilgamesh, who saw the wellspring, the founda-
    tions of the land,

Who knew [. . .], was wise in all things,
[He . . .] throughout,
Full understanding of it all he gained,
He saw what was secret and revealed what was
    hidden,
He brought back tidings from before the
    flood,

From a distant journey came home, weary, at
  peace,
Engraved all his hardships on a monument of
  stone,
He built the walls of ramparted Uruk,
The lustrous treasury of hallowed Eanna!
See its upper wall, whose facing gleams like
  copper,
Gaze at the lower course, which nothing will
  equal,
Mount the stone stairway, there from days of old,
Approach Eanna, the dwelling of Ishtar,
Which no future king, no human being will
  equal.
Go up, pace out the walls of Uruk,
Study the foundation terrace and examine the
  brickwork.
Is not its masonry of kiln-fired brick?
And did not seven masters lay its foundations?
One square mile of city, one square mile of
  gardens.
One square mile of clay pits, a half square mile of
  Ishtar's dwelling,
Three and a half square miles is the measure of
  Uruk!
[Search out] the foundation box of copper,
[Release] its lock of bronze,
Raise the lid upon its hidden contents,
Take up and read from the lapis tablet
Of him, Gilgamesh, who underwent many
  hardships.

[The narrator tells of the extraordinary characteris-
tics of Gilgamesh. An old version of the epic began
here.]

Surpassing all kings, for his stature renowned,
Heroic offspring of Uruk, a charging wild bull,
He leads the way in the vanguard,
He marches at the rear, defender of his comrades.
Mighty floodwall, protector of his troops,
Furious flood-wave smashing walls of stone,
Wild calf of Lugalbanda, Gilgamesh is perfect in
  strength,
Suckling of the subline wild cow, the woman
  Ninsun,

Towering Gilgamesh is uncannily perfect.
Opening passes in the mountains,
Digging wells at the highlands' verge,
Traversing the ocean, the vast sea, to the sun's
  rising,
Exploring the furthest reaches of the earth,
Seeking everywhere for eternal life,
Reaching in his might Utanapishtim the Distant
  One,
Restorer of holy places that the deluge had
  destroyed,
Founder of rites for the teeming peoples,
Who could be his like for kingly virtue?[1]
And who, like Gilgamesh, can proclaim, "I am
  king!"
Gilgamesh was singled out from the day of his
  birth,
Two-thirds of him was divine, one-third of him
  was human!
The Lady of Birth drew his body's image,
The God of Wisdom brought his stature to
  perfection.[2]

*   *   *

In the enclosure of Uruk he strode back and
  forth,
Lording it like a wild bull, his head thrust high.
The onslaught of his weapons had no equal.

---

[1] Mesopotamia rulers sometimes boasted of restoring ancient temples that had been destroyed and forgotten
long ago. Two lines up, the poet suggests that Gilgamesh
became a dutiful king of this kind. Mesopotamian
rulers also sometimes boasted of endowing temples
with new offerings. This pair of lines (Restorer . . .,
Founder . . .) sums up religious duties expected of a
good king by citing two extremes of benefactions: those
from the remote past and those beginning in his own
reign.

[2] According to one Mesopotamian tradition, the first human being was created by Mami, goddess of birth,
whom the gods thereupon rewarded with the title
"Mistress of All the Gods," and Enki, god of wisdom,
working together. Subsequent human beings were born
naturally. This passage means that Gilgamesh was physically a perfect human being, so much so that he resembled the first human created by the gods more than
the product of a normal birth.

His teammates stood forth by his game stick,
He was harrying the young men of Uruk beyond
    reason.
Gilgamesh would leave no son to his father,
Day and night he would rampage fiercely.

*   *   *

Bold, superb, accomplished, and mature!
Gilgamesh would leave no girl to her [mother]!
The warrior's daughter, the young man's spouse,
Goddesses kept hearing their plaints.[3]

*   *   *

They summoned the birth goddess, Aruru:

> You, Aruru, created [the boundless human
>   race],
> Now, create what Anu commanded,
> To his stormy heart, let that one be equal,
> Let them contend with each other, that Uruk
>   may have peace.

When Aruru heard this,
She conceived within her what Anu commanded.
Aruru wet her hands,
She pinched off clay, she tossed it upon the
    steppe,
She created valiant Enkidu in the steppe,
Offspring of potter's clay(?), with the force of the
    hero Ninurta.
Shaggy with hair was his whole body,
He was made lush with head hair, like a woman,
The locks of his hair grew thick as a grainfield.
He knew neither people nor inhabited land,
He dressed as animals do.
He fed on grass with gazelles,
With beasts he jostled at the water hole,
With wildlife he drank his fill of water.

[A distraught hunter seeks his father's advice as to
how to stop Enkidu's interference with his trapping.
The father counsels him to go to Gilgamesh, who

will give him a woman to seduce Enkidu from his
untamed way of life.]

A hunter, a trapping-man,
Encountered him at the edge of the water hole.
One day, a second, and a third he encountered
    him at the edge of the water hole.
When he saw him, the hunter stood stock-still
    with terror,
As for Enkidu, he went home with his beasts.
Aghast, struck dumb,
His heart in a turmoil, his face drawn,
With woe in his vitals,
His face like a traveler's from afar,

*   *   *

[Giving heed] to the advice of his father,
The hunter went forth [. . .].
He took the road, set off towards Uruk,
To [the king], Gilgamesh, [he said these words]:

> There is a certain fellow [who has come from
>   the uplands],
> He is mightiest in the land, strength is his,
> Like the force of heaven, so mighty is his
>   strentgh.
> He constantly ranges over the uplands,
> Constantly feeding on grass with his beasts,
> Constantly making his way to the edge of the
>   water hole.
> I am too frightened to approach him.
> He has filled in the pits I dug,
> He has torn out my traps I set,
> He has helped the beasts, wildlife of the steppe,
>   slip from my hands,
> He will not allow me to work the steppe.

Gilgamesh said to him, to the hunter:

> Go, hunter, take with you Shamhat the
>   harlot,
> When the wild beasts draw near the water
>   hole,
> Let her strip off her clothing, laying bare her
>   charms.
> When he sees her, he will approach her,
> His beasts that grew up with him on the
>   steppe will deny him.

---

[3] Certain goddesses were believed to pay particular attention to prayers of women. In this case, they are moved by the constant complaints of the women of Uruk that Gilgamesh was mistreating the women and men of the city.

Forth went the hunter, taking with him Shamhat
the harlot,
They took the road, going straight on their way.
On the third day they arrived at the appointed
place.
Hunter and harlot sat down to wait.
One day, a second day, they sat by the edge of the
water hole,
The beasts came to the water hole to drink,
The wildlife came to drink their fill of water.
But as for him, Enkidu, born in the uplands,
Who feeds on grass with gazelles,
Who drinks at the water hole with beasts,
Who, with wildlife, drinks his fill of water,
Shamhat looked upon him, a human-man,
A barbarous fellow from the midst of the steppe:

There he is, Shamhat, open your embrace,
Open your embrace, let him take your charms!
Be not bashful, take his vitality!
When he sees you, he will approach you,
Toss aside your clothing, let him lie upon
you,
Treat him, a human, to woman's work!
His wild beasts that grew up with him will
deny him,
As in his ardor he caresses you!

Shamhat loosened her garments.
She exposed her loins, he took her charms.
She was not bashful, she took his vitality.
She tossed aside her clothing and he lay upon
her,
She treated him, a human, to woman's work,
As in his ardor he caressed her.
Six days, seven nights was Enkidu aroused,
flowing into Shamhat.
After he had his fill of her delights,
He set off towards his beasts.
When they saw him, Enkidu, the gazelles shied
off,
The wild beasts of the steppe shunned his person.
Enkidu had spent himself, his body was limp,
His knees stood still, while his beasts went away.
Enkidu was too slow, he could not run as before,
But he had gained [reason] and expanded his
understanding.

*[Shamhat urges Enkidu to return with her to Uruk,
artfully piquing his interest with tales of the pleasures awaiting him there, then feigning second
thoughts as she describes Gilgamesh.]*

He returned, he sat at the harlot's feet,
The harlot gazed upon his face,
While he listened to what the harlot was saying.
The harlot said to him, to Enkidu:

You are handsome, Enkidu, you are become
like a god,
Why roam the steppe with wild beasts?
Come, let me lead you to ramparted Uruk,
To the holy temple, abode of Anu and Ishtar,
The place of Gilgamesh, who is perfect in
strength,
And so, like a wild bull, he lords it over the
young men.

As she was speaking to him, her words found
favor,
He was yearning for one to know his heart, a
friend.
Enkidu said to her, to the harlot:

Come, Shamhat, escort me
To the lustrous hallowed temple, abode of Anu
and Ishtar,
The place of Gilgamesh, who is perfect in
strength,
And so, like a wild bull, he lords it over the
young men.
I myself will challenge him, [I will speak out]
boldly,
[I will] raise a cry in Uruk: I am the mighty
one!
[I am come forward] to alter destinies!
He who was born in the steppe [is mighty],
strength is his!

[Shamhat speaks.]

[Come then], let him see your face,
[I will show you Gilgamesh], where he is I
know full well.
Come then, Enkidu, to ramparted Uruk,

Where fellows are resplendent in holiday
    clothing,
Where every day is set for celebration,
Where harps and drums are [played].
And the harlots too, they are fairest of form,
Rich in beauty, full of delights,
Even the great (gods) are kept from sleeping at
    night![4]
Enkidu, you who [have not] learned to live,
Oh, let me show you Gilgamesh, the joy-woe
    man.
Look at him, gaze upon his face,
He is radiant with virility, manly vigor is his,
The whole of his body is seductively gorgeous.
Mightier strength has he than you,
Never resting by day or night.
O Enkidu, renounce your audacity!
Gilgamesh is beloved of Shamash,
Anu, Enlil, and Ea broadened his wisdom.
Ere you come down from the uplands,
Gilgamesh will dream of you in Uruk.

*[The scene shifts to Uruk, where Gilgamesh is
telling his mother, Ninsun, his dreams. She explains
them to him.]*

Gilgamesh went to relate the dreams, saying to
    his mother:

Mother, I had a dream last night:
There were stars of heaven around me,
Like the force of heaven, something kept falling
    upon me!
I tried to carry it but it was too strong for me,
I tried to move it but I could not budge it.
The whole of Uruk was standing by it,
The people formed a crowd around it,
A throng was jostling towards it,
Young men were mobbed around it,
Infantile, they were groveling before it!
[I fell in love with it], like a woman I caressed it,
I carried it off and laid it down before you,
Then you were making it my partner.

The mother of Gilgamesh, knowing and wise,
Who understands everything, said to her son,
Ninsun [the wild cow], knowing and wise,
Who understands everything, said to
    Gilgamesh:

The stars of heaven around you,
Like the force of heaven, what kept falling
    upon you,
Your trying to move it but not being able to
    budge it,
Your laying it down before me,
Then my making it your partner,
Your falling in love with it, your caressing it
    like a woman,
Means there will come to you a strong one,
A companion who rescues a friend.
He will be mighty in the land, strength will be
    his,
Like the force of heaven, so mighty will be his
    strength.

*   *   *

Gilgamesh said to her, to his mother:

Let this befall according to the command of
    the great counselor Enlil,
I want a friend for my own counselor,
For my own counselor do I want a friend!

Even while he was having his dreams,
Shamhat was telling the dreams of Gilgamesh to
    Enkidu,
Each was drawn by love to the other.

FROM Tablet VIII

At the first glimmer of dawn,
Gilgamesh [lamented] his friend:

Enkidu, my friend, your mother the gazelle,
Your father the wild ass brought you into the
    world,
Onagers raised you on their milk,
And the wild beasts taught you all the grazing
    places.

---

[4] The Mesopotamians considered a small group of the
gods "great" or "superior," above all the others.

The pathways, O Enkidu, to the forest of
cedars,
May they weep for you, without falling silent,
night and day.
May the elders of the teeming city, ramparted
Uruk, weep for you,
May the crowd who blessed our departure
weep for you.
May the heights of highland and mountain
[weep for you],
[. . .]
May the lowlands wail like your mother.
May [the forest] of balsam and cedar weep for
you,
Which we slashed in our fury.
May bear, hyena, panther, leopard, deer, jackal,
Lion, wild bull, gazelle, ibex, the beasts and
creatures of the steppe, weep for you.
May the sacred Ulaya River weep for you, along
whose banks we once strode erect,
May the holy Euphrates weep for you,
Whose waters we libated from waterskins.
May the young men of ramparted Uruk weep
for you,
Who watched us slay the Bull of Heaven in
combat.
May the plowman weep for you [at his plow],
Who extolled your name in the sweet song of
harvest home.[1]
May they weep for you, [. . .] of the teeming
city of Uruk,
Who exalted your name at the first [. . .].
May the shepherd and herdsman weep for you,
Who held the milk and buttermilk to your
mouth,
May the [nurse] weep for you,
Who treated your rashes(?) with butter.
May the [. . .] weep for you,
Who held the ale to your mouth.
May the harlot weep for you,
Who massaged you with sweet-smelling oil.
May the wedding guests weep for you,

Who [. . .]
Like brothers may they weep for you,
Like sisters may they tear out their hair for
your sake.
[. . .] Enkidu, as your father, your mother,
I weep for you bitterly, [. . .]

Hear me, O young men, listen to me,
Hear me, O elders of [Uruk], listen to me!
I mourn my friend Enkidu,
I howl as bitterly as a professional keener.
Oh for the axe at my side, oh for the safeguard
by my hand,
Oh for the sword at my belt, oh for the shield
before me,
Oh for my best garment, oh for the raiment
that pleased me most!
An ill wind rose against me and snatched it away!
O my friend, swift wild donkey, mountain
onager, panther of the steppe!
O Enkidu my friend, swift wild donkey, moun-
tain onager, panther of the steppe!
You who stood by me when we climbed the
mountain,
Seized and slew the Bull of Heaven,
Felled Humbaba who [dwelt] in the forest of
cedar,
What now is this sleep that has seized you?
Come back to me! You hear me not.

But, as for him, he did not raise his head.
He touched his heart but it was not beating.
Then he covered his friend's face, like a bride's.
He hovered round him like an eagle,
Like a lioness whose cubs are in a pitfall,
He paced to and fro, back and forth,
Tearing out and hurling away the locks of his hair,
Ripping off and throwing away his fine clothes
like something foul.

*[Gilgamesh commissions a memorial statue of
Enkidu.]*

At the first glimmer of dawn,
Gilgamesh sent out a proclamation to the land:

Hear ye, blacksmith, lapidary, metalworker,
goldsmith, jeweler!

---

[1] Mesopotamian literature referred to work songs sung
when the crops were brought in from the harvest as
symbols of happiness and prosperity.

Make [an image] of my friend,
[Such as no one ever] made of his friend!
The limbs of my friend [. . .]
[Your beard] of lapis, your chest of gold,
Your skin of [. . .]

I will lay you down in the ultimate resting
   place,
In a perfect resting place I will surely lay you
   down.
I will settle you in peaceful rest in the dwelling
   sinister,
Rulers of the netherworld will do you homage.
I will have the people of Uruk shed bitter tears
   for you,
I will make the pleasure-loving people
   burdened down for you,
And, as for me, now that you are dead, I will
   let my hair grow matted,
I will put on a lion skin and roam the steppe!

*   *   *

FROM Tablet IX

Gilgamesh was weeping bitterly for Enkidu, his
   friend,
As he roamed the steppe:

Shall I not die too? Am I not like Enkidu?
Oh woe has entered my vitals!
I have grown afraid of death, so I roam the
   steppe.
Having come this far, I will go on swiftly
Towards Utanapishtim, son of Ubar-Tutu.

*   *   *

FROM Tablet X

Utanapishtim said to him, to Gilgamesh:

Why are your cheeks emaciated, your face cast
   down,
Your heart wretched, your features wasted,
Woe in your vitals,
Your face like a traveler's from afar,
Your features weathered by cold and sun,
   Why are you clad in a lion skin, roaming the
      steppe?

[Gilgamesh tells Utanapishtim his mission, wallowing in the luxury of self-pity on the difficulties of his quest.]

Gilgamesh said to him, to Utanapishtim:

My cheeks would not be emaciated, nor my
   face cast down,
Nor my heart wretched, nor my features
   wasted,
Nor would there be woe in my vitals,
Nor would my face be like a traveler's from
   afar,
Nor would my features be weathered by cold
   and sun,
Nor would I be clad in a lion skin, roaming the
   steppe,
But for my friend, swift wild donkey, mountain
   onager, panther of the steppe,
But for Enkidu, my friend, swift wild donkey,
   mountain onager, panther of the steppe,
He who stood by me as we ascended the
   mountain,
Seized and killed the bull that came down from
   heaven,
Felled Humbaba who dwelt in the forest of
   cedars,
Killed lions at the mountain passes,
My friend whom I so loved, who went with me
   through every hardship,
Enkidu, whom I so loved, who went with me
   through every hardship,
The fate of mankind has overtaken him.
Six days and seven nights I wept for him,
I would not give him up for burial,
Until a worm fell out of his nose.
I was frightened [. . .]
I have grown afraid of death, so I roam the
   steppe,
My friend's case weighs heavy upon me.
A distant road I roam over the steppe,
My friend Enkidu's case weighs heavy upon
   me!
A distant path I roam over the steppe,
How can I be silent? How can I hold my
   peace?
My friend whom I loved is turned into clay,

Enkidu, my friend whom I loved, is turned into
    clay!
Shall I too not lie down like him,
And never get up, forever and ever?

Gilgamesh said to him, to Utanapishtim:

So it is to go find Utanapishtim, whom they
    call the "Distant One,"
I traversed all lands,
I came over, one after another, wearisome
    mountains,
Then I crossed, one after another, all the seas.
Too little sweet sleep has smoothed my
    countenance,
I have worn myself out in sleeplessness,
My muscles ache for misery,
What have I gained my trials?
I had not reached the tavern keeper when my
    clothes were worn out,
I killed bear, hyena, lion, panther, leopard, deer,
    ibex, wild beasts of the steppe,
I ate their meat, I [. . .] their skins.
Let them close behind me the doors of woe,
[Let them seal them] with pitch and tar,
For my part, I [. . .] no amusement,
For me, [. . .]

*[Utanapishtim responds in a long speech, poorly
known because of damage to the manuscripts. He
chides Gilgamesh for his self-pity and ostentatious
mourning, all the more unseemly because the gods
had favored him. The village idiot, he points out,
wears rags and eats bad food, but no one accords
him merit for that. After a gap in the text,
Utanapishtim is found discoursing on the nature
of death.]*

Utanapishtim said to him, to Gilgamesh:

Why, O Gilgamesh, did you prolong woe,
You who are [formed] of the flesh of gods and
    mankind,
You for whom [the gods] acted like fathers and
    mothers?
When was it, Gilgamesh, you [. . .] to a fool?

*   *   *

FROM Tablet XI

Now then, who will convene the gods for your
    sake,
That you may find the eternal life you seek?
Come, come, try not to sleep for six days and
    seven nights.

*[Utanapishtim has challenged Gilgamesh to go
without sleep for a week; if he fails this test, how
could he expect to live forever? Even as he speaks,
Gilgamesh drifts off to sleep. Thus passes from the
scene the all-night rowdy of Table I.]*

As he sat there on his haunches,
Sleep was swirling over him like a mist.
Utanapishtim said to her, to his wife:

Behold this fellow who seeks eternal life!
Sleep swirls over him like a mist.

*[Utanapishtim's wife, taking pity on Gilgamesh,
urges her husband to awaken him and let him go
home. Utanapishtim insists on a proof of how long
he slept, lest Gilgamesh claim that he had only
dozed. She is to bake him fresh bread every day and
set it beside him, marking the wall for the day. The
bread spoils progressively as Gilgamesh sleeps for
seven days.]*

His wife said to him, to Utanapishtim the Distant
    One:

Do touch him that the man may wake up,
That he may return safe on the way whence he
    came,
That through the gate he came forth he may
    return to his land.

Utanapishtim said to her, to his wife:

Since the human race is duplicitous, he'll en-
    deavor to dupe you.
Come, come, bake his daily loaves, put them
    one after another by his head,
Then mark the wall for each day he has
    slept.

She baked his daily loaves for him, put them one
   after another by his head,
Then dated the wall for each day he slept.
The first loaf was dried hard,
The second was leathery, the third soggy,
The crust of the fourth turned white,
The fifth was gray with mold, the sixth was
   fresh,
The seventh was still on the coals when he
   touched him, the man woke up.

*[Gilgamesh wakes at last. Claiming at first that he
has scarcely dozed a moment, he sees the bread and
realizes that he has slept for the entire time he was
supposed to remain awake for the test. He gives up
in despair. What course is left for him? Utanapishtim does not answer directly but orders the boatman
to take him home. Further, the boatman himself is
never to return. Thus access to Utanapishtim is denied the human race forever. Gilgamesh is bathed
and given clothing that will stay magically fresh
until his return to Uruk.]*

Gilgamesh said to him, to Utanapishtim the
   Distant One:

Scarcely had sleep stolen over me,
When straightaway you touched me and roused
   me.

Utanapishtim said to him, to Gilgamesh:

[Up with you], Gilgamesh, count your daily
   loaves,
[That the days you have slept] may be known
   to you.
The first loaf is dried hard,
The second is leathery, the third soggy,
The crust of the fourth has turned white,
The fifth is gray with mold,
The sixth is fresh,
The seventh was still in the coals when I
   touched you and you woke up.

Gilgamesh said to him, to Utanapishtim the
   Distant One:

What then should I do, Utanapishtim, whither
   should I go,

Now that the Bereaver has seized my [flesh]?[1]
Death lurks in my bedchamber,
And wherever I turn, there is death!

Utanapishtim said to him, to Ur-Shanabi the
   boatman:

Ur-Shanabi, may the harbor [offer] you no
   [haven],
May the crossing point reject you,
Be banished from the shore you shuttled to.
The man you brought here,
His body is matted with filthy hair,
Hides have marred the beauty of his flesh.
Take him away, Ur-Shanabi, bring him to the
   washing place.
Have him wash out his filthy hair with water,
   clean as snow,
Have him throw away his hides, let the sea
   carry them off,
Let his body be rinsed clean.
Let his headband be new,
Have him put on raiment worthy of him.
Until he reaches his city,
Until he completes his journey,
Let his garments stay spotless, fresh and new.

Ur-Shanabi took him awy and brought him to the
   washing place.
He washed out his filthy hair with water, clean as
   snow,
He threw away his hides, the sea carried them off,
His body was rinsed clean.
He renewed his headband,
He put on raiment worthy of him.
Until he reached his city,
Until he completed his journey,
His garments would stay spotless, fresh and new.

*[Gilgamesh and Ur-Shanabi embark on their
journey to Uruk. As they push off from the shore,
Utanapishtim's wife intervenes, asking her husband
to give the hero something to show for his quest.
Gilgamesh brings the boat back to shore and waits
expectantly. Utanapishtim tells him of a plant of*

---

[1] "The Bereaver" is an epithet of death. It could also
mean something like "kidnapper."

*rejuvenation. Gilgamesh dives for the plant by open-
ing a shaft through the earth's surface to the water
below. He ties stones to his feet, a technique used in
traditional pearl diving in the Gulf. When he comes
up from securing the plant, he is on the opposite side
of the ocean, where he started from.]*

Gilgamesh and Ur-Shanabi embarked on the
    boat,
They launched the boat, they embarked upon it.
His wife said to him, to Utanapishtim the Distant
    One:

    Gilgamesh has come here, spent with exertion,
    What will you give him for his homeward
        journey?

At that he, Gilgamesh, lifted the pole,
Bringing the boat back by the shore.
Utanapishtim said to him, to Gilgamesh:

    Gilgamesh, you have come here, spent with
        exertion,
    What shall I give you for your homeward
        journey?
    I will reveal to you, O Gilgamesh, a secret
        matter,
    And a mystery of the gods I will tell you.
    There is a certain plant, its stem is like a
        thornbush,
    Its thorns, like the wild rose, will prick [your
        hand].
    If you can secure this plant, [. . .]
    [. . .]

No sooner had Gilgamesh heard this,
He opened a shaft, [flung away his tools].
He tied heavy stones [to his feet],
They pulled him down into the watery depths
    [. . .].
He took the plant though it pricked [his hand].
He cut the heavy stones [from his feet],
The sea cast him up on his home shore.

*[Gilgamesh resolves to take the plant to Uruk to
experiment on an old man. While Gilgamesh is
bathing on the homeward journey, a snake eats the
plant and rejuvenates itself by shedding its skin.
Gilgamesh gives up. Immense quantities of water
have flooded up through the shaft he dug and*

*covered the place. He has left behind his tools so
cannot dig another shaft. He has also lost the boat,
so there is no going back.]*

Gilgamesh said to him, to Ur-Shanabi the
    boatman:

    Ur-Shanabi, this plant is cure for heartache,
    Whereby a man will regain his stamina.
    I will take it to ramparted Uruk,
    I will have an old man eat some and so test the
        plant.
    His name shall be "Old Man Has Become
        Young-Again-Man."
    I myself will eat it and so return to my carefree
        youth.

At twenty double leagues they took a bite to eat,
At thirty double leagues they made their camp.

Gilgamesh saw a pond whose water was cool,
He went down into it to bathe in the water.
A snake caught the scent of the plant,
[Stealthily] it came up and carried the plant away,
On its way back it shed its skin.

Thereupon Gilgamesh sat down weeping,
His tears flowed down his face,
He said to Ur-Shanabi the boatman:

    For whom, Ur-Shanabi, have my hands been
        toiling?
    For whom has my heart's blood been poured
        out?
    For myself I have obtained no benefit,
    I have done a good deed for a reptile!
    Now, floodwaters rise against me for twenty
        double leagues,
    When I opened the shaft, I flung away the
        tools.
    How shall I find my bearings?
    I have come much too far to go back, and I
        abandoned the boat on the shore.

*[Upon completing his journey, Gilgamesh invites
Ur-Shanabi to inspect the walls of Uruk, using the
same words used by the narrator in Tablet I.]*

At twenty double leagues they took a bite to eat,
At thirty double leagues they made their camp.
When they arrived in ramparted Uruk,

TWO IMAGES OF SUMERIAN RULERSHIP (C. 2480 B.C.E.)

The first image (top) is a plaque of Ur-Nanshe, who ruled the Sumerian city-state of Lagash around 2480 B.C.E. He is shown both as a builder carrying a basket of bricks, with his family facing him (above), and enthroned (below). The second image (bottom), from a limestone monument known as the Vulture Stela, depicts Ur-Nanshe's successor Eannatum leading the troops of Lagash to victory against the rival city-state of Umma. The inscriptions on the stela record Lagash's victory and the terms it imposed on Umma. What do these images suggest about the status and responsibilities of Sumerian rulers? What do they suggest about the uses of cuneiform writing during the mid-third millennium B.C.E.?

Gilgamesh said to him, to Ur-Shanabi the
boatman:

Go up, UrShanabi, pace out the walls of Uruk.
Study the foundation terrace and examine the
   brickwork.
Is not its masonry of kiln-fired brick?
And did not seven masters lay its foundations?
One square mile of city, one square mile of
   gardens,
One square mile of clay pits, a half square mile
   of Ishtar's dwelling,
Three and a half square miles is the measure of
   Uruk!

*   *   *

REVIEW QUESTIONS

1. What kind of figure is Gilgamesh?
2. What becomes of his quest in this epic, and why?
3. What roles do the gods play in the story?
4. When his quest is completed, what is Gilgamesh's view of his fate?

Laws from Ancient Mesopotamia

Dating to the reign of Hammurabi of Babylon (the conventional dates for which are 1795–1750 B.C.E.), the Laws of Hammurabi are not the earliest Mesopotamian compilation of legal rulings known to us. They are, however, the longest and most diverse collection and undoubtedly constitute the single most informative document yet discovered regarding concepts of justice and social regulation in Mesopotamian society. Hammurabi's laws also provide extremely important evidence about the status and rights of women of various social classes in Babylonian society in the early second millennium B.C.E. The treatment of women according to those laws can be usefully compared to the treatment accorded them in a later body of legal rulings, the Middle Assyrian Laws, which date to a period roughly 500 years after Hammurabi's reign.

From *Law Collections from Mesopotamia and Asia Minor*, edited by Martha T. Roth, SBL Writings from the Ancient World Series, vol. 6 (Atlanta, Ga.: Scholars Press, 1995), pp. 76–135.

FROM The Laws of Hammurabi

When the august god Anu, king of the Anunnaku deities, and the god Enlil, lord of heaven and earth, who determines the destinies of the land, allotted supreme power over all peoples to the god Marduk, the firstborn son of the god Ea, exalted him among the Igigu deities, named the city of Babylon with its august name and made it supreme within the regions of the world, and established for him within it eternal kingship whose foundations are as fixed as heaven and earth, at that time, the gods Anu and Enlil, for the enhancement of the well-being of the people, named me by my name: Hammurabi, the pious prince, who venerates the gods, to make justice prevail in the land, to abolish the wicked and the evil, to prevent the strong from oppressing the weak, to rise like the sun-god Shamash over all humankind, to illuminate the land.

I am Hammurabi, the shepherd, selected by the god Enlil, he who heaps high abundance and plenty, who perfects every possible thing for the city Nippur, the city known as band-of-heaven-and-earth, the pious provider of the Ekur temple;

the capable king, the restorer of the city Eridu, the purifier of the rites of the Eabzu temple;

the onslaught of the four regions of the world, who magnifies the reputation of the city Babylon, who gladdens the heart of his divine lord Marduk, whose days are devoted to the Esagil temple;

*   *   *

When the god Marduk commanded me to provide just ways for the people of the land in order to attain appropriate behavior, I established truth and justice as the declaration of the land, I enhanced the well-being of the people.

*   *   *

1. If a man accuses another man and charges him with homicide but cannot bring proof against him, his accuser shall be killed.

*   *   *

2. If a man charges another man with practicing witchcraft but cannot bring proof against him, he who is charged with witchcraft shall go to the divine River Ordeal, he shall indeed submit to the divine River Ordeal; if the divine River Ordeal should overwhelm him, his accuser shall take full legal possession of his estate; if the divine River Ordeal should clear that man and should he survive, he who made the charge of witchcraft against him shall be killed; he who submitted to the divine River Ordeal shall take full legal possession of his accuser's estate.

3. If a man comes forward to give false testimony in a case but cannot bring evidence for his accusation, if that case involves a capital offense, that man shall be killed.

*   *   *

6. If a man steals valuables belonging to the god or to the palace, that man shall be killed, and also he who received the stolen goods from him shall be killed.

7. If a man should purchase silver, gold, a slave, a slave woman, an ox, a sheep, a donkey, or anything else whatsoever, from a son of a man or from a slave of a man without witnesses or a contract—or if he accepts the goods for safekeeping—that man is a thief, he shall be killed.

8. If a man steals an ox, a sheep, a donkey, a pig, or a boat—if it belongs either to the god or to the palace, he shall give thirtyfold; if it belongs to a commoner, he shall replace it tenfold; if the thief does not have anything to give, he shall be killed.

*   *   *

15. If a man should enable a palace slave, a palace slave woman, a commoner's slave, or a commoner's slave woman to leave through the main city-gate, he shall be killed.

16. If a man should harbor a fugitive slave or slave woman of either the palace or of a commoner in his house and not bring him out at the herald's public proclamation, that householder shall be killed.

17. If a man seizes a fugitive slave or slave woman in the open country and leads him back to his owner, the slave owner shall give him 2 shekels of silver.

18. If that slave should refuse to identify his owner, he shall lead him off to the palace, his circumstances shall be investigated, and they shall return him to his owner.

19. If he should detain that slave in his own house and afterward the slave is discovered in his possession, that man shall be killed.

20. If the slave should escape the custody of the one who seized him, that man shall swear an oath by the god to the owner of the slave, and he shall be released.

21. If a man breaks into a house, they shall kill him and hang him in front of that very breach.

22. If a man commits a robbery and is then seized, that man shall be killed.

*   *   *

53. If a man neglects to reinforce the embankment of the irrigation canal of his field and does not reinforce its embankment, and then a breach opens in its embankment and allows the water to carry away the common irrigated area, the man in whose embankment the breach opened shall replace the grain whose loss he caused.

54. If he cannot replace the grain they shall sell him and his property, and the residents of the common irrigated area whose grain crops the water carried away shall divide (the proceeds).

55. If a man opens his branch of the canal for irrigation and negligently allows the water to carry away his neighbor's field, he shall measure and deliver grain in accordance with his neighbor's yield.

*   *   *

102. If a merchant should give silver to a trading agent for an investment venture, and he incurs a loss on his journeys, he shall return silver to the merchant in the amount of the capital sum.

103. If enemy forces should make him abandon whatever goods he is transporting while on his business trip, the trading agent shall swear an oath by the god and shall be released.

104. If a merchant gives a trading agent grain, wool, oil, or any other commodity for local transactions, the trading agent shall return to the merchant the silver for each transaction; the trading agent shall collect a sealed receipt for each payment in silver that he gives to the merchant.

105. If the trading agent should be negligent and not take a sealed receipt for each payment in silver that he gives to the merchant, any silver that is not documented in a sealed receipt will not be included in the final accounting.

*   *   *

108. If a woman innkeeper should refuse to accept grain for the price of beer but accepts only silver measured by the large weight, thereby re-ducing the value of beer in relation to the value of grain, they shall charge and convict that woman innkeeper and they shall cast her into the water.

109. If there should be a woman innkeeper in whose house criminals congregate, and she does not seize those criminals and lead them off to the palace authorities, that woman innkeeper shall be killed.

*   *   *

117. If an obligation is outstanding against a man and he sells or gives into debt service his wife, his son, or his daughter, they shall perform service in the house of their buyer or of the one who holds them in debt service for three years; their release shall be secured in the fourth year.

118. If he should give a male or female slave into debt service, the merchant may extend the term beyond the three years, he may sell him; there are no grounds for a claim.

119. If an obligation is outstanding against a man and he therefore sells his slave woman who has borne him children, the owner of the slave woman shall weigh and deliver the silver which the merchant weighed and delivered as the loan and he shall thereby redeem his slave woman.

*   *   *

128. If a man marries a wife but does not draw up a formal contract for her, she is not a wife.

129. If a man's wife should be seized lying with another male, they shall bind them and throw them into the water; if the wife's master allows his wife to live, then the king shall allow his subject (i.e., the other male) to live.

130. If a man pins down another man's virgin wife who is still residing in her father's house, and they seize him lying with her, that man shall be killed; that woman shall be released.

131. If her husband accuses his own wife of adultery, although she has not been seized lying with another male, she shall swear to her innocence by an oath by the god, and return to her house.

132. If a man's wife should have a finger pointed against her in accusation involving another male,

although she has not been seized lying with another male, she shall submit to the divine River Ordeal for her husband.[1]

*   *   *

134. If a man should be captured and there are not sufficient provisions in his house, his wife may enter another's house; that woman will not be subject to any penalty.

135. If a man should be captured and there are not sufficient provisions in his house, before his return his wife enters another's house and bears children, and afterwards her husband returns and gets back to his city, that woman shall return to her first husband; the children shall inherit from their father.

136. If a man deserts his city and flees, and after his departure his wife enters another's house—if that man then should return and seize his wife, because he repudiated his city and fled, the wife of the deserter will not return to her husband.

*   *   *

138. If a man intends to divorce his first-ranking wife who did not bear him children, he shall give her silver as much as was her bridewealth and restore to her the dowry that she brought from her father's house, and he shall divorce her.

139. If there is no bridewealth, he shall give her 60 shekels of silver as a divorce settlement.

140. If he is a commoner, he shall give her 20 shekels of silver.

141. If the wife of a man who is residing in the man's house should decide to leave, and she appropriates goods, squanders her household possessions, or disparages her husband, they shall charge and convict her; and if her husband should declare his intention to divorce her, then he shall

divorce her; neither her travel expenses, nor her divorce settlement, nor anything else shall be given to her. If her husband should not declare his intention to divorce her, then her husband may marry another woman and that first woman shall reside in her husband's house as a slave woman.

142. If a woman repudiates her husband, and declares, "You will not have marital relations with me"—her circumstances shall be investigated by the authorities of her city quarter, and if she is circumspect and without fault, but her husband is wayward and disparages her greatly, that woman will not be subject to any penalty; she shall take her dowry and she shall depart for her father's house.

143. If she is not circumspect but is wayward, squanders her household possessions, and disparages her husband, they shall cast that woman into the water.

*   *   *

150. If a man awards to his wife a field, orchard, house, or movable property, and makes out a sealed document for her, after her husband's death her children will not bring a claim against her; the mother shall give her estate to whichever of her children she loves, but she will not give it to an outsider.

151. If a woman who is residing in a man's house should have her husband agree by binding contract that no creditor of her husband shall seize her for his debts—if that man has a debt incurred before marrying that woman, his creditors will not seize his wife; and if that woman has a debt incurred before entering the man's house, her creditors will not seize her husband.

*   *   *

153. If a man's wife has her husband killed on account of (her relationship with) another male, they shall impale that woman.

154. If a man should carnally know his daughter, they shall banish that man from the city.

155. If a man selects a bride for his son and his son carnally knows her, after which he himself

---

[1] The woman would take an oath swearing to her innocence before the river god. She then would be required to plunge into the river. If she survived, she was deemed innocent; if she drowned, it was deemed the punishment of the river god, in whose name she had falsely sworn. [Editor.]

then lies with her and they seize him in the act, they shall bind that man and cast him into the water.

156. If a man selects a bride for his son and his son does not yet carnally know her, and he himself then lies with her, he shall weigh and deliver to her 30 shekels of silver; moreover, he shall restore to her whatever she brought from her father's house, and a husband of her choice shall marry her.

157. If a man, after his father's death, should lie with his mother, they shall burn them both.

158. If a man, after his father's death, should be discovered in the lap of the father's principal wife who had borne children, that man shall be disinherited from the paternal estate.

*   *   *

162. If a man marries a wife, she bears him children, and that woman then goes to her fate, her father shall have no claim to her dowry; her dowry belongs only to her children.

163. If a man marries a wife but she does not provide him with children, and that woman goes to her fate—if his father-in-law then returns to him the bridewealth that that man brought to his father-in-law's house, her husband shall have no claim to that woman's dowry; her dowry belongs only to her father's house.

*   *   *

169. If he should be guilty of a grave offense deserving the penalty of disinheritance by his father, they shall pardon him for his first one; if he should commit a grave offense a second time, the father may disinherit his son.

*   *   *

188. If a craftsman takes a young child to rear and then teaches him his craft, he will not be reclaimed.

189. If he should not teach him his craft, that rearling shall return to his father's house.

190. If a man should not reckon the young child whom he took and raised in adoption as equal with his children, that rearling shall return to his father's house.

191. If a man establishes his household by reckoning as equal with any future children the young child whom he took and raised in adoption, but afterwards he has children of his own and then decides to disinherit the rearling, that young child will not depart empty-handed; the father who raised him shall give him a one-third share of his property as his inheritance and he shall depart; he will not give him any property from field, orchard, or house.

*   *   *

195. If a child should strike his father, they shall cut off his hand.

196. If an *awīlu* should blind the eye of another *awīlu*, they shall blind his eye.[2]

197. If he should break the bone of another *awīlu*, they shall break his bone.

198. If he should blind the eye of a commoner or break the bone of a commoner, he shall weigh and deliver 60 shekels of silver.

199. If he should blind the eye of an *awīlu*'s slave or break the bone of an *awīlu*'s slave, he shall weigh and deliver one-half of his value in silver.

200. If an *awīlu* should knock out the tooth of another *awīlu* of his own rank, they shall knock out his tooth.

201. If he should knock out the tooth of a commoner, he shall weigh and deliver 20 shekels of silver.

202. If an *awīlu* should strike the cheek of an *awīlu* who is of status higher than his own, he shall be flogged in the public assembly with 60 stripes of an ox whip.

203. If a member of the *awīlu*-class should strike the cheek of another member of the *awīlu*-class who is his equal, he shall weigh and deliver 60 shekels of silver.

204. If a commoner should strike the cheek of

---

[2] The most basic meaning of *awīlu* is "man." In this context it seems to represent a free man, probably an owner of private land and with a status higher than that of a "commoner." [Editor.]

another commoner, he shall weigh and deliver 10 shekels of silver.

* * *

209. If an *awīlu* strikes a woman of the *awīlu*-class and thereby causes her to miscarry her fetus, he shall weigh and deliver 10 shekels of silver for her fetus.

210. If that woman should die, they shall kill his daughter.

211. If he should cause a woman of the commoner-class to miscarry her fetus by the beating, he shall weigh and deliver 5 shekels of silver.

212. If that woman should die, he shall weigh and deliver 30 shekels of silver.

* * *

218. If a physician performs major surgery with a bronze lancet upon an *awīlu* and thus causes the *awīlu*'s death, or opens an *awīlu*'s temple with a bronze lancet and thus blinds the *awīlu*'s eye, they shall cut off his hand.

219. If a physician performs major surgery with a bronze lancet upon a slave of a commoner and thus causes the slave's death, he shall replace the slave with a slave of comparable value.

220. If he opens his (the commoner's slave's) temple with a bronze lancet and thus blinds his eye, he shall weigh and deliver silver equal to half his value.

* * *

226. If a barber shaves off the slave-hairlock of a slave not belonging to him without the consent of the slave's owner, they shall cut off that barber's hand.

227. If a man misinforms a barber so that he then shaves off the slave-hairlock of a slave not belonging to him, they shall kill that man and hang him in his own doorway; the barber shall swear, "I did not knowingly shave it off," and he shall be released.

* * *

These are the just decisions which Hammurabi, the able king, has established and thereby has di-

rected the land along the course of truth and the correct way of life.

I am Hammurabi, noble king. I have not been careless or negligent toward humankind, granted to my care by the god Enlil, and with whose shepherding the god Marduk charged me. I have sought for them peaceful places, I removed serious difficulties, I spread light over them. With the mighty weapon which the gods Zababa and Ishtar bestowed upon me, with the wisdom which the god Ea allotted to me, with the ability which the god Marduk gave me, I annihilated enemies everywhere, I put an end to wars, I enhanced the well-being of the land, I made the people of all settlements lie in safe pastures, I did not tolerate anyone intimidating them. The great gods having chosen me, I am indeed the shepherd who brings peace, whose scepter is just. My benevolent shade is spread over my city, I held the people of the lands of Sumer and Akkad safely on my lap. They prospered under my protective spirit, I maintained them in peace, with my skillful wisdom I sheltered them.

In order that the mighty not wrong the weak, to provide just ways for the waif and the widow, I have inscribed my precious pronouncements upon my stela and set it up before the statue of me, the king of justice, in the city of Babylon, the city which the gods Anu and Enlil have elevated, within the Esagil, the temple whose foundations are fixed as are heaven and earth, in order to render the judgments of the land, to give the verdicts of the land, and to provide just ways for the wronged.

* * *

FROM Middle Assyrian Laws

* * *

4. If either a slave or a slave woman should receive something from a man's wife, they shall cut off the slave's or slave woman's nose and ears; they shall restore the stolen goods; the man shall cut

off his own wife's ears. But if he releases his wife and does not cut off her ears, they shall not cut off the nose and ears of the slave or slave woman, and they shall not restore the stolen goods.

*   *   *

7. If a woman should lay a hand upon a man and they prove the charges against her, she shall pay 1,800 shekels of lead; they shall strike her 20 blows with rods.

8. If a woman should crush a man's testicle during a quarrel, they shall cut off one of her fingers. And even if the physician should bandage it, but the second testicle then becomes infected along with it and becomes . . . , or she should crush the second testicle during the quarrel—they shall gouge out both her

*   *   *

9. If a man lays a hand upon a woman, attacking her like a rutting bull, and they prove the charges against him and find him guilty, they shall cut off one of his fingers. If he should kiss her, they shall draw his lower lip across the blade of an ax and cut it off.

*   *   *

12. If a wife of a man should walk along the main thoroughfare and should a man seize her and say to her, "I want to have sex with you!"—she shall not consent but she shall protect herself; should he seize her by force and fornicate with her—whether they discover him upon the woman or witnesses later prove the charges against him that he fornicated with the woman—they shall kill the man; there is no punishment for the woman.

13. If the wife of a man should go out of her own house, and go to another man where he resides, and should he fornicate with her knowing that she is the wife of a man, they shall kill the man and the wife.

14. If a man should fornicate with another man's wife either in an inn or in the main thoroughfare, knowing that she is the wife of a man, they shall treat the fornicator as the man declares he wishes his wife to be treated. If he should fornicate with her without knowing that she is the wife of a man,

the fornicator is clear; the man shall prove the charges against his wife and he shall treat her as he wishes.

15. If a man should seize another man upon his wife and they prove the charges against him and find him guilty, they shall kill both of them; there is no liability for him. If he should seize him and bring him either before the king or the judges, and they prove the charges against him and find him guilty—if the woman's husband kills his wife, then he shall also kill the man; if he cuts off his wife's nose, he shall turn the man into a eunuch and they shall lacerate his entire face; but if he wishes to release his wife, he shall release the man.

16. If a man should fornicate with the wife of a man . . . by her invitation, there is no punishment for the man; the husband shall impose whatever punishment he chooses upon his wife. If he should fornicate with her by force and they prove the charges against him and find him guilty, his punishment shall be identical to that of the wife of the man.

*   *   *

23. If a man's wife should take another man's wife into her house and give her to a man for purposes of fornication, and the man knows that she is the wife of a man, they shall treat him as one who has fornicated with the wife of another man; and they treat the female procurer just as the woman's husband treats his fornicating wife. And if the woman's husband intends to do nothing to his fornicating wife, they shall do nothing to the fornicator or to the female procurer; they shall release them. But if the man's wife does not know what was intended, and the woman who takes her into her house brings the man in to her by deceit, and he then fornicates with her—if, as soon as she leaves the house, she should declare that she has been the victim of fornication, they shall release the woman, she is clear; they shall kill the fornicator and the female procurer. But if the woman should not so declare, the man shall impose whatever punishment on his wife he wishes; they shall kill the fornicator and the female procurer.

24. If a man's wife should withdraw herself from her husband and enter into the house of another

Assyrian, either in that city or in any of the nearby towns, to a house which he assigns to her, residing with the mistress of the household staying overnight three or four nights, and the householder is not aware that it is the wife of a man who is residing in his house, and later that woman is seized, the householder whose wife withdrew herself from him shall mutilate his wife and not take her back. As for the man's wife with whom his wife resided, they shall cut off her ears; if he pleases, her husband shall give 12,600 shekels of lead as her value, and, if he pleases, he shall take back his wife. However, if the householder knows that it is a man's wife who is residing in his house with his wife, he shall give "triple." And if he should deny that he knew of her status, he shall declare, "I did not know," they shall undergo the divine River Ordeal. And if the man in whose house the wife of a man resided should refuse to undergo the divine River Ordeal, he shall give "triple"; if it is the man whose wife withdrew herself from him who should refuse to undergo the divine River Ordeal, he in whose house she resided is clear; he shall bear the expenses of the divine River Ordeal. However, if the man whose wife withdrew herself from him does not mutilate his wife, he shall take back his wife; no sanctions are imposed.

*   *   *

37. If a man intends to divorce his wife, if it is his wish, he shall give her something; if that is not his wish, he shall not give her anything, and she shall leave emptyhanded.

*   *   *

40. Wives of a man, or widows, or any Assyrian women who go out into the main thoroughfare shall not have their heads bare. Daughters of a man with either a cloth or garments shall veil their heads. When they go about in the main thoroughfare during the daytime, they shall be veiled. A concubine who goes about in the main thoroughfare with her mistress is to be veiled. A married *qadiltu*-woman is to be veiled when she goes about in the main thoroughfare, but an unmarried

one is to leave her head bare in the main thoroughfare, she shall not be veiled. A prostitute shall not be veiled, her head shall be bare. Whoever sees a veiled prostitute shall seize her, secure witnesses, and bring her to the palace entrance. They shall not take away her jewelry, but he who has seized her takes her clothing; they shall strike her 50 blows with rods; they shall pour hot pitch over her head. And if a man should see a veiled prostitute and release her, and does not bring her to the palace entrance, they shall strike that man 50 blows with rods; the one who informs against him shall take his clothing; they shall pierce his ears, thread them on a cord, tie it at his back; he shall perform the king's service for one full month. Slave women shall not be veiled, and he who should see a veiled slave woman shall seize her and bring her to the palace entrance; they shall cut off her ears; he who seizes her shall take her clothing. If a man should see a veiled slave woman but release her and not seize her, and does not bring her to the palace entrance, and they then prove the charges against him and find him guilty, they shall strike him 50 blows with rods; they shall pierce his ears, thread them on a cord, tie it at his back; the one who informs against him shall take his garments; he shall perform the king's service for one full month.

*   *   *

53. If a woman aborts her fetus by her own action and they then prove the charges against her and find her guilty, they shall impale her, they shall not bury her. If she dies as a result of aborting her fetus, they shall impale her, they shall not bury her. If any persons should hide that woman because she aborted her fetus.* * *

*   *   *

55. If a man forcibly seizes and rapes a maiden who is residing in her father's house, who is not betrothed, whose womb is not opened, who is not married, and against whose father's house there is no outstanding claim—whether within the city or in the countryside, or at night whether in the main

thoroughfare, or in a granary, or during the city festival—the father of the maiden shall take the wife of the fornicator of the maiden and hand her over to be raped; he shall not return her to her husband, but he shall take (and keep) her; the father shall give his daughter who is the victim of fornication into the protection of the household of her fornicator. If he, the fornicator, has no wife, the fornicator shall give "triple" the silver as the value of the maiden to her father; her fornicator shall marry her; he shall not reject her. If the father does not desire it so, he shall receive "triple" silver for the maiden, and he shall give his daughter in marriage to whomever he chooses.

56. If a maiden should willingly give herself to a man, the man shall so swear; they shall have no claim to his wife; the fornicator shall pay "triple" the silver as the value of the maiden; the father shall treat his daughter in whatever manner he chooses.

*   *   *

59. In addition to the punishments for a man's wife that are written on the tablet, a man may whip his wife, pluck out her hair, mutilate her ears, or strike her, with impunity.

REVIEW QUESTIONS

1. Of the hundreds of records of litigation that exist from the era of Hammurabi and his successors, not one specifically states that a dispute was resolved in accordance with Hammurabi's laws; some, in fact, record rulings that directly contradict those laws. This has caused some scholars to question why Hammurabi had these laws compiled in the first place. Why do you think Hammurabi had his laws compiled? (Do the prologue and epilogue to the laws provide any clues?)

2. What principles of justice and compensation are evident in these laws, and what kinds of recourse did society have against wrongdoers?

3. What evidence of social classes in Babylonian society do they provide?

4. How did women's rights compare with those of men?

5. What do these laws tell us about Mesopotamian views about responsibility for sexual activity?

6. What do they tell us about power and authority within Mesopotamian families?

FROM *Lamentation over the Destruction of Sumer and Urim*

From early antiquity down to the present day, the region of what is now called Iraq has been both a cradle of great civilizations and empires and the subject of a series of catastrophic invasions that have laid low its cities and decimated its peoples. Among the most hauntingly evocative compositions in the literature of ancient Mesopotamia are the lamentations over the destruction of great cities of ancient Sumer—among them, Eridu, Nippur, and, as the following selection attests, the great city of Ur (Sumerian Urim), which the Hebrew Bible mentions as the original home of the Hebrew patriarch Abraham. Founded well before 3500 B.C.E., Ur was one of the greatest cities of ancient Sumer. Archaeological excavations there in the early twentieth century yielded some of the most spectacular discoveries ever made in the ancient Near East. Between circa 2100 and 2000 B.C.E., Ur was the royal capital of the Third Dynasty of Ur, whose kings assembled a highly organized bureaucracy to govern a realm that included much of what is now Iraq as well as part of Iran. Around 2000 B.C.E., the Ur Kingdom was brought to an end; its last king, Ibbi-Suen, was carried off into captivity and the city was ransacked, its temples desecrated. Modern historians have deduced that the fall of Ur resulted from a combination of factors: internal social stresses, pressure from "barbarian" outsiders, and invasion by the army of the neighboring kingdom of Elam (in what is now western Iran). But in this lamentation (and in other examples of this literary genre), as you will see, it is the Sumerian gods— especially the great deities Enlil, Enki, An, and Ninhursag—whose decision brings the devastation of both Ur and its temple (which is the house of the city's patron god Nanna-Suen) as well as the other great cities and temples of Sumer. But what the great gods can remove, they also can restore.

From The Electronic Text Corpus of Sumerian Literature, http://etcsl.orinst.ox.ac.uk/ cgi-bin?text=t.2.2.3.

To overturn the appointed times, to obliterate the divine plans, the storms gather to strike like a flood.

An, Enlil, Enki and Ninḫursaĝa have decided its fate—to overturn the divine powers of Sumer, to lock up the favourable reign in its home, to destroy the city, to destroy the house, to destroy the cattle-pen, to level the sheepfold; that the cattle should not stand in the pen, that the sheep should not multiply in the fold, that watercourses should carry brackish water, that weeds should grow in the fertile fields, that mourning plants should grow in the open country,

that the mother should not seek out her child, that the father should not say "O my dear wife!", that the junior wife should take no joy in his embrace, that the young child should not grow vigorous on his knee, that the wet-nurse should not sing lullabies; to change the location of kingship, to defile the seeking of oracles, to take kingship away from the Land, to cast the eye of the storm on all the land, to obliterate the divine plans by the order of An and Enlil;

after An had frowned upon all the lands, after Enlil had looked favourably on an enemy land, after Nintur had scattered the creatures that she had created, after Enki had altered the course of the

Tigris and Euphrates, after Utu had cast his curse on the roads and highways;

so as to obliterate the divine powers of Sumer, to change its preordained plans, to alienate the divine powers of the reign of kingship of Urim, to humiliate the princely son in his house E-kiš-nu-ĝal, to break up the unity of the people of Nanna, numerous as ewes; to change the food offerings of Urim, the shrine of magnificent food offerings; that its people should no longer dwell in their quarters, that they should be given over to live in an inimical place; that Šimaški and Elam, the enemy, should dwell in their place; that its shepherd, in his own palace, should be captured by the enemy, that Ibbi-Suen should be taken to the land Elam in fetters, that from Mount Zabu on the edge of the sea to the borders of Anšan, like a swallow that has flown from its house, he should never return to his city;

that on the two parallel banks of the Tigris and of the Euphrates bad weeds should grow, that no one should set out on the road, that no one should seek out the highway, that the city and its settled surroundings should be razed to ruin-mounds; that its numerous black-headed people should be slaughtered; that the hoe should not attack the fertile fields, that seed should not be planted in the ground, that the melody of the cowherds' songs should not resound in the open country, that butter and cheese should not be made in the cattle-pen, that dung should not be stacked on the ground, that the shepherd should not enclose the sacred sheepfold with a fence, that the song of the churning should not resound in the sheepfold;

to decimate the animals of the open country, to finish off all living things, that the four-legged creatures of Šakkan should lay no more dung on the ground, that the marshes should be so dry as to be full of cracks and have no new seed, that sickly-headed reeds should grow in the reedbeds and come to an end in a stinking morass, that there should be no new growth in the orchards, that it should all collapse by itself—so as quickly to subdue Urim like a roped ox, to bow its neck to the ground: the great charging wild bull, confident in its own strength, the primeval city of lordship and kingship, built on sacred ground.

Its fate cannot be changed. Who can overturn it? It is the command of An and Enlil. Who can oppose it?

An frightened the very dwellings of Sumer, the people were afraid. Enlil blew an evil storm, silence lay upon the city. Nintur bolted the door of the storehouses of the Land. Enki blocked the water in the Tigris and the Euphrates. Utu took away the pronouncement of equity and justice. Inana handed over victory in strife and battle to a rebellious land. Ninĝirsu poured Sumer away like milk to the dogs. Turmoil descended upon the Land, something that no one had ever known, something unseen, which had no name, something that could not be fathomed. The lands were confused in their fear. The god of the city turned away, its shepherd vanished.

The people, in their fear, breathed only with difficulty. The storm immobilised them, the storm did not let them return. There was no return for them, the storm did not retreat. This is what Enlil, the shepherd of the black-headed people, did: Enlil, to destroy the loyal households, to decimate the loyal men, to put the evil eye on the sons of the loyal men, on the first-born, Enlil then sent

down Gutium from the mountains. Their advance was as the flood of Enlil that cannot be withstood. The great wind of the countryside filled the countryside, it advanced before them. The extensive countryside was destroyed, no one moved about there.

The dark time was roasted by hailstones and flames. The bright time was wiped out by a shadow. {In the darkness, noses were heaped up, heads were smashed. The storm was a harrow coming from above, the city was struck by a hoe.} On that day, heaven rumbled, the earth trembled, the storm worked without respite. Heaven was darkened, it was covered by a shadow; the mountains roared. Utu lay down at the horizon, dust passed over the mountains. Nanna lay at the zenith, the people were afraid. The city's god left his dwelling and stood aside. The foreigners in the city even chased away its dead. Large trees were uprooted, the forest growth was ripped out. The orchards were stripped of their fruit, they were cleaned of their offshoots. The crop drowned while it was still on the stalk, the yield of the grain diminished.

They piled . . . up in heaps, they spread . . . out like sheaves. There were corpses floating in the Euphrates, weapons smashed heads. The father turned away from his wife saying "This is not my wife!" The mother turned away from her child saying "This is not my child!" He who had a productive estate neglected his estate saying "This is not my estate!" The rich man took an unfamiliar path away from his possessions. In those days the kingship of the Land was defiled. The tiara and crown that had been on the king's head were both spoiled. The lands that had followed the same path were split into disunity. The food offerings of Urim, the shrine of magnificent food offerings, were changed for the worse. Nanna traded away his people, numerous as ewes.

Its king sat immobilised in his own palace. Ibbi-Suen was sitting in anguish in his own palace. In E-namtila, his place of delight, he wept bitterly. The flood dashing a hoe on the ground was levelling everything. Like a great storm it roared over the earth—who could escape it?—to destroy the city, to destroy the house, so that traitors would lie on top of loyal men and the blood of traitors flow upon loyal men.

*   *   *

Kazallu, the city of teeming multitudes, was cast into confusion. Numušda took an unfamiliar path away from the city, his beloved dwelling. His wife Namrat, the beautiful lady, was lamenting bitterly. "Alas, the destroyed city, my destroyed house," she cried bitterly. Its river bed was empty, no water flowed. Like a river cursed by Enki its opening channel was dammed up. On the fields fine grains grew no more, people had nothing to eat. The orchards were scorched like an oven, its open country was scattered. The four-legged wild animals did not run about. The four-legged creatures of Šakkan could find no rest.

Lugal-Marda stepped outside his city. Ninzuana took an unfamiliar path away from her beloved dwelling. "Alas, the destroyed city, my destroyed house," she cried bitterly. Isin, the shrine that was not a quay, was split by onrushing waters. Ninisina, the mother of the Land, wept bitter tears. "Alas, the destroyed city, my destroyed house," she cried bitterly. Enlil smote Dur-an-ki with a mace. Enlil made lamentation in his city, the shrine Nibru. Mother Ninlil, the lady of the Ki-ur shrine, wept bitter tears. "Alas, the destroyed city, my destroyed house," she cried bitterly.

*   *   *

On that day the word of Enlil was an attacking storm. Who could fathom it? The word of Enlil was destruction on the right, was . . . on the left. This is what Enlil, the one who determines destinies, did: Enlil brought down the Elamites, the enemy, from the highlands. Nanše, the noble daughter, was settled outside the city. Fire approached Ninmarki in the shrine Gu-aba. Large boats were carrying off its silver and lapis lazuli. The lady, sacred Ninmarki, was despondent because of her perished goods. On that day he decreed a storm blazing like the mouth of a fire. The province of Lagaš was handed over to Elam. And then the queen also reached the end of her time.

Bau, as if she were human, also reached the end of her time: "Woe is me! Enlil has handed over the city to the storm. He has handed it over to the storm that destroys cities. He has handed it over to the storm that destroys houses." Dumuzid-abzu was full of fear in the house of Kinirša. Kinirša, the city to which she belongs, was ordered to be plundered. The city of Nanše, Niĝin, was delivered to the foreigners. Sirara, her beloved dwelling, was handed over to the evil ones. "Alas, the destroyed city, my destroyed house," she cried bitterly. Its sacred Ĝipar of *en* priesthood was defiled. Its *en* priest was snatched from the Ĝipar and carried off to enemy territory.

*   *   *

Enlil threw open the door of the grand gate to the wind. In Urim no one went to fetch food, no one went to fetch water. Its people rushed around like water being poured from a well. Their strength ebbed away, they could not even go on their way. Enlil afflicted the city with an evil famine. He afflicted the city with that which destroys cities, that which destroys houses. He afflicted the city with that which cannot be withstood with weapons. He afflicted the city with dissatisfaction and treachery. In Urim, which was like a solitary reed, there was not even fear. Its people, like fish being grabbed in a pond, sought to escape. Its young and old lay spread about, no one could rise.

At the royal station there was no food on top of the platform. The king who used to eat marvellous food grabbed at a mere ration. As the day grew dark, the eye of the sun was eclipsing, the people experienced hunger. There was no beer in the beer-hall, there was no more malt for it. There was no food for him in his palace, it was unsuitable to live in. Grain did not fill his lofty storehouse, he could not save his life. The grain-piles and granaries of Nanna held no grain. The evening meal in the great dining hall of the gods was defiled. Wine and syrup ceased to flow in the great dining hall. The butcher's knife that used to slay oxen and sheep lay hungry. Its mighty oven no longer cooked oxen and sheep, it no longer emitted the aroma of roasting meat. The sounds of the *bursaĝ* building, the pure . . . of Nanna, were stilled. The house which used to bellow like a bull was silenced. Its holy deliveries were no longer fulfilled, its . . . were alienated. The mortar, pestle and grinding stone lay idle; no one bent down over them.

The Shining Quay of Nanna was silted up. The sound of water against the boat's prow ceased, there was no rejoicing. Dust piled up in the *un-uribanda* of Nanna. The rushes grew, the rushes grew, the mourning reeds grew. Boats and barges ceased docking at the Shining Quay. Nothing moved on your watercourse which was fit for barges. The plans of the festivals at the place of the divine rituals were altered. The boat with first-fruit offerings of the father who begot Nanna no longer brought first-fruit offerings. Its food offerings could not be taken to Enlil in Nibru. Its watercourse was empty, barges could not travel.

*   *   *

Suen wept to his father Enlil: "O father who begot me, why have you turned away from my city which was built (?) for you? O Enlil, why have you turned away from my Urim which was built (?) for you? The boat with first-fruit offerings no longer brings first-fruit offerings to the father who begot him. Your food offerings can no longer be brought to Enlil in Nibru. The *en* priests of the countryside and city have been carried off by phantoms. Urim, like a city raked by a hoe, is to be counted as a ruin-mound. The Du-ur, Enlil's resting-place, has become a haunted shrine. O Enlil, gaze upon your city, an empty wasteland. Gaze upon your city Nibru, an empty wasteland."

"The dogs of Urim no longer sniff at the base of the city wall. The man who used to drill large wells scratches the ground in the market place. My father who begot me, enclose in your embrace my city which is all alone. Enlil, return to your embrace my Urim which is all alone. Enclose in your embrace my E-kiš-nu-ĝal which is all alone. May

you bring forth offspring in Urim, may you multiply its people. May you restore the divine powers of Sumer that have been forgotten."

Enlil then answered his son Suen: "There is lamentation in the haunted city, reeds of mourning grow there. {In its midst there is lamentation, reeds of mourning grow there.} In its midst the people pass their days in sighing. {My son, the noble son . . . , why do you concern yourself with crying?} Oh Nanna, the noble son . . . , why do you concern yourself with crying? The judgment uttered by the assembly cannot be reversed. The word of An and Enlil knows no overturning. Urim was indeed given kingship but it was not given an eternal reign. From time immemorial, since the Land was founded, until people multiplied, who has ever seen a reign of kingship that would take precedence for ever? The reign of its kingship had been long indeed but had to exhaust itself. O my Nanna, do not exert yourself in vain, abandon your city."

Then my king, the noble son, became distraught. Lord Ašimbabbar, the noble son, grieved. Nanna who loves his city left his city. Suen took an unfamiliar path away from his beloved Urim. In order to go as an exile from her city to foreign territory, Ningal quickly clothed herself and left the city. The Anuna stepped outside of Urim.

*   *   *

In the city, those who had not been felled by weapons succumbed to hunger. Hunger filled the city like water, it would not cease. This hunger contorted people's faces, twisted their muscles. Its people were as if drowning in a pond, they gasped for breath. Its king breathed heavily in his own palace. Its people dropped their weapons, their weapons hit the ground. They struck their necks with their hands and cried. They sought counsel with each other, they searched for clarification: "Alas, what can we say about it? What more can we add to it? How long until we are finished off by this catastrophe? Inside Urim there is death, outside it there is death. Inside it we are to be finished off by famine. Outside it we are to be finished off by Elamite weapons. In Urim the enemy oppresses us, oh, we are finished."

*   *   *

There was no eloquence in the Dubla-maḫ, the place where oaths used to be taken. The throne was not set up at its place of judgment, justice was not administered. Alamuš threw down his sceptre, his hands trembling. In the sacred bedchamber of Nanna musicians no longer played the *balaĝ* drum. The sacred box that no one had set eyes upon was seen by the enemy. The divine bed was not set up, it was not spread with clean hay. The statues that were in the shrine were cut down. The cook, the dream interpreter, and the seal keeper did not perform the ceremonies properly. They stood by submissively and were carried off by the foreigners. The priests of the holy *uzga* shrine and the sacred lustrations, the linen-clad priests, forsook the divine plans and sacred divine powers, they went off to a foreign city.

In his grief Suen approached his father. He went down on his knee in front of Enlil, the father who begot him: "O father who begot me, how long will the enemy eye be cast upon my account, how long . . . ? The lordship and the kingship that you bestowed . . . , Father Enlil, the one who advises with just words, the wise words of the Land . . . , your inimical judgment . . . , look into your darkened heart, terrifying like waves. O Father Enlil, the fate that you have decreed cannot be explained, as for my hairstyle (?) of lordship and the diadem with which I was crowned." . . . he put on a garment of mourning.

Enlil then provided a favourable response to his son Suen: "My son, the city built for you in joy and prosperity was given to you as your reign. Destroying the city, overthrowing its great wall and battlements: all this too is part of that reign. . . . the black, black days of the reign that has been your lot. As for dwelling in your home, the E-temen-ni-guru, that was properly built—indeed Urim shall be rebuilt in splendour, the people shall bow down to you. There is to be bounty at its base, there is to be grain. There is to be splendour at its top, the sun shall rejoice there. Let an abundance of grain embrace its table. May Urim, the city whose fate was pronounced by An, be restored for you." Having pronounced his blessing, Enlil raised his head toward the heavens: "May the land, south and highland, be organised for Nanna. May the roads of the mountains be set in order for Suen. Like a cloud hugging the earth, they shall submit to him. By order of An and Enlil it shall be conferred."

*   *   *

REVIEW QUESTIONS

1. What does this text suggest about the relationship between the gods and humankind?
2. Does this text offer some evidence as to what were considered the most important assets of a Sumerian city?

Letters of Royal Women of the Old Babylonian Period

Women's voices, though not completely silent, are all too infrequently heard in the documents of ancient Mesopotamia. Excavations earlier in this century recovered major portions of the palace archives (dating to the early second millennium B.C.E.)

of the northern Mesopotamian cities of Mari and Karana, including cuneiform tab-
lets containing letters to and from women of the royal houses of both places.

From *Mari and Karana: Two Old Babylonian Cities,* by Stephanie Dalley (Glenview, Ill.: Addison-Wesley Longman, 1984), pp. 104–9.

*   *   *

Speak to Iltani, thus Yasitna-abum your son. May Shamash and Marduk grant that my mother live forever for my sake. My mother called my name, and my heart came alive. Now, do send me a letter saying how you are, and give me new life. Whenever I reread your letter, the dust-storms of Adad are forgotten; my heart is replenished with life. The servant boy whom my mother sent to me is far too young. For that servant boy does not keep *me* regularly supplied; it is I who have to keep *him* regularly supplied! Whenever I go on a journey, not even so much as 2 litres of bread for my ration is carried behind me. May my mother send me another servant boy who will be able to carry 10 litres of bread for my ration behind me, and who will be able really to help.

*   *   *

Speak to my lady; thus Belassunu. Ever since the harvest I have written frequently to you, but you have never sent me a reply of any kind. The king had spoken to me saying, "Stay in Zarbat. As soon as I come, Usi-nawir will come with me, and he will let you plead your innocence." Now, why are you silent? He neither lets me plead my innocence nor lets me go. You are near the ruler where you are: write, that they may take me back to the ruler. What have I done wrong? Why have you frowned upon me, and not pleaded my cause? Who will deal with the matter, and who has turned to help me?

*   *   *

Speak to my lord; thus Iltani thy servant. My lord wrote to me about letting go the oxen, sheep and donkeys belonging to Tazabru, saying: "If you do not let them go, I shall cut you into twelve pieces." That is what my lord wrote to me. Why

has my lord written my death sentence to me? Only yesterday I spoke to my lord saying it was his own shepherd who had in the past kept his oxen and his sheep; he was pasturing them in Yashibatum. That is what I told my lord. Now, let my lord simply write that they are to take his oxen and sheep away from Yashibatum. If I have taken any of his oxen or sheep, may my lord inflict the punishment on me. Would I, without my lord's permission, would I have laid hands on and taken anything? Why then has my lord written my death sentence?

*   *   *

Speak to Iltani, my sister; thus Lamassani. I am well. The caravan comes regularly. You have never written to me to say how you are. I am still looking for a necklace of lapis lazuli, for which you wrote to me, and I shall send you a serving woman with it, but until now I have not found what you wrote for, and so I have not yet sent a slavegirl. Are you not aware that I am receiving short rations of barley? For in the city of Ashur, barley is expensive and linseed oil is expensive. Your son Sin-rimeni often comes and goes, but you have never mentioned me to him; you have not heaped honour on my head in the household where I am staying. As you must be aware, I am receiving short rations: please provide me with barley and linseed oil.

*   *   *

Speak to Iltani my sister, thus Amat-Shamash your sister. May my divine lord and lady grant that you live forever for my sake. Previously when Aqba-hammu came to Sippar I gave him cause to honour my priesthood, and he honoured me greatly, for he said to me: "When I go back to Karana, write to me and I shall send you a boat full of whatever you need. Offer a prayer for me to your divine lord." Now, I have written, and he has provided me with two servants. But you have not recalled my name; you never even sent me so much as a single jar of perfume; you never said: "Approach and offer a prayer for me to your divine lady." Instead you say: "What do you think I am for?" Apart from you, does a girl who has washed her husband's feet for one day not send her own sister provisions from then onwards? And the slaves whom my father gave me have grown old. Now, I have sent half a mina of silver to the king. Allow me my claim, and let him send to me slaves that have been captured recently, and who are trustworthy. Now, in recollection of you, I have sent to you five minas of first-rate wool and a basket of "shrimps."

*   *   *

Speak to the lady my mother, thus Erishti-Aya your daughter. May my divine lord and lady grant you long life for my sake. Why didn't you ever wear my dress, but sent it back to me, and made me dishonoured and accursed? I am your daughter, and you are the wife of a king. . . . Your husband and you put me into the cloister; but the soldiers who were taken captive pay me more respect than you! You should pay me respect, and then my divine lord and lady will honour you with the good opinion of the city and its inhabitants. I am sending you a nanny. Do send me something to make me happy, and then I will be happy. Don't neglect me.

*   *   *

Speak to my star, my father and my lord, thus your daughter Kiru. It really was a sign when I spoke to you in the courtyard saying: "You are going away, and so you will not be able to direct the country; the country will become hostile behind you." That is what I said to my father and lord, but he didn't listen to me. . . . Now, if I am truly a woman, may my lord and father pay heed to my words—I am always writing the words of the gods to my father!

*   *   *

About my worries I have written twice to my lord, and my lord has written to me saying: "Go into Ashlakka and don't cry." My lord wrote that to me, and now I have entered Ashlakka and my worries have been fully justified! The wife of Ibal-Addu is queen all right; that woman takes it upon herself to receive personally every delivery for Ashlakka city and its towns. She made me sit in a corner holding my head in my hands like any idiot woman. Food and drink were regularly put in front of her, while my eyes envied and my mouth watered. She put a strong guard on me, and took no notice at all of appeals in my lord's name. So my fears have been fulfilled here . . . May my lord send someone to fetch me back to my lord, that I may look upon my lord's face.

*   *   *

REVIEW QUESTIONS

1. What kinds of roles and responsibilities did these women have?
2. What were their relationships with the other members of their families and households?

FROM The Instructions of Ptah-hotep

In contrast to ancient Mesopotamia, no ancient Egyptian law code has survived, although various texts suggest that laws did indeed exist. This document, however, provides an excellent description of proper behavior in personal relations and, im-

plicitly, a sense of Egyptian social values, at least among the elite. Dating perhaps as early as the late Old Kingdom, this text is presented as the instructions of the vizier (the most important royal official under the king himself), Ptah-hotep, to his son.

From *Ancient Egyptian Literature,* vol. 1, *The Old and Middle Kingdoms,* by Miriam Lichtheim (Berkeley: University of California Press, 1973), pp. 205–9.

Instruction of the Mayor of the city, the Vizier Ptahhotep, under the Majesty of King Isesi, who lives for all eternity. The mayor of the city, the vizier Ptahhotep, said:

O king, my lord!
Age is here, old age arrived,
Feebleness came, weakness grows,
Childlike one sleeps all day.
Eyes are dim, ears deaf,
Strength is waning through weariness,
The mouth, silenced, speaks not,
The heart, void, recalls not the past,
The bones ache throughout.
Good has become evil, all taste is gone,
What age does to people is evil in everything.
The nose, clogged, breathes not,
Painful are standing and sitting.

May this servant be ordered to make a staff of old
    age,
So as to tell him the words of those who heard,
The ways of the ancestors,
Who have listened to the gods.
May such be done for you,
So that strife may be banned from the people,
And the Two Shores may serve you!
Said the majesty of this god:
Instruct him then in the sayings of the past,
May he become a model for the children of the
    great,
May obedience enter him,
And the devotion of him who speaks to him,
No one is born wise.

Beginning of the formulations of excellent discourse spoken by the Prince, Count, God's Father, God's beloved, Eldest Son of the King, of his body, Mayor of the city and Vizier, Ptahhotep, in instructing the ignorant in knowledge and in the standard of excellent discourse, as profit for him who will hear, as woe to him who would neglect them. He spoke to his son:

1. Don't be proud of your knowledge,
    Consult the ignorant and the wise;
    The limits of art are not reached,
    No artist's skills are perfect;
    Good speech is more hidden than greenstone,
    Yet may be found among maids at the
        grindstones.

2. If you meet a disputant in action,
    A powerful man, superior to you,
    Fold your arms, bend your back,
    To flout him will not make him agree with you.
    Make little of the evil speech
    By not opposing him while he's in action;
    He will be called an ignoramus,
    Your self-control will match his pile of words.

3. If you meet a disputant in action
    Who is your equal, on your level,
    You will make your worth exceed his by
        silence,
    While he is speaking evilly,
    There will be much talk by the hearers,
    Your name will be good in the mind of the
        magistrates.

4. If you meet a disputant in action,
    A poor man, not your equal,
    Do not attack him because he is weak,
    Let him alone, he will confute himself.
    Do not answer him to relieve your heart,
    Do not vent yourself against your opponent,
    Wretched is he who injures a poor man,
    One will wish to do what you desire,

You will beat him through the magistrates'
   reproof.

5. If you are a man who leads,
    Who controls the affairs of the many,
    Seek out every beneficent deed,
    That your conduct may be blameless.
    Great is justice, lasting in effect,
    Unchallenged since the time of Osiris.
    One punishes the transgressor of laws,
    Though the greedy overlooks this;
    Baseness may seize riches,
    Yet crime never lands its wares;
    In the end it is justice that lasts,
    Man says: "It is my father's ground."

6. Do not scheme against people,
    God punishes accordingly:
    If a man says: "I shall live by it,"
    He will lack bread for his mouth.
    If a man says: "I shall be rich,"
    He will have to say: "My cleverness has
      snared me."
    If he says: "I will snare for myself,"
    He will be unable to say: "I snared for my
      profit."
    If a man says: "I will rob someone,"
    He will end being given to a stranger.
    People's schemes do not prevail,
    God's command is what prevails;
    Live then in the midst of peace,
    What they give comes by itself.

7. If you are one among guests
    At the table of one greater than you,
    Take what he gives as it is set before you;
    Look at what is before you,
    Don't shoot many glances at him,
    Molesting him offends the *ka*.[1]
    Don't speak to him until he summons,
    One does not know what may displease;
    Speak when he has addressed you,
    Then your words will please the heart.

---

[1] The term *ka* represents a complex concept linked to an individual's life force.

The nobleman, when he is behind food,
Behaves as his *ka* commands him;
He will give to him whom he favors,
It is the custom when night has come.
It is the *ka* that makes his hands reach out,
The great man gives to the chosen man;
Thus eating is under the counsel of god,
A fool is who complains of it.

8. If you are a man of trust,
    Sent by one great man to another,
    Adhere to the nature of him who sent you,
    Give his message as he said it.
    Guard against reviling speech,
    Which embroils one great with another;
    Keep to the truth, don't exceed it,
    But an outburst should not be repeated.
    Do not malign anyone,
    Great or small, the *ka* abhors it.

9. If you plow and there's growth in the field,
    And god lets it prosper in your hand,
    Do not boast at your neighbors' side,
    One has great respect for the silent man:
    Man of character is man of wealth.
    If he robs he is like a crocodile in court.
    Don't impose on one who is childless,
    Neither decry nor boast of it;
    There is many a father who has grief,
    And a mother of children less content than
      another;
    It is the lonely whom god fosters,
    While the family man prays for a follower.

10. If you are poor, serve a man of worth,
    That all your conduct may be well with the
      god.
    Do not recall if he once was poor,
    Don't be arrogant toward him
    For knowing his former state;
    Respect him for what has accrued to him,
    For wealth does not come by itself.
    It is their law for him whom they love,
    His gain, he gathered it himself;
    It is the god who makes him worthy
    And protects him while he sleeps.

THE NARMER PALETTE (C. 3100 B.C.E.)

Found at Hierakonpolis in Upper Egypt and dating to around 3100 B.C.E., this schist palette bears images of a king named Narmer, whom some scholars identify with the king Menes who later Egyptian tradition identified as the first king to unify Upper and Lower Egypt. On one side of the palette (left), Narmer, wearing the crown of Upper Egypt, wields a mace against a captive. On the other side (right), where he wears the crown of Lower Egypt, Narmer inspects the aftermath of battle. Below, we see two animals with intertwined necks, a motif borrowed from the art of Iran and Mesopotamia. What images here suggest that Narmer claims to rule a unified Egypt? Was the process of unification peaceful? Do aspects of this image indicate the king's higher status? Is there evidence of Egyptian contact with Southwest Asia? How might that contact have been achieved?

11. Follow your heart as long as you live,
    Do no more than is required,
    Do not shorten the time of "follow-the-heart,"
    Trimming its moment offends the *ka*.
    Don't waste time on daily cares
    Beyond providing for your household;
    When wealth has come, follow your heart,
    Wealth does no good if one is glum!

12. If you are a man of worth
    And produce a son by the grace of god,
    If he is straight, takes after you,
    Takes good care of your possessions,
    Do for him all that is good,
    He is your son, your *ka* begot him,
    Don't withdraw your heart from him.
    But an offspring can make trouble:
    If he strays, neglects your counsel,
    Disobeys all that is said,
    His mouth spouting evil speech,
    Punish him for all his talk!
    They hate him who crosses you,
    His guilt was fated in the womb;
    He whom they guide can not go wrong,
    Whom they make boatless can not cross.

13. If you are in the antechamber,
    Stand and sit as fits your rank,
    Which was assigned you the first day.
    Do not trespass—you will be turned back,
    Keen is the face to him who enters announced,
    Spacious the seat of him who has been called.
    The antechamber has a rule,
    All behavior is by measure;
    It is the god who gives advancement,
    He who uses elbows is not helped.

14. If you are among the people,
    Gain supporters through being trusted;
    The trusted man who does not vent his
        belly's speech,
    He will himself become a leader.
    A man of means—what is he like?
    Your name is good, you are not maligned,
    Your body is sleek, your face benign,
    One praises you without your knowing.

He whose heart obeys his belly
Puts contempt of himself in place of love,
His heart is bald, his body unanointed;
The great-hearted is god-given,
He who obeys his belly belongs to the
    enemy.

15. Report your commission without faltering,
    Give your advice in your master's council.
    If he is fluent in his speech,
    It will not be hard for the envoy to report,
    Nor will he be answered, "Who is he to
        know it?"
    As to the master, his affairs will fail
    If he plans to punish him for it,
    He should be silent upon hearing: "I have
        told."

16. If you are a man who leads,
    Whose authority reaches wide,
    You should do outstanding things,
    Remember the day that comes after.
    No strife will occur in the midst of honors,
    But where the crocodile enters hatred arises.

17. If you are a man who leads,
    Listen calmly to the speech of one who
        pleads;
    Don't stop him from purging his body
    Of that which he planned to tell.
    A man in distress wants to pour out his heart
    More than that his case be won.
    About him who stops a plea
    One says: "Why does he reject it?"
    Not all one pleads for can be granted,
    But a good hearing soothes the heart.

18. If you want friendship to endure
    In the house you enter
    As master, brother, or friend,
    In whatever place you enter,
    Beware of approaching the women!
    Unhappy is the place where it is done,
    Unwelcome is he who intrudes on them.
    A thousand men are turned away from their
        good:

A short moment like a dream,
Then death comes for having known them.
Poor advice is "shoot the opponent,"
When one goes to do it the heart rejects it.
He who fails through lust of them,
No affair of his can prosper.

19. If you want a perfect conduct,
    To be free from every evil,
    Guard against the vice of greed:
    A grievous sickness without cure,
    There is no treatment for it.
    It embroils fathers, mothers,
    And the brothers of the mother,
    It parts wife from husband;
    It is a compound of all evils,
    A bundle of all hateful things.
    That man endures whose rule is rightness,
    Who walks a straight line;
    He will make a will by it,
    The greedy has no tomb.

20. Do not be greedy in the division,
    Do not covet more than your share;
    Do not be greedy toward your kin,
    The mild has a greater claim than the harsh.
    Poor is he who shuns his kin,
    He is deprived of interchange.
    Even a little of what is craved
    Turns a quarreler into an amiable man.

21. When you prosper and found your house,
    And love your wife with ardor,
    Fill her belly, clothe her back,
    Ointment soothes her body.
    Gladden her heart as long as you live,
    She is a fertile field for her lord.
    Do not contend with her in court,
    Keep her from power, restrain her—
    Her eye is her storm when she gazes—
    Thus will you make her stay in your
        house. * * *

22. Sustain your friends with what you have,
    You have it by the grace of god;
    Of him who fails to sustain his friends

One says, "a selfish *ka*."
One plans the morrow but knows not what
    will be,
The right *ka* is the *ka* by which one is
    sustained.
If praiseworthy deeds are done,
Friends will say, "welcome!"
One does not bring supplies to town,
One brings friends when there is need.

23. Do not repeat calumny,
    Nor should you listen to it,
    It is the spouting of the hot-bellied.
    Report a thing observed, not heard,
    If it is negligible, don't say anything,
    He who is before you recognizes worth.
    If a seizure is ordered and carried out,
    Hatred will arise against him who seizes;
    Calumny is like a dream against which one
        covers the face.

24. If you are a man of worth
    Who sits in his master's council,
    Concentrate on excellence,
    Your silence is better than chatter.
    Speak when you know you have a solution,
    It is the skilled who should speak in council;
    Speaking is harder than all other work,
    He who understands it makes it serve.

25. If you are mighty, gain respect through
        knowledge
    And through gentleness of speech.
    Don't command except as is fitting,
    He who provokes gets into trouble.
    Don't be haughty, lest you be humbled,
    Don't be mute, lest you be chided.
    When you answer one who is fuming,
    Avert your face, control yourself.
    The flame of the hot-heart sweeps across,
    He who steps gently, his path is paved.
    He who frets all day has no happy moment,
    He who's gay all day can't keep house. * * *

26. Don't oppose a great man's action,
    Don't vex the heart of one who is burdened;

If he gets angry at him who foils him,
The *ka* will part from him who loves him.
Yet he is the provider along with the god,
What he wishes should be done for him.
When he turns his face back to you after
    raging,
There will be peace from his *ka;*
As ill will comes from opposition,
So goodwill increases love.

27. Teach the great what is useful to him,
Be his aid before the people;
If you let his knowledge impress his lord,
Your sustenance will come from his *ka.*
As the favorite's belly is filled,
So your back will be clothed by it,
And his help will be there to sustain you.
For your superior whom you love
And who lives by it,
He in turn will give you good support.
Thus will love of you endure
In the belly of those who love you,
He is a *ka* who loves to listen.

28. If you are a magistrate of standing,
Commissioned to satisfy the many,
Hew a straight line.
When you speak don't lean to one side,
Beware lest one complain:
"Judges, he distorts the matter!"
And your deed turns into a judgment of you.

29. If you are angered by a misdeed,
Lean toward a man on account of his
    rightness;
Pass it over, don't recall it,
Since he was silent to you the first day.

30. If you are great after having been humble,
Have gained wealth after having been poor
In the past, in a town which you know,
Knowing your former condition,
Do not put trust in your wealth,
Which came to you as gift of god;
So that you will not fall behind one like you,
To whom the same has happened.

31. Bend your back to your superior,
Your overseer from the palace;
Then your house will endure in its
    wealth,
Your rewards in their right place.
Wretched is he who opposes a superior,
One lives as long as he is mild,
Baring the arm does not hurt it.
Do not plunder a neighbor's house,
Do not steal the goods of one near you,
Lest he denounce you before you are
    heard.
A quarreler is a mindless person,
If he is known as an aggressor
The hostile man will have trouble in the
    neighborhood.

*   *   *

33. If you probe the character of a friend,
Don't inquire, but approach him,
Deal with him alone,
So as not to suffer from his manner.
Dispute with him after a time,
Test his heart in conversation;
If what he has seen escapes him,
If he does a thing that annoys you,
Be yet friendly with him, don't attack,
Be restrained, don't let fly,
Don't answer with hostility,
Neither part from him nor attack him;
His time does not fail to come,
One does not escape what is fated.

34. Be generous as long as you live,
What leaves the storehouse does not
    return;
It is the food to be shared which is
    coveted,
One whose belly is empty is an accuser;
One deprived becomes an opponent,
Don't have him for a neighbor.
Kindness is a man's memorial
For the years after the function.

35. Know your helpers, then you prosper,
Don't be mean toward your friends,

They are one's watered field,
And greater then one's riches,
For what belongs to one belongs to another.
The character of a son-of-man is profit to
    him;
Good nature is a memorial.

36. Punish firmly, chastise soundly,
    Then repression of crime becomes an
        example;
    Punishment except for crime
    Turns the complainer into an enemy.

37. If you take to wife a *špnt*[2]
    Who is joyful and known by her town,
    If she is fickle and likes the moment,
    Do not reject her, let her eat,
    The joyful brings happiness.

Epilogue

If you listen to my sayings,
All your affairs will go forward;
In their truth resides their value,
Their memory goes on in the speech of men,
Because of the worth of their precepts;
If every word is carried on,
They will not perish in this land.
If advice is given for the good,
The great will speak accordingly;
It is teaching a man to speak to posterity,
He who hears it becomes a master-hearer;
It is good to speak to posterity,
It will listen to it.

If a good example is set by him who leads,
He will be beneficent for ever,
His wisdom being for all time.
The wise feeds his *ba*[3] with what endures,
So that it is happy with him on earth.
The wise is known by his wisdom,

The great by his good actions;
His heart matches his tongue,
His lips are straight when he speaks;
He has eyes that see,
His ears are made to hear what will profit his son,
Acting with truth he is free of falsehood.
Useful is hearing to a son who hears;
If hearing enters the hearer,
The hearer becomes a listener,
Hearing well is speaking well.
Useful is hearing to one who hears,
Hearing is better than all else,
It creates good will.
How good for a son to grasp his father's words,
He will reach old age through them.

He who hears is beloved of god,
He whom god hates does not hear.
The heart makes of its owner a hearer or non-
    hearer,
Man's heart is his life-prosperity-health!
The hearer is one who hears what is said,
He who loves to hear is one who does what is
    said.
How good for a son to listen to his father,
How happy is he to whom it is said:
"The son, he pleases as a master of hearing."
The hearer of whom this is said,
He is well-endowed
And honored by his father;
His remembrance is in the mouth of the living,
Those on earth and those who will be.

If a man's son accepts his father's words,
No plan of his will go wrong.
Teach your son to be a hearer,
One who will be valued by the nobles;
One who guides his speech by what he was told,
One regarded as a hearer.
This son excels, his deeds stand out,
While failure follows him who hears not.
The wise wakes early to his lasting gain,
While the fool is hard pressed.

The fool who does not hear,
He can do nothing at all;

---

[2] No single translation of *špnt* has been agreed upon.

[3] Like *ka*, the term *ba* is a complex concept intimately related to one's individuality. It is somewhat analogous to
our concept of "soul."

He sees knowledge in ignorance,
Usefulness in harmfulness.
He does all that one detests
And is blamed for it each day;
He lives on that by which one dies,
His food is distortion of speech.
His sort is known to the officials,
Who say: "A living death each day."
One passes over his doings,
Because of his many daily troubles.

A son who hears is a follower of Horus,
It goes well with him when he has heard.
When he is old, has reached veneration,
He will speak likewise to his children,
Renewing the teaching of his father.
Every man teaches as he acts,
He will speak to the children,
So that they will speak to their children:
Set an example, don't give offense,
If justice stands firm your children will live.

*   *   *

Conceal your heart, control your mouth,
Then you will be known among the officials;
Be quite exact before your lord,
Act so that one will say to him: "He's the son of
    that one."
And those who hear it will say:
"Blessed is he to whom he was born!"
Be deliberate when you speak,
So as to say things that count;

Then the officials who listen will say:
"How good is what comes from his mouth!"
Act so that your lord will say of you:
"How good is he whom his father taught;
When he came forth from his body,
He told him all that was in his mind,
And he does even more than he was told."

Lo, the good son, the gift of god,
Exceeds what is told him by his lord,
He will do right when his heart is straight.
As you succeed me, sound in your body,
The king content with all that was done,
May you obtain many years of life!
Not small is what I did on earth,
I had one hundred and ten years of life
As gift of the king,
Honors exceeding those of the ancestors,
By doing justice for the king,
Until the state of veneration!

*   *   *

REVIEW QUESTIONS

1. According to Ptah-hotep, what are the most important virtues in proper human relations?
2. Are those virtues to be applied differently to people of different rank and social class?
3. How much importance is ascribed to the ability to fight physically?

The Story of Sinuhe

*This Middle Kingdom novel was one of the most popular works of Egyptian litera-
ture. It tells the tale of an Egyptian official named Sinuhe who became fearful in
the wake of the king's assassination and fled into self-imposed exile in Asia where,
despite much success, he finds himself longing for his homeland.*

From *Ancient Egyptian Literature*, vol. 1, *The Old and Middle Kingdoms*, by Miriam Lichtheim
(Berkeley: University of California Press, 1973), pp. 62–76.

The Prince, Count, Governor of the domains of the sovereign in the lands of the Asiatics, true and beloved Friend of the King, the Attendant Sinuhe, says:

I was an attendant who attended his lord, a servant of the royal harem, waiting on the Princess, the highly praised Royal Wife of King Sesostris in Khenemsut, the daughter of King Amenemhet in Kanefru, Nefru, the revered.

Year 30, third month of the inundation, day 7: the god ascended to his horizon. The King of Upper and Lower Egypt, *Sehetepibre*, flew to heaven and united with the sun disk, the divine body merging with its maker. Then the residence was hushed; hearts grieved; the great portals were shut; the courtiers were head-on-knee; the people moaned.

His majesty, however, had despatched an army to the land of the Tjemeh, with his eldest son as its commander, the good god Sesostris. He had been sent to smite the foreign lands and to punish those of Tjehenu. Now he was returning, bringing captives of the Tjehenu and cattle of all kinds beyond number. The officials of the palace sent to the western border to let the king's son know the event that had occurred at the court. The messengers met him on the road, reaching him at night. Not a moment did he delay. The falcon flew with his attendants, without letting his army know it.

But the royal sons who had been with him on this expedition had also been sent for. One of them was summoned while I was standing there. I heard his voice, as he spoke, while I was in the near distance. My heart fluttered, my arms spread out, a trembling befell all my limbs. I removed myself in leaps, to seek a hiding place. I put myself between two bushes, so as to leave the road to its traveler.

I set out southward. I did not plan to go to the residence. I believed there would be turmoil and did not expect to survive it. I crossed Maaty near Sycamore; I reached Isle-of-Snefru. I spent the day there at the edge of the cultivation. Departing at dawn I encountered a man who stood on the road. He saluted me while I was afraid of him. At dinner time I reached "Cattle-Quay." I crossed in a barge without a rudder, by the force of the westwind. I passed to the east of the quarry, at the height of "Mistress of the Red Mountain." Then I made my way northward. I reached the "Walls of the Ruler," which were made to repel the Asiatics and to crush the Sand-farers. I crouched in a bush for fear of being seen by the guard on duty upon the wall.

I set out at night. At dawn I reached Peten. I halted at "Isle-of-Kem-Wer." An attack of thirst overtook me; I was parched, my throat burned. I said, "This is the taste of death." I raised my heart and collected myself when I heard the lowing sound of cattle and saw Asiatics. One of their leaders, who had been in Egypt, recognized me. He gave me water and boiled milk for me. I went with him to his tribe. What they did for me was good.

Land gave me to land. I traveled to Byblos; I returned to Qedem. I spent a year and a half there. Then Ammunenshi, the ruler of Upper Retenu, took me to him, saying to me: "You will be happy with me; you will hear the language of Egypt." He said this because he knew my character and had heard of my skill, Egyptians who were with him having borne witness for me. He said to me: "Why have you come here? Has something happened at the residence?" I said to him: "King Sehetepibre departed to the horizon, and one did not know the circumstances." But I spoke in half-truths: "When I returned from the expedition to the land of the Tjemeh, it was reported to me and my heart grew faint. It carried me away on the path of flight, though I had not been talked about; no one had spat in my face; I had not heard a reproach; my name had not been heard in the mouth of the herald. I do not know what brought me to this country; it is as if planned by god. As if a Delta-man saw himself in Yebu, a marsh-man in Nubia."

Then he said to me: "How then is that land without that excellent god, fear of whom was throughout the lands like Sakhmet in a year of plague?" I said to him in reply: "Of course his son has entered into the palace, having taken his father's heritage.

He is a god without peer,
No other comes before him;
He is lord of knowledge, wise planner, skilled
   leader,
One goes and comes by his will.

He was the smiter of foreign lands,
While his father stayed in the palace,
He reported to him on commands carried out.

He is a champion who acts with his arm,
A fighter who has no equal,
When seen engaged in archery,
When joining the melee.

Horn-curber who makes hands turn weak,
His foes can not close ranks;
Keen-sighted he smashes foreheads,
None can withstand his presence.

Wide-striding he smites the fleeing,
No retreat for him who turns him his back;
Steadfast in time of attack,
He makes turn back and turns not his back.

Stouthearted when he sees the mass,
He lets not slackness fill his heart;
Eager at the sight of combat,
Joyful when he works his bow.

Clasping his shield he treads under foot,
No second blow needed to kill;
None can escape his arrow,
None turn aside his bow.

The Bowmen flee before him,
As before the might of the goddess;
As he fights he plans the goal,
Unconcerned about all else.

Lord of grace, rich in kindness,
He has conquered through affection;
His city loves him more than itself,
Acclaims him more than its own god.

Men outdo women in hailing him,
Now that he is king;

Victor while yet in the egg,
Set to be ruler since his birth.

Augmenter of those born with him,
He is unique, god-given;
Happy the land that he rules!

Enlarger of frontiers,
He will conquer southern lands,
While ignoring northern lands,
Though made to smite Asiatics and tread on
   Sand-farers!

"Send to him! Let him know your name as one who inquires while being far from his majesty. He will not fail to do good to a land that will be loyal to him."

He said to me: "Well then, Egypt is happy knowing that he is strong. But you are here. You shall stay with me. What I shall do for you is good."

He set me at the head of his children. He married me to his eldest daughter. He let me choose for myself of his land, of the best that was his, on his border with another land. It was a good land called Yaa. Figs were in it and grapes. It had more wine than water. Abundant was its honey, plentiful its oil. All kinds of fruit were on its trees. Barley was there and emmer, and no end of cattle of all kinds. Much also came to me because of the love of me; for he had made me chief of a tribe in the best part of his land. Loaves were made for me daily, and wine as daily fare, cooked meat, roast fowl, as well as desert game. For they snared for me and laid it before me, in addition to the catch of my hounds. Many sweets were made for me, and milk dishes of all kinds.

I passed many years, my children becoming strong men, each a master of his tribe. The envoy who came north or went south to the residence stayed with me. I let everyone stay with me. I gave water to the thirsty; I showed the way to him who had strayed; I rescued him who had been robbed. When Asiatics conspired to attack the Rulers of Hill-Countries, I opposed their movements. For this ruler of Retenu made me carry out numerous missions as commander of his troops. Every hill tribe against which I marched I vanquished, so that it was driven from the pasture of its wells. I plundered its cattle, carried off its families, seized their food, and killed people by my strong arm, by my bow, by my movements and my skillful plans. I won his heart and he loved me, for he recognized my valor. He set me at the head of his children, for he saw the strength of my arms.

There came a hero of Retenu,
To challenge me in my tent.
A champion was he without peer,
He had subdued it all.
He said he would fight with me,
He planned to plunder me,
He meant to seize my cattle
At the behest of his tribe.

The ruler conferred with me and I said: "I do not know him; I am not his ally, that I could walk about in his camp. Have I ever opened his back rooms or climbed over his fence? It is envy, because he sees me doing your commissions. I am indeed like a stray bull in a strange herd, whom the bull of the herd charges, whom the longhorn attacks. Is an inferior beloved when he becomes a superior? No Asiatic makes friends with a Delta-man. And what would make papyrus cleave to the mountain? If a bull loves combat, should a champion bull retreat for fear of being equaled? If he wishes to fight, let him declare his wish. Is there a god who does not know what he has ordained, and a man who knows how it will be?"

At night I strung my bow, sorted my arrows, practiced with my dagger, polished my weapons. When it dawned Retenu came. It had assembled its tribes; it had gathered its neighboring peoples; it was intent on this combat.

He came toward me while I waited, having placed myself near him. Every heart burned for me; the women jabbered. All hearts ached for me thinking: "Is there another champion who could fight him?" He raised his battle-axe and shield, while his armful of missiles fell toward me. When I had made his weapons attack me, I let his arrows pass me by without effect, one following the other. Then, when he charged me, I shot him, my arrow sticking in his neck. He screamed; he fell on his nose; I slew him with his axe. I raised my war cry over his back, while every Asiatic shouted. I gave praise to Mont, while his people mourned him. The ruler Ammunenshi took me in his arms.

Then I carried off his goods; I plundered his cattle. What he had meant to do to me I did to him. I took what was in his tent; I stripped his camp. Thus I became great, wealthy in goods, rich in herds. It was the god who acted, so as to show mercy to one with whom he had been angry, whom he had made stray abroad. For today his heart is appeased.

A fugitive fled his surroundings—
I am famed at home.
A laggard lagged from hunger—
I give bread to my neighbor.
A man left his land in nakedness—
I have bright clothes, fine linen.
A man ran for lack of one to send—
I am rich in servants.
My house is fine, my dwelling spacious—
My thoughts are at the palace!

Whichever god decreed this flight, have mercy, bring me home! Surely you will let me see the place in which my heart dwells! What is more important than that my corpse be buried in the land in which I was born! Come to my aid! What if the happy event should occur! May god pity me! May he act so as to make happy the end of one whom he punished! May his heart ache for one whom he forced to live abroad! If he is truly appeased today, may he hearken to the prayer of one far away! May he return one whom he made roam the earth to the place from which he carried him off!

May Egypt's king have mercy on me, that I may live by his mercy! May I greet the mistress of the land who is in the palace! May I hear the commands of her children! Would that my body were young again! For old age has come; feebleness has overtaken me. My eyes are heavy, my arms weak; my legs fail to follow. The heart is weary; death is near. May I be conducted to the city of eternity! May I serve the Mistress of All! May she speak well of me to her children; may she spend eternity above me!

Now when the majesty of King Kheperkare was told of the condition in which I was, his majesty sent word to me with royal gifts, in order to gladden the heart of this servant like that of a foreign ruler. And the royal children who were in his palace sent me their messages. Copy of the decree brought to this servant concerning his return to Egypt:

Horus: Living in Births; the Two Ladies: Living in Births; the King of Upper and Lower Egypt; *Kheperkare*; the Son of Re: *Sesostris*, who lives forever. Royal decree to the Attendant Sinuhe:

This decree of the King is brought to you to let you know: That you circled the foreign countries, going from Qedem to Retenu, land giving you to land, was the counsel of your own heart. What had you done that one should act against you? You had not cursed, so that your speech would be reproved. You had not spoken against the counsel of the nobles, that your words should have been rejected. This matter—it carried away your heart. It was not in my heart against you. This your heaven in the palace lives and prospers to this day. Her head is adorned with the kingship of the land; her children are in the palace. You will store riches which they give you; you will live on their bounty. Come back to Egypt! See the residence in which you lived! Kiss the ground at the great portals, mingle with the courtiers! For today you have begun to age. You have lost a man's strength. Think of the day of burial, the passing into reveredness.

A night is made for you with ointments and wrappings from the hand of Tait. A funeral procession is made for you on the day of burial; the mummy case is of gold, its head of lapis lazuli. The sky is above you as you lie in the hearse, oxen drawing you, musicians going before you. The dance of the *mww*-dancers is done at the door of your tomb; the offering-list is read to you; sacrifice is made before your offering-stone. Your tomb-pillars, made of white stone, are among those of the royal children. You shall not die abroad! Not shall Asiatics inter you. You shall not be wrapped in the skin of a ram to serve as your coffin. Too long a roaming of the earth! Think of your corpse, come back!

This decree reached me while I was standing in the midst of my tribe. When it had been read to me, I threw myself on my belly. Having touched the soil, I spread it on my chest. I strode around my camp shouting: "What compares with this which is done to a servant whom his heart led astray to alien lands? Truly good is the kindness that saves me from death! Your *ka* will grant me to reach my end, my body being at home!"

Copy of the reply to this decree:

The servant of the Palace, Sinuhe, says: In very good peace! Regarding the matter of this flight which this servant did in his ignorance. It is your *ka*, O good god, lord of the Two Lands, which Re loves and which Mont lord of Thebes favors; and Amun lord of Thrones-of-the-Two-Lands, and Sobk-Re lord of Sumenu, and Horus, Hathor, Atum with his Ennead, and Sopdu-Neferbau-Semseru the Eastern Horus, and the Lady of Yemet—may she enfold your head—and the conclave upon the flood, and Min-Horus of the hill-countries, and Wereret lady of Punt, Nut, Haroeris-Re, and all the gods of Egypt and the isles of the sea—may they give life and joy to your nostrils, may they endue you with their bounty, may they give you eternity without limit, infinity without bounds! May the fear of you resound in lowlands and highlands, for you have subdued all that the sun encircles! This is the prayer of this servant for his lord who saves from the West.

The lord of knowledge who knows people knew in the majesty of the palace that this servant was afraid to say it. It is like a thing too great to repeat. The great god, the peer of Re, knows the heart of one who has served him willingly. This servant is in the hand of one who thinks about him. He is placed under his care. Your Majesty is the conquering Horus; your arms vanquish all lands. May then your Majesty command to have brought to you the prince of Meki from Qedem, the mountain chiefs from Keshu, and the prince of Menus from the lands of the Fenkhu. They are rulers of renown who have grown up in the love of you. I do not mention Retenu—it belongs to you like your hounds.

Lo, this flight which the servant made—I did not plan it. It was not in my heart; I did not devise it. I do not know what removed me from my place. It was like a dream. As if a Delta-man saw himself in Yebu, a marsh-man in Nubia. I was not afraid; no one ran after me. I had not heard a reproach; my name was not heard in the mouth of the herald. Yet my flesh crept, my feet hurried, my heart drove me; the god who had willed this flight dragged me away. Nor am I a haughty man. He who knows his land respects men. Re has set the fear of you throughout the land, the dread of you in every foreign country. Whether I am at the residence, whether I am in this place, it is you who covers this horizon. The sun rises at your pleasure. The water in the river is drunk when you wish. The air of heaven is breathed at your bidding. This servant will hand over to the brood which this servant begot in this place. This servant has been sent for! Your Majesty will do as he wishes! One lives by the breath which you give. As Re, Horus, and Hathor love your august nose, may Mont lord of Thebes wish it to live forever!

I was allowed to spend one more day in Yaa, handing over my possessions to my children, my eldest son taking charge of my tribe; all my possessions became his—my serfs, my herds, my fruit, my fruit trees. This servant departed southward. I halted at Horusways. The commander in charge of the garrison sent a message to the residence to let it be known. Then his majesty sent a trusted overseer of the royal domains with whom were loaded ships, bearing royal gifts for the Asiatics who had come with me to escort me to Horusways. I called each one by his name, while every butler was at his task. When I had started and set sail, there was kneading and straining beside me, until I reached the city of Itj-tawy.

When it dawned, very early, they came to summon me. Ten men came and ten men went to usher me into the palace. My forehead touched the ground between the sphinxes, and the royal children stood in the gateway to meet me. The courtiers who usher through the forecourt set me on the way to the audience-hall. I found his majesty on the great throne in a kiosk of gold.

Stretched out on my belly, I did not know myself before him, while this god greeted me pleasantly. I was like a man seized by darkness. My *ba* was gone, my limbs trembled; my heart was not in my body, I did not know life from death.

His majesty said to one of the courtiers: "Lift him up, let him speak to me." Then his majesty said: "Now you have come, after having roamed foreign lands. Flight has taken its toll of you. You have aged, have reached old age. It is no small matter that your corpse will be interred without being escorted by Bowmen. But don't act thus, don't act thus, speechless though your name was called!" Fearful of punishment I answered with the answer of a frightened man: "What has my lord said to me, that I might answer it? It is not disrespect to the god! It is the terror which is in my body, like that which caused the fateful flight! Here I am before you. Life is yours. May your Majesty do as he wishes!"

Then the royal daughters were brought in, and his majesty said to the queen: "Here is Sinuhe, come as an Asiatic, a product of nomads!" She uttered a very great cry, and the royal daughters shrieked all together. They said to his majesty: "Is it really he, O king, our lord?" Said his majesty: "It is really he!" Now having brought with them their necklaces, rattles, and sistra, they held them out to his majesty.

Your hands upon the radiance, eternal king,
Jewels of heaven's mistress!
The Gold gives life to your nostrils,
The Lady of Stars enfolds you!

Southcrown fared north, northcrown south,
Joined, united by your majesty's word.
While the Cobra decks your brow,
You deliver the poor from harm.
Peace to you from Re, Lord of Lands!
Hail to you and the Mistress of All!

Slacken your bow, lay down your arrow,
Give breath to him who gasps for breath!
Give us our good gift on this good day,
Grant us the son of northwind, Bowman born
   in Egypt!

He made the flight in fear of you,
He left the land in dread of you!
A face that sees you shall not pale,
Eyes that see you shall not fear!

His majesty said: "He shall not fear, he shall not dread!" He shall be a Companion among the nobles. He shall be among the courtiers. Proceed to the robing-room to wait on him!"

I left the audience-hall, the royal daughters giving me their hands. We went through the great portals, and I was put in the house of a prince. In it were luxuries: a bathroom and mirrors. In it were riches from the treasury; clothes of royal linen, myrrh, and the choice perfume of the king and of his favorite courtiers were in every room. Every servant was at his task. Years were removed from my body. I was shaved; my hair was combed. Thus was my squalor returned to the foreign land, my dress to the Sand-farers. I was clothed in fine linen; I was anointed with fine oil. I slept on a bed. I had returned the sand to those who dwell in it, the tree-oil to those who grease themselves with it.

I was given a house and garden that had belonged to a courtier. Many craftsmen rebuilt it, and all its woodwork was made anew. Meals were brought to me from the palace three times, four times a day, apart from what the royal children gave without a moment's pause.

A stone pyramid was built for me in the midst of the pyramids. The masons who build tombs constructed it. A master draughtsman designed in it. A master sculptor carved in it. The overseers of construction in the necropolis busied themselves with it. All the equipment that is placed in a tomb-shaft was supplied. Mortuary priests were given me. A funerary domain was made for me. It had fields and a garden in the right place, as is done for a Companion of the first rank. My statue was overlaid with gold, its skirt with electrum. It was his majesty who ordered it made. There is no commoner for whom the like has been done. I was in the favor of the king, until the day of landing came.

REVIEW QUESTIONS

1. What kind of image of the king does this story present?
2. What is the story's view of non-Egyptians?
3. What are the chief reasons why Sinuhe, as he grows older, wishes to return home?

FROM *The Book of the Dead*

Beginning in the late Old Kingdom, there were inscribed on the walls of the interior chambers of pyramids magical texts that were intended to ensure that the deceased king passed successfully into the next life. In the following centuries, these so-called Pyramid Texts were developed further, and the possibility of proceeding into the next world became less exclusively focused on the king and his immediate family and more inclusive of Egyptians of lesser rank (what some scholars have referred to as the "democratization of death"). From this process emerged the collection of texts that has come to be known (erroneously) as The Book of the Dead. *The following selection has been referred to as the "Protestation of Guiltlessness" or the "Negative*

Confession." It was to be recited by the deceased as he or she appeared for judgment before the god Osiris and his entourage.

From *Ancient Near Eastern Texts Relating to the Old Testament,* edited by James B. Pritchard, translated by H. L. Ginsberg (3d ed.; Princeton, N.J.: Princeton University Press, 1983).

*   *   *

What is said on reaching the Broad-Hall of the Two Justices, absolving X [the deceased] of every sin which he has committed, and seeing the faces of the gods:

Hail to thee, O great god, lord of the Two Justices! I have come to thee, my lord, I have been brought that I might see thy beauty. I know thee; I know thy name and the names of the forty-two gods who are with thee in the Broad-Hall of the Two Justices, who live on them who *preserve* evil and who drink their blood on that day of reckoning up character in the presence of Wennofer. Behold, "*Sati-mertifi,* Lord of Justice," is thy name. I have come to thee; I have brought thee justice; I have expelled deceit for thee.

I have not committed evil against men.

I have not mistreated cattle.

I have not committed sin in the place of truth.

I have not known that which is not.

I have not seen evil. . . .

My name has not reached the Master of the Barque.

I have not blasphemed a god.

I have not *done violence to* a poor man.

I have not done that which the gods abominate.

I have not defamed a slave to his superior.

I have not made anyone sick.

I have not made anyone weep.

I have not killed.

I have given no order to a killer.

I have not caused anyone suffering.

I have not cut down on the food-income in the temples.

I have not damaged the bread of the gods.

I have not taken the loaves of the blessed dead.

I have not had sexual relations with a boy.

I have not defiled myself.

I have neither increased or diminished the grain-measure.

I have not diminished the *aroura.*

I have not falsified a half-*aroura* of land.

I have not added to the weight of the balance.

I have not *weakened* the plummet of the scales.

I have not taken milk from the mouths of children.

I have not driven cattle away from their pasturage.

I have not snared the birds *of* the gods.

I have not caught fish in their marshes.

I have not held up the water in its season.

I have not built a dam against running water.

I have not quenched a fire at its proper time.

I have not neglected the appointed times and their meat-offerings.

I have not driven away the cattle of the god's property.

I have not stopped a god on his procession.

I am pure!—four times. My purity is the purity of that great *benu*-bird which is in Herakleopolis, because I am really that nose of the Lord of Breath, who makes all men to live, on that day of filling out the Eye of Horus in Heliopolis, in the second month of the second season, the last day, in the presence of the lord of this land. I am the one who has seen the filling out of the Eye in Heliopolis. Evil will never happen to me in this land or in this Broad-Hall of the Two Justices, because I know the names of these gods who are in it, the followers of the great god.

O Wide-of-Stride, who comes forth from Heliopolis, I have not committed evil.

O Embracer-of-Fire, who comes forth from Babylon, I have not stolen.

O Nosey, who comes forth from Hermopolis, I have not been covetous.

O Swallower-of-Shadows, who comes forth from the pit, I have not robbed.

O Dangerous-of-Face, who came forth from *Rostau*, I have not killed men.

O *Ruti*, who comes forth from heaven, I have not damaged the grain-measure.

O His-Eyes-are-of-Flint, who comes forth from the shrine, I have not caused *crookedness*.

O Flamer, who comes forth *backward*, I have not stolen the property of a god.

O Breaker-of-Bones, who comes forth from Herakleopolis, I have not told lies.

O *Commander-of-Fire*, who comes forth from Memphis, I have not taken away food.

O Dweller-in-the-Pit, who comes forth from the west, I have not been contentious.

O White-of-Teeth, who comes forth from the Faiyum, I have not trespassed.

O Eater-of-Blood, who comes forth from the execution-block, I have not slain the cattle of the god.

O Eater-of-Entrails, who comes forth from the Thirty, I have not *practised usury*.

O Lord-of-Justice, who comes forth from *Ma'ati*, I have not stolen the *bread-ration*.

O Wanderer, who comes forth from Bubastis, I have not *gossiped*.

O *Aadi*, who comes forth from Heliopolis, my mouth has not gone on unchecked.

O *Djudju*-serpent, who comes forth from Busiris, I have not argued with *some one summoned because of* his property.

O *Wamemti*-serpent, who comes forth from the place of judgment, I have not committed adultery.

O *Maa-Intef*, who comes forth from the Temple of Min, I have not defiled myself.

O Superior-of-the-Nobles, who comes forth from *Imau*, I have not caused terror.

O Wrecker, who comes forth from *the Saite Nome*, I have not trespassed.

O Mischief-Maker, who comes forth from the sanctuary, I have not been overheated.

O Child, who comes forth from the Heliopolitan Nome, I have not been unresponsive to a matter of justice.

O *Ser-kheru*, who comes forth from *Wensi*, I have not been quarrelsome.

O Bastet, who comes forth from the sanctum, I have not winked.

O His-Face-Behind-Him, who comes forth from *Tep-het-djat*, I have not *been perverted*; I have not had sexual relations with a boy.

O Hot-of-Leg, who comes forth from the twilight, I have not swallowed my heart.

O Dark-One, who comes forth from the darkness, I have not been abusive.

O Bringer-of-His-Peace, who comes forth from Sais, I have not been overenergetic.

O Lord-of-Faces, who comes forth from the Heroonpolite Nome, my heart has not been hasty.

O Plan-Maker, who comes forth from *Utenet*, I have not transgressed my color; I have not washed the god.

O Lord-of-Horns, who comes forth from Siut, my voice is not too much about matters.

O *Nefer-tem*, who comes forth from Memphis, I have not committed sins; I have not done evil.

O *Tem-sep*, who comes forth from Busiris, I have not been abusive against a king.

O Acting-with-His-Heart, who comes forth from *Tjebu*, I have not waded in water.

O Flowing-One, who comes forth from Nun, my voice has not been loud.

O Commander-of-the-People, who comes forth from *his shrine*, I have not been abusive against a god.

O *Neheb-nefert*, who comes forth from *the Saite Nome*, I have never made puffings-up.

O *Neheb-kau*, who comes forth from the town, I have not made *discriminations for* myself.

O High-of-Head serpent, who comes forth from the cavern, my portion has not been too large, *not even* in my own property.

O *In-af* serpent, who comes forth from the cemetery, I have not blasphemed against my local god.

WORDS TO BE SPOKEN BY X [the deceased]:

Hail to you, ye gods who are in this Broad-Hall of the Two Justices! I know you; I know your names. I shall not fall for dread of you. Ye have not reported guilt of mine up to this god in whose retinue ye are; no deed of mine has come *from* you. Ye have spoken truth about me in the presence of the All-Lord, because I acted justly in Egypt. I have not been abusive to a god. No deed of mine has come *from* a king who is in his day.

Hail to you who are in the Broad-Hall of the Two Justices, who have no deceit in your bodies, who live on truth and who eat of truth in the presence of Horus, who is in his sun disc. May ye rescue me from Babi, who lives on the entrails *of elders* on that day of the great reckoning. Behold me—I have come to you without sin, without guilt, without evil, without a witness against me, without one against whom I have taken action. I live on truth, and I eat of truth. I have done that which men said and that with which gods are content. I have satisfied a god with that which he desires. I have given bread to the hungry, water to the thirsty, clothing to the naked, and a ferry-boat to him who was marooned. I have provided divine offerings for the gods and mortuary offerings for the dead. So rescue me, you; protect me, you. Ye will not make report against me in the presence of the great god. I am one pure of mouth and pure of hands, one to whom "Welcome, welcome, in peace!" is said by those who see him, because I have heard those great words which the ass discussed with the cat in the house of *the hippopotamus,* when the witness was His-Face-Behind-Him and he gave out a cry. I have seen the splitting of the *ished*-tree in *Rostau.* I am one who has a concern for the gods, who knows the *nature* of their bodies. I have come here to testify to justice and to bring the scales to their proper position in the cemetery.

O thou who art high upon his standard, Lord of the *Atef*-Crown, whose name has been made "Lord of Breath," mayest thou rescue me from thy messengers who give forth uncleanliness and create *destruction,* who have no covering up of their faces, because I have effected justice for the Lord of Justice, being pure—my front is pure, my rear is clean, my middle is in the flowing water of justice; there is no part of me free of justice. . . .

. . . "I will not announce thee," says the door-keeper of the Broad-Hall of the Two Justices, "unless thou tellest my name." "Understander of Hearts, Searcher of Bodies is thy name." "Then to whom should I announce thee?" "To the god who is in his hour of service." "Thou shouldst tell it to the interpreter of the Two Lands." "Well, who is the interpreter of the Two Lands?" "It is Thoth."

"Come," says Thoth, "why hast thou come?" "I have come here to be announced." "What is thy condition?" "I am pure of sin. I have protected myself from the strife of those who are in their days. I am not among them." "Then to whom shall I announce thee? I shall announce thee to him whose ceiling is of fire, whose walls are living serpents, and whose pavement is water. Who is he?" "He is Osiris." "Then go thou. Behold, thou art announced. Thy bread is the Restored Eye; thy beer is the Restored Eye. Thou hast invocation-offerings upon earth in the Restored Eye." So spoke Osiris to *X,* the deceased.

Instructions for the Use of the Spell

TO BE DONE IN CONFORMANCE WITH WHAT TAKES PLACE IN THIS BROAD-HALL OF THE TWO JUSTICES. THIS SPELL IS TO BE RECITED WHEN ONE IS CLEAN AND PURE, CLOTHED IN FRESH GARMENTS, SHOD WITH WHITE SANDALS, PAINTED WITH STIBIUM, AND ANOINTED WITH MYRRH, TO WHOM CATTLE, FOWL, INCENSE, BREAD, BEER, AND VEGETABLES HAVE BEEN OFFERED. THEN MAKE THOU THIS TEXT IN WRITING ON A CLEAN PAVEMENT WITH OCHRE SMEARED WITH EARTH UPON WHICH PIGS AND OTHER SMALL CATTLE HAVE NOT TRODDEN. AS FOR HIM ON WHOSE BEHALF THIS BOOK IS MADE, HE SHALL BE PROSPEROUS AND HIS CHILDREN SHALL BE PROSPEROUS, WITHOUT *GREED,* BECAUSE HE SHALL BE A TRUSTED MAN OF THE KING AND HIS COURTIERS. LOAVES, JARS, BREAD, AND JOINTS OF MEAT SHALL BE GIVEN TO HIM FROM THE ALTAR OF *the great god.* HE CANNOT BE HELD BACK AT ANY DOOR OF THE WEST,

BUT HE SHALL BE USHERED IN WITH the Kings of Upper and Lower Egypt, and he shall be in the retinue of Osiris.

Right and true a million times.

REVIEW QUESTIONS

1. What does this text reveal about the Egyptians' concept of the next life and in particular, about the individual's eligibility for it? Can you detect any parallels in the beliefs of later religious systems?
2. How, ideally, was one to conduct oneself in order to appear blameless before the gods?
3. What does this text have to say about Egyptian social values?

Harper's Songs

The ancient Egyptians have often been characterized as morbidly fascinated by death and eagerly anticipating the next life, an attitude distinctly in contrast with that of most of modern Western society. The next readings are from a very unusual genre in Egyptian literature and present somewhat contrasting views of the afterlife. They may give us pause to reconsider.

From *Hymns, Prayers, and Songs: An Anthology of Ancient Egyptian Lyric Poetry,* translated by John L. Foster (Atlanta, Ga.: Scholars Press, 1995), pp. 168–69.

From the Tomb of King Intef

Song in the tomb of King Intef, vindicated, in front of the singer with the harp:

> He is prospering, this fine prince;
> death is a happy ending.

i

One generation passes, another stays behind—
such has it been since the men of ancient times.
The gods of long ago rest in their pyramids,
and the great and blessed likewise lie buried in their tombs.
Yet those who built great mansions, their places are no more.
What has become of them all?

I have heard the words of Imhotep, and Hordjedef too,
retold time and again in their narrations.
Where are their dwellings now?
Their walls are down,
Their places gone,
like something that has never been.

There is no return for them
to explain their present being,
To say how it is with them,
to gentle our hearts
until we hasten to the place where they have gone.

ii

So, let your heart be strong,
let these things fade from your thoughts.

Look to yourself,
and follow your heart's desire while you live!

Put myrrh on your head,
be clothed in fine linen,
Anoint yourself with the god's own perfumes,
heap up your happiness,
and let not your heart become weary.

Follow your heart's desire and what you
    find good;
act on your own behalf while on earth!
And let not your heart be troubled—
that day of mourning for you must come;
And Osiris, the Weary-Hearted, will not hear
    their wailing,
weeping does not save the heart from the grave.
So spend your days joyfully
and do not be weary with living!
No man takes his things with him,
and none who go can come back again.

*   *   *

From the Tomb of Neferhotep

Chanted by the singer with the harp for the God's
Father of Amun, Neferhotep, vindicated:
O all you excellent eminent dead, O Ennead, O
    Lady of Life
    in the West,
hear what has been composed
To sing the praises of the God's Father in
    honoring his soul,
what is helpful for the excellent dead man
Now that he is a living god for eternity,

elevated in the West.
May these words become a memorial in future
to anyone who passes by.

I have heard those songs in the tombs of ancient
    days
and what they say, exalting life on earth
and belittling the city of the dead.
Why is this, acting this way against the land
    of eternity
which is just and without terror?
It loathes disorder;
and no one arms himself against a neighbor
in this land without a rebel.
All our ancestors have come to rest within it
since the wastes at the beginning of time;
And those who shall come to be, millions
    on millions,
all go there.
There is no lingering in our Beloved Land,
not one fails to arrive there;
And the span of what was done on earth is the
    flicker of a dream
when they say, "Welcome, safe and sound!"
to the one who reaches the West.

*   *   *

REVIEW QUESTIONS

1. According to the harper's songs, how ought one
   to spend this life?
2. Do you believe that the ancient Egyptians were
   obsessed with death?

2 ❧ GODS AND EMPIRES IN THE ANCIENT NEAR EAST

Under the firm hand of the rulers of the Twelfth Dynasty, Egypt had reemerged as a unified, highly centralized monarchy served by an efficient corps of royal bureaucrats. By the seventeenth century B.C.E., however, that stability was shaken as "vile Asiatics" migrated from Palestine into the Nile Delta and asserted their own political authority as the Hyksos dynasties of Lower Egypt. With the onset of its Second Intermediate Period, then, Egypt was once again divided, but for the first time under the abominable yoke of "barbarian" conquerors. Once again, the unity of "The Two Lands" of Upper and Lower Egypt would be restored by the prowess of the rulers of Amun's city of Thebes, who expelled the foreigners, chased them back into Palestine, and subsequently, perhaps as insurance against a repetition of such an abomination, conquered and ruled most of the eastern Mediterranean seaboard from the Sinai to Syria as well as the region of Nubia, ranging into the interior of Africa.

The zenith of Egypt's New Kingdom empire coincides with the era of the Late Bronze Age, a cosmopolitan age of unprecedented internationalism. As reflected vividly in the diplomatic correspondence of the Amarna letters as well as in the preserved cargo of a shipwreck discovered off the coast of Turkey at Ulu Burun, kings from Babylonia to Cyprus negotiated favors and offered their daughters in marriage, while maritime traders plied the sea routes of the Aegean and eastern Mediterranean, carrying cargo such as ingots of bronze, tusks of ivory, disks of blue glass, and pottery containers filled with valuable oils and resins. Envoys and ambassadors trudged well-worn caravan tracks, bearing messages from kings offering alliances to other kings or from local princes offering their supplication to the pharaoh or informing him of depredations by hapiru *outlaws. At the top of royal wish lists was the gold of Nubia, which the pharaoh had the power to dispense to royal "brothers" in Babylonia, Assyria, Hatti, Mittani, Alashiya (Cyprus), or Ahhiyawa (perhaps Mycenaean Greece). Many pounds of that same gold were expended on the burial of a short-lived pharaoh named Tutankhamun, whose abandoned birth name of Tutankhaten testifies to the genius (or psychosis) of his predecessor, regarded by some experts as the first to espouse monotheism, a religious system based on a single God (in this instance, the sun as personified in its disk, or* aten*). Later Egyptians would condemn Akhenaten's "revolution" as heresy and attempt to eradicate his memory. Only well after the internationalism of the Late Bronze Age had been disrupted and Egypt itself had become a "broken reed" would the Hebrews (perhaps not totally unrelated to those* hapiru *outlaws of the Amarna letters) develop the concept of monotheism, a concept that eventually was to become one of the most central and enduring structures of civilization throughout the West, and the world.*

The period 1200–1100 B.C.E. *is a watershed in the history of the Ancient Near East. Before 1200, the region enjoyed a vibrant internationalism set against the backdrop of competing great kingdoms, some of them with substantial empires. By 1100, most of those great kingdoms had disappeared—in some instances suddenly, perhaps even catastrophically; among them were the Hittite kingdom of Anatolia, the Kassites of Babylonia, the kingdom of Alashiya on Cyprus, and Mycenaean Greece. Others were in decline—most notably, New Kingdom Egypt, whose empire in Syria and Palestine had waned and whose dynastic unity was dissolving. Scholars today still debate the impact of the invasion of the "Sea Peoples" on these events. In one prominent view, their invasions were the most catastrophic event to befall the Ancient Near East prior to the arrival of Alexander's armies. Others see their arrival, though certainly shattering, as but one event in a concatenation of causes, both external and internal, that brought down the great Late Bronze Age kingdoms, ushered in a new configuration of states and peoples, and contributed to the ascendancy of iron over bronze as the preferred metal of technology.*

Within the new configuration emerged peoples whose contributions to later Western and world civilizations were both profound and enduring. Among the Sea Peoples, the memory of the Philistines has endured the longest, perhaps because the region in which they settled took on their name, as "Palestine." The Hebrew Bible depicts them as a potent and incorrigible threat to the early Israelites, and the ensuing animosity undoubtedly has contributed to the modern (and surely unjustified) connotation of "philistine" as crude and unsophisticated. To their north, the long-established Canaanite craftsmen and traders of Tyre, Sidon, and Beirut whom the Greeks came to identify as "Phoenicians" established far-flung colonies and commercial routes along which their goods and reputation were carried to the Straits of Gibraltar and beyond. As part of their enterprise, they refined and disseminated a new technology (likely inspired by Egyptian hieroglyphs) that eventually would revolutionize both literacy and society—alphabetic writing. Meanwhile, emerging to the west of the Phoenicians were several "tribal" kingdoms of the Aramaeans, perhaps the most powerful of which was centered on the ancient city of Damascus. In time, Aramaean peoples spread across the Middle Eastern landscape as far away as Babylonia, bringing with them their language, Aramaic, and an alphabetic writing system that would eventually supplant the ancient cuneiform system. Aramaic became the official language of the Persian empire; it was the language spoken by Jesus Christ and it remained the dominant spoken language throughout the Middle East until supplanted by Arabic in the wake of the Arab/Islamic conquests many centuries later.

The ancient Hebrews, or Israelites, had an impact on the shaping of Western civilization that dwarfs their impact on the history and culture of their own time. They emerge from almost total obscurity late during the second millennium B.C.E., *in circumstances about which historians and archaeologists have yet to reach consensus and continually struggle to understand. According to the (hardly objective or verifiable) accounts in the Hebrew Bible, they came to dominate the area of modern Israel/Palestine under two kings, David and Solomon, whose reigns together encompass less than a century (approximately 1000–920* B.C.E.). *The civil war that erupted on Solomon's death left the previously united Hebrew monarchy irreparably divided into its two constituent parts: Israel in the north and Judah in the south.*

Within a few centuries, however, both of these kingdoms, and most of the rest of the Middle East as well, were overcome by the reasserted might of Mesopotamian and then Persian empires. The Assyrians destroyed Israel in 722 and by 650 had conquered virtually all of the Middle East, their kings celebrating their brutal conquests in vivid accounts that can shock even twenty-first-century sensibilities. One of their successors to imperial dominion, the Chaldaean king Nebuchadnezzar of Babylonia, captured Judah's capital, Jerusalem, in 587 and deported much of its population to Babylon—an event that began the Diaspora, the "dispersion" that has so dominated the experience of the Jewish people since that time. With Cyrus and his successors came the greatest of all ancient Near Eastern empires, that of the Achaemenid Persians, who developed a system and mentality of universal dominion that later empires emulated for centuries to come.

It was probably during the "Captivity" in Babylon that the displaced people of Judah (in Hebrew, yehudim—*the word came to be "Jews") undertook in earnest the process of compiling and editing their ancient laws and traditions. The body of writings that was developed over the next several centuries—the Hebrew Bible, condescendingly known in Christian tradition as the "Old Testament"—is, along with the "New Testament," arguably the most influential corpus of literature in human history. Without a doubt, it is the Ancient Near East's most significant contribution to the shaping of Western civilization, and its impact on the formation of later Islamic civilization worldwide, through its contribution to the teachings of the prophet Muhammad as reflected in the Qur'an, is likewise beyond measuring. Furthermore, for the nearly two millennia before the archaeological rediscovery of ancient Mesopotamian civilization in the mid-nineteenth century and the decipherment of the cuneiform and hieroglyphic* scripts, the Bible was the chief fount of knowledge of human history from the creation of the world (which some scholars, using Biblical evidence, dated to exactly 4004 B.C.E.) to the rise of the Greeks.

The theory of evolution and the modern discoveries of historians and archaeologists have undermined the historical value of much of the Bible's narrative. Obviously, then, it is not in the accuracy of their historical accounts that the Hebrews have had their greatest influence on later civilization. Rather, their singular contribution lies in the unique perspective that dominated their sense of their own history: their special relationship with a divine being who chose them as His own people and established with them a covenant that promised them His support and protection. In return, they pledged to accept only Him as their exclusive deity and to govern their behavior, both cultic and social, in accordance with a body of explicitly defined regulations handed down by Him, and Him alone. The "working out" of this covenant in the historical experience of the Hebrew people provided the developmental context for concepts that became central to the tradition of Western civilization: divinely revealed law as the basis of the relationship between God and humankind, and a monotheism founded on humankind's exclusive acceptance of a single, universal Supreme Being and Creator who demands justice and righteousness but is also capable of mercy and compassion. These concepts today remain at the heart of the faiths of the "children of Abraham," the shared monotheistic tradition of Judaism, Christianity, and Islam.

Akhenaton's *Hymn to the Aton*

The nature of the relationship between the king and the gods and the religious focus of the Egyptian royal court took on a significant (though short-lived) new direction during the reign of the New Kingdom pharaoh Amunhotep IV, better known to history by the name he assumed, Akhenaton ("Beloved of the Aton"). Referred to by some today as the heretic pharaoh, Akhenaton tried to redirect worship in the Egyptian royal court to an almost exclusive focus on the Aton, the personification of the sun's power as manifested in the sun disk. Many have seen in this an important precursor of the Hebrews' monotheism centered on their god, Yahweh; some, in fact, have claimed that the Hebrews derived their monotheism from learning of Akhenaton's reform during their captivity in Egypt (as described in the Hebrew Bible's

Book of Exodus). The following hymn is generally ascribed to Akhenaton himself and shows some interesting parallels to Psalm 104 in the Hebrew Bible.

From *Hymns, Prayers, and Songs: An Anthology of Ancient Egyptian Lyric Poetry,* translated by John L. Foster, SBL Writings from the Ancient World Series, vol. 8 (Atlanta, Ga.: Scholars Press, 1995), pp. 154–58.

In Praise of the living Horakhty who rejoices in the Horizon in his Name of the divine Light which is in the Sundisk, living eternally and forever, the living Aton, Great One who is in the Festival, Lord of all the sundisk circles, Lord of Heaven, Lord of Earth, Living on Maat, Lord of the Two Lands, Nefer-kheper-rê Wa-en-rê, Son of the Sun, Who lives on Maat, Lord of Appearances, Akhenaton, One Great in his Time; and the Great Royal Wife, whom he loves, Mistress of the Two Lands, Nefer-neferu-aten Nefertiti, living, healthy, flourishing forever and eternity. He says:

i

May you always appear thus gloriously in the
    horizon of the sky,
    O living Aton, origin of life!
Arisen from the eastern horizon,
    you have filled all earth with your splendor;
You are beautiful, great, dazzling, exalted above
        each land,
    yet your rays encompass the lands
        to the limits of all which you have created;
There in the Sun, you reach to their boundaries,
    making them bow to your Son, whom you
        love;
And though you are far, your rays are over the
        earth,
    and you are in the faces of those who watch
        your journeying.

ii

You go to rest in the western horizon,
    and earth is in a darkness like death,
With the sleepers in bedchambers, heads
        covered—

the eye cannot discern its companion;
All their goods might be carried off—
    though they are near—without their knowing.
Every lion comes forth from his doorway,
    insects and snakes bite and sting;
Darkness shrouds, earth is silent—
    he who created them is at rest in his tomb.

iii

Dawn rises shining on the horizon,
    gleams from the sundisk as day.
You scatter the darkness, bestow your sunbeams,
    and the Two Lands offer thanksgiving.
The Sunfolk awaken and stand on their feet,
    for you have raised them up;
Their bodies are bathed, they put on their
        clothing,
    their arms raised in praise at your appearing.
Throughout the land
    they take up their work.

iv

The herds are at peace in their meadows,
    trees and the vegetation grow green,
Birds fly from their nests,
    their wings spread wide in praise of your
        Person;
All the small beasts leap about on their feet,
    and all who fly up or settle to rest
        live because you have shone upon them.
Ships go downstream or upstream as well,
    each path lies open because of your
        presence;
The fish in the River dart about in your sight,
    and your beams are deep in the Great Green
        Sea.

v

It is you who create the seed in women,
　shape the fluids into human beings,
Make the son alive in the womb of his mother,
　soothe him, ending his tears,
Nurturer from the womb to those given breath
　to bring into life all that he has created.
He descends from the womb to breathe
　on the day of his birth,
And you open his mouth, determine his nature,
　and minister to his needs.

vi

The fledgling in the egg speaks in the shell,
　so you give him breath within it to succor
　　him;
And you have given to him his allotted time
　so that he might break out from the egg
To come forth peeping at that time
　and move about upon his own two feet
　　when he emerges from it.

vii

How various are the things you have created,
　and they are all mysterious to the sight!
O sole God, without another of your kind,
　you created the world according to your desire,
　　while you were alone,
With mankind and cattle and every sort of small
　　beast,
　all those upon land, those who go upon feet,
Those who are on high soaring upon their
　　wings,
　　the foreign lands of Khor and Kush,
　　and all that belongs to Egypt.

viii

You give each person his place in life,
　and you provide for his needs;
Each one has his sustenance,
　and his lifetime is reckoned for him.
Tongues are separated by words,

the natures of persons as well;
And their skins are made different
　so you can distinguish the peoples.

ix

You create Hapy, the Nile, in the Underworld
　to bring him, at your desire, to nourish the
　　people,
Just as you create them for yourself,
　Lord of them all, who is weary for them,
O Lord of all earth, who shines for them,
　O Aton of day, awesome in majesty.
All the foreign lands are far away,
　yet you make their lives possible,
For you have placed a Hapy in the sky
　that he might come down upon them—
Making waves upon the mountains like those of
　　the Great Green Sea
　to water the fields in their villages.

x

How well ordered it is, your governing,
　O Lord of Eternity, Hapy in heaven!
You belong to the foreign peoples,
　to the small beasts of each land who go upon
　　feet.
And Hapy comes from Below to beloved Egypt as
　　well,
　while your rays are nursing each meadow.
You shine, and they live,
　they grow strong for you;
You fashion the seasons to make all your creation
　　flourish—
　　the winter for cooling
　　and the heat which ripens;
And you have made the sky far off
　in order to shine down from it,
　　to watch over all you have created.

xi

You are one alone,
　shining forth in your visible Form as the living
　　Aton,

Glorious, giving light,
    far-off yet approaching nearby.
You create the numberless visible forms from
        yourself—
    you who are one alone—
Cities, towns, fields, the road, the River;
    and each eye looks to you as its shining
        example:
You are in the sun-disk of day,
    overseer of wherever you go and whatever
        shall be;
For you fashion their sight so that you may be
        complete—
    as they celebrate with one voice your
        creation.

xii

And you are in my heart;
    there is no other who knows you
Except for your son, Akhenaton,
    Nefer-kheper-rê Wa-en-rê.
Let him be wise with your counsel, your
        strength,
    that the world may approach your condition
        just as when you created it.
You have risen, and they are alive;
    you go to rest, and they die.

For you are the measure of Time itself,
    one lives by means of you.
Eyes shall be filled with beauty until your
        setting;
    all labor is set aside when you go to rest in the
        West.
Then rise! Let the creatures of earth thrive for the
        king!
    And let me hasten on with every footstep
        as I have since you founded the world.
And raise them up for your son
    who came forth from your very body.

The King of Upper and Lower Egypt, who lives on Truth, Lord of the Two Lands, Nefer-Kheper-Rê Wa-en-rê, son of the Sun, who lives on Truth, Lord of Appearances, Akhenaton, one exalted in his own lifetime; and the Great Royal Wife, whom he loves, Nefer-neferu-aton Nefertiti, who lives and flourishes for eternity and everlasting.

REVIEW QUESTIONS

1. What kinds of powers does this hymn ascribe to the Aton?
2. What is the king's relationship to his newly elevated god?

A Letter from Tell el-Amarna

Eager to establish firmly the supremacy of the Aton, Akhenaton decided to move his court to a virgin site. He built there a new capital that he named Akhetaton, the remains of which are located at Tell el-Amarna. In the early 1880s, Egyptian fellaheen (laborers) digging for decayed mud brick (an excellent fertilizer) in the tell came across a collection of clay tablets, inscribed in cuneiform, that turned out to be a portion of the diplomatic correspondence addressed to the Egyptian royal court. Written in the Akkadian language of Mesopotamia, most of these letters were from Egypt's vassals in Palestine and Syria, but many are letters from the kings of the other great powers of the ancient Near East during the mid-fourteenth century B.C.E. The following letter to pharaoh is from the king of Mittani, a Hurrian state in north-

ern Syria and Mesopotamia which, until the then-recent reemergence of the Hittites, had been Egypt's chief rival for control of Syria and Palestine.

From *The Amarna Letters*, edited and translated by William L. Moran (Baltimore: Johns Hopkins University Press, 1992), pp. 43–45.

Say to Nimmureya, Great King, the king of Egypt, my brother, my son-in-law, who loves me, and whom I love: Message of Tušratta, Great King, your father-in-law, who loves you, the king of Mittani, your brother. For me all goes well. For you may all go well. For your household, for my sister, for the rest of your wives, for your sons, for your chariots, for your horses, for your *warriors,* for your country, and for whatever else belongs to you, may all go very, very well.

As far back as the time of your ancestors, they always showed love to my ancestors. You yourself went even further and showed very great love to my father. Now, in keeping with our constant and mutual love, you have made it ten times greater than the love shown my father. May the gods grant it, and may Teššup, my lord, and Aman make *flour[ish]* for evermore, just as it is now, this mutual love of ours.

When my brother sent Mane, his messenger, saying, "Send your daughter here to be my wife and the mistress of Egypt," I caused my brother no distress and *immediately* I said, "Of course!" The one whom my brother requested I showed to Mane, and he saw her. When he saw her, he praised her greatly. I will *lead* her in safety to my brother's country. May Šauška and Aman make her the image of my brother's desire.

Keliya, my messenger, *brought* my brother's words to me, and when I heard them, they were very pleasing, and I rejoiced very, very much, saying, "*Certainly* there is this between us: we love each other." Now, with such words let us love each other forevermore.

When I wrote to my brother, I said, "Let us love each other very, very much, and between us let there be friendship." I also said to my brother, "May my brother treat me ten times better than he did my father."

I also asked my brother for much gold, saying, "May my brother grant me more than he did to my father and send it to me. You sent my father much gold. You sent him large gold jars and gold jugs. You sent him gold bricks as if they *were just the equivalent of* copper."

When I sent Keliya to my brother, I asked for much gold, saying, "May my brother treat me ten times better than he did my father, and may he send much gold that has not been worked."

May my brother send me much more than he did to my father. Thus did I say to my brother: "I am going to build a *mausoleum* for my grandfather." I also said, "In accordance with a avorable *answer,* I am going to make the paraphernalia." And thus did I also say: "The gold that my brother sends me may he send for the bride-price as well."

Now my brother has sent the gold. I say, "It may be little or not, not a little but much. Still, it has been worked. But though it has been worked, I rejoiced over it much, and whatever it was my brother sent, I am happy about it."

I now hereby write to my brother, and may my brother show me much more love than he did to my father. I hereby ask for gold from my brother, and the gold that I ask for from my brother is meant for a double purpose: one, for the *mausoleum,* and the other, for the bride-price.

May my brother send me in very great quantities gold that has not been worked, and may my brother send me much more gold than he did to my father. In my brother's country, gold is as plentiful as dirt. May the gods grant that, just as now gold is plentiful in my brother's country, he make it even ten times more plentiful than now. May the gold that I ask for not become a source of distress to my brother, and may my brother not cause me distress. May my brother send me in

THE EGYPTIAN KING AND SUBJECT PEOPLES (C. 1380 B.C.E.)

The New Kingdom was a period of Egyptian domination in Syria-Palestine and in the Nubian regions of Africa south of Egypt. This image from a Dynasty 18 tomb painting from Thebes shows the pharoah Amunhotep III and his queen, Tiye, seated on thrones in their palace. The dais on which their thrones sit is decorated with scenes of foreigners from Egypt's imperial dominions, bound and kneeling. The images on the king's footstool likewise are of foreigners. What do these images suggest about the Egyptian view of the relationship between king and empire? How are the foreigners depicted as different from Egyptians? How are they distinguished from each other?

very large quantities gold that has not been worked. Whatever my brother needs for his house, let him write and take it. I will give ten times more than what my brother asks for. This country is my brother's country, and this house is my brother's house.

I herewith send my messenger, Keliya, to my brother, and may my brother not detain him. May he let him go promptly so that he may be on his way and I hear my brother's greeting and rejoice exceedingly. Forevermore may I constantly hear the greeting of my brother. May Teššup, my lord, and Aman grant that these words that we shall be constantly writing achieve their *purpose,* and may they be, as long as they exist, just as they are now. Just as we love each other now, exactly as now, so may we love each other forevermore.

I herewith send as my brother's greeting-gift: 1 gold goblet, with inlays of genuine lapis lazuli in its handle, 1 *maninnu-*necklace, with a *counterweight,* 20 pieces of genuine lapis lazuli, and

19 pieces of gold, its centerpiece being of genuine lapis lazuli set in gold; 1 *maninnu-*necklace, with a *counterweight,* 42 genuine *ḫulalu-*stones, and 40 pieces of gold shaped like *arzallu-*stones, its centerpiece being of genuine *ḫulalu-*stone set in gold; 10 teams of horses; 10 wooden-chariots along with everything belonging to them; and 30 women (and) men.

REVIEW QUESTIONS

1. How does the king of Mittani address the pharaoh, and what does that imply about the nature of their relationship?
2. How does that compare to the view of Asiatics encountered in the preceding readings?
3. How were relations solidified between the great powers of the fourteenth century B.C.E.?
4. In particular, what is the role of royal women in international diplomacy?

FROM The Letters of Deir el-Medina

Tomb and temple inscriptions, as well as the more formal works of Egyptian literature, communicate an idealized view of authority, social values, and correct behavior. To that idealized perspective we can compare the straightforward, unvarnished, often emotionally charged letters recovered from the site of Deir el-Medina, near Thebes, where lived several generations of the foremen, artists, and artisans responsible for constructing and decorating the magnificent New Kingdom royal tombs in the Valley of the Kings.

From *Letters from Ancient Egypt,* translated by Edward Wente, SBL Writings from the Ancient World Series, vol. 1 (Atlanta, Ga.: Scholars Press, 1990), pp. 140–49.

On Fortunetelling

Kenhikhopeshef addresses the woman Inerwau:

What means your failing to go to the woman diviner on account of the two infants who died while in your charge? Inquire of the woman di-

viner about the death of the two infants, whether it was their fate or their destiny. And you shall inquire about them for me and get a view of my own life and their mother's life. As for whatever god shall be mentioned to you afterwards, you shall write me concerning his identity. You will be rendering service for one who knows her occupation.

On Illness

Addressed by the draftsman Pay to his son, the draftsman Preemhab:

Don't turn your back on me, for I'm not well. Don't be sparing in tears for me because I am in this darkness and my lord Amon has turned his back on me.

May you bring me a bit of honey for my eyes as well as ochre that has been freshly molded into sticks and genuine galena. . . . Be to it! Be to it! Am I not your father? Now I am incapacitated. I am searching for my eyesight, but it no longer exists.

*   *   *

". . . in Hikuptah . . . reached me," so you said. . . . You made for him good plans, and all that you said was heeded. And you caused there to be released . . . and said to me, "You should go to our house and enter a stall, being the one where the two boxes are standing next to the pigsty. Look opposite those two millstones, and you will find those two pits with the copper tools lying within them."

I did accordingly while I myself was with the . . . : 500 copper spikes, 30 large copper hoes, 50 large copper chisels, 60 large copper spikes for splitting stone, 25 copper adzes, 30 copper double-edged knives, and 40 copper. . . . And I discovered a jar of Coptos ware, which was capped with gypsum and sealed with two seal impressions and which was inscribed with a list of what was in it: 10 *deben*-weights of silver, 2 *mine*-weights of gold, 7 heart amulets, 7 chains of gold, and 20 gold signet rings. And Mose said to me, "Let the jar be opened, and we shall divide the items that are in it between the two of us, for no one knows of it, and you shall not inform your father about it." But I replied to him, "In no way! I will not break the seal," so I told him.

A further matter: Now when I withdrew the copper objects belonging to Pharaoh, l.p.h., saying, "I shall take them to the overseer of the trea-

sury of Pharaoh, l.p.h., and cause the servants to be released," the deputy officer of the northern quarter came and apprehended me.[1] And he said to me, "You discovered some . . . which were registered in the house of the master of works and were issued to the necropolis. Have them handed over so that I may take them to Pharaoh, l.p.h., namely, the things that were discovered and you appropriated. But I replied to him, "In no way! They are the tools of work which used to be under my grandfather's supervision. One came to look for them, but they couldn't be found. So our twelve servants were taken away in place of them. My father appealed to Pharaoh, and he had me set free, for I am a native of the necropolis community, who is enlisted at the place where they are. I shall take them (the copper objects) to the overseer of the treasury of Pharaoh, l.p.h., and our servants, whom they seized, shall be set free," so I said to him. And he caused it to be accomplished.

On Family

The scribe Turo greets his mother, the chantress of Amon [name lost]: In life, prosperity and health and in the favor of Amon-Re, King of the Gods! And further:

How are you? Further, I am calling upon Amon, Mut, Khonsu, and all the gods of Southern Heliopolis (Thebes) and upon Pre when he rises each day to keep you healthy, to keep you in the favor of the deified Western Promontory, the mistress, and to let me see you healthy each and every day. And further:

I am being sent as far as the east side to the vizier in order to collect dues of his agents who are in the fields. And . . . as last year's balance due. Now there is no loincloth for my rear, for my loincloth has been taken away. . . . apportioned to the granary of Pharaoh. Please give your

---

[1] In this and other letters, "l.p.h." is an abbreviation of the translation ("life, prosperity, health" for the king) of a standard formula that appears next to references to him in many Egyptian texts. [Editor.]

personal attention and have me provided that I may cause. . . . Don't make me walk helpless, or you will be made helpless, because . . .

Now as soon as I return from the errand, I will deliver his goods in grain. . . . Don't listen to what Wadjmose has said, or you may have to serve as a member of the crew!

* * *

The workman Horemwia, he addresses the citizeness Tanetdjesere, his daughter:

You are my good daughter. If the workman Baki throws you out of the house, I will take action! As for the house, it is what belongs to(?) Pharaoh, l.p.h., but you may dwell in the anteroom to my storehouse because it is I who built it. Nobody in the world shall throw you out of there.

* * *

Addressed by Takhentyshepse to her sister Iye: In life, prosperity and health! And further:

I shall send you the barley, and you shall have it ground for me and add emmer to it. And you shall make me bread with it, for I have been quarreling with Merymaat my husband. "I will divorce you," he keeps saying when he quarrels with me on account of my mother in questioning the amount of barley required for bread. "Now your mother does nothing for you," he keeps telling me and says, "Although you have brothers and sisters, they don't take care of you," he keeps telling me in arguing with me daily, "Now look, this is what you have done to me ever since I've lived here, whereas all people furnish bread, beer, and fish daily to their family members. In short, should you say anything, you will have to go back down to the Black Land." It is good if you take note.

* * *

I have written to you. It's none of my wife's business.

On Personal Relations

The draftsman Prehotep communicates to his superior, the scribe of the Place of Truth Kenhikhopeshef: In life, prosperity and health!

What's the meaning of this negative attitude that you are adopting toward me? I'm like a donkey to you. If there is work, bring the donkey! And if there is fodder, bring the ox! If there is beer, you never ask for me. Only if there is work to be done, will you ask for me.

Upon my head, if I am a man who is bad in his behavior with beer, don't ask for me. It is good for you to take notice in the Estate of Amon-Re, King of the Gods, l.p.h.

I am a man who is lacking beer in his house. I am seeking to fill my stomach by my writing to you.

* * *

To the scribe Nekhemmut: In life, prosperity and health and in the favor of your august god, Amon-Re, King of the Gods, your good lord, every day! And further:

What's the meaning of your getting into such a bad mood as you are in that nobody's speech can enter your ears as a consequence of your inflated ego? You are not a man since you are unable to make your wives pregnant like your fellowmen.

A further matter: You abound in being exceedingly stingy. You give no one anything. As for him who has no children, he adopts an orphan instead to bring him up. It is his responsibility to pour water onto your hands as one's own eldest son.

REVIEW QUESTIONS

1. What kinds of concerns appear in these letters?
2. How do these documents differ from those presented earlier in this chapter?
3. What kinds of roles did women play in the village society of Deir el-Medina?

CARGO FROM THE ULU BURUN SHIPWRECK (C. 1300 B.C.E.)

In 1982, the wreck of a fourteenth-century B.C.E. merchant ship, possibly of Canaanite origin, was discovered off the southwestern coast of Turkey at Ulu Burun. Its cargo included thousands of items representing as many as seven civilizations of the Late Bronze Age, including more than 200 four-handled ("oxhide") ingots of copper like the one shown above as well as many tools. The items shown are of copper and bronze and reflect designs originating in Egypt, Canaan, Cyprus, and Mycenaean Greece. What does this suggest about the nature of Late Bronze Age trade? What kinds of metal implements might be traded, and why?

EGYPTIAN BATTLE WITH THE SEA PEOPLES (C. 1150 B.C.E.)

This scene from a monumental relief at Medinet Habu in Thebes purports to depict the Egyptian defeat of the Sea Peoples' fleet in a battle that evidently was fought near the Nile Delta. Do the Egyptians seem in command of the situation? What kinds of weapons do they use? Do you see evidence of distinctive modes of dress and headgear? What do you believe is the intended effect on someone viewing this relief?

FROM The Book of Ezekiel:
Phoenician Trade in the Hebrew Bible

The documentary record that the Phoenicians left to us about their history and trade is frustratingly scant. Historians necessarily have had to rely on descriptions provided by other sources, most notably, the accounts of ancient Greek historians like Herodotus; later Roman authors' accounts of the Carthaginians, whose origins were Phoenician (which is why, in Latin, the Carthaginians are referred to as Poeni, or Punic); and references to the Phoenicians in the Hebrew Bible. As you might expect, none of these sources tends to be impartial. The following selection from the Book of Ezekiel (27: 1–33) is drawn from one of several prophecies against foreign nations and culminates in the prophesied destruction of the Phoenician city of Tyre, whose wealth and fame are described vividly.

From *Contemporary English Version* by American Bible Society (New York: American Bible Society, 1995).

The LORD said:

Ezekiel, son of man, sing a funeral song for Tyre, the city that is built along the sea and that trades with nations along the coast. Tell the people of Tyre that the following message is from me:

Tyre, you brag about
your perfect beauty,
and your control of the sea. You are a ship
built to perfection.
Builders used cypress trees
from Mount Hermon
to make your planks
and a cedar tree from Lebanon
for your tall mast.
Oak trees from Bashan
were shaped into oars;
pine trees from Cyprus were cut for your deck,
which was then decorated
with strips of ivory.
The builders used fancy linen
from Egypt for your sails,
so everyone could see you.

Blue and purple cloth
from Cyprus
was used
to shade your deck.
Men from Sidon and Arvad
did the rowing,
and your own skilled workers
were the captains.
Experienced men from Byblos
repaired any damages.
Sailors from all over
shopped
at the stores
in your port.
Brave soldiers from Persia,
Lydia, and Libya
served in your navy,
protecting you with shields
and helmets,
and making you famous.
Your guards came from
Arvad and Cilicia,
and men from Gamad
stood watch in your towers.
With their weapons

hung on your walls,
your beauty was complete.

Merchants from southern Spain traded silver, iron, tin, and lead for your products. The people of Greece, Tubal, and Meshech traded slaves and things made of bronze, and those from Beth-Togarmah traded work horses, war horses, and mules. You also did business with people from Rhodes, and people from nations along the coast gave you ivory and ebony in exchange for your goods. Edom traded emeralds, purple cloth, embroidery, fine linen, coral, and rubies. Judah and Israel gave you their finest wheat, fancy figs, honey, olive oil, and spices in exchange for your merchandise. The people of Damascus saw what you had to offer and brought you wine from Helbon and wool from Zahar. Vedan and Javan near Uzal traded you iron and spices. The people of Dedan supplied you with saddle blankets, while people from Arabia and the rulers of Kedar traded lambs, sheep, and goats. Merchants from Sheba and Raamah gave you excellent spices, precious stones, and gold in exchange for your products. You also did business with merchants from the cities of Haran, Canneh, Eden,

Sheba, Asshur, and Chilmad, and they gave you expensive clothing, purple and embroidered cloth, brightly colored rugs, and strong rope. Large, seagoing ships carried your goods wherever they needed to go. You were like a ship

loaded with heavy cargo
and sailing across the sea,

*   *   *

Nations that received
your merchandise
were always pleased;
kings everywhere got rich
from your costly goods.

*   *   *

REVIEW QUESTIONS

1. How well constructed were the ships of Tyre?
2. What commodities and goods were traded at Tyre? How farflung were Tyre's trade connections?

FROM The Book of I Kings: Solomon's Construction of Yahweh's Temple in Jerusalem

As recounted in the following selection from the First Book of Kings, 5–8, in the Hebrew Bible, the crowning achievement of the reign of the Israelite king Solomon was the building of the great temple of Yahweh in Jerusalem, perhaps some time during the later tenth century B.C.E. That temple was part of a larger palace complex, no archaeological evidence of which has yet been recovered. This helps explain why modern historians have been compelled to reassess the biblical accounts of the great power and extent of David's and Solomon's kingdom. Nonetheless, Solomon's First Temple, later destroyed by the Babylonians under Nebuchadnezzar in the sixth century B.C.E. (the Second Temple, rebuilt by Herod the Great in the first century

B.C.E., was also destroyed by the Romans in the first century C.E.),[1] became the central locus of ritual and worship in early Judaism and is an overriding reason for modern Israel's adamant refusal to restore Jerusalem to Arab control today.

From *Contemporary English Version* by American Bible Society (New York: American Bible Society, 1995).

King Hiram of Tyre had always been friends with Solomon's father David. When Hiram learned that Solomon was king, he sent some of his officials to meet with Solomon. Solomon sent a message back to Hiram: "Remember how my father David wanted to build a temple where the LORD his God could be worshiped? But enemies kept attacking my father's kingdom, and he never had the chance. Now, thanks to the LORD God, there is peace in my kingdom and no trouble or threat of war anywhere. The LORD God promised my father that when his son became king, he would build a temple for worshiping the LORD. So I've decided to do that. I'd like you to have your workers cut down cedar trees in Lebanon for me. I will pay them whatever you say and will even have my workers help them. We both know that your workers are more experienced than anyone else at cutting lumber."

Hiram was so happy when he heard Solomon's request that he said, "I am grateful that the LORD gave David such a wise son to be king of that great nation!" Then he sent back his answer: "I received your message and will give you all the cedar and pine logs you need. My workers will carry them down from Lebanon to the Mediterranean Sea. They will tie the logs together and float them along the coast to wherever you want them. Then they will untie the logs, and your workers can take them from there. To pay for the logs, you can provide the grain I need for my household." Hiram gave Solomon all the cedar and pine logs he needed. In return, Solomon gave Hiram about one hundred twenty-five thousand bushels of wheat and about one thousand one hundred gallons of pure olive oil each year. The LORD kept his promise and made Solomon wise. Hiram and Solomon signed a treaty and never went to war against each other.

Solomon ordered thirty thousand people from all over Israel to cut logs for the temple, and he put Adoniram in charge of these workers. Solomon divided them into three groups of ten thousand. Each group worked one month in Lebanon and had two months off at home. He also had eighty thousand workers to cut stone in the hill country of Israel, seventy thousand workers to carry the stones, and over three thousand assistants to keep track of the work and to supervise the workers. He ordered the workers to cut and shape large blocks of good stone for the foundation of the temple. Solomon's and Hiram's men worked with men from the city of Gebal, and together they got the stones and logs ready for the temple.

Solomon's workers started building the temple during Ziv, the second month of the year. It had been four years since Solomon became king of Israel, and four hundred eighty years since the people of Israel left Egypt. The inside of the LORD's temple was ninety feet long, thirty feet wide, and forty-five feet high. A fifteen-foot porch went all the way across the front of the temple. The windows were narrow on the outside but wide on the inside. Along the sides and back of the temple, there were three levels of storage rooms. The rooms on the bottom level were seven and a half feet wide, the rooms on the middle level were nine feet wide, and those on the top level were ten and a half feet wide. There were ledges on the outside of the temple that supported the beams of the storage rooms, so that nothing was built into the temple walls. Solomon did not want the noise of hammers and axes to be heard at the place where the temple was being built. So he had the workers shape the blocks of stone at the quarry.

---

[1]C.E. means "common era." [Editor.]

The entrance to the bottom storage rooms was on the south side of the building, and stairs to the other rooms were also there. The roof of the temple was made out of beams and cedar boards. The workers finished building the outside of the temple. Storage rooms seven and a half feet high were all around the temple, and they were attached to the temple by cedar beams.

The LORD told Solomon: "If you obey my commands and do what I say, I will keep the promise I made to your father David. I will live among my people Israel in this temple you are building, and I will not desert them."

So Solomon's workers finished building the temple. The floor of the temple was made out of pine, and the walls were lined with cedar from floor to ceiling. The most holy place was in the back of the temple, and it was thirty feet square. Cedar boards standing from floor to ceiling separated it from the rest of the temple. The temple's main room was sixty feet long, and it was in front of the most holy place. The inside walls were lined with cedar to hide the stones, and the cedar was decorated with carvings of gourds and flowers.

The sacred chest was kept in the most holy place. This room was thirty feet long, thirty feet wide, and thirty feet high, and it was lined with pure gold. There were also gold chains across the front of the most holy place. The inside of the temple, as well as the cedar altar in the most holy place, was covered with gold. Solomon had two statues of winged creatures made from olive wood to put in the most holy place. Each creature was fifteen feet tall and fifteen feet across. They had two wings, and the wings were seven and a half feet long. Solomon put them next to each other in the most holy place. Their wings were spread out and reached across the room. The creatures were also covered with gold. The walls of the two rooms were decorated with carvings of palm trees, flowers, and winged creatures. Even the floor was covered with gold. The two doors to the most holy place were made out of olive wood and were decorated with carvings of palm trees, flowers, and winged creatures. The doors and the carvings were covered with gold. The door frame came to a point at the top.

The two doors to the main room of the temple were made out of pine, and each one had two sections so they could fold open. The door frame was shaped like a rectangle and was made out of olive wood. The doors were covered with gold and were decorated with carvings of palm trees, flowers, and winged creatures. The inner courtyard of the temple had walls made out of three layers of cut stones with one layer of cedar beams.

Work began on the temple during Ziv, the second month of the year, four years after Solomon became king of Israel. Seven years later the workers finished building it during Bul, the eighth month of the year. It was built exactly as it had been planned. Solomon's palace took thirteen years to build.

Forest Hall was the largest room in the palace. It was one hundred fifty feet long, seventy-five feet wide, and forty-five feet high, and was lined with cedar from Lebanon. It had four rows of cedar pillars, fifteen in a row, and they held up forty-five cedar beams. The ceiling was covered with cedar. Three rows of windows on each side faced each other, and there were three doors on each side near the front of the hall. Pillar Hall was seventy-five feet long and forty-five feet wide. A covered porch supported by pillars went all the way across the front of the hall. Solomon's throne was in Justice Hall, where he judged cases. This hall was completely lined with cedar. The section of the palace where Solomon lived was behind Justice Hall and looked exactly like it. He had a similar place built for his wife, the daughter of the king of Egypt.

From the foundation all the way to the top, these buildings and the courtyard were made out of the best stones carefully cut to size, then smoothed on every side with saws. The foundation stones were huge, good stones—some of them fifteen feet long and others twelve feet long. The cedar beams and other stones that had been cut to size were on top of these foundation stones. The walls around the palace courtyard were made out of three layers of cut stones with one layer of cedar beams, just like the front porch and the inner courtyard of the temple.

Hiram was a skilled bronze worker from the city of Tyre. His father was now dead, but he also had been a bronze worker from Tyre, and his mother was from the tribe of Naphtali. King Solomon asked Hiram to come to Jerusalem and make the bronze furnishings to use for worship in the LORD's temple, and he agreed to do it. Hiram made two bronze columns twenty-seven feet tall and about six feet across. For the top of each column, he also made a bronze cap seven and a half feet high. The caps were decorated with seven rows of designs that looked like chains, with two rows of designs that looked like pomegranates. The caps for the columns of the porch were six feet high and were shaped like lilies. The chain designs on the caps were right above the rounded tops of the two columns, and there were two hundred pomegranates in rows around each cap. Hiram placed the two columns on each side of the main door of the temple. The column on the south side was called Jachin, and the one on the north was called Boaz. The lily-shaped caps were on top of the columns. This completed the work on the columns.

Hiram also made a large bowl called the Sea. It was seven and a half feet deep, about fifteen feet across, and forty-five feet around. Two rows of bronze gourds were around the outer edge of the bowl, ten gourds to every eighteen inches. The bowl itself sat on top of twelve bronze bulls with three bulls facing outward in each of four directions. The sides of the bowl were four inches thick, and its rim was like a cup that curved outward like flower petals. The bowl held about eleven thousand gallons.

Hiram made ten movable bronze stands, each one four and a half feet high, six feet long, and six feet wide. The sides were made with panels attached to frames decorated with flower designs. The panels themselves were decorated with figures of lions, bulls, and winged creatures. Each stand had four bronze wheels and axles and a round frame twenty-seven inches across, held up by four supports eighteen inches high. A small bowl rested in the frame. The supports were decorated with flower designs, and the frame with carvings.

The side panels of the stands were square, and the wheels and axles were underneath them. The wheels were about twenty-seven inches high and looked like chariot wheels. The axles, rims, spokes, and hubs were made out of bronze. Around the top of each stand was a nine-inch strip, and there were four braces attached to the corners of each stand. The panels and the supports were attached to the stands, and the stands were decorated with flower designs and figures of lions, palm trees, and winged creatures. Hiram made the ten bronze stands from the same mold, so they were exactly the same size and shape. Hiram also made ten small bronze bowls, one for each stand. The bowls were six feet across and could hold about two hundred thirty gallons. He put five stands on the south side of the temple, five stands on the north side, and the large bowl at the southeast corner of the temple. Hiram made pans for hot ashes, and also shovels and sprinkling bowls.

This is a list of the bronze items that Hiram made for the LORD's temple: two columns; two bowl-shaped caps for the tops of the columns; two chain designs on the caps; four hundred pomegranates for the chain designs; ten movable stands; ten small bowls for the stands; a large bowl; twelve bulls that held up the bowl; pans for hot ashes, and also shovels and sprinkling bowls. Hiram made these bronze things for Solomon near the Jordan River between Succoth and Zarethan by pouring melted bronze into clay molds. There were so many bronze things that Solomon never bothered to weigh them, and no one ever knew how much bronze was used.

Solomon gave orders to make the following temple furnishings out of gold: the altar; the table that held the sacred loaves of bread; ten lampstands that went in front of the most holy place; flower designs; lamps and tongs; cups, lamp snuffers, and small sprinkling bowls; dishes for incense; fire pans; and the hinges for the doors to the most holy place and the main room of the temple. After the LORD's temple was finished, Solomon put into its storage rooms everything that his father David had dedicated to the LORD, including the gold and the silver.

The sacred chest had been kept on Mount Zion, also known as the city of David. But

Solomon decided to have the chest moved to the temple while everyone was in Jerusalem, celebrating the Festival of Shelters during Ethanim, the seventh month of the year. Solomon called together the important leaders of Israel. Then the priests and the Levites carried to the temple the sacred chest, the sacred tent, and the objects used for worship. Solomon and a crowd of people walked in front of the chest, and along the way they sacrificed more sheep and cattle than could be counted.

The priests carried the chest into the most holy place and put it under the winged creatures, whose wings covered the chest and the poles used for carrying it. The poles were so long that they could be seen from right outside the most holy place, but not from anywhere else. And they stayed there from then on. The only things kept in the chest were the two flat stones Moses had put there when the LORD made his agreement with the people of Israel at Mount Sinai, after bringing them out of Egypt. Suddenly a cloud filled the temple as the priests were leaving the most holy place. The LORD's glory was in the cloud, and the light from it was so bright that the priests could not stay inside to do their work. Then Solomon prayed:

"Our LORD, you said that you
would live in a dark cloud.
Now I have built a glorious temple
where you can live forever."

Solomon turned toward the people standing there. Then he blessed them and said: "Praise the LORD God of Israel! Long ago he brought his people out of Egypt. He later kept his promise to make my father David the king of Israel. The LORD also said that he had not chosen the city where his temple would be built. So when David wanted to build a temple for the LORD God of Israel, the LORD said, 'It's good that you want to build a temple where I can be worshiped. But you're not the one to do it. Your son will build a temple to honor me.' The LORD has done what he promised. I am the king of Israel like my father, and I've built a temple for the LORD our God. I've also made a place in the temple for the sacred chest. And in that chest

are the two flat stones on which is written the solemn agreement the LORD made with our ancestors when he led them out of Egypt."

Solomon stood facing the altar with everyone standing behind him. Then he lifted his arms toward heaven and prayed: "LORD God of Israel, no other god in heaven or on earth is like you! You never forget the agreement you made with your people, and you are loyal to anyone who faithfully obeys your teachings. My father David was your servant, and today you have kept every promise you made to him. LORD God of Israel, you promised my father that someone from his family would always be king of Israel, if they do their best to obey you, just as he did. Please keep this promise you made to your servant David.

"There's not enough room in all of heaven for you, LORD God. How could you possibly live on earth in this temple I have built? But I ask you to answer my prayer. This is the temple where you have chosen to be worshiped. Please watch over it day and night and listen when I turn toward it and pray. I am your servant, and the people of Israel belong to you. So whenever any of us look toward this temple and pray, answer from your home in heaven and forgive our sins.

"Suppose someone accuses a person of a crime, and the accused has to stand in front of the altar in your temple and say, 'I swear I am innocent!' Listen from heaven and decide who is right. Then punish the guilty person and let the innocent one go free.

"Suppose your people Israel sin against you, and then an enemy defeats them. If they come to this temple and beg for forgiveness, listen from your home in heaven. Forgive them and bring them back to the land you gave their ancestors.

"Suppose your people sin against you, and you punish them by holding back the rain. If they turn toward this temple and pray in your name and stop sinning, listen from your home in heaven and forgive them. The people of Israel are your servants, so teach them to live right. And please send rain on the land you promised them forever.

"Sometimes the crops may dry up or rot or be eaten by locusts or grasshoppers, and your people will be starving. Sometimes enemies may surround their towns, or your people will become sick with deadly diseases. Listen when anyone in Israel truly feels sorry and sincerely prays with arms lifted toward your temple. You know what is in everyone's heart. So from your home in heaven answer their prayers, according to the way they live and what is in their hearts. Then your people will worship and obey you for as long as they live in the land you gave their ancestors. Foreigners will hear about you and your mighty power, and some of them will come to live among your people Israel. If any of them pray toward this temple, listen from your home in heaven and answer their prayers. Then everyone on earth will worship you, just like your people Israel, and they will know that I have built this temple to honor you.

"Our LORD, sometimes you will order your people to attack their enemies. Then your people will turn toward this temple I have built for you in your chosen city, and they will pray to you. Answer their prayers from heaven and give them victory.

"Everyone sins. But when your people sin against you, suppose you get angry enough to let their enemies drag them away to foreign countries. Later, they may feel sorry for what they did and ask your forgiveness. Answer them when they pray toward this temple I have built for you in your chosen city, here in this land you gave their ancestors. From your home in heaven, listen to their sincere prayers and do what they ask. Forgive your people no matter how much they have sinned against you. Make the enemies who defeated them be kind to them. Remember, they are the people you chose and rescued from Egypt that was like a blazing fire to them.

"I am your servant, and the people of Israel belong to you. So listen when any of us pray and cry out for your help. When you brought our ancestors out of Egypt, you told your servant Moses to say to them, 'From all people on earth, the LORD God has chosen you to be his very own.'"

When Solomon finished his prayer at the altar, he was kneeling with his arms lifted toward heaven. He stood up, turned toward the people, blessed them, and said loudly: "Praise the LORD! He has kept his promise and given us peace. Every good thing he promised to his servant Moses has happened. The LORD our God was with our ancestors to help them, and I pray that he will be with us and never abandon us. May the LORD help us obey him and follow all the laws and teachings he gave our ancestors. I pray that the LORD our God will remember my prayer day and night. May he help everyone in Israel each day, in whatever way we need it. Then every nation will know that the LORD is the only true God. Obey the LORD our God and follow his commands with all your heart, just as you are doing today."

Solomon and the people dedicated the temple to the LORD by offering twenty-two thousand cattle and one hundred twenty thousand sheep as sacrifices to ask the LORD's blessing. On that day, Solomon dedicated the courtyard in front of the temple and made it acceptable for worship. He offered the sacrifices there because the bronze altar in front of the temple was too small. Solomon and the huge crowd celebrated the Festival of Shelters at the temple for seven days. There were people from as far away as the Egyptian Gorge in the south and Lebo-Hamath in the north. Then on the eighth day, he sent everyone home. They said good-by and left, very happy, because of all the good things the LORD had done for his servant David and his people Israel.

*   *   *

REVIEW QUESTIONS

1. How are the wealth, skills, and products of the cities of Phoenicia represented in this selection?
2. Why did Solomon cause the temple to be built?
3. How is the temple intended to serve as a link between Yahweh and his people?

FROM *The Annals of Ashurnasirpal II of Assyria*

The ninth century B.C.E. witnessed the reemergence of Assyria under two powerful kings, Ashurnasirpal II and Shalmaneser III. Both kings waged far-flung military campaigns, the efficiency and brutality of which set the tone for the next 250 years of Assyrian conquest and empire. Ashurnasirpal's new capital city at Kalhu (Nimrud) on the Tigris River included a magnificent palace, the construction of which incorporated long cuneiform inscriptions celebrating his conquests and proclaiming his majesty and that of the chief Assyrian god, Ashur. The following selection includes the prologue to Ashurnasirpal's annals, followed by an account of his first year's campaign. As you read, you may find reason to agree with the assessment of the historian A. T. Olmstead, who characterized Ashurnasirpal's career as one of "calculated frightfulness."

From *Ancient Records of Assyria and Babylonia*, vol. I, by D. D. Luckenbill (Chicago: University of Chicago Press, 1926), pp. 138–45.

*   *   *

Unto Ninurta, the powerful, the almighty, the exalted, the chief of the gods, the valiant, the gigantic, the perfect, whose onslaught in battle cannot be equaled, the first(born) son, the destroyer of opposition, the first-born of Nudimmud, the hero of the Igigi, the powerful, the prince of the gods, the offspring of E-kur, who holds the bolt of heaven and earth, who opens the depths, who treads the broad earth, the god without whom the decisions of heaven and earth are not decided, the destroyer, the mighty one, the command of whose mouth is not void, pre-eminent in the (four) quarters (of the world), who gives scepter and law unto all cities, the impetuous ruler, the word of whose lips is not altered, (of) boundless strength, the master of the gods, the exalted, Utgallu, the lord of lords, whose hand controls the ends of heaven and earth, the king of battle, the strong one who conquers opposition, the triumphant, the perfect, the lord of the nether waters and of the oceans, the terrible, the merciless one whose onslaught is a storm (deluge), who overwhelms the land of enemies, who strikes down the wicked, the powerful god whose counsel is not void, the light of heaven and earth, who gives light unto the midst of the deep, who destroys the wicked, who brings to subjection the disobedient, who overthrows foes, whose name in the assembly of the gods no god can humble, the giver of life, the god Ab-u, to whom it is good to pray (?), who dwells in the city of Calah, the great lord, my lord, (I) Assur-nâsir-pal (do pray); the mighty king, king of the universe, the king without a rival, the king of the whole of the four quarters (of the world), the Sun of all peoples, favorite of Enlil and Ninurta, the beloved of Anu and Dagan, the worshiper of the great gods, the submissive one who is dear unto thy heart, the prince, the favorite of Enlil, whose priesthood is pleasing unto thy great godhead so that thou hast established his reign, the valiant hero who goes hither and yon trusting in Assur, his lord, and who is without a rival among the princes of the four quarters (of the world), the wonderful shepherd, who fears not opposition, the mighty flood who has no conqueror, the king who has brought into subjection those that were not submissive to him, who has brought under his sway the totality of all peoples, the mighty hero who treads on the neck of his foe, who tramples all enemies under foot, who shatters the might of the haughty, who goes about trusting in the great gods, his lords, whose hand has conquered all the countries, who has brought under his sway all the mountain (regions) and has received their tribute, who has taken hostages, and who has established might over all lands.

When Assur, the lord, who called me by my name and has made great my kingdom, intrusted his merciless weapon unto my lordly hand, (I) Assur-nâsir-pal, the exalted prince, who fears the great gods, the powerful despot, conqueror of cities and mountains to their farthest borders, the king of rulers, who consumes the wicked, who is crowned with glory, who fears not opposition, the strong, the exalted, the unsparing, who destroys opposition, the king of all princes, the lord of lords, the shepherd(?), the king of kings, the exalted priest, the chosen of the hero Ninurta, the worshiper of the great gods, the avenger (of his fathers), the king who trusting in Assur and Shamash, the gods, his helpers, walks righteously and has cut down haughty mountain(eers) and princes who were his enemies, like reeds of the marsh, bringing all lands into subjection under his feet, who provides the offerings for the great gods, the rightful prince who has been permanently intrusted (with the task) of maintaining the cults(?) of the temples of his land, the work of whose hands and the offering of whose sacrifices the great gods of heaven and earth love, and whose priesthood in the temples they have established for all time,—their weapons they presented as my (v., his) royal gift,—the radiance of whose arms and the awe-inspiring splendor of whose rule have made him supreme over the kings of the four quarters (of the world), who has battled with all the enemies of Assur north and south and has laid tribute and tax upon them, conqueror of the foes of Assur; son of Tukulti-Ninurta, priest of Assur, who overcame all his enemies and fixed the bodies of his foes upon stakes; grandson of Adad-Nirâri, the priest, the viceroy of the great gods, who brought about the overthrow of those that did not obey him and established his sway over all; the descendant of Assur-daân, who freed(?) cities and founded temples. And now at the command of the great gods my sovereignty, my dominion, and my power are manifesting themselves; I am regal, I am lordly, I am exalted, I am mighty, I am honored, I am glorified, I am pre-eminent, I am powerful, I am valiant, I am lion-brave, and I am heroic! (I), Assur-nâsir-pal, the mighty king, the king of Assyria, chosen of Sin, favorite of Anu, beloved of Adad, mighty one among the gods, I am the merciless weapon that strikes down the land of his enemies; I am a king, mighty in battle, destroying cities and highlands, first in war, king of the four quarters (of the world), who has conquered his foes, destroyed all his enemies, king of all the regions (of earth), of all princes, every one of them, the king who has trampled down all who were not submissive to him, and who has brought under his sway the totality of all peoples. These decrees of destiny came forth at the word of the great gods, and for my destiny they duly ordained them. In (every) desire of my heart and undertaking of my hand, Ishtar, the lady, who loves my priesthood, was gracious unto me and her heart prompted to the waging of war and battle.

At that time Assur-nâsir-pal, the exalted prince, who fears the great gods, the desire of whose heart Enlil has caused him to attain, and whose mighty hand has conquered all princes who were disobedient unto him, conqueror of his foes, who shattered the power of the mighty in difficult regions,—when Assur, my great lord, who called me by name and made great my kingship over the kings of the four quarters (of the world), had made my name exceeding great, and had intrusted his merciless weapon unto my lordly power, and in his wrath had commanded me to conquer, to subdue and to rule; trusting in Assur, my lord, I marched by difficult roads over steep mountains with the hosts of my army, and there was none who opposed me.

In the beginning of my kingship, in the first year of my reign, when Shamash the judge of the (four) regions (of the world) had spread his kindly shadow over me, and I had seated myself upon the royal throne in might, and (when) he had placed in my hand the scepter, which rules the peoples, I mobilized my chariots and armies, crossed over steep mountains by difficult roads which had not been prepared for the passage of chariots and troops, and marched to the land of Tumme. Libê, their fortified city, and the cities of Surra, Abuku, Arura, and Arubê, which lie among the mountains of Urini, Aruni and Etini, fortified cities, I captured. I slew great numbers of them; their spoil, their possessions and their cattle I carried off. The men escaped, and occupied a steep mountain; the mountain was exceeding steep and I did not go after them. The peak of the mountain rose like the point of an iron dagger, and no bird of heaven that flies comes to it. Like the nest of the eagle (vulture) their stronghold was situated within the mountain, whereinto none of the kings, my fathers, had penetrated. For three days the warrior searched out the mountain, his stout heart urging to battle; he climbed up on foot, he cast down the mountain, he destroyed their nest, he shattered their host. Two hundred of their fighting men I cut down with the sword; their heavy booty I carried off like a flock of sheep, with their blood I dyed the mountain red like wool; with the rest of them I darkened(?) the gullies and precipices of the mountain; their cities I destroyed, I devastated, I burned with fire. From the land of Tumme I departed, to the land of Kirruri I went down. Tribute from the lands of Kirruri, Simesi, Simera, Ulmania, Adaush, (from) the Hargeans and Harmaseans, —horses, mules, cattle, sheep, wine, vessels of copper, I received as their tribute and I imposed the carrying of the headpad(?) upon them.

While I was staying in the land of Kirruri, the awe-inspiring splendor of Assur, my lord, overwhelmed the men of the lands of Gilzani and Hubushkia; horses, silver, gold, lead, copper and vessels of copper they brought to me as their tribute. From the land of Kirruri I departed, and I entered by the pass of Hulun into the land of Kirhi, which lies inside. The cities of Hatu, Hataru, Nishtun, Irbidi, Mitkia, Arsania, Téla, and Halua, cities of the land of Kirhi which lie among the mighty mountains of Usu, Arua, and Arardi, I captured. Great numbers of them I slew, their spoil and their possessions I carried away. The men escaped and occupied a lofty mountain peak which was over against the city of Nishtun and

which was suspended like a cloud from heaven. Against these men, unto whom none among the kings my fathers had come near, my warriors flew like birds; 260 of their fighting men I cut down with the sword, I cut off their heads, and I formed them into pillars. The rest of them built a nest on the rocks of the mountain like a bird. Their spoil and their possessions I brought down from the mountain, and the cities which were in the midst of the mighty ranges, I destroyed, I devastated, I burned with fire. All the men who had fled from before my arms came down and embraced my feet. Tribute and tax, and the carrying of the head-pad(?) I imposed upon them. Bûbu, son of Bubâ, the governor of the city of Nishtun, I flayed in the city of Arbela and I spread his skin upon the city wall. At that time I fashioned an image of my own likeness, the glory of my power I inscribed thereon, and in the mountain of Eki, in the city of Assur-nâsir-pal, at the (river) source, I set it up.

In this (same) eponymy, on the twenty-fourth day of the month *Abu*, at the word of Assur and Ishtar, the great gods, my lords, I departed from Nineveh, against the cities which lie at the foot of the mighty mountains of Nipur and Pasate I marched. I captured the cities of Arkun, Ushhu and Pilazi and twenty cities of their neighborhood. Great numbers (of the inhabitants) I slew, their spoil and their possessions I carried off, their cities I burned with fire. All the men who had fled from before my arms, came down and embraced my feet, and I imposed forced labor upon them. From the cities at the foot of the mountains of Nipur and Pasate I departed, the Tigris I crossed, and I drew near to the land of Kutmuhi, I received tribute from the lands of Kutmuhi and Mushki—vessels of copper, cattle, sheep, and wine.

While I was staying in the land of Kutmuhi, they brought me the word: "The city of Sûru of Bît-Halupê has revolted, they have slain Hamatai, their governor, and Ahia-baba, the son of a nobody, whom they brought from Bît-Adini, they have set up as king over them." With the help of Adad and the great gods who have made great my kingdom, I mobilized (my) chariots and armies and marched along the bank of the Habur. During my advance I received much tribute from Shulmanu-haman-ilâni of the city of Gardiganni, from Ilu-Adad of the city of Katna—silver, gold, lead, vessels of copper, and garments of brightly colored wool, and garments of linen. To the city of Sûru of Bît-Halupê I drew near, and the terror of the splendor of Assur, my lord, overwhelmed them. The chief men and the elders of the city, to save their lives, came forth into my presence and embraced my feet, saying: "If it is thy pleasure, slay! If it is thy pleasure, let live! That which thy heart desireth, do!" Ahiababa, the son of nobody, whom they had brought from Bît-Adini, I took captive. In the valor of my heart and with the fury of my weapons I stormed the city. All the rebels they seized and delivered them up. My officers I caused to enter into his palace and his temples. His silver, his gold, his goods and his possessions, copper, iron, lead, vessels of copper, cups of copper, dishes of copper, a great hoard of copper, alabaster, tables with inlay, the women of his palaces, his daughters, the captive rebels together with their possessions, the gods together with their possessions, precious stone from the mountains, his chariot with equipment, his horses, broken to the yoke, trappings of men and trappings of horses, garments of brightly colored wool and garments of linen, goodly oil, cedar, and fine sweet-scented herbs, panels(?) of cedar, purple and crimson wool, his wagons, his cattle, his sheep, his heavy spoil, which like the stars of heaven could not be counted, I carried off. Azi-ilu I set over them as my own governor. I built a pillar over against his city gate, and I flayed all the chief men who had revolted, and I covered the pillar with their skins; some I walled up within the pillar, some I impaled upon the pillar on stakes, and oth-

ers I bound to stakes round about the pillar; many within the border of my own land I flayed, and I spread their skins upon the walls; and I cut off the limbs of the officers, of the royal officers who had rebelled. Ahiababa I took to Nineveh, I flayed him, I spread his skin upon the wall of Nineveh. My power and might I established over the land of Laké. While I was staying in the city of Sûru, (I received) tribute from all the kings of the land of Laké,—silver, gold, lead, copper, vessels of copper, cattle, sheep, garments of brightly colored wool, and garments of linen, and I increased the tribute and taxes and imposed them upon them. At that time, the tribute of Haiâani of the city of Hindani,—silver, gold, lead, copper, *umu*-stone, alabaster, purple wool, and (Bactrian) camels I received from him as tribute. At that time I fashioned a heroic image of my royal self, my power and my glory I inscribed thereon, in the midst of his palace I set it up. I fashioned memorial steles and inscribed thereon my glory and my prowess, and I set them up by his city gate.

*   *   *

REVIEW QUESTIONS

1. What is the relationship between the king and the gods? Do the king's conquests appear to be divinely sanctioned?
2. Would you characterize the Assyrians' attitude toward conquered peoples as benevolent?
3. To what kinds of techniques did the Assyrians resort in order to ensure their control?
4. What were the motives that underlay Ashurnasirpal's conquests?

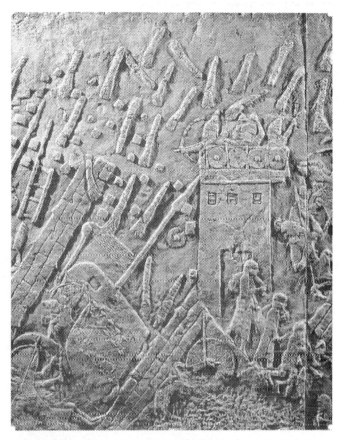

THE ASSYRIAN ATTACK ON LACHISH (701 B.C.E.)

The Assyrian onslaught at the Israelite city of Lachish is depicted on a portion of a wall relief in the palace of the Assyrian king Sennacherib at Nineveh. What kinds of military technology did the Assyrian army employ? Can you see evidence of one fate of the vanquished? What might be the practical uses of images such as these?

HERODOTUS

FROM *The Histories:* Customs of the Persians

The Greek historian Herodotus, who wrote during the fifth century B.C.E., has long been lauded as the father of history (although some would call him the grandfather and accord Thucydides the appellation father). Although modern historians are quite aware of Herodotus's own prejudices and gullibility, his The Histories *nonetheless remains our most important source for the history of the Persian invasions of Greece in 490 and 480-479 B.C.E. As background for that story, Herodotus also furnished a virtual travelogue of the peoples, places, and customs of the fifth century B.C.E. world. (In fact, his description of Egyptian customs remains an often-cited source on techniques of mummification.) In the following selection, Herodotus reports his knowledge of the customs of the Persians.*

From *Herodotus: The Histories,* edited by Walter Blanco and Jennifer Tolbert Roberts, translated by Walter Blanco (New York: Norton, 1992), pp. 48–50.

*   *   *

These are the customs I know the Persians to observe. They are not allowed to build statues, temples, and altars, and in fact they accuse those who do of silliness, in my opinion because unlike the Greeks, they don't think of the gods as having human form. It is their custom to climb to the mountaintops and sacrifice to Zeus, which is the name they give to the full circle of the sky. They sacrifice to the sun and the moon and the earth, as well as to fire, water, and air. At first, they sacrificed only to these, but they later learned to sacrifice to the Heavenly Aphrodite—they learned this from the Assyrians and the Arabians. The Assyrians call Aphrodite Mylitta, the Arabians call her Alilat, and the Persians call her Mitra.

This is the way the Persians sacrifice to the above-mentioned gods: they make no altars and light no fires when they are about to sacrifice. They don't pour libations or play the flute or wear garlands or sprinkle barley on their victims. Whenever someone wants to sacrifice to one of the gods, he leads the victim to a ritually pure place and invokes the god while wearing his tur-ban wreathed, preferably, with myrtle. It is not allowed for the sacrificer to pray, in private, for good things for himself. Instead, he prays for the well-being of all the Persians and of the king, for the sacrificer, after all, is included among all the Persians. When he has cut up the sacrificial victim into pieces and then boiled the meat, he spreads out the tenderest grass—preferably clover—and then places all of the meat on top of it. When he has arranged the meat piece by piece, a Magus stands near and chants a hymn on the origin of the gods—anyway, that's the kind of hymn they say it is. It is not their custom to perform a sacrifice without a Magus. The sacrificer waits a little while, then carries away the meat and does whatever he wants with it.

The day of all days they celebrate the most is their own birthday. On that day, the right thing to do is to serve a bigger meal than on any other day. On that day, their rich people serve up oxen, horses, camels, and donkeys that have been roasted whole in ovens, while their poor people serve smaller cattle, like sheep and goats. They eat few main dishes, but lots of appetizers, one after another, and for this reason the Persians say that the Greeks eat a main course and then stop when they are still hungry since after dinner nothing worth mentioning is brought out, though they wouldn't stop eating if it was. They love wine, but they are not allowed to vomit or to urinate in front of someone else. But though they have to be careful about that, they are accustomed to deliberate about their most important affairs when they are drunk, and then, on the next day, when they are sober, the master of the house they have been deliberating in proposes the decision that pleased them most. If they like it even when they are sober, they adopt it, but if not, they let it go. If they ever come to a provisional decision while sober, though, they then get drunk and reconsider it.

This is how you can tell if people who happen to meet each other on the street are social equals: instead of a verbal greeting, they kiss each other on the lips. If one is of slightly lower rank, they kiss each other's cheeks. If one is of a much lower rank, though, he prostrates himself and pays homage to the other. After themselves, Persians have the highest respect for the people who live closest to them, and next highest for those next closest, and so on. In accordance with this principle, they have the least respect for those who live farthest away. They consider themselves to be the best of people by far and others to share worth proportionally, so the people who live the farthest away are the worst. Subject nations ruled each other even under Median rule. That is, the Medes ruled over everything, but especially over those nearest to them, while those, in turn, ruled their neighbors, and so on. The Persians rank nations according to the same principle, by which each nation has a surrogate rule over the next one.

Nevertheless, the Persians are more inclined than other people to adopt foreign customs. For example, they wear Median clothes in the belief that they are more attractive than their own, and they wear Egyptian breastplates into war. They seek out and learn about all kinds of delights, and they even learned from the Greeks to have sex with boys. Each Persian man has many lawfully wedded wives, but many more mistresses.

Second only to being brave in battle, a man is considered manly if he has many sons to show for himself, and every year the king sends gifts to the man who shows off the most sons. They believe that there is strength in numbers. They educate their sons from the age of five to the age of twenty in only three things: horseback riding, archery, and telling the truth. The boy does not come into the presence of his father until he is five years old—until then he lives with the women. This is done so that if he should die while he is growing up he won't cause any grief to his father.

I approve of that custom, and I also approve of the one that forbids even the king to put someone to death on the basis of only one charge, and that forbids any Persian to do any of his household slaves any irreparable harm on the basis of one charge either. If, however, he finds on review that there are more and greater offenses than services, then he may give way to anger.

They say that no one has yet killed his own father or mother. It is inevitable, they say, that any such child who has ever been born will be found on investigation to have been either a changeling or a bastard. They say that it just isn't likely that a true parent will be killed by his own child.

Whatever they are not allowed to do, they are also not allowed to talk about. They consider lying to be the most disgraceful of all things. After that, it is owing money—for many reasons, but mostly, they say, because it is necessary for somebody who owes money to tell lies.

No citizen who is an albino or who has leprosy is allowed into the city or to mingle with other Persians. They say that he has committed some offense against the sun. Foreigners who catch these diseases are driven out of the country by posses. Even white doves are driven out, charged with the same offense.

They don't spit, urinate, or wash their hands in rivers, or allow anyone else to, for they especially revere rivers.

The Persians don't notice it, though we do, but this also happens to be true of them: their names, which refer to their physical characteristics or to their social importance, all end in the same letter, which the Dorians call san and which the Ionians call sigma. If you look into it, you will find that Persian names end in this letter—not some here and some there, but *all* of them.

I am able to say these things with certainty because I know them for a fact. There are things about the dead, though, which are concealed or referred to obliquely—for example that the corpse of a Persian man is not buried until it has been torn at by a bird or a dog. I know for sure, though, that the Magi practice this—because they do it openly—and that the Persians cover a corpse with wax before putting it in the ground. The Magi are very different from other people, including the Egyptian priests. The Egyptian priests refrain from killing any living thing, except what they ritually sacrifice. The Magi, however, will kill everything but dogs and people with their own hands. In fact,

they make a point of killing things, and go around killing ants and snakes and anything else that creeps, crawls, and flies. Well, that's how they've been practicing this custom since the beginning, so let it stay that way.

*　　*　　*

REVIEW QUESTIONS

1. How would you judge Herodotus's general opinion of Persian customs and values? Does he find things to admire about them?
2. Do any of his observations suggest to you that he might have been taken in by someone else's stories?

FROM The Torah: Laws

Modern scholars question the historicity of the Bible's account of the Hebrew Exodus, when thousands supposedly migrated from Egypt under the leadership of a man named Moses. The Egyptian records make no mention of such an event, nor is there any other evidence of it outside the biblical account. The impact of the Exodus story on the self-concept of the early Jewish people as a people who are chosen by God (who has identified himself by then as Yahweh) and whose fate is bound to their acceptance of him, is, however, immeasurable. As they made their way through the barren wilderness of the Sinai Desert, the Hebrews received from Yahweh a set of laws, the Decalogue or Ten Commandments. These laws were to govern both their relationship with him and their behavior among themselves. In subsequent books of the Pentateuch (the first five books of the Hebrew Bible, the authorship of which was traditionally ascribed to Moses), these laws were expanded and elaborated on to form the basis of the Torah, the corpus of biblical law. The Torah remains today the very core of Judaism and of Jewish self-identity as a people chosen by God.

From *Contemporary English Version* by American Bible Society (New York: American Bible Society, 1995).

FROM **The Book of Exodus**

Moses led the people out of the camp to meet God, and they stood at the foot of the mountain. Mount Sinai was covered with smoke because the LORD had come down in a flaming fire. Smoke poured out of the mountain just like a furnace, and the whole mountain shook. The trumpet blew louder and louder. Moses spoke, and God answered him with thunder. The LORD came down to the top of Mount Sinai and told Moses to meet him there. Then he said, "Moses, go and warn the people not to cross the boundary that you set at the foot of the mountain. They must not cross it to come and look at me, because if they do, many of them will die. Only the priests may come near me, and they must obey strict rules before I let them. If they don't, they will be punished." Moses replied, "The people cannot come up the mountain. You warned us to stay away because it is holy." Then the LORD told Moses, "Go down and bring Aaron back here with you. But the priests and people must not try to push their way through, or I will rush at them like a flood!" After Moses had gone back down, he told the people what the LORD had said.

God said to the people of Israel:

I am the LORD your God, the one who brought you out of Egypt where you were slaves.

Do not worship any god except me.

Do not make idols that look like anything in the sky or on earth or in the ocean under the earth. Don't bow down and worship idols. I am the LORD your God, and I demand all your love. If you reject me, I will punish your families for three or four generations. But if you love me and obey my laws, I will be kind to your families for thousands of generations.

Do not misuse my name. I am the LORD your God, and I will punish anyone who misuses my name. Remember that the Sabbath Day belongs to me. You have six days when you can do your work, but the seventh day of each week belongs to me, your God. No one is to work on that day—not you, your children, your slaves, your animals, or the foreigners who live in your towns. In six days I made the sky, the earth, the oceans, and everything in them, but on the seventh day I rested. That's why I made the Sabbath a special day that belongs to me.

Respect your father and your mother, and you will live a long time in the land I am giving you.

Do not murder.

Be faithful in marriage.

Do not steal.

Do not tell lies about others.

Do not want anything that belongs to someone else. Don't want anyone's house, wife or husband, slaves, oxen, donkeys or anything else.

*   *   *

The LORD told Moses to say to the people of Israel: "With your own eyes, you saw me speak to you from heaven. So you must never make idols of silver or gold to worship in place of me. Build an altar out of earth, and offer on it your sacrifices of sheep, goats, and cattle. Wherever I choose to be worshiped, I will come down to bless you. If you ever build an altar for me out of stones, do not use any tools to chisel the stones, because that would make the altar unfit. And don't build an altar that requires steps; you might expose yourself when you climb up."

The LORD gave Moses the following laws for his people:

If you buy a Hebrew slave, he must remain your slave for six years. But in the seventh year you must set him free, without cost to him. If he was single at the time you bought him, he alone must be set free. But if he was married at the time, both he and his wife must be given their freedom. If you give him a wife, and they have children, only the man himself must be set free; his wife and children remain the property of his owner.

But suppose the slave loves his wife and children so much that he won't leave without them. Then he must stand beside either the door or the doorpost at the place of worship, while his owner punches a small hole through one of his ears with a sharp metal rod. This makes him a slave for life. A young woman who was sold by her father doesn't gain her freedom in the same way that a man does. If she doesn't please the man who bought her to be his wife, he must let her be bought back. He cannot sell her to foreigners; this would break the contract he made with her. If he selects her as a wife for his son, he must treat her as his own daughter. If the man later marries another woman, he must continue to provide food and clothing for the one he bought and to treat her as a wife. If he fails to do any of these things, she must be given her freedom without cost.

Death is the punishment for murder. But if you did not intend to kill someone, and I, the LORD, let it happen anyway, you may run for safety to a place that I have set aside. If you plan in advance to murder someone, there's no escape, not even by holding on to my altar. You will be dragged off and killed. Death is the punishment for attacking your father or mother.

Death is the punishment for kidnapping. If you sell the person you kidnapped, or if you are caught with that person, the penalty is death.

Death is the punishment for cursing your father or mother.

Suppose two of you are arguing, and you hit the other with either a rock or your fist, without causing a fatal injury. If the victim has to stay in bed, and later has to use a stick when walking outside, you must pay for the loss of time and do what you can to help until the injury is completely healed. That's your only responsibility.

Death is the punishment for beating to death any of your slaves. However, if the slave lives a few days after the beating, you are not to be punished. After all, you have already lost the services of that slave who was your property.

Suppose a pregnant woman suffers a miscarriage as the result of an injury caused by someone who is fighting. If she isn't badly hurt, the one who injured her must pay whatever fine her husband demands and the judges approve. But if she is seriously injured, the payment will be life for life, eye for eye, tooth for tooth, hand for hand, foot for foot, burn for burn, cut for cut, and bruise for bruise. If you hit one of your slaves and cause the loss of an eye, the slave must be set free. The same law applies if you knock out a slave's tooth—the slave goes free.

A bull that kills someone with its horns must be killed and its meat destroyed, but the owner of the bull isn't responsible for the death.

Suppose you own a bull that has been in the habit of attacking people, but you have refused to keep it fenced in. If that bull kills someone, both you and the bull must be put to death by stoning. However, you may save your own life by paying whatever fine is demanded. This same law applies if the bull gores someone's son or daughter. If the bull kills a slave, you must pay the slave owner thirty pieces of silver for the loss of the slave, and the bull must be killed by stoning.

Suppose someone's ox or donkey is killed by falling into an open pit that you dug or left uncovered on your property. You must pay for the dead animal, and it becomes yours.

If your bull kills someone else's, yours must be sold. Then the money from your bull and the meat from the dead bull must be divided equally between you and the other owner.

If you refuse to fence in a bull that is known to attack others, you must pay for any animal it kills, but the dead animal will belong to you.

*   *   *

Suppose you borrow an animal from a neighbor, and it gets injured or dies while the neighbor isn't around. Then you must replace it. But if something happens to the animal while the owner is present, you do not have to replace it. If you had leased the animal, the money you paid the owner will cover any harm done to it.

Suppose a young woman has never been married and isn't engaged. If a man talks her into having sex, he must pay the bride price and marry her. But if her father refuses to let her marry the man, the bride price must still be paid. Death is the punishment for witchcraft.

Death is the punishment for having sex with an animal.

Death is the punishment for offering sacrifices to any god except me.

Do not mistreat or abuse foreigners who live among you. Remember, you were foreigners in Egypt.

Do not mistreat widows or orphans. If you do, they will beg for my help, and I will come to their rescue. In fact, I will get so angry that I will kill your men and make widows of their wives and orphans of their children.

Don't charge interest when you lend money to any of my people who are in need. Before sunset you must return any coat taken as security for a loan, because that is the only cover the poor have when they sleep at night. I am a merciful God, and when they call out to me, I will come to help them.

Don't speak evil of me or of the ruler of your people. Don't fail to give me the offerings of grain and wine that belong to me. Dedicate to me your first-born sons and the first-born of your cattle and sheep. Let the animals stay with their mothers for seven days, then on the eighth day give them to me, your God.

You are my chosen people, so don't eat the meat of any of your livestock that was killed by a wild animal. Instead, feed the meat to dogs.

Don't spread harmful rumors or help a criminal by giving false evidence.

Always tell the truth in court, even if everyone else is dishonest and stands in the way of justice. And don't favor the poor, simply because they are poor. If you find an ox or a donkey that has wandered off, take it back where it belongs, even if the owner is your enemy.

If a donkey is overloaded and falls down, you must do what you can to help, even if it belongs to someone who doesn't like you. Make sure that the poor are given equal justice in court. Don't bring false charges against anyone or sentence an innocent person to death. I won't forgive you if you do.

Don't accept bribes. Judges are blinded and justice is twisted by bribes.

Don't mistreat foreigners. You were foreigners in Egypt, and you know what it is like.

Plant and harvest your crops for six years, but let the land rest during the seventh year. The poor are to eat what they want from your fields, vineyards, and olive trees during that year, and when they have all they want from your fields, leave the rest for wild animals.

Work the first six days of the week, but rest and relax on the seventh day. This law is not only for you, but for your oxen, donkeys, and slaves, as well as for any foreigners among you.

*   *   *

FROM **The Book of Leviticus**

If you curse your father or mother, you will be put to death, and it will be your own fault.

If any of you men have sex with another man's wife, both you and the woman will be put to death.

Having sex with one of your father's wives disgraces him. So both you and the woman will be put to death, just as you deserve. It isn't natural to have sex with your daughter-in-law, and both of you will be put to death, just as you deserve. It's disgusting for men to have sex with one another, and those who do will be put to death, just as they deserve. It isn't natural for a man to marry both a mother and her daughter, and so all three of them will be burned to death. If any of you have sex with an animal, both you and the animal will be put to death, just as you deserve.

If you marry one of your sisters, you will be punished, and the two of you will be disgraced by being openly forced out of the community. If you have sex with a woman during her monthly period, both you and the woman will be cut off from the people of Israel. The sisters of your father and mother are your own relatives, and you will be punished for having sex with any of them. If you have sex with your uncle's wife, neither you nor she will ever have any children. And if you marry your sister-in-law, neither of you will ever have any children. Obey my laws and teachings. Or else the land I am giving you will become sick of you and throw you out. The nations I am chasing out did these disgusting things, and I hated them for it, so don't follow their example. I am the LORD your God, and I have promised you their land that is rich with milk and honey. I have chosen you to be different from other people. That's why you must make a difference between animals and birds that I have said are clean and unclean—this will keep you from becoming disgusting to me. I am the LORD, the holy God. You have been chosen to be my people, and so you must be holy too. If you claim to receive messages from the dead, you will be put to death by stoning, just as you deserve.

*   *   *

Suppose some of your people become so poor that they have to sell themselves and become your slaves. Then you must treat them as servants, rather than as slaves. And in the Year of Celebration they are to be set free, so they and their children may return home to their families and property. I brought them out of Egypt to be my servants, not to be sold as slaves. So obey me, and don't be cruel to the poor.

If you want slaves, buy them from other nations or from the foreigners who live in your own country, and make them your property. You can own them, and even leave them to your children when you die, but do not make slaves of your own people or be cruel to them.

*   *   *

Faithfully obey my laws, and I will send rain to make your crops grow and your trees produce fruit. Your harvest of grain and grapes will be so abundant, that you won't know what to do with it all. You will eat and be satisfied, and you will live in safety. I will bless your country with peace, and you will rest without fear. I will wipe out the dangerous animals and protect you from enemy attacks. You will chase and destroy your enemies, even if there are only five of you and a hundred of them, or only a hundred of you and ten thousand of them. I will treat you with such kindness that your nation will grow strong, and I will also keep my promises to you. Your barns will overflow with grain each year. I will live among you and never again look on you with disgust. I will walk with you—I will be your God, and you will be my people. I am the LORD your God, and I rescued you from Egypt, so that you would never again be slaves. I have set you free; now walk with your heads held high.

If you disobey me and my laws, and if you break our agreement, I will punish you terribly, and you will be ruined. You will be struck with incurable diseases and with fever that leads to blindness and depression. Your enemies will eat the crops you plant, and I will turn from you and let you be destroyed by your attackers. You will even run at the very rumor of attack. Then, if you still refuse to obey me, I will punish you seven times for each of your sins, until your pride is completely crushed. I will hold back the rain, so the sky above you will be like iron, and the ground beneath your feet will be like copper. All of your hard work will be for nothing—and there will be no harvest of grain or fruit.

If you keep rebelling against me, I'll punish you seven times worse, just as your sins deserve! I'll send wild animals to attack you, and they will gobble down your children and livestock. So few of you will be left that your roads will be deserted.

If you remain my enemies after this, I'll remain your enemy and punish you even worse. War will break out because you broke our agreement, and if you escape to your walled cities, I'll punish you with horrible diseases, and you will be captured by your enemies. You will have such a shortage of bread, that ten women will be able to bake their bread in the same oven. Each of you will get only a few crumbs, and you will go hungry.

Then if you don't stop rebelling, I'll really get furious and punish you terribly for your sins! In fact, you will be so desperate for food that you will eat your own children. I'll destroy your shrines and tear down your incense altars, leaving your dead bodies piled on top of your idols. And you will be disgusting to me. I'll wipe out your towns and your places of worship and will no longer be pleased with the smell of your sacrifices. Your land will become so desolate that even your enemies who settle there will be shocked when they see it. After I destroy your towns and ruin your land with war, I'll scatter you among the nations.

While you are prisoners in foreign lands, your own land will enjoy years of rest and refreshment, as it should have done each seventh year when you lived there. In the land of your enemies, you will tremble at the rustle of a leaf, as though it were a sword. And you will become so weak that you will stumble and fall over each other, even when no one is chasing you. Many of you will die in foreign lands, and others of you will waste away in sorrow as the result of your sins and the sins of your ancestors.

Then suppose you realize that I turned against you and brought you to the land of your enemies because both you and your ancestors had stubbornly sinned against me. If you humbly confess what you have done and start living right, I'll keep the promise I made to your ancestors Abraham, Isaac, and Jacob. I will bless your land and let it rest during the time that you are in a foreign country, paying for your rebellion against me and my laws.

No matter what you have done, I am still the LORD your God, and I will never completely reject you or become absolutely disgusted with you there in the land of your enemies. While nations watched, I rescued your ancestors from Egypt so that I would be their God. Yes, I am your LORD, and I will never forget our agreement.

*   *   *

FROM **The Book of Deuteronomy**

Suppose a man starts hating his wife soon after they are married. He might tell ugly lies about her, and say, "I married this woman, but when we slept together, I found out she wasn't a virgin."

If this happens, the bride's father and mother must go to the town gate to show the town leaders the proof that the woman was a virgin. Her father will say, "I let my daughter marry this man, but he started hating her and accusing her of not being a virgin. But he is wrong, because here is proof that she was a virgin!" Then the bride's parents will show them the bed sheet from the woman's wedding night.

The town leaders will beat the man with a whip because he accused his bride of not being a virgin. He will have to pay her father one hundred pieces of silver and will never be allowed to divorce her.

But if the man was right and there is no proof that his bride was a virgin, the men of the town will take the woman to the door of her father's house and stone her to death.

This woman brought evil into your community by sleeping with someone before she got married, and you must get rid of that evil by killing her.

People of Israel, if a man is caught having sex with someone else's wife, you must put them both to death. That way, you will get rid of the evil they have done in Israel.

If a man is caught in town having sex with an engaged woman who isn't screaming for help, they both must be put to death. The man is guilty of having sex with a married woman. And the woman is guilty because she didn't call for help, even though she was inside a town and people were nearby. Take them both to the town gate and stone them to death. You must get rid of the evil they brought into your community. If an engaged woman is raped out in the country, only the man will be put to death. Do not punish the woman at all; she has done nothing wrong, and certainly nothing deserving death. This crime is like murder, because the woman was alone out in the country when the man attacked her. She screamed, but there was no one to help her.

Suppose a woman isn't engaged to be married, and a man talks her into sleeping with him. If they are caught, they will be forced to get married. He must give her father fifty pieces of silver as a bride-price and can never divorce her. A man must not marry a woman who was married to his father. This would be a disgrace to his father.

REVIEW QUESTIONS

1. In the Torah, what is Yahweh's relationship to his chosen people?
2. How are these chosen people to set themselves apart from other peoples, and how are they to relate to them?
3. As reflected in these laws, what are the principal values and modes of acceptable behavior in Hebrew society?
4. What kinds of principles of compensation do these laws reflect, and how do they compare with the principles of compensation reflected in the laws of Hammurabi (see Chapter 1)?
5. What kinds of attitudes toward sexual behavior do these laws reflect, and how is that behavior regulated?
6. What status and rights do women possess in the context of these laws?
7. What does Yahweh promise in return for obedience to his laws? For disobedience to them?

FROM **The Book of Amos: Prophecies**

The works of the so-called literary prophets announced a new phase in the history of the covenant between Yahweh and his chosen people. Amos, a Judahite shepherd and fig grower who marks the first of this series of prophets, brought his message to the northern kingdom of Israel around 750 B.C.E., denouncing the sinfulness of that society and predicting its destruction. In the following selection, Amos reveals his visions that foretell Israel's doom.

From *Contemporary English Version* by American Bible Society (New York: American Bible Society, 1995).

*   *   *

Amaziah the priest at Bethel sent this message to King Jeroboam of Israel, "Amos is plotting against you in the very heart of Israel. Our nation cannot put up with his message for very long. Here is what he is saying:

'Jeroboam will be put to death,
and the people will be taken
to a foreign country.'"

Then Amaziah told me, "Amos, take your visions and get out! Go back to Judah and earn your living there as a prophet. Don't do any more preaching at Bethel. The king worships here at our national temple."

I answered:

I'm not a prophet! And I wasn't trained to be a prophet. I am a shepherd, and I take care of fig trees. But the LORD told me to leave my herds and preach to the people of Israel. And here you are, telling me not to preach! Now, listen to what the LORD says about you:

Your wife will become
a prostitute in the city,
your sons and daughters
will be killed in war,
and your land will be divided

among others.
You will die in a country
of foreigners,
and the people of Israel
will be dragged
from their homeland.

The LORD God showed me a basket of ripe fruit and asked, "Amos, what do you see?"

"A basket of ripe fruit," I replied.
Then he said,
"This is the end for my people Israel.
I won't forgive them again.
Instead of singing
in the temple,
they will cry and weep.
Dead bodies will be everywhere.
So keep silent!
I, the LORD, have spoken!"
You people crush those in need
and wipe out the poor.
You say to yourselves,
"How much longer before the end
of the New Moon Festival?
When will the Sabbath be over? Our wheat is
   ready,
and we want to sell it now.
We can't wait to cheat
and charge high prices

for the grain we sell.
We will use dishonest scales
and mix dust in the grain.
Those who are needy and poor
don't have any money.
We will make them our slaves
for the price
of a pair of sandals."
I, the LORD, won't forget
any of this,
though you take great pride
in your ancestor Jacob. Your country will tremble,
and you will mourn.
It will be like the Nile River
that rises and overflows,
then sinks back down.
On that day, I, the LORD God,
will make the sun
go down at noon,
and I will turn daylight
into darkness.
Your festivals and joyful singing
will turn into sorrow.
You will wear sackcloth and shave your heads,
as you would at the death
of your only son.
It will be a horrible day.
I, the LORD, also promise you
a terrible shortage,
but not of food and water.
You will hunger and thirst
to hear my message.
You will search everywhere—
from north to south,
from east to west.
You will go all over the earth,
seeking a message
from me, the LORD.
But you won't find one.
Your beautiful young women
and your young men
will faint from thirst.
You made promises
in the name of Ashimah,
the goddess of Samaria.
And you made vows in my name

at the shrines
of Dan and Beersheba. But you will fall
and never get up.
I saw a vision of the LORD
standing by the temple altar, and he said,
"Shake the columns
until the tops fall loose,
and the doorposts crumble.
Then make the pieces fall
on the people below.
I will take a sword and kill
anyone who escapes.
"If they dig deep into the earth
or climb to the sky,
I'll reach out and get them.
If they escape to the peaks
of Mount Carmel,
I'll search and find them.
And if they hide from me
at the bottom of the ocean,
I'll command a sea monster
to bite them.
I'll send a sword to kill them,
wherever their enemies
drag them off as captives.
I'm determined to hurt them,
not to help them."

When the LORD God All-Powerful
touches the earth,
it melts,
and its people mourn.
God makes the earth rise
and then fall,
just like the Nile River.
He built his palace in the heavens
and let its foundations
rest on the earth. He scoops up the ocean
and empties it on the earth.
His name is the LORD.

Israel, I am the LORD God,
and the Ethiopians are no less important to me
than you are.
I brought you out of Egypt,
but I also brought

the Philistines from Crete and the Arameans from
  Kir. My eyes have seen
what a sinful nation you are,
and I'll wipe you out.
But I will leave a few
of Jacob's descendants.
I, the LORD, have spoken!
At my command, all of you
will be sifted like grain.
Israelites who remain faithful
will be scattered
among the nations.
And the others will be trapped
like trash in a sifter.
Some of you are evil,
and you deny
that you will ever get caught.
But you will be killed.

In the future, I will rebuild
David's fallen kingdom.
I will build it from its ruins
and set it up again,
just as it used to be.
Then you will capture Edom
and the other nations
that are mine.
I, the LORD, have spoken,
and my words will come true.

You will have such a harvest
that you won't be able
to bring in all of your wheat
before plowing time.
You will have grapes left over
from season to season;
your fruitful vineyards
will cover the mountains.
I'll make Israel prosper again.
You will rebuild your towns
and live in them.
You will drink wine
from your own vineyards
and eat the fruit you grow.
I'll plant your roots deep
in the land I have given you,
and you won't ever
be uprooted again.
I, the LORD God, have spoken!

*   *   *

REVIEW QUESTIONS

1. According to Amos, why has Yahweh decided to punish Israel?
2. How thorough will that destruction be?
3. Does Yahweh offer any hope of salvation?

FROM The Book of Jeremiah: Prophecies

Given the resurgence of the great Mesopotamian powers of Assyria and then, follow-
ing Assyria's demise, Babylon, it was perhaps inevitable that Israel and then Judah
would be conquered. There emerged in Judah during the late seventh century B.C.E.
one of the greatest of the Hebrew prophets, Jeremiah, who foretold the destruction of
Judah as God's punishment of its people, who had failed to live up to their cove-
nant with him. Jeremiah, however, goes on to extend hope to the people of Judah in
the form of a new covenant that would focus, not on the unity and collective obedi-

ence of the Hebrew people but on the heartfelt commitment and renewal of the individual. Such a change in the focus of the covenant was to serve Judaism well in the coming years of the Diaspora.

From *Contemporary English Version* by American Bible Society (New York: American Bible Society, 1995).

*   *   *

The LORD told me to stand by the gate of the temple and to tell the people who were going in that the LORD All-Powerful, the God of Israel, had said: Pay attention, people of Judah! Change your ways and start living right, then I will let you keep on living in your own country. Don't fool yourselves! My temple is here in Jerusalem, but that doesn't mean I will protect you. I will keep you safe only if you change your ways. Be fair and honest with each other. Stop taking advantage of foreigners, orphans, and widows. Don't kill innocent people. And stop worshiping other gods. Then I will let you enjoy a long life in this land I gave your ancestors. But just look at what is happening! You put your trust in worthless lies. You steal and murder; you lie in court and are unfaithful in marriage. You worship idols and offer incense to Baal, when these gods have never done anything for you. And then you come into my temple and worship me! Do you think I will protect you so that you can go on sinning? You are thieves, and you have made my temple your hideout. But I've seen everything you have done.

Go to Shiloh, where my sacred tent once stood. Take a look at what I did there. My people Israel sinned, and so I destroyed Shiloh!

While you have been sinning, I have been trying to talk to you, but you refuse to listen. Don't think this temple will protect you. Long ago I told your ancestors to build it and worship me here, but now I have decided to tear it down, just as I destroyed Shiloh. And as for you, people of Judah, I'm going to send you away from my land, just as I sent away the people of Ephraim and the other northern tribes.

Jeremiah, don't pray for these people! I, the LORD, would refuse to listen. Do you see what the people of Judah are doing in their towns and in the streets of Jerusalem? Children gather firewood, their fathers build fires, and their mothers mix dough to bake bread for the goddess they call the Queen of Heaven. They even offer wine sacrifices to other gods, just to insult me. But they are not only insulting me; they are also insulting themselves by doing these shameful things. And now, I, the LORD All-Powerful, will flood Judah with my fiery anger until nothing is left—no people or animals, no trees or crops.

The LORD told me to say to the people of Judah:

I am the LORD All-Powerful, the God of Israel, but I won't accept sacrifices from you. So don't even bother bringing them to me. You might as well just cook the meat for yourselves.

At the time I brought your ancestors out of Egypt, I didn't command them to offer sacrifices to me. Instead, I told them, "If you listen to me and do what I tell you, I will be your God, you will be my people, and all will go well for you." But your ancestors refused to listen. They were stubborn, and whenever I wanted them to go one way, they always went the other. Ever since your ancestors left Egypt, I have been sending my servants the prophets to speak for me. But you have ignored me and become even more stubborn and sinful than your ancestors ever were!

Jeremiah, no matter what you do, the people won't listen. So you must say to them:

People of Judah, I am the LORD your God, but you have refused to obey me, and you didn't change when I punished you. And now, you no longer even pretend to be faithful to me.

*   *   *

. . . then bodies will lie scattered on the ground. Birds and wild animals will come and eat, and no one will be around to scare them off. When I am finished with your land, there will be deathly silence in the empty ruins of Jerusalem and the towns of Judah—no happy voices, no sounds of parties or wedding celebrations.

Then the bones of the dead kings of Judah and their officials will be dug up, along with the bones of the priests, the prophets, and everyone else in Jerusalem who loved and worshiped the sun, moon, and stars. These bones will be scattered and left lying on the ground like trash, where the sun and moon and stars can shine on them.

Some of you people of Judah will be left alive, but I will force you to go to foreign countries, and you will wish you were dead. I, the LORD God All-Powerful, have spoken.

*   *   *

You leaders of my people are like shepherds that kill and scatter the sheep. You were supposed to take care of my people, but instead you chased them away. So now I'll really take care of you, and believe me, you will pay for your crimes!

I will bring the rest of my people home from the lands where I have scattered them, and they will grow into a mighty nation. I promise to choose leaders who will care for them like real shepherds. All of my people will be there, and they will never again be frightened.

Someday I will appoint
an honest king
from the family of David,
a king who will be wise
and rule with justice.
As long as he is king,
Israel will have peace,
and Judah will be safe.
The name of this king will be
"The LORD Gives Justice."

A time will come when you will again worship me. But you will no longer call me the Living God who rescued Israel from Egypt. Instead, you will call me the Living God who rescued you from the land in the north and from all the other countries where I had forced you to go. And you will once again live in your own land.

When I think of the prophets,
I am shocked, and I tremble like someone drunk,
because of the LORD
and his sacred words.
Those unfaithful prophets
misuse their power
all over the country.
So God turned the pasturelands
into scorching deserts.

The LORD told me to say:
You prophets and priests
think so little of me, the LORD,
that you even sin
in my own temple!
Now I will punish you
with disaster,
and you will slip and fall
in the darkness.
I, the LORD, have spoken.
The prophets in Samaria
were disgusting to me,
because they preached
in the name of Baal
and led my people astray.
And you prophets in Jerusalem
are even worse.

You're unfaithful in marriage and never tell the truth. You even lead others to sin
instead of helping them
turn back to me.
You and the people of Jerusalem
are evil
like Sodom
and Gomorrah. You prophets in Jerusalem
have spread evil everywhere.
That's why I, the LORD, promise
to give you bitter poison
to eat and drink.

Don't listen to the lies
of these false prophets,
you people of Judah!
The message they preach
is something they imagined;
it did not come from me,
the LORD All-Powerful.
These prophets go to people
who refuse to respect me
and who are stubborn
and do whatever they want.
The prophets tell them,
"The LORD has promised
everything will be fine."
But I, the LORD, tell you
that these prophets
have never attended a meeting
of my council in heaven or heard me speak.
They are evil! So in my anger
I will strike them
like a violent storm.
I won't calm down,
until I have finished
what I have decided to do.
Someday you will understand
exactly what I mean.
I did not send these prophets
or speak to them,
but they ran to find you
and to preach their message.
If they had been in a meeting
of my council in heaven,
they would have told
you people of Judah
to give up your sins
and come back to me.
I am everywhere—
both near and far,
in heaven and on earth.
There are no secret places
where you can hide from me.

*   *   *

Israel, you belong to me, so don't be afraid.
You deserved to be punished;
that's why I scattered you

in distant nations.
But I am with you,
and someday I will destroy
those nations.
Then I will bring you
and your descendants
back to your land,
where I will protect you
and give you peace.
Then your fears will be gone.
I, the LORD, have spoken.

The LORD said:
My people, you are wounded
and near death.
You are accused of a crime
with no one to defend you,
and you are covered with sores
that no medicine can cure.
Your friends have forgotten you;
they don't care anymore.
Even I have acted like an enemy.
And because your sins
are horrible and countless,
I will be cruel
as I punish you.
So don't bother to cry out
for relief from your pain.
But if your enemies try to rob
or destroy you,
I will rob and destroy them,
and they will be led as captives
to foreign lands.
No one wants you as a friend
or cares what happens to you.
But I will heal your injuries,
and you will get well.

The LORD said:
Israel, I will be kind to you
and let you come home.
Jerusalem now lies in ruins,
but you will rebuild it,
complete with a new palace. Other nations
   will respect
and honor you.

Your homes will be filled
with children,
and you will celebrate,
singing praises to me.
It will be just like old times.
Your nation will worship me,
and I will punish anyone
who abuses you.
One of your own people
will become your ruler.
And when I invite him
to come near me
at the place of worship,
he will do so.
No one would dare to come near
without being invited.
You will be my people,
and I will be your God.
I, the LORD, have spoken.
I am furious!
And like a violent storm
I will strike those
who do wrong.
I won't calm down
until I have finished
what I have decided to do.
Someday, you will understand
what I mean.

The LORD said:
Israel, I promise
that someday all your tribes
will again be my people,
and I will be your God.
In the desert I was kind
to those who escaped death.
I gave them peace,
and when the time is right,
I'll do the same for you. I, the LORD, have
   spoken.

   Some time ago, the LORD appeared to me and
told me to say: Israel, I will always love you;

that's why I've been so patient
and kind.

You are precious to me,
and so I will rebuild
your nation.
Once again you will dance for joy
and play your tambourines.
You will plant vineyards
on the hills of Samaria
and enjoy the grapes.
Someday those who guard
the hill country of Ephraim
will shout, "Let's go to Zion
and worship the LORD our God."

The LORD says:
Celebrate and sing for Israel,
the greatest of nations.
Offer praises and shout,
"Come and rescue
your people, LORD!
Save what's left of Israel."
I, the LORD, will bring
my people back from Babylonia and everywhere
   else on earth.
The blind and the lame
will be there.
Expectant mothers
and women about to give birth
will come and be part
of that great crowd.
They will weep and pray
as I bring them home.
I will lead them
to streams of water.
They will walk on a level road and not stumble.
I am a father to Israel, my favorite children.
Listen to me, you nations
nearby or across the sea.
I scattered the people of Israel,
but I will gather them again.
I will protect them like a shepherd
guarding a flock;
I will rescue them from enemies
who could overpower them.
My people will come
to Mount Zion
and celebrate;

their faces will glow
because of my blessings.
I'll give them grain, grapes,
and olive oil,
as well as sheep and cattle.
Israel will be prosperous
and grow
like a garden
with plenty of water.
Young women and young men,
together with the elderly,
will celebrate and dance,
because I will comfort them
and turn their sorrow
into happiness.
I will bless my people
with more food

than they need,
and the priests will enjoy
the choice cuts of meat.
I, the LORD, have spoken.

* * *

REVIEW QUESTIONS

1. According to Jeremiah, what is God's opinion of the kings of Judah and the priests and prophets of Jerusalem?
2. What punishments does God promise?
3. Does God offer a promise of redemption?
4. Who will bring that redemption?

FROM The Book of Isaiah: Prophecies

The Book of Isaiah contains the writings of at least two different authors, separated in time by about 150 years: a prophet named Isaiah, from Jerusalem, whose career spanned the latter half of the eighth century B.C.E., and an unknown prophet, referred to now as the Second Isaiah, whose writings are included here. The Second Isaiah's career was in Babylon and dates to the later part of the exile there (587–39 B.C.E.). In the Second Isaiah's writings, Yahweh has assumed a role much larger than that of the exclusive God of a chosen people.

From *Contemporary English Version* by American Bible Society (New York: American Bible Society, 1995).

* * *

People of Israel,
I have chosen you
as my servant.
I am your Creator.
You were in my care
even before you were born.
Israel, don't be terrified!
You are my chosen servant,

my very favorite. I will bless the thirsty land
by sending streams of water;
I will bless your descendants
by giving them my Spirit.
They will spring up like grass or like willow
    trees
near flowing streams.
They will worship me
and become my people.
They will write my name

on the back of their hands. I am the LORD
  All-Powerful,
the first and the last,
the one and only God.
Israel, I have rescued you!
I am your King.
Can anyone compare with me?
If so, let them speak up
and tell me now.
Let them say what has happened
since I made my nation
long ago,
and let them tell
what is going to happen. Don't tremble with fear!
Didn't I tell you long ago?
Didn't you hear me?
I alone am God—
no one else is a mighty rock.
Those people who make idols
are nothing themselves,
and the idols they treasure
are just as worthless.
Worshipers of idols are blind,
stupid, and foolish.
Why make an idol or an image
that can't do a thing?
Everyone who makes idols
and all who worship them
are mere humans,
who will end up
sadly disappointed.
Let them face me in court
and be terrified.

*   *   *

People of Israel,
you are my servant,
so remember all of this.
Israel, I created you,
and you are my servant.
I won't forget you. Turn back to me!
I have rescued you
and swept away your sins
as though they were clouds.

Tell the heavens and the earth

to start singing!
Tell the mountains
and every tree in the forest
to join in the song!
The LORD has rescued his people;
now they will worship him.

Israel, I am your LORD.
I am your source of life,
and I have rescued you.
I created everything
from the sky above
to the earth below.
I make liars of false prophets
and fools of fortunetellers.
I take human wisdom
and turn it into nonsense.
I will make the message
of my prophets come true.
They are saying, "Jerusalem
will be filled with people,
and the LORD will rebuild
the towns of Judah."
I am the one who commands
the sea and its streams
to run dry.
I am also the one who says,
"Cyrus will lead my people
and obey my orders.
Jerusalem and the temple
will be rebuilt."

The LORD said to Cyrus, his chosen one:
I have taken hold
of your right hand
to help you capture nations
and remove kings from power.
City gates will open for you;
not one will stay closed.
As I lead you,
I will level mountains and break the iron bars
on bronze gates of cities.
I will give you treasures
hidden in dark
and secret places.
Then you will know that I,
the LORD God of Israel,

have called you by name.
Cyrus, you don't even know me!
But I have called you by name
and highly honored you because of Israel,
my chosen servant.
Only I am the LORD!
There are no other gods.
I have made you strong,
though you don't know me.
Now everyone from east to west
will learn that I am the LORD.
No other gods are real.
I create light and darkness,
happiness and sorrow.
I, the LORD, do all of this.

*   *   *

The clay doesn't ask,
"Why did you make me this way?
Where are the handles?"
Children don't have the right
to demand of their parents,
"What have you done
to make us what we are?"
I am the LORD, the Creator,
the holy God of Israel.
Do you dare question me
about my own nation
or about what I have done?
I created the world
and covered it with people;
I stretched out the sky
and filled it with stars.
I have done the right thing
by placing Cyrus in power,
and I will make the roads easy
for him to follow.
I am the LORD All-Powerful!
Cyrus will rebuild my city
and set my people free
without being paid a thing.
I, the LORD, have spoken.

*   *   *

Anyone who makes idols
will be confused

and terribly disgraced.
But Israel, I, the LORD,
will always keep you safe
and free from shame.

The LORD alone is God!
He created the heavens
and made a world
where people can live,
instead of creating
an empty desert.
The LORD alone is God;
there are no others.
The LORD did not speak
in a dark secret place
or command Jacob's descendants
to search for him in vain.
The LORD speaks the truth,
and this is what he says
to every survivor
from every nation:
"Gather around me!
Learn how senseless it is
to worship wooden idols
or pray to helpless gods.
"Why don't you get together
and meet me in court?
Didn't I tell you long ago
what would happen?
I am the only God!
There are no others.
I bring about justice,
and have the power to save.
"I invite the whole world
to turn to me and be saved.
I alone am God!
No others are real.
I have made a solemn promise,
one that won't be broken:
Everyone will bow down
and worship me.
They will admit that I alone
can bring about justice.
Everyone who is angry with me
will be terribly ashamed
and will turn to me.

I, the LORD, will give
victory and great honor
to the people of Israel."

City of Babylon,
You are delicate
and untouched,
but that will change.
Surrender your royal power
and sit in the dirt.
Start grinding grain!
Take off your veil.
Strip off your fancy clothes
and cross over rivers. You will suffer the shame
of going naked,
because I will take revenge,
and no one can escape. I am the LORD
   All-Powerful,
the holy God of Israel.
I am their Savior.
Babylon, be silent!
Sit in the dark.
No longer will nations
accept you as their queen.
I was angry with my people.
So I let you take their land
and bring disgrace on them.
You showed them no mercy,
but were especially cruel
to those who were old.
You thought that you
would be queen forever.
You didn't care what you did;
it never entered your mind
that you might get caught.
You think that you alone
are all-powerful,
that you won't be a widow
or lose your children.
All you care about is pleasure,
but listen to what I say.
Your magic powers and charms
will suddenly fail,
then you will be a widow
and lose your children.
You hid behind evil

like a shield and said,
"No one can see me!"
You were fooled by your wisdom
and your knowledge;
you felt sure that you alone
were in full control.
But without warning,
disaster will strike—
and your magic charms
won't help at all.
Keep using your magic powers
and your charms
as you have always done.
Maybe—just maybe—
you will frighten somebody!
You have worn yourself out,
asking for advice
from those who study the stars
and tell the future
month after month.
Go ask them how to be saved
from what will happen.
People who trust the stars
are as helpless
as straw
in a flaming fire.
No one can even keep warm, sitting by a fire
that feeds only on straw.
These are the fortunetellers
you have done business with
all of your life.
But they don't know
where they are going,
and they can't save you.

People of Israel,
you come from Jacob's family
and the tribe of Judah. You claim to worship me,
the LORD God of Israel,
but you are lying.
You call Jerusalem your home
and say you depend on me,
the LORD All-Powerful,
the God of Israel.
Long ago I announced
what was going to be,

then without warning,
I made it happen.
I knew you were stubborn
and hardheaded.
And I told you these things,
so that when they happened
you would not say,
"The idols we worship did this."
You heard what I said,
and you have seen it happen.
Now admit that it's true!
I will show you secrets
you have never known.

* * *

By the power of his Spirit
the LORD God has sent me
with this message:
People of Israel,
I am the holy LORD God,
the one who rescues you.
For your own good,
I teach you,
and I lead you
along the right path.
How I wish that you
had obeyed my commands!
Your success and good fortune
would then have overflowed
like a flooding river.
Your nation would be blessed
with more people
than there are grains of sand
along the seashore.
And I would never have let
your country be destroyed.
Now leave Babylon!
Celebrate as you go.
Be happy and shout
for everyone to hear,
"The LORD has rescued
his servant Israel!
He led us through the desert
and made water flow from a rock
to satisfy our thirst.
But the LORD has promised

that none who are evil
will live in peace."
Everyone, listen,
even you foreign nations
across the sea.
The LORD chose me
and gave me a name
before I was born.
He made my words pierce
like a sharp sword
or a pointed arrow;
he kept me safely hidden
in the palm of his hand.
The LORD said to me,
"Israel, you are my servant;
and because of you
I will be highly honored."
I said to myself,
"I'm completely worn out;
my time has been wasted.
But I did it for the LORD God,
and he will reward me."
Even before I was born,
the LORD God chose me
to serve him and to lead back
the people of Israel.
So the LORD has honored me
and made me strong.
Now the LORD says to me,
"It isn't enough for you
to be merely my servant.
You must do more than lead back
survivors
from the tribes
of Israel.
I have placed you here as a light
for other nations;
you must take my saving power
to everyone on earth."

Israel, I am the holy LORD God,
the one who rescues you.
You are slaves of rulers
and of a nation
who despises you. Now this is what I
   promise:

Kings and rulers will honor you
by kneeling at your feet.
You can trust me! I am your LORD,
the holy God of Israel,
and you are my chosen ones.

This is what the LORD says:
I will answer your prayers
because I have set a time
when I will help
by coming to save you.
I have chosen you
to take my promise of hope
to other nations. You will rebuild the country
from its ruins,
then people will come
and settle there.
You will set prisoners free
from dark dungeons
to see the light of day.
On their way home,
they will find plenty to eat,
even on barren hills.
They won't go hungry
or get thirsty;
they won't be bothered
by the scorching sun
or hot desert winds.
I will be merciful
while leading them along
to streams of water.
I will level the mountains
and make roads.
Then my people will return
from distant lands
in the north and the west
and from the city of Syene.

Tell the heavens and the earth
to celebrate and sing;
command every mountain
to join in the song.
The LORD's people have suffered,
but he has shown mercy
and given them comfort.
The people of Zion said,

"The LORD has turned away
and forgotten us."
The LORD answered,
"Could a mother forget a child
who nurses at her breast?
Could she fail to love an infant
who came from her own body?
Even if a mother could forget,
I will never forget you.
A picture of your city
is drawn on my hand.
You are always in my thoughts!
"Your city will be built faster
than it was destroyed—those who attacked it
will retreat and leave.
Look around! You will see
your people coming home.
As surely as I live,
I, the LORD, promise
that your city with its people
will be as lovely as a bride
wearing her jewelry."

Jerusalem is now in ruins!
Nothing is left of the city.
But it will be rebuilt
and soon overcrowded;
its cruel enemies
will be gone far away.
Jerusalem is a woman
whose children were born
while she was in deep sorrow over the loss of her
    husband.
Now those children
will come and seek room
in the crowded city,
and Jerusalem will ask,
"Am I really their mother?
How could I have given birth
when I was still mourning
in a foreign land?
Who raised these children?
Where have they come from?"
The LORD God says:
"I will soon give a signal
for the nations

to return your sons
and your daughters
to the arms of Jerusalem.
The kings and queens
of those nations
where they were raised
will come and bow down.
They will take care of you
just like a slave
taking care of a child.
Then you will know
that I am the LORD.
You won't be disappointed
if you trust me."

Has anyone believed us
or seen the mighty power
of the LORD in action?
Like a young plant or a root
that sprouts in dry ground,
the servant grew up
obeying the LORD.
He wasn't some handsome king.
Nothing about the way he looked
made him attractive to us.
He was hated and rejected;
his life was filled with sorrow
and terrible suffering.
No one wanted to look at him.
We despised him and said,
"He is a nobody!"
He suffered and endured
great pain for us,
but we thought his suffering
was punishment from God.
He was wounded and crushed
because of our sins;
by taking our punishment,
he made us completely well.
All of us were like sheep
that had wandered off.
We had each gone our own way,
but the LORD gave him
the punishment we deserved.
He was painfully abused,
but he did not complain.

He was silent like a lamb
being led to the butcher,
as quiet as a sheep
having its wool cut off.
He was condemned to death
without a fair trial.
Who could have imagined
what would happen to him?
His life was taken away
because of the sinful things
my people had done. He wasn't dishonest
    or violent,
but he was buried in a tomb
of cruel and rich people. The LORD decided
    his servant
would suffer as a sacrifice
to take away the sin
and guilt of others.
Now the servant will live
to see his own descendants. He did everything
the LORD had planned.
By suffering, the servant
will learn the true meaning
of obeying the LORD.
Although he is innocent,
he will take the punishment
for the sins of others,
so that many of them
will no longer be guilty.
The LORD will reward him
with honor and power
for sacrificing his life.
Others thought he was a sinner,
but he suffered for our sins
and asked God to forgive us.

REVIEW QUESTIONS

1. According to the Second Isaiah, what now is the dominion of the Hebrews' God?
2. What role has Israel now assumed in relation to the other nations of the earth?
3. Does a messiah figure emerge in this document?
4. What is God's view of Babylon?

An Aramaic Letter from Elephantine

*The exile of the Jews of Jerusalem to Babylon in 587 B.C.E. marked the beginning
of the Diaspora, the dispersion of the Jewish people from Judah throughout the
Near East and, in time, the globe. By the time of the Achaemenid Persian Empire,
a Jewish community had established itself at Elephantine in southern Egypt, where
the following letter was recovered. Written on papyrus in the Aramaic script and
dating to 410 B.C.E., it is addressed to the Persian governor of Judah from the
Jewish community.*

From *Ancient Near Eastern Texts Relating to the Old Testament*, edited by James B. Pritchard
(Princeton, N.J.: Princeton University Press, 1983).

To our lord Bagoas, governor of Judah, your servants Yedoniah and his colleagues, the priests who are in the fortress of Elephantine. May the God of Heaven seek after the welfare of our lord exceedingly at all times and give you favor before King Darius and the nobles a thousand times more than now. May you be happy and healthy at all times. Now, your servant Yedoniah and his colleagues depose as follows: In the month of Tammuz in the 14th year of King Darius, when Arsames departed and went to the king, the priests of the god Khnub, who is in the fortress of Elephantine, conspired with Vidaranag, who was commander-in-chief here, to wipe out the temple of the god Yaho from the fortress of Elephantine. So that wretch Vidaranag sent to his son Nefayan, who was in command of the garrison of the fortress of Syene, this order, "The temple of the god Yaho in the fortress of Yeb is to be destroyed." Nefayan thereupon led the Egyptians with the other troops. Coming with their weapons to the fortress of Elephantine, they entered that temple and razed it to the ground. The stone pillars that were there they smashed. Five "great" gateways built with hewn blocks of stone which were in that temple they demolished, but their doors *are standing,* and the hinges of those doors are of bronze; and *their* roof of cedarwood, all of it, with the . . . and whatever else was there, everything they

burnt with fire. As for the basins of gold and silver and other articles that were in that temple, they carried all of them off and made them their own.—Now, our forefathers built this temple in the fortress of Elephantine back in the days of the kingdom of Egypt, and when Cambyses came to Egypt he found it built. They knocked down all the temples of the gods of Egypt, but no one did an damage to this temple. But when this happened, we and our wives and our children wore sackcloth, and fasted, and prayed to Yaho the Lord of Heaven, who has let us see our desire upon that Vidaranag. The dogs took the fetter out of his feet, and any property he had gained was lost; and any men who have sought to do evil to this temple have all been killed and we have seen our desire upon them.—We have also sent a letter before now, when this evil was done to us, to our lord and to the high priest Johanan and his colleagues the priests in Jerusalem and to Ostanes the brother of Anani and the nobles of the Jews. Never a letter have they sent to us. Also, from the month of Tammuz, year 14 of King Darius, to this day, we have been wearing sackcloth and fasting, making our wives as widows, not anointing ourselves with oil or drinking wine. Also, from then to now, in the year 17 of King Darius, no meal-offering, incense, nor burnt offering have been offered in this temple. Now your servants Yedoniah, and his colleagues, and the Jews, the citizens of Elephantine, all say thus: If it please our lord, take thought of this temple to rebuild it, since they do not let us rebuild it. Look to your well-wishers and friends here in Egypt. Let a letter be sent from you to them concerning the temple of the god Yaho to build it in the fortress of Elephantine as it was built before; and the meal-offering, incense, and burnt offering will be offered in your name, and we shall pray for you at all times, we, and our wives, and our children, and the Jews who are here, all of them, if you do thus, so that that temple is rebuilt. And you shall have a merit before Yaho the God of Heaven more than a man who offers to him burnt offering and sacrifices worth a thousand talents of silver and because of gold.

Because of this we have written to inform you. We have also set the whole matter forth in a letter in our name to Delaiah and Shelemiah, the sons of Sanballat the governor of Samaria. Also, Arsames knew nothing of all that was done to us. On the 20th of Marheshwan, year 17 of King Darius.

REVIEW QUESTIONS

1. Why was this letter written? Does it provide any evidence of a relationship between the Elephantine community and that in Jerusalem?
2. What does it suggest about the conditions of the Jews living in the Diaspora (the Jewish communities outside Palestine) at this time?

3 ❧ THE GREEK EXPERIMENT

By the time that the uncharacteristically allied city-states of Hellas (Greece) had to face invasion by the massive forces of the Achaemenid Persian emperor Darius in 490 B.C.E., the much more ancient civilizations of Mesopotamia and Egypt (not to mention India and China) had been thriving for thousands of years. By 500 B.C.E., both Babylon and Egypt—in fact, the entire Near East— had fallen under the sway of the Persian Empire, which could boast of one of the more sophisticated imperial systems of antiquity and resources vastly superior to those of the upstarts from the Aegean, located on the empire's far western periphery. The Greeks themselves, from the Persian perspective, undoubtedly seemed to be a disorganized, belligerent, even barbarian people who represented no real threat to continued Persian dominion.

Nonetheless, only eleven years after the Persians' first invasion, the Greeks had vanquished and expelled not only the invasion of Darius but also a second, even more massive invasion under the son and successor of Darius, Xerxes. The Greeks' improbable success came to be seen as one of the first events in the process by which the West, over many centuries, defined itself as an entity distinct from and, in its eyes, generally superior to the East.

Scholars today recognize (as did ancient Greek writers) the tremendous debt the early Greeks owed to the older civilizations of the ancient Near East and Egypt. Indeed, to be aware of that debt, one need look no further than early Greek statuary and temple architecture, with their obviously Egyptian inspiration, or the Greek alphabet, borrowed from the Phoenicians, with whom the Greeks traded. However, within the unique context of early Greek society, political development, and culture, there emerged a number of concepts and issues that have remained at the heart of the ongoing development of Western civilization and have had significant impact on the non-Western civilizations that, in the past two centuries, have increasingly been confronted with the ideas and values of the West. What are the appropriate roles and rights of the individual in society? To what does the individual owe primary allegiance, the dictates of conscience or the laws of the state? How should a state be properly organized and governed, and by whom? What ought to be the respective roles of men and women in society? Do divine forces govern natural phenomena and human history? Indeed, do gods or a god even exist? Some have claimed that much of the history of Western culture subsequent to the era of the Greek city-states has centered on the continuing endeavor to answer these and other questions that the Greeks raised.

The Greeks took some giant steps in addressing these questions. In fact, they made perhaps their most significant contributions to that endeavor during the relatively brief "golden age" that accompanied Athens' rise to preeminence among the city-states after the defeat of the Persians. Classical Greek civilization achieved its loftiest heights in Athens during the decades prior to Athens' disastrous defeat by Sparta and its allies at the end of the Peloponnesian War. Less than seventy years later, Athens, Sparta, and the other previously independent city-states were compelled to cede their autonomy to the hegemony of the Macedonian king Philip II, whose son Alexander would inaugurate a new era during which the affairs of those city-states would take a back seat to the Hellenistic kingdoms. Nonetheless, the relatively brief zenith of the classical Greek city-states would, in time, be recognized as vastly out of proportion to their influence on the later course of Western civilization.

HOMER

FROM *The Odyssey*

The actual existence of the poet named Homer, and of the Trojan War about which he wrote, is still debated among scholars. The influence of the epic poems, the Iliad and the Odyssey, that the later Greeks attributed to him is not. For the warrior aristocracy whose interests and tastes these poems reflected and for whom they were recited as entertainment, Homer's tales of the Greeks' siege of Troy and of the exploits of Odysseus and his men on their way home after that siege provided a vivid model of heroic values and behavior in a world where the gods intruded their designs regularly into human affairs. In the following selection from the Odyssey, the main hero, Odysseus, on his long and dangerous journey back to Ithaca on the Greek mainland *after the Greeks have sacked Troy, has reached the land of Phaeacia. Its king, Alcinous, is determined to act as his worthy host.*

From *The Odyssey of Homer*, translated by Samuel Butler (Toronto: D. Van Nostrand, 1944), pp. 88–94.

Now when the child of morning, rosy-fingered Dawn, appeared, Alcinous and Odysseus both rose, and Alcinous led the way to the Phaeacian place of assembly, which was near the ships. When they got there they sat down side by side on a seat of polished stone, while Athene took the form of one of Alcinous' servants, and went round the town in order to help Odysseus to get home. She went up to the citizens, man by man, and said: "Aldermen and town councilors of the Phaeacians, come to the assembly all of you and listen to the stranger who has just come off a long voyage to the house of King Alcinous. He looks like an immortal god."

With these words she made them all want to come, and they flocked to the assembly till seats and standing room were alike crowded. Everyone was struck with the appearance of Odysseus, for Athene had beautified him about the head and shoulders, making him look taller and stouter than he really was, that he might impress the Phaeacians favorably as being a very remarkable man, and might come off well in the many trials of skill to which they would challenge him. Then, when they were got together, Alcinous spoke:

"Hear me," said he, "aldermen and town councilors of the Phaeacians, that I may speak even as I am minded. This stranger, whoever he may be, has found his way to my house from somewhere or other either east or west. He wants an escort and wishes to have the matter settled. Let us then get one ready for him, as we have done for others before him. Indeed, no one who ever yet came to my house has been able to complain of me for not speeding him on his way soon enough. Let us draw a ship into the sea—one that has never yet made a voyage—and man her with two and fifty of our smartest young sailors. Then when you have made

fast your oars each by his own seat, leave the ship and come to my house to prepare a feast. I will supply you with everything. I am giving these instructions to the young men who will form the crew. As regards you aldermen and town councilors, you will join me in entertaining our guest in the cloisters. I can take no excuses, and we will have Demodocus to sing to us; for there is no bard like him, whatever he may choose to sing about."

Alcinous then led the way, and the others followed after, while a servant went to fetch Demodocus. The fifty-two picked oarsmen went to the seashore as they had been told, and when they got there they drew the ship into the water, got her mast and sails inside her, bound the oars to the thole-pins with twisted thongs of leather, all in due course, and spread the white sails aloft. They moored the vessel a little way out from land, and then came on shore and went to the house of King Alcinous. The outhouses, yards, and all the precincts were filled with crowds of men in great multitudes both old and young; and Alcinous killed them a dozen sheep, eight full-grown pigs, and two oxen. These they skinned and dressed so as to provide a magnificent banquet.

A servant presently led in the famous bard Demodocus, whom the muse had dearly loved, but to whom she had given both good and evil, for though she had endowed him with a divine gift of song, she had robbed him of his eyesight. Pontonous set a seat for him among the guests, leaning it up against a bearing-post. He hung the lyre for him on a peg over his head, and showed him where he was to feel for it with his hands. He also set a fair table with a basket of victuals by his side, and a cup of wine from which he might drink whenever he was so disposed.

The company then laid their hands upon the

good things that were before them, but as soon as they had had enough to eat and drink, the muse inspired Demodocus to sing the feats of heroes, and more especially a matter that was then in the mouths of all men, to wit, the quarrel between Odysseus and Achilles, and the fierce words that they heaped on one another as they sat together at a banquet. But Agamemnon was glad when he heard his chieftains quarreling with one another, for Apollo had foretold him this at Pytho when he crossed the stone floor to consult the oracle. Here was the beginning of the evil that by the will of Zeus fell both upon Danaans and Trojans.

Thus sang the bard, but Odysseus drew his purple mantle over his head and covered his face, for he was ashamed to let the Phaeacians see that he was weeping. When the bard left off singing, he wiped the tears from his eyes, uncovered his face, and, taking his cup, made a drink offering to the gods; but when the Phaeacians pressed Demodocus to sing further, for they delighted in his lays, then Odysseus again drew his mantle over his head and wept bitterly. No one noticed his distress except Alcinous, who was sitting near him, and heard the heavy sighs that he was heaving. So he at once said, "Aldermen and town councilors of the Phaeacians, we have had enough now, both of the feast and of the minstrelsy that is its due accompaniment. Let us proceed therefore to the athletic sports so that our guest on his return home may be able to tell his friends how much we surpass all other nations as boxers, wrestlers, jumpers, and runners."

With these words he led the way, and the others followed after. A servant hung Demodocus' lyre on its peg for him, led him out of the cloister, and set him on the same way as that along which all the chief men of the Phaeacians were going to see the sports; a crowd of several thousands of people followed them, and there were many excellent competitors for all the prizes. Acroneos, Ocyalus, Elatreus, Nauteus, Prymneus, Anchialus, Eretmeus, Ponteus, Proreus, Thoon, Anabesineus, and Amphialus son of Polyneus son of Tecton. There was also Euryalus son of Naubolus, who was like Ares himself, and was the best looking man among the Phaeacians except Laodamas. Three sons of Alcinous—Laodamas, Halios, and Clytoneus—competed also.

The foot races came first. The course was set out for them from the starting post, and they raised a dust upon the plain as they all flew forward at the same moment. Clytoneus came in first by a long way; he left everyone else behind him by the length of the furrow that a couple of mules can plow in a fallow field. They then turned to the painful art of wrestling, and here Euryalus proved to be the best man. Amphialus excelled all the others in jumping, while at throwing the disc there was no one who could approach Elatreus. Alcinous' son Laodamas was the best boxer, and he it was who presently said, when they had all been diverted with the games, "Let us ask the stranger whether he excels in any of these sports. He seems very powerfully built; his thighs, calves, hands, and neck are of prodigious strength, nor is he at all old, but he has suffered much lately, and there is nothing like the sea for making havoc with a man, no matter how strong he is."

"You are quite right, Laodamas," replied Euryalus, "go up to your guest and speak to him about it yourself."

When Laodamas heard this he made his way into the middle of the crowd and said to Odysseus, "I hope, sir, that you will enter yourself for some one or other of our competitions if you are skilled in any of them—and you must have gone in for many a one before now. There is nothing that does anyone so much credit all his life long as the showing himself a proper man with his hands and feet. Have a try therefore at something, and banish all sorrow from your mind. Your return home will not be long delayed, for the ship is already drawn into the water, and the crew is found."

Odysseus answered, "Laodamas, why do you taunt me in this way? My mind is set rather on cares than contests; I have been through infinite trouble, and am come among you now as a suppliant, praying your king and people to further me on my return home."

Then Euryalus reviled him outright and said: "I gather, then, that you are unskilled in any of the many sports that men generally delight in. I suppose you are one of those grasping traders that go about in ships as captains or merchants, and who think of nothing but of their outward freights and homeward cargoes. There does not seem to be much of the athlete about you."

"For shame, sir!" answered Odysseus, fiercely. "You are an insolent fellow—so true is it that the gods do not grace all men alike in speech, person, and understanding. One man may be of weak presence, but heaven has adorned him with such a good conversation that he charms everyone who sees him; his honeyed moderation carries his hearers with him so that he is leader in all assemblies of his fellows, and wherever he goes he is looked up to. Another may be as handsome as a god, but his good looks are not crowned with discretion. This is your case. No god could make a finer looking fellow than you are, but you are a fool. Your ill-judged remarks have made me exceedingly angry, and you are quite mistaken, for I excel in a great many athletic exercises. Indeed, so long as I had youth and strength, I was among the first athletes of the age. Now, however, I am worn out by labor and sorrow, for I have gone through much both on the field of battle and by the waves of the weary sea. Still, in spite of all this I will compete, for your taunts have stung me to the quick."

So he hurried up without even taking his cloak off, and seized a disc, larger, more massive and much heavier than those used by the Phaeacians when disc-throwing among themselves. Then, swinging it back, he threw it from his brawny hand, and it made a humming sound in the air as he did so. The Phaeacians quailed beneath the rushing of its flight as it sped gracefully from his hand, and flew beyond any mark that had been made yet. Athene, in the form of a man, came and marked the place where it had fallen. "A blind man, sir," said she, "could easily tell your mark by groping for it—it is so far ahead of any other. You may make your mind easy about this contest, for no Phaeacian can come near to such a throw as yours."

Odysseus was glad when he found he had a friend among the lookers-on, so he began to speak more pleasantly. "Young men," said he, "come up to that throw if you can, and I will throw another disc as heavy or even heavier. If anyone wants to have a bout with me let him come on, for I am exceedingly angry. I will box, wrestle, or run, I do not care what it is, with any man of you all except Laodamas, but not with him because I am his guest, and one cannot compete with one's own personal friend. At least I do not think it a prudent or a sensible thing for a guest to challenge his host's family at any game, especially when he is in a foreign country. He will cut the ground from under his own feet if he does. But I make no exception as regards anyone else, for I want to have the matter out and know which is the best man.

"I am a good hand at every kind of athletic sport known among mankind. I am an excellent archer. In battle I am always the first to bring a man down with my arrow, no matter how many more are taking aim at him alongside of me. Philoctetes was the only man who could shoot better than I could when we Achaeans were before Troy and in practice. I far excel everyone else in the whole world, of those who still eat bread upon the face of the earth, but I should not like to shoot against the mighty dead, such as Heracles, or Eurytus the Oechalian—men who could shoot against the gods themselves. This in fact was how Eurytus came prematurely by his end, for Apollo was angry with him and killed him because he challenged him as an archer. I can throw a dart farther than anyone else can shoot an arrow. Running is the only point in respect of which I am afraid some of the Phaeacians might beat me, for I have been brought down very low at sea; my provisions ran short, and therefore I am still weak."

They all held their peace except King Alcinous, who began: "Sir, we have had much pleasure in hearing all that you have told us, from which I understand that you are willing to show your prowess, as having been displeased with some insolent remarks that have been made to you by one of our athletes, and which could never have been uttered by anyone who knows how to talk with propriety. I hope you will apprehend my meaning, and will explain to anyone of your chief men who may be dining with yourself and your family when you get home, that we have an hereditary aptitude for accomplishments of all kinds. We are not particularly remarkable for our boxing, nor yet as wrestlers, but we are singularly fleet of foot and are excellent sailors. We are extremely fond of good dinners, music, and dancing; we also like frequent changes of linen, warm baths, and good beds. So now, please, some of you who are the best dancers set about dancing, that our guest on his return home may be able to tell his friends how much we surpass all other nations as sailors, runners, dancers, and minstrels. Demodocus has left his lyre at my house, so run some one or other of you and fetch it for him."

*   *   *

REVIEW QUESTIONS

1. What does this selection reveal about the Greek ideal of masculine behavior?
2. What does it reveal about attitudes concerning hospitality?

PROTO-CANAANITE	EARLY LETTER NAMES AND MEANINGS	PHOENICIAN	EARLY GREEK	EARLY MONUMENTAL LATIN	MODERN ENGLISH CAPITALS
⊘	*alp* oxhead	𐤀	△	⋏	A
⊓	*bêt* house	𐤁	𐊡	B	B
L	*gaml* throwstick	⅂	𐊱	<	C
⋈	*digg* fish	⊲	△	D	D
Ψ Ψ	*hô(?)* man calling	∃	∃	Ⅎ	E
⃒	*wô (waw)* mace	Y	𐊥	⸀	F
	zê(n) ?	I	I		
Ⅲ	*ḥê(t)* fence?	目	日	H	H
	ṭê(t) spindle?	⊗	⊗		
⋔	*yad* arm	Z	⋜	l	I
Ⅲ	*kapp* palm	𐊟	𐊨	K	K
∿	*lamd* ox-goad	𐊣	⌐	↳	L
∿	*mêm* water	𐊳	𐊎	M	M
⌁	*naḥš* snake	𐊷	𐊲	N	N
⬤	*cên* eye	O	O	O	O
⊔	*pi't* corner?	𐤐	⌐	Γ	P
Ψ	*sa(d)* plant	𐋉	M		
8	*qu(p)* ?	𐊤	𐊤	Oᴌ	Q
𐊥	*ra'š* head of man	𐊣	𐊥	R	R
W	*tann* composite bow	W	𐊰	⟩	S
X +	*tô (taw)* owner's mark	✗	X	T	T

ORIGINS OF THE GREEK ALPHABET (C. 500 B.C.E.)

This chart illustrates the evolution of the writing system that we refer to as the alphabet. How great is the Greek (and later Roman) debt to the Phoenicians and earlier Canaanites? Can you identify the origin of the word alphabet?

116

HESIOD

FROM *Works and Days*

The partly autobiographical Works and Days *of Hesiod (c. 700 B.C.E.) reflects a world quite different from that of Homer's heroes. Indeed, in one part of this work Hesiod describes five ages of mankind that begin with a golden age of men who "lived like gods" but that decline thereafter, culminating in an age of bronze that coincides with the Homeric heroes ("a god-like race of hero-men") and then his own age, that of a race of iron, oppressed by hard labor and sorrow. As the following readings suggest, humankind's lot and the values of the time are in many ways quite different from those of Homer's world.*

From *Works and Days*, translated by Hugh G. Evelyn-White in *Homeric Hymns and Homerica* (Cambridge, Mass.: Harvard University Press, 1936), pp. 361–62.

*   *   *

FROM **"On Work and Wealth"**

To you, foolish Perses, I will speak good sense. Badness can be got easily and in shoals: the road to her is smooth, and she lives very near us. But between us and Goodness the gods have placed the sweat of our brows: long and steep is the path that leads to her, and it is rough at the first; but when a man has reached the top, then indeed she is easy, though before that she was hard.

That man is altogether best who considers all things himself and marks what will be better afterwards and at the end; and he, again, is good who listens to a good adviser; but whoever neither thinks for himself nor keeps in mind what another man tells him, he is an unprofitable man. But do you at any rate, always remembering my charge, work, well-born Perses, that Hunger may hate you, and venerable Demeter richly crowned may love you and fill your barn with food; for Hunger is altogether a meet comrade for the sluggard. Both gods and men are angry with a man who lives idle, for in nature he is like the stingless drones who waste the labor of the bees, eating without working; but let it be your care to order your work properly, that in the right season your barns may be full of victual. Through work men grow rich in flocks and substance, and working they are much better loved by the immortals. Work is no disgrace: it is idleness which is a disgrace. But if you work, the idle will soon envy you as you grow rich, for fame and renown attend on wealth. And whatever be your lot, work is best for you, if you turn your misguided mind away from other men's property to your work and attend to your livelihood as I bid you. An evil shame is the needy man's companion, shame which both greatly harms and prospers men: shame is with poverty, but confidence with wealth.

Wealth should not be seized: god-given wealth is much better; for if a man take great wealth violently and perforce, or if he steal it through his tongue, as often happens when gain deceives men's sense and dishonor tramples down honor, the gods soon blot him out and make that man's house low, and wealth attends him only for a little time. Alike with him who does wrong to a suppliant or a guest, or who goes up to his brother's bed and commits unnatural sin in lying with his wife, or who infatuately offends against fatherless children, or who abuses his old father at the cheerless threshold of old age and attacks him with harsh words, truly Zeus himself is angry, and at the last lays on him a heavy requital for his evildoing. But do you turn your foolish heart altogether away from these things, and, as far as you are able, sacrifice to the deathless gods purely and cleanly, and burn rich meats also, and at other times propitiate them with libations and incense, both when you go to bed and when the holy light has come back, that they may be gracious to you in heart and spirit, and so you may buy another's holding and not another yours.

. . . He who adds to what he has, will keep off bright-eyed hunger; for if you add only a little to a little and do this often, soon that little will become great. What a man has by him at home does not trouble him: it is better to have your stuff at home, for whatever is abroad may mean loss. It is a good thing to draw on what you have; but it grieves your heart to need something and not to have it, and I bid you mark this. Take your fill when the cask is first opened and when it is nearly spent, but midways be sparing: it is poor saving when you come to the lees.

Let the wage promised to a friend be fixed; even with your brother smile—and get a witness; for trust and mistrust, alike ruin men.

Do not let a flaunting woman coax and cozen and deceive you: she is after your barn. The man who trusts womankind trusts deceivers.

There should be an only son, to feed his father's house, for so wealth will increase in the home; but if you leave a second son you should die old. Yet Zeus can easily give great wealth to a greater number. More hands mean more work and more increase.

If your heart within you desires wealth, do these things and work with work upon work.

*　　*　　*

"Pandora"

For the gods have hidden and keep hidden what
　could be men's livelihood.
It could have been that easily in one day you
　could work out
enough to keep you for a year, with no more
　working.
Soon you could have hung up your steering oar
　in the smoke of the fireplace,
and the work the oxen and patient mules do
　would be abolished,
but Zeus in the anger of his heart hid it away
because the devious-minded Prometheus had
　cheated him;
and therefore Zeus thought up dismal sorrows
　for mankind.
He hid fire; but Prometheus, the powerful son of
　Iapetos,
stole it again from Zeus of the counsels, to give
　to mortals.
He hid it out of the sight of Zeus who delights
　in thunder
in the hollow fennel stalk. In anger the cloud-
　gatherer spoke to him:
"Son of Iapetos, deviser of crafts beyond all others,
you are happy that you stole the fire, and
　outwitted my thinking;
but it will be a great sorrow to you, and to men
　who come after.
As the price of fire I will give them an evil, and
　all men shall fondle
this, their evil, close to their hearts, and take
　delight in it."
　So spoke the father of gods and mortals; and
　laughed out loud.
He told glorious Hephaistos to make haste, and
　plaster
earth with water, and to infuse it with a human voice
and vigor, and make the face like the immortal
　goddesses,
the bewitching features of a young girl;
　meanwhile Athene
was to teach her her skills, and how to do the
　intricate weaving,
while Aphrodite was to mist her head in golden
　endearment
and the cruelty of desire and longings that wear
　out the body,

From *Works and Days*, translated by Richard Lattimore, (Ann Arbor: University of Michigan Press, 1959).

but to Hermes, the guide, the slayer of Argos, he
    gave instructions
to put in her the mind of a hussy, and a
    treacherous nature.
    So Zeus spoke. And all obeyed Lord Zeus, the
    son of Kronos.
The renowned strong smith modeled her figure
    of earth, in the likeness
of a decorous young girl, as the son of Kronos
    had wished it.
The goddess gray-eyed Athene dressed and
    arrayed her; the Graces,
who are goddesses, and hallowed Persuasion put
    necklaces
of gold upon her body, while the Seasons, with
    glorious tresses,
put upon her head a coronal of spring flowers,
and Pallas Athene put all decor upon her body.
But into her heart Hermes, the guide, the slayer
    of Argos,
put lies, and wheedling words of falsehood, and
    a treacherous nature,
made her as Zeus of the deep thunder wished,
    and he, the gods' herald,
put a voice inside her, and gave her the name of
    woman,
Pandora, because all the gods who have their
    homes on Olympos
had given her each a gift, to be a sorrow to men
who eat bread. Now when he had done with this
    sheer, impossible
deception, the Father sent the gods' fleet
    messenger, Hermes,
to Epimetheus, bringing her, a gift, nor did
    Epimetheus
remember to think how Prometheus had told
    him never
to accept a gift from Olympian Zeus, but always
    to send it
back, for fear it might prove to be an evil for mankind.
He took the evil, and only perceived it when he
    possessed her.
Since before this time the races of men had been
    living on earth

free from all evils, free from laborious work, and
    free from
all wearing sicknesses that bring their fates down
    on men
(for men grow old suddenly in the midst of
    misfortune;)
but the woman, with her hands lifting away the
    lid from the great jar,
scattered its contents, and her design was sad
    troubles for mankind.
Hope was the only spirit that stayed there in the
    unbreakable
closure of the jar, under its rim, and could not
    fly forth
abroad, for the lid of the great jar closed down
    first and contained her;
this was by the will of cloud-gathering Zeus of
    the aegis;
but there are other troubles by thousands that
    hover about men,
for the earth is full of evil things, and the sea is
    full of them;
there are sicknesses that come to men by day,
    while in the night
moving of themselves they haunt us, bringing
    sorrow to mortals,
and silently, for Zeus of the counsels took the
    voice out of them.

So there is no way to avoid what Zeus has
    intended.

REVIEW QUESTIONS

1. What kind of society does Hesiod's writing reflect?
2. How might one succeed in it?
3. According to Hesiod, what is the underlying
cause of man's misery, and what is the relationship of women to it?

Spartan Society and Values

Among all the Greek city-states, Sparta was distinguished by the military ethic that governed virtually every aspect of its society. The life of the Spartan citizen was geared toward maintaining a constant state of military preparedness. For this achievement, no sacrifice was too great, as was heroically demonstrated by the Spartans who defended the pass at Thermopylae against the Persians in 480 B.C.E. The following selections shed light on the values and organization of Spartan society. The first, "The Spartan Creed," is the work of the Spartan poet Tyrtaeus, whose poetry continued to inspire Spartan warriors long after his death. The second selection is a description of Spartan laws and customs by Xenophon, an Athenian follower of the philosopher Socrates. Xenophon is known best for his work, the Anabasis, *which describes the retreat, led by him, of a mercenary army stranded in Persian territory circa 400 B.C.E.*

Tyrtaeus
"The Spartan Creed"

I would not say anything for a man nor take
    account of him
for any speed of his feet or wrestling skill he
    might have,
not if he had the size of a Cyclops and strength
    to go with it,
not if he could outrun Bóreas, the North Wind
    of Thrace,
not if he were more handsome and gracefully
    formed than Tithónos,
or had more riches than Midas had, or Kínyras too,
not if he were more of a king than Tantalid
    Pelops,
or had the power of speech and persuasion
    Adrastos had,
not if he had all splendors except for a fighting
    spirit.
For no man ever proves himself a good man in
    war
unless he can endure to face the blood and the
    slaughter,

go close against the enemy and fight with his
    hands.
Here is courage, mankind's finest possession,
    here is
the noblest prize that a young man can endeavor
    to win,
and it is a good thing his city and all the people
    share with him
when a man plants his feet and stands in the
    foremost spears
relentlessly, all thought of foul flight completely
    forgotten,
and has well trained his heart to be steadfast and
    to endure,
and with words encourages the man who is
    stationed beside him.
Here is a man who proves himself to be valiant
    in war.
With a sudden rush he turns to flight the rugged
    battalions
of the enemy, and sustains the beating waves of
    assault.
And he who so falls among the champions and
    loses his sweet life,
so blessing with honor his city, his father, and
    all his people,
with wounds in his chest, where the spear that
    he was facing has transfixed

From *Greek Lyrics*, translated by Richmond Lattimore (Chicago: University of Chicago Press, 1960).

that massive guard of his shield, and gone
  through his breastplate as well,
why, such a man is lamented alike by the young
  and the elders,
and all his city goes into mourning and grieves
  for his loss.

His tomb is pointed to with pride, and so are
  his children,
and his children's children, and afterward all the
  race that is his.
His shining glory is never forgotten, his name is
  remembered,
and he becomes an immortal, though he lies
  under the ground,
when one who was a brave man has been killed
  by the furious War God
standing his ground and fighting hard for his
  children and land.
But if he escapes the doom of death, the
  destroyer of bodies,
and wins his battle, and bright renown for the
  work of his spear,
all men give place to him alike, the youth and
  the elders,
and much joy comes his way before he goes
  down to the dead.
Aging, he has reputation among his citizens. No
  one
tries to interfere with his honors or all he deserves;
all men withdraw before his presence, and yield
  their seats to him,
the youth, and the men his age, and even those
  older than he.
Thus a man should endeavor to reach this high
  place of courage
with all his heart, and, so trying, never be
  backward in war.

Xenophon
FROM **"The Laws and Customs
of the Spartans"**

*   *   *

But reflecting once how Sparta, one of the least
populous of states, had proved the most powerful
and celebrated city in Greece, I wondered by what
means this result had been produced. When I proceeded, however, to contemplate the institutions
of the Spartans, I wondered no longer.

Lycurgus, who made the laws for them, by
obedience to which they have flourished, I not
only admire, but consider to have been in the fullest sense a wise man; for he rendered his country
preëminent in prosperity, not by imitating other
states, but by making ordinances contrary to those
of most governments.

With regard, for example, to the procreation
of children, that I may begin from the beginning,
other people feed their young women, who are
about to produce offspring, and who are of the
class regarded as well brought up, on the most
moderate quantity of vegetable food possible, and
on the least possible quantity of meat, while they
either keep them from wine altogether, or allow
them to use it only when mixed with water; and
as the greater number of the men engaged in
trades are sedentary, so the rest of the Greeks
think it proper that their young women should sit
quiet and spin wool. But how can we expect that
women thus treated should produce a vigorous
progeny? Lycurgus, on the contrary, thought that
female slaves were competent to furnish clothes;
and, considering that the production of children
was the noblest duty of the free, he enacted, in the
first place, that the female should practice bodily
exercises no less than the male sex; and he thus
appointed for the women contests with one another, just as for the men, expecting that when

From *Xenophon's Minor Works,* translated by J. S. Watson
(Bell: Bohn Classical Library, 1878).

both parents were rendered strong a stronger offspring would be born from them.

Observing, too, that the men of other nations, when women were united to husbands, associated with their wives during the early part of their intercourse without restraint, he made enactments quite at variance with this practice; for he ordained that a man should think it shame to be seen going in to his wife, or coming out from her. When married people meet in this way, they must feel stronger desire for the company of one another, and whatever offspring is produced must thus be rendered far more robust than if the parents were satiated with each other's society.

In addition to these regulations, he also took from the men the liberty of marrying when each of them pleased, and appointed that they should contract marriages only when they were in full bodily vigour, deeming this injunction also conducive to the production of an excellent offspring. Seeing also that if old men chanced to have young wives, they watched their wives with the utmost strictness, he made a law quite opposed to this feeling; for he appointed that an old man should introduce to his wife whatever man in the prime of life he admired for his corporeal and mental qualities, in order that she might have children by him. If, again, a man was unwilling to associate with his wife, and yet was desirous of having proper children, he made a provision also with respect to him, that whatever women he saw likely to have offspring, and of good disposition, he might, on obtaining the consent of her husband, have children by her. Many similar permissions he gave; for the women are willing to have two families, and the men to receive brothers to their children, who are equal to them in birth and standing, but have no claim to share in their property.

Let him who wishes, then, consider whether Lycurgus, in thus making enactments different from those of other legislators, in regard to the procreation of children, secured for Sparta a race of men eminent for size and strength.

Having given this account of the procreation of children, I wish also to detail the education of those of both sexes. Of the other Greeks, those who say that they bring up their sons best set slaves over them to take charge of them, as soon as the children can understand what is said to them, and send them, at the same time, to schoolmasters, to learn letters, and music, and the exercises of the palaestra. They also render their children's feet delicate by the use of sandals, and weaken their bodies by changes of clothes; and as to food, they regard their appetite as the measure of what they are to take. But Lycurgus, instead of allowing each citizen to set slaves as guardians over his children, appointed a man to have the care of them all, one of those from whom the chief magistrates are chosen; and he is called the paedonomus. He invested this man with full authority to assemble the boys, and, if he found that any one was negligent of his duties, to punish him severely. He assigned him also some of the grown-up boys as whip-carriers, that they might inflict whatever chastisement was necessary; so that great dread of disgrace, and great willingness to obey, prevailed among them.

Instead, also, of making their feet soft with sandals, he enacted that they should harden them by going without sandals; thinking that, if they exercised themselves in this state, they would go up steep places with far greater ease, and descend declivities with greater safety; and that they would also leap, and skip, and run faster unshod, if they had their feet inured to doing so, than shod. Instead of being rendered effeminate, too, by a variety of dresses, he made it a practice that they should accustom themselves to one dress throughout the year; thinking that they would thus be better prepared to endure cold and heat.

As to food, he ordained that they should exhort the boys to take only such a quantity as never to be oppressed with overeating, and not to be strangers to living somewhat frugally; supposing that, being thus brought up, they would be the better able, if they should be required, to support toil under a scarcity of supplies, would be the more likely to persevere in exertion, should it be imposed on them, on the same quantity of provisions, and would be less desirous of sauces, more easily satisfied with any kind of food, and pass their lives in greater health. He also considered that the fare which rendered the body slender would be more conducive to increasing its stature than that which expanded it with nutriment. Yet that the boys might not suffer too much from hunger, Lycurgus, though he did not allow them to take what they wanted without trouble, gave them liberty to steal certain things to relieve the cravings of nature; and he made it honourable to steal as many cheeses as possible. That he did not give them leave to form schemes for getting food because he was at a loss what to allot them, I suppose no one is ignorant; as it is evident that he who designs to steal must be wakeful during the night, and use deceit, and lay plots; and, if he would gain anything of consequence, must employ spies. All these things, therefore, it is plain that he taught the children from a desire to render them more dexterous in securing provisions, and better qualified for warfare.

Some one may say, "Why, then, if he thought it honourable to steal, did he inflict a great number of whiplashes on him who was caught in the act?" I answer, that in other things which men teach, they punish him who does not follow his instructions properly; and that the Spartans accordingly punished those who were detected as having attempted to steal in an improper manner. These boys he gave in charge to others to whip them at the altar of Diana Orthia; designing to show by this enactment that it is possible for a person, after enduring pain for a short time, to enjoy pleasure with credit for a long time. It is also shown by this punishment that, where there is need of activity, the inert person benefits himself the least, and occasions himself most trouble.

In order, too, that the boys, in case of the paedonomus being absent, may never be in want of a president, he appointed that whoever of the citizens may happen at any time to be present is to assume the direction of them, and to enjoin whatever he may think advantageous for them, and punish them if they do anything wrong. By doing this, Lycurgus has also succeeded in rendering the boys much more modest; for neither boys nor men respect any one so much as their rulers. And

that if, on any occasion, no full-grown man happen to be present, the boys may not even in that case be without a leader, he ordained that the most active of the grown-up youths take the command of each band; so that the boys there are never without a superintendent.

It appears to me that I must say something also of the boys as objects of affection; for this has likewise some reference to education. Among the other Greeks, a man and boy either form a union, as among the Boeotians, and associate together, or, as among the Eleians, the men gain the favour of the youths by means of attentions bestowed upon them; but there are some of the Greeks who prohibit the suitors for the boys' favours from having the least conversation with them. But Lycurgus, acting contrary to all these people also, thought proper, if any man, being himself such as he ought to be, admired the disposition of a youth, and made it his object to render him a faultless friend, and to enjoy his society, to bestow praise upon him, and regarded this as the most excellent kind of education; but if any man showed that his affections were fixed only on the bodily attractions of a youth, Lycurgus, considering this as most unbecoming, appointed that at Lacedaemon suitors for the favours of boys should abstain from intimate connexion with them, not less strictly than parents abstain from such intercourse with their children, or children of the same family from that with one another. That such a state of things is disbelieved by some, I am not surprised; for in most states the laws are not at all adverse to the love of youths; but Lycurgus, for his part, took such precautions with reference to it.

*   *   *

Lycurgus, then, having found the Spartans, like the other Greeks, taking their meals at home, and knowing that most were guilty of excess at them, caused their meals to be taken in public, thinking that his regulations would thus be less likely to be transgressed. He appointed them such a quantity of food, that they should neither be overfed nor feel stinted. Many extraordinary supplies are also furnished from what is caught in hunting, and for these the rich sometimes contribute bread; so that the table is never without provisions, as long as they design the meal to last, and yet is never expensive.

Having put a stop likewise to all unnecessary drinking, which weakens alike the body and the mind, he gave permission that every one should drink when he was thirsty, thinking that the drink would then be most innoxious and most pleasant. When they take their meals together in this manner, how can any one ruin either himself or his family by gluttony or drunkenness? In other states, equals in age generally associate together, and with them modesty has but very little influence; but Lycurgus, at Sparta, mixed citizens of different ages, so that the younger are for the most part instructed by the experience of the older. It is a custom at these public meals, that whatever any one has done to his honour in the community is related; so that insolence, or disorder from intoxication, or any indecency in conduct or language, has there no opportunity of showing itself. The practice of taking meals away from home is also attended with these advantages, that the people are obliged to walk in taking their departure homewards, and to be careful that they may not stagger from the effects of wine, knowing that they will not remain where they dined, and that they must conduct themselves in the night just as in the day; for it is not allowable for any one who is still liable to military duty to walk with a torch.

As Lycurgus observed, too, that those who, after taking food, exercise themselves, become well-complexioned, plump, and robust, while those who are inactive are puffy, unhealthy-looking, and feeble, he did not neglect to give attention to that point; and as he perceived that when any one engages in labour from his own inclination, he proves himself to have his body in efficient condition, he ordered that the oldest in each place of exercise should take care that those belonging to it should never be overcome by taking too much food. With regard to this matter, he appears to me to have been by no means mistaken; for no one would easily find men more healthy, or more able-bodied, than the Spartans; for they exercise themselves alike in their legs, in their hands, and in their shoulders.

*   *   *

From acquiring money by unjust means, he prohibited them by such methods as the following. He instituted, in the first place, such a kind of money, that, even if but ten minae came into a house, it could never escape the notice either of masters or of servants; for it would require much room, and a carriage to convey it. In the next place, gold and silver are searched after, and, if they are discovered anywhere, the possessor of them is punished. How, then, could gain by traffic be an object of pursuit, in a state where the possession of money occasions more pain than the use of it affords pleasure?

That at Sparta the citizens pay the strictest obedience to the magistrates and laws, we all know. I suppose, however, that Lycurgus did not attempt to establish such an excellent order of things, until he had brought the most powerful men in the state to be of the same mind with regard to it. I form my opinion on this consideration, that, in other states, the more influential men are not willing even to appear to fear the magistrates, but think that such fear is unbecoming free men but in Sparta, the most powerful men not only put themselves under the magistrates, but even count it an honour to humble themselves before them, and to obey, when they are called upon, not walking, but running; supposing that if they themselves are the first to pay exact obedience, others will follow their example; and such has been the case. It is probable, also, that the chief men established the offices of the Ephors in conjunction with Lycurgus, as they must have been certain that obedience is of the greatest benefit, alike in a state, and in an army, and in a family; and they doubtless considered that the greater power magistrates have, the greater effect will they produce on the citizens in enforcing obedience. The Ephors, accordingly, have full power to impose a fine on whomsoever they please, and to exact the fine without delay; they have power also to degrade magistrates even while they are in office, and to put them in prison, and to bring them to trial for their life. Being possessed of such authority, they do not, like the magistrates in other states, always permit those who are elected to offices to rule during the whole year as they choose, but, like despots and presidents in gymnastic contests, punish on the instant whomsoever they find acting at all contrary to the laws.

Though there were many other excellent contrivances adopted by Lycurgus, to induce the citizens to obey the laws, the most excellent of all appears to me to be, that he did not deliver his laws to the people until he had gone, in company with the most eminent of his fellow-citizens, to Delphi, and consulted the god whether it would be more beneficial and advantageous for Sparta to obey the laws which he had made. As the god replied that it would be more beneficial in every way, he at once delivered them, deciding that it would be not only illegal, but impious, to disobey laws sanctioned by the oracle.

It is deserving of admiration, too, in Lycurgus, that he made it a settled principle in the community, that an honourable death is preferable to a dishonourable life; for whoever pays attention to the subject will find that fewer of those who hold this opinion die than of those who attempt to escape danger by flight. Hence we may say with truth, that safety attends for a much longer period on valour than on cowardice; for valour is not only attended with less anxiety and greater pleasure, but is also more capable of assisting and supporting us. It is evident, too, that good report accompanies valour; for almost everybody is willing to be in alliance with the brave.

How he contrived that such sentiments should be entertained, it is proper not to omit to mention. He evidently, then, intended a happy life for the brave, and a miserable one for the cowardly. In other communities, when a man acts as a coward, he merely brings on himself the name of coward, but the coward goes to the same market, and sits or takes exercise, if he pleases, in the same place with the brave men; at Sparta, however, every one would be ashamed to admit a coward into the same tent with him, or to allow him to be his opponent in a match at wrestling. Frequently, too, a person of such character, when they choose opposite parties to play at ball, is left without any place, and in forming a chorus he is thrust into the least hon-

ourable position. On the road he must yield the way to others, and at public meetings he must rise up, even before his juniors. His female relatives he must maintain at home, and they too must pay the penalty of his cowardice, since no man will marry them. He is also not allowed to take a wife, and must at the same time pay the customary fine for being a bachelor. He must not walk about with a cheerful expression, or imitate the manners of persons of blameless character; else he will have to receive whipping from his betters. Since, then, such disgrace is inflicted on cowards, I do not at all wonder that death is preferred at Sparta to a life so dishonourable and infamous.

Lycurgus seems to me to have provided also, with great judgment, how virtue might be practised even to old age; for by adding to his other enactments the choice of senators at an advanced stage of life, he caused honour and virtue not to be disregarded even in old age.

It is worthy of admiration in him, too, that he attached consideration to the old age of the well-deserving; for by making the old men arbiters in the contest for superiority in mental qualifications, he rendered their old age more honourable than the vigour of those in the meridian of life. This contest is deservedly held in the greatest esteem among the people, for gymnastic contests are attended with honour, but they concern only bodily accomplishments; the contest for distinction in old age involves a decision respecting merits of the mind. In proportion, therefore, as the mind is superior to the body, so much are contests for mental eminence more worthy of regard than those concerning bodily superiority.

Is it not highly worthy of admiration, also, in Lycurgus, that when he saw that those who are disinclined to practice virtue are not qualified to increase the power of their country, he obliged all the citizens of Sparta to cultivate every kind of virtue publicly. As private individuals, accordingly, who practise virtue, are superior in it to those who neglect it, so Sparta is naturally superior in virtue to all other states, as it is the only one that engages in a public cultivation of honour and virtue. Is it not also deserving of commendation, that, when other states punish any person that injures another, Lycurgus inflicted no less punishment on any one that openly showed himself unconcerned with becoming as good a man as possible? He thought, as it appears, that by those who make others slaves, or rob them, or steal anything, the individual sufferers only are injured, but that by the unprincipled and cowardly whole communities are betrayed; so that he appears to me to have justly imposed the heaviest penalties on such characters.

He also imposed on his countrymen an obligation, from which there is no exception, of practising every kind of political virtue; for he made the privileges of citizenship equally available to all those who observed what was enjoined by the laws, without taking any account either of weakness of body or scantiness of means; but if any one was too indolent to perform what the laws prescribed, Lycurgus appointed that he should be no longer counted in the number of equally privileged citizens.

That these laws are extremely ancient is certain; for Lycurgus is said to have lived in the time of the Heracleidae; but, ancient as they are, they are still very new to other communities; for, what is the most wonderful of all things, all men extol such institutions, but no state thinks proper to imitate them.

The regulations which I have mentioned are beneficial alike in peace and in war; but if any one wishes to learn what he contrived better than other legislators with reference to military proceedings, he may attend to the following particulars.

In the first place, then, the Ephors proclaim the age limits for the citizen draft to the army; artisans (non-citizens) are also called by the same order to serve supplying the troops. For the Spartans provide themselves in the field with an abundance of all those things which people use in a city; and of whatever instruments an army may require in common, orders are given to bring some on waggons, and others on beasts of burden, as by this arrangement anything left behind is least likely to escape notice.

For engagements in the field he made the following arrangements. He ordered that each soldier should have a purple robe and a brass shield; for he thought that such a dress had least resemblance to that of women, and was excellently adapted for the field of battle, as it is soonest made splendid, and is longest in growing soiled. He permitted also those above the age of puberty to let their hair grow, as he thought that they thus appeared taller, more manly, and more terrifying in the eyes of the enemy. . . .

*   *   *

REVIEW QUESTIONS

1. According to these readings, what was the pre-eminent role of the individual citizen within Spartan society?
2. What was the purpose of education among the Spartans?
3. What was the proper role of women in Spartan society, and why?
4. What were the values that governed Spartan life?

HIPPOCRATES

FROM "On Airs, Waters, and Places"

One of the classical Greek philosopher-scientists whose names have become almost household words today is Hippocrates of Cos, the "father of medicine" by whose name modern physicians are obligated (in the "Hippocratic oath") to apply rational, humane treatment to the care and healing of their patients. Hippocrates himself was born around 460 B.C.E. on the Aegean island of Cos. During his career, he established a school of medical thought that focused on natural medicine, attention to personal hygiene, and simple common sense in emphasizing a rational (rather than magical, superstition-bound) approach to the study and care of the human body. By the second century C.E., Greek and Latin writers ascribed to Hippocrates a substantial body of written works dealing with human physiology; the diagnosis of illness; and the influence of lifestyle, diet, and environment on health. Scholars today continue to debate their authorship, but their contribution to later Western (and Islamic) civilizations is incalculable, not only in the realm of medicine, but also—as the selection below reflects—in shaping later, often destructive assumptions that linked supposedly innate superiorities and inferiorities of other human societies to their environment, climate, and lifestyle. In some instances, the judgments that the "Hippocratic" authors reached parallel more modern notions of ethnocentrism and racism—other elements of later Western thought that, like rationalism and democracy, can be traced to Classical roots.

In the following selection, Hippocrates first defines the criteria for assessing the impact of environment on human health—among them, winds, water quality, terrain, and personal habits and lifestyle of the inhabitants. Then, the author uses these criteria to assess and contrast the qualities of peoples inhabiting different regions of the world known to him.

From The Internet Classics Archive, http://classics.mit.edu//Hippocrated/airwatpl.html.

Part 1

Whoever wishes to investigate medicine properly, should proceed thus: in the first place to consider the seasons of the year, and what effects each of them produces for they are not at all alike, but differ much from themselves in regard to their changes. Then the winds, the hot and the cold, especially such as are common to all countries, and then such as are peculiar to each locality. We must also consider the qualities of the waters, for as they differ from one another in taste and weight, so also do they differ much in their qualities. In the same manner, when one comes into a city to which he is a stranger, he ought to consider its situation, how it lies as to the winds and the rising of the sun; for its influence is not the same whether it lies to the north or the south, to the rising or to the setting sun. These things one ought to consider most attentively, and concerning the waters which the inhabitants use, whether they be marshy and soft, or hard, and running from elevated and rocky situations, and then if saltish and unfit for cooking; and the ground, whether it be naked and deficient in water, or wooded and well watered, and whether it lies in a hollow, confined situation, or is elevated and cold; and the mode in which the inhabitants live, and what are their pursuits, whether they are fond of drinking and eating to excess, and given to indolence, or are fond of exercise and labor, and not given to excess in eating and drinking.

Part 2

From these things he must proceed to investigate everything else. For if one knows all these things well, or at least the greater part of them, he cannot miss knowing, when he comes into a strange city, either the diseases peculiar to the place, or the particular nature of common diseases, so that he will not be in doubt as to the treatment of the diseases, or commit mistakes, as is likely to be the case provided one had not previously considered these matters. And in particular, as the season and the year advances, he can tell what epidemic diseases will attack the city, either in summer or in winter, and what each individual will be in danger of experiencing from the change of regimen. For knowing the changes of the seasons, the risings and settings of the stars, how each of them takes place, he will be able to know beforehand what sort of a year is going to ensue. Having made these investigations, and knowing beforehand the seasons, such a one must be acquainted with each particular, and must succeed in the preservation of health, and be by no means unsuccessful in the practice of his art. And if it shall be thought that these things belong rather to meteorology, it will be admitted, on second thoughts, that astronomy contributes not a little, but a very great deal, indeed, to medicine. For with the seasons the digestive organs of men undergo a change.

*   *   *

Part 12

I wish to show, respecting Asia and Europe, how, in all respects, they differ from one another, and concerning the figure of the inhabitants, for they are different, and do not at all resemble one another. To treat of all would be a long story, but I will tell you how I think it is with regard to the greatest and most marked differences. I say, then, that Asia differs very much from Europe as to the nature of all things, both With regard to the productions of the earth and the inhabitants, for everything is produced much more beautiful and large in Asia; the country is milder, and the dispositions of the inhabitants also are more gentle and affectionate. The cause of this is the temperature of the seasons, because it lies in the middle of the risings of the sun towards the east, and removed from the cold (and heat), for nothing tends to growth and mildness so much as when the climate has no predominant quality, but a general equality of temperature prevails. It is not everywhere the same with regard to Asia, but such parts of the country as lie intermediate between the heat and the cold, are the best supplied with fruits and trees, and have the most genial climate, and enjoy the purest waters, both celestial and terrestrial. For neither are they much burnt up by the heat, nor dried up by the drought and want of rain, nor do they suffer from the cold; since they are well watered from abundant showers and snow, and the fruits of the season, as might be supposed, grow in abundance, both such as are raised from seed that has been sown, and such plants as the earth produces of its own accord, the fruits of which the inhabitants make use of, training them from their wild state and transplanting them to a suitable soil; the cattle also which are reared there are vigorous, particularly prolific, and bring up young of the fairest description; the inhabitants too, are well fed, most beautiful in shape, of large stature, and differ little from one another either as to figure or size; and the country itself, both as regards its constitution and mildness of the seasons, may be said to bear a close resemblance to the spring. Manly courage, endurance of suffering, laborious enterprise, and high spirit, could not be produced in such a state of things either among the native inhabitants or those of a different country, for there pleasure necessarily reigns. For this reason, also, the forms of wild beasts there are much varied. Thus it is, as I think, with the Egyptians and Libyans.

Part 13

But concerning those on the right hand of the summer risings of the sun as far as the Palus Maeotis (for this is the boundary of Europe and Asia), it is with them as follows: the inhabitants there differ far more from one another than those I have treated of above, owing to the differences of the seasons and the nature of the soil. But with regard to the country itself, matters are the same there as among all other men; for where the seasons undergo the greatest and most rapid changes, there the country is the wildest and most unequal; and you will find the greatest variety of mountains, forests, plains, and meadows; but where the seasons do not change much there the country is the most even; and, if one will consider it, so is it also with regard to the inhabitants; for the nature of some is like to a country covered with trees and well watered; of some, to a thin soil deficient in water; of others, to fenny and marshy places; and of some again, to a plain of bare and parched land. For the seasons which modify their natural frame of body are varied, and the greater the varieties of them the greater also will be the differences of their shapes.

Part 14

I will pass over the smaller differences among the nations, but will now treat of such as are great either from nature, or custom; and, first, concerning the Macrocephali. There is no other race of men which have heads in the least resembling theirs. At first, usage was the principal cause of the length of their head, but now nature cooperates with usage. They think those the most noble who have the longest heads. It is thus with regard to the usage: immediately after the child is born, and while its head is still tender, they fashion it with their hands, and constrain it to assume a lengthened shape by applying bandages and other suitable contrivances whereby the spherical form of the head is destroyed, and it is made to increase in length. Thus, at first, usage operated, so that this constitution was the result of force: but, in the course of time, it was formed naturally; so that usage had nothing to do with it; for the semen comes from all parts of the body, sound from the sound parts, and unhealthy from the unhealthy parts. If, then, children with bald heads are born to parents with bald heads; and children with blue eyes to parents who have blue eyes; and if the children of parents having distorted eyes squint also for the most part; and if the same may be said of other forms of the body, what is to prevent it from happening that a child with a long head should be produced by a parent having a long head? But now these things do not happen as they did formerly, for the custom no longer prevails owing to their intercourse with other men. Thus it appears to me to be with regard to them.

Part 15

As to the inhabitants of Phasis [along the eastern shore at the Black Sea], their country is fenny, warm, humid, and wooded; copious and severe rains occur there at all seasons; and the life of the inhabitants is spent among the fens; for their dwellings are constructed of wood and reeds, and are erected amidst the waters; they seldom practice walking either to the city or the market, but sail about, up and down, in canoes constructed out of single trees, for there are many canals there. They drink the hot and stagnant waters, both when rendered putrid by the sun, and when swollen with rains. The Phasis itself is the most stagnant of all rivers, and runs the smoothest; all the fruits which spring there are unwholesome, feeble and imperfect growth, owing to the redundance of water, and on this account they do not ripen, for much vapor from the waters overspreads the country. For these reasons the Phasians have shapes different from those of all other men; for they are large in stature, and of a very gross habit of body, so that not a joint nor vein is visible; in color they are sallow, as if affected with jaundice. Of all men they have the roughest voices, from their breathing an atmosphere which is not clear, but misty and humid; they are naturally rather languid in supporting bodily fatigue. The seasons undergo but little change either as to heat or cold; their winds for the most part are southerly, with the exception of one peculiar to the country, which sometimes blows strong, is violent and hot, and is called by them the wind cenchron. The north wind scarcely reaches them, and when it does blow it is weak and gentle. Thus it is with regard to the different nature and shape of the inhabitants of Asia and Europe.

Part 16

And with regard to the pusillanimity and cowardice of the inhabitants, the principal reason the Asiatics are more unwarlike and of gentler disposition than the Europeans is, the nature of the seasons, which do not undergo any great changes either to heat or cold, or the like; for there is neither excitement of the understanding nor any strong change of the body whereby the temper might be ruffled and they be roused to inconsiderate emotion and passion, rather than living as they do always in the state. It is changes of all kinds which arouse understanding of mankind, and do not allow them to get into a torpid condition. For these reasons, it appears to me, the Asiatic race is feeble, and further, owing to their laws; for monarchy prevails in the greater part of Asia, and where men are not their own masters nor independent, but are the slaves of others, it is not a matter of consideration with them how they may acquire military discipline, but how they may seem not to be warlike, for the dangers are not equally shared, since they must serve as soldiers, perhaps endure fatigue, and die for their masters, far from their children, their wives, and other friends; and whatever noble and manly actions they may perform lead only to the aggrandizement of their masters, whilst the fruits which they reap are dangers and death; and, in addition to all this, the lands of such persons must be laid waste by the enemy and want of cul-

ture. Thus, then, if any one be naturally warlike and courageous, his disposition will be changed by the institutions. As a strong proof of all this, such Greeks or barbarians in Asia as are not under a despotic form of government, but are independent, and enjoy the fruits of their own labors, are of all others the most warlike; for these encounter dangers on their own account, bear the prizes of their own valor, and in like manner endure the punishment of their own cowardice. And you will find the Asiatics differing from one another, for some are better and others more dastardly; of these differences, as I stated before, the changes of the seasons are the cause. Thus it is with Asia.

Part 17

In Europe there is a Scythian race, called Sauromatae, which inhabits the confines of the Palus Maeotis, and is different from all other races. Their women mount on horseback, use the bow, and throw the javelin from their horses, and fight with their enemies as long as they are virgins; and they do not lay aside their virginity until they kill three of their enemies, nor have any connection with men until they perform the sacrifices according to law. Whoever takes to herself a husband, gives up riding on horseback unless the necessity of a general expedition obliges her. They have no right breast; for while still of a tender age their mothers heat strongly a copper instrument constructed for this very purpose, and apply it to the right breast, which is burnt up, and its development being arrested, all the strength and fullness are determined to the right shoulder and arm.

Part 18

As the other Scythians have a peculiarity of shape, and do not resemble any other, the same observation applies to the Egyptians, only that the latter are oppressed by heat and the former by cold. What is called the Scythian desert is a prairie, rich in meadows, high-lying, and well watered; for the rivers which carry off the water from the plains are large. There live those Scythians which are called

Nomades, because they have no houses, but live in wagons. The smallest of these wagons have four wheels, but some have six; they are covered in with felt, and they are constructed in the manner of houses, some having but a single apartment, and some three; they are proof against rain, snow, and winds. The wagons are drawn by yokes of oxen, some of two and others of three, and all without horns, for they have no horns, owing to the cold. In these wagons the women live, but the men are carried about on horses, and the sheep, oxen, and horses accompany them; and they remain on any spot as long as there is provender for their cattle, and when that fails they migrate to some other place. They eat boiled meat, and drink the milk of mares, and also eat hippace, which is cheese prepared from the milk of the mare. Such is their mode of life and their customs.

Part 19

In respect of the seasons and figure of body, the Scythian race, like the Egyptian, have a uniformity of resemblance, different from all other nations; they are by no means prolific, and the wild beasts which are indigenous there are small in size and few in number, for the country lies under the Northern Bears, and the Rhiphaean mountains, whence the north wind blows; the sun comes very near to them only when in the summer solstice, and warms them but for a short period, and not strongly; and the winds blowing from the hot regions of the earth do not reach them, or but seldom, and with little force; but the winds from the north always blow, congealed, as they are, by the snow, ice, and much water, for these never leave the mountains, which are thereby rendered uninhabitable. A thick fog covers the plains during the day, and amidst it they live, so that winter may be said to be always present with them; or, if they have summer, it is only for a few days, and the heat is not very strong. Their plains are high-lying and naked, not crowned with mountains, but extending upwards under the Northern Bears. The wild beasts there are not large, but such as can be sheltered underground; for the cold of winter and the barrenness of the country prevent their growth, and because they have no covert nor shelter. The changes of the seasons, too, are not great nor violent, for, in fact, they change gradually; and therefore their figures resemble one another, as they all equally use the same food, and the same clothing summer and winter, respiring a humid and dense atmosphere, and drinking water from snow and ice; neither do they make any laborious exertions, for neither body nor mind is capable of enduring fatigue when the changes of the seasons are not great. For these reasons their shapes are gross and fleshy, with ill-marked joints, of a humid temperament, and deficient in tone: the internal cavities, and especially those of the intestines, are full of humors; for the belly cannot possibly be dry in such a country, with such a constitution and in such a climate; but owing to their fat, and the absence of hairs from their bodies, their shapes resemble one another, the males being all alike, and so also with the women, for the seasons being of a uniform temperature, no corruption or deterioration takes place in the concretion of the semen, unless from some violent cause, or from disease.

Part 20

I Will give you a strong proof of the humidity (laxity?) of their constitutions. You will find the greater part of the Scythians, and all the Nomades, with marks of the cautery on their shoulders, arms, wrists, breasts, hip-joints, and loins, and that for no other reason but the humidity and flabbiness of their constitution, for they can neither strain with their bows, nor launch the javelin from their shoulder owing to their humidity and atony: but when they are burnt, much of the humidity in their joints is dried up, and they become better braced, better fed, and their joints get into a more suitable condition. They are flabby and squat at first, because, as in Egypt, they are not swathed (?); and then they pay no attention to horsemanship, so that they may be adepts at it; and because of their sedentary mode of life; for the males, when they cannot be carried about on horseback, sit the most of their time in the wagon, and rarely practise walking, because of their frequent migrations and shiftings of situation; and as to the women, it is amazing how flabby and sluggish they are. The Scythian race are tawny from the cold, and not from the intense heat of the sun, for the whiteness of the skin is parched by the cold, and becomes tawny.

Part 21

It is impossible that persons of such a constitution could be prolific, for, with the man, the sexual desires are not strong, owing to the laxity of his constitution, the softness and coldness of his belly, from all which causes it is little likely that a man should be given to venery; and besides, from being jaded by exercise on horseback, the men become weak in their desires. On the part of the men these are the causes; but on that of the women, they are embonpoint and humidity; for the womb cannot take in the semen, nor is the menstrual discharge such as it should be, but scanty and at too long intervals; and the mouth of the womb is shut up by fat and does not admit the semen; and, moreover, they themselves are indolent and fat, and their bellies cold and soft. From these causes the Scythian race is not prolific. Their female servants furnish a strong proof of this; for they no sooner have connection with a man than they prove with child, owing to their active course of life and the slenderness of body.

Part 22

And, in addition to these, there are many eunuchs among the Scythians, who perform female work, and speak like women. Such persons are called effeminates. The inhabitants of the country attribute the cause of their impotence to a god, and venerate and worship such persons, every one dreading that the like might befall himself; but to me it appears that such affections are just as much divine as all others are, and that no one disease is either more divine or more human than another, but that all are alike divine, for that each has its own nature, and that no one arises without a natural cause. But

I will explain how I think that the affection takes its rise. From continued exercise on horseback they are seized with chronic defluxions in their joints owing to their legs always hanging down below their horses; they afterwards become lame and stiff at the hip-joint, such of them, at least, as are severely attacked with it. They treat themselves in this way: when the disease is commencing, they open the vein behind either ear, and when the blood flows, sleep, from feebleness, seizes them, and afterwards they awaken, some in good health and others not. To me it appears that the semen is altered by this treatment, for there are veins behind the ears which, if cut, induce impotence; now, these veins would appear to me to be cut. Such persons afterwards, when they go in to women and cannot have connection with them, at first do not think much about it, but remain quiet; but when, after making the attempt two, three, or more times, they succeed no better, fancying they have committed some offence against the god whom they blame for the affection, they put on female attire, reproach themselves for effeminacy, play the part of women, and perform the same work as women do. This the rich among the Scythians endure, not the basest, but the most noble and powerful, owing to their riding on horseback; for the poor are less affected, as they do not ride on horses. And yet, if this disease had been more divine than the others, it ought not to have befallen the most noble and the richest of the Scythians alone, but all alike, or rather those who have little, as not being able to pay honors to the gods, if, indeed, they delight in being thus rewarded by men, and grant favors in return; for it is likely that the rich sacrifice more to the gods, and dedicate more votive offerings, inasmuch as they have wealth, and worship the gods; whereas the poor, from want, do less in this way, and, moreover, upbraid the gods for not giving them wealth, so that those who have few possessions were more likely to bear the punishments of these offences than the rich. But, as I formerly said, these affections are divine just as much as others, for each springs from a natural cause, and this disease arises among the Scythians from such a cause as I have stated. But it attacks other men in like manner, for whenever men ride much and very frequently on horseback, then many are affected with rheums in the joints, sciatica, and gout, and they are inept at venery. But these complaints befall the Scythians, and they are the most impotent of men for the aforesaid causes, and because they always wear breeches, and spend the most of their time on horseback, so as not to touch their privy parts with the hands, and from the cold and fatigue they forget the sexual desire, and do not make the attempt until after they have lost their virility. Thus it is with the race of the Scythians.

Part 23

The other races in Europe differ from one another, both as to stature and shape, owing to the changes of the seasons, which are very great and frequent, and because the heat is strong, the winters severe, and there are frequent rains, and again protracted droughts, and winds, from which many and diversified changes are induced. These changes are likely to have an effect upon generation in the coagulation of the semen, as this process cannot be the same in summer as in winter, nor in rainy as in dry weather; wherefore, I think, that the figures of Europeans differ more than those of Asiatics; and they differ very much from one another as to stature in the same city; for vitiations of the semen occur in its coagulation more frequently during frequent changes of the seasons, than where they are alike and equable. And the same may be said of their dispositions, for the wild, and unsociable, and the passionate occur in such a constitution; for frequent excitement of the mind induces wildness, and extinguishes sociableness and mildness of disposition, and therefore I think the inhabitants of Europe more courageous than those of Asia; for a climate which is always the same induces indolence, but a changeable climate, laborious exertions both of body and mind; and from rest and indolence cowardice is engendered, and from laborious exertions and pains, courage. On this account the inhabitants of Europe are than the Asiatics, and also owing to their institutions, because they are not governed by kings like the latter, for where men

are governed by kings there they must be very cowardly, as I have stated before; for their souls are enslaved, and they will not willingly, or readily undergo dangers in order to promote the power of another; but those that are free undertake dangers on their own account, and not for the sake of others; they court hazard and go out to meet it, for they themselves bear off the rewards of victory, and thus their institutions contribute not a little to their courage.

Such is the general character of Europe and Asia.

Part 24

And there are in Europe other tribes, differing from one another in stature, shape, and courage: the differences are those I formerly mentioned, and will now explain more clearly. Such as inhabit a country which is mountainous, rugged, elevated, and well watered, and where the changes of the seasons are very great, are likely to have great variety of shapes among them, and to be naturally of an enterprising and warlike disposition; and such persons are apt to have no little of the savage and ferocious in their nature; but such as dwell in places which are low-lying, abounding in meadows and ill ventilated, and who have a larger proportion of hot than of cold winds, and who make use of warm waters- these are not likely to be of large stature nor well proportioned, but are of a broad make, fleshy, and have black hair; and they are rather of a dark than of a light complexion, and are less likely to be phlegmatic than bilious; courage and laborious enterprise are not naturally in them, but may be engendered in them by means of their institutions. And if there be rivers in the country which carry off the stagnant and rain water from it, these may be wholesome and clear; but if there be no rivers, but the inhabitants drink the waters of fountains, and such as are stagnant and marshy, they must necessarily have prominent bellies and enlarged spleens. But such as inhabit a high country, and one that is level, windy, and well-watered, will be large of stature, and like to one another; but their minds will be rather unmanly and gentle.

Those who live on thin, ill-watered, and bare soils, and not well attempered in the changes of the seasons, in such a country they are likely to be in their persons rather hard and well braced, rather of a blond than a dark complexion, and in disposition and passions haughty and self-willed. For, where the changes of the seasons are most frequent, and where they differ most from one another, there you will find their forms, dispositions, and nature the most varied. These are the strongest of the natural causes of difference, and next the country in which one lives, and the waters; for, in general, you will find the forms and dispositions of mankind to correspond with the nature of the country; for where the land is fertile, soft, and well-watered, and supplied with waters from very elevated situations, so as to be hot in summer and cold in winter, and where the seasons are fine, there the men are fleshy, have ill-formed joints, and are of a humid temperament; they are not disposed to endure labor, and, for the most part, are base in spirit; indolence and sluggishness are visible in them, and to the arts they are dull, and not clever nor acute. When the country is bare, not fenced, and rugged, blasted by the winter and scorched by the sun, there you may see the hardy, slender, with well-shaped joints, well-braced, and shaggy; sharp, industry and vigilance accompany such a constitution; in morals and passions they are haughty and opinionative, inclining rather to the fierce than to the mild; and you will find them acute and ingenious as regards the arts, and excelling in military affairs; and likewise all the other productions of the earth corresponding to the earth itself. Thus it is with regard to the most opposite natures and shapes; drawing conclusions from them, you may judge of the rest without any risk of error.

REVIEW QUESTIONS

1. Which human groups does Hippocrates consider to be superior? On what basis?
2. Can you discern any parallels between what Hippocrates writes and more recent concepts of "race" and racial inferiority?

HERODOTUS

FROM *The Histories*

The Second Persian Invasion of Greece

The Greeks' repelling of the Persian invasions of 490 and 480 to 479 B.C.E. can be regarded as one of the earliest events through which the West began to define itself as distinct from the East. Our knowledge of the invasions is derived almost entirely from the account by Herodotus, who wrote only a few decades after the actual events. His description of the war against the Persians is preceded by long discourses (often of questionable reliability) on the history and customs of other peoples who were involved in the war. The following excerpts, however, focus on the fierce resistance of the Spartans during the second invasion, led by the Persian king Xerxes. In the first selection, Xerxes asks the expatriate Spartan Demaratus how the Greeks can possibly stand up to Persia's might. (This is after Herodotus has given an account-

ing of the composition of the Persian army. According to his figures, it numbered a fantastic—and impossible—2,641,610 warriors.) The following selection is Herodotus' account of the heroic stand of the Spartans, under their king, Leonidas, at the mountain pass at Thermopylae.

From *Herodotus: The Histories,* edited by Walter Blanco and Jennifer Tobert Roberts, translated by Walter Blanco (New York: Norton, 1992), pp. 157–77, 191–97.

*   *   *

After the army had been counted and put in battle order, Xerxes wanted to ride past his troops and review them, which he did. He rode past the forces of each nation in his chariot, asking questions while his scribes wrote down the answers until he had gone from one end of the army to the other and reviewed both infantry and cavalry. After he had done this, the ships were dragged down into the sea and Xerxes transferred from his chariot to a Sidonian ship. He sat under a golden awning and sailed along the prows of the ships, asking questions and having answers written down just as he had done with the army. The captains had taken their ships back about four hundred feet from shore, lined them up with their prows facing land, and dropped anchor after posting the marines at their battle stations in full gear. Xerxes conducted his naval review while sailing between the ships' prows and the shore.

When he had sailed past his fleet and disembarked from his ship, Xerxes summoned Demaratus, son of Ariston, who was accompanying him on the campaign against Greece. As Demaratus approached, Xerxes called out to him and said, "Demaratus, there's something it would give me great pleasure to ask you about right now. You are a Greek, and as far as I can tell from you and the other Greeks who have had conversations with me, your city is by no means the smallest or the weakest. Tell me this, now, are the Greeks going to take up arms and resist? Because I believe that neither all the Greeks nor all the other people who live to the west put together are going to be able to resist my assault—unless they are united, that

is. Still, I want to hear from you what you have to say about it."

When Xerxes had finished, Demaratus answered. "Should I tell you the truth, Your Majesty, or just something pleasing?" And Xerxes commanded him to tell the truth—he wouldn't like him any less than before.

When he heard this, Demaratus said, "Since you demand that I tell the truth by all means, Your Majesty, and not something you will later find to be a lie, why then, poverty is congenital to Greece, but bravery is an import, bought with skill and strict rules, and Greece uses bravery to fend off both poverty and despotism. Now, while I praise all Greeks who live in Dorian lands, I'm not really talking about all of them, but solely about the Lacedaemonians. First: there is no way they will ever accept any terms of slavery you bring to Greece. Second: they will oppose you in battle even if all the other Greeks come around to your way of thinking. Don't bother finding out whether there will be enough of them to do it. If there are a thousand, they will fight you, and they will fight you if there are fewer and fight you if there are more."

After Xerxes heard this, he said through his laughter. "What nonsense you talk, Demaratus! A thousand men fighting with an army like this! But come, now, tell me. You say that you yourself used to be king over these people. How would you like to fight with ten men right now? But really, if your citizens are all such as you describe them, then under your laws it would be fitting for you, as their king, to fight with twice that number. If each of them is worth ten men from my army, then I look for you to be worth twenty. That way you can make good on what you've said. Because if they are all like you and the other Greeks who come to talk to me—like you, that is, in size and shape—and you all brag in this way, then see to it that your boast isn't made in vain. Come now, look at it reasonably. How could a thousand, or ten thousand, or fifty thousand men who are all equally free and not ruled by one man stand up to an army this size? Because if there are five thousand of them we will outnumber them by more than a thousand to one! If, like us, they were ruled by one man, they would either surpass themselves through fear of him or they would, under the lash, go up against forces that outnumbered them. But if they are left to their own devices, they won't do either. Anyway, I think that even if the numbers were the same, it would be hard for the Greeks to fight with just the Persians. We, too, have this quality you speak of. There isn't much of it—it's rare, but there are some of my Persian bodyguard who want to take on three Greeks at a time. You've never come up against them, and that's why you can talk so much drivel."

Demaratus answered, "I knew from the beginning, Your Majesty, that if I told you the truth, you wouldn't like what I had to say. But since you forced me to tell you the whole truth, I told you what the Spartans are like. You, though, more than anyone, know how much I love them now—they who stripped me of my rank and my privileges, who drove me from the city of my fathers and made me an exile while your father welcomed me and gave me an income and a home. A rational man is much more likely to appreciate goodwill than to reject it. As for me, I don't claim to be able to fight with ten men or with two. I wouldn't even willingly fight with one. But if I had to, or if a great cause spurred me on, then I would gladly fight—especially with one of those men who say they're a match for three Greeks. In the same way, when the Lacedaemonians fight one at a time, they are no worse than any other men, but when they fight together, they are the best in the world. Because though they're free, they aren't totally free. Custom is the despot who stands over them, and they secretly fear it more than your people fear you. They do whatever it commands,

and its command is always the same: not to run away from any force, however large, but to stay in formation and either prevail or die. If I seem to be talking drivel to you, then I'll keep quiet from now on. I spoke just now only because you made me, but let it be as you think best, Your Majesty."

Although Demaratus answered him in this way, Xerxes didn't get at all angry. Instead, he turned it into a joke and genially sent Demaratus away.

*   *   *

The Spartans sent Leonidas with an advance guard so that the other allies would go to war after seeing them do so and not use any delay on Sparta's part as an excuse for also collaborating with the Persians. Later, after celebrating the Carneian festival, which prevented them from going to battle immediately, they would station a guard in Sparta and march out on the double in full strength. Their allies had the same idea. The Olympic Games were taking place at the same time as these events, so the allies, too, sent their advance guards, never thinking that the battle of Thermopylae would be decided so quickly.

These, then, were their intentions. Meanwhile, when the Greeks at Thermopylae saw the Persians approaching the pass, they panicked and talked about retreat. In general, the Peloponnesians thought they should return to the Peloponnese and guard the Isthmus, but when the Phocians and Locrians became extremely agitated over this idea, Leonidas voted to stay where they were and to dispatch messengers calling on the allies to come to the rescue since they were too few to hold off the Persian army.

While the Greek commanders were discussing their plans, Xerxes sent out a mounted spy to see how many Greeks there were and what they were doing. He had already heard while still in Thessaly that a small army had gathered at Thermopylae, and that it was led by Lacedaemonians under the command of Leonidas, a descendant of Heracles. The horseman could not observe or even see the whole camp as he rode toward it, because some of the men were posted out of sight inside the wall, which they had rebuilt and were guarding. He did see the men outside the wall, though, and their weapons lying nearby. During that watch, the Spartans happened to be stationed outside. He saw some of the men exercising, others combing their long hair. He was amazed at what he saw. He noted their numbers and, after carefully observing everything he could, trotted back unmolested. Nobody pursued him; nobody paid any attention to him at all. When he returned, he told Xerxes everything he had seen.

Xerxes heard it, but he couldn't understand that what they were doing was getting ready to kill or be killed. They seemed to him to be acting so absurdly that he sent for Demaratus, son of Ariston, who was in the camp. When he arrived, Xerxes asked him about everything in detail; he was eager to find out just what the Lacedaemonians were doing. Demaratus said, "I already told you about these men as we were setting out against Greece. You laughed at me for seeing that things would turn out just as they have. I keep trying to tell you the truth, Your Majesty, but it's a struggle. Listen to me now. Those men came here to fight with us for this pass, and that's what they are getting ready to do. It's their way. They comb their hair whenever they are about to risk their lives. But know this: if you defeat these men and the force that remains in Sparta, there are no other people on earth who will take up arms against you, because you are about to face the noblest king and the bravest men in all of Greece."

What he said seemed to Xerxes to be absolutely incredible, and Xerxes asked him for the second time how so few men could do battle with his army. Demaratus said, "Consider me a liar, Your Majesty, if things don't turn out as I say."

That's what he said, but Xerxes didn't believe him.

He let four days go by, expecting the Greeks to run away at any moment. When they had not only not left on the fifth day but seemed to be staying out of sheer reckless effrontery; Xerxes became furious and sent the Medes and Cissians out to attack them, with orders to bring them back into his presence alive. Waves of Medians rushed the Greeks. Many men fell, and others followed in

their wake, but none retreated from the overwhelming disaster. The Medes made it clear to everyone and not least to the king himself that he had many troops but few real men. Nevertheless, the battle lasted all day long.

The Medes finally retreated after being thoroughly manhandled. The Persians were the next to attack—the men Xerxes called his Immortals. They were under the command of Hydarnes, and indeed they thought that they would easily prevail, but it was no different for them when they mixed it up with the Greeks from what it had been for the Medes. It was just the same because they were fighting at very close quarters, using spears shorter than the Greeks', and were unable to take advantage of their numerical superiority. The Lacedaemonians fought a battle to remember! Among these men who knew nothing of warfare, they showed in all sorts of ways that they really knew how to fight—like when they turned their backs and pretended to run away, the barbarians would see them running and would chase after them shouting and making noise, and then the Greeks would wheel around and face the barbarians just as they were about to be overtaken and slaughter countless numbers of them.

A few of the Spartans fell there, too.

The Persians couldn't take the pass after attacking it company by company and in every other way, and they finally retreated.

They say that the king, who was observing these assaults, jumped up from his throne three times in fear for his army. That, then, is how the battle went on that day; and the barbarians fought with no more success the next day, either. They attacked in the belief that the small number of Greeks must have suffered so many casualties that they wouldn't even be able to raise their arms to resist. The Greeks, however, stood in formations of tribes and regiments and took turns in the fighting—all except the Phocians, who had been posted on the mountain to guard the trail. The Persians retreated when they didn't see anything different from what they had found the day before.

Xerxes was at a loss as to how to deal with this situation when a Malian, Ephialtes, son of Eurydemus, came to talk to the king in the hope of receiving a large gift. He told Xerxes about the trail leading through the mountains to Thermopylae and thereby doomed the Greek defenders at the pass. Ephialtes later fled to Thessaly in fear of the Lacedaemonians, but at a meeting at Pylae, the Amphyctionic delegates—the Pylagorac—offered a reward for the fugitive. When he returned to Anticyra some time later, he was killed by Athenades, a man from Trachis. Now, Athenades killed Ephialtes for a different reason (which I will talk about in a later narrative), but the Lacedaemonians honored him for it nonetheless.

*   *   *

Xerxes was delighted with what Ephialtes had offered to do, and soon became positively overjoyed. He immediately dispatched Hydarnes and his Immortals, who left camp at dusk, at around the time the lamps are lit.

Malian locals discovered this trail and then guided the Thessalians over it to attack the Phocians after the Phocians had walled up the pass to hold off an invasion. That's how long the Malians have known about this deadly trail! The trail begins where the Asopus issues through the gorge, and its name is the same as the mountain's—the Anopaea. The Anopaea trail runs along the mountain ridge and leaves off at Alpeni, the first town on the Malian side of Locris, at a place called Black Ass Rock and the Cercopian Butts. This is the narrowest part of the pass.

The Persians crossed the Asopus and made their way over the trail through the night, keeping the Oeta Mountains on the right and the mountains of Trachis on the left. They reached the top of the mountain with the glimmering of dawn. As I have already said, a thousand heavily armed Phocians were stationed there to guard the trail and defend their own homeland. The Phocians had voluntarily given their oath to Leonidas to guard that mountain trail, and we know very well who was guarding the pass below.

The Persians could go up the mountain unnoticed because it was covered with oak trees, so the Phocians only found out that the Persians had already gotten up there when, on that perfectly

still day, they heard the loud noise of fallen leaves crackling under the tramp of feet. The Phocians sprang up and were putting on their battle gear as the barbarians came in sight. The Persians were astonished to see men putting on their armor. They had thought they would meet with no opposition, and yet here was an army! Hydarnes dreaded that the Phocians might be Spartans, so he asked Ephialtes where they were from. When he was sure of their nationality, he arrayed his Persians for battle. After being showered with arrows thick and fast, the Phocians thought the attack was aimed at them, and they ran up to the very top of the mountain ready to fight to the death; but they were mistaken, because the Persians under Ephialtes and Hydarnes paid no further attention to them and hurried down the mountain.

Meanwhile, Megistias the seer had examined the sacrificial animals and told the Greeks at Thermopylae that they would die at dawn. Also, deserters had told them during the night that the Persians were circling around behind them. Finally, their lookouts ran down from the mountaintops with the news at the dawn's early light. The Greeks then held a meeting, and their opinions were divided between those who would not leave their positions and those who took the opposite view. The two sides parted company: some retreated and scattered into their respective cities; others prepared to take their stand there with Leonidas.

It is said that Leonidas himself sent the others away, concerned lest they be destroyed—while as for him and the Spartans who were with him, they couldn't rightly abandon the post they had come to guard in the first place. I myself am inclined to the view that when Leonidas saw that his allies were balking, unwilling to stay with him and risk their lives, he must have ordered them to retreat, though he himself couldn't go home honorably. He would stay to leave eternal fame behind him, and see to it that Sparta's prosperity was not snuffed out. You see, the Spartans had consulted the Delphic oracle as soon as the war broke out, and the Pythian priestless had prophesied that either the Lacedaemonian people would be uprooted by the barbarians or their king would die. She uttered the prophecy in the following hexameter verses:

But for you, O dwellers in Sparta's wide land,
Either your glorious city shall be sacked by the
    men of Persia
Or, if not, she will mourn the action of Heracles,
The dead ruler over all the land of Lacedaemon.
The strength of bulls and lions cannot resist the
    foe,
For he has the strength of Zeus. No, he will not
    leave off,
I say, until he tears city or king limb from limb.

Leonidas dismissed the allies with this prophecy in mind, and because he wanted to be the only Spartan to win such fame; they did not go home in disarray over a difference of opinion.

For me, not the least evidence for this view is the well-known fact that Leonidas also tried to dismiss the army seer I mentioned—Megistias the Acarnanian, who they say descended from Melampus, and who foretold the future from his sacrificial animals. But although he had been dismissed to keep him from being killed with everyone else, he didn't leave; instead, he sent home his only son, who had gone to war with him.

The allies who had been dismissed obeyed Leonidas and left. Only the Thespians and the Thebans stayed with the Lacedaemonians. The Thebans remained without wanting to because Leonidas, regarding them as hostages, held them against their will. The Thespians, on the other hand, were very willing to stay. Refusing to abandon Leonidas or desert his men, they stayed behind and died along with them. The Thespian commander was Demophilus, son of Diadromes.

Xerxes poured out drink offerings at sunrise. He waited until about midmorning and then began the attack. This plan had been arranged in advance with Ephialtes, because the descent from the mountain would be much quicker, with much less ground to cover, than the march around and the climb up had been. The barbarians under Xerxes moved forward while the Greeks under Leonidas advanced like men who are going out to their deaths; and this time they went much farther out into the wider part of the pass than they had at first. In the first days of battle, concerned with protecting the defending wall, they would only make forays into the narrowest part and fight there. This time, as the two sides grappled with each other beyond the narrow neck of the pass, very many barbarians fell while their company commanders whipped each and every man, driving them constantly forward. Many of them fell into the sea and drowned; many others trampled each other alive; no one cared about the dying. And because they knew that death was coming from the troops who had circled the mountain, the Greeks fought the barbarians with all the strength they had, fought recklessly out of their minds.

Most of their spears were broken by now, so they slaughtered Persians with their swords. That brave man Leonidas fell in the struggle, and other renowned Spartans along with him. I have learned the names of these noble men, as I have learned the names of all the three hundred Spartans who perished. And, indeed, many brave Persians died there, too, two sons of Darius among them—Abrocomes and Hyperanthes, Darius' children by Phratagune, daughter of Artanes. This Artanes was the brother of King Darius, and the son of Hystaspes, son of Arsames. When he married his daughter to Darius, Artanes gave up his whole estate along with her since she was his only child.

Thus two brothers of Xerxes died in the battle.

There was a tremendous crush of Persians and Lacedaemonians around the body of Leonidas, until by sheer courage the Greeks dragged him away after beating back the enemy four times. The fight continued until Ephialtes arrived. The nature of the battle changed as soon as the Greeks realized that he was there. They fell back to the narrow part of the pass and, after ducking behind the wall, massed together on the hillock behind it and dug in—all except the Thebans. This mound is in the pass where the stone lion now stands in honor of Leonidas. The men defended themselves on this hillock with daggers, if they still had them, or with their hands and teeth, while some of the Persians came at them head-on after pulling down and demolishing the wall and others surrounded them and stood there burying them under arrows, spears, and stones.

They say that Dieneces the Spartan stood out even in this company of Lacedaemonians and Thespians. Just before the battle with the Persians, he heard some Trachinian say that when the barbarians shot their arrows the sky was so full of them that the sun was blotted out—that's how many Persians there were. Dieneces wasn't fazed at all. He pooh-poohed the Persian numbers, and is reported to have said that his Trachinian friend had brought good news, because if the Persians blotted out the sun they could have their battle in the shade rather than in the sunlight. They say Dieneces the Spartan left this and other witticisms to be remembered by. After him, they say, two Lacedaemonian brothers, Alpheus and Maron, sons of Orsiphantus, distinguished themselves. The most outstanding Thespian was named Dithyrambus, son of Harmatides.

The men were buried where they fell, along with those who had died before the departure of the men Leonidas had dismissed. There is an epitaph over the mass grave which says:

IN THIS PLACE FOUR THOUSAND
PELOPONNESIANS FOUGHT
FOUR MILLION MEN

That epitaph was for all the men. These words commemorate the Spartans alone:

STRANGER GO TELL THE
LACEDAEMONIANS THAT WE WHO LIE
HERE OBEYED THEIR ORDERS

*   *   *

REVIEW QUESTIONS

1. According to Herodotus, why does Xerxes decide to invade Greece? Do he or his generals fear the Greeks at all?
2. What special attributes of the Greeks make it possible for them to resist and eventually defeat the Persian forces?
3. Do the Persians, and Xerxes specifically, possess any flaws that ensure their eventual defeat?
4. How does Herodotus' account of the Spartans at Thermopylae compare with the readings preceding this one?

THUCYDIDES

FROM *The Peloponnesian Wars*

The costly Peloponnesian War of 431–404 B.C.E. was the culmination of years of growing tension between Sparta and its league of allies, on the one hand, and the Athenian empire on the other. Our principal historical source for that war is the history written by the Athenian Thucydides, who tended to be much more rigorous than Herodotus in his assessment and use of historical evidence. In the first selection that follows, Thucydides recreates the speech given by the Athenian leader Pericles to honor those Athenians who fell in battle during the war's first year. It has come to be

regarded as one of the classic statements of the values of a democracy. The second se-
lection is Thucydides' account of the negotiations several years later between the en-
voys of the invading Athenian forces and the local authorities of Melos, an Aegean
island that Athens was seeking to add to its empire.

From *Thucydides: The Peloponnesian Wars,* translated by Benjamin Jowett, revised by P. A.
Brunt (New York: Washington Square Press, 1991).

Pericles' Funeral Speech

During the same winter, in accordance with traditional custom, the funeral of those who first fell
in this war was celebrated by the Athenians at the
public charge. The ceremony is as follows: Three
days before the celebration they erect a tent in
which the bones of the dead are laid out, and every
one brings to his own dead any offering which he
pleases. At the time of the funeral, the bones are
placed in chests of cypress wood, which are conveyed on hearses; there is one chest for each tribe.
They also carry a single empty litter decked with
a pall for all whose bodies had not been found
and recovered. The procession is accompanied by
anyone who chooses, whether citizen or foreigner;
and the female relatives of the deceased are present at the funeral and make lamentation. The
public sepulcher is situated in the most beautiful
suburb of the city; there they always bury those
who fall in war; only after the battle of Marathon,
in recognition of their preeminent valor, the dead
were interred on the field. When the remains have
been laid in the earth, a man, chosen by the city
for his reputed sagacity of judgment and eminent
prestige, delivers the appropriate eulogy over
them; after which the people depart. This is the
manner of interment, and the ceremony was repeated from time to time throughout the war.
Over the first who were buried, Pericles was chosen to speak. At the fitting moment he advanced
from the sepulcher to a lofty stage, which had been
erected in order that he might be heard as far away
as possible by the crowd, and spoke somewhat as
follows:

"Most of those who have spoken here before
me commend the law-giver who added this oration to our other funeral customs, thinking it right
for an oration to be delivered at the funeral of
those killed in wars. But I would have thought it
enough that when men have been brave in action,
they should also be publicly honored in action,
and with such a ceremony as this state funeral,
which you are now witnessing. Then the reputation of many would not have been imperiled by
one man and their merits believed or not, as he
speaks well or ill. For it is difficult to say neither
too little nor too much when belief in the truth is
hard to confirm. The friend of the dead who
knows the facts may well think that the words of
the speaker fall short of his wishes and knowledge;
another who is not well informed, when he hears
of anything which surpasses his own nature, may
be envious and suspect exaggeration. Mankind is
tolerant of the praises of others so long as each
hearer thinks himself capable of doing anything
he has heard; but when the speaker rises above
this, jealousy and incredulity are at once aroused.
However, since our ancestors have set the seal of
their approval upon the practice, I must obey the
law and, to the utmost of my power, endeavor to
satisfy the wishes and beliefs of you all.

"I will speak of our ancestors first, for it is
right and seemly that on such an occasion as this we
should also render this honor to their memory. Men
of the same stock, ever dwelling in this land, in successive generations to this very day, by their valor
handed it down as a free land. They are worthy of
praise, and still more are our fathers, who added
to their inheritance, and after many a struggle

bequeathed to us, their sons, the great empire we possess. Most of it those of our own number who are still in the settled time of life have strengthened further and have richly endowed our city in every way and made her most self-sufficient for both peace and war. Of the military exploits by which our various possessions were acquired or of the energy with which we or our fathers resisted the onslaught of barbarians or Hellenes I will not speak, for the tale would be long and is familiar to you. But before I praise the dead, I shall first proceed to show by what kind of practices we attained to our position, and under what kind of institutions and manner of life our empire became great. For I conceive that it would not be unsuited to the occasion that this should be told, and that this whole assembly of citizens and foreigners may profitably listen to it.

"Our institutions do not emulate the laws of others. We do not copy our neighbors: rather, we are an example to them. Our system is called a democracy, for it respects the majority and not the few; but while the law secures equality to all alike in their private disputes, the claim of excellence is also recognized; and when a citizen is in any way distinguished, he is generally preferred to the public service, not in rotation, but for merit. Nor again is there any bar in poverty and obscurity of rank to a man who can do the state some service. It is as free men that we conduct our public life, and in our daily occupations we avoid mutual suspicions; we are not angry with our neighbor if he does what he likes; we do not put on sour looks at him which, though harmless, are not pleasant. While we give no offense in our private intercourse, in our public acts we are prevented from doing wrong by fear; we respect the authorities and the laws, especially those which are ordained for the protection of the injured as well as those unwritten laws which bring upon the transgressor admitted dishonor.

"Furthermore, none have provided more relaxations for the spirit from toil; we have regular games and sacrifices throughout the year; our homes are furnished with elegance; and the delight which we daily feel in all these things banishes melancholy. Because of the greatness of our city, the fruits of the whole earth flow in upon us so that we enjoy the goods of other countries as freely as our own.

"Then, again, in military training we are superior to our adversaries, as I shall show. Our city is thrown open to the world, and we never expel a foreigner or prevent him from seeing or learning anything which, if not concealed, it might profit an enemy to see. We rely not so much upon preparations or stratagems, as upon our own courage in action. And in the matter of education, whereas from early youth they are always undergoing laborious exercises which are to make them brave, we live at ease and yet are equally ready to face perils to which our strength is equal. And here is the evidence. The Lacedæmonians march against our land not by themselves, but with all their allies: we invade a neighbor's country alone; and although our opponents are fighting for their homes and we are on a foreign soil, we seldom have any difficulty in overcoming them. Our enemies have never yet felt our strength in full; the care of a navy divides our attention, and on land we are obliged to send our own citizens to many parts. But if they meet and defeat some part of our army, they boast of having routed us all, and when defeated, of having been vanquished by our whole force.

"If then we prefer to meet danger with a light heart but without laborious training and with a courage which is instilled by habit more than by laws, we are the gainers; we do not anticipate the pain, although, when the hour comes, we show ourselves no less bold than those who never allow themselves to rest. Nor is this the only cause for marveling at our city. We are lovers of beauty without extravagance and of learning without loss of vigor. Wealth we employ less for talk and ostentation than when there is a real use for it. To avow poverty with us is no disgrace: the true disgrace is in doing nothing to avoid it. The same persons attend at once to the concerns of their households and of the city, and men of diverse employments have a very fair idea of politics. If a man takes no interest in public affairs, we alone do not commend him as quiet but condemn him as useless; and if few of us are originators, we are all sound judges of a policy. In our opinion action does not suffer from discussion but, rather, from the want of that instruction which is gained by discussion preparatory to the action required. For we have an exceptional gift of acting with audacity after calculating the prospects of our enterprises, whereas other men are bold from ignorance but hesitate upon reflection. But it would be right to esteem those men bravest in spirit who have the clearest understanding of the pains and pleasures of life and do not on that account shrink from danger. In doing good, again, we are unlike others; we make our friends by conferring, not by receiving favors. Now a man who confers a favor is the firmer friend because he would keep alive the memory of an obligation by kindness to the recipient; the man who owes an obligation is colder in his feelings because he knows that in recruiting the service, he will not be winning gratitude but only paying a debt. We alone do good to our neighbors, not so much upon a calculation of interest, but in the fearless confidence of freedom.

"To sum up, I say that the whole city is an education for Hellas and that each individual in our society would seem to be capable of the greatest self-reliance and of the utmost dexterity and grace in the widest range of activities. This is no passing boast in a speech, but truth and fact, and verified by the actual power of the city which we have won by this way of life. For when put to the test, Athens alone among her contemporaries is superior to report. No enemy who comes against her is indignant at the reverses which he sustains at the hands of such men; no subject complains that his masters do not deserve to rule. And we shall assuredly not be without witnesses; there are mighty monuments of our power which will make us the wonder of this and of succeeding ages; we shall not need the praises of Homer or of any other whose poetry will please for the moment, but whose reconstruction of the facts the truth will damage. For we have compelled every land and sea to open a path to our daring and have everywhere planted eternal memorials of our triumphs and misfortunes. Such

is the city these men fought and died for and nobly disdained to lose, and every one of us who survive would naturally wear himself out in her service.

"This is why I have dwelt upon the greatness of Athens, showing you that we are contending for a higher prize than those who enjoy no like advantages, and establishing by manifest proof the merit of these men whom I am now commemorating. Their loftiest praise has been already spoken; for in descanting on the city, I have honored the qualities which earned renown for them and for men such as they. And of how few Hellenes can it be said as of them, that their deeds matched their fame! In my belief an end such as theirs proves a man's worth; it is at once its first revelation and final seal. For even those who come short in other ways may justly plead the valor with which they have fought for their country; they have blotted out evil with good, and their public services have outweighed the harm they have done in their private actions. None of these men were enervated by wealth or hesitated to resign the pleasures of life; none of them put off the evil day in the hope, natural to poverty, that a man, though poor, may yet become rich. But deeming that vengeance on their enemies was sweeter than any of these things and that they could hazard their lives in no nobler cause, they accepted the risk and resolved on revenge in preference to every other aim. They resigned to hope the obscure chance of success, but in the danger already visible they thought it right to act in reliance upon themselves alone. And when the moment for fighting came, they held it nobler to suffer death than to yield and save their lives; it was the report of dishonor from which they fled, but on the battlefield their feet stood fast; and while for a moment they were in the hands of fortune, at the height, less of terror than of glory, they departed.

"Such was the conduct of these men; they were worthy of Athens. The rest of us must pray for a safer issue to our courage and yet disdain to show any less daring towards our enemies. We must not consider only what words can be uttered on the utility of such a spirit. Anyone might discourse to you at length on all the advantages of resisting the enemy bravely, but you know them just as well yourselves. It is better that you should actually gaze day by day on the power of the city until you are filled with the love of her; and when you are convinced of her greatness, reflect that it was acquired by men of daring who knew their duty and feared dishonor in the hour of action, men who if they ever failed in an enterprise, even then disdained to deprive the city of their prowess but offered themselves up as the finest contribution to the common cause. All alike gave their lives and received praise which grows not old and the most conspicuous of sepulchers—I speak not so much of that in which their remains are laid as of that in which their glory survives to be remembered forever, on every fitting occasion in word and deed. For every land is a sepulcher for famous men; not only are they commemorated by inscriptions on monuments in their own country, but even in foreign lands there dwells an unwritten memorial of them, graven not so much on stone as in the hearts of men. Make them your examples now; and, esteeming courage to be freedom and freedom to be happiness, do not weigh too nicely the perils of war. It is not the unfortunate men with no hope of blessing, who would with best reason be unsparing of their lives, but the prosperous, who, if they survive, are always in danger of a change for the worse, and whose situation would be most transformed by any reverse. To a man of spirit it is more painful to be oppressed like a weakling than in the consciousness of strength and common hopes to meet a death that comes unfelt.

"Therefore I do not now commiserate the parents of the dead who stand here; I shall rather comfort them. They know that their life has been passed amid manifold vicissitudes and that those men may be deemed fortunate who have gained most honor, whether an honorable death, like the men we bury here, or an honorable sorrow like yours, and whose days have been so measured that the term of their happiness is likewise the term of their life. I know how hard it is to make you feel this when the good fortune of others will often remind you of the happiness in which you, like

them, once rejoiced. Sorrow is felt at the want not of those blessings which a man never knew, but of those which were a part of his life before they were taken from him. Some of you are of an age at which you may have other children, and that hope should make you bear your sorrow better; not only will the children who may hereafter be born make you forget those you have lost, but the city will be doubly a gainer; she will not be left desolate, and she will be safer. For a man's counsel cannot have equal weight or worth when he has no children like the rest to risk in the general danger. To those of you who have passed their prime, I say: 'Congratulate yourselves that you have been happy during the greater part of your days; remember that what remains will not last long, and let it be lightened by the glory of these men.' For only the love of honor is ever young; and it is not so much profit, as some say, but honor which is the delight of men when they are old and useless.

"To you who are the sons and brothers of the departed, I see that the struggle to emulate them will be arduous. For all men praise the dead; and, however pre-eminent your virtue may be, you would hardly be thought their equals, but somewhat inferior. The living have their rivals and detractors; but when a man is out of the way, the honor and good will which he receives is uncontested. And, if I am also to speak of womanly virtues to those of you who will now be widows, let me sum them up in one short admonition: 'Your glory will be great if you show no more than the infirmities of your nature, a glory that consists in being least the subjects of report among men, for good or evil.'

"I have spoken in obedience to the law, making use of such fitting words as I had. The tribute of deeds has been paid in part, for the dead have been honorably interred; it remains only that their children shall be maintained at the public charge until they are grown up: this is the solid prize with which, as with a garland, Athens crowns these men and those left behind after such contests. For where the rewards of virtue are greatest, there men do the greatest services to their cities. And now, when you have duly lamented, everyone his own dead, you may depart."

Such was the order of the funeral celebrated in this winter, with the end of which ended the first year of this war.

*   *   *

The Melian Dialogue

The Athenians next made an expedition against the island of Melos with thirty ships of their own, six Chian, and two Lesbian, twelve hundred hoplites and three hundred archers and twenty mounted archers of their own, and about fifteen hundred hoplites furnished by their allies in the islands. The Melians are colonists of the Lacedæmonians who would not submit to Athens like the other islanders. At first they were neutral and passive. But when the Athenians tried to coerce them by ravaging their lands, they were driven into open hostilities. The generals, Cleomedes the son of Lycomedes and Tisias the son of Tisimachus, encamped with the Athenian forces on the island. But before they did the country any harm, they sent envoys to negotiate with the Melians. Instead of bringing these envoys before the people, the Melians desired them to explain their errand to the minority who held the magistracies. They spoke as follows:

"Since we are denied a public audience on the ground that the multitude might be deceived by hearing our seductive arguments without refutation if they were set forth in a single uninterrupted oration (for we are perfectly aware that this is what you mean in bringing us before the select few), we ask you who are seated here to proceed with even further caution, to reply on each point, instead of speaking continuously yourselves, and to take up at once any statement of ours of which you do not approve, and so reach your decision. Say first of all how you like our proposal."

The Melian representatives answered: "The quiet interchange of explanations is reasonable, and we do not object to that. But at this very time you are actually engaged in acts of war, which obviously belie your words. We see that you mean to decide the discussion yourselves and that at the end of it, if (as is likely) the justice of our cause prevail and we therefore refuse to yield, we may expect war; if we are convinced by you, slavery."

ATH.: "Of course, if you are going to base your calculations on conjectures of the future or if you meet us with any other purpose than that of looking your circumstances in the face and thinking how to save your city, we might as well have done; but if this is your intention, we will proceed."

MEL.: "It is natural and excusable that men in our position should resort to many arguments and considerations. But we admit that this conference has met to consider the question of our preservation; and therefore let the argument proceed in the manner which you propose, if you think that best."

ATH.: "Well, then, we Athenians will use no fine words; we will not say at length, without carrying conviction, that we have a right to rule because we overthrew the Persians or that we are attacking you now because we are suffering any injury at your hands. And you should not expect to convince us by arguing that, although a colony of the Lacedæmonians, you have taken no part in their expeditions or that you have never done us any wrong. You must act with realism on the basis of what we both really think, for we both alike know that in human reckoning the question of justice only enters where there is equal power to enforce it and that the powerful exact what they can and the weak grant what they must."

MEL.: "Well, then, since you thus set aside justice and make expediency the subject of debate, in our judgment it is certainly of advantage that you respect the common good, that to every man in peril fair treatment be accorded, and that any plea which he has urged, even if failing of the point a little, should help his cause. Your interest in this principle is quite as great as ours, since if you fall, you might incur the heaviest vengeance and be an example to mankind."

ATH.: "The end of our empire, even if it should fall, does not dismay us; for ruling states such as Lacedæmon are not cruel to their vanquished enemies. But we are not now contending with the Lacedæmonians; the real danger is from our subjects, who may of their own motion rise up and overcome their masters. But this is a danger which you may leave to us. We will show that we have come in the interests of our empire and that in what we are about to say, we are only seeking the preservation of your city. We wish to subdue you without effort and to preserve you to our mutual advantage."

MEL.: "It may be your advantage to be our masters, but how can it be ours to be your slaves?"

ATH.: "By submission you would avert the most terrible sufferings, and we should profit from not destroying you."

MEL.: "But must we be your enemies? Would you not receive us as friends if we are neutral and remain at peace with you?"

ATH.: "No, your enmity does not injure us as much as your friendship; for your enmity is in the eyes of our subjects a demonstration of our power, your friendship of our weakness."

MEL.: "But do your subjects think it fair not to distinguish between cities in which you have no connection and those which are chiefly your own colonies, and in some cases have revolted and been subdued?"

ATH.: "Why, they believe that neither lack pleas of right, but that by reason of their power some escape us and that we do not attack them out of fear. So that your subjection would give us security, as well as an extension of empire, all the more as you are islanders, and insignificant islanders."

MEL.: "But do you not think that there is security in our proposal? For once more, since you drive us from the plea of justice and urge us to submit to you our interest, we must show you what is for our advantage and try to convince you, if it really coincides with yours: Will you not be making enemies of all who are now neutrals? When they see how you are treating us, they will expect you some day to turn against them; and if so, are you not strengthening the enemies whom you already have and bringing upon you others who, if they could help it, would never dream of being your enemies at all?"

ATH.: "We consider that our really dangerous enemies are not any of the peoples inhabiting the mainland who are secure in their freedom and will defer indefinitely any measures of precaution against us, but islanders who, like you, are under no control, and all who are already irritated by the necessity of submission to our empire; for without calculating, they would be most likely to plunge themselves, as well as us, into a danger for all to foresee."

MEL.: "Surely then, if you and your subjects will brave all this danger, you to preserve your empire and they to be quit of it, how base and cowardly would it be for us, as we are still free, not to do and suffer anything rather than be your slaves."

ATH.: "Not if you deliberate with sound sense; you are in an unequal contest; not about your good character and avoiding dishonor: you must think of saving yourselves by not resisting far superior forces."

MEL.: "But we know that the fortune of war is sometimes impartial and not always on the side of numbers. If we yield, hope is at once gone, but if we act, we can still hope to stand unbowed."

ATH.: "Hope comforts men in danger; and when they have ample resources, it may be hurtful, but is not ruinous. But when her spendthrift nature has induced them to stake their all, they see her as she is only in the moment of their ruin; when their eyes are opened, and they would at last take precautions, they are left with nothing. You are weak, and a single turn of the scale may be your ruin: do not desire to be deluded; or to be like the common herd of men; when they still, humanly speaking, have a chance of survival but find themselves, in their extremity, destitute of real grounds for confidence, they resort to illusions, to prophecies and oracles and the like, which ruin men by the hopes which they inspire in them."

MEL.: "You may be sure that we think it hard to struggle against your power and against fortune if she does not mean to be impartial. But still we trust that we shall not have the worst of the fortune that comes from heaven because we stand as righteous men against your injustice, and we are satisfied that our deficiency in power will be compensated by the alliance of the Lacedæmonians; they are bound to help us, if only because we are their kinsmen and for the sake of their own honor. And therefore our confidence is not so utterly unreasonable."

ATH.: "As for the gods, we expect to have quite as much of their favor as you: for we are not claiming or doing anything which goes beyond what men believe of the gods and desire in human relationships. For we believe of the gods by repute, and of men by clear evidence, that by a necessity of nature, wherever they have the power, they will rule. This law was not made by us, and we are not the first who have acted upon it; we did but inherit it, and shall bequeath it to all time; we obey it in the knowledge that you and all mankind, with our strength would act like us. So much for the gods; we have no reason to fear any lack of their favor. And then as to the Lacedæmonians—when you imagine that out of very shame they will assist you, we congratulate you on your blissful ignorance, but we do not admire your folly. No men do each other more services, by their own local standards, than the Lacedæmonians; but as for their conduct to the rest of the world, much might be said, but it could be most clearly expressed in a few words—of all men whom we know, they are the most conspicuous for identifying pleasure with honor and expediency with justice. But how inconsistent is such a character with your present unreasonable hope of deliverance!"

MEL.: "That is the very reason why we are now particularly reliant on them; they will look to their interest, and therefore will not be willing to betray the Melians, their own colonists, lest they should be distrusted by their friends in Hellas and play into the hands of their enemies."

ATH.: "Then you do not think that the path of expediency is safe, whereas justice and honor involve action and danger, which none are more generally averse to facing than the Lacedæmonians."

MEL.: "No, we believe that they would be ready to face dangers for our sake, and will think them safer where we are concerned. If action is required, we are close to the Peloponnese; and they can better trust our loyal feeling because we are their kinsmen."

ATH.: "Yes, but what gives men security in joining in a conflict is clearly not the good will of those who summon help but a decided superiority in real power. To this none look more keenly than the Lacedæmonians; so little confidence have they in their own resources that they only attack their neighbors when they have numerous allies, and therefore they are not likely to find their way by themselves to an island, when we are masters of the sea."

MEL.: "But they might send others; the Cretan sea is a large place, and the masters of the sea will have more difficulty in seizing vessels than those who would elude detection in making their escape. And if the attempt should fail, they might invade Attica itself and find their way to allies of yours whom Brasidas did not reach; and then you will have to make efforts, not for the conquest of a land which is not yours, but nearer home, for the preservation of your confederacy and of your own territory."

ATH.: "Some of this may happen; we have actually experienced it, and you are not unaware that never once have the Athenians retired from a siege through fear of others. You told us that you would deliberate on the safety of your city; but we remark that, in this long discussion, you have uttered not a word which would justify men in expecting deliverance. Your strongest grounds are hopes deferred; and what power you have, compared with that already arrayed against you, is too little to save you. What you have in mind is most unreasonable, unless you ultimately come to a sounder decision after we have withdrawn. For surely you will not fall back on a sense of honor, which has been the ruin of so many, when danger and dishonor were staring them in the face. Many men with their eyes still open to the consequences have found the word *honor* too much for them and have let a mere name lure them on, until with their own acquiescence it has drawn down upon them real and irretrievable calamities; through their own folly they have incurred a worse dishonor than fortune would have inflicted upon them. If you are wise, you will not run this risk; you will think it not unfitting to yield to the greatest of cities, which invites you to become her ally on reasonable terms, keeping your own land and merely paying tribute; you will find no honor, when you have a choice between two alternatives, safety and war, in obstinately preferring the worse. To maintain one's rights against equals, to be politic with superiors and to be moderate toward inferiors is generally the right course. Reflect once more when we have withdrawn, and say to yourselves over and over again that you are deliberating about your one and only country, which a single decision will save or destroy."

The Athenians left the conference; the Melians, after consulting among themselves, resolved to persevere in their refusal and gave the following answer: "Men of Athens, our resolution is unchanged; and we will not in a moment surrender that liberty which our city, founded seven hundred years ago, still enjoys; we will trust to the good fortune which, by the favor of the gods, has hitherto preserved us, and for human help, to the Lacedæmonians; and we will endeavor to save ourselves. We are ready, however, to be your friends and the enemies neither of you nor of the Lacedæmonians and we ask you to leave our country when you have made such a peace as appears to be in the interest of both parties."

This was the substance of the Melian answer; the Athenians said as they quitted the conference: "Well, we must say, judging from the decision at which you have arrived, that you are the only men who find things to come plainer than what lies before their eyes: your wishes make you see the secrets of the future as present realities; you put your faith in the Lacedæmonians, in fortune and in your hopes; none have more than you at stake, and none will be more utterly ruined."

REVIEW QUESTIONS

1. What, in Pericles' estimation, are the benefits of democracy?
2. What are the reasons for Athens' greatness?
3. How do the values of Athenian democracy compare with those of Spartan society?
4. How evident are Athens' democratic values in the Athenians' negotiations with the citizens of Melos?

XENOPHON

FROM *Oeconomicus*

While the modern democracies of the early twenty-first century C.E. rightfully trace their pedigrees back to classical Athens, it bears remembering that participation in Athenian democracy was restricted to male citizens of that polis. Resident aliens, women, and slaves had no voice. That women were excluded from political activity is hardly surprising given the social restrictions that were placed on them, not to mention the inferior status they had within their own households. In the following reading, the philosopher Socrates (of whom Xenophon was a student) questions one of his students, Ischomachos, about how he has educated his wife.

From *Xenophon's Socratic Discourse: An Interpretation of the Oeconomicus*, edited by Leo Strauss (Ithaca, N.Y.: Cornell University Press, 1970), pp. 32–38.

*   *   *

" 'As to what you asked me, Socrates,' he said, 'I never spend time indoors. Indeed,' he said, 'my wife is quite able by herself to manage the things within the house.'

" 'It would please me very much, Ischomachos,' I said, 'if I might also inquire about this— whether you yourself educated your wife to be the way she ought to be, or whether, when you took her from her mother and father, she already knew how to manage the things that are appropriate to her.'

" 'How, Socrates,' he said, 'could she have known anything when I took her, since she came to me when she was not yet fifteen, and had lived previously under diligent supervision in order that she might see and hear as little as possible and ask the fewest possible questions? Doesn't it seem to you that one should be content if she came knowing only how to take the wool and make clothes, and had seen how the spinning work is distributed among the female attendants? For as to matters of the stomach, Socrates,' he said, 'she came to me very finely educated; and to me, at any rate, that seems to be an education of the greatest importance both for a man and a woman.'

" 'By the gods, Ischomachos,' I said, 'relate to me what you first began teaching her. I'd listen to you relating these things with more pleasure than if you were telling me about the finest contest in wrestling or horsemanship.'

"And Ischomachos replied: 'Well, Socrates,' he said, 'when she had gotten accustomed to me and had been domesticated to the extent that we could have discussions, I questioned her somewhat as follows. "Tell me, woman, have you thought yet why it was that I took you and your parents gave you to me? That it was not for want of someone else to spend the night with—this is obvious, I know, to you too. Rather, when I considered for myself, and your parents for you, whom we might take as the best partner for the household and children, I chose you, and your parents, as it appears, from among the possibilities chose me. Should a god grant us children, we will then con-sider, with respect to them, how we may best educate them; for this too is a good common to us —to obtain the best allies and the best supporters in old age; but for the present this household is what is common to us. As to myself, everything of mine I declare to be in common, and as for you, everything you've brought you have deposited in common. It's not necessary to calculate which of us has contributed the greater number of things, but it is necessary to know this well, that which ever of us is the better partner will be the one to contribute the things of greater worth." To this, Socrates, my wife replied: "What can I do to help you?" she said. "What is my capacity? But everything depends on you: my work, my mother told me, is to be moderate." "By Zeus, woman," I said "my father told me the same thing. But it's for moderate people—for man and woman alike —not only to keep their substance in the best condition but also to add as much as possible to it by fine and just means." "Then what do you see," said my wife, "that I might do to help in increasing the household?" "By Zeus," I said, "just try to do in the best manner possible what the gods have brought you forth to be capable of and what the law praises." "And what are these things?" she said. . . . "Since, then, work and diligence are needed both for the indoor and for the outdoor things, it seems to me," ' he had said, ' "that the god directly prepared the woman's nature for indoor works and indoor concerns. For he equipped the man, in body and in soul, with a greater capacity to endure cold and heat, journey and expeditions, and so has ordered him to the outdoor works; but in bringing forth, for the woman, a body that is less capable in these respects," ' he said that he had said, ' "the god has, it seems to me, ordered her to the indoor works. But knowing that he had implanted in the woman, and ordered her to, the nourishment of newborn children, he also gave her a greater affection for the newborn infants than he gave to the man. Since he had also ordered the woman to the guarding of the thing brought in, the god, understanding that a fearful soul is not worse at guarding, also gave the woman a greater share of fear than the man. And knowing too that the one who had the outdoor works would need to defend himself should someone act unjustly, to him he gave a greater share of boldness. But because it's necessary for both to give and to take, he endowed both with memory and diligence in like degree, so that you can't distinguish whether the male or the female kind has the greater share of these things. As for self-control in the necessary things, he endowed both with this too in like degree; and the god allowed the one who proved the better, whether the man or the woman, to derive more from this good. Since, then, the nature of each has not been brought forth to be naturally apt for all of the same things, each has need of the other, and their pairing is more beneficial to each, for where one falls short the other is capable. Now," I said, "O woman, as we know what has been ordered to each of us by the god, we must, separately, do what's appropriate to each. The law too praises these things," ' he said that he had said, ' "in pairing man and woman; and as the god made them partners in children, so too does the law appoint them partners. . . . It will be necessary," I said, "for you to remain indoors and to send out those of the servants whose work is outside; as for those whose work is to be done inside, these are to be in your charge; you must receive what is brought in and distribute what needs to be expended, and as for what needs to be set aside, you must use forethought and guard against expending in a month what was intended to last a year. When wool is brought to you, it must be your concern that clothes be made for whoever needs them. And it must be your concern that the dry grain be fine and fit for eating. There is one thing, however," I said, "among the concerns appropriate to you, that will perhaps seem less agreeable: whenever any of the servants become ill, it must be your concern that all be attended." "By Zeus," said my wife, "that will be most agreeable, at least if those who have been well tended are going to be grateful and feel more good will than before." I admired her reply,' said Ischomachos, 'and spoke: "Isn't it through this kind of forethought that the leader of the hive so disposes the other bees to her that when she leaves the hive, not one of the bees

supposes they must let her go, but rather they all follow? . . . But the most pleasant thing of all: if you look to be better than I and make me your servant, you will have no need to fear that with advancing age you will be honored any less in the household, and you may trust that as you grow older, the better a partner you prove to be for me, and for the children the better a guardian of the household, by so much more will you be honored in the household. . . ." I seem to remember saying such things to her, Socrates, at the time of our first discussion.' "

" 'Did you notice, Ischomachos,' I said, 'that she was stirred to diligence by these things?'

" 'Yes, by Zeus,' said Ischomachos. 'I know she once became very upset, and blushed deeply, when she was unable to give me one of the things I had brought in when I asked for it. Seeing she was irritated, I spoke. "Don't be discouraged, woman," I said, "because you can't give me what I happen to ask for. It is indeed clear poverty not to have a thing to use when it's needed; at the same time our present want—to look for something and be unable to find it—is certainly a less painful thing than not to look for it at all, knowing it's not there. But you aren't at fault in this," I said; "rather I am, since I handed over these things to you without giving orders as to where each kind of thing should be put, so that you would know where to put them and where to find them again. There is nothing, woman, so useful or fine for human beings as order. . . . That an ordered arrangement of implements is a good, then, and that it is easy to find in the house an advantageous place for each kind of thing, has been established. But how fine it looks, too, when shoes of any kind are set out in a regular manner; it is fine to see clothes of any kind when they are sorted, as also bedcovers, bronze kettles, and things pertaining to the table, and—what of all things would be most ridiculed, not indeed by the solemn man but by the wit—even pots have a graceful look when distinctly arranged." ' "

" 'What then, Ischomachos?' I said. 'Did your wife seem to listen at all to what you were trying so seriously to teach her?'

" 'What else did she do if not promise to be diligent, manifest her very great pleasure, as though she had found some easy means out of a difficulty, and ask me to order things separately as quickly as possible in the way I had stated?'

" 'How, then, Ischomachos,' I said, 'did you separately order them for her?'

" 'What else seemed best to me if not to show her first the capacity of the house? For it is not adorned with decorations, Socrates; the rooms were planned and built simply with a view to their being the most advantageous receptacles for the things that would be in them, so that each calls for what is suitable to it. The bedroom, being in an interior part of the house, invites the most valuable bedcovers and implements; the dry parts of the dwelling, the grain; the cool places, the wine; and the well-lighted places, the works and implements that need light. And I displayed to her the areas for the daily use of human beings, furnished so as to be cool in summer and warm in winter. And I displayed to her the house as a whole, and how it lies open to the south—obviously, so as to be well exposed to the sun in winter and well shaded in summer. Then I pointed out to her the women's apartments, separated from the men's by a bolted door, so that nothing may be taken out that shouldn't be and so that the servants may not produce offspring without our knowledge. For the useful ones, for the most part, feel even more good will once they have had children, but when wicked ones are paired together, they become only more resourceful in their bad behavior. When we had gone through these things,' he said, 'we then proceeded to separate our belongings according to tribes. We began first,' he said, 'by collecting whatever we use for sacrifices. After this we distinguished the woman's ornaments for festivals, the man's dress for festivals and war, bedcovers for the women's apartments, bedcovers for the men's apartments, shoes for women, shoes for men. Another tribe consisted of arms, another of instruments for spinning, another of instruments for breadmaking, another of instruments for cooking, another of the things for bathing, another of the things for kneading bread, another of the things

for the table; and all these things were further divided according to whether they were used every day or only for festivals. We also set apart the expenses for each month from the amount that had been calculated and reserved for the whole year; for in this way we could better see how things would come out at the end. And when we had sorted our belongings according to tribes, we took each kind of thing to its appropriate place. After this, as to the implements the servants use from day to day—those for the making of bread, for cooking, for spinning, and others of this sort—we pointed out to those who would be using them where each must go, handed them over, and gave orders that they be kept secure. Those we use for festivals, for entertaining foreigners, or only from time to time we handed over to the housekeeper, and after pointing out to her their places and counting and making lists of the various kinds of things, we told her to give each what he needed of them, to remember what she had given someone, and when she had got it back, to return it to the place she had taken it from. We chose as housekeeper the one who upon examination seemed to us the most self-controlled as regards food, wine, sleep, and intercourse with men, and who, in addition, seemed to have a good memory and the forethought to avoid punishment for negligence and to consider how, by gratifying us in some way, she might be honored by us in return. We taught her also to feel good will toward us, sharing our delights when we were delighted in some way, and when there was something painful, inviting her aid. We further educated her to be eager to increase the household, making her thoroughly acquainted with it and giving her a share in its prosperity. And we inspired justice in her, honoring the just more than the unjust and displaying to her that they live richer and freer lives than the unjust. We then installed her in the place. But in addition to all these things, Socrates,' he said, 'I told my wife that there would be no benefit in any of this unless she herself was diligent in seeing that the order is preserved in each thing. I taught her that in the cities subject to good laws the citizens do not think it enough merely to have fine laws, but in addition choose guardians of the laws to examine them, to praise the one who acts lawfully, and to punish the one who acts contrary to the laws. Then,' he said 'I suggested that my wife consider herself a guardian of the laws regarding the things in the house; that she inspect the implements whenever it seems best to her, just as a garrison commander inspects his guards; that she test the fitness of each thing, just as the council tests the fitness of horses and horsemen; and that, like a queen, she praise and honor the deserving, to the limit of her capacity, and rebuke and punish the one who needs such things. In addition,' he said, 'I taught her that she could not be justly annoyed if I gave her many more orders in regard to our possessions than I gave to the servants, displaying to her that the servants share in their master's wealth only to the extent that they carry it, attend to it, or guard it, and that no one of them is allowed to use it unless the lord gives it to him, whereas everything is the master's to use as he wishes. To the one deriving the greatest benefit from its preservation and the greatest harm from its destruction belongs the greatest concern for a thing—this I declared to her.'

" 'What then?' I said. 'After your wife had heard these things, Ischomachos, did she at all obey you?'

" 'What else did she do,' he said, 'if not tell me I didn't understand her correctly if I supposed that in teaching her to be concerned with our substance I had ordered her to do something hard. For as she told me,' he said, 'it would have been much harder if I had ordered her to neglect her own things than if she were required to concern herself with the goods of the household. For just as it seems natural,' he said, 'for a sensible woman to be concerned for her offspring rather than to neglect them, so, she said, it's more pleasant for a sensible woman to be concerned for those of the possessions that delight her because they are her own than to neglect them.' "

"On hearing that his wife had replied to him in this way," said Socrates, "I spoke. 'By Hera, Ischomachos,' I said, 'you display your wife's manly understanding.'

" 'There are other instances of her high-mindedness that I am willing to relate to you,' said Ischomachos, 'instances of her obeying me quickly in some matter after hearing it only once.'

" 'In what sort of thing?' I said. 'Speak; for to me it is much more pleasant to learn of the virtue of a living woman than to have had Zeuxis display for me the fine likeness of a woman he had painted.'

"Ischomachos then speaks. 'And yet once, Socrates,' he said, 'I saw she had applied a good deal of white lead to her face, that she might seem to be fairer than she was, and some dye, so that she would look more flushed than was the truth, and she also wore high shoes, that she might seem taller than she naturally was. "Tell me, woman," I said, "would you judge me more worthy to be loved as a partner in wealth if I showed you our substance itself, didn't boast of having more substance than is really mine, and didn't hide any part of our substance, or if instead I tried to deceive you by saying I have more substance than is really mine and by displaying to you counterfeit money, necklaces of gilt wood, and purple robes that lose their color, and asserting they are genuine?" She broke in straightway. "Hush," she said; "don't you become like that; if you did, I could never love you from my soul." "Haven't we also come together, woman," I said, "as partners in one another's bodies?" "Human beings say so, at least," she said. "Would I then seem more worthy to be loved," I said, "as a partner in the body, if I tried to offer you my body after concerning myself that it be healthy and strong, so that I would really be well complexioned, or if instead I smeared myself with vermilion, applied flesh color beneath the eyes, and then displayed myself to you and embraced you, all the while deceiving you and offering you vermilion to see and touch instead of my own skin?" "I wouldn't touch vermilion with as much pleasure as I would you," she said, "or see flesh color with as much pleasure as your own, or see painted eyes with as much pleasure as your healthy ones." "You must believe, woman," ' Ischomachos said that he had said, " 'that I too am not more pleased by the color of white lead or dye than by your color, but just as the gods have made horses most pleasant to horses, oxen to oxen, and sheep to sheep, so human beings suppose the pure body of a human being is most pleasant. Such deceits may in some way deceive outsiders and go undetected, but when those who are always together try to deceive one another they are necessarily found out. For either they are found out when they rise from their beds and before they have prepared themselves, or they are detected by their sweat or exposed by tears, or they are genuinely revealed in bathing." '

" 'By the gods,' I said, 'what did she reply to this?'

" 'What else,' he said, 'was her reply, if not that she never did anything of the sort again and tried always to display herself suitably and in a pure state. At the same time she asked me if I could not advise her how she might really come to sight as fine and not merely seem to be. I advised her, Socrates,' he said, 'not always to sit about like a slave but to try, with the gods' help, to stand at the loom like a mistress, to teach others what she knew better than they, and to learn what she did not know as well; and also to examine the breadmaker, to watch over the housekeeper in her distribution of things, and to go about and investigate whether each kind of thing is in the place it should be. In this way, it seemed to me, she could both attend to her concerns and have the opportunity to walk about. And I said it would be good exercise to moisten and knead the bread and to shake out and fold the clothes and bedcovers. I

said that if she exercised in this way, she would take more pleasure in eating, would become healthier, and so would come to sight as better complexioned in truth. And a wife's looks, when in contrast to a waiting maid she is purer and more suitably dressed, become attractive, especially when she gratifies her husband willingly instead of serving him under compulsion. On the other hand, women who always sit about in pretentious solemnity lend themselves to comparison with those who use adornments and deceit. And now, Socrates,' he said, 'know well, my wife still arranges her life as I taught her then and as I tell you now.' "

*   *   *

REVIEW QUESTIONS

1. What kinds of attitudes toward women underlie Ischomachos' treatment of his wife?
2. How do women and men differ, in his eyes?
3. What are his wife's responsibilities in the household?
4. What can you deduce from this reading about the internal configuration of a Greek dwelling (at least, that of someone of Ischomachos' social standing)?
5. Can you discern any contrasts between the role of women as presented here and their role in Spartan society as described in the earlier selection by Xenophon?

SOPHOCLES

FROM *Antigone*

One of the foremost features of the culture of classical Athens was its focus on the rights, responsibilities, and potential of the individual and its celebration of human intellect and personality. Nowhere is this more evident than in the surviving works of the greatest of the Athenian tragedians, Aeschylus, Sophocles, and Euripides. Sophocles wrote his play Antigone, *from which the following excerpts are taken, shortly before 441 B.C.E. Like so many of the plays of this era,* Antigone *focuses on the nobility of spirit of the human being when faced with terrible conflict. Indeed, one well-known analysis of its impact characterizes it as the only work of literature that expresses "all the principal constants of conflict in the condition of man . . . : the confrontation of men and women; of age and of youth; of society and of the individual; of the living and the dead; of men and of god(s)."*

From *The Antigone of Sophocles*, translated by George Herbert Palmer (Boston: Houghton Mifflin, 1927).

THE PERSONS

CREON, King of Thebes
EURYDICE, his wife
HAEMON, his son, betrothed to Antigone
ANTIGONE, ⎫
ISMENE, ⎬ his nieces, daughters of Oedipus and Jocasta, former King and Queen of Thebes
WATCHMAN
MESSENGER
SECOND MESSENGER
BOY AND GUARDS, silent persons
CHORUS OF THEBAN ELDERS

The Scene throughout is at Thebes, in front of the palace. The Play begins at daybreak.

ANTIGONE: Ismene, my own sister, of all the woes begun in Oedipus can you imagine any that Zeus will not complete within our lives? There is no grief or crime, no degradation or dishonor, not to be found among the woes of you and me. And what is this new edict issued lately by our captain, people say, to the whole city? Do you know, and did you hear? Or have you failed to learn how on our friends fall evils from our foes?

ISMENE: To me, Antigone, have come no tidings of our friends, for good or ill, since we two lost two brothers, slain in mutual strife the self-same day. I know the Argive host retreated this last night, but I know nothing further—whether we gain or lose.

ANTIGONE: I guessed as much, and therefore brought you here alone outside the gate to learn the truth.

ISMENE: What is it, then? You seem to hint at some dark tale.

ANTIGONE: Yes. In his order for the burial of our brothers has not Creon honored the one, outraged the other? To Eteocles, they say, he paid each proper rite and custom and laid him in the ground, to be in honor with the dead below. But as for poor dead Polynices' body, they say he has proclaimed among our people that none shall hide it in a grave and mourn, but let it lie unwept, unburied, welcome provision for the birds who watch for such-like prey. These are, they say, the orders our good Creon has proclaimed for you and me—yes, even for me!—and now comes hither to make plain his will to such as do not know. Nor does he treat the matter lightly. But let one do what he forbids, and death by public stoning shall await him in the city. So it stands now, and you must quickly show if you are rightly born or the base child of noble parents.

ISMENE: But, my poor sister, if it has come to this, what further can I do to help or hinder?

ANTIGONE: Think, will you share my toil and strife?

ISMENE: In what bold deed? What is your plan?

ANTIGONE: To try if you with this hand's help will raise that body.

ISMENE: What! Bury him? In opposition to the State?

ANTIGONE: My brother, though, and yours. If you refuse, I will be found no traitor.

ISMENE: Reckless! When Creon too forbids?

ANTIGONE: 'T is not for him to keep me from my own.

ISMENE: Alas! consider, sister, how our father died, hated and scorned, because of self-exposed offences doing his eyes a violence with his own hand. And then his mother and his wife—ah, double title!—with twisted cord ended her life in shame. A third disaster came. Our pair of brothers in a single day, like wretched suicides, wrought out one common ruin by each other's hand. And now once more, when we are the only ones still left, think what a far worse fate we two shall meet if we, defying law, transgress our rulers' will and power. Nay, rather let us bear in mind that we are women, so not fit to strive with men. Moreover, since we are the subjects of those stronger than ourselves, we must obey these orders and orders harsher still. I, then, beseeching those beneath the earth to grant me pardon, seeing I am compelled, will bow to those in power. To act beyond one's sphere shows little wisdom.

ANTIGONE: I will not urge you. No! Nor if hereafter you desire, shall you with my consent give any aid. Be what you will, and I will bury him. Good it would be to die in doing so. Dearly shall I lie with him, with my dear, after my pious sin. And longer must I satisfy those there below than people here, for there I shall lie ever. But you, if you think well, keep disregarding what the gods regard!

ISMENE: I mean no disregard. But to defy the State—it is not in me.

ANTIGONE: Make that, then, your excuse! I will go raise a grave over my dearest brother.

ISMENE: O my poor sister, how I fear for you!

ANTIGONE: Be not disturbed for me. Let your own course be true.

ISMENE: At least do not reveal what you have done. Keep it a secret. I will hide it too.

ANTIGONE: Ha? Speak it out! Far more my enemy if silent than if telling it to all!

ISMENE: Hot heart and chilling deeds!

ANTIGONE: I know I please those I most ought to please.

ISMENE: If you succeed. But you desire what cannot be.

ANTIGONE: Why, then, when strength shall fail me, I will cease.

ISMENE: Best not pursue at all what cannot be.

ANTIGONE: Speak thus, and I shall hate you. And he who died will hate you,—rightly too. Nay, leave me and my rash design to meet our doom, for I shall meet none equal to not dying nobly.

ISMENE: Go, then, if go you must. And yet of this be sure, that mad as is your going, dearly are you loved by those you love.

*   *   *

[*Enter* CREON.]

CREON: Sirs, our city's welfare, though shaken in a heavy surge, the gods have safely righted. Therefore by mandate I have brought you hither, parted from all the rest, because I know full well how in the time of Laïus you steadily respected the power of the throne. So also in the days when Oedipus upheld the State. And even when he fell, you stood around the children of his house with faithful hearts. Since, then, these two have fallen in one day by double doom, smiting and smitten in their own hand's guilt, I take possession of all power and of the throne through being next of kin to the two dead.

It is impossible fully to learn what a man is in heart and mind and judgment until he proves himself by test of office and of laws. For to my thinking he who ordering a great state catches at plans not through their being best, and then through fear holds his lips locked, appears and ever has appeared most base. Him who regards his friend more than his land I count no man at all. I therefore,—all-seeing Zeus bear witness!—never shall keep silence when I see woe coming on my citizens instead of weal. Nor would I ever make that man my friend who is my country's foe; because I know how it is she who saves us, and when we sail with her secure we find true friends.

Such are the principles by which I make this city prosper. And in accord herewith I now have issued public edict touching the sons of Oedipus: ordering that Eteocles, who fell fighting for this city after winning all distinction with his spear, be laid within a grave and given whatever honors meet the brave dead below. But for his brother Polynices, who coming back from exile tried by fire utterly to destroy his native land and his ancestral gods, tried even to taste the blood of his own kin or force them into bondage—this man we have proclaimed throughout the city none shall honor with a grave and none lament, but that his corpse be left unburied, for the birds and dogs to eat, disgraced for all to see. Such is my will. Never by act of mine shall bad men have more honor than the just. But he who is well minded toward this state alike in life or death by me is honored.

*   *   *

CREON: You there, now turning to the ground your face, do you acknowledge or deny you did this thing?

ANTIGONE: I say I did it. I deny not that I did.

CREON: (*To Watchman.*) Then go your way, clear of a heavy charge. [*Exit.*] (*To Antigone.*) Tell me, not at full length but briefly, did you know my edict against doing this?

ANTIGONE: I did. How could I help it? It was plain.

CREON: Yet you presumed to transgress laws?

ANTIGONE: Yes, for it was not Zeus who gave this edict; nor yet did Justice, dwelling with the gods below, make for men laws like these. I did

not think such force was in your edicts that the unwritten and unchanging laws of God you, a mere man, could traverse. These are not matters of to-day or yesterday, but are from everlasting. No man can tell at what time they appeared. In view of them I would not, through fear of human will, meet judgment from the gods. That I shall die, I knew,—how fail to know it?—though you had never made an edict. And if before my time I die, I count it gain. For he who lives like me in many woes, how can he fail to find in death a gain? So then for me to meet this doom is not a grief at all. But when my mother's child had died if I had kept his corpse unburied, then I should have grieved. For this I do not grieve. And if I seem to you to have been working folly, it may be he who charges folly is the fool.

CHORUS: Plain is the headstrong temper of this child of headstrong father. She knows not how to bend in times of ill.

CREON: Yet know that spirits very stiff may soonest fail. The strongest iron, baked in the fire overhard, you may see oftenest snap and break. By a little bit, I find, high-mettled steeds are managed. There is no place for pride in one who is dependent. She first set out in crime when she transgressed the established laws; and after that comes further crime in boasting here, laughing at having done so. I am no longer man, she is the man, if such power rests in her unchallenged. Be she my sister's child, or closer to my blood than all who bow before our household Zeus, she and her kin shall not escape the direst doom.

Yes, for I count her sister an equal plotter of this burial. Summon her hither! Even now I saw her in the house raving and uncontrolled. It often happens that the stealthy heart is caught before the act, when in the dark men fashion crooked deeds. But it is hateful, too, when one found out in wrong will give his guilt fine names.

ANTIGONE: Do you desire more than having caught to kill me?

CREON: No, nothing. Having that, I have the whole.

ANTIGONE: Then why delay? For nothing in your words can give me pleasure—and may they never please! So also you mine naturally displease. Yet how could I have gained glory more glorious than by now laying my own brother in the grave? All here would speak approval, did not terror seal their lips. Rulers, so fortunate in much besides, have this advantage too—that they can do and say whatever they may please.

CREON: Of all the race of Cadmus you alone see it so.

ANTIGONE: These also do, but curb their tongues through fear of you.

CREON: And are you not ashamed to act so unlike them?

ANTIGONE: 'T is no disgrace to honor one's own kin.

CREON: Was not he also of your blood who fell, his rival?

ANTIGONE: Mine, by one mother and one father too.

CREON: Why then pay honors which dishonor him?

ANTIGONE: He who is dead would not describe it so.

CREON: Yes, if you give like honor to his impious foe.

ANTIGONE: It was no slave who died. It was his brother.

CREON: Wasting the land. And he defending it.

ANTIGONE: But these are rites called for by Death itself.

CREON: The good and bad should not be like in lot.

ANTIGONE: Who knows if that is pity below?

CREON: A hated man is not beloved, though dead.

ANTIGONE: I take no part in hate. 'T is mine to love.

CREON: Down to the grave, then, if you needs must love, and love those there! But while I live, no woman masters me.

*   *   *

CHORUS: But here is Haemon, the youngest of your sons. Does he come grieving for the fate of his intended bride Antigone, vexed at his vanished nuptials?

[*Enter* HAEMON.]

*   *   *

CREON: Soon we shall know, better than seers could say. My son, because you heard the immutable decree passed on your promised bride, you are not here incensed against your father? Are we not dear to you, do what we may?

HAEMON: My father, I am yours; and with just judgment you may direct, and I shall follow. No marriage shall be counted greater gain than your wise guidance.

CREON: Yes, so it should be settled in your heart, my son, always to take your stand behind your father's judgment. Therefore men pray to rear obedient children and to have them in their homes, to recompense the foe with ill and honor as their father does the friend. If one begets unprofitable children, what shall we say but that he breeds pains for himself, loud laughter for his foes? Do not, my son, at pleasure's bidding, give up your wits for any woman. But know embraces soon grow cold when she who shares the home is false. What ulcer can be worse than the false friend? Then spurn the girl as if she were your foe, and let her seek a husband in the house of Hades. For having found her only, out of all the State, openly disobedient, recreant to that State I will not be, but I will have her life.

Let her appeal to Zeus, the god of kindred; but if I train my kin to be disorderly, I surely shall all those outside my kin. He who in private matters is a faithful man will prove himself upright in public too. But one who wantonly forces the law, and thinks to dictate to the rulers, wins no praise from me. No, whosoever is established by the State should be obeyed, in matters trivial and just or in their opposites. And the obedient man, I should be confident, would govern well and easily be governed, and posted in the storm of spears would hold his ground, a true and loyal comrade. Than lawlessness there is no greater ill. It ruins states, overturns homes, and joining with the spearthrust breaks the ranks in rout. But in the steady lines what saves most lives is discipline. Therefore we must defend the public order and not at all subject it to a woman. Better be pushed aside, if need be, by a man than to be known as women's subjects.

CHORUS: Unless through age we are at fault, you seem to say with reason what you say.

HAEMON: Father, the gods plant wisdom in mankind, which is of all possessions highest. In what respects you have not spoken rightly I cannot say, and may I never learn; and still it may be possible for some one else to be right too. I naturally watch in your behalf all that men do or say or find to blame. For your eye terrifies the common man and checks the words you might not wish to hear; but it is mine to hear things uttered in the dark. I know how the whole city mourns this maid, as one who of all women least deservedly for noblest deeds meets basest death. "She who, when her brother had fallen in the fight and lay unburied, did not leave him to be torn by savage dogs and birds, is she not worthy to receive some golden honor?" Such guarded talk runs covertly about.

For me, my father, nothing I possess is dearer than your welfare. For what can bring to children greater glory than a successful father's noble name, or to a father than his son's renown? Do not then carry in your heart one fixed belief that what you say and nothing else is right. For he who thinks that he alone is wise, or that he has a tongue and mind no other has, will when laid open be found empty. However wise a man may be, it is no shame to learn, learn much, and not to be too firm. You see along the streams in winter how many trees bend down and save their branches; while those that stand up stiff go trunk and all to ruin. So he who tightly draws his vessel's sheet and will not slack, upsets the boat and ends his course with benches upside down. Be yielding, then, and admit change. For if from me, though younger, an opinion be allowed, I count it best that man should be by nature wise. But if that cannot be,—and usually the scale does not incline so— then it is well to learn from good advisers.

CHORUS: My lord, you ought, when Haemon speaks aright, to learn of him; and Haemon, you of him. For both have spoken well.

CREON: At our age shall we learn from one so young?

HAEMON: Only the truth. Young though I am, do not regard my years more than the facts.

CREON: The fact, you mean, of being gentle to the unruly.

HAEMON: I would not ask for gentleness to wicked persons.

CREON: But is not she tainted with some such ill?

HAEMON: With one accord the men of Thebes say no.

CREON: And shall the city tell me how to rule?

HAEMON: Surely you see how childish are such words!

CREON: Govern this land for others than myself?

HAEMON: No city is the property of one alone.

CREON: Is not the city reckoned his who rules?

HAEMON: Excellent ruling,—you alone, the land deserted!

CREON: He fights, it seems, the woman's battle.

HAEMON: If you are she. Indeed my care is all for you.

CREON: Perverted boy, pressing a cause against your father!

HAEMON: Because I see you causelessly do wrong.

CREON: Do I do wrong in reverencing my office?

HAEMON: It is not reverence to trample on the rights of gods.

CREON: A hateful heart that bends before a woman!

HAEMON: But never will you find me subservient to the base.

CREON: Why, all your argument is urged for her.

HAEMON: Yes, and for you and me, and for the gods below.

CREON: You shall not marry her this side the grave.

HAEMON: So then she dies; but if she dies, destroys another.

CREON: Will you assail me with your threats, audacious boy?

HAEMON: Is it a threat to combat silly schemes?

CREON: To your sorrow you shall teach, while yourself in need of teaching.

HAEMON: But that you are my father, I had counted you ill-taught.

CREON: Be a plaything for your mistress, but trifle not with me!

HAEMON: Will you then speak, and when you speak not listen?

CREON: And has it come to this? But, by Olympus, you shall not lightly heap reproach on insult. Bring me that piece of malice, straight-way to die before my eyes in presence of her bridegroom!

HAEMON: Not in my presence. Do not think it! She shall not die while I am near. And you youself shall see my face no more. Rave on then here with those who will submit!

[*Exit.*]

*   *   *

CHORUS: So you will put them both to death?

CREON: Not her who had no finger in the business. You say well.

CHORUS: And by what doom do you intend to slay the other?

CREON: Leading her where the ways are clear of humankind, I will shut her up alive in a stone cell, allowing only so much food for expiation that the whole city may escape the stain. And if she calls upon the Grave,—the only god she honors—she may obtain deliverance from death; or else will learn, though late, that honor done the Grave is labor lost.

[*Exit.*]

*   *   *

ANTIGONE: Men of my land, you see me taking my last walk here, looking my last upon the sunshine—never more. No, Hades, who brings all to bed, leads me alive along the strand of Acheron, missing my part in wedding song. Never did bridal hymn hymn me. But I shall be the bride of Acheron.

CHORUS: And yet you will in glory and with praise pass to the secret places of the dead. Not smitten with slow disease, nor meeting the sword's portion, but self-possessed, alone among mankind you go to the Grave alive.

ANTIGONE: I have heard of the pitiful end of the stranger from Phrygia, the daughter of Tantalus, on Mount Sipylus; o'er whom like clinging ivy a rocky growth would creep, and from her wasting form the showers and snow, 't is said, are never absent, but drop upon her neck down from her weeping brows. Most like to her, God brings me to my rest.

CHORUS: Nay, nay! She was a god and sprung from gods. But we are mortals and of human birth. Yet for a mortal maid to win a godlike lot is high renown, whether one live or die.

ANTIGONE: Ah, I am mocked! Why, by our country's gods, taunt me when not yet gone but here before you? O thou my city, and ye great ones of my city, thou spring of Dircé, and thou grove of charioted Thebes, I call on you to witness how all unwept of friends and by what cruel laws I go to that sepulchral mound for an unheard-of burial. Ah, poor me! Having no home with mankind or with corpses, with living or with dead!

CHORUS: Onward pressing to the utmost verge of daring, on the deep foundation stone of Right you fell, my child,—a grievous fall. A father's penalty you pay.

ANTIGONE: Ah, there you touched my bitterest pang, my father's thrice-told woe, and all the doom of the great line of Labdacus. Alas, the horrors of my mother's bed! And the embraces—his very self begetting—of that father and that hapless mother from whom I here, distracted, once was born! To them I go, accursed, unwedded, now to dwell. Alas for you, my brother, who made an ill-starred marriage and in your death stripped me, alive, of all.

CHORUS: In pious actions there is piety. Yet power, when his whose right it is, may nowise be transgressed. Your self-willed temper slew you.

ANTIGONE: Unwept, unfriended, with no bridal song, poor I am led along the appointed way. Never again that sacred ball of fire may I, alas! behold. Yet for my tearless lot not a friend grieves.

CREON: Do you not know that groans and dirges before death would never cease, were it allowed to voice them? Away with her forthwith! And when, as I commanded, you have shut her in the vaulted tomb, leave her alone in solitude, to die if so she must, or let her live her life prisoned in such a home. Thus we are clear of what befalls the maid. Only from dwelling in the light above shall she be hindered.

ANTIGONE: O grave! O bridal chamber! Hollow home, forever holding me! whither I go to join my own; for far the greater number Persephassa has received among the dead, all gone! Last of them I, and most unhappy far, now go below before I reach the limit of my life; yet going, dearly cherish it among my hopes to have my coming welcome to my father, welcome to you, my mother, welcome too to you, my brother. When you all died, with my own hand I washed you, did you service, and poured libations at your graves. But, Polynices, for ministering to your corpse this is my recompense.

Rightly I honored you, the wise will think. Yet had I children, or were my husband mouldering in death, I might not in defiance of my townsmen have taken up the task. And wherefore so? I might have had another husband, had mine died, a child too by another man when I had lost my own; but mother and father hidden in the grave, there is no brother ever to be born. Yet when upon such grounds I held you first in honor, to Creon's eye I seemed to sin and to be over-bold, my brother dear. And now he leads me forth, a captive, deprived of bridal bed and song,—without experience of marriage or the rearing of a child,—that so poor I, cut off from friends but still alive, enter the caverned chambers of the dead.

What ordinance of heaven have I transgressed? Yet why in misery still look to gods or call on them for aid, when even this name of impious I got by piety! No, if such acts are pleasing to the gods, I may by suffering come to know my sin. But if these others rather sin, may they not suffer greater ill than they now wrongly wreak on me.

CHORUS: Still the same winds' same blasts of passion sway her.

CREON: Therefore her guards shall smart for their delay.

ANTIGONE: Ah me! The signal comes that death is nigh!

CHORUS: I cannot bid you hope it will not follow.

ANTIGONE: O city in the land of Thebes! Home of my fathers! And ye, ancestral gods! Men seize me and I cannot stay. Behold, O lords of Thebes, how I, last remnant of the royal line, now suffer, and from whom—I who revered the right.

[ANTIGONE *is led away.*]

*   *   *

[*Enter a messenger.*]

MESSENGER: Ye dwellers at the palace of Cadmus and Amphion, there is no human life, however placed, that I can praise or blame. For fortune raises, fortune overthrows, him who is now in good or evil fortune. No seer can tell the destinies of man. Creon was enviable once, I thought, through having saved this land of Cadmus from its foes. Winning full sovereignty he ruled the land, blest too in noble issue. Now all is gone. For when man parts with happiness, I count him not alive, but a mere breathing corpse. Let him have riches in his house, great riches if you will, and live in royal state; if happiness be absent, I would not pay a puff of smoke for all the rest, when weighed with joy.

CHORUS: What new disaster to our kings come you to tell?

MESSENGER: Dead! And the living caused the death.

CHORUS: Who is the slayer? Who has fallen? Speak!

MESSENGER: Haemon is gone. With violence his blood is shed.

CHORUS: What? By his father's hand, or by his own?

MESSENGER: His own, incensed against his father for the murder.

*   *   *

CHORUS: But lo! Our lord himself draws near, bringing in his arms clear proof—if we may say so—of wrong not wrought by others but by his erring self.

[*Enter* CREON, *bearing the body of* HAEMON.]

*   *   *

CREON: Alas, the sins of a presumptuous soul, stubborn and deadly! Ah, ye who see slayers and slain of kindred blood! Woe for my ill-starred plans! Alas, my boy, so young in life and young in sorrow! Woe! Woe! Thou, dead and gone? And by my folly, not thy own!

CHORUS: Ah me! It seems you see the right too late!

CREON: Unhappy I have learned it now. But then some god possessed me, smote on my head a heavy blow, drove me along a brutish path, and so—alas!—o'erthrew my joy and trampled it. Woe, woe, for the wearisome works of man!

[*Enter a second messenger.*]

SECOND MESSENGER: My lord, 't is having and still getting. You bear one sorrow in your arms; enter the house, and there you soon should see another.

CREON: What is there yet more sorrowful than this?

SECOND MESSENGER: The queen is dead, true mother of the dead here. Poor lady, she has fallen by wounds dealt even now.

CREON: Alas, alas! Insatiate gulf of death! Why, why thus cause my ruin? And cruel messenger, speeding my pain, what is the tale you tell? Why, one already dead you slay anew! What say you, boy? What tidings do you bring? Ah, must the slaughterous ending of my wife follow the death of him?

[*The Scene opens, and the body of* EURYDICE *is disclosed.*]

CHORUS: Here you may see! It shall be hid no longer.

CREON: Ah me! A fresh, a second grief poor I behold. What more has fate in waiting? Just now I took my child in my arms—alas!—and face to face behold another corse. Woe! Woe! unhappy mother! Woe, my child!

SECOND MESSENGER: Crazed, clinging to the altar, and closing her dark eyes, she fist bemoaned the glorious grave of Megareus who died before, then this one's end; and with her last breath called down ill on you, the murderer of your children.

CREON: Alas! Alas! Fear thrills me. Will none strike home with two-edged sword? Poor I am steeped in sore distress.

SECOND MESSENGER: You were accused by her who died of causing both the deaths.

CREON: And by what sort of violence did she depart?

SECOND MESSENGER: Her own hand smote herself below the heart, soon as she learned the lamentable ending of her son.

CREON: Ah me! To no one else can this be shifted from my guilty self. 'T was I indeed that killed thee, wretched I! I say the truth, 't was I. Take me, my servants, take me straightway hence, to be no more than nothing.

CHORUS: Wise wishes these, if any way is wise in evil. Briefest is best, when evil clogs our feet.

CREON: Come, then, appear, fairest of fates that brings my final day! O come, best boon, and let me never see another day!

CHORUS: Time will determine that. The present needs our care. Let them whose right it is direct the rest!

CREON: All I desire is summed up in that prayer.

CHORUS: Pray no more now. From his appointed woe man cannot fly.

CREON: Then take away the useless man who by no will of his killed thee, my child, and thee too lying here. Alas poor me, who know not which to look on, where to turn! All in my hands was at cross purposes, and on my head fell fate I could not guide.

CHORUS: Wisdom is far the greater part of peace. The gods will have their dues. Large language, bringing to the proud large chastisement, at last brings wisdom.

*   *   *

REVIEW QUESTIONS

1. What is the dilemma with which Antigone is confronted?
2. Where, in her eyes, must her principal allegiance lie?
3. How does the fact that Antigone is a woman affect her treatment by Creon?
4. How do you think this play would have been received by a Spartan audience?

VASE DEPICTING A SLAVE, PERHAPS IN A SCENE FROM A GREEK PLAY (C. 450 B.C.E.)

Slaves at Athens included a variety of nationalities and were at the bottom of the socio-economic hierarchy. What does the depiction in this vase painting suggest about attitudes toward slaves? How do the physical features and clothing of this slave differ from what you have observed in other works of classical Greek art?

PLATO

FROM "Apology"

Our knowledge of the life, personality, and teachings of the late-fifth-century B.C.E. Athenian philosopher and social critic Socrates is derived almost entirely from the dialogues composed by his most famous student, Plato. In them, Plato recreates Socrates' method of using questions and answers (what today we still refer to as the "Socratic method") to examine and test commonly held opinions. In the following excerpt from the "Apology" (a word that in ancient Greek referred to a defense of one's actions or beliefs, not an expression of contrition or regret), Socrates, on trial before an Athenian jury for allegedly subverting the youth of Athens by converting them to gods of his own invention, defends his career as a teacher. (His eloquence and intellect, in the end, did not save him from condemnation and subsequent execution in 399 B.C.E.)

From *The Last Days of Socrates*, translated by Hugh Tredennick (New York: Penguin Books, 1969), pp. 48–52, 72–76.

*   *   *

Here perhaps one of you might interrupt me and say "But what is it that you do, Socrates? How is it that you have been misrepresented like this? Surely all this talk and gossip about you would never have arisen if you had confined yourself to ordinary activities, but only if your behaviour was abnormal. Tell us the explanation, if you do not want us to invent it for ourselves." This seems to me to be a reasonable request, and I will try to explain to you what it is that has given me this false notoriety; so please give me your attention. Perhaps some of you will think that I am not being serious; but I assure you that I am going to tell you the whole truth.

I have gained this reputation, gentlemen, from nothing more or less than a kind of wisdom. What kind of wisdom do I mean? Human wisdom, I suppose. It seems that I really am wise in this limited sense. Presumably the geniuses whom I mentioned just now are wise in a wisdom that is more than human; I do not know how else to account for it. I certainly have no knowledge of such wisdom, and anyone who says that I have is a liar

and wilful slanderer. Now, gentlemen, please do not interrupt me if I seem to make an extravagant claim; for what I am going to tell you is not my own opinion; I am going to refer you to an unimpeachable authority. I shall call as witness to my wisdom (such as it is) the god at Delphi.

You know Chaerephon, of course. He was a friend of mine from boyhood, and a good democrat who played his part with the rest of you in the recent expulsion and restoration. And you know what he was like; how enthusiastic he was over anything that he had once undertaken. Well, one day he actually went to Delphi and asked this question of the god—as I said before, gentlemen, please do not interrupt—he asked whether there was anyone wiser than myself. The priestess replied that there was no one. As Chaerephon is dead, the evidence for my statement will be supplied by his brother, who is here in court.

Please consider my object in telling you this. I want to explain to you how the attack upon my reputation first started. When I heard about the oracle's answer, I said to myself "What does the god mean? Why does he not use plain language? I am only too conscious that I have no claim to wisdom, great or small; so what can he mean by asserting that I am the wisest man in the world? He cannot be telling a lie; that would not be right for him."

After puzzling about it for some time, I set myself at last with considerable reluctance to check the truth of it in the following way. I went to interview a man with a high reputation for wisdom, because I felt that here if anywhere I should succeed in disproving the oracle and pointing out to my divine authority "You said that I was the wisest of men, but here is a man who is wiser than I am."

Well, I gave a thorough examination to this person—I need not mention his name, but it was one of our politicians that I was studying when I had this experience—and in conversation with him I formed the impression that although in many people's opinion, and especially in his own, he appeared to be wise, in fact he was not. Then when I began to try to show him that he only thought he was wise and was not really so, my efforts were resented both by him and by many of the other people present. However, I reflected as I walked away: "Well, I am certainly wiser than this man. It is only too likely that neither of us has any knowledge to boast of; but he thinks that he knows something which he does not know, whereas I am quite conscious of my ignorance. At any rate it seems that I am wiser than he is to this small extent, that I do not think that I know what I do not know."

After this I went on to interview a man with an even greater reputation for wisdom, and I formed the same impression again; and here too I incurred the resentment of the man himself and a number of others.

From that time on I interviewed one person after another. I realized with distress and alarm that I was making myself unpopular, but I felt compelled to put my religious duty first; since I was trying to find out the meaning of the oracle, I was bound to interview everyone who had a reputation for knowledge. And by Dog, gentlemen! (for I must be frank with you) my honest impression was this: it seemed to me, as I pursued

my investigation at the god's command, that the people with the greatest reputations were almost entirely deficient, while others who were supposed to be their inferiors were much better qualified in practical intelligence.

I want you to think of my adventures as a sort of pilgrimage undertaken to establish the truth of the oracle once for all. After I had finished with the politicians I turned to the poets, dramatic, lyric, and all the rest, in the belief that here I should expose myself as a comparative ignoramus. I used to pick up what I thought were some of their most perfect works and question them closely about the meaning of what they had written, in the hope of incidentally enlarging my own knowledge. Well, gentlemen, I hesitate to tell you the truth, but it must be told. It is hardly an exaggeration to say that any of the bystanders could have explained those poems better than their actual authors. So I soon made up my mind about the poets too: I decided that it was not wisdom that enabled them to write their poetry, but a kind of instinct or inspiration, such as you find in seers and prophets who deliver all their sublime messages without knowing in the least what they mean. It seemed clear to me that the poets were in much the same case; and I also observed that the very fact that they were poets made them think that they had a perfect understanding of all other subjects, of which they were totally ignorant. So I left that line of inquiry too with the same sense of advantage that I had felt in the case of the politicians.

Last of all I turned to the skilled craftsmen. I knew quite well that I had practically no technical qualifications myself, and I was sure that I should find them full of impressive knowledge. In this I was not disappointed; they understood things which I did not, and to that extent they were wiser than I was. But, gentlemen, these professional experts seemed to share the same failing which I had noticed in the poets; I mean that on the strength of their technical proficiency they claimed a perfect understanding of every other subject, however important; and I felt that this error more than outweighed their positive wisdom. So I made myself spokesman for the oracle, and asked myself whether I would rather be as I was—neither wise with their wisdom nor stupid with their stupidity —or possess both qualities as they did. I replied through myself to the oracle that it was best for me to be as I was.

The effect of these investigations of mine, gentlemen, has been to arouse against me a great deal of hostility, and hostility of a particularly bitter and persistent kind, which has resulted in various malicious suggestions, including the description of me as a professor of wisdom. This is due to the fact that whenever I succeed in disproving another person's claim to wisdom in a given subject, the bystanders assume that I know everything about that subject myself. But the truth of the matter, gentlemen, is pretty certainly this: that real wisdom is the property of God, and this oracle is his way of telling us that human wisdom has little or no value. It seems to me that he is not referring literally to Socrates, but has merely taken my name as an example, as if he would say to us "The wisest of you men is he who has realized, like Socrates, that in respect of wisdom he is really worthless."

That is why I still go about seeking and searching in obedience to the divine command, if I think that anyone is wise, whether citizen or stranger; and when I think that any person is not wise, I try to help the cause of God by proving that he is not. This occupation has kept me too busy to do much either in politics or in my own affairs; in fact, my service to God has reduced me to extreme poverty.

* * *

Well, gentlemen, for the sake of a very small gain in time you are going to earn the reputation—and the blame from those who wish to disparage our city—of having put Socrates to death, "that wise man"—because they will say I am wise even if I am not, these people who want to find fault with you. If you had waited just a little while, you would have had your way in the course of nature. You can see that I am well on in life and near to death. I am saying this not to

all of you but to those who voted for my execution, and I have something else to say to them as well.

No doubt you think, gentlemen, that I have been condemned for lack of the arguments which I could have used if I had thought it right to leave nothing unsaid or undone to secure my acquittal. But that is very far from the truth. It is not a lack of arguments that has caused my condemnation, but a lack of effrontery and impudence, and the fact that I have refused to address you in the way which would give you most pleasure. You would have liked to hear me weep and wail, doing and saying all sorts of things which I regard as unworthy of myself, but which you are used to hearing from other people. But I did not think then that I ought to stoop to servility because I was in danger, and I do not regret now the way in which I pleaded my case; I would much rather die as the result of this defence than live as the result of the other sort. In a court of law, just as in warfare, neither I nor any other ought to use his wits to escape death by any means. In battle it is often obvious that you could escape being killed by giving up your arms and throwing yourself upon the mercy of your pursuers; and in every kind of danger there are plenty of devices for avoiding death if you are unscrupulous enough to stick at nothing. But I suggest, gentlemen, that the difficulty is not so much to escape death; the real difficulty is to escape from doing wrong, which is far more fleet of foot. In this present instance, I, the slow old man, have been overtaken by the slower of the two, but my accusers, who are clever and quick, have been overtaken by the faster: by iniquity. When I leave this court I shall go away condemned by you to death, but they will go away convicted by Truth herself of depravity and wickedness. And they accept their sentence even as I accept mine. No doubt it was bound to be so, and I think that the result is fair enough.

Having said so much, I feel moved to prophesy to you who have given your vote against me; for I am now at that point where the gift of prophecy comes most readily to men: at the point of death. I tell you, my executioners, that as soon as I am dead, vengeance shall fall upon you with a punishment far more painful than your killing of me. You have brought about my death in the belief that through it you will be delivered from submitting your conduct to criticism; but I say that the result will be just the opposite. You will have more critics, whom up till now I have restrained without your knowing it; and being younger they will be harsher to you and will cause you more annoyance. If you expect to stop denunciation of your wrong way of life by putting people to death, there is something amiss with your reasoning. This way of escape is neither possible nor creditable; the best and easiest way is not to stop the mouths of others, but to make yourselves as good men as you can. This is my last message to you who voted for my condemnation.

As for you who voted for my acquittal, I should very much like to say a few words to reconcile you to the result, while the officials are busy and I am not yet on my way to the place where I must die. I ask you, gentlemen, to spare me these few moments; there is no reason why we should not exchange fancies while the law permits. I look upon you as my friends, and I want you to understand the right way of regarding my present position.

Gentlemen of the jury—for *you* deserve to be so called—I have had a remarkable experience. In the past the prophetic voice to which I have become accustomed has always been my constant companion, opposing me even in quite trivial things if I was going to take the wrong course. Now something has happened to me, as you can see, which might be thought and is commonly considered to be a supreme calamity; yet neither when I left home this morning, nor when I was taking my place here in the court, nor at any point in any part of my speech did the divine sign oppose me. In other discussions it has often checked me in the middle of a sentence; but this time it has never opposed me in any part of this business in anything that I have said or done. What do I suppose to be the explanation? I will tell you. I suspect that this thing that has happened to me is a blessing, and we are quite mistaken in supposing

death to be an evil. I have good grounds for thinking this, because my accustomed sign could not have failed to oppose me if what I was doing had not been sure to bring some good result.

We should reflect that there is much reason to hope for a good result on other grounds as well. Death is one of two things. Either it is annihilation, and the dead have no consciousness of anything; or, as we are told, it is really a change: a migration of the soul from this place to another. Now if there is no consciousness but only a dreamless sleep, death must be a marvellous gain. I suppose that if anyone were told to pick out the night on which he slept so soundly as not even to dream, and then to compare it with all the other nights and days of his life, and then were told to say, after due consideration, how many better and happier days and nights than this he had spent in the course of his life—well, I think that the Great King himself, to say nothing of any private person, would find these days and nights easy to count in comparison with the rest. If death is like this, then, I call it gain; because the whole of time, if you look at it in this way, can be regarded as no more than one single night. If on the other hand death is a removal from here to some other place, and if what we are told is true, that all the dead are there, what greater blessing could there be than this, gentlemen? If on arrival in the other world, beyond the reach of our so-called justice, one will find there the true judges who are said to preside in those courts, Minos and Rhadamanthys and Aeacus and Triptolemus and all those other half-divinities who were upright in their earthly life, would that be an unrewarding journey? Put it in this way: how much would one of you give to meet Orpheus and Musaeus, Hesiod and Homer? I am willing to die ten times over if this account is true. It would be a specially interesting experience for me to join them there, to meet Palamedes and Ajax the son of Telamon and any other heroes of the old days who met their death through an unfair trial, and to compare my fortunes with theirs—it would be rather amusing, I think—; and above all I should like to spend my time there, as here, in examining and searching people's minds, to find out who is really wise among them, and who only thinks that he is. What would one not give, gentlemen, to be able to question the leader of that great host against Troy, or Odysseus, or Sisyphus, or the thousands of other men and women whom one could mention, to talk and mix and argue with whom would be unimaginable happiness? At any rate I presume that they do not put one to death there for such conduct; because apart from the other happiness in which their world surpasses ours, they are now immortal for the rest of time, if what we are told is true.

You too, gentlemen of the jury, must look forward to death with confidence, and fix your minds on this one belief, which is certain: that nothing can harm a good man either in life or after death, and his fortunes are not a matter of indifference to the gods. This present experience of mine has not come about mechanically; I am quite clear that the time had come when it was better for me to die and be released from my distractions. That is why my sign never turned me back. For my own part I bear no grudge at all against those who condemned me and accused me, although it was not with this kind intention that they did so, but be cause they thought that they were hurting me; and that is culpable of them. However, I ask them to grant me one favour. When my sons grow up, gentlemen, if you think that they are putting money or anything else before goodness, take your revenge by plaguing them as I plagued you; and if they fancy themselves for no reason, you must scold them just as I scolded you, for neglecting the important things and thinking that they are good for something when they are good for nothing. If you do this, I shall have had justice at your hands, both I myself and my children.

Now it is time that we were going, I to die and you to live; but which of us has the happier prospect is unknown to anyone but God.

REVIEW QUESTIONS

1. What does Socrates identify as his mission?
2. Why might Socrates' activities have seemed subversive to some of the citizens of Athens?
3. What is his attitude toward his own death, and why?

4 ⌘ THE EXPANSION OF GREECE

While Aristotle was composing his works Ethics *and* Politics, *his former pupil Alexander, the young king of Macedonia, was in the process of rendering his former tutor's discourse on the proper structure of the polis somewhat obsolete. Between 336 and his death in 322 B.C.E., Alexander achieved success almost beyond imagining: the subjugation of the vast Persian Empire, followed by further conquests that took his armies as far east as India. Yet, almost immediately on Alexander's death, his empire began to fragment, and in less than 300 years the Ptolemid, Seleucid, and Antigonid kingdoms all had succumbed to the ascending empires of the Romans from the west and the Parthians from the east. Political and military dominion, then, proved to be ephemeral. Not so fleeting, however, were the influence of Greek culture and urban institutions on the Near East (and the reciprocal influence of Near Eastern and Egyptian cultures on the Greeks) and the devastating impact of the invaders from the west on the previously established state structures of the areas they conquered.*

Historians, and the times during which they write, create history as much as do the great figures and civilizations about which they write. Nowhere is this more evident than in the history of Western perceptions of both Alexander and the new world order that he is claimed to have inaugurated. Until relatively recently, the West has made itself quite comfortable with an idealized image of Alexander the Great as a heroic figure whose conquests were aimed at harmoniously fusing Greek culture with the cultures of the Persian Empire. Likewise, Hellenistic civilization was regarded as mixed, essentially Greek in its inspiration but enriched by its contact with the older Near Eastern cultures. The rise of this point of view, understandably enough, coincided largely with the European colonial ascendancy over the Near and Far East and Africa that began during the nineteenth century C.E. With the disappearance of that colonialism over the past few decades, however, and as previously subject peoples have raised their own voices, there has come a dramatic reevaluation of Hellenistic civilization. The idealized image of a cultural fusion has been replaced with an image of that civilization as more emphatically Greek and of the Greek ruling class of the Hellenistic kingdoms as a colonial presence that was quite determined to maintain its superiority and preserve a large degree of separation from the indigenous peoples. Meanwhile, the political traditions of the regions over which the Greeks ruled continued largely as they had for centuries.

As the Hellenistic world order of large kingdoms took shape, it is not surprising that the traditional institutions and parochial perspectives of the polis were found wanting. This is nowhere more evident than in the development of religion and philosophy in the Hellenistic era. Much of Greek religion had been bound directly to formal cult and ritual within the polis. As the expansion of Greek colonization into the Near Eastern world began to sever the links to the traditional religion of the polis, another kind of religious experience, the mystery religions, became increasingly popular because of their more universal appeal and their promise of salvation and mystical union with a divine presence. In many ways, the spread of these mystery religions established a milieu that later promoted the spread of Christianity in the eastern Mediterranean.

Much of the philosophical thought of Plato and Aristotle had resonated greatest within the political context of the traditional city-state. Although much of the thought of the great Hellenistic philosophers derived from their classical predecessors, it also liberated itself from the confines of the city-state, developing an increasingly universal appeal. Long after the absorption of the Hellenistic kingdoms into the Roman and Parthian empires, the Hellenistic schools of philosophy, and in particular, the Stoic teachings of a divine, universal natural law and the basic brotherhood of human beings, provided rich intellectual capital for the continued development of the legal, political, and spiritual traditions of the West.

In both the broad sweep of its cultural expansion and the increasingly universal appeal of the philosophical doctrines and systems of religious belief of the time, the new world order of the Hellenistic period can justifiably be regarded as the first truly cosmopolitan age. The widespread Greek cultural legacy endowed to the Near East set the stage for the eventual success, during the subsequent era of the Roman Empire, of what became the most successful of the cosmopolitan religions: Christianity.

PLATO

FROM *The Republic*

After the death of his teacher, Socrates, Plato established the Academy, a school of philosophical instruction in an olive grove on the outskirts of Athens. (The fame of this school is apparent in the modern application of the terms academy *and* academic *to institutions of higher learning.) Among the works that Plato produced there was* The Republic, *commonly regarded as one of the most influential works of political philosophy ever written. Perhaps the central problem that Plato addresses is how to achieve a just society within the framework of the city-state. The following selection, which includes his famous Allegory of the Cave, offers some of his ideas on how to achieve that end.*

From *The Republic*, by Plato, translated by Richard W. Sterling and William C. Scott (New York: Norton, 1985), pp. 146–151, 209–115.

*   *   *

Book V

*   *   *

Now, then, can you think of any of the human arts in which men do not generally excel women? Let's not make a long story out of it by bringing up weaving and baking cakes and boiling vegetables, matters in which women take pride and would be mortified should a man best them in these skills.

You are surely correct in saying that the one sex excels the other in every respect. But it is also true that individually many women are more skilled than many men, even if your general proposition is true.

Then we must conclude that sex cannot be the criterion in appointments to government positions. No office should be reserved for a man just because he is a man or for a woman just because she is a woman. All the capabilities with which nature endows us are distributed among men and women alike. Hence women will have the rightful opportunity to share in every task, and so will men, even though women are the weaker of the two sexes.

Agreed.

Could we then assign all the tasks to the men and none to the women?

How could we propose such thing as that?

Well, then, we shall want to say instead that one woman has the capacity to be a doctor and another not, that one woman is naturally musical and another is unmusical.

Certainly.

Could we deny that there are some women who are warlike and natural athletes while others love neither war nor gymnastic?

I don't think we can.

Again, are there not women who love wisdom and those who do not? Are not some women high-spirited and some not?

There are all these kinds of women, too.

Hence it must also be true that one woman is fit to be a guardian and another unfit. For these are the same criteria we used when we were selecting men as guardians, are they not?

Yes.

As guardians of the state, then, women and men are naturally the same, except that one is weaker and the other stronger.

Apparently.

It follows that women with the requisite qualities must be chosen to live and guard together with men of like qualities since they have the necessary competence and are naturally kin.

By all means.

And the same natures ought to perform the same functions?

Yes.

So we have closed the circle. We agree that we do nothing against nature by educating the guardians' wives in music and gymnastic.

We are agreed.

Since we have legislated in harmony with nature, we have not proposed anything impractical or unattainable. On the contrary, we may say that if anything contradicts nature, it is the way things are done today.

So it appears.

Now we designed our inquiry to test whether our proposals would turn out to be both possible and desirable?

Yes.

Well, I take it we have just established that they are possible.

Yes.

Then we must see if we can agree that they are also desirable.

Clearly.

In preparing a woman to be a guardian, then, we won't prescribe one kind of education for women guardians and another for the men because their natures are the same.

No. There should be no differentiation.

Let me ask you a question.

About what?

About men. Do you think some are better and some worse, or are all alike?

They are certainly not all alike.

Then which do you think will become the better men in the city we are building: the guardians who are being educated in the manner we have prescribed or the cobblers who received instruction in the cobbler's art?

An absurd question.

I understand your answer. You mean that the guardians are the best of our citizens.

By far.

And will not the women guardians be the best of the women?

Yes.

And can we wish for the state anything better than that it should nurture the best possible men and women?

Nothing.

And the education we have prescribed in music and gymnastic will produce this outcome?

Without fail.

Therefore the institutions we have proposed for the state are not only possible, they are the best possible.

Quite so.

Then wearing virtue as a garment, the guardians' wives must go naked and take part alongside their men in war and the other functions of government, and no other duties will be required of them. Owing to the weakness of their gender, however, they shall perform the less burdensome tasks. When they are at their exercises for the body's benefit, any man who laughs at their nakedness will be "gathering unripe fruit," for he does not know what he ridicules nor where his laughter leads. He is ignorant of the fairest words ever spoken: what is beneficial must be beautiful; only the harmful is ugly.

You are right.

Having successfully reached this point in our legislation for women, we could compare ourselves with a swimmer who has surmounted a wave without being drowned by it. Our argument that men and women guardians should pursue all things in common turns out to be consistent in itself, since we have found our proposals to be both possible and beneficial.

That was no small wave, either.

You won't think it was so big when you see what the next one looks like.

Go ahead, then, and let me see.

Here it is. I think that everything we have said so far leads up to the following law.

What law?

That all the women shall belong to all the men and that none shall cohabit privately; that the children should also be raised in common and no child should know its parent nor the parent its child.

A far greater wave, indeed. Your proposal raises questions about both practicability and utility that will provoke the greatest misgivings.

I shouldn't think anyone would want to debate its utility. The desirability of having wives and children in common, were it possible, ought to be self-evident. But I suppose the main subject of dispute would be whether or not it would be possible to establish such a community.

I expect both aspects of the proposal will produce plenty of debate.

I see that you want to entangle me in both questions at once. I hoped for your consent in the matter of utility, so that I could escape from having to discuss it. Then I would only have to consider the question of feasibility.

Your escape efforts have been detected. You won't be allowed to run away, and you will be obliged to defend your case on both counts.

I will pay your penalty. But first, relent a little. Let me go on holiday, like men with lazy minds are wont to do, so that they may entertain themselves with their own thoughts as they walk alone. These men pursue their desires without pausing to inquire how they might be achieved. All such considerations they dismiss in order to spare themselves the trouble of weighing the possible against the impossible. They assume that what they wish is already at hand, giving their imaginations free rein in concocting the details and relishing in advance what they will do when everything is in place. So do idle minds become more idle still. I now yield to this same weakness. I would like to postpone the feasibility issue for later consideration. With your permission, I shall assume the feasibility of my proposal and proceed to inquire how the rulers will arrange the particulars in practice. At the same time, I shall seek to demonstrate that nothing could be more beneficial to our city and its guardians than a successful implementation of our proposal. Let us consider this first, and then we can address the other issue.

Permission granted. Proceed as you suggest.

I suppose that worthy rulers will be prepared to command and worthy helpers ready to obey. In some of their commands the rulers will obey the laws. In those matters of detail that we have left to their discretion their commands will imitate the spirit of the laws.

Presumably they will.

As their lawgiver, you will have selected these men. You will apply the same criteria to select women whose natures are as similar as possible to those of the men. They will live in common houses and eat at common meals. There will be no private property. They will live together, learn together, and exercise together. The necessities of nature, I presume, would see to it that they will also mate with one another. Or is necessity too strong a word?

Not if you mean the necessities of love. They attract and compel most people with far greater force than all geometric necessities posited by the mathematicians.

You are right, Glaucon. But irregularity in sexual relations or in any other matters has no place in a happy city; the rules will not tolerate it.

They would be right.

Then it is evident that we must make marriage a sacred relationship, so far as may be. And those marriages that attain the highest degree of sanctity will produce the best results.

Agreed.

What will produce the best results? You can help me, Glaucon, for I have seen hunting dogs and a number of pedigreed cocks at your house. Have you noticed something about how they mate and breed?

What?

Well, first of all, even though all of them are thoroughbreds, some prove out better than others?

True.

So are you indiscriminate in how you breed them, or do you breed from the best?

From the best.

And which age do you select for the breeding? The young or the old or, so far as possible, those in their prime?

Those in their prime.

And if you failed to supervise the breeding in this way, you would have to expect that the quality of your stock of birds and hounds would deteriorate?

Certainly.

Would it be the same with horses and other animals?

Without doubt.

Well, then, old friend, if the same holds true for human beings, we can see how urgent is our need for rulers with the highest skills.

It does hold true, but what of it?

I say this because the rulers will have to employ many of the kinds of drugs we spoke of earlier. Remember we said that those who can be healed by submitting their bodies to diet and regimen do not need drugs and can be attended by an ordinary doctor. But we know that where it is necessary to prescribe drugs, a physician with greater imagination and audacity will be indispensable.

True, but what is your point?

I mean that the rulers will probably have to resort to frequent doses of lies and mystifications for the benefit of their subjects. You will recall that we said these kinds of lies could be advantageous if used after the manner of medical remedies.

And we were right.

And the right use of this sort of medicine will very often be imperative in matters of marriage and the begetting of children.

How so?

It follows necessarily from the conclusion we reached a moment ago. The best of the men must mate with the best of the women as often as possible. Inferior should mate with inferior as seldom as possible. In order to safeguard the quality of the stock the children of the best unions must be retained for nurture by the rulers, but the others not. And how all this will be managed must be known to none but the rulers, so that the guardian flock will not be divided by dissension.

* * *

Book VII

Here allegory may show us best how education—or the lack of it—affects our nature. Imagine men living in a cave with a long passageway stretching between them and the cave's mouth, where it opens wide to the light. Imagine further that since childhood the cave dwellers have had their legs and necks shackled so as to be confined to the same spot. They are further constrained by blinders that prevent them from turning their heads; they can see only directly in front of them. Next, imagine a light from a fire some distance behind them and burning at a higher elevation. Between the prisoners and the fire is a raised path along whose edge there is a low wall like the partition at the front of a puppet stage. The wall conceals the puppeteers while they manipulate their puppets above it.

So far I can visualize it.

Imagine, further, men behind the wall carrying all sorts of objects along its length and holding them above it. The objects include human and animal images made of stone and wood and all other material. Presumably, those who carry them sometimes speak and are sometimes silent.

You describe a strange prison and strange prisoners.

Like ourselves. Tell me, do you not think those men would see only the shadows cast by the fire on the wall of the cave? Would they have seen anything of themselves or of one another?

How could they if they couldn't move their heads their whole life long?

Could they see the objects held above the wall behind them or only the shadows cast in front?

Only the shadows.

If, then, they could talk with one another, don't you think they would impute reality to the passing shadows?

Necessarily.

Imagine an echo in their prison, bouncing off the wall toward which the prisoners were turned. Should one of those behind the wall speak, would the prisoners not think that the sound came from the shadows in front of them?

No doubt of it.

By every measure, then, reality for the prisoners would be nothing but shadows cast by artifacts.

It could be nothing else.

Imagine now how their liberation from bondage and error would come about if something like the following happened. One prisoner is freed from his shackles. He is suddenly compelled to stand up, turn around, walk, and look toward the light. He suffers pain and distress from the glare of the light. So dazzled is he that he cannot even discern the very objects whose shadows he used to be able to see. Now what do you suppose he would answer if he were told that all he had seen before was illusion but that now he was nearer reality, observing real things and therefore seeing more truly? What if someone pointed to the objects being carried above the wall, questioning him as to what each one is? Would he not be at a loss? Would he not regard those things he saw formerly as more real than the things now being shown him?

He would.

Again, let him be compelled to look directly at the light. Would his eyes not feel pain? Would he not flee, turning back to those things he was able to discern before, convinced that they are in every truth clearer and more exact than anything he has seen since?

He would.

Then let him be dragged away by force up the rough and steep incline of the cave's passageway, held fast until he is hauled out into the light of the sun. Would not such a rough passage be painful? Would he not resent the experience? And when he came out into the sunlight, would he not be dazzled once again and unable to see what he calls realities?

He could not see even one of them, at least not immediately.

Habituation, then, is evidently required in order to see things higher up. In the beginning he would most easily see shadows; next, reflections in the water of men and other objects. Then he would see the objects themselves. From there he would go on to behold the heavens and the heavenly phenomena—more easily the moon and stars by night than the sun by day.

Yes.

Finally, I suppose, he would be able to look on the sun itself, not in reflections in the water or in fleeting images in some alien setting. He would look at the sun as it is, in its own domain, and so be able to see what it is really like.

Yes.

It is at this stage that he would be able to conclude that the sun is the cause of the seasons and of the year's turning, that it governs all the visible world and is in some sense also the cause of all visible things.

This is surely the next step he would take.

Now, supposing he recalled where he came from. Supposing he thought of his fellow prisoners and of what passed for wisdom in the place they were inhabiting. Don't you think he would feel pity for all that and rejoice in his own change of circumstance?

He surely would.

Suppose there had been honors and citations those below bestowed upon one another. Suppose prizes were offered for the one quickest to identify the shadows as they go by and best able to remember the sequence and configurations in which they appear. All these skills, in turn, would enhance the ability to guess what would come next. Do you think he would covet such rewards? More, would he envy and want to emulate those who hold power over the prisoners and are in turn reverenced by them? Or would he not rather hold fast to Homer's words that it is "better to be the poor servant of a poor master," better to endure anything, than to believe those things and live that way?

I think he would prefer anything to such a life.

Consider, further, if he should go back down again into the cave and return to the place he was before, would not his eyes now go dark after so abruptly leaving the sunlight behind?

They would.

Suppose he should then have to compete once more in shadow watching with those who never left the cave. And this before his eyes had become accustomed to the dark and his dimmed vision still required a long period of habituation. Would he not be laughed at? Would it not be said that he had made the journey above only to come back with his eyes ruined and that it is futile even to attempt the ascent? Further, if anyone tried to release the prisoners and lead them up and they could get their hands on him and kill him, would they not kill him?

Of course.

Now, my dear Glaucon, we must apply the allegory as a whole to all that has been said so far. The prisoners' cave is the counterpart of our own visible order, and the light of the fire betokens the power of the sun. If you liken the ascent and exploration of things above to the soul's journey through the intelligible order, you will have understood my thinking, since that is what you wanted to hear. God only knows whether it is true. But, in any case, this is the way things appear to me: in the intelligible world the last thing to be seen—and then only dimly—is the idea of the good. Once seen, however, the conclusion becomes irresistible that it is the cause of all things right and good, that in the visible world it gives birth to light and its sovereign source, that in the intelligible world it is itself sovereign and the author of truth and reason, and that the man who will act wisely in private and public life must have seen it.

I agree, insofar as I can follow your thinking.

Come join me, then, in this further thought. Don't be surprised if those who have attained this high vision are unwilling to be involved in the affairs of men. Their souls will ever feel the pull from above and yearn to sojourn there. Such a preference is likely enough if the assumptions of our allegory continue to be valid.

Yes, it is likely.

By the same token, would you think it strange if someone returning from divine contemplation to the miseries of men should appear ridiculous? What if he were still blinking his eyes and not yet readjusted to the surrounding darkness before being compelled to testify in court about the shadows of justice or about the images casting the shadows? What if he had to enter into debate about the notions of such matters held fast by people who had never seen justice itself?

It would not be strange.

Nonetheless, a man with common sense would know that eyesight can be impaired in two different ways by dint of two different causes, namely, transitions from light into darkness and from darkness into light. Believing that the soul also meets with the same experience, he would not thoughtlessly laugh when he saw a soul perturbed and having difficulty in comprehending something. Instead he would try to ascertain whether the cause of its faded vision was the passage from a brighter life to unaccustomed darkness or from the deeper darkness of ignorance toward the world of light, whose brightness then dazzled the soul's eye. He will count the first happy, and the second he will pity. Should he be minded to laugh, he who comes from below will merit it more than the one who descends from the light above.

A fair statement.

If this is true, it follows that education is not what some professors say it is. They claim they can transplant the power of knowledge into a soul that has none, as if they were engrafting vision into blind eyes.

They do claim that.

But our reasoning goes quite to the contrary. We assert that this power is already in the soul of everyone. The way each of us learns compares with what happens to the eye: it cannot be turned away from darkness to face the light without turning the whole body. So it is with our capacity to know; together with the entire soul one must turn away from the world of transient things toward the world of perpetual being, until finally one learns to endure the sight of its most radiant manifestation. This is what we call goodness, is it not?

Yes.

Then there must be some art that would most easily and effectively turn and convert the soul in the way we have described. It would lay no claim to produce sight in the soul's eye. Instead it would assume that sight is already there but wrongly directed; wrongly the soul is not looking where it should. This condition it would be the purpose of the art to remedy.

Such an art might be possible.

Wisdom, then, seems to be of a different order than those other things that are also called virtues of the soul. They seem more akin to the attributes of the body, for when they are not there at the outset, they can be cultivated by exercise and habit. But the ability to think is more divine. Its power is constant and never lost. It can be useful and benign or malevolent and useless, according to the purposes toward which it is directed. Or have you never observed in men who are called vicious but wise how sharp-sighted the petty soul is and how quickly it can pick out those things toward which it has turned its attention? All this shows that we have to do not with poor eyesight but with a soul under compulsion of evil, so that the keener his vision, the more harm he inflicts.

I have seen these things.

Consider then what would happen if such a soul had been differently trained from childhood or had been liberated early from the love of food and similar pleasures that are attached to us at birth like leaden weights. Supposing, I say, he were freed from all these kinds of things that draw the soul's vision downward. If he were then turned and converted to the contemplation of real things, he would be using the very same faculties of vision and be seeing them just as keenly as he now sees their opposites.

That is likely.

And must we not draw other likely and necessary conclusions from all that has been said so far? On the one hand, men lacking education and experience in truth cannot adequately preside over a city. Without a sense of purpose or duty in life they will also be without a sense of direction to govern their public and private acts. On the other hand, those who prolong their education endlessly are also unfit to rule because they become incapable of action. Instead, they suffer themselves to believe that while still living they have already been transported to the Islands of the Blessed.

So our duty as founders is to compel the best natures to achieve that sovereign knowledge we described awhile ago, to scale the heights in order to reach the vision of the good. But after they have reached the summit and have seen the view, we must not permit what they are now allowed to do.

What is that?

Remain above, refusing to go down again among those prisoners to share their labors and their rewards, whatever their worth may be.

Must we wrong them in this way, making them live a worse life when a better is possible?

My friend, you have forgotten again that the law is concerned not with the happiness of any particular class in the city but with the happiness of the city as a whole. Its method is to create harmony among the citizens by persuasion and compulsion, making them share the benefits that each is able to bestow on the community. The law itself produces such men in the city, not in order to let them do as they please but with the intention of using them to bind the city together.

True, I did forget.

Consider further, Glaucon, that in fact we won't be wronging the philosophers who come among us. When we require them to govern the city and be its guardians, we shall vindicate our actions. For we shall say to them that it is quite understandable that men of their quality do not participate in the public life of other cities. After all, there they develop autonomously without favor from the government. It is only just that self-educated men, owing nothing to others for their enlightenment, are not eager to pay anyone for it. But you have been begotten by us to be like kings and leaders in a hive of bees, governing the city for its good and yours. Your education is better and more complete, and you are better equipped to participate in the two ways of life. So down you must go, each in turn, to where the others live and habituate yourselves to see in the dark. Once you have adjusted, you will see ten thousand times better than those who regularly dwell there. Because you have seen the reality of beauty, justice, and goodness, you will be able to know idols and shadows for what they are. Together and wide awake, you and we will govern our city, far differently from most cities today whose inhabitants are ruled darkly as in a dream by men who will fight with each other over shadows and use faction in order to rule, as if that were some great good. The truth is that the city where those who rule are least eager to do so will be the best governed and the least plagued by dissension. The city with the contrary kind of rulers will be burdened with the contrary characteristics.

I agree.

When we tell them this, will our students disobey us? Will they refuse to play their role in the affairs of state even when they know that most of the time they will be able to dwell with one another in a better world?

Certainly not. These are just requirements, and they are just men. Yet they will surely approach holding office as an imposed necessity, quite in the opposite frame of mind from those who now rule our cities.

Indeed, old friend. A well-governed city becomes a possibility only if you can discover a better way of life for your future rulers than holding office. Only in such a state will those who rule be really rich, not in gold but with the wealth that yields happiness: a life of goodness and wisdom. But such a government is impossible if men behave like beggars, turning to politics because of what is lacking in their private lives and hoping to find

their good in the public business. When office and the power of governing are treated like prizes to be won in battle the result must be a civil war that will destroy the city along with the office seekers.

True.

Is there any life other than that of true philosophers that looks with scorn on political office?

None, by Zeus.

That is why we require that those in office should not be lovers of power. Otherwise there will be a fight among rival lovers.

Right.

Who else would you compel to guard the city? Who else than those who have the clearest understanding of the principles of good government and who have won distinction in another kind of life preferable to the life of politics?

No one else.

*   *   *

REVIEW QUESTIONS

1. In Plato's view, to whom ought the governing of the state be entrusted?
2. How were these individuals to be educated for such responsibility?
3. Were women to have any possible role in directing the state? How do Plato's views in this regard contrast with the attitudes expressed in Xenophon's *Oeconomicus*?
4. How do Plato's ideas compare with the values underlying the democratic system of Athens?
5. Do you see any influence of the Spartan system in Plato's ideas?
6. Does Plato draw any contrasts between the material and immaterial realms?

ARISTOTLE

FROM *Politics*

After twenty years as a student of Plato at the Academy and a subsequent three-year stint as a tutor for Alexander, the young son of King Philip II of Macedonia, Aristotle established his own school, the Lyceum, at Athens and taught there until almost the end of his life. Much of his work is a continuation of Plato's, although, in contrast to Plato's emphasis on the primacy of a world of universal forms or ideas, Aristotle asserted that those ideal forms could not exist independently of the world of matter that could be directly experienced and observed by human senses. His two most important surviving works are the Ethics *and the* Politics. *The* Ethics *is his investigation of human character in order to determine what produces a good character and, therefore, happiness. Aristotle also believed, however, that the greatest degree of human happiness could be achieved only in the context of a properly ordered and governed city-state, the formation and characteristics of which are the focus of the* Politics.

From *The Politics of Aristotle*, edited by H. W. C. Davis, translated by Benjamin Jowett (Oxford, Eng.: Oxford University Press, 1905), pp. 258–61, 264–68.

*   *   *

He who thus considers things in their first growth and origin, whether a state or anything else, will obtain the clearest view of them. In the first place (1) there must be a union of those who cannot exist without each other; for example, of male and female, that the race may continue; and this is a union which is formed, not of deliberate purpose, but because, in common with other animals and with plants, mankind have a natural desire to leave behind them an image of themselves. And (2) there must be a union of natural ruler and subject, that both may be preserved. For he who can foresee with his mind is by nature intended to be lord and master, and he who can work with his body is a subject, and by nature a slave; hence master and slave have the same interest. . . .

Of household management we have seen that there are three parts—one is the rule of a master

over slaves, which has been discussed already, another of a father, and the third of a husband. A husband and father rules over wife and children, both free, but the rule differs, the rule over his children being a royal, over his wife a constitutional rule. For although there may be exceptions to the order of nature, the male is by nature fitter for command than the female, just as the elder and full-grown is superior to the younger and more immature. . . .

Now it is obvious that the same principle applies generally, and therefore almost all things rule and are ruled according to nature. But the kind of rule differs; the freeman rules over the slave after another manner from that in which the male rules over the female, or the man over the child; although the parts of the soul are present in all of them, they are present in different degrees. For the slave has no deliberative faculty at all; the woman has, but it is without authority, and the child has, but it is immature. So it must necessarily be with the moral virtues also; all may be supposed to partake of them, but only in such manner and degree as is required by each for the fulfillment of his duty. . . . The courage of a man is shown in commanding, of a woman in obeying. . . . All classes must be deemed to have their special attributes; as the poet says of women, "Silence is a woman's glory," but this is not equally the glory of man. . . .

*   *   *

Next let us consider what should be our arrangements about property; should the citizens of the perfect state have possessions in common or not? . . .

There is always a difficulty in men living together and having things in common, but especially in their having common property. . . . The present arrangement, if improved as it might be by good customs and laws, would be far better, and would have the advantages of both systems. Property should be in a certain sense common, but, as a general rule, private. For when everyone has his separate interest, men will not complain of one another, and they will make more progress, because everyone will be attending to his own business. Yet among good men, and as regards use, "friends," as the proverb says, "will have all things common." . . . For although every human has his own property, some things he will place at the disposal of his friends, while of others he shares the use of them. . . .

Again, how immeasurably greater is the pleasure, when a man feels a thing to be his own! For love of self is a feeling implanted by nature and not given in vain, although selfishness is rightly condemned. This, however is not mere love of self, but love of self in excess, like the miser's love of money; for all, or almost all, men love money, and other such objects in a measure. Furthermore, there is the greatest pleasure in doing a kindness or service to friends or guests or companions, which can only be done when a man has private property. These advantages are lost by the excessive unification of the state. . . . No one, when men have all things in common, will any longer

set an example of liberality or do any liberal action; for liberality consists in the use a man makes of his own property.

Such legislation may have a specious appearance of benevolence. Men readily listen to it, and are easily induced to believe that in some wonderful manner everybody will become everybody's friend, especially when someone is heard denouncing the evils now existing in states, suits about contracts, convictions for perjury, flatteries of rich men, and the like, which are said to arise out of the possession of private property. These evils, however, are due to a very different cause—the wickedness of human nature. Indeed, we see that there is much more quarreling among those who have all things in common, though there are not many of them when compared with the vast numbers who have private property.

Again, we ought to reckon, not only the evils from which the citizens will be saved, but also the advantages which they will lose. The life which they are to lead appears to be quite impracticable. The error of Socrates must be attributed to the false notion of unity from which he starts. Unity there should be, both of the family and of the state, but in some respects only. For there is a point at which a state may attain such a degree of unity as to be no longer a state, or at which, without actually ceasing to exist, it will become an inferior state, like harmony passing into unison, or rhythm which has been reduced to a single foot. The state, as I was saying, is a plurality, which should be united and made into a community by education. . . . Let us remember that we should not disregard the experience of ages. . . .

*   *   *

. . . We have next to consider whether there is only one form of government or many; and if many, what they are, and how many; and what are the differences between them.

A constitution is the arrangement of powers in a state, especially of the supreme power, and the constitution is the government. For example, in democracies the people are supreme, but in oligarchies, the few; therefore, we say that the two constitutions are different; and so in other cases. First let us consider what is the purpose of a state and how many forms of government there are by which human society is regulated. We have already said, earlier in this treatise, when drawing a distinction between household management and the rule of a governor, that man is by nature a political animal. And therefore men, even when they do not require one another's help, desire to live together all the same, and are in fact brought together by their common interests in proportion as they severally attain to any measure of well-being. Well-being is certainly the chief end of individuals and of states. . . .

The conclusion is evident: governments which have a regard to the common interest are constituted in accordance with strict principles of justice, and are therefore true forms; but those which regard only the interest of the rulers are all defective and perverted forms. For they are despotic, whereas a state is a community of free men.

Having determined these points, we have next to consider how many forms of constitution there are, and what they are; and in the first place what are the true forms, for when they are determined the perversions of them will at once be apparent. The words constitution and government have the same meaning; and the government, which is the supreme authority in states, is necessarily in the hands either of one, or of a few, or of many. The true forms of government, therefore, are those in which the one, or the few, or the many, govern with a view to the common interest; but governments which rule with a view to the private interest, whether of the one, or of the few, or of the many, are perversions. For citizens, if they are truly citizens, ought all to participate in the advantages of a state. We call that form of government in which one rules, and which regards the common interest, kingship or royalty; that in which more than one, but not many, rule, aristocracy. It is so called, either because the rulers are the best men, or because they have at heart the best interest of the state and of the citizens. But when the citizens at large administer the state for the common interest, the government is called

by the generic name—constitutional government. And there is a reason for this use of language. One man or a few may excel in virtue; but of virtue there are many kinds. As the number of rulers increases it becomes more difficult for them to attain perfection in every kind, though they may in military virtue, for this is found in the masses. Hence, in a constitutional government the fighting men have the supreme power, and those who possess arms are citizens.

Of the above-mentioned forms, the perversions are as follows: of royalty, tyranny; of aristocracy, oligarchy; of constitutional government, democracy. For tyranny is a kind of monarchy which has in view the interest of the monarch only; oligarchy has in view the interest of the wealthy; democracy, of the needy; none of them the common good of all.

*   *   *

. . . But a state exists for the sake of a good life, and not for the sake of life only. If life only were the object, slaves and brute animals might form a state, but they cannot, for they have no share in happiness or in a life of free choice. Nor does a state exist merely for the sake of alliance and security from injustice, nor yet for the sake of trade and mutual intercourse; for then the Tyrrhenians and the Carthaginians, and all who have commercial treaties with one another, would be citizens of one state. . . . Those who care for good government take into consideration the larger questions of virtue and vice in states. Whence it may be further inferred that virtue must be the serious care of a state which truly deserves the name. Otherwise the community becomes a mere alliance, which differs only in place from alliances of which the members live apart. And law is only a convention, "a surety to one another of justice," as the sophist Lycophron says, and has no real power to make the citizens good and just. . . .

Clearly then a state is not a mere society, having a common place, established for the prevention of crime and for the sake of trade. These are conditions without which a state cannot exist; but all of them together do not constitute a state, which is a community of families and aggregations of families in well-being for the sake of a perfect and self-sufficing life. Such a community can only be established among those who live in the same place and intermarry. Hence arise in states family connections, brotherhoods, common sacrifices, amusements which draw men together. They are created by friendship, for friendship is the motive of society. The end is the good life, and these are the means towards it. And the state is the union of families and villages having for an end a perfect and self-sufficing life, by which we mean a happy and honorable life.

Our conclusion, then, is that political society exists for the sake of noble actions, and not of mere companionship. And they who contribute most to such a society have a greater share in it than those who have the same or a greater freedom or nobility of birth but are inferior to them in political virtue; or than those who exceed them in wealth but are surpassed by them in virtue. . . .

We maintain that the true forms of government are three, and that the best must be that which is administered by the best, and in which there is one man, or a whole family, or many persons, excelling in virtue, and both rulers and subjects are fitted, the one to rule, the others to be ruled, in such a manner as to attain the most eligible life. We showed at the commencement of our inquiry that the virtue of the good man is necessarily the same as the virtue of the citizen of the perfect state. Clearly then in the same manner, and by the same means through which a man becomes truly good, he will frame a state which will be truly good whether aristocratical, or under kingly rule, and the same education and the same habits will be found to make a good man a good statesman and king. . . .

*   *   *

We have now to inquire what is the best constitution for most states, and the best life for most men, neither assuming a standard of virtue which is above ordinary persons, nor an education which is exceptionally favored by nature and circumstances, nor yet an ideal state which is an inspiration only, but having regard to the life in which the majority are able to share, and to the form of government which states in general can attain. . . . If it was truly said in the *Ethics* that the happy life is the life according to unimpeded virtue and that virtue is a mean, then the life which is a mean and a mean attainable by everyone must be best. And the same criteria of virtue and vice are characteristic of cities and of constitutions; for the constitution is in pattern the life of the city.

Now in all states there are three elements; one class is very rich, another very poor, and a third in the mean. It is admitted that moderation and the mean are best, and therefore it will clearly be best to possess the gifts of fortune in moderation; for in that condition of life men are most ready to listen to reason. . . . Those who have too much of the goods of fortune, strength, wealth, friends, and the like, are neither willing nor able to submit to authority. The evil begins at home; for when they are boys, by reason of the luxury in which they are brought up, they never learn, even at school, the habit of obedience. On the other hand, the very poor, who are in the opposite extreme, are too degraded. So that the one class cannot obey, and can only rule despotically; the other knows not how to command and must be ruled like slaves. Thus arises a city, not of freemen, but of masters and slaves, the one despising, the other envying. Nothing can be more fatal to friendship and good fellowship in states than this; for good fellowship starts from friendship. When men are at enmity with one another, they would rather not even share the same path.

But a city ought to be composed, as far as possible, of equals and similars; and these are generally the middle classes. Wherefore a city which is composed of middle-class citizens is necessarily best constituted with respect to what we call the natural elements of a state. And this class of citizens is most secure in a state, for they do not, like the poor, covet their neighbors' goods; nor do others covet theirs, as the poor covet the goods of the rich. And as they neither plot against others nor are themselves plotted against, they pass through life safely. . . .

Thus it is manifest that the best political community is formed by citizens of the middle class, and that those states are likely to be well administered in which the middle class is large, and if possible larger than both the other classes, or at any rate than either singly, for the addition of the middle class turns the scale and prevents either of the extremes from being dominant. Great then is the good fortune of a state in which the citizens have a moderate and sufficient property. For where some possess much and the rest nothing, there may arise an extreme democracy, or a pure oligarchy; or a tyranny may grow out of either extreme—out of either the most rampant democracy or out of an oligarchy. But it is not so likely to arise out of a middle and nearly equal condition.

Democracies are safer and more permanent than oligarchies, because they have a middle class which is more numerous and has a greater share in the government. For when there is no middle class and the poor greatly exceed in number, troubles arise and the state soon comes to an end. A proof of the superiority of the middle class is that the best legislators have been of a middle rank; for example, Solon, as his own verses testify, and Lycurgus, for he was not a king. . . .

What then is the best form of government, and what makes it the best is evident. Of other states, since we say there are many kinds of democracy and oligarchy, it is not difficult to see which has the first and which the second or any other place in the order of excellence, now that we have determined which is best. For that which is nearest to the best must of necessity be the better, and that which is furthest from it the worse, if we are judging absolutely and not with reference to given conditions. I say "with reference to given conditions," since a particular government may be preferable for some, but another form may be better for others.

*   *   *

REVIEW QUESTIONS

1. In Aristotle's view, what constitutes a state?
2. What is the purpose of the state?
3. Ought women to have any role in the governing of the state?
4. What is Aristotle's view of democracy?
5. Do you find any of Aristotle's views pertinent to government and society of the late twentieth and early twenty-first century C.E.?

ISOCRATES

FROM "Panegyricus"

When Alexander launched the Greco-Macedonian invasion of the Persian Empire in 335 B.C.E., he did not pull his motives out of thin air. His father, Philip, had been preparing such an invasion himself, motivated by reasons about which historians still debate. Even before Philip, however, a rationale for a great military campaign against the Persian king by a united force of Greek city-states ("Hellenes") had been formulated most vigorously by the Athenian orator Isocrates (436–338 B.C.E.). Though not a confident orator in his own right, Isocrates was a prolific writer of speeches, with as many as sixty of his speeches known to the Romans centuries later (of which, twenty-one have survived).

Although he may be better known for his speech "To Philip," in which he exhorts the Macedonian king to lead an expedition against the Persians, in an earlier work, "Panegyricus," Isocrates lays out an eloquent case, rationalized with substantial historical argumentation, for why the Greek city-states, under the aegis of Athens, should attack and conquer lands in the Persian Empire. In particular, as the following selection reflects, Isocrates goes to considerable lengths to establish two points: (1) the superiority of the Hellenes and Europe, and Athens especially; and (2) the inferiority of "barbarians" of Asia, and the Persians especially. In such works by Isocrates and other Greek writers of similar ilk, some historians discern the genesis of the process whereby Asia came to be identified as "Them" by the West's self-constructed "Us"— a dichotomy that still lurks beneath cultural attitudes and government policies even today.

From *Isocrates with an English Translation*, translated by George Norlin (3 vols.; Cambridge, Mass.: William Heinemann, 1980).

*   *   *

. . . , if it is the most experienced and the most capable who in any field of action deserve to be honored, it is without question our right to recover the hegemony which we [Athens] formerly possessed; for no one can point to another state which so far excels in warfare on land as our city is superior in fighting battles on the sea. But, in the next place, if there are any who do not regard this as a fair basis of *judgement,* since the reversals of fortune are frequent (for sovereignty never remains in the same hands), and who believe that the hegemony, like any other prize, should be held by those who first won this honor, or else by those who have rendered the most service to the *Hellenes,* I think that these also are on our side; for the farther back into the past we go in our examination of both these titles to leadership, the farther behind shall we leave those who dispute our claims. For it is admitted that our city is the oldest and the greatest in the world and in the eyes of all men the most renowned. But noble as is the foundation of our claims, the following grounds give us even a clearer title to distinction: for we did not become dwellers in this land by driving others out of it, nor by finding it uninhabited, nor by coming together here a motley horde composed of many races; but we are of a lineage so noble and

so pure that throughout our history we have continued in possession of the very land which gave us birth, since we are sprung from its very soil and are able to address our city by the very names which we apply to our nearest kin; for we alone of all the *Hellenes* have the right to call our city at once nurse and fatherland and mother. And yet, if men are to have good ground for pride and make just claims to leadership and frequently recall their ancestral glories, they must show that their race boasts an origin as noble as that which I have described.

So great, then, are the gifts which were ours from the beginning and which fortune has bestowed upon us. But how many good things we have contributed to the rest of the world we could estimate to best advantage if we should recount the history of our city from the beginning and go through all her achievements in detail; for we should find that not only was she the leader in the hazards of war, but that the social order in general in which we dwell, with which we share the rights of citizenship and through which we are able to live, is almost wholly due to her. It is, however, necessary to single out from the number of her benefactions, not those which because of their slight importance have escaped attention and been passed over in silence, but those which because of their great importance have been and still are on the lips and in the memory of all men everywhere.

*　　*　　*

Nor did our city, after she had played her part in bringing to pass the most important benefits, neglect what remained to be done; on the contrary she made it but the beginning of her benefactions to find for those who were in want that sustenance which men must have who are to provide well also for their other needs; but considering that an existence limited to this alone was not enough to make men desire to live, she gave such careful thought to their remaining wants as well that of the good things which are now at the service of mankind—in so far as we do not have them from the gods but owe them to each other—there is not one in which our city has had no part, and most of them are due to her alone. For, finding the *Hellenes* living without laws and in scattered abodes, some oppressed by tyrannies, others perishing through anarchy, she delivered them from these evils by taking some under her protection and by setting to others her own example; for she was the first to lay down laws and establish a polity. This is apparent from the fact that those who in the beginning brought charges of homicide, and desired to settle their mutual differences by reason and not by violence, tried their cases under our laws. Yes, and the arts also, both those which are useful in producing the necessities of life and those which have been devised to give us pleasure, she has either invented or stamped with her approval, and has then presented them to the rest of the world to enjoy.

Moreover, she has established her polity in general in such a spirit of welcome to strangers and friendliness to all men, that it adapts itself both to those who lack means and to those who wish to enjoy the means which they possess, and that it fails to be of service neither to those who are prosperous nor to those who are unfortunate in their own cities; nay, both classes find with us what they desire, the former the most delightful pastimes, the latter the securest refuge. Again, since the different populations did not in any case possess a country that was self-sufficing, each lacking in some things and producing others in excess of their needs, and

since they were greatly at a loss where they should dispose of their surplus and whence they should import what they lacked, in these difficulties also our city came to the rescue; for she established the *Piraeus* as a market in the center of *Hellas*—a market of such abundance that the articles which it is difficult to get, one here, one there, from the rest of the world, all these it is easy to procure *from Athens*.

*　　*　　*

Philosophy, moreover, which has helped to discover and establish all these institutions, which has educated us for public affairs and made us gentle towards each other, which has distinguished between the misfortunes that are due to ignorance and those which spring from necessity, and taught us to guard against the former and to bear the latter nobly—philosophy, I say, was given to the world by our city. And *Athens* it is that has honored eloquence, which all men crave and envy in its possessors; for she realized that this is the one endowment of our nature which singles us out from all living creatures, and that by using this advantage we have risen above them in all other respects as well; she saw that in other activities the fortunes of life are so capricious that in them often the wise fail and the foolish succeed, whereas beautiful and artistic speech is never allotted to ordinary men, but is the work of an intelligent mind, and that it is in this respect that those who are accounted wise and ignorant present the strongest contrast; and she knew, furthermore, that whether men have been liberally educated from their earliest years is not to be determined by their courage or their wealth or such advantages, but is made manifest most of all by their speech, and that this has proved itself to be the surest sign of culture in every one of us, and that those who are skilled in speech are not only men of power in their own cities but are also held in honor in other states. And so far has our city distanced the rest of mankind in thought and in speech that her pupils have become the teachers of the rest of the world; and she has brought it about that the name *Hellenes* suggests no longer a race but an intelligence, and that the title *Hellenes* is applied rather to those who share our culture than to those who share a common blood.

But in order that I may not appear to be dwelling at length on the details when I have proposed to speak on the general subject nor to be extolling the city for these accomplishments because I lack ground for praising her conduct in war, let what I have said suffice for those who glory in such services. But I think that honor is due to our ancestors no less for their wars than for their other benefactions; for not slight, nor few, nor obscure, but many and dread and great, were the struggles they sustained, some for their own territories, some for the freedom of the rest of the world; for at all times, without ceasing, they have offered the city as a common refuge and as a champion to the *Hellenes* whenever oppressed. And it is for this very reason that we are sometimes charged with adopting a foolish policy in that we are accustomed to cultivate the weaker peoples—as though such charges do not support those who desire to sing our praises. For it was not because we failed to appreciate how much more advantageous great alliances are in point of security that we pursued this policy in regard to the weak; no, although we realized much more exactly than our rivals the consequences of such a course, we nevertheless preferred to stand by the weaker even against our interests rather than to unite with the stronger in oppressing others for our own advantage.

*   *   *

For when all the allies were in a state of dejection, and the *Peloponnesians* were fortifying the Isthmus and selfishly seeking their own safety; when the other states had submitted to the barbarians and were fighting on the *Persian* side, save only those which were overlooked because of their insignificance; when twelve hundred ships of war were bearing down upon them, and an innumerable army was on the point of invading *Attica*; when no light of deliverance could be glimpsed in any quarter, but, on the contrary, the *Athenians* had been abandoned by their allies and cheated of their every hope; and when it lay in their power not only to escape from their present dangers but also to enjoy the signal honors which the King held out to them, since he conceived that if he could get the support of the Athenian fleet he could at once become master of the *Peloponnesus* also, then our ancestors scorned to accept his gifts; nor did they give way to anger against the *Hellenes* for having betrayed them and rush gladly to make terms with the barbarians; nay, by themselves they made ready to battle for freedom, while they forgave the rest for choosing bondage. For they considered that while it was natural for the weaker states to seek their security by every means, it was not possible for those states which asserted their right to stand at the head of *Hellas* to avoid the perils of war; on the contrary, they believed that just as it is preferable for men who are honorable to die nobly rather than to live in disgrace, so too it is better for cities which are illustrious to be blotted out from the sight of mankind rather than to be seen in a state of bondage. It is evident that they were of this mind; for when they were not able to marshal themselves against both the land and the sea forces at once, they took with them the entire population, abandoned the city, and sailed to the neighboring island, in order that they might encounter each force in turn.

And yet how could men be shown to be braver or more devoted to *Hellas* than our ancestors, who, to avoid bringing slavery upon the rest of the *Hellenes*, endured to see their city made desolate, their land ravaged, their sanctuaries rifled, their temples burned, and all the forces of the enemy closing in upon their own country? But in truth even this did not satisfy them; they were ready to give battle on the sea—they alone against twelve hundred ships of war. They were not, indeed, allowed to fight alone; for the *Peloponnesians*, put to shame by our courage, and thinking, moreover, that if the *Athenians* should first be destroyed, they could not themselves be saved from destruction, and that if the *Athenians* should succeed, their own cities would be brought into disrepute, they were constrained to share the dangers. Now the clamors that arose during the action, and the shoutings and the cheers—things which are common to all those who fight on ships—I see no reason why I should take time to describe; my task is to speak of those matters which are distinctive and give claim to leadership, and which confirm the arguments which I have already advanced. In short, our city was so far superior while she stood unharmed that even after she had been laid waste she contributed more ships to the battle for the deliverance of *Hellas* than all the others put together who fought in the engagement; and no one is so prejudiced against us that he would not acknowledge that it was by winning the sea fight that we conquered in the war, and that the credit for this is due to *Athens*.

Who then should have the hegemony, when a campaign against the barbarians is in prospect? Should it not be they who distinguished themselves above all others in the former war? Should it not be they who many times bore, alone, the brunt of battle, and in the joint struggles of the *Hellenes* were awarded the prize of valor? Should it not be they who abandoned their own country to save the rest of *Hellas*, who in ancient times founded most of the Hellenic cities, and who later delivered them from the greatest disasters? Would it not be an outrage upon us, if, having taken the largest share in the evils of war, we should be adjudged worthy of a lesser share in its honors, and if, having at that time been placed in the lead in the cause of all the *Hellenes*, we should now be compelled to follow the lead of others?

*   *   *

And none of these things has happened by accident, but all of them have been due to natural causes; for it is not possible for people who are reared and governed as are the *Persians*, either to have a part in any other form of virtue or to set up on the field of battle trophies of victory over their foes. For how could either an able general or a good soldier be produced amid such ways of life as theirs? Most of their population is a mob without discipline or experience of dangers, which has lost all stamina for war and has been trained more effectively for servitude than are the slaves in our country. Those, on the other hand, who stand highest in repute among them have never governed their lives by dictates of equality or of common interest or of loyalty to the state; on the contrary, their whole existence consists of insolence toward some, and servility towards others—a manner of life than which nothing could be more demoraliz-

ing to human nature. Because they are rich, they pamper their bodies; but because they are subject to one man's power, they keep their souls in a state of abject and cringing fear, parading themselves at the door of the royal palace, prostrating themselves, and in every way schooling themselves to humility of spirit, falling on their knees before a mortal man, addressing him as a divinity, and thinking more lightly of the gods than of men. So it is that those of the *Persians* who come down to the sea, whom they term satraps, do not dishonor the training which they receive at home, but cling steadfastly to the same habits: they are faithless to their friends and cowardly to their foes; their lives are divided between servility on the one hand and arrogance on the other; they treat their allies with contempt and pay court to their enemies.

*   *   *

. . . who of those that have fought against them has not come off with success, and who of those that have fallen under their power has not perished from their atrocities?

*   *   *

Then why should we cherish the friendship of men who punish their benefactors and so openly flatter those who do them injury? Who is there among us whom they have not wronged? When have they given the *Hellenes* a moment's respite from their treacherous plots? What in our world is not hateful to them who did not shrink in the earlier war from rifling even the images and temples of the gods, and burning them to the ground? Therefore, the *Ionians* deserve to be commended because, when their sanctuaries had been burned, they invoked the wrath of Heaven upon any who should disturb the ruins or should desire to restore their shrines as they were of old; and they did this, not because they lacked the means to rebuild them, but in order that there might be left a memorial to future generations of the impiety of the barbarians, and that none might put their trust in men who do not scruple to commit such sins against our holy temples, but that all might be on their guard against them and fear them, seeing that they waged that war not against our persons only, but even against our votive offerings to the gods.

Of my own countrymen also I have a similar tale to tell. For towards all other peoples with whom they have been at war, they forget their past enmities the moment they have concluded peace, but toward the Asiatics they feel no gratitude even when they receive favors from them; so eternal is the wrath which they cherish against the barbarians. Again, our fathers condemned many to death for defection to the *Medes*; in our public assemblies even to this day, before any other business is transacted, the *Athenians* call down curses upon any citizen who proposes friendly overtures to the *Persians*; and, at the celebration of the Mysteries, the *Eumolpidae* and the Kerykes, because of our hatred of the *Persians*, give solemn warning to the other barbarians also, even as to men guilty of murder, that they are for ever banned from the sacred rites. So ingrained in our nature is our hostility to them that even in the matter of our stories we linger most fondly over those which tell of the *Trojan* and the *Persian* wars, because through them we learn of our enemies' misfortunes; and you will find that our warfare against the barbarians has inspired our hymns, while that against the *Hellenes* has brought forth our dirges; and that the former are sung at our festivals, while we recall the latter on occasions of sorrow. Moreover, I think that even the poetry of Homer has won a greater renown because he has nobly glorified the men who fought against the barbarians, and that on this account our ancestors determined to give his art a place of honor in our *musical contests* and in the education of our youth, in order that we, hearing his verses over and over again, may learn by heart the enmity which stands from of old between us and them, and that we, admiring the valor of those who were in the war against *Troy*, may conceive a passion for like deeds.

⚸   ⚸   ⚸

I shall show still more clearly both the dishonor which we have suffered, and the advantage which the King has gained by putting the matter in this way: All the world which lies beneath the firmament being divided into two parts, the one called *Asia*, the other *Europe*, he has taken half of it by the Treaty, as if he were apportioning the earth with *Zeus*, and not making compacts with men.

REVIEW QUESTIONS

1. How would you rank Isocrates as a "spin doctor"?
2. From what you have learned from other sources, can you critique Isocrates' rendition of the history of the Greek encounter with the Persians?

PLUTARCH

FROM "Life of Alexander"

The biographies produced by Plutarch are an important (though by no means entirely objective or accurate) source of knowledge of the lives of many great figures of the Greek and Roman past. The following selections reveal something of ancient opinion concerning Alexander's character amd intentions. To a great extent, they also communicate a view of him that dominated much thinking until relatively recent times.

*　　*　　*

Philonicus the Thessalian brought the horse Bucephalusto Philip, offering to sell him for thirteen talents; but when they went into the field to try him, they found him so very vicious and unmanageable, that he reared up when they endeavored to mount him, and would not so much as endure the voice of any of Philip's attendants. Upon which, as they were leading him away as wholly useless and untractable, Alexander, who stood by, said, "What an excellent horse do they lose, for want of skill and boldness to manage him!" Philip at first took no notice of what he said; but when he heard him repeat the same thing several times, and saw he was very frustrated to see the horse sent away, "Do you criticize," said Philip, "those who are older than yourself, as if you knew more, and were better able to manage him then they?" "I could manage this horse," replied Alexander, "better than others do." "And if you do not," said Philip, "what will you forfeit for your rashness?" "I will pay," answered Alexander, "the whole price of the horse." At this the whole company fell laughing; and as soon as the wager was settled among them, he immediately ran to the horse, and, taking hold of the bridle, turned him directly towards the sun, having, it seems, observed that he was disturbed at and afraid of the motion of his own shadow; then letting him go forward a little, still keeping the reins in his hand, and stroking him gently when he began to grow eager and fiery, . . . with one nimble leap, Alexander securely mounted him, and when he was seated, by little and little drew in the bridle, and curbed him without either striking or spurring him. Presently, when he found him free from all rebelliousness, and only impatient for the course, he let him go at full speed, inciting him now with a commanding voice, and urging him also with his heel. Philip and his friends looked on at first in silence and anxiety for the result, but when he came back rejoicing and triumphing for what he had performed, they all burst out into acclamations of applause; and his father, shedding tears, it is said, for joy, kissed him as he came down from his horse, and in his transport said, "O my son, carve out a kingdom equal to and worthy of yourself, for Macedonia is too small for you."

*　　*　　*

After the company had drunk a good deal somebody began to sing the verses of a man named Pranichus . . . which had been written to humiliate and make fun of some Macedonian commanders who had recently been defeated by the barbarians. The older members of the party took offense at this and showed their resentment of both the poet and the singer, but Alexander and those sitting near him listened with obvious pleasure and told the man to continue. Thereupon Cleitus, who had already drunk too much and was rough and hot-tempered by nature, became angrier than ever and shouted that it was not right for Macedonians to be insulted in the presence of barbarians and enemies, even if they had met with misfortune, for they were better men than those who were laughing at them. Alexander retorted that if Cleitus was trying to disguise cowardice as misfortune, he must be pleading his own case. At this Cleitus sprang to his feet and shouted back, "Yes, it was my cowardice that saved your life, you who call yourself the son of the gods, when you were turning your back to Spithridates' sword. And it is the blood of these Macedonians and their wounds which have made you so great that you disown your father Philip and claim to be the son of Ammon!"

These words made Alexander furious. "You scum," he cried out, "do you think that you can keep on speaking of me like this, and stir up trouble among the Macedonians and not pay for it?"

From *Readings in Ancient History,* vol. 1, edited by William S. Davis (Boston: Allyn and Bacon, 1912).

From *The Age of Alexander,* translated by Ian Scott-Kilvert (New York: Penguin Books, 1973), pp. 257–58, 307–9.

"Oh, but we Macedonians do pay for it," Cleitus retorted. "Just think of the rewards we get for all our efforts. It's the dead ones who are happy, because they never lived to see Macedonians being beaten with Median rods, or begging the Persians for an audience with our own king." Cleitus blurted out all this impulsively, whereupon Alexander's friends jumped up and began to abuse him, while the older men tried to calm down both sides. . . . But Cleitus refused to take back anything and he challenged Alexander to speak out whatever he wished to say in front of the company, or else not invite to his table freeborn men who spoke their minds: it would be better for him to spend his time among barbarians and slaves, who would prostrate themselves before his white tunic and his Persian girdle. At this Alexander could no longer control his rage: he hurled one of the apples that lay on the table at Cleitus, hit him, and then looked around for his dagger. One of his bodyguards, Aristophanes, had already moved it out of harm's way, and the others crowded around him and begged him to be quiet. But Alexander leaped to his feet and shouted out in the Macedonian tongue for his bodyguard to turn out, a signal that this was an extreme emergency. . . . As Cleitus still refused to give way, . . . Alexander seized a spear from one of his guards, faced Cleitus as he was drawing aside the curtain of the doorway, and ran him through. With a roar of pain and a groan, Cleitus fell, and immediately the king's anger left him. When he came to himself and saw his friends standing around him speechless, he snatched the weapon out of the dead body and would have plunged it into his own throat if the guards had not forestalled him by seizing his hands and carrying him by force to his chamber.

There he spent the rest of the night and the whole of the following day sobbing in an agony of remorse. At last he lay exhausted by his grief, uttering deep groans but unable to speak a word, until his friends, alarmed at his silence, forced their way into his room. He paid no attention to what any of them said, except that when Aristan-

der the diviner reminded him . . . that these events had long ago been ordained by fate, he seemed to accept this assurance.

*   *   *

Now Fortune argues that Alexander belongs to her and to her alone. However, this ought to be denied in the name of philosophy and even more so because of the wrath and indignation of Alexander at the notion that he received as a gift of Fortune that empire which he purchased with a copious expenditure of his blood and repeated wounds,

And many sleepless nights he spent
And bloody days consumed while making war,

contending with invincible forces, nations without number, impassable rivers, and rocks above the range of bow and arrow, helped only by good judgment, perseverance, courage and self-control.

And I imagine he might address Fortune when she claimed these deeds for herself in these words: "Do not depreciate my honor, or strip me of my fame . . . my body bears many indications that Fortune was my adversary, not my ally. First I was struck in the head by a stone and clubbed on the neck in the Illyrian land. Later, at the Granicus, my head was broken by the lone knife of a barbarian, and at Issus my thigh was gashed with a sword. Before Gaza my ankle was pierced by an arrow, when I fell heavily, dislocating my shoulder. At Maracanda my shin was broken by an arrow. Then came blows and the ravages of famine in the Indian lands. Among the Aspasians I was shot in the shoulder by an arrow; in the land of the Gandridae in the leg; among the Malli a missile from a bow reached me, burying its iron point in my breast, and when I had also been struck by a club along the neck, the ladders that had been raised against the walls gave way, and Fortune,

From *De Alexandri Magni Fortuna aut Virtute*, Oration I, in *Sources in Western Civilization: Ancient Greece*, translated by Truesdell S. Brown (New York: Free Press, 1965).

taking delight in such a deed, penned me up there alone, not to contend with famous adversaries but with unknown barbarians. And if Ptolemy had not covered me with his shield and if Limnaeus had not died in front of me after intercepting countless missiles, and if the Macedonians had not torn down the walls in their rage, then that nameless barbarian village would have been Alexander's tomb."

And in this same expedition gales, droughts, deep rivers, rocks higher than a bird can fly, monstrous beasts, savage customs, a succession of petty rulers and constant betrayals were also encountered. But even before the expedition itself, Greece fought back after the ways of Philip. The Thebans shook the dust of Chaeronea from their weapons, rising up after disaster while Athens extended a helping hand. All Macedon was ripe for rebellion, looking secretly to Amyntas and the sons of Aeropus. The Illyrians erupted and the state of affairs in Scythia threatened her troubled neighbors. Persian gold, diffused in every direction by popular orators, stirred up the Peloponnese. Philip's treasury was empty and there was even a deficit of two hundred talents, as Onesicritus relates. With such an appalling lack of money and with the government still in confusion a young man just barely beyond boyhood had the audacity to entertain thoughts of Babylon and Susa, and even of an empire embracing all mankind—and this, mind you, with thirty thousand foot and four thousand horse. Those at least are the figures given by Aristobulus; according to King Ptolemy there were thirty thousand foot and five thousand horse, while Anaximenes gives 43,500 foot and 5,500 horse. The great and magnificent sum which Fortune had provided for his traveling chest was seventy talents, as Aristobulus tells it, but Duris says he had only supplies for thirty days.

Then Alexander must have been an unthinking hothead to challenge such a formidable power with his meager resources? Not at all. Did anyone ever start out for war with greater or better preparation for succeeding than nobility of character, intelligence, self-mastery and courage—with which philosophy had equipped him for his journey? He crossed over against the Persians with greater resources furnished by his teacher Aristotle than by his father Philip. In fact there are writers who allege that Alexander once said that he had brought the *Iliad* and the *Odyssey* along as a provision for the army; and we believe them, honoring Homer. And if anyone maintains that he only used Homer for relaxation after toil and as a pleasant way of diverting his leisure moments, but that his real provision for the journey lay in the philosophic doctrines, in discourses on fearlessness and valor, on self-mastery and on highmindedness we look on this with scorn. For obviously Alexander wrote nothing about syllogisms or propositions, and he never held forth in the Lyceum or presented a thesis for debate in the Academy, while such a view would restrict philosophy to things of this sort as though it were made up of words rather than deeds. Yet there were famous philosophers like Pythagoras, or Socrates, or Arcesilaus or Carneades who wrote nothing. And these men were not occupied with such great wars, or civilizing barbarian princes, or establishing Greek cities among savage peoples, nor did they continue pressing on against lawless and ignorant tribes in order to instruct them in law and peace. Instead, though they did have the time, they abandoned writing to the sophists. Then why are they believed to have been philosophers? Because of what they said, how they lived and what they taught. Then let Alexander be judged on the same basis and he will be revealed as a philosopher by what he said, by what he did and by what he taught.

But first and, if you will, most surprising, look at Alexander's pupils and compare them with those of Socrates and Plato. Now they were teaching adaptable scholars who spoke the same language, for even if they knew nothing else they all understood Greek. Despite this, there were many of them whom they failed to convince: the Critiases, Alcibiadeses and Clitophons went astray, spitting out their doctrines as a horse gets rid of a bit. But then look at Alexander's instruction: he taught marriage to the Hyrcanians, he showed the Arachosians how to farm, he persuaded the Sogdianians to support their fathers instead of killing them, and induced the Persians to respect their mothers and not to marry them. What an admirable philosophy, which caused the Indians to bow down before the gods of Greece, the Scythians to bury their dead instead of devouring them! We are astonished at the ability of Carneades if he hellenizes Clitomachus, who was a Carthaginian by birth formerly named Hasdrubal, and we also admire Zeno for his skill if he induces Diogenes of Babylon to become a philosopher. But thanks to Alexander Homer was read in Asia, and the sons of Persia, Susiana, and Gedrosia sang the choruses of Euripides and Sophocles. Now Socrates was brought to judgment for introducing foreign gods by informers in Athens, but Alexander caused Bactra and the Caucasus to worship the gods of Greece. While Plato drew up a single form of government which was so strict he could induce no one to adopt it, Alexander, by founding more than seventy cities among the barbarian tribes, and seeding Asia with Greek outposts, suppressed their savage and uncivilized customs. Although a few of us read about the laws of Plato, countless numbers have adopted and continue to use the laws of Alexander. Those whom Alexander conquered were more fortunate than those who escaped, because there was no one to correct their foolish way of life, while the conquerer forced his subjects to live in prosperity. Therefore Themistocles' remark when he received munificent gifts from the [Persian] king during his exile and obtained three tribute-paying cities—one to furnish him with grain, one with wine and the other with condiments: "Oh, my children, had we not been ruined, we would have been ruined indeed!"—was a remark that might have been made even more appropriately by those whom Alexander conquered. For they would not have been civilized unless they had been conquered. And Egypt would not have had its Alexandria, or Mesopotamia its Seleuceia, or India its Bucephalia, nor would the Caucasus have had a Greek city founded there, yet it is by means of such cities that savagery is gradually extinguished and bad customs changed into good ones. Now if philosophers really set such store by refining and altering rough and ignorant disposi-

tions, then Alexander, who is seen transforming countless races and natural savages, ought truly to be regarded as a very great philosopher.

Now the much-admired *Republic* of Zeno, the founder of the Stoic school, adds up to this one thing: that we ought not to live in cities or in demes, each distinguished by its own regulations, but we should look on all men as fellow citizens and demesmen, having one life and one world, feeding together like a single herd sharing a common pasture. Zeno, however, wrote this as a dream, a philosophic image of a well-governed state, while Alexander expressed his views by deeds. He did not follow Aristotle's advice to treat the Greeks as a leader, the barbarians as a master, cultivating the former as friends and kinsmen, and treating the latter as animals or plants. Had he done so his kingdom would have been filled with warfare, banishments and secret plots, but he regarded himself as divinely sent to mediate and govern the world. And those whom he failed to win over by persuasion he overpowered in arms, bringing them together from every land, combining, as it were in a loving cup, their lives, customs, marriages and manner of living; he bade them all look on the inhabited world as their native land, on his camp as their citadel and protection, on good men as their kinsmen and evildoers as aliens, and not to distinguish Greek from barbarian by the chlamys, or the shield, or the sword, or the sleeved tunic but to associate Hellenism with virtue and barbarism with evildoing; and to regard their clothing, food, marriages and manners as common to all, blended together by their blood and their children.

Now Demaratus of Corinth, the mercenary and a friend of Philip's, wept tears of joy when he saw Alexander in Susa, exclaiming that those Greeks who had died earlier had been robbed of great happiness since they had not seen Alexander sitting on Darius' throne. But I, by Zeus, do not envy those who saw a spectacle which is associated with Fortune and lesser kings, but I think I would have been more pleased at the fair and blessed sight of the marriage procession when, bringing together one hundred Persian brides and one hundred Greek and Macedonian grooms into a single tent bedecked with gold, with a single hearth and a single table, he was the first, crowned with flowers, to raise the hymeneal song, singing as it were a song of friendship, while he joined together the greatest and most powerful peoples into one community by wedlock: the bridegroom of one, but for everyone at once a bride-giver, a father and a sponsor. I would gladly have said: "O barbarous and foolish Xerxes, your great efforts in putting a bridge across the Hellespont were wasted, for intelligent rulers do not join Asia to Europe in this way with planks, or floats or lifeless and unfeeling fetters; but they unite the races by true laws, and chaste marriages and common off-spring." . . .

. . . For he did not cross Asia like a robber, nor did he have it in mind to ravage and despoil it for the booty and loot presented by such an unheard-of stroke of fortune—the way Hannibal treated Italy later on, or the way the Treres acted earlier in Ionia or the Scythians in Media. Instead he conducted himself as he did out of a desire to subject all the races in the world to one rule and one form of government, making all mankind a single people. Had not the divinity that sent Alexander recalled his soul so soon, there would have been a single law, as it were, watching over all mankind, and all men would have looked to one form of justice as their common source of light. But now, that portion of the world that never beheld Alexander has remained as if deprived of the sun.

Now, at the outset, the very purpose of his expedition commends the man as a philosopher for aiming not at wealth and luxury for himself but at bringing peace, harmony and mutual fellowship to all men. Secondly, let us examine what he said, since other kings and rulers reveal their character by the spirit of their pronouncements. . . . When he talked to Diogenes himself, in Corinth, he was so captivated and overwhelmed by the man's way of life and reputation that he would often refer to him later, saying: "If I were not Alexander, I would like to be Diogenes!" By this he meant: . . . "If I did not intend to blend the customs of the Greeks and the barbarians; to cross every continent and tame it; to search out the farthest points of land and sea; to make Ocean the boundary of Macedon; and if I did not mean to transplant the peace and the justice of Greece to every people, even then I would not waste my energies in useless luxury, but I would emulate the frugality of Diogenes. But now, Diogenes, excuse me. I am imitating Heracles, rivalling Perseus and following in the footsteps of Dionysus, the ancestor of my line. I wish to bring the chorus of victorious Greeks to India once more, and to renew the memory of Bacchic revels among the wild mountainous peoples beyond the Caucasus. And there are said to be holy men in those parts who live under laws of their own, a rough and naked sect devoting their lives to the god. They are even more self-denying than Diogenes, in that they require no wallet, for they do not save any food since the land continually provides them with a fresh supply. Flowing rivers furnish them with drink, trees shed their foliage over them and herbs of the field serve them as a bed. Thanks to me they will come to know of Diogenes, and Diogenes of them. I, too, must coin money, and stamp the form of a Greek constitution on a barbarian mold."

Well, then, do his deeds appear to be primarily the result of chance? Power in war? Government by force? Do they not rather suggest the great courage and justice, the great self-control and mildness of one who does everything in an orderly and intelligent manner and in accordance with a sober and sagacious plan?

REVIEW QUESTIONS

1. How would you characterize Plutarch's view of Alexander?
2. Is it completely unbiased?
3. What kind of leader does Alexander appear to be?
4. Does he have any apparent flaws?
5. What, according to Plutarch, were the motives underlying Alexander's conquests?

ERATOSTHENES' MAP OF THE WORLD (C. 200 B.C.E.)

As shown in this reconstruction, the world map created by the Hellenistic geographer Eratosthenes (c. 275–195 B.C.E.) shows the use of lines corresponding to latitude and longitude and is considerably advanced for its time. How might Eratosthenes' research have benefited from Alexander's campaigns? How well developed was the Hellenistic sense of Africa, Asia, and Europe?

HELLENISTIC ARCHITECTURE IN THE NEAR EAST (C. 175 C.E.)

In the wake of Alexander's conquests, Greek culture and tastes were adopted by many of the native elites in the Near East. This "treasury" (perhaps a royal mausoleum in actuality) was carved into the sandstone of the city of Petra, now in modern Jordan. In the third and second centuries B.C.E., Petra was the capital of the Nabataean kings, much of whose wealth and power derived from Petra's importance as a major hub for long-distance caravan trade. How does the style of the architecture compare with that of Greek public buildings? What would have inspired non-Greeks to adopt Greek styles?

FROM **The First Book of Maccabees**

Relatively few documents have survived that provide evidence of the response of Near Eastern peoples to their conquest by Alexander's armies and their subsequent inclusion in the Ptolemid and Seleucid kingdoms. Perhaps the most eloquent and informative sources are from the Hebrew Bible. The following selection is from the First Book of Maccabees. Probably written around 100 B.C.E., it chronicles the rebellion begun in 167 B.C.E. by the priest Mattathias, and then continued by his sons Judas, Jonathan, and Simon (all of whom came to be known as Maccabee, possibly meaning "designated by God"), against the Seleucid rulers of Syria. After years of struggle, the rebels succeeded in securing the independent Hasmonean kingdom of Judea, which later was incorporated into the Roman Empire.

From *New American Bible with Revised New Testament and Revised Psalms* (Washington D.C.: Confraternity of Christian Doctrine, 1991).

*   *   *

After Antiochus had defeated Egypt in the year one hundred and forty-three, he returned and went up to Israel and to Jerusalem with a strong force. He insolently invaded the sanctuary and took away the golden altar, the lampstand for the light with all its fixtures, the offering table, the cups and the bowls, the golden censers, the curtain, the crowns, and the golden ornament on the façade of the temple. He stripped off everything, and took away the gold and silver and the precious vessels; he also took all the hidden treasures he could find. Taking all this, he went back to his own country, after he had spoken with great arrogance and shed much blood.

And there was great mourning for Israel, in
   every place where they dwelt,
and the rulers and the elders groaned.
Virgins and young men languished,
and the beauty of the women was disfigured.
Every bridegroom took up lamentation,
she who sat in the bridal chamber mourned,
And the land was shaken on account of its
   inhabitants,
and all the house of Jacob was covered with
   shame.

Two years later, the king sent the Mysian commander to the cities of Judah, and he came to Jerusalem with a strong force. He spoke to them deceitfully in peaceful terms, and won their trust. Then he attacked the city suddenly, in a great onslaught, and destroyed many of the people in Israel. He plundered the city and set fire to it, demolished its houses and its surrounding walls, took captive the women and children, and seized the cattle. Then they built up the City of David with a high, massive wall and strong towers, and it became their citadel. There they installed a sinful race, perverse men, who fortified themselves inside it, storing up weapons and provisions, and depositing there the plunder they had collected from Jerusalem. And they became a great threat.

*   *   *

Then the king wrote to his whole kingdom that all should be one people, each abandoning his particular customs. All the Gentiles conformed to the command of the king, and many Israelites were in favor of his religion; they sacrificed to idols and profaned the sabbath.

The king sent messengers with letters to Jerusalem and to the cities of Judah, ordering them to follow customs foreign to their land: to prohibit holocausts, sacrifices, and libations in the sanctuary, to profane the sabbaths and feast days, to desecrate the sanctuary and the sacred ministers, to build pagan altars and temples and shrines, to sacrifice swine and unclean animals, to leave their sons uncircumcised, and to let themselves be defiled with every kind of impurity and abomination, so that they might forget the law and change all their observances. Whoever refused to act according to the command of the king should be put to death.

Such were the orders he published throughout his kingdom. He appointed inspectors over all the people, and he ordered the cities of Judah to offer sacrifices, each city in turn. Many of the people, those who abandoned the law, joined them and committed evil in the land. Israel was driven into hiding, wherever places of refuge could be found.

On the fifteenth day of the month Chislev, in the year one hundred and forty-five, the king erected the horrible abomination upon the altar of holocausts, and in the surrounding cities of Judah they built pagan altars. They also burnt incense at the doors of houses and in the streets. Any scrolls of the law which they found they tore up and burnt. Whoever was found with a scroll of the covenant, and whoever observed the law, was condemned to death by royal decree. So they used their power against Israel, against those who were caught, each month, in the cities. On the twenty-fifth day of each month they sacrificed on the altar erected over the altar of holocausts. Women who had had their children circumcised were put to death, in keeping with the decree, with the babies hung from their necks; their families also and those who had circumcised them were killed. But many in Israel were determined and resolved in their hearts not to eat anything unclean; they preferred to die rather than to be defiled with unclean food or to profane the holy covenant; and they did die. Terrible affliction was upon Israel.

*   *   *

Many who sought to live according to righteousness and religious custom went out into the desert to settle there, they and their sons, their wives and their cattle, because misfortunes pressed so hard on them.

It was reported to the officers and soldiers of the king who were in the City of David, in Jerusalem, that certain men who had flouted the king's order had gone out to the hiding places in the desert. Many hurried out after them, and having caught up with them, camped opposite and prepared to attack them on the sabbath. "Enough of this!" the pursuers said to them. "Come out and obey the king's command, and your lives will be spared." But they replied, "We will not come out, nor will we obey the king's command to profane the sabbath." Then the enemy attacked them at once; but they did not retaliate; they neither threw stones, nor blocked up their own hiding places. They said, "Let us all die without reproach; heaven and earth are our witnesses that you destroy us unjustly." So the officers and soldiers attacked them on the sabbath, and they died with their wives, their children and their cattle, to the number of a thousand persons.

When Mattathias and his friends heard of it, they mourned deeply for them. "If we all do as our kinsmen have done," they said to one another, "and do not fight against the Gentiles for our lives and our traditions, they will soon destroy us from the earth." On that day they came to this decision: "Let us fight against anyone who attacks us on the sabbath, so that we may not all die as our kinsmen died in the hiding places."

*   *   *

Mattathias and his friends went about and tore down the pagan altars; they also enforced circumcision for any uncircumcised boys whom they found in the territory of Israel. They put to flight the arrogant, and the work prospered in their hands. They saved the law from the hands of the Gentiles and of the kings and did not let the sinner triumph.

*   *   *

Then his son Judas, who was called Maccabeus, took his place. All his brothers and all who had joined his father supported him, and they carried on Israel's war joyfully.

*   *   *

Then Judas and his brothers began to be feared, and dread fell upon the Gentiles about them. His fame reached the king, and all the Gentiles talked about the battles of Judas.

When Antiochus heard about these events, he was angry; so he ordered a muster of all the forces of his kingdom, a very strong army.

*   *   *

So the following year Lysias gathered together sixty thousand picked men and five thousand cavalry, to subdue them. They came into Idumea and camped at Beth-zur, and Judas met them with ten thousand men. Seeing that the army was strong, he prayed thus: "Blessed are you, O Savior of Israel, who broke the rush of the mighty one by the hand of your servant David and delivered the camp of the Philistines into the hand of Jonathan, the son of Saul, and his armor-bearer. Give this army into the hands of your people Israel; make them ashamed of their troops and their cavalry. Strike them with fear, weaken the boldness of their strength, and let them tremble at their own destruction. Strike them down by the sword of those who love you, that all who know your name may hymn your praise."

Then they engaged in battle, and about five thousand of Lysias' men fell in hand-to-hand fighting. When Lysias saw his ranks beginning to give way, and the increased boldness of Judas, whose men were ready either to live or to die bravely, he withdrew to Antioch and began to recruit mercenaries so as to return to Judea with greater numbers.

Then Judas and his brothers said, "Now that our enemies have been crushed, let us go up to purify the sanctuary and rededicate it." So the whole army assembled, and went up to Mount Zion. They found the sanctuary desolate, the altar desecrated, the gates burnt, weeds growing in the courts as in a forest or on some mountain, and the priests' chambers demolished. Then they tore their clothes and made great lamentation; they sprinkled their heads with ashes and fell with their faces to the ground. And when the signal was given with trumpets, they cried out to Heaven.

Judas appointed men to attack those in the citadel, while he purified the sanctuary. He chose blameless priests, devoted to the law; these purified the sanctuary and carried away the stones of the Abomination to an unclean place. They deliberated what ought to be done with the altar of holocausts that had been desecrated. The happy thought came to them to tear it down, lest it be a lasting shame to them that the Gentiles had defiled it; so they tore down the altar. They stored the stones in a suitable place on the temple hill, until a prophet should come and decide what to do with them. Then they took uncut stones, according to the law, and built a new altar like the former one. They also repaired the sanctuary and the interior of the temple and purified the courts. They made new sacred vessels and brought the lampstand, the altar of incense, and the table into the temple. Then they burned incense on the altar and lighted the lamps on the lampstand, and these illuminated the temple. They also put loaves on the table and hung up curtains. Thus they finished all the work they had undertaken.

Early in the morning on the twenty-fifth day of the ninth month, that is, the month of Chislev, in the year one hundred and forty-eight, they arose and offered sacrifice according to the law on the new altar of holocausts that they had made. On the anniversary of the day on which the Gentiles had defiled it, on that very day it was reconsecrated with songs, harps, flutes, and cymbals. All the people prostrated themselves and adored and praised Heaven, who had given them success.

For eight days they celebrated the dedication of the altar and joyfully offered holocausts and sacrifices of deliverance and praise. They ornamented the façade of the temple with gold crowns and shields; they repaired the gates and the priests' chambers and furnished them with doors. There was great joy among the people now that the disgrace of the Gentiles was removed. Then Judas and his brothers and the entire congregation of Israel decreed that the days of the dedication of the altar should be observed with joy and gladness on the anniversary every year for eight days, from the twenty-fifth day of the month Chislev.

*   *   *

REVIEW QUESTIONS

1. According to the First Book of Maccabees, what was the impact of Greek conquest on the Jews of Israel?
2. What provoked them to resist Hellenistic domination?
3. Where lay the conflicts between the values of the Jews and those of their conquerors?
4. How does this account of Greek domination contrast with the ideals of Alexander as described by Plutarch?

EPICURUS

Principal Doctrines

With the exception of Stoicism, no Hellenistic philosophy has had more influence on the intellectual history of Western civilization than Epicureanism. Although later thinkers mistakenly perceived Epicureanism as a philosophy that espoused hedonistic pleasure seeking, in fact its founder, the Athenian philosopher Epicurus (341–270 B.C.E.), advocated a prudent pursuit of pleasure in the quest for peace of mind. Attaining that state entailed, among other things, an avoidance of excessive involvement in public affairs—very much in keeping with the escapism that in so many ways characterized the Hellenistic approach to life. The following selection provides the principal doctrines of his teaching.

From *Greek and Roman Philosophy after Aristotle*, by Jason L. Saunders (New York: Free Press, 1994).

1. A blessed and eternal being has no trouble himself and brings no trouble upon any other being; hence he is exempt from movements of anger and partiality, for every such movement implies weakness.

2. Death is nothing to us; for the body, when it has been resolved into its elements, has no feeling, and that which has no feeling is nothing to us.

3. The magnitude of pleasure reaches its limit in the removal of all pain. When pleasure is present, so long as it is uninterrupted, there is no pain either of body or of mind or of both together.

4. Continuous pain does not last long in the flesh; on the contrary, pain, if extreme, is present a very short time, and even that degree of pain which barely outweighs pleasure in the flesh does not last for many days together. Illnesses of long duration even permit of an excess of pleasure over pain in the flesh.

5. It is impossible to live a pleasant life without living wisely and well and justly, and it is impossible to live wisely and well and justly without living pleasantly. Whenever any one of these is lacking, when, for instance, the man is not able to live wisely, though he lives well and justly, it is impossible for him to live a pleasant life.

6. In order to obtain security from other men any means whatsoever of procuring this was a natural good.

7. Some men have sought to become famous and renowned, thinking that thus they would make themselves secure against their fellow-men. If,

then, the life of such persons really was secure, they attained natural good; if, however, it was insecure, they have not attained the end which by nature's own prompting they originally sought.

8. No pleasure is in itself evil, but the things which produce certain pleasures entail annoyances many times greater than the pleasures themselves.

9. If all pleasure had been capable of accumulation, if this had gone on not only by recurrence in time, but all over the frame or, at any rate, over the principal parts of man's nature, there would never have been any difference between one pleasure and another, as in fact there is.

10. If the objects which are productive of pleasures to profligate persons really freed them from fears of the mind,—the fears, I mean, inspired by celestial and atmospheric phenomena, the fear of death, the fear of pain; if, further, they taught them to limit their desires, we should never have any fault to find with such persons, for they would then be filled with pleasures to overflowing on all sides and would be exempt from all pain, whether of body or mind, that is, from all evil.

11. If we had never been molested by alarms at celestial and atmospheric phenomena, nor by the misgiving that death somehow affects us, nor by neglect of the proper limits of pains and desires, we should have had no need to study natural science.

12. It would be impossible to banish fear on matters of the highest importance, if a man did not know the nature of the whole universe, but lived in dread of what the legend tells us. Hence without the study of nature there was no enjoyment of unmixed pleasures.

13. There would be no advantage in providing security against our fellow-men, so long as we were alarmed by occurrences over our heads or beneath the earth or in general by whatever happens in the boundless universe.

14. When tolerable security against our fellow-men is attained, then on a basis of power sufficient to afford support and of material prosperity arises in most genuine form the security of a quiet private life withdrawn from the multitude.

15. Nature's wealth at once has its bounds and is easy to procure; but the wealth of vain fancies recedes to an infinite distance.

16. Fortune but seldom interferes with the wise man; his greatest and highest interests have been, are, and will be, directed by reason throughout the course of his life.

17. The just man enjoys the greatest peace of mind, while the unjust is full of the utmost disquietude.

18. Pleasure in the flesh admits no increase when once the pain of want has been removed; after that it only admits of variation. The limit of pleasure in the mind, however, is reached when we reflect on the things themselves and their congeners which cause the mind the greatest alarms.

19. Unlimited time and limited time afford an equal amount of pleasure, if we measure the limits of that pleasure by reason.

20. The flesh receives as unlimited the limits of pleasure; and to provide it requires unlimited time. But the mind, grasping in thought what the end and limit of the flesh is, and banishing the terrors of futurity, procures a complete and perfect life, and has no longer any need of unlimited time. Nevertheless it does not shun pleasure, and even in the hour of death, when ushered out of existence by circumstances, the mind does not lack enjoyment of the best life.

21. He who understands the limits of life knows how easy it is to procure enough to remove the pain of want and make the whole of life complete and perfect. Hence he has no longer any need of things which are not to be won save by labor and conflict.

22. We must take into account as the end all that really exists and all clear evidence of sense to which we refer our opinions; for otherwise everything will be full of uncertainty and confusion.

23. If you fight against all your sensations, you will have no standard to which to refer, and thus no means of judging even those judgments which you pronounce false.

24. If you reject absolutely any single sensation without stopping to discriminate with respect to that which awaits confirmation between matter of

opinion and that which is already present, whether in sensation or in feelings or in any presentative perception of the mind, you will throw into confusion even the rest of your sensations by your groundless belief and so you will be rejecting the standard of truth altogether. If in your ideas based upon opinion you hastily affirm as true all that awaits confirmation as well as that which does not, you will not escape error, as you will be maintaining complete ambiguity whenever it is a case of judging between right and wrong opinion.

25. If you do not on every separate occasion refer each of your actions to the end prescribed by nature, but instead of this in the act of choice or avoidance swerve aside to some other end, your acts will not be consistent with your theories.

26. All such desires as lead to no pain when they remain ungratified are unnecessary, and the longing is easily got rid of, when the thing desired is difficult to procure or when the desires seem likely to produce harm.

27. Of all the means which are procured by wisdom to ensure happiness throughout the whole of life, by far the most important is the acquisition of friends.

28. The same conviction which inspires confidence that nothing we have to fear is eternal or even of long duration, also enables us to see that even in our limited conditions of life nothing enhances our security so much as friendship.

29. Of our desires some are natural and necessary; others are natural, but not necessary; others, again, are neither natural nor necessary, but are due to illusory opinion.

30. Those natural desires which entail no pain when not gratified, though their objects are vehemently pursued, are also due to illusory opinion; and when they are not got rid of, it is not because of their own nature, but because of the man's illusory opinion.

31. Natural justice is a symbol or expression of expediency, to prevent one man from harming or being harmed by another.

32. Those animals which are incapable of making covenants with one another, to the end that they may neither inflict nor suffer harm, are without either justice or injustice. And those tribes which either could not or would not form mutual covenants to the same end are in like case.

33. There never was an absolute justice, but only an agreement made in reciprocal intercourse in whatever localities now and again from time to time, providing against the infliction or suffering of harm.

34. Injustice is not in itself an evil, but only in its consequence, viz. the terror which is excited by apprehension that those appointed to punish such offences will discover the injustice.

35. It is impossible for the man who secretly violates any article of the social compact to feel confident that he will remain undiscovered, even if he has already escaped ten thousand times; for right on to the end of his life he is never sure he will not be detected.

36. Taken generally, justice is the same for all, to wit, something found expedient in mutual intercourse; but in its application to particular cases of locality or conditions of whatever kind, it varies under different circumstances.

37. Among the things accounted just by conventional law, whatever in the needs of mutual intercourse is attested to be expedient, is thereby stamped as just, whether or not it be the same for all; and in case any law is made and does not prove suitable to the expediencies of mutual intercourse, then this is no longer just. And should the expediency which is expressed by the law vary and only for a time correspond with the prior conception, nevertheless for the time being it was just, so long as we do not trouble ourselves about empty words, but look simply at the facts.

38. Where without any change in circumstances the conventional laws, when judged by their consequences, were seen not to correspond with the notion of justice, such laws were not really just; but wherever the laws have ceased to be expedient in consequence of a change in circumstances, in that case the laws were for the time being just when they were expedient for the mutual intercourse of the citizens, and subsequently ceased to be just when they ceased to be expedient.

39. He who best knew how to meet fear of external foes made into one family all the creatures he could; and those he could not, he at any rate did not treat as aliens; and where he found even this impossible, he avoided all intercourse, and, so far as was expedient, kept them at a distance.

40. Those who were best able to provide themselves with the means of security against their neighbors, being thus in possession of the surest guarantee, passed the most agreeable life in each other's society; and their enjoyment of the fullest intimacy was such that, if one of them died before his time, the survivors did not lament his death as if it called for commiseration.

REVIEW QUESTIONS

1. What is Epicurus' view of the gods' role in the cosmos?
2. What is the role of human senses?
3. Does his view conflict with that of Plato?

LUCRETIUS

FROM *On the Nature of Things*

Among the chief tenets of Epicureanism was the belief in a completely materialistic interpretation of the cosmos. Thus, human beings had nothing to fear from non-existent supernatural powers or from eternal misery after this life. The epitaph of the otherwise obscure philosopher Diogenes of Oenoanda sums up the Epicurean creed with marvelous succinctness: "Nothing to fear in God, nothing to feel in death, good can be attained, evil can be endured." A much more eloquent discourse on the Epicurean view of death and of Epicurean beliefs in general is to be found in On the Nature of Things *by the first-century* B.C.E. *Roman poet Lucretius.*

From *The Way Things Are,* translated by Rolfe Humphries (Bloomington: Indiana University Press, 1968), pp. 596–603.

*   *   *

Death
Is nothing to us, has no relevance
To our condition, seeing that the mind
Is mortal. Just as, long ago, we felt
Not the least touch of trouble when the wars
Were raging all around the shaken earth
And from all sides the Carthaginian hordes
Poured forth to battle, and no man ever knew
Whose subject he would be in life or death,

Which doom, by land or sea, would strike him
    down,
So, when we cease to be, and body and soul,
Which joined to make us one, have gone their
    ways,
Their separate ways, nothing at all can shake
Our feelings, not if earth were mixed with sea
Or sea with sky. Perhaps the mind or spirit,
After its separation from our body,
Has some sensation; what is that to us?
Nothing at all, for what we knew of being,

Essence, identity, oneness, was derived
From body's union with spirit, so, if time,
After our death, should some day reunite
All of our present particles, bring them back
To where they now reside, give us once more
The light of life, this still would have no meaning
For us, with our self-recollection gone.
As we are now, we lack all memory
Of what we were before, suffer no wound
From those old days. Look back on all that
    space
Of time's immensity, consider well
What infinite combinations there have been
In matter's ways and groupings. How easy, then,
For human beings to believe we are
Compounded of the very selfsame motes,
Arranged exactly in the selfsame ways
As once we were, our long-ago, our now
Being identical. And yet we keep
No memory of that once-upon-a-time,
Nor can we call it back; somewhere between
A break occurred, and all our atoms went
Wandering here and there and far away
From our sensations. If there lies ahead
Tough luck for any man, he must be there,
Himself, to feel its evil, but since death
Removes this chance, and by injunction stops
All rioting of woes against our state,
We may be reassured that in our death
We have no cause for fear, we cannot be
Wretched in nonexistence. Death alone
Has immortality, and takes away
Our mortal life. It does not matter a bit
If we once lived before.
                So, seeing a man
Feel sorry for himself, that after death
He'll be a rotting corpse, laid in a tomb,
Succumb to fire, or predatory beasts,
You'll know he's insincere, just making noise,
With rancor in his heart, though he believes,
Or tries to make us think so, that death ends all.

*   *   *

Some older man, a senior citizen,
Were plaintiff, wretcheder than he ought to be,
Lamenting death, would Nature not be right

To cry him down, with even sharper voice,
"Why, you old scoundrel, take those tears of yours
Somewhere away from here, cut out the whining.
You have had everything from life, and now
You find you're going to pieces. You desire,
Always, what isn't there; what is, you scorn,
So life has slipped away from you, incomplete,
Unsatisfactory, and here comes death,
An unexpected summoner, to stand
Beside you, long before you want to leave,
Long, long, before you think you've had enough.
Let it all go, act as becomes your age,
Be a great man, composed; give in; you must."
Such a rebuke from Nature would be right,
For the old order yields before the new,
All things require refashioning from others.
No man goes down to Hell's black pit; we need
Matter for generations yet to come,
Who, in their turn, will follow you, as men
Have died before you and will die hereafter.
So one thing never ceases to arise
Out of another; life's a gift to no man
Only a loan to him. Look back at time—
How meaningless, how unreal!—before our birth.
In this way Nature holds before our eyes
The mirror of our future after death.
Is this so grim, so gloomy? Is it not
A rest more free from care than any sleep?
Now all those things which people say exist
In Hell, are really present in our lives.
The story says that Tantalus, the wretch,
Frozen in terror, fears the massive rock
Balanced in air above him. It's not true.
What happens is that in our lives the fear,
The silly, vain, ridiculous fear of gods,
Causes our panic dread of accident.
No vultures feed on Tityos, who lies
Sprawled out for them in Hell; they could not
    find
In infinite eternities of time
What they are searching for in that great bulk,
Nine acres wide, or ninety, or the spread
Of all the globe. No man can ever bear
Eternal pain, nor can his body give
Food to the birds forever. We do have
A Tityos in ourselves, and lie, in love,

Torn and consumed by our anxieties,
Our fickle passions. Sisyphus, too, is here
In our own lives; we see him as the man
Bent upon power and office, who comes back
Gloomy and beaten after every vote.
To seek for power, such an empty thing,
And never gain it, suffering all the while,
This is to shove uphill the stubborn rock
Which over and over comes bouncing down
    again
To the flat levels where it started from.
Or take another instance: when we feed
A mind whose nature seems unsatisfied,
Never content, with all the blessings given
Through season after season, with all the charms
And graces of life's harvest, this, I'd say,
Is to be like those young and lovely girls,
The Danaids, trying in vain to fill
Their leaky jars with water. Cerberus,
The Furies, and the dark, and the grim jaws
Of Tartarus, belching blasts of heat—all these
Do not exist at all, and never could.
But here on earth we do fear punishment
For wickedness, and in proportion dread
Our dreadful deeds, imagining all too well
Being cast down from the Tarpeian Rock,
Jail, flogging, hangmen, brands, the rack, the
    knout;
And even though these never touch us, still
The guilty mind is its own torturer
With lash and rowel, can see no end at all
To suffering and punishment, and fears
These will be more than doubled after death.
Hell does exist on earth—in the life of fools.

You well might think of saying to yourself:
"Even good Ancus closed his eyes on the light—
A better man than you will ever be,
You reprobate—and many lords and kings
Rulers of mighty nations, all have died.
Even that monarch, who once paved the way
Making the sea a highway for his legions
Where foot and horse alike could march dry-
    shod
While the deep foamed and thundered at the
    outrage,

Even he, great Xerxes, died and left the light,
And Scipio, the thunderbolt of war,
Terror of Carthage, gave his bones to earth
As does the meanest lackey. Add to these
Philosophers and artists, all the throng
Blessed by the Muses; Homer's majesty
Lies low in the same sleep as all the rest.
Democritus, warned by a ripe old age
That, with his memory, his powers of mind
Were also failing, gave himself to death;
And Epicurus perished, that great man
Whose genius towered over all the rest,
Making their starry talents fade and die
In his great sunlight. Who are you, forsooth,
To hesitate, resent, protest your death?
Your life is death already, though you live
And though you see, except that half your time
You waste in sleep, and the other half you snore
With eyes wide open, forever seeing dreams,
Forever in panic, forever lacking wit
To find out what the trouble is, depressed,
Or drunk, or drifting aimlessly around."

Men seem to feel some burden on their souls,
Some heavy weariness; could they but know
Its origin, its cause, they'd never live
The way we see most of them do, each one
Ignorant of what he wants, except a change,
Some other place to lay his burden down.
One leaves his house to take a stroll outdoors
Because the household's such a deadly bore,
And then comes back, in six or seven minutes—
The street is every bit as bad. Now what?
He has his horses hitched up for him, drives,
Like a man going to a fire, full-speed,
Off to his country-place, and when he gets there
Is scarcely on the driveway, when he yawns,
Falls heavily asleep, oblivious
To everything, or promptly turns around,
Whips back to town again. So each man flees
Himself, or tries to, but of course that pest
Clings to him all the more ungraciously.
He hates himself because he does not know
The reason for his sickness; if he did,
He would leave all this foolishness behind,
Devote his study to the way things are,

The problem being his lot, not for an hour,
But for all time, the state in which all men
Must dwell forever and ever after death.
Finally, what's this wanton lust for life
To make us tremble in dangers and in doubt?
All men must die, and no man can escape.
We turn and turn in the same atmosphere
In which no new delight is ever shaped
To grace our living; what we do not have
Seems better than everything else in all the world
But should we get it, we want something else.
Our gaping thirst for life is never quenched.
We have to know what luck next year will bring,
What accident, what end. But life, prolonged,
Subtracts not even one second from the term
Of death's continuance. We lack the strength
To abbreviate that eternity. Suppose
You could contrive to live for centuries,

As many as you will. Death, even so,
Will still be waiting for you; he who died
Early this morning has as many years
Interminably before him, as the man,
His predecessor, has, who perished months
Or years, or even centuries ago.

*   *   *

REVIEW QUESTIONS

1. From an Epicurean standpoint, what is an appropriate attitude toward death?
2. Should death hold any terror for humans?
3. Can you discern from this selection something of the Epicurean view concerning matter and the composition of the cosmos?

EPICTETUS

FROM *The Manual:* Stoicism

The school of philosophy known as Stoicism, founded by Zeno of Citium, undoubtedly has had a more profound impact on the Western intellectual tradition than any other of the Hellenistic schools. In particular, its emphasis on a universal natural order governed by a divine plan greatly influenced the later development of both Roman imperial law and Christian thought. The literary remains of the early development of Stoic philosophy are quite fragmentary. Much better preserved is the systematic presentation of Stoic principles in The Manual of Epictetus *(60 C.E.–?), as set down probably by his student Arrian.*

From *The Manual of Epictetus*, translated by P. E. Matheson (Oxford, Eng.: Clarendon Press).

1. Of all existing things some are in our power, and others are not in our power. In our power are thought, impulse, will to get and will to avoid, and, in a word, everything which is our own doing. Things not in our power include the body, property, reputation, office, and, in a word, every-thing which is not our own doing. Things in our power are by nature free, unhindered, untrammelled; things not in our power are weak, servile, subject to hindrance, dependent on others. Remember then that if you imagine that what is naturally slavish is free, and what is naturally an-

other's is your own, you will be hampered, you will mourn, you will be put to confusion, you will blame gods and men; but if you think that only your own belongs to you, and that what is another's is indeed another's, no one will ever put compulsion or hindrance on you, you will blame none, you will accuse none, you will do nothing against your will, no one will harm you, you will have no enemy, for no harm can touch you.

Aiming then at these high matters, you must remember that to attain them requires more than ordinary effort; you will have to give up some things entirely, and put off others for the moment. And if you would have these also—office and wealth—it may be that you will fail to get them, just because your desire is set on the former, and you will certainly fail to attain those things which alone bring freedom and happiness.

Make it your study then to confront every harsh impression with the words, "You are but an impression, and not at all what you seem to be." Then test it by those rules that you possess; and first by this—the chief test of all—"Is it concerned with what is in our power or with what is not in our power?" And if it is concerned with what is not in our power, be ready with the answer that it is nothing to you.

2. Remember that the will to get promises attainment of what you will, and the will to avoid promises escape from what you avoid; and he who fails to get what he wills is unfortunate, and he who does not escape what he wills to avoid is miserable. If then you try to avoid only what is unnatural in the region within your control, you will escape from all that you avoid; but if you try to avoid disease or death or poverty you will be miserable.

Therefore let your will to avoid have no concern with what is not in man's power; direct it only to things in man's power that are contrary to nature. But for the moment you must utterly remove the will to get; for if you will to get something not in man's power you are bound to be unfortunate; while none of the things in man's power that you could honourably will to get is yet within your reach. Impulse to act and not to act,

these are your concern; yet exercise them gently and without strain, and provisionally.

3. When anything, from the meanest thing upwards, is attractive or serviceable or an object of affection, remember always to say to yourself, "What is its nature?" If you are fond of a jug, say you are fond of a jug; then you will not be disturbed if it be broken. If you kiss your child or your wife, say to yourself that you are kissing a human being, for then if death strikes it you will not be disturbed.

4. When you are about to take something in hand, remind yourself what manner of thing it is. If you are going to bathe put before your mind what happens in the bath—water pouring over some, others being jostled, some reviling, others stealing; and you will set to work more securely if you say to yourself at once: "I want to bathe, and I want to keep my will in harmony with nature," and so in each thing you do; for in this way, if anything turns up to hinder you in your bathing, you will be ready to say, "I did not want only to bathe, but to keep my will in harmony with nature, and I shall not so keep it, if I lose my temper at what happens."

5. What disturbs men's minds is not events but their judgements on events. For instance, death is nothing dreadful, or else Socrates would have thought it so. No, the only dreadful thing about it is men's judgement that it is dreadful. And so when we are hindered, or disturbed, or distressed, let us never lay the blame on others, but on ourselves, that is, on our own judgements. To accuse others for one's own misfortunes is a sign of want of education; to accuse oneself shows that one's education has begun; to accuse neither oneself nor others shows that one's education is complete.

6. Be not elated at an excellence which is not your own. If the horse in his pride were to say, "I am handsome," we could bear with it. But when you say with pride, "I have a handsome horse," know that the good horse is the ground of your pride. You ask then what you can call your own. The answer is—the way you deal with your impressions. Therefore when you deal with your

impressions in accord with nature, then you may be proud indeed, for your pride will be in a good which is your own.

7. When you are on a voyage, and your ship is at anchorage, and you disembark to get fresh water, you may pick up a small shellfish or a truffle by the way, but you must keep your attention fixed on the ship, and keep looking towards it constantly, to see if the Helmsman calls you; and if he does, you have to leave everything, or be bundled on board with your legs tied like a sheep. So it is in life. If you have a dear wife or child given you, they are like the shellfish or the truffle, they are very well in their way. Only, if the Helmsman call, run back to your ship, leave all else, and do not look behind you. And if you are old, never go far from the ship, so that when you are called you may not fail to appear.

8. Ask not that events should happen as you will, but let your will be that events should happen as they do, and you shall have peace.

9. Sickness is a hindrance to the body, but not to the will, unless the will consent. Lameness is a hindrance to the leg, but not to the will. Say this to yourself at each event that happens, for you shall find that though it hinders something else it will not hinder you.

10. When anything happens to you, always remember to turn to yourself and ask what faculty you have to deal with it. If you see a beautiful boy or a beautiful woman, you will find continence the faculty to exercise there; if trouble is laid on you, you will find endurance; if ribaldry, you will find patience. And if you train yourself in this habit your impressions will not carry you away.

11. Never say of anything, "I lost it," but say, "I gave it back." Has your child died? It was given back. Has your wife died? She was given back. Has your estate been taken from you? Was not this also given back? But you say, "He who took it from me is wicked." What does it matter to you through whom the Giver asked it back? As long as He gives it you, take care of it, but not as your own; treat it as passers-by treat an inn.

12. If you wish to make progress, abandon reasonings of this sort: "If I neglect my affairs I shall

have nothing to live on;" "If I do not punish my son, he will be wicked." For it is better to die of hunger, so that you be free from pain and free from fear, than to live in plenty and be troubled in mind. It is better for your son to be wicked than for you to be miserable. Wherefore begin with little things. Is your drop of oil spilt? Is your sup of wine stolen? Say to yourself, "This is the price paid for freedom from passion, this is the price of a quiet mind." Nothing can be had without a price. When you call your slave-boy, reflect that he may not be able to hear you, and if he hears you, he may not be able to do anything you want. But he is not so well off that it rests with him to give you peace of mind.

*   *   *

14. It is silly to want your children and your wife and your friends to live for ever, for that means that you want what is not in your control to be in your control, and what is not your own to be yours. In the same way if you want your servant to make no mistakes, you are a fool, for you want vice not to be vice but something different. But if you want not to be disappointed in your will to get, you can attain to that.

Exercise yourself then in what lies in your power. Each man's master is the man who has authority over what he wishes or does not wish, to secure the one or to take away the other. Let him then who wishes to be free not wish for anything or avoid anything that depends on others; or else he is bound to be a slave.

*   *   *

16. When you see a man shedding tears in sorrow for a child abroad or dead, or for loss of property, beware that you are not carried away by the impression that it is outward ills that make him miserable. Keep this thought by you: "What distresses him is not the event, for that does not distress another, but his judgement on the event." Therefore do not hesitate to sympathize with him so far as words go, and if it so chance, even to groan with him; but take heed that you do not also groan in your inner being.

17. Remember that you are an actor in a play, and the Playwright chooses the manner of it: if he wants it short, it is short; if long, it is long. If he wants you to act a poor man you must act the part with all your powers; and so if your part be a cripple or a magistrate or a plain man. For your business is to act the character that is given you and act it well; the choice of the cast is Another's.

18. When a raven croaks with evil omen, let not the impression carry you away, but straightway distinguish in your own mind and say, "These portents mean nothing to me; but only to my bit of a body or my bit of property or name, or my children or my wife. But for me all omens are favourable if I will, for, whatever the issue may be, it is in my power to get benefit therefrom."

19. You can be invincible, if you never enter on a contest where victory is not in your power. Beware then that when you see a man raised to honour or great power or high repute you do not let your impression carry you away. For if the reality of good lies in what is in our power, there is no room for envy or jealousy. And you will not wish to be praetor, or prefect or consul, but to be free; and there is but one way to freedom—to despise what is not in our power.

20. Remember that foul words or blows in themselves are no outrage, but your judgement that they are so. So when any one makes you angry, know that it is your own thought that has angered you. Wherefore make it your first endeavour not to let your impressions carry you away. For if once you gain time and delay, you will find it easier to control yourself.

21. Keep before your eyes from day to day death and exile and all things that seem terrible, but death most of all, and then you will never set your thoughts on what is low and will never desire anything beyond measure.

*   *   *

26. It is in our power to discover the will of Nature from those matters on which we have no difference of opinion. For instance, when another man's slave has broken the wine-cup we are very ready to say at once, "Such things must happen."

Know then that when your own cup is broken, you ought to behave in the same way as when your neighbour's was broken. Apply the same principle to higher matters. Is another's child or wife dead? Not one of us but would say, "Such is the lot of man;" but when one's own dies, straightway one cries, "Alas! miserable am I." But we ought to remember what our feelings are when we hear it of another.

27. As a mark is not set up for men to miss it, so there is nothing intrinsically evil in the world.

*   *   *

29. . . . Man, consider first what it is you are undertaking; then look at your own powers and see if you can bear it. Do you want to compete in the pentathlon or in wrestling? Look to your arms, your thighs, see what your loins are like. For different men are born for different tasks. Do you suppose that if you do this you can live as you do now—eat and drink as you do now, indulge desire and discontent just as before? Nay, you must sit up late, work hard, abandon your own people, be looked down on by a mere slave, be ridiculed by those who meet you, get the worst of it in everything—in honour, in office, in justice, in every possible thing. This is what you have to consider: whether you are willing to pay this price for peace of mind, freedom, tranquillity. If not, do not come near; do not be, like the children, first a philosopher, then a tax-collector, then an orator, then one of Caesar's procurators. These callings do not agree. You must be one man, good or bad; you must develop either your Governing Principle, or your outward endowments; you must study either your inner man, or outward things—in a word, you must choose between the position of a philosopher and that of a mere outsider.

*   *   *

31. For piety towards the gods know that the most important thing is this: to have right opinions about them—that they exist, and that they govern the universe well and justly—and to have set yourself to obey them, and to give way to all that happens, following events with a free will, in the belief

that they are fulfilled by the highest mind. For thus you will never blame the gods, nor accuse them of neglecting you. But this you cannot achieve, unless you apply your conception of good and evil to those things only which are in our power, and not to those which are out of our power. For if you apply your notion of good or evil to the latter, then, as soon as you fail to get what you will to get or fail to avoid what you will to avoid, you will be bound to blame and hate those you hold responsible. For every living creature has a natural tendency to avoid and shun what seems harmful and all that causes it, and to pursue and admire what is helpful and all that causes it. It is not possible then for one who thinks he is harmed to take pleasure in what he thinks is the author of the harm, any more than to take pleasure in the harm itself. That is why a father is reviled by his son, when he does not give his son a share of what the son regards as good things; thus Polynices and Eteocles were set at enmity with one another by thinking that a king's throne was a good thing. That is why the farmer, and the sailor, and the merchant, and those who lose wife or children revile the gods. For men's religion is bound up with their interest. Therefore he who makes it his concern rightly to direct his will to get and his will to avoid, is thereby making piety his concern. But it is proper on each occasion to make libation and sacrifice and to offer first-fruits according to the custom of our fathers, with purity and not in slovenly or careless fashion, without meanness and without extravagance.

*   *   *

32. * * * Lay down for yourself from the first a definite stamp and style of conduct, which you will maintain when you are alone and also in the society of men. Be silent for the most part, or, if you speak, say only what is necessary and in a few words. Talk, but rarely, if occasion calls you, but do not talk of ordinary things—of gladiators, or horse-races, or athletes, or of meats or drinks— these are topics that arise everywhere—but above all do not talk about men in blame or compliment or comparison. If you can, turn the conversation of your company by your talk to some fitting sub-

ject; but if you should chance to be isolated among strangers, be silent. Do not laugh much, nor at many things, nor without restraint.

Refuse to take oaths, altogether if that be possible, but if not, as far as circumstances allow.

Refuse the entertainments of strangers and the vulgar. But if occasions arise to accept them, then strain every nerve to avoid lapsing into the state of the vulgar. For know that, if your comrade has a stain on him, he that associates with him must needs share the stain, even though he be clean in himself.

For your body take just so much as your bare need requires, such as food, drink, clothing, house, servants, but cut down all that tends to luxury and outward show.

Avoid impurity to the utmost of your power before marriage, and if you indulge your passion, let it be done lawfully. But do not be offensive or censorious to those who indulge it, and do not be always bringing up your own chastity. If some one tells you that so and so speaks ill of you, do not defend yourself against what he says, but answer, "He did not know my other faults, or he would not have mentioned these alone."

It is not necessary for the most part to go to the games; but if you should have occasion to go, show that your first concern is for yourself; that is, wish that only to happen which does happen, and him only to win who does win, for so you will suffer no hindrance. But refrain entirely from applause, or ridicule, or prolonged excitement. And when you go away do not talk much of what happened there, except so far as it tends to your improvement. For to talk about it implies that the spectacle excited your wonder.

Do not go lightly or casually to hear lectures; but if you do go, maintain your gravity and dignity and do not make yourself offensive. When you are going to meet any one, and particularly some man of reputed eminence, set before your mind the thought, "What would Socrates or Zeno have done?" and you will not fail to make proper use of the occasion.

When you go to visit some great man, prepare your mind by thinking that you will not find him in, that you will be shut out, that the doors will be slammed in your face, that he will pay no heed to you. And if in spite of all this you find it fitting for you to go, go and bear what happens and never say to yourself, "It was not worth all this"; for that shows a vulgar mind and one at odds with outward things.

In your conversation avoid frequent and disproportionate mention of your own doings or adventures; for other people do not take the same pleasure in hearing what has happened to you as you take in recounting your adventures.

Avoid raising men's laughter; for it is a habit that easily slips into vulgarity, and it may well suffice to lessen your neighbour's respect.

It is dangerous too to lapse into foul language; when anything of the kind occurs, rebuke the offender, if the occasion allow, and if not, make it plain to him by your silence, or a blush or a frown, that you are angry at his words.

34. When you imagine some pleasure, beware that it does not carry you away, like other imaginations. Wait a while, and give yourself pause. Next remember two things: how long you will enjoy the pleasure, and also how long you will afterwards repent and revile yourself. And set on the other side the joy and self-satisfaction you will feel if you refrain. And if the moment seems come to realize it, take heed that you be not overcome by the winning sweetness and attraction of it; set in the other scale the thought how much better is the consciousness of having vanquished it.

35. When you do a thing because you have determined that it ought to be done, never avoid being seen doing it, even if the opinion of the multitude is going to condemn you. For if your action is wrong, then avoid doing it altogether, but if it is right, why do you fear those who will rebuke you wrongly?

*   *   *

37. If you try to act a part beyond your powers, you not only disgrace yourself in it, but you neglect the part which you could have filled with success.

38. As in walking you take care not to tread on a nail or to twist your foot, so take care that you do not harm your Governing Principle. And if we guard this in everything we do, we shall set to work more securely.

39. Every man's body is a measure for his property, as the foot is the measure for his shoe. If you stick to this limit, you will keep the right measure; if you go beyond it, you are bound to be carried away down a precipice in the end; just as with the shoe, if you once go beyond the foot, your shoe puts on gilding, and soon purple and embroidery. For when once you go beyond the measure there is no limit.

40. Women from fourteen years upwards are called "madam" by men. Wherefore, when they see that the only advantage they have got is to be marriageable, they begin to make themselves smart and to set all their hopes on this. We must take pains then to make them understand that they are really honoured for nothing but a modest and decorous life.

41. It is a sign of a dull mind to dwell upon the cares of the body, to prolong exercise, eating, drinking, and other bodily functions. These things are to be done by the way; all your attention must be given to the mind.

42. When a man speaks evil or does evil to you, remember that he does or says it because he thinks it is fitting for him. It is not possible for him to follow what seems good to you, but only what seems good to him, so that, if his opinion is wrong, he suffers, in that he is the victim of deception. In the same way, if a composite judgement which is true is thought to be false, it is not the judgement that suffers, but the man who is deluded about it. If you act on this principle you will be gentle to him who reviles you, saying to yourself on each occasion, "He thought it right."

*   *   *

44. It is illogical to reason thus, "I am richer than you, therefore I am superior to you," "I am more eloquent than you, therefore I am superior to you." It is more logical to reason, "I am richer than you, therefore my property is superior to yours," "I am more eloquent than you, therefore my speech is superior to yours." You are something more than property or speech.

* * *

46. On no occasion call yourself a philosopher, nor talk at large of your principles among the multitude, but act on your principles. For instance, at a banquet do not say how one ought to eat, but eat as you ought. Remember that Socrates had so completely got rid of the thought of display that when men came and wanted an introduction to philosophers he took them to be introduced; so patient of neglect was he. And if a discussion arise among the multitude on some principle, keep silent for the most part; for you are in great danger of blurting out some undigested thought. And when someone says to you, 'You know nothing,' and you do not let it provoke you, then know that you are really on the right road. For sheep do not bring grass to their shepherds and show them how much they have eaten, but they digest their fodder and then produce it in the form of wool and milk. Do the same yourself; instead of displaying your principles to the multitude, show them the results of the principles you have digested.

* * *

The signs of one who is making progress are: he blames none, praises none, complains of none, accuses none, never speaks of himself as if he were somebody, or as if he knew anything. And if any one compliments him he laughs in himself at his compliment; and if one blames him, he makes no defence. He goes about like a convalescent, careful not to disturb his constitution on its road to recovery, until it has got firm hold. He has got rid of the will to get, and his will to avoid is directed no longer to what is beyond our power but only to what is in our power and contrary to nature. In all things he exercises his will without strain. If men regard him as foolish or ignorant he pays no heed. In one word, he keeps watch and guard on himself as his own enemy, lying in wait for him.

* * *

REVIEW QUESTIONS

1. As presented in this work, according to what principles is the practitioner of Stoicism to live his life?
2. Why do things happen as they do, and what should the proper Stoic's attitude be?
3. How do the principles of Stoicism contrast with those of Epicureanism?

HELLENISTIC AUTHORS

Short Poems

Many short poems by various, often obscure (for us, at least) authors survive from the Hellenistic era. As the selections provided below reveal, the concerns that they reflect are not limited to the human beings of 2000 years ago.

Asclepiades of Samos

Although she's a girl, Dorkion
Is wise to the ways of the boys.
Like a chubby kid, she knows how
To throw over her shoulder, from
Under her broadbrimmed hat, the quick
Glance of Public Love, and let her
Cape show a glimpse of her bare butt.

Didyme waved her wand at me.
I am utterly enchanted.
The sight of her beauty makes me
Melt like wax before the fire. What
Is the difference if she is black?
So is coal, but alight, it shines like roses.

Leonidas of Tarentum

These were my end: a fierce down-squall from
   the east,
And night, and the waves of Oriôn's stormy setting:
And I, Kallaischros, yielded my life
Far on the waste of the lonely Libyan sea.

And now I roll with drifting currents, the prey
Of fishes:
           and this gravestone lies
If it says that it marks the place of my burial.

Anonymous

Boy, hold my wreath for me.
The night is black,
             the path is long,
And I am completely and beautifully drunk.

Nevertheless I will go
To Themison's house and sing beneath his window.
You need not come with me:
               though I may
  stumble,
He is a steady lamp for the feet of love.

Philodemos

  In the middle of the night
  I stole from my husband's bed
  And came to you, soaked with rain.
  And now, are we going to
  Sit around, and not get down
  To business, and not bill and coo,
  And love like lovers ought to love?

Here it's rose-time again, chick-peas in season,
cabbages, Sosylus, first heads of the year,
fillets of smelt, fresh-salted cheese,
tender and furled up lettuce leaves . . .
but we don't go way out to the point, Sosylus,
or picnic, as we used to, on the overlook.
Antigenes and Bacchios had the old party spirit,
but today we dump them in their graves.

Anonymous

At sixty I, Dionysios of Tarsos, lie here,
Never having married:
             and I wish my father had
  not.

Marcus Argentarius

1

Welcome, old friend, long-necked bottle,
Dearest companion of my table
And of the winejar, with your soft gurgle
And your sweetly chuckling mouth: welcome;
You secret witness of my poverty

Asclepiades of Samos, from *Poems from the Greek Anthology,* translated by Kenneth Rexroth (Ann Arbor: The University of Michigan Press, 1962).

Leonidas of Tarentum, Anonymous, Philodemos, and *Anonymous,* from *Poems from the Greek Anthology,* translated by Dudley Fitts (New York: New Directions, 1938).

Anonymous from *Poems from the Greek Anthology,* translated and edited by Peter Jay (London: Allen Lane, 1973).

Marcus Argentarius (1), translated by Fleur Adcock, from *The Greek Anthology and Other Ancient Greek Epigrams,* edited by Peter Jay (London: Allen Lane, 1973), (2) and (3) from *Poems from the Greek Anthology,* translated by Dudley Fitts (New York: New Directions, 1938).

(Which you've done little enough to aid)
At last I hold you in my hand again.
But I wish you had come to me undiluted,
Pure as a virgin to her bridegroom's bed.

2

Lately thumbing the pages of Works and Days,
I saw my Pyrrhé coming.
                              Goodbye book!
"Why in the world should I cobweb my days," I
    cried,
"With the works of Old Man Hesiod?"

3

It was this way:

I'd been going for weeks with this girl,
Alkippê her name was; well, so
One night I manage to get her up to my room.
That's all right,
Though our hearts are cloppety-clopping like
    mad
For fear we'll be caught together.
                              Well,
Everything's fine, you know what I mean, when
All of a sudden the door pops
And in pokes her old mother's sheep-head:
"Remember, daughter," she bleats, "you and I
    go halves!"

Dioskorides

Hiero's former Nurse
Silenis, who liked wine
Straight & plentiful
Rests in these vine-fields,
May her old body
Buried amid vines
Feed in death the vats
She loved in life.

Dioskorides and *Meleager*, translated by Peter Whigham,
from *The Greek Anthology and Other Ancient Greek Epigrams*, edited by Peter Jay (London: Allen Lane, 1973).

Meleager

Whose the hand unloosed Clearista's zone
at bride-night, in her bride-room?
Death, in guise of the bridegroom.

Evening, & flutes & clapping hands
clamour at bridal door.
At dawn the funeral wail. No more
the Hymen song. The very lights
    that lit the bridal bed
light now Clearista's journey to the dead.

Glaukos

Time was when once upon a time, such toys
As balls or pet birds won a boy, or dice.
Now it's best china, or cash. Lovers of boys,
Try something else next time. Toys cut no ice.

Krinagoras

Back from the west, back from the war, Marcellus,
carrying his loot, at the rocky frontier post
first shaved his tawny beard—as the fatherland
had wished: it sent a boy, got back a man.

Lucilius

Doubly unfortunate are those who dwell in
    Hell—
    Eutychides the Lyric Poet,
out of breath at last, has had burned with him
    twelve lyres and twenty-five
albums of songs, which poor Charon will have to
    ferry over the charcoal waters.

Glaukos, translated by Peter Jay, from *The Greek Anthology and Other Ancient Greek Epigrams,* edited by Peter
Jay (London: Allen Lane, 1973).

Krinagoras, translated by Alistair Elliot, from *The Greek
Anthology and Other Ancient Greek Epigrams,* edited by
Peter Jay (London: Allen Lane, 1973).

Lucilius and *Nikarchos,* translated by Peter Porter, from
The Greek Anthology and Other Ancient Greek Epigrams,
edited by Peter Jay (London: Allen Lane, 1973).

Alas, where will music-lovers take refuge now
  Eutychides will be singing for eternity?

Nikarchos

Agelaus was kind to Acestorides,
  who, if he'd lived, would have been lame.
Agelaus decided to operate.

REVIEW QUESTION

1. To what extent do the themes of these brief poems echo the concerns expressed in the writings of Epicurean and Stoic philosophers?

Nikarchos from *Poems from the Greek Anthology,* translated by Peter Porter, edited by Peter Jay (London: Allen Lane, 1973).

5 ✑ ROMAN CIVILIZATION

During the same period that the Greeks and Persians were doing battle at Marathon and Thermopylae and Alexander was launching his invasion of the Near East, a new power that in time was to supersede them both had begun gradually to emerge in the west. The rise of Rome is one of the most compelling stories of Western civilization: an insignificant settlement, confronted by dangerous enemies and often wracked by internal turmoil, succeeds not only in surviving but also in becoming first the master of Italy, then of the Mediterranean. In only a few centuries, Rome fashioned an empire that extended from Spain to Mesopotamia.

During the march to empire, of course, the Romans sustained casualties. Among them were their early system of government, a republic, and a society that was regulated by a strict code of law and by a tradition that emphasized respect for paternal authority and duty to family, state, and gods. In time, however, the republican system that had brought Rome to greatness was ripped apart by the demands of overseas dominion, to be replaced by rival, power-hungry generals and, eventually, by an emperor whose status, in time, went from that of princeps *("first citizen") to* dominus et deus *("lord and god"). As Roman government was inexorably changed, so Roman society and values were transformed by the massive infusion of luxury brought by imperial possessions and the influence of Greek culture and philosophical ideas on venerable Roman traditions and behavior. Indeed, of the many parallels that have been drawn between the rise of Rome and the rise of the United States to global domination two millennia later, none has been more jarring, and perhaps more potentially instructive, than the perception of decline brought by the transformation of traditional values in the wake of involvement with the outside world. For both Rome and the United States, one can discern changes brought by the influence of foreign cultures and ideas as their respective dominions expanded; in both cases, the challenge of such changes brought a response, in the form of attempts to reassert the primacy of traditional values and attitudes. This process is no-where more evident in the Roman world than in the introduction and rapid spread of Christianity and the official Roman response to it. For both Roman and U.S. societies, the balance sheet of benefits and liabilities will surely be discussed for years to come.*

Whatever the conclusions historians and others may reach in such matters, it remains indisputable that the Pax Romana *("Roman peace") over which the Roman emperors presided gave Western civilization the longest period of continuous peace and stability that it had ever seen or has seen since. In the names of our months and the nine planets of our solar system, in the names of some of our important governmental institutions (senate, consulate, diocese), in the architectural style and grandeur of some of our most important public buildings, we find constant reminders that, even with its slavery, gladiatorial games, and vomitoria, the age of imperial Rome remains the great golden age of Western civilization.*

FROM The Twelve Tables

Issued by a commission of Roman magistrates in 449 B.C.E., this codification of early Roman law was originally inscribed on twelve bronze plaques that were set up in the Forum in Rome. Our single most important source on the society and economy of early Rome, the Twelve Tables reflect, in relatively unvarnished fashion, the values that dominated life during the early years of the Roman Republic. (To borrow a modern expression, there was not much "kidding around.")

From *Roman Civilization: Selected Readings*, vol. 2, edited by Naphtali Lewis and Meyer Reinhold (New York: Columbia University Press, 1953), pp. 54–67.

Table I
Preliminaries to and Rules for a Trial

If plaintiff summons defendant to court, he shall go. If he does not go, plaintiff shall call witness thereto. Then only shall he take defendant by force.

If defendant shirks or takes to his heels, plaintiff shall lay hands on him.

If disease or age is an impediment, he [who summons defendant to court] shall grant him a team; he shall not spread with cushions the covered carriage if he does not so desire.

For a landowner, a landowner shall be surety; but for a proletarian person, let any one who is willing be his protector. . . .

When parties make a settlement of the case, the judge shall announce it. If they do not reach a settlement, they shall state the outline of their case in the meeting place or Forum before noon.

They shall plead it out together in person. After noon, the judge shall adjudge the case to the party present. If both be present, sunset shall be the time limit [of proceedings].

Table II
Further Enactments on Trials

Action under solemn deposit: 500 *as* pieces is the sum when the object of dispute under solemn deposit is valued at 1,000 in bronze or more, fifty pieces when less. Where the controversy concerns the liberty of a human being, fifty pieces shall be the solemn deposit under which the dispute should be undertaken.

If any of these be impediment for judge, referee, or party, on that account the day of trial shall be broken off.

Whoever is in need of evidence, he shall go on every third day to call out loudly before witness' doorway.

Table III
Execution; Law of Debt

When a debt has been acknowledged, or judgment about the matter has been pronounced in court, thirty days must be the legitimate time of grace. After that, the debtor may be arrested by laying on of hands. Bring him into court. If he does not satisfy the judgment, or no one in court offers himself as surety in his behalf, the creditor may take the defaulter with him. He may bind him either in stocks or in fetters; he may bind him with a weight no more than fifteen pounds, or with less if he shall so desire. The debtor, if he wishes, may live on his own. If he does not live on his own, the person who shall hold him in bonds shall give him one pound of grits for each day. He may give more if he so desires.

Unless they make a settlement, debtors shall be held in bonds for sixty days. During that time they shall be brought before the praetor's court in the meeting place on three successive market days,

and the amount for which they are judged liable shall be announced; on the third market day they shall suffer capital punishment or be delivered up for sale abroad, across the Tiber.

On the third market day creditors shall cut pieces. Should they have cut more or less than their due, it shall be with impunity.

Against a stranger, title of ownership shall hold good forever.

Table IV
Patria Potestas: Rights of Head of Family

Quickly kill . . . a dreadfully deformed child.

If a father thrice surrender a son for sale, the son shall be free from the father.

A child born ten months after the father's death will not be admitted into a legal inheritance.

Table V
Guardianship; Succession

Females shall remain in guardianship even when they have attained their majority . . . except Vestal Virgins.

Conveyable possessions of a woman under guardianship of agnates cannot be rightfully acquired by *usucapio*, save such possessions as have been delivered up by her with a guardian's sanction.

According as a person shall will regarding his [household], chattels, or guardianship of his estate, this shall be binding.

If a person dies intestate, and has no self-successor, the nearest agnate kinsman shall have possession of deceased's household.

If there is no agnate kinsman, deceased's clansmen shall have possession of his household.

To persons for whom a guardian has not been appointed by will, to them agnates are guardians.

If a man is raving mad, rightful authority over his person and chattels shall belong to his agnates or to his clansmen.

A spendthrift is forbidden to exercise administration over his own goods. . . . A person who, being insane or a spendthrift, is prohibited from administering his own goods shall be under trusteeship of agnates.

The inheritance of a Roman citizen-freedman shall be made over to his patron if the freedman has died intestate and without self-successor.

Items which are in the category of debts are not included in the division when they have with automatic right been divided into portions of an inheritance.

Debt bequeathed by inheritance is divided proportionally amongst each heir with automatic liability when the details have been investigated.

Table VI
Acquisition and Possession

When a party shall make bond or conveyance, the terms of the verbal declaration are to be held binding. * * *

A person who has been ordained a free man [in a will, on condition] that he bestow a sum of 10,000 pieces on the heir, though he has been sold by the heir, shall win his freedom by giving the money to the purchaser.

It is sufficient to make good such faults as have been named by word of mouth, and that for any flaws which the vendor had expressly denied, he shall undergo penalty of double damage.]* * *

Any woman who does not wish to be subjected in this manner to the hand of her husband should be absent three nights in succession every year, * * *

A person shall not dislodge from a framework a [stolen] beam which has been fixed in buildings or a vineyard. . . . Action [is granted] for double damages against a person found guilty of fixing such [stolen] beam.

Table VII
Rights Concerning Land

Ownership within a five-foot strip [between two pieces of land] shall not be acquired by long usage.

The width of a road [extends] to eight feet where it runs straight ahead, sixteen round a bend. . . .

Persons shall mend roadways. If they do not keep them laid with stone, a person may drive his beasts where he wishes.

If rainwater does damage . . . this must be restrained according to an arbitrator's order.

If a water course directed through a public place shall do damage to a private person, he shall have right of suit to the effect that damage shall be repaired for the owner.

Branches of a tree may be lopped off all round to a height of more than 15 feet. . . . Should a tree on a neighbor's farm be bent crooked by a wind and lean over your farm, action may be taken for removal of that tree.

It is permitted to gather up fruit falling down on another man's farm.

Table VIII
Torts or Delicts

If any person has sung or composed against another person a song such as was causing slander or insult to another, he shall be clubbed to death.

If a person has maimed another's limb, let there be retaliation in kind unless he makes agreement for settlement with him.

If he has broken or bruised a freeman's bone with his hand or a club, he shall undergo penalty of 300 *as* pieces; if a slave's, 150.

If he has done simple harm [to another], penalties shall be 25 *as* pieces.

If a four-footed animal shall be said to have caused loss, legal action . . . shall be either the surrender of the thing which damaged, or else the offer of assessment for the damage.

For pasturing on, or cutting secretly by night, another's crops acquired by tillage, there shall be capital punishment in the case of an adult malefactor . . . he shall be hanged and put to death as a sacrifice to Ceres. In the case of a person under the age of puberty, at the discretion of the praetor either he shall be scourged or settlement shall be made for the harm done by paying double damages.

Any person who destroys by burning any building or heap of corn deposited alongside a house shall be bound, scourged, and put to death by burning at the stake, provided that he has committed the said misdeed with malice aforethought; but if he shall have committed it by accident, that is, by negligence, it is ordained that he repair the damage, or, if he be too poor to be competent for such punishment, he shall receive a lighter chastisement.

Any person who has cut down another person's trees with harmful intent shall pay 25 *as* pieces for every tree.

If theft has been done by night, if the owner kill the thief, the thief shall be held lawfully killed.

It is forbidden that a thief be killed by day . . . unless he defend himself with a weapon; even though he has come with a weapon, unless he use his weapon and fight back, you shall not kill him. And even if he resists, first call out.

In the case of all other thieves caught in the act, if they are freemen, they should be flogged and adjudged to the person against whom the theft has been committed, provided that the malefactors have committed it by day and have not defended themselves with a weapon; slaves caught in the act of theft should be flogged and thrown from the Rock; boys under the age of puberty should, at the praetor's discretion, be flogged, and the damage done by them should be repaired.

If a person pleads on a case in theft in which the thief has not been caught in the act, the thief must compound for the loss by paying double damages. ✶ ✶ ✶

No person shall practice usury at a rate more than one twelfth . . . A usurer is condemned for quadruple amount. ✶ ✶ ✶

If a patron shall have defrauded his client, he must be solemnly forfeited.

Whosoever shall have allowed himself to be called as witness or shall have been scales-balancer, if he does not as witness pronounce his testimony, he must be deemed dishonored and incapable of acting as witness.

Penalty . . . for false witness . . . a person who has been found guilty of giving false witness shall be hurled down from the Tarpeian Rock. . . .

No person shall hold meetings by night in the city.

Members [of associations] . . . are granted . . . the right to pass any binding rule they like for themselves provided that they cause no violation of public law.

Table IX
Public Law

✶   ✶   ✶

The penalty shall be capital punishment for a judge or arbiter legally appointed who has been found guilty of receiving a bribe for giving a decision.

He who shall have roused up a public enemy, or handed over a citizen to a public enemy, must suffer capital punishment.

Putting to death . . . of any man who has not been convicted, whosoever he might be, is forbidden.

Table X
Sacred Law

A dead man shall not be buried or burned within the city.

One must not do more than this [at funerals]; one must not smooth the pyre with an axe. ✶ ✶ ✶

Women must not tear cheeks or hold chorus of "Alas!" on account of funeral.

When a man is dead one must not gather his bones in order to make a second funeral. An exception [in the case of] death in war or in a foreign land. . . .

Anointing by slaves is abolished, and every kind of drinking bout.

Let there be no costly sprinkling . . . no long garlands . . . no incense boxes. . . .

When a man wins a crown himself or through a chattel or by dint of valor, the crown bestowed on him . . . [may be laid in the grave] with impunity [on the man who won it] or on his father.

To make more than one funeral for one man and to make and spread more than one bier for him . . . this should not occur . . . and a person must not add gold. . . .

But him whose teeth shall have been fastened together with gold, if a person shall bury or burn him along with that gold, it shall be with impunity.

No new pyre or personal burning-mound must be erected nearer than sixty feet to another person's buildings without consent of the owner]

*   *   *

Table XI
Supplementary Laws

Intermarriage shall not take place between plebeians and patricians.

*   *   *

REVIEW QUESTIONS

1. What can you deduce from this selection about early Roman justice?
2. What are the roles and the rights of the family in early Roman law?
3. How important was corporal punishment in Roman law?

PLUTARCH

FROM *Lives*

By the early second century B.C.E., *Rome's conquests outside Italy, along with its increased exposure to Greek culture, began to have a significant impact on Rome's traditional values. In particular, there began to emerge leaders whose individualistic behavior challenged ancient traditions that subjugated the interests of the individual to those of family and state. Plutarch's biography of Cato the Elder (234–149* B.C.E.*), however, presents the life of a Roman leader steeped in traditional values and opposed to the inroads that Greek culture was making into Roman society.*

From *Lives*, by Plutarch, translated by Bernadotte Perrin, vol. 2 (Cambridge, Mass.: Harvard University Press, 1914).

*   *   *

FROM Marcus Cato the Elder

The family of Marcus Cato, it is said, was of Tusculan origin, though he lived, previous to his career as soldier and statesman, on an inherited estate in the country of the Sabines. His ancestors commonly passed for men of no note whatever, but Cato himself extols his father, Marcus, as a brave man and good soldier. He also says that his grandfather, Cato, often won prizes for soldierly valour, and received from the state treasury, because of his bravery, the price of five horses which had been killed under him in battle. The Romans used to call men who had no family distinction, but were coming into public notice through their own achievements, "new men," and such they called Cato. But he himself used to say that as far as office and distinction went, he was indeed new, but having regard to ancestral deeds of valour, he was oldest of the old. His third name was not Cato at first, but Priscus. Afterwards he got the surname of Cato for his great abilities. The Romans call a man who is wise and prudent, *catus*.

*   *   *

His physical body—since he laboured from the very first with his own hands, held to a temperate way of life, and performed military duties —was very serviceable, vigorous, and healthy. His eloquence—a second body, as it were, and an instrument with which to perform not only necessary, but also high and noble services—he developed and perfected in the villages and towns about Rome. There he served as advocate for all who needed him, and got the reputation of being, first a zealous pleader, and then a capable orator. Thenceforth the weight and dignity of his character revealed themselves more and more to those who had dealings with him; they saw that he was bound to be a man of great affairs, and have a leading place in the state. For he not only gave his services in legal contests without fee of any sort, but did not appear to cherish even the reputation won in such contests. For he was more desirous of high reputation in battles and campaigns against the enemy, and while he was yet a mere youth had his breast covered with honourable wounds. He says himself that he made his first campaign when he was seventeen years old, at the time when Hannibal was consuming Italy with the flames of his successes.

In battle, he showed himself effective in hand combat, sure and steadfast of foot, and with a fierce expression. With threatening speech and harsh cries he would advance upon the foe, for he rightly thought, and tried to show others, that often-times such action terrifies the enemy more than does the sword. On the march, he carried his own armour on foot, while a single servant followed in charge of his camp provisions. With this man, it is said, he was never angry, and never scolded him when he served up a meal; he actually assisted in most of such preparations, provided he was free from his military duties. Water was what he drank on his campaigns, except that once in a while, in a raging thirst, he would call for vinegar, or, when his strength was failing, would add a little wine.

Near his fields was the cottage which had once belonged to Manius Curius, a hero of three triumphs. To this he would often go, and the sight of the small farm and the simple dwelling led him to think of their former owner, who, though he had become the greatest of the Romans, had subdued the most warlike nations, and driven Pyrrhus out of Italy. Nevertheless, he tilled this little patch of ground with his own hands and occupied this cottage, after three triumphs. Here it was that the ambassadors of the Samnites once found him seated at his hearth cooking turnips, and offered him much gold; but he dismissed them, saying that a man whom such a meal satisfied had no need of gold, and for his part he thought that a more honourable thing than the possession of gold was the conquest of its possessors. Cato would go away with his mind full of these things, and on viewing again his own house and lands and servants and way of life, would increase the labours of his hands and reduce his extravagances.

*   *   *

The influence which Cato's oratory won for him increased, and men called him a Roman Demosthenes; but his manner of life was even more talked about and carried abroad. For his oratorical ability set before young men not only a goal which many already were striving eagerly to attain, but a man who worked with his own hands, as his fathers did, and was contented with a cold breakfast, a frugal dinner, simple clothing, and a humble dwelling—one who thought more of rejecting the extras of life than of possessing them. The Roman commonwealth had now grown too large to keep its earlier integrity. The conquest of many kingdoms and peoples had brought a large mixture of customs, and the adoption of ways of life of every sort. It was natural, therefore, that men should admire Cato, when they saw that, whereas other men were broken down by labors and weakened by pleasures, he was victor over both. And this too, not only while he was still young and ambitious, but even in his old age, after consulship and triumph. Then, like some victorious athlete, he persisted in the regimen of his training, and kept his mind unaltered to the last.

He tells us that he never wore expensive clothing; that he drank the same wine as his slaves; that as for fish and meats, he would buy enough for his dinner from the public stalls—and even this for Rome's sake, that he might strengthen his body for military service. He once inherited an embroidered Babylonian robe, but sold it at once; not a single one of his farm-houses had plastered walls; he never paid much for a slave, since he did not want them to be delicately beautiful, but sturdy workers, such as grooms and herdsmen. And these he thought it his duty to sell when they got old, instead of feeding them when they were useless; and that in general, he thought nothing cheap that one could do without. He said also that he bought lands where crops were raised and cattle herded, not those where lawns were sprinkled and paths swept for pleasure.

These things were thought by some to be the result of the man's stinginess; but others excused them in the belief that he lived in this way only to correct and moderate the extravagance of others. However, for my part, I regard his treatment of his slaves like beasts of burden, using them to the utmost, and then, when they were old, driving them off and selling them, as the mark of a very mean nature, which recognizes no tie between man and man but that of profit. . . . A kindly man will take good care even of his horses when they are worn out with age, and of his dogs, too, not only in their puppyhood, but when their old age needs nursing. . . .

We should not treat living creatures like shoes or pots and pans, casting them aside when they are bruised and worn out with service; but, if for no other reason, than for the sake of practice in kindness to our fellow men, we should accustom ourselves to mildness and gentleness in our dealings with other creatures. I certainly would not sell even an ox that had worked for me, just because he was old, much less an elderly man, removing him from his habitual place and customary life, as it were from his native land, for a paltry price, useless as he is to those who sell him and as he will be to those who buy him. But Cato, boasting of such things, says that he left in Spain even the horse which had carried him through his military campaign, that he might not tax the city with the cost of its transportation home. Whether these things should be set down to greatness of spirit or littleness of mind, is an open question.

But in other matters, his self-restraint was beyond measure admirable. For instance, when he was in command of an army, he took for himself and his staff not more than three bushels of wheat a month, and for his beasts of burden, less than a bushel and a half of barley a day. He received Sardinia to govern as his province; and whereas his predecessors used to charge the public treasury for their tents, couches, and clothing, . . . his simple economy stood out in an incredible contrast. He made no demands whatever upon the public treasury, and made his circuit of the cities on foot, followed by a single public officer, who carried his robe and cup for libations to the gods. And yet, though in such matters he showed himself mild and lenient to those under his authority, in other ways he displayed a dignity and severity proper to the administration of justice. He carried out the edicts of the government in a direct and masterful way so that the Roman power never inspired its subjects with greater fear or affection.

*   *   *

He dealt with the Athenians through an interpreter. He could have spoken to them directly, but he always clung to his native ways, and mocked at those who were lost in admiration of anything that was Greek.

*   *   *

Ten years after his consulship, Cato was a candidate for the censorship. This office towered, as it were, above every other civic honour, and was, in a way, the high point of a political career. The variety of its powers was great, including that of examining into the lives and manners of the citizens. Its creators thought that no one should be left to his own ways and desires, without inspection and review, either in his marrying, having children, ordering his daily life, or in the entertainment of his friends. Thinking that these things revealed a man's real character more than did his public and political career, they set men in office to watch, warn, and chastise, that no one should turn to vices and give up his native and customary way of life. They chose to this office one of the so-called patricians, and one of the plebeians. These officers were called censors, and they had authority to degrade a knight, or to expel a senator who led a wild and disorderly life. They also revised the assessments of property, and arranged the citizens in lists [for military service] according to their social and political classes. There were other great powers also connected with the office.

Therefore, when Cato became a candidate, nearly all the best known and most influential men of the senatorial party united to oppose him. The men of noble parentage among them were moved by jealousy, thinking that nobility of birth would be trampled if men of lowly origin forced their way up to the summits of honour and power; while those who were conscious of base practices and of a departure from ancestral customs, feared the severity of the man, which was sure to be harsh and unyielding in the exercise of power. Therefore, after due consultation and preparation, they put up in opposition to Cato seven candidates for the office, who sought the favour of the people with promises of mild conduct in office, supposing that they wanted to be ruled with a lax and indulgent hand. Cato, on the contrary, showed no inclination to be agreeable whatever, but plainly threatened wrong-doers in his speeches, and loudly cried that the city had need

of a great purification. He urged the people, if they were wise, not to choose the most agreeable physician, but the one who was most in earnest. He himself, he said, was such a physician, and so was Valerius Flaccus, of the patricians. With him as colleague, and him alone, he thought he could cut the excessive luxury and effeminacy of the time. As for the rest of the candidates, he saw that they were all trying to force their way into the office in order to administer it badly, since they feared those who would administer it well. And so truly great were the Roman voters, and so worthy of great leaders, that they did not fear Cato's rigour and haughty independence, but rejected those candidates who, it was believed, would do everything to please them, and elected Flaccus to the office along with Cato.

*   *   *

As censor, Cato paid not the slightest heed to his accusers, but grew still more strict. He cut off the pipes by which people conveyed part of the public water supply into their private houses and gardens; he upset and demolished all buildings that encroached on public land; he reduced the cost of public works to the lowest, and forced the rent of public lands to the highest possible figure. All these things brought much hatred upon him.

*   *   *

Still, it appears that the people approved of his censorship to an amazing extent. At any rate, after erecting a statue to his honour in the temple of Health, they commemorated in the inscription upon it, not the military commands nor the triumph of Cato, but, as the inscription may be translated, the fact "that when the Roman state was tottering to its fall, he was made censor, and by helpful guidance, wise restraints, and sound teachings, restored it again." . . .

*   *   *

He was also a good father, a considerate husband, and a household manager of no little talent; nor did he give only a fitful attention to this, as a matter of little or no importance. Therefore, I

think I ought to give suitable instances of his conduct in these relations. He married a wife who was
of higher birth than she was rich, thinking that,
although the rich and the high-born may be alike
given to pride, still, women of high birth have
such a horror of what is disgraceful that they are
more obedient to their husbands in all that is honourable. He used to say that the man who struck
his wife or child, laid violent hands on the holiest
of holy things. Also that he thought it more praiseworthy to be a good husband than a great senator,
and there was nothing more to admire in Socrates
of old than that he was always kind and gentle
with his shrewish wife and stupid sons. After the
birth of his own son, no business could be so urgent, unless it had a public character, as to prevent
him from being present when his wife bathed and
wrapped the babe. For the mother nursed it herself, and often gave her breast also to the infants
of her slaves, that so they might come to cherish
a brotherly affection for her son. As soon as the
boy showed signs of understanding, his father
took him under his own charge and taught him
to read, although he had an accomplished slave,
Chilo by name, who was a school-teacher, and
taught many boys. Still, Cato thought it not right,
as he tells us himself, that his son should be
scolded by a slave, or have his ears tweaked when
he was slow to learn, still less that he should be
indebted to his slave for such a priceless thing as
education. He was therefore himself not only the
boy's reading-teacher, but his tutor in law, and his
athletic trainer, and he taught his son not merely
to hurl the javelin and fight in armour and ride
the horse, but also to box, to endure heat and
cold, and to swim strongly through the eddies and
billows of the Tiber. His "History of Rome," as he
tells us himself, he wrote out with his own hand
and in large characters, that his son might have in
his own home an aid to acquaintance with his
country's ancient traditions. He declares that his
son's presence put him on guard against making
indecencies of speech as if in the presence of the
Vestal Virgins, and that he never bathed with him.
This, indeed, would seem to have been a general
taboo with the Romans, for even fathers-in-law

avoided bathing with their sons-in-law, because
they were ashamed to uncover their nakedness.
Afterwards, however, when they had learned from
the Greeks their freedom in going naked before
men, they in their turn infected the Greeks with
the practice of doing so even before women.

* * *

He owned many slaves, and usually bought
those prisoners of war who were young and still
capable of being reared and trained. Not one of
his slaves ever entered another man's house unless
sent there by Cato or his wife, and when any of
them was asked what Cato was doing, he always
answered that he did not know. A slave of his was
expected either to be busy about the house, or to
be asleep, and he preferred the sleepy ones. He
thought these gentler than the wakeful ones, and
that those who had enjoyed the gift of sleep were
better for any kind of service than those who
lacked it. In the belief that his slaves were led into
most mischief by their sexual passions, he required
that the males should have sex with the female
slaves of the house at a fixed price, but should
never approach any other woman.

At the outset, when Cato was still poor and in
military service, he found no fault at all with what
was served up to him, declaring that it was shameful for a man to quarrel with a servant over food
and drink. But afterwards, when his circumstances
were improved and he used to entertain his friends
and colleagues at table, no sooner was the dinner
over than he would flog those slaves who had been
unsatisfactory in preparing or serving it. He was
always arranging that his slaves should have feuds
and disagreements among themselves; harmony
among them made him suspicious and fearful of
them. He had those who were suspected of some
capital offence brought to trial before all their fellow servants, and, if convicted, put to death.

* * *

He used to lend money also to those of his
slaves who wished it, and they would buy boys
with it, and after training and teaching them for
a year, at Cato's expense, would sell them again.

Many of these boys Cato would retain for himself, counting to the credit of the slave the highest price bid for his boy by outsiders. He tried to persuade his son also to such investments, by saying that it was not the part of a man, but of a widow woman, to lessen his property. But surely Cato was going too far when he said that a man should be admired and glorified like a god if the final inventory of his property showed that he had added to it more than he had inherited.

When he was now well on in years, there came as delegates from Athens to Rome, Carneades the Academic, and Diogenes the Stoic philosopher, to beg the reversal of a certain decision against the Athenian people, which imposed upon them a heavy fine. Upon the arrival of these philosophers, the most studious of the city's youth hastened to wait upon them, and became their devoted and admiring listeners. The charm of Carneades especially, which had boundless power, and a fame not inferior to its power, won large and sympathetic audiences, and filled the city, like a rushing mighty wind, with the noise of his praises. Report spread far and wide that a Greek of amazing talent, who disarmed all opposition by the magic of his eloquence, had infused a tremendous passion into the youth of the city—in consequence of which they gave up their other pleasures and pursuits and were "possessed" about philosophy. The other Romans were pleased at this, and glad to see their young men lay hold of Greek culture and associate with such admirable men. But Cato, at the very outset, when this zeal for discussion came into the city, was distressed—fearing that the young men, by giving this direction to their ambition, should come to love a reputation based on mere words more than one achieved by military deeds. And when the fame of the visiting philosophers rose yet higher in the city, and their first speeches before the Senate were interpreted, at his own instance and request, by so conspicuous a man as Gaius Acilius, Cato determined, on some excuse or other, to rid the city of them all. So he rose in the Senate and condemned the city officials for keeping for so long a time a delegation composed of men who could easily secure anything they wished, so persuasive were they. "We ought," he said, "to make up our minds one way or another, and vote on what the delegation proposes, in order that these men may return to their schools and lecture to the sons of Greece, while the youth of Rome give ear to their laws and officials, as before."

This he did, not, as some think, out of personal hostility to Carneades, but because he was wholly opposed to philosophy, and made mock of all Greek culture and training, out of patriotic Roman zeal. He says, for instance, that Socrates was a mighty talker, who attempted, as best he could, to be his country's tyrant, by abolishing its customs, and by enticing his fellow citizens into opinions contrary to the laws. * * * And seeking to prejudice his son against Greek culture, he declared, in the tone of a prophet or a seer, that Rome would lose her empire when she had become infected with Greek literature. But time has certainly shown the emptiness of this pessimistic declaration, for while the city was at the height of its empire, she made every form of Greek learning and culture her own.

* * *

REVIEW QUESTIONS

1. What were the virtues that Cato prized most highly?
2. What were his reasons for opposing the spread of Greek culture?
3. How did he treat his slaves?
4. What were his attitudes toward women?

DIODORUS SICULUS

FROM *On Slavery in the Later Republic*

Rome's imperial conquests, besides exposing Roman values to alien influences, also produced a huge supply of captives who generally were reduced to slavery. The following selection describes the conditions of slaves set to work in the silver and gold mines of Spain, and then describes an especially destructive slave revolt on Sicily between 135 and 132 B.C.E.

From *On Slavery in the Later Republic, The Library of History*, vol. 3, by Diodorus Siculus, translated by C. H. Oldfather (Cambridge, Mass.: Harvard University Press, 1939), pp. 114–16.

*   *   *

. . . After the Romans had made themselves masters of Iberia, a multitude of Italians have swarmed to the mines and taken great wealth away with them, such was their greed. For they purchase a multitude of slaves whom they turn over to the overseers of the working of the mines; and these men, opening shafts in a number of places and digging deep into the ground, seek out the seams of earth which are rich in silver and gold; and not only do they go into the ground a great distance, but they also push their diggings many stades in depth and run galleries off at every angle, turning this way and that, in this manner bringing up from the depths the ore which gives them the profit they are seeking. . . .

But to continue with the mines, the slaves who are engaged in the working of them produce for their masters revenues in sums defying belief, but they themselves wear out their bodies both by day and by night in the diggings under the earth, dying in large numbers because of the exceptional hardships they endure. For no respite or pause is granted them in their labours, but compelled beneath blows of the overseers to endure the severity of their plight, they throw away their lives in this wretched manner, although certain of them who

can endure it, by virtue of their bodily strength and their persevering souls, suffer such hardships over a long period; indeed death in their eyes is more to be desired than life, because of the magnitude of the hardships they must bear.

There was never a sedition of slaves so great as that which occurred in Sicily, whereby many cities met with grave calamities, innumerable men and women, together with their children, experienced the greatest misfortunes, and all the island was in danger of falling into the power of fugitive slaves. . . .

. . . The Servile War broke out for the following reason. The Sicilians, having shot up in prosperity and acquired great wealth, began to purchase a vast number of slaves, to whose bodies, as they were brought in droves from the slave markets, they at once applied marks and brands. The young men they used as cowherds, the others in such ways as they happened to be useful. But they treated them with a heavy hand in their service, and granted them the most meagre care, the bare minimum for food and clothing. . . .

The slaves, distressed by their hardships, and frequently outraged and beaten beyond all reason, could not endure their treatment. Getting together as opportunity offered, they discussed the possibility of revolt, until at last they put their plans into action. . . . The beginning of the whole revolt took place as follows.

There was a certain Damophilus of Enna, a man of great wealth but insolent of manner; he had abused his slaves to excess, and his wife Megallis vied even with her husband in punishing the slaves and in her general inhumanity towards them. The slaves, reduced by this degrading treatment to the level of brutes, conspired to revolt and to murder their masters. Going to Eunus they asked him whether their resolve had the favour of the gods. He, resorting to his usual mummery, promised them the favour of the gods, and soon persuaded them to act at once. Immediately, therefore, they brought together four hundred of their fellow slaves and, having armed themselves in such ways as opportunity permitted, they fell upon the city of Enna, with Eunus at their head and working his miracle of the flames of fire for their benefit. When they found their way into the houses they shed much blood, sparing not even suckling babes. Rather they tore them from the breast and dashed them to the ground, while as for the women—and under their husbands' very eyes—but words cannot tell the extent of their outrages and acts of lewdness! By now a great multitude of slaves from the city had joined them, who, after first demonstrating against their own masters their utter ruthlessness, then turned to the slaughter of others. When Eunus and his men learned that Damophilus and his wife were in the garden that lay near the city, they sent some of their band and dragged them off, both the man and his wife, fettered and with hands bound behind their backs, subjecting them to many outrages along the way. Only in the case of the couple's daughter were the slaves seen to show consideration throughout, and this was because of her kindly nature, in that to the extent of her power she was always compassionate and ready to succour the slaves. Thereby it was demonstrated that the others were treated as they were, not because of some "natural savagery of slaves," but rather in revenge for wrongs previously received.

The men appointed to the task, having dragged Damophilus and Megallis into the city, as we said, brought them to the theatre, where the crowd of rebels had assembled. But when Damophilus attempted to devise a plea to get them off safe and was winning over many of the crowd with his words, Hermeias and Zeuxis, men bitterly disposed towards him, denounced him as a cheat, and without waiting for a formal trial by the assembly the one ran him through the chest with a sword, the other chopped off his head with an axe. Thereupon Eunus was chosen king, not for his manly courage or his ability as a military leader, but solely for his marvels and his setting of the revolt in motion. . . .

Established as the rebels' supreme commander, he called an assembly and put to death all the citizenry of Enna except for those who were skilled in the manufacture of arms: these he put in chains and assigned them to this task. He gave Megallis to the maidservants to deal with as they might wish; they subjected her to torture and threw her over a precipice. He himself murdered his own masters, Antigenes and Pytho. Having set a diadem upon his head, and arrayed himself in full royal style, he proclaimed his wife queen (she was a fellow Syrian and of the same city) and appointed to the royal council such men as seemed to be gifted with superior intelligence. . . .

. . . In three days Eunus had armed, as best he could, more than six thousand men, besides others in his train who had only axes and hatchets, or slings, or sickles, or fire-hardened stakes, or even kitchen spits; and he went about ravaging the countryside. Then, since he kept recruiting untold numbers of slaves, he ventured even to do battle with Roman generals, and on joining combat repeatedly overcame them with his superior numbers, for he now had more than ten thousand soldiers.

Soon after, engaging in battle with a general arrived from Rome, Lucius Hypsaeus, who had eight thousand Sicilian troops, the rebels were victorious, since they now numbered twenty thousand. Before long their band reached a total of two hundred thousand, and in numerous battles with the Romans they acquitted themselves well, and failed but seldom. As word of this was bruited about, a revolt of one hundred and fifty slaves, banded together, flared up in Rome, of more than a thousand in Attica, and of yet others in Delos and many other places. But thanks to the speed with which forces were brought up and to the severity of their punitive measures, the magistrates of these communities at once disposed of the rebels and brought to their senses any who were wavering on the verge of revolt. In Sicily, however, the trouble grew. Cities were captured with all their inhabitants, and many armies were cut to pieces by the rebels, until Rupilius, the Roman commander, recovered Tauromenium for the Romans by placing it under strict siege and confining the rebels under conditions of unspeakable duress and famine: conditions such that, beginning by eating the children, they progressed to the women, and did not altogether abstain even from eating one another. . . .

Finally, after Sarapion, a Syrian, had betrayed the citadel, the general laid hands on all the runaway slaves in the city, whom, after torture, he threw over a cliff. From there he advanced to Enna, which he put under siege in much the same manner, bringing the rebels into extreme straits and frustrating their hopes. . . . Rupilius captured this city also by betrayal, since its strength was impregnable to force of arms. Eunus, taking with him his bodyguards, a thousand strong, fled in unmanly fashion. . . .

. . . He met such an end as befitted his knavery, and died at Morgantina. Thereupon Rupilius, traversing the whole of Sicily with a few picked troops, sooner than had been expected rid it of every nest of robbers.

*   *   *

REVIEW QUESTIONS

1. According to Diodorus, to what kinds of treatment were slaves subjected in the second century B.C.E.?
2. How does Cato the Elder's treatment of his slaves compare with the conditions of slaves in the mines?

CICERO

FROM *On the Laws*

Whereas Cato the Elder epitomizes the traditionalists' resistance to the advances of Greek culture in the late Roman Republic, Cicero (106–43 B.C.E.) is that era's foremost representative of Greek ideals. A foremost legal expert and compelling orator, he was a leading political figure during the era of the rise of Julius Caesar and was eventually executed after Caesar's assassination for advocating the restoration of the power of the Roman Senate. His most significant influence on the later Western intellectual tradition, however, lies in his prolific production as a writer. It was largely through his works that Greco-Roman thought was transmitted to later eras. The following selection is from Cicero's On the Laws, *in which, through the mechanism of dialogue that was used so well by earlier Greek philosophers, he propounds his concept of the ideal state.*

From *De Legibus* (*On the Laws*), by Cicero, translated by Clinton W. Keyes (Cambridge, Mass.: Harvard University Press, 1928), pp. 311–91.

*   *   *

ATTICUS: Yet if you ask what I expect of you, I consider it a logical thing that, since you have already written a treatise on the constitution of the ideal State, you should also write one on its laws. For I note that this was done by your beloved Plato, whom you admire, revere above all others, and love above all others.

MARCUS: Is it your wish, then, that, as he discussed the institutions of States and the ideal laws, . . . sometimes walking about, sometimes resting —you recall his description—we, in like manner, strolling or taking our ease among these stately poplars on the green and shady river bank, shall discuss the same subjects along somewhat broader lines than the practice of the courts calls for? * * *

MARCUS: And you are wise, for you must understand that in no other kind of discussion can one bring out so clearly what Nature's gifts to man are, what a wealth of most excellent possessions the human mind enjoys, what the purpose is, to strive after and accomplish which we have been born and placed in this world, what it is that unites men, and what natural fellowship there is among them. For it is only after all these things have been made clear that the origin of Law and Justice can be discovered.

ATTICUS: Then you do not think that the science of law is to be derived from the praetor's edict, as the majority do now, or from the Twelve Tables, as people used to think, but from the deepest mysteries of philosophy?

MARCUS: Quite right; for in our present conversation, Pomponius, we are not trying to learn how to protect ourselves legally, or how to answer clients' questions. Such problems may be important, and in fact they are; for in former times

many eminent men made a specialty of their solution, and at present one person performs this duty with the greatest authority and skill. But in our present investigation we intend to cover the whole range of universal Justice and Law in such a way that our own civil law, as it is called, will be confined to a small and narrow corner. For we must explain the nature of Justice, and this must be sought for in the nature of man; we must also consider the laws by which States ought to be governed; then we must deal with the enactments and decrees of nations which are already formulated and put in writing; and among these the civil law, as it is called, of the Roman people will not fail to find a place. * * *

MARCUS: . . . now let us investigate the origins of Justice.

Well then, the most learned men have determined to begin with Law, and it would seem that they are right, if, according to their definition, Law is the highest reason, implanted in Nature, which commands what ought to be done and forbids the opposite. This reason, when firmly fixed and fully developed in the human mind, is Law. And so they believe that Law is intelligence, whose natural function it is to command right conduct and forbid wrongdoing. . . . Now if this is correct, as I think it to be in general, then the origin of Justice is to be found in Law, for Law is a natural force; it is the mind and reason of the intelligent man, the standard by which Justice and Injustice are measured. But since our whole discussion has to do with the reasoning of the populace, it will sometimes be necessary to speak in the popular manner, and give the name of law to that which in written form decrees whatever it wishes, either by command or prohibition. For such is the crowd's definition of law. But in determining what Justice is, let us begin with that supreme Law which had its origin ages before any written law existed or any State had been established. ✳ ✳ ✳

✳   ✳   ✳

MARCUS: I will not make the argument long. Your admission leads us to this: that animal which we call man, endowed with foresight and quick intelligence, complex, keen, possessing memory, full of reason and prudence, has been given a certain distinguished status by the supreme God who created him; for he is the only one among so many different kinds and varieties of living beings who has a share in reason and thought, while all the rest are deprived of it. But what is more divine, I will not say in man only, but in all heaven and earth, than reason? And reason, when it is full grown and perfected, is rightly called wisdom. Therefore, since there is nothing better than reason, and since it exists both in man and God, the first common possession of man and God is reason. But those who have reason in common must also have right reason in common. And since right reason is Law, we must believe that men have Law also in common with the gods. Further, those who share Law must also share Justice; and those who share these are to be regarded as members of the same commonwealth. If indeed they obey the same authorities and powers, this is true in a far greater degree; but as a matter of fact they do obey this celestial system, the divine mind, and the God of transcendent power. Hence we must now conceive of this whole universe as one commonwealth of which both gods and men are members.

✳   ✳   ✳

MARCUS: The points which are now being briefly touched upon are certainly important; but out of all the material of the philosophers' discussions, surely there comes nothing more valuable than the full realization that we are born for Justice, and that right is based, not upon men's opinions, but upon Nature. This fact will immediately be plain if you once get a clear conception of man's fellowship and union with his fellow-men. For no single thing is so like another, so exactly its counterpart, as all of us are to one another. Nay, if bad habits and false beliefs did not twist the weaker minds and turn them in whatever direction they are inclined, no one would be so like his own self as all men would be like all others. And so, however we may define man, a single definition will apply to all. This is a sufficient proof that there is no difference in kind between man and man; for if there were, one definition could not be applicable to all men; and indeed reason, which alone raises us above the level of the beasts and enables us to draw inferences, to prove and disprove, to discuss and solve problems, and to come to conclusions, is certainly common to us all, and, though varying in what it learns, at least in the capacity to learn it is invariable. For the same things are invariably perceived by the senses, and those things which stimulate the senses, stimulate them in the same way in all men; and those rudimentary beginnings of intelligence to which I have referred, which are imprinted on our minds, are imprinted on all minds alike; and speech, the mind's interpreter, though differing in the choice of words, agrees in the sentiments expressed. In fact, there is no human being of any race who, if he finds a guide, cannot attain to virtue.

✳   ✳   ✳

MARCUS: The next point, then, is that we are so constituted by Nature as to share the sense of Justice with one another and to pass it on to all men. And in this whole discussion I want it understood that what I shall call Nature is that which is implanted in us by Nature; that, however, the corruption caused by bad habits is so great that the sparks of fire, so to speak, which Nature has kindled in us are extinguished by this corruption, and the vices which are their opposites spring up and are established. But if the judgments of men were in agreement with Nature, so that . . . they considered "nothing alien to them which concerns mankind," then Justice would be equally observed by all. For those creatures who have received the gift of reason from Nature have also received right reason, and therefore they have also received the gift of Law, which is right reason applied to command and prohibition. And if they have received Law, they have received Justice also. Now all men have received reason; therefore all men have received Justice. . . .

Now all this is really a preface to what remains to be said in our discussion, and its purpose is to make it more easily understood that Justice is inherent in Nature. After I have said a few words more on this topic, I shall go on to the civil law, the subject which gives rise to all this discourse. . . .

But you see the direction this conversation is to take; our whole discourse is intended to promote the firm foundation of States, the strengthening of cities, and the curing of the ills of peoples. For that reason I want to be especially careful not to lay down first principles that have not been wisely considered and thoroughly investigated. Of course I cannot expect that they will be universally accepted, for that is impossible; but I do look for the approval of all who believe that everything which is right and honourable is to be desired for its own sake, and that nothing whatever is to be accounted a good unless it is praiseworthy in itself, or at least that nothing should be considered a great good unless it can rightly be praised for its own sake.

*   *   *

MARCUS: Once more, then, before we come to the individual laws, let us look at the character and nature of Law, for fear that, though it must be the standard to which we refer everything, we may now and then be led astray by an incorrect use of terms, and forget the rational principles on which our laws must be based.

QUINTUS: Quite so, that is the correct method of exposition.

MARCUS: Well, then, I find that it has been the opinion of the wisest men that Law is not a product of human thought, nor is it any enactment of peoples, but something eternal which rules the whole universe by its wisdom in command and prohibition. Thus they have been accustomed to say that Law is the primal and ultimate mind of God, whose reason directs all things either by compulsion or restraint. Wherefore that Law which the gods have given to the human race has been justly praised; for it is the reason and mind of a wise lawgiver applied to command and prohibition.

*   *   *

MARCUS: So in the very beginning we must persuade our citizens that the gods are the lords and rulers of all things, and that what is done, is done by their will and authority; that they are likewise great benefactors of man, observing the character of every individual, what he does, of what wrong he is guilty, and with what intentions and with what piety he fulfils his religious duties; and that they take note of the pious and the impious. For surely minds which are imbued with such ideas will not fail to form true and useful opinions. Indeed, what is more true than that no one ought to be so foolishly proud as to think that, though reason and intellect exist in himself, they do not exist in the heavens and the universe, or that those things which can hardly be understood by the highest reasoning powers of the human intellect are guided by no reason at all? In truth, the man that is not driven to gratitude by the orderly courses of the stars, the regular alternation of day and night, the gentle progress of the seasons, and the produce of the earth brought forth for our sustenance—how can such an one be accounted a man at all? And since all things that possess reason stand above those things which are without reason, and since it would be sacrilege to say that anything stands above universal Nature, we must admit that reason is inherent in Nature. Who will deny that such beliefs are useful when he remembers how often oaths are used to confirm agreements, how important to our well-being is the sanctity of treaties, how many persons are deterred from crime by the fear of divine punishment, and how sacred an association of citizens becomes when the immortal gods are made members of it, either as judges or as witnesses?

REVIEW QUESTIONS

1. According to Cicero, what is the source of all law?
2. What is the relationship of civil law to law as Cicero defines it?

3. Do you find in this selection any evidence of a Stoic concept of universal human brotherhood and equality?

JUVENAL

FROM *The Sixteen Satires*

As Rome's power and wealth increased, the values and concerns of its people were affected and transformed. The next three readings testify, in one way or another, to that transformation. The first selection, which is drawn from the "Third" and "Sixth Satires" of Juvenal (c. 55–130 c.e.), sharply criticizes the excessive wealth and growing corruption of Roman society.

From *The Sixteen Satires,* by Juvenal, translated by Peter Green (New York: Penguin Books, 1974), pp. 87–91, 142–44.

*   *   *

Yet a musical wife's not so bad as some
    presumptuous
Flat-chested busybody who rushes around the
    town
Gate-crashing all-male meetings, talking back
    straight-faced
To a uniformed general—*and* in her husband's
    presence.
She knows all the news of the world, what's
    cooking in Thrace
Or China, just what the stepmother did with her
    stepson
Behind closed doors, who's fallen in love, which
    gallant
Is all the rage. She'll tell you who got the widow
Pregnant, and in which month; she knows each
    woman's
Pillow endearments, and all the positions she
    favors.

She's the first to spot any comet presaging trouble
For some eastern prince, in Armenia, maybe, or
    Parthia.
She's on to the latest gossip and rumors as soon
    as
They reach the city-gates, or invents her own,
    informing
Everyone she meets that Niphates has overflowed
And is inundating whole countries—towns are
    cut off,
She says, and the land is sinking: flood and
    disaster!
    Yet even this is not so insufferable
As her habit, when woken up, of grabbing some
    poor-class
Neighbor and belting into him with a whip. If
    her precious
Sleep is broken by barking, "Fetch me the cudgels,"
She roars, "and be quick about it!" The dog gets
    a thrashing,
But its master gets one first. She's no joke to cross,

A SCENE FROM A ROMAN-ERA ITALIAN HARBOR (C. 80 C.E.)

This scene is from a wall painting discovered at the small town of Stabiae, near Pompeii, which was destroyed by the eruption of Mt. Vesuvius in 79 C.E. What does this reflect about the organization and sophistication of maritime trade in the Roman Empire? Was much expense devoted to the construction and decoration of the harbor's facilities? Why might such a painting have been commissioned?

And her face is a grisly fright. Not till the evening
Does she visit the baths: only then are her oil-
    jars and
The rest of her clobber transferred there. First
    she works out
With the weights and dumb-bells. Then, when
    her arms are aching,
The masseur takes over, craftily slipping one hand
Along her thigh, and tickling her up till she comes.
Lastly she makes for the sweat-room. She loves
    to sit there
Amid all that hubbub, perspiring. Meanwhile at
    home
Her unfortunate guests are nearly dead with
    hunger.
At last she appears, all flushed, with a three-
    gallon thirst,
Enough to empty the brimming jar at her
    feet
Without assistance. She knocks back two straight
    pints
On an empty stomach, to sharpen her appetite:
    then
Throws it all up again, souses the floor with
    vomit
That flows in rivers across the terrazzo. She
    drinks
And spews by turns, like some big snake that's
    tumbled
Into a wine-vat, till her gilded jordan brims
Right over with sour and vinous slops. Quite
    sickened,
Eyes shut, her husband somehow holds down his
    bile.
    Worse still is the well-read menace, who's
    hardly settled for dinner
Before she starts praising Virgil, making a moral
    case
For Dido (death justifies all), comparing,
    evaluating
Rival poets, Virgil and Homer suspended
In opposite scales, weighed up one against the
    other.
Critics surrender, academics are routed, all
Fall silent, not a word from lawyer or
    auctioneer—

Or even another woman. Such a rattle of talk,
You'd think all the poets and bells were being
    clashed together
When the moon's in eclipse. . . .
                    So avoid a dinner-partner
With an argumentative style, who hurls well-
    rounded
Syllogisms like slingshots, who has all history
    pat:
Choose someone rather who doesn't understand
    all she reads.
I hate these authority-citers, the sort who are
    always thumbing
Some standard grammatical treatise, whose every
    utterance
Observes all the laws of syntax, who with
    antiquarian zeal
Quote poets I've never heard of. Such matters
    are men's concern.
If she wants to correct someone's language, she
    can always
Start with her unlettered girl-friends.

                *   *   *

From here we strolled down
To the nymph's new, modernized grotto. (What
    a gain in sanctity
And atmosphere there would be if grassy banks
Surrounded the pool, if no flash marble affronted
Our native limestone!) Here Umbricius stood,
    and
Opened his heart to me.
"There's no room in this city,"
He said, "for the decent professions: they don't
    show any profit.
My resources have shrunk since yesterday, and
    tomorrow
Will eat away more of what's left. So I am going
Where Daedalus put off his weary wings, while
    as yet
I'm in vigorous middle age, while active years
    are left me,
While my white hairs are still few, and I need no
    stick
To guide my tottering feet. So farewell Rome, I
    leave you

To sanitary engineers and municipal architects,
   men
Who by swearing black is white land all the juicy
   contracts
Just like that—a new temple, swamp-drainage,
   harbour-works,
River-clearance, undertaking, the lot—then
   pocket the cash
And fraudulently file their petition in
   bankruptcy.
Once these fellows were horn-players, stumping
   the provinces
In road-shows, their puffed-out cheeks a familiar
   sight
To every country village. But now they stage
   shows themselves,
Of the gladiatorial sort, and at the mob's
   thumbs-down
Will butcher a loser for popularity's sake, and
Pass on from that to erecting public privies.
   Why not?
These are such men as Fortune, by way of a joke,
Will sometimes raise from the gutter and make
   Top People.
What can I do in Rome? I never learnt how
To lie. If a book is bad, I cannot puff it, or
   bother
To ask around for a copy; astrological clap-trap
Is not in my stars. I cannot and will not promise
To encompass any man's death by way of
   obliging his son.
I have never meddled with frogs' guts; the task
   of carrying
Letters and presents between adulterous lovers
I resign to those who know it. I refuse to
   become
An accomplice in theft—which means that no
   governor
Will accept me on his staff. It's like being a
   cripple
With a paralysed right hand. Yet who today is
   favoured
Above the conspirator, his head externally
   seething
With confidential matters, never to be revealed?

Harmless secrets carry no obligations, and he
Who shares them with you feels no great call
   thereafter
To keep you sweet. But if Verres promotes a man
You can safely assume that man has the screws
   on Verres
And could turn him in tomorrow. Not all the
   gold
Washed seaward with the silt of tree-lined Tagus
Is worth the price you pay, racked by insomnia,
   seeing
Your high-placed friends all cringe at your
   approach—and
For what? Too-transient prizes, unwillingly
   resigned."
  "Now let me turn to that race which goes
   down so well
With our millionaires, but remains *my* special
   pet aversion,
And not mince my words. I cannot, citizens,
   stomach
A Greek-struck Rome. Yet what fraction of these
   sweepings
Derives, in fact, from Greece? For years now
   Syrian
Orontes has poured its sewerage into our native
   Tiber—
Its lingo and manners, its flutes, its outlandish
   harps
With their transverse strings, its native
   tambourines,
And the whores who hang out round the race-
   course. (That's where to go
If you fancy a foreign piece in one of those
   saucy toques.)
Our beloved Founder should see how his
   homespun rustics
Behave today, with their dinner-pumps—
   trechedipna
They call them—not to mention their
   niceteria
(Decorations to you) hung round their *ceromatic*
   (that's
Well-greased) wrestlers' necks. Here's one from
   Sicyon,

Another from Macedonia, two from Aegean
    islands—
Andros, say, or Samos—two more from Caria,
All of them lighting out for the City's classiest
    districts
And burrowing into great houses, with a long-
    term plan
For taking them over. Quick wit, unlimited
    nerve, a gift
Of the gab that outsmarts a professional public
    speaker—
These are their characteristics. What do you take
That fellow's profession to be? He has brought a
    whole bundle
Of personalities with him—schoolmaster,
    rhetorician,
Surveyor, artist, masseur, diviner, tightrope-
    walker,
Magician or quack, your versatile hungry
    Greekling
Is all by turns. Tell him to fly—he's airborne.
The inventor of wings was no Moor or Slav,
    remember,
Or Thracian, but born in the very heart of
    Athens."
    "When such men as these wear the purple,
    when some creature
Blown into Rome along with the figs and
    damsons
Precedes me at dinner-parties, or for the
    witnessing
Of manumissions and wills—*me,* who drew my
    first breath
On these Roman hills, and was nourished on
    Sabine olives!—
Things have reached a pretty pass. What's more,
    their talent
For flattery is unmatched. They praise the
    conversation
Of their dimmest friends; the ugly they call
    handsome,
So that your scrag-necked weakling finds himself
    compared
To Hercules holding the giant Antaeus aloft
Way off the earth. They go into ecstasies over

Some shrill and scrannel voice that sounds like a
    hen
When the cock gets at her. We can make the
    same compliments, but
It's they who convince. On the stage they remain
    supreme
In female parts, courtesan, matron or slave-girl,
With no concealing cloak: you'd swear it was a
    genuine
Woman you saw, and not a masked
    performer.
Look there, beneath that belly: no bulge, all
    smooth, a neat
Nothingness—even a hint of the Great Divide.
    Yet back home
These queens and dames pass unnoticed. Greece
    is a nation
Of actors. Laugh, and they split their sides. At
    the sight
Of a friend's tears, they weep too—though quite
    unmoved.
If you ask for a fire in winter, the Greek puts on
    his cloak;
If you say 'I'm hot,' *he* starts sweating. So you
    see
We are not on an equal footing: he has the great
    advantage
Of being able on all occasions, night and day,
To take his cue, his mask, from others. He's
    always ready
To throw up his hands and applaud when a
    friend delivers
A really resounding belch, or pisses right on the
    mark,
With a splendid drumming sound from the
    upturned golden basin."
    "Besides, he holds nothing sacred, not a soul
    is safe
From his randy urges, the lady of the house, her
Virgin daughter, her daughter's still unbearded
Husband-to-be, her hitherto virtuous son—
And if none of these are to hand, he'll cheerfully
    lay
His best friend's grandmother. (Anything to
    ferret

Domestic secrets out, and get a hold over
    people.)
  And while we are on the subject of Greeks,
    let us consider
Academics and their vices—not the gymnasium
    crowd
But big philosophical wheels, like that Stoic
    greybeard
Who narked on his friend and pupil, and got
    him liquidated.
He was brought up in Tarsus, by the banks of
    that river
Where Bellerophon fell to earth from the
    Gorgon's flying nag.
No room for honest Romans when Rome's ruled
    by a junta
Of Greek-born secret agents, who—like all their
    race—
Never share friends or patrons. One small dose
    of venom
(Half Greek, half personal) dropped in that
    ready ear
And I'm out, shown the back-door, my years of
    obsequious
Service all gone for nothing. Where can a
    hanger-on
Be ditched with less fuss than in Rome?

        *   *   *

Here a citizen, free-born,
Must stand aside on the pavement for some
    wealthy tycoon's slave:
He can afford to squander a senior officer's
    income
On classy amateur harlots, just for the privilege
Of laying them once or twice. But when *you*
    fancy
A common-or-garden tart, you dither and
    hesitate:
Can I afford to accost her?

        *   *   *

The poor man's an eternal
Butt for bad jokes, with his torn and dirt-caked
    top-coat,

His grubby toga, one shoe agape where the
    leather's
Split—those clumsy patches, that coarse and tell-
    tale stitching
Only a day or two old. The hardest thing to bear
In poverty is the fact that it makes us ridiculous.
"Out of those front-row seats," we're told. "You
    ought to be
Ashamed of yourselves—your incomes are far
    too small, and
The law's the law. Make way for some pander's
    son,
Spawned in an unknown brothel, let your place
    be occupied
By that natty auctioneer's offspring, with his
    high-class companions
The trainer's brat and the son of the gladiator
Applauding beside him." Such were the fruits of
    that pinhead
Otho's Reserved Seat Act. What prospective son-
    in-law
Ever passed muster here if he was short on cash
To match the girl's dowry? What poor man ever
    inherits
A legacy, or is granted that meanest of
    sinecures—
A job with the Office of Works? All lower-
    income citizens
Should have marched out of town, in a body,
    years ago.
Nobody finds it easy to get to the top if meagre
Resources cripple his talent. But in Rome the
    problem's worse
Than anywhere else. Inflation hits the rental
Of your miserable apartment, inflation distends
The ravenous maws of your slaves; your humble
    dinner
Suffers inflation too. You feel ashamed to eat
Off earthenware dishes—yet if you were
    transported
To some rural village, you'd be content enough
And happily wear a cloak of coarse blue
    broadcloth
Complete with hood. Throughout most of Italy—
    we

Might as well admit it—no one is seen in a toga
Till the day he dies. Even on public holidays,
When the same old shows as last year are
    cheerfully staged
In the grassgrown theatre, when peasant
    children, sitting
On their mothers' laps, shrink back in terror at
    the sight
Of those gaping, whitened masks, you will still
    find the whole
Audience—top row or bottom—dressed exactly
    alike;
Even the magistrates need no better badge of
    status
Than a plain white tunic. But here in Rome we
    must toe
The line of fashion, living beyond our means,
    and
Often on borrowed credit: every man jack of us
Is keeping up with his neighbours. To cut a long
    story short,
Nothing's for free in Rome. * * *
    "What countryman ever bargained, besides,
    for his house collapsing
About his ears? Such things are unheard-of in
    cool
Praeneste, or rural Gabii, or Tivoli perched on
    its hillside,
Or Volsinii, nestling amid its woodland ridges.
    But here
We live in a city shored up, for the most part,
    with gimcrack
Stays and props: that's how our landlords arrest
The collapse of their property, papering over
    great cracks
In the ramshackle fabric, reassuring the
    tenants
They can sleep secure, when all the time the
    building
Is poised like a house of cards. I prefer to live
    where
Fires and midnight panics are not quite such
    common events.
By the time the smoke's got up to your third-
    floor apartment

(And you still asleep) your downstairs neighbour
    is roaring
For water, and shifting his bits and pieces to
    safety.
If the alarm goes at ground-level, the last to fry
Will be the attic tenant, way up among the
    nesting
Pigeons, with nothing but tiles between himself
    and the weather.
What did friend Cordus own? One truckle bed,
    too short
For even a midget nympho; one marble-topped
    sideboard
On which stood six little mugs; beneath it, a
    pitcher
And an up-ended bust of Chiron; one ancient
    settle
Crammed with Greek books (though by now
    analphabetic mice
Had gnawed their way well into his texts of the
    great poets).
Cordus could hardly be called a property-owner,
    and yet
What little the poor man had, he lost. Today the
    final
Straw on his load of woe (clothes worn to
    tatters, reduced
To begging for crusts) is that no one will offer
    him lodging
Or shelter, not even stand him a decent meal.
    But if
Some millionaire's mansion is gutted, women
    rend their garments,
Top people put on mourning, the courts go into
    recess:
Then you hear endless complaints about the
    hazards
Of city life, these deplorable outbreaks of fire;
Then contributions pour in while the shell is still
    ash-hot—
Construction materials, marble, fresh-gleaming
    sculptured nudes.
Up comes A with bronzes (genuine antique works
By a real Old Master) acquired, as part of his
    booty,

From their hallowed niche in some Asiatic
    temple;
B provides bookshelves, books, and a study bust
    of Minerva;
C a sackful of silver. So it goes on, until
This dandified bachelor's losses are all
    recouped—
And more than recouped—with even rarer
    possessions,
And a rumour (well-founded) begins to circulate
That he fired the place himself, a deliberate piece
    of arson."

*   *   *

"Insomnia causes more deaths amongst
    Roman invalids
Than any other factor (the most common
    complaints, of course,
Are heartburn and ulcers, brought on by over-
    eating.)
How much sleep, I ask you, can one get in
    lodgings here?
Unbroken nights—and this is the root of the
    trouble—
Are a rich man's privilege. The waggons
    thundering past
Through those narrow twisting streets, the oaths
    of draymen
Caught in a traffic-jam—these alone would
    suffice
To jolt the doziest sea-cow of an Emperor into
Permanent wakefulness. If a business
    appointment
Summons the tycoon, *he* gets there fast, by litter,
Tacking above the crowd. There's plenty of
    room inside:
He can read, or take notes, or snooze as he jogs
    along—
Those drawn blinds are most soporific. Even so
He outstrips us: however fast we pedestrians
    hurry
We're blocked by the crowds ahead, while those
    behind us
Tread on our heels. Sharp elbows buffet my ribs,
Poles poke into me; one lout swings a crossbeam

Down on my skull, another scores with a barrel.
My legs are mud-encrusted, big feet kick me, a
    hobnailed
Soldier's boot lands squarely on my toes. Do you
    see
All that steam and bustle? The great man's
    hangers-on
Are getting their free dinner, each with his own
Kitchen-boy in attendance. Those outsize dixies,
And all the rest of the gear one poor little slave
Must balance on his head, while he trots along
To keep the charcoal glowing, would tax the
    strength
Of a musclebound general. Recently-patched
    tunics
Are ripped to shreds. Here's the great trunk of a
    fir-tree
Swaying along on its waggon, and look, another
    dray
Behind it, stacked high with pine-logs, a nodding
    threat
Over the heads of the crowd. If that axle
    snapped, and a
Cartload of marble avalanched down on them,
    what
Would be left of their bodies? Who could
    identify bits
Of ownerless flesh and bone? The poor man's
    flattened corpse
Would vanish along with his soul. And
    meanwhile, all unwitting,
The folk at home are busily scouring dishes,
Blowing the fire to a glow, clattering over
    greasy
Flesh-scrapers, filling up oil-flasks, laying out
    clean towels.
But all the time, as his houseboys hasten about
    their chores,
Himself is already sitting—the latest arrival—
By the bank of the Styx, and gawping in holy
    terror
At its filthy old ferryman. No chance of a
    passage over
That mud-thick channel for him, poor devil,
    without so much

As a copper stuck in his mouth to pay for the ride."
   "There are other nocturnal perils, of various
      sorts,
Which you should consider. It's a long way up
   to the rooftops,
And a falling tile can brain you—not to
   mention all
Those cracked or leaky pots that people toss out
   through windows.
Look at the way they smash, the weight of them,
   the damage
They do to the pavement! You'll be thought
   most improvident,
A catastrophe-happy fool, if you don't make
   your will before
Venturing out to dinner. Each open upper
   casement
Along your route at night may prove a death-
   trap:
So pray and hope (poor you!) that the local
   housewives
Drop nothing worse on your head than a pailful
   of slops."
   Then there's the drunken bully, in an
      agonized state
For lack of a victim, who lies there tossing and
   turning
The whole night through, like Achilles after the
   death
Of his boy-friend Patroclus. [This lout is
   doomed to insomnia
Unless he gets a fight.] Yet however flown with
   wine
Our young hothead may be, he carefully keeps
   his distance
From the man in a scarlet cloak, the man
   surrounded
By torches and big brass lamps and a numerous
   bodyguard.
But for me, a lonely pedestrian, trudging home
   by moonlight
Or with hand cupped round the wick of one
   poor guttering candle,
He has no respect whatever. This is the way the
   wretched

Brawl comes about (if you can term it a brawl
When you do the fighting and I'm just cast as
   punchbag).
He blocks my way. "Stop," he says. I have no
   option
But to obey—what else can one do when
   attacked
By a huge tough, twice one's size and fighting-
   mad as well?
   "Where have *you* sprung from?" he shouts.
      "Ugh, what a stench
Of beans and sour wine! I know your sort,
   you've been round
With some cobbler-crony, scoffing a boiled
   sheep's head
And a dish of spring leeks. What? Nothing to
   say for yourself?
Speak up, or I'll kick your teeth in! Tell me,
   where's your pitch?
What synagogue do you doss in?" It makes not
   a jot of difference
Whether you try to answer, or back away from
   him
Without saying a word, you get beaten up just
   the same—
And then your irate "victim" takes *you* to court
   on a charge
Of assault and battery. Such is the poor man's
   "freedom":
After being slugged to a pulp, he may beg, as a
   special
Favour, to be left with his last few remaining
   teeth.

   *   *   *

REVIEW QUESTIONS

1. On the basis of this selection, what were some
   of the major dangers and irritations of life in
   Rome?
2. What is Juvenal's attitude toward the bearers of
   Greek culture?
3. What kinds of women do his satires deal with?

OVID

FROM *The Loves*

Written in a style in distinct contrast to Juvenal's biting satires, Ovid's works about love (or lust) reflect what some might regard as a certain shallowness in Roman social relations. Eventually, Emperor Augustus found his work so morally repugnant that he banished Ovid from Rome.

From *Amores*, by Ovid, translated by Guy Lee (London: John Murray, 1968), pp. 728–31.

*   *   *

Your husband? Going to the same dinner as us?
I hope it chokes him.

So I'm only to gaze at you, darling? Play
    gooseberry
while another man enjoys your touch?

You'll lie there snuggling up to him? He'll put
    his arm
round your neck whenever he wants?

No wonder Centaurs fought over Hippodamia
when the wedding wine began to flow.

I don't live in the forest nor am I part horse
but I find it hard to keep my hands off you.

However here's my plan. Listen carefully.
Don't throw my words of wisdom to the winds.

Arrive before him—not that I see what good
arriving first will do but arrive first all the same.

When he takes his place on the couch and you
    go to join him
looking angelic, secretly touch my foot.

Watch me for nods and looks that talk
and unobserved return my signals

in the language of eyebrows and fingers
with annotations in wine.

Whenever you think of our love-making
stroke that rosy cheek with your thumb.

If you're cross with me, darling,
press the lobe of your ear

but turn your ring round if you're pleased
with anything I say or do.

When you feel like cursing your fool of a
    husband
touch the table as if you were praying.

If he mixes you a drink, beware—tell him to
    drink it himself,
then quietly ask the waiter for what you want.

I'll intercept the glass as you hand it back
and drink from the side you drank from.

Refuse all food he has tasted first—
it has touched his lips.

Don't lean your gentle head against his shoulder
and don't let him embrace you

or slide a hand inside your dress
or touch your breasts. Above all don't kiss him.

If you do I'll cause a public scandal,
grab you and claim possession.

I'm bound to see all this. It's what I shan't see
that worries me—the goings on under your
    cloak.

Don't press your thigh or your leg against his
or touch his coarse feet with your toes.

I know all the tricks. That's why I'm worried.
I hate to think of him doing what I've done.

We've often made love under your cloak,
    sweetheart,
in a glorious race against time.

You won't do that, I know. Still,
to avoid all doubt don't wear one.

Encourage him to drink but mind—no kisses.
Keep filling his glass when he's not looking.

If the wine's too much for him and he drops off
we can take our cue from what's going on
    around us.

When you get up to leave and we all follow
move to the middle of the crowd.

You'll find me there—or I'll find you
so touch me anywhere you can.

But what's the good? I'm only temporizing.
Tonight decrees our separation.

Tonight he'll lock you in and leave me
desolated at your door.

Then he'll kiss you, then go further,
forcing his right to our secret joy.

But you *can* show him you're acting under
    duress.
Be mean with your love—give grudgingly—in
    silence.

He won't enjoy it if my prayers are answered.
And if they're not, at least assure me you won't.

But whatever happens tonight tell me tomorrow
you didn't sleep with him—and stick to that
    story.

*   *   *

REVIEW QUESTIONS

1. Does Ovid seem to have any moral scruples about adultery?
2. Would Cato the Elder have approved?

APULEIUS

FROM *The Golden Ass*

Also known as "Metamorphoses," Apuleius' semi-autobiographical story (dating to the second century C.E.) recounts the misadventures of a young man named Lucius, who had resorted to the arts of magic to further his sexual desires, only to end up turning himself (literally) into an ass. He was saved from his predicament only through the intercession of the goddess Isis, whose cult had become immensely popular throughout the Mediterranean world by the time of the early Roman Empire. This selection suggests why her cult appealed to so many.

From *The Golden Ass*, translated by Robert Graves (New York: Farrar, Straus & Giroux, 1951), pp. 263–70.

Her long thick hair fell in tapering ringlets on her lovely neck, and was crowned with an intricate chaplet in which was woven every kind of flower. Just above her brow shone a round disc, like a mirror, or like the bright face of the moon, which told me who she was. Vipers rising from the left-hand and right-hand partings of her hair supported this disc, with ears of corn bristling beside them. Her many-coloured robe was of finest linen; part was glistening white, part crocus-yellow, part glowing red and along the entire hem a woven bordure of flowers and fruit clung swaying in the breeze. But what caught and held my eye more than anything else was the deep black lustre of her mantle. She wore it slung across her body from the right hip to the left shoulder, where it was caught in a knot resembling the boss of a shield; but part of it hung in innumerable folds, the tasselled fringe quivering. It was embroidered with glittering stars on the hem and everywhere else, and in the middle beamed a full and fiery moon.

In her right hand she held a bronze rattle, of the sort used to frighten away the God of the Sirocco; its narrow rim was curved like a sword-belt and three little rods, which sang shrilly when she shook the handle, passed horizontally through it. A boat-shaped gold dish hung from her left hand, and along the upper surface of the handle writhed an asp with puffed throat and head raised ready to strike. On her divine feet were slippers of palm leaves, the emblem of victory.

All the perfumes of Arabia floated into my nostrils as the Goddess deigned to address me: 'You see me here, Lucius, in answer to your prayer. I am Nature, the universal Mother, mistress of all the elements, primordial child of time, sovereign of all things spiritual, queen of the dead, queen also of the immortals, the single manifestation of all gods and goddesses that are. My nod governs the shining heights of Heaven, the wholesome sea-breezes, the lamentable silences of the world below. Though I am worshipped in many aspects, known by countless names, and propitiated with all manner of different rites, yet the whole round earth venerates me. The primeval Phrygians call me Pessinuntica, Mother of the gods; the Athenians, sprung from their own soil, call me Cecropian Artemis; for the islanders of Cyprus I am Paphian Aphrodite; for the archers of Crete I am Dictynna; for the trilingual Sicilians, Stygian Proserpine; and for the Eleusinians their ancient Mother of the Corn.

'Some know me as Juno, some as Bellona of the Battles; others as Hecate, others again as Rhamnubia, but both races of Aethiopians, whose lands the morning sun first shines upon, and the Egyptians who excel in ancient learning and worship me with ceremonies proper to my godhead, call me by my true name, namely, Queen Isis. I have come in pity of your plight, I have come to favour and aid you. Weep no more, lament no longer; the hour of deliverance, shone over by my watchful light, is at hand.

*   *   *

* * * Only remember, and keep these words of mine locked tight in your heart, that from now onwards until the very last day of your life you are dedicated to my service. It is only right that you should devote your whole life to the Goddess who makes you a man again. Under my protection you will be happy and famous, and when at the destined end of your life you descend to the land of ghosts, there too in the subterrene hemisphere you shall have frequent occasion to adore me. From the Elysian fields you will see me as queen of the profound Stygian realm, shining through the darkness of Acheron with a light as kindly and tender as I show you now. Further, if you are found to deserve my divine protection by careful obedience to the ordinances of my religion and by perfect chastity, you will become aware that I, and I alone, have power to prolong your life beyond the limits appointed by destiny.'

With this, the vision of the invincible Goddess faded and dissolved.

*   *   *

I rose at once, wide awake, bathed in a sweat of joy and fear. Astonished beyond words at this clear manifestation of her godhead, I splashed myself with sea water and carefully memorized her orders, intent on obeying them to the letter. Soon a golden sun arose to rout the dark shadows of night, and at once the streets were filled with people walking along as if in a religious triumph. Not only I, but the whole world, seemed filled with delight. The animals, the houses, even the weather itself reflected the universal joy and serenity, for a calm sunny morning had succeeded yesterday's frost, and the song-birds, assured that spring had come, were chirping their welcome to the queen of the stars, the Mother of the seasons, the mistress of the universe. The trees, too, not only the orchard trees but those grown for their shade, roused from their winter sleep by the warm breezes of the south and tasselled with green leaves, waved their branches with a pleasant rustling noise; and the crash and thunder of the surf was stilled, for the gales had blown themselves out, the dark clouds were gone and the calm sky shone with its own deep blue light.

Presently the vanguard of the grand procession came in view. It was composed of a number of people in fancy dress of their own choosing; a man wearing a soldier's sword-belt; another dressed as a huntsman, a thick cloak caught up to his waist with hunting knife and javelin; another who wore gilt sandals, a wig, a silk dress and expensive jewellery and pretended to be a woman. Then a man with heavy boots, shield, helmet and sword, looking as though he had walked straight out of the gladiators' school; a pretended magistrate with purple robe and rods of office; a philosopher with cloak, staff, clogs and billy-goat beard; a bird-catcher, car-

rying lime and a long reed; a fisherman with another long reed and a fish-hook. Oh, yes, and a tame she-bear, dressed like a woman, carried in a sedan chair; and an ape in a straw hat and a saffron-coloured Phrygian cloak with a gold cup grasped in its paws—a caricature of Jupiter's beautiful cup-bearer Ganymede. Finally an ass with wings glued to its shoulders and a doddering old man seated on its rump; you would have laughed like anything at that pair, supposed to be Pegasus and Bellerophon. These fancy-dress comedians kept running in and out of the crowd, and behind them came the procession proper.

At the head walked women crowned with flowers, who pulled more flowers out of the folds of their beautiful white dresses and scattered them along the road; their joy in the Saviouress appeared in every gesture. Next came women with polished mirrors tied to the backs of their heads, which gave all who followed them the illusion of coming to meet the Goddess, rather than marching before her. Next, a party of women with ivory combs in their hands who made a pantomime of combing the Goddess's royal hair, and another party with bottles of perfume who sprinkled the road with balsam and other precious perfumes; and behind these a mixed company of women and men who addressed the Goddess as 'Daughter of the Stars' and propitiated her by carrying every sort of light—lamps, torches, wax-candles and so forth.

Next came musicians with pipes and flutes, followed by a party of carefully chosen choir-boys singing a hymn in which an inspired poet had explained the origin of the procession. The temple pipers of the great god Serapis were there, too, playing their religious anthem on pipes with slanting mouth-pieces and tubes curving around their right ears; also a number of beadles and whifflers crying: 'Make way there, way for the Goddess!' Then followed a great crowd of the Goddess's initiates, men and women of all classes and every age, their pure white linen clothes shining brightly. The women wore their hair tied up in glossy coils under gauze head-dresses; the men's heads were completely shaven, representing the Goddess's bright earthly stars, and they carried rattles of brass, silver and even gold, which kept up a shrill and ceaseless tinkling.

The leading priests, also clothed in white linen drawn tight across their breasts and hanging down to their feet, carried the oracular emblems of the deity. The High Priest held a bright lamp, which was not at all like the lamps we use at night banquets; it was a golden boat-shaped affair with a tall tongue of flame mounting from a hole in the centre. The second priest held an *auxiliaria*, or sacrificial pot, in each of his hands—the name refers to the Goddess's providence in helping her devotees. The third priest carried a miniature palm-tree with gold leaves, also the serpent wand of Mercury. The fourth carried the model of a left hand with the fingers stretched out, which is an emblem of justice because the left hand, with its natural slowness and lack of any craft or subtlety, seems more impartial than the right. He also held a golden vessel, rounded in the shape of a woman's breast, from the nipple of which a thin stream of milk fell to the ground. The fifth carried a winnowing fan woven with golden rods, not osiers. Then came a man, not one of the five, carrying a wine-jar.

Next in the procession followed those deities that deigned to walk on human feet. Here was the frightening messenger of the gods of Heaven, and of the gods of the dead: Anubis with a face black on one side, golden on the other, walking erect and holding his herald's wand in one hand, and in the other a green palm-branch. Behind, danced a man

carrying on his shoulders, seated upright, the statue of a cow, representing the Goddess as the fruitful Mother of us all. Then along came a priest with a box containing the secret implements of her wonderful cult. Another fortunate priest had an ancient emblem of her godhead hidden in the lap of his robe: this was not made in the shape of any beast, wild or tame, or any bird or human being, but the exquisite beauty of its workmanship no less than the originality of its design called for admiration and awe. It was a symbol of the sublime and ineffable mysteries of the Goddess, which are never to be divulged: a small vessel of burnished gold, upon which Egyptian hieroglyphics were thickly crowded, with a rounded bottom, a long spout, and a generously curving handle along which sprawled an asp, raising its head and displaying its scaly, wrinkled, puffed-out throat.

At last the moment had come when the blessing promised by the almighty Goddess was to fall upon me.

REVIEW QUESTIONS

1. What does Isis demand from Lucius in return for her help?
2. How is it apparent that Isis' cult has achieved broad popularity?
3. Why might people of the early Roman Empire have been attracted to this cult?

COLUMELLA

Management of a Large Estate

The extravagant banquets that the Roman elite hosted required considerable resources in food and a suitable number and variety of slaves to perform all of the necessary tasks. The next selection is the only surviving work of a man, evidently himself the owner of a sizable estate, who lived in Spain during the first century C.E. It describes in considerable detail how an agricultural estate should be organized and managed.

From *Roman Civilization: Selected Readings*, vol. 2, edited by Naphtali Lewis and Meyer Reinhold (New York: Columbia University Press, 1953), pp. 54–67.

The size of the villa and the number of its parts should be proportioned to the whole enclosure, and it should be divided into three groups: the *villa urbana,* the *villa rustica,* and the *villa fructuaria.* The manor house should be divided in turn into winter apartments and summer apartments, in such a way that the winter bedrooms face the southeast, and the winter dining room faces the west. The summer bedrooms, on the other hand, should look toward the south, but the dining rooms of that season should look toward the southeast. The baths should face the northwest, that they may be lighted from midday up to evening. The promenades should have a southern exposure, so as to receive both the maximum of sun in winter and the minimum in summer. But in the part devoted to farm uses there will be placed a spacious and high kitchen, that the rafters may be free from the danger of fire, and that it may offer a convenient place for the slave household to stop in at every season of the year. It will be best that cubicles for unfettered slaves be built facing the south; for those who are in chains there should be an underground prison, as wholesome as possible, receiving light through a number of narrow windows built so high from the ground that they cannot be reached with the hand.

For cattle there should be stables which will not be troubled by either heat or cold; for animals broken to work, two sets of stalls—one for winter, another for summer; and for the other animals which it is proper to keep within the farmstead there should be places partly covered, partly open to the sky, and surrounded with high walls so that the animals may rest in the one place in winter, in the other in summer, secure against attacks by wild animals. But stables should be roomy and so arranged that no moisture can flow in and that whatever is made there may run off quickly, to prevent the rotting of either the bases of the walls or the hoofs of the cattle. Ox stalls should be ten feet wide, or nine at least—a size which will allow room for the animal to lie down and for the oxherd to move around in it when performing his duties. The feedracks should not be too high for the ox or pack animal to feed from without inconvenience while standing. Quarters should be provided for the overseer alongside the entrance, so that he may have oversight of all who come in and go out; and for the steward over the entrance for the same reason, and also so that he may keep close watch on the overseer; and near both of these there should be a storehouse in which all farm gear may be collected, and within it a closet for the storing of the iron implements.

Cells for the herdsmen and shepherds should be adjacent to their animals, so that they may conveniently run out to care for them. And yet all should be quartered as close as possible to one another, so that the diligence of the overseer may not be overtaxed in making the rounds of the several places, and also that they may be witnesses of one another's industry and diligence.

The storehouse part is divided into rooms for oil, for presses, for wine, for the boiling down of must; lofts for hay and chaff; and storerooms and grain bins—in such a manner that those on the ground floor take care of liquid products, such as oil and wine for marketing, while dry products, such as grain, hay, leaves, chaff, and other fodder, should be stored in lofts. But the grain lofts, as I have said, should be reached by ladders and should receive ventilation through small openings on the north side; for that exposure is the coolest and the least humid, and both these factors contribute to the preservation of stored grain. The same reason holds true in the placing of the wine room on the ground floor; and it should be far removed from the baths, oven, dunghill, and other filthy places which give off a foul odor, and no less so from cisterns and running water, from which is derived a moisture that spoils the wine. . . .

The press rooms especially and the storerooms for oil should be warm, because every liquid is more readily thinned with heat and thickened by great cold; and if oil freezes, which seldom happens, it becomes rancid. But as it is natural heat that is wanted, arising from the climate and the exposure, there is no need of fire or flame, as the taste of oil is spoiled by smoke and soot. For this reason the pressing room should be lighted from the southern side, so that we may not find it necessary to employ fires and lamps when the olives are being pressed.

The cauldron room, in which boiled wine is made, should be neither narrow nor dark, so that the attendant who is boiling down the must may move around without inconvenience. The smoke room, too, in which timber not long cut may be seasoned quickly, can be built in a section of the farmhouse adjoining the farmhouse baths (it is important also that there be such places in which the household may bathe—but only on holidays; for the frequent use of baths is not conducive to physical vigor). Storerooms for wine will be situated to advantage over these places from which smoke is usually rising, for wines age more rapidly when they are brought to an early maturity by a certain kind of smoke. For this reason there should be another loft to which they may be removed, to keep them from becoming tainted, on the other hand, by too much smoking.

As for the situation of the farmhouse and the arrangement of its several parts, enough has been said. It will be necessary, next, that the farmhouse have the following near it: an oven and a mill, of such size as may be required by the number of tenant farmers; at least two ponds, one to serve for geese and cattle, the other in which we may soak lupines, elm withes, twigs, and other things suitable for our needs. There should also be two manure pits, one to receive the fresh dung and

keep it for a year, and a second from which the old is hauled; but both of them should be built shelving with a gentle slope, in the manner of fish ponds, and built up and packed hard with earth, so as not to let the moisture drain away. . . .

The threshing floor is to be placed, if possible, in such manner that it can be viewed from above by the master, or at least by the farm manager. Such a floor is best when paved with hard stone, because the grain is thus threshed out quickly, since the ground does not give way under the beating of the hoofs and threshing sledges, and the winnowed grain is cleaner and is free from small stones and clods, which a dirt floor nearly always casts up during the threshing. . . .

The orchards, too, and the gardens should be fenced all around and should lie close by, in a place to which there may flow all manure-laden seepage from barnyard and baths, and the watery lees squeezed from olives; for both vegetables and trees thrive on nutriment of this sort, too.

After all these things have been obtained or constructed, the master must give special attention, among other things, to laborers; and these are either tenant farmers or slaves. He should be civil in dealing with his tenant farmers, should show himself affable, and should be more exacting in the matter of work than of payments, as this gives less offense yet is, generally speaking, more profitable. For when land is carefully tilled, it usually brings a profit, and never a loss except when it is assailed by unusually severe weather or robbers; and therefore the tenant does not venture to ask for reduction of his rent. But the master should not be insistent on his rights in every particular to which he has bound his tenant, such as the exact day for payment of money, or the matter of demanding firewood and other trifling contributions; attention to such matters causes country folk more trouble than expense. . . . I myself remember having heard Publius Volusius, an old man who had been consul and was very wealthy, declare that estate to be most fortunate which had natives of the place as tenant farmers and which held them by reason of long association, even from the cradle, as if born on their own father's property. So I am decidedly of the opinion that repeated re-letting of a farm is a bad thing, but that a worse thing is the tenant farmer who lives in town and prefers to till the land through his slaves rather than by his own hand. Saserna used to say that from a man of this sort the return was usually a lawsuit instead of income, and that for this reason we should take pains to keep with us tenants who are country-bred and at the same time diligent farmers, when we are not able to till the land ourselves or when it is not feasible to cultivate it with our own household; though this does not happen except in districts which are desolated by the severity of the climate and the barrenness of the soil. But when the climate is moderately healthful and the soil moderately good, a man's personal attention never fails to yield a larger return from his land than does that of a tenant. Even reliance on an overseer yields a larger return, except in the event of extreme carelessness or greed on the part of that slave. There is no doubt that in general both these offenses are either committed or fostered through the fault of the master, inasmuch as he has the authority to prevent such a person from being placed in charge of his affairs or to see to it that he is removed if so placed. On far-distant estates, however, which it is not easy for the owner to visit, it is better for every kind of land to be under free farmers than under slave overseers, but this is particularly true of grain land. To such land a tenant farmer can do no great harm, as he can to vineyards and trees, while slaves do it tremendous damage: they let out oxen for hire, and they keep them and other animals poorly fed; they do not plow the ground carefully, and they charge the account with far more seed than they have actually sown; what they have committed to the earth they do not foster so that it will make the proper growth; and when hey have brought it to the threshing floor, every day during the threshing they lessen the quantity either by trickery or by carelessness. For they themselves steal it and do not guard against the thieving of others, and even when it is stored away, they do not enter it honestly in their accounts. The result is that both manager and hands

are offenders, and the land pretty often gets a bad name. Therefore my opinion is that an estate of this sort should be leased if, as I have said, it cannot have the presence of the owner.

The next point is with regard to slaves—over what duty it is proper to place each, and to what sort of tasks to assign them. So my advice at the start is not to appoint an overseer from the sort of slaves who are physically attractive, and certainly not from that class which has been engaged in the voluptuous occupations of the city. This lazy and sleepy-headed class of slaves, accustomed to idling, to the Field of Mars, the circus and the theaters, to gambling, to taverns, to bawdy houses, never ceases to dream of these follies; and when they carry them over into their farming, the master suffers not so much loss in the slave himself as in his whole estate. A man should be chosen who has been hardened by farm work from his infancy, one who has been tested by experience. . . . He should be of middle age and of strong physique, skilled in farm operations or at least very painstaking, so that he may learn the more readily; for it is not in keeping with this business of ours for one man to give orders and another to give instruction, nor can a man properly exact work when he is being tutored by an underling as to what is to be done and in what way. Even an illiterate person, if only he have a retentive mind, can manage affairs well enough. Cornelius Celsus says that an overseer of this sort brings money to his master oftener than he does his book, because, being illiterate, he is either less able to falsify accounts or is afraid to do so through a second party, because that would make another aware of the deception.

But be the overseer what he may, he should be given a woman companion to keep him within bounds and moreover in certain matters to be a help to him. . . . He must be urged to take care of the equipment and the iron tools, and to keep in repair and stored away twice as many as the number of slaves requires, so that there will be no need of borrowing from a neighbor; for the loss in slave labor exceeds the cost of articles of this sort. In the care and clothing of the slave household he should have an eye to usefulness rather than appearance, taking care to keep them fortified against wind, cold, and rain, all of which are warded off with long-sleeved leather tunics, garments of patchwork, or hooded cloaks. If this be done, no weather is so unbearable but that some work may be done in the open. He should be not only skilled in the tasks of husbandry but should also be endowed, as far as the servile disposition allows, with such qualities of mind that he may exercise authority without laxness and without cruelty, and always humor some of the better hands, at the same time being forbearing even with those of lesser worth, so that they may rather fear his sternness than detest his cruelty. . . .

In the case of the other slaves, the following are, in general, the precepts to be observed, and I do not regret having held to them myself: to talk rather familiarly with the country slaves, provided only that they have not conducted themselves unbecomingly, more frequently than I would with town slaves; and when I perceived that their unending toil was lightened by such friendliness on the part of the master, I would even jest with them at times and allow them also to jest more freely. Nowadays I make it a practice to call them into consultation on any new work, as if they were more experienced, and to discover by this means what sort of ability is possessed by each of them and how intelligent he is. Furthermore, I observe that they are more willing to set about a piece of work on which they think that their opinions have been asked and their advice followed. Again, it is the established custom of all men of caution to inspect the slaves in the prison, to find out whether they are carefully chained, whether the places of confinement are quite safe and properly guarded, whether the overseer has put anyone in fetters or removed his shackles without the master's knowledge. . . . And the investigation of the householder should be the more painstaking in the interest of slaves of this sort, that they may not be treated unjustly in the matter of clothing or other allowances, inasmuch as, being subject to a greater number of people, such as overseers, taskmasters, and jailers, they are the more liable to

unjust punishment, and again, when smarting under cruelty and greed, they are more to be feared. Accordingly, a careful master inquires not only of them, but also of those who are not in bonds, as being more worthy of belief, whether they are receiving what is due them under his instructions. He also tests the quality of their food and drink by tasting it himself and examines their clothing, mittens, and foot covering. In addition, he should give them frequent opportunities for making complaints against those persons who treat them cruelly or dishonestly. In fact, I now and then avenge those who have just cause for grievance, as well as punish those who incite the slaves to revolt or who slander their taskmasters; and, on the other hand, I reward those who conduct themselves with energy and diligence. Also, to women who are unusually prolific, and who ought to be rewarded for the bearing of a certain number of offspring, I have granted exemption from work and sometimes even freedom after they have reared many children: a mother of three children received exemption from work, a mother of more, her freedom as well. Such justice and consideration on the part of the master contributes greatly to the increase of his estate. . . .

This, too, I believe: that the duties of the slaves should not be confused to the point where all take a hand in every task. For this is by no means to the advantage of the husbandman, either because no one regards any particular task as his own or because, when he does make an effort, he is performing a service that is not his own but common to all, and therefore shirks his work to a great extent; and yet fault cannot be fastened upon any one man because many have a hand in it. For this reason plowmen must be distinguished from vine dressers, and vine dressers from plowmen, and both of these from men of all work. Furthermore, squads should be formed, not to exceed ten men each, which the ancients called *decuriae* and approved of highly, because that limited number was most conveniently guarded while at work and the size was not disconcerting to the person in charge as he led the way. Therefore, if the field is of considerable extent, such squads should be distributed over sections of it and the work should be so apportioned that men will not be by ones or twos, because they are not easily watched when scattered; and yet they should not number more than ten, lest, on the other hand, when the band is too large, each individual may think that the work does not concern him. This arrangement not only stimulates rivalry, but also discloses the slothful; for, when a task is enlivened by competition, punishment inflicted on the laggards appears just and free from censure.

REVIEW QUESTIONS

1. What kinds of crops are produced on the estate?
2. Who performs most of the work?
3. How are the workers to be managed and treated?
4. How does the treatment of slaves on this estate compare with the treatment of slaves in the mines of Spain (as described in the earlier selection by Diodorus Siculus)?
5. How do living conditions on a country estate compare with those in Rome?

JOSEPHUS

FROM *The Jewish War*

A major component of the rich religious diversity of the Roman empire was Judaism, from which would emerge the religion that would come to dominate later European civilization, Christianity. At the same time, the Jews of Judaea (modern Palestine/ Israel) actively resented Roman rule and on several occasions rose in rebellion, only to be crushed by Roman troops and eventually, in 70 C.E., to see their great temple in Jerusalem sacked and destroyed. The following selections from the works of the Jewish historian Flavius Josephus, a participant in this war, illustrate the diversity and vitality within Judaism in the mid-first century C.E., as well as the awesomeness and brutality of Roman imperial domination.

From Josephus, *The Jewish War*, translated by G. A. Williamson (New York: Penguin Books, 1981), pp. 133–38, 156–62 (original translation published 1959).

*   *   *

Among the Jews there are three schools of thought, whose adherents are called Pharisees, Sadducees, and Essenes respectively. The Essenes profess a severer discipline: they are Jews by birth and are peculiarly attached to each other. They eschew pleasure-seeking as a vice and regard temperance and mastery of the passions as virtue. Scorning wedlock, they select other men's children while still pliable and teachable, and fashion them after their own pattern—not that they wish to do away with marriage as a means of continuing the race, but they are afraid of the promiscuity of women and convinced that none of the sex remains faithful to one man. Contemptuous of wealth, they are communists to perfection, and none of them will be found to be better off than the rest: their rule is that novices admitted to the sect must surrender their property to the order, so that among them all neither humiliating poverty nor excessive wealth is ever seen, but each man's possessions go into the pool and as with brothers their entire property belongs to them all. Oil they regard as polluting, and if a man is unintentionally smeared with it he scrubs himself clean; for they think it desirable to keep the skin dry and always to wear white. Men to supervise the community's affairs are elected by show of hands, chosen for their tasks by universal suffrage.

They possess no one city but everywhere have large colonies. When adherents arrive from elsewhere, all local resources are put at their disposal as if they were their own, and men they have never seen before entertain them like old friends. And so when they travel they carry no baggage at all, but only weapons to keep off bandits. In every town one of the order is appointed specially to look after strangers and issue clothing and provisions. In dress and personal appearance they are like children in the care of a stern tutor. Neither garments nor shoes are changed till they are dropping to pieces or worn out with age. Among themselves nothing is bought or sold: everyone gives what he has to anybody in need and receives from him in return something he himself can use; and even without giving anything in return they are free to share the possessions of anyone they choose.

They show devotion to the Deity in a way all their own. Before the sun rises they do not utter a word on secular affairs, but offer to Him some traditional prayers as if beseeching Him to appear. After this their supervisors send every man to the craft he understands best, and they work assiduously till an hour before noon, when they again meet in one place and donning linen loincloths wash all over with cold water. After this purification they assemble in a building of their own which no one outside their community is allowed to enter; they then go into the refectory in a state of ritual cleanliness as if it was a holy temple and sit down in silence. Then the baker gives them their loaves in turn, and the cook sets before each man one plateful of one kind of food. The priest says

grace before meat: to taste the food before this prayer is forbidden. After breakfast he offers a second prayer; for at beginning and end they give thanks to God as the Giver of life. Then removing their garments as sacred they go back to their work till evening. Returning once more they take supper in the same way, seating their guests beside them if any have arrived. Neither shouting nor disorder ever desecrates the house: in conversation each gives way to his neighbour in turn. To people outside the silence within seems like some dread mystery; it is the natural result of their unfailing sobriety and the restriction of their food and drink to a simple sufficiency.

In general they take no action without orders from the supervisors, but two things are left entirely to them—personal aid, and charity; they may of their own accord help any deserving person in need or supply the penniless with food. But gifts to their own kinsfolk require official sanction. Showing indignation only when justified, they keep their tempers under control; they champion good faith and serve the cause of peace. Every word they speak is more binding than an oath; swearing they reject as something worse than perjury, for they say a man is already condemned if he cannot be believed without God being named. They are wonderfully devoted to the work of ancient writers, choosing mostly books that can help soul and body; from them in their anxiety to cure disease they learn all about medicinal roots and the properties of stones.

Persons desirous of joining the sect are not immediately admitted. For a whole year a candidate is excluded but is required to observe the same rule of life as the members, receiving from them a hatchet, the loin-cloth mentioned above, and white garments. When he has given proof of his temperance during this period, he is associated more closely with the rule and permitted to share the purer waters of sanctification, though not yet admitted to the communal life. He has demonstrated his strength of purpose, but for two more years his character is tested, and if he is then seen to be worthy, he is accepted into the society. But before touching the communal food he must swear terrible oaths, first that he will revere the Godhead, and secondly that he will deal justly with men, will injure no one either of his own accord or at another's bidding, will always hate the wicked and co-operate with the good, and will keep faith at all times and with all men—especially with rulers, since all power is conferred by God. If he himself receives power, he will never abuse his authority and never by dress or additional ornament outshine those under him; he will always love truth and seek to convict liars, will keep his hands from stealing and his soul innocent of unholy gain, and will never hide anything from members of the sect or reveal any of their secrets to others, even if brought by violence to the point of death. He further swears to impart their teaching to no man otherwise than as he himself received it, to take no part in armed robbery, and to preserve the books of the sect and in the same way the names of the angels. Such are the oaths by which they make sure of their converts.

*   *   *

They are divided into four grades, according to the stage they have reached in their preparation; and so far are the juniors inferior to the seniors that if they touch them the persons touched must wash as though contaminated by an alien. They are long-lived, most of them passing the century, owing to the simplicity of their daily life, I suppose, and the regular routine. They despise danger and conquer pain by sheer will-power: death, if it comes with honour, they value more than life without end. Their spirit was tested to the utmost by the war with the Romans, who racked and twisted, burnt and broke them, subjecting them to every torture yet invented in order to make them blaspheme the Lawgiver or eat some forbidden food, but could not make them do either, or ever once fawn on their tormentors or shed a tear. Smiling in their agony and gently mocking those who tortured them, they resigned their souls in the joyous certainty that they would receive them back.

It is indeed their unshakable conviction that bodies are corruptible and the material composing them impermanent, whereas souls remain immortal for ever. Coming forth from the most rarefied ether they are trapped in the prison-house of the body as if drawn down by one of nature's spells; but once freed from the bonds of the flesh, as if released after years of slavery, they rejoice and soar aloft. Teaching the same doctrine as the sons of Greece, they declare that for the good souls there waits a home beyond the ocean, a place troubled by neither rain nor snow nor heat, but refreshed by the zephyr that blows ever gentle from the ocean. Bad souls they consign to a darksome, stormy abyss, full of punishments that know no end. I think the Greeks had the same notion when they assigned to their brave men, whom they call heroes or demigods, the Islands of the Blest, and to the souls of the wicked the place of the impious in Hades, where according to their stories certain people undergo punishment—Sisyphus and Tantalus, Ixion and Tityus, and the like. They tell these tales firstly because they believe souls to be immortal, and secondly in the hope of encouraging virtue and discouraging vice, since the good become better in their lifetime through the hope of a reward after death, and the propensities of the bad are restrained by the fear that, even if they are not caught in this life, after their dissolution they will undergo eternal punishment. This then is the religious teaching of the Essenes about the soul, providing an inescapable inducement to those who have once tasted their wisdom.

Some of them claim to foretell the future, after a lifelong study of sacred literature, purifications of different kinds, and the aphorisms of prophets; rarely if ever do their predictions prove wrong.

There is a second order of Essenes, which agrees with the other in its way of life, customs, and rules, and differs only in its views on marriage. They think that the biggest thing in life—the continuance of the race—is forfeited by men who do not marry, and further, if everyone followed their example mankind would rapidly disappear. However, they put their brides on probation for three years, and do not marry them till the regularity of their periods proves them capable of child-bearing. When conception has taken place intercourse ceases—proof that the object of the marriage was not pleasure but the begetting of children. When women bathe they wear a dress just as the men wear a loincloth. Such are the customs of the order.

Of the two schools named first, the Pharisees are held to be the most authoritative exponents of the Law and count as the leading sect. They ascribe everything to Fate or to God: the decision whether or not to do right rests mainly with men, but in every action Fate takes some part. Every soul is imperishable, but only the souls of good men pass into other bodies, the souls of bad men being subjected to eternal punishment. The Sadducees, the second order, deny Fate altogether and hold that God is incapable of either committing sin or seeing it; they say that men are free to choose between good and evil, and each individual must decide which he will follow. The permanence of the soul, punishments in Hades, and rewards they deny utterly. Again, Pharisees are friendly to one another and seek to promote concord with the general public, but Sadducees, even towards each other, show a more disagreeable spirit, and in their relations with men like themselves they are as harsh as they might be to foreigners.

*   *   *

[Later in his account, Josephus describes the atrocities perpetrated against the Jews of Judaea by the brutal and corrupt Roman procurator Florus. He then recounts how the Roman-backed king of Judaea, Agrippa, appealed to the people of Jerusalem to refrain from rising in revolt against the power of Rome.]

'Consider these pretexts one at a time, and see how feeble are your grounds for war. First, the charges against the procurators. You should flatter, not provoke, the authorities; when for trifling errors you pile on reproaches, it is yourselves you hurt by your denunciation of the offenders; instead of injuring you secretly and shamefacedly they plunder you openly. Nothing damps an aggressor like patient submission, and the meekness of the persecuted puts the persecutor to shame. I grant that the ministers of Rome are unbearably harsh; does it follow that all the Romans are persecuting

you, including Caesar? Yet it is on them that you are going to make war! It is not by their wish that an unscrupulous governor comes from Rome, and western eyes cannot see the goings-on in the east; it is not easy in Rome even to get up-to-date news of what happens here. It would be absurd because of the trifling misdemeanours of one man to go to war with a whole nation, and such a nation—a nation that does not even know what it is all about! Our grievances can be quickly put right; the same procurator will not be here for ever, and his successors are almost sure to be more reasonable. But once set on foot, war cannot easily be either broken off or fought to a conclusion without disaster.

'As for your new passion for liberty, it comes too late; you ought to have made a supreme effort to retain it long ago. For the experience of slavery is a painful one, and to escape it altogether any effort is justified; but the man who has once submitted and then revolts is a refractory slave, not a lover of liberty. Thus the time when we ought to have done everything possible to keep the Romans out was when the country was invaded by Pompey. But our ancestors and their kings, with material, physical, and mental resources far superior to yours, faced a mere fraction of the Roman army and put up no resistance; will you, who have learnt submission from your fathers and are so ill provided compared with those who first submitted, stand up to the whole Roman Empire?

'Think of the Athenians. To preserve the liberty of Greece they once consigned their city to the flames. When proud Xerxes sailed across land and marched across water and counting the seas no barrier led an army too big for Europe to hold, they chased him away in a single ship like a runaway slave. Near little Salamis they broke the might of Asia—and today they are slaves of Rome, and the city that once lorded it over Greece takes her orders from Italy! Think of the Spartans; after Thermopylae and Plataea, after Agesilaus who swept across Asia, they are happy under the same masters. Think of the Macedonians. They still dream of Philip and see visions of the goddess who with Alexander sowed for them the seeds of world-empire; yet they endure this complete transformation and loyally serve the new recipients of Fortune's favours. Other nations by the thousand, bursting with greater determination to assert their liberty, no longer resist. Will you alone refuse to serve the masters of the whole world?

'Where are the men, where are the weapons you count on? Where is the fleet that is to sweep the Roman seas? Where are the funds to pay for your expeditions? Do you think you are going to war with Egyptians and Arabs? Look at the far-flung empire of Rome and contrast your own impotence. Why, our forces have been worsted even by our neighbours again and again, while their arms have triumphed over the whole world! And even the world is not big enough to satisfy them; the Euphrates is not far enough to the east, or the Danube to the north, or Libya and the desert beyond to the south, or Cadiz to the west; but beyond the Ocean they have sought a new world, carrying their arms as far as Britain, that land of mystery. Why not face facts? Are you richer than the Gauls, stronger than the Germans, cleverer than the Greeks, more numerous than all the nations of the world? What gives you confidence to defy the power of Rome?

'It is terrible to be enslaved, it will be said. How much worse for Greeks, who surpass every nation under the sun in nobility and fill such a wide domain, and yet bow before the *fasces* of a Roman governor, as do the Macedonians, who have a better right than you to demand their liberty! And what of the five hundred cities of Asia? Do they not without a garrison bow before one governor and the consular *fasces*? Need I mention the Heniochi, the Colchians, and the Tauric race, the peoples near the Bosporus, the Black Sea, and the Sea of Azov? At one time they recognized not even a native ruler, and now they submit to 3,000 legionaries, while forty warships keep the peace on the sea where before none but pirates sailed. How justly Bithynia, Cappadocia, Pamphylia, Lycia, and Cilicia might demand liberty! Yet without armed pressure they pay their dues.

'Then there are the Thracians, spread over a country five days' march in width and seven in length, more rugged and much more defensible

than yours, a country whose icy blasts are enough to halt an invader. Yet 2,000 Roman guards suffice to maintain order. Their neighbours the Illyrians, whose land extends from Dalmatia to the Danube frontier, need only two legions to keep them quiet; in fact Illyrians unite with Romans to halt Dacian raids. The Dalmatians again, who have so often tried to shake off the yoke and have always been driven by defeat to rally their forces and revolt again, now live peaceably under one Roman legion!

'But if any people might reasonably be tempted to rebel by its peculiar advantages, that people is the Gauls, provided as they are with such marvellous natural defences, on the east the Alps, on the north the Rhine, on the south the Pyrenees, and on the west the Ocean. Yet in spite of these immense obstacles, in spite of their huge total of three hundred and five tribes, in spite of the prosperity that wells up from their soil and enables them to flood the whole world with their goods, they submit to being the milch cow of Rome and receiving from her hands what they themselves have produced! And this they tolerate, not from effeminacy or racial inferiority—they fought for eighty years to save their liberty—but because they are overawed by the might of Rome and still more by her destiny, which wins her more victories than do her arms. So Gaul is kept in order by 1,200 soldiers—hardly more men than she has cities!

'Then Spain—in the fight for independence the gold from her soil could not save her, nor could the vast stretch of land and sea that separates her from Rome, nor the tribes of Lusitania and Cantabria with their passion for fighting, nor the neighbouring Ocean that terrifies even the natives with its tides. Crossing the cloud-capped Pyrenees and advancing their arms beyond the Pillars of Hercules, the Romans enslaved Spain too. Yet to guard this remote and almost invincible nation requires but one legion!

'Which of you has not heard of the Germans, with their inexhaustible manpower? You have, I am sure, seen their magnificent physique on many occasions, for on every side Roman masters have German slaves; yet this people occupies an immense area, their physique is surpassed by their pride, from the bottom of their hearts they despise death, and when enraged they are more dangerous than the fiercest of wild beasts. Yet the Rhine is the limit of their aggression and the Romans with eight legions have tamed them, enslaving the prisoners and driving the entire nation to seek refuge in flight.

'Consider the defences of the Britons, you who feel so sure of the defences of Jerusalem. They are surrounded by the Ocean and inhabit an island as big as the land which we inhabit; yet the Romans crossed the sea and enslaved them, and four legions keep that huge island quiet. But why should I say more about that, when even the Parthians, the most warlike race of all, rulers of so many nations and protected by such vast forces, send hostages to Rome, and on Italian soil may be seen, humbly submitting for the sake of peace, the aristocrats of the east.

'Almost every nation under the sun bows down before the might of Rome; and will you alone go to war, not even considering the fate of the Carthaginians, who boasted of great Hannibal and their glorious Phoenician ancestors, but fell beneath Scipio's hand? The Cyrenians (Spartans by descent), the Marmaridae (a race that extends to the waterless desert), Syrtes, whose very mention terrifies, Nasamonians, Moors, Numidians with their vast numbers—none of them could resist Roman skill at arms. This third of the whole world, whose nations could hardly be counted, bounded by the Atlantic and the Pillars of Hercules, and supporting the millions of Ethiopia as far as the Indian Ocean, is subdued in its entirety; and apart from the regular crops which for eight months of the year feed the whole population of Rome, these peoples pay tribute of every kind, and for the needs of the Empire willingly submit to taxation; and unlike you they take no offence when given orders, though only a single legion is quartered in their midst.

'But why should we go so far for evidence of the Roman power when we can find it in Egypt, our nearest neighbour? She stretches as far as Ethiopia and Arabia Felix; she is the port for India; she has a population of seven and a half million

(excluding the citizens of Alexandria), as is shown by the poll-tax returns. But she does not repudiate the rule of Rome—yet what a stimulus to revolt she has in Alexandria with its size, its population and its wealth! a city three and a half miles long and over a mile wide, which pays Rome every month more tribute than you pay in a year, and apart from money sends her corn for four months, and which is protected on every side by trackless deserts or harbourless seas or rivers or marshes. Yet none of these things proved equal to the fortune of Rome, and two legions stationed in the city curb the remotest parts of Egypt and the nobility of Macedon as well.

'Whom, I ask you, will you find in the uninhabited wilds to be your allies in this war? for in the inhabited world all are Romans—unless you extend your hopes beyond the Euphrates and imagine that your kinsmen from Adiabene will come to your aid! But they will not without good reason get involved in a full-scale war, and if they should decide on anything so foolish, the Parthian king would put a stop to it; for he is anxious to preserve his armistice with the Romans, and will consider it a breach of the truce if any of his tributaries takes the field against them.

'So there is no refuge left except to make God your ally. But He too is ranged on the Roman side, for without His help so vast an empire could never have been built up. Think too how difficult it would be, even if you were fighting feeble opponents, to preserve the purity of your religion, and how you will be forced to transgress the very laws which furnish your chief hope of making God your ally, and so will alienate Him. If you observe the custom of the Sabbath with its complete cessation of activity, you will promptly be crushed, as were your ancestors by Pompey, who was most active in pressing the siege on the days when the besieged were passive. But if in the war you transgress your ancestral Law I don't see what you have left to fight for, since your one desire is that none of your ancestral customs should be broken. How will you be able to call the Deity to your aid, if you deliberately deny Him the service that is due?

'Everyone who engages in war relies on either

divine or human help; but when, as is probable, both are denied, the aggressor is bringing certain destruction on himself. What prevents you from killing your wives and children with your own hands and from consigning your ancestral home, the most beautiful in the world, to the flames? By such madness you would at least avoid the shame of defeat! It is wise, my friends, it is wise, while the vessel is still in harbour, to foresee the approaching storm, and not to sail out into the middle of the hurricane to sure destruction. For those on whom disaster falls out of the blue are at least entitled to pity, but a man who plunges into destruction with his eyes open earns only contempt.

'Possibly some of you suppose that you are making war in accordance with agreed rules, and that when the Romans have won they will be kind to you, and will not think of making you an example to other nations by burning down your Holy City and destroying your entire race. I tell you, not even if you survive will you find a place of refuge, since every people recognizes the lordship of Rome or fears that it will have to do so. Again, the danger threatens not only ourselves here but also those who live in other cities; for there is not a region in the world without its Jewish colony. All these, if you go to war, will be massacred by your opponents, and through the folly of a few men every city will run with Jewish blood. There would be an excuse for such a massacre; but if it did not take place, think how wicked it would be to take up arms against such kindly people! Pity your wives and children, or at least pity your mother city and

its sacred precincts. Spare the Temple and preserve for your use the Sanctuary with its sacred treasures. For the Romans will no longer keep their hands off when they have captured these, since for sparing them hitherto they have received no thanks at all. I call to witness all you hold sacred, the holy angels of God, and the Fatherland we all share, that I have not kept back anything that is for your safety; if you make a right decision, you will share with me the blessings of peace, but if you are carried away by your passions, you will go without me to your doom.'

*   *   *

REVIEW QUESTIONS

1. Can you identify possible points of conflict in religious belief and practice within Judaism in the first century C.E.?
2. Can you identify parallels between aspects of Jewish belief and beliefs of non-Jewish groups of this time?
3. Can you identify reasons that the Jews of Judaea might resent and rebel against Roman imperial authority?
4. Many historians have observed similarities and contrasts between Roman imperial rule and American global hegemony in the early twenty-first century. Does Josephus' account of Agrippa's speech provide some basis for such observations?

TACITUS

FROM *Germania*

As the Romans' empire expanded, they came into contact with various peoples. None of them was to have a more significant or enduring influence on the shaping of Western civilization than the Germans, whose chieftains eventually would sup-

plant Roman authority in western Europe. That at least some Romans had an ink-
ling of the Germans' later importance is evident in the Germania *of the Roman*
historian Tacitus, who wrote this work at the end of the first century C.E.

From *The Agricola and Germany of Tacitus*, translated by A. J. Church and W. J. Brodribb
(Basingstoke, Eng.: Macmillan, 1877).

*   *   *

For my own part, I agree with those who think that the tribes of Germany are free from all taint of intermarriages with foreign nations, and that they appear as a distinct, unmixed race, like none but themselves. Hence, too, the same physical peculiarities throughout so vast a population. All have fierce blue eyes, red hair, huge frames, fit only for a sudden exertion. They are less able to bear laborious work. Heat and thirst they cannot in the least endure; to cold and hunger their climate and their soil inure them.

Their country, though somewhat various in appearance, yet generally either bristles with forests or reeks with swamps; it is more rainy on the side of Gaul, bleaker on that of Noricum and Pannonia. It is productive of grain, but unfavourable to fruit-bearing trees; it is rich in flocks and herds, but these are for the most part undersized, and even the cattle have not their usual beauty or noble head. It is number that is chiefly valued; they are in fact the most highly prized, indeed the only riches of the people. Silver and gold the gods have refused to them, whether in kindness or in anger I cannot say. I would not, however, affirm that no vein of German soil produces gold or silver, for who has ever made a search? They care but little to possess or use them. You may see among them vessels of silver, which have been presented to their envoys and chieftains, held as cheap as those of clay. The border population, however, value gold and silver for their commercial utility, and are familiar with, and show preference for, some of our coins. The tribes of the interior use the simpler and more ancient practice of the barter of commodities. They like the old and well-known money, coins milled, or showing a two-horse

chariot. They likewise prefer silver to gold, not from any special liking, but because a large number of silver pieces is more convenient for use among dealers in cheap and common articles.

Even iron is not plentiful with them, as we infer from the character of their weapons. But few use swords or long lances. They carry a spear with a narrow and short head, but so sharp and easy to wield that the same weapon serves, according to circumstances, for close or distant conflict. As for the horse-soldier, he is satisfied with a shield and spear; the foot-soldiers also scatter showers of missiles, each man having several and hurling them to an immense distance, and being naked or lightly clad with a little cloak. There is no display about their equipment: their shields alone are marked with very choice colours. A few only have corslets, and just one or two here and there a metal or leathern helmet. Their horses are remarkable neither for beauty nor for fleetness. Nor are they taught various evolutions after our fashion, but are driven straight forward, or so as to make one wheel to the right in such a compact body that none is left behind another. On the whole, one would say that their chief strength is in their infantry, which fights along with the cavalry; admirably adapted to the action of the latter is the swiftness of certain foot-soldiers, who are picked from the entire youth of their country, and stationed in front of the line. Their number is fixed,—a hundred from each canton; and from this they take their name among their countrymen, so that what was originally a mere number has now become a title of distinction. Their line of battle is drawn up in a wedge-like formation. To give ground, provided you return to the attack, is considered prudence rather than cowardice. The bodies of their slain they carry off even

A MUMMY FROM THE TIME OF THE ROMAN EMPIRE (100 C.E.)

This painted and gilded case contains the mummy of a man with the very un-Egyptian name Artemidorus, who died evidently in his early twenties, shortly after 100 C.E. To what extent are classical and Egyptian artistic elements and symbolism mixed in the decoration of this case? Do you see evidence for the survival of ancient Egyptian religious beliefs and traditions under Roman rule? What is your assessment of the skill of the artist who painted Artemidorus' portrait?

in indecisive engagements. To abandon your shield is the basest of crimes; nor may a man thus disgraced be present at the sacred rites, or enter their council; many, indeed, after escaping from battle, have ended their infamy with the halter.

They choose their kings by birth, their generals for merit. These kings have not unlimited or arbitrary power, and the generals do more by example than by authority. If they are energetic, if they are conspicuous, if they fight in the front, they lead because they are admired. But to reprimand, to imprison, even to flog, is permitted to the priests alone, and that not as a punishment, or at the general's bidding, but, as it were, by the mandate of the god whom they believe to inspire the warrior. They also carry with them into battle certain figures and images taken from their sacred groves. And what most stimulates their courage is, that their squadrons or battalions, instead of being formed by chance or by a fortuitous gathering, are composed of families and clans. Close by them, too, are those dearest to them, so that they hear the shrieks of women, the cries of infants. *They* are to every man the most sacred witnesses of his bravery—*they* are his most generous applauders. The soldier brings his wounds to mother and wife, who shrink not from counting or even demanding them and who administer both food and encouragement to the combatants.

Tradition says that armies already wavering and giving way have been rallied by women who, with earnest entreaties and bosoms laid bare, have vividly represented the horrors of captivity, which the Germans fear with such extreme dread on behalf of their women, that the strongest tie by which a state can be bound is the being required to give, among the number of hostages, maidens of noble birth. They even believe that the sex has a certain sanctity and prescience, and they do not despise their counsels, or make light of their answers. In Vespasian's days we saw Veleda, long regarded by many as a divinity. In former times, too, they venerated Aurinia, and many other women, but not with servile flatteries, or with sham deification.

* * *

Augury and divination by lot no people practise more diligently. The use of the lots is simple. A little bough is lopped off a fruit-bearing tree, and cut into small pieces; these are distinguished by certain marks, and thrown carelessly and at random over a white garment. In public questions the priest of the particular state, in private the father of the family, invokes the gods, and, with his eyes towards heaven, takes up each piece three times, and finds in them a meaning according to the mark previously impressed on them. If they prove unfavourable, there is no further consultation that day about the matter; if they sanction it, the confirmation of augury is still required. For they are also familiar with the practice of consulting the notes and the flight of birds. It is peculiar to this people to seek omens from horses. Kept at the public expense, in these same woods and groves, are white horses, pure from the taint of earthly labour; these are yoked to a sacred car, and accompanied by the priest and the king, or chief of the tribe, who note their neighings and snortings. No species of augury is more trusted, not only by the people and by the nobility, but also by the priests, who regard themselves as the ministers of the gods, and the horses as acquainted with their will. They have also another method of observing auspices, by which they seek to learn the result of an important war. Having taken, by whatever means, a prisoner from the tribe with whom they are at war, they pit him against a picked man of their own tribe, each combatant using the weapons of their country. The victory of the one or the other is accepted as an indication of the issue.

About minor matters the chiefs deliberate, about the more important the whole tribe. Yet even when the final decision rests with the people, the affair is always thoroughly discussed by the chiefs. They assemble, except in the case of a sudden emergency, on certain fixed days, either at new or at full moon; for this they consider the most auspicious season for the transaction of business. Instead of reckoning by days as we do, they reckon by nights, and in this manner fix both their ordinary and their legal appointments. Night they regard as bringing on day. Their freedom has this disadvantage, that they do not meet simultaneously or as they are bidden, but two or three days are wasted in the delays of assembling. When the multitude think proper, they sit down armed. Silence is proclaimed by the priests, who have on these occasions the right of keeping order. Then the king or the chief, according to age, birth, distinction in war, or eloquence, is heard, more because he has influence to persuade than because he has power to command. If his sentiments displease them, they reject them with murmurs; if they are satisfied, they brandish their spears. The most complimentary form of assent is to express approbation with their weapons.

In their councils an accusation may be preferred or a capital crime prosecuted. Penalties are distinguished according to the offence. Traitors and deserters are hanged on trees; the coward, the unwarlike, the man stained with abominable vices, is plunged into the mire of the morass, with a hurdle put over him. This distinction in punishment means that crime, they think, ought, in being punished, to be exposed, while infamy ought to be buried out of sight. Lighter offences, too, have penalties proportioned to them; he who is convicted, is fined in a certain number of horses or of cattle. Half of the fine is paid to the king or to the state, half to the person whose wrongs are avenged and to his relatives. In these same councils they also elect the chief magistrates, who administer law in the cantons and the towns. Each of these has a hundred associates chosen from the people, who support him with their advice and influence.

They transact no public or private business without being armed. It is not, however, usual for anyone to wear arms till the state has recognised his power to use them. Then in the presence of the council one of the chiefs, or the young man's father, or some kinsman, equips him with a shield and a spear. These arms are what the "toga" is

with us, the first honour with which youth is invested. Up to this time he is regarded as a member of a household, afterwards as a member of the commonwealth. Very noble birth or great services rendered by the father secure for lads the rank of a chief; such lads attach themselves to men of mature strength and of long approved valour. It is no shame to be seen among a chief's followers. Even in his escort there are gradations of rank, dependent on the choice of the man to whom they are attached. These followers vie keenly with each other as to who shall rank first with his chief, the chiefs as to who shall have the most numerous and the bravest followers. It is an honour as well as a source of strength to be thus always surrounded by a large body of picked youths; it is an ornament in peace and a defence in war. And not only in his own tribe but also in the neighbouring states it is the renown and glory of a chief to be distinguished for the number and valour of his followers, for such a man is courted by embassies, is honoured with presents, and the very prestige of his name often settles a war.

When they go into battle, it is a disgrace for the chief to be surpassed in valour, a disgrace for his followers not to equal the valour of the chief. And it is an infamy and a reproach for life to have survived the chief, and returned from the field. To defend, to protect him, to ascribe one's own brave deeds to his renown, is the height of loyalty. The chief fights for victory; his vassals fight for their chief. If their native state sinks into the sloth of prolonged peace and repose, many of its noble youths voluntarily seek those tribes which are waging some war, both because inaction is odious to their race, and because they win renown more readily in the midst of peril, and cannot maintain a numerous following except by violence and war. Indeed, men look to the liberality of their chief for their war-horse and their blood-stained and victorious lance. Feasts and entertainments, which, though inelegant, are plentifully furnished, are their only pay. The means of this bounty come from war and rapine. Nor are they as easily persuaded to plough the earth and to wait for the year's produce as to challenge an enemy and earn the honour of wounds. Nay, they actually think it tame and stupid to acquire by the sweat of toil what they might win by their blood.

Whenever they are not fighting, they pass much of their time in the chase, and still more in idleness, giving themselves up to sleep and to feasting, the bravest and the most warlike doing nothing, and surrendering the management of the household, of the home, and of the land, to the women, the old men, and all the weakest members of the family. They themselves lie buried in sloth, a strange combination in their nature that the same men should be so fond of idleness, so averse to peace. It is the custom of the states to bestow by voluntary and individual contribution on the chiefs a present of cattle or of grain, which, while accepted as a compliment, supplies their wants. They are particularly delighted by gifts from neighbouring tribes, which are sent not only by individuals but also by the state, such as choice steeds, heavy armour, trappings, and neckchains. We have now taught them to accept money also.

It is well known that the nations of Germany have no cities, and that they do not even tolerate closely contiguous dwellings. They live scattered and apart, just as a spring, a meadow, or a wood has attracted them. Their villages they do not arrange in our fashion, with the buildings connected and joined together, but every person surrounds his dwelling with an open space, either as a precaution against the disasters of fire, or because they do not know how to build. No use is made by them of stone or tile; they employ timber for all purposes, rude masses without ornament or attractiveness. Some parts of their buildings they stain more carefully with a clay so clear and bright that it resembles painting, or a coloured design. They are wont also to dig out subterranean caves, and pile on them great heaps of dung, as a shelter from winter and as a receptacle for the year's produce, for by such places they mitigate the rigour of the cold. And should an enemy approach, he lays waste the open country, while what is hidden and buried is either not known to exist, or else

escapes him from the very fact that it has to be searched for.

They all wrap themselves in a cloak which is fastened with a clasp, or, if this is not forthcoming, with a thorn, leaving the rest of their persons bare. They pass whole days on the hearth by the fire. The wealthiest are distinguished by a dress which is not flowing, like that of the Sarmatae and Parthi, but is tight, and exhibits each limb. They also wear the skins of wild beasts; the tribes on the Rhine and Danube in a careless fashion, those of the interior with more elegance, as not obtaining other clothing by commerce. These select certain animals, the hides of which they strip off and vary them with the spotted skins of beasts, the produce of the outer ocean, and of seas unknown to us. The women have the same dress as the men, except that they generally wrap themselves in linen garments, which they embroider with purple, and do not lengthen out the upper part of their clothing into sleeves. The upper and lower arm is thus bare, and the nearest part of the bosom is also exposed.

Their marriage code, however, is strict, and indeed no part of their manners is more praiseworthy. Almost alone among barbarians they are content with one wife, except a very few among them, and then not from sensuality, but because their noble birth procures for them many offers of alliance. The wife does not bring a dower to the husband, but the husband to the wife. The parents and relatives are present, and pass judgment on the marriage-gifts, gifts not meant to suit a woman's taste, nor such as a bride would deck herself with, but oxen, a caparisoned steed, a shield, a lance, and a sword. With these presents the wife is espoused, and she herself in her turn brings her husband a gift of arms. This they count their strongest bond of union, these their sacred mysteries, these their gods of marriage. Lest the woman should think herself to stand apart from aspirations after noble deeds and from the perils of war, she is reminded by the ceremony which inaugurates marriage that she is her husband's partner in toil and danger, destined to suffer and to dare with him alike both in peace and in war.

The yoked oxen, the harnessed steed, the gift of arms, proclaim this fact. She must live and die with the feeling that she is receiving what she must hand down to her children neither tarnished nor depreciated, what future daughters-in-law may receive, and may be so passed on to her grandchildren.

Thus with their virtue protected they live uncorrupted by the allurements of public shows or the stimulant of feastings. Clandestine correspondence is equally unknown to men and women. Very rare for so numerous a population is adultery, the punishment for which is prompt, and in the husband's power. Having cut off the hair of the adulteress and stripped her naked, he expels her from the house in the presence of her kinsfolk, and then flogs her through the whole village. The loss of chastity meets with no indulgence; neither beauty, youth, nor wealth will procure the culprit a husband. No one in Germany laughs at vice, nor do they call it the fashion to corrupt and to be corrupted. Still better is the condition of those states in which only maidens are given in marriage, and where the hopes and expectations of a bride are then finally terminated. They receive one husband, as having one body and one life, that they may have no thoughts beyond, no further-reaching desires, that they may love not so much the husband as the married state. To limit the number of their children or to destroy any of their subsequent offspring is accounted infamous, and good habits are here more effectual than good laws elsewhere.

In every household the children, naked and filthy, grow up with those stout frames and limbs which we so much admire. Every mother suckles her own offspring, and never entrusts it to servants and nurses. The master is not distinguished from the slave by being brought up with greater delicacy. Both live amid the same flocks and lie on the same ground till the freeborn are distinguished by age and recognised by merit. The young men marry late, and their vigour is thus unimpaired. Nor are the maidens hurried into marriage; the same age and a similar stature is required; well-matched and vigorous they wed,

and the offspring reproduce the strength of the parents. Sisters' sons are held in as much esteem by their uncles as by their fathers; indeed, some regard the relation as even more sacred and binding, and prefer it in receiving hostages, thinking thus to secure a stronger hold on the affections and a wider bond for the family. But every man's own children are his heirs and successors, and there are no wills. Should there be no issue, the next in succession to the property are his brothers and his uncles on either side. The more relatives he has, the more numerous his connections, the more honoured is his old age; nor are there any advantages in childlessness.

It is a duty among them to adopt the feuds as well as the friendships of a father or a kinsman. These feuds are not implacable; even homicide is expiated by the payment of a certain number of cattle and of sheep, and the satisfaction is accepted by the entire family, greatly to the advantage of the state, since feuds are dangerous in proportion to a people's freedom.

No nation indulges more profusely in entertainments and hospitality. To exclude any human being from their roof is thought impious; every German, according to his means, receives his guest with a well-furnished table. When his supplies are exhausted, he who was but now the host becomes the guide and companion to further hospitality, and without invitation they go to the next house. It matters not; they are entertained with like cordiality. No one distinguishes between an acquaintance and a stranger, as regards the rights of hospitality. It is usual to give the departing guest whatever he may ask for, and a present in return is asked with as little hesitation. They are greatly charmed with gifts, but they expect no return for what they give, nor feel any obligation for what they receive.

On waking from sleep, which they generally prolong to a late hour of the day, they take a bath, oftenest of warm water, which suits a country where winter is the longest of the seasons. After their bath they take their meal, each having a separate seat and table of his own. Then they go armed to business, or no less often to their festal meetings. To pass an entire day and night in drinking disgraces no one. Their quarrels, as might be expected with intoxicated people, are seldom fought out with mere abuse, but commonly with wounds and bloodshed. Yet it is at their feasts that they generally consult on the reconciliation of enemies, on the forming of matrimonial alliances, on the choice of chiefs, finally even on peace and war, for they think that at no time is the mind more open to simplicity of purpose or more warmed to noble aspirations. A race without either natural or acquired cunning, they disclose their hidden thoughts in the freedom of the festivity. Thus the sentiments of all having been discovered and laid bare, the discussion is renewed on the following day, and from each occasion its own peculiar advantage is derived. They deliberate when they have no power to dissemble; they resolve when error is impossible.

A liquor for drinking is made out of barley or other grain, and fermented into a certain resemblance to wine. The dwellers on the river-bank also buy wine. Their food is of a simple kind, consisting of wild-fruit, fresh game, and curdled milk. They satisfy their hunger without elaborate preparation and without delicacies. In quenching their thirst they are not equally moderate. If you indulge their love of drinking by supplying them with as much as they desire, they will be overcome by their own vices as easily as by the arms of an enemy.

One and the same kind of spectacle is always exhibited at every gathering. Naked youths who practise the sport bound in the dance amid swords and lances that threaten their lives. Experience gives them skill, and skill again gives grace; profit or pay are out of the question; however reckless their pastime, its reward is the pleasure of the spectators. Strangely enough they make games of hazard a serious occupation even when sober, and so venturesome are they about gaining or losing, that, when every other resource has failed, on the last and final throw they stake the freedom of their own persons. The loser goes into voluntary slavery; though the younger and stronger, he suffers himself to be bound and sold. Such is their stub-born persistency in a bad practice; they themselves call it honour. Slaves of this kind the owners part with in the way of commerce, and also to relieve themselves from the scandal of such a victory.

The other slaves are not employed after our manner with distinct domestic duties assigned to them, but each one has the management of a house and home of his own. The master requires from the slave a certain quantity of grain, of cattle, and of clothing, as he would from a tenant, and this is the limit of subjection. All other household functions are discharged by the wife and children. To strike a slave or to punish him with bonds or with hard labour is a rare occurrence. They often kill them, not in enforcing strict discipline, but on the impulse of passion, as they would an enemy, only it is done with impunity. The freedmen do not rank much above slaves, and are seldom of any weight in the family, never in the state, with the exception of those tribes which are ruled by kings. There indeed they rise above the freedborn and the noble; elsewhere the inferiority of the freedman marks the freedom of the state.

Of lending money on interest and increasing it by compound interest they know nothing—a more effectual safeguard than if it were prohibited.

Land proportioned to the number of inhabitants is occupied by the whole community in turn, and afterwards divided among them according to rank. A wide expanse of plains makes the partition easy. They till fresh fields every year, and they have still more land than enough; with the richness and extent of their soil, they do not laboriously exert themselves in planting orchards, inclosing meadows, and watering gardens. Corn is the only produce required from the earth; hence even the year itself is not divided by them into as many seasons as with us. Winter, spring, and summer have both a meaning and a name; the name and blessings of autumn are alike unknown.

In their funerals there is no pomp; they simply observe the custom of burning the bodies of illustrious men with certain kinds of wood. They do not heap garments or spices on the funeral pile. The weapons of the dead man and in some cases his horse are consigned to the fire. A turf mound forms the tomb. Monuments with their lofty elaborate splendour they reject as oppressive to the dead. Tears and lamentations they soon dismiss; grief and sorrow but slowly. It is thought becoming for women to bewail, for men to remember, the dead.

Such on the whole is the account which I have received of the origin and manners of the entire German people.

*   *   *

REVIEW QUESTIONS

1. As described by Tacitus, what were some of the principal values that governed German society?
2. How did those values compare with values of imperial Roman society as evidenced in some of the preceding readings?
3. Can you discern parallels or contrasts between Tacitus' views on Germans and the earlier views (see Chapter 3) of Hippocrates on the people of Europe?

6 ❧ CHRISTIANITY AND THE TRANSFORMATION OF THE ROMAN WORLD

By 300 C.E., the emperor Diocletian and his colleagues had reorganized the Roman Empire, which now appeared more prosperous and stable than it had been for decades. Paganism, a convenient but misleading name for the broad spectrum of ancient, nonmonotheistic beliefs, remained dominant, and Diocletian soon began a vigorous persecution of the Christian sect. By about 600 C.E., this world had profoundly changed. The Roman Empire had disappeared in the West, replaced by numerous barbarian kingdoms. Starting with the conversion of the emperor Constantine in 312 C.E., Christianity gradually triumphed over paganism in the Roman Empire, becoming the official religion before the collapse of the empire. Missionary work among the barbarian tribes succeeded in bringing new peoples like the Goths and Franks into the Christian fold. The barbarian kingdoms and the Christian Church, through its bishops and monasteries, transformed the legacies of the ancient world, religion, and classical culture and created the new society of early medieval Europe.

Constantine's conversion remains one of the most important events in late antiquity. The emperor's understanding of his new faith included the idea that he was an authority in religious matters and a leader of the church in this world. As emperor and high priest of the Roman state cult, Constantine retained the same legal rights over Christianity that earlier rulers had exercised over pagan cults. Of all the aspects of Roman culture, its legal system, based on imperial decrees and legal commentaries, was one of the main bequests to subsequent societies. The fifth-century C.E. Theodosian Code and the great compilations made under Emperor Justinian in the next century show the Christian Roman emperors trying to incorporate the recently tolerated (313 C.E.) and soon enough only official religion (391 C.E.) into a legal system originally attuned to pagan values.

In the centuries before Christianity emerged from persecution, the new faith found adherents because of its promise of salvation, the supportive and caring nature of early Christian communities, and the witnessing of generations of martyrs. For nearly three centuries Christianity existed in a context of bouts of persecution and indifference, as Rome's pagan subjects, Christians, and Jews were in conflict over the most basic beliefs. In addition to the texts collected into the New Testament and approved by church leaders, many other documents reveal both the spirit of the early martyrs and the effects of martyrdom on the people who witnessed it.

One of Christianity's distinctive institutions originating in Egypt was the monastery, and the Benedictine Rule demonstrates how a community dedicated to poverty, chastity, and obedience organized a common life for people wanting to escape the secular world and its temptations. Not everyone was called to be a nun or monk, but her or his style of life, as well as that of the more isolated hermits, defined perfection, especially after the opportunities for martyrdom waned. The late empire's internal decay encouraged people to abandon the world, but it also attracted its most serious external threat, the waves of barbarians from the north and east. Tribes like the Franks and Visigoths, seeking protection inside the frontiers from more fearsome peoples like the Huns, ended up wrecking an empire they probably wanted to preserve for their own benefit. But as Rome was unable to defend its western frontiers, more doubts surfaced about the vitality and meaning of classical values.

St. Augustine of Hippo in North Africa was perhaps the most significant voice of the late Roman world. His many books continued to influence theologians in the medieval and early modern periods and beyond. Augustine tried to account for the sack of Rome in 410 C.E. in terms that strengthened Christian beliefs and denied pagans the chance to blame the new religion for the empire's defeats. Augustine, laying the foundations for doctrines on original sin and predestination of the saved and damned, also took on one of the empire's most important social and economic institutions, slavery, and fit it into Christian belief. Augustine also wrote a spiritual autobiography, The Confessions, *that served as a model of self-reflection and awareness for many centuries. The Christian Church preserved some of the traditions and texts of ancient culture as most of this world crumbled.*

FROM The Gospel of Matthew

Among the eastern religions that gained popularity during the early empire was Judaism, especially that version of it espoused by the Christians, followers of the teachings of an itinerant Jewish preacher named Yeshua (in Latin, Jesus), whose career in Judaea ended with his death by crucifixion sometime around 30 C.E. The chief records of his life and teachings are contained in the gospels, a number of which were composed in the decades after his death (including a gospel of James and a gospel of Thomas) but only four of which, those of Mark, Matthew, Luke, and John, were later accepted as authoritative.

From *Contemporary English Version* by American Bible Society (New York: American Bible Society, 1995).

*   *   *

Years later, John the Baptist started preaching in the desert of Judea. He said, "Turn back to God! The kingdom of heaven will soon be here." John was the one the prophet Isaiah was talking about, when he said,

"In the desert someone
is shouting,
'Get the road ready
for the Lord!
Make a straight path
for him.'"

John wore clothes made of camel's hair. He had a leather strap around his waist and ate grasshoppers and wild honey.

From Jerusalem and all Judea and from the Jordan River Valley crowds of people went to John. They told how sorry they were for their sins, and he baptized them in the river.

Many Pharisees and Sadducees also came to be baptized. But John said to them:

You bunch of snakes! Who warned you to run from the coming judgment? Do something to show that you have really given up your sins. And don't start telling yourselves that you belong to Abraham's family. I tell you that God can turn these stones into children for Abraham. An ax is ready to cut the trees down at their roots. Any tree that doesn't produce good fruit will be chopped down and thrown into a fire.

I baptize you with water so that you will give up your sins. But someone more powerful is going to come, and I am not good enough even to carry his sandals. He will baptize you with the Holy Spirit and with fire. His threshing fork is in his hand, and he is ready to separate the wheat from the husks. He will store the wheat in a barn and burn the husks in a fire that never goes out.

Jesus left Galilee and went to the Jordan River to be baptized by John. But John kept objecting and said, "I ought to be baptized by you. Why have you come to me?"

Jesus answered, "For now this is how it should be, because we must do all that God wants us to do." Then John agreed.

So Jesus was baptized. And as soon as he came out of the water, the sky opened, and he saw the Spirit of God coming down on him like a dove. Then a voice from heaven said, "This is my own dear Son, and I am pleased with him."

When Jesus saw the crowds, he went up on the side of a mountain and sat down. Jesus' disciples gathered around him, and he taught them:

God blesses those people
who depend only on him.
They belong to the kingdom
of heaven! God blesses those people
who grieve.
They will find comfort!
God blesses those people
who are humble.
The earth will belong
to them!
God blesses those people
who want to obey him more than to eat or
   drink.
They will be given
what they want!
God blesses those people
who are merciful.
They will be treated
with mercy!
God blesses those people
whose hearts are pure.
They will see him!
God blesses those people
who make peace.
They will be called
his children!
God blesses those people
who are treated badly
for doing right.
They belong to the kingdom
of heaven.

God will bless you when people insult you, mistreat you, and tell all kinds of evil lies about you because of me. Be happy and excited! You will have a great reward in heaven. People did these same things to the prophets who lived long ago.

You are like salt for everyone on earth. But if salt no longer tastes like salt, how can it make food salty? All it is good for is to be thrown out and walked on.

You are like light for the whole world. A city built on top of a hill cannot be hidden, and no one would light a lamp and put it under a clay pot. A lamp is placed on a lampstand, where it can give light to everyone in the house. Make your light shine, so that others will see the good that you do and will praise your Father in heaven.

Don't suppose that I came to do away with the Law and the Prophets. I did not come to do away with them, but to give them their full meaning. Heaven and earth may disappear. But I promise you that not even a period or comma will ever disappear from the Law. Everything written in it must happen. If you reject even the least important command in the Law and teach others to do the same, you will be the least important person in the kingdom of heaven. But if you obey and teach others its commands, you will have an important place in the kingdom. You must obey God's commands better than the Pharisees and the teachers of the Law obey them. If you don't, I promise you that you will never get into the kingdom of heaven.

You know that our ancestors were told, "Do not murder" and "A murderer must be brought to trial." But I promise you that if you are angry with someone, you will have to stand trial. If you call someone a fool, you will be taken to court. And if you say that someone is worthless, you will be in danger of the fires of hell. So if you are about to place your gift on the altar and remember that someone is angry with you, leave your gift there in front of the altar. Make peace with that person, then come back and offer your gift to God.

Before you are dragged into court, make friends with the person who has accused you of doing wrong. If you don't, you will be handed over to the judge and then to the officer who will put you in jail. I promise you that you will not get out until you have paid the last cent you owe.

You know the commandment which says, "Be faithful in marriage." But I tell you that if you look at another woman and want her, you are already unfaithful in your thoughts. If your right eye causes you to sin, poke it out and throw it away. It is better to lose one part of your body, than for your whole body to end up in hell. If your right hand causes you to sin, chop it off and throw it away! It is better to lose one part of your body, than for your whole body to be thrown into hell.

You have been taught that a man who divorces his wife must write out divorce papers for her. But

I tell you not to divorce your wife unless she has committed some terrible sexual sin. If you divorce her, you will cause her to be unfaithful, just as any man who marries her is guilty of taking another man's wife.

You know that our ancestors were told, "Don't use the Lord's name to make a promise unless you are going to keep it." But I tell you not to swear by anything when you make a promise! Heaven is God's throne, so don't swear by heaven. The earth is God's footstool, so don't swear by the earth. Jerusalem is the city of the great king, so don't swear by it. Don't swear by your own head. You cannot make one hair white or black. When you make a promise, say only "Yes" or "No." Anything else comes from the devil.

You know that you have been taught, "An eye for an eye and a tooth for a tooth." But I tell you not to try to get even with a person who has done something to you. When someone slaps your right cheek, turn and let that person slap your other cheek. If someone sues you for your shirt, give up your coat as well. If a soldier forces you to carry his pack one mile, carry it two miles. When people ask you for something, give it to them. When they want to borrow money, lend it to them.

You have heard people say, "Love your neighbors and hate your enemies." But I tell you to love your enemies and pray for anyone who mistreats you. Then you will be acting like your Father in heaven. He makes the sun rise on both good and bad people. And he sends rain for the ones who do right and for the ones who do wrong. If you love only those people who love you, will God reward you for that? Even tax collectors love their friends. If you greet only your friends, what's so great about that? Don't even unbelievers do that? But you must always act like your Father in heaven.

*   *   *

When you pray, don't be like those show-offs who love to stand up and pray in the meeting places and on the street corners. They do this just to look good. I can assure you that they already have their reward.

When you pray, go into a room alone and close the door. Pray to your Father in private. He knows what is done in private, and he will reward you.

When you pray, don't talk on and on as people do who don't know God. They think God likes to hear long prayers. Don't be like them. Your Father knows what you need before you ask.

You should pray like this:

Our Father in heaven,
help us to honor
your name.
Come and set up
your kingdom,
so that everyone on earth
will obey you,
as you are obeyed
in heaven.
Give us our food for today. Forgive us for
doing wrong,
as we forgive others.
Keep us from being tempted
and protect us from evil.

If you forgive others for the wrongs they do to you, your Father in heaven will forgive you. But if you don't forgive others, your Father will not forgive your sins.

When you go without eating, don't try to look gloomy as those show-offs do when they go without eating. I can assure you that they already have their reward. Instead, comb your hair and wash your face. Then others won't know that you are going without eating. But your Father sees what is done in private, and he will reward you.

Don't store up treasures on earth! Moths and rust can destroy them, and thieves can break in and steal them. Instead, store up your treasures in heaven, where moths and rust cannot destroy them, and thieves cannot break in and steal them. Your heart will always be where your treasure is.

Your eyes are like a window for your body. When they are good, you have all the light you need. But when your eyes are bad, everything is dark. If the light inside you is dark, you surely are in the dark.

You cannot be the slave of two masters! You will like one more than the other or be more loyal to one than the other. You cannot serve both God and money.

I tell you not to worry about your life. Don't worry about having something to eat, drink, or wear. Isn't life more than food or clothing? Look at the birds in the sky! They don't plant or harvest. They don't even store grain in barns. Yet your Father in heaven takes care of them. Aren't you worth more than birds?

Can worry make you live longer? Why worry about clothes? Look how the wild flowers grow. They don't work hard to make their clothes. But I tell you that Solomon with all his wealth wasn't as well clothed as one of them. God gives such beauty to everything that grows in the fields, even though it is here today and thrown into a fire tomorrow. He will surely do even more for you! Why do you have such little faith? Don't worry and ask yourselves, "Will we have anything to eat? Will we have anything to drink? Will we have any clothes to wear?" Only people who don't know God are always worrying about such things. Your Father in heaven knows that you need all of these. But more than anything else, put God's work first and do what he wants. Then the other things will be yours as well.

Don't worry about tomorrow. It will take care of itself. You have enough to worry about today.

Don't condemn others, and God won't condemn you. God will be as hard on you as you are on others! He will treat you exactly as you treat them.

You can see the speck in your friend's eye, but you don't notice the log in your own eye. How can you say, "My friend, let me take the speck out of your eye," when you don't see the log in your own eye? You're nothing but show-offs! First, take the log out of your own eye. Then you can see how to take the speck out of your friend's eye.

Don't give to dogs what belongs to God. They will only turn and attack you. Don't throw pearls down in front of pigs. They will trample all over them.

Ask, and you will receive. Search, and you will find. Knock, and the door will be opened for you.

Everyone who asks will receive. Everyone who searches will find. And the door will be opened for everyone who knocks. Would any of you give your hungry child a stone, if the child asked for some bread? Would you give your child a snake if the child asked for a fish? As bad as you are, you still know how to give good gifts to your children. But your heavenly Father is even more ready to give good things to people who ask.

Treat others as you want them to treat you. This is what the Law and the Prophets are all about.

Go in through the narrow gate. The gate to destruction is wide, and the road that leads there is easy to follow. A lot of people go through that gate. But the gate to life is very narrow. The road that leads there is so hard to follow that only a few people find it.

Watch out for false prophets! They dress up like sheep, but inside they are wolves who have come to attack you. You can tell what they are by what they do. No one picks grapes or figs from thornbushes. A good tree produces good fruit, and a bad tree produces bad fruit. A good tree cannot produce bad fruit, and a bad tree cannot produce good fruit. Every tree that produces bad fruit will be chopped down and burned. You can tell who the false prophets are by their deeds.

Not everyone who calls me their Lord will get into the kingdom of heaven. Only the ones who obey my Father in heaven will get in. On the day of judgment many will call me their Lord. They will say, "We preached in your name, and in your name we forced out demons and worked many miracles." But I will tell them, "I will have nothing to do with you! Get out of my sight, you evil people!"

Anyone who hears and obeys these teachings of mine is like a wise person who built a house on solid rock. Rain poured down, rivers flooded, and winds beat against that house. But it did not fall, because it was built on solid rock.

Anyone who hears my teachings and doesn't obey them is like a foolish person who built a house on sand. The rain poured down, the rivers flooded, and the winds blew and beat against that house. Finally, it fell with a crash.

When Jesus finished speaking, the crowds were surprised at his teaching. He taught them like someone with authority, and not like their teachers of the Law of Moses.

*   *   *

1. As expressed in the Sermon on the Mount, what were the chief features of Jesus' teaching?
2. How does he offer his teachings as a break from earlier traditions?
3. What is the kingdom of heaven?

CONSTANTINE

FROM An Oration

Constantine the Great (ruled 312–337 C.E.) converted to Christianity in 312 C.E., unified the empire under his rule by 324 C.E., and began the process of turning the Roman Empire into a Christian state. He also founded its new eastern capital at Constantinople and summoned the first great ecumenical council of the church at Nicaea in 325 C.E. This document is the final part of a speech Constantine probably gave to a local church council in Antioch in the spring of 325 C.E. This oration displays the emperor's bombastic style and his opinions about the new religion and God he chose to adopt.

From *Eusebius*, vol. 1, *Nicene and Post-Nicene Fathers of the Christian Church*, edited by Henry Wace and Philip Schaff (1890), pp. 578–80.

*   *   *

Chapter XXII

To thee, Piety, I ascribe the cause of my own prosperity, and of all that I now possess. To this truth the happy issue of all my endeavors bears testimony: brave deeds, victories in war, and triumphs over conquered foes. This truth the great city itself allows with joy and praise. The people, too, of that much-loved city accord in the same sentiment, though once, deceived by ill-grounded hopes, they chose a ruler unworthy of themselves, a ruler who speedily received the chastisement which his audacious deeds deserved. But be it far from me now to recall the memory of these events, while holding converse with thee, Piety, and essaying with earnest endeavor to address thee with holy and gentle words. Yet will I say one thing, which haply shall not be unbefitting or unseemly. A furious, a cruel, and implacable war was maintained by the tyrants against thee, Piety, and thy holy churches: nor were there wanting some in Rome itself who exulted at a calamity so grievous to the public weal. Nay, the battlefield was prepared; when thou didst stand forth, and present thyself a voluntary victim, supported by faith in God. Then indeed it was that the cruelty of ungodly men, which raged incessantly like a devouring fire, wrought for thee a wondrous and ever memorable glory. Astonishment seized the spectators themselves, when they beheld the very executioners who tortured the bodies of their holy victims wearied out, and disgusted at the cruelties; the bonds loosened, the engines of torture powerless, the flames extinguished, while the sufferers preserved their constancy unshaken even for a moment. What, then, hast thou gained by these atrocious deeds, most impious of men? And what was the cause of thy insane fury? Thou wilt say, doubtless, these acts of thine were done in honor of the gods. What gods are these? or what worthy conception hast thou of the Divine nature? Thinkest thou the gods are subject to angry passions as thou art? Were it so indeed, it had been better for thee to wonder at their strange determination than obey their harsh command, when they urged thee to the unrighteous slaughter of innocent men. Thou wilt allege, perhaps, the customs of thy ancestors, and the opinion of mankind in general, as the cause of this conduct. I grant the fact: for those customs are very like the acts themselves, and proceed from the self same source of folly. Thou thoughtest, it may be, that some special power resided in images formed and fashioned by human art; and hence thy reverence, and diligent care lest they should be defiled: those mighty and highly exalted gods, thus dependent on the care of men!

Chapter XXIII

Compare our religion with your own. Is there not with us genuine concord, and unwearied love of others? If we reprove a fault, is not our object to admonish, not to destroy; our correction for safety, not for cruelty? Do we not exercise, not only sincere faith towards God, but fidelity in the relations of social life? Do we not pity the unfortunate? Is not ours a life of simplicity, which disdains to cover evil beneath the mask of fraud and hypocrisy? Do we not acknowledge the true God, and his undivided sovereignty? This is real godliness: this is religion sincere and truly undefiled: this is the life of wisdom; and they who have it are travelers, as it were, on a noble road which leads to eternal life. For he who has entered on such a course, and keeps his soul pure from the pollutions of the body, does not wholly die: rather may he be said to complete the service appointed him by God, than to die. Again, he who confesses allegiance to God is not easily overborne by insolence or rage, but nobly stands under the pressure of necessity and the trial of his constancy is, as it were, a passport to the favor of God. For we cannot doubt that the Deity is pleased with excellence in human conduct. For it would be absurd indeed if the powerful and the humble alike acknowledge gratitude to those from whose services they receive benefit, and repay them by services in return, and yet that he who is supreme and sovereign of all, nay, who is Good itself, should be negligent in this respect. Rather does he follow us throughout the course of our lives, is near us in every act of goodness, accepts, and at once rewards our virtue and obedience; though he defers the full recompense to that future period, when the actions of our lives shall pass under his review, and when those who are clear in that account shall receive the reward of everlasting life, while the wicked shall be visited with the penalties due to their crimes.

Chapter XXIV

To thee, Decius, I now appeal, who has trampled with insult on the labors of the righteous: to thee, the hater of the Church, the punisher of those who lived a holy life: what is now thy condition after death? How hard and wretched thy present circumstances! Nay, the interval before thy death gave proof enough of thy miserable fate, when, overthrown with all thine army on the plains of Scythia, thou didst expose the vaunted power of Rome to the contempt of the Goths. Thou, too, Valerian, who didst manifest the same spirit of cruelty towards the servants of God, hast afforded an example of righteous judgment. A captive in the enemies' hands, led in chains while yet arrayed in the purple and imperial attire, and at last thy skin stripped from thee, and preserved by command of Sapor the Persian king, thou hast left a perpetual trophy of thy calamity. And thou, Aurelian, fierce perpetrator of every wrong, how signal was thy fall, when, in the midst of thy wild career in Thrace, thou wast slain on the public highway, and didst fill the furrows of the road with thine impious blood!

Chapter XXV

Diocletian, however, after the display of relentless cruelty as a persecutor, evinced a consciousness of his own guilt, and, owing to the affliction of a disordered mind, endured the confinement of a mean and separate dwelling. What, then, did he gain by his active hostility against our God? Simply this, I believe, that he passed the residue of his life in continual dread of the lightning's stroke. Nicomedia attests the fact; eyewitnesses, of whom I myself am one, declare it. The palace, and the emperor's private chamber were destroyed, consumed by lightning, devoured by the fire of heaven. Men of understanding hearts had indeed predicted the issue of such conduct; for they could not keep silence, nor conceal their grief at such unworthy deeds; but boldly and openly expressed their feeling, saying one to another: "What madness is this? and what an insolent abuse of power, that man should dare to fight against God; should deliberately insult the most holy and just of all religions; and plan, without the slightest provocation, the destruction of so great a multitude of righteous persons? O rare example of moderation to his subjects! Worthy instructor of his army in the care and protection due to their fellow-citizens! Men who had never seen the backs of a retreating army plunged their swords into the breasts of their own countrymen!" So great was the effusion of blood shed, that if shed in battle with barbarian enemies, it had been sufficient to purchase a perpetual peace. At length, indeed, the providence of God took vengeance on these unhallowed deeds; but not without severe damage to the state. For the entire army of the emperor of whom I have just spoken, becoming subject to the authority of a worthless person, who had violently usurped the supreme authority at Rome (when the providence of God restored freedom to that great

city), was destroyed in several successive battles. And when we remember the cries with which those who were oppressed, and who ardently longed for their native liberty, implored the help of God; and their praise and thanksgiving to him on the removal of the evils under which they had groaned, when that liberty was regained, and free and equitable intercourse restored: do not these things every way afford convincing proofs of the providence of God, and his affectionate regard for the interests of mankind?

Chapter XXVI

When men commend my services, which owe their origin to the inspiration of Heaven, do they not clearly establish the truth that God is the cause of the exploits I have performed? Assuredly they do: for it belongs to God to do whatever is best, and to man, to perform the commands of God. I believe, indeed, the best and noblest course of action is, when, before an attempt is made, we provide as far as possible for a secure result: and surely all men know that the holy service in which these hands have been employed has originated in pure and genuine faith towards God; that whatever has been done for the common welfare has been effected by active exertion combined with supplication and prayer; the consequence of which has been as great an amount of individual and public benefit as each could venture to hope for himself and those he holds most dear. They have witnessed battles, and have been spectators of a war in which the providence of God has granted victory to this people: they have seen how he has favored and seconded our prayers. For righteous prayer is a thing invincible; and no one fails to attain his object who addresses holy supplication to God: nor is a refusal possible, except in the case of wavering faith; for God is ever favorable, ever ready to approve of human virtue. While, therefore, it is natural for man occasionally to err, yet God is not the cause of human error. Hence it becomes all pious persons to render thanks to the Saviour of all, first for our own individual security, and then for the happy posture of public affairs: at the same time intreating the favor of Christ with holy prayers and constant supplications, that he would continue to us our present blessings. For he is the invincible ally and protector of the righteous: he is the supreme judge of all things, the prince of immortality, the Giver of everlasting life.

REVIEW QUESTIONS

1. How does Constantine account for his own successes?
2. Describe Constantine's understanding of Christianity.
3. What difference did the emperor's conversion make to the ordinary men and women of the empire?

FROM The Theodosian Code: Roman Law

The Theodosian Code is a collection of imperial decrees put together in the early fifth century C.E. to arrange by topic the Roman legal tradition. The Roman Empire had no formal constitution, and its legal system depended on senatorial laws and precedent-setting decisions by emperors in particular cases. The selections here from Book 16 are decisions on how the Christian Church and its officials should function in the empire's legal and tax policies. Both Church and state were also concerned about the heretics, people who believed the "wrong" things.

From *The Theodosian Code and Novels and the Sirmondian Constitutions*, by Claude Pharr (Princeton, N.J.: Princeton University Press, 1980), pp. 440–51.

Book 16

TITLE 1
THE CATHOLIC FAITH

1. Emperors Valentinian and Valens Augustuses to Symmachus, Prefect of the City

If any judge or apparitor should appoint men of the Christian religion as custodians of temples, he shall know that neither his life nor his fortunes will be spared.

Given on the fifteenth day before the kalends of December at Milan in the year of the consulship of Valentinian and Valens Augustuses.—November 17, 365; 364.

2. Emperors Gratian, Valentinian, and Theodosius Augustuses: An Edict to the People of the City of Constantinople

It is Our will that all the peoples who are ruled by the administration of Our Clemency shall practice that religion which the divine Peter the Apostle transmitted to the Romans, as the religion which he introduced makes clear even unto this day. It is evident that this is the religion that is followed by the Pontiff Damasus and by Peter, Bishop of Alexandria, a man of apostolic sanctity; that is, according to the apostolic discipline and the evangelic doctrine, we shall believe in the single Deity of the Father, the Son, and the Holy Spirit, under the concept of equal majesty and of the Holy Trinity.

SAN PAOLO FUORI LE MURI, ROME (C. 385 C.E.)

Interior of a classic late Roman nave. The building was begun in 385; it was largely rebuilt after a fire in 1823. The Christian Roman emperors intended to make a statement about their church. What were they trying to say?

We command that those persons who follow this rule shall embrace the name of Catholic Christians. The rest, however, whom We adjudge demented and insane, shall sustain the infamy of heretical dogmas, their meeting places shall not receive the name of churches, and they shall be smitten first by divine vengeance and secondly by the retribution of Our own initiative, which We shall assume in accordance with the divine judgment.

Given on the third day before the kalends of March at Thessalonica in the year of the fifth consulship of Gratian Augustus and the first consulship of Theodosius Augustus.—February 28, 380.

3. The same Augustuses to Auxonius, Proconsul of Asia

We command that all churches shall immediately be surrendered to those bishops who confess that the Father, the Son, and the Holy Spirit are of one majesty and virtue, of the same glory, and of one splendor; to those bishops who produce no dissonance by unholy distinction, but who affirm the concept of the Trinity by the assertion of three Persons and the unity of the Divinity; to those bishops who appear to have been associated in the communion of Nectarius, Bishop of the Church of Constantinople, and of Timotheus, Bishop of the City of Alexandria in Egypt; to those bishops also who, in the regions of the Orient, appear to be communicants with Pelagius, Bishop of Laodicea, and with Diodorus, Bishop of Tarsus; also, in the Proconsular Province of Asia and in the Diocese of Asia, with Amphilochius, Bishop of Iconium, and with Optimus, Bishop of Antioch; in the Diocese of Pontus, with Helladius, Bishop of Caesarea, and with Otreius of Melitene, and with Gregorius, Bishop of Nyssa; with Terennius, Bishop of Scythia, and with Marmarius, Bishop of Martianopolis. Those bishops who are of the communion and fellowship of such acceptable priests must be permitted to obtain the Catholic churches. All, however, who dissent from the communion of the faith of those who have been expressly mentioned in this special enumeration shall be expelled from their churches as manifest

heretics and hereafter shall be altogether denied the right and power to obtain churches, in order that the priesthood of the true Nicene faith may remain pure, and after the clear regulations of Our law, there shall be no opportunity for malicious subtlety.

Given on the third day before the kalends of August at Heraclea in the year of the consulship of Eucherius and Syagrius.—July 30, 381.

4. Emperors Valentinian, Theodosius, and Arcadius Augustuses to Eusignius, Praetorian Prefect

We bestow the right of assembly upon those persons who believe according to the doctrines which in the times of Constantius of sainted memory were decreed as those that would endure forever, when the priests had been called together from all the Roman world and the faith was set forth at the Council of Ariminum by these very persons who are now known to dissent, a faith which was also confirmed by the Council of Constantinople. The right of voluntary assembly shall also be open to those persons for whom We have so ordered. If those persons who suppose that the right of assembly has been granted to them alone should attempt to provoke any agitation against the regulation of Our Tranquillity, they shall know that, as authors of sedition and as disturbers of the peace of the Church, they shall also pay the penalty of high treason with their life and blood. Punishment shall no less await those persons who may attempt to supplicate Us surreptitiously and secretly, contrary to this Our regulation.

Given on the tenth day before the kalends of February at Milan in the year of the consulship of Emperor Designate Honorius and of Evodius.—January 23, 386.

TITLE 2
BISHOPS, CHURCHES, AND CLERICS

1. Emperor Constantine Augustus

We have learned that clerics of the Catholic Church are being so harassed by a faction of heretics that they are being burdened by nominations and by service as tax receivers, as public custom demands, contrary to the privileges granted them. It is Our pleasure, therefore, that if Your Gravity should find any person thus harassed, another person shall be chosen as a substitute for him and that henceforth men of the aforesaid religion shall be protected from such outrages.

Given on the day before the kalends of November in the year of the third consulship of Constantine Augustus and of Licinius Caesar.—October 31, 313(?).

2. The same Augustus to Octavianus, Governor of Lucania and of Bruttium

Those persons who devote the services of religion to divine worship, that is, those who are called clerics, shall be exempt from all compulsory public services whatever, lest, through the sacrilegious malice of certain persons, they should be called away from divine services.

Given on the twelfth day before the kalends of November in the year of the fifth consulship of Constantine Augustus and the consulship of Licinius Caesar.—October 21, 319; 313.

INTERPRETATION: This law by special ordinance directs that no person whatsoever by sacrilegious ordinance shall presume to make tax collectors or tax gatherers of clerics. The law commands that such clerics shall be free from every compulsory public service, that is, from every duty and servitude, and shall zealously serve the Church.

3. The same Augustus to Bassus, Praetorian Prefect

A constitution was issued which directs that thenceforth no decurion or descendant of a decurion or even any person provided with adequate resources and suitable to undertake compulsory public services shall take refuge in the name and the service of the clergy, but that in the place of deceased clerics thereafter only those persons shall be chosen as substitutes who have slender fortunes and who are not held bound to such compulsory

municipal services. But We have learned that those persons also are being disturbed who became associated with the clergy before the promulgation of the aforesaid law. We command, therefore, that the latter shall be freed from all annoyance, and that the former, who in evasion of public duties have taken refuge in the number of the clergy after the issuance of the law, shall be completely separated from that body, shall be restored to their orders and to the municipal councils, and shall perform their municipal duties.

Posted on the fifteenth day before the kalends of August in the year of the sixth consulship of Constantine Augustus and the consulship of Constantius Caesar.—July 18, 320; 329.

4. The same Augustus to the People

Every person shall have the liberty to leave at his death any property that he wishes to the most holy and venerable council of the Catholic Church. Wills shall not become void. There is nothing which is more due to men than that the expression of their last will, after which they can no longer will anything, shall be free and the power of choice, which does not return again, shall be unhampered.

Posted on the fifth day before the nones of July at Rome in the year of the second consulship of Crispus and Constantine Caesars.—July 3, 321.

5. The same Augustus to Helpidius

Whereas We have learned that certain ecclesiastics and others devoting their services to the Catholic sect have been compelled by men of different religions to the performance of lustral sacrifices, We decree by this sanction that, if any person should suppose that those who devote their services to the most sacred law may be forced to the ritual of an alien superstition, he shall be beaten publicly with clubs, provided that his legal status so permits. If, however, the consideration of his honorable rank protects him from such an outrage, he shall sustain the penalty of a very heavy fine, which shall be vindicated to the municipalities.

Given on the eighth day before the kalends of June at Sirmium in the year of the consulship of Severus and Rufinus.—May (December) 25, 323.

6. The same Augustus to Ablavius, Praetorian Prefect

Exemption from compulsory public services shall not be granted by popular consent, nor shall it be granted indiscriminately to all who petition under the pretext of being clerics, nor shall great numbers be added to the clergy rashly and beyond measure, but rather, when a cleric dies, another shall be selected to replace the deceased, one who has no kinship with a decurion family and who has not the wealth of resources whereby he may very easily support the compulsory public services. Thus, if there should be a dispute about the name of any person between a municipality and the clergy, if equity claims him for public service and if he is adjudged suitable for membership in the municipal council through either lineage or wealth, he shall be removed from the clergy and shall be delivered to the municipality. For the wealthy must assume secular obligations, and the poor must be supported by the wealth of the churches.

Posted on the kalends of June in the year of the seventh consulship of Constantine Augustus and the consulship of Constantius Caesar.—June 1, 326; 329.

7. The same Augustus to Valentinus, Governor of Numidia

Lectors of the divine scriptures, subdeacons, and the other clerics who through the injustice of heretics have been summoned to the municipal councils shall be absolved, and in the future, according to the practice of the Orient, they shall by no means be summoned to the municipal councils, but they shall possess fullest exemption.

Given on the nones of February at Sofia (Serdica) in the year of the consulship of Gallicanus and Symmachus.—February 5, 330.

8. Emperor Constantius Augustus to the Clergy, Greetings

According to the sanction which you are said to have obtained previously, no person shall obligate you and your slaves to new tax payments, but you shall enjoy exemption. Furthermore, you shall not be required to receive quartered persons, and if any of you, for the sake of a livelihood, should wish to conduct a business, they shall possess tax exemption.

Given on the sixth day before the kalends of September in the year of the consulship of Placidus and Romulus.—August 27, 343.

9. The same Augustus to Severianus, Proconsul of Achaea

All clerics must be exempt from compulsory services as decurions and from every annoyance of municipal duties. Their sons, moreover, must continue in the Church, if they are not held obligated to the municipal councils.

Given on the third day before the ides of April in the year of the consulship of Limenius and Catullinus.—April 11, 349.

10. Emperors Constantius and Constans Augustuses to all the Bishops throughout the various provinces.

In order that organizations in the service of the churches may be filled with a great multitude of people, tax exemption shall be granted to clerics and their acolytes, and they shall be protected from the exaction of compulsory public services of a menial nature. They shall by no means be subject to the tax payments of tradesmen, since it is manifest that the profits which they collect from stalls and workshops will benefit the poor. We decree also that their men who engage in trade shall be exempt from all tax payments. Likewise, the exaction of services for the maintenance of the supplementary postwagons shall cease. This indulgence We grant to their wives, children, and servants, to males and females equally, for We command that they also shall continue exempt from tax assessments.

Given on the seventh day before the kalends of June at Constantinople in the year of the sixth consulship of Constantius and the consulship of Constans.—May 26, 353; 320; 346.

11. The same Augustuses to Longinianus, Prefect of Egypt

We formerly sanctioned that bishops and clerics of the Catholic faith who possess nothing at all and are useless with respect to patrimony shall not be summoned to compulsory public services as decurions. But We learn that they are being disturbed in their life of perfection, to no public advantage. Therefore, We direct that their sons also who are not financially responsible and who are found to be below the legal age shall sustain no molestation.

Given on the fourth day before the kalends of March in the year of the seventh consulship of Constantius Augustus and the consulship of Constans Augustus.—February 26, 354; 342.

12. The same Augustuses to their dear friend Severus, Greetings

By a law of Our Clemency We prohibit bishops to be accused in the courts, lest there should be an unrestrained opportunity for fanatical spirits to accuse them, while the accusers assume that they will obtain impunity by the kindness of the bishops. Therefore, if any person should lodge any complaint, such complaint must unquestionably be examined before other bishops, in order that an opportune and suitable hearing may be arranged for the investigation of all concerned.

Given as a letter on the ninth day before the kalends of October.—September 23. Received on the nones of October in the year of the consulship of Arbitio and Lollianus.—October 7, 355.

INTERPRETATION: It is specifically prohibited that any person should dare to accuse a bishop before secular judges, but he shall not delay to submit to the hearing of bishops whatever he supposes may be due him according to the nature of the case, so that the assertions which he makes against the bishop may be decided in a court of other bishops.

13. The same Augustus and Julian Caesar to Leontius

We command that the privileges granted to the Church of the City of Rome and to its clerics shall be firmly guarded.

Given on the fourth day before the ides of November at Milan in the year of the ninth consulship of Constantius Augustus and the second consulship of Julian Caesar.—November 10, 357; 356.

14. The same Augustus and Julian Caesar to Bishop Felix

Clerics shall be protected from every injustice of an undue suit and from every wrong of an unjust exaction, and they shall not be summoned to compulsory public services of a menial nature. Moreover, when tradesmen are summoned to some legally prescribed tax payment, all clerics shall cease to be affected by such a disturbance; for if they have accumulated anything by thrift, foresight, or trading, but still in accordance with honesty, this must be administered for the use of the poor and needy, and whatever they have been able to acquire and collect from their workshops and stalls they shall regard as having been collected for the profit of religion.

(1) Moreover, with respect to their men who are employed in trade, the statutes of the sainted Emperor, that is, of Our father, provided with manifold regulations that the aforesaid clerics should abound in numerous privileges. (2) Therefore, with respect to the aforesaid clerics, the requirement of extraordinary services and all molestation shall cease. (3) Moreover, they and their resources and substance shall not be summoned to furnish supplementary postwagons.

(4) All clerics shall be assisted by the prerogative of this nature, namely, that wives of clerics and also their children and attendants, males and females equally, and their children, shall continue to be exempt forever from tax payments and free from such compulsory public services.

Given on the eighth day before the ides of December at Milan—December 6. Read into the records on the fifth day before the kalends of January in the year of the ninth consulship of Constantius Augustus and the second consulship of Julian Caesar.—December 28, 357; 356. Or: Read in court proceedings, acta, 2, 8, 1, n. 4.

*   *   *

29. Emperors Arcadius and Honorius Augustuses to Hierius, Vicar of Africa

We direct that whatever statutes were enacted by Our Fathers at different times with respect to the sacrosanct churches shall remain inviolate and unimpaired. None of their privileges, therefore, shall be altered, and protection shall be granted to all those persons who serve the churches, for We desire that reverence shall be increased in Our time rather than that any of the privileges which were formerly granted should be altered.

Given on the tenth day before the kalends of April at Milan in the year of the consulship of Olybrius and Probinus.—March 23, 395.

30. The same Augustuses to Theodorus, Praetorian Prefect

We decree nothing new by the present sanction; rather, We confirm those privileges that appear to have been granted formerly. We prohibit, therefore, under threat of punishment, that privileges which were formerly obtained through reverence for religion shall be curtailed, so that those who serve the Church may also enjoy fully those special benefits which the Church enjoys.

Given on the day before the kalends of February at Milan in the year of the consulship of Caesarius and Atticus.—January 31, 397.

31. The same Augustuses to Theodorus, Praetorian Prefect

If any person should break forth into such sacrilege that he should invade Catholic churches and should inflict any outrage on the priests and ministers, or on the worship itself and on the place of worship, whatever occurs shall be brought to the notice of the authorities by letters of the municipal senates, magistrates, and curators, and by official reports of the apparitors who are called rural police, so that the names of those who could be recognized may be revealed. Moreover, if the offense is said to have been perpetrated by a multitude, some, if not all, can nevertheless be recognized, and by their confession the names of their accomplices may be disclosed. Thus the governor of the province shall know that the outrage to the priests and ministers of the Catholic Church, to the divine worship, and to the place of worship itself must be punished with a capital sentence against the aforesaid convicted or confessed criminals. The governor shall not wait until the bishop shall demand the avenging of his own injury, since the bishop's sanctity leaves nothing to him except the glory of forgiving. It shall be not only permissible but even laudable for all persons to prosecute as a public crime the atrocious outrages committed against priests and ministers and to exact punishment from such criminals. But if it should be impossible to bring to court a violent multitude by the operation of civil apparitors and by the help of the municipal senates and landholders, in case the multitude protects itself by arms or by the difficulty of the places, the African judges shall prefix the contents of this law to letters which they shall send to the Respectable Count of Africa, and they shall demand the aid of the armed apparitors, in order that the perpetrators of such crimes may not escape.

Given on the seventh day before the kalends of May at Milan in the year of the fourth consulship of Honorius Augustus and the consulship of Eutychianus.—April 25, 398; January 15, 409.

32. The same Augustuses to Caesarius, Praetorian Prefect

If perchance the bishops should suppose that they are in need of clerics, they will more properly ordain them from the number of monks. They shall not incur disfavor by holding those persons who are bound by public and private accounts but shall have those already approved.

Given on the seventh day before the kalends of August in the year of the fourth consulship of Honorius Augustus and the consulship of Eutychianus.—July 26, 398(?).

*   *   *

TITLE **3**

MONKS

1. Emperors Valentinian, Theodosius, and Arcadius Augustuses to Tatianus, Praetorian Prefect

If any persons should be found in the profession of monks, they shall be ordered to seek out and to inhabit desert places and desolate solitudes.

Given on the fourth day before the nones of September at Verona in the year of the fourth consulship of Valentinian Augustus and the consulship of Neoterius.—September 2, 390.

2. The same Augustuses to Tatianus, Praetorian Prefect

We direct that the monks to whom the municipalities had been forbidden, since they are strengthened by judicial injustices, shall be restored to their original status, and the aforesaid law shall be repealed. Thus indeed, We revoke such a decree of Our Clemency, and We grant them free ingress into the towns.

Given on the fifteenth day before the kalends of May at Constantinople in the year of the second consulship of Arcadius Augustus and the consulship of Rufinus.—April 17, 392.

REVIEW QUESTIONS

1. What did the emperors and their officials want from the church?
2. What benefits did the church expect from the state?
3. What are the assumptions and logic of Roman legal thought?

IGNATIUS OF ANTIOCH

Letter to the Romans

Around the year 110 c.e., Ignatius of Antioch in Syria wrote a series of letters to communities of Christians. In these letters, he argued against heretics and the Gnostics; in this one to the Romans, he made a personal statement about his approaching martyrdom. The letter shows the Christian community immediately after the age of the Apostles and is a precious early source, not much later than the New Testament.

From *Early Christian Fathers*, by Cyril C. Richardson (Louisville, Ky.: Westminster/John Knox Press, 1953), pp. 102–6.

G reetings in Jesus Christ, the Son of the Father, from Ignatius, the "God-inspired," to the church that is in charge of affairs in Roman quarters and that the Most High Father and Jesus Christ, his only Son, have magnificently embraced in mercy and love. You have been granted light both by the will of Him who willed all that is, and by virtue of your believing in Jesus Christ, our God, and of loving him. You are a credit to God: you deserve your renown and are to be congratulated. You deserve praise and success and are privileged to be without blemish. Yes, you rank first in love, being true to Christ's law and stamped with the Father's name. To you, then, sincerest greetings in Jesus Christ, our God, for you cleave to his every commandment—observing not only their letter but their spirit—being permanently filled with God's grace and purged of every stain alien to it.

Since God has answered my prayer to see you godly people, I have gone on to ask for more. I mean, it is as a prisoner for Christ Jesus that I hope to greet you, if indeed it be God's will that I should deserve to meet my end. Things are off to a good start. May I have the good fortune to meet my fate without interference! What I fear is your generosity which may prove detrimental to me. For you can easily do what you want to, whereas it is hard for me to get to God unless you let me alone. I do not want you to please men, but to please God, just as you are doing. For I shall never again have such a chance to get to God, nor can you, if you keep quiet, get credit for a finer deed. For if you quietly let me alone, people will see in me God's Word. But if you are enamored of my mere body, I shall, on the contrary, be a meaningless noise. Grant me no more than to be a sacrifice for God while there is an altar at hand. Then you can form yourselves into a choir and sing praises to the Father in Jesus Christ that God gave the bishop of Syria the privilege of reaching the sun's setting when he summoned him from its rising. It is a grand thing for my life to set on the world, and for me to be on my way to God, so that I may rise in his presence.

You never grudged anyone. You taught others. So I want you to substantiate the lessons that you bid them heed. Just pray that I may have strength of soul and body so that I may not only talk about martyrdom, but really want it. It is not that I want merely to be called a Christian, but actually to *be* one. Yes, if I prove to be one, then I can have the name. Then, too, I shall be a convincing Christian only when the world sees me no more. Nothing you can see has real value. Our God Jesus Christ, indeed, has revealed himself more clearly by returning to the Father. The greatness of Christianity lies in its being hated by the world, not in its being convincing to it.

I am corresponding with all the churches and bidding them all realize that I am voluntarily dying for God—if, that is, you do not interfere. I plead with you, do not do me an unseasonable kindness. Let me be fodder for wild beasts—that is how I can get to God. I am God's wheat and I am being ground by the teeth of wild beasts to make a pure loaf for Christ. I would rather that you fawn on the beasts so that they may be my tomb and no scrap of my body be left. Thus, when I have fallen asleep, I shall be a burden to no one. Then I shall be a real disciple of Jesus Christ when the world sees my body no more. Pray Christ for me that by these means I may become God's sacrifice. I do not give you orders like Peter and Paul. They were apostles: I am a convict. They were at liberty: I am still a slave. But if I suffer, I shall be emancipated by Jesus Christ; and united to him, I shall rise to freedom.

Even now as a prisoner, I am learning to forgo my own wishes. All the way from Syria to Rome I am fighting with wild beasts, by land and sea, night and day, chained as I am to ten leopards (I mean to a detachment of soldiers), who only get worse the better you treat them. But by their injustices I am becoming a better disciple, "though not for that reason am I acquitted." What a thrill I shall have from the wild beasts that are ready for me! I hope they will make short work of me. I shall coax them on to eat me up at once and not to hold off, as sometimes happens, through fear. And if they are reluctant, I shall force them to it. Forgive me—I know what is good for me. Now is the moment I am beginning to be a disciple. May nothing seen or unseen begrudge me making my way to Jesus Christ. Come fire, cross, battling with wild beasts, wrenching of bones, mangling of limbs, crushing of my whole body, cruel tortures of the devil—only let me get to Jesus Christ! Not the wide bounds of earth nor the kingdoms of this world will avail me anything. "I would rather die" and get to Jesus Christ, than reign over the ends of the earth. That is whom I am looking for—the One who died for us. That is whom I want—the One who rose for us. I am going through the pangs of being born. Sympathize with me, my brothers! Do not stand in the way of my coming to life—do not wish death on me. Do not give back to the world one who wants to be God's; do not trick him with material things. Let me get into the clear light and manhood will be mine. Let me imitate the Passion of my God. If anyone has Him in him, let him appreciate what I am longing for, and sympathize with me, realizing what I am going through.

The prince of this world wants to kidnap me and pervert my godly purpose. None of you, then, who will be there, must abet him. Rather be on my side—that is, on God's. Do not talk Jesus Christ and set your heart on the world. Harbor no envy. If, when I arrive, I make a different plea, pay no attention to me. Rather heed what I am now writing to you. For though alive, it is with a passion for death that I am writing to you. My Desire has been crucified and there burns in me no passion for material things. There is living water in me, which speaks and says inside me, "Come to the Father." I take no delight in corruptible food or in the dainties of this life. What I want is God's bread, which is the flesh of Christ, who came from David's line; and for drink I want his blood: an immortal love feast indeed!

I do not want to live any more on a human plane. And so it shall be, if you want it to. Want it to, so that you will be wanted! Despite the brevity of my letter, trust my request. Yes, Jesus Christ will clarify it for you and make you see I am really in earnest. He is the guileless mouth by which the Father has spoken truthfully. Pray for me that I reach my goal. I have written prompted, not by human passion, but by God's will. If I suffer, it will be because you favored me. If I am rejected, it will be because you hated me.

Remember the church of Syria in your prayers. In my place they have God for their shepherd. Jesus Christ alone will look after them—he, and your love. I blush to be reckoned among them, for I do not deserve it, being the least of them and an afterthought. Yet by his mercy I shall be something, if, that is, I get to God.

With my heart I greet you; and the churches which have welcomed me, not as a chance passerby, but in the name of Jesus Christ, send their love. Indeed, even those that did not naturally lie on my route went ahead to prepare my welcome in the different towns. I am sending this letter to you from Smyrna by those praiseworthy Ephesians. With me, along with many others, is Crocus—a person very dear to me. I trust you have had word about those who went ahead of me from Syria to Rome for God's glory. Tell them I am nearly there. They are all a credit to God and to you; so you should give them every assistance. I am writing this to you on the twenty-fourth of August. Farewell, and hold out to the end with the patience of Jesus Christ.

Review Questions

1. What did Ignatius hope to accomplish by his death?
2. How does he describe his attitude toward death?
3. How might a contemporary pagan react to the sentiments in this letter?

The Martyrdom of Polycarp

Around the year 156 C.E., Polycarp, a leader of the church in Smyrna in Asia Minor, was martyred. A group of his followers composed the following account of his arrest, trial, and execution. This is one of the earliest documents on martyrdom, which was experienced by many men and women in the phases of persecution in the Roman Empire. Authentic texts on martyrdom were an important means by which the early churches kept alive the memory of martyrs, especially for those who did not see the actual events described in the acts.

From *Early Christian Fathers*, by Cyril C. Richardson (Louisville, Ky.: Westminster/John Knox Press, 1953), pp. 149–58.

The church of God that sojourns at Smyrna to the church of God that sojourns at Philomelium, and to all those of the holy and Catholic Church who sojourn in every place: may mercy, peace, and love be multiplied from God the Father and our Lord Jesus Christ.

We write you, brethren, the things concerning those who suffered martyrdom, especially the blessed Polycarp, who put an end to the persecution by sealing it, so to speak, through his own witness. For almost everything that led up to it happened in order that the Lord might show once again a martyrdom conformable to the gospel. For he waited to be betrayed, just as the Lord did, to the end that we also might be imitators of him, "not looking only to that which concerns ourselves, but also to that which concerns our neighbors." For it is a mark of true and steadfast love for one not only to desire to be saved oneself, but all the brethren also.

Blessed and noble, indeed, are all the martyrdoms that have taken place according to God's will; for we ought to be very reverent in ascribing to God power over all things. For who would not admire their nobility and patient endurance and love of their Master? Some of them, so torn by scourging that the anatomy of their flesh was visible as far as the inner veins and arteries, endured with such patience that even the bystanders took pity and wept; others achieved such heroism that not one of them uttered a cry or a groan, thus showing all of us that at the very hour of their tortures the most noble martyrs of Christ were no longer in the flesh, but rather that the Lord stood by them and conversed with them. And giving themselves over to the grace of Christ they despised the tortures of this world, purchasing for themselves in the space of one hour the life eternal. To them the fire of their inhuman tortures was cold; for they set before their eyes escape from the fire that is everlasting and never quenched, while with the eyes of their heart they gazed upon the good things reserved for those that endure patiently, "which things neither ear has heard nor eye has seen, nor has there entered into the heart of man." But they were shown to them by the Lord, for they were no longer men, but were already angels. Similarly, those condemned to the wild beasts endured fearful punishments, being made to lie on sharp shells and punished with other forms of various torments, in order that the devil might bring them, if possible, by means of the prolonged punishment, to a denial of their faith.

Many, indeed, were the machinations of the devil against them. But, thanks be to God, he did not prevail against them all. For the most noble Germanicus encouraged their timidity through his own patient endurance—who also fought with the beasts in a distinguished way. For when the proconsul, wishing to persuade him, bade him have pity on his youth, he forcibly dragged the wild beast toward himself, wishing to obtain more quickly a release from their wicked and lawless life. From this circumstance, all the crowd, marveling at the heroism of the God-loving and God-fearing race of the Christians, shouted: "Away with the atheists! Make search for Polycarp!"

But a Phrygian, named Quintus, lately arrived from Phrygia, took fright when he saw the wild beasts. In fact, he was the one who had forced himself and some others to come forward voluntarily. The proconsul by much entreaty persuaded him to take the oath and to offer the sacrifice. For this reason, therefore, brethren, we do not praise those who come forward of their own accord, since the gospel does not teach us so to do.

The most admirable Polycarp, when he first heard of it, was not perturbed, but desired to remain in the city. But the majority induced him to withdraw, so he retired to a farm not far from the city and there stayed with a few friends, doing nothing else night and day but pray for all men and for the churches throughout the world, as was his constant habit. And while he was praying, it so happened, three days before his arrest, that he had a vision and saw his pillow blazing with fire, and turning to those who were with him he said, "I must be burned alive."

And while those who were searching for him continued their quest, he moved to another farm, and forthwith those searching for him arrived. And when they did not find him, they seized two young slaves, one of whom confessed under torture. For it was really impossible to conceal him, since the very ones who betrayed him were of his own household. And the chief of the police, who chanced to have the same name as Herod, was zealous to bring him into the arena in order that he might fulfill his own appointed lot of being made a partaker with Christ; while those who betrayed him should suffer the punishment of Judas himself.

Taking, therefore, the young slave on Friday about suppertime, the police, mounted and with their customary arms, set out as though "hasting after a robber." And late in the evening they came up with him and found him in bed in the upper room of a small cottage. Even so he could have escaped to another farm, but he did not wish to do so, saying, "God's will be done." Thus, when he heard of their arrival, he went downstairs and talked with them, while those who looked on marveled at his age and constancy, and at how there should be such zeal over the arrest of so old a man. Straightway he ordered food and drink, as much as they wished, to be set before them at that hour, and he asked them to give him an hour so that he might pray undisturbed. And when they consented, he stood and prayed—being so filled with the grace of God that for two hours he could

not hold his peace, to the amazement of those who heard. And many repented that they had come to get such a devout old man.

When at last he had finished his prayer, in which he remembered all who had met with him at any time, both small and great, both those with and those without renown, and the whole Catholic Church throughout the world, the hour of departure having come, they mounted him on an ass and brought him into the city. It was a great Sabbath. And there the chief of the police, Herod, and his father, Nicetas, met him and transferred him to their carriage, and tried to persuade him, as they sat beside him, saying, "What harm is there to say 'Lord Caesar,' and to offer incense and all that sort of thing, and to save yourself?"

At first he did not answer them. But when they persisted, he said, "I am not going to do what you advise me."

Then when they failed to persuade him, they uttered dire threats and made him get out with such speed that in dismounting from the carriage he bruised his shin. But without turning around, as though nothing had happened, he proceeded swiftly, and was led into the arena, there being such a tumult in the arena that no one could be heard. But as Polycarp was entering the arena, a voice from heaven came to him, saying, "Be strong, Polycarp, and play the man." No one saw the one speaking, but those of our people who were present heard the voice.

And when finally he was brought up, there was a great tumult on hearing that Polycarp had been arrested. Therefore, when he was brought before him, the proconsul asked him if he were Polycarp. And when he confessed that he was, he tried to persuade him to deny the faith, saying, "Have respect to your age"—and other things that customarily follow this, such as, "Swear by the fortune of Caesar; change your mind; say, 'Away with the atheists!' "

But Polycarp looked with earnest face at the whole crowd of lawless heathen in the arena, and motioned to them with his hand. Then, groaning and looking up to heaven, he said, "Away with the atheists!"

But the proconsul was insistent and said: "Take the oath, and I shall release you. Curse Christ."

Polycarp said: "Eighty-six years I have served him, and he never did me any wrong. How can I blaspheme my King who saved me?"

And upon his persisting still and saying, "Swear by the fortune of Caesar," he answered, "If you vainly suppose that I shall swear by the fortune of Caesar, as you say, and pretend that you do not know who I am, listen plainly: I am a Christian. But if you desire to learn the teaching of Christianity, appoint a day and give me a hearing."

The proconsul said, "Try to persuade the people."

But Polycarp said, "You, I should deem worthy of an account; for we have been taught to render honor, as is befitting, to rulers and authorities appointed by God so far as it does us no harm; but as for these, I do not consider them worthy that I should make defense to them."

But the proconsul said: "I have wild beasts. I shall throw you to them, if you do not change your mind."

But he said: "Call them. For repentance from the better to the worse is not permitted us; but it is noble to change from what is evil to what is righteous."

And again he said to him, "I shall have you consumed with fire, if you despise the wild beasts, unless you change your mind."

But Polycarp said: "The fire you threaten burns but an hour and is quenched after a little; for you do not know the fire of the coming judgment and everlasting punishment that is laid up for the impious. But why do you delay? Come, do what you will."

And when he had said these things and many more besides he was inspired with courage and joy, and his face was full of grace, so that not only did it not fall with dismay at the things said to im, but on the contrary, the proconsul was astonished, and sent his own herald into the midst of the arena to proclaim three times: "Polycarp has confessed himself to be a Christian."

When this was said by the herald, the entire crowd of heathen and Jews who lived in Smyrna shouted with uncontrollable anger and a great cry: "This one is the teacher of Asia, the father of the Christians, the destroyer of our gods, who teaches many not to sacrifice nor to worship."

Such things they shouted and asked the Asiarch Philip that he let loose a lion on Polycarp. But he said it was not possible for him to do so, since he had brought the wild-beast sports to a close. Then they decided to shout with one accord that he burn Polycarp alive. For it was necessary that the vision which had appeared to him about his pillow should be fulfilled, when he saw it burning while he was praying, and turning around had said prophetically to the faithful who were with him, "I must be burned alive."

Then these things happened with such dispatch, quicker than can be told—the crowds in so great a hurry to gather wood and faggots from the workshops and the baths, the Jews being especially zealous, as usual, to assist with this. When the fire was ready, and he had divested himself of all his clothes and unfastened his belt, he tried to take off his shoes, though he was not heretofore in the habit of doing this because each of the faithful always vied with one another as to which of them would be first to touch his body. For he had always been honored, even before his martyrdom, for his holy life. Straightway then, they set about him the material prepared for the pyre. And when they were about to nail him also, he said: "Leave me as I am. For he who grants me to endure the fire will enable me also to remain on the pyre unmoved, without the security you desire from the nails."

So they did not nail him, but tied him. And with his hands put behind him and tied, like a noble ram out of a great flock ready for sacrifice, a burnt offering ready and acceptable to God, he looked up to heaven and said:

Lord God Almighty, Father of thy beloved and blessed Servant Jesus Christ, through whom we have received full knowledge of thee, "the God of angels and powers and all creation" and of the whole race of the righteous who live in thy presence: I bless thee, because thou hast deemed me worthy of this day and hour, to take my part in the number of the martyrs, in the cup of thy Christ, for "resurrection to eternal life" of soul and body in the immortality of the Holy Spirit; among whom may I be received in thy presence this day as a rich and acceptable sacrifice, just as thou hast prepared and revealed beforehand and fulfilled, thou that art the true God without any falsehood. For this and for everything I praise thee, I bless thee, I glorify thee, through the eternal and heavenly High Priest, Jesus Christ, thy beloved Servant, through whom be glory to thee with him and Holy Spirit both now and unto the ages to come. Amen.

And when he had concluded the Amen and finished his prayer, the men attending to the fire lighted it. And when the flame flashed forth, we saw a miracle, we to whom it was given to see. And we are preserved in order to relate to the rest what happened. For the fire made the shape of a vaulted chamber, like a ship's sail filled by the wind, and made a wall around the body of the martyr. And he was in the midst, not as burning flesh, but as bread baking or as gold and silver refined in a furnace. And we perceived such a sweet aroma as the breath of incense or some other precious spice.

At length, when the lawless men saw that his body could not be consumed by the fire, they commanded an executioner to go to him and stab him with a dagger. And when he did this a dove and a great quantity of blood came forth, so that the fire was quenched and the whole crowd marveled that there should be such a difference between the unbelievers and the elect. And certainly the most admirable Polycarp was one of these elect, in whose times among us he showed himself an apostolic and prophetic teacher and bishop of the Catholic Church in Smyrna. Indeed, every utterance that came from his mouth was accomplished and will be accomplished.

But the jealous and malicious evil one, the adversary of the race of the righteous, seeing the greatness of his martyrdom and his blameless life from the beginning, and how he was crowned with the wreath of immortality and had borne away an incontestable reward, so contrived it that his corpse should not be taken away by us, although many desired to do this and to have fellowship with his holy flesh. He instigated Nicetas, the father of Herod and brother of Alce, to plead with the magistrate not to give up his body, "else," said he, "they will abandon the Crucified and begin worshiping this one." This was done at the instigation and insistence of the Jews, who also watched when we were going to take him from the fire, being ignorant that we can never forsake Christ, who suffered for the salvation of the whole world of those who are saved, the faultless for the sinners, nor can we ever worship any other. For we worship this One as Son of God, but we love the martyrs as disciples and imitators of the Lord, deservedly so, because of their unsurpassable devotion to their own King and Teacher. May it be also our lot to be their companions and fellow disciples!

The captain of the Jews, when he saw their contentiousness, set it [his body] in the midst and burned it, as was their custom. So we later took up his bones, more precious than costly stones and more valuable than gold, and laid them away in a suitable place. There the Lord will permit us, so far as possible, to gather together in joy and gladness to celebrate the day of his martyrdom as a birthday, in memory of those athletes who have gone before, and to train and make ready those who are to come hereafter.

Such are the things concerning the blessed Polycarp, who, martyred at Smyrna along with twelve others from Philadelphia, is alone remembered so much the more by everyone, that he is even spoken of by the heathen in every place. He was not only a noble teacher, but also a distinguished martyr, whose martyrdom all desire to imitate as one according to the gospel of Christ. By his patient endurance he overcame the wicked magistrate and so received the crown of immortality; and he rejoices with the apostles and all the righteous to glorify God the Father Almighty and to bless our Lord Jesus Christ, the Saviour of our souls and Helmsman of our bodies and Shepherd of the Catholic Church throughout the world.

You requested, indeed, that these things be related to you more fully, but for the present we have briefly reported them through our brother Marcion. When you have informed yourselves of these things, send this letter to the brethren elsewhere, in order that they too might glorify the Lord, who makes his choices from his own servants. To him who is able by his grace and bounty to bring us to his everlasting Kingdom, through his Servant, the only-begotten Jesus Christ, be glory, honor, might, majesty, throughout the ages. Greet all the saints. Those with us greet you and also Evarestus, who wrote this, with his whole household.

The blessed Polycarp was martyred on the second day of the first part of the month Xanthicus, the seventh day before the kalends of March, a great Sabbath, at two o'clock P.M. He was arrested by Herod, when Philip of Tralles was high priest, and Statius Quadratus was proconsul, but in the everlasting reign of our Lord Jesus Christ. To him be glory, honor, majesty, and the eternal throne, from generation to generation. Amen.

We bid you farewell, brethren, as you live by the word of Jesus Christ according to the gospel, with whom be glory to God the Father and Holy Spirit, unto the salvation of his holy elect; just as the blessed Polycarp suffered martyrdom, in whose footsteps may it be our lot to be found in the Kingdom of Jesus Christ.

These things Gaius copied from the papers of Irenaeus, a disciple of Polycarp; he also lived with Irenaeus. And Isocrates, wrote it in Corinth from the copy of Gaius. Grace be with all.

I, Pionius, again wrote it from the aforementioned copy, having searched for it according to a revelation of the blessed Polycarp, who appeared to me, as I shall explain in the sequel. I gathered it together when it was almost worn out with age, in order that the Lord Jesus Christ might bring me also with his elect unto his heavenly Kingdom. To him be glory with the Father and Holy Spirit unto the ages of ages. Amen.

Another Epilogue from the Moscow Manuscript

These things Gaius copied from the papers of Irenaeus. He also lived with Irenaeus, who had been a disciple of the holy Polycarp. For this Irenaeus, at the time of the martyrdom of Bishop Polycarp, was in Rome and taught many; and many of his excellent and orthodox writings are in circulation, in which he mentions Polycarp, for he was taught by him. He ably refuted every heresy and handed down the ecclesiastical and Catholic rule, as he had received it from the saint. He says this also: that once when Marcion, after whom the Marcionites are called, met the holy Polycarp and said, "Do you know us, Polycarp?" he said to Marcion, "I know you; I know the first-born of Satan." And this fact is also found in the writings of Irenaeus, that on the day and at the hour when Polycarp was martyred in Smyrna, Irenaeus, being in the city of Rome, heard a voice like a trumpet saying, "Polycarp has suffered martyrdom."

From these papers of Irenaeus, then, as was said above, Gaius made a copy, and from Gaius' copy Isocrates made another in Corinth. And I, Pionius, again from the copies of Isocrates wrote according to the revelation of holy Polycarp, when I searched for it, and gathered it together when it was almost worn out with age, in order that the Lord Jesus Christ might bring me with his elect unto his heavenly Kingdom. To whom be glory with the Father and the Son and the Holy Spirit unto the ages of ages. Amen.

REVIEW QUESTIONS

1. What threat did Polycarp pose to the Roman state?
2. What does this document reveal about relations among Christians, Jews, and pagans?
3. How did Polycarp's friends portray him as the ideal martyr?

St. Benedict

from *The Rule*

St. Benedict (ca. 480–547 C.E.), the author of The Rule of Saint Benedict *and founder of the monastery of Monte Cassino in southern Italy, drew on Egyptian and Syrian practices for his guidelines for a religious community. By withdrawing from the world and its temptations, the monks wanted to fight the devil and secure their own salvation. The monastery was in theory a self-sustaining community where all members prayed and worked. The following sections of the rule discuss some central values: obedience, silence, and humility.*

From *The Rule of Saint Benedict,* by Cardinal Gasquet (Whitestone, N.Y.: Cooper Square, 1966).

Chapter V
On Obedience

The first degree of humility is prompt obedience. This is required of all who, whether by reason of the holy servitude to which they are pledged, or through fear of hell, or to attain to the glory of eternal life, hold nothing more dear than Christ. Such disciples delay not in doing what is ordered by their superior, just as if the command had come from God. Of such our Lord says, *At the hearing of the ear he hath obeyed me.* And to the teachers He likewise says, *He that heareth you, heareth me.*

For this reason such disciples, surrendering forthwith all they possess, and giving up their own will, leave unfinished what they were working at, and with the ready foot of obedience in their acts follow the word of command. Thus, as it were, at the same moment comes the order of the master and the finished work of the disciple: with the speed of the fear of God both go jointly forward and are quickly effected by such as ardently desire to walk in the way of eternal life. These take the narrow way, of which the Lord saith, *Narrow is the way which leads to life.* That is, they live not as they themselves will, neither do they obey their own desires and pleasures; but following the command and direction of another and abiding in

their monasteries, their desire is to be ruled by an abbot. Without doubt such as these carry out that saying of our Lord, *I came not to do my own will, but the will of Him Who sent me.*

This kind of obedience will be both acceptable to God and pleasing to men, when what is ordered is not done out of fear, or slowly and coldly, grudgingly, or with reluctant protest. Obedience shown to superiors is indeed given to God, Who Himself hath said, *He that heareth you, heareth Me.* What is commanded should be done by those under obedience, with a good will, since *God loveth a cheerful giver.* If the disciple obey unwillingly and murmur in word as well as in heart, it will not be accepted by God, Who considereth the heart of a murmurer, even if he do what was ordered. For a work done in this spirit shall have no reward; rather shall the doer incur the penalty appointed for murmurers if he amend not and make not satisfaction.

Chapter VI
On Silence

Let us do as the prophet says, *I have said, I will keep my ways, that I offend not with my tongue. I have been watchful over my mouth: I held my peace and humbled myself and was silent from speaking even good things.* Here the prophet shows that, for the sake of silence, we are at times to abstain even from good talk. If this be so, how much more needful is it that we refrain from evil words, on account of the penalty of the sin! Because of the importance of silence, therefore, let leave to speak be seldom given, even to perfect disciples, although their talk be of good and holy matters and tending to edification, since it is written, *In much speaking, thou shalt not escape sin.* The master, indeed, should speak and teach: the disciple should hold his peace and listen.

Whatever, therefore, has to be asked of the prior, let it be done with all humility and with reverent submission. But as to coarse, idle words, or such as move to laughter, we utterly condemn and ban them in all places. We do not allow any disciple to give mouth to them.

Chapter VII
On Humility

Brethren, Holy Scripture cries out to us, saying, *Every one who exalteth himself shall be humbled, and he who humbleth himself shall be exalted.* In this it tells us that every form of self-exaltation is a kind of pride, which the prophet declares he carefully avoided, where he says, *Lord, my heart is not exalted, neither are my eyes lifted up; neither have I walked in great things, nor in wonders above myself.* And why? *If I did not think humbly, but exalted my soul: as a child weaned from his mother, so wilt Thou reward my soul.*

Wherefore, brethren, if we would scale the summit of humility, and swiftly gain the heavenly height which is reached by our lowliness in this present life, we must set up a ladder of climbing deeds like that which Jacob saw in his dream, whereon angels were descending and ascending. Without doubt that descending and ascending is to be understood by us as signifying that we descend by exalting ourselves and ascend by humbling ourselves. But the ladder itself thus set up is our life in this world, which by humility of heart is lifted by our Lord to heaven. Our body and soul

we may indeed call the sides of the ladder in which our divine vocation has set the divers steps of humility and discipline we have to ascend.

The first step of humility, then, is reached when a man, with the fear of God always before his eyes, does not allow himself to forget, but is ever mindful of all God's commandments. He remembers, moreover, that such as contemn God fall into hell for their sins, and that life eternal awaits such as fear Him. And warding off at each moment all sin and defect in thought and word, of eye, hand or foot, of self-will, let such a one bestir himself to prune away the lusts of the flesh.

Let him think that he is seen at all times by God from heaven; and that wheresoever he may be, all his actions are visible to the eye of God and at all times are reported by the angels. The prophet shows us this when he says that God is ever present to our thoughts: *God searcheth the hearts and reins.* And again, *The Lord knoweth the thoughts of men that they are vain.* He also saith, *Thou hast understood my thoughts afar off;* and again, *The thought of man shall confess Thee.* In order, then, that the humble brother may be careful to avoid wrong thoughts let him always say in his heart, *Then shall I be without spot before Him, if I shall keep me from my iniquity.*

We are forbidden to do our own will, since Scripture tells us, *Leave thy own will and desire.* And again, *We beg of God in prayer that His will may be done in us.*

Rightly are we taught therefore not to do our own will, if we take heed of what the Scripture teaches: *There are ways which to men seem right, the end whereof plungeth even into the deep pit of hell.* And again, when we fear what is said about the negligent, *They are corrupted, and made abominable in their pleasures.* But in regard of the desires of the flesh we ought to believe that God is present with us; as the prophet says, speaking to the Lord, *O Lord, all my desire is before Thee.*

We have therefore to beware of evil desires, since death stands close at the door of pleasure. It is for this reason that Scripture bids us, *Follow not thy concupiscences.* If, therefore, the eyes of the Lord behold both the good and the bad; if He be ever looking down from heaven upon the sons of men to find one who thinks of God or seeks Him; and if day and night what we do is made known to Him—for these reasons, by the angels appointed to watch over us, we should always take heed, brethren, lest God may sometime or other see us, as the prophet says in the Psalm, *inclined to evil and become unprofitable servants.* Even though He spare us for a time, because He is loving and waits for our conversion to better ways, let us fear that He may say to us hereafter, *These things thou hast done and I held my peace.*

The second step of humility is reached when any one not loving self-will takes no heed to satisfy his own desires, but copies in his life what our Lord said, *I came not to do My own will, but the will of Him Who sent Me.* Scripture likewise proclaims that self-will engendereth punishment, and necessity purchaseth a crown.

The third step of humility is reached when a man, for the love of God, submits himself with all obedience to a superior, imitating our Lord, of whom the apostle saith, *He was made obedient even unto death.*

The fourth step of humility is reached when any one in the exercise of his obedience patiently and with a quiet mind bears all that is inflicted on him, things contrary to nature, and even at times unjust, and in suffering all these he neither wearies nor gives over the work, since the Scripture says, *He only that persevereth to the end shall be saved;* also *Let thy heart be comforted, and expect the Lord.* And in order to show that for our Lord's sake the faithful man ought to bear all things, no matter how contrary to nature they may be, in the person of the sufferers, says, *For thee we suffer death all the day long; we are esteemed as sheep for the slaughter.* Secure in the hope of divine reward they rejoice, saying, *But in all things we overcome by the help of Him Who hath loved us.*

Elsewhere also Scripture says, *Thou hast proved us, O Lord; Thou hast tried us, as silver is tried, with fire. Thou hast brought us into the snare; Thou hast laid tribulation upon our backs.* And to show that we ought to be subject to a prior it goes on, *Thou hast placed men over our heads.* And, more-

over, they fulfil the Lord's command by patience in adversity and injury, who, *when struck on one cheek, offer the other;* when one *taketh away their coat leave go their cloak also,* and who being compelled to carry a burden one mile, go two; who, with Paul the apostle, suffer false brethren, and bless those who speak ill of them.

The fifth step of humility is reached when a monk manifests to his abbot, by humble confession, all the evil thoughts of his heart and his secret faults. The Scripture urges us to do this where it says, *Reveal thy way to the Lord and hope in Him.* It also says, *Confess to the Lord, because He is good, because His mercy endureth for ever.* And the prophet also says, *I have made known unto Thee mine offence, and mine injustices I have not hidden. I have said, I will declare openly against myself mine injustices to the Lord; and Thou hast pardoned the wickedness of my heart.*

The sixth step of humility is reached when a monk is content with all that is mean and vile; and in regard to everything enjoined him accounts himself a poor and worthless workman, saying with the prophet, *I have been brought to nothing, and knew it not. I have become as a beast before Thee, and I am always with Thee.*

The seventh step of humility is reached when a man not only confesses with his tongue that he is most lowly and inferior to others, but in his inmost heart believes so. Such a one, humbling himself, exclaims with the prophet, *I am a worm and no man, the reproach of men and the outcast of the people. I have been exalted and am humbled and confounded* And again, *It is good for me that Thou hast humbled me, that I may learn Thy commandments.*

The eighth step of humility is reached when a monk does nothing but what the common rule of the monastery, or the example of his seniors, enforces.

The ninth step of humility is reached when a monk restrains his tongue from talking, and, practising silence, speaks not till a question be asked him, since Scripture says, *In many words thou shalt not avoid sin,* and *a talkative man shall not be directed upon the earth.*

The tenth step of humility is attained to when one is not easily and quickly moved to laughter, for it is written, *The fool lifteth his voice in laughter.*

The eleventh step of humility is reached when a monk, in speaking, do so quietly and without laughter, humbly, gravely and in a few words and not with a loud voice, for it is written, *A wise man is known by a few words.*

The twelfth step of humility is reached when a monk not only has humility in his heart, but even shows it also exteriorly to all who behold him. Thus, whether he be in the oratory at the "Work of God," in the monastery, or in the garden, on a journey, or in the fields, or wheresoever he be, sitting, standing or walking, always let him, with head bent and eyes fixed on the ground, bethink himself of his sins and imagine that he is arraigned before the dread judgment of God. Let him be ever saying to himself, with the publican in the Gospel, *Lord, I a sinner am not worthy to lift mine eyes to heaven;* and with the prophet, *I am bowed down and humbled on every side.*

When all these steps of humility have been mounted the monk will presently attain to that love of God which is perfect and casteth out fear. By means of this love everything which before he had observed not without fear, he shall now begin to do by habit, without any trouble and, as it were, naturally. He acts now not through fear of hell, but for the love of Christ, out of a good habit and a delight in virtue. All this our Lord will vouchsafe to work by the Holy Ghost in His servant, now cleansed from vice and sin.

REVIEW QUESTIONS

1. What did we learn about the lives of the women and men who lived according to this rule?
2. Why is humility such a central monastic value?
3. How does the monastic life define sin and struggle against it?

AMMIANUS MARCELLINUS

FROM *The History*

Ammianus Marcellinus (c. 330–after 392 C.E.) was the last of a series of Roman authors whose vigorous classical style shaped a distinctive imperial history centered on Rome and the frontiers. In these passages Ammianus describes a powerful politician, Petronius Probus, whose career typified late Roman imperial administration. Ammianus was also an early source on the new threats the barbarians posed to the empire.

From *Ammianus Marcellinus: The Later Roman Empire,* edited by Walter Hamilton (New York: Penguin Books, 1986), pp. 345–46, 410–16.

*   *   *

Career and Character of Probus
(368 C.E.)

During this period Vulcatius Rufinus died in office, and Probus was recalled from Rome to succeed him as praetorian prefect. Probus was known all over the Roman world for his high birth, powerful influence, and vast riches; he owned estates in almost every part of the empire, but whether they were honestly come by or not is not for a man like me to say. In his case Fortune, who, to use the language of poetry, carried him on her swift wings, took a double form. Sometimes she exhibited him as a benevolent man engaged in promoting the careers of his friends; at others he appeared as a pernicious schemer who worked off his deadly grudges by inflicting injury. Throughout his life he exercised enormous influence owing to the gifts he bestowed and the constant succession of offices he filled. There were times when he showed fear of those who stood up to him, but he took a high line with those who were afraid of him. When he felt that he was on strong ground he hectored in the elevated style of tragedy, but in panic he could be more abject than any down-at-heel comedian. Probus languished like a fish out of water if he was not in office. This he was driven to seek by the lawless behaviour of his countless dependants, whose excessive greed could never be satisfied in an innocent way, and who thrust their master into public life so as to be able to gain their ends with impunity. It must be admitted that he had sufficient principle never to order a client or slave to break the law, but if he heard that any had committed a crime he would defend him in the teeth of justice itself, without any investigation of the matter or regard for right and honour. This is a fault reprobated by Cicero when he says: 'What is the difference between prompting a deed and approving it when it is done? Or what difference does it make whether I wished it to happen or am glad that it has happened?'

Probus was by nature suspicious and petty. He could wear a sour smile, and sometimes employed flattery when he meant to injure. He had a common defect of characters of his type that is conspicuously bad, especially when its possessor believes that he can conceal it: he was so implacable and inflexible that once he had decided to injure a man he was deaf to all entreaties. Nothing could induce him to pardon an offence, and his ears seemed stopped with lead rather than the proverbial wax.

Even at the height of wealth and honour he was nervous and worried, and in consequence always subject to slight ailments. This was the course of events in the western part of the empire.

*   *   *

Omens of the Death of Valens and of the Imminent Gothic Disaster

Meanwhile a rapid turn of fortune's wheel, which is perpetually alternating adversity and prosperity, was arming Bellona and her attendant Furies and bringing sad calamity upon the East. Its approach was plainly foreshadowed by omens and portents. Besides many true predictions from seers and augurs, dogs howled in answer to wolves, night-birds burst into doleful shrieks, and gloomy dawns dimmed the bright light of morning. At Antioch, where quarrels and riots among the populace were common, it became the habit for anyone who thought himself wronged to shout boldly: 'Burn Valens alive.' Criers could be heard constantly urging people to collect combustibles to set fire to the Baths of Valens, which had been built at the instance of the emperor himself. This indicated almost in so many words the manner of his death. In addition, the ghostly likeness of the king of Armenia and the pathetic shades of the victims in the recent affair of Theodorus made the night hideous with dirge-like howls, and inspired dire terror. A heifer was found lying dead with its throat cut, and this was a sign of widespread misery and death among the public. Lastly, when the old walls of Chalcedon were being taken down to provide material for a bath at Constantinople, the removal of the stone revealed a square block hidden in the fabric, on which were inscribed in Greek the following verses, a clear indication of what was to come:

When through the city's street with garlands
  crowned
Fresh maidens whirl rejoicing in the dance,
And what was once a city wall shall serve—
O what a mournful change—to guard a bath,
Then countless hordes of men from lands afar
Shall cross fair Ister's river, lance in hand,
And lay all Scythia and Mysia waste;
Next on Paeonia turn their mad career,
To spread there likewise nought but death and
  strife.

The Nature of the Huns and Alans

The seed-bed and origin of all this destruction and of the various calamities inflicted by the wrath of Mars, which raged everywhere with unusual fury, I find to be this. The people of the Huns, who are mentioned only cursorily in ancient writers and who dwell beyond the Sea of Azov (Palus Maeotis) near the frozen ocean, are quite abnormally savage. From the moment of birth they make deep gashes in their children's cheeks, so that when in due course hair appears its growth is checked by the wrinkled scars; as they grow older this gives them the unlovely appearance of beardless eunuchs. They have squat bodies, strong limbs, and thick necks, and are so prodigiously ugly and bent that they might be two-legged animals, or the figures crudely carved from stumps which are seen on the parapets of bridges. Still, their shape, however disagreeable, is human; but their way of life is so rough that they have no use for fire or seasoned food, but live on the roots of wild plants and the half-raw flesh of any sort of animal, which they warm a little by placing it between their thighs and the backs of their horses. They have no buildings to shelter them, but avoid anything of the kind as carefully as we avoid living in the neighbourhood of tombs; not so much as a hut thatched with reeds is to be found among them.

They roam at large over mountains and forests, and are inured from the cradle to cold, hunger, and thirst. On foreign soil only extreme necessity can persuade them to come under a roof, since they believe that it is not safe for them to do so. They wear garments of linen or of the skins of field-mice stitched together, and there is no difference between their clothing whether they are at home or abroad. Once they have put their necks into some dingy shirt they never take it off or change it till it rots and falls to pieces from incessant wear. They have round caps of fur on their heads, and protect their hairy legs with goatskins. Their shapeless shoes are not made on a last and make it hard to walk easily. In consequence they are ill-fitted to fight on foot, and remain glued to their horses, hardy but ugly beasts, on which they sometimes sit like women to perform their everyday business. Buying or selling, eating or drinking, are all done by day or night on horseback, and they even bow forward over their beasts' narrow necks to enjoy a deep and dreamy sleep. When they need to debate some important matter they conduct their conference in the same posture. They are not subject to the authority of any king, but break through any obstacle in their path under the improvised command of their chief men.

They sometimes fight *by challenging their foes to single combat,* but when they join battle they advance in packs, uttering their various warcries. Being lightly equipped and very sudden in their movements they can deliberately scatter and gallop about at random, inflicting tremendous slaughter; their extreme nimbleness enables them to force a rampart or pillage an enemy's camp before one catches sight of them. What makes them the most formidable of all warriors is that they shoot from a distance arrows tipped with sharp splinters of bone instead of the usual heads; these are joined to the shafts with wonderful skill. At close quarters they fight without regard for their lives, and while their opponents are guarding against sword-thrusts they catch their limbs in lassos of twisted cloth which make it impossible for them to ride or walk. None of them ploughs or ever touches a plough-handle. They have no fixed abode, no home or law or settled manner of life, but wander like refugees with the wagons in which they live. In these their wives weave their filthy clothing, mate with their husbands, give birth to their children, and rear them to the age of puberty. No one if asked can tell where he comes from, having been conceived in one place, born somewhere else, and reared even further off. You cannot make a truce with them, because they are quite unreliable and easily swayed by any breath of rumour which promises advantage; like unreasoning beasts they are entirely at the mercy of the maddest impulses. They are totally ignorant of the distinction between right and wrong, their speech is shifty and obscure, and they are under no restraint from religion or superstition. Their greed for gold is prodigious, and they are so fickle and prone to anger that often in a single day they will quarrel with their allies without any provocation, and then make it up again without anyone attempting to reconcile them.

This wild race, moving without encumbrances and consumed by a savage passion to pillage the property of others, advanced robbing and slaughtering over the lands of their neighbours till they reached the Alans. The Alans are the ancient Massagetae, and at this point it is relevant to discuss their origin and situation. This is a problem that has perplexed geographers, who have, however, *after much discussion found a reliable solution.*

The Danube, swollen by the waters of a number of tributaries, flows past the territory of the Sarmatians, which extends as far as the river Don (Tanais), the boundary between Europe and Asia. Beyond this the Alans inhabit the immense deserts of Scythia, deriving their name from the mountains. By repeated victories they gradually wore down the people next to them, and, like the Persians, incorporated them into a single nation bearing their own name. Of these the Nervi occupy the interior of the country near high peaks whose steep sides are frozen hard and swept by north winds. Next to them are the savage tribes of the Vidini and Geloni, who flay the skin from their dead enemies and make coverings of it for themselves and their chargers. On the borders of the

Geloni are the Agathyrsi, who tattoo their bodies and colour their hair with a blue dye; the common people display only small spots widely spaced, but in the nobles they are larger and closer together. Beyond them, we are told, roam the Melanchlaenae and Anthropophagi, who live on human flesh. On account of this abominable habit all their neighbours have given them a wide berth and removed to distant regions. In consequence the entire north-eastern tract as far as China has remained uninhabited. In another direction, near the country of the Amazons, the Alans approach the East and form populous and widespread communities. These stretch into Asia, and I have been told that they reach as far as the Ganges, the river which intersects India and empties into the southern sea.

Thus the Alans, whose various tribes there is no point in enumerating, extend over both parts of the earth. But, although they are widely separated and wander in their nomadic way over immense areas, they have in course of time come to be known by one name and are all compendiously called Alans, because their character, their wild way of life, and their weapons are the same everywhere. They have no huts and make no use of the plough, but live upon meat and plenty of milk. They use wagons covered with a curved canopy of bark, and move in these over the endless desert. When they come to a grassy place they arrange their carts in a circle and feed like wild animals; then, having exhausted the forage available, they again settle what one might call their mobile towns upon their vehicles, and move on. In these wagons the males couple with the women and their children are born and reared; in fact, these wagons are their permanent dwellings and, wherever they go, they look upon them as their ancestral home.

They drive their cattle before them and pasture them with their flocks, and they pay particular attention to the breeding of horses. The plains there are always green and there are occasional patches of fruit-trees, so that, wherever they go, they never lack food and fodder. This is because the soil is damp and there are numerous rivers. Those whose age or sex makes them unfit to fight stay by the wagons and occupy themselves in light work, but the younger men, who are inured to riding from earliest boyhood, think it beneath their dignity to walk and are all trained in a variety of ways to be skilful warriors. This is why the Persians too, who are of Scythian origin, are such expert fighters.

Almost all Alans are tall and handsome, with yellowish hair and frighteningly fierce eyes. They are active and nimble in the use of arms and in every way a match for the Huns, but less savage in their habits and way of life. Their raiding and hunting expeditions take them as far as the Sea of Azov and the Crimea, and also to Armenia and Media. They take as much delight in the dangers of war as quiet and peaceful folk in ease and leisure. They regard it as the height of good fortune to lose one's life in battle; those who grow old and die a natural death are bitterly reviled as degenerate cowards. Their proudest boast is to have killed a man, no matter whom, and their most coveted trophy is to use the flayed skins of their decapitated foes as trappings for their horses.

No temple or shrine is to be found among them, not so much as a hut thatched with straw, but their savage custom is to stick a naked sword in the earth and worship it as the god of war, the presiding deity of the regions over which they range. They have a wonderful way of foretelling the future. They collect straight twigs of osier, and at an appointed time sort them out uttering a magic formula, and in this way they obtain clear knowledge of what is to come. They are all free from birth, and slavery is unknown among them. To this day they choose as their leaders men who have proved their worth by long experience in war. Now I must return to what remains of my main theme.

The Huns and Alans Expel the Goths from Their Homes

The Huns, overrunning the territory of those Alans who border on the Greuthungi and are commonly called the Don Alans, killed and stripped many of them, and made a pact of friendship with the survivors. This success emboldened them to make a sudden inroad on the rich and extensive realm of Ermenrich, a warlike king whose many heroic exploits had made him a terror to his neighbours. Ermenrich was hard hit by the violence of this unexpected storm. For some time he endeavoured to stand his ground, but exaggerated reports circulated of the dreadful fate which awaited him, and he found release from his fears by taking his own life. He was succeeded as king by Vithimir, who resisted the Alans for a time, relying on the help of other Huns whom he had hired to support him. But after many defeats he was overwhelmed by superior force and lost his life in battle. The guardianship of his young son Videric was undertaken by Alatheus and Saphrax, experienced commanders of proved courage, but their plans were frustrated by circumstances, and they had to abandon any hope of successful resistance. So they prudently withdrew to the line of the river Dniester (Danastius), which waters the wide plains between the Danube and the Dnieper (Borysthenes).

Athanaric the chief of the Thervingi, against whom, as I have already said, Valens had recently taken the field to punish him for sending help to Procopius, heard of these unexpected events and attempted to maintain his ground, being resolved to put forth all his strength if he should be attacked like the rest. Accordingly he took up his position in a good spot near the banks of the Dniester but some distance from the defensive works of the Greuthungi, and sent Munderic, who later commanded on the Arabian frontier, together with Lagariman and some other notables twenty miles ahead to watch for the approach of the enemy, while he himself marshalled his army undisturbed. But things turned out very differently from what he expected. The Huns, who are good guessers, suspected that there was a larger force further off. So they paid no attention to the troops they had seen, who had lain down to rest as if they had no enemy near them. Then the Huns forded the river by moonlight, and took what was undoubtedly the best course. They forestalled the possibility of any warning reaching the enemy by making a rapid assault on Athanaric himself, and before he could recover from the surprise of their first onset drove him with some losses on their own part to take refuge in rugged mountain country. This new situation and the fear that there was worse to follow constrained him to erect a high rampart extending from the Pruth (Gerasus) to the Danube and skirting the territory of the Taifali. He believed that this hastily but carefully constructed barrier would ensure his security. But while he was pushing on this important work he was hard pressed by the rapid advance of the Huns, who would have overwhelmed him if the weight of booty they were carrying had not forced them to desist.

A report, however, now spread widely among the other Gothic tribes that a hitherto unknown race of men had appeared from some remote corner of the earth, uprooting and destroying everything in its path like a whirlwind descending from high mountains. Weakened by lack of the neces-

sities of life the greater part of the people abandoned Athanaric, and looked for a dwelling far from all knowledge of the barbarians. After much debate where to settle they fixed upon Thrace as the most eligible refuge for two reasons, first, because of its fertility, and second, because it is separated by the broad stream of the Danube from the regions exposed to the thunderbolts of the alien Mars. This decision met with unanimous support.

*   *   *

REVIEW QUESTIONS

1. What does the career of Probus reveal about corruption in the Roman state?
2. What aspects of barbarian life did Ammianus admire?
3. Why are these barbarians such a threat to the empire?

GREGORY OF TOURS

FROM *History of the Franks*

Gregory, bishop of Tours (538–594 C.E.), was descended from a long line of provincial nobles and bishops in Gaul. He wrote History of the Franks, *which relates how the Franks and other tribes conquered and settled a key area of the Roman Empire, as seen through the eyes of a Gallo-Roman aristocrat. These selections discuss how and why Clovis converted to Roman Christianity in 496 C.E. and his role in solidifying the Merovingian dynasty. Barbarian tribes did not yet produce historians or documents, so we must depend on the views of outsiders like Gregory for details on their earliest history.*

From *History of the Franks by Gregory of Tours*, edited by Ernest Brehaut (New York: Columbia University Press, 1944), pp. 36–45.

*   *   *

After these events Childeric died and Clovis his son reigned in his stead. In the fifth year of his reign Siagrius, king of the Romans, son of Egidius, had his seat in the city of Soissons which Egidius, who has been mentioned before, once held. And Clovis came against him with Ragnachar, his kinsman, because he used to possess the kingdom, and demanded that they make ready a battle-field. And Siagrius did not delay nor was he afraid to resist. And so they fought against each other and Siagrius, seeing his army crushed, turned his back and fled swiftly to king Alaric at Toulouse. And Clovis sent to Alaric to send him back, otherwise he was to know that Clovis would make war on him for his refusal. And Alaric was afraid that he would incur the anger of the Franks on account of Siagrius, seeing it is the fashion of the Goths to be terrified, and he surrendered him in chains to Clovis' envoys. And Clovis took him and gave orders to put him under guard, and when he had got his kingdom he directed that he be executed secretly. At that time many churches were despoiled by Clovis' army, since he was as yet involved in heathen error. Now the army had taken from a certain church a vase of wonderful size and beauty, along with the remainder of the utensils for the service of the church. And the bishop of the church sent messengers to the king asking that the vase at least be returned, if he could not get back any more of the sacred dishes. On hearing this the king said to the messenger: "Follow us as far as Soissons, because all that has been taken is to be divided there and when the lot assigns me that dish I will do what the father asks." Then when he came to Soissons and all the booty was set in their midst, the king said: "I ask of you, brave warriors, not to refuse to grant me in addition to my share, yonder dish," that is, he was speaking of the vase just mentioned. In answer to the speech of the king those of more sense replied: "Glorious king, all that we see is yours, and we ourselves are subject to your rule. Now do what seems well-pleasing to you; for no one is able to resist your power." When they said this a foolish,

envious and excitable fellow lifted his battle-ax and struck the vase, and cried in a loud voice: "You shall get nothing here except what the lot fairly bestows on you." At this all were stupefied, but the king endured the insult with the gentleness of patience, and taking the vase he handed it over to the messenger of the church, nursing the wound deep in his heart. And at the end of the year he ordered the whole army to come with their equipment of armor, to show the brightness of their arms on the field of March. And when he was reviewing them all carefully, he came to the man who struck the vase, and said to him: "No one has brought armor so carelessly kept as you; for neither your spear nor sword nor ax is in serviceable condition." And seizing his ax he cast it to the earth, and when the other had bent over somewhat to pick it up, the king raised his hands and drove his own ax into the man's head. "This," said he, "is what you did at Soissons to the vase." Upon the death of this man, he ordered the rest to depart, raising great dread of himself by this action. He made many wars and gained many victories. In the tenth year of his reign he made war on the Thuringi and brought them under his dominion.

Now the king of the Burgundians was Gundevech, of the family of king Athanaric the persecutor, whom we have mentioned before. He had four sons; Gundobad, Godegisel, Chilperic and Godomar. Gundobad killed his brother Chilperic with the sword, and sank his wife in water with a stone tied to her neck. His two daughters he condemned to exile; the older of these, who became a nun, was called Chrona, and the younger Clotilda. And as Clovis often sent embassies to Burgundy, the maiden Clotilda was found by his envoys. And when they saw that she was of good bearing and wise, and learned that she was of the family of the king, they reported this to King Clovis, and he sent an embassy to Gundobad without delay asking her in marriage. And Gundobad was afraid to refuse, and surrendered her to the men, and they took the girl and brought her swiftly to the king. The king was very glad when he saw her, and married her, having already by a concubine a son named Theodoric.

He had a first-born son by queen Clotilda, and as his wife wished to consecrate him in baptism, she tried unceasingly to persuade her husband, saying: "The gods you worship are nothing, and they will be unable to help themselves or any one else. For they are graven out of stone or wood or some metal. And the names you have given them are names of men and not of gods, as Saturn, who is declared to have fled in fear of being banished from his kingdom by his son; as Jove himself, the foul perpetrator of all shameful crimes, committing incest with men, mocking at his kinswomen, not able to refrain from intercourse with his own sister as she herself says: *Jovisque et soror et conjunx.* What could Mars or Mercury do? They are endowed rather with the magic arts than with the power of the divine name. But he ought rather to be worshipped who created by his word heaven and earth, the sea and all that in them is out of a state of nothingness, who made the sun shine, and adorned the heavens with stars, who filled the waters with creeping things, the earth with living things and the air with creatures that fly, at whose nod the earth is decked with growing crops, the trees with fruit, the vines with grapes, by whose hand mankind was created, by whose generosity all that creation serves and helps man whom he created as his own." But though the queen said this the spirit of the king was by no means moved to belief, and he said: "It was at the command of our gods that all things were created and came forth, and it is plain that your God has no power and, what is more, he is proven not to belong to the family of the gods." Meantime the faithful queen made her son ready for baptism; she gave command to adorn the church with hangings and curtains, in order that he who could not be moved by persuasion might be urged to belief by this mystery. The boy, whom they named Ingomer, died after being baptized, still wearing the white garments in which he became regenerate. At this the king was violently angry, and reproached the queen harshly, saying: "If the boy had been dedicated in the name of my gods he would certainly

have lived; but as it is, since he was baptized in the name of your God, he could not live at all." To this the queen said: "I give thanks to the omnipotent God, creator of all, who has judged me not wholly unworthy, that he should deign to take to his kingdom one born from my womb. My soul is not stricken with grief for his sake, because I know that, summoned from this world as he was in his baptismal garments, he will be fed by the vision of God."

After this she bore another son, whom she named Chlodomer at baptism; and when he fell sick, the king said: "It is impossible that anything else should happen to him than happened to his brother, namely, that being baptized in the name of your Christ, he should die at once." But through the prayers of his mother, and the Lord's command, he became well.

The queen did not cease to urge him to recognize the true God and cease worshiping idols. But he could not be influenced in any way to this belief, until at last a war arose with the Alamanni, in which he was driven by necessity to confess what before he had of his free will denied. It came about that as the two armies were fighting fiercely, there was much slaughter, and Clovis's army began to be in danger of destruction. He saw it and raised his eyes to heaven, and with remorse in his heart he burst into tears and cried: "Jesus Christ, whom Clotilda asserts to be the son of the living God, who art said to give aid to those in distress, and to bestow victory on those who hope in thee, I beseech the glory of thy aid, with the vow that if thou wilt grant me victory over these enemies, and I shall know that power which she says that people dedicated in thy name have had from thee, I will believe in thee and be baptized in thy name. For I have invoked my own gods, but, as I find, they have withdrawn from aiding me; and therefore I believe that they possess no power, since they do not help those who obey them. I now call upon thee, I desire to believe thee, only let me be rescued from my adversaries." And when he said this, the Alamanni turned their backs, and began to disperse in flight. And when they saw that their king was killed, they submitted to the dominion of Clovis, saying: "Let not the people perish further, we pray; we are yours now." And he stopped the fighting, and after encouraging his men, retired in peace and told the queen how he had had merit to win the victory by calling on the name of Christ. This happened in the fifteenth year of his reign.

Then the queen asked saint Remi, bishop of Rheims, to summon Clovis secretly, urging him to introduce the king to the word of salvation. And the bishop sent for him secretly and began to urge him to believe in the true God, maker of heaven and earth, and to cease worshiping idols, which could help neither themselves nor any one else. But the king said: "I gladly hear you, most holy father; but there remains one thing: the people who follow me cannot endure to abandon their gods; but I shall go and speak to them according to your words." He met with his followers, but before he could speak the power of God anticipated him, and all the people cried out together: "O pious king, we reject our mortal gods, and we are ready to follow the immortal God whom Remi preaches." This was reported to the bishop, who was greatly rejoiced, and bade them get ready the baptismal font. The squares were shaded with tapestried canopies, the churches adorned with white curtains, the baptistery set in order, the aroma of incense spread, candles of fragrant odor burned brightly, and the whole shrine of the baptistery was filled with a divine fragrance: and the Lord gave such grace to those who stood by that they thought they were placed amid the odors of paradise. And the king was the first to ask to be baptized by the bishop. Another Constantine advanced to the baptismal font, to terminate the disease of ancient leprosy and wash away with fresh water the foul spots that had long been borne. And when he entered to be baptized, the saint of God began with ready speech: "Gently bend your neck, Sigamber; worship what you burned; burn what you worshipped." The holy bishop Remi was a man of excellent wisdom and especially trained in rhetorical studies, and of such surpassing holiness that he equalled the miracles of Silvester. For there is extant a book of his life which tells that he raised a dead man. And so the king confessed

all-powerful God in the Trinity, and was baptized in the name of the Father, Son and holy Spirit, and was anointed with the holy ointment with the sign of the cross of Christ. And of his army more than 3000 were baptized. His sister also, Albofled, was baptized, who not long after passed to the Lord. And when the king was in mourning for her, the holy Remi sent a letter of consolation which began in this way: "The reason of your mourning pains me, and pains me greatly, that Albofled your sister, of good memory, has passed away. But I can give you this comfort, that her departure from the world was such that she ought to be envied rather than mourned." Another sister also was converted, Lanthechild by name, who had fallen into the heresy of the Arians, and she confessed that the Son and the holy Spirit were equal to the Father, and was anointed.

At that time the brothers Gundobad and Godegisel were kings of the country about the Rhone and the Saône together with the province of Marseilles. And they, as well as their people, belonged to the Arian sect. And since they were fighting with each other, Godegisel, hearing of the victories of King Clovis, sent an embassy to him secretly, saying: "If you will give me aid in attacking my brother, so that I may be able to kill him in battle or drive him from the country, I will pay you every year whatever tribute you yourself wish to impose." Clovis accepted this offer gladly, and promised aid whenever need should ask. And at a time agreed upon he marched his army against Gundobad. On hearing of this, Gundobad, who did not know of his brother's treachery, sent to him, saying: "Come to my assistance, since the Franks are in motion against us and are coming to our country to take it. Therefore let us be united against a nation hostile to us, lest because of division we suffer in turn what other peoples have suffered." And the other said: "I will come with my army, and will give you aid." And these three, namely, Clovis against Gundobad and Godegisel, were marching their armies to the same point, and they came with all their warlike equipment to the stronghold named Dijon. And they fought on the river Ouche, and Godegisel joined

Clovis, and both armies crushed the people of Gundobad. And he perceived the treachery of his brother, whom he had not suspected, and turned his back and began to flee, hastening along the banks of the Rhone, and he came to the city of Avignon. And Godegisel having won the victory, promised to Clovis a part of his kingdom, and departed quietly and entered Vienne in triumph, as if he now held the whole kingdom. King Clovis increased his army further, and set off after Gundobad to drag him from his city and slay him. He heard it, and was terrified, and feared that sudden death would come to him. However he had with him Aridius, a man famed for energy and wisdom, and he sent for him and said: "Difficulties wall me in on every side, and I do not know what to do, because these barbarians have come upon us to slay us and destroy the whole country." To this Aridius answered: "You must soften the fierceness of this man in order not to perish. Now if it is pleasing in your eyes, I will pretend to flee from you and to pass over to his side, and when I come to him, I shall prevent his harming either you or this country. Only be willing to do what he demands of you by my advice, until the Lord in his goodness deigns to make your cause successful." And Gundobad said: "I will do whatever you direct." When he said this, Aridius bade him goodby and departed, and going to King Clovis he said: "Behold I am your humble servant, most pious king, I come to your protection, leaving the wretched Gundobad. And if your goodness condescends to receive me, both you and your children shall have in me a true and faithful servant." Clovis received him very readily, and kept him by him, for he was entertaining in story-telling, ready in counsel, just in judgment, and faithful in what was put in his charge. Then when Clovis with all his army sat around the walls of the city, Aridius said: "O King, if the glory of your loftiness should kindly consent to hear the few words of my lowliness, though you do not need counsel, yet I would utter them with entire faithfulness, and they will be advantageous to you and to the cities through which you purpose to go. Why," said he, "do you keep your army here, when your enemy sits in a very strong place? If you ravage the fields, lay waste the meadows, cut down the vineyards, lay low the olive-yards, and destroy all the produce of the country, you do not, however, succeed in doing him any harm. Send an embassy rather and impose tribute to be paid you every year, so that the country may be safe and you may rule forever over a tributary. And if he refuses, then do whatever pleases you." The king took this advice, and commanded his army to return home. Then he sent an embassy to Gundobad, and ordered him to pay him every year a tribute. And he paid it at once and promised that he would pay it for the future.

Later he regained his power, and now contemptuously refused to pay the promised tribute to king Clovis, and set his army in motion against his brother Godegisel, and shut him up in the city of Vienne and besieged him. And when food began to be lacking for the common people, Godegisel was afraid that the famine would extend to himself, and gave orders that the common people be expelled from the city. When this was done, there was driven out, among the rest, the artisan who had charge of the aqueduct. And he was indignant that he had been cast out from the city with the rest, and went to Gundobad in a rage to inform him how to burst into the city and take vengeance on his brother. Under his guidance an army was led through the aqueduct, and many with iron crowbars went in front, for there was a vent in the aqueduct closed with a great stone, and when this had been pushed away with crowbars, by direction of the artisan, they entered the city, and surprised from the rear the defenders who were shooting arrows from the wall. The trumpet was sounded in the midst of the city, and the besiegers seized the gates, and opened them and entered at the same time, and when the people between these two battle lines were being slain by each army, Godegisel sought refuge in the church of the heretics, and was slain there along with the Arian bishop. Finally the Franks who were with Godegisel gathered in a tower. But Gundobad ordered that no harm should be done to a single one of them, but seized them and sent them in exile to king Alaric at Toulouse, and he slew the

Burgundian senators who had conspired with Godegisel. He restored to his own dominion all the region which is now called Burgundy. He established milder laws for the Burgundians lest they should oppress the Romans.

*   *   *

REVIEW QUESTIONS

1. According to Gregory, what qualities does a barbarian king need to succeed?
2. Why did Clovis become a Christian?
3. What is the significance of his conversion?

ST. AUGUSTINE

FROM *City of God* AND *Confessions*

St. Augustine (354–430 C.E.) was the most important Latin father of the church. Educated in Carthage and for a time a professor of rhetoric in Milan, Augustine abandoned his early beliefs in a famous conversion to Christianity in 386 C.E. He then sought a career in the church and was eventually selected to be bishop of Hippo in North Africa. His best-known works are his autobiographical Confessions *and the* City of God, *an immense book composed in the years after the Visigothic sack of Rome in 410 C.E. These passages come from the introduction, where Augustine explains the thesis of his book and his analysis of freedom, sin, and slavery. The short passage from his* Confessions *describes a youthful crime that troubled Augustine for the rest of his life.*

From *City of God*, by St. Augustine, translated by Henry Bettenson (New York: Penguin Books, 1972), pp. 5–9, 874–76. From *Confessions* by St. Augustine, translated by R. S. Pine-Coffin (New York: Penguin, 1961), pp. 47–49.

City of God, Book I

Here, my dear Marcellinus, is the fulfilment of my promise, a book in which I have taken upon myself the task of defending the glorious City of God against those who prefer their own gods to the Founder of that City. I treat of it both as it exists in this world of time, a stranger among the ungodly, living by faith, and as it stands in the security of its everlasting seat. This security it now awaits in steadfast patience, until 'justice returns to judgement'; but it is to attain it hereafter in virtue of its ascendancy over its enemies, when the final victory is won and peace established. The task is long and arduous; but God is our helper.

I know how great is the effort needed to convince the proud of the power and excellence of humility, an excellence which makes it soar above all the summits of this world, which sway in their temporal instability, overtopping them all with an eminence not arrogated by human pride, but granted by divine grace. For the King and Founder of this City which is our subject has revealed in the Scripture of his people this statement of the divine Law, 'God resists the proud, but he gives grace to the humble.' This is God's prerogative;

but man's arrogant spirit in its swelling pride has claimed it as its own, and delights to hear this verse quoted in its own praise: 'To spare the conquered, and beat down the proud.'

Therefore I cannot refrain from speaking about the city of this world, a city which aims at dominion, which holds nations in enslavement, but is itself dominated by that very lust of domination. I must consider this city as far as the scheme of this work demands and as occasion serves.

1. THE ENEMIES OF CHRISTIANITY WERE SPARED BY THE BARBARIANS AT THE SACK OF ROME, OUT OF RESPECT FOR CHRIST.

From this world's city there arise enemies against whom the City of God has to be defended, though many of these correct their godless errors and become useful citizens of that City. But many are inflamed with hate against it and feel no gratitude for the benefits offered by its Redeemer. The benefits are unmistakable; those enemies would not today be able to utter a word against the City if, when fleeing from the sword of their enemy, they had not found, in the City's holy places, the safety on which they now congratulate themselves. The barbarians spared them for Christ's sake; and now these Romans assail Christ's name. The sacred places of the martyrs and the basilicas of the apostles bear witness to this, for in the sack of Rome they afforded shelter to fugitives, both Christian and pagan. The bloodthirsty enemy raged thus far, but here the frenzy of butchery was checked; to these refuges the merciful among the enemy conveyed those whom they had spared outside, to save them from encountering foes who had no such pity. Even men who elsewhere raged with all the savagery an enemy can show, arrived at places where practices generally allowed by laws of war were forbidden and their monstrous passion for violence was brought to a sudden halt; their lust for taking captives was subdued.

In this way many escaped who now complain of this Christian era, and hold Christ responsible for the disasters which their city endured. But they

do not make Christ responsible for the benefits they received out of respect for Christ, to which they owed their lives. They attribute their deliverance to their own destiny; whereas if they had any right judgement they ought rather to attribute the harsh cruelty they suffered at the hands of their enemies to the providence of God. For God's providence constantly uses war to correct and chasten the corrupt morals of mankind, as it also uses such afflictions to train men in a righteous and laudable way of life, removing to a better state those whose life is approved, or else keeping them in this world for further service.

Moreover, they should give credit to this Christian era for the fact that these savage barbarians showed mercy beyond the custom of war—whether they so acted in general in honour of the name of Christ, or in places specially dedicated to Christ's name, buildings of such size and capacity as to give mercy a wider range. For this clemency our detractors ought rather to give thanks to God; they should have recourse to his name in all sincerity, so as to escape the penalty of everlasting fire, seeing that so many of them assumed his name dishonestly, to escape the penalty of immediate destruction. Among those whom you see insulting Christ's servants with such wanton insolence there are very many who came unscathed through that terrible time of massacre only by passing themselves off as Christ's servants. And now with ungrateful pride and impious madness they oppose his name in the perversity of their hearts, so that they may incur the punishment of eternal darkness; but then they took refuge in that name, though with deceitful lips, so that they might continue to enjoy this transitory light.

2. THAT VICTORS SHOULD SPARE THE VANQUISHED OUT OF RESPECT FOR THEIR GODS IS SOMETHING UNEXAMPLED IN HISTORY.

We have the records of many wars, both before the foundation of Rome and after its rise to power. Let our enemies read their history, and then produce instances of the capture of any city by foreign enemies when those enemies spared any whom they found taking refuge in the temples of their gods. Let them quote any barbarian general who gave instructions, at the storming of a town, that no one should be treated with violence who was discovered in this temple or that. Aeneas saw Priam at the altar,

> polluting with his blood
> The fire which he had consecrated.

And Diomedes and Ulysses

> Slew all the warders of the citadel
> And snatched with bloody hands the sacred
>   image;
> Nor shrank to touch the chaplets virginal
> Of the dread goddess.

And there is no truth in the statement that comes after,

> The Grecian hopes then failed, and ebbed away.

For what in fact followed was the Greek victory, the destruction of Troy by fire and sword, the slaughter of Priam at the altar.

And it was not because Troy lost Minerva that Troy perished. What loss did Minerva herself first incur, that led to her own disappearance? Was it, perhaps, the loss of her guards? There can be no doubt that their death made her removal possible—the image did not preserve the men; the men were preserving the image. Why then did they worship her, to secure her protection for their country and its citizens? She could not guard her own keepers.

3. THE FOLLY OF THE ROMANS IN CONFIDING THEIR SAFETY TO THE HOUSEHOLD GODS WHO HAD FAILED TO PROTECT TROY.

There you see the sorts of gods to whom the Romans gladly entrusted the preservation of their city. Pitiable folly! Yet the Romans are enraged by such criticisms from us, while they are not incensed at the authors of such quotations; in fact they pay money to become acquainted with their works, and they consider that those who merely instruct them in these works merit an official sal-

ary and an honoured position in the community. Virgil certainly is held to be a great poet; in fact he is regarded as the best and the most renowned of all poets, and for that reason he is read by children at an early age—they take great draughts of his poetry into their unformed minds, so that they may not easily forget him, for, as Horace remarks,

> New vessels will for long retain the taste
> Of what is first poured into them.

Now in Virgil Juno is introduced as hostile to the Trojans, and when she urges Aeolus, king of the winds, against them, she says,

> A race I hate sails the Etruscan sea
> Bringing to Italy Troy's vanquished gods,
> And Troy itself.

Ought the Romans, as prudent men, to have entrusted the defence of Rome to gods unable to defend themselves? Juno no doubt spoke like a woman in anger, heedless of what she was saying. But consider what is said by Aeneas himself, who is so often called "the pious."

> Panthus, the priest of Phoebus and the citadel,
> Snatching his conquered gods and his young
>   grandson
> Rushes in frenzy to the door.

He does not shrink from calling the gods "conquered," and he speaks of them as being entrusted to him, rather than the other way round, when he is told, "To thee, Troy now entrusts her native gods."

If Virgil speaks of such gods as "vanquished," and tells how, after their overthrow, they only succeeded in escaping because they were committed to the care of a man, what folly it is to see any wisdom in committing Rome to such guardians, and in supposing that it could not be sacked while it retained possession of them. To worship "vanquished" gods as protectors and defenders is to rely not on divinities but on defaulters. It is not sensible to assume that Rome would have escaped this disaster had these gods not first perished; the sensible belief is that those gods would have perished long before, had not Rome made every effort to preserve them. Anyone who gives his mind to it can see that it is utter folly to count on invincibility by virtue of the possession of defenders who have been conquered and to attribute destruction to the loss of such guardian deities as these. In fact, the only possible cause of destruction was the choice of such perishable defenders. When the poets wrote and sang of "vanquished gods," it was not because it suited their whim to lie—they were men of sense, and truth compelled them to admit the facts.

But I must deal with this subject in fuller detail in a more convenient place. For the present I will return to the ingratitude of those who blasphemously blame Christ for the disasters which their moral perversity deservedly brought upon them, and I will deal with the subject as briefly as I can. They were spared for Christ's sake, pagans though they were; yet they scorn to acknowledge this. With the madness of sacrilegious perversity they use their tongues against the name of Christ; yet with those same tongues they dishonestly claimed that name in order to save their lives, or else, in places sacred to him, they held their tongues through fear. They were kept safe and protected there where his name stood between them and the enemy's violence. And so they issue from that shelter to assail him with curses of hate.

*   *   *

15. MAN'S NATURAL FREEDOM; AND THE SLAVERY CAUSED BY SIN.

This relationship is prescribed by the order of nature, and it is in this situation that God created man. For he says, "Let him have lordship over the fish of the sea, the birds of the sky . . . and all the reptiles that crawl on the earth." He did not wish the rational being, made in his own image, to have dominion over any but irrational creatures, not man over man, but man over the beasts. Hence the first just men were set up as shepherds of flocks, rather than as kings of men, so that in this

way also God might convey the message of what was required by the order of nature, and what was demanded by the deserts of sinners—for it is understood, of course, that the condition of slavery is justly imposed on the sinner. That is why we do not hear of a slave anywhere in the Scriptures until Noah, the just man, punished his son's sin with this word; and so that son deserved this name because of his misdeed, not because of his nature. The origin of the Latin word for slave, *servus*, is believed to be derived from the fact that those who by the laws of war could rightly be put to death by the conquerors, became *servi*, slaves, when they were preserved, receiving this name from their preservation. But even this enslavement could not have happened, if it were not for the deserts of sin. For even when a just war is fought it is in defence of his sin that the other side is contending; and victory, even when the victory falls to the wicked, is a humiliation visited on the conquered by divine judgement, either to correct or to punish their sins. We have a witness to this in Daniel, a man of God, who in captivity confesses to God his own sins and the sins of his people, and in devout grief testifies that they are the cause of that captivity. The first cause of slavery, then, is sin, whereby man was subjected to man in the condition of bondage; and this can only happen by the judgement of God, with whom there is no injustice, and who knows how to allot different punishments according to the deserts of the offenders.

Now, as our Lord above says, "Everyone who commits sin is sin's slave," and that is why, though many devout men are slaves to unrighteous masters, yet the masters they serve are not themselves free men; 'for when a man is conquered by another he is also bound as a slave to his conqueror.' And obviously it is a happier lot to be slave to a human being than to a lust; and, in fact, the most pitiless domination that devastates the hearts of men, is that exercised by this very lust for domination, to mention no others. However, in that order of peace in which men are subordinate to other men, humility is as salutary for the servants as pride is harmful to the masters. And yet by nature, in the condition in which God created man, no man is the slave either of man or of sin. But it remains true that slavery as a punishment is also ordained by that law which enjoins the preservation of the order of nature, and forbids its disturbance; in fact, if nothing had been done to contravene that law, there would have been nothing to require the discipline of slavery as a punishment. That explains also the Apostle's admonition to slaves, that they should be subject to their masters, and serve them loyally and willingly. What he means is that if they cannot be set free by their masters, they themselves may thus make their slavery, in a sense, free, by serving not with the slyness of fear, but with the fidelity of affection, until all injustice disappears and all human lordship and power is annihilated, and God is all in all.

16. EQUITY IN THE RELATION OF MASTER AND SLAVE.

This being so, even though our righteous fathers had slaves, they so managed the peace of their households as to make a distinction between the situation of children and the condition of slaves in respect of the temporal goods of this life; and yet in the matter of the worship of God—in whom we must place our hope of everlasting goods—they were concerned, with equal affection, for all the members of their household. This is what the order of nature prescribes, so that this is the source of the name *paterfamilias*, a name that has become so generally used that even those who exercise unjust rule rejoice to be called by this title. On the other hand, those who are genuine "fathers of their household" are concerned for the welfare of all in their households in respect of the worship and service of God, as if they were all their children, longing and praying that they may come to the heavenly home, where it will not be a necessary duty to give orders to men, because it will no longer be a necessary duty to be concerned for the welfare of those who are already in the felicity of that immortal state. But until that home is reached, the fathers have an obligation to ex-ercise the authority of masters greater than the duty of slaves to put up with their condition as servants.

However, if anyone in the household is, through his disobedience, an enemy to the domestic peace, he is reproved by a word, or by a blow, or any other kind of punishment that is just and legitimate, to the extent allowed by human society; but this is for the benefit of the offender, intended to readjust him to the domestic peace from which he had broken away. For just as it is not an act of kindness to help a man, when the effect of the help is to make him lose a greater good, so it is not a blameless act to spare a man, when by so doing you let him fall into a greater sin. Hence the duty of anyone who would be blameless includes not only doing no harm to anyone but also restraining a man from sin or punishing his sin, so that either the man who is chastised may be corrected by his experience, or others may be deterred by his example. Now a man's house ought to be the beginning, or rather a small component part of the city, and every beginning is directed to some end of its own kind, and every component part contributes to the completeness of the whole of which it forms a part. The implication is quite apparent, that domestic peace contributes to the peace of the city— that is, the ordered harmony of those who live together in a house in the matter of giving and obeying orders, contributes to the ordered harmony concerning authority and obedience obtaining among the citizens. Consequently it is fitting that the father of a household should take his rules from the law of the city, and govern his household in such a way that it fits in with the peace of the city.

Confessions

4

It is certain, O Lord, that theft is punished by your law, the law that is written in men's hearts and cannot be erased however sinful they are. For no thief can bear that another thief should steal from him, even if he is rich and the other is driven to it by want. Yet I was willing to steal, and steal I did, although I was not compelled by any lack, unless it were the lack of a sense of justice or a distaste for what was right and a greedy love of doing wrong. For of what I stole I already had plenty, and much better at that, and I had no wish to enjoy the things I coveted by stealing, but only to enjoy the theft itself and the sin. There was a pear-tree near our vineyard, loaded with fruit that was attractive neither to look at nor to taste. Late one night a band of ruffians, myself included, went off to shake down the fruit and carry it away, for we had continued our games out of doors until well after dark, as was our pernicious habit. We took away an enormous quantity of pears, not to eat them ourselves, but simply to throw them to the pigs. Perhaps we ate some of them, but our real pleasure consisted in doing something that was forbidden.

Look into my heart, O God, the same heart on which you took pity when it was in the depths of the abyss. Let my heart now tell you what prompted me to do wrong for no purpose, and why it was only my own love of mischief that made me do it. The evil in me was foul, but I loved it. I loved my own perdition and my own faults, not the things for which I committed wrong, but the wrong itself. My soul was vicious and broke away from your safe keeping to seek its own destruction looking for no profit in disgrace but only for disgrace itself.

5

The eye is attracted by beautiful objects, by gold and silver and all such things. There is great pleasure, too, in feeling something agreeable to the touch, and material things have various qualities to please each of the other senses. Again, it is gratifying to be held in esteem by other men and to have the power of giving them orders and gaining the mastery over them. This is also the reason why revenge is sweet. But our ambition to obtain all these things must not lead us astray from you, O Lord, nor must we depart from what your law allows.

The life we live on earth has its own attractions as well, because it has a certain beauty of its own in harmony with all the rest of this world's beauty. Friendship among men, too, is a delightful bond, uniting many souls in one. All these things and their like can be occasions of sin because, good though they are, they are of the lowest order of good, and if we are too much tempted by them we abandon those higher and better things, your truth, your law, and you yourself, O Lord our God. For these earthly things, too, can give joy, though not such joy as my God, who made them all, can give, because *honest men will rejoice in the Lord; upright hearts will not boast in vain.*

When there is an inquiry to discover why a crime has been committed, normally no one is satisfied until it has been shown that the motive might have been either the desire of gaining, or the fear of losing, one of those good things which I said were of the lowest order. For such things are attractive and have beauty, although they are paltry trifles in comparison with the worth of God's blessed treasures. A man commits murder and we ask the reason. He did it because he wanted his victim's wife or estates for himself, or so that he might live on the proceeds of robbery, or because he was afraid that the other might defraud him of something, or because he had been wronged and was burning for revenge. Surely no one would believe that he would commit murder for no reason but the sheer delight of killing? Sallust tells us that Catiline was a man of insane ferocity, "who chose to be cruel and vicious without apparent reason"; but we are also told that his purpose was "not to allow his men to lose heart or waste their skill through lack of practice." If we ask the reason for this, it is obvious that he meant that once he had made himself master of the government by means of this continual violence, he would obtain honour, power, and wealth and would no longer go in fear of the law because of his crimes or have to face difficulties through lack of funds. So even Catiline did not love crime for crime's sake. He loved something quite different, for the sake of which he committed his crimes.

6

If the crime of theft which I committed that night as a boy of sixteen were a living thing, I could speak to it and ask what it was that, to my shame, I loved in it. I had no beauty because it was a robbery. It is true that the pears which we stole had beauty, because they were created by you, the good God, who are the most beautiful of all beings and the Creator of all things, the supreme Good and my own true Good. But it was not the pears that my unhappy soul desired. I had plenty of my own, better than those, and I only picked them so that I might steal. For no sooner had I picked them than I threw them away, and tasted nothing in them but my own sin, which I relished and enjoyed. If any part of one of those pears passed my lips, it was the sin that gave it flavour.

*   *   *

REVIEW QUESTIONS

1. How does Augustine interpret the meaning of the sack of Rome?
2. How does he justify slavery?
3. What light does he shed on the daily life of Roman slaves?
4. What troubled Augustine about the memory of stealing the pears?

MOSAICS OF JUSTINIAN AND THEODORA, CHURCH OF SAN VITA, RAVENNA (C. 500 C.E.)

Justinian (top) holds a communion dish, Theodora (bottom) a chalice. The emperor commissioned these mosaics for an important church in Ravenna, capital of a part of Byzantine Italy. What does this mosaic suggest about the position of the imperial family in the church?

7 ∼ ROME'S THREE HEIRS: THE BYZANTINE, ISLAMIC, AND EARLY MEDIEVAL WORLDS

Roman control over most of the western Mediterranean collapsed in the fifth century, and soon Rome itself became the capital of an Ostrogothic kingdom in Italy. A world formerly centered on the Middle Sea began to take a different shape. In the eastern Mediterranean, the Roman Empire endured. This state, smaller after the rise of Islam and the loss of North Africa, Egypt, Syria, and the Holy Land, became the Byzantine Empire, a largely Greek kingdom on the shores of the Aegean Sea. Ancient culture continued to evolve here in the setting of Eastern Orthodox Christianity and a nearly incessant struggle for survival against Slavic, Muslim, and eventually western Christian neighbors.

The Arabian Peninsula, largely neglected by the neighboring Roman and Persian Empires, unified in the seventh century under the influence of Muhammad of Mecca. The new religion of Islam, partially drawing on and extending Jewish and Christian traditions but containing a specific revelation and message for the Arabian peoples, unified Arabia with a mission. Armies spread the new faith as they quickly extended Muslim conquests across Africa to the west and crossed to the Iberian Peninsula, and the religion spread through Mesopotamia, Persia, and northern India to the east eventually to the Philippines. The collected revelations of Muhammad, in the form of the Qur'an, brought a knowledge of the religion as well as Arabic language to all the new peoples converted into the world of Islam. Islamic scholars and schools preserved much of ancient Greek, Syrian, and Persian culture and soon contributed new insights in the sciences and history. Much of the West's knowledge of ancient Greek thought came through translations of Arabic sources.

In northwestern Europe, the barbarian kingdoms, converted to Christianity, became the center of a third culture, not Greek Christian or Muslim, but eventually a Latin Christendom, shaped by the Roman heritage and Germanic culture. European monasteries preserved and copied classical Latin and early Christian texts that became the core of early medieval culture. The religious frontiers between the Eastern Orthodox, Roman Catholic, and Muslim worlds in Europe masked deep ethnic divisions and eventual splits in the apparent unity of the faiths. All three cultures preserved parts of the classical legacy while despising paganism and some ancient values not suited to the newer religions.

For a time in the sixth century, the Emperor Justinian seemed poised to re-store imperial authority in large parts of the West, but his failures and the rise of Islam resulted in a more compact Byzantine state. For nearly a thousand years, Byzantine culture produced distinctive artistic works and writers. In the West there was no longer a Roman emperor until the coronation of Charle-magne in 800. The resurgent Frankish state in the West helped to halt the ad-vance of Islam in Europe and extended the frontiers of Christendom into pagan Germanic and Slavic lands to the east. Government depended on the personality of individual rulers, and in Charlemagne the Franks benefited from the rule of an ideal king who was also interested in sponsoring the revival of learning and the arts. Anglo-Saxon England, remaining outside the Carolingian Empire, also contributed monks and missionaries, as well as a distinctive literature, to this early medieval culture. A renewed wave of Viking, Hungarian, and Muslim at-tacks in the late eighth and ninth centuries disrupted the Carolingian and Anglo-Saxon states.

In the Muslim world, the caliphate of Baghdad presided over a golden age of Arabic culture under Harun al Rashid (786–809). This ruler established contacts with the Christian West and sent Charlemagne an elephant, an animal not seen in Europe since the Romans and a marvel of the age, and a clock, which did not last as long as the elephant. By about the year 1000, three centers of power had replaced the Roman Empire of late antiquity. Islamic rulers held sway over the southern and eastern shores of the Mediterranean, and in the East a Greek state calling itself a Roman Empire still endured. In the West a distinctly me-dieval Latin Christendom emerged from the end of Rome and the subsequent barbarian kingdoms, but this world was insecure and beset by powerful enemies on all sides.

PROCOPIUS

FROM *Secret History*

Procopius, a sixth-century Byzantine writer active in the reign of Justinian (527–565), suppressed some of his true opinions from the public by including them in his lively Secret History. *In these selections Procopius explains his purpose in writing history and attacks Justinian, whose ambitions to reestablish Roman authority in the West exhausted his empire.*

From *Procopius: Secret History*, edited by Richard Atwater (Ann Arbor: University of Michigan Press, 1978), pp. 40–44.

*   *   *

In what I have written on the Roman wars up to the present point, the story was arranged in chronological order and as completely as the times then permitted. What I shall write now follows a different plan, supplementing the previous formal chronicle with a disclosure of what really happened throughout the Roman Empire. You see, it was not possible, during the life of certain persons, to write the truth of what they did, as a historian should. If I had, their hordes of spies would have found out about it, and they would have put me to a most horrible death. I could not even trust my nearest relatives. That is why I was compelled to hide the real explanation of many matters glossed over in my previous books.

These secrets it is now my duty to tell and reveal the remaining hidden matters and motives. Yet when I approach this different task, I find it hard indeed to have to stammer and retract what I have written before about the lives of Justinian and Theodora. Worse yet, it occurs to me that what I am now about to tell will seem neither probable nor plausible to future generations, especially as time flows on and my story becomes ancient history. I fear they may think me a writer of fiction, and even put me among the poets.

However, I have this much to cheer me, that my account will not be unendorsed by other testimony: so I shall not shrink from the duty of completing this work.

*   *   *

Character and Appearance of Justinian

Now this went on not only in Constantinople, but in every city: for like any other disease, the evil, starting there, spread throughout the entire Roman Empire. But the Emperor was undisturbed by the trouble, even when it went on continually under his own eyes at the hippodrome. For he was very complacent and resembled most the silly ass, which follows, only shaking its ears, when one drags it by the bridle. As such Justinian acted, and threw everything into confusion.

As soon as he took over the rule from his uncle, his first measure was to spend the public money without restraint, now that he had control of it. He gave much of it to the Huns who, from time to time, entered the state; and in consequence the Roman provinces were subject to constant incursions, for these barbarians, having once tasted Roman wealth, never forgot the road that led to it. And he threw much money into the sea in the form of moles, as if to master the eternal roaring of the breakers. For he jealously hurled stone breakwaters far out from the mainland against the onset of the sea, as if by the power of wealth he could outmatch the might of ocean.

He gathered to himself the private estates of Roman citizens from all over the Empire: some by accusing their possessors of crimes of which they were innocent, others by juggling their owners' words into the semblance of a gift to him of their property. And many, caught in the act of murder and other crimes, turned their possessions over to him and thus escaped the penalty for their sins.

Others, fraudulently disputing title to lands happening to adjoin their own, when they saw they had no chance of getting the best of the argument, with the law against them, gave him their equity in the claim so as to be released from court. Thus, by a gesture that cost him nothing, they gained his favor and were able illegally to get the better of their opponents.

I think this is as good a time as any to describe the personal appearance of the man. Now in physique he was neither tall nor short, but of average height; not thin, but moderately plump; his face was round, and not bad looking, for he had good color, even when he fasted for two days. To make a long description short, he much resembled Domitian, Vespasian's son. He was the one whom the Romans so hated that even tearing him into pieces did not satisfy their wrath against him, but a decree was passed by the Senate that the name of this Emperor should never be written, and that no statue of him should be preserved. And so this name was erased in all the inscriptions at Rome and wherever else it had been written, except only where it occurs in the list of emperors; and nowhere may be seen any statue of him in all the Roman Empire, save one in brass, which was made for the following reason.

Domitian's wife was of free birth and otherwise noble; and neither had she herself ever done wrong to anybody, nor had she assented in her husband's acts. Wherefore she was dearly loved; and the Senate sent for her, when Domitian died, and commanded her to ask whatever boon she wished. But she asked only this: to set up in his memory one brass image, wherever she might desire. To this the Senate agreed. Now the lady, wishing to leave a memorial to future time of the savagery of those who had butchered her husband, conceived this plan: collecting the pieces of Domitian's body, she joined them accurately together and sewed the body up again into its original semblance. Taking this to the statue makers, she ordered them to produce the miserable form in brass. So the artisans forthwith made the image, and the wife took it, and set it up in the street which leads to the Capitol, on the right hand side as one goes there from the Forum: a monument to Domitian and a revelation of the manner of his death until this day.

Justinian's entire person, his manner of expression and all of his features might be clearly pointed out in this statue.

Now such was Justinian in appearance; but his character was something I could not fully describe. For he was at once villainous and amenable; as people say colloquially, a moron. He was never truthful with anyone, but always guileful in what he said and did, yet easily hoodwinked by any who wanted to deceive him. His nature was an unnatural mixture of folly and wickedness. What in olden times a peripatetic philosopher said was also true of him, that opposite qualities combine in a man as in the mixing of colors. I will try to portray him, however, insofar as I can fathom his complexity.

This Emperor, then, was deceitful, devious, false, hypocritical, two-faced, cruel, skilled in dissembling his thought, never moved to tears by either joy or pain, though he could summon them artfully at will when the occasion demanded, a liar always, not only offhand, but in writing, and when he swore sacred oaths to his subjects in their very hearing. Then he would immediately break his agreements and pledges, like the vilest of slaves, whom indeed only the fear of torture drives to confess their perjury. A faithless friend, he was a treacherous enemy, insane for murder and plunder, quarrelsome and revolutionary, easily led to anything evil, but never willing to listen to good counsel, quick to plan mischief and carry it out, but finding even the hearing of anything good distasteful to his ears.

How could anyone put Justinian's ways into words? These and many even worse vices were disclosed in him as in no other mortal: nature seemed to have taken the wickedness of all other men combined and planted it in this man's soul. And besides this, he was too prone to listen to accusations; and too quick to punish. For he decided such cases without full examination, naming the punishment when he had heard only the accuser's side of the matter. Without hesitation he wrote decrees for the plundering of countries, sacking of cities, and slavery of whole nations, for no cause whatever. So that if one wished to take all the calamities which had befallen the Romans before this time and weigh them against his crimes, I think it would be found that more men had been murdered by this single man than in all previous history.

He had no scruples about appropriating other people's property, and did not even think any excuse necessary, legal or illegal, for confiscating what did not belong to him. And when it was his, he was more than ready to squander it in insane display, or give it as an unnecessary bribe to the barbarians. In short, he neither held on to any money himself nor let anyone else keep any: as if his reason were not avarice, but jealousy of those who had riches. Driving all wealth from the country of the Romans in this manner, he became the cause of universal poverty.

Now this was the character of Justinian, so far as I can portray it.

*   *   *

REVIEW QUESTIONS

1. What difference does Procopius see between official and secret history?
2. How does this account square with the version of Justinian's reign in the textbook?

FROM *Digenis Akritis*

This Byzantine epic poem concerns the legendary hero Digenis Akritis (Double-Descent Frontiersman). The setting is Cappadocia, on the contested frontier between Greek Christian and Muslim Syrian lands in the ninth or tenth centuries. This selection tells the story of the hero's father, a Muslim emir who fell in love with a captured Christian woman. The emir changed his faith and married the woman. The emir's mother sends a letter to berate her renegade son. Hence, the emphasis in this part of the epic is on the hero's parents and their conflicting loyalties. The hero, as his name implies, is a product of this mixed relationship.

From *Digenis Akritis*, edited and translated by Elizabeth Jeffreys (Cambridge, Eng.: Cambridge University Press, 1998), pp. 25–43.

The Second Book, concerning the Birth of the Frontiersman

Since they gave oaths that they would accept him
  as a brother-in-law,
the emir immediately took his youngsters
and returned to Roman territory, for the sake of
  his beloved.
When he reached the area of Roman territory,
he set free all those whom he had taken prisoner,

giving each sufficient provisions for the journey.
  The girl's brothers wrote everything to their
    mother,
the finding of the girl, the emir's desire,
how he had renounced his faith, his kinsmen and
    his country,
saying, "Much beloved mother, do not be dis-
    tressed,
for we shall have a very good-looking and hand-
    some brother-in-law.
Prepare all that is required for the wedding."
  When she heard this, she gave thanks to God,
saying, "Thanks be to your benevolence, Christ,
thanks be to your might, hope of the hopeless;
you can accomplish whatever you wish, nothing
    is impossible for you.
For you have made this enemy gentle,
and you have rescued my daughter from death.
But, my longed-for daughter, light of my eyes,
when shall I see you alive, when shall I hear your
    voice?
See, I have prepared your wedding and what is
    required.
Will the bridegroom be your equal in beauty?
Will he share the views of high-born Romans?
I fear, my lovely child, that he may be lacking in
    affection,
being a heathen, he may have a fierce temper, and
    there may be no point in my living."
This is what the general's lady sang as she
    rejoiced.
  The emir and with him the girl's brothers,
all rejoicing, set off on their way wearily.
When they came near their own house
a great retinue and their kinsmen came out to
    greet them,
then so did the general's lady with great magnifi-
    cence.
The boundless joy that arose then,
who can describe it completely or picture it
    completely?
For the children embraced their mother with
    fervour,
and the mother rejoiced truly in her children;
and seeing that her son-in-law was exceedingly
    handsome,
she gave thanks to God with all her heart,

saying, "Lord Christ, no one whose hope is in
    you
has ever failed to achieve what they desire."
  When they reached the house, they celebrated
    the wedding
and administered holy baptism to the son-in-law.
The universal joy grew and grew,
for the emir rejoiced since he had won his
    beloved;
for there is no joy greater than passionate love
(and the more the lover is enflamed by lack of
    success,
the more he rejoices when he wins his beloved).
  After the union the girl conceived
and bore Basil Digenis Akritis, the Frontiersman
    of Double Descent,
and the emir's desire increased yet more.
  But the emir's mother sent a letter from Syria,
full of lamentation, reproach and blame:
"Most beloved child, how could you have forgot-
    ten your mother,
blinded my eyes and extinguished my light?
How could you renounce your kinsmen and faith
    and country
and become a reproach to all Syria?
We are abominated by all men
as deniers of the faith, as law-breakers
and for not having observed well the Prophet's
    words.
What has happened to you, my child? How have
    you forgotten these things?
How could you not remember your father's
    deeds,
how many Romans he slew, how many he carried
    off as slaves?
Did he not fill prisons with generals and
    toparchs?
Did he not plunder many of the themes in
    Roman territory
and carry off beautiful high-born girls as
    prisoners?
Was he not pressured, like you, to become a
    renegade?
For when the Roman armies encircled him,
the generals swore him most terrible oaths
that he would be honoured as a patrikios by
    the emperor

and become a protostrator, if he were to throw
   down his sword.
But he kept the Prophet's commandments,
spurned renown and paid no attention to wealth,
and they hewed him limb from limb and took
   away his sword.
But you, not even under compulsion, have abandoned everything at once,
your faith, your kinsmen and me, your mother.
My brother, your uncle, Moursis Karoïs,
made an expedition to Smyrna, to the sea-board;
he plundered Ankyra, the city of Abydos,
Aphrike, Taranta and Hexakomia,
and when he had won these victories he returned
   to Syria.
You too, most miserable man, have made a
   campaign.
When you were about to be honoured by all
   Syria,
you destroyed everything for the love of a
   pig-eater
and have become accursed in every mosque.
If you do not leave quickly and come to Syria,
the emirs intend to behead me,
and kill your children since their father is
   a rebel,
and to give to others your delightful girls,
who are lamenting for you and are losing
   patience.
My sweetest child, pity your mother;
do not send me in my old age to Hades in
   sorrow,
do not allow your children to be slain unjustly,
do not ignore the tears of your delightful girls
and let God in his greatness remove you from
   the world.
Look, I have sent you, as you see, choice horses.
Mount the chestnut, lead the black,
let the bay follow and no one will catch you.
Bring the Roman girl too, if you are upset because of her,
but if you disobey me, may you be accursed."
   Picked Arabs took the letter
and came with great speed to Roman territory.
There was a place, Lakkopetra, far from the
   house.
They encamped there, so as not to be seen,

and told the emir by means of the letter-carrier:
"There is moonlight shining all night, let us make
   our journey if you wish."
   When the emir saw his mother's letter,
he was filled greatly with the compassion a son
   feels for his mother,
he pitied his children and their mothers.
Jealousy seized him, should they embrace others,
for a former passion is never forgotten
though love of the girl had quite blotted it out,
for the more intense pain blots out the lesser.
And he was left wondering what he was to do.
   Going into their chamber, he said to his beloved,
"I wish to entrust some secret information to
   you,
but I am afraid, my dearest, that it may not be to
   your liking.
See, the time has come for me to know for
   certain
if the love you have for me is quite pure."
   When she heard this, she was pierced to
   the heart
and, sighing deeply, spoke as follows:
"My most sweet husband, my lord and defender,
when have I heard any word from you that is not
   to my liking?
What circumstances will separate me from your
   desire?
Indeed, even if I have to die, I shall not renounce
   you,
for circumstances are a test of affection."
   "No question of death, dearest," the emir replied,
"may what you expect and decide never happen,
   my soul.
But I have received a letter from my mother in
   Syria,
and she is in danger because of me, so I wish
   to go.
If you, my dear soul, come with me
(I do not wish to be separated from you even for
   one hour),
we shall also return once more with great
   speed."
   "With pleasure, my sweetheart," the girl replied,
"do not grieve because of this, I will go wherever
   you command."
   But God performed an unexpected wonder

and brought the secret plan to light through
   a dream.
For the girl's youngest brother had a dream,
and on rising from sleep called his brothers
and told them the dream he had had in the night.
   "I was seated," he said, "up in the house,
and I was watching hawks at Lakkopetra,
and a fierce falcon pursuing a dove.
As he pursued it and neared success,
both came into the chamber
where our brother-in-law lives with our sister.
Suddenly I leapt up and ran to seize her;
my soul was troubled and I woke from sleep."
   Then the eldest brother interpreted the vision:
"Hawks, so they say, stand for abductors,
and as for the falcon whom you saw, I fear that
   our brother-in-law
might do some harm to the dove, our sister.
But let us go to where you had your dream,
where you saw the hawks flying."
   They mounted immediately and went to
   the rock,
and found the Arabs with the horses.
On seeing them they were amazed and astonished
   at the vision,
saying, "Welcome, our brother-in-law's youngsters.
Why are you encamped here, avoiding our
   house?"
   They could make no denial and confessed,
revealing what was certain; nothing was hidden.
For unexpected fear brings out the truth,
but when it is expected it leads to excuses.
Gathering them up immediately, they came to
   their brother-in-law
and reproached him for being malicious.
Indeed, the youngest, who was very hot-headed,
said, "Don't reject what you had in mind,
though you must understand, Saracen, that you
   will not see Syria.
But since you have proved to be a law-breaker
   and an enemy,
leave our sister, renounce your child,
take what you brought and go back to where you
   came from."
   On hearing this and seeing the evidence,

the emir could make no denial and remained
   utterly silent,
full of shame, fear and distress.
For he was ashamed to be caught as a thief, he
   was afraid since he was a foreigner,
and he grieved because he could not endure separation from his dearest.
Not knowing what to do, he came to the girl,
for from her alone he had hoped to find consolation,
not realising what God had revealed in a dream.
And "Why did you do this?" he cried out in tears,
"Is this your love and is this what you promised?
Did I not entrust my whole plan to you?
Did you not agree joyfully to accompany me?
Surely I didn't insist or compel you?
On the contrary, you insisted that you should
   accompany me,
that we should enjoy the journey together and
   then return.
But you, having no fear of God before your eyes,
have insisted that your brothers kill me.
Do you not remember what I did with you at
   the beginning?
I seized you as my prisoner, but I honoured you
   as my lady.
I had intended to keep you as a slave, but instead
   you made me the slave.
I renounced my parents and my faith for your
   sake,
and for love of you I came to Roman territory,
but you have thought of death in return for this,
   girl.
See, my beauty, that you do not break the oaths
   between us,
do not renounce the love which was ours through
   passion.
If your brothers use force and overpower me,
without fail I shall draw my sword and kill
   myself,
and God will judge between the two of us.
May all scions of noble families reproach you
because you could not keep your husband's
   secret,
but delivered him to his death, as Delilah did
   with Samson."

The emir said all this sorrowfully to the girl,
for he supposed that she had revealed his plan;
for love that is dishonoured brings harsh words.
When the girl heard it she became dumb,
completely unable to utter a word;
she remained despondent for many hours.
For every wrong-doer is capable of finding excuses,
but the one who has done no wrong is silent, not
　　knowing what to say.
Scarcely coming to herself by evening,
"Why do you reproach me without reason?" she
　　cried out in tears.
"Why, my husband, do you accuse the one who
　　longs for you so much?
It is unthinkable for me—may this never hap-
　　pen—to reveal your plan.
If I did that, may the earth swallow me up alive,
so that I may become an example to all the world
of one who makes public her husband's secrets."
　　And seeing the emir increasing his lament
she went almost out of her mind with grief
(for excess of grief brings delirium,
in which state many people attempt unlawful
　　deeds),
she feared he might kill himself with his sword.
She went out to her brothers, tearing her hair:
"Sweetest brothers, why do you harass without
　　reason
a man who had done no wrong? See, he is about
　　to die;
see, he will kill himself out of madness.
My brothers, before God, do not let your guest be
　　wronged;
he has renounced kinsmen and his faith for my
　　sake,
he has never wished to act against you.
Now, out of fear of his mother's curse,
he is going off to Syria and is returning with her.
He told me of his plan, he also showed me the
　　letter.
And how did you, out of respect for our mother's
　　curse,
dare to go alone against thousands
and to join battle for my sake in the pass,
not fearing death but your mother's curse?
He fears this too, he wants to make the journey."

The girl said all this to her brothers,
shedding hot tears and tearing at her hair.
They could not bear to see their sister lamenting
and cried out together, kissing her,
"We all think of you as our soul and delight.
Since you too want to send our brother-in-law
　　off,
may he take God as his witness that he will
　　return quickly,
and let us wish him all success on his journey."
　　And they all went in immediately to their
　　brother-in-law
and asked pardon for what had been said earlier.
"And do not, brother-in-law, hold against us
　　words spoken in ignorance,
for we were not the cause but the fault is surely
　　yours,
as you did not inform us of what you planned
　　to do."
　　And he forgave them and embraced them all.
Facing towards the east and raising his hands
　　on high,
"Christ," he declared, "Son of God and Word,
who has guided me to the light of your knowl-
　　edge of God,
who has freed me from darkness and futile error,
who knows the secrets and reckonings of my
　　heart,
if ever I forget my dearest spouse
or our delightful offspring, our beloved child,
and do not return swiftly from my mother,
may I become food for wild beasts and birds
　　on the mountain,
and be no longer reckoned on the side of the
　　Christians."
　　And from that moment he began to prepare for
　　the journey
and made everything ready within fifteen days;
his departure became known to everyone,
and the whole host of kinsmen and friends gath-
　　ered together.
And then the love between the two could be seen,
for the emir took the girl by the hand
and went alone with her inside the chamber,
and heartfelt tears fell like showers;
their sighs re-echoed each other's.

"Give me your word, my lady, give me your ring;
let me wear it, my noble wife, until I return."
The girl sighed and said to the emir,
"Take care, my golden lord, that you do not break
    your oaths,
and God will repay you, if you embrace another
    woman;
for God is a just judge who settles accounts
    appropriately."
 "If I do that, my dearest," the emir replied,
"or nullify the love which is ours through passion
or grieve your heart, my most high-born wife,
the earth will gape and receive me, may Hades
    swallow me up,
and may I not have rejoiced in you, my sweet-
    perfumed darling."
    Embracing closely, they kissed insatiably,
so that the moment was drawn out;
they became soaked with their many tears
and were scarcely able to part from each other,
and had no modesty before the host of those
    gathered there.
For physical love brings shamelessness,
and all who have learned of love know this.
Then, taking his child in his arms
and lamenting, he said this in the hearing of all,
"Surely God will make me worthy of seeing you,
my sweetest child, on horseback in my presence?

Surely, my son of double descent, I shall teach
    you to use the spear,
so that all your kinsmen may boast of you?"
And all wept as they saw the emir.
    Then, each mounting a swift and altogether
        noble horse,
the youngsters left the house
and after them the emir, riding his charger.
The host of kinsmen and friends was large
and they accompanied him for three miles.
And embracing them all, he made them return,
while he himself set off on the journey, together
    with his youngsters.

REVIEW QUESTIONS

1. What ideas about the social functions of honor
   emerge from this poem?
2. What does it mean in this time and place to be
   a renegade?
3. Conflicting loyalties to creed and the family
   seem important in this epic. What does it teach
   us about the values of love and shame?
4. In fact, the emir's mother herself converts and
   becomes a renegade too. Does this change your
   opinion of her letter?

MUHAMMAD

FROM The Qur'an

*The prophet Muhammad (c. 570–632) brought the message of Islam first to the
Arab peoples of his home city, Mecca. Muslims, those who submitted to the will of
the one God, Allah, believe that the revelations committed to Muhammad and the
prophet's teachings were collected shortly after his death and compose the Qur'an.
Following are two suras (chapters) from the Qur'an, an excerpt from number 2, the
Cow, and number 47, Muhammad; they are typical of the style and content of the
Qur'an.*

From *Al-Quran: A Contemporary Translation*, by Ahmed Ali (Princeton, N.J.: Princeton University Press, 2001), pp. 31–39.

Cow

O men, eat only the things of the earth
that are lawful and good.
Do not walk in the footsteps of Satan,
your acknowledged enemy.
He will ask you to indulge in evil, indecency,
and to speak lies of God you cannot even
    conceive.
When it is said to them:
"Follow what God has revealed,"
they reply: "No, we shall follow only what
our fathers had practiced,"—
even though their fathers had no wisdom
    or guidance!
The semblance of the infidels
is that of a man
who shouts to one that cannot hear
more than a call and a cry.
They are deaf, dumb and blind,
and they fail to understand.
O believers, eat what is good of the food
We have given you, and be grateful to God,
if indeed you are obedient to Him.
Forbidden to you are carrion and blood,
and the flesh of the swine,
and that which has been
consecrated (or killed)
in the name of any other than God.
If one is obliged by necessity
to eat it without intending to transgress,
or reverting to it, he is not guilty of sin;
for God is forgiving and kind.
Those who conceal any part of the Scriptures
that God has revealed, and thus make
a little profit thereby,
take nothing but fire as food;
and God will not turn to them on the Day
    of Resurrection,
nor nourish them for growth;
and their doom will be painful.
They are those who bartered away
good guidance for error, and pardon for
    punishment:
How great is their striving for the Fire!
That is because God has revealed
the Book containing the truth;

but those who are at variance about it
have gone astray in their contrariness.

Piety does not lie in turning your face
to East or West:
Piety lies in believing in God,
the Last Day and the angels,
the Scriptures and the prophets,
and disbursing your wealth out of love for God
among your kin and the orphans,
the wayfarers and mendicants,
freeing the slaves, observing your devotional
    obligations,
and in paying the zakat and fulfilling a pledge
    you have given,
and being patient in hardship, adversity,
and times of peril.
These are the men who affirm the truth,
and they are those who follow the straight path.
O believers, ordained for you is retribution
for the murdered,
(whether) a free man (is guilty)
of (the murder of) a free man, or a slave of
    a slave,
or a woman of a woman.
But he who is pardoned some of it by his brother
should be dealt with equity,
and recompense (for blood) paid with a grace.
This is a concession from your Lord and
    a kindness.
He who transgresses in spite of it
shall suffer painful punishment.
In retribution there is life (and preservation).
O men of sense, you may haply take heed for
    yourselves.
It is ordained that when any one of you
nears death, and he owns goods and chattels,
he should bequeath them equitably
to his parents and next of kin.
This is binding on those who are upright and
    fear God.
And any one who changes the will, having heard
    it,
shall be guilty and accountable;
for God hears all and knows every thing.
He who suspects wrong or partiality
on the part of the testator

and brings about a settlement,
does not incur any guilt,
for God is verily forgiving and merciful.

O believers, fasting is enjoined on you
as it was on those before you,
so that you might become righteous.
Fast a (fixed) number of days,
but if someone is ill or is travelling
(he should complete) the number of days (he
    had missed);
and those who find it hard to fast
should expiate by feeding a poor person.
For the good they do with a little harship is
    better for men.
And if you fast it is good for you,
if you knew.
Ramadan is the month in which the Qur'an
    was revealed
as guidance to man and clear proof of the
    guidance,
and criterion (of falsehood and truth).
So when you see the new moon you should fast
    the whole month;
but a person who is ill or travelling
(and fails to do so) should fast on other days,
as God wishes ease and not hardship for you,
so that you complete the (fixed) number (of
    fasts),
and give glory to God
for the guidance, and be grateful.
When My devotees enquire of you about Me,
I am near, and answer the call
of every supplicant when he calls.
It behoves them to hearken to Me
and believe in Me
that they may follow the right path.
You are allowed to sleep with your wives
on the nights of the fast:
They are your dress as you are theirs.
God is aware you were cheating yourselves,
so He turned to you and pardoned you.
So now you may have intercourse with them,
and seek what God has ordained for you.
Eat and drink until the white thread
of dawn appears clear from the dark line,
then fast until the night falls;

and abstain from your wives (when you have
    decided)
to stay in the mosques for assiduous devotion.
These are the bounds fixed by God,
so keep well within them.
So does God make His signs clear to men
that they may take heed for themselves.
And do not consume each other's wealth in vain,
nor offer it to men in authority with intent
of usurping unlawfully and knowingly
a part of the wealth of others.

They ask you of the new moons.
Say: "These are periods set for men (to reckon)
    time,
and for pilgrimage."
Piety does not lie in entering the house through
    the back door,[1]
for the pious man is he who follows the straight
    path.
Enter the house through the main gate,[2]
and obey God. You may haply find success.
Fight those in the way of God who fight you,
but do not be aggressive:
God does not like aggressors.
And fight those (who fight you) wheresoever you
    find them,
and expel them from the place
they had turned you out from.
Oppression is worse than killing.
Do not fight them by the Holy Mosque
unless they fight you there.
If they do, then slay them:
Such is the requital for unbelievers.
But if they desist, God is forgiving and kind.
Fight them till sedition comes to end,
and the law of God (prevails).
If they desist, then cease to be hostile,
except against those who oppress.
(Fighting during) the holy month

---

[1] It means the same thing as is meant by the English expression 'through the back door,' i.e., clandestinely.
Here it has more than one implication, as the verse
deals with the new moon and reckoning "periods," e.g.,
the period of fasting, a woman's monthly courses, etc.

[2] That is, seek attainment through the right way.

(if the sanctity) of the holy month (is violated)
is (just) retribution.
So if you are oppressed,
oppress those who oppress you to the same
    degree,
and fear God, and know that God
is with those who are pious
and follow the right path.
Spend in the way of God,
and do not seek destruction at your own hands.
So do good;
for God loves those who do good.
Perform the pilgrimage and holy visit ('Umra,
    to Mecca)
in the service of God.
But if you are prevented, send an offering
which you can afford as sacrifice,
and do not shave your heads until
the offering has reached the place of sacrifice.
But if you are sick or have ailment of the scalp
(preventing the shaving of hair),
then offer expiation by fasting
or else giving alms or a sacrificial offering.
When you have security, then those of you who
    wish
to perform the holy visit along with the pilgrim
    age,
should make a sacrifice according to their means.
But he who has nothing,
should fast for three days during the pilgrimage
and seven on return, completing ten.
This applies to him whose family does not live
near the Holy Mosque.
Have fear of God, and remember that God
is severe in punishment.

Known are the months of pilgrimage.
If one resolves to perform the pilgrimage in
    these months,
let him not indulge in concupiscence, sin or
    quarrel.
And the good you do shall be known to God.
Provide for the journey,
and the best of provisions is piety.
O men of understanding, obey Me.
It is no sin to seek the favours of your Lord
    (by trading).

When you start from 'Arafat in a concourse,
remember God at the monument that is sacred
(al-Mash'ar al-haram),
and remember Him as He has shown you the way,
for in the olden days you were a people astray.
Then move with the crowd impetuously,
and pray God to forgive you your sins.
God is surely forgiving and kind.
When you have finished the rites and ceremonies,
remember God as you do your fathers,
in fact with a greater devotion.
There are some who say:
"Give us, O Lord, in the world;"
but they will forego their share in the life
    to come.
But some there are who pray:
"Give us of good in the world, O Lord,
and give us of good in the life to come,
and suffer us not to suffer the torment of Hell."
They are those who will surely have their share
of whatsoever they have earned;
for God is swift at the reckoning.
Remember God during the stated days,
but if a person comes away after two days,
it will not be a sin; and if one tarries,
he will not transgress, if he keep away from evil.
Follow the law of God, and remember
that you will have to gather before Him in
    the end.
There is a man who talks well
of the world to your pleasing,
and makes God witness to what is in his heart,
yet he is the most contentious;
For when his back is turned
he goes about spreading disorder in the land,
destroying fields and flocks;
but God does not love disorder.
Whenever he is told: "Obey God,"
his arrogance leads him to more sin;
and sufficient for him shall be Hell:
How evil a place of wide expanse!
And there is a man who is willing to sell
even his soul to win the favour of God;
and God is compassionate to His creatures.
O believers, come to full submission to God.
Do not follow in the footsteps of Satan
your acknowledged foe.

If you falter even after Our signs
have reached you, then do not forget
that God is all-powerful and all-wise.
Are they waiting for God to appear
in the balconies of clouds
with a host of angels,
and the matter to be settled?
But all things rest
with God in the end.

Ask the children of Israel
how many a clear sign We had given them.
But if one changes the favour of God
after having received it, then remember,
God is severe in revenge.
Enamoured are the unbelievers
of the life of this world,
and scoff at the faithful.
But those who keep from evil and follow the
    straight path
will have a higher place than they
on the Day of Reckoning;
for God gives in measure without number
whomsoever He will.
Men belonged to a single community,
and God sent them messengers
to give them happy tidings and warnings,
and sent the Book with them containing the truth
to judge between them in matters of dispute;
but only those who received it differed
after receiving clear proofs,
on account of waywardness
(and jealousies) among them.
Then God by His dispensation showed those
    who believed
the way to the truth about which they were
    differing;
for God shows whom He please
the path that is straight.
Do you think you will find your way to Paradise
even though you have not known
what the others before you have gone through?
They had suffered affliction and loss,
and were shaken and tossed about
so that even the Apostle
had to cry out with his followers:
"When will the help of God arrive?"

Remember, the help of God is ever at hand.
They ask you of what they should give in charity.
Tell them: "What you can spare of your wealth
as should benefit the parents, the relatives,
the orphans, the needy, the wayfarers,
for God is not unaware of the good deeds that
    you do."
Enjoined on you is fighting,
and this you abhor.
You may dislike a thing
yet it may be good for you;
or a thing may haply please you
but may be bad for you.
Only God has knowledge, and you do not know.

They ask you of war in the holy month.
Tell them: "To fight in that month is a great sin.
But a greater sin in the eyes of God
is to hinder people from the way of God,
and not to believe in Him,
and to bar access to the Holy Mosque
and turn people out of its precincts;
and oppression is worse than killing.
They will always seek war against you
till they turn you away from your faith, if
    they can.
But those of you who turn back on their faith
and die disbelieving
will have wasted their deeds
in this world and the next.
They are inmates of Hell,
and shall there abide for ever.
Surely those who believe,
and those who leave their homes
and fight in the way of God,
may hope for His benevolence,
for God is forgiving and kind.
They ask you of (intoxicants,) wine and gambling.
Tell them: "There is great enervation though
    profit in them[3]
for men; but their enervation is greater than
    benefit.
And they ask you what they should give.

---

[3] The basic meaning of *ithm* is drunkenness or enervation (*Taj* and Ibn Faris) of which the wine of Paradise
is free.

Tell them: "The utmost you can spare."
So does God reveal His signs: You may haply reflect
On this world and the next.
And they ask you about the orphans.
Tell them: "Improving their lot is much better;
    and if
you take interest in their affairs, they are your
    brethren;
and God is aware who are corrupt and who
    are honest;
and if He had pleased
He could surely have imposed on you hardship,
for God is all-powerful and all-wise.
Do not marry idolatrous women
unless they join the faith.
A maid servant who is a believer
is better than an idolatress
even though you may like her.
And do not marry your daughters to idolaters
until they accept the faith.
A servant who is a believer is better than
    an idolater
even though you may like him.
They invite you to Hell, but God
calls you to Paradise and pardon by His grace.
And He makes His signs manifest that men
may haply take heed.

*   *   *

Muhammad

In the name of Allah, most benevolent, ever-
    merciful.

THOSE WHO DISBELIEVE
and obstruct (others) from the way of God
will have wasted their deeds.
But those who believe and do the right,
and believe what has been revealed to
    Muhammad,
which is the truth from their Lord,
will have their faults condoned by Him
and their state improved.
That is because those who refuse to believe
only follow what is false; but those who believe
follow the truth from their Lord.

That is how God gives men precepts of wisdom.
So, when you clash with the unbelievers,
smite their necks until you overpower them,
then hold them in bondage.
Then either free them graciously
or after taking a ransom,
until war shall have come to end.
If God had pleased
He could have punished them (Himself),
but He wills to test some of you through some
    others.
He will not allow the deeds
of those who are killed in the cause of God
to go waste.
He will show them the way,
and better their state,
And will admit them into gardens
with which he has acquainted them.
O you who believe, if you help (in the cause of)
    God
He will surely come to your aid,
and firmly plant your feet.
As for the unbelievers, they will suffer misfortunes,
and their deeds will be rendered ineffective.
That is so as they were averse
to what has been revealed by God,
and their actions will be nullified.
Have they not journeyed in the land
and seen the fate of those before them?
Destroyed they were utterly by God;
and a similar (fate) awaits the unbelievers.
This is so for God is the friend of those who
    believe
while the unbelievers have no friend.

Verily God will admit those who believe and do
    the right
into gardens with streams of water running by.
But the unbelievers revel and carouse
and subsist like beasts, and Hell will be their
    residence.
How many were the habitations,
mightier than your city which has turned you out,
which We destroyed;
and they did not have a helper.
Can one who stands on a clear proof from his
    Lord,

be like one enamoured of his evil deeds
and follows his inane desires?
The semblance of Paradise promised the pious
    and devout
(is that of a garden) with streams of water that
    will not go rank,
and rivers of milk whose taste will not undergo a
    change,
and rivers of wine delectable to drinkers,
and streams of purified honey,
and fruits of every kind in them, and forgiveness
    of their Lord.
Are these like those who will live for ever in the
    Fire
and be given boiling water to drink
which will cut their intestines to shreds?
There are some who listen to you; but as soon
    as they go
from you they say to those who were given
    knowledge:
"What is this he is saying now?"
They are those whose hearts
have been sealed by God, and they follow their
    own lusts.
But those who are rightly guided will be given
greater guidance by Him, and they will have
    their intrinsic piety.
Do they wait for any thing but the Hour (of
    change),
that it may come upon them suddenly?
Its signs have already appeared.
How then will they be warned when it has come
    upon them?
Know then, therefore, there is no god but He,
and ask forgiveness for your sins
and those of believing men and women.
God knows your wanderings
and your destination.

Those who believe say: "How is it no Surah was
    revealed?"
But when a categorical Surah is revealed
that mentions war, you should see those
who are sceptical
staring at you like a man in the swoon of death.
Alas the woe for them!

Obedience and modest speech (would have been
    more becoming).
And when the matter has been determined
it is best for them to be true to God.
Is it possible that if placed in authority
you will create disorder in the land
and sever your bonds of relationship?
They are those who were condemned by God,
whose ears were blocked by Him and their eyes
    blinded.
Do they not ponder
on what the Qur'an says?
Or have their hearts been sealed with locks?
Those who turn their backs
after the way of guidance has been opened
    to them,
have been surely tempted by Satan
and beguiled by illusory hopes.
This was so because they said to those
who disdain what God has revealed:
"We shall obey you in some things."
But God knows their secret intentions well.
How will it be when the angels draw out their
    souls
striking their faces and their backs?
Because they followed what displeases God,
and they were averse to pleasing Him.
So We nullified their deeds.

Do they whose minds are filled with doubt, think
that God will not expose their malice?
Had We pleased We could have shown them
    to you
that you could know them by their marks,
and recognise them from the way
they twist their words.
Yet God knows all your deeds.
We shall try you in order to know
who are the fighters among you,
and who are men of fortitude,
and verify your histories.
Surely those who do not believe, and obstruct
    others
from the path of God, and oppose the Prophet
after the way of guidance has been opened
    to them,

will not hurt God in the least,
and He will nullify all that they have done.
O you who believe, obey God and the Prophet,
and do not waste your deeds.
Those who do not believe and obstruct others
from the way of God, and die disbelieving,
will not be pardoned by God.
So do not become weak-kneed and sue for
    peace,
for you will have the upper hand
as God is with you and will not overlook your deeds.
Verily the life of this world
is no more than a sport and frivolity.
If you believe and fear God,
He will give you your reward,
and will not ask for your possessions.
If He asks for all you possess and insist upon it,
you will become niggardly,
and it will bring out your malevolence.
Beware! You are called to spend in the way of
    God,

yet some among you close their fists.
But he who is niggardly is so for his own self:
God is above need, and it is you who are needy.
If you turn away then God
will bring other people in your place
who, moreover, will not be like you.

*   *   *

REVIEW QUESTIONS

1. What aspects of Muslim belief are the most important in these suras?
2. What seems to be the relationship between Islam and the peoples of the Book, Christians and Jews?
3. What are the rewards and obligations of the faithful?
4. What ideas about violence and disorder appear in these suras?

AL-ṬABARĪ

FROM *The History*

al-Ṭabarī (?838–923) was one of the most-respected scholars in early Islam. This prolific author, who worked and taught in Baghdad, wrote on Islamic law and religion as well as producing his monumental history, an immense work covering the subject from its beginnings to his own times. al-Ṭabarī's history carefully noted the sources he used. This excerpt describes the conquest of Jerusalem by the Caliph ʿUmar in 637.

From *The History of al-Ṭabarī*, vol. 12, translated by Yohanan Friedmann (New York: State University of New York Press, 1992), pp. 189–99.

* * *

The Conquest of Jerusalem

According to Sālim b. ʿAbdallāh: When ʿUmar reached al-Jābiyah, a Jew said to him: "O Commander of the Faithful, you will not return to your country before God has granted you victory over Jerusalem." While in al-Jābiyah ʿUmar b. al-Khaṭṭāb saw an approaching detachment of horsemen. When they came close, they drew their swords, but ʿUmar said: "These are people who are coming to seek an assurance of safety. Grant it to them." They drew near and it became clear that they were people from Jerusalem. They made peace with ʿUmar on the condition that they would pay the poll tax and opened up Jerusalem for him. When ʿUmar was granted victory over Jerusalem, he summoned that same Jew, and it was said to him: "He is, indeed, in possession of knowledge." ʿUmar asked the Jew about the false Messiah, for he was wont to ask about him a great deal. The Jew said to him: "What are you asking about him, O Commander of the Faithful? You, the Arabs, will kill him ten odd cubits in front of the gate of Lydda."

According to Sālim: When ʿUmar entered Syria, a Jew from Damascus met him and said: "Peace be upon you, O Fārūq! You are the master of Jerusalem. By God, you will not return before God conquers Jerusalem!"

[The people of Jerusalem] caused distress to ʿAmr and he caused distress to them, but he could not conquer Jerusalem, nor could he conquer al-Ramlah.

While ʿUmar was camping in al-Jābiyah, the Muslims seized their weapons in alarm. ʿUmar asked: "What is it?", and they replied: "Do you not see the horsemen and the swords?" ʿUmar looked and saw a detachment of horsemen brandishing their swords. He said: "They are seeking an assurance of safety. Do not be afraid, but grant it to them." They granted them an assurance of safety and [it became clear that] these were people from Jerusalem. They gave to ʿUmar . . . and asked him to give them in writing [the peace terms] for Jerusalem and its region and for al-Ramlah and its region. Palestine was divided into two parts: one part was with the people of Jerusalem, and the other with the people of al-Ramlah. The people of Palestine were [organized in] ten provinces, and Palestine was equal to Syria in its entirety.

The Jew witnessed the conclusion of the peace treaty. ʿUmar asked him about the false Messiah. The Jew said: "He is from the sons of Benjamin. By God, you Arabs will kill him ten odd cubits from the gate of Lydda."

According to Khālid and ʿUbādah: The peace treaty concerning Palestine was concluded by the populace of Jerusalem and al-Ramlah. The reason for this was that Arṭabūn and al-Tadhāriq had left for Egypt when ʿUmar came to al-Jābiyah; they were subsequently killed in one of the summer expeditions.

It was said that the reason for ʿUmar's coming to Syria was the following: Abū ʿUbaydah besieged Jerusalem. Its people asked him to conclude peace with them on the conditions of the Syrian cities and asked that ʿUmar b. al-Khaṭṭāb be responsible for the treaty. Abū ʿUbaydah wrote to ʿUmar about it, and ʿUmar made the journey from Medina.

According to ʿAdī b. Sahl: When the Muslims of Syria asked ʿUmar to help them against the people of Palestine, he appointed ʿAlī as his deputy and set out to reinforce them. ʿAlī said: "Where are going by yourself? You are heading toward a rabid enemy." ʿUmar said: "I hasten to fight the enemy before the death of al-ʿAbbās. If you lose al-ʿAbbās, evil will untwist you like the ends of a rope." ʿAmr and Shuraḥbīl joined ʿUmar in al-Jābiyah when the peace [with the people of Palestine] was concluded. They witnessed the writing [of the treaty].

According to Khālid and ʿUbādah: ʿUmar made peace with the people of Jerusalem in al-Jābiyah. He wrote for them the peace conditions. He wrote one letter to all the provinces (of Palestine) except to the people of Jerusalem:

DOME OF THE ROCK, JERUSALEM (C. 690 C.E.)

Built in the 690s and restored in the sixteenth century, the dome sits over the traditional site where Abraham nearly sacrificed Isaac and where the prophet Muhammad on his horse began his ascent to Paradise. The building is on the Temple Mount, the traditional location of Solomon's Temple, and is near the Church of the Holy Sepulchre. What is distinctive about Muslim art? What does the building imply about the connections between Islam and Jerusalem?

In the name of God, the Merciful, the Compassionate. This is the assurance of safety (*amān*) which the servant of God, ᶜUmar, the Commander of the Faithful, has granted to the people of Jerusalem. He has given them an assurance of safety for themselves, for their property, their churches, their crosses, the sick and the healthy of the city, and for all the rituals that belong to their religion. Their churches will not be inhabited [by Muslims] and will not be destroyed. Neither they, nor the land on which they stand, nor their cross, nor their property will be damaged. They will not be forcibly converted. No Jew will live with them in Jerusalem. The people of Jerusalem must pay the poll tax like the people of the [other] cities, and they must expel the Byzantines and the robbers. As for those who will leave the city, their lives and property will be safe until they reach their place of safety; and as for those who remain, they will be safe. They will have to pay the poll tax like the people of Jerusalem. Those of the people of Jerusalem who want to leave with the Byzantines, take their property, and abandon their churches and their crosses will be safe until they reach their place of safety. Those villagers (*ahl al-arḍ*) who were in Jerusalem before the killing of so-and-so may remain in the city if they wish, but they must pay the poll tax like the people of Jerusalem. Those who wish may go with the Byzantines, and and those who wish may return to their families. Nothing will be taken from them before their harvest is reaped. If they pay the poll tax according to their obligations, then the contents of this letter are under the covenant of God, are the responsibility of His Prophet, of the caliphs, and of the faithful. The persons who attest to it are Khālid b. al-Walīd, ᶜAmr b. al-ᶜĀṣī, ᶜĀbd al-Raḥmān b. ᶜAwf, and Muᶜāwiyah b. Abī Sufyān. This letter was written and prepared in the year 15/636–37.

The rest of the letters were identical to the letter of Lydda [which follows]:

In the name of God, the Merciful, the Compassionate. This is what the servant of God, ᶜUmar, the Commander of the Faithful, awarded to the people of Lydda and to all the people of Palestine who are in the same category. He gave them an assurance of safety for themselves, for their property, their churches, their crosses, their sick and their healthy, and all their rites. Their churches will not be inhabited [by the Muslims] and will not be destroyed. Neither their churches, nor the land where they stand, nor their rituals, nor their crosses, nor their property will be damaged. They will not be forcibly converted, and none of them will be harmed. The people of Lydda and those of the people of Palestine who are in the same category must pay the poll tax like the people of the Syrian cities. The same conditions, in their entirety, apply to them if they leave (Lydda).

He then sent to them [an army] and divided Palestine between two men; he put ᶜAlqamah b. Ḥakīm in charge of one half and stationed him in al-Ramlah, and he put ᶜAlqamah b. Mujazziz in charge of the other half and stationed him in Jerusalem. Each of them stayed in his province with the soldiers who were with him.

According to Sālim: [ᶜUmar] appointed ᶜAlqamah b. Mujazziz governor of Jerusalem and appointed ᶜAlqamah b. al-Ḥakīm governor of al-Ramlah. He placed the soldiers who were with ᶜAmr (b. al-ᶜĀṣī) at their disposal. He ordered ᶜAmr and Shuraḥbīl to join him in al-Jābiyah. When they reached al-Jābiyah, they found ᶜUmar riding. They kissed his knee, and ᶜUmar embraced them, holding them to his chest.

According to ᶜUbādah and Khālid: Having sent the assurance of safety to the people of Jerusalem and having stationed the army there, ᶜUmar set out from al-Jābiyah to Jerusalem. He saw that his horse had injuries on its hooves. So he dismounted, and a jade was brought to him and he rode it. The jade shook him, however, so ᶜUmar dismounted, hit the jade's face with his mantle, and said: "May God make ugly him who taught you this!" Then he called for his horse to be brought to him, after he had left him unridden for a few days, and treated his hooves. He mounted his horse and rode until he reached Jerusalem.

According to Abū Ṣafiyyah, an elder from Banū Shaybān: When ʿUmar came to Syria, he was brought a jade and rode it. The jade moved in an unstable manner, inclining from side to side. ʿUmar dismounted, hit the jade's face, and said: "May God not teach him who taught you this sort of pride!" He had not ridden a jade before that or after that.

Jerusalem and its entire region were conquered by ʿUmar, except for Ajnādayn, which was conquered by ʿĀmr (b. al-ʿĀṣi), and Caesarea, which was conquered by Muʿawiyah (b. Abī Sufyan).

According to Abū ʿUthmān and Abū Ḥārithah: Jerusalem and its region were conquered in the month of Rabīʿ al-Ākhir of the year 16/May 637.

According to Abū Maryam, the client of Salāmah, who said: I witnessed the conquest of Jerusalem with ʿUmar: He set out from al-Jābiyah, leaving it behind until he came to Jerusalem. He then went on and entered the mosque. Then he went on toward the *miḥrāb* of David, while we were with him; he entered it, recited the prostration of David, and prostrated himself, and we prostrated ourselves with him.

According to Rajāʾ b. Ḥaywah——persons who were present at the event: When ʿUmar came from al-Jābiyah to Jerusalem and drew near the gate of the mosque, he said: "Watch out for Kaʿb on my behalf!" When the gate was opened for him, he said: "O God, I am ready to serve you in what you love most." Then he turned to the *miḥrāb*, the *miḥrāb* of David, peace be upon him. It was at night, and he prayed there. It was not long before dawn broke, and then ʿUmar ordered the *muʾadhdhin* to sound the call for prayer. Then he moved forward, led the prayer, and recited Sūrat Ṣād with the people. During the prayer he prostrated himself. Then he stood up and read with them in the second (*rakʿah*) the beginnning of Sūrat Banī Isrāʾīl. Then he prayed another *rakʿah* and went away. He said: "Bring Kaʿb to me." Kaʿb was brought to him. ʿUmar said: "Where do you think we should establish the place of prayer?" Kaʿb said: "Toward the Rock." ʿUmar said: "O Kaʿb, you

are imitating the Jewish religion! I have seen you taking off your shoes." Kaʿb said: "I wanted to touch this ground with my feet." ʿUmar said: "I have seen you. Nay, we shall place the *qiblah* in the front of it; the Messenger of God likewise made the front part of our mosques the *qiblah*. Take care of your own affairs; we were not commanded to venerate the Rock, but we were commanded to venerate the Kaʿbah."

ʿUmar made the front part of the mosque its *qiblah*. Then he stood up from his place of prayer and went to the rubbish in which the Romans buried the temple (*bayt al-maqdis*) at the time of the sons of Israel. (When he came to the Byzantines, they had uncovered a part but left the rest [under the rubbish].) He said: "O people, do what I am doing." He knelt in the midst of the rubbish and put it by the handful into the lower part of his mantle. He heard behind him the proclama-tion "God is most great!" He disliked improper behavior in any matter and said: "What is this?" The people said: "Kaʿb proclaimed 'God is most great!' and the people proclaimed it following him." ʿUmar said: "Bring him to me!" Kaʿb said: "O Commander of the Faithful, five hundred years ago a prophet predicted what you have done today." ʿUmar asked: "In what way?" Kaʿb said:

The Byzantines (*Rūm*) attacked the sons of Israel, were given victory over them, and buried the temple. Then they were given another victory, but they did not attend to the temple until the Persians attacked them. The Persians oppressed the sons of Israel. Later the Byzantines were given victory over the Persians. Then you came to rule. God sent a prophet to the [city buried in] rubbish and said: "Rejoice O Jerusalem (*Ūrī shalam*)! Al-Fārūq will come to you and cleanse you." Another prophet was sent to Constantinople. He stood on a hill belonging to the city and said: "O Constantinople, what did your people do to My House? They ruined it, presented you as if you were similar to My throne and made interpretations contrary to My purpose. I have determined to make you one day unfortified (and defenseless). Nobody will seek shelter from you, nor rest in your shade. [I shall make you unfortified] at the hands of Banū al-Qādhir, Sabā, and Waddān."

By the time it was evening nothing remained of the rubbish.

An identical tradition was transmitted according to Rabīʿah al-Shāmī. He added: "Al-Fārūq came to you with my obedient army. They will take revenge upon the Byzantines on behalf of your people." Regarding Constantinople he said: "I shall leave you unfortified and exposed to the sun; nobody will seek shelter from you, and you will not cast your shade on anyone."

According to Anas b. Mālik:

I was present in Jerusalem with ʿUmar. While he was giving food to the people one day, a monk from Jerusalem came to him without knowing that wine had been prohibited. The monk said: "Do you want a drink which will be permissible according to our books [even] when wine is prohibited?"

ʿUmar asked him to bring it and said: "From what has it been prepared?" The monk informed him that he had cooked it from juice until only one-third of it remained. ʿUmar dipped his finger into it, then stirred it in the vessel, divided it into two halves, and said: "This is syrup (ṭilāʾ)." He likened it to resin (qaṭirān), drank from it, and ordered the amīrs of the Syrian provinces to prepare it. He wrote to the newly established garrison towns (amṣār), saying: "I have been brought a beverage cooked from juice until two-thirds of it were gone and one-third remained. It is like syrup. Cook it and provide it to the Muslims."

According to Abū ʿUthmān and Abū Ḥārithah: Arṭabūn went to Egypt when ʿUmar came to al-Jābiyah. Those who rejected the peace agreement and wanted [to go with him] joined him. Then, when the people of Egypt made a peace agreement [with the Muslims] and defeated the Byzantines, he took to the sea and survived afterward. He com-

manded the summer expeditions of the Byzantines and confronted the commander of the Muslim summer expeditions. Arṭabūn and a man from the tribe of Qays, whose name was Durays, exchanged blows, and Arṭabūn cut the Qaysī's hand. The Qaysī killed him and recited:

> Though Arṭabūn of the Byzantines maimed my hand,
> there is still some use to it, praise be to God.
> Two fingers and a stump, with which I hold straight
> the front part of the spear when people are struck with fear.
> Though Arṭabūn of the Byzantines cut my hand,
> I left his limbs cut to pieces, in return.

Ziyād b. Ḥanẓalah recited:

> I remembered the long wars against the Byzantines,
> when we spent a year full of journeys.
> When we were in the land of Ḥijāz and
> a month's journey separated us, with anxieties in between;
> When Arṭabūn of the Byzantines defended his country,
> a noble chieftain tackled him here and struggled with him;
> When al-Fārūq saw that the time [was right] for the conquest of Arṭabūn's land,
> he brought forward God's soldiers to attack him.
> When they became aware of al-Fārūq and feared his assault,
> they came to him and said: "You are of those whom we shall befriend."
> Syria threw its buried treasures at his feet,
> as well as a life of abundance with countless gains.
> He put whatever was between east and west at our disposal,
> as inheritance for posterity, gathered by his two-humped camels.

Many a beast of burden that had been unable
   to carry its load,
[now] carried a burden while being well into
   pregnancy.

*   *   *

REVIEW QUESTIONS

1. How do you explain ʿUmar's easy success in conquering Syria and Palestine?
2. What role does Jerusalem play for Muslims, Christians, and Jews in the region?
3. What are al-Ṭabarī's strengths and weaknesses as a historian?

BEDE

FROM *A History of the English Church and People*

The Venerable Bede (died 735), to use his common name, was an Anglo-Saxon monk who wrote on many religious, scientific, and historical subjects. He was especially interested in problems of chronology and time, in an age when an accurate calendar was a considerable accomplishment. In this selection from his most famous book, A History of the English Church and People, *Bede describes the conversion of Edwin of Northumbria.*

From *Bede: A History of the English Church and People,* edited by Leo Sherley-Price (New York: Penguin Books, 1968), pp. 126–29.

*   *   *

Chapter 13

When he heard this, the king answered that it was his will as well as his duty to accept the Faith that Paulinus taught, but said that he must still discuss the matter with his principal advisers and friends, so that, if they were in agreement with him, they might all be cleansed together in Christ the Fount of Life. Paulinus agreed, and the king kept his promise. He summoned a council of the wise men, and asked each in turn his opinion of this strange doctrine and this new way of worshipping the godhead that was being proclaimed to them.

Coifi, the Chief Priest, replied without hesitation: "Your Majesty, let us give careful considera-tion to this new teaching; for I frankly admit that, in my experience, the religion that we have hitherto professed seems valueless and powerless. None of your subjects has been more devoted to the service of our gods than myself; yet there are many to whom you show greater favour, who receive greater honours, and who are more successful in all their undertakings. Now, if the gods had any power, they would surely have favoured myself, who have been more zealous in their service. Therefore, if on examination you perceive that these new teachings are better and more effectual, let us not hesitate to accept them."

Another of the king's chief men signified his agreement with this prudent argument, and went on to say: "Your Majesty, when we compare the present life of man on earth with that time of which we have no knowledge, it seems to me like the swift flight of a single sparrow through the banqueting-hall where you are sitting at dinner on a winter's day with your thanes and counsellors. In the midst there is a comforting fire to warm the hall; outside, the storms of winter rain or snow are raging. This sparrow flies swiftly in through one door of the hall, and out through another. While he is inside, he is safe from the winter storms; but after a few moments of comfort, he vanishes from sight into the wintry world from which he came. Even so, man appears on earth for a little while; but of what went before this life or of what follows, we know nothing. Therefore, if this new teaching has brought any more certain knowledge, it seems only right that we should follow it." The other elders and counsellors of the king, under God's guidance, gave similar advice.

Coifi then added that he wished to hear Paulinus' teaching about God in greater detail; and when, at the king's bidding, this had been given, he exclaimed: "I have long realized that there is nothing in our way of worship; for the more diligently I sought after truth in our religion, the less I found. I now publicly confess that this teaching clearly reveals truths that will afford us the blessings of life, salvation, and eternal happiness. Therefore, Your Majesty, I submit that the temples and altars that we have dedicated to no advantage be immediately desecrated and burned." In short, the king granted blessed Paulinus full permission to preach, renounced idolatry, and professed his acceptance of the Faith of Christ. And when he asked the Chief Priest who should be the first to profane the altars and shrines of the idols, together with the enclosures that surrounded them, Coifi replied: "I will do this myself; for now that the true God has granted me knowledge, who more suitably than I can set a public example and destroy the idols that I worshipped in ignorance?" So he formally renounced his empty superstitions and asked the king to give him arms and a stallion—for hitherto it had not been lawful for the Chief Priest to carry arms or to ride anything but a mare—and, thus equipped, he set out to destroy the idols. Girded with a sword and with a

spear in his hand, he mounted the king's stallion and rode up to the idols. When the crowd saw him, they thought he had gone mad; but without hesitation, as soon as he reached the temple, he cast into it the spear he carried and thus profaned it. Then, full of joy at his knowledge of the worship of the true God, he told his companions to set fire to the temple and its enclosures and destroy them. The site where these idols once stood is still shown, not far east of York, beyond the river Derwent, and is known today as Goodmanham. Here it was that the Chief Priest, inspired by the true God, desecrated and destroyed the altars that he had himself dedicated.

Chapter 14

So King Edwin, with all the nobility of his kingdom and a large number of humbler folk, accepted the Faith and were washed in the cleansing waters of Baptism in the eleventh year of his reign, which was the year of our Lord 627, and about one hundred and eighty years after the first arrival of the English in Britain. The king's Baptism took place at York on Easter Day, the 12th of April, in the church of Saint Peter the Apostle, which the king had hastily built of timber during the time of his instruction and preparation for Baptism; and in this city he established the see of his teacher and bishop Paulinus. Soon after his Baptism, at Paulinus' suggestion, he gave orders to build on the same site a larger and more noble basilica of stone, which was to enclose the little oratory he had built before. The foundations were laid, and the walls of a square church began to rise around this little oratory; but before they reached their appointed height, the cruel death of the king left the work to be completed by Oswald his successor. Thenceforward for six years, until the close of Edwin's reign, Paulinus preached the word in that province with the king's full consent and approval, and as many as were predestined to eternal life believed and were baptized. Among these were Osfrid and Eadfrid, sons of King Edwin, who were both born to him in exile of Coenburg, daughter of Cearl, King of the Mercians.

At a later date, other children of his by Queen Ethelberga were also baptized: these included a son, Ethelhun; a daughter, Ethelthryd; and another son, Wuscfrea. The two former were snatched from life while still wearing their white baptismal robes, and were buried in the church at York. Yffi, son of Osfrid, was also baptized, and many others of noble and princely rank. Indeed, so great was the fervour of faith and desire for baptism among the Northumbrian people that Paulinus is said to have accompanied the king and queen to the royal residence at Ad-Gefrin and remained there thirty-six days constantly occupied in instructing and baptizing. During this period, he did nothing from dawn to dusk but proclaim Christ's saving message to the people, who gathered from all the surrounding villages and countryside; and when he had instructed them, he washed them in the cleansing waters of Baptism in the nearby River Glen. This residence was abandoned by the later kings, who built another at a place called Maelmin.

These events took place in the province of Bernicia.

*   *   *

REVIEW QUESTIONS

1. Is there a core of credible pagan belief in the story of the sparrow?
2. If so, what is it?
3. How does Edwin's conversion compare to that of Clovis?

FROM The Lombard Laws: Rothair's Edict

In 568 the Lombards, another Germanic tribe, invaded Italy and overthrew the Ostrogothic kingdom, and also took some areas away from Byzantine control. The Lombards settled down to rule a complex peninsula with Roman, Gothic, and Greek laws still in place, and the papacy in Rome with its own developing sense of canon law. Rothair's Edict (643) is the earliest legal text from the Lombard kingdom in Italy. These sections of the law outline some of the most serious crimes and punishments.

From *The Lombard Laws*, edited by Katherine Fischer Drew (Philadelphia: University of Pennsylvania Press, 1973).

*   *   *

9. If in the presence of the king one man accuses another of an offense which would involve the loss of his life, then the accused may offer satisfactory oath and clear himself. If in such a case the man accused is present together with him who accused him of the offense, then the accused may refute the charge, if he can, by means of the *camfio*, that is, by judicial duel. If the accusation is proved against him, he shall lose his life or pay such an amount as composition as pleases the king. If the charge is not proved against him, and it is recognized that he has been accused wrongfully, then he who accused him and was not able to prove it shall pay the amount of his wergeld as composition, half to the king and half to him charged with the offense.

10. If any freeman plots against another man's life and that one does not die as a result, then the plotter shall pay twenty solidi as composition.

11. On plots involving death. If freemen without the king's consent plot another man's death, but that one does not die as a result of the agreement, then each of them shall pay twenty solidi as composition, as stated above. But if that one conspired against dies as a result of the plot, then the doer of the deed shall pay the victim's wergeld,[1] according as he is valued, as composition.

12. If two or three or more freemen commit a homicide together, and wish to associate themselves so that as one they may pay composition for that one the man killed according as he is valued, such an agreement is permitted to them. If one of them separates himself from the others and is not able to clear himself as the law provides, namely, he is not able to prove that he inflicted none of the blows against that man who was killed, then he is as guilty as the others who paid the composition. If he does clear himself, however, he shall be free of blame in connection with the homicide. If he is accused of being in the counsel of the conspirators, he shall pay twenty solidi as composition, as stated above, unless he can clear himself of involvement in the conspiracy.

13. He who kills his lord, shall be killed himself. The man who tries to defend this murderer who killed his lord shall pay 900 solidi as composition, half to the king and half to the relatives of the dead man. And he who refuses aid in avenging the man's death, if his aid is sought, shall pay fifty solidi as composition, half to the king and half to the man to whom he refused aid.

14. On murder. If anyone secretly kills a freeman or a man or woman slave, if one or two persons commit the homicide, he or they shall pay 900 solidi as composition. If more than two were involved, each shall pay the wergeld of the man killed, if he was a native-born freeman, according to his rank. If it was a slave or freedman who was killed, each shall pay composition according to his

value. If they plunder the dead body, that is, if they commit *plodraub*, each shall pay eighty solidi as composition for this.

15. On grave breaking. He who breaks into the grave of a dead man and despoils the body and throws it out shall pay 900 solidi to the relatives of the dead. And if there are no near relatives, then the king's gastald or schultheis shall exact this penalty and collect it for the king's court.

16. On despoiling the dead. He who finds a human corpse in a river or beside it and despoils the body and hides it shall pay eighty solidi as composition to the relatives of the dead man. If he found and stripped the body, however, and immediately after made it known to those in the vicinity that he did it for the sake of reward and not for the purpose of robbery, then he shall return those things which he had found on the body and no further guilt shall be imputed to him.

17. If one of our men wishes to come to us, let him come in safety and return to his home unharmed; let none of his enemies presume to cause any injury or harm to him on the journey. It shall be done thus in order that he who hastens to come to the king may come openly and receive no injury or damage of any sort on that journey while coming to the king and returning. He who does cause such injury shall pay compensation as is provided below in this code.

18. He who, in order to avenge some injury or damage, attacks with arms one of his enemies who is on his way to the king, shall pay 900 solidi, half to the king and half to him who bore the injury.

19. He who falls upon another with armed hand in order to vindicate some injury, or who leads an armed band containing up to four men into a village, shall die for his unlawful presumption or shall at least pay 900 solidi as composition, half to the king and half to him who was wronged. Each of those with him, if freemen, shall pay eighty solidi as composition, half to the king and half to him who was wronged. And, in addition, if they have burned houses in that village or killed any man there, then they shall pay composition, according as the damage is assessed, to him whose houses were burned or whose relative or slave was killed.

---

[1] Wergeld is the value of human life, based on rank, and paid as compensation. [Editor.]

20. If any soldier refuses to go to his duke for justice, he shall pay twenty solidi as composition to the king and to his duke.

21. Anyone who refuses to go out with the army or with the guard shall pay twenty solidi as composition to the king and to his duke.

22. Any soldier who refuses aid to his duke when that one is pursuing justice, shall pay twenty solidi as composition to the king and to the duke.

23. If a duke treats his men unjustly, the gastald shall aid the injured man. The gastald shall find out the truth and bring the case to justice in the presence of the king or at least before the duke.

24. It any gastald treats his man contrary to reason, then the duke shall aid the injured man and find out the truth.

25. If anyone attempts to obtain his property from another soldier, and that one does not return it to him, then he shall go to his duke. And if the duke or the judge appointed for that place by the king will not serve him with truth and justice, then he the duke or judge shall pay twenty solidi as composition to the king and to him who brought the case, and the case shall continue.

26. On road-blocking, that is *orbitaria*. Anyone who places himself in the road before a free woman or girl, or inflicts some injury upon her, shall pay 900 solidi as composition, half to the king and half to her who suffered the injury or to him who is her legal guardian.

27. Anyone who blocks the road to a freeman shall pay him twenty solidi as composition, provided no physical injury was caused. But he who causes injury shall pay twenty solidi as composition to him before whom the road was blocked and he shall also pay compensation for any wounds or injuries that he inflicted according to the schedule provided below.

28. Anyone who blocks the road to another's man or woman slave or to his *aldius* or freedman shall pay twenty solidi as composition to that one's lord.

29. He who in defense closes his field or meadow or other enclosure to any man by placing himself so that it cannot be entered is not guilty as is that one who blocks the road to a man simply walking along, because in this particular case he is protecting his own property.

30. On throwing someone from his horse. He who intentionally throws a freeman from his horse to the ground by any means shall pay the aggrieved party eighty solidi as composition. And if he causes that one some injury, he shall in addition pay composition for the injuries as is provided in this code.

31. Concerning him who in disguise does violence. He who unjustly does violence to a freeman as a walopaus shall pay the injured party eighty solidi as composition. A walopaus is one who secretly puts on another's clothing or disguises his head or face.

32. If a freeman is found in someone else's courtyard at night and does not willingly give his hands to be bound, he may be killed and no compensation may be sought by his relatives. But if he gives his hands to be bound and they have been bound, he still must pay eighty solidi for himself, because it is not consistent with reason that a man should silently or secretly enter someone else's courtyard at night; if he has some useful purpose, he should call out before he enters.

33. If a slave is found at night in someone else's courtyard and does not give his hands to be bound he may be killed and no compensation may be sought by his lord. But if the slave holds out his hands and they have been bound, he may free himself with a payment of forty solidi.

34. That one who in anger shoots an arrow or hurls a lance into another's courtyard from outside of the wall and wounds someone within the yard shall pay twenty solidi as composition. In addition, he must pay composition for any wounds or injuries inflicted as provided in this code.

35. On breach of the peace. He who creates a disturbance in a church shall pay forty solidi to that venerable place in addition to him who suffered the wounds or injuries. The abovementioned forty solidi shall be collected by the schultheis or judge of the district and laid on the holy altar of that church where the offense occurred.

36. He who dares to create a disturbance within the king's palace when the king is present shall lose his life unless he can redeem his life from the king.

37. The freeman who creates a disturbance in that district where the king is present, although he does not strike a blow, shall pay twelve solidi to the king's palace. But he who raises a disturbance and also strikes a blow, shall pay twenty-four solidi to the fisc. In addition, he shall pay composition for any wounds or injuries which he caused as provided below.

*   *   *

REVIEW QUESTIONS

1. What is the Lombard conception of justice?
2. How does this style of punishment help to keep the peace?
3. What are the assumptions of Lombard legal reasoning?

EINHARD

FROM *The Life of Charlemagne*

Einhard's biography of Charlemagne, composed shortly after the emperor's death in 814, is an excellent source on this remarkable ruler's career. Charlemagne's numerous accomplishments made him a fitting subject for the first biography of a secular ruler since the fall of the Roman Empire. Although Einhard patterned his biography on Roman models, he presents an accurate portrait of his friend the emperor. This chapter covers Charlemagne's private life, which the author distinguishes from the accomplishments of his father, Pepin, and his wars, mainly against the Muslims in Spain and the Saxons in Germany, and also against the Avars around what is today Austria and Hungary.

From *Two Lives of Charlemagne*, edited by Lewis Thorpe (New York: Penguin Books, 1969), pp. 73–82.

*   *   *

The Emperor's Private Life

What has gone before is a fair picture of Charlemagne and all that he did to protect and enlarge his kingdom, and indeed to embellish it. I shall now speak of his intellectual qualities, his extraordinary strength of character, whether in prosperity or adversity, and all the other details of his personal and domestic life.

After the death of his father, at the time when he was sharing the kingship with Carloman, Charlemagne bore with such patience this latter's hatred and jealousy that everyone was surprised that he never lost his temper with his brother.

Then, at the bidding of his mother, he married the daughter of Desiderius, the King of the Longobards. Nobody knows why, but he dismissed this wife after one year. Next he married Hildigard, a woman of most noble family, from the Swabian race. By her he had three sons, Charles,

Pepin and Lewis, and the same number of daughters, Rotrude, Bertha and Gisela. He had three more daughters, Theoderada, Hiltrude and Rothaide, two of these by his third wife, Fastrada, who was from the race of Eastern Franks or Germans, and the last by a concubine whose name I cannot remember. Fastrada died and he married Luitgard, from the Alamanni, but she bore him no children. After Luitgard's death, he took four concubines: Madelgard, who bore him a daughter Ruothilde; Gersvinda, of the Saxon race, by whom he had a daughter Adaltrude; Regina, who bore him Drogo and Hugo; and Adallinda, who became the mother of Theodoric.

Charlemagne's own mother, Bertrada, lived with him in high honour to a very great age. He treated her with every respect and never had a cross word with her, except over the divorce of King Desiderius' daughter, whom he had married on her advice. Bertrada died soon after Hildigard, living long enough to see three grandsons and as many granddaughters in her son's house. Charlemagne buried her with great honour in the church of Saint Denis, where his father lay.

He had a single sister, Gisela by name, who from her childhood onwards had been dedicated to the religious life. He treated her with the same respect which he showed his mother. She died a few years before Charlemagne himself, in the nunnery where she had spent her life.

Charlemagne was determined to give his children, his daughters just as much as his sons, a proper training in the liberal arts which had formed the subject of his own studies. As soon as they were old enough he had his sons taught to ride in the Frankish fashion, to use arms and to hunt. He made his daughters learn to spin and weave wool, use the distaff and spindle, and acquire every womanly accomplishment, rather than fritter away their time in sheer idleness.

Of all his children he lost only two sons and one daughter prior to his own death. These were his eldest son Charles, Pepin whom he had made King of Italy, and Rotrude, the eldest of his daughters, who had been engaged to Constantine, the Emperor of the Greeks. Pepin left one son, called Bernard, and five daughters, Adelhaid, Atula, Gundrada, Berthaid and Theoderada. Charlemagne gave clear proof of the affection which he bore them all, for after the death of Pepin he ordered his grandson Bernard to succeed and he had his granddaughters brought up with his own girls. He bore the death of his two sons and his daughter with less fortitude than one would have expected, considering the strength of his character; for his emotions as a father, which were very deeply rooted, made him burst into tears.

When the death of Hadrian, the Pope of Rome and his close friend, was announced to him, he wept as if he had lost a brother or a dearly loved son. He was firm and steady in his human relationships, developing friendship easily, keeping it up with care and doing everything he possibly could for anyone whom he had admitted to this degree of intimacy.

He paid such attention to the upbringing of his sons and daughters that he never sat down to table without them when he was at home, and never set out on a journey without taking them with him. His sons rode at his side and his daughters followed along behind. Hand-picked guards watched over them as they closed the line of march. These girls were extraordinarily beautiful and greatly loved by their father. It is a remarkable fact that, as a result of this, he kept them with him in his household until the very day of his death, instead of giving them in marriage to his own men or to foreigners, maintaining that he could not live without them. The consequence was that he had a number of unfortunate experiences, he who had been so lucky in all else that he undertook. However, he shut his eyes to all that happened, as if no suspicion of any immoral conduct had ever reached him, or as if the rumour was without foundation.

I did not mention with the others a son called Pepin who was born to Charlemagne by a concubine. He was handsome enough, but a hunchback. At a moment when his father was wintering in Bavaria, soon after the beginning of his campaign against the Huns, this Pepin pretended to be ill and conspired with certain of the Frankish leaders who had won him over to their cause by pretending to offer him the kingship. The plot was discovered and the conspirators were duly punished. Pepin was tonsured and permitted to take up, in the monastery of Prüm, the life of a religious for which he had already expressed a vocation.

Earlier on there had been another dangerous conspiracy against Charlemagne in Germany. All the plotters were exiled, some having their eyes put out first, but the others were not maltreated physically. Only three of them were killed. These resisted arrest, drew their swords and started to defend themselves. They slaughtered a few men in the process and had to be destroyed themselves, as there was no other way of dealing with them.

The cruelty of Queen Fastrada is thought to have been the cause of both these conspiracies, since it was under her influence that Charlemagne seemed to have taken actions which were fundamentally opposed to his normal kindliness and good nature. Throughout the remainder of his life he so won the love and favour of all his fellow human beings, both at home and abroad, that no one ever levelled against him the slightest charge of cruelty or injustice.

He loved foreigners and took great pains to make them welcome. So many visited him as a result that they were rightly held to be a burden not only to the palace, but to the entire realm. In his magnanimity he took no notice at all of this criticism, for he considered that his reputation for hospitality and the advantage of the good name which he acquired more than compensated for the great nuisance of their being there.

The Emperor was strong and well built. He was tall in stature, but not excessively so, for his height was just seven times the length of his own feet. The top of his head was round, and his eyes were piercing and unusually large. His nose was slightly longer than normal, he had a fine head of white hair and his expression was gay and good-humoured. As a result, whether he was seated or standing, he always appeared masterful and dignified. His neck was short and rather thick, and his stomach a trifle too heavy, but the proportions of the rest of his body prevented one from noticing these blemishes. His step was firm and he was manly in all his movements. He spoke distinctly, but his voice was thin for a man of his physique. His health was good, except that he suffered from frequent attacks of fever during the last four years of his life, and towards the end he was lame in one foot. Even then he continued to do exactly as he wished, instead of following the advice of his doctors, whom he came positively to dislike after they advised him to stop eating the roast meat to which he was accustomed and to live on stewed dishes.

He spent much of his time on horseback and out hunting, which came naturally to him, for it would be difficult to find another race on earth who could equal the Franks in this activity. He took delight in steam-baths at the thermal springs, and loved to exercise himself in the water whenever he could. He was an extremely strong swimmer and in this sport no one could surpass him. It was for this reason that he built his palace at Aachen and remained continuously in residence there during the last years of his life and indeed until the moment of his death. He would invite not only his sons to bathe with him, but his nobles and friends as well, and occasionally even a crowd of his attendants and bodyguards, so that sometimes a hundred men or more would be in the water together.

He wore the national dress of the Franks. Next to his skin he had a linen shirt and linen drawers; and then long hose and a tunic edged with silk. He wore shoes on his feet and bands of cloth wound round his legs. In winter he protected his chest and shoulders with a jerkin made of otter skins or ermine. He wrapped himself in a blue cloak and always had a sword strapped to his side, with a hilt and belt of gold or silver. Sometimes he would use a jewelled sword, but this was only on great feast days or when ambassadors came from foreign peoples. He hated the clothes of other countries, no matter how becoming they might be, and he would never consent to wear them. The only exception to this was one day in Rome when Pope Hadrian entreated him to put on a long tunic and a Greek mantle, and to wear shoes made in the Roman fashion; and then a second time, when Leo, Hadrian's successor, persuaded him to do the same thing. On feast days he walked in procession in a suit of cloth of gold, with jewelled shoes, his cloak fastened with a golden brooch and with a crown of gold and precious stones on his head. On ordinary days his dress differed hardly at all from that of the common people.

He was moderate in his eating and drinking, and especially so in drinking; for he hated to see drunkenness in any man, and even more so in himself and his friends. All the same, he could not go long without food, and he often used to complain that fasting made him feel ill. He rarely gave banquets and these only on high feast days, but then he would invite a great number of guests. His main meal of the day was served in four courses, in addition to the roast meat which his hunters used to bring in on spits and which he enjoyed more than any other food. During his meal he would listen to a public reading or some other entertainment. Stories would be recited for him, or the doings of the ancients told again. He took great pleasure in the books of Saint Augustine and especially in those which are called *The City of God.*

He was so sparing in his use of wine and every other beverage that he rarely drank more than three times in the course of his dinner. In summer, after his midday meal, he would eat some fruit and take another drink; then he would remove his shoes and undress completely, just as he did at night, and rest for two or three hours. During the night he slept so lightly that he would wake four or five times and rise from his bed. When he was dressing and putting on his shoes he would invite his friends to come in. Moreover, if the Count of the Palace told him that there was some dispute which could not be settled without the Emperor's personal decision, he would order the disputants to be brought in there and then, hear the case as if he were sitting in tribunal and pronounce a judgement. If there was any official business to be transacted on that day, or any order to be given to one of his ministers, he would settle it at the same time.

He spoke easily and fluently, and could express with great clarity whatever he had to say. He was not content with his own mother tongue, but took the trouble to learn foreign languages. He learnt Latin so well that he spoke it as fluently as his own tongue; but he understood Greek better than he could speak it. He was eloquent to the point of sometimes seeming almost garrulous.

He paid the greatest attention to the liberal arts; and he had great respect for men who taught them, bestowing high honours upon them. When he was learning the rules of grammar he received tuition from Peter the Deacon of Pisa, who by then was an old man, but for all other subjects he was taught by Alcuin, surnamed Albinus, another Deacon, a man of the Saxon race who came from Britain and was the most learned man anywhere to be found. Under him the Emperor spent much time and effort in studying rhetoric, dialectic and especially astrology. He applied himself to math-ematics and traced the course of the stars with great attention and care. He also tried to learn to write. With this object in view he used to keep writing-tablets and notebooks under the pillows on his bed, so that he could try his hand at forming letters during his leisure moments; but, although he tried very hard, he had begun too late in life and he made little progress.

Charlemagne practised the Christian religion with great devotion and piety, for he had been brought up in this faith since earliest childhood. This explains why he built a cathedral of such great beauty at Aachen, decorating it with gold and silver, with lamps, and with lattices and doors of solid bronze. He was unable to find marble columns for his construction anywhere else, and so he had them brought from Rome and Ravenna.

VISION OF THE HEAVENLY JERUSALEM (C. 900 C.E.)   MAIUS

An illumination by Maius for a manuscript by Beatus of Liébana, tenth-century Spain. Beatus of Liébana wrote a commentary on the Apocalypse for which the illuminator/artist Maius did 110 miniatures. This page shows the Heavenly Jerusalem as an early medieval city, surrounded by the twelve apostles. Inside the city are St. John the Evangelist with his book, the Lamb of God, and an angel measuring the city. Do any features of this miniature connect it to Christian Spain? Illustrating a book by hand was an immense labor. Why did medieval monks and nuns go to all this trouble?

As long as his health lasted, he went to church morning and evening with great regularity, and also for early-morning Mass, and the late-night hours. He took the greatest pains to ensure that all church ceremonies were performed with the utmost dignity, and he was always warning the sacristans to see that nothing sordid or dirty was brought into the building or left there. He donated so many sacred vessels made of gold and silver, and so many priestly vestments, that when service time came even those who opened and closed the doors, surely the humblest of all church dignitaries, had no need to perform their duties in their everyday clothes.

He made careful reforms in the way in which the psalms were chanted and the lessons read. He was himself quite an expert at both of these exercises, but he never read the lesson in public and he would sing only with the rest of the congregation and then in a low voice.

He was most active in relieving the poor and in that form of really disinterested charity which the Greeks call *eleemosyna*. He gave alms not only in his own country and in the kingdom over which he reigned, but also across the sea in Syria, Egypt, Africa, Jerusalem, Alexandria and Carthage. Wherever he heard that Christians were living in want, he took pity on their poverty and sent them money regularly. It was, indeed, precisely for this reason that he sought the friendship of kings beyond the sea, for he hoped that some relief and alleviation might result for the Christians living under their domination.

Charlemagne cared more for the church of the holy Apostle Peter in Rome than for any other sacred and venerable place. He poured into its treasury a vast fortune in gold and silver coinage and in precious stones. He sent so many gifts to the Pope that it was impossible to keep count of them. Throughout the whole period of his reign nothing was ever nearer to his heart than that, by his own efforts and exertion, the city of Rome should regain its former proud position. His ambition was not merely that the church of Saint Peter should remain safe and protected thanks to

him, but that by means of his wealth it should be more richly adorned and endowed than any other church. However much he thought of Rome, it still remains true that throughout his whole reign of forty-seven years he went there only four times to fulfil his vows and to offer up his prayers.

These were not the sole reasons for Charlemagne's last visit to Rome. The truth is that the inhabitants of Rome had violently attacked Pope Leo, putting out his eyes and cutting off his tongue, and had forced him to flee to the King for help. Charlemagne really came to Rome to restore the Church, which was in a very bad state indeed, but in the end he spent the whole winter there. It was on this occasion that he received the title of Emperor and Augustus. At first he was far from wanting this. He made it clear that he would not have entered the cathedral that day at all, although it was the greatest of all the festivals of the Church, if he had known in advance what the Pope was planning to do. Once he had accepted the title, he endured with great patience the jealousy of the so called Roman Emperors, who were most indignant at what had happened. He overcame their hostility only by the sheer strength of his personality, which was much more powerful than theirs. He was for ever sending messengers to them, and in his dispatches he called them his brothers.

Now that he was Emperor, he discovered that there were many defects in the legal system of his own people, for the Franks have two separate codes of law which differ from each other in many points. He gave much thought to how he could best fill the gaps, reconcile the discrepancies, correct the errors and rewrite the laws which were ill-expressed. None of this was ever finished; he added a few sections, but even these remained incomplete. What he did do was to have collected together and committed to writing the laws of all the nations under his jurisdiction which still remained unrecorded.

At the same time he directed that the age-old narrative poems, barbarous enough, it is true, in which were celebrated the warlike deeds of the kings of ancient times, should be written out and so preserved. He also began a grammar of his native tongue.

*   *   *

REVIEW QUESTIONS

1. According to Einhard, what are the qualities of a strong Germanic king?
2. What do we learn about the role of women at the upper levels of Carolingian society?
3. Einhard does not want to reveal the emperor's weaknesses, but what might they be?

Monastic Clamors, Curses, and Excommunications

Monastic culture relied on prayer and God's help to protect its people and possessions in an increasingly violent world. The spiritual weapons at the church's disposal consisted mainly of words, in the form of ritual cursing and excommunication of enemies. These short excerpts illustrate a clamor, a collective plea to God for help against troubles and enemies, a curse on enemies, an excommunication, and another curse.

From *Benedictine Maledictions: Liturgical Cursing in Romanesque France*, by Lester Little (Ithaca, N.Y.: Cornell University Press, 1993), pp. 25, 36, 41, 43.

A Clamor from Chartres, about 1020

*   *   *

In the spirit of humility and with contrite soul we come before your sacred altar and your most holy body and blood, Lord Jesus, redeemer of the world, and we acknowledge ourselves guilty against you on account of our sins, for which we are justly afflicted. To you, Lord Jesus, we come; to you, prostrate, we clamor, because iniquitous and proud men, emboldened by their own followers, invade, plunder, and lay waste the lands of this your sanctuary and of other churches subject to it. They compel your poor ones who till these lands to live in pain and hunger and nakedness; they kill both by the sword and by torment. And our belongings as well, by which we are supposed to live and which blessed souls bequeathed to this

place for their own salvation, they seize and violently take away from us. This your church, Lord, which in ancient times you founded and raised up in honor of the blessed and glorious ever-virgin Mary, sits in sadness. There is no one who can console it or liberate it except you, our God. So rise up, Lord Jesus, in support of us. Comfort us and help us. Attack those who are attacking us, and break the pride of those who afflict your place and us. You know, Lord, who they are and what their names are; their bodies and their hearts have been known to you alone from before they were born. Wherefore, Lord, judge them as you know how in your strength. Make them aware, to the extent that it pleases you, of their misdeeds, and free us by your mercy. Do not despise us, Lord, who call out to you in affliction, but because of the glory of your name and the mercy with which you founded this place and dedicated it in honor of your mother, visit us in peace and bring us out of our present distress.

*   *   *

A Curse from Reims, about 900

In the name of the Lord and by the power of the Holy Spirit and the authority divinely granted bishops by blessed Peter, prince of the apostles, we separate them from the bosom of holy mother church and we condemn them with an anathema of perpetual malediction, that they might not have help from any man or contact with any Christian. May they be cursed in town and cursed in the fields. May their barns be cursed and may their bones be cursed. May the fruit of their loins be cursed as well as the fruit of their lands, their herds of cattle and their flocks of sheep. May they be cursed going in and coming out. May they be cursed at home and may they be fugitives outside their homes. May they drain out through their bowels, like the faithless and unhappy Arius. May there come upon them all those maledictions by which the Lord through Moses threatened transgressors of the divine law.

*   *   *

A Curse by Pope Benedict VIII in 1014

May they be cursed in the four corners of the earth. May they be cursed in the East, disinherited in the West, interdicted in the North, and excommunicated in the South. May they be cursed in the day and excommunicated at night. May they be cursed at home and excommunicated while away, cursed in standing and excommunicated in sitting, cursed in eating, drinking and sleeping, excommunicated in waking, cursed when they work and excommunicated when they rest. May they be cursed in the spring and excommunicated in the summer, cursed in the autumn and excommunicated in the winter.

*   *   *

An Excommunication from Compiègne

By the authority of the Father and of the Son and of the Holy Spirit and of the Blessed Mary ever virgin and of the blessed apostles Peter and Paul and of the holy martyrs Cornelius and Cyprianus, we excommunicate them from the company of all Christians, and we bar them from the thresholds of the holy church of God so that they undergo eternal punishments with Dathan and Abiron and with those who said to the Lord God: "Stay away from us, we do not wish to know of your ways." And so may their lights be extinguished forever and ever unless they come forward and make amends.

*   *   *

REVIEW QUESTIONS

1. What type of justice is at work here?
2. What is the church trying to accomplish through these rituals?
3. How might the targets have responded?

"The Wanderer": Anglo-Saxon Poetry

"The Wanderer," known from a copy made about 975 C.E., is an example of an Anglo-Saxon elegiac lament, a poem in which a warrior must search for a new lord to follow. Like the great epic Beowulf, *this poem illustrates some of the spirit of Germanic culture with a thin or nonexistent veneer of Christianity.*

From "The Wanderer," translated by E. Talbot Donaldson (New York: Norton, 1993).

He who is alone often lives to find favor, mildness of the Lord, even though he has long had to stir with his arms the frost-cold sea, troubled in heart over the water-way had to tread the tracks of exile. Fully-fixed is his fate."

So spoke the earth-walker, remembering hardships, fierce war-slaughters—the fall of dear kinsmen.

"Often before the day dawned I have had to speak of my cares, alone: there is now none among the living to whom I dare clearly express the thought of my heart. I know indeed that it is a fine custom for a man to lock tight his heart's coffer, keep closed the hoard-case of his mind, whatever his thoughts may be. Words of a weary heart may not withstand fate, nor those of an angry spirit bring help. Therefore men eager for fame shut sorrowful thought up fast in their breast's coffer.

"Thus I, wretched with care, removed from my homeland, far from dear kinsmen, have had to fasten with fetters the thoughts of my heart—ever since the time, many years ago, that I covered my gold-friend in the darkness of the earth; and from there I crossed the woven waves, winter-sad, downcast for want of a hall, sought a giver of treasure—a place, far or near, where I might find one in a mead-hall who should know of my people, or would comfort me friendless, receive me with gladness. He who has experienced it knows how cruel a companion sorrow is to the man who has no beloved protectors. Exile's path awaits him, not twisted gold—frozen thoughts in his heart-case, no joy of earth. He recalls the hall-warriors and the taking of treasure, how in youth his gold-friend made him accustomed to feasting. All delight has gone.

"He who has had long to forgo the counsel of a beloved lord knows indeed how, when sorrow and sleep together bind the poor dweller-alone, it will seem to him in his mind that he is embracing and kissing his liege lord and laying his hands and his head on his knee, as it some times was in the old days when he took part in the gift-giving. Then he wakens again, the man with no lord, sees the yellow waves before him, the sea-birds bathe, spread their feathers, frost and snow fall, mingled with hail.

"Then the wounds are deeper in his heart, sore for want of his dear one. His sorrow renews as the memory of his kinsmen moves through his mind: he greets them with glad words, eagerly looks at them, a company of warriors. Again they fade, moving off over the water; the spirit of these fleeting ones brings to him no familiar voices. Care renews in him who must again and again send his weary heart out over the woven waves.

"Therefore I cannot think why the thoughts of my heart should not grow dark when I consider all the life of men through this world—with what terrible swiftness they forgo the hall-floor, bold young retainers. So this middle-earth each day fails and falls. No man may indeed become wise before he has had his share of winters in this world's kingdom. The wise man must be patient, must never be too hot-hearted, nor too hasty of speech, nor too fearful, nor too glad, nor too greedy for wealth, nor ever too eager to boast before he has thought clearly. A man must wait, when he speaks in boast, until he knows clearly, sure-minded, where the thoughts of his heart may turn.

"The wise warrior must consider how ghostly it will be when all the wealth of this world stands waste, just as now here and there through this middle-earth wind-blown walls stand covered with frost-fall, storm-beaten dwellings. Wine-halls totter, the lord lies bereft of joy, all the company has fallen, bold men beside the wall. War took away some, bore them forth on their way; a bird carried one away over the deep sea; a wolf shared one with Death; another a man sad of face hid in an earth-pit.

"So the Maker of mankind laid waste this dwelling-place until the old works of giants stood idle, devoid of the noise of the stronghold's keepers. Therefore the man wise in his heart considers carefully this wallplace and this dark life, remembers the multitude of deadly combats long ago, and speaks these words: 'Where has the horse gone? Where the young warrior? Where is the giver of treasure? What has become of the feasting seats? Where are the joys of the hall? Alas, the bright cup! Alas, the mailed warrior! Alas, the prince's glory! How that time has gone, vanished beneath night's cover, just as if it never had been!

The wall, wondrous high, decorated with snake-likenesses, stands now over traces of the beloved company. The ash-spears' might has borne the earls away—weapons greedy for slaughter, Fate the mighty; and storms beat on the stone walls, snow, the herald of winter, falling thick binds the earth when darkness comes and the night-shadow falls, sends harsh hailstones from the north in hatred of men. All earth's kingdom is wretched, the world beneath the skies is changed by the work of the fates. Here wealth is fleeting, here friend is fleeting, here man is fleeting, here woman is fleeting—all this earthly habitation shall be emptied.' "

So spoke the man wise in heart, sat apart at the council. He is good who keeps his word; a man must never utter too quickly his breast's passion, unless he knows first how to achieve remedy, as a leader with his courage. It will be well with him who seeks favor, comfort from the Father in heaven, where for us all stability resides.

REVIEW QUESTIONS

1. What are the values of this warrior society?
2. What are the qualities of a good follower?
3. If the dominant tone is pessimistic, then what human or supernatural powers can counteract the gloomy side of life?

FROM *Egil's Saga:* **Viking Literature**

Egil's Saga is one of the best examples of Viking literature. This tale is about Egil Skallagrimsson and his life in Norway and Iceland in the ninth and tenth centuries C.E. *The great Icelandic historian Snorri Sturluson (1179–1241) is the probable composer of the saga. Egil's life, however, contains many realistic adventures that illustrate Scandinavian life before 1000* C.E. *The first excerpt concerns Egil's friend Einar, and the second describes Egil's old age and death. Both episodes take place in Iceland.*

From *The Sagas of Icelanders*, by Paul Kellogg and Jane Smiley, translated by Bernard Scudder (New York: Viking Penguin, 2000), pp. 165–67, 180–84.

*   *   *

81

There was a man named Einar, the son of Helgi Ottarsson and the great-grandson of Bjorn the Easterner who settled in Breidafjord. Einar was the brother of Osvif the Wise. Even at an early age, Einar was large and strong and a man of great accomplishments. He began composing poetry when he was young and was fond of learning.

One summer at the Althing, Einar went to Egil Skallagrimsson's booth and they began talking. The conversation soon turned to poetry and they both took great delight in the discussion.

After that, Einar made a habit of talking to Egil and a great friendship developed between them. Einar had just come back from a voyage abroad. Egil asked Einar about recent news and his friends in Norway, and also about the men he regarded as his enemies. He also often asked about the leading men there. Einar asked in return about Egil's voyages and exploits; Egil enjoyed talking about them and they got on well together. Einar asked Egil to tell him where his toughest ordeal had been, and Egil spoke a verse:

> I fought alone with eight,
> and twice with eleven.
> I fed the wolf with corpses,
> killed them all myself.
> Fiercely we swapped
> blades that shiver through shields.[1]
> From the tree of my arm
> I tossed the plated fire of death.[2]

Egil and Einar promised each other friendship when they parted. Einar spent a long time in other countries with men of rank. He was generous but usually had scant means, and he was a firm character and a noble man. He was one of Earl Hakon Sigurdarson's men.

At that time there was much unrest in Norway. Earl Hakon was at war with Eirik's sons and many people fled the country. King Harald Eiriksson died in Denmark, at Hals in Limfjord, when he was betrayed. He fought against Harald, the son of Canute, who was called Gold-Harald, and against Earl Hakon.

Arinbjorn the Hersir died with Harald Eiriksson in that battle. When Egil heard of Arinbjorn's death, he composed this verse:

> Their numbers are dwindling, the famous
> warriors who met with weapons
> and spread gifts like the gold of day.
> Where will I find generous men,
> who beyond the sea that, nailed with islands,
> girds the earth, showered snows of silver
> on to my hands where hawks perch,
> in return for my words of praise?

The poet Einar Helgason was nicknamed Skalaglamm (Bowl-rattle). He composed a drapa about Earl Hakon called Lack of Gold, which was very long. For a long time the earl was angry with Einar and refused to listen to it. Then Einar spoke a verse:

> I made mead for the battle-father[3]
> while everyone slept, about the noble
> warrior who rules the lands—
> and now I regret it.
> I think that the spreader of treasure,
> the renowned leader, considers few
> poets worse than me; I was
> too eager to come to see him.

And he spoke another verse:

> Let us seek to meet the earl who dares
> to make meals for the wolf with his sword,
> adorn the ship's oar-sides
> with ornate victory shields;
> the warrior who swings his sword
> like a serpent inflicting wounds
> will not turn his hand
> to rebuff me when I find him.

---

[1] *blades that shiver through shields*: swords
[2] *plated fire of death*: sword

[3] *mead*: poetry; *battle-father*: Odin, god of poetry and battle

The earl did not want Einar to leave then, but listened to his poem and afterwards gave him as a reward a shield, which was an outstanding treasure. It was adorned with legends, and between the carvings it was overlaid with gold and embossed with jewels. Then Einar went to Iceland to stay with his brother Osvif.

In the autumn, Einar rode over to Borg and stayed there. Egil was not at home, having gone north, but was expected shortly. Einar stayed three nights waiting for him; it was not the custom to stay more than three nights on a visit. Einar then prepared to leave, and when he was ready to go he went to Egil's bed and hung up his precious shield there, and told the people of the household that it was a present for Egil.

After that, Einar rode away, and Egil came home the same day. When he went to his bed he saw the shield and asked who owned such a treasure. He was told that Einar Skalaglamm had been there and given him the shield as a present.

Then Egil said, "That scoundrel! Does he expect me to stay awake making a poem about his shield? Fetch my horse, I will ride after him and kill him."

Then he was told that Einar had ridden away early that morning—"He will have reached Dalir by now."

Then Egil made a drapa, which begins with this verse:

It is time to light up with praise
the bright bulwark I was given.[4]
The sender of generosity's message
reached me at my home.
I will steer the reins well
of the sea-king's horse,[5]
my dwarf's ship of verse.[6]
Listen to my words.

Egil and Einar remained friends all their lives. It is said of the fate of the shield that Egil took it

---

[4] *bright bulwark*: shield
[5] *sea-king's horse*: ship
[6] *dwarf's ship*: poetry

with him when he went north to Vidimyri with Thorkel Gunnvaldsson, who was going to fetch his bride there, and Bjorn the Red's sons Scarf and Helgi. The shield was dilapidated by then; it had been thrown into a tub of whey. Afterwards Egil had the fittings taken off, and there were twelve ounces of gold in the overlays.

*   *   *

88

Egil Skallagrimsson lived a long life, but in his old age he grew very frail, and both his hearing and sight failed. He also suffered from very stiff legs. Egil was living at Mosfell with Grim and Thordis then.

One day Egil was walking outdoors alongside the wall when he stumbled and fell.

Some women saw this, laughed at him and said, "You're completely finished, Egil, now that you fall over of your own accord."

Grim replied, "Women made less fun of us when we were younger. And I expect they find little of value in our womanizing now."

Egil said that things had reached that pass, and he spoke a verse:

My head bobs like a bridled horse
it plunges baldly into woe.
my middle leg both droops and drips
while both my ears are dry.

Egil went completely blind. One winter day when the weather was cold, he went to warm himself by the fire. The cook said it was astonishing for a man who had been as great as Egil to lie around under people's feet and stop them going about their work.

"Don't grudge me that I warm myself through by the fire," said Egil. "We should make room for each other."

"Stand up," she said, "and go off to your bed and leave us to get on with our work."

Egil stood up, went off to his bed and spoke this verse:

Blind I wandered to sit by the fire,
asked the flame-maiden for peace;
such affliction I bear on the border

where my eyebrows cross.
Once when the land-rich king
took pleasure in my words
he granted me the hoard
that giants warded, gold.

Another time Egil went over to the fire to keep warm, and someone asked him if his legs were cold and told him not to stretch them out too close to the fire.

"I will do that," said Egil, "but I don't find it easy to control my legs now that I cannot see. Being blind is dismal."

Then Egil spoke a verse:

Time seems long in passing
as I lie alone,
a senile old man
on the king's guard.[7]
My legs are two
frigid widows,
those women
need some flame.

This was at the start of Earl Hakon the Powerful's reign. Egil Skallagrimsson was in his eighties then and still active apart from his blindness.

In the summer, when everyone was preparing to ride to the Thing, Egil asked Grim to ride there with him. Grim was reluctant.

When Grim spoke to Thordis, he told her what Egil had asked of him.

"I want you to find out what lies behind this request of his," he said.

Thordis went to see her kinsman Egil, who by that time had no greater pleasure in life than talking to her.

When she saw him she asked, "Is it true that you want to ride to the Thing, kinsman? I'd like you to tell me what you're planning."

"I will tell you what I've been thinking," he said. "I want to go to the Thing with the two chests full of English silver that King Athelstan gave to me. I'm going to have the chests carried to the Law Rock when the crowd there is at its

biggest. Then I'll toss the silver at them and I'll be very much surprised if they all share it out fairly amongst themselves. I expect there'll be plenty of pushing and shoving. It might even end with the whole Thing breaking out in a brawl."

Thordis said, "That sounds like a brilliant plan. It will live for as long as people live in Iceland."

Then Thordis went to talk to Grim and tell him about Egil's plan.

"He must never be allowed to get away with such a mad scheme," said Grim.

When Egil brought up the subject of riding to the Thing with Grim he would have none of it, so Egil stayed at home while the Thing was held. He was displeased and wore a rather grumpy look.

The cattle at Mosfell were kept in a shieling, and Thordis stayed there while the Thing took place.

One evening when everyone was going to bed at Mosfell, Egil called in two of Grim's slaves.

He told them to fetch him a horse, "because I want to go to bathe in the pool."

When he was ready he went out, taking his chests of silver with him. He mounted the horse, crossed the hayfields to the slope that begins there and disappeared.

In the morning, when all the people got up, they saw Egil wandering around on the hill east of the farm, leading a horse behind him. They went over to him and brought him home.

But neither the slaves nor the chests of treasure ever returned, and there are many theories about where Egil hid his treasure. East of the farm is a gully leading down from the mountain. It has been noticed that English coins have been found in the gully when the river recedes after floods caused by sudden thaws. Some people believe Egil must have hidden his treasure there. Then there are large and exceptionally deep marshes below the hayfields at Mosfell, and it is claimed that Egil threw his treasure into them. On the south side of the rivers are hot springs with big pits nearby, where some people believe Egil must have hidden his treasure, because a will-o'-the-wisp is often seen there. Egil himself said he had killed Grim's

---

[7] *king's guard:* his back? a bed? his chest?

slaves and hidden his treasure somewhere, but he never told a single person where it was.

In the autumn Egil caught the illness that eventually led to his death. When he died, Grim had his body dressed in fine clothes and taken over to Tjaldanes, where a mound was made that Egil was buried in, along with his weapons and clothes.

89

Grim from Mosfell was baptized when Christianity was made the law in Iceland and he had a church built at Mosfell. It is said that Thordis had Egil's bones moved to the church. This is supported by the fact that when a cemetery was dug, after the church that Grim had had built at Hrisbru was taken down and set up at Mosfell, human bones were found under the site of the altar. They were much larger than normal human bones, and on the basis of old accounts people are certain they must have belonged to Egil.

Skafti Thorarinsson the Priest, a wise man, was there at the time. He picked up Egil's skull and put it on the wall of the churchyard. The skull was astonishingly large and even more incredible for its weight. It was all ridged on the outside, like a scallop shell. Curious to test its thickness, Skafti took a fair-sized hand-axe in one hand and struck the skull with it as hard as he could, to try to break it. A white mark was left where he struck the skull, but it neither dented nor cracked. This goes to prove that such a skull would not have been easy for weak men to damage when it was covered with hair and skin. Egil's bones were buried by the edge of the churchyard at Mosfell.

90

Thorstein, Egil's son, was baptized when Christianity came to Iceland and he had a church built at Borg. He was a devout and orderly man. He grew to an old age, died of illness and was buried at Borg in the church he had had built there.

A great family is descended from Thorstein which includes many prominent men and poets. Thorstein's descendants belong to the Myrar clan, as do all other descendants of Skallagrim. For a long time it was a family trait to be strong and warlike, and some members were men of great wisdom. It was a family of contrasts. Some of the best-looking people ever known in Iceland belonged to it, such as Thorstein Egilsson, his nephew Kjartan Olafsson, Hall Gudmundarson and Thorstein's daughter Helga the Fair, whose love Gunnlaug Serpent-tongue and Hrafn the Poet contested. But most members of the Myrar clan were exceptionally ugly.

Of Thorstein's sons, Thorgeir was the strongest but Skuli was the greatest. He lived at Borg after his father's day and spent a long time on Viking raids. He was at the stem of Earl Eirik's ship Iron-prow in the battle where King Olaf Tryggvason was killed. Skuli fought seven battles on his Viking raids and was considered to be outstandingly resolute and brave. He went to Iceland afterwards and farmed at Borg, where he lived until his old age, and many people are descended from him. And here this saga ends.

REVIEW QUESTIONS

1. What are the roles of poetry and poets in Icelandic society?
2. What attitudes toward wealth and gifts emerge from this saga?
3. These excerpts reveal a society in transition from traditional Norse religious beliefs to Christianity. What does the saga show about these two systems of belief?

8   THE EXPANSION OF EUROPE: ECONOMY, SOCIETY, AND POLITICS IN THE HIGH MIDDLE AGES, 1000–1300

The centuries of the High Middle Ages witnessed tremendous economic growth, which began in agriculture, the basis of the medieval economy. All societies in Europe, North Africa, and the Middle East remained overwhelmingly rural and depended on villages of peasants to produce the food and supplies needed to sustain urban life and to pay the taxes for the emerging national governments. Better technology for vital tools like plows and harnesses, accurate record keeping and attention to land, and perhaps benign weather, all contributed to the improved yields in crops and flocks. Great landowners, especially the bishops and monasteries, kept records of their manors, the great estates where peasants lived and worked. Manors did not exist everywhere and were not uniform across Europe, but they were a widespread feature of rural life. Rulers and landowners needed to mix coercion and incentives to keep their serfs (peasants tied to the land) in the countryside and to recruit farmers for the new lands being reclaimed from the forests, swamps, and even the sea. The feudal warrior class and the church depended on the peasantry for subsistence and in return were supposed to protect peasants in this world and the next and to keep the peace necessary for growth.

About the year 1000, Christian Europe had only a few small cities, while the Muslim world contained many large ones in Spain, Sicily, and the Middle East. Most European cities rapidly increased in population in the following centuries, a growth that depended on adequate food supplies, either produced locally or acquired through trade. People living in towns also needed certain rights and liberties to transact business, and urban people wanted secure land ownership; personal liberty, including freedom of travel; and a sound coinage. Merchants did not want to resort to feuds and vendettas to settle their disputes. Kings and lords were prepared to grant some liberties to towns in exchange for money. Urban wealth largely resulted from trade and a modest level of artisan manufactures, especially cloth. The most lucrative trade with the Muslim world required reliable contracts to encourage merchants to invest or risk their lives in overseas trade. These contracts rested on a legal framework partly inherited from the Romans but also borrowed from the Byzantines and Muslims and invented in the new trading centers. As certain families amassed fortunes in trade and the rest benefited from a general increase in prosperity, the use of written documents in business and family life became more common throughout urban society. Literacy, once mainly useful to the church, became a valuable money-making skill and produced jobs for copyists and notaries who provided the written word to a basically illiterate society still dependent on memory. An ability to manipulate numbers was also valuable in a world where rationality about words or sums was remaking the older, simpler society of those who prayed, fought, and farmed.

Monarchs ruled over states that contained proud and quarrelsome nobles tied to kings by reciprocal feudal links of vassalage, urban people engaged in a variety of businesses and crafts, and the great majority of the population which remained as peasants working the land. States became more bureaucratic and had laws, taxes, and courts, all of which required written records. The personality and energy of individual rulers, however, were still important, as the career of the saintly Louis IX of France illustrates. A bad or simply weak ruler, like John of England, had to yield rights to other centers of power—a process described in the Magna Carta. Fighting wars and dispensing justice remained the main tasks of medieval government, and good outcomes like victory and less crime were the best measures of its success. Whether a free city or an emerging kingdom, a government was above all expected to defend its existence. Good tax records and laws were the best means to accomplish this goal. Better-organized states and the reformed church had the authority to define more closely all liberties and duties, and this was not usually good news for women or for religious or ethnic minorities. The origins of persecution and subjugation rested in the better records and bureaucracies produced by the improving economy.

The Charter of Liberties for St. Omer

William of Normandy, count of Flanders, issued this famous charter of liberties to the citizens of St. Omer in 1127. Such charters were the foundations of urban freedom, and they reveal what city people needed to conduct their businesses. William also benefited from this arrangement, and the charter embodies the results of some hard bargaining between the merchants and their lord.

From *Medieval Culture and Society*, by David Herlihy (New York: HarperCollins, 1968), pp. 178–84.

I, William, by the grace of God, Count of the Flemings, not wishing to reject the petition of the citizens of St. Omer—especially as they have willingly received my petition about the consulate of Flanders, and because they have always been more honest and faithful than other Flemings to me—grant them the laws and customs written below in perpetuity, and command that these laws remain inviolate.

1. First, that to every man I will show peace, and I will maintain and defend them as my own men without deceit. And I concede that their aldermen can make right judgment concerning all men, including myself. I grant liberty to those aldermen such as the most favored aldermen of my lands enjoy.

2. If any citizen of St. Omer lend money to anyone, and the borrower freely acknowledges this in the presence of lawful men who hold inheritances in the city, if the debt is unpaid on the agreed date, he or his goods may be detained until all is paid. If he is unwilling to pay, or denies the agreement, he shall be detained until he pays the debt, if he is convicted on the testimony of two aldermen or two sworn men.

3. If anyone is accused under the law of the Church, he need not leave St. Omer to do justice elsewhere, but may do what is right in the city, in the presence of the bishop or his archdeacon or his priest, and by the judgment of the clerics and aldermen. He need answer to no one, except for these three reasons: that is, desecration of a church or temple, an injury of a cleric, or rape and violation of a woman. If a complaint is lodged against him for other reasons, the case should be heard in the presence of the judges and my prévôt. Thus it was decreed in the presence of Count K. Charles and Bishop John.

4. I concede to them the liberty which they enjoyed at the time of my ancestors, that is, that they never must leave their territory on campaign, saving only if a hostile army invade Flanders. Then they must defend me and my land.

5. All those who have their guild and belong to it and reside within the circle of the city, I free from all tolls at the port of Dixmude and Gravelines; and throughout all the land of Flanders I free them of the tax called *sewerp*. I grant them the toll which the men of Arras pay at Bapaume.

6. If any of them go into the land of the emperor for trading, he shall not be required by any of my men to pay the tax known as *hansa*.

7. If it should happen that at any time I should acquire land outside of Flanders, or if a treaty of peace should be made between me and my uncle Henry, king of England, I shall free them of all tolls in the land acquired or in the entire realm of the English, or I shall make them free of all customs by the terms of such a treaty.

8. In every market of Flanders, if anyone raises a complaint against them, they shall undergo the judgment of the aldermen concerning every complaint without a duel. They shall henceforth be free from the duel.

9. All who live within the walls of St. Omer, or who shall live there in the future, I make free from the *cavagium,* that is, from the head tax, and from payments to the court officials.

10. Their money which after the death of Count K. was taken from them, and which because of the fidelity which they hold towards me is still not given them, I shall repay within the year, or I shall have justice done for them according to the judgment of the aldermen.

11. Moreover, they have asked the king of France and Ralph of Péronne that wherever they go in their lands they should be free from all toll, transit duties and passage; this I too wish to grant them.

12. I command that their commune remain undisturbed, just as they created it by oath. I shall let it be dissolved by no one. I concede to them all right and right justice, as it is best available in my land, that is, in Flanders. I wish them to be free henceforth of all customary taxes, as the best and freer townsmen of Flanders. I shall ask of them no scot, no taille, and make no request for their money.

13. I give my mint at St. Omer, from which I have had 30 pounds per year, and whatever I ought to

have from it, for the repayment of their losses and the sustenance of their guild. These townsmen should keep the money for all my life stable and good, so that their city may be improved.

14. The guards who every night in the year protect the castle of St. Omer, and who, besides their salary and support as was established in olden times in oats and cheese and in goatskins, are accustomed to demand unjustly and violently one loaf and one or two pennies from each house in the city, at the feasts of St. Omer and St. Bertin and at Christmas, should dare no longer to take anything besides their salary and support.

15. Whoever comes to Nieuport from any place should have permission to come to St. Omer with his goods in whatever ship he pleases.

16. If I make peace with Stephan count of Boulogne, I shall in that peace make them free from toll and *sewerp* at Wissant and in all his lands.

17. I grant for their use the pasture adjacent to the city of St. Omer in the forest which is called Lo and in the marshes and meadows, moors and uncultivated lands, except in the land of the lepers, as it was at the time of Count Robert the Bearded.

18. I make free from all tolls the houses which are under the supervision of the advocate of the abbey of St. Bertin, namely those which are inhabited. Each one shall give 12 pennies at the feast of St. Michael, 12 pennies as bread tax, and 12 pennies as beer tax. Deserted houses shall pay nothing.

19. If any stranger should attack any citizen of St. Omer and bring injury or insult upon him or violently rob him of his property, and with this injury should escape his hands, and is afterwards summoned by the castellan or by his wife or by his steward, if he disdains to come to make satisfaction within three days or should neglect to do so, the commune shall together take the injury of their brother upon themselves. In taking vengeance, if a home should be destroyed or burned, or if anyone should be injured or killed, he who accomplished the vengeance should not incur any danger

of person or property nor should he know or fear my displeasure concerning this. If however, whoever made the injury should soon be taken, he shall be judged according to the laws and customs of the city and shall be punished according to the degree of the crime, that is, he shall render an eye for eyes, a tooth for a tooth, and a head for a head.

20. Concerning the death of Eustache of Steenvoorde, whoever may disturb and molest any citizen of St. Omer should be held guilty of the betrayal and death of Count K., since whatever was done was done out of fidelity to me. And as I swore and gave faith, thus I wish them to be reconciled and hold peace towards his relatives.

The following persons under oath promised to uphold this commune and to observe the abovementioned customs and agreements: Louis, the king of the French; William, the count of Flanders Ralph of Péronne; Hugh Oatfield; Osto the castellan and William his brother; Robert of Béthune and William his son; Anselm of Hesdin; Stephan, the count of Boulogne; Masasses, the count of Guines; Walter of Lillers; Balduin of Ghent; Ywain his brother; Roger the castellan of Lille, and Robert his son; Rasse of Gavere; Daniel of Termonde; Helias of Saint-Saens; Henry of Bourbourg; Eustache the advocate and Arnulf his son; the castellan of Ghent, Gervais; Peter the steward; Stephan of Steninghem.

This privilege was confirmed by Count William and the abovementioned barons, by faith and oath approved and accepted. In the year of the Lord's Incarnation 1127, 18 kalends of May, the fifth day of the week, the feast of the saints Tiburtius and Valerian.

REVIEW QUESTIONS

1. From this charter, what liberties appear to be the crucial ones to urban people?
2. What did William get from this charter?
3. How did St. Omer govern itself?

FROM *The Anonymous Treatise on Husbandry*

This treatise or manual (originally in French), dating from the late thirteenth century, was intended to be a guide for an official, a steward, in charge of managing a monastic estate or manor. The job of this farm manager was to keep track of resources, to maximize income, and to oversee the lesser officials—the bailiff and the reeve— usually a senior peasant tenant. These selections concern husbandry—the work of raising crops and animals. A handbook for managers is an imperfect window on the actual farmers and their lives. Women and men did this work under a good manager's watchful gaze. These excerpts introduce the manager to agricultural lore about livestock. They serve as a window on to the practical business of farming in thirteenth-century England.

From *Walter of Henley and Other Treatises on Estate Management and Accounting*, by Dorothea Oschinsky (Oxford, Eng.: Clarendon Press, 1971).

*   *   *

c.9 You ought then to see your stock, how much and what kind were kept on the manor during the previous year and appear on the last account. And whether any kind of stock was brought after that into the manor either by gift or by purchase, remittance, heriot, weif, or acquisition, by chance or in any other way.

And you ought then to see how many head there are of each kind of beast and of small stock, and of what age they are, so that you can obtain information about those which are of the age of being mated. And see how many male and how many female of each kind of beast or fowl there are so that you may know how to charge the accountant correctly for their issue in the manner shown below.

c.10 The reeve ought to answer for the issue of the mares of the manor, that is to say for each mare one foal in the year. And if there is any mare which has no foal an inquiry ought to be made whether this is due to bad keeping or lack of food, too much work or through lack of a stallion, or whether the mare is barren and that the reeve could have changed her—and in time—for another but did not do so. In these cases he ought to be charged fully for the foal or the value.

c.11 And if there are any dead birds or beasts on the manor it ought to be inquired whether the death occurred through the fault of their keeper, or of the bailiff or reeve; whether they could have saved them or could have made some improvements and did not do so. If so, they pay out of their own pocket. And if the animals died through misadventure such as murrain which happens at times, then the reeve ought to answer for fleeces, hides, and carcasses and for the issue; and he ought to use these to his lord's advantage as best he knows how and is able.

c.12 And if you wish to send oxen or cows or aged cattle or any such beasts away from the fields and into the woods let your men find out where rain water is standing within hollow trees, or boughs of cut down wood or in any other part of bole or trunk or tree and make the beasts take a long drink of this water three or four times on the first day there when they begin to eat of the woodland herbage. And that will save them from dying of liver fluke.

c.13 And you ought to have in every place where there is a dairy some person in charge, be it a man or a woman. And if it were a man he ought to do the same things a dairymaid would do. And, because of the benefits which he has from milk he ought to take one quarter of corn every sixteen weeks where other servants have one quarter for every twelve weeks.

And the dairymaid ought to winnow all the corn, and half of her pay shall be for paying the woman who will help her.

c.14 And they ought to winnow four quarters of wheat and of rye for one penny and six quarters of barley, peas, and beans for one penny, and eight quarters of oats for one penny. And always and with every kind of corn she ought to winnow five quarters stricken of every four heaped.

c.15 And so one ought to thresh a quarter of wheat and rye for two pence, a quarter of barley, beans, and peas for 1½ pence, and one quarter of oats for one penny. And always he ought to count five quarters stricken for every four heaped.

c.16 And the dairymaid ought to look after all the small stock which are kept on the manor such as sucking pigs, peacocks and their issue, geese and their issue, capons, cocks, and hens and their issue in chickens and eggs.

c.17 And be it known that the sow ought to bear pigs twice a year and at each farrowing she ought to bear at least seven piglets. And every goose ought to produce five goslings in the year and every hen one hundred and fifteen eggs and seven chickens. Of these, three ought to be made capons and if there are too many female birds they ought to be exchanged for male birds while they are still young so that each hen is reckoned to yield four hens and three capons a year. And for every five geese you ought to keep one gander and for every five hens one cock. And every cow ought to bear one calf in the year and every ewe one lamb.

c.18 And if there be a cow or ewe which did not bear that year, an inquiry ought to be made through whose fault this was, whether the fault lay with the bailiff, the reeve, or the keeper, whether it happened through bad supervision, through lack of food or neglect in mating or whether the reeve could have changed the cow or the ewe for another one in time but did not. And if the officers are found guilty of any of this then they ought to be charged with the entire issue or its value.

And also, if any beast died in any way through their fault they ought to answer for the live beast or its value.

c.19 If there is a manor in which there is no dairy then it is always advisable to have a woman there for much less money than a man would take, to take care of the small stock and of all that is kept on the manor and to answer for all the issues there just as the dairymaid would do, that is for sows and their piglets, for peacocks and their chicks, and if there are some, for geese and their goslings and for capons, cocks, hens and their chickens and eggs. And she ought to be responsible for half of the winnowing of the corn just as the dairymaid would be.

c.20 And if you wish to farm out your stock you ought to take 4 shillings a year, clear, for the milk yield of each cow, and this will pay for the tithe, and the cow and the calf will remain yours. And the sow will yield 6 shillings and six pence a year, clear; this will pay the tithe and the sow will remain yours. And the ewe will yield 6d. for milk in the year; this will pay for the tithe of the milk, and the lamb and the sheep will remain yours. Each goose ought to answer for 9d. a year clear, and this will pay for the tithe and will save the goose for you. And each hen 10d. and save the hen for you (after paying for the tithe).

c.21 You ought to know that a mare carries her foal from the hour of conception until the birth 49 weeks. And a cow carries her calf from the hour of conception until the birth 40 weeks. And the ewe carries her lamb from the hour of conception until birth for 21 weeks, and the sow carries her piglets from the hour of conception until the birth for 16 weeks. And a sow may farrow five times in two years if she is well looked after. And a hen will sit easily three times in the year, once between Michaelmas and Martinmas and twice between Easter and Michaelmas. And a goose may well sit twice a year if she is well looked after.

c.22 Ten quarter of apples and pears ought to yield easily one tun of cyder; and one quarter of nuts ought to yield four gallons of oil. And seven quarter of oats ought to answer three quarter, stricken measure, of flour.

c.23 And you may well keep a lamb during all the time when it is suckled, on three gallons of milk, of his mother's milk.

c.24 And each cow ought to yield ten pence in the season—from the day of Michaelmas until the first day of May—one cow more another less. And it must be understood that cows do not all yield the same and that some give more and others less milk and some are in milk for a shorter period than others, and dry up sooner, nor yield heifers as much milk at the first calving as at the next, but, taking one with another, this is as much as they ought to yield by right. And from the first day of May until the day of Michaelmas inclusive, which is one hundred and fifty-two days, the yield of the milk of one cow ought to be worth one farthing a day, three shilling and two pence for this season. And the yield of each cow ought to be on this reckoning four shilling a year, for her milk alone and apart from the calf.

*　　*　　*

c.34 And you ought to know that heifers do not give as much milk in their first year of bearing as they do later when they are mature cows and therefore one ought not to expect as high a yield from them as from cows. But you ought to see how many heifers you have among the cows and keep the record of their milk separate according to whether they have calved earlier or later in the season; because heifers do not give milk except after they have calved and wean their young, from then until Michaelmas, and cows answer for the whole year from one Michaelmas to the next.

c.35 One does not render account on the roll for bees or their issue, or swans or peacocks or for their issue, or for goats or their issue because many people do not have or raise any of these, and do not enter on the account donkeys which carry corn or their issue nor wild ducks or domestic ducks in the yard or their issue or any wild beast or wild bird.

c.36 Each hive of bees ought to answer for two swarms a year as their issue, one with another, because some give nothing while some give three or four in the year. In some places one feeds them all the winter and in some places one does not give them anything to eat, that is to say to the old ones which have remained in the hive one year or two. But the young ones which have been hatched during the summer do not know so well how to find food in winter nor had they the time to save like the old ones who have worked throughout the year and therefore it is advisable to take more care with the young than with the old. And you may well support eight swarms all the winter with one gallon of honey and each swarm ought to yield one gallon of honey and wax per year.

And it is more profitable to leave them to work undisturbed for two or three years than to take away the wax and honey which they made each year; that way the hives and the bees will yield more in issue, wax, and honey.

*　　*　　*

REVIEW QUESTIONS

1. What can we learn from this document about the relationships between farm animals and people?
2. What does this document reveal about a gender division of labor in the countryside?
3. What can we conclude about the social function of bees and their products?
4. How far have the rules of the marketplace and knowledge of numbers penetrated farming life?

Medieval Commercial Contracts and Reports

Urban society and trade required reliable contracts. These documents, from Genoa, illustrate two basic types of contracts. The famous commenda and societas contracts were partnerships in which the parties contributed varying amounts of capital and labor to a joint enterprise and divided the profits accordingly. The letter from an Italian merchant in France to his colleagues back in Siena reveals the work and worries of a merchant.

From *Medieval Trade in the Mediterranean World*, by Robert S. Lopez and Irving W. Raymond (New York: Columbia University Press, 1955), pp. 179, 181, 190–93, 388–92.

*　　*　　*

The Genoese Commenda and Societas

Genoa, September 29, 1163

Witnesses: Simone Bucuccio, Ogerio Peloso, Ribaldo di Sauro, and Genoardo Tasca. Stabile and Ansaldo Garraton have formed a *societas* in which, as they mutually declared, Stabile contributed £88 Genoese and Ansaldo £44. Ansaldo carries this *societas*, in order to put it to work, to Tunis or to wherever goes the ship in which he shall go—namely, [the ship] of Baldizzone Grasso and Girardo. On his return he will place the proceeds in the power of Stabile or of his messenger for [the purpose of] division. After deducting the capital, they shall divide the profits in half. Done in the chapter house, September 29, 1163, eleventh indiction.

In addition, Stabile gave his permission to send that money to Genoa by whatever ship seems most convenient to him to Ansaldo.

*　　*　　*

Genoa, October 7, 1163

Witnesses: Bernizone Serra, Raimondo, Crispino and Pietro Vinattiere. I, Ingo Bedello, declare publicly that I am carrying £41 s.6 Genoese of goods belonging to Guglielmotto Ciriolo invested in silk and paper to Tunis, and from there to Genoa where I shall place the proceeds in the power of Guglielmotto or of his messenger. And he is not under obligation to contribute toward expenses in regard to them except in furnishing the original money. Ingo on his return will place the proceeds in the power of Guglielmotto or of his messenger and, after deducting the capital, he is to have one fourth of the profit. And Gugliel motto himself reserved as his right that there will be no expense for him in it. Done in the chapter house, October 7, 1163, eleventh indiction.

*　　*　　*

Barcelona, August 9, 1252

Be it known to all that I, Arnau Fabriz, am carrying in *comanda* from you, Bernat Fuentes, though you are absent, and from your partners in this present voyage which I am making in the ship of Ferrer Descoll and partners to Overseas Territory or wherever the said ship shall make port in this present voyage for the purpose of commerce, "£140 s.4 d.5 Barcelonese invested in five pieces of cloth of Saint-Quentin and in six Saracens. And I promise you to sell all of this well and faithfully there, and to invest in good faith the proceeds obtained from it in useful merchandise just as I see and understand best. And after this voyage is made I promise to return into your possession and into that of your partners said merchandise, that is, the capital and the profit, just as God shall have granted to preserve them, so acting, however, that after deducting your said capital for you I am to have one fourth of all the profit that God shall have granted in this *comanda* of yours. But you are to have the three remaining parts of the said profit in addition to your said capital, your *comanda* itself, however, going and being held there and returning anywhere at your risk and fortune. This was done on the fifth day before the Ides of August, in the year of the Lord, 1252.

*   *   *

Intermediate Forms of Partnership

Marseilles, May 8, 1248

The same day and place. Bonenfant, son of the late Jacob, and Bonseigneur, son of Astruc, and Bonafous, son of the late Chaim, wishing to go on a voyage to Valencia in the vessel of Bertram Belpel, which is named "Leopard," have formed a *societas* among themselves in the manner written below, to wit, that the profits of all *comandae* made by the three of them or by one of them, no matter how many the *comandae* are, are to be common to them in equal shares in the aforesaid voyage; and all investments of the said *comandae* made by them or by one of them, and the investments of those amounts of money which any one of them shall carry in the aforesaid voyage, are to be common to them: with this reservation, that whoever of them shall have extra money of his own in the said *companhia* is to receive that extra share of the profits, according as it is coming to him, by the solidus and by the pound. And all the aforesaid men have promised, by stipulation, each of them to the others, to be faithful and law-abiding one to the other, and to tell each other the truth, and to keep faith throughout the voyage mentioned above, pledging to each other, etc., waiving, etc. And for greater security they all swore on the Mosaic Law, touched by them physically with the hand, to undertake and to fulfill all the aforesaid. Witnesses: R. Boneti, Jehan Gauselin, G. Peire Salvi.

*   *   *

Genoa, January 19, 1308

In the name of the Lord, amen. Percivalle Grillo, son of Andreolo; Daniele Grillo; Meliano Grillo; Benedetto Contardo and Nicola Contardo, brothers, sons of the late Luchetto Contardo; Manuele Bonifacio; Antonino Grillo, son of Andreolo, acknowledge to each other that they have formed and made a *societas* for the purpose of maintaining a bank in the city of Genoa and of engaging in commerce and business in Genoa and throughout other and different parts of the world, according to what shall seem proper and shall be the pleasure of the partners themselves, to continue, God willing, for the next two succeeding years. This *societas* they acknowledge to be of £9,450 Genoese, in which sum they acknowledge to each other that each of them has or has deposited as below, viz.: said Percivalle, £3,500; said Daniele, £2,000; said Meliano, £1,000; the aforesaid Benedetto Contardo and Nicola, his brother, £2,000; said Manuele Bonifacio, £450; and said Antonio Grillo, £500. This capital they acknowledge to be in the hands of said Percivalle in money, in credits, in exchange to be received in France, and in a vein of iron in Elba. And the aforesaid partners have waived the exception and legal right by which they could speak against or oppose the aforesaid. And said Percivalle is to use this money in business and commerce in Genoa in said bank which he maintains, in the buying and selling of wares, and in exchange both in France and throughout other and different parts of the world, by sea and by land, personally and through his factors and messengers, according as God may dispose better for him, up to the time limit mentioned above, at the risk and fortune of the partners. And he has promised said partners of his to act in good faith and efficiently for the increase and preservation of said *societas*. And the aforesaid partners promised each other to guard and to preserve the goods and wares and money which may come into the hands of any one of them from the aforesaid *societas*, and not to defraud one another in anything. The profit which God may grant in the aforesaid *societas* shall be allocated to each of them pro rata to his capital;

and if any accident befall said *societas* or the goods of said *societas*—may God be our help—it shall be allocated similarly to each of them pro rata to his capital. And they have promised each other in good faith to come to the accounting of the capital and profit of said *societas* at the end of the time limit; and each of them is to deduct his capital and to divide among them the profit pro rata to the capital of each one. The aforesaid *societas* and each and all of the above conditions the aforesaid partners promised each other, etc. Firm, etc., and for it, etc. And said Benedetto acknowledges that he is more than twenty-four years old, and said Nicola acknowledges that he is more than nineteen years old, and said Antonio acknowledges that he is more than nineteen years old, and said Antonio acknowledges that he is more than nineteen years old. And they swore by the sacred Gospels of God, putting their hands on the Scriptures, to undertake and to observe everything as above stated and not to do anything or to act contrary in any way by reason of their being minors or by any other cause. And they made the aforesaid agreement with the counsel of the witnesses written below, whom for this purpose they call their relatives, neighbors, and counselors. Done in Genoa in the Church of Santa Maria delle Vigne, in the year of the Nativity of the Lord 1308, fifth indiction, January 19, about nones. Witnesses: Arnaldo of Spigno, dealer in poultry; Manfredo; and Pagano of Moneglia, dealer in poultry.

*   *   *

Reports from the Fairs of Champagne

Siena, July 5, 1260

In the name of the Lord, amen. Reply to the letters from France brought by the first messenger of the May fair of Provins, year 1260.

Dear Giacomo di Guido Cacciaconti:

Giacomo and Giovannidi Gregorio, Vincente di Aldobrandino Vincenti and the other partners send you greetings. And we are informing you that we have safely received the letters which you sent us by the messenger of the gild merchant from the May fair of Provins of this year. And through these letters we perfectly understand what were your instructions, and we shall get busy on what will be our business here. Therefore we beg you to be on the alert and to make it your concern to work and get busy on what you have to do. And especially we beg you to be careful in investing and in lending what you have in your hands and what you will have in the future to good and reliable payers, so that we can have it back at any time we may need it or we may want it back. And to do this we ask from God our Lord mercy, that He grant you the grace to do it so that honor may come to you personally and that the partnership may come out in good standing. Amen.

You ought to know, Giacomo, that we shall write accurately all that we have to write, and especially what you will instruct us by your letters, such as your receipts, your payments, and the loans you will make. Just as you will instruct us by your letters at each fair, so at each fair shall we write and enter it in our book. The receipts we shall post to your receipts, the payments we shall post to your payments, and the loans we shall write to the loans, just as we have always done up to the present time. Therefore, any money which you collect or which comes into your hands, when you have instructed us once by letter about it, do not repeat it any more; for as soon as you have instructed us about it, we post it at once—whatever you tell us are receipts among the receipts, and we post the payments to the payments, and the loans to the loans. And we do so for every letter. Therefore, if you should instruct us through more than one letter, you see that it would not be a good thing to do; for just as many times as you instruct us, so many times we shall post it in the book in our customary way. Therefore do take care. And we mention this in connection with the £3 Provisine, which Testa Tebaldi takes and Tederigo Lei gives. For you received out of them 34 soldi less 4 deniers, and you have sent me instructions about this through several letters. For if we had not remembered that we had posted them once to your receipts, we certainly would have posted them a second time. Therefore take care—do not instruct us about it more than once.

And just as we instructed you in the other letter, so we repeat in this that you must not be astonished that we have sold and are selling Provisines; for you ought to know, Giacomo, that we are under great expense and extremely busy because of the war we are having against Florence. And you ought to know that we have to have money to spend and to make war; on account of this, we see that we cannot raise money from any source more advantageous for us than by selling Provisines. And should you say that we ought to obtain a loan here, it would do us no good: for you ought to know that money costs from 5 to 6 deniers a pound from one merchant to another, and it costs those who are not merchants from 10 to 12 deniers a pound in *corsa,* although it is in the same state. Now you see what the conditions of lending are here. Therefore do not feel too badly that we are selling Provisines, since we had rather be in debt in France than be in debt here or sell sterling. For it is worth far more to us so long as we can get Provisines at the price they cost you today than it would be to sell the sterling or to borrow here; because we draw greater interest in England than we would in France, and in order to raise a loan here today we should have to pay a price greater than would be any profit that we could get in France. Therefore be satisfied with what we are doing, and do not be astonished at all about it. And you ought to know, Giacomo, that if in the country of France one could profit more than one can profit there today, we should do well, since you would have a great many Provisines, so that you would well get whatever arrangement you may wish, and we would certainly get our share of whatever profit might be made in that land; and about that be of good cheer.

And we understand from you through your letter that you have gone, both without and with Tolomeo Pelacane, to see the dean of Saint Etienne of Troyes about the business of Lyons-on-the-Rhone, and that you spoke and argued a good deal with the procurator of that archbishop of Lyons-on-the-Rhone, and you could not persuade him to come to any conclusion or agreement that was good for us; nor could you persuade him unless we sent you a letter from the papal Curia against him. In this matter you ought to know that we have had and are still having a great deal of trouble, because of the war and making expeditions and cavalry raids, so that we have not been able to devote our attention to obtaining the letter. Therefore you ought to know that as soon as we have a breathing spell to devote our attention to it we shall do so, and we shall see to it that you get the said letter against them.

And we also understand from you through that letter of yours that you and Tolomeo Pelacane had been to see Bonico Maniardi and had told him that you wanted to go to Lyons to learn if you could get any agreement at all from that person, and the said Bonico answered that you could go all right but that he would not pay one bit of the expenses unless Mino Pieri instructed him to do so; for he told you that Mino had not sent a word of instruction about the matter. This astonishes us, for we were in agreement about it here with Mino Pieri, and Mino told us he would instruct him to pay us whatever was his share of our expenses. And in this letter we cannot tell you anything further about it, because Mino Pieri is with the army at Montepulciano while we are writing this letter. Through other letters we shall get in touch with him; and if he has not instructed about it, we certainly shall tell him to instruct him, and we shall communicate to you what he will answer us.

And we also understand from you through a note of yours that we are expected to beg Orlando Bonsignore that he should instruct his partners over there that whenever you wish to borrow from his partners they should consent to it, for that would be a great boon to us. In this regard we tell you that the said Orlando Bonsignore was not in Siena when this letter was written, but he was with the army at Montepulciano. Therefore, when he returns, we shall get in touch with him and remind him about it; and we definitely believe that he will do what we wish about it.

You ought to know, Giacomo, that I, Vincente, will give 60 to Madonna Pacina, just as you have instructed me. And Niccolò, son of Messer Nicola, wants us to beg you for his love that if you have not sold for him his Kirkoswald *biffa*, you get it sold. He would have instructed you about this in a letter if he had not been with the army at Montepulciano; for he went there before the letters were written, and he begged me, Vincente, that I should write you about it in this letter.

And also we let you know that we have sold £106 Provisine to Giacomo Ubertini, changer, to be paid at the fair of Saint John, year 1260; and we sold them at the rate of s.33 a dozen, and we have been paid. Therefore you shall pay them at his order to Rimbotto Buonaiuti at the latter's pleasure; and when you make the payment to him, have a record made of it in the book of the Officials of the Merchants, as is customary to do.

And also we have sold £24 Provisine to Accorso Guarguaglia and his partnership, to be paid at the said fair of Saint John, at the rate of 31 a dozen, and we have been paid. Therefore you shall pay them to Gregorio Rigoli at his pleasure at that fair; and when you pay them, have a record made of it in the book of the Officials of the Merchants, as is customary to do.

On the other hand, we want to let you know about the developments in Tuscany. For you ought to know, Giacomo, that we are today under great expense and extremely busy because of the war we are having against Florence. And you ought to know that it will take plenty out of our pocket; but we shall lick Florence so badly that we shall never

have to guard ourselves from her any more, if God protects from evil the lord King Manfred, to whom may God grant long life, amen. . . .

You ought to know, Giacomo, that after this letter was written up to this point we had news that Montepulciano had come to terms and had pledged loyalty to the lord king—King Manfred—and to Siena. And she will make expeditions and cavalry raids against whomever we wish, will hold our friends as friends, and our enemies as enemies. And when that was done, lord Count Giordano left Montepulciano with all the expedition he had and went against Arezzo; and we believe that he will have the town at his will. Well, things up to now have been like this; for the future they will be the same and better, if it please God.

Dispatched Monday, the fifth day of July.

To Giacomo di Guido Cacciaconti, and let it not be given to anyone else.

*   *   *

REVIEW QUESTIONS

1. What is a contract?
2. What were the levels of risks and rewards in the various styles of medieval partnerships?
3. Which ones required the most trust, and which did the law help to enforce?
4. How did merchants make money?

ANNA COMNENA

FROM *The Alexiad*

Anna Comnena (1083–after 1148), an imperial princess, wrote an admiring biography of her father, The Alexiad. *In this selection, she is describing how Emperor Alexius engaged his mother, Anna Dalassena, in the governance of the Byzantine Empire, and there is also a digression on Anna Dalassena's own qualities. Byzantine royal families allowed women a wide scope for participating in government. Alexius spent much of his reign defending the empire from Turkish advances in Asia Minor, and his request for help from the West was one of the motivations for the First Crusade, the centerpiece of Anna's history.*

From *The Alexiad of Anna Comnena*, edited by E. R. A. Sewter (New York: Penguin Books, 1969), pp. 116–23.

*   *   *

Gradually and surreptitiously he involved her more and more in state affairs; on occasions he even declared openly that without her brains and good judgement the Empire would not survive. By these means he bound her more closely to himself, but prevented her from attaining her own goal and frustrated it. She had in mind the last stage of life and dreamed of monasteries in which she would drag out her remaining years in the contemplation of wisdom. Such was her intention, the constant aim of her prayers. Despite this longing in her heart, despite the total preoccupation with a higher life, she also loved her son to a quite exceptional degree and wished somehow to bear with him the storms that buffeted the Empire (if I may apply seafaring metaphor to the manifold troubles and tumults to which it was exposed). She desired to guide the ship of state on the best possible course, in fair weather or in tempest (when waves crashed on to it from all sides), especially since the young man had only just taken his seat in the stern and put his hand to the tiller, with no previous experience of storms, winds and waves of such violence. She was constrained, therefore, by a mother's affection for her son, and governed with him, sometimes even grasping the reins (to change the metaphor) and alone driving the chariot of power—and without accident or error. The truth is that Anna Dalassena was in any case endowed with a fine intellect and possessed besides a really first-class aptitude for governing. On the other hand, she was distracted from it by her love for God. When in the month of August (in the same indiction) Robert's crossing to Epirus compelled Alexius to leave the capital, he brought

to light and put into operation his cherished plan: the whole executive power was entrusted to his mother alone and the decision was confirmed publicly in a chrysobull. As it is the historian's duty not merely to summarize the deeds and decrees of good men, but as far as he can to give some details of the former and transmit the latter in full, I myself will set out the terms of this document, omitting only the subtle refinements of the scribe. It ran thus: "When danger is foreseen or some other dreadful occurrence is expected, there is no safeguard stronger than a mother who is understanding and loves her son, for if she gives counsel, her advice will be reliable; if she offers prayers, they will confer strength and certain protection. Such at any rate has been the experience of myself, your emperor, in the case of my own revered mother, who has taught and guided and sustained me throughout, from my earliest years. She had a place in aristocratic society, but her first concern was for her son and his faith in her was preserved intact. It was well known that one soul animated us, physically separated though we were, and by the grace of Christ that happy state has persisted to this day. Never were those cold words, 'mine' and 'yours,' uttered between us, and what was even more important, the prayers she poured out during all that time reached the ears of the Lord and have raised me now to the imperial throne. After I took in my hand the imperial sceptre, she found it intolerable that she was not bearing an equal share in my labours, to the interests both of your emperor and of the whole people. But now I am preparing with God's help to do battle with Rome's enemies; with much forethought an army is being recruited and thoroughly equipped; not the least of my cares, however, has been the provision of an efficient organization in financial and civil affairs. Fortunately, an impregnable bulwark for good government has been found—in the appointment of my revered mother, of all women most honoured, as controller of the entire administration. I, your emperor, therefore decree explicitly in this present chrysobull the following: because of her vast experience of secular affairs (despite the very low value she sets upon such matters), whatever she decrees in writing (whether the case be referred to her by the logothete, or by his subordinate officers, or by any other person who prepares memoranda or requests or judgements concerning remissions of public debts) shall have permanent validity as if I myself, your Serene Emperor, had issued them or after dictating them had had them committed to writing. Whatever decisions or orders are made by her, written or unwritten, reasonable or unreasonable, provided that they bear her seal (the Transfiguration and the Assumption), shall be regarded as coming from myself, by the fact that they carry the 'In the month . . .' of the current logothete. Moreover, with regard to promotions and successions to the tribunals and fiscs, and in the matter of honours, offices and donations of immovable property, my saintly mother shall have full power to take whatever action shall seem good to her. Further, if any persons are promoted to the tribunals or succeed to the fiscs and are honoured with the highest or medium or lowest dignities, they shall thereafter retain these positions on a permanent basis. Again, increases of salary, additional gifts, reductions of tax, economies and diminution of payments shall be settled by her without question. In brief, nothing shall be reckoned invalid which she commands either in writing or by word of mouth, for her words and her decisions shall be reckoned as my own and none of them shall be annulled. In years to come they shall have the force of law permanently. Neither now nor in the future shall my mother be subjected to inquiry or undergo any examination whatsoever at the hands of anybody, whoever he may be. The same provision shall also hold good for her ministers and the chancellor of the time, whether their actions seem to be reasonable or ridiculous. It shall be absolutely impossible in the future to demand account of any action taken by them under the terms of this present chrysobull."

The reader may be surprised by the honour conferred on his mother by the emperor in this matter, since he yielded her precedence in everything, relinquishing the reins of government, as it were, and running alongside as she drove the imperial chariot; only in the title of emperor did he share with her the privileges of his rank. And this despite the fact that he had already passed his boyhood years and was of an age which in the case of men like him is particularly susceptible to the lust for power. Wars against the barbarians, with all their attendant trials and tribulations he was prepared to face himself, but the entire administration of affairs, the choice of civil magistrates, the accounts of the imperial revenues and expenditure he left to his mother. At this point the reader may well censure him for transferring the government of the Empire to the gynacconitis, but had he known this woman's spirit, her surpassing virtue, intelligence and energy, his reproaches would soon have turned to admiration. For my grandmother had an exceptional grasp of public affairs, with a genius for organization and government; she was capable, in fact, of managing not only the Roman Empire, but every other empire under the sun as well. She had vast experience and a wide understanding of the motives, ultimate consequences, interrelations good and bad of various courses of action, penetrating quickly to the right solution, adroitly and safely carrying it out. Her intellectual powers, moreover, were paralleled by her command of language. She was indeed a most persuasive orator, without being verbose or long-winded. Nor did the inspiration of the argument readily desert her, for if she began on a felicitous note, she was also most successful in ending her speeches with just the right words. She was already a woman of mature years when she was called upon to exercise imperial authority, at a time of life when one's mental powers are at their best, when one's judgement is fully developed and knowledge of affairs is widest—all qualities that lend force to good administration and government. It is natural that persons of this age should not merely speak with greater wisdom than the young (as the tragic playwright says), but also act in a more expedient way. In the past, when Anna Dalassena was still looked upon as a younger woman, she had impressed everyone as "having an old head on young shoulders"; to the observant her face alone revealed Anna's inherent virtue and gravity. But, as I was saying, once he had seized power my father reserved for himself the struggles and hard labour of war, while she became so to speak an onlooker, but he made her sovereign and like a slave said and did whatever she commanded. He loved her exceedingly and depended on her for advice (such was his affection for her). His right hand he devoted to her service; his ears listened for her bidding. In all things he was entirely subservient, in fact, to her wishes. I can sum up the whole situation thus: he was in theory the emperor, but she had real power. She was the legislator, the complete organizer and governor, while he confirmed her arrangements, written and unwritten, the former by his signature, the latter by his spoken approval. One might say that he was indeed the instrument of her power—he was not emperor, for all the decisions and ordinances of his mother satisfied him, not merely as an obedient son, but as an attentive listener to her instruction in the art of ruling. He was convinced that she had attained perfection in everything and easily excelled all men of that generation in prudence and understanding of affairs.

Such were the events that marked the beginning of the reign. One could hardly at that stage call Alexius emperor once he had entrusted to her the supreme authority. Another person might yield here to the claims of panegyric and extol the native land of this remarkable woman; he might trace her descent from the Adriani Dalasseni and Charon, while he embarked on the ocean of their achievements. But I am writing history and my fitting task is not to describe her through the family and kinsmen, but by reference to her character, her virtue, and the events which form the proper

subject of history. To return once more to my grandmother, I must add this: not only was she a very great credit to her own sex, but to men as well; indeed, she contributed to the glory of the whole human race. The women's quarters in the palace had been the scene of utter depravity ever since the infamous Constantine Monomachos had ascended the throne and right up to the time when my father became emperor had been noted for foolish love intrigues, but Anna effected a reformation; a commendable decorum was restored and the palace now enjoyed a discipline that merited praise. She instituted set times for the singing of sacred hymns, stated hours for breakfast; there was now a special period in which magistrates were chosen. She herself set a firm example to everybody else, with the result that the palace assumed the appearance rather of a monastery under the influence of this really extraordinary woman and her truly saintly character; for in self-control she surpassed the famous women of old, heroines of many a legend, as the sun outshines all stars. As for her compassion for the poor and her generosity to the needy, no words could do justice to them. Her house was a refuge for penniless relatives, but no less for strangers. Priests and monks she honoured in particular: they shared her meals and no one ever saw her at table without some of them as guests. Her outward serenity, true reflection of character, was respected by angels but terrorized even the demons, and pleasure-loving fools, victims of their own passions, found a single glance from her more than they could bear; yet to the chaste she seemed gentle and gay. She knew exactly how to temper reserve and dignity; her own reserve never gave the impression of harshness or cruelty, nor did her tenderness seem too soft or unrestrained—and this, I fancy, is the true definition of propriety: the due proportion of warm humanity and strict moral principle. She was by nature thoughtful and was always evolving new ideas, not, as some folk whispered, to the detriment of the state; on the contrary, they were wholesome schemes which restored to full vigour the already corrupted empire and revived, as far as one could, the ruined fortunes of the people. In spite of her preoccupation with matters of government, she by no means neglected the duties incumbent on a religious woman, for the greater part of the night was spent by her in the chanting of sacred hymns and she wore herself out with continual prayers and vigils. Nevertheless, at dawn or even at second cock-crow, she was applying herself anew to state business, attending to the choice of magistrates and answering the petitions of suppliants with the help of her secretary Gregory Genesius. Now if some orator had decided to make this the subject of a panegyric, he would no doubt have exalted her and praised her to the skies (as is the way of encomiasts) for her deeds and thoughts and superiority to all others; the famous ones of old, both men and women, who were renowned for their virtue would certainly have been thrown into the shade. But such licence is not for the writer of history. Those who know her virtue, therefore, her dignified character, her never-failing sagacity and the loftiness and sublimity of her spirit, must not blame my history, if I have done less than justice to her great qualities.

* * *

REVIEW QUESTIONS

1. What do we learn about the role of women at the highest levels of Byzantine society?
2. How does their position compare to their role in the West?
3. What are Anna Comnena's skills as a historian and writer?

FROM **The Anonymous Mainz Account**

The summoning of the First Crusade by Pope Urban II at Clermont in 1095 resulted in widespread enthusiasm in western Europe for an armed expedition to the Muslim east to recover Jerusalem. Some crusaders passing through the Rhineland engaged in massacres of the Jewish populations, most notably in the city of Mainz. This Jewish account of the massacre, though anonymous, is close to the original events and bears all the marks of an eyewitness to what occurred. The author quotes and paraphrases extensively from Hebrew Scripture, and these passages remain in quotation marks. This narrative evokes the horrors in the spring of 1096 for the old Jewish communities in the Rhineland and provides a foretaste of similar massacres of Muslims and Jews that occurred at the conquest of Jerusalem in 1099.

From *European Jewry and the First Crusade,* by Robert Chazan (Berkeley: University of California Press, 1987), pp. 225–27, 232–42. Bracketed insertions are Chazan's, insertions in braces are editorial.

Spring, 1096

I shall begin the account of the former persecution. May the Lord protect us and all Israel from persecution.

It came to pass in the year one thousand twenty-eight after the destruction of the Temple that this evil befell Israel. There first arose the princes and nobles and common folk in France, who took counsel and set plans to ascend and "to rise up like eagles" and to do battle and "to clear a way" for journeying to Jerusalem, the Holy City, and for reaching the sepulcher of the Crucified, "a trampled corpse" "who cannot profit and cannot save for he is worthless." They said to one another: "Behold we travel to a distant land to do battle with the kings of that land. 'We take our souls in our hands' in order to kill and to subjugate all those kingdoms that do not believe in the Crucified. How much more so [should we kill and subjugate] the Jews, who killed and crucified him." They taunted us from every direction. They took counsel, ordering that either we turn to their abominable faith or they would destroy us "from infant to suckling." They—both princes and common folk—placed an evil sign upon their garments, a cross, and helmets upon their heads.

When the [Jewish] communities in France heard, they were seized by consternation, fear, and trembling . . . They wrote letters and sent emissaries to all the [Jewish] communities along the Rhine River, [asking that they] fast and deprive themselves and seek mercy from [God "who] dwells on high," so that he deliver them [the Jews] from their [the crusaders'] hands. When the letters reached the saintly ones who were in that land, they—those men of God, "the pillars of the universe," who were in Mainz—wrote in reply to France. Thus was it written in them [their letters]: "All the [Jewish] communities have decreed a fast. We have done our part. May God save us and save you from 'all distress and hardship.' We are greatly fearful for you. We, however, have less reason to fear [for ourselves], for we have heard not even a rumor [of such developments]." Indeed we did not hear that a decree had been issued and that "a sword was to afflict us mortally."

When the crusaders began to reach this land, they sought funds with which to purchase bread. We gave them, considering ourselves to be fulfilling the verse: "Serve the king of Babylon, and live." All this, however, was of no avail, for our sins brought it about that the burghers in every city to which the crusaders came were hostile to us, for their [the burghers'] hands were also with them [the crusaders] to destroy vine and stock all along the way to Jerusalem.

It came to pass that, when the crusaders came, battalion after battalion, like the army of Sennacherib, some of the princes in the empire said: "Why do we sit thus? Let us also go with them. For every man who sets forth on this journey and undertakes to ascend to the impure sepulcher dedicated to the Crucified will be assured paradise." Then the crusaders along with them [the princes] gathered from all the provinces until they became as numerous "as the sands of the sea," including both princes and common folk. They circulated a report . . . "Anyone who kills a single Jew will have all his sins absolved." Indeed there was a certain nobleman, Ditmar by name, who announced that he would not depart from this empire until he would kill one Jew—then he would depart. Now when the holy community in Mainz heard this, they decreed a fast. "They cried out mightily to the Lord" and they passed night and day in fasting. Likewise they recited dirges both morning and evening, both small and great. Nonetheless our God "did not turn away from his awesome wrath" against us. For the crusaders with their insignia came, with their standards before our houses. When they saw one of us, they ran after him and pierced him with a spear, to the point that we were afraid even to cross our thresholds.

It came to pass on the eighth of the month of Iyyar {May 3, 1096}, on the Sabbath, the measure of justice began to manifest itself against us. The crusaders and burghers arose first against the saintly ones, the pious of the Almighty in Speyer. They took counsel against them, [planning] to seize them together in the synagogue. But it was revealed to them and they arose [early] on the Sabbath morning and prayed rapidly and left the synagogue. When they [the crusaders and burghers] saw that their plan for seizing them together was foiled, they rose against them [the Jews] and killed eleven of them. From there the decree began to fulfill that which is said: "Begin at my sanctuary." When Bishop John heard, he came with a large force and helped the [Jewish] community wholeheartedly and brought them indoors and saved them from their [the crusaders' and burghers'] hands. He seized some of the burghers and "cut off their hands." He was a pious one among the nations. Indeed God brought about well-being and salvation through him. R. Moses ben Yekutiel the *parnas*, {a leader}, "stood on the breach" and extended himself on their behalf. Through him all those forcibly converted who remained "here and there" in the empire of Henry returned [to Judaism]. Through the emperor, Bishop John removed the remnant of the community of Speyer to his fortified towns, and the Lord turned to them, for the sake of his great Name. The bishop hid them until the enemies of the Lord passed. They [the Jews] remained there, fasting and weeping and mourning. "They despaired deeply," for every day the crusaders and the gentiles and Emicho—may his bones be ground up—and the common folk gathered against them, to seize them and to destroy them. Through R. Moses the *parnas*, Bishop John saved them, for the Lord inclined his heart to save them without bribery. This was from the Lord, in order to give us there "a remnant and a residue" through him.

*   *   *

It came to pass that, when the saintly ones, the pious of the Almighty, the holy community in Mainz, heard that some of the community of Speyer had been killed and the community of Worms [had been attacked] twice, then their spirit collapsed and "their hearts melted and turned to water." They cried out to the Lord and said: " 'Ah Lord God of Israel! Are you wiping out the remnant of Israel?' 'Where are all your wondrous deeds about which our ancestors told us, saying: "Truly the Lord brought you up from Egypt." But now you have abandoned us, delivering us into the hands of the gentiles for destruction.' " Then all the leaders of Israel gathered from the community and came to the archbishop and his ministers and servants and said to them: "What are we to do with regard to the report which we have heard concerning our brethren in Speyer and Worms who have been killed?" They said to them: "Heed our advice and bring all your moneys into our treasury and into the treasury of the archbishop. Then you and your wives and your children and all your retinue bring into the courtyard of the archbishop. Thus will you

be able to be saved from the crusaders." They contrived and gave this counsel in order to surrender us and to gather us up and to seize us "like fish enmeshed in a fatal net." In addition, the archbishop gathered his ministers and servants—exalted ministers, nobles and grandees—in order to assist us and to save us from the crusaders. For at the outset it was his desire to save us, but ultimately he failed.

It came to pass on a certain day that a gentile woman came and brought with her a goose that she had raised since it was a gosling. This goose went everywhere that the gentile woman went. She said to all passersby: "Behold this goose understands that I intend to go on the crusade and wishes to go with me." Then the crusaders and burghers gathered against us, saying to us: "Where is your source of trust? How will you be saved? Behold the wonders that the Crucified does for us!" Then all of them came with swords and spears to destroy us. Some of the burghers came and would not allow them [to do so]. At that time they stood . . . and killed along the Rhine River, until they killed one of the crusaders. Then they said: "All these things the Jews have caused." Then they almost gathered [against us]. When the saintly ones saw all these things, their hearts melted. They [the Christians] spoke harshly with them, [threatening] to assault and attack us. When they [the Jews] heard their words, they said—from great to small: "If only we might die by the hand of the Lord, rather than die at the hands of the enemies of the Lord. For he is a merciful God, the only king in his universe."

They left their houses empty and came to the synagogue only on the sabbath, that last sabbath prior to our disaster, when "a few" entered to pray. R. Judah ben R. Isaac entered there to pray on that Sabbath. They wept copiously, to the point of exhaustion, for they saw that this was the decree of the King of kings. There was a venerable scholar, R. Baruch ben R. Isaac, and he said to us: "Know that a decree has truly and surely been enacted against us, and we will not be able to be saved. For tonight we—I and my son-in-law Judah—heard the souls praying here loudly, [with a sound] like weeping. When we heard the sound, we thought that perhaps they [those praying] came from the courtyard of the archbishop and that some of the community had returned to pray in the synagogue at midnight out of pain and anguish. We ran to the door of the synagogue, but it was closed. We heard the sound, but we comprehended nothing. We returned home shaken, for our house was close to the synagogue." When we heard these words, we fell on our faces and said: " 'Ah Lord God! Are you wiping out the remnant of Israel?' " They went and recounted these incidents to their brethren in the courtyard of the burgrave and in the courtyard of the archbishop. They likewise wept copiously.

It came to pass on the new moon of Sivan that the wicked Emicho—may his bones be ground up on iron millstones—came with a large army outside the city, with crusaders and common folk. For he also said: "It is my desire to go on the crusade." He was our chief persecutor. He had no mercy on the elderly, on young men and young women, on infants and sucklings, nor on the ill. He made the people of the Lord "like dust to be trampled." "Their young men he put to the sword and their pregnant women he ripped open." They camped outside the city for two days. Then the heads of the [Jewish] community said: "Let us send him money, along with our letters, so that the [Jewish] communities along the way will honor him. Perhaps the Lord will treat us with his great loving-kindness." For previously they had liberally spent their moneys, giving the archbishop and the burgrave and their ministers and their servants and the burghers approximately four hundred marks, so that they might aid them. It availed them nothing. We were unlike Sodom and Gomorrah, for in their case ten [righteous] were sought in order to save them. For us neither twenty nor ten were sought.

*   *   *

It came to pass at midday that the wicked Emicho—may his bones be ground up—he and all his army—came, and the burghers opened up to him the gates. Then the enemies of the Lord said one to another: "Behold the gates have been opened by themselves. All this the Crucified has done for us, so that we might avenge his blood on the Jews." They came with their standards to the archbishop's gate, where the children of the sacred covenant were—an army as numerous "as the sands on the seashore." When the saintly and God-fearing saw the huge multitude, they trusted in and cleaved to their Creator. They donned armor and strapped on weapons—great and small—with R. Kalonymous ben Meshullam at their head.

There was a pious one, one of the great men of the generation, Rabbi Menahem ben Rabbi David the *levi*. He said: "All the congregation, sanctify the revered and awesome Name unreservedly." They all replied: . . . [He said]: "All of you must do as did the sons of our ancestor Jacob when he sought to reveal to them the time of redemption, at which point the Divine Presence left him. [Jacob said]: 'Perhaps I too am sullied as was my grandfather Abraham [from whom proceeded Ishmael] or like my father Isaac [from whom proceeded Esau.'] [His sons said to him: 'Hear O Israel! The Lord is our God; the Lord is one.'] [Do] as did our ancestors when they answered and said, as they received the Torah at this very time on Mount Sinai: 'We shall do and hear.' " They then called out loudly: "Hear O Israel! The Lord is our God, the Lord is one." They all then drew near to the gate to do battle with the crusaders and with the burghers. They did battle one with another around the gate. Our sins brought it about that the enemy overcame them and captured the gate. The men of the archbishop, who had promised to assist, fled immediately, in order to turn them over to the enemy, for they are "splintered reeds." Then the enemy came into the courtyard and found R. Isaac ben R. Moses [and others and struck them] a mortal sword blow. Not so for the fifty-three souls who fled with R. Kalonymous through the chambers of the archbishop, exiting into a long room called . . . and remaining there.

*   *   *

When the children of the sacred covenant saw that the decree had been issued and that the enemy had overcome them, they all cried out—young men and old men, young women and children, menservants and maidservants—and wept for themselves and their lives. They said: "We shall suffer the yoke of awe of the sacred. For the moment the enemy will kill us with the easiest of the four deaths—by the sword. But we shall remain alive; our souls [will repose] in paradise, in the radiance of the great light, forever." They all said acceptingly and willingly: "Ultimately one must not question the ways of the Holy One blessed be he and blessed be his Name, who gave us his Torah and commanded us to put to death and to kill ourselves for the unity of his holy Name. Blessed are we if we do his will and blessed are all those who are killed and slaughtered and who die for the unity of his Name. Not only are they privileged to enter the world to come and sit in the circle of the saintly, 'the pillars of the universe.' What is more, they exchange a world of darkness for a world of light, a world of pain for a world of happiness, a transitory world for a world that is eternal and everlasting."

*   *   *

It came to pass that, when the enemy came to the chambers and broke down the doors and found them convulsing, still writhing in their blood, they took their money and stripped them naked. They struck those remaining and left not "a remnant or a residue." Thus they did in all the chambers where there were children of Israel, [children of] the sacred covenant, with the exception of one chamber which was too strong. The enemy did battle against it till evening. When the saintly ones [in that chamber] saw that the enemy was mightier than they were, the men and the women rose up and slaughtered the children. Subsequently, they slaughtered one another. Some fell on their swords or knives. The saintly women threw rocks through the windows. The enemy in turn struck them with rocks. They [the Jewish women] endured all these rocks, until their flesh and faces became shredded. They cursed and blasphemed the crusaders in the name of the Crucified, the profane and despised, the son of lust: "Upon whom do you rely? 'Upon a trampled corpse!' " Then the crusaders advanced to break down the door.

There was a notable lady, Rachel the daughter of R. Isaac ben R. Asher. She said to her companions: "I have four children. On them as well have no mercy, lest these uncircumcised come and seize them and they remain in their pseudo-faith. With them as well you must sanctify the holy Name." One of her companions came and took the knife. When she saw the knife, she cried loudly and bitterly. She beat her face, crying and saying: " 'Where is your steadfast love, O Lord?' " She took Isaac her small son—indeed he was very lovely—and slaughtered him. She . . . said to her companions: "Wait! Do not slaughter Isaac before Aaron." But the lad Aaron, when he saw that his brother had been slaughtered, cried out: "Mother, Mother, do not slaughter me!" He then went and hid himself under a bureau. She took her two daughters, Bella and Matrona, and sacrificed them to the Lord God of Hosts, who commanded us not to abandon pure awe of him and to remain loyal to him. When the saintly one finished sacrificing her three children before our Creator, she then lifted her voice and called out to her son: "Aaron, Aaron, where are you? I shall not have pity or mercy on you either." She pulled him by the leg from under the bureau, where he had hidden, and sacrificed him before the sublime and exalted God. She then put them under her two sleeves, two on one side and two on the other, near her heart. They convulsed near her, until the crusaders seized the chamber. They found her sitting and mourning them. They said to her: "Show us the money which you have under your sleeves." When they saw the slaughtered children, they smote her and killed her. With regard to them and to her it is said: "Mother and babes were dashed to death together." She died with them, as did the [earlier] saintly one with her seven sons. With regard to her it is said: "The mother of the child is happy." The crusaders killed all those in the chamber and stripped them naked. They were still writhing and convulsing in their blood, as they stripped them. "See, O Lord, and behold, how abject I have become."

Subsequently they threw them from the chambers through the windows naked, heap upon heap and mound upon mound, until they formed a high heap. Many of the children of the sacred covenant, as they were thrown, still had life and would signal with their fingers: "Give us water that we might drink." When the crusaders saw this, they would ask them: "Do you wish to sully yourselves [with the waters of the baptism]?" They would shake their heads and would look at their Father in heaven as a means of saying no and would point with their fingers to the Holy One blessed be he. The crusaders then killed them.

All these things were done by those whom we have designated by name. The rest of the community all the more proclaimed the unity of the sacred Name, and all fell in the hands of the Lord.

Then the crusaders began to exult in the name of the Crucified. They lifted their standards and came to the remnant of the community, to the courtyard of the burgrave. They besieged them as well and did battle against them and seized the entranceway to the courtyard and smote them also.

There was a certain man, named Moses ben Helbo. He called to his sons and said to them: "My sons Simon and Helbo. At this moment hell and paradise are open [before you]. Into which do you wish to enter?" They answered him and said: "Bring us into paradise." They stretched forth their necks. The enemy smote them, the father along with the sons.

There was a Torah scroll there in the chamber. The crusaders came into the chamber, found it, and tore it to shreds. When the saintly and pure daughters of royalty [the Jewish women] saw that the Torah had been torn, they called out loudly to their husbands: "Behold, behold the holy Torah. The enemy is tearing it." Then they all, the men and the women, said together: "Woe for the holy Torah,

'perfect in beauty,' 'the delight of our eyes.' We used to bow before it in the synagogue; we used to kiss it; we used to honor it. How has it now fallen into the hands of the unclean and uncircumcised." When the men heard the words of the saintly women, "they became exceedingly zealous" for the Lord our God and for the holy and beloved Torah. There was there a young man named R. David ben Rabbi Menahem. He said to them: "My brethren, rend your garments over the honor of the Torah." They rent their garments as our teacher commanded. They then found a crusader in a chamber and they all—both men and women—rose up and stoned him. He fell and died. Now when the burghers and crusaders saw that he had died, they did battle against them. They went up on the roof over the place where the children of the covenant were, broke the roof, shot at them with arrows, and pierced them with spears.

*   *   *

I know not how much is missing here. May God save us from this exile. The end of the former persecutions.

REVIEW QUESTIONS

1. Why did the Jews of Speyer escape the worst consequences endured by the Jews of Mainz?
2. What does the story about the goose reveal about crusader mentality, and does it seem credible?
3. How did the Jews respond to this violence?
4. What emerges from this account about the motives of the crusaders?

The Magna Carta: English Constitutional Law

The Magna Carta, or Great Charter of Liberties, is one of the most famous of me-dieval documents. Various disasters, including the loss of almost all his possessions in France, placed King John in a weak position by 1215, when his bishops, nobles, and other powerful men, all in revolt, extracted this contract from him. The charter is a curious mix of lofty ideals and practical details about how John should govern his realm and not infringe on the liberties of his subjects, who were by no means all equal.

From *Select Documents of English Constitutional History*, edited by George Burton Adams and H. Morse Stephens (Basingstoke, Eng.: Macmillan, 1901).

John, by the grace of God, king of England, lord of Ireland, duke of Normandy and Aquitaine, count of Anjou, to the archbishops, bishops, ab-bots, earls, barons, justiciars, foresters, sheriffs, reeves, servants, and all bailiffs and his faithful peo-ple greeting. Know that by the suggestion of God and for the good of our soul and those of all our predecessors and of our heirs, to the honor of God and the exaltation of holy church, and the im-provement of our kingdom, by the advice of our venerable fathers Stephen, archbishop of Canter-bury, primate of all England and Cardinal of the Holy Roman Church, Henry, archbishop of Dublin, William of London, Peter of Winchester, Joscelyn of Bath and Glastonbury, Hugh of Lincoln, Walter of Worcester, William of Coventry, and Benedict of Rochester, bishops; of Master Pandulf, subdeacon and member of the household of the lord Pope, of Brother Aymeric, master of the Knights of the Tem-ple in England; and of the noblemen William Mar-shall, earl of Pembroke, William, earl of Salisbury, William, earl Warren, William, earl of Arundel, Alan of Galloway, con-stable of Scotland, Warren Fitz-Gerald, Peter Fitz-Herbert, Hubert de Burgh, seneschal of Poitou, Hugh de Nevil, Matthew Fitz-Herbert, Thomas Bassett, Alan Bassett, Philip d'Albini, Robert de Ropesle, John Marshall, John Fitz-Hugh, and others of our faithful.

1. In the first place we have granted to God, and by this our present charter confirmed, for us and our heirs forever, that the English church shall be free, and shall hold its rights entire and its liberties uninjured; and we will that it thus be observed; which is shown by this, that the freedom of elec-tions, which is considered to be most important and especially necessary to the English church, we, of our pure and spontaneous will, granted, and by our charter confirmed, before the contest between us and our barons had arisen; and obtained a con-firmation of it by the lord Pope Innocent III.; which we will observe and which we will shall be observed in good faith by our heirs forever.

We have granted moreover to all free men of our kingdom for us and our heirs forever all the liberties written below, to be had and holden by themselves and their heirs from us and our heirs.

2. If any of our earls or barons, or others holding from us in chief by military service shall have died, and when he has died his heir shall be of full age and owe relief, he shall have his inheri-tance by the ancient relief; that is to say, the heir or heirs of an earl for the whole barony of an earl a hundred pounds; the heir or heirs of a baron for a whole barony a hundred pounds; the heir or heirs of a knight, for a whole knight's fee, a hun-dred shillings at most; and who owes less let him give less according to the ancient custom of fiefs.

3. If moreover the heir of any one of such shall be under age, and shall be in wardship, when he

comes of age he shall have his inheritance without relief and without a fine.

4. The custodian of the land of such a minor heir shall not take from the land of the heir any except reasonable products, reasonable customary payments, and reasonable services, and this without destruction or waste of men or of property; and if we without destruction or waste of men or of property; and if we shall have committed the custody of the land of any such a one to the sheriff or to any other who is to be responsible to us for its proceeds, and that man shall have caused destruction or waste from his custody we will recover damages from him, and the land shall be committed to two legal and discreet men of that fief, who shall be responsible for its proceeds to us or to him to whom we have assigned them; and if we shall have given or sold to any one the custody of any such land, and he has caused destruction or waste there, he shall lose that custody, and it shall be handed over to two legal and discreet men of that fief who shall be in like manner responsible to us as is said above.

5. The custodian moreover, so long as he shall have the custody of the land, must keep up the houses, parks, warrens, fish ponds, mills, and other things pertaining to the land, from the proceeds of the land itself; and he must return to the heir, when he has come to full age, all his land, furnished with ploughs and implements of husbandry according as the time of wainage requires and as the proceeds of the land are able reasonably to sustain.

6. Heirs shall be married without disparity, so nevertheless that before the marriage is contracted, it shall be announced to the relatives by blood of the heir himself.

7. A widow, after the death of her husband, shall have her marriage portion and her inheritance immediately and without obstruction, nor shall she give anything for her dowry or for her marriage portion, or for her inheritance which inheritance her husband and she held on the day of the death of her husband; and she may remain in the house of her husband for forty days after his death, within which time her dowry shall be assigned to her.

8. No widow shall be compelled to marry so long as she prefers to live without a husband, provided she gives security that she will not marry without our consent, if she holds from us, or without the consent of her lord from whom she holds, if she holds from another.

9. Neither we nor our bailiffs will seise any land or rent, for any debt, so long as the chattels of the debtor are sufficient for the payment of the debt; nor shall the pledges of a debtor be distrained so long as the principal debtor himself has enough for the payment of the debt; and if the principal debtor fails in the payment of the debt, not having the wherewithal to pay it, the pledges shall be responsible for the debt; and if they wish, they shall have the lands and the rents of the debtor until they shall have been satisfied for the debt which they have before paid for him, unless the principal debtor shall have shown himself to be quit in that respect towards those pledges.

10. If any one has taken anything from the Jews, by way of a loan, more or less, and dies before that debt is paid, the debt shall not draw interest so long as the heir is under age, from whomsoever he holds; and if that debt falls into our hands, we will take nothing except the chattel contained in the agreement.

11. And if any one dies leaving a debt owing to the Jews, his wife shall have her dowry, and shall pay nothing of that debt; and if there remain minor children of the dead man, necessaries shall be provided for them corresponding to the holding of the dead man; and from the remainder shall be paid the debt, saving the service of the lords. In the same way debts are to be treated which are owed to others than the Jews.

12. No scutage or aid shall be imposed in our kingdom except by the common council of our kingdom, except for the ransoming of our body, for the making of our oldest son a knight, and for once marrying our oldest daughter, and for these purposes it shall be only a reasonable aid; in the same way it shall be done concerning the aids of the city of London.

13. And the city of London shall have all its ancient liberties and free customs, as well by land as by water. Moreover, we will and grant that all other cities and boroughs and villages and ports shall have all their liberties and free customs.

14. And for holding a common council of the kingdom concerning the assessment of an aid otherwise than in the three cases mentioned above, or concerning the assessment of a scutage we shall cause to be summoned the archbishops, bishops, abbots, earls, and greater barons by our letters individually; and besides we shall cause to be summoned generally, by our sheriffs and bailiffs all those who hold from us in chief, for a certain day, that is at the end of forty days at least, and for a certain place; and in all the letters of that summons, we will express the cause of the summons, and when the summons has thus been given the business shall proceed on the appointed day, on the advice of those who shall be present, even if not all of those who were summoned have come.

15. We will not grant to any one, moreover, that he shall take an aid from his free men, except for ransoming his body, for making his oldest son a knight, and for once marrying his oldest daughter and for these purposes only a reasonable aid shall be taken.

16. No one shall be compelled to perform any greater service for a knight's fee, or for any other free tenement than is owed from it.

17. The common pleas shall not follow our court, but shall be held in some certain place.

18. The recognition of *novel disseisin, mort d'ancestor,* and *darrein presentment* shall be held only in their own counties and in this manner: we, or if we are outside of the kingdom our principal justiciar, will send two justiciars through each county four times a year, who with four knights of each county, elected by the county, shall hold in the county, and on the day and in the place of the county court, the aforesaid assizes of the county.[1]

---

[1]Note that *novel disseisin* is the recovery of recently seized land; *mort d'ancestor* is an inheritance claim; and *darrein presentment* is a last nomination to a church office. [Editor.]

19. And if the aforesaid assizes cannot be held within the day of the county court, a sufficient number of knights and free-holders shall remain from those who were present at the county court on that day to give the judgments, according as the business is more or less.

20. A free man shall not be fined for a small offence, except in proportion to the measure of the offence; and for a great offence he shall be fined in proportion to the magnitude of the offence, saving his freehold; and a merchant in the same way, saving his merchandise; and the villain shall be fined in the same way, saving his wainage, if he shall be at our mercy; and none of the above fines shall be imposed except by the oaths of honest men of the neighborhood.

21. Earls and barons shall only be fined by their peers, and only in proportion to their offence.

22. A clergyman shall be fined, like those before mentioned, only in proportion to his lay holding, and not according to the extent of his ecclesiastical benefice.

23. No vill or man shall be compelled to make bridges over the rivers except those which ought to do it of old and rightfully.

24. No sheriff, constable, coroners, or other bailiffs of ours shall hold pleas of our crown.

25. All counties, hundreds, wapentakes, and trithings shall be at the ancient rents and without any increase, excepting our demesne manors.

26. If any person holding a lay fief from us shall die, and our sheriff or bailiff shall show our letters-patent of our summons concerning a debt which the deceased owed to us, it shall be lawful for our sheriff or bailiff to attach and levy on the chattels of the deceased found on his lay fief, to the value of that debt, in the view of legal men, so nevertheless that nothing be removed thence until the clear debt to us shall be paid; and the remainder shall be left to the executors for the fulfilment of the will of the deceased; and if nothing is owed to us by him, all the chattels shall go to the deceased, saving to his wife and children their reasonable shares.

27. If any free man dies intestate, his chattels shall be distributed by the hands of his near relatives and friends, under the oversight of the church,

saving to each one the debts which the deceased owed to him.

28. No constable or other bailiff of ours shall take any one's grain or other chattels, without immediately paying for them in money, unless he is able to obtain a postponement at the goodwill of the seller.

29. No constable shall require any knight to give money in place of his ward of a castle if he is willing to furnish that ward in his own person or through another honest man, if he himself is not able to do it for a reasonable cause; and if we shall lead or send him into the army he shall be free from ward in proportion to the amount of time during which he has been in the army through us.

30. No sheriff or bailiff of ours or any one else shall take horses or wagons of any free man for carrying purposes except on the permission of that free man.

31. Neither we nor our bailiffs will take the wood of another man for castles, or for anything else which we are doing, except by the permission of him to whom the wood belongs.

32. We will not hold the lands of those convicted of a felony for more than a year and a day, after which the lands shall be returned to the lords of the fiefs.

33. All the fish-weirs in the Thames and the Medway, and throughout all England shall be done away with, except those on the coast.

34. The writ which is called *præcipe* shall not be given for the future to any one concerning any tenement by which a free man can lose his court.

35. There shall be one measure of wine throughout our whole kingdom, and one measure of ale, and one measure of grain, that is the London quarter, and one width of dyed cloth and of russets and of halbergets, that is two ells within the selvages; of weights, moreover it shall be as of measures.

36. Nothing shall henceforth be given or taken for a writ of inquisition concerning life or limbs, but it shall be given freely and not denied.

37. If any one holds from us by fee farm or by socage or by burgage, and from another he holds

land by military service, we will not have the guardianship of the heir or of his land which is of the fief of another, on account of that fee farm, or socage, or burgage; nor will we have the custody of that fee farm, or socage, or burgage, unless that fee farm itself owes military service. We will not have the guardianship of the heir or of the land of any one, which he holds from another by military service on account of any petty serjeanty which he holds from us by the service of paying to us knives or arrows, or things of that kind.

38. No bailiff for the future shall put any one to his law on his simple affirmation, without credible witnesses brought for this purpose.

39. No free man shall be taken or imprisoned or dispossessed, or outlawed, or banished, or in any way destroyed, nor will we go upon him, nor send upon him, except by the legal judgment of his peers or by the law of the land.

40. To no one will we sell, to no one will we deny, or delay right or justice.

41. All merchants shall be safe and secure in going out from England and coming into England and in remaining and going through England, as well by land as by water, for buying and selling, free from all evil tolls, by the ancient and rightful customs, except in time of war, and if they are of a land at war with us; and if such are found in our land at the beginning of war, they shall be attached without injury to their bodies or goods, until it shall be known from us or from our principal justiciar in what way the merchants of our land are treated who shall be then found in the country which is at war with us; and if ours are safe there, the others shall be safe in our land.

42. It is allowed henceforth to any one to go out from our kingdom, and to return, safely and securely, by land and by water, saving their fidelity to us, except in time of war for some short time, for the common good of the kingdom; excepting persons imprisoned and outlawed according to the law of the realm, and people of a land at war with us, and merchants, of whom it shall be done as is before said.

43. If any one holds from any escheat, as from the honor of Wallingford, or Nottingham, or Bou-

logne, or Lancaster, or from other escheats which
are in our hands and are baronies, and he dies,
his heir shall not give any other relief, nor do to
us any other service than he would do to the
baron, if that barony was in the hands of the
baron; and we will hold it in the same way as
the baron held it.

44. Men who dwell outside the forest shall not
henceforth come before our justiciars of the forest,
on common summons, unless they are in a plea
of, or pledges for any person or persons who are
arrested on account of the forest.

45. We will not make justiciars, constables, sheriffs
or bailiffs except of such as know the law of the
realm and are well inclined to observe it.

46. All barons who have founded abbeys for which
they have charters of kings of England, or ancient
tenure, shall have their custody when they have
become vacant, as they ought to have.

47. All forests which have been afforested in our
time shall be disafforested immediately; and so it
shall be concerning river banks which in our time
have been fenced in.

48. All the bad customs concerning forests and
warrens and concerning foresters and warreners,
sheriffs and their servants, river banks and their
guardians shall be inquired into immediately in
each county by twelve sworn knights of the same
county, who shall be elected by the honest men of
the same county, and within forty days after the
inquisition has been made, they shall be entirely
destroyed by them, never to be restored, provided
that we be first informed of it, or our justiciar, if
we are not in England.

49. We will give back immediately all hostages and
charters which have been liberated to us by Englishmen as security for peace or for faithful service.

50. We will remove absolutely from their baili-
wicks the relatives of Gerard de Athyes, so that for
the future they shall have no bailiwick in England
Engelard de Cygony, Andrew, Peter and Gyon de
Chancelles, Gyon de Cygony, Geoffrey de Martin
and his brothers, Philip Mark and his brothers, and
Geoffrey his nephew and their whole retinue.

51. And immediately after the reëstablishment
of peace we will remove from the kingdom all
foreign-born soldiers, cross-bow men, serjeants,
and mercenaries who have come with horses and
arms for the injury of the realm.

52. If any one shall have been dispossessed or removed by us without legal judgment of his peers,
from his lands, castles, franchises, or his right we
will restore them to him immediately; and if contention arises about this, then it shall be done according to the judgment of the twenty-five barons,
of whom mention is made below concerning the
security of the peace. Concerning all those things,
however, from which any one has been removed
or of which he has been deprived without legal
judgment of his peers by King Henry our father,
or by King Richard our brother, which we have in
our hand, or which others hold, and which it is
our duty to guarantee, we shall have respite till the
usual term of crusaders; excepting those things
about which the suit has been begun or the inquisition made by our writ before our assumption
of the cross; when, however, we shall return from
our journey or if by chance we desist from the
journey, we will immediately show full justice in
regard to them.

53. We shall, moreover, have the same respite and
in the same manner about showing justice in regard to the forests which are to be disafforested
or to remain forests, which Henry our father or
Richard our brother made into forests; and concerning the custody of lands which are in the fief
of another, custody of which we have until now
had on account of a fief which any one has held
from us by military service; and concerning the
abbeys which have been founded in fiefs of others
than ourselves, in which the lord of the fee has
asserted for himself a right; and when we return
or if we should desist from our journey we will
immediately show full justice to those complaining in regard to them.

54. No one shall be seised nor imprisoned on the
appeal of a woman concerning the death of any
one except her husband.

55. All fines which have been imposed unjustly
and against the law of the land, and all penalties
imposed unjustly and against the law of the land
are altogether excused, or will be on the judgment

of the twenty-five barons of whom mention is made below in connection with the security of the peace, or on the judgment of the majority of them, along with the aforesaid Stephen, archbishop of Canterbury, if he is able to be present, and others whom he may wish to call for this purpose along with him. And if he should not be able to be present, nevertheless the business shall go on without him, provided that if any one or more of the aforesaid twenty-five barons are in a similar suit they should be removed as far as this particular judgment goes, and others who shall be chosen and put upon oath, by the remainder of the twenty-five shall be substituted for them for this purpose.

56. If we have dispossessed or removed any Welshmen from their lands, or franchises, or other things, without legal judgment of their peers, in England, or in Wales, they shall be immediately returned to them; and if a dispute shall have arisen over this, then it shall be settled in the borderland by judgment of their peers, concerning holdings of England according to the law of England, concerning holdings of Wales according to the law of Wales, and concerning holdings of the borderland according to the law of the borderland. The Welsh shall do the same to us and ours.

57. Concerning all those things, however, from which any one of the Welsh shall have been removed or dispossessed without legal judgment of his peers, by King Henry our father, or King Richard our brother, which we hold in our hands, or which others hold, and we are bound to warrant to them, we shall have respite till the usual period of crusaders, those being excepted about which suit was begun or inquisition made by our command before our assumption of the cross. When, however, we shall return or if by chance we shall desist from our journey, we will show full justice to them immediately, according to the laws of the Welsh and the aforesaid parts.

58. We will give back the son of Lewellyn immediately, and all the hostages from Wales and the charters which had been liberated to us as a security for peace.

59. We will act toward Alexander, king of the Scots, concerning the return of his sisters and his hostages, and concerning his franchises and his right, according to the manner in which we shall act toward our other barons of England, unless it ought to be otherwise by the charters which we hold from William his father, formerly king of the Scots, and this shall be by the judgment of his peers in our court.

60. Moreover, all those customs and franchises mentioned above which we have conceded in our kingdom, and which are to be fulfilled, as far as pertains to us, in respect to our men; all men of our kingdom as well clergy as laymen, shall observe as far as pertains to them, in respect to their men.

61. Since, moreover, for the sake of God, and for the improvement of our kingdom, and for the better quieting of the hostility sprung up lately between us and our barons, we have made all these concessions; wishing them to enjoy these in a complete and firm stability forever, we make and concede to them the security described below; that is to say, that they shall elect twenty-five barons of the kingdom, whom they will, who ought with all their power to observe, hold, and cause to be observed, the peace and liberties which we have conceded to them, and by this our present charter confirmed to them; in this manner, that if we or our justiciar, or our bailiffs, or any one of our servants shall have done wrong in any way toward any one, or shall have transgressed any of the articles of peace or security; and the wrong shall have been shown to four barons of the aforesaid twenty-five barons, let those four barons come to us or to our justiciar, if we are out of the kingdom, laying before us the transgression, and let them ask that we cause that transgression to be corrected without delay. And if we shall not have corrected the transgression or, if we shall be out of the kingdom, if our justiciar shall not have corrected it within a period of forty days, counting from the time in which it has been shown to us or to our justiciar, if we are out of the kingdom; the aforesaid four barons shall refer the matter to the remainder of the twenty-five barons, and let these twenty-five barons with the whole community of the country distress and injure us in every way they can; that is to say by the seizure of our

castles, lands, possessions, and in such other ways as they can until it shall have been corrected according to their judgment, saving our person and that of our queen, and those of our children; and when the correction has been made, let them devote themselves to us as they did before. And let whoever in the country wishes take an oath that in all the above-mentioned measures he will obey the orders of the aforesaid twenty-five barons, and that he will injure us as far as he is able with them, and we give permission to swear publicly and freely to each one who wishes to swear, and no one will we ever forbid to swear. All those, moreover, in the country who of themselves and their own will are unwilling to take an oath to the twenty-five barons as to distressing and injuring us along with them, we will compel to take the oath by our mandate, as before said. And if any one of the twenty-five barons shall have died or departed from the land or shall in any other way be prevented from taking the above-mentioned action, let the remainder of the aforesaid twenty-five barons choose another in his place, according to their judgment, who shall take an oath in the same way as the others. In all those things, moreover, which are committed to those five and twenty barons to carry out, if perhaps the twenty-five are present, and some disagreement arises among them about something, or if any of them when they have been summoned are not willing or are not able to be present, let that be considered valid and firm which the greater part of those who are present arrange or command, just as if the whole twenty-five had agreed in this; and let the aforesaid twenty-five swear that they will observe faithfully all the things which are said above, and with all their ability cause them to be observed. And we will obtain nothing from any one, either by ourselves or by another by which any of these concessions and liberties shall be revoked or diminished; and if any such thing shall have been obtained, let it be invalid and void, and we will never use it by ourselves or by another.

62. And all ill-will, grudges, and anger sprung up between us and our men, clergy and laymen, from the time of the dispute, we have fully renounced and pardoned to all. Moreover, all transgressions committed on account of this dispute, from Easter in the sixteenth year of our reign till the restoration of peace, we have fully remitted to all, clergy and laymen, and as far as pertains to us, fully pardoned. And moreover we have caused to be made for them testimonial letters-patent of lord Stephen, archbishop of Canterbury, lord Henry, archbishop of Dublin, and of the aforesaid bishops and of Master Pandulf, in respect to that security and the concessions named above.

63. Wherefore we will and firmly command that the Church of England shall be free, and that the men in our kingdom shall have and hold all the aforesaid liberties, rights and concessions, well and peacefully, freely and quietly, fully and completely, for themselves and their heirs, from us and our heirs, in all things and places, forever, as before said. It has been sworn, moreover, as well on our part as on the part of the barons, that all these things spoken of above shall be observed in good faith and without any evil intent. Witness the above named and many others. Given by our hand in the meadow which is called Runnymede, between Windsor and Staines, on the fifteenth day of June, in the seventeenth year of our reign.

REVIEW QUESTIONS

1. What liberties were most important to English nobles?
2. What rights did the church and the English people get from this charter?
3. What powers remained to the king?

JEAN DE JOINVILLE

FROM *The Life of Saint Louis*

Jean de Joinville was a French noble who knew King Louis IX of France (1226–1270) and went on a crusade to Egypt with him in 1248. Long after the king's death in 1270, while on a crusade in North Africa, Joinville dictated these reminiscences as part of a successful campaign to have the church canonize Louis as a saint. Joinville admired his king and stressed his outstanding qualities as a king and warrior. In this section of the biography, Joinville is remembering the holiness that the king displayed during his lifetime, but there is much more here about Louis's character.

From *Joinville and Villehardouin: Chronicles of the Crusades*, edited by M. R. B. Shaw (New York: Penguin Books, 1963), pp. 167–75.

Chapter 1
The Servant of God

In the name of God Almighty, I, Jean, Lord of Joinville, Seneschal of Champagne, dictate the life of our good King, Saint Louis, in which I shall record what I saw and heard both in the course of the six years in which I was on pilgrimage in his company oversea, and after we returned to France. But before I speak to you of his great deeds and his outstanding valour, I will tell you what I myself observed of his good teaching and his saintly conversation, so that it may be set down in due order for the edification of those to whom this book is read.

This saintly man loved our Lord with all his heart, and in all his actions followed His example. This is apparent from the fact that as our Lord died for the love he bore His people, even so King Louis put his own life in danger, and that several times, for the very same reason. It was danger too that he might well have avoided, as I shall show you later.

The great love King Louis bore his people is shown by what he said, as he lay dangerously ill at Fontainebleau, to his eldest son, my Lord Louis. "My dear son," he said, "I earnestly beg you to make yourself loved by all your people. For I would rather have a Scot come from Scotland to govern the people of this kingdom well and justly than that you should govern them ill in the sight of all the world." This upright king, moreover, loved truth so well that, as I shall show you later, he would never consent to lie to the Saracens with regard to any covenant he made with them.

He was so temperate in his appetite that I never heard him, on any day of my life, order a special dish for himself, as many men of wealth and standing do. On the contrary, he would always eat with good grace whatever his cooks had prepared to set before him. He was equally temperate in his speech. I never, on any single occasion, heard him speak evil of any man; nor did I ever hear him utter the name of the Devil—a name in very common use throughout the kingdom—which practice, so I believe, is not pleasing to God.

He used to add water to his wine, but did so reasonably, according as the strength of the wine allowed it. While we were in Cyprus he asked me why I did not mix my wine with water. I replied that this was on the advice of my doctors, who had told me that I had a strong head and a cold stomach, so that I could not get drunk. He answered that they had deceived me; for if I did not learn to mix my wine with water while I was still young, and wished to do so in my old age, gout and stomach troubles would take hold on me, and I should never be in good health. Moreover, if I went on drinking undiluted wine when I was old, I should get drunk every night, and it was too revolting a thing for any brave man to be in such a state.

The king once asked me if I wished to be honoured in this world, and to enter paradise when I died. I told him I did. "If so," said he, "you should avoid deliberately saying or doing anything which, if it became generally known, you would be ashamed to acknowledge by saying 'I did this,' or 'I said that.' " He also told me not to contradict or call in question anything said in my presence— unless indeed silence would imply approval of something wrong, or damaging to myself, because harsh words often lead to quarrelling, which has ended in the death of countless numbers of men.

He often said that people ought to clothe and arm themselves in such a way that men of riper age would never say they had spent too much on dress, or young men say they had spent too little. I repeated this remark to our present king when speaking of the elaborately embroidered tabards that are in vogue today. I told him that, during the whole of our voyage oversea, I had never seen such embroidered tabards, either on the king or on any one else. He said to me that he had several such garments, with his own arms embroidered on them, and they had cost him eight hundred *livres parisis.* I told him that he would have put his money to better use if he had given it to God, and had his clothes made of good plain taffeta bearing his arms, as his father had done.

King Louis once sent for me and said: "You have such a shrewd and subtle mind that I hardly dare speak to you of things concerning God. So I have summoned these two monks to come here, because I want to ask you a question." Then he said: "Tell me, seneschal, what is your idea of God?" "Your Majesty," I replied, "He is something so good that there cannot be anything better." "Indeed," said he, "you've given me a very good answer; for it's precisely the same as the definition given in this book I have here in my hand.

"Now I ask you," he continued, "which you would prefer: to be a leper or to have committed some mortal sin?" And I, who had never lied to him, replied that I would rather have committed thirty mortal sins than become a leper. The next day, when the monks were no longer there, he called me to him, and making me sit at his feet said to me: "Why did you say that to me yesterday?" I told him I would still say it. "You spoke without thinking, and like a fool," he said. "You ought to know there is no leprosy so foul as being in a state of mortal sin; for the soul in that condition is like the Devil; therefore no leprosy can be so vile. Besides, when a man dies his body is healed of its leprosy; but if he dies after committing a mortal sin, he can never be sure that, during his lifetime, he has repented of it sufficiently for God to forgive him. In consequence, he must be greatly afraid lest that leprosy of sin should last as long as God dwells in paradise. So I beg you," he added, "as earnestly as I can, for the love of God, and for love of me, to train your heart to prefer any evil that can happen to the body, whether it be leprosy or any other disease, rather than let mortal sin take possession of your soul."

At another time King Louis asked me if I washed the feet of the poor on Maundy Thursday. "Your Majesty," I exclaimed, "what a terrible idea! I will never wash the feet of such low fellows." "Really," said he, "that is a very wrong thing to say; for you should never scorn to do what our Lord Himself did as an example for us. So I beg you, first for the love of God and then for love of me, to accustom yourself to washing the feet of the poor."

This good king so loved all manner of people who believed in God and loved Him that he appointed Gilles le Brun, who was not a native of his realm, as High Constable of France, because he was held in such high repute for his faith in God and devotion to His service. For my part, I believe he well deserved that reputation. Another man, Maître Robert de Sorbon, who was famed for his goodness and his learning, was invited, on that account, to dine at the royal table.

It happened one day that this worthy priest was sitting beside me at dinner, and we were talking to each other rather quietly. The king reproved us and said: "Speak up, or your companions may think you are speaking ill of them. If at table you talk of things that may give us pleasure, say them aloud, or else be silent."

When the king was feeling in a mood for fun, he would fire questions at me, as for instance: "Seneschal, can you give me reasons why a wise and upright layman is better than a friar?" Thereupon a discussion would begin between Maître Robert and myself. When we had disputed for some length of time the king would pronounce judgement. "Maître Robert," he would say, "I would willingly be known as a wise and upright man, provided I were so in reality—and you can have all the rest. For wisdom and goodness are such fine qualities that even to name them leaves a pleasant taste in the mouth."

On the other hand, he always said that it was a wicked thing to take other people's property. "To 'restore,'" he would say, "is such a hard thing to do that even in speaking of it the word itself rasps one's throat because of the r's that are in it. These r's are, so to speak, like the rakes of the Devil, with which he would draw to himself all those who wish to 'restore' what they have taken from others. The Devil, moreover, does this very subtly; for he works on great usurers and great robbers in such a way that they give to God what they ought to *restore* to men."

On one occasion the king gave me a message to take to King Thibaut, in which he warned his son-in-law to beware lest he should lay too heavy a burden on his soul by spending an excessive amount of money on the house he was building for the Predicants of Provins. "Wise men," said the king, "deal with their possessions as executors ought to do. Now the first thing a good executor does is to settle all debts incurred by the deceased and restore any property belonging to others, and only then is he free to apply what money remains to charitable purposes."

One Whitsunday the saintly king happened to þe at Corbeil, where all the knights had assembled. He had come down after dinner into the court

below the chapel, and was standing at the doorway talking to the Comte de Bretagne, the father of the present count—may God preserve him!—when Maître Robert de Sorbon came to look for me, and taking hold of the hem of my mantle led me towards the king. So I said to Maître Robert: "My good sir, what do you want with me?" He replied: "I wish to ask you whether, if the king were seated in this court and you went and sat down on his bench, at a higher place than he, you ought to be severely blamed for doing so?" I told him I ought to be. "Then," he said "you certainly deserve a reprimand for being more richly dressed than the king, since you are wearing a fur-trimmed mantle of fine green cloth, and he wears no such thing." "Maître Robert," I answered, "I am, if you'll allow me to say so, doing nothing worthy of blame in wearing green cloth and fur, for I inherited the right to such dress from my father and mother. But you, on the other hand, are much to blame, for though both your parents were commoners, you have abandoned their style of dress, and are now wearing finer woollen cloth than the king himself." Then I took hold of the skirt of his surcoat and of the surcoat worn by the king, and said to Maître Robert: "See if I'm not speaking the truth." At this the king began to take Maître Robert's part, and say all in his power to defend him.

A little later on the king beckoned to his son, the Prince Philippe—the father of our present king—and to King Thibaut. Then, seating himself at the entrance to his oratory, he patted the ground and said to the two young men: "Sit down here, quite close to me, so that we shan't be overheard." "But, my lord," they protested, "we should not dare to sit so close to you." Then the king said to me, "Seneschal, you sit here." I obeyed, and sat down so close to him that my clothes were touching his. He made the two others sit down next, and said to them: "You have acted very wrongly, seeing you are my sons, in not doing as I commanded the moment I told you. I beg you to see this does not happen again." They assured him it would not.

Then the king said to me that he had called us together to confess that he had wrongly defended Maître Robert against me. "But," said he, "I saw he was so taken aback that he greatly needed my help. All the same you must not attach too great importance to anything I may have said in his defence. As the seneschal rightly says, you ought to dress well, and in a manner suited to your condition, so that your wives will love you all the more and your men have more respect for you. For, as a wise philosopher has said, our clothing and our armour ought to be of such a kind that men of mature experience will not say that we have spent too much on them, nor younger men say we have spent too little."

I will tell you here of one of the lessons King Louis taught me on our voyage back from the land oversea. It so happened that our ship was driven on to the rocks off the island of Cyprus by a wind known as the *garbino,* which is not one of the four great winds. At the shock our ship received the sailors were so frantic with despair that they rent their clothes and tore their beards. The king sprang out of bed barefoot—for it was night—and with nothing on but his tunic went and lay with arms outstretched to form a cross before the body of Our Lord on the altar, as one who expected nothing but death.

The day after this alarming event, the king called me aside to talk with him alone, and said to me: "Seneschal, God has just shown us a glimpse of His great power; for one of these little winds, so little indeed that it scarcely deserves a name, came near to drowning the King of France, his children, his wife, and his men. Now Saint Anselm says that such things are warnings from our Lord, as if God meant to say to us: 'See how easily I could have brought about your death if that had been My will.' 'Lord God,' says the saint, 'why dost Thou thus threaten us? For when Thou dost, it is not for Thy own profit, nor for Thy advantage— seeing that if Thou hadst caused us all to be lost Thou wouldst be none the poorer, nor any the richer either if Thou hadst caused us to be saved. Therefore the warning Thou sendest us is not for

Thy own benefit, but for ours, if so be we know how to profit by it.'

"Let us therefore," said the king, "take this warning God has sent us in such a way that if we feel there is anything in our hearts or our bodies that is displeasing to Him, we shall get rid of it without delay. If, on the other hand, we can think of anything that will please Him, we ought to see about doing it with equal speed. If we act thus our Lord will give us blessings in this world, and in the next greater bliss than we can tell. But if we do not act as we ought, He will deal with us as a good lord deals with his unfaithful servant. For if the latter will not amend his ways after he has been given warning, then his lord punishes him with death, or with penalties even harder to bear."

So I, Jean de Joinville, say: "Let the king who now reigns over us beware; for he has escaped from perils as great as those to which we were then exposed, or even greater. Therefore, let him turn from doing wrong, and in such a way that God will not smite him cruelly, either in himself or in his possessions."

In the conversations he had with me, this saintly king did every thing in his power to give me a firm belief in the principles of Christianity as given us by God. He used to say that we ought to have such an unshaken belief in all the articles of faith that neither fear of death nor of any harm that might happen to our bodies should make us willing to go against them in word or deed. "The Enemy," he would add, "works so subtly that when people are at the point of death he tries all he can to make them die with some doubt in their minds on certain points of our religion. For this cunning adversary is well aware that he cannot take away the merit of any good works a man has done; and he also knows that a man's soul is lost to him if he dies in the true faith.

"Therefore," the king would say, "it is our duty so to defend and guard ourselves against this snare as to say to the Enemy, when he sends us such a temptation: 'Go away! You shall not lure me from my steadfast belief in the articles of my faith. Even if you had all my limbs cut off, I would still live and die a true believer.' Whoever acts thus overcomes the Devil with the very same weapons with which this enemy of mankind had proposed to destroy him."

King Louis would also say that the Christian religion as defined in the creed was something in which we ought to believe implicitly, even though our belief in it might be founded on hearsay. On this point he asked me what was my father's name. I told him it was Simon. So he asked me how I knew it, and I replied that I thought I was certain of it, and believed it without question, because I had my mother's word for it. "Then," said he, "you ought to have a sure belief in all the articles of our faith on the word of the Apostles, which you hear sung of a Sunday in the Creed."

On one occasion the king repeated to me what Guillaume, Bishop of Paris, had told him about a certain eminent theologian who had come to see him. This man told the bishop that he wished to speak with him. "Speak as freely as you like, sir," said the bishop. However, when the theologian tried to speak to him he only burst into tears. So the bishop said: "Say what you have to say, sir; don't be disheartened; no one can be such a sinner that God can no longer forgive him." "Indeed, my lord," said the theologian, "I cannot control my tears. For I fear I must be an apostate, since I cannot compel my heart to believe in the sacrament of the altar, in the way that Holy Church teaches. Yet I know very well that this is a temptation of the Enemy."

"Pray tell me, sir," said the bishop, "do you feel any pleasure when the Enemy exposes you to this temptation?" "On the contrary, my lord," said the theologian, "it worries me as much as anything can." "Now," said the bishop, "I will ask you whether you would accept any gold or silver if it were offered you on condition you allowed your mouth to utter anything derogatory to the sacrament of the altar, or the other sacraments of Holy Church?" "My lord," said the other, "I can assure you that nothing in the world would induce me to do so. I would rather have one of my limbs torn from my body than consent to say such a thing."

"I will now," said the bishop, "take a different approach. You know that the King of France is at war with the King of England; you also know that the castle nearest the boundary-line between their two domains is the castle of Rochelle in Poitou. So I will ask you a question: Suppose the king had set you to guard the castle of Rochelle, and had put me in charge of the castle of Montlhéri, which is in the very centre of France, where the land is at peace, to which of us do you think the king would feel most indebted at the end of the war— to you who had guarded La Rochelle without loss, or to me who had remained in safety at Montlhéri?" "Why, in God's name, my lord," cried the theologian, "to me, who had guarded La Rochelle, and not lost it to the enemy."

"Sir," said the bishop, "my heart is like the castle of Montlhéri; for I have neither temptation nor doubts concerning the sacrament of the altar. For this reason I tell you that if God owes me any grace because my faith is secure and untroubled, He owes four times as much to you, who have kept your heart from defeat when beset by tribulations, and have moreover such good-will towards Him that neither worldly advantage, nor fear of any harm that might be done to your body, could tempt you to renounce Him. So I tell you to be comforted; for your state is more pleasing to Our Lord than mine." When the theologian heard this, he knelt before the bishop, at peace with himself, and well satisfied.

The king once told me how several men from among the Albigenses had gone to the Comte de Montfort, who at the time was guarding their land for his Majesty, and asked him to come and look at the body of our Lord, which had become flesh and blood in the hands of the priest. The count had answered: "Go and see it for yourselves, you who do not believe it. As for me, I believe it firmly, in accordance with Holy Church's teaching on the sacrament of the altar. And do you know," he added, "what I shall gain for having, in this mortal life, believed what Holy Church teaches us? I shall have a crown in heaven, and a finer one than the angels, for they see God face to face and consequently cannot but believe."

ILLUMINATED BIBLE, FRANCE (C. 1230)

This illuminated page from a Bible shows Queen Blanche and her son Louis IX of France. Below are an editor who is selecting texts and dictating and a scribe who is writing. How does this picture complement Joinville's description of King Louis IX of France? What do the figures at the bottom of the page suggest about literacy in thirteenth-century France?

EKKEHARD AND UTA, NAUMBERG CATHEDRAL STATUES (C. 1250)

The Naumberg Master, an unknown artist of the first rank, created a series of statues for the interior of Naumberg Cathedral in Germany. The noble couple Ekkehard and Uta, patrons of the church, were not sculpted from life, but they represent marvelous, idealized yet distinctive portraits of believable people. How do the characteristics of the noble class emerge from these statues?

King Louis also spoke to me of a great assembly of clergy and Jews which had taken place at the monastery of Cluny. There was a poor knight there at the time to whom the abbot had often given bread for the love of God. This knight asked the abbot if he could speak first, and his request was granted, though somewhat grudgingly. So he rose to his feet, and leaning on his crutch, asked to have the most important and most learned rabbi among the Jews brought before him. As soon as the Jew had come, the knight asked him a question. "May I know, sir," he said, "if you believe that the Virgin Mary, who bore our Lord in her body and cradled Him in her arms, was a virgin at the time of His birth, and is in truth the Mother of God?"

The Jew replied that he had no belief in any of those things. Thereupon the knight told the Jew that he had acted like a fool when—neither believing in the Virgin, nor loving her—he had set foot in that monastery which was her house. "And by heaven," exclaimed the knight, "I'll make you pay for it!" So he lifted his crutch and struck the Jew such a blow with it near the ear that he knocked him down. Then all the Jews took to flight, and carried their sorely wounded rabbi away with them. Thus the conference ended.

The abbot went up to the knight and told him he had acted most unwisely. The knight retorted that the abbot had been guilty of even greater folly in calling people together for such a conference, because there were many good Christians there who, before the discussion ended, would have gone away with doubts about their own religion through not fully understanding the Jews. "So I tell you," said the king, "that no one, unless he is an expert theologian, should venture to argue with these people. But a layman, whenever he hears the Christian religion abused, should not attempt to defend its tenets, except with his sword, and that he should thrust into the scoundrel's belly, and as far as it will enter."

*　　*　　*

REVIEW QUESTIONS

1. According to Joinville, what kind of man was Louis?
2. How did his personality shape the way he ruled?
3. Why does Joinville admire Louis?
4. What do we learn of the king's attitudes toward his social inferiors and Jews?

FROM *Las Siete Partidas:* Castilian Law Code

Las Siete Partidas is a great law code compiled for the kingdom of Castile early in the reign of Alfonso the Wise (1252–1284), a learned ruler interested in history, science, and the law. This selection concerns how the law regulated the Jews, who were a small minority of the population in Castile but much more numerous there than in most other parts of Christian Europe.

From *Las Siete Partidas*, edited by Samuel Parsons Scott (Chicago: American Bar Association by Commerce Clearing House, 1931).

*   *   *

Title XXIV
Concerning the Jews

Jews are a people who, although they do not believe in the religion of Our Lord Jesus Christ, yet, the great Christian sovereigns have always permitted them to live among them. Wherefore, since in the preceding Title we spoke of Diviners, and other men who allege that they know things that are to come, which is a kind of contempt of God, since they desire to make themselves equal to Him by learning his acts and his secrets; we intend to speak here of the Jews, who insult His name and deny the marvelous and holy acts which He performed when he sent His Son, Our Lord Jesus Christ, into the world to save sinners. We shall explain what the word Jew means; whence it derived this name; for what reasons the Church and the great Christian world permitted the Jews to live among them; in what way Jews should pass their lives among Christians; what things they should not use, or do, according to our religion; and what Jews those are who can be subjected to force on account of the wicked acts that they have performed, or the debt which they owe. Also why Jews who become Christians should not be subject to compulsion; what advantage a Jew, by becoming a Christian obtains over other Jews who do not; what penalty those deserve who cause him injury or dishonor; and to what punishment Christians, who become Jews, and also Jews who force their Moorish slaves to embrace their religion, are liable.

LAW I
WHAT THE WORD JEW MEANS, AND WHENCE THIS TERM IS DERIVED.

A party who believes in, and adheres to the law of Moses is called a Jew, according to the strict signification of the term, as well as one who is circumcised, and observes the other precepts commanded by his religion. This name is derived from the tribe of Judah which was nobler and more powerful than the others, and, also possessed another advantage, because the king of the Jews had to be selected from that tribe, and its members always received the first wounds in battle. The reason that the church, emperors, kings and princes, permitted the Jews to dwell among them and with Christians, is because they always lived, as it were, in captivity, as it was constantly in the minds of men that they were descended from those who crucified Our Lord Jesus Christ.

LAW II
IN WHAT WAY JEWS SHOULD PASS THEIR LIVES AMONG CHRISTIANS; WHAT THINGS THEY SHOULD NOT MAKE USE OF OR PRACTICE, ACCORDING TO OUR RELIGION; AND WHAT PENALTY THOSE DESERVE WHO ACT CONTRARY TO ITS ORDINANCES.

Jews should pass their lives among Christians quietly and without disorder, practicing their own religious rites, and not speaking ill of the faith of Our Lord Jesus Christ, which Christians acknowledge. Moreover, a Jew should be very careful to avoid preaching to, or converting any Christian, to the end that he may become a Jew, by exalting his own belief and disparaging ours. Whoever violates this law shall be put to death and lose all his property. And because we have heard it said that in some places Jews celebrated, and still celebrate Good Friday, which commemorates the Passion of Our Lord Jesus Christ, by way of contempt; stealing children and fastening them to crosses, and making images of wax and crucifying them, when they cannot obtain children; we order that, hereafter, if in any part of our dominions anything like this is done, and can be proved, all persons who were present when the act was committed shall be seized, arrested and brought before the king; and after the king ascertains that they are guilty, he shall cause them to be put to death in a disgraceful manner, no matter how many there may be.

We also forbid any Jew to dare to leave his house or his quarter on Good Friday, but they must all remain shut up until Saturday morning; and if they violate this regulation, we decree that they shall not be entitled to reparation for any injury or dishonor inflicted upon them by Christians.

LAW III
NO JEW CAN HOLD ANY OFFICE OR EMPLOYMENT BY WHICH HE MAY BE ABLE TO OPPRESS CHRISTIANS.

Jews were formerly highly honored, and enjoyed privileges above all other races, for they alone were called the People of God. But for the reason that they disowned Him who had honored them and given them privileges; and instead of showing Him reverence humiliated Him, by shamefully putting Him to death on the cross; it was proper and just that, on account of the great crime and wickedness which they committed, they should forfeit the honors and privileges which they enjoyed; and therefore from the day when they crucified Our Lord Jesus Christ they never had either king or priests among themselves, as they formerly did. The emperors, who in former times were lords of all the world, considered it fitting and right that, on account of the treason which they committed in killing their lord, they should lose all said honors and privileges, so that no Jew could ever afterwards hold an honorable position, or a public office by means of which he might, in any way, oppress a Christian.

LAW IV
HOW JEWS CAN HAVE A SYNAGOGUE AMONG CHRISTIANS.

A synagogue is a place where the Jews pray, and a new building of this kind cannot be erected in any part of our dominions, except by our order. Where, however, those which formerly existed there are torn down, they can be built in the same spot where they originally stood; but they cannot be made any larger or raised to any greater height, or be painted. A synagogue constructed in any other manner shall be lost by the Jews, and shall belong to the principal church of the locality where it is built. And for the reason that a synagogue is a place where the name of God is praised, we forbid any Christian to deface it, or remove anything from it, or take anything out of it by force; except where some malefactor takes refuge there; for they have a right to remove him by force in order to bring him before the judge. Moreover, we forbid Christians to put any animal into a synagogue, or loiter in it, or place any hindrance in the way of the Jews while they are there performing their devotions according to their religion.

LAW V
NO COMPULSION SHALL BE BROUGHT TO BEAR UPON THE JEWS ON SATURDAY, AND WHAT JEWS CAN BE SUBJECT TO COMPULSION.

Saturday is the day on which Jews perform their devotions, and remain quiet in their lodgings, and do not make contracts or transact any business; and for the reason that they are obliged by their religion, to keep it, no one should on that day summon them or bring them into court. Wherefore we order that no judge shall employ force or any constraint upon Jews on Saturday, in order to bring them into court on account of their debts; or arrest them; or cause them any other annoyance; for the remaining days of the week are sufficient for the purpose of employing compulsion against them, and for making demands for things which can be demanded of them, according to law. Jews are not bound to obey a summons served upon them on that day; and, moreover, we decree that any decision rendered against them on Saturday shall not be valid; but if a Jew should wound, kill, rob, steal, or commit any other offense like these for which he can be punished in person and property, then the judge can arrest him on Saturday.

We also decree that all claims that Christians have against Jews, and Jews against Christians, shall be decided and determined by our judges in the district where they reside, and not by their old men. And as we forbid Christians to bring Jews into court or annoy them on Saturday; so we also decree that Jews, neither in person, nor by their attorneys, shall have the right to bring Christians into court, or annoy them on this day. And in addition to this, we forbid any Christian, on his own responsibility, to arrest or wrong any Jew either in his person or property, but where he has any complaint against him he must bring it before our judges; and if anyone should be so bold as to use violence against the Jews, or rob them of anything, he shall return them double the value of the same.

LAW VI
JEWS WHO BECOME CHRISTIANS SHALL NOT BE
SUBJECT TO COMPULSION; WHAT ADVANTAGE A
JEW HAS WHO BECOMES A CHRISTIAN; AND
WHAT PENALTY OTHER JEWS DESERVE WHO DO
HIM HARM.

No force or compulsion shall be employed in any way against a Jew to induce him to become a Christian; but Christians should convert him to the faith of Our Lord Jesus Christ by means of the texts of the Holy Scriptures, and by kind words, for no one can love or appreciate a service which is done him by compulsion. We also decree that if any Jew or Jewess should voluntarily desire to become a Christian, the other Jews shall not interfere with this in any way, and if they stone, wound, or kill any such person, because they wish to become Christians, or after they have been baptized, and this can be proved; we order that all the murderers, or the abettors of said murder or attack, shall be burned. But where the party was not killed, but wounded, or dishonored; we order that the judges of the neighborhood where this took place shall compel those guilty of the attack, or who caused the dishonor, to make amends to him for the same; and also that they be punished for the offence which they committed, as they think they deserve; and we also order that, after any Jews become Christians, all persons in our dominions shall honor them; and that no one shall dare to reproach them or their descendants, by way of insult, with having been Jews; and that they shall possess all their property, sharing the same with their brothers, and inheriting it from their fathers

and mothers and other relatives, just as if they were Jews; and that they can hold all offices and dignities which other Christians can do.

LAW VII
WHAT PENALTY A CHRISTIAN DESERVES WHO
BECOMES A JEW.

Where a Christian is so unfortunate as to become a Jew, we order that he shall be put to death just as if he had become a heretic; and we decree that his property shall be disposed of in the same way that we stated should be done with that of heretics.

LAW VIII
NO CHRISTIAN, MAN OR WOMAN SHALL LIVE
WITH A JEW.

We forbid any Jew to keep Christian men or women in his house, to be served by them; although he may have them to cultivate and take care of his lands, or protect him on the way when he is compelled to go to some dangerous place. Moreover, we forbid any Christian man or woman to invite a Jew or a Jewess, or to accept an invitation from them, to eat or drink together, or to drink any wine made by their hands. We also order that no Jews shall dare to bathe in company with Christians, and that no Christian shall take any medicine or cathartic made by a Jew; but he can take it by the advice of some intelligent person, only where it is made by a Christian, who knows and is familiar with its ingredients.

LAW IX
WHAT PENALTY A JEW DESERVES WHO HAS
INTERCOURSE WITH A CHRISTIAN WOMAN.

Jews who live with Christian women are guilty of great insolence and boldness, for which reason we decree that all Jews who, hereafter, may be convicted of having done such a thing shall be put to death. For if Christians who commit adultery with married women deserve death on that account, much more do Jews who have sexual intercourse with Christian women, who are spiritually the wives of Our Lord Jesus Christ because of the faith and the baptism which they receive in His name; nor do we consider it proper that a Christian woman who commits an offense of this kind shall escape without punishment. Wherefore we order that, whether she be a virgin, a married woman, a widow, or a common prostitute who gives herself to all men, she shall suffer the same penalty which we mentioned in the last law in the Title concerning the Moors, to which a Christian woman is liable who has carnal intercourse with a Moor.

LAW X
WHAT PENALTY JEWS DESERVE WHO HOLD CHRISTIANS AS SLAVES.

A Jew shall not purchase, or keep as a slave a Christian man or woman, and if anyone violates this law the Christian shall be restored to freedom and shall not pay any portion of the price given for him, although the Jew may not have been aware when he bought him, that he was a Christian; but if he knew that he was such when he purchased him, and makes use of him afterwards as a slave, he shall be put to death for doing so. Moreover, we forbid any Jew to convert a captive to his religion, even though said captive may be a Moor, or belong to some other barbarous race. If anyone violates this law we order that the said slave who has become a Jew shall be set at liberty, and removed from the control of the party to whom he or she belonged. If any Moors who are the captives of Jews become Christians, they shall at once be freed, as is explained in the Fourth Partida of this book, in the Title concerning Liberty, in the laws which treat of this subject.

LAW XI
JEWS SHALL BEAR CERTAIN MARKS IN ORDER THAT THEY MAY BE KNOWN.

Many crimes and outrageous things occur between Christians and Jews because they live together in cities, and dress alike; and in order to avoid the offenses and evils which take place for this reason, we deem it proper, and we order that all Jews male and female living in our dominions shall bear some distinguishing mark upon their heads so that people may plainly recognize a Jew, or a Jewess; and any Jew who does not bear such a mark, shall pay for each time he is found without it ten maravedis of gold; and if he has not the means to do this he shall publicly receive ten lashes for his offence.

REVIEW QUESTIONS

1. In *Las Siete Partidas,* what aspects of Jewish life were Christians most eager to control?
2. What does it tell us about Christian-Jewish interactions?
3. In what ways does it both protect and oppress Jews?

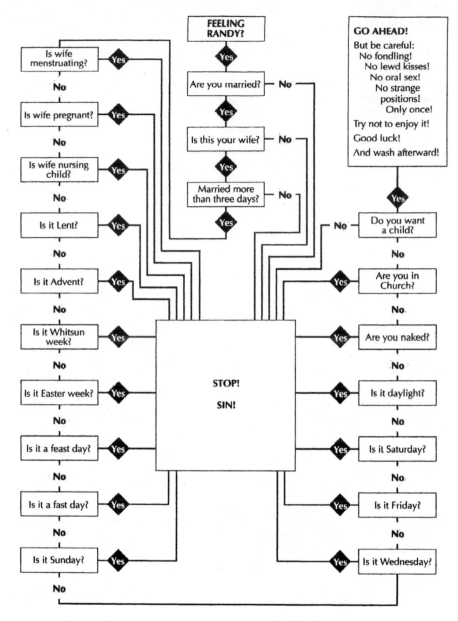

FEELING RANDY?

Yes

Is wife menstruating? — Yes

No

Is wife pregnant? — Yes

No

Is wife nursing child? — Yes

No

Is it Lent? — Yes

No

Is it Advent? — Yes

No

Is it Whitsun week? — Yes

No

Is it Easter week? — Yes

No

Is it a feast day? — Yes

No

Is it a fast day? — Yes

No

Is it Sunday? — Yes

No

Are you married? — No

Yes

Is this your wife? — No

Yes

Married more than three days? — No

Yes

STOP! SIN!

GO AHEAD!
But be careful:
No fondling!
No lewd kisses!
No oral sex!
No strange positions!
Only once!
Try not to enjoy it!
Good luck!
And wash afterward!

Yes

Do you want a child? — No

No

Are you in Church? — Yes

No

Are you naked? — Yes

No

Is it daylight? — Yes

No

Is it Saturday? — Yes

No

Is it Friday? — Yes

No

Is it Wednesday? — Yes

THE MEDIEVAL SEXUAL DECISION-MAKING PROCESS (C. 1275)

Medieval penitentials were manuals that described penances for transgressions against the teachings of the church. Canon law, the rules of the Catholic Church across Christendom, contained an increasingly elaborate sest of laws regulating sexual conduct. The following chart is a decision tree that a modern historian has constructed to show the kinds of questions a believer was supposed to ask himself or herself before engaging in sexual relations. What attitudes toward human sexuality emerge from this decision tree? What is the purpose of sex? What is the most positive interpretation that can be placed on the chart? Whom does it protect? Is the chart taking a too cynical approach to this important moral matter?

9   THE HIGH MIDDLE AGES: RELIGIOUS AND INTELLECTUAL DEVELOPMENTS, 1000–1300

As the economic and social vitality of the High Middle Ages strengthened the institutions of church, monarchy, and city governments, medieval people faced the problem of determining the right relationship among these different centers of power. The processes of crusade, mission, and colonization expanded the frontiers of Western Christendom and brought Europeans into conflicts with their neighbors. In the early eleventh century, the papacy was a weak institution and no universities existed in Europe. By 1300, the pope in Rome had become the center of a huge ecclesiastical bureaucracy, and new religious orders like the Cistercians, Franciscans, and Dominicans and an intricate system of canon law buttressed the church's authority. The university, perhaps the most distinctive and certainly the most durable legacy of the Middle Ages, supplied the church with an educated clergy trained in the new disciplines of theology and canon law. Medicine and civil law also benefited from the birth of higher education. Faith and logic and civil and canon law occupied university professors and their students, while across Europe millions of women and men looked to their local churches and traditions for answers on how they should live. Similar institutions developed in Muslim lands, and the great schools in Cairo may have served as models for the oldest colleges in Paris.

The movement for reforming the church in the eleventh century, instigated by monastic spirituality and a few dutiful German emperors, raised the issues of clerical celibacy, simony, and the proper relations between the church and the secular world of warriors and kings. Pope Gregory VII, a leader of the reform movement, began the investiture controversy with the emperor Henry IV. This dispute concerned the appointment of church officials and their investiture with the symbols of office, and the limits of their duties to secular lords. A series of powerful popes like Urban II, Innocent III, and Gregory IX increased the church's authority by successfully claiming that the church should not be subordinate to any earthly power. The church's jurisdiction over sin gave the clergy wide authority over many familial, moral, and even economic activities.

Pope Boniface VIII's papacy (1294–1303) represents the most extreme claim of papal supremacy in the world. One of the papacy's best tools for uniting Western Christendom behind its teachings was the Crusades, a series of holy wars the popes proclaimed and attempted to direct against Muslims and others. Eventually, the church used the Crusades as a way to fight heretics and even the political opponents of the church.

As Europeans fought against Muslims in Spain, North Africa, and the Middle East, some church leaders and kings also tried to foster the conversion of non-Christians and to find allies against the Muslims. (The journeys of the Venetian Polo family to China later in the century were motivated by a desire for profits from the eastern trade.) The church also accepted new styles of religious life that some charismatic teachers offered. St. Francis is the best-known founder of a new order, but other spiritual leaders like St. Clare and St. Dominic attracted followers. The older Benedictine monasteries and convents remained centers of learning and reform. St. Elizabeth's life embodied many of the new styles of thirteenth-century piety.

At the local level, creative minds were also finding new answers to old questions about faith, health, and miracles. What was happening at the universities often seemed remote from the daily lives of peasants. St. Thomas Aquinas, the most accomplished theologian of the thirteenth century, applied the recently revived tools of Aristotelian logic to the same basic concerns in order to harmonize faith and reason, the goal of scholasticism. Many artistic developments accompanied all this religious and intellectual fervor, and the great cathedrals and churches rising across Europe are testimony to the society's prosperity and values. In literature, the transition from epic to romance reflects changing noble tastes; the new courtly literature reflects both the older heroic tastes and some of the new refinements and complex attitudes toward women.

Gregory VII

"To Herman of Metz, in Defense of the Papal Policy toward Henry IV"

Pope Gregory VII (1073–1085) wrote this letter to Herman of Metz to justify his decision to excommunicate Emperor Henry IV of Germany and to explain his views on the role of the church in the world. The pope's dispute with Henry IV concerned the emperor's claim to appoint bishops and abbots. The pope considered these ap-

pointments to be in the church's jurisdiction, and other reformers were also troubled by churchmen who became vassals of a secular lord. Homage and fealty for fiefs gave the appearance that the secular power was superior to the spiritual. This letter is a concise statement of the reform movement's position.

From *The Correspondence of Pope Gregory VII*, edited by Ephriam Emerton (New York: Columbia University Press, 1969), pp. 166–75.

Gregory to his beloved brother in Christ, Hermann, bishop of Metz, greeting . . .

We know you to be ever ready to bear labor and peril in defense of the truth, and doubt not that this is a gift from God. It is a part of his unspeakable grace and his marvelous mercy that he never permits his chosen ones to wander far or to be completely cast down; but rather, after a time of persecution and wholesome probation, makes them stronger than they were before. On the other hand, just as among cowards one who is worse than the rest is broken down by fear, so among the brave one who acts more bravely than the rest is stirred thereby to new activity. We remind you of this by way of exhortation that you may stand more joyfully in the front ranks of the Christian host, the more confident you are that they are the nearest to God the conqueror.

You ask us to fortify you against the madness of those who babble with accursed tongues about the authority of the Holy Apostolic See not being able to excommunicate King Henry as one who despises the law of Christ, a destroyer of churches and of the empire, a promoter and partner of heresies, nor to release anyone from his oath of fidelity to him; but it has not seemed necessary to reply to this request, seeing that so many and such convincing proofs are to be found in Holy Scripture. Nor do we believe that those who abuse and contradict the truth to their utter damnation do this as much from ignorance as from wretched and desperate folly. And no wonder! It is ever the way of the wicked to protect their own iniquities by calling upon others like themselves; for they think it of no account to incur the penalty of falsehood.

To cite but a few out of the multitude of proofs: Who does not remember the words of our Lord and Savior Jesus Christ: "Thou art Peter and on this rock I will build my Church, and the gates of hell shall not prevail against it. And I will give thee the keys of the kingdom of heaven and whatsoever thou shalt bind on earth shall be bound in heaven and whatsoever thou shalt loose on earth shall be loosed in heaven." Are kings excepted here? Or are they not of the sheep which the Son of God committed to St. Peter? Who, I ask, thinks himself excluded from this universal grant of the power of binding and loosing to St. Peter unless, perchance, that unhappy man who, being unwilling to bear the yoke of the Lord, subjects himself to the burden of the Devil and refuses to be numbered in the flock of Christ? His wretched liberty shall profit him nothing; for if he shakes off from his proud neck the power divinely granted to Peter, so much the heavier shall it be for him in the day of judgment.

This institution of the divine will, this foundation of the rule of the Church, this privilege granted and sealed especially by a heavenly decree to St. Peter, chief of the Apostles, has been accepted and maintained with great reverence by the holy fathers, and they have given to the Holy Roman Church, as well in general councils as in their other acts and writings, the name of "universal mother." They have not only accepted her expositions of doctrine and her instructions in our holy religion, but they have also recognized her judicial decisions. They have agreed as with one spirit and one voice that all major cases, all especially important affairs and the judgments of all churches ought to be referred to her as to their head and mother, that from her there shall be no appeal, that her judgments may not and cannot be reviewed or reversed by anyone.

Thus Pope Gelasius, writing to the emperor Anastasius, gave him these instructions as to the right theory of the principate of the Holy and Apostolic See, based upon divine authority:

Although it is fitting that all the faithful should submit themselves to all priests who perform their sacred functions properly, how much the more should they accept the judgment of that prelate who has been appointed by the supreme divine ruler to be superior to all priests and whom the loyalty of the whole later Church has recognized as such. Your Wisdom sees plainly that no human capacity whatsoever can equal that of him whom the word of Christ raised above all others and whom the reverend Church has always confessed and still devotedly holds as its Head.

So also Pope Julius, writing to the eastern bishops in regard to the powers of the same Holy and Apostolic See, says:

You ought, my brethren, to have spoken carefully and not ironically of the Holy Roman and Apostolic Church, seeing that our Lord Jesus Christ addressed her respectfully, saying, "Thou art Peter and upon this rock I will build my church, and the gates of hell shall not prevail against it; and I will give thee the keys of the kingdom of heaven." For it has the power, granted by a unique privilege, of opening and shutting the gates of the celestial kingdom to whom it will.

To whom, then, the power of opening and closing Heaven is given, shall he not be able to judge the earth? God forbid! Do you remember what the most blessed Apostle Paul says: "Know ye not that we shall judge angels? How much more things that pertain to this life?"

So Pope Gregory declared that kings who dared to disobey the orders of the Apostolic See should forfeit their office. He wrote to a certain senator and abbot in these words:

If any king, priest, judge or secular person shall disregard this decree of ours and act contrary to it, he shall be deprived of his power and his office and shall learn that he stands condemned at the bar of God for the wrong that he has done. And unless he shall restore what he has wrongfully taken and shall have done fitting penance for his unlawful acts he shall be excluded from the sacred body and blood of our Lord and Savior Jesus Christ and at the last judgment shall receive condign punishment.

Now then, if the blessed Gregory, most gentle of doctors, decreed that kings who should disobey his orders about a hospital for strangers should be not only deposed but excommunicated and condemned in the last judgment, how can anyone blame us for deposing and excommunicating Henry, who not only disregards apostolic judgments, but so far as in him lies tramples upon his mother the Church, basely plunders the whole kingdom and destroys its churches—unless indeed it were one who is a man of his own kind?

As we know also through the teaching of St. Peter in his letter touching the ordination of Clement, where he says: "If any one were friend to those with whom he is not on speaking terms, that man is among those who would like to destroy the Church of God and, while he seems to be with us in the body, he is against us in mind and heart, and he is a far worse enemy than those who are without and are openly hostile. For he, under the forms of friendship, acts as an enemy and scatters and lays waste the Church." Consider then, my best beloved, if he passes so severe a judgment upon him who associates himself with those whom the pope opposes on account of their actions, with what severity he condemns the man himself to whom the pope is thus opposed.

But now, to return to our point: Is not a sovereignty invented by men of this world who were ignorant of God subject to that which the providence of Almighty God established for his own glory and graciously bestowed upon the world? The Son of God we believe to be God and man,

·sitting at the right hand of the Father as High Priest, head of all priests and ever making intercession for us. He despised the kingdom of this world wherein the sons of this world puff themselves up and offered himself as a sacrifice upon the cross.

Who does not know that kings and princes derive their origin from men ignorant of God who raised themselves above their fellows by pride, plunder, treachery, murder—in short, by every kind of crime—at the instigation of the Devil, the prince of this world, men blind with greed and intolerable in their audacity? If, then, they strive to bend the priests of God to their will, to whom may they more properly be compared than to him who is chief over all the sons of pride? For he, tempting our High Priest, head of all priests, son of the Most High, offering him all the kingdoms of this world, said: "All these will I give thee if thou wilt fall down and worship me."

Does anyone doubt that the priests of Christ are to be considered as fathers and masters of kings and princes and of all believers? Would it not be regarded as pitiable madness if a son should try to rule his father or a pupil his master and to bind with unjust obligations the one through whom he expects to be bound or loosed, not only on earth but also in heaven? Evidently recognizing this the emperor Constantine the Great, lord over all kings and princes throughout almost the entire earth, as St. Gregory relates in his letter to the emperor Mauritius, at the holy synod of Nicaea took his place below all the bishops and did not venture to pass any judgment upon them but, even addressing them as gods, felt that they ought not to be subject to his judgment but that he ought to be bound by their decisions.

Pope Gelasius, urging upon the emperor Anastasius not to feel himself wronged by the truth that was called to his attention said: "There are two powers, O august Emperor, by which the world is governed, the sacred authority of the priesthood and the power of kings. Of these the priestly is by so much the greater as they will have to answer for kings themselves in the day of divine judgment;" and a little further: "Know that

you are subject to their judgment, not that they are to be subjected to your will."

In reliance upon such declarations and such authorities, many prelates have excommunicated kings or emperors. If you ask for illustrations: Pope Innocent excommunicated the emperor Arcadius because he consented to the expulsion of St. John Chrysostom from his office. Another Roman pontiff deposed a king of the Franks, not so much on account of his evil deeds as because he was not equal to so great an office, and set in his place Pippin, father of the emperor Charles the Great, releasing all the Franks from the oath of fealty which they had sworn to him. And this is often done by Holy Church when it absolves fighting men from their oaths to bishops who have been deposed by apostolic authority. So St. Ambrose, a holy man but not bishop of the whole Church, excommunicated the emperor Theodosius the Great for a fault which did not seem to other prelates so very grave and excluded him from the Church. He also shows in his writings that the priestly office is as much superior to royal power as gold is more precious than lead. He says: "The honor and dignity of bishops admit of no comparison. If you liken them to the splendor of kings and the diadem of princes, these are as lead compared to the glitter of gold. You see the necks of kings and princes bowed to the knees of priests, and by the kissing of hands they believe that they share the benefit of their prayers." And again: "Know that we have said all this in order to show that there is nothing in this world more excellent than a priest or more lofty than a bishop."

Your Fraternity should remember also that greater power is granted to an exorcist when he is made a spiritual emperor for the casting out of devils, than can be conferred upon any layman for the purpose of earthly dominion. All kings and princes of this earth who live not piously and in their deeds show not a becoming fear of God are ruled by demons and are sunk in miserable slavery. Such men desire to rule, not guided by the love of God, as priests are, for the glory of God and the profit of human souls, but to display their intolerable pride and to satisfy the lusts of their mind. Of these St. Augustine says in the first book of his Christian doctrine: "He who tries to rule over men—who are by nature equal to him—acts with intolerable pride." Now if exorcists have power over demons, as we have said, how much more over those who are subject to demons and are limbs of demons! And if exorcists are superior to these, how much more are priests superior to them!

Furthermore, every Christian king when he approaches his end asks the aid of a priest as a miserable suppliant that he may escape the prison of hell, may pass from darkness into light and may appear at the judgment seat of God freed from the bonds of sin. But who, layman or priest, in his last moments has ever asked the help of any earthly king for the safety of his soul? And what king or emperor has power through his office to snatch any Christian from the might of the Devil by the sacred rite of baptism, to confirm him among the sons of God and to fortify him by the holy chrism? Or—and this is the greatest thing in the Christian religion—who among them is able by his own word to create the body and blood of the Lord? or to whom among them is given the power to bind and loose in Heaven and upon earth? From this it is apparent how greatly superior in power is the priestly dignity.

Or who of them is able to ordain any clergyman in the Holy Church—much less to depose him for any fault? For bishops, while they may ordain other bishops, may in no wise depose them except by authority of the Apostolic See. How, then, can even the most slightly informed person doubt that priests are higher than kings? But if kings are to be judged by priests for their sins, by whom can they more properly be judged than by the Roman pontiff?

In short, all good Christians, whosoever they may be, are more properly to be called kings than are evil princes; for the former, seeking the glory of God, rule themselves rigorously; but the latter, seeking their own rather than the things that are of God, being enemies to themselves, oppress others tyrannically. The former are the body of the true Christ; the latter, the body of the Devil. The former rule themselves that they may reign forever with the supreme ruler. The power of the latter brings it to pass that they perish in eternal damnation with the prince of darkness who is king over all the sons of pride.

It is no great wonder that evil priests take the part of a king whom they love and fear on account of honors received from him. By ordaining any person whomsoever, they are selling their God at a bargain price. For as the elect are inseparably united to their Head, so the wicked are firmly bound to him who is head of all evil—especially against the good. But against these it is of no use to argue, but rather to pray God with tears and groans that he may deliver them from the snares of Satan, in which they are caught, and after trial may lead them at last into knowledge of the truth.

So much for kings and emperors who, swollen with the pride of this world, rule not for God but for themselves. But since it is our duty to exhort everyone according to his station, it is our care with God's help to furnish emperors, kings and other princes with the weapons of humility that thus they may be strong to keep down the floods and waves of pride. We know that earthly glory and the cares of this world are wont especially to cause rulers to be exalted, to forget humility and, seeking their own glory, strive to excel their fellows. It seems therefore especially useful for emperors and kings, while their hearts are lifted up in the strife for glory, to learn how to humble themselves and to know fear rather than joy. Let them therefore consider carefully how dangerous, even awesome is the office of emperor or king, how very few find salvation therein, and how those who are saved through God's mercy have become far less famous in the Church by divine judgment than many humble persons. From the beginning of the world to the present day we do not find in all authentic records emperors or kings whose lives were as distinguished for virtue and piety as were those of a countless multitude of men who despised the world—although we believe that many of them were saved by the mercy of God. Not to speak of Apostles and Martyrs, who among emperors and kings was famed for his miracles as were St. Martin, St. Antony and St. Benedict? What emperor or king ever raised the dead, cleansed lepers or opened the eyes of the blind? True, Holy Church praises and honors the emperor Constantine, of pious memory, Theodosius and Honorius, Charles and Louis, as lovers of justice, champions of the Christian faith and protectors of churches, but she does not claim that they were illustrious for the splendor of their wonderful works. Or to how many names of kings or emperors has Holy Church ordered churches or altars to be dedicated or masses to be celebrated?

Let kings and princes fear lest the higher they are raised above their fellows in this life, the deeper they may be plunged in everlasting fire. Wherefore it is written: "The mighty shall suffer mighty torments." They shall render unto God an account for all men subject to their rule. But if it is no small labor for the pious individual to guard his own soul, what a task is laid upon princes in the care of so many thousands of souls! And if Holy Church imposes a heavy penalty upon him who takes a single human life, what shall be done to those who send many thousands to death for the glory of this world? These, although they say with their lips, *mea culpa*, for the slaughter of many, yet in their hearts they rejoice at the increase of their glory and neither repent of what they have done nor regret that they have sent their brothers into the world below. So that, since they do not repent with all their hearts and will not restore what they have gained by human bloodshed, their penitence before God remains without the fruits of a true repentance.

Wherefore they ought greatly to fear, and they should frequently be reminded that, as we have said, since the beginning of the world and throughout the kingdoms of the earth very few kings of saintly life can be found out of an innumerable multitude, whereas in one single chair of successive bishops—the Roman—from the time of the blessed Apostle Peter nearly a hundred are counted among the holiest of men. How can

this be, except because the kings and princes of the earth, seduced by empty glory, prefer their own interests to the things of the Spirit, whereas pious pontiffs, despising vainglory, set the things of God above the things of the flesh. The former readily punish offenses against themselves but are not troubled by offenses against God; the latter quickly forgive those who sin against them but do not easily pardon offenders against God. The former, far too much given to worldly affairs, think little of spiritual things; the latter, dwelling eagerly upon heavenly subjects, despise the things of this world.

All Christians, therefore, who desire to reign with Christ are to be warned not to reign through ambition for wordly power. They are to keep in mind the admonition of that most holy pope Gregory in his book on the pastoral office: "Of all these things what is to be followed, what held fast, except that the man strong in virtue shall come to his office under compulsion? Let him who is without virtue not come to it even though he be urged thereto." If, then, men who fear God come under compulsion with fear and trembling to the Apostolic See where those who are properly ordained become stronger through the merits of the blessed Apostle Peter, with what awe and hesitation should men ascend the throne of a king where even good and humble men like Saul and David become worse! What we have said above is thus stated in the decrees of the blessed pope Symmachus—though we have learned it by experience: "He, that is St. Peter, transmitted to his successors an unfailing endowment of merit together with an inheritance of innocence;" and again: "For who can doubt that he is holy who is raised to the height of such an office, in which if he is lacking in virtue acquired by his own merits, that which is handed down from his predecessor is sufficient. For either he raises men of distinction to bear this burden or he glorifies them after they are raised up."

Wherefore let those whom Holy Church, of its own will and with deliberate judgment, not for fleeting glory but for the welfare of multitudes, has called to royal or imperial rule—let them be obedient and ever mindful of the blessed Gregory's declaration in that same pastoral treatise: "When a man disdains to be the equal of his fellow men, he becomes like an apostate angel. Thus Saul, after his period of humility, swollen with pride, ran into excess of power. He was raised in humility, but rejected in his pride, as God bore witness, saying: 'Though thou wast little in thine own sight, wast thou not made the head of the tribes of Israel?'" and again: "I marvel how, when he was little to himself he was great before God, but when he seemed great to himself he was little before God." Let them watch and remember what God says in the Gospel: "I seek not my own glory," and, "He who would be first among you, let him be the servant of all." Let them ever place the honor of God above their own; let them embrace justice and maintain it by preserving to everyone his right; let them not enter into the counsels of the ungodly, but cling to those of religion with all their hearts. Let them not seek to make Holy Church their maid-servant or their subject, but recognizing priests, the eyes of God, as their masters and fathers, strive to do them becoming honor.

If we are commanded to honor our fathers and mothers in the flesh, how much more our spiritual parents! If he that curseth his father or his mother shall be put to death, what does he deserve who curses his spiritual father or mother? Let not princes, led astray by carnal affection, set their own sons over that flock for whom Christ shed his blood if a better and more suitable man can be found. By thus loving their own son more than God they bring the greatest evils upon the Church. For it is evident that he who fails to provide to the best of his ability so great and necessary an advantage for our holy mother, the Church, does not love God and his neighbor as befits a Christian man. If this one virtue of charity be wanting, then whatever of good the man may do will lack all saving grace.

But if they do these things in humility, keeping their love for God and their neighbor as they ought, they may count upon the mercy of him who said: "Learn of me, for I am meek and lowly of heart." If they humbly imitate him, they shall pass from their servile and transient reign into the kingdom of eternal liberty.

*   *   *

REVIEW QUESTIONS

1. What does Pope Gregory VII think is the right relationship between the church and secular authority?
2. How effectively does he use evidence to support his case?
3. How might a supporter of Henry IV answer the pope's arguments?

POPE BONIFACE VIII

Papal Bull *Unam Sanctam*

Pope Boniface VIII (1294–1303) quarreled with Philip IV of France about papal authority over the French church and the crown's power to tax the church. In this papal bull, November 1302, the pope reformulated the church's view on the sources and extent of its authority. Ultimately, the king of France accused the pope of her-

esy and sent officials to arrest Boniface, who narrowly escaped, with his health and prestige severely damaged.

From *The Crisis of Church and State 1050–1300*, edited by Brian Tierney (Upper Saddle River, N.J.: Prentice-Hall, 1964), pp. 188–89.

That there is one holy, Catholic and apostolic church we are bound to believe and to hold, our faith urging us, and this we do firmly believe and simply confess; and that outside this church there is no salvation or remission of sins, as her spouse proclaims in the Canticles, "One is my dove, my perfect one. She is the only one of her mother, the chosen of her that bore her"; which represents one mystical body whose head is Christ, while the head of Christ is God. In this church there is one Lord, one faith, one baptism. At the time of the Flood there was one ark, symbolizing the one church. It was finished in one cubit and had one helmsman and captain, namely Noah, and we read that all things on earth outside of it were destroyed. This church we venerate and this alone, the Lord saying through his prophet, "Deliver, O God, my soul from the sword, my only one from the power of the dog." He prayed for the soul, that is himself, the head, and at the same time for the body, which he called the one church on account of the promised unity of faith, sacraments and charity of the church. This is that seamless garment of the Lord which was not cut but fell by lot. Therefore there is one body and one head of this one and only church, not two heads as though it were a monster, namely Christ and Christ's vicar, Peter and Peter's successor, for the Lord said to this Peter, "Feed my sheep." He said "My sheep" in general, not these or those, whence he is understood to have committed them all to Peter. Hence, if the Greeks or any others say that they were not committed to Peter and his successors, they necessarily admit that they are not of Christ's flock, for the Lord says in John that there is one sheepfold and one shepherd.

We are taught by the words of the Gospel that in this church and in her power there are two swords, a spiritual one and a temporal one. For when the apostles said "Here are two swords," meaning in the church since it was the apostles who spoke, the Lord did not reply that it was too many but enough. Certainly anyone who denies that the temporal sword is in the power of Peter has not paid heed to the words of the Lord when he said, "Put up thy sword into its sheath." Both then are in the power of the church, the material sword and the spiritual. But the one is exercised for the church, the other by the church, the one by the hand of the priest, the other by the hand of kings and soldiers, though at the will and suffrance of the priest. One sword ought to be under the other and the temporal authority subject to the spiritual power. For, while the apostle says, "There is no power but from God and those that are ordained of God," they would not be ordained unless one sword was under the other and, being inferior, was led by the other to the highest things. For, according to the blessed Dionysius, it is the law of divinity for the lowest to be led to the highest through intermediaries. In the order of the universe all things are not kept in order in the same fashion and immediately but the lowest are ordered by the intermediate and inferiors by superiors. But that the spiritual power excels any earthly one in dignity and nobility we ought the more openly to confess in proportion as spiritual things excel temporal ones. Moreover we clearly perceive this from the giving of tithes, from benediction and sanctification, from the acceptance of this power and from the very government of things. For, the truth bearing witness, the spiritual power has to institute the earthly power and to judge it if it has not been good. So is verified the prophecy of Jeremias concerning the church and the power of the church, "Lo, I have set thee this day over the nations and over kingdoms" etc.

Therefore, if the earthly power errs, it shall be judged by the spiritual power, if a lesser spiritual power errs it shall be judged by its superior, but if the supreme spiritual power errs it can be judged only by God not by man, as the apostle witnesses, "The spiritual man judgeth all things and he himself is judged of no man." Although this authority was given to a man and is exercised by a man it is not human but rather divine, being given to Peter at God's mouth, and confirmed to him and to his successors in him, the rock whom the Lord acknowledged when he said to Peter himself "Whatsoever thou shalt bind" etc. Whoever therefore resists this power so ordained by God resists the ordinance of God unless, like the Manicheans, he imagines that there are two begin-nings, which we judge to be false and heretical, as Moses witnesses, for not "in the beginnings" but "in the beginning" God created heaven and earth. Therefore we declare, state, define and pronounce that it is altogether necessary to salvation for every human creature to be subject to the Roman Pontiff.

REVIEW QUESTIONS

1. What does Pope Boniface VIII see as the right relation between the church and secular power?
2. How do his arguments and evidence differ from those of his predecessor Gregory VII?
3. What, in practice, did the last sentence of this bull mean?

FROM *Interrogation of Beatrice of Planisolles*

Beatrice de Planisolles, a member of the minor nobility in Languedoc, was accused of the Cathar heresy and tried in 1320 before the court of Jacques Fournier, bishop of Pamiers and later Pope Benedict XII. The events she describes in some cases go back more than two decades. The official church considered Cathars to be heretics rejecting most of the tenets of Catholic Christianity. The testimony here concerns what Beatrice has to say about the priest Pierre Clergue, the rector of Montaillou, a village in the Pyrenees and apparently one of the last Cathar strongholds to have survived the Crusades and inquisitions of the thirteenth century. Clergue was a not-so-secret Cathar, and Beatrice's testimony is second-hand information about Cathar beliefs, further filtered by the procedures of the inquisition. Beatrice was probably trying to save her life, but what she said about Cathar beliefs had to conform to what the inquisitors already knew, so most scholars credit the sincerity of this confession obtained under duress.

From *Other Middle Ages: Witnesses at the Margins of Medieval Society*, edited by Michael Goodich (Philadelphia: University of Pennsylvania Press, 1998), pp. 205–11.

*   *   *

On August 8, 1320, continuing her confession, she said that with respect to marriage Pierre said that many of the rules do not proceed from God's will. God did not decide that a man ought not to take as a wife his biological sister or another blood relative, because in the beginning of the world brothers knew their own sisters. But when several brothers had one or two beautiful sisters, each wanting to have one or both, many murders took place between them. The church therefore decided that a brother should not know his own sister or any relative carnally. But in God's eyes it is as much of a sin to know another woman as to know own's own sister or another relative, since this sin is as great with one woman as with another, with the exception that it is not as great a sin between a man and his own wife . . . since married persons do not confess to having known each other and one does so without shame.

He said that marriage is perfect and complete when one pledges one's faith to another; what takes place in church between married persons—for example, the nuptial blessing—is mere worthless secular pomp, and was instituted by the church only for the sake of worldly pomp. The rector told the speaker that a man or woman may perform any sin while they live in the world and do as they please. It is enough for a man or woman to be accepted into the sect of the good Christians at the end of their lives for them to be saved and absolved of all sins they may have committed in their lives, because Christ told the apostles that he who abandons father, mother, wife, and children, and whatever they have to follow Him, will possess the kingdom of Heaven [Matthew 19.27, James 5]. Peter had replied to Christ, "If we abandon all and follow you, and thus have the Kingdom of Heaven, what will happen to those who are weak and cannot follow you?" The Lord replied to Peter that his friends would come to place their hands on the heads of the weak and they would be cured, and those who were cured would follow Him and thus possess the Kingdom of Heaven.

The rector said that these "friends of God" were the good Christians and those whom others call heretics; through the imposition of their hands, if men or women are near death, they are saved and absolved of whatever sins they may have committed. In order to prove that it might be better for the world if a brother were permitted to marry his sister, he said, "Look, we are four brothers, I am a priest and I don't want to marry. If my brothers Guillaume and Bernard had married our sisters Esclarmonde and Guillemette, our lineage would

not have been destroyed, because our sisters had to give a dowry. Otherwise, the house would have remained intact. With the assistance of the one woman whom our brother Raimond brought into the house, we would have had enough women, and the family would have been wealthier than it is. It would therefore be better for a brother to take his sister than a strange woman, or even that a sister should take her brother as a husband, since when she leaves her paternal home with a dowry to marry a stranger, the house may be ruined."

As a consequence of these and similar remarks, the speaker said that she consented to have relations with him one night in her home during the octave of saints Peter and Paul [July 6]; he knew her carnally for about a year and a half, and then two or three times a week at night she lay with him in her home near the chateau of Montaillou. She even came to the rector's house for two nights in order to have relations with him. One night during Christmas the priest knew her carnally and celebrated mass the next day, although no other priest was present.[1] When once this same Christmas night he wanted to have relations with her, she said to him, "How can you want to commit such a grave sin on such a holy night?" He replied that it is as grave a sin to have sex with a woman on Christmas night as it is on any other night. When on this occasion and on the other frequent occasions he celebrated mass the day after she had relations with him, he did not confess to any priest, because none were present. She often asked him how he dared to celebrate mass when he had committed such a grave sin the previous night without confessing to a priest; he replied that the only true confession is the one made to God, who knows about a sin before it has even been committed, and only he can absolve one of sin. The confession, on the other hand, made to a priest who only knows about this sin when it has been revealed to him and who cannot absolve one of sin, is not valid; it is only undertaken for show and pomp, since only God can absolve from sin and no man has such power.

---

[1] This was presumably in order to impose absolution, as the priest was in a state of sin.

The priest told the speaker that she should not confess to any priest about the sin she had committed with him because it is enough to confess to God, who knows all her sins and can absolve her, something no other man can do. In order to convince her to believe that no pope nor bishop nor priest under him has the power to absolve from sin, he argued that Saint Peter was not "apostolic" when he was alive, but only after he died and his bones were thrown into a well where they lay for many years. When his bones were found they were washed and were put in the throne on which the Roman pontiffs have their seat.[2] But since these bones of St. Peter do not have the power to absolve from sin, when they had been placed in the throne and "made apostolic," neither was Peter himself thereby made apostolic, nor did the Roman pontiffs who sit on the throne thereby receive the apostolic power to absolve from sin. Only the good Christians who are persecuted and suffer death like saints Lawrence, Stephen, and Bartholomew can absolve from sin. The bishops and priests subject to the Roman church, who are heretics and persecute good Christians, do not have the power to absolve from sin; for this power was taken from them by God and only given to the good Christians, who knew and predicted that they would undergo persecution.

She asked the priest, if it is true that since no confession made to a priest is of value, priests cannot absolve from sin, nor does the satisfaction meted out by them have any value, why does he hear confessions, absolve, and impose satisfaction? He replied that, although what he and other priests do is invalid, they do so because otherwise they will lose their incomes and nothing will be given to them unless they do what the church prescribes. Good Christians and others received by them after having adored[3] them can absolve others from sin. It is not necessary for those who have been absolved by them of their sins to confess their sins.

They must rather give themselves to God and to the good Christians who will absolve them by placing their hands over their heads, and they will be absolved of all their sins. . . .

The priest then said that only God made the spirits and could not have made what is corrupted and destroyed, since the works of God are eternal, whereas the bodies we see and feel, the heavens and the earth and all that is in them, except for the spirits, were made by the Devil, the governor of the world. Because the Devil did this, everything will be corrupted, since he cannot do anything which is stable and permanent.

The priest told the speaker that when in the beginning God made a man who walked and spoke, after the Devil saw this, he made the body of another man who could neither walk nor talk. God then said to the Devil, "Why don't you make your man walk and talk?" The Devil replied that he couldn't, but asked God to make his man walk and talk. God replied that he would willingly do so provided whatever he placed in the Devil's man would belong to God. The Devil replied that whatever was placed by God in this man would indeed belong to Him. God then breathed into the mouth of the man made by the Devil, and the man began to walk and talk. As a result, man's soul belongs to God and his body to the Devil.

The priest told her that God had made all the spirits in heaven, which had then committed the sin of pride, wanting to be equal to God. Because of this sin, they fell from heaven into the air and the earth where they dwell, and enter into the bodies which they encounter indiscriminately whenever they can, so they enter equally into the bodies of brute beasts and human beings, with the exception that they can't speak when they inhabit the bodies of brute beasts. The spirits found in the bodies of brute beasts possess reason and knowledge, so that because of this it appears that they avoid what is injurious to them and desire and pursue what is useful. For this reason it is an equal sin to kill a brute beast as it is to kill a person, since both brute beasts and humans possess the spirit of reason and knowledge. All said spirits must enter some human body in which to do penance for the

---

[2] St. Peter's in Rome.

[3] This refers to the Cathar ceremony of *melioramentum*.

sin of pride; and this must happen before the world comes to an end. These spirits can do penance for this sin only while they dwell in human bodies, but not while in the bodies of brute beasts.

The priest said that those spirits that have sinned in this way are very happy if they are able to enter into the body of a good Christian. Immediately upon leaving their bodies they return to heaven, from whence they had fallen. But if they have not left the body of a good Christian, but rather that of another man or woman, when they exit that body they enter into the body of another man or woman if they can, and they enter nine bodies if they haven't succeeded again in entering the bodies of a good male or female Christian. Once entering such a body they immediately afterward exit and return to heaven from which they had fallen. But if after successively entering nine bodies such a spirit has not entered that of a good Christian man or woman, after leaving the ninth one such a spirit is lost forever and cannot be penitent afterward. This is generally the case, although those spirits which have consented to the betrayal of Christ, such as Judas and other Jews, after having exited their bodies, are immediately damned, unable to do penance afterward or to enter other bodies in order to do penance. But those spirits which were present at the betrayal of Christ and did not agree to that betrayal will in the end enter nine bodies, like the other spirits.

The priest told her that only those spirits which enter the bodies of good Christians will be saved, and no others, whether they be good Christians, Jews, or Saracens; and all good Christians and all who adore them, believe in them, and are accepted into their sect will be saved. Because of this his own mother Mengarde will be saved, for she did many good things for said good Christians. Na Roca and Raimond Roche his son, who were imprisoned for a while for the crime of heresy, received all their food from her house. Because these two persons were heretics and believers, his mother had been good to them.

The priest said that when such spirits were in heaven and sinned by rebelling against God, they were divided. Some of them had conspired to re-

volt against God and were the first to be expelled from heaven. Their sin was so serious that God had refused to receive their penance, and they would be destroyed in Hell. They are the demons. In contrast, the other spirits who did not plan to rebel against God nor openly showed contempt, but had rather wanted merely to follow those who had planned the rebellion, fell down to the earth and air, became incarnate in human and animal bodies, and may be saved or damned, as noted above.

The priest said that the good Christians do not believe that God makes the seeds which generate, flower, and grow those things which are born on earth. If this were the case, then God could equally make seeds grow on a naked stone, just as takes place in arable soil. Those seeds thrown on a stone could grow as well as those thrown on the ground. This rather takes place because of the enrichment of the soil, not because God has acted in some way.

The priest said that the good Christians do not believe that Christ was incarnate in the blessed Virgin or descended into her in order to take human flesh from her, since even before the blessed Mary was born, Christ existed from eternity.[4] He merely "adumbrated" himself in the blessed Mary, taking nothing from her. The word *adumbration* means that, if a man were inside a cask, he receives nothing inside the shadow of that cask from the cask itself, but is only contained therein. In the same way Christ dwelled within the Virgin Mary, receiving nothing from her, but was only in her as the contents is held within its container.

The priest said that when Christ ate with his disciples he never ate or drank, although he appeared to eat and drink.

Because Christ was crucified on the cross, no one should venerate or adore the cross, because so much vituperation was hurled at Christ when he was on it.

Swearing falsely on a book of the Gospels is not a lie, but only if one swears in God's name.

The Church of God exists only where there is a good Christian, because he is the Church of God,

---

[4] See John 8.58: "Jesus said unto them, Verily verily, I say unto you, Before Abraham was, I am."

but otherwise there is no church of God, nor are other persons the Church of God.

When good Christians are burned because of their faith, they are martyrs of Christ.

When good Christians receive someone into their sect, they should afterward neither eat nor drink, except cold water. When they die weakly in this way because they don't want to eat, they become the saints of God.

The fire in which the good Christians burn does not consume them, because God helps them not to be burned by that fire, and they do not suffer much.

* * *

REVIEW QUESTIONS

1. Given the circumstances of this confession, how much of what Beatrice said should we believe?
2. According to this confession what were the major beliefs of Cathars?
3. Why was the Cathar faith such a threat to the Catholic Church?

SALISBURY CATHEDRAL (1258) WITH SPIRE (1330)

Salisbury Cathedral is a classic example of English Gothic architecture. What are the characteristic features of Gothic architecture? What possible connections are there between these features and the messages the medieval church tried to communicate to the laity?

FROM *Carmina Burana*

Carmina Burana ("Songs of Beuren," the place in Bavaria where the manuscript was found) is a collection of about 350 songs and poems on a variety of subjects. This thirteenth-century manuscript preserves the greatest known collection of medieval Latin poetry. The texts reflect the world of late-twelfth-century university and courtly life. All the works in the manuscript are anonymous, though some authors have been identified from other sources. The poems are a window on many aspects of medieval social history. The first piece here, attributed by some to Walter of Châtillon, concerns the decline in morals, and the second the game of chess.

From *Selections from the Carmina Burana*, translated by David Parlett (New York: Penguin Books, 1986), pp. 56–57, 169–72.

*   *   *

CB3 Mouldering Morals

Ecce torpet probitas,
virtus sepelitur . . .

Morals lie a-mouldering,
   virtue's all a-tatter,
liberality grows lean,
   parsimony fatter,
only lies are genuine—
   truth's another matter.
   Laws are for the breaking:
all illicitly allow
   any undertaking.

Mammon lords it over all,
   misers run the nation—
none but wouldn't gladly crawl
   for a small donation,
counting on their wherewithal
   for their reputation.
   Laws are for the breaking:
understanding underwrites
   any undertaking.

What's the hardest verb to learn?
   G I V E is. Give—gave—given.

Few words are of less concern
   to those who have striven
after wealth—who, more they earn,
   more to crave are driven.
   Laws are for the breaking:
moneymakers can't keep count
   of the amount they're making.

Self-control is on the wane,
   prurience uprears:
faithless vows are poured in vain
   into faithless ears:
Jove to Juno's found to feign,
   Dido to Aeneas.
   Laws are for the breaking:
who forsake fidelity
   are themselves forsaking.

If you seek to be precise
   don't describe as "living"
fools who, once involved in vice,
   sin without misgiving.
Life? The word must ill suffice
   for their self-deceiving.
   Laws are for the breaking—
all overtly overlook
   any undertaking.

*   *   *

CB210 Verses on Chess

Qui cupit egregium   scachorum noscere ludum,
   Audiat: ut potui   carmine composui . . .

All who desire instruction
in chess, most noble distraction,
   hark: I've written you these
   ditties of expertise.

First, a few lines to settle
the scene of this sportive battle.
   The board measures eight by eight
   and bi-coloured squares alternate.

White is the usual colour
of one, and red is the other—
   failing red, black or blue
   or any old colour will do.

Rooks in the first position
threaten their warlike commission:
   on each next square, a knight
   champs at the bit for a fight.

On the third square stands a bishop
on guard against royal mishap:
   king on the fourth is seen
   standing next to his queen.

Then follow, up to the border,
the same men but in reverse order—
   and on the subsequent row
   little pawns, raring to go.

They proceed down the wide ways
capturing, right or left, sideways,
   adverse pieces that stand
   on each diagonal hand.

Should any pawn's expedition
reach to the eighthmost position
   it drops the pawn's routine,
   takes on that of a queen.

Having thus changed its sex, it
fights for its monarch—protects it,
   orders and regulates:
   here conquers, and there abates.

Pawns, as the first to engage in
battle, fall first to its raging,
   leaving a pathway clear
   for those in wait at the rear.

Rooks, let loose by their slaughter,
roam over every quarter,
   marching wherever they may
   if nothing stands in their way.

Major pieces take major,
threaten the minor with danger—
   yet even they may fall
   prey to the weakest of all.

Bearing the signs of his knighting,
swift, wise, and clever at fighting,
   see the bold knight advance
   seizing his every chance.

Capturing innocent pieces
who lack his subtle caprices:
   worrying this way and that,
   here lays low—there is laid flat.

As for the bishop, his three-pointed
headgear leaves courage disjointed:
   hither and thither he goes
   felling invigilant foes.

Dominant pieces put paid to
minor pieces—yet they, too,
   yield to the weakest of all.
   Pawns are the quickest to fall.

No king can ever be taken
although by his partner forsaken:
   queenless, her king and lord
   has to remain on the board.

Often a king, though surrounded
by aides, is "checkmated" or grounded:
   if he has nowhere to flee
   that is the finish of he.

*   *   *

REVIEW QUESTIONS

1. How is the rise of a money economy affecting the traditional values of this society?
2. How do the rules of chess reflect the social realities of medieval Europe?

ST. FRANCIS

FROM *The Rule of 1223* AND *The Testament*

Francis of Assisi (1182–1226) was an inspired preacher whose famous conversion from secular life put him on the path to founding the Friars Minor (the Little Brothers), the Franciscans. Francis abandoned the worlds of commerce and warfare and devoted himself to preaching and acts of charity toward the sick and poor. Supported by Pope Innocent III, Francis tried to imitate the life of Christ through preaching, poverty, and humility. The Rule of 1223 *and his* Testament *show the charismatic Francis trying to take his small band of followers into the institutional world of the organized church so that his community would outlive him.*

From *St. Francis of Assisi: Writings and Early Biographies*, edited by Raphael Brown (Quincy: Franciscan Herald Press, 1973), pp. 57–64, 67–70.

FROM *The Rule of 1223*

CHAPTER 1
IN THE NAME OF THE LORD BEGINS
THE LIFE OF THE FRIARS MINOR

The Rule and life of the Friars Minor is this, namely, to observe the Holy Gospel of our Lord Jesus Christ by living in obedience, without property, and in chastity. Brother Francis promises obedience and reverence to his holiness Pope Honorius and his lawfully elected successors and to the Church of Rome. The other friars are bound to obey Brother Francis and his successors.

CHAPTER 2
OF THOSE WHO WISH TO TAKE UP THIS LIFE
AND HOW THEY ARE TO BE RECEIVED

If anyone wants to profess our Rule and comes to the friars, they must send him to their provincial minister, because he alone, to the exclusion of others, has permission to receive friars into the Order. The ministers must carefully examine all candidates on the Catholic faith and the sacraments of the Church. If they believe all that the Catholic faith teaches and are prepared to profess it loyally, holding by it steadfastly, to the end of their lives, and if they are not married; or if they are married and their wives have already entered a convent or after taking a vow of chastity have by the authority of the bishop of the diocese been granted this permission; and the wives are of such an age that no suspicion can arise concerning them: let the ministers tell them what the holy Gospel says, that they should go and sell all that belongs to them and endeavour to give it to the poor. If they cannot do this, their good will is sufficient.

The friars and their ministers must be careful not to become involved in the temporal affairs of newcomers to the Order, so that they may dispose of their goods freely, as God inspires them. If they ask for advice, the ministers may refer them to some God-fearing persons who can advise them how to distribute their property to the poor.

When this has been done, the ministers should clothe the candidates with the habit of probation, namely, two tunics without a hood, a cord and trousers, and a caperon reaching to the cord, unless the ministers themselves at any time decide that something else is more suitable. After the year of the novitiate, they should be received to obedience, promising to live always according to this life and Rule. It is absolutely forbidden to leave the Order, as his holiness the Pope has laid down. For the Gospel tells us, *No one, having put his hand to the plough and looking back, is fit for the kingdom of God.*

The friars who have already vowed obedience may have one tunic with a hood and those who wish may have another without a hood. Those who are forced by necessity may wear shoes. All the friars are to wear poor clothes and they can use pieces of sackcloth and other material to mend them, with God's blessing.

I warn all the friars and exhort them not to condemn or look down on people whom they see wearing soft or gaudy clothes and enjoying luxuries in food or drink; each one should rather condemn and despise himself.

CHAPTER 3
OF THE DIVINE OFFICE AND FASTING, AND HOW THE FRIARS ARE TO TRAVEL ABOUT THE WORLD

The clerics are to recite the Divine Office according to the rite of the Roman Curia, except the psalter; and so they may have breviaries. The lay brothers are to say twenty-four *Our Fathers* for Matins and five for Lauds; for Prime, Terce, Sext, and None, for each of these, they are to say seven; for Vespers twelve and for Compline seven. They should also say some prayers for the dead.

All the friars are to fast from the feast of All Saints until Christmas. Those who voluntarily fast for forty days after Epiphany have God's blessing, because this is the period our Lord sanctified by his holy fast. However, those who do not wish to do so, should not be forced to it. All the friars are bound to keep the Lenten fast before Easter, but they are not bound to fast at other times, except on Fridays. However, in case of manifest necessity, they are not obliged to corporal fasting.

And this is my advice, my counsel, and my earnest plea to my friars in our Lord Jesus Christ that, when they travel about the world, they should not be quarrelsome or take part in disputes with words or criticize others; but they should be gentle, peaceful, and unassuming, courteous and humble, speaking respectfully to everyone, as is expected of them. They are forbidden to ride on horseback, unless they are forced to it by manifest necessity or sickness. *Whatever house* they *enter,* they should *first say, "Peace to this house,"* and in the words of the Gospel they *may eat what is set before* them.

CHAPTER 4
THE FRIARS ARE FORBIDDEN TO ACCEPT MONEY

I strictly forbid all the friars to accept money in any form, either personally or through an intermediary. The ministers and superiors, however, are bound to provide carefully for the needs of the sick and the clothing of the other friars, by having recourse to spiritual friends, while taking into account differences of place, season, or severe climate, as seems best to them in the circumstances. This does not dispense them from the prohibition of receiving money in any form.

CHAPTER 5
THE MANNER OF WORKING

The friars to whom God has given the grace of working should work in a spirit of faith and devotion and avoid idleness, which is the enemy of the soul, without however extinguishing the spirit of prayer and devotion, to which every temporal consideration must be subordinate. As wages for their labour they may accept anything necessary for their temporal needs, for themselves or their brethren, except money in any form. And they should accept it humbly as is expected of those who serve God and strive after the highest poverty.

CHAPTER 6
THAT THE FRIARS ARE TO APPROPRIATE NOTHING FOR THEMSELVES; ON SEEKING ALMS; AND ON THE SICK FRIARS

The friars are to appropriate nothing for themselves, neither a house, nor a place, nor anything else. As *strangers and pilgrims* in this world, who serve God in poverty and humility, they should beg alms trustingly. And there is no reason why they should be ashamed, because God made himself poor for us in this world. This is the pinnacle of the most exalted poverty, and it is this, my dearest brothers, that has made you heirs and kings of the kingdom of heaven, poor in temporal things, but rich in virtue. This should be your portion, because it leads to the land of the living. And to this poverty, my beloved brothers, you must cling with all your heart, and wish never to have anything else under heaven, for the sake of our Lord Jesus Christ.

Wherever the friars meet one another, they should show that they are members of the same family. And they should have no hesitation in making known their needs to one another. For if a mother loves and cares for her child in the flesh, a friar should certainly love and care for his spiritual brother all the more tenderly. If a friar falls ill, the others are bound to look after him as they would like to be looked after themselves.

CHAPTER 7
OF THE PENANCE TO BE IMPOSED ON FRIARS WHO FALL INTO SIN

If any of the friars, at the instigation of the enemy, fall into mortal sin, they must have recourse as soon as possible, without delay, to their provincial ministers, if it is a sin for which recourse to them has been prescribed for the friars. If the ministers are priests, they should impose a moderate penance on such friars; if they are not priests, they should see that a penance is imposed by some priest of the Order, as seems best to them before God. They must be careful not to be angry or upset because a friar has fallen into sin, because anger or annoyance in themselves or in others makes it difficult to be charitable.

CHAPTER 8
THE ELECTION OF THE MINISTER GENERAL OF THE ORDER AND THE PENTECOST CHAPTER

The friars are always bound to have a member of the Order as Minister General, who is the servant of the whole fraternity, and they are strictly bound to obey him. At his death the provincial ministers and the custodes are to elect a successor at the Pentecost Chapter, at which the provincial ministers are bound to assemble in the place designated by the Minister General. This chapter should be held once every three years, or at a longer or shorter interval, if the Minister General has so ordained.

If at any time it becomes clear to all the provincial ministers and custodes that the Minister General is incapable of serving the friars and can be of no benefit to them, they who have the power to elect must elect someone else as Minister General.

After the Pentecost Chapter, the provincial ministers and custodes may summon their subjects to a chapter in their own territory once in the same year, if they wish and it seems worthwhile.

CHAPTER 9
OF PREACHERS

The friars are forbidden to preach in any diocese, if the bishop objects to it. No friar should dare to preach to the people unless he has been examined and approved by the Minister General of the Order and has received from him the commission to preach.

Moreover, I advise and admonish the friars that in their preaching, their words should be examined and chaste. They should aim only at the advantage and spiritual good of their listeners, telling them briefly about vice and virtue, punishment and glory, because our Lord himself kept his words short on earth.

CHAPTER 10
ON ADMONISHING AND CORRECTING THE FRIARS

The ministers, who are the servants of the other friars, must visit their subjects and admonish them, correcting them humbly and charitably, without commanding them anything that is against their conscience or our Rule. The subjects, however, should remember that they have renounced their own wills for God's sake. And so I strictly command them to obey their ministers in everything that they have promised God and is not against their conscience and our Rule. The friars who are convinced that they cannot observe the Rule spiritually, wherever they may be, can and must have recourse to their ministers. The ministers, for their part, are bound to receive them kindly and charitably, and be so sympathetic towards them that the friars can speak and deal with them as employers with their servants. That is the way it ought to be; the ministers should be the servants of all the friars.

With all my heart, I beg the friars in our Lord Jesus Christ to be on their guard against pride, boasting, envy, and greed, against the cares and anxieties of this world, against detraction and complaining. Those who are illiterate should not be anxious to study. They should realize instead that the only thing they should desire is to have the spirit of God at work within them, while they pray to him unceasingly with a heart free from self-interest. They must be humble, too, and patient in persecution or illness, loving those who persecute us by blaming us or bringing charges against us, as our Lord tells us, *Love your enemies, pray for those who persecute and calumniate you. Blessed are those who suffer persecution for justice' sake, for theirs is the kingdom of heaven. He who has persevered to the end will be saved.*

CHAPTER 11
THE FRIARS ARE FORBIDDEN TO ENTER THE MONASTERIES OF NUNS

I strictly forbid all the friars to have suspicious relationships or conversations with women. No one may enter the monasteries of nuns, except those who have received special permission from the Apostolic See. They are forbidden to be sponsors of men or women lest scandal arise amongst or concerning the friars.

CHAPTER 12
OF THESE WHO WISH TO GO AMONG THE SARACENS AND OTHER UNBELIEVERS

If any of the friars is inspired by God to go among the Saracens or other unbelievers, he must ask permission from his provincial minister. The ministers, for their part, are to give permission only to those whom they see are fit to be sent.

The ministers, too, are bound to ask the Pope for one of the cardinals of the holy Roman Church to be governor, protector, and corrector of this fraternity, so that we may be utterly subject and submissive to the Church. And so, firmly established in the Catholic faith, we may live always according to the poverty, and the humility, and the Gospel of our Lord Jesus Christ, as we have solemnly promised.

*   *   *

FROM *The Testament*

This is how God inspired me, Brother Francis, to embark upon a life of penance. When I was in sin, the sight of lepers nauseated me beyond measure; but then God himself led me into their company, and I had pity on them. When I had once become acquainted with them, what had previously nauseated me became a source of spiritual and physical consolation for me. After that I did not wait long before leaving the world.

And God inspired me with such faith in his churches that I used to pray with all simplicity, saying, "We adore you, Lord Jesus Christ, here and in all your churches in the whole world, and we bless you, because by your holy cross you have redeemed the world."

God inspired me, too, and still inspires me with such great faith in priests who live according to the laws of the holy Church of Rome, because of their dignity, that if they persecuted me, I should still be ready to turn to them for aid. And if I were as wise as Solomon and met the poorest priests of the world, I would still refuse to preach against their will in the parishes in which they live. I am determined to reverence, love and honour priests and all others as my superiors. I refuse to consider their sins, because I can see the Son of God in them and they are better than I. I do this because in this world I cannot see the most high Son of God with my own eyes, except for his most holy Body and Blood which they receive and they alone administer to others.

Above everything else, I want this most holy Sacrament to be honoured and venerated and reserved in places which are richly ornamented. Whenever I find his most holy name or writings containing his words in an improper place, I make a point of picking them up, and I ask that they be picked up and put aside in a suitable place. We should honour and venerate theologians, too, and the ministers of God's word, because it is they who give us spirit and life.

When God gave me some friars, there was no one to tell me what I should do; but the Most High himself made it clear to me that I must live the life of the Gospel. I had this written down briefly and simply and his holiness the Pope confirmed it for me. Those who embraced this life gave everything they had to the poor. They were satisfied with one habit which was patched inside and outside, and a cord, and trousers. We refused to have anything more.

Those of us who were clerics said the Office like other clerics, while the lay brothers said the *Our Father*, and we were only too glad to find shelter in abandoned churches. We made no claim to learning and we were submissive to everyone. I worked with my own hands and I am still determined to work; and with all my heart I want all the other friars to be busy with some kind of work that can be carried on without scandal. Those who do not know how to work should learn, not because they want to get something for their efforts, but to give good example and to avoid idleness. When we receive no recompense for our work, we can turn to God's table and beg alms from door to door. God revealed a form of greeting to me, telling me that we should say, "God give you peace."

The friars must be very careful not to accept churches or poor dwellings for themselves, or anything else built for them, unless they are in harmony with the poverty which we have promised in the Rule; and they should occupy these places only as strangers and pilgrims.

In virtue of obedience, I strictly forbid the friars, wherever they may be, to petition the Roman Curia, either personally or through an intermediary, for a papal brief, whether it concerns a church or any other place, or even in order to preach, or because they are being persecuted. If they are not welcome somewhere, they should flee to another country where they can lead a life of penance, with God's blessing.

I am determined to obey the Minister General of the Order and the guardian whom he sees fit to give me. I want to be a captive in his hands so that I cannot travel about or do anything against his command or desire, because he is my superior. Although I am ill and not much use, I always want to have a cleric with me who will say the Office for me, as is prescribed in the Rule.

All the other friars, too, are bound to obey their guardians in the same way, and say the Office according to the Rule. If any of them refuse to say the Office according to the Rule and want to change it, or if they are not true to the Catholic faith, the other friars are bound in virtue of obedience to bring them before the custos nearest the place where they find them. The custos must keep any such friar as a prisoner day and night so that he cannot escape from his hands until he personally hands him over to his minister. The minister, then, is strictly bound by obedience to place him in the care of friars who will guard him day and night like a prisoner until they present him before his lordship the Bishop of Ostia, who is the superior, protector, and corrector of the whole Order.

The friars should not say, this is another Rule. For this is a reminder, admonition, exhortation, and my testament which I, Brother Francis, worthless as I am, leave to you, my brothers, that we may observe in a more Catholic way the Rule we have promised to God. The Minister General and all the other ministers and custodes are bound in virtue of obedience not to add anything to these words or subtract from them. They should always have this writing with them as well as the Rule and at the chapters they hold, when the Rule is read, they should read these words also.

In virtue of obedience, I strictly forbid any of my friars, clerics or lay brothers, to interpret the Rule or these words, saying, "This is what they mean." God inspired me to write the Rule and these words plainly and simply, and so you too must understand them plainly and simply, and live by them, doing good to the last.

And may whoever observes all this be filled in heaven with the blessing of the most high Father, and on earth with that of his beloved Son, together with the Holy Spirit, the Comforter, and all the powers of heaven and all the saints. And I, Brother Francis, your poor worthless servant, add my share internally and externally to that most holy blessing. Amen.

REVIEW QUESTIONS

1. How did Francis expect the brothers to live without property?
2. In what ways are his teachings a support or a threat to the organized church?
3. What was Francis worried about as he dictated his last will and testament?

HILDEGARD OF BINGEN

Letter to the Clergy of Mainz

Hildegard of Bingen (1098–1179) was a German abbess whose creative genius extended to preaching, founding convents, and above all writing down her visionary prophesies. She was also a prolific composer of sacred songs and plays. Hildegard's remarkable career as an abbess demonstrates one of the few opportunities women

GOLD AND SILVER JEWELED BOOK COVER,
WEINGARTEN ABBEY, GERMANY (C. 1200–1232)

This binding, or book cover, has the Virgin and Child at the center, the apostles (with their distinctive creatures) in the corners, and other saints and angels. The cover protected the monastery's sacramentary. The binding also contains relics of the Virgin Mary and Saints George, Oswald, Bartholomew, Thomas, Peter, Paul, and James, as the writing along the edges reveals. This book cover is also a reliquary—an object containing pieces of the saints. What is the significance and power of a relic? Can you tell a book by its cover? What does this cover say?

*had to be in charge of an institution in the medieval world. In this letter to the
male clergy of Mainz, Hildegard is objecting to the interdict her convent is experiencing because of a dispute over a burial.*

From *The Letters of Hildegard of Bingen,* edited by Joseph L. Baird (Oxford, Eng.: Oxford
University Press, 1994), pp. 76–79.

By a vision, which was implanted in my soul by God the Great Artisan before I was born, I have been compelled to write these things because of the interdict by which our superiors have bound us, on account of a certain dead man buried at our monastery, a man buried without any objection, with his own priest officiating. Yet only a few days after his burial, these men ordered us to remove him from our cemetery. Seized by no small terror, as a result, I looked as usual to the True Light, and, with wakeful eyes, I saw in my spirit that if this man were disinterred in accordance with their commands, a terrible and lamentable danger would come upon us like a dark cloud before a threatening thunderstorm.

Therefore, we have not presumed to remove the body of the deceased inasmuch as he had confessed his sins, had received extreme unction and communion, and had been buried without objection. Furthermore, we have not yielded to those who advised or even commanded this course of action. Not, certainly, that we take the counsel of upright men or the orders of our superiors lightly, but we would not have it appear that, out of feminine harshness we did injustice to the sacraments of Christ, with which this man had been fortified while he was still alive. But so that we may not be totally disobedient we have, in accordance with their injunction, ceased from singing the divine praises and from participation in Mass, as had been our regular monthly custom.

As a result, my sisters and I have been greatly distressed and saddened. Weighed down by this burden, therefore, I heard these words in a vision: It is improper for you to obey human words ordering you to abandon the sacraments of the Garment of the Word of God, Who, born virgin-ally of the Virgin Mary, is your salvation. Still, it is incumbent upon you to seek permission to participate in the sacraments from those prelates who laid the obligation of obedience upon you. For ever since Adam was driven from the bright region of paradise into the exile of this world on account of his disobedience, the conception of all people is justly tainted by that first transgression. Therefore, in accordance with God's inscrutable plan, it was necessary for a man free from all pollution to be born in human flesh, through whom all who are predestined to life might be cleansed from corruption and might be sanctified by the communion of his body so that he might remain in them and they in him for their fortification. That person, however, who is disobedient to the commands of God, as Adam was, and is completely forgetful of Him must be completely cut off from participation in the sacrament of His body, just as he himself has turned away from Him in disobedience. And he must remain so until, purged through penitence, he is permitted by the authorities to receive the communion of the Lord's body again. In contrast, however, a person who is aware that he has incurred such a restriction not as a result of anything that he has done, either consciously or deliberately, may be present at the service of the life-giving sacrament, to be cleansed by the Lamb without sin, Who, in obedience to the Father, allowed Himself to be sacrificed on the altar of the cross that he might restore salvation to all.

In that same vision I also heard that I had erred in not going humbly and devoutly to my superiors for permission to participate in the communion, especially since we were not at fault in receiving that dead man into our cemetery. For, after all, he had been fortified by his own priest with proper Christian procedure, and, without objection from anyone, was buried in our cemetery, with all Bingen joining in the funeral procession. And so God has commanded me to report these things to you, our lords and prelates. Further, I saw in my vision also that by obeying you we have been celebrating the divine office incorrectly, for from the time of your restriction up to the present, we have ceased to sing the divine office, merely reading it instead. And I heard a voice coming from the Living Light concerning the various kinds of praises, about which David speaks in the psalm: "Praise Him with sound of trumpet: praise Him with psaltery and harp," and so forth up to this point: "Let every spirit praise the Lord." These words use outward, visible things to teach us about inward things. Thus the material composition and the quality of these instruments instruct us how we ought to give form to the praise of the Creator and turn all the convictions of our inner being to the same. When we consider these things carefully, we recall that man needed the voice of the living Spirit, but Adam lost this divine voice through disobedience. For while he was still innocent, before his transgression, his voice blended fully with the voices of the angels in their praise of God. Angels are called spirits from that Spirit which is God, and thus they have such voices by virtue of their spiritual nature. But Adam lost that angelic voice which he had in paradise, for he fell asleep to that knowledge which he possessed before his sin, just as a person on waking up only dimly remembers what he had seen in his dreams. And so when he was deceived by the trick of the devil and rejected the will of his Creator, he became wrapped up in the darkness of inward ignorance as the just result of his iniquity.

God, however, restores the souls of the elect to that pristine blessedness by infusing them with the light of truth. And in accordance with His eternal plan, He so devised it that whenever He renews the hearts of many with the pouring out of the prophetic spirit, they might, by means of His interior illumination, regain some of the knowledge which Adam had before he was punished for his sin.

And so the holy prophets, inspired by the Spirit which they had received, were called for this purpose: not only to compose psalms and canticles (by which the hearts of listeners would be inflamed) but also to construct various kinds of musical instruments to enhance these songs of praise with melodic strains. Thereby, both through the form and quality of the instruments, as well as through the meaning of the words which accompany them, those who hear might be taught, as we said above, about inward things, since they have been admonished and aroused by outward things. In such a way, these holy prophets get beyond the music of this exile and recall to mind that divine melody of praise which Adam, in company with the angels, enjoyed in God before his fall.

Men of zeal and wisdom have imitated the holy prophets and have themselves, with human skill, invented several kinds of musical instruments, so that they might be able to sing for the delight of their souls, and they accompanied their singing with instruments played with the flexing of the fingers, recalling, in this way, Adam, who was formed by God's finger, which is the Holy Spirit. For, before he sinned, his voice had the sweetness of all musical harmony. Indeed, if he had remained in his original state, the weakness of mortal man would not have been able to endure the power and the resonance of his voice.

But when the devil, man's great deceiver, learned that man had begun to sing through God's inspiration and, therefore, was being transformed to bring back the sweetness of the songs of heaven, mankind's homeland, he was so terrified at seeing his clever machinations go to ruin that he was greatly tormented. Therefore, he devotes himself continually to thinking up and working out all kinds of wicked contrivances. Thus he never ceases from confounding confession and the sweet beauty of both divine praise and spiritual hymns, eradicating them through wicked suggestions, impure thoughts, or various distractions from the heart of man and even from the mouth of the Church itself, wherever he can, through dissension, scandal, or unjust oppression.

Therefore, you and all prelates must exercise

the greatest vigilance to clear the air by full and thorough discussion of the justification for such actions before your verdict closes the mouth of any church singing praises to God or suspends it from handling or receiving the divine sacraments. And you must be especially certain that you are drawn to this action out of zeal for God's justice, rather than out of indignation, unjust emotions, or a desire for revenge, and you must always be on your guard not to be circumvented in your decisions by Satan, who drove man from celestial harmony and the delights of paradise.

Consider, too, that just as the body of Jesus Christ was born of the purity of the Virgin Mary through the operation of the Holy Spirit so, too, the canticle of praise, reflecting celestial harmony, is rooted in the Church through the Holy Spirit. The body is the vestment of the spirit, which has a living voice, and so it is proper for the body, in harmony with the soul, to use its voice to sing praises to God. Whence, in metaphor, the prophetic spirit commands us to praise God with clashing cymbals and cymbals of jubilation, as well as other musical instruments which men of wisdom and zeal have invented, because all arts pertaining to things useful and necessary for mankind have been created by the breath that God sent into man's body. For this reason it is proper that God be praised in all things.

And because sometimes a person sighs and groans at the sound of singing, remembering, as it were, the nature of celestial harmony, the prophet, aware that the soul is symphonic and thoughtfully reflecting on the profound nature of the spirit, urges us in the psalm to confess to the Lord with the harp and to sing a psalm to Him with the ten-stringed psaltery. His meaning is that the harp, which is plucked from below, relates to the discipline of the body; the psaltery, which is plucked from above, pertains to the exertion of the spirit; the ten chords, to the fulfillment of the law.

Therefore, those who, without just cause, impose silence on a church and prohibit the singing of God's praises and those who have on earth unjustly despoiled God of His honor and glory will lose their place among the chorus of angels, unless they have amended their lives through true penitence and humble restitution. Moreover, let those who hold the keys of heaven beware not to open those things which are to be kept closed nor to close those things which are to be kept open, for harsh judgment will fall upon those who rule, unless, as the apostle says, they rule with good judgment.

And I heard a voice saying thus: Who created heaven? God. Who opens heaven to the faithful? God. Who is like Him? No one. And so, O men of faith, let none of you resist Him or oppose Him, lest He fall on you in His might and you have no helper to protect you from His judgment. This time is a womanish time, because the dispensation of God's justice is weak. But the strength of God's justice is exerting itself, a female warrior battling against injustice, so that it might fall defeated.

REVIEW QUESTIONS

1. What role does Hildegard assign to music in worship?
2. Why is music such a big part of her argument about the interdict?
3. What are the sources of Hildegard's authority to challenge the decisions of the Mainz clergy?

STEPHEN OF BOURBON

FROM *On the Seven Gifts of the Holy Spirit*

The Dominican preacher and author Stephen of Bourbon (?1180–1262) preserves in a theological work this account of what he learned while hearing confessions in the diocese of Lyons in southern France. Only from an educated and observant friar do we learn the story of St. Guinefort. The official, institutional church still did not control the variety of religious practices on the local level.

From *The Holy Greyhound*, by Jean Claude Schmitt (Cambridge, Eng.: Cambridge University Press, 1983), pp. 4–6.

*   *   *

On the Worship of the Dog Guinefort

Sixthly, I should speak of offensive superstitions, some of which are offensive to God, others to our fellow men. Offensive to God are those which honour demons or other creatures as if they were divine: it is what idolatry does, and it is what the wretched women who cast lots do, who seek salvation by worshipping elder trees or making offerings to them; scorning churches and holy relics, they take their children to these elder trees, or to anthills, or to other things in order that a cure may be effected.

This recently happened in the diocese of Lyons where, when I preached against the reading of oracles, and was hearing confession, numerous women confessed that they had taken their children to Saint Guinefort. As I thought that this was some holy person, I continued with my enquiry and finally learned that this was actually a greyhound, which had been killed in the following manner.

In the diocese of Lyons, near the enclosed nuns' village called Neuville, on the estate of the Lord of Villars, was a castle, the lord of which and his wife had a baby boy. One day, when the lord and lady had gone out of the house, and the nurse had done likewise, leaving the baby alone in the cradle, a huge serpent entered the house and approached the baby's cradle. Seeing this, the greyhound, which had remained behind, chased the serpent and, attacking it beneath the cradle, upset the cradle and bit the serpent all over, which defended itself, biting the dog equally severely. Finally, the dog killed it and threw it well away from the cradle. The cradle, the floor, the dog's mouth and head were all drenched in the serpent's blood. Although badly hurt by the serpent, the dog remained on guard beside the cradle. When the nurse came back and saw all this she thought that the dog had devoured the child, and let out a scream of misery. Hearing it the child's mother also ran up, looked, thought the same thing and screamed too. Likewise the knight, when he arrived, thought the same thing and drew his sword and killed the dog. Then, when they went closer to the baby they found it safe and sound, sleeping peacefully. Casting around for some explanation, they discovered the serpent, torn to pieces by the dog's bites, and now dead. Realising then the true facts of the matter, and deeply regretting having unjustly killed so useful a dog they threw it into a well in front of the manor door, threw a great pile of stones on top of it, and planted trees beside it, in memory of the event. Now, by divine will, the manor was destroyed and the estate, reduced to a desert, was abandoned by its inhabitants. But the peasants, hearing of the dog's conduct and of how it had been killed, although innocent, and for a deed for which it might have expected praise, visited the place, honoured the dog as a martyr, prayed to it when they were sick or in need of something, and many there fell victim to the enticements and illusions of the devil, who in this way used to lead men into error. Above all, though, it was women with sick or weak children who took them to this place. They would go and seek out an old woman in a fortified town a league distant, and she taught them the rituals they should enact in order to make offerings to demons, and in order to invoke them, and she led them to the place. When they arrived, they would make offerings of salt and other things; they would hang their babies' swaddling-clothes on the bushes roundabout; they would drive nails into the trees which had grown in this place; they would pass the naked babies between the trunks of two trees —the mother, on one side, held the baby and threw it nine times to the old woman, who was on the other side. Invoking the demons, they called upon the fauns in the forest of Rimite to take the sick, feeble child which, they said, was theirs, and to return their child that the fauns had taken away, fat and well, safe and sound.

Having done this, the infanticidal mothers took their children and laid them naked at the foot of the tree on straw from the cradle; then, using the light they had brought with them, they lit two candles, each an inch long, one on each side of the child's head and fixed them in the trunk above it. Then they withdrew until the candles had burnt out, so as not to see the child or hear him crying. Several people have told us that while the candles were burning like this they burnt and killed several babies. One woman also told me that she had just invoked the fauns and was withdrawing from the scene when she saw a wolf come out of the forest towards the baby. If maternal love had not made her feel pity and go back for him, the wolf, or as she put it, the devil in the shape of a wolf, would have devoured the baby.

When a mother returned to her child and found it still alive, she carried it out into the fast-flowing waters of a nearby river, called the Chalaronne, and plunged it in nine times; if it came through without dying on the spot, or shortly afterwards, it had a very strong constitution.

We went to this place, we called together all the people on the estate, and we preached against everything that had been said. We had the dead dog disinterred, and the sacred wood cut down and burnt, along with the remains of the dog. And I had an edict passed by the lords of the estate, warning that anyone going thenceforth to that place for any such reason would be liable to have his possessions seized and then sold.

*   *   *

REVIEW QUESTIONS

1. How could these people believe that a dog could be a saint?
2. What was the social meaning of the ritual of leaving sick children in the forest?
3. Does Stephen really understand what the mothers were doing with their sick children?

JACOBUS DE VORAGINE

FROM *The Golden Legend*

Jacobus de Voragine's The Golden Legend *was the most widely known European collection of medieval saints' lives. Jacobus (c. 1226–1298) was a well-educated Dominican friar who eventually became archbishop of Genoa. Most of the saints in the collection were martyrs and heroes of the early church, but a few, like St. Elizabeth, lived in Jacobus' century. The author borrowed and adapted these biographies of the saints from numerous sources, but his plain and vivid style made the collection accessible across Europe. St. Elizabeth's life reveals the opportunities and constraints facing women in thirteenth-century society.*

From *The Golden Legend*, by Jacobus de Voragine, translated by William Granger Ryan (Princeton, N.J.: Princeton University Press, 1993), vol. 2, pp. 306–13.

Life of St. Elizabeth of Hungary

*　　*　　*

Elizabeth, illustrious daughter of the king of Hungary, was noble by birth and still more noble by her faith and her devotion to religion. She ennobled her already noble lineage by her example, shed light on it by her miracles, and embellished it with the grace of her holiness. The Author of nature somehow raised her above nature. As a child growing up surrounded by regal privileges and pleasures, she either spurned the things children love, or directed them to God's service, showing how much her tender childhood was strengthened by her simplicity, and how sweet was the devotion of her earliest years. As a child she applied herself to serious concerns, shunning idle games, avoiding worldly success and prosperity, and advancing always in reverence toward God. When she was only five years old, she spent so much time praying in church that her companions and her maids could hardly get her out to play. Her servants and playmates noticed that when one of them in the course of a game went into the chapel, Elizabeth followed her, profiting by the opportunity to get into the church; and when she entered, she would kneel down or lie full length on the floor. She had not yet learned to read but often spread the Psalter open before her, pretending to read so that no one would disturb her. Sometimes she stretched herself on the ground beside other girls, playing at measuring herself against them, but also to display reverence for God. When playing the game of rings or any other game, she put her whole trust in God. When as a little girl she won something in a game or acquired a new possession in some other way, she divided it among poor children, urging them to say frequently the Our Father and the Hail Mary.

Elizabeth grew in age and even more in the intensity of her devotion. She chose the Blessed Virgin, mother of God, as her patroness and advocate, and Saint John the Evangelist as the guardian of her chastity. When papers with the names of the several apostles written on them were placed on the altar and then distributed at random among the girls, Elizabeth prayed three times and always received the paper with Saint Peter's name on it as she wanted to, because her devotion to that saint was so fervent that she would never deny anything to anyone who asked in his name. For fear that worldly successes might attract flattery to her, she daily gave away some token of her prosperity. When she won in some game, she called a halt and said: "I don't want to play any more! I leave the rest for the sake of God!" When invited to dance with other girls she would dance one round, then would say: "Let's let one round be enough and give up the rest for God," thus tempering the girls' taste for such vain pastimes. She abhorred too much show in dress and loved modesty in all such matters.

Elizabeth imposed upon herself the daily recitation of a certain number of prayers, and if she was too busy to complete the number during the day and was put to bed by her maids, she stayed awake until she had fulfilled her promise to her heavenly spouse. She observed solemn feast days with so much devotion that she would not allow her long sleeves to be stitched on her dress under any pretext until after the celebration of mass. She forbade herself the wearing of gloves before noon on Sunday, wishing thereby both to defer to the sacred solemnity and to satisfy her own devotion. For this same purpose it was her custom to impose such practices upon herself by vow, so that no one would be able to dissuade her from carrying out her intention. She assisted at liturgical services with such reverence that when the gospel was read, or the host consecrated, she removed her sleeves if they had been stitched on, and put aside her necklaces and any ornaments she was wearing on her head.

She lived out her state of virginity prudently and innocently, but was compelled to enter the state of marriage in obedience to her father's order. Thus she gained the thirtyfold fruit, keeping the faith of the Trinity and obeying the Ten Commandments. She consented to conjugal intercourse, not out of libidinous desire but out of respect for her father's command, and in order to procreate and raise children for the service of God. Thus, while bound by the law of the conjugal bed, she was not bound to enjoyment. This is obvious from the fact that she made a vow in Master Conrad's hands, that if she survived her husband she would practice continence for the rest of her life.

Elizabeth therefore was married to the landgrave of Thuringia, as befitted her royal dignity but also as God's providence ordained, namely, that she might thus lead many to the love of God and might give instruction to the ignorant.[1] Although her state of life was changed, there was no change in the way she intended to live. How great her devotion and humility toward God was, how strict her austerity and self-denial, how abundant her generosity and compassion for the poor, it will be the purpose of what follows to demonstrate.

She was so fervently devoted to prayer that she sometimes hurried to arrive in church ahead of her maids, as if wishing by some secret prayer to win a particular favor from God. She often rose during the night to pray, though her husband begged her to spare herself and give her body some rest. She had an arrangement with one of her maids who was closer to her than the others, that if by chance she overslept, the maid would wake her up by touching her foot. Once by mistake she touched the landgrave's foot. He woke up with a start but understood what had happened, and patiently put up with it and pretended not to have noticed anything. In order to make her prayers a rich sacrifice to God, Elizabeth often sprinkled them with a profusion of tears, but she shed her tears happily and without any unseemly change of countenance, weeping with sorrow and rejoicing at the sorrow; and this beautified her visage with gladness.

So profound was her humility that for the love of God she never shunned menial or lowly work, but did it with unbounded devotion. She once took an ugly sick man and clasped his filthy head to her bosom, then cut his hair and washed his head, while her maids stood by laughing. On Rogation Days she always walked in the procession barefoot and wearing a plain woolen garment. At the station churches she sat among the poorest women to hear the sermon, as if she too were poor and of low estate. When she went to be churched after childbirth, she never made a show of jewelry

---

[1] Landgrave was a title equivalent to "count."

or gold-embroidered gowns, as other women did.[2] Following the example of Mary the immaculate mother, she carried her child in her arms and humbly offered him at the altar with a lamb and a candle, thus showing her distaste for wordly pomp and modeling her behavior after that of the Blessed Mother. Then, when she returned to her house, she gave the clothing she had worn in church to some poor woman.

As a further manifestation of her humility, Elizabeth, unsurpassed though she was in freedom and high station, submitted herself in obedience to a priest called Master Conrad. Conrad was a very poor man but was known for his knowledge and piety. With her husband's consent and the marriage right safeguarded, she pledged herself to obey Master Conrad so unreservedly that she would fulfill any order of his with reverence and joy. Her purpose was to gain merit and to imitate the example of her Savior, who became obedient even unto death. For instance, on one occasion Master Conrad had ordered her to attend a service at which he was to preach, but the marchioness of Meissen came to visit and Elizabeth missed the service. Conrad took her disobedience so amiss that he would not forgive it until, stripped to her shift, she was soundly flogged, along with some of her servants who had committed some fault.

Elizabeth took on herself so much abstinence and privation that her body was wasted with vigils and disciplines and fasting. Frequently she avoided her husband's bed and went without sleep in order to spend the night in contemplation and to pray to her heavenly Father in secret. When sleep overcame her, she slept on mats strewn on the floor. When her husband was away she passed the whole night in prayer with her heavenly spouse. Often, too, she had her serving women flog her in her bedroom, in return for the scourging her Savior had borne for her and to quell all carnal desire.

Such was Elizabeth's temperance in matters of food and drink that at her husband's table, laden

as it was with a variety of tasty dishes, she sometimes ate nothing but a bit of bread. Master Conrad forbade her to eat any food about which she had the slightest qualm of conscience, and she obeyed this behest so meticulously that however abundant the delicious foods might be, she and her servingmaids partook of coarser fare. At other times she sat at table and divided and moved the food around on her plate, so as to seem to be eating and to ward off any notion that she was superstitious: thus, by her urbanity, she put all the guests at their ease. When they were traveling and she was worn out with the length and labors of the journey, and she and her husband were offered foods that might not have been honestly acquired, she accepted none of them and patiently ate stale black bread soaked in hot water, as her maids did. For this reason, indeed, her husband had assigned funds to her, sufficient to provide for her living and that of some few of her women, who chose to follow her example in everything. Frequently, too, she refused what was served at the royal table and asked for the provisions of ordinary people. The landgrave was tolerant of all of this and said that he would gladly do the same himself if he were not afraid of upsetting the whole household.

Elizabeth's position was one of the highest dignity, but her whole desire was to share poverty with the poor, so that she might make return to Christ for his poverty and the world might have no claim on her. Sometimes, when she was alone with her servingwomen, she put on cheap, dingy clothing, covered her head with a shabby kerchief, and said to them: "This is how I will go about when I have attained the state of poverty." She checked her own appetite with a tight rein of abstinence but was openhanded in her generosity to the poor, never letting anyone go hungry and supplying the needs of all so liberally that she was acclaimed as the mother of the poor.

Blessed Elizabeth put her utmost effort into the performance of the seven works of mercy, hoping to inherit the everlasting kingdom and to reign there perpetually, and to possess the Father's blessing with the saints gathered at his right hand. She clothed the naked and provided raiment for

---

[2] "To be churched" refers to the practice in which after giving birth, a woman came to the church to offer thanksgiving and to receive a special blessing.

the burial of poor people and strangers, as well as for infants at their christening. Often she lifted children of the poor from the baptismal font and sewed clothing for them with her own hands: having become their godmother, she then did more for them. On one occasion she gave a rather elegant dress to a poor woman, who was so overwhelmed with joy at the sight of such a magnificent gift that she fell to the ground and was thought to be dead. Blessed Elizabeth, seeing her lying there, was sorry she had given her so fine a present, fearing that she had thus been the cause of her death, but she prayed for her and the woman stood up fully recovered. Often, too, she spun wool in company with her servants, in order to receive the glorious fruit of these good labors, giving an example of true humility, and an alms to God out of the toil of her own body.

She fed the hungry. Once, when the landgrave had gone to the court of Emperor Frederick, then being held at Cremona, Elizabeth collected the whole year's crop from his barns, called in the poor from all sides, and provided for their daily needs, because the cost of living had risen and they were threatened with famine. When poor people ran out of money, she often sold her jewelry in order to help them. Indeed she regularly drew from her own resources and those of her faithful servingwomen to have something put aside for the poor.

She gave drink to the thirsty. Once she was serving beer to poor people, and after everyone had been served, the jug was still as full as it had been before she started.

She provided shelter for pilgrims and poor people. She had a very large house built at the foot of the high hill on which her castle stood, and there took care of numbers of the ill and infirm despite the difficulty of getting up and down the hill. While with them she saw to all their needs and exhorted them to patience. Bad air always distressed her, but for God's love, even in the heat of summer, she did not shrink from the smells and sores of the sick, but applied remedies to their wounds, dried them with the veil from her head, and treated them with her own hands, although her maids could hardly bear to watch her.

In this same house Elizabeth saw to it that children of poor women were well fed and cared for. She was so gentle and kind to them that they all called her Mother and, when she came into the house, followed her around as if she were in fact their mother, and crowded about her to be as close to her as possible. She also bought some small dishes and cups and rings and other glass toys for the children to play with. She was riding up the hill, carrying these things in the fold of her cloak, when they came loose and fell to the rocks below, but not one of the toys was broken.

Elizabeth visited the sick. Her compassion for their sufferings ruled her heart so much that she often went looking for their lodgings and visited them solicitously, entering their poor abodes as if she were at home, not deterred by the strangeness of the locale or bothered by the distance she had to go. She provided for their needs and spoke words of consolation to them, thus earning reward in five ways, namely, by honoring them with her visit, by the fatigues of the journey, by the warmth of her compassion, by her words of consolation, and by the generosity of her donations.

She concerned herself with the burial of the poor, devotedly going to their funerals, covering their bodies with clothes that she herself had made, and on one occasion cutting up the large linen veil she was wearing and wrapping the corpse of a poor person with part of it. She prepared them for interment with her own hands and piously stayed for the rites at the grave.

The piety of her husband deserves praise for his part in all these doings. He had many interests to attend to but was devout in honoring God, and, since he could not personally get involved in such activities, gave his wife the freedom and the means to do whatever served the honor of God and made for the salvation of his soul. Blessed Elizabeth wanted very much to see her husband turn the use of his arms to the defense of the faith, and by her salutary exhortations persuaded him to go to the Holy Land. There the landgrave, a faithful prince, devout and renowned for the integrity and sincerity of his faith, lost his life and received the reward of his good works.

Elizabeth now piously embraced the state of widowhood, taking care not to be defrauded of the reward of a widow's continence and to gain the sixtyfold fruit by observing the Decalogue together with the seven works of mercy. But as soon as the news of her husband's death spread throughout Thuringia, she was denounced by some of the landgrave's vassals as a prodigal, wasteful woman and was shamefully banned from her country. Thus her patience was brought fully to light, and her long-standing desire for poverty was fulfilled.

She went by night to the house of an innkeeper and was given shelter where the pigs usually rested, and for this she gave thanks to God. In the morning she went to the house of the Friars Minor and asked them to sing a *Te Deum*, in thanksgiving for the troubles that had befallen her. The following day she was ordered to go with her children into the house of one of her enemies, where she was given a very small room to live in. The man and woman whose house it was treated her so meanly that she bade farewell only to the walls, saying: "I would gladly give my good wishes to these people, if they had been kind to me." Having no place else to go she went back to the innkeeper's house, sending her children to various places to be cared for. She had to go along a path filled with mud, with only stepping-stones to walk on, and came face to face with an old woman whom she had befriended many times; but the old woman would not let her pass and she fell into the mud. Nothing daunted, she came up rejoicing and laughing, and shook the mud out of her clothes.

Now her aunt, who was an abbess, took pity on Elizabeth's poverty and brought her to the bishop of Bamberg, who was her uncle. He received her with due honor and shrewdly gave her hospitality in his house, planning to get her married again. The servingwomen who had vowed continence with her learned of the bishop's intention and wept as they reported it to blessed Elizabeth; but she reassured them, saying: "I trust in the Lord, for love of whom I have vowed perpetual continence. He will keep my resolution firm, will ward off all violence, and will defeat the schemes

of men. If perchance my uncle wishes to wed me to another, I will set my mind against him and contradict him verbally; and if no other way of escape is left to me, I will cut off my nose, because no one would have me, thus disfigured."

By the bishop's order she was taken against her will to a castle, to stay there until she consented to marry, and she wept and commended her chastity to the Lord. But now, by God's will, her husband's bones were returned from overseas, and the bishop had Elizabeth brought back to give loving welcome to her spouse's remains. The bishop met the landgrave's bones in a procession of honor, and blessed Elizabeth gave them welcome with devotion and much shedding of tears. She then turned to the Lord and said: "I give you thanks, O God, for deigning to console miserable me by the reception of the bones of my spouse whom you loved. You know, O Lord, that I loved him dearly, as he loved you, yet for love of you I deprived myself of his presence and sent him to relieve your Holy Land. Delightful as it would be for me to live with him still, even were we reduced to go begging through the whole world, yet I would not give one hair of my head to have him back against your will, nor to recall him to this mortal life. I commend him and me to your grace."

Now, lest she lose the hundredfold fruit which is given to those who strive for evangelical perfection and are transferred from the left hand of misery to the right hand of glory, Elizabeth put on religious dress, namely, robes of plain gray, low-grade material. She observed perpetual continence after her husband's death, embraced voluntary poverty, and would have begged from door to door had not Master Conrad forbidden her. Her habit was so shabby that her gray cloak had to be lengthened and the holes in the sleeves of her tunic patched with cloth of a different color. When her father, the king of Hungary, heard of the destitution in which she was living, he sent a knight to persuade her to return to her paternal home. When the knight saw her dressed in such poor attire, sitting humbly and spinning thread, he was overcome with confusion and wonder, and exclaimed: "Never has a king's daughter been seen in such tawdry clothes, nor any royal personage spinning wool!"

Blessed Elizabeth absolutely refused to return with the knight, preferring to live in poverty with the poor rather than to be surrounded with riches with the rich. Then in order that her spirit might move totally to God and her devotion be unhampered by distraction or impediment, she prayed the Lord to fill her with contempt for all temporal goods, to take from her heart her love for her children, and to grant her indifference and constancy in the face of every insult. When she had finished her prayer, she heard the Lord saying to her: "Your prayer has been favorably heard." Elizabeth told her women: "The Lord has heard my voice graciously, because I regard all temporal things as dung, I care for my children no more than for others around me, I make light of all contempt and disrespect, and it seems to me that I no longer love any but God alone."

Master Conrad often imposed disagreeable and contrary things upon her, and separated from her company any persons to whom she seemed to feel a particular attachment. Thus he sent away from her two servingmaids who had grown up with her and were her loyal and dear friends: many tears were shed on both sides over this separation. The holy man took these measures in order to break her will and allow her to direct her whole desire to God, and to guard her from being reminded of her past glory by any of her servants. In all these matters she was quick in obedience and steadfast in patience, in order to possess her own soul by patience, and by obedience to be crowned with victory.

Blessed Elizabeth also said: "For God's sake I fear mortal man as much as I ought to fear the heavenly judge. Therefore I choose to give my obedience to Master Conrad, a poor, undistinguished man, rather than to some bishop, so that every occasion of worldly consolation may be taken away from me." Once when she had yielded to the earnest request of some nuns and had visited their convent without obtaining permission from her spiritual master, he had her flogged so severely that the marks of the lashes were still visible three weeks later. To her women she said, for their consolation as well as for her own: "The sedge grass lies flat when the river is in flood, and when the water recedes, the sedge straightens up. So, when some affliction befalls us, we should bow to it humbly and, when it passes, be lifted up by spiritual joy to God." Her humility was such that she would not allow her servants to address her as "lady" but insisted that they use the singular forms, as is usual when speaking to inferiors.[3] She washed the dishes and other kitchen utensils, and, lest her maids prevent her from doing so, had them carried to different places. She also said: "Could I have found a more menial way of life, I would have chosen it."

For the rest, in order to possess the best part with Mary, Elizabeth gave herself diligently to contemplative prayer. In this prayer she had special graces to shed tears, to have frequent visions of heaven, and to light the fire of love in others. At times when she was happiest she shed tears of joyous devotion, so that happy tears seemed to flow from her eyes as from a serene fountain. She seemed to be weeping and rejoicing at the same time, never letting tears change or mar her face. She said of those who looked gloomy when they wept: "Do they want to frighten the Lord away? Let them give to God what they have to give him with joy and good cheer!"

*   *   *

Elizabeth, having reached the summit of perfection through Mary's contemplative prayer, did not give up Martha's laborious activity, as we have shown by her devotion to the seven works of mercy. Indeed, after taking the veil of religion, she practiced those works as assiduously as before. She had received two thousand marks for her dowry. Now she gave some of that to the poor and with the rest built a large hospital at Marburg. This made people regard her as a prodigal spendthrift, and many called her insane. When she gladly accepted these insults, they accused her of being so happy because she had put the memory of her husband out of her heart too quickly.

---

[3] Singular forms are thou, thee, thy, etc.

After the hospital was built, she committed herself to serving the poor like a simple serving-woman. She ministered solicitously to their needs, bathing them, putting them to bed, covering them, and cheerfully saying to her own maids: "How fortunate we are, to be able to bathe our Lord and cover him!" In waiting on the sick she humbled herself so completely that when a poor child who had only one eye and was covered with scabs came into the hospital, she took him in her arms to the privy seven times in one night and willingly washed his bedclothes. Again there was a woman with a horrible leprosy whom she bathed and put to bed, cleansing and bandaging her sores, applying remedies, trimming her fingernails, and kneeling at her feet to loosen her shoes. She prevailed upon the sick to confess their sins and to receive holy communion, and when one old woman flatly refused, she had her whipped to change her mind.

When Elizabeth was not busy with caring for the sick, she spun wool that was sent to her from a monastery, and divided the money she earned among the needy. At a time when everyone was poor, Elizabeth received five hundred marks from her dowry and set about distributing the money to those in need. She lined them all up, tied an apron on, and began the distribution, having made a rule that if anyone changed place in the line in order to receive a second time, that person's hair would be cut off. It happened that a girl named Radegund, who was admired for the beauty of her tresses, came to the hospital, not to receive an alms but to visit her sister who was ill. Since she did not get on line, she was brought to blessed Elizabeth for breaking the rule, and Elizabeth ordered her hair cut off, despite her sobs and her struggles. Then some of those present said that the girl was not at fault, but Elizabeth said: "At least from now on she won't be able to flaunt her curls at dances or indulge in similar vanities." She asked Radegund if she had ever thought of entering the religious life, and the girl answered that she would have done so long since if she were not so proud of her hair. Elizabeth: "It is dearer to me that you have lost your hair than if my son

had been raised to the Empire!" Radegund took the religious habit and stayed on with Elizabeth, leading a praiseworthy life.

A poor woman gave birth to a daughter, and blessed Elizabeth lifted the baby from the sacred font and gave her her own name. Then she saw to the mother's needs and gave her the sleeves taken from her maid's coat to keep the infant warm. She also gave her shoes to the mother. Three weeks later the woman deserted her child and secretly went off with her husband. When Elizabeth got word of this, she had recourse to prayer, and the man and wife were unable to go a step farther, but had to come back to her and beg her forgiveness. She reproached them for their ingratitude, as they deserved, then turned the baby over to them to be cared for, and provided them with the necessary means.

The time was drawing near when the Lord intended to call his beloved out of the prison of this world, and to receive her, who had despised the kingdom of mortals, into the kingdom of the angels. Christ appeared to her and said: "Come, my beloved, to the eternal dwelling prepared for you!" She was brought low with fever and lay with her face turned toward the wall, and those who stood around her heard her humming a sweet melody. When one of her maids asked her what this meant, she answered: "A little bird perched between me and the wall, and sang so sweetly that I too had to sing." Throughout her illness she was always cheerful and prayed all the time. The day before she died she said to her attendants: "What would you do if the devil came near you?" After an interval she cried out three times: "Go away!" as if chasing the devil. Then she said: "It is almost midnight, the hour when Christ chose to be born and when he lay in his crib." And as the moment of her departure drew near, she said: "Now is the time when almighty God calls those who are his friends to the celestial nuptials!" Another interval, and she breathed her last and slept in peace, in the year of our Lord 1231.

Although her venerable body lay unburied for four days, no unpleasant odor came from it, but rather a pleasant aroma that refreshed everyone.

Then flocks of small birds that had never been seen there before clustered on the roof of the church. Their melodies were so sweet and their harmonies so varied that their music, which, as it were, accompanied the saint's obsequies, won the admiration of all who heard it. Loud was the mourning of the poor, deep the devotion of all the people. Some cut off wisps of her hair; others clipped shreds from her graveclothes, to be kept as precious relics. Her body was placed in a monument from which oil is said to have flowed afterwards.

*　　*　　*

REVIEW QUESTIONS

1. What are the characteristic attributes of a thirteenth-century female saint?
2. What were the signs that Elizabeth was in fact a saint?
3. Elizabeth was a member of the nobility. How did her social status determine the opportunities she had, as opposed to women from other social classes?

St. Thomas Aquinas

FROM *Summa Theologica*

Thomas Aquinas (c. 1225–1274) was a Dominican theologian, university professor, and author of the Summa Theologica, *the most influential theological work of the Middle Ages.* Theology *was a new term devised to define the recent academic subject of applying the tools of reason to religious truths. This confidence in human ability to understand a reasonable universe working according to God's logical plans and laws is central to the values of medieval humanism. In these sections of the* Summa Theologica, *Thomas is analyzing proofs of God's existence, and the meaning of humanity's creation. This translation, faithful to the content of the original, rearranges for a modern audience a very formal style of scholastic argument.*

From *St. Thomas Aquinas: Summa Theologica*, edited by Timothy S. McDermott (Westminster, Md.: Christian Classics, 1989), pp. 12–13, 144–49.

*　　*　　*

There Is a God. There are Five Ways of Proving There is a God:

The first and most obvious way is based on change. We see things changing. Now anything changing is being changed by something else. (For things changing are on the way to realization, whereas things causing change are already realized: they are realizing something else's potential, and for that they must themselves be real. The actual heat of a fire causes wood, already able to be hot, to become actually hot, and so causes change in the wood. Now the actually hot cannot at the same time be potentially hot, but only potentially cold. So what changes cannot as such be causing the change, but must be being changed by something else.) This something else, if itself changing, is being changed by yet another thing; and this last by another. Now we must stop somewhere, otherwise there will be no first cause of the change, and, as a result, no subsequent causes. (Only when acted upon by a first cause do intermediate causes produce a change; if a hand does not move the stick, the stick will not move anything else.) We arrive then at some first cause of change not itself being changed by anything, and this is what everybody understands by *God*.

The second way is based on the very notion of cause. In the observable world causes derive their causality from other causes; we never observe, nor ever could, something causing itself, for this would mean it preceded itself, and this is not possible. But the deriving of causality must stop somewhere; for in the series of causes an earlier member causes an intermediate and the intermediate a last (whether the intermediate be one or many). Now eliminate a cause and you also eliminate its effects: you cannot have a last cause, nor an intermediate one, unless you have a first. Given no stop in the series of causes, no first cause, there will be no intermediate causes and no last effect; which contradicts observation. So one is forced to suppose some first cause, to which everyone gives the name *God*.

The third way is based on what need not be and on what must be, and runs as follows. Some of the things we come across can be but need not be, for we find them springing up and dying away, thus sometimes in being and sometimes not. Now everything cannot be like this, for a thing that need not be, once was not; and if everything need not be, once upon a time there was nothing. But if that were true there would be nothing even now, because something that does not exist can only be brought into being by something already existing. If

nothing was in being nothing could be brought into being, and nothing would be in being now, which contradicts observation. Not everything therefore is the sort of thing that need not be; some things must be, and these may or may not owe this necessity to something else. But just as a series of causes must have a stop, so also a series of things which must be and owe this to other things. One is forced to suppose something which must be, and owes this to nothing outside itself; indeed it itself is the cause that other things must be.

The fourth way is based on the gradation observed in things. Some things are better, truer, more excellent than others. Such comparative terms describe varying degrees of approximation to a superlative; for example, things are hotter and hotter the nearer they approach what is hottest. Something therefore is the truest and best and most excellent of things, and hence the most fully in being; for Aristotle says that the truest things are the things most fully in being. Now *when many things possess some property in common, the one most fully possessing it causes it in the others: fire,* as Aristotle says, *the hottest of all things, causes all other things to be hot.* Something therefore causes in all other things their being, their goodness, and whatever other perfection they have. And this is what we call *God*.

The fifth way is based on the guidedness of nature. Goal-directed behaviour is observed in all bodies obeying natural laws, even when they lack awareness. Their behaviour hardly ever varies and practically always turns out well, showing that they truly tend to goals and do not merely hit them by accident. But nothing lacking awareness can tend to a goal except it be directed by someone with awareness and understanding; the arrow, for example, requires an archer. Everything in nature, therefore, is directed to its goal by someone with understanding, and this we call *God*.

*   *   *

The Genesis of Man

God formed man from the slime of the earth and breathed into his face the breath of life, and man became a living soul. Only what possesses existence and is subject of its own existence—substance—properly exists; all supervening properties exist not as themselves possessing existence but as forms under which a substance exists. Whiteness's existence is really the existence of something as white. This is true of all non-subsistent forms; so, properly speaking, it is not such forms but the things of which they are forms that come into existence. The soul however is a subsistent form and can properly be said both to exist and to come into existence. But since it does not come from pre-existent matter (only bodies do that) it must come by a new creation. Only God can create. All secondary agents presuppose material provided by a primary agent, which they then transform. Since the human soul does not come into existence by transformation of pre-existent matter, it must be produced by God's immediate creation. The soul however is only part of man, and naturally perfect only when united to its body, so it was fittingly created in its body, not before it. If it was a natural species of thing the soul would be a sort of angel; but by nature it is the form of a body, the formal element in an animal. Forms in matter are caused by forms in matter, when composite material things generate one another. The only immaterial thing that can produce something material without needing previous material is God; he alone can create new matter. So Adam's body was formed by God immediately, there being no preceding human body that could generate a body of like species to itself. Because the senses are mainly concentrated in the face, other animals have faces close to the ground to look for food and provender; but men have raised faces so that their senses, especially the finest and most discriminating sense of sight, may experience sense-objects in every direction of heaven and earth. Man's upright carriage also releases his hands for various useful purposes. And since he does not have to use his mouth for gathering food, it is not oblong and hard as in other animals but adapted for speech, the special work of reason. So man's upright carriage is not like that of the plants, for they have their roots (which are their mouths) in the earth.

It is not good for man to be alone; let us make him a help that is like himself. The help God makes for man is not for any sort of work (for there other men would be more help than a woman) but for producing children. In plants, which have no nobler function in life than propagation, the active and passive abilities to propagate are joined at all times. In the higher animals however there is more to life than that, so the active male and passive female partners mate only at certain times, constituting the sort of unity a plant is always. Aristotle called the female *a male manqué.* The particular nature of the active male seed intends to produce a perfect likeness of itself, and when females are conceived this is due to weak seed, or unsuitable material, or external influences like the dampness of the south wind. But this is because nature as a whole intends women; and in this sense they are not manqué but intended by God, the author of nature as a whole. The type of subordination in which servants are managed in their master's interests came in after sin; but the subordination seen in households or cities, where management is for the benefit of the subordinates themselves, would have obtained even without sin. And such is the natural inequality and subordination of women to men, who are by nature more reasonable and discerning. [Some say God should not have produced Eve to be an occasion of sin for Adam, but] if God removed from the world everything which man has made an excuse for sin, the world would be a poor place. What is a general good must not be sacrificed because of some particular abuse, especially since God is powerful enough to turn any evil to good account. Forming Eve from Adam's rib signified companionship, not domination (so not from his head) nor yet subjection (so not from his feet); and it also symbolized the establishment of the church by the sacraments of blood and water flowing from the side of Christ sleeping on the cross.

Let us make man after our own image and likeness. An image not only resembles, it expresses: however like each other two eggs may be, one does not express the other and is not its image. But the resemblance man bears God derives from God as from an original, so scripture describes man as made to God's image; where the preposition *to* signifies approach to something at a distance, the original in this case being infinitely distant from the image. An image must also resemble its original in species, or in some attribute like shape peculiar to that species, where likeness in species means likeness down to the last thing differentiating the species. Things in general resemble God in existing, some things also in being alive, and some finally in intellectual discernment: the closest likeness to God in creation. Properly speaking then, only creatures with intellect are made to God's image. And the point at which such creatures most closely resemble God is when they imitate his self-understanding and love. So there are three levels to the imaging of God by man: the very nature of mind gives to all men a natural aptitude for understanding and loving God; grace adds to some men an actual if imperfect understanding and love of God; and the glory of heaven brings this to perfection. The principal constituent of God's image in man, mind, is found in both male and female human beings; which is why Genesis says *To God's image he created him (namely, mankind); male and female he created them.* A secondary image of God as beginning and end of creation is however to be found only in male man, the beginning and end of woman: and this is what made St Paul say that *the man is the image and glory of God, and the woman the glory of man, for Adam was not from Eve but Eve from Adam, and Adam was not for Eve, but Eve for Adam.*

That man is made in the image of God's nature implies that all three persons of God are represented in him. In other creatures, and in other parts of man than his mind, there is not the same image or likeness in species to God, but only the sort of trace that all causes leave even in effects unlike in species. Thus we talk of tracks left by animals as traces, fires leave traces of themselves in ashes, and armies traces in the ravaged countryside. An image of the uncreated Trinity can be found in creatures with reason, who utter a word in their minds, and in whose wills a love issues, so representing God in species. In other creatures there is no such word-source or word or love; but a trace of the fact that source, word and love exist in its maker. For a creature's shaping and conditioning indicate that it *comes from* somewhere; its specific form indicates its maker's *word* as a house's shape indicates its architect's idea; and its functional order indicates its maker's *love* as a house's uses indicate what its architect willed. A first image of the Trinity in our minds is found in our activities of thinking out and formulating an inner word from the information we have, and then bursting out from this in a love. But since such activities exist implicitly in their sources [memory, understanding and will], a secondary image of the Trinity exists in our powers and dispositions to act. The kind of word and love we have in our heart varies according to what it is we are conceiving and loving: stone or horse. So God's image is to be found in the conceiving of a word that expresses what we know of God and a love flowing from that; in other words, in the soul attending directly to God. Though the mind can also attend indirectly to God (as to an object seen in a mirror) when, as Augustine says, it remembers and understands and loves itself, and perceives there a trinity: not God indeed, but an image of God; and then moves through that to God.

God made man right. No one can wilfully turn away from happiness, for man wants happiness by nature. So no one seeing God for what he is can wilfully turn his back on God. Plainly then, since Adam sinned, he had not seen God for what he is. The disembodied state of the soul after death differs from its present embodied state in being unnatural; but Adam's state of innocence and man's state after sin differ as integrated and disintegrated states of a soul which has preserved its natural way of existence unimpaired. In the state of innocence, just as now, man's soul was adapted to controlling and perfecting and giving life to his body, but in so fully integrated a way that his body was completely at the service of his soul without hindrance. And since the way of understanding appropriate to a soul that must control and perfect the body's animal life is by recourse to sense-experience, this was also Adam's way of understanding. The things that were made in the beginning were made not only to be themselves but to start other things existing, and that is why they were produced in a state of perfection. Adam was created mature in body, capable of immediate procreation, and mature in soul, capable of immediate education and instruction of others. So he knew all that men normally have to learn, everything implicit in the first self-evident premises, all natural knowledge: *he gave all animals their names.* And since controlling his own and other people's lives also involved knowing life as destined to a goal beyond nature, Adam needed to know the supernatural things required to direct life in that state of innocence, just as nowadays we need the faith. But Adam did not know other things not naturally knowable but not required for directing life: such as men's thoughts, or the indeterminate future, or details like the number of pebbles in some river.

The integrated state of Adam in which his reason was submissive to God, his lower powers to his reason, and his body to his soul, seems to imply that he possessed God's grace from the start; for this is an integration not written into man's nature, otherwise it would have remained after sin. The primary submissiveness of Adam's reason to God must have been more than natural, and therefore due to a gift of grace; for effects cannot be more potent than their cause. In us feeling is partly but not wholly subject to reason: sometimes our feelings pre-empt and hamper reasoned assessment, whilst at other times they presuppose it. In the state of innocence the lower appetites were completely subject to reason, and all feelings presupposed reasoned assessment. Virtues are what

dispose our reason towards God and our lower powers towards the standards set by reason; so the very rightness of man's first state required him to possess all virtue. Some virtues, like charity and justice, contain no implication of imperfection, and others, like faith and hope, imply imperfections which were compatible with Adam's state (not yet seeing God and not in full enjoyment of him); so these existed in Adam without qualification, both the dispositions and the acts that proceed from them. But virtues like repentance and compassion that imply imperfections incompatible with Adam's state could only exist inactively, as dispositions to act when required, in the way Aristotle says shame exists in an earnest man.

Let him rule the fishes of the sea and the birds of the sky and the beasts of the earth. In nature the less perfect serve the more perfect: plants feed on the earth, animals on plants, and men on both plants and animals. Moreover, the instincts of animals to behave in certain particular ways is a sort of sharing in man's universal practical sense which can reason out all behaviour. So the subordination of animals to man is natural. To think wild and aggressive animals were originally peaceable, not only to men but also to other animals, is quite irrational. How could man by sinning change the nature of animals from vegetarian to carnivorous? Hostility between animals is natural, but it no more made them insubordinate to man then than it makes them insubordinate to God and his providence now. Man would have been an instrument of that providence then, just as he is now with domesticated animals, giving his tame hawks hens to eat. Instinctively geese follow a leader and bees obey a queen: all animals share by nature in the practical sense we have by reason. And at that time all animals would have obeyed man of their own accord, as the ones he has domesticated do today. Man was master of other things to the measure that he was master of himself. He shares reason with the angels, sense-powers with other animals, natural vital powers with plants, and the body itself with all non-living things. Reason is master, not subject (so man never had mastery over angels); feelings of aggression and desire man masters to some extent by reason's command (and so in the state of innocence he could command animals); but his own body and vital forces man masters not by command but by use (and so in the state of innocence he could not command plants and non-living things to change their behaviour, but would have had no trouble using their behaviour for his purposes). Of course, disparities existed in that first state: disparities first of all in sex and age, but also in moral and intellectual proficiency (men being free to work to different extents at doing and willing and knowing things), and again in physical strength (since this is influenced by food and climate and the stars one is born under). But none of this would have implied natural defect or sin. Free men exist for their own ends, as Aristotle says; whereas slaves serve others. Such slavery can't exist without suffering: everyone values his own good, and does not willingly cede it exclusively to another. But men can be subordinate to one another and yet remain free, if the good being served is their own or a common good. Such subordination would have existed in the state of innocence, since man is by nature a social animal, and people living a social life need some single authority to look to their common good. If some men are more knowledgeable and just than others the right thing is to use that to the others' benefit.

Death entered the world through sin. Before sin then, man must have been immortal. Not because he was immaterial like angels, or made of a kind of matter that cannot lose its form like the stars of heaven, nor because of some inherent disposition preserving him from his natural mortality like the glorified in heaven, but because God gave his soul supernatural ability to preserve his body from decay as long as it itself remained submissive to God. In the state of innocence man preserved his body from external injury by his own wits, helped by God's providence which so cared for him that nothing dangerous took him by surprise. As Augustine says *Adam was provided with food against hunger, with drink against thirst, and with the tree of life against the ravages of old age.* But the tree of life couldn't be the sole source of immortality. For one thing the tree of life couldn't give the soul its ability to preserve the body from injury; and for another, the potency of any material thing is finite and the effects of the tree of life would wear off in time, after which man would either move on to a life in the spirit or need another dose.

Increase and multiply and fill the earth. Unless there had been reproduction in the state of innocence to propagate the human race, man would have urgently needed to sin, seeing it would have brought such good. For among corruptible things, in which only the species lasts for ever, nature's main aim is the good of the species and its reproduction. Only among incorruptible substances is nature interested in individuals. So man needed to reproduce for the sake of his perishable body; though as regards his imperishable soul man needed nature (or better the author of nature, who alone creates human souls) to be interested in a multitude of individuals for their own sakes. So in the state of innocence reproduction was needed not for conservation of the species but for multiplication of individuals. In the present state of things, when owners multiply, property must be divided up, since, as Aristotle says, common property breeds discord. But in the state of innocence men's wills would have been well enough disposed for them to use their common property in a manner suited to each without danger of discord; as we indeed often see good men doing nowadays.

Some early theologians seeing intercourse besmirched by lust in our present state, thought reproduction would have happened without intercourse in the state of innocence. But this is unreasonable. It is in man's nature, like that of other animals, both before and after sin, to reproduce by intercourse, and nature has provided him with the organs needed for the purpose. In our present state the natural mating of male and female is somewhat disfigured by unbalanced desire, but this would not have happened in the state of innocence where the lower powers obeyed reason. Because animals lack reason, people sometimes say that men become like animals during intercourse, when reason is unable to balance the pleasure and heat of desire. But in the state of innocence nothing would have escaped reason in that way. Yet the pleasure would not have been any less; in fact it would have been greater given the greater purity of nature and sensitivity of body men then had. Rule by reason requires not that the pleasure should be less, but that the desire for it should be within reasonable bounds. Men who eat moderately can take as much pleasure in their food as gluttons do, but their desire doesn't wallow in the pleasure. In the state of innocence there would have been no great esteem for sexual abstinence, which we esteem nowadays not because it reduces fruitfulness but because it tempers lust.

Things beyond nature only faith can teach, and for faith we need authority. So, without God's authority, we can only assert what is in the nature of things. Now scripture tells us God created man right, so that his limbs, for example, would obey his properly ordered will. But a properly ordered will tends only to the behaviour appropriate to one's age. So newly-born infants would only have had power to move their limbs appropriately to their age, sucking the breast and so on. Weakness of seed or unsuitable material are not the only causes of females being conceived, but also external circumstances such as the direction of the wind or an idea in the mind. And this would have been particularly likely in the state of innocence, when the body was more subordinate to the mind, so that the sex of the child could have been decided by the parent. The integrated state in which man was created was a state of our nature, not deriving from the natural constitution of man, but from a gift of God given to human nature as a whole. We know this because its opposite, inherited sin, attaches to nature as a whole and passes from parent to child. When authority is silent we can only believe what accords with nature. Now men naturally learn by sense-experience, so those born in a state of innocence would also have acquired their knowledge over a period of time by discovery and instruction, though without the difficulties we have. And, as infants, they would no more have had mature use of their reason than they had of their bodily limbs.

People who locate Paradise at the equator do so because they think the evenness of day and night produces a temperate climate there, never too cold and never too hot. Aristotle however expressly says that the region is so hot that it is uninhabitable; and this seems more likely, seeing that even countries where the sun never passes directly overhead have excessively hot climates from mere proximity to the sun. In any case we believe Paradise to be situated in the most temperate locality, whether that be on the equator or elsewhere.

*   *   *

REVIEW QUESTIONS

1. What ideas tie together Thomas's five ways of proving there is a God?
2. How does Thomas see the natural relationship between men and women?
3. For Thomas, what is humanity's proper place in nature, and why?

FROM *The Poem of the Cid*

The Poem of the Cid describes the life of Rodrigo Díaz, Mio Cid, "my lord" in Arabic, or El Campeador, "the Battler." This Castilian noble and his eleventh-century exploits, notably the conquest of Valencia in 1094, became the core of a legendary heroic poem, written down in this form in 1207. In this final part of the poem, Rodrigo, with the help of King Alfonso of Leon, directs his champions to fight the evil Infantes of Carrión, the Cid's treacherous sons-in-law and instigators of his exile.

From *The Poem of the Cid*, translated by Rita Hamilton and Janet Perry (New York: Penguin Books, 1984), pp. 203, 205, 207, 209, 211, 213, 215.

*   *   *

The King raised his hand and, making the sign of the cross, he said "I swear by St. Isidore, whom we venerate in León, that there is not such a man as you in all our land." The Cid rode up and kissed the hand of his lord, King Alfonso. "You ordered me" he said "to show the paces of my swift horse, Babieca, who has no peer in the world today. I give him to you as a present, my lord; order him to be led away." The King answered: "I will not accept your gift. If I took this horse from you he would not have so good a master. Such a horse is fit for such a man as you—to defeat Moors in battle and follow them in pursuit. May anyone who takes him from you be deprived of God's aid! You with your horse gain great honour for us." Then they said farewell, and the court broke up. The Campeador gave wise advice to those who were to take part in the combat: "Martín Antolínez and you, Pedro Bermúdez," he said, "and you, Muño Gustioz, hold firm in the field like brave men, so that in Valencia I may hear good reports of your conduct." Martín Antolínez answered: "Why do you say this? We have undertaken this duty and it is for us to see it through. You may hear of us as dead but not as defeated." The Cid was glad to hear him speak like that, and he took leave of all his friends there. The Cid then set out for Valencia, and the King for Carrión. The three weeks of grace came to an end, and the Cid's followers arrived punctually to fulfil the duty laid on them by their lord. They were under the protection of Alfonso as king of León. After a delay of two days the Infantes of Carrión came, well equipped with arms and horses. All their relatives had plotted with them that, if they could find the Campeador's men unprotected in the field, they would kill them and so dishonour their lord. It was a wicked plot but it was not carried out for fear of King Alfonso of León. That night they all held vigil beside their arms and prayed to God for victory. The night had passed and dawn was about to break, when a great crowd of nobles assembled to witness the combat, which they were eager to behold. Above all, King Alfonso was there to see that justice was done and no wrong. The Cid's three men donned their armour, ready for the fray as champions of one lord. In another place the Infantes were arming while Count García Ordóñez plied them with advice. They then approached the King with the request that the swords, Colada and Tizón, should not be used in the fight by the Campeador's champions. They deeply regretted having handed them over. The King, however, refused to grant their request, saying: "When we held our court you made no objection to their use. If you have good swords they will prove to your advantage, and the same applies to the Cid's men. Rise and enter the field, Infantes of Carrión; it is your obligation to fight like men. The Campeador's champions will not be found wanting. If you are successful in the combat you will gain great honour, and if you are defeated do not blame us, for everyone knows that you brought this on yourselves." The Infantes began to repent bitterly of what they had done. They would rather for all Carrión that it had been left undone. All three champions of the Campeador were armed and ready when King Alfonso went to inspect them. They said to him: "We kiss your hands as our king and lord, asking that you should see justice done between them and us. Protect us in right but not in wrong. The Infantes of Carrión are here surrounded by their henchmen, and we do not know what plots they may be hatching. Our liege lord gave us into your care. Keep us from unjust attack for the love of God." The King replied: "This I shall assuredly do." When their fine swift horses were led forward they made the sign of the cross over their saddles and swung into their seats. Their bucklers with strong bosses hung from their necks and they grasped in their hands the shafts of their lances from which three pennons fluttered. Around them stood a crowd of sturdy fighters. Then they rode out into the lists, and all three of the Cid's men were determined that each and every one of them would strike his adversary a hard blow. On the other side were the Infantes of Carrión, accompanied by many members of their family. The King appointed umpires to decide all points of dispute, so that there might be no argument. As they all stood ready in the field, King Alfonso spoke as follows: "Hear what I say to you, Infantes of Carrión. You might have fought this combat in Toledo, but you refused to do so. These three knights, followers of the Cid Campeador, I have brought under safe-conduct to the lands of Carrión. Do what is right and attempt no wrong. I shall take severe measures against any man who proposes to do wrong, and he will find no refuge in all my territory." His words struck unpleasantly

on the young men's ears. The umpires and the King marked out the bounds, the bystanders were cleared from the field. It was explained to all six combatants that any one of them who crossed the bounds would be considered beaten. The bystanders were ordered not to approach within six lance-lengths of the boundary. They drew lots for position and it was arranged that neither party should have the sun against them. The umpires then left the two parties facing each other. The Cid's champions approached the Infantes of Carrión, and they also advanced, each man intent on his own special adversary. They clasped their shields against their breasts, lowered their pennoned lances, bent down their heads over their saddle-bows and set spurs to their horses; the earth trembled as they galloped forward. Each one was intent on his man; three against three were joined in battle. The onlookers thought they would all fall dead at the same time. Pedro Bermúdez, the first to challenge, met Fernando González face to face, each striking the other's shield fearlessly. Fernando pierced Don Pedro's shield, but not deeply enough to reach the flesh, and his spear broke in two places with the shock. Pedro Bermúdez held firm and did not topple over. He received one blow but gave another in return, which broke off the boss of Fernando's shield and pierced the shield itself, which proved no protection. The lance struck through the breast near to the heart. His three layers of mail saved him, for two were pierced, but the third held. The lance drove it with the padded tunic and shirt a hand's breadth into the flesh, and the blood poured from his mouth. Every strap of the horse's caparison snapped, and his rider was knocked to the ground over his croup. The onlookers thought he had received his death wound. Pedro Bermúdez laid aside his lance and seized his sword. When Fernando González saw the sword he recognized Tizón and, before the blow fell, he cried: "I am defeated." The umpires acknowledged the admission, and Pedro Bermúdez stayed his hand.

Martín Antolínez and Diego González attacked each other with their lances so fiercely that both these were broken. When Martín Antolínez put hand to his sword, the whole field flashed—so clear and bright it was. With a side blow he struck away the top of Diego's helmet, cutting all the straps which held it on to the mailed hood; reaching the coif, he carried coif and hood away and, shaving the hair, touched the flesh. One part of the helmet fell to the ground and the rest remained in place. When the great sword, Colada, struck this blow, Diego González saw that he would be doomed to die and he pulled his horse's rein to turn his face away. Martín Antolínez was ready with his sword, but he struck with the flat and not with the sharp edge. Diego González held a sword in his hand but did not use it, and then he shouted out: "Help me, great God! Protect me from this sword!" He reined in his horse, guiding it away from the sword, and drew it over the boundary line. Martín Antolínez remained victorious in the field. Then the King said: "Come to my side; you have won this battle in fair fight." The umpires confirmed the King's words.

Two of the challengers had vanquished their opponents, and now you will hear how Muño Gustioz made out with Ansur González. They too exchanged mighty blows. Strong and valiant, Ansur González struck Muño Gustioz's shield and pierced his armour beyond it, but the lance failed to reach the flesh. After this first blow, Muño Gustioz struck another, which pierced the shield and penetrated the armour through the boss; Ansur could not ward it off, and the lance pierced his armour. Muño struck him on one side, not near the heart, but he thrust his lance and pennon through the flesh an arm's length out on the other side; he gave him a twist and removed Ansur from the saddle. Then, withdrawing his lance, he cast him to the ground. The shaft, blade and pennon came out stained red with blood. All thought he had received his death blow. When Muño had recovered his lance he stood over Ansur González.

Gonzalo Ansúrez cried: "Do not strike him, for God's sake!" The fight was ended when this was done. The umpires said: "We confirm the admission." King Alfonso ordered the field to be cleared. The arms of the vanquished which were left there became his property. The Campeador's champions departed with honour, for they had, by God's grace, won the fight. There was great sorrow throughout the lands of Carrión. The King dispatched the Cid's followers by night so that they might have no fear of an attack. Like prudent men they travelled day and night and arrived safely in Valencia, where they joined the Cid. They had proved the Infantes of Carrión traitors and so fulfilled the obligation laid on them by their lord, who was greatly rejoiced to hear it. The Infantes of Carrión had suffered deep disgrace. May such a fate or worse befall anyone who treats a noble lady shamefully and then abandons her! We shall now leave the subject of the Infantes of Carrión, hard hit by the punishment they have received, and speak about the Cid. There was great rejoicing in Valencia over the honour won by the Cid's followers. Their lord, Ruy Díaz, grasped his beard and said: "I thank God in His Heaven that my daughters are avenged! Let them now be considered quit of the estates of Carrión. I can give them in marriage without let or hindrance." The Princes of Navarre and Aragon began negotiations and arranged a meeting for that purpose with King Alfonso of León. The marriages with Doña Elvira and Doña Sol were duly solemnised. Their first marriages brought them honour, but these were better still. See what honour accrued to the Cid when his daughters became Queens of Navarre and Aragon. Today the Kings of Spain are related to him and all gain lustre from the fame of the fortunate Campeador. He passed from this life on the day of Pentecost. May Christ pardon him as He may pardon us all, righteous and sinners alike. These are the exploits of the Cid Campeador, and here our story ends.

To the writer of this book may God give His Paradise, Amen! Per Abbat wrote it down in the month of May, in the year of Our Lord 1207. [The poem has been read out, give us some wine; if you have no pennies, throw down some pledges there, for you will get a good return on them.]

REVIEW QUESTIONS

1. In this poem, what assumptions about justice are behind trial by combat?
2. What values of the warrior aristocracy are apparent in this poem?

10 ✣ THE LATER MIDDLE AGES, 1300–1500

By about 1300, Europe's economic and demographic growth seemed to stall. Medieval society reached limits on its geographic frontiers, could not count on increased agricultural yields from depleted soils, and no longer experienced big productivity gains from improved technologies in artisan manufacturing. Signs of trouble, famines and increased mortality, appeared long before the devastating plague of 1348, which killed one-third of the population in Europe and the Middle East and was especially lethal in the great cities like Cairo and Florence. The long fourteenth century, calamitous for its repeated epidemics and wars like the century-long episodic conflict between France and England, is a bridge between the confident thirteenth century and the first signs of recovery in the late fifteenth century. The Later Middle Ages is an awkward but necessary term for the period roughly from 1300 to 1500. The new values and artistic tastes associated with the Renaissance in Italy usually stand apart from the wider world of feudal monarchies and lingering medieval culture in northern Europe.

Yet basic similarities in religion and the economy united this world, and above all the plague was no respecter of historical periods. Much of Europe experienced the same religious, economic, social, and psychological responses to repeated outbreaks of plague. The basic institutions of late medieval life—the family, papacy, monarchies, and universities—endured the shocks of high levels of mortality, proving the strength of late medieval people and their culture. These same institutions offered few practical explanations for the new killer, leading to a crisis in belief and a search for scapegoats that focused on traditional targets: the Jews and the lepers.

Giovanni Boccaccio, an eyewitness to the plague's course through Florence where it killed more than half the population, recorded in his introduction to the Decameron *the impressions of a survivor. Whether the disease was the one known to modern biologists as bubonic plague or some unknown killer, its effects on society, movingly described by Boccaccio, occurred in a setting where the eco-*

nomic shocks of high mortality led to declining prices and rents, and the paradox of higher wages for the remaining workers. The mood of the survivors—a strange mix of hyperconsumerism, greed, fear, and suspicion—produced a culture preoccupied with piety, melancholy, and death. The plague struck down priests, students, monks, and nuns in higher than average numbers, and the church, with the papacy in Avignon and on the verge of schism, faced new challenges to its authority. Theologians like John Wyclif and Jan Hus raised fundamental questions about the sacraments and how the church functioned in the world. The papacy itself was usually at the center of controversies, especially when the great schism resulted in three competing popes by 1409. Pius II's account of his election as pope in 1458 shows the strengths and weaknesses of the mid-fifteenth-century church.

In the eastern Mediterranean, the Ottoman state was advancing into the Balkans and finally destroyed the last remnant of the Byzantine Empire by taking Constantinople in 1453. The Russian church and people came to see themselves as the third Rome, heirs to the Greek world and bulwark against the Muslims and Tartars. Another distinctive feature of this period is the rise of a vernacular culture, as more literature appeared outside the traditional Latin of the universities. Authors like Dante in Italian, Chaucer in English, and Christine de Pisan in French captured the spirit of late medieval society. The small reading audience and the larger numbers who were read to wanted literature and art that responded to the crises and questions of late medieval life. The old epics and courtly romances still appealed to many, but so much death required new approaches and explanations.

In the last phase of the Hundred Years' War, the dramatic career of France's heroic Jeanne d'Arc reveals a complex mix of the miraculous, nationalism, and misogyny at work as a teenage woman saved the French cause but paid a great price. The Later Middle Ages witnessed the irony of destructive wars fought by smaller armies and navies in the midst of continued devastating outbreaks of plague.

IBN KHALDÛN

FROM *The Muqaddimah*

The North African scholar Ibn Khaldûn (1332–1406) wrote The Muqaddimah, *the first systematic explanation of history as a useful subject for research and analytical writing. In these excerpts, Ibn Khaldûn discusses the complex subject of history and truth, and the even more difficult topic of interpreting the Qur'an in its historical context.*

From *Ibn Khaldûn: The Muqaddimah*, vol. 1, by Franz Rosenthal (Princeton, N.J.: Princeton University Press, 1967), pp. 6–17.

History is a discipline widely cultivated among nations and races. It is eagerly sought after. The men in the street, the ordinary people, aspire to know it. Kings and leaders vie for it.

Both the learned and the ignorant are able to understand it. For on the surface history is no more than information about political events, dynasties, and occurrences of the remote past, elegantly presented and spiced with proverbs. It serves to entertain large, crowded gatherings and brings to us an understanding of human affairs. It shows how changing conditions affect human affairs, how certain dynasties came to occupy an ever wider space in the world, and how they settled the earth until they heard the call and their time was up.

The inner meaning of history, on the other hand, involves speculation and an attempt to get at the truth, subtle explanation of the causes and origins of existing things, and deep knowledge of the how and why of events. History, therefore, is firmly rooted in philosophy. It deserves to be accounted a branch of philosophy.

The outstanding Muslim historians made exhaustive collections of historical events and wrote them down in book form. But, then, persons who had no right to occupy themselves with history introduced into those books untrue gossip which they had thought up or freely invented, as well as false, discredited reports which they had made up or embellished. Many of their successors followed in their steps and passed that information on to us as they had heard it. They did not look for, or pay any attention to, the causes of events and conditions, nor did they eliminate or reject nonsensical stories.

Little effort is being made to get at the truth. The critical eye, as a rule, is not sharp. Errors and unfounded assumptions are closely allied and familiar elements in historical information. Blind trust in tradition is an inherited trait in human beings. Occupation with the scholarly disciplines on the part of those who have no right is widespread. But the pasture of stupidity is unwholesome for mankind. No one can stand up against the authority of truth, and the evil of falsehood is to be fought with enlightening speculation. The reporter merely dictates and passes on the material. It takes critical insight to sort out the hidden truth; it takes knowledge to lay truth bare and polish it so that critical insight may be applied to it.

Many systematic historical works have been composed, and the history of nations and dynasties in the world has been compiled and written down. But there are very few historians who have become so well known as to be recognized as authorities, and who have replaced the products of their predecessors by their own works. They can almost be counted on the fingers of the hands; they are hardly more numerous than the vowels in grammatical constructions which are just three. There are, for instance, Ibn Isḥâq; aṭ-Ṭabarî; Ibn al-Kalbî; Muḥammad b. 'Umar al-Wâqidî; Sayf b. 'Umar al-Asadî; al-Mas'ûdî, and other famous historians who are distinguished from the general run of historians.

It is well known to competent persons and reliable experts that the works of al-Mas'ûdî and al-Wâqidî are suspect and objectionable in certain respects. However, their works have been distinguished by universal acceptance of the information they contain and by adoption of their methods and their presentation of material. The discerning critic is his own judge as to which part of their material he finds spurious, and which he gives credence to. Civilization, in its different conditions, contains different elements to which historical information may be related and with which reports and historical materials may be checked.

Most of the histories by these authors cover everything because of the universal geographical extension of the two earliest Islamic dynasties and because of the very wide selection of sources of which they did or did not make use. Some of these authors, such as al-Mas'ûdî and historians of his type, gave an exhaustive history of the pre-Islamic dynasties and nations and of other pre-Islamic affairs in general. Some later historians, on the other hand, showed a tendency toward greater restriction, hesitating to be so general and comprehensive. They brought together the happenings of their own period and gave exhaustive historical information about their own part of the world. They restricted themselves to the history of their own dynasties and cities. This was done by Ibn Ḥayyân, the historian of Spain and the Spanish Umayyads, and by Ibn ar-Raqîq, the historian of Ifrîqiyah and the dynasty in Kairouan (al-Qayra-wân).

The later historians were all tradition-bound and dull of nature and intelligence, or did not try not to be dull. They merely copied the older historians and followed their example. They disregarded the changes in conditions and in the customs of nations and races that the passing of time had brought about. Thus, they presented historical information about dynasties and stories of events from the early period as mere forms without substance, blades without scabbards, as knowledge that must be considered ignorance, because it is not known what of it is extraneous and what is genuine. Their information concerns happenings the origins of which are not known. It concerns species the genera of which are not taken into consideration, and whose specific differences are not verified. With the information they set down they merely repeated historical material which is, in any case, widely known, and followed the earlier historians who worked on it. They neglected the importance of change over the generations in their treatment of the historical material, because they had no one who could interpret it for them. Their works, therefore, give no explanation for it. When they then turn to the description of a particular dynasty, they report the historical information about it mechanically and take care to preserve it as it had been passed on down to them, be it imaginary or true. They do not turn to the beginning of the dynasty. Nor do they tell why it unfurled its banner and was able to give prominence to its emblem, or what caused it to come to a stop when it had reached its term. The student, thus, has still to search for the beginnings of conditions and for the principles of organization of the various dynasties. He must himself investigate why the various dynasties brought pressures to bear upon each other and why they succeeded each other. He must search for a convincing explanation of the elements that made for mutual separation or contact among the dynasties. All this will be dealt with in the Introduction to this work.

Other historians, then, came with too brief a presentation of history. They went to the extreme of being satisfied with the names of kings, without any genealogical or historical information, and with only a numerical indication of the length of reigns. This was done by Ibn Rashîq in the *Mîzân al-'amal*, and by those lost sheep who followed his method. No credence can be given to what they say. They are not considered trustworthy, nor is their material considered worthy of transmission, for they caused useful material to be lost and damaged the methods and customs acknowledged as sound and practical by historians.

When I had read the works of others and probed into the recesses of yesterday and today, I shook myself out of that drowsy complacency and sleepiness. Although not much of a writer, I exhibited my own literary ability as well as I could, and, thus, composed a book on history. In this book I lifted the veil from conditions as they arise in the various generations. I arranged it in an orderly way in chapters dealing with historical facts and reflections. In it I showed how and why dynasties and civilization originate. I based the work on the history of the two races that constitute the population of the Maghrib at this time and people its various regions and cities, and on that of their ruling houses, both long- and short-lived, including the rulers and allies they had in the past. These two races are the Arabs and the Berbers. They are the two races known to have resided in the Maghrib for such a long time that one can hardly imagine they ever lived elsewhere, for its inhabitants know no other human races.

I corrected the contents of the work carefully and presented it to the judgment of scholars and the elite. I followed an unusual method of arrangement and division into chapters. From the various possibilities, I chose a remarkable and original method. In the work, I commented on civilization, on urbanization, and on the essential characteristics of human social organization, in a way that explains to the reader how and why things are as they are, and shows him how the men who constituted a dynasty first came upon the historical scene. As a result, he will wash his hands of any blind trust in tradition. He will become aware of the conditions of periods and races that were before his time and that will be after it.

I divided the work into an introduction and three books:

The Introduction deals with the great merit of historiography, offers an appreciation of its

various methods, and cites errors of the historians.

The First Book deals with civilization and its essential characteristics, namely, royal authority, government, gainful occupations, ways of making a living, crafts, and sciences, as well as with the causes and reasons thereof.

The Second Book deals with the history, races, and dynasties of the Arabs, from the beginning of creation down to this time. This will include references to such famous nations and dynasties contemporaneous with them, as the Nabataeans, the Syrians, the Persians, the Israelites, the Copts, the Greeks, the Byzantines, and the Turks.

The Third Book deals with the history of the Berbers and of the Zanâtah who are part of them; with their origins and races; and, in particular, with the royal authority and dynasties in the Maghrib.

Later on, there was my trip to the East, in order to find out about the manifold illumination it offers and to fulfill the religious duty and custom of circumambulating the Kaᶜbah and visiting Medina, as well as to study the systematic works and tomes on Eastern history. As a result, I was able to fill the gaps in my historical information about the non-Arab (Persian) rulers of those lands, and about the Turkish dynasties in the regions over which they ruled. I added this information to what I had written here before in this connection. I inserted it into the treatment of the nations of the various districts and rulers of the various cities and regions that were contemporary with those Persian and Turkish races. In this connection I was brief and concise and preferred the easy goal to the difficult one. I proceeded from general genealogical tables to detailed historical information.

Thus, this work contains an exhaustive history of the world. It forces stubborn stray wisdom to return to the fold. It gives causes and reasons for happenings in the various dynasties. It turns out to be a vessel for philosophy, a receptacle for historical knowledge. The work contains the history of the Arabs and the Berbers, both the sedentary groups and the nomads. It also contains references to the great dynasties that were contemporary with them, and, moreover, clearly indicates memorable lessons to be learned from early conditions and from subsequent history. Therefore, I called the work "Book of Lessons and Archive of Early and Subsequent History, Dealing with the Political Events Concerning the Arabs, Non-Arabs, and Berbers, and the Supreme Rulers Who Were Contemporary with Them."

I omitted nothing concerning the origin of races and dynasties, concerning the synchronism of the earliest nations, concerning the reasons for change and variation in past periods and within religious groups, concerning dynasties and religious groups, towns and hamlets, strength and humiliation, large numbers and small numbers, sciences and crafts, gains and losses, changing general conditions, nomadic and sedentary life, actual events and future events, all things expected to occur in civilization. I treated everything comprehensively and exhaustively and explained the arguments for and causes of its existence.

As a result, this book has become unique, as it contains unusual knowledge and familiar if hidden wisdom. Still, after all has been said, I am conscious of imperfection when I look at the scholars of past and contemporary times. I confess my inability to penetrate so difficult a subject. I wish that men of scholarly competence and wide knowledge would look at the book with a critical, rather than a complacent eye, and silently correct and overlook the mistakes they come upon. The capital of knowledge that an individual scholar has to offer is small. Admission of one's shortcomings saves from censure. Kindness from colleagues is hoped for. It is God whom I ask to make our deeds acceptable in His sight. He suffices me. He is a good protector.

Introduction

It should be known that history is a discipline that has a great number of different approaches. Its useful aspects are very many. Its goal is distinguished.

History makes us acquainted with the conditions of past nations as they are reflected in their national character. It makes us acquainted with the biographies of the prophets and with the dynasties and policies of rulers. Whoever so desires may thus achieve the useful result of being able to imitate historical examples in religious and worldly matters.

The writing of history requires numerous sources and greatly varied knowledge. It also requires a good speculative mind and thoroughness. Possession of these two qualities leads the historian to the truth and keeps him from slips and errors. If he trusts historical information in its plain transmitted form and has no clear knowledge of the principles resulting from custom, the fundamental facts of politics, the nature of civilization, or the conditions governing human social organization, and if, furthermore, he does not evaluate remote or ancient material through comparison with near or contemporary material, he often cannot avoid stumbling and slipping and deviating from the highroad of truth. Historians, Qur'ân commentators and leading transmitters have committed frequent errors in the stories and events they reported. They accepted them in the plain transmitted form, without regard for its value. They did not check them with the principles underlying such historical situations, nor did they compare them with similar material. Also, they did not probe more deeply with the yardstick of philosophy, with the help of knowledge of the nature of things, or with the help of speculation and historical insight. Therefore, they strayed from the truth and found themselves lost in the desert of baseless assumptions and errors.

This is especially the case with figures, either of sums of money or of soldiers, whenever they occur in stories. They offer a good opportunity for false information and constitute a vehicle for nonsensical statements. They must be controlled and checked with the help of known fundamental facts.

For example, al-Masᶜûdî and many other historians report that Moses counted the army of the Israelites in the desert. He had all those able to carry arms, especially those twenty years and older, pass muster. There turned out to be 600,000 or more. In this connection, al-Masᶜûdî forgets to take into consideration whether Egypt and Syria could possibly have held such a number of soldiers. Every realm may have as large a militia as it can hold and support, but no more. This fact is attested by well-known customs and familiar conditions. Moreover, an army of this size cannot march or fight as a unit. The whole available territory would be too small for it. If it were in battle formation, it would extend two, three, or more times beyond the field of vision. How, then, could two such parties fight with each other, or one battle formation gain the upper hand when one flank does not know what the other flank is doing! The situation at the present day testifies to the correctness of this statement. The past resembles the future more than one drop of water another.

Furthermore, the realm of the Persians was much greater than that of the Israelites. This fact is attested by Nebuchadnezzar's victory over them. He swallowed up their country and gained complete control over it. He also destroyed Jerusalem, their religious and political capital. And he was merely one of the officials of the province of Fârs. It is said that he was the governor of the western border region. The Persian provinces of the two ᶜIrâqs, Khurâsân, Transoxania, and the region of Derbend on the Caspian Sea were much larger than the realm of the Israelites. Yet, the Persian army did not attain such a number or even approach it. The greatest concentration of Persian troops, at al-Qâdisîyah, amounted to 120,000 men, all of whom had their retainers. This is according to Sayf who said that with their retainers they amounted to over 200,000 persons. According to ᶜÂ'ishah and az-Zuhrî, the troop concentration with which Rustum advanced against Saᶜd at al-Qâdisîyah amounted to only 60,000 men, all of whom had their retainers.

*   *   *

It should be known that the Qur'ân was revealed in the language of the Arabs and according to their rhetorical methods. All Arabs understood it and knew the meaning of the individual words and composite statements. It was revealed in chapters and verses, in order to explain the oneness of God and the religious duties according to the various occasions.

Some passages of the Qur'ân concern articles of faith. Others concern the duties of the limbs of the body. Some are early and are followed by other, later passages that abrogate the earlie ones.

The Prophet used to explain these things, as it is said: "So that you may explain to the people that which was revealed to them." He used to explain the unclear statements in the Qur'ân and to distinguish the abrogating statements from those abrogated by them, and to inform the men around him in this sense. The men around him, thus, became acquainted with the subject. They knew why individual verses had been revealed, and the situation that had required them, directly on Muhammad's authority. Thus, the verse of the Qur'ân, "When God's help comes and the victory," refers to the announcement of the Prophet's death, and similar things.

These explanations were transmitted on the authority of the men around Muhammad and were circulated by the men of the second generation after them on their authority. They continued to be transmitted among the early Muslims, until knowledge became organized in scholarly disciplines and systematic scholarly works were written. At that time, most of these explanations were committed to writing. The traditional information concerning them, which had come down from the men around Muhammad and the men of the second generation, was transmitted farther. That material reached at-Tabarî, al-Wâqidî, ath-Tha'âlibî, and other Qur'ân interpreters. They committed to writing as much of the traditional information as God wanted them to do.

The linguistic sciences then became technical discussions of the lexicographical meaning of words, the rules governing vowel endings, and style in word combinations. Systematic works were written on these subjects. Formerly, these subjects had been habits with the Arabs. No recourse to oral and written transmission had been necessary with respect to them. Now, that state of affairs was forgotten, and these subjects were learned from the books of philologists. They were needed for the interpretation of the Qur'ân, because the Qur'ân is in Arabic and follows the stylistic technique of the Arabs. Qur'ân interpretation thus came to be handled in two ways.

One kind of Qur'ân interpretation is traditional. It is based upon information received from the early Muslims. It consists of knowledge of the abrogating verses and of the verses that are abrogated by them, of the reasons why a given verse was revealed, and of the purposes of individual verses. All this can be known only through traditions based on the authority of the men around Muhammad and the men of the second generation. The early scholars had already made complete compilations on the subject. However, their works and the information they transmit contain side by side important and unimportant matters, accepted and rejected statements. The reason is that the Arabs had no books or scholarship. The desert attitude and illiteracy prevailed among them. When they wanted to know certain things that human beings are usually curious to know, such as the reasons for the existing things, the beginning of creation, and the secrets of existence, they consulted the earlier People of the Book about it and got their information from them. The People of the Book were the Jews who had the Torah, and the Christians who followed the religion of the Jews. Now, the people of the Torah who lived among the Arabs at that time were themselves Bedouins. They knew only as much about these matters as is known to ordinary People of the Book in contrast to learned rabbis. The majority of those Jews were Himyarites who had adopted Judaism. When they became Muslims, they clung to the information they possessed, such as information about the beginning of creation and information of the type of forecasts and predictions. That information had no connection with the Jewish or Christian religious laws they were preserving as theirs. Such men were Ka'b al-ahbâr, Wahb b. Munabbih, 'Abdallâh b. Sallâm,

and similar people. The Qur'ân commentaries were filled with material of such tendencies transmitted on their authority. It is information that entirely depends on them. It has no relation to religious laws, such that one might claim for it the soundness that would make it necessary to act in accordance with it. The Qur'ân interpreters were not very rigorous in this respect. They filled the Qur'ân commentaries with such material, which originated, as we have stated, with the people of the Torah who lived in the desert and were not capable of verifying the information they transmitted. However, they were famous and highly esteemed, because they were people of rank in their religion and religious group. Therefore, their interpretation has been accepted from that time onwards.

Later, scholars applied themselves to verification and critical investigation. Abû Muhammad b. 'Atîyah, a recent Maghribî scholar, made his appearance. He abridged all the commentaries and selected the most likely interpretations. He set that material down in a good book, which is in general circulation among the inhabitants of the Maghrib and of Spain. Al-Qurtubî adopted his method in this respect in another work, which is well known in the East.

The other kind of Qur'ân interpretation has recourse to linguistic knowledge, such as lexicography and the stylistic form used for conveying meaning through the appropriate means and methods. This kind of Qur'ân interpretation rarely appears separately from the first kind. The first kind is the one that is wanted essentially. The second kind made its appearance only after language and the philological sciences had become crafts. However, it has become preponderant, as far as certain Qur'ân commentaries are concerned.

The commentary in which this discipline is best represented is the *Kitâb al-Kashshâf* by az-Zamakhsharî, of Khuwârizm in the 'Irâq. However, its author is a Mu'tazilah in his dogmatic views. Therefore, he uses the various methods of rhetoric, arguing in favor of the pernicious doctrines of the Mu'tazilah, wherever he believed they occurred in the verses of the Qur'ân. Competent orthodox scholars have, therefore, come to disregard his work and to warn everyone against its pitfalls. However, they admit that he is on firm ground in everything relating to language and style. If the student of the work is acquainted with the orthodox dogmas and knows the arguments in their defense, he is no doubt safe from its fallacies. Therefore, he should seize the opportunity to study it, because it contains remarkable and varied linguistic information.

Recently, a work by an ᶜIrâqî scholar, Sharaf-ad-dîn aṭ-Ṭîbî, of Tabrîz in the non-Arab ᶜIrâq, has reached us. It is a commentary on the work of az-Zamakhsharî. Aṭ-Ṭîbî follows az-Zamakhsharî's work literally, but opposes its Muᶜtazilah dogmas and arguments, showing their lack of validity and always explaining that an eloquent style exists in a given verse but it reflects the opinions of orthodox Muslims, and not the dogmas of the Muᶜtazilah. He does that very well, and he also possesses all the various disciplines of rhetoric *balâghah*.

"And He knows more than any scholar."

*   *   *

REVIEW QUESTIONS

1. On the basis of Ibn Khaldûn's principles, how can we determine the truth and accuracy of a historical work?
2. Is there a difference between truth and accuracy in history?
3. How does Ibn Khaldûn handle his chief religious text, the Qur'an?

GIOVANNI BOCCACCIO

FROM *The Decameron*

Giovanni Boccaccio (1313–1374), a poet, scholar, and humanist, put together by 1351 this collection of one hundred tales, The Decameron, *to entertain the survivors of the plague and divert them from their troubles. The framework of these stories is the ten Florentines (seven women and three men) who fled the city to escape death and passed the time by telling stories on set themes. In the introduction, Boccaccio describes how his home city, Florence, experienced and survived the first terrible outbreak of plague in the spring of 1348.*

From *The Decameron*, edited by Giovanni Boccaccio, translated by G. H. McWilliams (New York: Penguin Books, 1995), pp. 5–13.

FROM Introduction

I say, then, that the sum of thirteen hundred and forty-eight years had elapsed since the fruitful Incarnation of the Son of God, when the noble city of Florence, which for its great beauty excels all others in Italy, was visited by the deadly pestilence. Some say that it descended upon the human race through the influence of the heavenly bodies, others that it was a punishment signifying God's righteous anger at our iniquitous way of life. But whatever its cause, it had originated some years

THE TRIUMPH OF DEATH (C. 1340)   FRANCESCO TRAINI (?)

This painting is part of a series of frescos decorating the Camposanto, the famous cemetery of Pisa. The frescos are by local tradition attributed to the Pisan painter Francesco Traini. This fresco about death was probably painted just before the arrival of the bubonic plague in Pisa in 1348, and it incorporates images of death formed in the years of famine and epidemics of the early fourteenth century. What overall impression of death does this fresco convey? In particular, find the image of Death and consider her role in the fresco. One of the many striking parts of this fresco is the detail in which the three riders confront the three corpses. What can we learn about the mentality of a people who commissioned this fresco to decorate a cemetery?

earlier in the East, where it had claimed countless lives before it unhappily spread westward, growing in strength as it swept relentlessly on from one place to the next.

In the face of its onrush, all the wisdom and ingenuity of man were unavailing. Large quantities of refuse were cleared out of the city by officials specially appointed for the purpose, all sick persons were forbidden entry, and numerous instructions were issued for safeguarding the people's health, but all to no avail. Nor were the countless petitions humbly directed to God by the pious, whether by means of formal processions or in all other ways, any less ineffectual. For in the early spring of the year we have mentioned, the plague began, in a terrifying and extraordinary manner, to make its disastrous effects apparent. It did not take the form it had assumed in the East, where if anyone bled from the nose it was an obvious portent of certain death. On the contrary, its earliest symptom, in men and women alike, was the appearance of certain swellings in the groin or the armpit, some of which were egg-shaped whilst others were roughly the size of the common apple. Sometimes the swellings were large, sometimes not so large, and they were referred to by the populace as *gavòccioli*. From the two areas already mentioned, this deadly *gavòcciolo* would begin to spread, and within a short time it would appear at random all over the body. Later on, the symptoms of the disease changed, and many people began to find dark blotches and bruises on their arms, thighs, and other parts of the body, sometimes large and few in number, at other times tiny and closely spaced. These, to anyone unfortunate enough to contract them, were just as infallible a sign that he would die as the *gavòcciolo* had been earlier, and as indeed it still was.

Against these maladies, it seemed that all the advice of physicians and all the power of medicine were profitless and unavailing. Perhaps the nature of the illness was such that it allowed no remedy: or perhaps those people who were treating the illness (whose numbers had increased enormously because the ranks of the qualified were invaded by people, both men and women, who had never received any training in medicine), being ignorant of its causes, were not prescribing the appropriate cure. At all events, few of those who caught it ever recovered, and in most cases death occurred within three days from the appearance of the symptoms we have described, some people dying more rapidly than others, the majority without any fever or other complications.

But what made this pestilence even more severe was that whenever those suffering from it mixed with people who were still unaffected, it would rush upon these with the speed of a fire racing through dry or oily substances that happened to come within its reach. Nor was this the full extent of its evil, for not only did it infect healthy persons who conversed or had any dealings with the sick, making them ill or visiting an equally horrible death upon them, but it also seemed to transfer the sickness to anyone touching the clothes or other objects which had been handled or used by its victims.

It is a remarkable story that I have to relate. And were it not for the fact that I am one of many people who saw it with their own eyes, I would scarcely dare to believe it, let alone commit it to paper, even though I had heard it from a person whose word I could trust. The plague I have been describing was of so contagious a nature that very often it visibly did more than simply pass from one person to another. In other words, whenever an animal other than a human being touched anything belonging to a person who had been stricken or exterminated by the disease, it not only caught the sickness, but died from it almost at once. To all of this, as I have just said, my own eyes bore witness on more than one occasion. One day, for instance, the rags of a pauper who had died from the disease were thrown into the street, where they attracted the attention of two pigs. In their wonted fashion, the pigs first of all gave the rags a thorough mauling with their snouts, after which they took them between their teeth and shook them against their cheeks. And within a short time they began to writhe as though they had been poisoned, then they both dropped dead to the ground, spread-eagled upon the rags that had brought about their undoing.

These things, and many others of a similar or even worse nature, caused various fears and fantasies to take root in the minds of those who were still alive and well. And almost without exception, they took a single and very inhuman precaution, namely to avoid or run away from the sick and their belongings, by which means they all thought that their own health would be preserved.

Some people were of the opinion that a sober and abstemious mode of living considerably reduced the risk of infection. They therefore formed themselves into groups and lived in isolation from everyone else. Having withdrawn to a comfortable abode where there were no sick persons, they locked themselves in and settled down to a peaceable existence, consuming modest quantities of delicate foods and precious wines and avoiding all excesses. They refrained from speaking to outsiders, refused to receive news of the dead or the sick, and entertained themselves with music and whatever other amusements they were able to devise.

Others took the opposite view, and maintained that an infallible way of warding off this appalling evil was to drink heavily, enjoy life to the full, go round singing and merrymaking, gratify all of one's cravings whenever the opportunity offered, and shrug the whole thing off as one enormous joke. Moreover, they practised what they preached to the best of their ability, for they would visit one tavern after another, drinking all day and night to immoderate excess; or alternatively (and this was their more frequent custom), they would do their drinking in various private houses, but only in the ones where the conversation was restricted to subjects that were pleasant or entertaining. Such places were easy to find, for people behaved as though their days were numbered, and treated their belongings and their own persons with equal abandon. Hence most houses had become common property, and any passing stranger could make himself at home as naturally as though he were the rightful owner. But for all their riotous manner of living, these people always took good care to avoid any contact with the sick.

In the face of so much affliction and misery, all respect for the laws of God and man had virtually broken down and been extinguished in our city. For like everybody else, those ministers and executors of the laws who were not either dead or ill were left with so few subordinates that they were unable to discharge any of their duties. Hence everyone was free to behave as he pleased.

There were many other people who steered a middle course between the two already mentioned, neither restricting their diet to the same degree as the first group, nor indulging so freely as the second in drinking and other forms of wantonness, but simply doing no more than satisfy their appetite. Instead of incarcerating themselves, these people moved about freely, holding in their hands a posy of flowers, or fragrant herbs, or one of a wide range of spices, which they applied at frequent intervals to their nostrils, thinking it an excellent idea to fortify the brain with smells of that particular sort; for the stench of dead bodies, sickness, and medicines seemed to fill and pollute the whole of the atmosphere.

Some people, pursuing what was possibly the safer alternative, callously maintained that there was no better or more efficacious remedy against a plague than to run away from it. Swayed by this argument, and sparing no thought for anyone but themselves, large numbers of men and women abandoned their city, their homes, their relatives, their estates and their belongings, and headed for the countryside, either in Florentine territory or, better still, abroad. It was as though they imagined that the wrath of God would not unleash this plague against men for their iniquities irrespective of where they happened to be, but would only be aroused against those who found themselves within the city walls; or possibly they assumed that the whole of the population would be exterminated and that the city's last hour had come.

Of the people who held these various opinions, not all of them died. Nor, however, did they all survive. On the contrary, many of each different persuasion fell ill here, there, and everywhere, and having themselves, when they were fit and well, set an example to those who were as yet unaffected, they languished away with virtually no one to nurse them. It was not merely a question of one citizen avoiding another, and of people almost invariably neglecting their neighbours and rarely or never visiting their relatives, addressing them only from a distance; this scourge had implanted so great a terror in the hearts of men and women that brothers abandoned brothers, uncles their nephews, sisters their brothers, and in many cases wives deserted their husbands. But even worse, and almost incredible, was the fact that fathers and mothers refused to nurse and assist their own children, as though they did not belong to them.

Hence the countless numbers of people who fell ill, both male and female, were entirely dependent upon either the charity of friends (who were few and far between) or the greed of servants, who remained in short supply despite the attraction of high wages out of all proportion to the services they performed. Furthermore, these latter were men and women of coarse intellect and the majority were unused to such duties, and they did little more than hand things to the invalid when asked to do so and watch over him when he was dying. And in performing this kind of service, they frequently lost their lives as well as their earnings.

As a result of this wholesale desertion of the sick by neighbours, relatives and friends, and in view of the scarcity of servants, there grew up a practice almost never previously heard of, whereby when a woman fell ill, no matter how gracious or beautiful or gently bred she might be, she raised no objection to being attended by a male servant, whether he was young or not. Nor did she have any scruples about showing him every part of her body as freely as she would have displayed it to a woman, provided that the nature of her infirmity required her to do so; and this explains why those women who recovered were possibly less chaste in the period that followed.

Moreover a great many people died who would perhaps have survived had they received some assistance. And hence, what with the lack of

appropriate means for tending the sick, and the virulence of the plague, the number of deaths reported in the city whether by day or by night was so enormous that it astonished all who heard tell of it, to say nothing of the people who actually witnessed the carnage. And it was perhaps inevitable that among the citizens who survived there arose certain customs that were quite contrary to established tradition.

It had once been customary, as it is again nowadays, for the women relatives and neighbours of a dead man to assemble in his house in order to mourn in the company of the women who had been closest to him; moreover his kinsfolk would forgather in front of his house along with his neighbours and various other citizens, and there would be a contingent of priests, whose numbers varied according to the quality of the deceased; his body would be taken thence to the church in which he had wanted to be buried, being borne on the shoulders of his peers amidst the funeral pomp of candles and dirges. But as the ferocity of the plague began to mount, this practice all but disappeared entirely and was replaced by different customs. For not only did people die without having many women about them, but a great number departed this life without anyone at all to witness their going. Few indeed were those to whom the lamentations and bitter tears of their relatives were accorded; on the contrary, more often than not bereavement was the signal for laughter and witticisms and general jollification—the art of which the women, having for the most part suppressed their feminine concern for the salvation of the souls of the dead, had learned to perfection. Moreover it was rare for the bodies of the dead to be accompanied by more than ten or twelve neighbours to the church, nor were they borne on the shoulders of worthy and honest citizens, but by a kind of gravedigging fraternity, newly come into being and drawn from the lower orders of society. These people assumed the title of sexton, and demanded a fat fee for their services, which consisted in taking up the coffin and hauling it swiftly away, not to the church specified by the dead man in his will, but usually to the nearest at hand. They would be preceded by a group of four or six clerics, who between them carried one or two candles at most, and sometimes none at all. Nor did the priests go to the trouble of pronouncing solemn and lengthy funeral rites, but, with the aid of these so-called sextons, they hastily lowered the body into the nearest empty grave they could find.

As for the common people and a large proportion of the bourgeoisie, they presented a much more pathetic spectacle, for the majority of them were constrained, either by their poverty or the hope of survival, to remain in their houses. Being confined to their own parts of the city, they fell ill daily in their thousands, and since they had no one to assist them or attend to their needs, they inevitably perished almost without exception. Many dropped dead in the open streets, both by day and by night, whilst a great many others, though dying in their own houses, drew their neighbours' attention to the fact more by the smell of their rotting corpses than by any other means. And what with these, and the others who were dying all over the city, bodies were here, there and everywhere.

Whenever people died, their neighbours nearly always followed a single, set routine, prompted as much by their fear of being contaminated by the decaying corpse as by any charitable feelings they may have entertained towards the deceased. Either on their own, or with the assistance of bearers whenever these were to be had, they extracted the bodies of the dead from their houses and left them lying outside their front doors, where anyone going about the streets, especially in the early morning, could have observed countless numbers of them. Funeral biers would then be sent for, upon which the dead were taken away, though there were some who, for lack of biers, were carried off on plain boards. It was by no means rare for more than one of these biers to be seen with two or three bodies upon it at a time; on the contrary, many were seen to contain a husband and wife, two or three brothers and sisters, a father and son, or some other pair of close relatives. And times without number it happened that two priests would be on their way to bury someone, holding a cross before them, only to find that bearers carrying three or four additional biers would fall in behind them; so that whereas the priests had thought they had only one burial to attend to, they in fact had six or seven, and sometimes more. Even in these circumstances, however, there were no tears or candles or mourners to honour the dead; in fact, no more respect was accorded to dead people than would nowadays be shown towards dead goats. For it was quite apparent that the one thing which, in normal times, no wise man had ever learned to accept with patient resignation (even though it struck so seldom and unobtrusively), had now been brought home to the feeble-minded as well, but the scale of the calamity caused them to regard it with indifference.

Such was the multitude of corpses (of which further consignments were arriving every day and almost by the hour at each of the churches), that there was not sufficient consecrated ground for them to be buried in, especially if each was to have its own plot in accordance with long-established custom. So when all the graves were full, huge trenches were excavated in the churchyards, into which new arrivals were placed in their hundreds, stowed tier upon tier like ships' cargo, each layer of corpses being covered over with a thin layer of soil till the trench was filled to the top.

But rather than describe in elaborate detail the calamities we experienced in the city at that time, I must mention that, whilst an ill wind was blowing through Florence itself, the surrounding region was no less badly affected. In the fortified towns, conditions were similar to those in the city itself on a minor scale; but in the scattered hamlets and the countryside proper, the poor unfortunate peasants and their families had no physicians or servants whatever to assist them, and collapsed by the wayside, in their fields, and in their cottages at all hours of the day and night, dying more like animals than human beings. Like the townspeople, they too grew apathetic in their ways, disregarded their affairs, and neglected their possessions. Moreover they all behaved as though each day was to be their last, and far from making provision for the future by tilling their lands, tending their flocks, and adding to their previous labours, they tried in every way they could think of to squander the assets already in their possession. Thus it came about that oxen, asses, sheep, goats, pigs, chickens, and even dogs (for all their deep fidelity to man) were driven away and allowed to roam freely through the fields, where the crops lay abandoned and had not even been reaped, let alone gathered in. And after a whole day's feasting, many of these animals, as though possessing the power of reason, would return glutted in the evening to their own quarters, without any shepherd to guide them.

But let us leave the countryside and return to the city. What more remains to be said, except that the cruelty of heaven (and possibly, in some measure, also that of man) was so immense and so devastating that between March and July of the year in question, what with the fury of the pestilence and the fact that so many of the sick were inadequately cared for or abandoned in their hour of need because the healthy were too terrified to approach them, it is reliably thought that over a hundred thousand human lives were extinguished within the walls of the city of Florence? Yet before this lethal catastrophe fell upon the city, it is doubtful whether anyone would have guessed it contained so many inhabitants.

Ah, how great a number of splendid palaces, fine houses, and noble dwellings, once filled with retainers, with lords and with ladies, were bereft of all who had lived there, down to the tiniest child! How numerous were the famous families, the vast estates, the notable fortunes, that were seen to be left without a rightful successor! How many gallant gentlemen, fair ladies, and sprightly youths, who would have been judged hale and hearty by Galen, Hippocrates and Aesculapius (to say nothing of others), having breakfasted in the morning with their kinsfolk, acquaintances and friends, supped that same evening with their ancestors in the next world!

The more I reflect upon all this misery, the deeper my sense of personal sorrow; hence I shall refrain from describing those aspects which can suitably be omitted, and proceed to inform you that these were the conditions prevailing in our city, which was by now almost emptied of its inhabitants. * * *

*   *   *

REVIEW QUESTIONS

1. According to Boccaccio, how did contemporaries explain the nature of the plague?
2. What were the worst social effects of the plague in Florence?
3. How were the unafflicted and the survivors likely to respond to their own continued life in the face of so much death?

GEOFFREY CHAUCER

FROM *The Canterbury Tales*

The English poet Geoffrey Chaucer (c. 1340–1400) never completed his famous late work, The Canterbury Tales, *a collection of stories in verse form told by a group of pilgrims on their way to the shrine of St. Thomas Beckett in Canterbury. This format gave Chaucer the chance to retell some old stories, including a few from Boc-*

caccio. "The Pardoner's Tale," the story by a minor church official, is one of
Chaucer's best and most revealing pieces.

From *The Canterbury Tales: Nine Tales and the General Prologue*, by Geoffrey Chaucer, edited
by V. A. Kolve and Glending Olson, A Norton Critical Edition (New York: Norton, 1989),
pp. 192–207.

The Prologue

"Lordinges," quod he, "in chirches whan I preche,
I peyne me° to han an hauteyn° speche,   *take pains / elevated*
And ringe it out as round as gooth° a belle,   *sounds*
For I can al by rote° that I telle.   *know all by memory*
My theme° is alwey oon,° and evere was—   *text / always the same*
Radix malorum est Cupiditas.[1]

 First I pronounce° whennes° that I come,   *proclaim / whence, from where*
And thanne my bulles[2] shewe I, alle and somme.°   *one and all*
Oure lige lordes seel[3] on my patente,°   *license*
That shewe I first, my body° to warente,°   *person / authorize*
That no man be so bold, ne preest ne clerk,°   *neither priest nor scholar*
Me to destourbe of Cristes holy werk;
And after that thanne telle I forth my tales.
Bulles of popes and of cardinales,
Of patriarkes,° and bishoppes I shewe,   *heads of churches*
And in Latyn I speke a wordes fewe
To saffron with my predicacioun,[4]
And for to stire° hem to devocioun.   *stir*
Thanne shewe I forth my longe cristal stones,°   *glass cases*
Y-crammed ful of cloutes° and of bones—   *rags*
Reliks been they, as wenen they echoon.[5]
Thanne have I in latoun[6] a sholder-boon
Which that was of an holy Jewes shepe.
'Goode men,' seye I, 'tak of my wordes kepe:°   *heed*
If that this boon be wasshe° in any welle,   *washed, dunked*
If cow, or calf, or sheep, or oxe swelle,°   *swell (up)*

---

[1] "Avarice (the love of money) is the root of all evil."

[2] Bulls, writs of indulgence for sin, purchasable in lieu
of other forms of penance.

[3] Bishop's seal.

[4] "With which to season my preaching." (Saffron is a
yellow spice.)

[5] "They are (saints') relics, or so they all suppose."

[6] Latten, a metal like brass.

That any worm hath ete, or worm y-stonge,[7]
Tak water of that welle, and wash his tonge,
And it is hool° anon;° and forthermore,   *healed / at once*
Of pokkes° and of scabbe and every sore   *pox*
Shal every sheep be hool,° that of this welle   *healed*
Drinketh a draughte. Tak kepe° eek° what I telle: *heed / also*
If that the good-man that the bestes° oweth°   *animals / owns*
Wol every wike,° er° that the cok him croweth,   *week / before*
Fastinge,° drinken of this welle a draughte—   *(While) fasting*
As thilke° holy Jewe[8] bure eldres taughte—   *that same*
His bestes and his stoor° shal multiplye.   *stock*

And, sires, also it heleth° jalousye: *heals*
For though a man be falle in jalous rage,
Let maken with this water his potage,[9]
And nevere shal he more his wyf mistriste,°   *mistrust*
Though he the sooth° of hir defaute° wiste°—   *truth / erring / should know*
Al° had she taken° preestes two or three.   *Even if / taken (as lovers)*

Heer is a miteyn° eek, that ye may see: *mitten*
He that his hond wol putte in this miteyn,
He shal have multiplying of his greyn°   *grain*
Whan he hath sowen, be it whete° or otes,°   *wheat / oats*
So that he offre pens, or elles grotes.[10]

Good men and wommen, o° thing warne° I yow: *one / tell*
If any wight° be in this chirche now,   *person*
That hath doon sinne horrible, that he
Dar° nat for shame of it y-shriven[11] be,   *Dare*
Or any womman, be she yong or old,
That hath y-maked hir housbonde cokewold,°   *a cuckold*
Swich° folk shul have no power ne no grace   *Such*
To offren° to my reliks in this place.   *To offer (money)*
And whoso findeth him out of swich blame,°   *not deserving such blame*
He wol com up and offre a° Goddes name,   *make an offering in*
And I assoille° him by the auctoritee°   *(will) absolve / authority*
Which that by bulle y-graunted was to me.'

By this gaude° have I wonne,° yeer° by yeer,   *trick / earned / year*
An hundred mark sith I was pardoner.[12]

---

[7] "Who has eaten any (poisonous) worm, or whom a snake
has stung (bitten)."

[8] Jacob.

[9] "Have his soup made with this water."

[10] "Provided that he offers (to me) pennies or else groats
(coins worth fourpence)."

[11] Confessed and absolved.

[12] "A hundred marks (coins worth thirteen shillings fourpence) since I became a pardoner."

I stonde lyk a clerk° in my pulpet,   *scholar*
And whan the lewed° peple is doun y-set,   *ignorant, unlearned*
I preche, so as ye han herd bifore,
And telle an hundred false japes° more.   *tricks, stories*
Thanne peyne I me° to strecche forth the nekke,   *I take pains*
And est and west upon the peple I bekke°   *nod*
As doth a dowve,° sittinge on a berne.°   *dove / in a barn*
Myn hondes and my tonge goon so yerne°   *rapidly*
That it is joye to see my bisinesse.
Of avaryce and of swich° cursednesse   *such*
Is al my preching, for° to make hem free°   *in order / generous*
To yeven hir pens, and namely unto me.[13]
For myn entente° is nat but for to winne,°   *intention / profit*
And nothing° for correccioun of sinne: *not at all*
I rekke° nevere, whan that they ben beried,°   *care / buried*
Though that hir soules goon a-blakeberied![14]
For certes,° many a predicacioun°   *certainly / sermon*
Comth ofte tyme of yvel° entencioun: *evil*
Som for plesaunce° of folk and flaterye,   *the entertainment*
To been avaunced by ypocrisye,[15]
And som for veyne glorie,° and som for hate.   *vainglory*
For whan I dar non other weyes debate,[16]
Than wol I stinge him[17] with my tonge smerte°   *sharp*
In preching, so that he shal nat asterte°   *leap up (to protest)*
To been° defamed falsly, if that he   *At being*
Hath trespased to° my brethren[18] or to me.   *wronged*
For, though I telle noght his propre° name,   *own*
Men shal wel knowe that it is the same
By signes and by othere circumstances.
Thus quyte° I folk that doon us displesances;°   *requite / offenses*
Thus spitte I out my venim under hewe°   *hue, coloring*
Of holynesse, to semen° holy and trewe.   *seem*
   But shortly° myn entente I wol devyse:°   *briefly / describe*
I preche of no thing but for coveityse.°   *out of covetousness*
Therfore my theme is yet, and evere was,
Radix malorum est cupiditas.
Thus can I preche agayn° that same vyce   *against*
Which that I use,° and that is avaryce.   *practice*

---

[13] "In giving their pence, and particularly to me."
[14] Blackberrying, i.e., wandering.
[15] To seek advancement through hypocrisy.
[16] "For when I dare enter into contest (argument) no other way."
[17] Some enemy.
[18] Fellow pardoners.

But though myself be gilty in that sinne,
Yet can I maken other folk to twinne°   *part*
From avaryce, and sore° to repente.   *ardently*
But that is nat my principal entente:
I preche nothing but for coveityse.
Of this matere° it oughte y-nogh suffyse.   *subject*
   Than telle I hem ensamples many oon°   *examples many a one*
Of olde stories longe tyme agoon,°   *past*
For lewed° peple loven tales olde;   *unlearned*
Swich° thinges can they wel reporte° and holde.°   *Such / repeat / remember*
What, trowe ye, the whyles I may preche[19]
And winne° gold and silver for° I teche,   *obtain / because*
That I wol live in povert° wilfully?°   *poverty / willingly*
Nay, nay, I thoghte° it nevere, trewely!   *considered*
For I wol preche and begge in sondry° londes;   *various*
I wol nat do no labour with myn hondes,
Ne make baskettes,[20] and live therby,
By cause I wol nat beggen ydelly.°   *without profit*
I wol non of the Apostles counterfete:°   *imitate*
I wol have money, wolle,° chese, and whete,   *wool*
Al° were it yeven of° the povereste page,°   *Even if / given by / servant*
Or of° the povereste widwe° in a village,   *by / poorest widow*
Al sholde hir children sterve for famyne.[21]
Nay! I wol drinke licour° of the vyne,   *liquor, wine*
And have a joly wenche in every toun.
But herkneth,° lordinges, in conclusioun: *listen*
Youre lyking is that I shall telle a tale.
Now have I dronke a draughte of corny° ale,   *malty*
By God, I hope I shal yow telle a thing
That shal by resoun° been at° youre lyking.   *with reason / to*
For though myself be a ful vicious° man,   *evil, vice-ridden*
A moral tale yet I yow telle can,

Which I am wont to preche for to winne.[22]
Now holde youre pees,° my tale I wol beginne."   *peace*

The Tale

In Flaundres whylom was° a compaignye   *once (there) was*
Of yonge folk, that haunteden folye—

---

[19] "What? do you believe (that) as long as I can preach."

[20] St. Paul was said to have been a basket maker.

[21] "Even though her children should die of hunger."

[22] "Which I am in the habit of preaching, in order to make
some money."

As ryot, hasard, stewes, and tavernes,[23]
Where as° with harpes, lutes, and giternes,°   *There where / guitars*
They daunce and pleyen at dees° bothe day and night,   *dice*
And eten also and drinken over hir might,°   *beyond their capacity*
Thurgh which they doon the devel sacrifyse°   *make sacrifice to the devil*
Withinne that develes temple,[24] in cursed wyse,°   *way*
By superfluitee° abhominable.   *excess*
Hir othes° been so grete and so dampnable,°   *oaths, curses / condemnable*
That it is grisly for to here hem swere.
Our blissed Lordes body they totere°—   *tear apart*
Hem thoughte° Jewes rente° him noght y-nough—   *It seemed to them / tore*
And ech° of hem at otheres sinne lough.°   *each / laughed*
And right anon thanne comen tombesteres°   *female tumblers, dancers*
Fetys and smale, and yonge fruytesteres,[25]
Singeres with harpes, baudes,° wafereres,°   *bawds / girls selling cakes*
Whiche been the verray° develes officeres   *the very*
To kindle and blowe the fyr of lecherye
That is annexed° unto glotonye: *joined (as a sin)*
The Holy Writ take I to my witnesse
That luxurie° is in wyn and dronkenesse.   *lechery*
     Lo, how that dronken Loth° unkindely°   *Lot / unnaturally*
Lay by his doghtres two, unwitingly;°   *unknowingly*
So dronke he was, he niste° what he wroghte.°   *knew not / did*
     Herodes,° whoso wel the stories soghte,°   *Herod / should seek out*
Whan he of wyn was repleet° at his feste,   *replete, full*
Right at his owene table he yaf° his heste°   *gave / command*
To sleen the Baptist John ful giltelees.°   *guiltless (innocent)*
     Senek° seith a good word doutelees: *Seneca*
He seith, he can no difference finde
Bitwix a man that is out of his minde
And a man which that is dronkelewe,°   *drunken*
But that woodnesse, y-fallen in a shrewe,[26]
Persevereth lenger° than doth dronkenesse.   *Continues longer*
O glotonye,° ful of cursednesse!   *gluttony*
O cause first° of oure confusioun!°   *first cause / ruin*
O original° of oure dampnacioun,   *origin*
Til Crist had boght us with his blood agayn!

---

[23] "Of young folk who gave themselves up to folly—(such) as excessive revelry, gambling with dice, (visiting) brothels and taverns."

[24] The tavern.

[25] "Shapely and slender, and young girls selling fruit."

[26] "Except that madness, having afflicted a miserable man."

Lo, how dere,° shortly for to sayn,°   *costly / to speak briefly*
Aboght was thilke cursed vileinye;[27]
Corrupt° was al this world for glotonye!   *Corrupted*
Adam oure fader and his wyf also
Fro Paradys to labour and to wo
Were driven for that vyce, it is no drede.°   *doubt*
For whyl that Adam fasted, as I rede,°   *read*
He was in Paradys; and whan that he
Eet of the fruyt defended° on the tree,   *forbidden*
Anon° he was outcast to wo and peyne.°   *Immediately / pain*
O glotonye, on thee wel oghte us pleyne![28]

    O, wiste a man° how manye maladyes   *(if) a man knew*
Folwen of° excesse and of glotonyes,   *Follow on*
He wolde been the more mesurable°   *measured, temperate*
Of his diete, sittinge at his table.
Allas! the shorte throte, the tendre mouth,[29]
Maketh that,° est and west, and north and south,   *Causes*
In erthe, in eir,° in water, men to swinke°   *air / labor*
To gete a glotoun deyntee° mete and drinke!   *dainty*
Of this matere,° O Paul, wel canstow trete:°   *subject / canst thou treat*
"Mete° unto wombe,° and wombe eek unto mete,   *Meat / belly*
Shal God destroyen bothe," as Paulus seith.[30]
Allas! a foul thing is it, by my feith,
To seye this word, and fouler is the dede,
Whan man so drinketh of the whyte and rede[31]
That of his throte he maketh his privee,°   *privy (toilet)*
Thurgh thilke° cursed superfluitee.°   *that same / excess*

    The apostel,[32] weping, seith ful pitously,
"Ther walken manye of whiche yow told have I"—
I seye it now weping with pitous voys—
"They been enemys of Cristes croys,°   *cross*
Of which the ende is deeth: wombe° is her° god!"   *belly / their*
O wombe! O bely! O stinking cod,[33]
Fulfild of donge and of corrupcioun![34]
At either ende of thee foul is the soun.°   *sound*

---

[27] "Bought was that same cursed, evil deed."

[28] "Oh, gluttony, we certainly ought to complain against you."

[29] "The brief pleasure of swallowing, the mouth accustomed to delicacies."

[30] 1 Corinthians 6:13.

[31] Wines.

[32] St. Paul. See Philippians 3:18–19.

[33] "Bag," i.e., the stomach.

[34] "Filled up with dung and with decaying matter."

How° greet labour and cost is thee to finde!°	*What / to provide for*
Thise cookes, how they stampe,° and streyne,° and grinde,	*pound / strain*
And turnen substaunce into accident,[35]	
To fulfille al thy likerous talent!°	*lecherous (here, gluttonous) appetite*
Out of the harde bones knokke they	
The mary,° for they caste noght° awey	*marrow / nothing*
That may go thurgh the golet° softe and swote;°	*gullet / sweet*
Of spicerye° of leef, and bark, and rote°	*spices / root(s)*
Shal been his sauce y-maked by delyt,°	*to give pleasure*
To make him yet a newer° appetyt.	*renewed*
But certes, he that haunteth swich delyces[36]	
Is deed, whyl that° he liveth in tho° vyces.	*while / those*
A lecherous thing is wyn, and dronkenesse	
Is ful of stryving° and of wrecchednesse.	*quarreling*
O dronke man, disfigured is thy face,	
Sour is thy breeth, foul artow° to embrace,	*art thou*
And thurgh thy dronke nose semeth the soun°	*sound*
As though thou seydest ay° "Sampsoun, Sampsoun";[37]	*ever*
And yet, God wot,° Sampsoun drank nevere no wyn.	*knows*
Thou fallest,[38] as it were a stiked swyn;°	*stuck pig*
Thy tonge is lost, and al thyn honest cure,°	*care for decency*
For dronkenesse is verray sepulture°	*the true tomb*
Of mannes wit° and his discrecioun.°	*understanding / discretion*
In whom that° drinke hath dominacioun,	*In him whom*
He can no conseil° kepe, it is no drede.°	*secrets / doubt*
Now kepe yow fro the whyte and fro the rede—	
And namely° fro the whyte wyn of Lepe[39]	*especially*
That is to selle° in Fishstrete° or in Chepe.°	*for sale / Fish Street / Cheapside*
This wyn of Spaigne crepeth subtilly	
In othere wynes growinge faste by,[40]	
Of° which ther ryseth swich fumositee,°	*From / vapor*
That whan a man hath dronken draughtes three	
And weneth° that he be at hoom in Chepe,	*thinks*
He is in Spaigne, right at the toune of Lepe,	

---

[35] "And turn substance into accident" (a scholastic joke: *substaunce* means "essence, essential qualities"; *accident*, "external appearances").

[36] "But truly, he that gives himself up to such pleasures."

[37] A witty kind of onomatopoeia—the snoring sound seems to say "Samson," who was betrayed.

[38] Down.

[39] Near Cadiz.

[40] The wines sold as French are often mixed with the cheaper wines of Spain.

Nat at The Rochel,° ne at Burdeux toun;°   *La Rochelle / Bordeaux*
And thanne wol he seye, "Sampsoun, Sampsoun."
 But herkneth,° lordinges, o° word I yow preye,   *listen / one*
That alle the sovereyn actes,° dar I seye,   *supreme deeds*
Of victories in the Olde Testament,
Thurgh verray° God, that is omnipotent,   *true*
Were doon in abstinence and in preyere:
Loketh the Bible, and ther ye may it lere.°   *learn*
 Loke Attila,[41] the grete conquerour,
Deyde° in his sleep, with shame and dishonour,   *Died*
Bledinge ay° at his nose in dronkenesse: *continually*
A capitayn shoulde live in sobrenesse.
And over al this, avyseth yow right wel°   *be well advised*
What was comaunded unto Lamuel°—   *Lemuel*
Nat Samuel, but Lamuel, seye I—
Redeth the Bible, and finde it expresly
Of wyn-yeving to hem that han justyse.[42]
Namore of this, for it may wel suffyse.
 And now that I have spoke of glotonye,
Now wol I yow defenden° hasardrye.°   *forbid / gambling at dice*
Hasard is verray moder° of lesinges,°   *the true mother / lies*
And of deceite and cursed forsweringes,°   *perjuries*
Blaspheme of Crist, manslaughtre, and wast° also   *waste*
Of catel° and of tyme; and forthermo,   *goods*
It is repreve° and contrarie of honour   *a reproach*
For to ben holde a commune hasardour.°   *gambler*
And ever the hyer° he is of estaat°   *higher / in social rank*
The more is he y-holden desolaat:°   *considered debased*
If that a prince useth° hasardrye,   *practices*
In alle governaunce and policye
He is, as by commune opinioun,
Y-holde the lasse in reputacioun.
 Stilbon, that was a wys° embassadour,   *wise*
Was sent to Corinthe in ful greet honour,
For Lacidomie° to make hire alliaunce.°   *Lacedaemon (Sparta) / their alliance*
And whan he cam, him happede par chaunce°   *it happened by chance*
That alle the grettest° that were of that lond,   *greatest (men)*
Pleyinge atte° hasard he hem fond.   *at (the)*
For which, as sone as it mighte be,°   *could be*
He stal him° hoom agayn to his contree,   *stole away*
And seyde, "Ther wol I nat lese° my name,°   *lose / (good) name*
Ne I wol nat take on me so greet defame,°   *dishonor*

---

[41] The Hun.

[42] Concerning the giving of wine to those responsible for the
law (see Proverbs 31.4–5).

Yow for to allye° unto none hasardours.°	*to ally / gamblers*
Sendeth othere wyse embassadours—	
For by my trouthe, me were levere dye°	*I would rather die*
Than I yow sholde to hasardours allye.	
For ye that been so glorious in honours	
Shul nat allyen yow with hasardours	
As by my wil, ne as by my tretee."°	*negotiations*
This wyse philosophre, thus seyde he.	
Loke eek° that to the king Demetrius	*also*
The king of Parthes,° as the book seith us,[43]	*Parthia*
Sente him a paire of dees° of gold in scorn,	*dice*
For he hadde used hasard ther-biforn;	
For which he heeld his glorie or his renoun°	*renown*
At no value or reputacioun.	
Lordes may finden other maner pley	
Honeste° y-nough to dryve the day awey.	*Honorable*
Now wol I speke of othes° false and grete	*oaths, curses*
A word or two, as olde bokes trete.	
Gret swering° is a thing abhominable,	*cursing*
And false swering[44] is yet more reprevable.°	*reproachable*
The heighe° God forbad swering at al—	*high*
Witnesse on Mathew—but in special	
Of swering seith the holy Jeremye,°	*Jeremiah*
"Thou shalt swere sooth° thyn othes° and nat lye,	*truly / oaths*
And swere in dome,° and eek in rightwisnesse;"°	*(good) judgment / righteousness*
But ydel° swering is a cursednesse.°	*vain / wickedness*
Bihold and see, that in the first table°	*tablet (of Moses)*
Of heighe Goddes hestes° honurable,	*commandments*
How that the seconde heste of him is this:	
"Tak nat my name in ydel° or amis."°	*in vain / amiss (wrongly)*
Lo, rather° he forbedeth swich° swering	*earlier (in the list) / such*
Than homicyde or many a cursed thing—	
I seye that, as by ordre,° thus it stondeth—	*in terms of the order*
This knoweth, that his hestes understondeth,[45]	
How that the second heste of God is that.	
And forther over,° I wol thee telle al plat°	*moreover / flatly*
That vengeance shal nat parten° from his hous	*depart*
That° of his othes is to° outrageous.	*Who / too*
"By Goddes precious herte," and "By his nayles,"	

---

[43] The *Policraticus* of John of Salisbury, which also contains the preceding story.

[44] I.e., Of oaths.

[45] "[He] knows this, who understands His commandments."

And "By the blode of Crist that is in Hayles,[46]
Seven is my chaunce,[47] and thyn is cink° and treye;"°   *five / three*
"By Goddes armes, if thou falsly pleye,
This dagger shal thurghout thyn herte go!"
This fruyt cometh of the bicched bones two—[48]
Forswering,° ire,° falsnesse, homicyde.   *Perjury / anger*
Now for the love of Crist that for us dyde,
Lete° youre othes, bothe grete and smale.   *Cease*
But, sires, now wol I telle forth my tale.

    Thise ryotoures° three of which I telle,   *rioters, revelers*
Longe erst er° pryme° rong of any belle,   *before / 9 A.M.*
Were set hem° in a taverne for to drinke;   *Had set themselves down*
And as they sat, they herde a belle clinke
Biforn a cors° was° caried to his grave.   *corpse / (which) was (being)*
That oon of hem gan callen to his knave,
"Go bet," quod he, "and axe redily,[49]
What cors is this that passeth heer forby;°   *by here*
And looke that thou reporte his name wel."[50]

    "Sire," quod this boy, "it nedeth never-a-del.°   *it isn't at all necessary*
It was me told, er° ye cam heer two houres.   *before*
He was, pardee,[51] an old felawe° of youres;   *companion*
And sodeynly he was y-slayn to-night,
For-dronke,° as he sat on his bench upright.   *Dead drunk*
Ther cam a privee° theef men clepeth° Deeth,   *secret / call*
That in this contree° al the peple sleeth,°   *region / kills*
And with his spere he smoot his herte atwo,[52]
And wente his wey withouten wordes mo.°   *more*
He hath a thousand slayn this pestilence.°   *(during) this plague*
And maister, er° ye come in his presence,   *before*
Me thinketh° that it were necessarie   *It seems to me*
For to be war° of swich an adversarie: *aware, careful*
Beth redy for to mete him everemore.°   *always*

---

[46] An abbey in Gloucestershire supposed to possess (as a high relic) some of Christ's blood.

[47] Throw.

[48] This fruit, i.e., result, comes from the two cursed dice. (Dice were made of bone; hence "bones" here.)

[49] The one of them proceeded to call to his servant-boy, "Go quickly," he said, "and ask straightway."

[50] Correctly.

[51] A weak form of the oath "by God," based on the French *par dieu.*

[52] "And with his spear he struck his heart in two." (Death was often shown in the visual arts as a hideous skeleton menacing men with a spear or arrow.)

Thus taughte me my dame,° I sey namore."   *mother*
"By Seinte Marie," seyde this taverner,°   *tavernkeeper*
"The child seith sooth, for he hath slayn this yeer,
Henne° over a myle, withinne a greet village,   *Hence, from here*
Bothe man and womman, child, and hyne,° and page;°   *laborer / servant*
I trowe° his habitacioun be there.   *believe*
To been avysed° greet wisdom it were,   *forewarned*
Er that° he dide a man a dishonour."   *Before*

   "Ye,° Goddes armes," quod° this ryotour,°   *Aye, yes / said / reveler*
"Is it swich peril with him for to mete?
I shal him seke by wey° and eek° by strete,   *road / also*
I make avow to° Goddes digne° bones!   *avow (it) by / worthy*
Herkneth, felawes, we three been al ones:°   *all of one mind*
Lat ech° of us holde up his hond til other,°   *each / to the other*
And ech of us bicomen otheres° brother,   *the others'*
And we wol sleen° this false traytour Deeth.   *slay*
He shal be slayn, he that so manye sleeth,
By Goddes dignitee,° er it be night."   *worthiness*

   Togidres° han thise three hir trouthes plight°   *Together / plighted their troth*
To live and dyen ech of hem for other,°   *one another*
As though he were his owene y-boren° brother.   *born*
And up they sterte,° al dronken in this rage,°   *leaped / passion*
And forth they goon towardes that village
Of which the taverner hadde spoke biforn,
And many a grisly ooth thanne han they sworn,
And Cristes blessed body they to-rente°—   *tore apart*
Deeth shal be deed, if that they may him hente.°   *seize*

   Whan they han goon nat fully half a myle,
Right° as they wolde han troden° over a style,°   *Just / stepped / stile*
An old man and a povre° with hem mette.   *poor (one)*
This olde man ful mekely° hem grette,°   *meekly / greeted them*
And seyde thus, "Now, lordes, God yow see!"°   *may God protect you*

   The proudest of thise ryotoures three
Answerde agayn, "What, carl,° with sory grace!°   *Hey, fellow / confound you*
Why artow al forwrapped save thy face?[53]
Why livestow° so longe in so greet age?"   *livest thou*
This olde man gan loke in° his visage,   *scrutinized*

   And seyde thus, "For° I ne can nat finde   *Because*
A man, though that I walked into Inde,°   *India*
Neither in citee nor in no village,
That wolde chaunge his youthe for myn age;
And therfore moot° I han myn age stille,   *must*
As longe time as it is Goddes wille.

---

[53] "Why art thou all wrapped up, except for thy face?"

Ne Deeth, allas! ne wol nat han my lyf.
Thus walke I, lyk° a restelees caityf,°   *like / captive*
And on the ground, which is my modres° gate,   *mother's*
I knokke with my staf bothe erly and late,
And seye, 'Leve° moder, leet me in!   *Dear*
Lo, how I vanish,° flesh, and blood, and skin!   *waste away*
Allas! whan shul my bones been at reste?
Moder, with yow wolde I chaunge° my cheste°   *exchange / chest (of clothes)*
That in my chambre longe tyme hath be,°   *been*
Ye, for an heyre clout° to wrappe me!'   *haircloth (for burial)*
But yet to me she wol nat do that grace,
For which ful pale and welked° is my face.   *withered*
     But sires, to yow it is no curteisye[54]
To speken to an old man vileinye,°   *rudeness*
But° he trespasse° in worde or elles° in dede.   *Unless / offend / else*
In Holy Writ ye may yourself wel rede,°   *read*
'Agayns° an old man, hoor° upon his heed,   *Before / hoary, white*
Ye sholde aryse.' Wherfor I yeve yow reed:[55]
Ne dooth unto an old man noon harm now,
Namore than that ye wolde men did to yow
In age, if that ye so longe abyde.°   *remain (alive)*
And God be with yow, wher ye go° or ryde;   *walk*
I moot° go thider as° I have to go."   *must / thither where*
     "Nay, olde cherl, by God, thou shalt nat so,"
Seyde this other hasardour° anon;°   *gambler / at once*
"Thou partest° nat so lightly, by Seint John!   *departest*
Thou spak right now of thilke° traitour Deeth   *that same*
That in this contree alle oure frendes sleeth.
Have heer my trouthe,° as° thou art his espye,°   *pledge / since / spy*
Telle wher he is, or thou shalt it abye,°   *pay for*
By God, and by the holy sacrament!
For soothly thou art oon of his assent°   *in league with him*
To sleen us yonge folk, thou false theef!"
     "Now, sires," quod he, "if that yow be so leef°   *desirous*
To finde Deeth, turne up this croked° wey,   *crooked*
For in that grove I lafte° him, by my fey,°   *left / faith*
Under a tree, and there he wol abyde:°   *stay*
Nat for youre boost he wole him nothing hyde.[56]
See ye that ook?° right ther ye shul him finde.   *oak*
God save yow, that boghte agayn° mankinde,   *redeemed*
     And yow amende!"° Thus seyde this olde man.   *make you better*

---

[54] "But, sirs, it is not courteous of you."

[55] "'You should stand up (in respect).' Therefore I give you
     (this) advice."

[56] "He won't conceal himself at all because of your boasting."

And everich° of thise ryotoures° ran,   *each / revelers*
Til he cam to that tree, and ther they founde
Of florins° fyne of golde y-coyned° rounde   *florins, coins / coined*
Wel ny an° eighte busshels, as hem thoughte.°   *nearly / it seemed to them*
No lenger thanne° after Deeth they soughte,   *No longer then*
But ech° of hem so glad was of that sighte—   *each*
For that the florins been so faire and brighte—
That doun they sette hem by this precious hord.
The worste of hem he spake the firste word.

   "Brethren," quod he, "take kepe° what that I seye: *heed*
My wit° is greet, though that I bourde° and pleye.   *understanding / jest*
This tresor° hath Fortune unto us yiven°   *treasure / given*
In mirthe and jolitee° our lyf to liven,   *merriment*
And lightly as it comth, so wol we spende.
Ey! Goddes precious dignitee!° who wende°   *worthiness / would have supposed*
To-day that we sholde han so fair a grace?°   *favor*
But° mighte this gold be caried fro this place   *If only*
Hoom to myn hous—or elles unto youres—
For wel ye woot° that al this gold is oures—   *know*
Thanne were we in heigh felicitee.°   *supreme happiness*
But trewely, by daye it may nat be.°   *be (done)*
Men wolde seyn that we were theves stronge,°   *flagrant*
And for oure owene tresor doon us honge.°   *have us hanged*
This tresor moste y-caried be by nighte,
As wysly° and as slyly° as it mighte.°   *prudently / craftily / can (be)*
Wherfore I rede° that cut° among us alle   *advise / lots, straws*
Be drawe,° and lat se wher the cut wol falle;   *drawn, pulled*
And he that hath the cut with herte blythe
Shal renne° to the toune, and that ful swythe,°   *run / quickly*
And bringe us breed and wyn ful prively.°   *secretly*
And two of us shul kepen° subtilly°   *guard / carefully*
This tresor wel; and if he wol nat tarie,°   *tarry*
Whan it is night we wol this tresor carie,
By oon assent, where as us thinketh best."[57]
That oon of hem the cut broughte in his fest,°   *fist*
And bad hem drawe, and loke wher it wol falle;
And it fil on the yongeste of hem alle,
And forth toward the toun he wente anon.
And also sone as° that he was agon,   *as soon as*
That oon of hem° spak thus unto that other: *The one of them*
"Thou knowest wel thou art my sworne brother;
Thy profit° wol I telle thee anon.   *Something to thy advantage*
Thou woost° wel that oure felawe is agon,°   *knowest / gone*
And heer is gold, and that° ful greet plentee,   *that (in)*

---

[57] "By common assent, wherever seems to us best."

That shal departed° been among us three.   *divided*
But natheles,° if I can shape° it so   *nonetheless / arrange*
That it departed were among us two,
Hadde I nat doon a freendes torn° to thee?"   *turn*
   That other answerde, "I noot° how that may be: *know not*
He woot how that the gold is with us tweye.
What shal we doon? what shal we to him seye?"
   "Shal it be conseil?"° seyde the firste shrewe;°   *a secret / wretch*
"And I shal tellen in a wordes fewe
What we shal doon, and bringe it wel aboute."
"I graunte,"° quod that other, "out of doute,[58]   *grant (it)*
That, by my trouthe, I wol thee nat biwreye."°   *betray*
   "Now," quod the firste, "thou woost° wel
   we be tweye,°   *knowest / two*
And two of us shul strenger° be than oon.   *stronger*
Looke whan that he is set,° that right anoon°   *has sat down / right away*
Arys° as though thou woldest with him pleye;   *Arise (get up)*
And I shal ryve° him thurgh the sydes tweye°   *stab / through his two sides*
Whyl that thou strogelest° with him as in game,°   *strugglest / as if in play*
And with thy dagger looke° thou do the same;   *take heed*
And thanne shall al this gold departed° be,   *divided*
My dere freend, bitwixen me and thee.
Thanne may we bothe oure lustes° al fulfille,   *desires*
And pleye at dees° right at oure owene wille."   *dice*
And thus acorded° been thise shrewes° tweye   *agreed / cursed fellows*
To sleen the thridde, as ye han herd me seye.
   This yongest, which that wente unto the toun,
Ful ofte in herte he rolleth up and doun[59]
The beautee of thise florins newe and brighte.
"O Lord!" quod he, "if so were that I mighte
Have al this tresor to myself allone,
Ther is no man that liveth under the trone°   *throne*
Of God that sholde live so mery as I!"
And atte laste° the feend,° our enemy,   *at (the) last / devil*
Putte in his thought that he shold poyson beye,°   *buy poison*
With which he mighte sleen his felawes tweye°—   *two companions*
For-why the feend fond him in swich lyvinge[60]
That he had leve° him to sorwe bringe: *permission (from God)*
For this was outrely° his fulle entente,°   *completely / purpose*
To sleen hem bothe, and nevere to repente.
And forth he gooth—no lenger wolde he tarie—

---

[58] You can be sure.

[59] Thinks on.

[60] "Because the fiend [the devil] found him living in such
a way."

Into the toun, unto a pothecarie,°   *apothecary, pharmacist*
And preyed° him that he him wolde selle   *asked*
Som poyson, that° he mighte his rattes quelle,°   *so that / kill his rats*
And eek° ther was a polcat° in his hawe,°   *also / weasel / yard*
That, as he seyde, his capouns° hadde y-slawe,°   *capons / killed*
And fayn° he wolde wreke him,° if he mighte,   *gladly / avenge himself*
On vermin, that destroyed° him by nighte.   *were ruining*
    The pothecarie answerde, "And thou shalt have
A thing that, also° God my soule save,   *so (may)*
In al this world ther nis no° creature,   *is not any*
That ete or dronke hath of this confiture°   *mixture*
Noght but the mountance of a corn of whete,[61]
That he ne shal his lyf anon° forlete.°   *at once / lose*
Ye,° sterve° he shal, and that in lasse whyle°   *Yes / die / shorter time*
Than thou wolt goon a paas° nat but° a myle,   *walk at normal pace / only*
This poyson is so strong and violent."
    This cursed man hath in his hond y-hent°   *grasped*
This poyson in a box, and sith° he ran   *afterward*
Into the nexte strete unto a man
And borwed [of] him large botels° three,   *bottles (probably of leather)*
And in the two his poyson poured he—
The thridde he kepte clene for his° drinke—   *his (own)*
For al the night he shoop him° for to swinke°   *was preparing himself / work*
In caryinge of the gold out of that place.
And whan this ryotour, with sory grace,[62]
Hadde filled with wyn his grete botels three,
To his felawes agayn repaireth° he.   *returns*
    What nedeth it to sermone° of it more?   *speak*
For right as they hadde cast° his deeth bifore,   *planned*
Right so they han him slayn, and that anon.°   *immediately*
And whan that this was doon, thus spak that oon:
"Now lat us sitte and drinke, and make us merie,
And afterward we wol his body berie."°   *bury*
And with that word it happed° him, par cas,°   *befell / by chance*
To take the botel ther° the poyson was,   *where*
And drank, and yaf° his felawe drink also,   *gave*
For which anon they storven° bothe two.   *died*
    But certes, I suppose that Avicen
Wroot nevere in no canon, ne in no fen,

Mo wonder signes of empoisoning[63]
Than hadde thise wrecches two, er° hir° ending.   *before / their*

---

[61] "No more than the quantity of a grain of wheat."
[62] Blessed by evil.
[63] "But truly, I would guess that Avicenna—an Arab physician and author—never described, in any treatise or
chapter, more terrible symptoms of poisoning."

Thus ended been thise homicydes two,
And eek° the false empoysoner° also.°   *also / poisoner / as well*
   O cursed sinne of alle cursednesse!
O traytours° homicyde, O wikkednesse!   *traitorous*
O glotonye, luxurie,° and hasardrye!   *lechery*
Thou blasphemour of Crist with vileinye°   *vile speech*
And othes grete, of usage° and of pryde!   *out of habit*
Allas! mankinde, how may it bityde°   *happen*
That to thy Creatour which that thee wroghte,
And with his precious herte-blood thee boghte,°   *redeemed*
Thou art so fals and so unkinde,° allas!   *unnatural*
   Now, goode men, God forgeve° yow youre trespas,   *may God forgive*
And ware yow fro° the sinne of avaryce.   *make you beware of*
Myn holy pardoun may yow alle waryce°—   *cure*
So that ye offre nobles or sterlinges,[64]
Or elles silver broches, spones,° ringes.   *spoons*
Boweth youre heed° under this holy bulle!   *head*
Cometh up, ye wyves, offreth of youre wolle!°   *wool*
Youre names I entre heer in my rolle° anon:°   *roll, list / at once*
Into the blisse of hevene shul ye gon.
I yow assoile,° by myn heigh power—   *absolve*
Yow that wol offre°—as clene and eek as cleer°   *make an offering / pure*
As ye were born.—And, lo, sires, thus I preche.
And Jesu Crist, that is our soules leche,°   *healer, doctor*
So graunte° yow his pardon to receyve,   *May He grant*
For that is best; I wol yow nat deceyve.
   But sires, o° word forgat I in my tale: *a, one*
I have relikes and pardon in my male°   *pouch*
As faire as any man in Engelond,
Whiche were me yeven° by the Popes hond.   *given*
If any of yow wol of devocioun°   *out of devotion*
Offren and han myn absolucioun,
Cometh forth anon, and kneleth heer adoun,
And mekely receyveth my pardoun;
Or elles, taketh pardon as ye wende,°   *travel*
Al newe and fresh, at every myles ende—
So that ye offren alwey newe and newe[65]
Nobles or pens,° which that be gode and trewe.   *pence*
It is an honour to everich° that is heer   *every one*
That ye mowe° have a suffisant° pardoneer   *may / capable*
T'assoille° yow, in contree as ye ryde,   *To absolve*

---

[64] "As long as you offer nobles [gold coins] or silver pennies."
[65] "As long as you make offering anew each time (of)."

For aventures whiche that may bityde.[66]	
Peraventure° ther may falle oon or two	By chance
Doun of his hors, and breke his nekke atwo.°	in two
Look which a seuretee° is it to you alle	what a security
That I am in youre felaweship y-falle,	
That may assoille yow, bothe more and lasse,°	great and small
Whan that the soule shal fro the body passe.	
I rede° that oure Host heer shal biginne,	advise
For he is most envoluped° in sinne.	enveloped, wrapped up
Com forth, sire Hoste, and offre first anon,°	first now
And thou shalt kisse the reliks everichon,°	every one
Ye, for a grote:° unbokel° anon thy purs."	groat (four pence) / unbuckle
"Nay, nay," quod° he, "thanne have I Cristes curs!	said
Lat be," quod he, "it shal nat be, so theech!°	as I hope to prosper
Thou woldest make me kisse thyn olde breech°	breeches
And swere it were a relik of a seint,	
Thogh it were with thy fundement° depeint!°	fundament (rectum) / stained
But by the croys° which that Seint Eleyne° fond,	(true) Cross / St. Helena
I wolde I hadde thy coillons° in myn hond	testicles
In stede of relikes or of seintuarie.[67]	
Lat cutte hem of! I wol thee helpe hem carie.[68]	
Thay shul be shryned° in an hogges tord!"°	enshrined / turd
This Pardoner answerde nat a word;	
So wrooth° he was, no word ne wolde he seye.	wroth, angered
"Now," quod our Host, "I wol no lenger pleye	
With thee, ne with noon other angry man."	
But right anon the worthy Knight bigan,	
"Whan that he saugh that al the peple lough,°	laughed
"Namore of this, for it is right y-nough!°	quite enough
Sire Pardoner, be glad and mery of chere;°	mood
And ye, sire Host, that been to me so dere,	
I prey yow that ye kisse the Pardoner.	
And Pardoner, I prey thee, drawe thee neer,	
And, as we diden, lat us laughe and pleye."	
Anon° they kiste, and riden forth hir weye.°	At once / (on) their way

* * *

---

[66] "In respect to things which may befall."
[67] Holy things.
[68] "Have them cut off! I'll help thee carry them."

REVIEW QUESTIONS

1. How does the pardoner himself illustrate the problems of the late medieval church?
2. What is the image of death in this disease-ridden world?
3. In what ways does the pardoner's tale reflect the realities of postplague conditions?

JAN HUS

FROM *The Church*

Jan Hus (c. 1373–1415) was a Czech preacher and writer active in Prague. Hus, influenced by the writings of the English theologian John Wyclif (c. 1330–1384), called for radical reforms in the church. Summoned under safe conduct to the Council of Constance, he was nevertheless accused of heresy, convicted, and burned at the stake. Hus became a national martyr in his native Bohemia, which remained for centuries in rebellion against the Catholic Church. This chapter from his book The Church *concerns his opinions on the papacy.*

From *The Church by John Hus*, edited by David S. Schaff (New York: Scribner's, 1915).

Chapter XIII
The Pope Not the Head of the Church but Christ's Vicar

Further, the aforesaid doctors lay down in their writing that "the pope is head of the Roman church and the college of cardinals the body, and that they are very successors and princes of the apostle Peter and the college of Christ's other apostles in ecclesiastical office for the purpose of discerning and defining all catholic and church matters, correcting and purging all errors in respect to them and, in all these matters, to have the care of all the churches and of all the faithful of Christ. For in order to govern the church throughout the whole world it is fitting there should always continue to be such manifest and true successors in the office of Peter, the prince of the apostles, and of the college of the other apostles of Christ. And such successors cannot be found or procured on the earth other than the pope, the existing head, and the college of cardinals, the existing body, of the aforesaid Roman church."

These follies, long drawn out, which, I think, proceeded for the most part from the brain of Stanislaus, overcome and terrified by the Roman

curia, involve many points. And in regard to these, I note that in their writing the church is taken to mean all Christian pilgrims. They seem to admit this when they say that "the body of the clergy in the kingdom of Bohemia, not only with the whole body of clergy in the world but also with the whole body of Christendom, always feels and believes as the faith dictates, just as the Roman church does." Or, secondly, these doctors call the pope, together with his cardinals, alone the Roman church, when they say that they believe just as the Roman church believes and not otherwise, the pope being the head of this Roman church and the cardinals the body. In these ways only, so far as I can see, do the doctors designate the church in their writing.

I assume that the pope stands for that spiritual bishop who, in the highest way and in the most similar way, occupies the place of Christ, just as Peter did after the ascension. But if any person whatsoever is to be called pope—whom the Western church accepts as Roman bishop—appointed to decide as the final court ecclesiastical cases and to teach the faithful whatever he wishes, then there is an abuse of the term, because according to this view, it would be necessary in cases to concede that the most unlettered layman or a female, or a heretic and antichrist, may be pope. This is plain, for Constantine II, an unlettered layman, was suddenly ordained a priest and through ambition made pope and then was deposed and all the things which he ordained were declared invalid, about A. D. 707. And the same is plain from the case of Gregory, who was unlettered and consecrated another in addition to himself. And as the people were displeased with the act, a third pope was superinduced. Then these quarrelling among themselves, the emperor came to Rome and elected another as sole pope. As for a female, it is plain in the case of Agnes, who was called John Anglicus, and of her Castrensis, * * * writes: "A certain woman sat in the papal chair two years and five months, following Leo. She is said to have been a girl, called Agnes, of the nation of Mainz, was led about by her paramour in a man's dress in Athens and named John Anglicus. She made such progress in different studies that, coming to Rome, she read the trivium to an audience of great teachers. Finally, elected pope, she was with child by her paramour, and, as she was proceeding from St. Peter's to the Lateran, she had the pains of labor in a narrow street between the Colosseum and St. Clement's and gave birth to a child. Shortly afterward she died there and was buried. For this reason it is said that all the popes avoid this street. Therefore, she is not put down in the catalogue of popes."

As for a heretic occupying the papal chair we have an instance in Liberius, of whom Castrensis writes, * * * that at Constantius's command he was exiled for three years because he wished to favor the Arians. At the counsel of the same Constantius, the Roman clergy ordained Felix pope who, during the sessions of a synod condemned and cast out two Arian presbyters, Ursacius and Valens, and when this became known, Liberius was recalled from exile, and being wearied by his long exile and exhilarated by the reoccupation of the papal chair, he yielded to heretical depravity; and when Felix was cast down, Liberius with violence held the church of Peter and Paul and St. Lawrence so that the clergy and

priests who favored Felix were murdered in the church, and Felix was martyred, Liberius not preventing.

As for antichrist occupying the papal chair, it is evident that a pope living contrary to Christ, like any other perverted person, is called by common consent antichrist. In accordance with John 2: 22, many are become antichrists. And the faithful will not dare to deny persistently that it is possible for the man of sin to sit in the holy place. Of him the Saviour prophesied when he said: "When ye see the abomination of desolation, which is spoken of by Daniel, standing in the holy place." * * * The apostle also says: "Let no man beguile you in any wise, for it will not be except the falling away come first and the man of sin be revealed, the son of perdition; he that opposeth and exalteth himself against all that is called God or is worshipped; so that he sitteth in the temple of God setting himself forth as God," * * * And it is apparent from the *Chronicles* how the papal dignity has sunk.

For the emperor Constantine, about A. D. 301, thought and commanded that the highest bishop should be called by all pope and in his dotation that name also sprang up. The emperor Phocas likewise, about the year 600, at the instance of the clergy confirmed this same thing, as may be read in his *Annals*. Therefore, Castrensis * * * describes how the excellency of the Roman empire helped the papacy of the Roman pontiff above others. He says: "The Nicene council conferred this prerogative on the Roman pontiff, that, just as Augustus had rank above other kings, so the Roman pontiff should be held as bishop, and the pope be called chief father—*principalis pater.*" The origin, however, of this name and this excellency is to be found in the dotation of the church, as is indicated in the *Decretum*, 96, *Dist. Constant.*

These things being noted, in order to remove ambiguity, I assume that the doctors in their writing designate by the Roman church that church of which the Saviour said to Peter: "On this rock I will build my church." * * * The holy writers and the Decretals speak of it as the Roman church.

* * * And in the Clementines, *de Jurejurando,* * * * it is said: "The Romans, princes, professors of the orthodox faith, venerate with warm faith and pure devotion the holy Roman church, whose head is Christ, our Saviour, and the Roman pontiff, the Saviour's vicar." And in the *Sextus* it is said: "Our alma mater, the church" and in the *Extravagante* of Boniface VIII, "The holy Roman church." And the same is true of the other statements made in other places and alleged above.

In regard to these follies of the Unlearned—*indoctorum*—I find these points: (1) The pope is the head of the holy Roman church. (2) The college of cardinals is the body of the holy Roman church. (3) The pope is manifestly and truly the successor of the prince of the apostles, Peter. (4) Cardinals are manifest and true successors of the college of Christ's other apostles. (5) For the government of the church throughout the whole world, there should always be manifest and true successors of the same kind in the office of the prince of the apostles and in the office of Christ's other apostles. (6) Such successors are not to be found or procured on the earth, other than the pope, the existing head and the college of cardinals, the existing body of the church.

Against all these six points, the argument in brief runs thus: all truth in the religion of Christ is to be followed and only that is truth which is known by the bodily senses, or discovered by an infallible intelligence, or made known through revelation, or laid down in sacred Scripture. But none of these six points is truth known by the bodily senses or discovered by an infallible intelligence or known through revelation, or laid down in divine Scripture. Therefore, no one of these six points is truth in the religion of Jesus Christ which is to be followed. The major premise is seen in what St. Augustine says, *Enchiridion,* * * * "these things chiefly, yea almost exclusively, are to be followed in religion, and he who contradicts them is altogether a stranger to the name of Christ or he is a heretic. * * * These things are to be defended by the reason whether they start from the bodily senses or are discovered by the intelligence of the mind. But these things, which we have not been

aware of through the bodily senses or been able to reach with the mind, nor now are able—these are beyond doubt to be believed on the testimony of those witnesses by whom the Scriptures, deservedly called divine, were written, because, assisted with divine help, they were able to see these things or to foresee them either through the bodily senses or through the mind." Thus much St. Augustine.

The minor premise, however, the doctors are unable to disprove unless one of these six points should be revealed to them by divine revelation. For neither by the bodily senses, nor by the reason, nor from sacred Scripture do these points appear. Yea, the doctors in making these points authoritative, so that they must be believed, are seen to be anathema by the authority of Augustine himself which they adduce in their writing. If any one venerate any other scriptures than those which the catholic church has received or has handed down to be held as authoritative, let him be anathema. This is clear because these doctors have offered their own writings as authoritative and to be believed and the catholic church has not received them for they are found neither in the divine law nor in the code of canons. Therefore, it follows that these doctors are themselves anathema, and it is clear that religious faith is not held by them so far as these points are concerned unless they prove them plainly or show them to be founded in sacred Scripture or in clear reasoning, for Augustine says, *Ep. ad Hieron., Decretum, Dist.* 9: 5 "I have learned to give only to those writers, who are now called canonical, honor and regard, so that I would not dare to believe that any of them erred in writing. But other writers I will read as far as they seem to excel by sanctity or true doctrine but I will not regard as true what they say because they have felt it to be true, but because they have been able to convince me by other writers, or by canonical or probable reasons, that they do not differ from the truth."

Inasmuch as these doctors are not writers of sacred Scripture—it being granted that they excel by their sanctity—the faithful are not, therefore, to think a thing is true because they feel it to be true unless by other writers of Scripture or for canonical or probable reasons they prove that these points do not deviate from the truth. Then, similarly, as to the point that the pope is always and uniformly to be regarded as the head of the Roman church, and that the church is the bride of Christ built upon Christ "against which the gates of hell cannot prevail," we must argue thus: No pope is the most exalted person of the catholic church but Christ himself; therefore no pope is the head of the catholic church besides Christ. The conclusion is valid reasoning from description to the thing described. Inasmuch as the head of the church is the capital or chief person of the church, yea, inasmuch as the head is a name of dignity and of office—dignity in view of predestination, and office in view of the administration of the whole church—it follows that no one may reasonably assert of himself or of another without revelation that he is the head of a particular holy church, although if he live well he ought to hope that he is a member of the holy catholic church, the bride of Christ. Therefore, we should not contend in regard to the reality of the incumbency whether any one, whoever he may be, living with us is the head of a particular holy church but, on the ground of his works, we ought assume that, if he is a superior, ruling over a particular holy church, then he is the superior in that particular church, and this ought to be assumed of the Roman pontiff, unless his works gainsay it, for the Saviour said: "Beware of false prophets which come unto you in sheep's clothing but inwardly they are ravening wolves. By their fruits ye shall know them." * * *

Likewise, it is not necessary to believe that every Roman pontiff whatsoever is the head of any particular holy church unless God has predestinated him. This is clear because otherwise the Christian faith would be perverted and a Christian would have to believe a lie. For the church was deceived in the case of Agnes, and for the sake of His own, and without doubt for the better, God permits that he who is chosen pope should not forthwith and without reverent hesitancy be regarded as holy or such as he assumes himself to

be. Hence I could wish that the doctors would openly teach the people whether for the whole clergy that lived at that time and held Agnes to be a true pope, Agnes was really the head of the church; or, if the church was at that time without a head—*acephalous*—with only a nominal pope in the church militant for two years and five months, the faithful for that reason ought not to think that it is not of the substance of the catholic faith to believe expressly that Liberius, Joanna, Boniface, Clement, or Urban were predestinate or members of holy mother church—in view of the judgment given above.

In the same way, it is not of necessity to salvation for all Christians, living together, that they should believe expressly that any one is head of any church whatsoever unless his evangelical life and works plainly moved them to believe this. For it would be all too much presumption to affirm that we are heads of any particular church which perhaps might be a part of holy mother church. How, therefore, may any one of us without revelation presume to assert of himself or of another that he is the head, since it is said truly, Ecclesiasticus 9, that "no one knows, so far as predestination goes, whether one is worthy of love or hatred."

Likewise, if we examine in the light of the feeling and influence with which we influence inferiors and, on the other hand, examine by the mirror of Scripture, according to which we should regulate our whole life, then we would choose rather to be called servants and ministers of the church than its heads. For it is certain that if we do not fulfil the office of a head, we are not heads, as Augustine, *de decem chordis* says: that a perverse husband is not the head of his wife, much less is a prelate of the church, who alone from God could have a dignity of this kind, the head of a particular church in case he fall away from Christ.

Therefore, after Augustine has shown that a truly Christian wife ought to mourn over the fornication of her husband, not for carnal reasons, but out of love and for the chastity due to the man Christ—he says consequentially that Christ speaks in the hearts of good women, where the husband does not hear, and he goes on to say: "Mourn over the injuries done by thy husband, but do not imitate them that he may rather imitate you in that which is good. For in that wherein he does wrong, do not regard him as thy head but me, thy Lord." And he proves that this ought to be the case and says: "If he is the head in that wherein he does wrong and the body follow its head, they both go over the precipice. But that the Christian may not follow this bad head, let him keep himself to the head of the church, Christ, to whom he owes his chastity, to whom he yields his honor, no longer a single man but now a man wedded to his mother, the church." Blessed, therefore, be the head of the church, Christ, who cannot be separated from his bride which is his mystical body, as the popes have often been separated from the church by heresy.

But some of the aforesaid doctors say that the pope is the bodily head of the church militant and this head ought always to be here with the church, but in this sense Christ is not the bodily head. Here is meant that the same difficulty remains, namely, that they prove the first part of the statement. For it remains for them to prove that the pope is the head of holy church, a thing they have not proved. And, before that, it remains for them to prove that Christ is not the bodily head of the church militant, inasmuch as Christ is a bodily person, because the man who is the head of the church militant, who is Christ, is present through all time with his church unto the consummation of the age, in virtue of his divine personality. Similarly, he is present by grace, giving his body to the church to be eaten in a sacramental and spiritual way. Wherefore, is not that bridegroom, who is the head of the church, much more present with us than the pope, who is removed from us two thousand miles and incapable of influencing of himself our feeling or movements? Let it suffice, therefore, to say, that the pope may be the vicar of Christ and may be so to his profit, if he is a faithful minister predestinated unto the glory of the head, Jesus Christ.

*   *   *

REVIEW QUESTIONS

1. What sources of authority in the church does Hus accept or deny?
2. How do his arguments compare to the ones Gregory VII and Boniface VIII raised in defense of papal authority?
3. In what ways was Hus a threat or an asset to the organized church?

DANTE ALIGHIERI

FROM *The Divine Comedy*

Dante Alighieri (1265–1321) a Florentine poet and part-time politician who was exiled for his views on the political role of the papacy, completed his masterpiece, The Divine Comedy, *toward the end of his life. Dante's earlier poetry centered on Beatrice, the great love of his life, and her early death changed the direction of his artistic development. Praised as divine after his death, the* Comedy, *beginning sadly in hell and ending happily in heaven, consists of one hundred cantos in a then-new poetic style. This complex poem is a window on the values of its age, because Dante allows himself to comment on many aspects of history as he tours hell, purgatory, and paradise, seeing many famous people of the past. Canto V describes the fate of the carnal in hell, as seen by Dante and his guide and master, the Roman poet Virgil.*

From *The Divine Comedy*, by Dante Alighieri, translated by John Ciardi (New York: Norton, 1954), pp. 25–29.

*   *   *

Canto V

CIRCLE TWO

THE CARNAL

The Poets leave Limbo and enter the Second Circle. Here begin the torments of Hell proper, and here, blocking the way, sits Minos, the dread and semi-bestial judge of the damned who assigns to each soul its eternal torment. He orders the Poets back; but Virgil silences him as he earlier silenced Charon, and the Poets move on.

They find themselves on a dark ledge swept by a great whirlwind, which spins within it the souls of the Carnal, those who betrayed reason to their appetites. Their sin was to abandon themselves to the tempest of their passions: so they are swept forever in the tempest of Hell, forever denied the light of reason and of God. Virgil identifies many among them. Semiramis is there, and Dido, Cleopatra, Helen, Achilles, Paris, and Tristan. Dante sees Paolo and Francesca swept together, and in the name of love he calls to them to tell their sad story. They pause from their eternal flight to come to him, and Francesca tells their history while Paolo weeps at her side. Dante is so stricken by compassion at their tragic tale that he swoons once again.

So we went down to the second ledge alone;
a smaller circle[1] of so much greater pain
the voice of the damned rose in a bestial moan.

There Minos[2] sits, grinning, grotesque, and hale.
He examines each lost soul as it arrives
and delivers his verdict with his coiling tail.

That is to say, when the ill-fated soul
appears before him it confesses all,[3]
and that grim sorter of the dark and foul

decides which place in Hell shall be its end,
then wraps his twitching tail about himself
one coil for each degree it must descend.

The soul descends and others take its place:
each crowds in its turn to judgment, each
     confesses,
each hears its doom and falls away through space.

"O you who come into this camp of woe,"
cried Minos when he saw me turn away

---

[1] The pit of Hell tapers like a funnel. The circles of ledges accordingly grow smaller as they descend.

[2] Like all the monsters Dante assigns to the various offices of Hell, Minos is drawn from classical mythology. He was the son of Europa and of Zeus, who descended to her in the form of a bull. Minos became a mythological king of Crete, so famous for his wisdom and justice that after death his soul was made judge of the dead. Virgil presents him fulfilling the same office at Aeneas' descent to the underworld. Dante, however, transforms him into an irate and hideous monster with a tail. The transformation may have been suggested by the form Zeus assumed for the rape of Europa—the monster is certainly bullish enough here—but the obvious purpose of the brutalization is to present a figure symbolic of the guilty conscience of the wretches who come before it to make their confessions. Dante freely reshapes his materials to his own purposes.

[3] Just as the souls appeared eager to cross Acheron, so they are eager to confess even while they dread. Dante is once again making the point that sinners elect their Hell by an act of their own will.

without awaiting his judgment, "watch where
you go

once you have entered here, and to whom you
turn!
Do not be misled by that wide and easy
passage!"
And my Guide to him: "That is not your
concern;

it is his fate to enter every door.
This has been willed where what is willed
must be,
and is not yours to question. Say no more."

Now the choir of anguish, like a wound,
strikes through the tortured air. Now I have
come
to Hell's full lamentation,[4] sound beyond
sound.

I came to a place stripped bare of every light
and roaring on the naked dark like seas
wracked by a war of winds. Their hellish
flight

of storm and counterstorm through time
foregone,
sweeps the souls of the damned before its
charge.
Whirling and battering it drives them on,

and when they pass the ruined gap of Hell[5]
through which we had come, their shrieks begin
anew.
There they blaspheme the power of God
eternal.

And this, I learned, was the never ending flight
of those who sinned in the flesh, the carnal and
lusty
who betrayed reason to their appetite.

As the wings of wintering starlings bear them on
in their great wheeling flights, just so the blast
wherries these evil souls through time foregone.

Here, there, up, down, they whirl and, whirling,
strain
with never a hope of hope to comfort them,
not of release, but even of less pain.

As cranes go over sounding their harsh cry,
leaving the long streak of their flight in air,
so come these spirits, wailing as they fly.

And watching their shadows lashed by wind, I
cried:
"Master, what souls are these the very air
lashes with its black whips from side to side?"

"The first of these whose history you would
know,"
he answered me, "was Empress of many
tongues.[6]
Mad sensuality corrupted her so

that to hide the guilt of her debauchery
she licensed all depravity alike,
and lust and law were one in her decree.

---

[4] It is with the second circle that the real tortures of Hell begin.
[5] At the time of the Harrowing of Hell a great earthquake shook the underworld shattering rocks and cliffs. Ruins resulting from the same shock are noted in Canto XII, 34, and Canto XXI, 112 ff. At the beginning of Canto XXIV, the Poets leave the *bolgia* of the

Hypocrites by climbing the ruined slabs of a bridge that was shattered by this earthquake.
    Here begin the punishments for the various sins of incontinence (the sins of the She-Wolf). Those are punished who sinned by excess of sexual passion. Since this is the most natural sin and the sin most nearly associated with love, its punishment is the lightest of all to be found in Hell proper. The Carnal are whirled and buffeted endlessly through the murky air (symbolic of the beclouding of their reason by passion) by a great gale (symbolic of their lust).
[6] Semiramis, a legendary queen of Assyria who assumed full power at the death of her husband, Ninus.

She is Semiramis of whom the tale is told
how she married Ninus and succeeded him
to the throne of that wide land the Sultans
   hold.

The other is Dido;[7] faithless to the ashes
of Sichaeus, she killed herself for love.
The next whom the eternal tempest lashes

is sense-drugged Cleopatra. See Helen there,
from whom such ill arose. And great
   Achilles,[8]
who fought at last with love in the house of
   prayer.

And Paris. And Tristan." As they whirled above
he pointed out more than a thousand shades
of those torn from the mortal life by love.

I stood there while my Teacher one by one
named the great knights and ladies of dim time;
and I was swept by pity and confusion.

At last I spoke: "Poet, I should be glad
to speak a word with those two swept together[9]
so lightly on the wind and still so sad."

And he to me: "Watch them. When next they pass,
call to them in the name of love that drives
and damns them here. In that name they will
   pause."

Thus, as soon as the wind in its wild course
brought them around, I called: "O wearied
   souls!
if none forbid it, pause and speak to us."

As mating doves that love calls to their nest
glide through the air with motionless raised
   wings,
borne by the sweet desire that fills each
   breast—

Just so those spirits turned on the torn sky
from the band where Dido whirls across the air;
such was the power of pity in my cry.

"O living creature, gracious, kind, and good,
going this pilgrimage through the sick night,
visiting us who stained the earth with blood,

were the King of Time our friend, we would
   pray His peace
on you who have pitied us. As long as the wind
will let us pause, ask of us what you please.

---

[7] Queen and founder of Carthage. She had vowed to remain faithful to her husband, Sichaeus, but she fell in love with Aeneas. When Aeneas abandoned her she stabbed herself on a funeral pyre she had had prepared. According to Dante's own system of punishments, she should be in the Seventh Circle with the suicides. The only clue Dante gives to the tempering of her punishment is his statement that "she killed herself for love." Dante always seems readiest to forgive in that name.

[8] Achilles is placed among this company because of his passion for Polyxena, the daughter of Priam. For love of her, he agreed to desert the Greeks and to join the Trojans, but when he went to the temple for the wedding (according to the legend Dante has followed), he was killed by Paris.

[9] Paolo and Francesca (PAH-oe-loe: Frahn-CHAY-ska). Dante's treatment of these two lovers is certainly the tenderest and most sympathetic accorded any of the sinners in Hell, and legends immediately began to grow about this pair.

The facts are these. In 1275 Giovanni Malatesta (Djoe-VAH-nee Mahl-ah-TEH-stah) of Rimini, called Giovanni the Lame, a somewhat deformed but brave and powerful warrior, made a political marriage with Francesca, daughter of Guido da Polenta of Ravenna. Francesca came to Rimini and there an amour grew between her and Giovanni's younger brother Paolo. Despite the fact that Paolo had married in 1269 and had become the father of two daughters by 1275, his affair with Francesca continued for many years. It was sometime between 1283 and 1286 that Giovanni surprised them in Francesca's bedroom and killed both of them.

Around these facts the legend has grown that Paolo was sent by Giovanni as his proxy to the marriage, that Francesca thought he was her real bridegroom and accordingly gave him her heart irrevocably at first sight. The legend obviously increases the pathos, but nothing in Dante gives it support.

The town where I was born lies by the shore
where the Po descends into its ocean rest
with its attendant streams in one long murmur.

Love, which in gentlest hearts will soonest
    bloom
seized my lover with passion for that sweet
    body
from which I was torn unshriven to my
    doom.

Love, which permits no loved one not to
    love,
took me so strongly with delight in him
that we are one in Hell, as we were above.[10]

Love led us to one death. In the depths of
    Hell
Caïna waits for him[11] who took our lives."
This was the piteous tale they stopped to tell.

And when I had heard those world-offended
    lovers
I bowed my head. At last the Poet spoke:
"What painful thoughts are these your lowered
    brow covers?"

When at length I answered, I began: "Alas!
What sweetest thoughts, what green and young
    desire
led these two lovers to this sorry pass."

Then turning to those spirits once again,
I said: "Francesca, what you suffer here
melts me to tears of pity and of pain.

But tell me: in the time of your sweet sighs
by what appearances found love the way
to lure you to his perilous paradise?"

And she: "The double grief of a lost bliss
is to recall its happy hour in pain.
Your Guide and Teacher knows the truth of this.

But if there is indeed a soul in Hell
to ask of the beginning of our love
out of his pity, I will weep and tell:

On a day for dalliance we read the rhyme
of Lancelot,[12] how love had mastered him.
We were alone with innocence and dim time.[13]

Pause after pause that high old story drew
our eyes together while we blushed and paled;
but it was one soft passage overthrew

our caution and our hearts. For when we read
how her fond smile was kissed by such a lover,
he who is one with me alive and dead

breathed on my lips the tremor of his kiss.
That book, and he who wrote it, was a pander.[14]
That day we read no further." As she said this,

---

[10] At many points of *The Inferno* Dante makes clear the principle that the souls of the damned are locked so blindly into their own guilt that none can feel sympathy for another, or find any pleasure in the presence of another. The temptation of many readers is to interpret this line romantically: i.e., that the love of Paolo and Francesca survives Hell itself. The more Dantean interpretation, however, is that they add to one another's anguish (a) as mutual reminders of their sin, and (b) as insubstantial shades of the bodies for which they once felt such great passion.

[11] Giovanni Malatesta was still alive at the writing. His fate is already decided, however, and upon his death, his soul will fall to Caïna, the first ring of the last circle, where lie those who performed acts of treachery against their kin.

[12] The story exists in many forms. The details Dante makes use of are from an Old French version.

[13] The original simply reads "We were alone, suspecting nothing." "Dim time" is rhyme-forced, but not wholly outside the legitimate implications of the original, I hope. The old courtly romance may well be thought of as happening in the dim ancient days. The apology, of course, comes after the fact: one does the possible, then argues for justification, and there probably is none.

[14] *Galeotto*, the Italian word for "pander," is also the Italian rendering of the name of Gallehault, who in the French Romance Dante refers to here, urged Lancelot and Guinevere on to love.

the other spirit, who stood by her, wept
so piteously, I felt my senses reel
and faint away with anguish. I was swept

by such a swoon as death is, and I fell,
as a corpse might fall, to the dead floor of Hell.

*   *   *

REVIEW QUESTIONS

1. Why is Dante so affected by the story of Paolo and Francesca, the lovers slain by a jealous husband?
2. Why is literature so dangerous?
3. Why are there so many women in this part of hell?

CHRISTINE DE PISAN

FROM *The Book of the City of Ladies*

Christine de Pisan (1365–after 1429) was the highly educated daughter of a Venetian physician at the court of Charles VI of France. Widowed at an early age, Christine became a writer to support her family, becoming the first French woman of letters. Her most famous work, The Book of the City of Ladies, *is both a historical treatise on women and a defense of them. In this selection, the allegorical figure of Lady Rectitude introduces the subject of virtuous women.*

From *The Book of the City of Ladies*, by Christine de Pizan, translated by Earl Jeffrey Richards (New York: Persea Books, 1982), pp. 206–15.

*   *   *

Rectitude Says That Many Women Are Loved for Their Virtues More Than Other Women for Their Prettiness.

"If we assumed that women who wished to be loved tried, for this reason, to be pretty, conceited, cute, and vain, then I can show you that such action will not make wise and worthwhile men love them more quickly or better and that, in fact, honest, virtuous, and simple women will more readily and more deeply be loved by men who love honor than pretty women, even if we suppose that these honest women are less beautiful. One could answer that, since women attract men with virtue and integrity and since it is bad that men be attracted, it would be better if women were less good. But of course this argument has no validity at all, for one should not neglect the cultivation and advancement of the good in spite of however much fools abuse it, and everyone must do his duty by acting well regardless of what might happen. I will give you an example to prove that women are loved for their virtue and integrity. First I could tell you about the many women who are saints in Paradise who were desired by men because of their honesty.

"Consider Lucretia, whom I spoke to you about before and who was raped: her great integrity was the reason why Tarquin became enamored, much more so than because of her beauty. For once, when her husband was dining with this Tarquin (who afterward raped her) and with many other knights, the subject of their conversation turned to their wives, and each one claimed that his own was the best. In order to discover the truth and to prove which one of their wives was worthy of the highest praise, they got up and rode home, and those women found occupied in the most honest occupation and activity were to be the most celebrated and honored. Lucretia, of all these wives, turned out to be the most honestly occupied, for her husband found her, such a wise and upright woman, clothed in a simple gown, sitting at home among her women servants, working in wool, and discoursing on various subjects. This same Tarquin, the king's son, arrived there with her husband and saw her outstanding honesty, her smile and fair conduct, and her serene manner. He was so captivated by her that he began to plan the folly which he committed later."

Here She Speaks of Queen Blanche, the Mother of Saint Louis, and of Other Good and Wise Ladies Loved for Their Virtue.

"The most noble Queen Blanche, mother of Saint Louis, was similarly loved for great learning, prudence, virtue, and goodness by Thibault, the count of Champagne. Even though she had already passed the flower of her youth, this noble count—hearing the wise and good queen speak to him so judiciously after he had gone to war against Saint Louis, sensibly reproving him, telling him he ought not to have acted this way, considering the good deeds her son had done for him—looked at her intently, amazed by her enormous goodness and virtue, and was so overwhelmed by love that he did not know what to do. He did not dare confess his love for fear of death, for he realized that she was so good that she would never consent to his proposition. From that time onward he suffered much grief because of the mad desire which oppressed him. Nevertheless, he told her then not to fear his continuing to wage war against the king and that he wished to be her subject totally, that she should be certain that everything he possessed, body and soul, was entirely subject to her command. So he loved her all his life, from that hour on, and he never stopped loving her in spite of the slight chance he had of ever winning her love. He made his laments to Love in his poems, where he praised his lady most graciously. These beautiful poems of his were put to music in a charming way. He had them inscribed in his bedroom in Provins and also in Troyes, and they appear there to this day. And so I could tell you about many others."

And I, Christine, replied, "Indeed, my lady, I have seen in my own experience several cases similar to the one you mention, for I know of virtuous and wise women who, from what they have confessed to me in lamenting their distress, have been propositioned more frequently after their peak of beauty and youthfulness than when they were in their greatest flower. Concerning this, they have told me, 'Gods! What can this possibly mean? Do these men see in me some foolish behavior which would give them the slightest glimmer of hope that I would agree to commit such foolishness?' But I realize now, from what you say, that their outstanding goodness caused them to be loved. And this is very much against the opinion of many people who claim that an honest woman who intends to be chaste will never be desired or propositioned unless she herself so wishes."

Christine Speaks, and Rectitude Responds in Her Reply to Those Men Who Claim That Women Are Naturally Greedy.

"I do not know what more to tell you, my dear lady, for all my questions are answered. It seems to me that you have disproven the slanders put forth by so many men against women. Likewise, what they so often claim is not true, that greed is, among feminine vices, a very natural thing."

She answered, "My dear friend, let me assure you that greed is no more natural in women than it is in men, and God only knows whether men are less greedy! You can see that the latter is in fact the case because considerably more evil occurs and recurs in the world because of the rapacity of different men than because of the greed of women. But, just as I told you before, the fool sees his neighbor's peccadillo and fails to see his own enormous crime. Since one commonly sees women taking delight in collecting cloth and thread and such trifles which go into a household, women are thought to be greedy. I can, however, assure you that there are many women who, were they to possess anything, would not be greedy or stingy in bestowing honors and giving generously where what they have could be used well, just as one poor person would do for an even poorer person in need. Women are usually kept in such financial straits that they guard the little that they can have, knowing they can recover this only with the greatest pain. So some people consider women greedy because some women have foolish husbands, great wastrels of property and gluttons, and the poor women, who know well that their households need what their husbands spend foolishly and that in the end their poor children will have to pay for it, are unable to refrain from speaking to their husbands and from urging them to spend less. Thus, such behavior is not at all avarice or greed, but is a sign of great prudence. Of course I am referring to those women who act with discretion. One sees so much quarreling in these marriages because the husbands do not like such urging and so blame their wives for something which they should praise them for. It is clear from the alms which these women so freely give that the vice of avarice is not to be found in them. God knows how many prisoners, even in the lands of the Saracens, how many destitute and needy noblemen and others have been and are every day, in this world here below, comforted and helped by women and their property."

And I, Christine, then said, "Indeed, my lady, your remarks remind me that I have seen women show themselves honorable in prudent generosity, and today I am acquainted with women who rejoice when they can say, 'See, the money is put to good use there, and no greedy man can hoard it away in some coffer.' For although Alexander the Great was said to be generous, I can tell you that I never saw any examples of it."

Rectitude then began to laugh and said, "Indeed, my friend, the ladies of Rome were not greedy when their city was gravely afflicted with war, when the public treasury was completely spent on warriors. The Romans had terrible trouble finding money to finance a large army which they had to raise. But the ladies, with their liberality—even the widows—collected all their jewels and property together, sparing nothing, and freely gave them to the princes of Rome. The ladies received great praise for this deed, and afterward their jewels were given back to them, and quite rightly so, for they had saved Rome."

Here She Speaks of the Rich and Generous Lady Named Busa.

"In the *Faits des Romains* the generosity of a rich and upright woman named Busa, or Paulina, is described. She lived in Apuleia during the time when Hannibal was ravaging the Romans with fire and arms, despoiling almost all of Italy of men and goods. Many Romans retreated after the great defeat at the battle of Cannae, where Hannibal won such a noble victory, and they fled the battlefield wounded or injured. But this valiant Lady Busa received as many as she could take in, until she sheltered some ten thousand in her household, for she was extremely wealthy and had them cared for at her expense. All of them, having been helped by her wealth as much as by the aid and comfort she afforded them, were able to return to Rome and put the army back on its feet, for which she was highly praised. So do not doubt, dear friend, that I could tell you more about the endless generosity, bounty, and liberality of women.

"And even without going back to look for historical examples, how many other examples of the generosity of ladies from your own time could be mentioned! Was not the generosity great which was shown by the Dame de la Rivière, named Marguerite, who is still alive and was formerly the wife of Monsieur Burel de la Rivière, first chamberlain of the wise King Charles? On one occasion among others it happened that this lady, as she was always wise, valiant, and well-bred, was attending a very fine celebration which the duke of Anjou, later king of Sicily, was holding in Paris. At this celebration there were a large number of noble ladies and knights and gentlemen in fine array. This lady, who was young and beautiful, realized while she watched the noble knights assembled there, that a most noteworthy knight of great fame among those then living, named Emerion de Poumiers, was missing from the company of knights. She, of course, allowed that this Sir Emerion was too old to remember her, but his goodness and valiance made the lady remember him, and she felt there could be no more beautiful an ornament for such an assembly than so noteworthy and famous a man, even if he were old, so she inquired where the missing knight was. She was told that he was in prison in the Châtelet in Paris because of a debt of five hundred francs that he had incurred during his frequent travels in arms. 'Ah!' said the noble lady, 'what a shame for this kingdom to suffer a single hour of such a man imprisoned for debt!' Whereupon she removed the gold chaplet which she was wearing on her rich and fair head and replaced it with a chaplet of periwinkle on her blond hair. She gave the gold chaplet to a certain messenger and said, 'Go and give this chaplet as a pledge for what he owes, and let him be freed immediately and come here.' This was done and she was highly praised for it."

She Speaks Here of the Princesses and Ladies of France.

Then I, Christine, spoke again. "My lady, since you have recalled a lady from my own time and since you have come to the history of the ladies of France and of those ladies still living, let me ask you whether you think it is a good idea to lodge some of them in our City. For why should they be forgotten, and foreign women as well?"

She replied, "I can answer you, Christine, that there are certainly a great many virtuous ladies of France, and I would be more than pleased if they were among our citizens. First of all, the noble queen of France, Isabella of Bavaria, will not be refused, reigning now by the grace of God, and in whom there is not a trace of cruelty, extortion, or any other evil vice, but only great love and good will toward her subjects.

"We can equally praise the fair, young, good, and wise duchess of Berry, wife of Duke John, son of the late King John of France and brother of wise King Charles. In the flower of her youth this noble duchess conducted herself so chastely, so sensibly, and so wisely that all the world praised and reputed her for her excellent virtue.

"What could I say about Valentina Visconti, the duchess of Orléans, wife of Duke Louis, son of Charles, the wise king of France, and daughter of the duke of Milan? What more could be said about such a prudent lady? A lady who is strong and constant in heart, filled with devotion to her lord and good teaching for her children, well-informed in government, just toward all, sensible in her conduct, and virtuous in all things—and all this is well known.

"What more could be said concerning the duchess of Burgundy, wife of Duke John, son of Philip, the son of the late King John of France? Is she not extraordinarily virtuous, loyal to her lord, kind in heart and manners, excellent in her morals and lacking a single vice?

"Is not the countess of Clermont, daughter of the duke of Berry mentioned above from his first marriage, and wife of Count John of Clermont, son of the duke of Bourbon and heir to the duchy, is she not everything which every lofty princess must be, devoted to her love, well-bred in everything, beautiful, wise, and good? In short, her virtues shine forth in her good conduct and honorable bearing.

"And what about that one woman among others whom you love singularly as much for the goodness of her virtues as for the favors she has extended to you and to whom you are much beholden, the noble duchess of Holland and countess of Hainault, daughter of the late Duke Philip of Burgundy mentioned above, and sister of the present duke? This lady should be ranked among the most perfect ladies, loyal-hearted, most prudent, wise in government, charitable, supremely devoted to God, and, in short, wholly good.

"Should not the duchess of Bourbon also be recalled among princesses known for their honor and laudability in all things?

"What more shall I tell you? I would need much time to recount all their great virtues.

"The good and beautiful countess of Saint-Pol, noble and upright, daughter of the duke of Bar, second cousin of the king of France, should also be ranked among the good women.

"Similarly the woman whom you love, Anne, daughter of the late count of La Marche and sister of the present duke, married to Ludwig of Bavaria, brother of the queen of France, does not discredit the company of women endowed with grace and praise, for her excellent virtues are well-known to God and the world.

"In spite of the slanderers, there are so many good and beautiful women among the ranks of countesses, baronesses, ladies, maidens, bourgeois women, and all classes that God should be praised who upholds them all. May He correct those women with shortcomings! Do not think otherwise, for I assure you of its truth, even if many jealous and slanderous people say the opposite."

And I, Christine, replied, "My lady, hearing this from you is a supreme joy for me."

She answered, "My dear friend, it seems to me I have now more than adequately executed my office in the City of Ladies. I have built it up with beautiful palaces and many fair inns and mansions. I have populated it for your sake with noble ladies and with such great numbers of women from all classes that it is already completely filled. Now let my sister Justice come to complete the rest, and this should satisfy you."

Christine Addresses Herself to All Princesses and to All Women.

"Most excellent, revered, and honored princesses of France and of all lands, and all ladies and maidens, and, indeed, all women who have loved and do love and will love virtue and morality, as well as all who have died or who are now living or who are to come, rejoice and exult in our new City which, thanks to God, is already formed and almost finished and populated. Give thanks to God who has led me to undertake this great labor and the desirable task of establishing for you honorable lodging within city walls as a perpetual residence for as long as the world endures. I have come this far hoping to reach the conclusion of my work with the aid and comfort of Lady Justice, who, in accordance with her promise, will unfailingly help me until the City is finished and wholly completed. Now, my most honored ladies, pray for me."

*   *   *

REVIEW QUESTIONS

1. How does Christine de Pisan use history to make her case for women?
2. What does Christine see as the correct way for men and women to relate in society?

THE ARNOLFINI MARRIAGE (1434)   JAN VAN EYCK

The Flemish painter Jan van Eyck was one of the great artists in oil paint in fifteenth-century northern Europe. The Arnolfini couple are exchanging marriage vows. The use of light, color, perspective, and imagery are especially remarkable and fresh in this painting. What does this image tell us about fifteenth-century conceptions of marriage in Flanders? (Keep in mind that you are looking at an Italian merchant and his wife.) What is the dog doing in the picture?

FROM *The Trial of Jeanne d'Arc*

Jeanne d'Arc appeared on the scene in 1429 as French fortunes in the Hundred Years' War were at their lowest. Taking command of the Dauphin's army, and then lifting the siege of Orleans, she had him crowned as Charles VII at Rheims and revived the French cause. Captured by the Burgundians and then sold to their English allies, Jeanne was tried as a heretic and eventually burned at the stake in Rouen in May of 1431. Although she was dead before the age of twenty, Jeanne's career is a remarkable episode in the history of France and of late medieval women. The following excerpts from her trial include some of Jeanne's own words and reveal the concerns of the prosecutors.

From *The Trial of Jeanne d'Arc*, edited by W. P. Barrett (London: Routledge and Paul, 1931), pp. 50–51, 68–70, 73–74, 125–26, 318–19.

*   *   *

First Inquiry after the Oath

When she had thus taken the oath the said Jeanne was questioned by us about her name and her surname. To which she replied that in her own country she was called Jeannette, and after she came to France, she was called Jeanne. Of her surname she said she knew nothing. Consequently she was questioned about the district from which she came. She replied she was born in the village of Domrémy, which is one with the village of Greux; and in Greux is the principal church.

Asked about the name of her father and mother, she replied that her father's name was Jacques d'Arc, and her mother's Isabelle.

Asked where she was baptized, she replied it was in the church of Domrémy.

Asked who were her godfathers and godmothers, she said one of her godmothers was named Agnes, another Jeanne, another Sibylle; of her godfathers, one was named Jean Lingué, another Jean Barrey: she had several other godmothers, she had heard her mother say.

Asked what priest had baptized her, she replied that it was master Jean Minet, as far as she knew.

Asked if he was still living, she said she believed he was.

Asked how old she was, she replied she thought nineteen. She said moreover that her mother taught her the Paternoster, Ave Maria, and Credo; and that no one but her mother had taught her her Credo.

*   *   *

Asked whether the voice which spoke to her was that of an angel, or of a saint, male or female, or straight from God, she answered that the voice was the voice of St. Catherine and of St. Margaret. And their heads were crowned in a rich and precious fashion with beautiful crowns. "And to tell this," she said, "I have God's permission. If you doubt it, send to Poitiers where I was examined before."

Asked how she knew they were these two saints, and how she knew one from the other, she answered she knew well who they were, and easily distinguished one from the other.

Asked how she knew one from the other, she answered she knew them by the greeting they gave her. She said further that a good seven years have passed since they undertook to guide her. She said also she knows the saints because they tell her their names.

Asked if the said saints are dressed in the same cloth, she answered: "I will tell you no more now; I have not leave to reveal it. If you do not believe me, send to Poitiers!" She said also that there were some revelations made directly to the king of France, and not to those who question her.

Asked if the saints are the same age, she answered that she had not leave to say.

Asked if the saints spoke at the same time, or one after another, she answered: "I have not leave to tell you; nevertheless I have always had counsel from both."

Asked which one appeared first, she answered: "I did not recognize them immediately; I knew well enough once, but I have forgotten; if I had leave I would gladly tell you. It is written down in the register at Poitiers." She added that she had received comfort from St. Michael.

Asked which of the apparitions came to her first, she answered that St. Michael came first.

Asked whether it was a long time ago that she first heard the voice of St. Michael, she answered: "I do not speak of St. Michael's voice, but of his great comfort."

Asked which was the first voice which came to her when she was about thirteen, she answered that it was St. Michael whom she saw before her eyes; and he was not alone, but accompanied by many angels from heaven. She said also that she came into France only by the instruction of God.

Asked if she saw St. Michael and these angels corporeally and in reality, she answered: "I saw them with my bodily eyes as well as I see you; and when they left me, I wept; and I fain would have had them take me with them too."

Asked in what form St. Michael appeared, she answered: "There is as yet no reply to that, for I have not had leave to answer."

Asked what St. Michael said to her the first time, she answered: "You will get no further reply to-day." She said the voices told her to answer boldly. She said she had indeed once told her king everything that had been revealed to her, since it concerned him. She said, however, that she had not yet leave to reveal what St. Michael said. She added that she wished her examiner had a copy of the book at Poitiers, provided that God desired it.

Asked if the voices told her not to tell her revelations without their permission, she answered: "I will not answer you further about that; and what I have permission to, that I will gladly answer. If the voices forbade me, I did not understand."

Asked what sign she gives that this revelation comes from God, and that it is St. Catherine and St. Margaret who speak to her, she answered: "I have told you often enough that it is St. Catherine and St. Margaret; believe me if you will."

Asked if it is forbidden for her to tell, she answered: "I have not quite understood whether that is permitted or not."

Asked how she can distinguish such points as she will answer, and such as she will not, she answered that on some points she had asked permission, and on some points she had received it. Furthermore she said she would rather be torn asunder by horses than have come to France without God's leave.

Asked if God ordered her to wear a man's dress, she answered that the dress is a small, nay, the least thing. Nor did she put on man's dress by the advice of any man whatsoever; she did not put it on, nor did she do aught, but by the command of God and the angels.

Asked whether it seemed to her that this command to assume male attire was lawful, she answered: "Everything I have done is at God's command; and if He had ordered me to assume a different habit, I should have done it, because it would have been His command."

Asked if she did it at the order of Robert de Baudricourt she said no.

Asked if she thought she had done well to take man's dress, she answered that everything she did at God's command she thought well done, and hoped for good warrant and succour in it.

Asked if, in this particular case, by taking man's dress, she thought she had done well, she answered that she had done nothing in the world but by God's commands.

Asked whether, when she saw the voice coming to her, there was a light, she answered that there was a great deal of light on all sides, as was most fitting. She added to the examiner that not all the light came to him alone!

*   *   *

Asked whether, when she went to Orleans, she had a standard or banner, in French *estandart ou banière*, and what colour it was, she answered she had a banner, with a field sown with lilies; the world was depicted on it, and two angels, one at each side; it was white, of white linen or boucassin, and on it were written, she thought, these names, JHESUS MARIA; and it was fringed with silk.

Asked if these names JHESUS MARIA were written above, or below, or at the side, she answered, at the side, she believed.

Asked which she preferred, her standard or her sword, she answered she much preferred her standard to her sword.

Asked who persuaded her to have this painting on her standard, she answered: "I have told you often enough that I have done nothing but by God's command." She said also that she herself bore the standard, when attacking the enemy, so as not to kill anyone; she never has killed anyone, she said.

Asked what force her king gave her when he set her to work, she answered that he gave her 10 or 12,000 men; and she went first to Orleans, to the fortress of Saint-Loup, and then to the fortress of the Bridge.

Asked to which fortress she ordered her men to retire, she says she does not remember. She added that she was confident of raising the siege of Orleans, for it had been revealed to her, and she had told the king so before going there.

Asked whether, when the assault was to be made, she did not tell her men that she would receive arrows, crossbolts and stones hurled by catapults or cannons, she answered no; there were a hundred wounded, or more. But she had indeed told her men not to fear and they would raise the siege. She said also that at the assault upon the fortress of the Bridge she was wounded in the neck by an arrow or crossbolt; but she received great comfort from St. Margaret, and was better in a fortnight. But she did not on account of that give up her riding or work.

Asked if she knew beforehand that she would be wounded, she answered that she did indeed, and she had told her king so; but that notwithstanding she would not give up her work. And it was revealed to her by the voices of the two saints, namely the blessed Catherine and Margaret. She added that she herself was the first to plant the ladder against the said fortress of the Bridge; and as she was raising the ladder she was wounded in the neck with the crossbolt, as she had said.

*   *   *

Asked on the subject of the woman's dress offered her so that she might hear Mass, she answered that she would not put it on till it should please Our Lord. And if it be that she must be brought to judgment she requests the Lords of the Church to grant her the mercy of a woman's dress and a hood for her head; she would die rather than turn back from what Our Lord commanded her; she firmly believed God would not let her be brought so low, or be presently without His help or miracle.

Asked why, if she wore man's dress at God's bidding, she asked for a woman's robe in the event of her death, she answered: "It is enough for me that it be long."

Asked if her godmother, who saw the fairies, was held to be a wise woman, she answered that she was held and reputed to be an honest woman, and not a witch or sorceress.

Asked whether her saying she would take a woman's dress if they would let her go would please God, she answered that if she were given permission to go in woman's dress she would immediately put on man's dress and do what Our Lord bade her. So she had formerly answered: and nothing would induce her to swear not to take up arms or to wear man's dress, to accomplish our Lord's will.

Asked about the age of the garments worn by St. Catherine and St. Margaret, she answered: "You already have my reply on this matter, and you will get none other from me. I have answered you as best I can."

Asked if she did not believe heretofore that the fairies were evil spirits, she answered she knew nothing of that.

Asked how she knew that St. Catherine and St. Margaret hated the English, she answered: "They love those whom God loves, and hate whom He hates."

Asked if God hated the English, she answered that of God's love or His hatred for the English, or of what He would do to their souls, she knew nothing, but she was certain that, excepting those who died there, they would be driven out of France, and God would send victory to the French and against the English.

Asked if God was for the English when they were prospering in France, she answered that she knew not whether God hated the French, but she believed it was His will to suffer them to be beaten for their sins, if they were in a state of sin.

*　　*　　*

The Trial for Relapse

On Monday following, the day after Holy Trinity Sunday, we the said judges repaired to Jeanne's prison to observe her state and disposition. ＊ ＊ ＊

Now because the said Jeanne was wearing a man's dress, a short mantle, a hood, a doublet and other garments used by men (which at our order she had recently put off in favour of woman's dress), we questioned her to find out when and for what reason she had resumed man's dress and rejected woman's clothes. Jeanne said she had but recently resumed man's dress and rejected woman's clothes.

Asked why she had resumed it, and who had compelled her to wear it, she answered that she had taken it of her own will, under no compulsion, as she preferred man's to woman's dress.

She was told that she had promised and sworn not to wear man's dress again, and answered that she never meant to take such an oath.

Asked for what reason she had assumed male costume, she answered that it was more lawful and convenient for her to wear it, since she was among men, than to wear woman's dress. She said she had resumed it because the promises made to her had not been kept, which were to permit her to go to Mass and receive her Saviour, and to take off her chains.

Asked whether she had not abjured and sworn in particular not to resume this male costume, she answered that she would rather die than be in chains, but if she were allowed to go to Mass, if her chains were taken off and she were put in a gracious prison and were given a woman as companion, she would be good and obey the Church.

As we her judges had heard from certain people that she had not yet cut herself off from her illusions and pretended revelations, which she had previously renounced, we asked her whether she had not since Thursday heard the voices of St. Catherine and St. Margaret. She answered yes.

Asked what they told her, she answered that they told her God had sent her word through St. Catherine and St. Margaret of the great pity of this treason by which she consented to abjure and recant in order to save her life; that she had damned herself to save her life. She said that before Thursday they told her what to do and say then, which she did. Further her voices told her, when she was on the scaffold or platform before the people, to answer the preacher boldly. The said Jeanne declared that he was a false preacher, and had accused her of many things she had not done. She said that if she declared God had not sent her she would damn herself, for in truth she was sent from God. She said that her voices had since told her that she had done a great evil in declaring that what she had done was wrong. She said that what she had declared and recanted on Thursday was done only for fear of the fire.

Asked if she believed her voices to be St. Catherine and St. Margaret, she answered yes, and they came from God.

Asked to speak truthfully of the crown which is mentioned above, she replied: "In everything, I told you the truth about it in my trial, as well as I could."

*　　*　　*

REVIEW QUESTIONS

1. Why do the prosecutors seem preoccupied with the issues of Jeanne's dress and appearance?

2. How can she be tried for heresy?
3. How can we explain Jeanne's effect on contemporaries?

The Distribution of Wealth in Tuscany in 1427

In 1427, the republic of Florence instituted a new and complex system of taxation that assessed payment not on income but on wealth, minus some deductions. The records from this tax, called the catasto, *provide a very detailed portrait of households in Florence, as well as the towns, smaller cities, and countryside of Tuscany. The following table breaks down wealth by real property, mainly land; movables, things like animals and furniture; and shares in the public debt, minus the deductions for items like the family's house, tools, and a per capita exemption. This table provides a snapshot of the households of Florence; nowhere else in Europe provides such a detailed look at its population. The historians David Herlihy and Christiane Klapisch-Zuber created computer files for the individual returns and produced this table.*

From *Tuscans and Their Families,* by David Herlihy and Christiane Klapisch-Zuber (New Haven, Conn.: Yale University Press, 1985), p. 94.

Regional Distribution of Wealth in Tuscany according to Residence, 1427*

	Florence	Six Large Cities	Fifteen Towns	Countryside	Total
Nmbr Hhlds	9,946	6,724	5,994	37,266	59,890
Percent	16.2	11.2	10.0	62.2	100.0
Nmbr Persons	37,245	26,315	24,809	175,840	264,210
Percent	14.1	10.0	9.4	66.5	100.0
Real Property	4,128,024	1,137,466	614,446	2,178,253	8,058,189
Percent	51.2	14.1	7.6	17.0	100.0
Movables	3,467,707	585,357	170,245	223,792	4,447,101
Percent	78.0	13.2	3.8	5.0	100.0
Public Debt	2,573,378	3,438	1,888	1,337	2,580,041
Percent	99.7	0.1	0.1	0.1	100.0
Total Wealth	10,169,109	1,726,261	786,579	2,403,382	15,085,331
Percent	67.4	11.4	5.2	15.0	100.0
Deductions	2,504,041	332,763	135,341	321,205	3,293,350
Percent	76.0	10.1	4.1	9.8	100.0
Taxable Wealth	7,665,068	1,393,498	651,238	2,082,177	11,791,981
Percent	65.0	11.8	5.5	17.1	100.0

* Values are in gold florins. Figures do not include the personal deduction of 200 florins per person allowed at Florence and 50 florins at Pisa.

REVIEW QUESTIONS

1. Where was wealth concentrated, and what trends might have accounted for this distribution?
2. All of Florentine Tuscany contained about a 250,000 people, and Renaissance Florence itself fewer than 40,000. What do these numbers reveal about the plague and its consequences?
3. Florence, with one-sixth of the households, had over three-quarters of the deductions. What might have accounted for this disparity?

POPE PIUS II

FROM *Commentaries*

Aeneas Silvio Piccolomini (1405–1464) was born into an important aristocratic family in Siena. He received a fine humanist education and pursued a career in the church, where he rose in the ranks of papal diplomats. He became archbishop of Siena in 1450, a cardinal in 1456, and to his surprise was elected pope in 1458, taking the name Pius II. He spent most of his pontificate in a fruitless and very frustrating effort to organize a Crusade against the Ottoman Turks. This excerpt from his autobiography, the Commentaries—*a work not published in his lifetime— is a unique account of a papal election—his own. In this work, the pope writes about himself in the third person, as Aeneas. Rodrigo Borgia, the Spanish cardinal, was later elected Pope Alexander VI (1492–1503).*

From *Memoirs of a Renaissance Pope*, edited by Leona C. Gabel, translated by Florence A. Gragg (New York: Putnam, 1959), pp. 79–88.

* * *

Ten days after Calixtus's death the other eighteen cardinals entered the conclave, while the whole city waited in suspense for the outcome; though indeed it was common talk that Aeneas, Cardinal of Siena, would be pope, since no one was held in higher esteem.

The conclave was held in the apostolic palace at St. Peter's, where two halls and two chapels were set apart for it. In the larger chapel were constructed cells in which the cardinals might eat and sleep; the smaller, called the chapel of San Niccolò, was reserved for discussion and the election of the pope. The halls were places where all might walk about freely.

On the day of their entrance nothing was done about the election. On the next day certain capitulations were announced, which they agreed should be observed by the new pope, and each swore that he would abide by them, should the lot fall on him. On the third day after mass, when they came to the scrutiny, it was found that Filippo, Cardinal of Bologna, and Aeneas, Cardinal of Siena, had an equal number of votes, five apiece. No one else had more than three. On that ballot, whether from strategy or dislike, no one voted for Guillaume, Cardinal of Rouen.

The cardinals were accustomed, after the result of the scrutiny was announced, to sit and talk together in case any wished to change his mind and transfer the vote he had given one to another (a method called "by accession"), for in this way they more easily reach an agreement. This procedure was omitted after the first scrutiny owing to the opposition of those who had received no votes and therefore could not now be candidates for accession. They adjourned for luncheon and then there were many private conferences. The richer and more influential members of the college summoned the rest and sought to gain the papacy for themselves or their friends. They begged, promised, threatened, and some, shamelessly casting aside all decency, pleaded their own causes and claimed the papacy as their right. Among these were Guillaume, Cardinal of Rouen, Pietro, Cardinal of San Marco, and Giovanni, Cardinal of Pavia; nor did the Cardinal of Lerida neglect his own interests. Each had a great deal to say for himself. Their rivalry was extraordinary, their energy unbounded. They took no rest by day or sleep by night.

Rouen, however, did not fear these men so much as he did Aeneas and the Cardinal of Bologna, toward whom he saw the majority of the votes inclining. But he was especially afraid of Aeneas, whose silence he had no doubt would prove far more effective than the barkings of the rest. Therefore he would summon now some, now others, and upbraid them as follows: "What is Aeneas to you? Why do you think him worthy of the papacy? Will you give us a lame, poverty-stricken pope? How shall a destitute pope restore a destitute church, or an ailing pope an ailing church? He has but recently come from Germany. We do not know him. Perhaps he will even transfer the Curia thither. And look at his writings! Shall we set a poet in Peter's place? Shall we govern the Church by the laws of the heathen? Or do you think Filippo of Bologna is to be preferred?—a stiff-necked fellow, who has not the wit to rule himself, and will not listen to those who show him the right course. I am the senior cardinal. You know I am not without wisdom. I am learned in pontifical law and can boast of royal blood. I am rich in friends and resources with which I can succor the impoverished Church. I hold also not a few ecclesiastical benefices, which I shall distribute among you and the others, when I resign them."

He would then add many entreaties and if they had no effect, he would resort to threats. If anyone brought up his past simony as an indication that in his hands the papacy would be for sale, he did not deny that his past life had been tainted with that stain but swore that in the future his hands should be clean. He was supported by Alain, Cardinal of Avignon, who lent him every assistance in his power, not so much because he was a Frenchman siding with a Frenchman as because, at the elevation of Guillaume, he expected to obtain his house in Rome, the church of Rouen, and the vice chancellorship. Not a few were won over by Rouen's splendid promises and were caught like flies by their gluttony. And the tunic of Christ without Christ was being sold.

Many cardinals met in the privies as being a secluded and retired place. Here they agreed as to how they might elect Guillaume pope and they bound themselves by written pledges and by oath. Guillaume trusted them and was presently promising benefices and preferment and dividing provinces among them. A fit place for such a pope to be elected! For where could one more appropriately enter into a foul covenant than in privies? Guillaume could certainly count on the two Greeks, the Cardinals of Genoa, San Sisto, Avignon, Colonna, and Pavia. The Vice-Chancellor, the Cardinals of Bologna, Orsini, and Sant' Anastasia were doubtful and seemed likely to accede to him if pushed a little. Indeed they had almost given him definite grounds for hope. Since it now appeared that eleven were agreed, they did not doubt that they would at once get the twelfth. For when it has come to this point, some one is always at hand to say, "I too make you pope," to win the favor that utterance always brings. They thought therefore that the thing was as good as done and were only waiting for daylight to go to the scrutiny.

Some time after midnight the Cardinal of Bologna went hurriedly to Aeneas's cell and waking him said, "Look here, Aeneas! Don't you know that we already have a pope? Some of the cardinals have met in the privies and decided to elect Guillaume. They are only waiting for daylight. I advise you to get up and go and offer him your vote before he is elected, for fear that if he is elected with you against him, he will make trouble for you. I intend to take care not to fall into the old trap. I know what it means to have the pope your enemy. I have had experience with Calixtus, who never gave me a friendly look, because I had not voted for him. It seems to me expedient to curry favor beforehand with the man who is going to be pope. I offer you the advice I am taking myself."

Aeneas answered, "Filippo, away with you and your advice! No one shall persuade me to vote for a man I think utterly unworthy to be the successor of St. Peter. Far from me be such a sin! I will be clean of that crime and my conscience shall not prick me. You say it is hard not to have the pope well-disposed to you. I have no fears on that score. I know he will not murder me because I have not voted for him. 'But,' you say, 'he will not love you, will not make you presents, will not help you. You will feel the pinch of poverty.' Poverty is not hard for one accustomed to it. I have led a life of indigence heretofore; what matter if I die indigent? He will not take from me the Muses, who are all the sweeter in humble fortunes.

"But I am not the man to believe that God will allow the Church, His Bride, to perish in the hands of the Cardinal of Rouen. For what is more alien to the profession of Christ than that His Vicar should be a slave to simony and lewdness? The Divine Mercy will not endure that this palace, which has been the dwelling of so many Holy Fathers, shall become a den of thieves or a brothel of whores. The apostleship is bestowed by God, not by men. Those who have conspired to commit the papacy to Rouen are men; and men's schemes are vain—who does not know it? Well has their conspiracy been made in the privies! Their plots too will have to retire and, like the Arian heresy, their most foul contrivings will end in a most foul place. Tomorrow will show that the Bishop of Rome is chosen by God not by men. As for you, if you are a Christian, you will not choose as Christ's Vicar him whom you know to be a limb of the devil." With these words he frightened Filippo from going over to Rouen.

Next Aeneas went at daybreak to Rodrigo, the Vice-Chancellor, and asked whether he had sold himself to Rouen. "What would you have me do?" he answered. "The thing is settled. Many of the cardinals have met in the privies and decided to elect him. It is not for my advantage to remain with a small minority out of favor with a new pope. I am joining the majority and I have looked out for my own interests. I shall not lose the chancellorship; I have a note from Rouen assuring me of that. If I do not vote for him, the others will elect him anyway and I shall be stripped of my office." Aeneas said to him, "You young fool! Will you then put an enemy of your nation in the Apostle's chair? And will you put faith in the note of a man who is faithless? You will have the note; Avignon will have the chancellorship. For what has been promised you has been promised him also and solemnly affirmed. Will faith be kept with him or with you? Will a Frenchman be more friendly to a Frenchman or to a Catalan? Will he be more concerned for a foreigner or for his own countryman? Take care, you inexperienced boy! Take care, you fool! And if you have no thought for the Church of Rome, if you have no regard for the Christian religion and despise God, for Whom you are preparing such a vicar, at least take thought for yourself, for you will find yourself among the hindmost, if a Frenchman is pope."

The Vice-Chancellor listened patiently to these words of his friend and completely abandoned his purpose.

After this Aeneas, meeting the Cardinal of Pavia, said to him, "I hear that you too are with those who have decided to elect Rouen. Is this true?" He replied, "You have heard correctly. I have agreed to give him my vote so that I may not be left alone. For his victory is already certain; so many have declared for him." Aeneas said, "I thought you a different man from what I find you. Only see how much you have degenerated from your ancestors! Your father's brother (or was he your mother's?), Branda, Cardinal of Piacenza, when the papacy was beyond the mountains in Germany (for John XXIII, when he appointed the Council of Constance, had carried the Roman Curia across the Alps) never rested till he brought the Holy See back to Italy. It was owing to his diplomacy, devotion, and genius that on the withdrawal of the contestants for the papacy, Martin V, a Roman of the house of Colonna, was elected pope. Branda brought the Apostolic Curia back from Germany to Italy; you, his nephew, are going to transfer it from Italy to France. But Rouen will prefer his own nation to Italy and a Frenchman will be off to France with the supreme office.

"You say, 'He is under oath. He will not go outside this province without the decree of the senate and if he wishes to go, we will not consent.' What cardinal will dare oppose him when he is once seated on the apostolic throne? You will be the first, when you have secured some rich benefice, to say, 'Go where you will, Holy Father.' And what is our Italy without the Bishop of Rome? We still have the Apostleship though we have lost the Imperium, and in this one light we see light. Shall we be deprived of this with your sympathy, persuasion, help? A French pope will either go to France—and then our dear country is bereft of its splendor; or he will stay among us—and Italy, the queen of nations, will serve a foreign master, while we shall be the slaves of the French. The kingdom of Sicily will come into the hands of the French. The French will possess all the cities and strongholds of the Church. You might have taken warning from Calixtus, during whose papacy there was nothing the Catalans did not get. After trying the Catalans are you so eager to try the French? You

will soon be sorry if you do! You will see the college filled with Frenchmen and the papacy will never again be wrested from them. Are you so dull that you do not realize that this will lay a yoke upon your nation forever?

"And what shall I say of this man's life? Are you not ashamed to entrust Christ's office to a slippery fellow who would sell his own soul? A fine bridegroom you are planning for the bride of Christ! You are trusting a lamb to a wolf. Where is your conscience? your zeal for justice? your common sense? Have you so far fallen below your true self? I suppose we have not often heard you say that it would be the Church's ruin if it fell into Rouen's hands? and that you would rather die than vote for this very man? What is the reason for this change? Has he suddenly been transformed from a demon to an angel of light? Or have you been changed from an angel of light to the devil, that you love his lust and filth and greed? What has become of your love for your country and your continual protestations that you preferred Italy above all other nations? I used to think that if everyone else fell away from devotion to her, you never would. You have failed me; nay, more, you have failed yourself and Italy, your country, unless you come to your senses."

The Cardinal of Pavia was stunned by these words and, overcome alike with grief and shame, he burst into tears. Then stifling his sobs he said, "I am ashamed, Aeneas. But what am I to do? I have given my promise. If I do not vote for Rouen, I shall be charged with treachery." Aeneas answered, "So far as I can see, it has come to the point where you will be guilty of treachery whichever way you turn. You now have to choose whether you prefer to betray Italy, your country, and the Church or the Bishop of Rouen." Convinced by these arguments Pavia decided it was less shameful to fail Rouen.

When Pietro, Cardinal of San Marco, learned of the conspiracy of the French and had lost hope of getting the papacy himself, actuated alike by patriotism and hatred of Rouen, he began to go to the Italian cardinals urging and warning them not to abandon their country; and he did not rest until he had gathered all the Italians except Colonna in the cell of the Cardinal of Genoa, revealed the conspiracy that had been made in the privies, and showed them that the Church would be ruined and Italy a slave forever, if Rouen should obtain the papacy. He implored them individually to show themselves men, to consult for the good of Mother Church and unhappy Italy, to put aside their enmities for one another and choose an Italian rather than a foreigner for pope. If they listened to him, they would prefer Aeneas to all others. There were present seven cardinals: Genoa, Orsini, Bologna, San Marco, Pavia, Siena, and Sant' Anastasia. All approved Pavia's words except Aeneas, who thought himself unworthy of so exalted an office.

The next day they went as usual to mass and then began the scrutiny. A golden chalice was placed on the altar and three cardinals, the Bishop of Ruthen, the Presbyter of Rouen, and the Deacon of Colonna, were set to watch it and see that there should be no cheating. The other cardinals took their seats and then, rising in order of rank and age, each approached the altar and deposited in the chalice a ballot on which was written the name of his choice for pope. When Aeneas came up to put in his ballot, Rouen, pale and trembling, said, "Look, Aeneas! I commend myself to you"—certainly a rash thing to say when it was not allowable to change what he had written. But ambition overcame prudence. Aeneas said, "Do you commend yourself to a worm like me?" and without another word he dropped his ballot in the cup and went back to his place.

When all had voted, a table was placed in the middle of the room and the three cardinals mentioned above turned out upon it the cupful of votes. Then they read aloud the ballots one after another and noted down the names written on them. And there was not a single cardinal who did not likewise make notes of those named, that there might be no possibility of trickery. This proved to be to Aeneas's advantage, for when the votes were counted and the teller, Rouen, announced that Aeneas had eight, though the rest said nothing about

another man's loss, Aeneas did not allow himself to be defrauded. "Look more carefully at the ballots," he said to the teller, "for I have nine votes." The others agreed with him. Rouen said nothing, as if he had merely made a mistake.

This was the form of the ballot: The voter wrote with his own hand, "I, Peter (or John or whatever his name was) choose for pope Aeneas, Cardinal of Siena, and Jaime, Cardinal of Lisbon"; for it is permitted to vote for one or two or more, on the understanding that the one first named is the one preferred, but if he does not have enough votes to be elected, the next is to be counted in his place, that an agreement may more easily be reached. But a thing advantageous in itself some men pervert to base ends, as Latino Orsini did on that day. He named seven in the hope that those he named might be influenced by that good turn either to accede to him in that scrutiny or to vote for him in another; although he who has the reputation of a cheat does not gain much by tricks.

When the result of the scrutiny was made known, it was found, as we have said before, that nine cardinals (Genoa, Orsini, Lerida, Bologna, San Marco, Santi Quattro Coronati, Zamora, Pavia, and Portugal) had voted for Aeneas; the Cardinal of Rouen had only six votes, and the rest were far behind. Rouen was petrified when he saw himself so far outstripped by Aeneas and all the rest were amazed, for never within the memory of man had anyone polled as many as nine votes by scrutiny. Since no one had received enough votes for election, they decided to resume their seats and try the method that is called "by accession," to see if perhaps it might be possible to elect a pope that day. And here again Rouen indulged in empty hopes. All sat pale and silent in their places as if entranced. For some time no one spoke, no one opened his lips, no one moved any part of his body except the eyes, which kept glancing all about. It was a strange silence and a strange sight, men sitting there like their own statues; no sound to be heard, no movement to be seen. They remained thus for some moments, those inferior in rank waiting for their superiors to begin the accession.

Then Rodrigo, the Vice-Chancellor, rose and said, "I accede to the Cardinal of Siena," an utterance which was like a dagger in Rouen's heart, so pale did he turn. A silence followed and each man looking at his neighbor, began to indicate his sentiments by gestures. By this time it looked as if Aeneas would be pope and some, fearing this result, left the conclave, pretending physical needs, but really with the purpose of escaping the fate of that day. Those who thus withdrew were the Cardinals of Ruthen and San Sisto. However, as no one followed them, they soon returned. Then Jacopo, Cardinal of Sant' Anastasia, said, "I accede to the Cardinal of Siena." At this all appeared even more stunned, like people in a house shaken by unprecedented earthquakes, and lost the power of speech.

Aeneas now lacked but one vote, for twelve would elect a pope. Realizing this, Cardinal Prospero Colonna thought that he must get for himself the glory of announcing the pope. He rose and was about to pronounce his vote with the customary dignity, when he was seized by the Cardinals of Nicaea and Rouen and sharply rebuked for wishing to accede to Aeneas. When he persisted in his intention, they tried to get him out of the room by force, resorting even to such means to snatch the papacy from Aeneas. But Prospero, who, though he had voted for the Cardinal of Rouen on his ballot, was nevertheless bound to Aeneas by ties of old friendship, paid no attention to their abuse and empty threats. Turning to the other cardinals, he said, "I too accede to the Cardinal of Siena and I make him pope." When they heard this, the courage of the opposition failed and all their machinations were shattered.

All the cardinals immediately fell at Aeneas's feet and saluted him as Pope. Then they resumed their seats and ratified his election without a dissenting vote. At this point Bessarion, Cardinal of Nicaea, speaking for himself and for the others who had voted for the Cardinal of Rouen, said, "Your Holiness, we approve your election, which we do not doubt is of God. We thought before and still think that you are worthy of this office. The reason we did not vote for you was your infirmity. We thought your gout the one thing against you; for the Church needs an active man who has the physical strength to take long journeys and meet the dangers which we fear threaten us from the Turks. You on the contrary need rest. It was this consideration that won us to the side of the Cardinal of Rouen. If you were physically strong, there is no one we should have preferred. But, since God is satisfied, we must needs be satisfied too. God Himself, who has chosen you, will make good the defect in your feet and will not punish our ignorance. We revere you as Pope, we elect you again, so far as is in our power, and we will serve you faithfully."

Aeneas answered, "Your Eminence of Nicaea, your opinion of us, as we understand it, is much higher than our own, when you attribute to us no defect except that in our feet. We are not ignorant that our imperfection is more general and we realize that our failings, which might justly have caused us to be rejected as pope, are almost innumerable. As to any virtues which might raise us to this post, we know of none; and we should declare ourselves utterly unworthy and should refuse the honor offered us, if we did not fear the judgment of Him Who has called us. For what is done by two thirds of the sacred college, that is surely of the Holy Ghost, which may not be resisted. Therefore we obey the divine summons and we praise you, Your Eminence of Nicaea, and those who voted with you. If, following the dictates of your conscience, you thought we ought not to be elected as being inadequate, you will still be welcomed by us, who attribute our calling not to this man or that but to the whole college and to God Himself, from Whom cometh every good and perfect gift."

With these words he took off the garments he was wearing and put on the white tunic of Christ. When asked by what name he wished to be called, he answered, "Pius," and he was at once addressed as Pius II. Then after swearing to observe the capitulations that had been announced in the college two days before, he took his place by the altar and was again reverenced by the cardinals, who kissed his feet, hands, and cheek. After that the election of a pope was proclaimed to the people from a high window and it was announced that he who had been Cardinal of Siena was now Pope Pius II.

*   *   *

REVIEW QUESTIONS

1. What were the divisions among the eighteen cardinals, and who were the ones with a chance of becoming pope?
2. Are there any signs in this candid account of the election that Aeneas is hiding something about his own ambitions?
3. In the end, what factors counted the most in Aeneas's election?

11 COMMERCE, CONQUEST, AND COLONIZATION, 1300–1600

The commercial revolution of the Middle Ages built on and fostered a desire by Europeans to extend trading networks beyond their homelands. Trade was not the only motive for travel. Religious pilgrimages and missions, Crusades, and a desire to pillage their neighbors still motivated some people to venture beyond the frontiers of Western Christendom—their Europe. Successful trade depended on reliable knowledge about the world. Better maps and accounts of travels made it possible for people to find their way over the vast stretches of Asia to China or across the Atlantic to Vinland. The most adventurous travel was by sea, and better ships, sails, ropes, compasses, and astrolabes made it easier to sail long distances out of the sight of land. Traveling by galleys in the Mediterranean was a little easier than sailing in the Atlantic. The great inland sea, the Mediterranean, whose waters touched Africa, Asia, and Europe, witnessed the first advances in sailing techniques, and also the first experiments in European colonization on islands like Crete and Cyprus. Muslim merchants continued to dominate the trading networks in the Indian Ocean.

After 1250, Europeans increasingly visited, traded with, and eventually colonized the various "new worlds" that lay in all directions. These places were, of course, not new to their indigenous inhabitants. Northern travel was the least promising because of the difficult Arctic climate, yet the Scandinavians had established a precarious settlement on Greenland in around 1000 that lasted until about 1450. Plague, climatic changes, and the hardships of making a living in the Arctic may explain the eventual retreat of the Vikings from parts of the north. Yet memories persisted about the mysterious Vinland. Modern excavations have proved that Vikings visited and for a time lived on North American soil. English and French fishing ships continued to visit the Grand Banks for its wonderful supplies of cod. In the 1490s, both states resumed efforts to explore the North Atlantic. English kings supported the voyages of John and Sebastian Cabot out of Bristol to find a northern passage to China and the fabled riches of the East.

Beginning in the mid-thirteenth century, missionaries like William of Ru-bruck and intrepid merchants like the Polos of Venice followed the Silk Road across central Asia to China, "the east beyond the east." A small trade contin-ued along this route to Europe until the mid-fourteenth century, when plague and changes in the Mongol Empire made travel across Asia more difficult. Ac-counts of the East and its immense riches in spices, precious gems and gold, and silk continued to intrigue Europeans. Muslim travelers like Ibn Battuta displayed a similar curiosity about Muslim states across Asia. In the fifteenth century, Chinese explorers made it all the way to Madagascar off the coast of southern Africa. The impulse to explore so far from home waned when the emperors stopped supporting these trading voyages. If Europeans wanted regular trade with China, they needed to find new, safe routes not controlled by the emerging Islamic Ottoman and Mamluk Empires in the East. The Ottoman conquest of Constantinople in 1453 choked off trade routes to the East and encouraged west-ern Europeans like Columbus to look for new ways of reaching Asia. When the Turks absorbed the Mamluk state in 1517, they became an important presence in the Indian Ocean and found the Portuguese already there.

The Portuguese, facing the Atlantic, the Ocean Sea, began to explore the west coast of Africa in search of gold. In the fourteenth century, Portuguese and Italian sailors found the islands—the Azores and Madeira, both uninhabited, and the Canaries, peopled by the Canarians. Spanish and French traders and explorers also took an interest in the opportunities for trade and settlement, but only the Portuguese continued to sail south beyond the Saharan coast. Mer-chants and sailors from Lisbon hoped to confirm ancient speculations that it was possible to circumnavigate Africa and find a way to the Indian Ocean. Explora-tions of the West African coast opened up a lucrative trade in gold and slaves that made tiny Portugal a world power. The patronage of the infante Henry the Navigator (1394–1460) established a seafaring tradition that enabled Bartolo-meu Dias to round the Cape of Good Hope in 1488. Vasco de Gama sailed for India in 1497 and eventually rewarded his investors with fabulous profits in spices. The opening up of sub-Saharan Africa to trade was not yet followed by significant colonization, as Europeans did not thrive in the tropics.

Only after reaching the "new worlds" of Asia and Africa did Europeans again "discover" the last new world, the Americas. It is important to recognize that Europeans had some previous experiences with colonies and new peoples be-fore Columbus. The Italian-born Christopher Columbus (c. 1450–1506) con-vinced Isabella of Castile and Ferdinando of Aragon to gamble on a sea route across the perilous Atlantic to the East. Until his dying day, Columbus remained convinced that the people he called Indians lived off the coast of Asia, though he must have been puzzled by his repeated failures to reach the Chinese and Japa-nese. Still, Columbus's accomplishments as a sailor were striking. His search for wealth and trade was frustrated, however, and he laid the foundations for trad-

ing in slaves and exploiting the Indians and their lands in the search for gold that reached its bloody conclusion with Hernando Cortéz in Mexico in 1519 and and the Pizarros in Peru in 1533. In the sixteenth century, the Spanish, and soon the Portuguese in Brazil, began to establish permanent colonies in their new territories. Soon other European powers, notably the Dutch, English, and French, would follow in their wake, first as explorers, traders, pirates, and slave traders.

At the same time, a demographic catastrophe occurred in the Americas as the new diseases like smallpox which the Europeans brought with them wiped out a high percentage, in some places perhaps as much as 90 percent, of the Indians. As the Indians completely disappeared in some places and were greatly reduced in numbers in others, colonists planning to make money in the mines or the newly established sugar plantations increasingly relied on African slaves for labor. Supplying slaves to the last new world became an increasingly lucrative trade for the Portuguese, and soon enough for the Dutch and English as well. This first global economy, involving trade networks that stretched from Lisbon to Nanking, from the Senegal River in Africa to Vera Cruz in Mexico, enriched some Europeans and laid the foundations for colonial empires on which the sun never set.

WILLIAM OF RUBRUCK

FROM *On the Mongols*

William of Rubruck, a Franciscan monk from Flanders, was sent in 1253 to the Mongols by Louis IX of France, then on crusade in the East. The Mongol Empire, established by Chingis, or Genghis, Chan (1167–1227) and extended by successors like Mangu (1251–1259), had sent scouting parties as far west as Poland and Hungary. In the first section of this account, William describes Mongol culture to the French king. In the second section, he is at the Mongol capital of Caracorum in Mongolia, seeking another audience with Mangu.

From *Mission to Asia*, edited by Christopher Dawson (Cambridge, Mass.: Medieval Academy of America, 1980), pp. 95–98, 100–6, 194–97.

*   *   *

Commerce and Conquest

The married women make for themselves really beautiful carts which I would not know how to describe for you except by a picture; in fact I would have done you paintings of everything if I only knew how to paint. A wealthy Mongol or Tartar may well have a hundred or two hundred such carts with chests. Baatu has twenty-six wives and each of these has a large house, not counting the other small ones which are placed behind the large one and which are, as it were, chambers in which their attendants live; belonging to each of these houses are a good two hundred carts. When they pitch their houses the chief wife places her dwelling at the extreme west end and after her the others according to their rank, so that the last wife will be at the far east end, and there will be the space of a stone's throw between the establishment of one wife and that of another. And so the orda of a rich Mongol will look like a large town and yet there will be very few men in it.

One woman will drive twenty or thirty carts, for the country is flat. They tie together the carts, which are drawn by oxen or camels, one after the other, and the woman will sit on the front one driving the ox while all the others follow in step. If they happen to come on a bad bit of track they loose them and lead them across it one by one. They go at a very slow pace, as a sheep or an ox might walk.

When they have pitched their houses with the door facing south, they arrange the master's couch at the northern end. The women's place is always on the east side, that is, on the left of the master of the house when he is sitting on his couch looking towards the south; the men's place is on the west side, that is, to his right.

On entering a house the men would by no means hang up their quiver in the women's section. Over the head of the master there is always an idol like a doll or little image of felt which they call the master's brother, and a similar one over the head of the mistress, and this they call the mistress's brother; they are fastened on to the wall. Higher up between these two is a thin little one which is, as it were, the guardian of the whole house. The mistress of the house places on her right side, at the foot of the couch, in a prominent position, a goat-skin stuffed with wool or other material, and next to it a tiny image turned towards her attendants and the women. By the entrance on the women's side is still another idol with a cow's udder for the women who milk the cows, for this is the women's job. On the other side of the door towards the men is another image with a mare's udder for the men who milk the mares.

When they have foregathered for a drink they first sprinkle with the drink the idol over the master's head, then all the other idols in turn; after this an attendant goes out of the house with a cup and some drinks; he sprinkles thrice towards the south, genuflecting each time; this is in honour of fire; next towards the east in honour of the air, and after that to the west in honour of water; they cast it to the north for the dead. When the master is holding his cup in his hand and is about to drink, before he does so he first pours some out on the earth as its share. If he drinks while seated on a horse, before he drinks he pours some over the neck or mane of the horse. And so when the attendant has sprinkled towards the four quarters of the earth he returns into the house; two servants with two cups and as many plates are ready to carry the drink to the master and the wife sitting beside him upon his couch. If he has several wives, she with whom he sleeps at night sits next to him during the day, and on that day all the others have to come to her dwelling to drink, and the court is held there, and the gifts which are presented to the master are placed in the treasury of that wife. Standing in the entrance is a bench with a skin of milk or some other drink and some cups.

In the winter they make an excellent drink from rice, millet, wheat and honey, which is clear like wine. Wine, too, is conveyed to them from distant regions. In the summer they do not bother about anything except cosmos. Cosmos is always to be found inside the house before the entrance door, and near it stands a musician with his instrument. Our lutes and viols I did not see there but many other instruments such as are not known among us. When the master begins to drink, then one of the attendants cries out in a loud voice "Ha!" and the musician strikes his instrument. And when it is a big feast they are holding, they all clap their hands and also dance to the sound of the instrument, the men before the master and the women before the mistress. After the master has drunk, then the attendant cries out as before and the instrument-player breaks off. Then they drink all round, the men and the women, and sometimes vie with each other in drinking in a really disgusting and gluttonous manner.

When they want to incite anyone to drink they seize him by the ears and pull them vigorously to make his gullet open, and they clap and dance in front of him. Likewise when they want to make a great feast and entertainment for anyone, one man takes a full cup and two others stand, one on his right and one on his left, and in this manner the three, singing and dancing, advance right up to him to whom they are to offer the cup, and they sing and dance before him; when he stretches out his hand to take the cup they suddenly leap back, and then they advance again as before; and in this way they make fun of him, drawing back the cup three or four times until he is in a really lively mood and wants it: then they give him the cup and sing and clap their hands and stamp with their feet while he drinks.

The Food of the Tartars

As for their food and victuals I must tell you they eat all dead animals indiscriminately and with so many flocks and herds you can be sure a great many animals do die. However, in the summer as long as they have any cosmos, that is mare's milk, they do not care about any other food. If during that time an ox or a horse happens to die, they dry the flesh by cutting it into thin strips and hanging it in the sun and the wind, and it dries immediately without salt and without any unpleasant smell. Out of the intestines of horses they make sausages which are better than pork sausages and they eat these fresh; the rest of the meat they keep for the winter. From the hide of oxen they make large jars which they dry in a wonderful way in the smoke. From the hind part of horses' hide they make very nice shoes.

They feed fifty or a hundred men with the flesh of a single sheep, for they cut it up in little bits in a dish with salt and water, making no other sauce; then with the point of a knife or a fork especially made for this purpose—like those with which we are accustomed to eat pears and apples cooked in wine—they offer to each of those standing round one or two mouthfuls, according to the number of guests. Before the flesh of the sheep is served, the master first takes what pleases him; and also if he gives anyone a special portion then the one receiving it has to eat it himself and may give it to no one else. But if he cannot eat it all he may take it away with him or give it to his servant, if he is there, to keep for him; otherwise he may put it away in his *captargac*, that is, a square bag which they carry to put all such things in: in this they also keep bones when they have not the time to give them a good gnaw, so that later they may gnaw them and no food be wasted.

*　　*　　*

The Animals They Eat, Their Clothes and Their Hunting

The great lords have villages in the south from which millet and flour are brought to them for the winter; the poor provide for themselves by trading sheep and skins; and the slaves fill their bellies with dirty water and are content with this. They also catch mice, of which many kinds abound there; mice with long tails they do not eat but give to their birds; they eat dormice and all kinds of mice with short tails. There are also many marmots there which they call *sogur* and these congregate in one burrow in the winter, twenty or thirty of them together, and they sleep for six months; these they catch in great quantities.

Also to be found there are conies with a long tail like a cat and having at the tip of the tail black and white hairs. They have many other little animals as well which are good to eat, and they are very clever at knowing the difference. I saw no deer there, I saw few hares, many gazelles; wild asses I saw in great quantities and these are like mules. I also saw another kind of animal which is called *arcali* and which has a body just like a ram's and horns twisted like a ram's but of such a size that I could scarce lift the two horns with one hand; and they make large cups out of these horns.

They have hawks, gerfalcons and peregrine falcons in great numbers and these they carry on their right hand, and they always put a little thong round the hawk's neck. This thong hangs down the middle of its breast and by it they pull down with the left hand the head and breast of the hawk when they cast it at its prey, so that it is not beaten back by the wind or carried upwards. They procure a large part of their food by the chase.

When they want to hunt wild animals they gather together in a great crowd and surround the district in which they know the animals to be, and gradually they close in until between them they shut in the animals in a circle and then they shoot at them with their arrows.

I will tell you about their garments and their clothing. From Cathay and other countries to the east, and also from Persia and other districts of the south, come cloths of silk and gold and cotton materials which they wear in the summer. From Russia, Moxel, Great Bulgaria and Pascatu, which is Greater Hungary, and Kerkis, which are all districts towards the north, and full of forests, and from many other regions in the north which are subject to them, valuable furs of many kinds are brought for them, such as I have never seen in our part of the world; and these they wear in winter. In the winter they always make at least two fur garments, one with the fur against the body, the other with the fur outside to the wind and snow, and these are usually of the skins of wolves or foxes or monkeys, and when they are sitting in

their dwelling they have another softer one. The poor make their outer ones of dog and goat.

They also make trousers out of skins. Moreover, the rich line their garments with silk stuffing which is extraordinarily soft and light and warm. The poor line their clothes with cotton material and with the softer wool which they are able to pick out from the coarser. With the coarse they make felt to cover their dwellings and coffers and also for making bedding. Also with wool mixed with a third part horse-hair they make their ropes. From felt they make saddle pads, saddle cloths and rain cloaks, which means they use a great deal of wool. You have seen the men's costume.

How the Men Shave and the Women Adorn Themselves

The men shave a square on the top of their heads and from the front corners of this they continue the shaving in strips along the sides of the head as far as the temples. They also shave their temples and neck to the top of the cervical cavity and their forehead in front to the top of the frontal bone, where they leave a tuft of hair which hangs down as far as the eyebrows. At the sides and the back of the head they leave the hair, which they make into plaits, and these they braid round the head to the ears.

The costume of the girls is no different from that of the men except that it is somewhat longer. But on the day after she is married a woman shaves from the middle of her head to her forehead, and she has a tunic as wide as a nun's cowl, and in every respect wider and longer, and open in front, and this they tie on the right side. Now in this matter the Tartars differ from the Turks, for the Turks tie their tunics on the left, but the Tartars always on the right.

They also have a head-dress which they call *bocca*, which is made out of the bark of a tree or of any other fairly light material which they can find; it is large and circular and as big as two hands can span around, a cubit and more high and square at the top like the capital of a column. This *bocca* they cover with costly silk material, and it is hollow inside, and on the capital in the middle or on the side they put a rod of quills or slender canes, likewise a cubit and more in length; and they decorate this rod at the top with peacock feathers and throughout its length all round with little feathers from the mallard's tail and also with precious stones. The wealthy ladies wear such an ornament on the top of their head and fasten it down firmly with a hood which has a hole in the top for this purpose, and in it they stuff their hair, gathering it up from the back on to the top of the head in a kind of knot and putting over it the *bocca* which they then tie firmly under the chin. So when several ladies ride together and are seen from a distance, they give the appearance of soldiers with helmets on their heads and raised lances; for the *bocca* looks like a helmet and the rod on top like a lance.

All the women sit on their horses like men, astride, and they tie their cowls with a piece of sky-blue silk round the waist, and with another strip they bind their breasts, and they fasten a piece of white stuff below their eyes which hangs down to the breast.

The women are wondrous fat and the less nose they have the more beautiful they are considered. They disfigure themselves hideously by painting their faces. They never lie down on a bed to give birth to their children.

The Duties of the Women and Their Work

It is the duty of the women to drive the carts, to load the houses on to them and to unload them, to milk the cows, to make the butter and *grut,* to dress the skins and to sew them, which they do with thread made out of tendons. They split the tendons into very thin threads and then twist these into one long thread. They also sew shoes and socks and other garments. They never wash their clothes, for they say that that makes God angry and that it would thunder if they hung them out to dry; they even beat those who do wash them and take them away from them. They are extraordinarily afraid of thunder. At such a time they turn all strangers out of their dwellings and wrap themselves in black felt in which they hide until it has passed over. They never wash their dishes, but when the meat is cooked, they wash out the bowl in which they are going to put it with some boiling broth from the cauldron which they afterwards pour back. The women also make the felt and cover the houses.

The men make bows and arrows, manufacture stirrups and bits and make saddles; they build the houses and carts, they look after the horses and milk the mares, churn the cosmos, that is the mares' milk, and make the skins in which it is kept, and they also look after the camels and load them. Both sexes look after the sheep and goats, and sometimes the men, sometimes the women, milk them. They dress skins with the sour milk of ewes, thickened and salted.

When they want to wash their hands or their head, they fill their mouth with water and, pouring this little by little from their mouth into their hands, with it they wet their hair and wash their head.

As for their marriages, you must know that no one there has a wife unless he buys her, which means that sometimes girls are quite grown up before they marry, for their parents always keep them until they sell them. They observe the first and second degrees of consanguinity, but observe no degrees of affinity; they have two sisters at the same time or one after the other. No widow among them marries, the reason being that they believe that all those who serve them in this life will serve them in the next, and so of a widow they believe that she will always return after death to her first husband. This gives rise to a shameful custom among them whereby a son sometimes takes to wife all his father's wives, except his own mother; for the orda of a father and mother always falls to the youngest son and so he himself has to provide for all his father's wives who come to him with his father's effects; and then, if he so wishes, he uses them as wives, for he does not consider an injury has been done to him if they return to his father after death.

And so when anyone has made an agreement with another to take his daughter, the father of the girl arranges a feast and she takes flight to relations where she lies hid. Then the father declares: "Now my daughter is yours; take her wherever you find her." Then he searches for her with his friends until he finds her; then he has to take her by force and bring her, as though by violence, to his house.

Of Their Justice and Judgments, Death and Burial

Concerning their penal laws I can tell you that when two men fight no one dares to interfere, even a father dare not help his son, but he who comes off the worse may appeal to the court of the lord and if the other touches him after the appeal, he is put to death. But he must go immediately without any delay and the one who has suffered the injury leads the other like a captive.

They inflict capital punishment on no one unless he has been caught in the act or confesses; but when a man is accused by a number of people, they torture him well, so that he confesses. Murder they punish by the death sentence, and also cohabiting with a woman not one's own. By one's own I mean wife or servant, for it is lawful for a man to use his slave as he will. Robbery on a grand scale they likewise punish by death. For a petty theft, such as one sheep, so long as a man has not been caught doing it often, they beat him cruelly, and if they deal him a hundred strokes, then they have to have a hundred rods. I am speaking of those who are beaten as a result of the court's sentence. Similarly they put to death false ambassadors, that is to say men who pretend they are ambassadors but are not; also sorceresses, of whom however I will tell you more later, for they consider them to be witches.

When anyone dies they mourn, wailing in a loud voice, and then they are free from paying taxes until the year is up. And if anyone is present at the death of an adult, he does not enter the dwelling of Mangu Chan for a year; if it is a child who dies he does not enter it for a month.

Near the grave of a dead man they always leave a dwelling, if he is of the nobility, that is of the family of Chingis, who was their first father and lord. The burial place of him who dies is not known; and always around those places where they bury their nobles there is a camp of men who guard the tombs. It has not come to my knowledge that they bury treasure with the dead. The Comans make a great mound over the dead man and set up a statue to him, facing the east and holding a cup in its hand in front of its navel. They also make pyramids for the rich, that is, little pointed houses; and in some places I saw large towers of baked tiles, and in others stone houses, although stones are not to be found there. I saw a man recently dead for whom they had hung up, between tall poles, the skins of sixteen horses, four facing each quarter of the earth, and they had put cosmos there for him to drink and meat for him to eat, and in spite of this they said of him that he had been baptised. Further east I saw other tombs, namely large areas strewn with stones, some round, some square and then four tall stones upright round the plot facing the four quarters of the earth.

When anyone is ill he takes to his bed and places a sign above his dwelling that there is a sick person there and that no one may enter. And so nobody visits the invalid except the one who looks after him. When anyone from one of the great ordas is sick, they place guards at a distance round the orda and they do not allow anyone to cross these bounds, for they are afraid an evil spirit or wind may come in with those entering. They summon their soothsayers as if they were their priests.

*   *   *

Friar William's Last Audience with Mangu

On the day of Pentecost Mangu Chan summoned me and the *tuin* with whom I had debated to his presence; before I went in the interpreter, Master William's son, told me we would have to return to our own country and that I was not to offer any objection for he had learned this was settled. When I came before the Chan I had to kneel down with the *tuin* beside me together with his interpreter. Then the Chan said to me: "Tell me if it is true that the other day when I sent my scribes to you, you said I was a *tuin*." I replied: "My lord, I did not say that, but, if you allow me, I will tell you the words I used." I then repeated to him what I had said and he answered: "I well thought you had not said it, for that was not the sort of thing you ought to say, but your interpreter translated badly." And he stretched out towards me the staff on which he was leaning, saying "Fear not." I smiled and said quietly: "If I were afraid I would not have come here." He enquired of the interpreter what I had said and he repeated it to him.

He then began to make a profession of his faith to me. "We Mongols," said he, "believe that there is but one God, by Whom we live and by Whom we die and towards Him we have an upright heart." I said, "God Himself will grant this for it cannot come about but by His gift." He asked what I had said and the interpreter told him. Afterwards the Chan continued: "But just as God gave different fingers to the hand so has He given different ways to men. To you God has given the Scriptures and you Christians do not observe them. You do not find in the Scriptures that a man ought to disparage another, now do you?" he said. "No," I replied, "but from the beginning I made it clear to you that I had no wish to wrangle with anyone." "My words do not apply to you," said he. "Similarly you do not find that a man ought to turn aside from justice for the sake of money." "No, my Lord," I said, "and for a truth I have not come to these parts in order to gain money, rather have I refused that which was offered to me." There was a scribe present, who bore witness to the fact that I had refused a *iascot* and some pieces of silk. "My words do not apply to you," he said. "As I was saying, God has given you the Scriptures and you do not keep them; to us, on the other hand, He has given soothsayers, and we do what they tell us, and live in peace." He drank four times, I believe, before he finished saying these things.

And while I was listening closely to hear if there was still more he wished to declare concerning his faith, he began to speak of my return saying: "You have stayed here a long time, it is my wish that you go back. You have said that you dare not take my envoys with you; are you willing to take a message and letter from me?"

From then onwards I had neither the opportunity nor the time to put the Catholic Faith before him, for a man may not say more in his presence than he desires, unless he be an envoy; an envoy can say whatever he will, and they always enquire whether he wishes to say still more. I, however, was not allowed to continue speaking, but had to listen to him and reply to the questions he put.

I then answered him that if he would have his message explained to me and put down in writing, I would gladly take it to the best of my ability. He next asked if I desired gold or silver or costly garments. I said: "Such things we do not accept, but we have no provisions and without your aid cannot leave your country." He answered: "I will arrange for you to have all that you need as far as my territory stretches, do you wish for more?" I replied, "That is sufficient for me." He then enquired: "How far do you wish to be conducted?" I said: "We can manage for ourselves when we reach the land of the King of Armenia. If I were given a guide as far as that I would be satisfied." He answered: "I will have you accompanied thus far, after that you can fend for yourselves." And he added, "There are two eyes in a head, yet although they are two, nevertheless they have but one sight, and whither the vision of one is directed so is that of the other; you came from Baatu, it therefore behoves you to return by way of him."

When he had said this I asked his leave to say a few words. "You may speak," he answered. Then I said: "My Lord, we are not warlike men, we would like to see those holding dominion over the world who would govern it most justly according to the will of God. Our duty is to teach men to live according to the will of God; for this reason did we come to these parts and we would gladly have remained here if you had allowed it. Since it is your good pleasure that we return, it must needs be; I will go back and carry your letter to the best of my ability in accordance with your commands. I would like to ask of your Eminence that, when I have taken your letter, I may be granted your permission to return to you, especially as you have some poor serfs at Bolac who speak our language and need a priest to teach them and their children their faith, and I would gladly abide with them." He replied: "Provided your masters send you back to me." I then said: "My Lord, I do not know what my masters have in mind, but I have permission from them to go wherever I will, where there is need to preach the word of God; and it seems to me that it is most necessary in these parts, therefore whether he send back an envoy to you or not, given your permission I would return."

He kept silent and sat for a long time as if turning things over in his mind, and the interpreter told me not to speak any more. However, I anxiously awaited his reply. At last he spoke: "You have a long journey ahead of you, fortify yourself with food so that you may be strong enough to reach your own country." And he had me given something to drink. I then left his presence, and never afterwards returned. If I had had the power of working miracles like Moses, he might have humbled himself.

*   *   *

REVIEW QUESTIONS

1. If William were a spy or an anthropologist, what valuable insights would he offer about Mongol culture?
2. In particular, according to William, how does the role of women in Mongol society compare with that of European women?
3. What ideas about religion determine the ways Mangu and William think about it?

IBN BATTUTA

FROM *The Travels*

Ibn Battuta (1304–c. 1377), from Tangier in Morocco, was an extraordinary traveler whose journeys took him as far as China and India. He wrote extensive accounts of his travels; here he describes Muslim Cairo in its prime before the plague.

From *The Travels of Ibn Battuta*, A.D. *1325–1354*, edited by H. A. R. Gibb (London: Hakluyt Society, 1958), pp. 41–53.

*   *   *

Commerce

I arrived at length at the city of Miṣr, mother of cities and seat of Pharaoh the tyrant, mistress of broad provinces and fruitful lands, boundless in multitude of buildings, peerless in beauty and splendour, the meeting-place of comer and goer, the stopping-place of feeble and strong. Therein is what you will of learned and simple, grave and gay, prudent and foolish, base and noble, of high estate and low estate, unknown and famous; she surges as the waves of the sea with her throngs of folk and can scarce contain them for all the capacity of her situation and sustaining power. Her youth is ever new in spite of length of days, and the star of her horoscope does not move from the mansion of fortune; her conquering capital (*al-Qāhira*) has subdued the nations, and her kings have grasped the forelocks of both Arab and non-Arab. She has as her peculiar possession the majestic Nile, which dispenses her district from the need of entreating the distillation [of the rain]; her territory is a month's journey for a hastening traveller, of generous soil, and extending a friendly welcome to strangers.

Ibn Juzayy remarks: Of Cairo the poet says—

No common town is Cairo, by thy life! Nay, she
Is heaven on earth for those with eyes to see;
Her youth those boys and maids with lustrous
   eyes,
Kawthar her Nile, her Rawḍa Paradise.

*   *   *

It is said that in Cairo there are twelve thousand water-carriers who transport water on camels, and thirty thousand hirers of mules and donkeys, and that on its Nile there are thirty-six thousand vessels belonging to the Sultan and his subjects, which sail upstream to Upper Egypt and downstream to Alexandria and Damietta, laden with goods and commodities of all kinds. On the bank of the Nile opposite Cairo is the place known as al-Rawḍa ['the Garden'], which is a pleasure park and promenade, containing many beautiful gardens. The people of Cairo are fond of pleasure and amusement. I once witnessed a fête there which was held for al-Malik al-Nāṣir's recovery from a fracture which he had suffered in his hand. All the merchants decorated their bazaars and had rich stuffs, ornaments, and silken fabrics hung up in their shops for several days.

The Mosque of ʿAmr b. al-ʾĀṣ, and the Colleges, Hospital, and Convents

The Mosque of ʿAmr b. al-ʿĀṣ is a noble mosque, highly venerated and widely celebrated. The Friday service is held in it, and the road runs right through it from east to west. To the west of it is the cell where the Imām Abū ʿAbdallāh al-Shāfiʿī used to teach. As for the madrasas in Cairo, they are too many for anyone to count; and as for the Māristān, which is "between the two castles" near the mausoleum of al-Malik al-Manṣūr Qalāʾūn, no description is adequate to its beauties. It is equipped with innumerable conveniences and medicaments, and its revenue is reported to be a thousand dinars a day. The convents too are numerous. The people there call them *khawāniq*, the singular being *khānqa*, and the amīrs in Cairo vie with one another in building them.

Each convent in Cairo is affected to the use of a separate congregation of poor brethren, most of whom are Persians, men of good education and adepts in the "way" of Sufism. Each has a shaikh and a warden, and the organization of their affairs is admirable. It is one of their customs in the matter of their food that the steward of the house comes in the morning to the faqīrs, each of whom then specifies what food he desires. When they assemble for meals, each person is given his bread and soup in a separate dish, none sharing with another. They eat twice a day. They receive winter clothing and summer clothing and a monthly allowance varying from twenty to thirty dirhams each. Every Thursday night they are given sugar cakes, soap to wash their clothes, the price of admission to the bath-house, and oil to feed their lamps. These men are celibate; the married men have separate convents. Amongst the stipulations required of them are attendance at the five daily prayers, spending the night in the convent, and assembly in mass in a chapel within the convent. Another of their customs is that each one of them sits upon a prayer-carpet reserved for his exclusive use. When they pray the dawn prayer they recite the chapters of *Victory*, of *the Kingdom*, and of '*Amma*. After this copies of the Holy Qur'ān are brought, divided into sections, and each faqīr takes a section. After 'sealing' the Qur'ān and reciting a *dhikr*, the Qur'ān-readers give a recital according to the custom of the Easterners. They hold a similar service following the mid-afternoon prayer.

They have a regular ritual for the admission of newcomers. The applicant comes to the gate of the convent and takes up his stand there, with his waist girt, a prayer mat on his shoulder, the staff in his right hand and the jug in his left. The gatekeeper informs the steward of the convent that he is there. The steward then comes out to him and asks him from what country he has come, what convents he has stayed in on his way, and who was his spiritual director (*shaikh*). When he has ascertained the truth of his answers, he admits him into the convent, spreads his prayer-mat for him in a place befitting his station, and shows him the lavatory. The newcomer renews his ablutions and, returning to his mat, ungirds his waist, and prays two prostrations, then he clasps the hand of the shaikh and those of the others present, and takes his seat amongst them. Another custom of theirs is that on Fridays the servant collects all their prayer-mats and takes them to the mosque, where he spreads them in readiness for their coming. The faqīrs come out in a body, accompanied by their shaikh, proceed to the mosque, and pray each on his own mat. When they have finished the prayer they recite the Qur'ān according to their custom, and thereafter return in a body to the convent, accompanied by their shaikh.

The Qarāfa of Cairo and Its Sanctuaries

At [Old] Cairo too is [the cemetery called] al-Qarāfa, a place of vast repute for blessed power, whose special virtue is affirmed in a tradition related by al-Qurṭubī amongst others, for it is a part of the amount al-Muqaṭṭam, of which God has promised that it shall be one of the gardens of Paradise. These people build in the Qarāfa beautiful domed chapels and surround them by walls, so that they look like houses, and they construct chambers in them and hire the services of Qur'ān-readers, who recite night and day in beautiful voices. There are some of them who build a religious house or a madrasa by the side of the mausoleum. They go out every Thursday evening to spend the night there with their children and womenfolk and make a circuit of the famous sanctuaries. They go out also to spend the night there on the night of mid-Sha'bān, and the market-people take out all kinds of eatables.

Among the celebrated sanctuaries is the imposing holy shrine where rests the head of al-Ḥusain b. 'Alī * * *. Beside it is a vast convent, of wonderful workmanship, on the doors of which there are silver rings, and plates also on them of the same metal. This shrine is paid its full meed of respect and veneration.

Amongst the monuments is the tomb of the Lady (*Sayyida*) Nafīsa, daughter of Zaid b. 'Alī b. al-Ḥusain b. 'Alī (upon them be peace). She was a woman answered in prayer and zealous in her devotions. This mausoleum is of elegant construction and resplendent brightness, and beside it is a convent which is visited by a great concourse during the days of the feast dedicated to her. Another is the tomb of the Imām Abū 'Abdallāh Muḥammad b. Idrīs al-Shāfi'ī, close by which is a large convent. The mausoleum enjoys an immense revenue and is surmounted by the famous dome, of admirable workmanship and marvellous construction, an exceedingly fine piece of architecture and exceptionally lofty, the diameter of which exceeds thirty cubits. The Qarāfa of Cairo contains also an incalculable number of graves of men eminent for learning and religion, and in it lie a goodly number of the Companions and of the leading figures of both earlier and later generations (God be pleased with them). ＊ ＊ ＊

＊   ＊   ＊

The Egyptian Nile

The Egyptian Nile surpasses all rivers of the earth in sweetness of taste, breadth of channel and magnitude of utility. Cities and villages succeed one another along its banks without interruption and have no equal in the inhabited world, nor is any river known whose basin is so intensively cultivated as that of the Nile. There is no river on earth but it which is called a sea; God Most High has said "If thou fearest for him, cast him into the *yamm*," thus calling it *yamm*, which means "sea" (*bahr*). It is related in an unimpeachable Tradition that the Prophet of God (God's blessing and peace upon him) reached on the night of his Ascension the Lote-Tree of the Extremity, and lo, at its base were four streams, two outer streams and two inner streams. He asked Gabriel (peace be upon him) what streams these were, and he replied 'The two inner streams flow through Paradise, and as for the two outer streams they are the Nile and Euphrates'. It is also related in the Traditions of the Prophet that the Nile, Euphrates, Saihān and Jaihān are, each one, rivers of Paradise. The course of the Nile is from south to north, contrary to all the great rivers. One extraordinary thing about it is that it begins to rise in the extreme hot weather, at the time when rivers generally diminish and dry up, and begins to subside at the time when rivers increase in volume and overflow. The river of Sind [Indus] resembles it in this respect, and will be mentioned later. The first beginning of the Nile flood is in Hazīrān, that is June; and when its rise amounts to sixteen cubits, the land-tax due to the Sultan is payable in full. If it rises another cubit, there is plenty in that year, and complete well-being. But if it reaches eighteen cubits it does damage to the cultivated lands and causes an outbreak of plague. If it falls short of sixteen by a cubit, the Sultan's land-tax is diminished, and if it is two cubits short the people make solemn prayers for rain and there is the greatest misery.

The Nile is one of the five great rivers of the world, which are the Nile, Euphrates, Tigris, Saihūn [Syr Darya] and Jaihūn [Amu Darya]; five other rivers rival these, the river of Sind, which is called Panj Āb [i.e. Five Rivers], the river of Hindustān which is called the Kank [or Gang, i.e. Ganges]—to it the Hindus go on pilgrimage, and when they burn their dead they throw the ashes of them into it, and they say that it comes from Paradise—the river Jūn, also in Hindustān, the river Itil [Volga] in the Qifjaq [Kipchak] steppe, on the shore of which is the city of al-Sarā, and the river Sarū in the land of al-Khitā [Cathay], on the banks of which is the city of Khān-Bāliq [Peking], whence it descends to the city of al-Khansā [Hang-chow] and from there to the city of al-Zaitūn [Zayton] in the land of China. We shall speak of all these in their proper places, if God will. Some distance below Cairo the Nile divides into three sections, and none of these streams can be crossed except by boat, winter or summer. The inhabitants of every township have canals led off the Nile; when it is in flood it fills these and they inundate the cultivated fields.

The Pyramids and Berbās

These are among the marvels which have been celebrated through the course of ages, and there is much talk and theorizing amongst men about them, their significance and the origin of their construction. They aver that all branches of knowledge which came into existence before the Deluge were derived from Hermes the Ancient, who lived in the remotest part of the Sa'īd [Upper Egypt]; he is also called by the name of Khanūkh [Enoch] that is Idrīs (on him be peace). It is said that he was the first to speculate on the movements of the spheres and the celestial bodies, and the first to construct temples and glorify God in them; and that he warned men of the coming of the Deluge, and fearing for the disappearance of knowledge and destruction of the practical arts built the pyramids and berbas, in which he depicted all the practical arts and their tools, and made diagrams of the sciences, in order that they might remain immortalized. It is said also that the seat of learning and kingship in Egypt was the city of Manūf [Memphis], which is one *barīd* from al-Fusṭāṭ. When Alexandria was built, the people removed to it, and it became the seat of learning and kingship until the coming of Islām, when 'Amr b. al-'Āṣ (God be pleased with him) laid out the city of al-Fusṭāṭ, which remains the capital of Egypt to this day.

The pyramids is an edifice of solid hewn stone, of immense height and circular plan, broad at the base and narrow at the top, like the figure of a cone. They have no doorways and the manner of their erection is unknown. One of the tales related about them is that a certain king of Egypt before the Flood dreamed a dream which filled him with terror and determined him to build these pyramids on the western side of the Nile, as a depository for the sciences and for the bodies of the kings. He asked the astrologers whether they would be opened in the future at any spot, and they told him that an opening would be made on the north side, and informed him of the exact spot where the opening would begin, and of the sum of money which would be expended in making the opening. He then ordered to be deposited in that place the sum of money which they had told him would be spent in breaching it. By pressing forward its construction, he completed it in sixty years, and wrote this inscription upon them: "We erected these pyramids in the space of sixty years; let him who will, pull them down in the space of six hundred years; yet to pull down is easier than to build." Now when the Caliphate devolved upon the Commander of the Faithful al-Ma'mūn, he proposed to pull them down, and although one of the Egyptian shaikhs advised him not to do so he persisted in his design and ordered that they should be breached from the north side. So they set about lighting fires up against them and then sprinkling them with vinegar and battering them with a mangonel, until the breach which is still to be seen in them was opened up. There they found,

facing the hole, a sum of money which the Commander of the Faithful ordered to be weighted. He then calculated what had been spent on making the breach, and finding the two sums equal, was greatly astonished. At the same time they found the breadth of the wall to be twenty cubits.

The Sultan of Egypt

The Sultan of Egypt at the time of my entry was al-Malik al-Nāṣir Abu'l-Fatḥ Muḥammad, son of al-Malik al-Manṣūr Saif al-Dīn Qalā'ūn al-Ṣāliḥī. Qalā'ūn was known as al-Alfī ['the Thousand-man'] because al-Malik al-Ṣāliḥ bought him for a thousand dinars of gold. He came originally from Qifjaq [Kipchak]. Al-Malik al-Nāṣir (God's mercy upon him was a man of generous character and great virtues, and sufficient proof of his nobility is furnished by his devotion to the service of the two holy sanctuaries of Mecca and Madīna and the works of beneficence which he does every year to assist the pilgrims, in furnishing camels loaded with provisions and water for those without means and the helpless, and for carrying those who cannot keep up with the caravan or are too weak to walk on foot, both on the Egyptian pilgrim-road and on that from Damascus. He also built a great convent at Siryāqus, in the outskirts of Cairo. But the convent built by our lord the Commander of the Faithful and Defender of the Faith, the refuge of the poor and needy, Caliph of God upon earth, whose zeal in the Holy War transcends its obligations, Abū 'Inān (God be his strength and aid, and grant him the signal victory, and prosper him), in the outskirts of his sublime residence, the luminous city (God guard it), has no equal to it in the inhabited world for perfection of architecture, beauty of construction, and plaster carving such as none of the Easterners can accomplish. We shall speak in due course of the schools, hospitals, and convents which he (God be his strength) has founded in his land (God guard it and preserve it by the prolongation of his reign).

*　　*　　*

REVIEW QUESTIONS

1. How does old Cairo compare to a contemporary European city?

2. What did Ibn Battuta think was important about a city?

3. What did he actually know about the pyramids and the Nile?

DOUKAS

FROM *Decline and Fall of Byzantium to the Ottoman Turks*

Doukas (also appears as Ducas), a fifteenth-century Byzantine historian, descended from a noble Greek family. For a time he worked for the Genoese colonial administration at New Phocaea in Asia Minor. Doukas wrote his history to illustrate what he hoped were temporary Ottoman triumphs over the Greek world. The historian was present at the Ottoman siege of Lesbos in 1462, during which he disappeared from the historical record, probably through death or enslavement. This section of Doukas's history concerns the conquest of Constantinople in 1453.

From *Decline and Fall of Byzantium to the Ottoman Turks,* by Doukas, translated by Harry J. Magoulias (Detroit, Mich.: Wayne State University Press, 1975), pp. 220–27, 240–41.

*   *   *

When all preparations had been completed according to plan, Mehmed sent an envoy to the emperor inside the City with the following message, "The preparations for the assault have been concluded. It is now time to consummate what we planned long ago. Let us leave the outcome of this undertaking to God. What say you? Do you wish to quit the City and go wherever you like together with your officials and their possessions, leaving behind the populace unharmed by us and by you? Or do you choose to resist and to lose your life and belongings, and to have the Turks take the populace captive and scatter them throughout the earth?" The emperor and the senate answered, "If you so wish, as your fathers did before you, you too, by the grace of God, can live peacefully with

us. They regarded my parents as their fathers, and as such honored them, and they looked upon this City as their fatherland. In time of difficulty, they entered within her walls and were saved. No one who resisted her lived long. Keep the fortresses and the lands which have been unjustly seized from us as justly yours. Extract as much tribute annually as we are able to pay you, and depart in peace. Can you be certain that victory instead of defeat awaits you? The right to surrender the City to you belongs neither to me nor to anyone who dwells therein. Rather than to have our lives spared, it is our common resolve willingly to die."

When the tyrant heard this reply, he despaired of a peaceful surrender of the City. He therefore instructed the heralds to announce to the entire army the day on which the assault would be launched. He also affirmed on oath that he desired for himself no gain other than the buildings and walls of the City. As for the treasures and captives to be taken, he declared, "Let those be your reward." The troops shouted their approval.

As night fell, he sent heralds around the camp with instructions that large torches and fires should be lighted at every tent. And once the torches were burning, they were all to chant and shout in their foul and impious tongue. This strange spectacle was indeed incredible. As the torches poured their light over land and sea, brighter than the sun, they illuminated the entire City, Galata, all the islands, ships and boats as far as Skutari. The entire surface of the water flashed so brightly that it was like lightning. Would that it had been lightning, the lightning which not only produces light but also burns and utterly consumes everything! The Romans thought that fire had fallen on the camp and ran up to the breach in the wall. When they saw the Turks dancing and heard their joyous shouts, they foresaw the future. With a contrite heart they prayed to God, "Spare us, O Lord, from Thy just wrath and deliver us from the hands of the enemy." The spectacle and din affected the citizens so much that they appeared to be half-dead, unable to breathe either in or out.

Giovanni labored throughout the night. He ordered all the brushwood in the City gathered and placed at the breach. He also constructed a second fosse within for protection where the walls had been destroyed. The Romans realized that their movements were conspicuous and that they could not pass through the gate to oppose the Turks at the outer fortifications because the fallen walls exposed them. There were, however, some old men who knew of an underground sallyport located at the lower end of the palace that, many years before, had been sealed shut. When the emperor was informed of its existence, he commanded that it be opened. The soldiers could now sally through because it was screened by solid walls, and they gave battle to the Turks in the enclosure. The name of this hidden door was Kerkoporta.

On Sunday, the tyrant began to engage in full

scale warfare. Right into the evening and through the night he gave no rest to the Romans. That Sunday was the Feast of All Saints, the twenty-seventh day of May.

From daybreak he engaged in light skirmishes until the ninth hour [3 p.m.], and after the ninth hour he arrayed the army from the palace to the Golden Gate. He also deployed the eighty ships from the Xyloporta Gate to the Plataea Gate. The remaining ships, which were stationed at the Double Columns, began an encircling maneuver, starting from the Horaia Gate and continuing past the Acropolis of Demetrios the Great and the small postern located at the Hodegetria monastery. Sailing past the Great Palace and crossing the harbor, they completed the encirclement as far as Vlangas. In addition to all kinds of equipment, each vessel carried a scaling ladder equal to the height of the walls.

Just as the sun set, the call to battle rang out. The battle array was most formidable indeed! The tyrant himself was on horseback on Monday evening. Exactly opposite the fallen walls he gave battle with his faithful slaves, young and all-powerful, fighting like lions, more than ten thousand of them. To the rear and on both flanks there were more than one hundred thousand fighting cavalrymen. To the south of these and as far as the harbor of the Golden Gate there were another hundred thousand troops and more. From the spot where the ruler was standing to the extremities of the palace there were another fifty thousand soldiers. The troops on the ships and at the bridge were beyond number.

The City's defenders were deployed in the following manner: The emperor and Giovanni Giustiniani were stationed at the fallen walls, outside the stockade in the enclosure, with about three thousand Latins and Romans. The grand duke was posted at the Imperial Gate with about five hundred troops. At the sea walls and along the battlements from the Xyloporta Gate to the Horaia Gate, more than five hundred crossbowmen and archers were arrayed. Making the complete circuit from the Horaia Gate to the Golden Gate there was stationed in each bastion a single archer, crossbowman, or gunner. They spent the entire night on watch with no sleep at all.

The Turks with Mehmed rushed to the walls, carrying a great number of scaling ladders which had been constructed beforehand. Behind the lines, the tyrant, brandishing an iron mace, forced his archers to the walls by using both flattery and threats. The City's defenders fought back bravely with all the strength they could muster. Giovanni and his men, supported by the emperor in arms, together with all his troops, fought back courageously.

But just as Fortune's feats of arms were about to snatch victory from Turkish hands, from the very middle of the embattled Roman troops, God removed their general, a mighty warrior of gigantic stature. He was wounded just before dawn by lead shot which went through the back of his arm, penetrating his iron breastplate which had been forged in the manner of Achilles' weapons. Unable to relieve the pain of the wound, he cried out to the emperor, "Stand your ground bravely, and I will retire to the ship to attend to my wound. Then I will quickly return." It was in that hour that the words spoken by Jeremias to the Jews were fulfilled, "Thus shall ye say to Sedekias: Thus saith the Lord God of Israel. Behold, I will turn back the weapons of war *which are in your hands,* wherewith ye fight against the king of Babylon and the Chaldeans that have besieged you from outside the wall; and I will gather them into the midst of this city. And I will fight against you with an outstretched hand *or* with an *uplifted* arm with wrath and anger and *great irritation.* And I will smite the dwellers in this city, both men and cattle with grievous death, and they shall die. I will not spare them, and I will not have compassion upon them!"[1] When the emperor beheld Giovanni in retreat, he lost heart and so did his companions. Yet they continued the fight with all their strength.

The Turks gradually made their way to the walls, and, using their shields for cover, threw up

their scaling ladders. Thwarted, however, by stone-throwers from above, they achieved nothing. Their assault, therefore, was repulsed. All the Romans with the emperor held their ground against the enemy, and all their strength and purpose were exerted to prevent the Turks from entering through the fallen walls. Unbeknown to them, however, God willed that the Turks would be brought in by another way. When they saw the sallyport, to which we referred above, open, some fifty of the tyrant's renowned slaves leaped inside. They climbed to the top of the walls and zealously slew anyone they met and struck down the sentinels who discharged missiles from above. It was a sight filled with horror! Some of the Romans and Latins who were preventing the Turks from attaching scaling ladders to the walls were cut to pieces, while others, closing their eyes, jumped from the wall and ended their lives horribly by smashing their bodies. Unimpeded, the Turks threw up the scaling ladders and ascended like soaring eagles.

The Romans and the emperor did not know what had happened because the entry of the Turks took place at a distance; indeed, their paramount concern was the enemy before them. The fierce Turkish warriors outnumbered the Romans twenty to one. The Romans, moreover, were not as experienced in warfare as the ordinary Turks. Their attention and concern, therefore, were focused on the Turkish ground attack. Then suddenly arrows fell from above, slaughtering many Romans. When they looked up and saw the Turks, they fled behind the walls. Unable to enter through the Gate of Charisios because of the press of the multitude, only those got through who were stronger and able to trample down the weaker. When the tyrant's troops witnessed the rout of the Romans, they shouted with one voice and pursued them inside, trampling upon the wretches and slaughtering them. When they reached the gate, they were unable to get through because it was blocked by the bodies of the dead and the dying. The majority entered through the breaches in the walls and they cut down all those they met.

---

[1] Jeremiah 21: 3–6. Doukas's additions are in italics.

The emperor, despairing and hopeless, stood with sword and shield in hand and poignantly cried out, "Is there no one among the Christians who will take my head from me?" He was abandoned and alone. Then one of the Turks wounded him by striking him flush, and he, in turn, gave the Turk a blow. A second Turk delivered a mortal blow from behind and the emperor fell to the earth. They slew him as a common soldier and left him, because they did not know he was the emperor.

Only three Turks perished and all the rest made their way inside. It was the first hour of the day [6 a.m.], and the sun had not yet risen. As they entered the City and spread out from the Gate of Charisios to the palace, they slew those who resisted and those who fled. Some two thousand fighting men were slaughtered. The Turks were apprehensive because they had estimated that within the City there must be at least fifty thousand soldiers. Consequently, they slew the two thousand. Had they known that the total number of armed troops did not exceed eight thousand men, they would not have killed any of them. This nation is a lover of money and if a patricide fell into their hands, they would release him for gold. How much truer this would be for him who had done no wrong but had instead been wronged by them. After the conflict I met many Turks who related the following to me, "Fearful of those ahead of us, we slew as many as we met. Had we known that there was such a dearth of men in the City, we would have sold them all like sheep."

Some of the Azabs, that is, the tyrant's retinue who are also called Janissaries, overran the palace. Others swarmed over the Monastery of the Great Forerunner called Petra and the Monastery of Chora in which was found the icon of my Immaculate Mother of God. O tongue and lips, how can I relate what happened there to the icon because of your sins? While the apostates were anxious to go elsewhere for more plunder, one of the infidels, extending his befouled hands, hacked the icon into four pieces with an axe. Casting lots, each received his equal share and its accompany-

ing ornament. After they seized the monastery's precious vessels, they rode off.

Breaking into the protostrator's home, they broke open the coffers full of treasures amassed long ago. In so doing, they aroused the noblewomen from their sleep. It was the twenty-ninth day of May, and the morning sleep of the youths and maidens was sweet indeed; they slept unafraid and carefree as they had done yesterday and the day before.

Then a great horde of mounted infidels charged down the street leading to the Great Church. The actions of both Turks and Romans made quite a spectacle! In the early dawn, as the Turks poured into the City and the citizens took flight, some of the fleeing Romans managed to reach their homes and rescue their children and wives. As they moved, bloodstained, across the Forum of the Bull and passed the Column of the Cross [Forum of Constantine], their wives asked, "What is to become of us?" When they heard the fearful cry, "The Turks are slaughtering Romans within the City's walls," they did not believe it at first. They cursed and reviled the ill-omened messenger instead. But behind him came a second, and then a third, and all were covered with blood, and they knew that the cup of the Lord's wrath had touched their lips. Monks and nuns, therefore, and men and women, carrying their infants in their arms and abandoning their homes to anyone who wished to break in, ran to the Great Church. The thoroughfare, overflowing with people, was a sight to behold!

Why were they all seeking refuge in the Great Church? Many years before they had heard from some false prophets that the City was fated to be surrendered to the Turks who would enter with great force, and that the Romans would be cut down by them as far as the Column of Constantine the Great. Afterwards, however, an angel, descending and holding a sword, would deliver the empire and the sword to an unknown man, extremely plain and poor, standing at the Column. "Take this sword," the angel would say, "and avenge the people of the Lord." Then the Turks would take flight and the Romans would follow hard upon them, cutting them down. They would drive them from the City and from the West, and from the East as far as the borders of Persia, to a place called Monodendrion. Because they fully expected these prophecies to be realized, some ran and advised others to run also. This was the conviction of the Romans who long ago had contemplated what their present action would be, contending, "If we leave the Column of the Cross behind us, we will avoid future wrath." This was the cause then of the flight into the Great Church. In one hour's time that enormous temple was filled with men and women. There was a throng too many to count, above and below, in the courtyards and everywhere. They bolted the doors and waited, hoping to be rescued by the anonymous savior.

O miserable Romans! O wretches! The temple which only yesterday you called a cave and altar of heretics, and not one of you would enter so as not to be defiled because the liturgy was offered by clerics who had embraced Church Union, and now, because of the impending wrath you push your way inside, seeking to be saved. But not even the impending just wrath could move your hearts to peace. And even if, in such a calamity, an angel were to descend from heaven and say to you, "If you will accept the Union and a state of peace in the Church, I will expel the enemy from the City," even then you would not assent. And if you did assent, it would only be a lie! They who but a few days before had said, "It would be better to fall into the hands of the Turks than into the clutches of the Franks," knew this was true.

Pillaging, slaughtering, and taking captives on the way, the Turks reached the temple before the termination of the first hour. The gates were barred, but they broke them with axes. They entered with swords flashing and, beholding the myriad populace, each Turk caught and bound his own captive. There was no one who resisted or who did not surrender himself like a sheep. Who can recount the calamity of that time and place? Who can describe the wailing and the cries of the babes, the mothers' tearful screams and the fathers' lamentations? The commonest Turk sought the most tender maiden. The lovely nun, who heretofore belonged only to the one God, was now seized and bound by another master. The rapine caused the tugging and pulling of braids of hair, the exposure of bosoms and breasts, and outstretched arms. The female slave was bound with her mistress, the master with his slave, the archimandrite with the doorkeeper, tender youths with virgins, who had never been exposed to the sun and hardly ever seen by their own fathers, were dragged about, forcibly pushed together and flogged. The despoiler led them to a certain spot, and placing them in safekeeping, returned to take a second and even a third prize. The abductors, the avengers of God, were in a great hurry. Within one hour they had bound everyone, the male captives with cords and the women with their own veils. The infinite chains of captives who like herds of kine and flocks of sheep poured out of the temple and the temple sanctuary made an extraordinary spectacle! They wept and wailed and there was none to show them mercy.

What became of the temple treasures? What shall I say and how shall I say it? My tongue is stuck fast in my larynx. I am unable to draw breath through my sealed mouth. In that same hour the dogs hacked the holy icons to pieces, removing the ornaments. As for the chains, candelabra, holy altar coverings, and lamps, some they destroyed and the rest they seized. All the precious and sacred vessels of the holy sacristy, fashioned from gold and silver and other valuable materials, they collected in an instant, leaving the temple desolate and naked; absolutely nothing was left behind.

*   *   *

Three days after the Fall, Mehmed released the ships so that they might sail to their own province and city. They carried so much cargo that they almost sank from the weight. What cargo did they carry? Costly apparel, silver, gold, copper and tin vessels, and books beyond number. They were filled to capacity with captives—priests and lay-men, nuns and monks. The tents at the fosse were also teeming with captives and with the multifar-ious articles enumerated above. It was indeed spectacular to see a barbarian wearing an episcopal *sakkos,*[2] and another girded about with a golden stole and leading around dogs that were arrayed in fabrics embroidered with golden lambs instead of in coarse blankets. Others were sitting and feasting, eating a variety of fruits from the sacred patens in front of them, and drinking unwatered wine from the sacred chalices. Innumerable books were loaded onto the wagons and hauled in all directions; they were dispersed throughout East and West. For a single gold coin, ten books were sold—the works of Aristotle and Plato, books of theological content and on every subject. Gold and silver were pulled from the Evangelistaries which were adorned with many different jewels; some were sold and the rest were thrown away. All the icons were thrown to the flames and the meats they ate were roasted by the fire that was kindled.

On the fifth day Mehmed visited Galata. Or-dering a census taken of all the inhabitants, he found that many of the homes had been bolted because the Latins had fled in the ships. He or-dered the homes opened and an inventory taken of their belongings. He stipulated that should the owners return within a period of three months, they would be allowed to repossess their posses-sions, but if they failed to return, all would then be confiscated by the ruler. Afterwards, he com-manded the entire army with the assistance of the outlying villages to demolish and raze the walls of Galata. Once this was accomplished they would be dismissed. His orders were executed. The land walls were overthrown but the walls along the har-bor were allowed to stand.

In order to prepare enough lime to rebuild the fallen walls of the City, Mehmed ordered the lime-slakers to work the whole month of August. After five thousand families were registered from both the eastern and western provinces, Mehmed in-structed them and their entire households to take up residence in the City by September on penalty of death. He next appointed his slave Sulayman *eparch.* He converted the Great Church into an al-tar for his God and Muhammad, but left the other churches desolate. He returned triumphant to Adrianople with innumerable captives and booty.

He departed from the City on the eighteenth day of June, taking with him in wagons and on horseback all the noblewomen and their daughters. The wife of the grand duke died en route near the village of Mesene and she was buried there. She was renowned for her charity and compassion for the indigent and for being a prudent woman who exercised restraint over the many passions of the spirit.

Mehmed's majestic triumphal entry into Adri-anople was followed—and what a spectacle it was—by all the noble-women and Christian gov-ernors and rulers streaming in and greeting him with "Hail!" With what heart and intent did their lips and mouths say this? Afraid that they might suffer the same fate as the City, they involuntarily made their submission with gifts. The tyrant was sitting on his throne, haughty and proud, boasting about the fall of the City. The Christian rulers stood there trembling and wondering what the fu-ture held in store for them.

First, he demanded of the Serb ambassador the annual payment of twelve thousand gold coins to the Turkish throne. The despots of the Pelopon-nesos were instructed to appear in person annually with gifts to make their obeisance and to submit the payment of ten thousand gold coins. The lord of Chios was to make an annual payment of six thousand gold coins and the lord of Mitylene three thousand gold coins annually. The emperor of Trebizond and all those who resided along the Black Sea were to come annually with gifts to make obeisance and to pay the tribute.

*   *   *

---

[2] An episcopal garment.

REVIEW QUESTIONS

1. How does Doukas explain the reason for the fall of Constantinople?
2. What difference did the end of the Byzantine state make to the history of the eastern Mediterranean? Why did the Byzantines receive so little help from the West?
3. What signs of bias appear in Doukas's account of the Turks and Sultan Mehmed?

AŞIKPAŞAZADE

FROM *History of the House of Osman*

Aşikpaşazade (also appears as Ashiq Pasha-Zade) (1400–after 1484), the grandson of a famous Turkish poet of the fourteenth century, descended from a dervish family. In his youth, he participated in Ottoman campaigns in the Balkans. He wrote in the 1480s his history of the Ottoman sultans beginning with the founder of the family line Osman. This excerpt from his chronicle describes the fall of Constantinople and the end of the vizier Halil Pasha from a Turkish perspective.

From *Islam: From the Prophet Muhammad to the Capture of Constantinople, Volume 1: Politics and War*, edited and translated by Bernard Lewis (New York: Oxford University Press, 1974), pp. 144–48.

*   *   *

The Capture of Constantinople

WHAT SULTAN MEḤMED KHAN GĀZI DID WHEN HE HAD RETURNED FROM KARAMAN, AND WHAT BUILDINGS HE RAISED

He wanted to cross to Rumeli at Gallipoli, but they said to him, "O mighty Sultan! Infidel ships have come and have closed the straits at Gallipoli."

So they took the Sultan and led him to Kojaeli. They made camp at Akčahisar, on the shore of the Bosphorus above Istanbul.

There, where his father had crossed, he crossed to Rumeli and made camp opposite Akčahisar.

He said to Halīl Pasha, "Lala, here I need a fortress!" In short, he gave orders at once and had the fortress built, and it was completed.

Then he despatched Akčayluoglu Meḥmed Bey, saying, "Make haste and besiege Istanbul."

Meḥmed Bey came, cleared the people from the city gates, and drove away the sheep and goats from the adjoining villages. The Emperor was told, "The Turk has struck us to the heart and pulled our house down on our heads."

The Emperor said, "Neighborliness between them and us is like the neighborliness of the falcon and the crow."

Then he said, "If there is any way of saving ourselves from this Turk, we must appeal again to our friend Halīl Pasha. Now we must send Halīl Pasha some little fish."

He filled the bellies of these fish with florins and sent them to Halīl Pasha. The Emperor had a vizier whose name was Master Luke.[1] He said, "Ha! Halīl Pasha will swallow the fish and it won't do you any good. He is no longer concerned about helping you. Look to your own resources."

They brought Halīl the fish. He ate the fish and put the contents in his money chest. Then he acted for the infidels. He went to the Sultan and spoke many words to him about the infidels. The Sultan said, "Ha Lala, let the summer come and then we shall see. What God commands, that we shall do."

They had been busy for some time with preparations for the conquest of the city. When all was ready and summer came, Sultan Mehmed said, "We shall spend this summer in Istanbul."

They came and made camp around the walls of Istanbul. From the land side and with ships on the sea they enclosed the city all around. There were 400 ships on the sea, and 70 ships sailed over Galata across the dry land. The warriors stood ready and unfurled their flags. At the foot of the walls they went into the sea and made a bridge over the water. They attacked.

The fighting went on, day and night, for fifty days. On the fifty-first day the Sultan ordered free plunder. They attacked. On the fifty-first day, a Tuesday, the citadel was captured. There was good booty and plunder. Gold and silver and jewels and fine stuffs were brought and stacked in the camp market. They began to sell them. They made the people of the city slaves and killed their Emperor, and the *gāzīs* embraced their pretty girls. On Wednesday they arrested Halīl Pasha and his sons and his officers and put them in prison. Theirs is a long story, but I have cut it short, because all this is well known, concerning what they did to Halīl Pasha.

In short, on the first Friday after the conquest, they recited the communal prayer in Santa Sofia, and the Islamic invocation was read in the name of Sultan Mehmed Khan Gāzī, the son of Sultan Murād Khan Gāzī, the son of Sultan Mehmed Khan Gāzī, the son of Sultan Bāyezīd Khan, the son of Murād Hünkâr Gāzī, the son of Orkhan Gāzī Khan, the son of Osmān Gāzī Khan, the son of Ertugrul Gāzī Khan, the son of Sultan Süleymānshāh Gāzī Khan of the house of Gökalp, the son of Oguz Khan. I have set forth their family tree in the first chapter.

This victory was achieved by Sultan Mehmed Khan in the year 857 of the Hijra [1453].

HOW ISTANBUL WAS DESTROYED WHEN IT WAS CAPTURED AND HOW IT AGAIN BECAME A FLOURISHING CITY

When Sultan Mehmed Khan Gāzī had captured Istanbul, he made his servant Süleymān Bey city commandant. Then he sent messengers to all his lands saying, "Whoever wishes, let him come, and let him become owner of houses, vineyards, and gardens in Istanbul." And they gave them to all who came.

This was, however, not enough to repopulate the city. This time, therefore, the Sultan gave orders to dispatch families, both rich and poor, from every province. The Sultan's servants were sent with orders to the qāḍīs and the military commandants of every province and, in accordance with these orders, conscripted and brought very many families. These newcomers were also given houses, and this time the city began to flourish.

On the houses which were given to these newcomers a rental [*muqāṭaʿa*] was imposed, which bore heavily upon them. They said, "Did you remove us from our own property and bring us here just to pay rent for these infidel houses?" And some abandoned their wives and children and ran away.

Sultan Mehmed had a servant called Kula Shahin who had served his father and grandfather and had been a vizier. Kula Shahin said to the Pādishāh, "O mighty Sultan! Your father and your grandfather conquered so many lands but in none did they impose a rental. It would be more fitting for my Sultan not to do this."

The Pādishāh accepted what he said and forewent the rental. He issued orders, "Every house which you assign, assign as freehold [*mülk*]."

---

[1] The Byzantine *Megadux* Lucas Notaras.

Henceforth, with every house which was assigned, they gave a letter that it was to be their freehold. In this way the city again began to flourish. They began to build mosques. Some of them built dervish convents, some of them private houses, and the city returned to its previous state.

Then a new vizier, who was the son of an infidel, came to the Pādishāh and became the Pādishāh's close confidant. The father and friends of this vizier were infidels, old residents of Istanbul. They came to him and said, "Hey, what are you doing? The Turks have repopulated this city. Have you no loyalty? They have taken your father's home and our home and make free with it before our eyes. But you are the confidant of the Pādishāh; therefore, do all you can so that these people should give up the rebuilding of this city, and then it will remain in our hands as before."

The vizier said, "We shall reimpose that rental which they had imposed at the time. Then these people will stop building private houses, and in this way the city will again fall in ruins and finally be left in the hands of our community."

One day this vizier found an occasion to persuade the Pādishāh, and he reintroduced the rental. . . . Whatever this scheming infidel said, he did, and they wrote it down.

Question: Who then was this vizier?

Answer: It was the Greek Meḥmed Pasha, whom he later had strangled like a dog.

Question: What buildings did Sultan Meḥmed Khan Gāzī build in Istanbul?

He built eight *medreses*, with a great cathedral mosque in their midst, and facing the mosque a fine hospice and a hospital, and at the side of the eight *medreses* he built eight more small *medreses*, to house the students. Apart from this, he had a fine mausoleum built over the grave of the holy Eyyūb-ī Ensārī, with a hospice, a *medrese*, and a mosque nearby.

*   *   *

Because of this rental people began to flee the rebuilding of Istanbul. . . . The imposing of this rental, which still stands, was the fault of this Greek Mehmed.

*   *   *

REVIEW QUESTIONS

1. How does this account of the conquest of Constantinople compare with the one by Doukas?
2. Why is it easier to criticize the vizier than the sultan? What is the role of the vizier in the Ottoman Empire?

"The Tale of the White Cowl": A Russian Tale

The Russian story "The Tale of the White Cowl" was written down in this form in Novogorod by church officials sometime in the late fifteenth century. The white cowl, a simple woolen hood, passed from the classical first Rome, briefly to the Byzantine state, and finally to the Russian people, after 1453 the only remaining defenders of eastern Orthodoxy. Russia became the easternmost state that traced some of its culture back to the Mediterranean world.

From *Medieval Russia's Epics, Chronicles and Tales*, edited by Serge A. Zenkovsky (New York: Dutton, 1963).

At that time the Patriarch of Constantinople was Philotheus, who was distinguished by his strict fasting and his virtuous ways. Once, he had a vision in the night of a youth from whom emanated light and who told him:

"Blessed teacher, in the olden times the Roman Emperor, Constantine, who, through the vision of the Holy Apostles Peter and Paul, was enlightened by God, decided to give Blessed Pope Sylvester the White Cowl to glorify the Holy Apostolic Church. Later, the unfaithful popes of the Latin heresies wanted to profane and destroy this cowl, but I appeared to the evil pope, and now this pope has sent this cowl to you. When the messengers arrive with it, you must accept it with all honors. Then send the White Cowl to the Russian land, to the city of Novgorod the Great with your written blessing. And there this cowl will be worn on the head of Vasily, Archbishop of Novgorod so that he may glorify the Holy Apostolic Cathedral of Holy Sophia and laud the Orthodox. There, in that land, the faith of Christ is verily glorified. And the popes, because of their shamelessness, will receive the vengeance of God." And having spoken these words, the youth became invisible.

The patriarch awoke filled with awe and joy, and was unable to sleep throughout the remainder of the night. And he contemplated this vision. In the morning he ordered that the bells should sound the Matins, and when day came he summoned the Church council and revealed his vision. And all praised God, perceiving that a holy angel had appeared to the patriarch. Yet they did not fully understand the meaning of the message. When they were still in council and were filled with awe due to their great joy, there arrived a servant of the patriarch, and he announced to them that messengers had arrived from the Pope of Rome. The patriarch ordered that they be brought before him. The messengers came, bowed lowly to the patriarch, and gave him the message. The patriarch read the message and pondered it, praising God. He announced its contents to Emperor John who was reigning at that time and whose name was Kantakuzen. And then he went

with the entire council to meet the bringers of the divine treasure which lay in an ark. He accepted it with all honors, broke the seal, and took from the ark the Holy White Cowl. He kissed it with reverence, and looked upon it with wonderment both for its creation and for the wonderful fragrance that emanated from it.

At that time the patriarch had diseased eyes and constant headaches, but when he placed the White Cowl upon his head, these afflictions immediately ceased to be. And he rejoiced with great joy and rendered glory to Christ, our Lord, to Constantine's blessed memory for his creating this wonderful cowl for Blessed Pope Sylvester. And he put the Holy Cowl on the golden salver that was also sent by the pope. He placed them in the great church in an honorable place until he could make a decision with the emperor's counseling.

After the White Cowl was sent from Rome, the evil pope, who was counseled by heretics, became angered against the Christian faith and was driven to a frenzy, extremely regretting his allowing the White Cowl to be sent to Constantinople. And he wrote an evil letter to the patriarch, in which he demanded the return of the White Cowl on the golden salver. The patriarch read this letter and, understanding the pope's evil and cunning design, sent him a letter in return that was based on Holy Scripture, and in it he called the pope both evil and godless, the apostate and precursor of the Antichrist. And the patriarch cursed the pope in the name of our Lord, Jesus Christ, the Holy Apostles, and the Church Fathers. And this letter came to the pope.

When the pope had read the letter and learned that the patriarch intended to send the White Cowl with great honor to the Russian land, to the city of Novgorod the Great, he uttered a roar. And his face changed and he fell ill, for he, the infidel, disliked the Russian land and could not even bear to hear of this land where the Christian faith was professed.

Patriarch Philotheus, having seen that the White Cowl was illumined with grace, began to ponder how he might keep it in Constantinople and wear it on his own head. He consulted with the emperor about the matter several times, and wanted to write to the other patriarchs and metropolitans to summon them to a council. After Matins one Sunday, the patriarch returned to his chambers and, after the usual prayers, lay down to rest. But he slept but lightly, and in this sleep he saw that two men, who were unknown to him, came through the door. And from them there emanated light. One of them was armed as a warrior and had an imperial crown upon his head. The other wore a bishop's vestments and was distinguished by his venerable white hair.

The latter spoke to the patriarch, saying: "Patriarch! Stop pondering your wearing of the White Cowl on your own head. If this were to be, our Lord, Jesus Christ, would have so predestined it from the founding of this city. And for a long time did divine enlightenment come from heaven, and then God's voice came to me and I learned that Rome had to betray God and embrace their Latin heresies. That is the reason I did not wish to wear this cowl upon my head, and thus I instructed other popes not to do so. And this imperial city of Constantinople will be taken by the sons of Hagar because of its sins, and all holy shrines will be defiled and destroyed. Thus has it been predestined since the founding of this city.

"The ancient city of Rome will break away from the glory and faith of Christ because of its pride and ambition. In the new Rome, which will be the City of Constantinople, the Christian faith will also perish through the violence of the sons of Hagar. In the third Rome, which will be the land of Russia, the Grace of the Holy Spirit will be revealed. Know then, Philotheus, that all Christians will finally unite into one Russian nation because of its orthodoxy. Since ancient times and by the will of Constantine, Emperor of the Earth, the imperial crown of the imperial city is predestined to be given to the Russian tsar. But the White Cowl, by the will of the King of Heaven, Jesus Christ, will be given to the archbishop of Novgorod the Great. And this White Cowl is more honorable than the crown of the tsar, for it is an imperial crown of the archangelic spiritual order.

Thus, you must send this Holy White Cowl to the Russian land, to the city of Novgorod the Great, as you were told to do in the vision of the angel. You should believe and trust in what I say. And when you send it to the Russian land, the Orthodox Faith will be glorified and the cowl will be safe from seizure by the infidel sons of Hagar and from the intended profanation by the Latin pope. And the grace, glory, and honor which were taken from Rome, as well as the Grace of the Holy Spirit, will be removed from the imperial city of Constantinople after its capture by the sons of Hagar. And all holy relics will be given to the Russian land in the predestined moment. And the Russian tsar will be elevated by God above other nations, and under his sway will be many heathen kings. And the power of the patriarch of this imperial ruling city will pass to the Russian land in the predestined hour. And that land will be called Radiant Russia, which, by the Grace of God, will be glorified with blessings. And its majesty will be strengthened by its orthodoxy, and it will become more honorable than the two Romes which preceded it."

And saying this, the man of the vision who was dressed in a bishop's vestment wished to leave, but the patriarch, seized by great awe, fell before the bishop and said: "Who are you, my lord? Your vision has seized me with great awe; my heart has been frightened by your words, and I tremble to my very bones."

The man in the bishop's vestments answered: "Don't you know who I am? I am Pope Sylvester, and I came to you because I was ordered by God to reveal to you the great mystery which will come to pass in the predestined time." Then, pointing to the other man in the vision, he added: "This is blessed Emperor Constantine of Rome to whom I gave rebirth in the holy font and whom I won over to the faith of our Lord, Jesus Christ. He was the first Christian emperor, my child in Christ, who created and gave me the White Cowl in place of the imperial crown." And saying this, he blessed the patriarch, and became invisible.

Waking up, the patriarch was seized with awe, remembering the words about the White Cowl and the conquest of Constantinople by the pagan sons of Hagar. And he wept for a long time. When the hour of the divine Mass arrived, the patriarch went to the church, fell before the icon of the Holy Mother of God, and remained lying there for some time. Then he arose, took the White Cowl with great reverence, kissed it piously, placed it upon his head, and then put it to his eyes and his heart. And his adoration for this cowl increased even more. And doing this, he wept. His clerics, who were around him and saw that he wept inconsolably, did not dare to inquire as to why he was weeping. Finally the patriarch ceased crying and told his clerics in detail of the vision of Pope Sylvester and Emperor Constantine. Having heard these words, the clerics wept sorrowfully, and exclaimed, "Thy will be done!"

The patriarch, mourning the forthcoming misfortunes of the city of Constantinople and fearing to trespass the divine will, told them that he must fulfill the will of the Lord and do with the White Cowl as he was commanded to do. After having deliberated with blessed Emperor John, he took the White Cowl and the golden salver, put them in the aforementioned ark, sealed it with his seal, and, as he was commanded by the holy angel and Blessed Pope Sylvester, put in his epistle with his blessings, and in it he commanded Archbishop Vasily and all other bishops who would follow Vasily to wear the White Cowl upon their heads. He added many other honorable and marvelous gifts from his clergy for the bishopric of Novgorod the Great. And he also sent vestments with their embroidered crosses for the glorification of the Holy Apostolic Church. And all this was placed in another ark. And he gave these arks to a bishop named Eumeny, and sent him forth with both joy and sorrow.

In the bishopric of the city of Novgorod the Great was Archbishop Vasily who distinguished himself by his fasting and virtuous ways. Once, in the night, he prayed to God and then lay down to rest, but he slept but lightly, and had a dream in which he saw the angel of God. This angel of God, who had a handsome appearance and radiant face, appeared before him in the garb of a monk and

with the White Cowl upon his head. With his finger he pointed to his head and in a low voice announced: "Vasily! This White Cowl which you see on my head is from Rome. In olden times the Christian Emperor Constantine created it in honor of Sylvester, Pope of Rome. He gave it to this pope to wear upon his head. But God Almighty did not permit the White Cowl to remain there because of their Latin heresies. Tomorrow morning you must go from the city with your clergymen and meet the bishop and messengers sent by the patriarch. And they will bring an ark, and in this ark you will find the White Cowl upon a golden salver. Accept it with all honors, for this White Cowl symbolizes the radiant Resurrection which came to pass on the third day. And from now, you and all other archbishops of this city will wear it on your heads. And I have come to you to assure you before hand that all is as God wills it and to assuage any doubts you may have." And saying this, the angel became invisible.

Waking up, Archbishop Vasily was seized with awe and joy, pondering the meaning of the vision. The next morning he sent his clerics outside the city, to the crossroads, to see whether the messengers really would appear. In the vicinity of the city the servant of Archbishop Vasily met a Greek bishop who was unknown to him and who traveled to the city of Novgorod. They made a low obeisance and returned to the archbishop and told them all they had seen. The bishop then sent his messenger into the city to summon the clerics and the entire population. And he ordered the tolling of the bells, and both he and his clerics donned their vestments.

The procession had not gone far from the Cathedral of Holy Sophia when they met the aforementioned bishop, sent by the patriarch and bearing the ark that had been sealed by the patriarch, and which contained the venerable gifts, came to Archbishop Vasily, made a low obeisance before him, and gave him the epistles of the patriarch. They blessed and greeted each other in Christ's name. Archbishop Vasily accepted the epistles of the patriarch and the arks bearing the venerable gifts. And he went with them to the Cathedral of Holy Sophia, the Wisdom of God. There he put them in the middle of the church in an honorable place, and ordered that the patriarchal epistles be read aloud. When the Orthodox people, who were in the cathedral, heard these writings read aloud, they rendered glory to God and rejoiced with great joy. Archbishop Vasily opened one of the arks and removed the cover. And a wonderful fragrance and miraculous radiance spread through the church. Archbishop Vasily and all present were in wonderment, witnessing these happenings. And Bishop Eumeny, who was sent by the patriarch, wondered about these blessed deeds of God that he had witnessed. And they all rendered glory to God, and celebrated the service of thanksgiving.

Archbishop Vasily took the White Cowl from the ark and saw that it appeared exactly like the one he had seen on the angel's head in his vision. And he kissed it with reverence. At that same moment there came a sonorous voice from the icon of the Lord, which was in the cupola of the church, saying, "Holy, holy" And after a moment of silence there came the same voice, which thrice announced, "Ispola cti despota." And when the archbishop and all those present heard these voices, they were seized with awe and joy. And they said, "The Lord have mercy upon us!" And the archbishop then ordered that all present in the church be silent, and he revealed to them his vision of the angel and his words concerning the White Cowl. And he told of his vision as it had happened and in detail, even as it was told to him by the angel in the night.

Giving thanks to God for sending this cowl, the archbishop went forth from the church, preceded by the deacons in holy vestments carrying tapers and singing hymns. And they proceeded with serenity and piety. And the people crowded round, jostling each other and jumping so that they might see the White Cowl on the arch-bishop's head. And all were in wonderment. Thus, in this way, thanks to the Grace of our Lord, Jesus Christ, and to the blessing of his Holiness Philotheus, Patriarch of of Constantinople, the White Cowl became a symbol upon the heads of the archbishops of Novgorod. And Archbishop Vasily was overcome with great joy, and for seven days he feasted all priests, deacons, and clerics of the city of Novgorod the Great. And he also offered food and drink to the poor, to monks, and to prisoners. And he asked that the prisoners be released. During the divine service he placed the holy and venerable gifts of the patriarch in the Cathedral of Holy Sophia and with the blessings of all clerics. And the golden salver, on which the White Cowl was placed, was also deposited in the Cathedral of Holy Sophia during the Mass.

The messengers of the patriarch who brought the Holy White Cowl were also shown great honor and they received many gifts. The archbishop sent gifts to the Emperor and Patriarch of Constantinople and sent the messengers forth with great honors. Thereafter, multitudes arrived from many cities and kingdoms to look upon, as if it were a miracle, the archbishop in the White Cowl. And they were in wonderment about it, and told of it in many lands. This Holy White Cowl was created by the first pious Christian Emperor, Constantine, for Blessed Pope Sylvester in the year 297. And this is the history of the Holy White Cowl up to this day.

REVIEW QUESTIONS

1. What were the Russian attitudes toward the Roman Catholic Church, the Muslims, and the Eastern Orthodox Church?
2. Given these attitudes, why is anyone in Russia interested in portraying it as a third Rome?

ALVISE DA MOSTO

Voyage to Africa

Alvise da Mosto (died 1483), also known as Cadamosto, was a member of a promi-
nent family in the Venetian nobility. Alvise passed his early years as a merchant,
visiting Flanders and Portugal. In 1454, he accompanied a Portuguese expedition en-
gaged in trade and exploration south of the Sahara. The account of this voyage and
another one the following year constitutes one of the earliest European descriptions
of black Africa. This excerpt contains Alvise's first impressions of the empire of Mali
(here called Melli) in central Africa, inhabited by the people he called the Azanegi
(Tuaregs) and the Wolof people, a large tribe south of the Senegal River.

From *The Voyages of Cadamosto*, translated and edited by G. R. Crone (London: Hakluyt
Society, 1937), pp. 20–33.

*   *   *

You should know that these people have no
knowledge of any Christians except the Portuguese, against whom they have waged war for
[thirteen or] fourteen years, many of them having
been taken prisoners, as I have already said, and
sold into slavery. It is asserted that when for the
first time they saw sails, that is, ships, on the sea
(which neither they nor their forefathers had ever
seen before), they believed that they were great
sea-birds with white wings, which were flying, and
had come from some strange place: when the sails
were lowered for the landing, some of them,
watching from far off, thought that the ships were
fishes. Others again said that they were phantoms
that went by night, at which they were greatly terrified. The reason for this belief was because these
caravels within a short space of time appeared at
many places, where attacks were delivered, especially at night, by their crews. Thus one such assault might be separated from the next by a
hundred or more miles, according to the plans of
the sailors, or as the winds, blowing hither and
thither, served them. Perceiving this, they said
amongst themselves, "If these be human creatures,

how can they travel so great a distance in one
night, a distance which we could not go in three
days?" Thus, as they did not understand the art of
navigation, they all thought that the ships were
phantoms. This I know is testified to by many
Portuguese who at that time were trading in caravels on this coast, and also by those who were
captured on these raids. And from this it may be
judged how strange many of our ways appeared
to them, if such an opinion could prevail.

Beyond the said mart of Edon [Oden], six days
journey further inland, there is a place called
Tagaza, that is to say in our tongue "cargador,"
where a very great quantity of rock-salt is mined.
Every year large caravans of camels belonging to
the above mentioned Arabs and Azanaghi, leaving
in many parties, carry it to Tanbutu [Timbuktu];
thence they go to Melli, the empire of the Blacks,
where, so rapidly is it sold, within eight days of its
arrival all is disposed of at a price of two to three
hundred *mitigalli* a load, according to the quantity
[a *mitigallo* is worth about a ducat]: then with the
gold they return to their homes.

In this empire of Melli it is very hot, and the
pasturage is very unsuitable for fourfooted animals: so that of the majority which come with the

caravans no more than twenty-five out of a hundred return. There are no quadrupeds in this country, because they all die, and many also of the Arabs and Azanaghi sicken in this place and die, on account of the great heat. It is said that on horseback it is about forty days from Tagaza to Tanbutu, and thirty from Tanbutu to Melli.

I enquired of them what the merchants of Melli did with this salt, and was told that a small quantity is consumed in their country. Since it is below the meridional and on the equinoctial, where the day is constantly about as long as the night, it is extremely hot at certain seasons of the year: this causes the blood to putrefy, so that were it not for this salt, they would die. The remedy they employ is as follows: they take a small piece of the salt, mix it in a jar with a little water, and drink it every day. They say that this saves them. The remainder of this salt they carry away on a long journey in pieces as large as a man can, with a certain knack, bear on his head.

You must know that when this salt is carried to Melli by camel it goes in large pieces [as it is dug out from the mines], of a size most easily carried on camels, two pieces on each animal. Then at Melli, these Blacks break it in smaller pieces, in order to carry it on their heads, so that each man carries one piece, and thus they form a great army of men on foot, who transport it a great distance. Those who carry it have two forked sticks, one in each hand: when they are tired, they plant them in the ground, and rest their load upon them. In this way they carry it until they reach certain waters: I could not learn from them whether it is fresh or sea water, so that I do not know if it is a river or the sea, though they consider it to be the sea. [I think however it must be a river, for if it were the sea, in such a hot country there would be no lack of salt.] These Blacks are obliged to carry it in this way, because they have no camels or other beasts of burden, as these cannot live in the great heat. It may be imagined how many men are required to carry it on foot, and how many are those who consume it every year. Having reached these waters with the salt, they proceed in this fashion: all those who have the salt

pile it in rows, each marking his own. Having made these piles, the whole caravan retires half a day's journey. Then there come another race of Blacks who do not wish to be seen or to speak. They arrive in large boats, from which it appears that they come from islands, and disembark. Seeing the salt, they place a quantity of gold opposite each pile, and then turn back, leaving salt and gold. When they have gone, the negroes who own the salt return: if they are satisfied with the quantity of gold, they leave the salt and retire with the gold. Then the Blacks of the gold return, and remove those piles which are without gold. By the other piles of salt they place more gold, if it pleases them, or else they leave the salt. In this way, by long and ancient custom, they carry on their trade without seeing or speaking to each other. Although it is difficult to believe this, I can testify that I have had this information from many merchants, Arab as well as Azanaghi, and also from persons in whom faith can be placed.

How the Emperor Sought to Take One of These Traders Prisoner

Reflecting upon this, I asked the merchants how it came to be that the Emperor of Melli, who, they said, was so great a lord, had not wished so to proceed as to find out by love or by other means what people these were who did not wish to speak or to be seen. They replied that, not many years previously, an Emperor of Melli determined at all costs to get one of them in his power, and having taken counsel about it, ordered some of his men to leave a few days before the salt caravan, and proceed to the place where it was customary to pile the salt, to dig trenches near by, in which to conceal themselves. When the Blacks returned to set the gold by the salt, they were to attack them and to take two or three, whom they were to convey under close guard to Melli. To be brief, this was done. They seized four, the others taking to flight: of the four they released three, surmising that one would satisfy the desires of the lord, and not wishing to anger these Blacks more. They spoke to this man in several Negro languages, but he would not reply, or speak at all, neither would he eat. He lived four days and then died. For this reason these Blacks of Melli are of the opinion, after the experience they had with him who would not speak, that they are dumb. Others think that they behave thus from disdain [of doing what their ancestors had never done]. This death vexed all the Blacks of Melli, for on account of it their lord could not achieve his intention. On returning to him they related the incident in due order.

Then the lord was very displeased with them, and asked what the Blacks looked like. They replied they were very black in colour, with well-formed bodies, a span higher than they themselves. The lower lip, more than a span in width, hung down, huge and red, over the breast, displaying the inner part glistening like blood.[1] The upper lip was as small as their own. This form of the lips displayed the gums and teeth, the latter, they said, being bigger than their own: they had two large teeth on each side, and large black eyes. Their appearance is terrifying, and the gums exude blood, as do the lips.

Because of this incident, none of the emperor's men have since been willing to embroil themselves in similar affairs, since, as a result of the capture and death of this one Negro, it was three years before the others would resume the customary exchange of gold for salt. It was thought that their lips became putrid, being in a warmer country than ours: so that these Blacks, having borne much sickness and death [for this space of time], and having no other way of obtaining the salt to cure themselves, resumed the accustomed trade. On this account, it is our opinion, being unable to live without salt, they set off their plight against our action, just as the Emperor did not care whether these Blacks spoke or not, so long as he had the profit of the gold. This is what I understood from this incident, and since it is related by so many we can accept it. Because I have seen and understood such things in the world, I am one of those who

are willing to believe this and other matters to be possible.

The gold thus brought to Melli is divided in three parts: one portion goes with the caravan which takes the road from Melli to a place that is called Cochia. This is the route which runs towards Soria [and il Cairo]: the second and third portions go with a caravan from Melli to Tanbutu. There they are separated: one portion goes to Atoet, whence it is carried to Tunis in Barbary through all the coast beyond: the other part goes to the above mentioned Hoden, whence it spreads towards Orā and Hona, towns in Barbary within the Strecto de Zibelterra, Afezes, Amarochos, Arzib, Azafi, and Amessa, towns in Barbary beyond the Straits. In these places it is bought by us Italians and other Christians from the Moors with the various merchandize we give them.

To return to my first subject, this is the best thing that is brought from the said land and country of the Azanaghi, that is, the brown men. Of that portion of the gold which is brought every year to Hoden, as described already, some quantity is carried to the sea coast, and sold to the Spaniards who are continuously stationed on the said island of Argin for the trade of merchandize, in exchange for other things.

In this land of the brown men, no money is coined, and they have never used it. Nor, formerly, was money to be found in any of their towns. Their sole method is to barter article for article, or two articles for one, and by such means they live. It is true that I understand that inland these Azanaghi, and also the Arabs in some of their districts, are wont to employ white cowries, of those small kinds which are brought to Venice from the Levant. They give certain numbers of these according to the things they have to buy. I should explain that the gold they sell they give by the weight of a *mitigallo;* according to the practice in Barbary, this *mitigallo* is of the value of a ducat, more or less.

*   *   *

---

[1] This suggests the use of the labret, which is still worn by the Lobi women.

The Rio de Senega, Which Divides the Desert from the Fertile Land

When we had passed in sight of this Cauo Bianco, we sailed on our journey to the river called the Rio de Senega, the first river of the Land of the Blacks, which debouches on this coast. This river separates the Blacks from the brown people called Azanaghi, and also the dry and arid land, that is, the above mentioned desert, from the fertile country of the Blacks. The river is large; its mouth being over a mile wide, and quite deep. There is another mouth a little distance beyond, with an island between. Thus it enters the sea by two mouths, and before each of them about a mile out to sea are shoals and broad sand-banks. In this place the water increases and decreases every six hours, that is, with the rise and fall of the tide. The tide ascends the river more than sixty miles, according to the information I have had from Portuguese who have been [many miles] up it [in caravels]. He who wishes to enter this river must go in with the tide, on account of the shoals and banks at the mouth. From Cauo Bianco it is 380 miles to the river: all the coast is sandy to within about twenty miles of the mouth. It is called Costa de Antte rotte, and is of the Azanaghi, or brown men.

It appears to me a very marvellous thing that beyond the river all men are very black, tall and big, their bodies well formed; and the whole country green, full of trees, and fertile: while on this side, the men are brownish, small, lean, ill-nourished, and small in stature: the country sterile and arid. This river is said to be a branch of the river Nile, of the four royal rivers: it flows through all Ethiopia, watering the country as in Egypt: passing through "lo caiero," it waters all the land of Egypt. This river has many other very large branches, in addition to that of Senega, and they are great rivers on this coast of Ethiopia, of which more will be related later.

The Lords Who Rule on the Coast of Capo Verde

The country of these first Blacks of the Kingdom of Senega is at the beginning of the first Kingdom of Ethiopia. It is all low-lying country, and many people live on the banks of this river. They are called Zilofi. For a great distance beyond, it is low country, and beyond the river likewise, except for Cauo Verde, which is the highest land on all this coast, for 400 miles beyond this Cauo Verde, and for 900 miles on this side of the said cape, the whole coast is flat. [And the people who dwell along its banks are called Gilofi. And all this coast and the known country behind is all lowland as far as the river, and also beyond this river to Capo Verde. This Cape is the highest land on the whole coast, that is for four hundred miles beyond the said Cape.]

The King of Senega in my time was called Zuchalin [Zucolin—a youth of twenty-two years. This Kingdom does not descend by inheritance] but in this land there are divers lesser lords, who [three or four of whom] through jealousy, at times agree among themselves, and set up a King of their own, if he is in truth of noble parentage. This King rules as long as is pleasing to the said lords [that is, according to the treatment they receive from him]. Frequently [they banish him by force: and as frequently] the King makes himself so powerful that he can defend himself against them. Thus his position is not stable and firm, as is that of the Soldan of Babilonia: but he is always in dread of deposition [death or exile].

You must know that this King is lord of a very poor people, and has no city in his country, but villages with huts of straw only. [They do not know how to build houses with walls:] they have no lime with which to build walls, and there is great lack of stones. This Kingdom, also, is very small; it extends no more than two hundred miles along the coast, and, from the information I had, about the same distance inland or a little more. The king lives thus: he has no fixed income [from taxes]: save that each year the lords of the country, in order to stand well with him, present him with horses, which are much esteemed owing to their scarcity, forage, beasts such as cows and goats, vegetables, millet, and the like. The King supports himself by raids, which result in many slaves from his own as well as neighbouring countries. He employs these slaves [in many ways, mainly] in cultivating the land allotted to him: but he also sells many to the Azanaghi [and Arab] merchants in return for horses and other goods, and also to Christians, since they have begun to trade with these Blacks.

The King is permitted to have as many wives as he wishes, as also are all the chiefs and men of this country, that is, as many as they can support. Thus this King has always thirty of them, though he favours one more than another, according to those from whom they are descended. This is his manner of living with his wives: he has certain villages and places, in some of which he keeps eight or ten of them. Each has a house of her own, with young servants to attend her, and slaves to cultivate the possessions and lands assigned by the lord, [with the fruits of which they are able to support themselves]. They have also a certain number of beasts, such as cows and goats, for their use; in this way his wives have the land sown and the beasts tended, and so gain a living. When the King arrives at one of these villages, he goes to the house of one of his wives, for they are obliged to provide, out of this produce, for him and those accompanying him. Every morning, at sunrise, each prepares three or four dishes of various foods, either meat, fish, or other Moorish foods according to their practice. These are sent by their slaves to be put at the disposal of their lord, so that within an hour forty or fifty dishes are assembled; when the time at which the lord wishes to eat has arrived, he picks out whatever tempts him, and gives the remainder to those in his train. But he never gives his people abundance to eat, so that they are always hungry. In this fashion he journeys from place to place without giving any thought to his victuals, and lodges sometimes with one wife, sometimes with another, so that he begets numerous sons, for when one is pregnant he leaves

her alone. All the other chiefs of this country live in this same fashion.

The Customs of the Blacks, and Their Beliefs

The faith of these first Blacks is Muhammadanism: they are not however, as are the white Moors, very resolute in this faith, especially the common people. The chiefs adhere to the tenets of the Muhammadans because they have around them priests of the Azanaghi or Arabs, [who have reached this country]. These give them some instruction in the laws of Muhammad, enlarging upon the great disgrace of being rulers and yet living without any divine law, and behaving as do their people and lowly men, who live without laws; and since they have converse with none but these Azanaghi and Arab priests, they are converted to the law of Muhammad. But since they have had converse with Christians, they believe less in it, for our customs please them, and they also realise our wealth and ingenuity in everything as compared with theirs. They say that the God, who has bestowed so many benefits, has shown his great love for us, which could only be if his law were good—but that, none the less, theirs is still the law of God, through which they will find salvation, as we through ours.

These people dress thus: almost all constantly go naked, except for a goatskin fashioned in the form of drawers, with which they hide their shame. But the chiefs and those of standing wear a cotton garment—for cotton grows in these lands. Their women spin it into cloth of a span in width. They are unable to make wider cloth because they do not understand how to card it for weaving. When they wish to make a larger piece, they sew four or five of these strips together. These garments are made to reach half way down the thigh, with wide sleeves to the elbow. They also wear breeches of this cotton, which are tied across, and reach to the ankles, and are otherwise so large as to be from thirty to thirty-five, or even forty *palmi* round the top; when they are girded round the waist, they are much crumpled and form a sack in front, and the hinder part reaches to the ground, and waggles like a tail—the most comical thing to be seen in the world. They would come in these wide petticoats with these tails and ask us if we had ever seen a more beautiful dress or fashion: for they hold it for certain that they are the most beautiful garments in the world. Their women, both married and single, all go covered with girdles, below which they wear a sheet of these cotton strips bound across, half way down their legs. Men and women always go barefoot. They wear nothing on their heads: the hair of both sexes is fashioned into neat tresses arranged in various styles, though their hair by nature is no longer than a span. You must know also that the men of these lands perform many women's tasks, such as spinning, washing clothes and such things. It is always very hot there, and the further one goes inland, the greater the heat: by comparison, it is no colder in these parts in January than it is in April in our country of Italy.

Men Clean in Their Persons and Filthy in Eating

The men and women are clean in their persons, since they wash themselves all over four or five times a day: but in eating they are filthy, and ill-mannered. In matters of which they have no experience they are credulous and awkward, but in those to which they are accustomed they are the equal of our skilled men. They are talkative, and never at a loss for something to say: in general they are great liars and cheats: but on the other hand, charitable, receiving strangers willingly, and providing a night's lodging and one or two meals without any charge.

*   *   *

REVIEW QUESTIONS

1. What does da Mosto's account reveal about the earliest phases of the African slave trade?
2. His description of the silent trade is the first extended account we have of this remarkable type of barter. How plausible is this account, and what might it teach the economic historian about markets?
3. Alvise da Mosto was also the first European ethnographer of the Wolof. What types of bias and questions did he bring to his view of the Wolof? What contrasts are there in the way he described them to the way William of Rubruck described the Mongols?

CHRISTOPHER COLUMBUS

Letter on His First Voyage

Christopher Columbus (c. 1450–1506) was born somewhere around Genoa and from an early age made his living as a sailor. Columbus saw much of the Mediterranean and Atlantic world and acquired real skill as a mapmaker and navigator. Self-taught in geography, Columbus developed a theory of the globe's size that made sailing across the Atlantic to China and Japan a daring but plausible adventure. After he had spent years looking for a patron among the rulers of Europe, at last in

SAPI-PORTUGUESE SALT CELLAR, IVORY (C. 1500)

Portuguese traders in West Africa commissioned art works from the indigenous Sapi people. Merchants then sold these imaginative ivory carvings across Europe; this salt cellar ended up in Italy. Why would a European collector have purchased this object? How does the style of Sapi art differ from contemporary works of art created by Europeans?

1492, Isabella of Castile took the lead along with her husband Ferdinando of Aragon in sponsoring Columbus's first voyage. This letter is one of his earliest accounts of this trip—but we do not know to whom the letter was sent.

From *Selected Documents Illustrating the Four Voyages of Christopher Columbus,* translated and edited by Cecil Jane (London: Hakluyt Society, 1930), pp. 3–18.

Sir, As I know that you will be pleased at the great victory with which Our Lord has crowned my voyage, I write this to you, from which you will learn how in thirty-three days, I passed from the Canary Islands to the Indies with the fleet which the most illustrious king and queen, our sovereigns, gave to me. And there I found very many islands filled with people innumerable, and of them all I have taken possession for their highnesses, by proclamation made and with the royal standard unfurled, and no opposition was offered to me. To the first island which I found, I gave the name *San Salvador,* in emembrance of the Divine Majesty, Who has marvellously bestowed all this; the Indians call it "Guanahani." To the second, I gave the name *Isla de Santa María de Concepción;* to the third, *Fernandina;* to the fourth, *Isabella;* to the fifth, *Isla Juana,* and so to each one I gave a new name.

When I reached Juana, I followed its coast to the westward, and I found it to be so extensive that I thought that it must be the mainland, the province of Catayo. And since there were neither towns nor villages on the seashore, but only small hamlets, with the people of which I could not have speech, because they all fled immediately, I went forward on the same course, thinking that I should not fail to find great cities and towns. And, at the end of many leagues, seeing that there was no change and that the coast was bearing me northwards, which I wished to avoid, since winter was already beginning and I proposed to make from it to the south, and as moreover the wind was carrying me forward, I determined not to wait for a change in the weather and retraced my path as far as a certain harbour known to me. And from that point, I sent two men inland to learn if there were a king or great cities. They travelled three

days' journey and found an infinity of small hamlets and people without number, but nothing of importance. For this reason, they returned.

I understood sufficiently from other Indians, whom I had already taken, that this land was nothing but an island. And therefore I followed its coast eastwards for one hundred and seven leagues to the point where it ended. And from that cape, I saw another island, distant eighteen leagues from the former, to the east, to which I at once gave the name "Española." And I went there and followed its northern coast, as I had in the case of Juana, to the eastward for one hundred and eighty-eight great leagues in a straight line. This island and all the others are very fertile to a limitless degree, and this island is extremely so. In it there are many harbours on the coast of the sea, beyond comparison with others which I know in Christendom, and many rivers, good and large, which is marvellous. Its lands are high, and there are in it very many sierras and very lofty mountains, beyond comparison with the island of Teneriffe. All are most beautiful, of a thousand shapes, and all are accessible and filled with trees of a thousand kinds and tall, and they seem to touch the sky. And I am told that they never lose their foliage, as I can understand, for I saw them as green and as lovely as they are in Spain in May, and some of them were flowering, some bearing fruit, and some in another stage, according to their nature. And the nightingale was singing and other birds of a thousand kinds in the month of November there where I went. There are six or eight kinds of palm, which are a wonder to behold on account of their beautiful variety, but so are the other trees and fruits and plants. In it are marvellous pine groves, and there are very large tracts of cultivatable lands, and there is honey, and there are birds of many kinds and fruits in great diversity. In the interior are mines of metals, and the population is without number. Española is a marvel.

The sierras and mountains, the plains and arable lands and pastures, are so lovely and rich for planting and sowing, for breeding cattle of every kind, for building towns and villages. The harbours of the sea here are such as cannot be believed to exist unless they have been seen, and so with the rivers, many and great, and good waters, the majority of which contain gold. In the trees and fruits and plants, there is a great difference from those of Juana. In this island, there are many spices and great mines of gold and of other metals.

The people of this island, and of all the other islands which I have found and of which I have information, all go naked, men and women, as their mothers bore them, although some women cover a single place with the leaf of a plant or with a net of cotton which they make for the purpose. They have no iron or steel or weapons, nor are they fitted to use them, not because they are not well built men and of handsome stature, but because they are very marvellously timorous. They have no other arms than weapons made of canes, cut in seeding time, to the ends of which they fix a small sharpened stick. And they do not dare to make use of these, for many times it has happened that I have sent ashore two or three men to some town to have speech, and countless people have come out to them, and as soon as they have seen my men approaching they have fled, even a father not waiting for his son. And this, not because ill has been done to anyone; on the contrary, at every point where I have been and have been able to have speech, I have given to them of all that I had, such as cloth and many other things, without receiving anything for it; but so they are, incurably timid. It is true that, after they have been reassured and have lost their fear, they are so guileless and so generous with all they possess, that no one would believe it who has not seen it. They never refuse anything which they possess, if it be asked of them; on the contrary, they invite anyone to share it, and display as much love as if they would

give their hearts, and whether the thing be of value or whether it be of small price, at once with whatever trifle of whatever kind it may be that is given to them, with that they are content. I forbade that they should be given things so worthless as fragments of broken crockery and scraps of broken glass, and ends of straps, although when they were able to get them, they fancied that they possessed the best jewel in the world. So it was found that a sailor for a strap received gold to the weight of two and a half *castellanos,* and others much more for other things which were worth much less. As for new *blancas,* for them they would give everything which they had, although it might be two or three *castellanos'* weight of gold or an *arroba* or two of spun cotton. . . . They took even the pieces of the broken hoops of the wine barrels and, like savages, gave what they had, so that it seemed to me to be wrong and I forbade it. And I gave a thousand handsome good things, which I had brought, in order that they might conceive affection, and more than that, might become Christians and be inclined to the love and service of their highnesses and of the whole Castilian nation, and strive to aid us and to give us of the things which they have in abundance and which are necessary to us. And they do not know any creed and are not idolaters; only they all believe that power and good are in the heavens, and they are very firmly convinced that I, with these ships and men, came from the heavens, and in this belief they everywhere received me, after they had overcome their fear. And this does not come because they are ignorant; on the contrary, they are of a very acute intelligence and are men who navigate all those seas, so that it is amazing how good an account they give of everything, but it is because they have never seen people clothed or ships of such a kind.

And as soon as I arrived in the Indies, in the first island which I found, I took by force some of them, in order that they might learn and give me information of that which there is in those parts, and so it was that they soon understood us, and we them, either by speech or signs, and they have been very serviceable. I still take them with me, and they are always assured that I come from Heaven, for all the intercourse which they have had with me; and they were the first to announce this wherever I went, and the others went running from house to house and to the neighbouring towns, with loud cries of, 'Come! Come to see the people from Heaven!' So all, men and women alike, when their minds were set at rest concerning us, came, so that not one, great or small, remained behind, and all brought something to eat and drink, which they gave with extraordinary affection. In all the island, they have very many canoes, like rowing *fustas,* some larger, some smaller, and some are larger than a *fusta* of eighteen benches. They are not so broad, because they are made of a single log of wood, but a *fusta* would not keep up with them in rowing, since their speed is a thing incredible. And in these they navigate among all those islands, which are innumerable, and carry their goods. One of these canoes I have seen with seventy and eighty men in her, and each one with his oar.

In all these islands, I saw no great diversity in the appearance of the people or in their manners and language. On the contrary, they all understand one another, which is a very curious thing, on account of which I hope that their highnesses will determine upon their conversion to our holy faith, towards which they are very inclined.

I have already said how I have gone one hundred and seven leagues in a straight line from west to east along the seashore of the island Juana, and as a result of that voyage, I can say that this island is larger than England and Scotland together, for, beyond these one hundred and seven leagues, there remain to the westward two provinces to which I have not gone. One of these provinces they call "Avan," and there the people are born with tails; and these provinces cannot have a length of less than fifty or sixty leagues, as I could understand from those Indians whom I have and who know all the islands.

The other, Española, has a circumference greater than all Spain, from Colibre, by the sea-coast, to Fuenterabia in Vizcaya, since I voyaged along one side one hundred and eighty-eight great leagues in a straight line from west to east. It is a land to be desired and, seen, it is never to be left. And in it, although of all I have taken possession for their highnesses and all are more richly endowed than I know how, or am able, to say, and I hold them all for their highnesses, so that they may dispose of them as, and as absolutely as, of the kingdoms of Castile, in this Española, in the situation most convenient and in the best position for the mines of gold and for all intercourse as well with the mainland here as with that there, belonging to the Grand Khan, where will be great trade and gain, I have taken possession of a large town, to which I gave the name *Villa de Navidad,* and in it I have made fortifications and a fort, which now will by this time be entirely finished, and I have left in it sufficient men for such a purpose with arms and artillery and provisions for more than a year, and a *fusta,* and one, a master of all sea-craft, to build others, and great friendship with the king of that land, so much so, that he was proud to call me, and to treat me as, a brother. And even if he were to change his attitude to one of hostility towards these men, he and his do not know what arms are and they go naked, as I have already said, and are the most timorous people that there are in the world, so that the men whom I have left there alone would suffice to destroy all that land, and the island is without danger for their persons, if they know how to govern themselves.

In all these islands, it seems to me that all men are content with one woman, and to their chief or king they give as many as twenty. It appears to me that the women work more than the men. And I have not been able to learn if they hold private property; what seemed to me to appear was that, in that which one had, all took a share, especially of eatable things.

In these islands I have so far found no human monstrosities, as many expected, but on the contrary the whole population is very well-formed, nor are they Negroes as in Guinea, but their hair is flowing, and they are not born where there is intense force in the rays of the sun; it is true that the sun has there great power, although it is distant from the equinoctial line twenty-six degrees. In these islands, where there are high mountains, the cold was severe this winter, but they endure it, being used to it and with the help of meats which they eat with many and extremely hot spices. As I have found no monsters, so I have had no report of any, except in an island "Quaris," the second at the coming into the Indies, which is inhabited by a people who are regarded in all the islands as very fierce and who eat human flesh. They have many canoes with which they range through all the islands of India and pillage and take as much as they can. They are no more malformed than the others, except that they have the custom of wearing their hair long like women, and they use bows and arrows of the same cane stems, with a small piece of wood at the end, owing to lack of iron which they do not possess. They are ferocious among these other people who are cowardly to an excessive degree, but I make no more account of them than of the rest. These are those who have intercourse with the women of "Matinino," which is the first island met on the way from Spain to the Indies, in which there is not a man. These women engage in no feminine occupation, but use bows and arrows of cane, like those already mentioned, and they arm and protect themselves with plates of copper, of which they have much.

In another island, which they assure me is larger than Española, the people have no hair. In it, there is gold incalculable, and from it and from the other islands, I bring with me Indians as evidence.

In conclusion, to speak only of that which has been accomplished on this voyage, which was so hasty, their highnesses can see that I will give them as much gold as they may need, if their highnesses will render me very slight assistance; moreover, spice and cotton, as much as their highnesses shall command; and mastic, as much as they shall order to be shipped and which, up to now, has been found only in Greece, in the island of Chios, and the Seignory sells it for what it pleases; and aloe wood, as much as they shall order to be shipped, and slaves, as many as they shall order to be

shipped and who will be from the idolaters. And I believe that I have found rhubarb and cinamon, and I shall find a thousand other things of value, which the people whom I have left there will have discovered, for I have not delayed at any point, so far as the wind allowed me to sail, except in the town of Navidad, in order to leave it secured and well established, and in truth, I should have done much more, if the ships had served me, as reason demanded.

This is enough . . . and the eternal God, our Lord, Who gives to all those who walk in His way triumph over things which appear to be impossible, and this was notably one; for, although men have talked or have written of these lands, all was conjectural, without suggestion of ocular evidence, but amounted only to this, that those who heard for the most part listened and judged it to be rather a fable than as having any vestige of truth. So that, since Our Redeemer has given this victory to our most illustrious king and queen, and to their renowned kingdoms, in so great a matter, for this all Christendom ought to feel delight and make great feasts and give solemn thanks to the Holy Trinity with many solemn prayers for the great exaltation which they shall have, in the turning of so many peoples to our holy faith, and afterwards for temporal benefits, for not only Spain but all Christians will have hence refreshment and gain.

This, in accordance with that which has been accomplished, thus briefly.

Done in the caravel, off the Canary Islands, on the fifteenth of February, in the year one thousand four hundred and ninety-three.

At your orders.   El Almirante.

After having written this, and being in the sea of Castile, there came on me so great a south-south-west wind, that I was obliged to lighten ship. But I ran here to-day into this port of Lisbon, which was the greatest marvel in the world, whence I decided to write to their highnesses. In all the Indies, I have always found weather like May; where I went in thirty-three days and I had returned in twenty-eight, save for these storms which have detained me for fourteen days, beating about in this sea. Here all the sailors say that never has there been so bad a winter nor so many ships lost.

Done on the fourth day of March.

REVIEW QUESTIONS

1. What can we learn about Columbus's personality and motives from this letter?
2. Columbus also provided here the first Western account of the people he called Indians. What do we learn about his interests and abilities as an ethnographer?

MANUEL I

"The Letter Which the King, Our Lord, Wrote to the King and Queen of Castile, His Kin, Concerning the News of India"

In 1501, King Manuel I of Portugal wrote this letter to his relatives Isabella of Castile and Ferdinando of Aragon. The king was clearly proud of the journey Pedro Alvarez Cabral had made to India the previous year. As this letter explains, Cabral's fleet also "discovered" Brazil (here called Santa Cruz) during this voyage. The letter describes Cabral's visit to Kilwa (here Quilon) in East Africa as well. But most of the letter concerns Cabral's long stay in Calicut in India.

From *The Voyage of Pedro Álvares Cabral to Brazil and India*, translated by William Brooks Greenlee (London: Hakluyt Society, 1937), pp. 43–52.

Most high and most excellent and most powerful Sovereigns, Father and Mother: During these past days, after the first news arrived from India, I did not write at once to Your Majesties concerning the matters there because Pedro Alvarez Cabral, my chief captain of the fleet, which I had sent there, had not yet returned. And after his arrival I also delayed in doing so because two ships of his company had not yet come. One of these he had sent to Çofalla, a gold-mine which was discovered recently, not to establish trade, but only to have true information of what was there; because of the two ships which went there for this purpose, one was lost at sea, and the other was separated from the fleet in stormy weather and did not go there. And after the aforesaid ships had arrived, and I was on the point of notifying Your Majesties, Pero Lopes de Padilha told me that you would be glad to have news of what had happened there. The following is briefly everything which took place. My aforesaid captain with thirteen ships departed from Lisbon the 9th of March of last year, and during the octave of Easter he reached a land which he newly discovered, to

CONQUEST OF MEXICO, FLORENTINE CODEX (C. 1555)

The Franciscan friar Bernardino de Sahagún (d. 1590) directed a team of Nahua aides who produced the Florentine Codex. This book is an account of Cortéz's expedition of 1519, which resulted in the destruction of the Aztec Empire. The book is in Nahuatl and is accompanied by over 100 illustrations. Scholars have debated the extent to which the text and pictures allowed the Nahua to express their own views on these events. Sahagún began collecting information in the 1540s, and this chapter may have been composed around 1555. The illustrations accompanying the text may also have been sketched by Nahua people. These six pictures show characteristic battle scenes; in the last one, the Mexicans have captured a Spanish cannon. Guns and steel certainly played a role in the Spanish conquest of Mexico. What evidence do these pictures provide of this? Perhaps even more striking were the roles of horses and large dogs (not pictured here). What advantages did these animals provide the Spaniards?

which he gave the name of Santa Cruz. In it he found the people nude as in the first innocence, gentle, and peaceable. It seemed that Our Lord miraculously wished it to be found, because it is very convenient and necessary for the voyage to India, because he repaired his ships and took water there. And on account of the long voyage which he had to make, he did not stop to obtain information about the said land; he only sent me a ship from there to notify me how he found it; and he pursued his route by way of the Cape of Good Hope. In that gulf, before arriving at it, he encountered great storms, in which, during one single day, four ships foundered together before his eyes, of which not a single person escaped. At this time, also, another of his ships disappeared, of which no news has been received up to this time. And that in which he went, with the others which remained, passed through great danger. And thus he went his way to make port at the kingdom of Quiloa, which belongs to the Moors, under whose sovereignty is the said mine of Çotalla, because he carried my letters and messages for its king, to establish peace with him, and a treaty concerning purchases and trade at the said mine. And before reaching the aforesaid kingdom, he found two ships with a great quantity of gold, which he took possession of, and because they belonged to the said King of Quiloa, after doing them much honour, he let them go. He was very well received by that king, who came in person to converse with my said captain on the sea, and entered with him in his boat, and he sent him presents; and after receiving my letters and messages, he agreed to the treaty. And since the ships which were destined for that mine were among those which were lost, no trade was begun there at that time, because the merchandise which the other ships carried was not suitable for what was needed for that land. And he departed from there and went to another kingdom, Melinde, for which he also was carrying my letters and messages, because its king, who likewise is a Moor, had done good deeds to Dom Vasco, who first went there to discover it. This king likewise visited him on the sea and also sent him presents, and confirmed and

established peace and friendship with him, and gave him the pilots whom he needed for his voyage. These kingdoms extend from the Red Sea in this direction, and in the interior they border on Gentiles, and these Gentiles border on the land of Prester John, whom they call the *abechy*. In their language this means "branded with iron," because, as a matter of fact, they do this, and they are branded with iron as a sign that they are baptized in water. From there he departed for Calecut, which is seven hundred leagues beyond. This city, as I believe you must already know, is of the Gentiles who worship many things and believe that there is only one God. And it is very populous, and there are in it many Moors who, until now, always traded there in spices, because it is thus like Bruges in Flanders, the principal trading place for the things of India, which come to it from outside; and in it there are only cassiafistula and ginger. He arrived at this city five months after having departed from Lisbon. And he was very honourably received by the king, who came to a house beside the sea to speak to him, with all his lords and many other people. And there he gave him my messages and established with him my peace and concord. Concerning this agreement the aforesaid king ordered a letter written on a sheet of silver with his seal inlaid in gold, for this is the custom in his land in matters of great importance, and other letters written on leaves of trees which resemble palms, on which they ordinarily write. And from these trees and their fruit are made the following things: sugar, honey, oil, wine, water, vinegar, charcoal, and cordage for ships, and for everything else, and matting of which they make some sails for ships, and it serves them for everything which they need. And the aforesaid fruit, in addition to what is thus made of it, is their chief food, particularly at sea. After the agreement had thus been made with the said king, my factor sent on shore the entire establishment which I had ordered for the above-mentioned factory, and at once he began to trade with his merchandise and to load the ships with spices. In the meantime, the King of Calecut sent word to my captain that a very large and well-armed ship which had annoyed him on previous occasions, belonging to another king, his enemy, had sent word to him that it was passing before his port, without any fear of him, and he begged him to order it to be captured, enlarging on the matter, as it greatly concerned his estate and honour.

And the said captain, in view of the good treatment which he and also my factor were beginning to receive, and in order to confirm further peace and friendship, agreed to do it. And in order to show him the strength of our people in ships and artillery, he sent against it only the smallest ship which he had, with a large bombard. And it overtook them within the harbour of another king, his neighbour, and before his eyes and those of all his people he captured it, and brought it to Calecut with 400 bowmen and some artillery and with seven elephants, trained in warfare, on board (there these would be worth thirty thousand cruzados, for they gave five thousand for only one of them), and with other merchandise of spices. This ship my captain ordered to be presented to him, and he gave it to him with everything which came in it, and he came to the shore with all his state and pomp to see it, since it was to them a very great surprise that so small a ship with so few men should take so large a ship with so many people, and to receive the message which the said captain was sending him concerning it. And the Moors, especially those of Mecca, who were there, seeing that they were in this concord and friendship, and that two ships were already loaded with spices, and seeing also the great loss which they were suffering, sought all the means that they could to put discord between my factor and the king. And they stirred up a tumult on land to hinder them; and because all the merchandise was in the hands of the Moors they hid it, and secretly sent it elsewhere. When he learned this, the aforesaid captain sent word to the King of Calecut, complaining to him and asking him to fulfil what he had agreed, which was that in twenty days he would give him merchandise with which to load the said ships, and that until they were loaded, he would not give authority to load to any others. And the king answered him that he would at once order all the

merchandise which there was in the land to be given to him, and that if any ship should be loaded in his harbour without the knowledge of his officials, he gave him the authority and power to detain it until he sent his said officials, so that they might arrange to turn it over to him. As soon as the Moors learned of this, they agreed to load a ship publicly with great diligence, using still greater care in hiding the merchandise than they had previously done, and this, in order to give an excuse for an outbreak to begin, for they are powerful. And the city is of many nationalities and of extensive population, in which the king can, with difficulty, attend to the tumults of the populace. And when my factor saw that the ship was being loaded, he asked the said captain to detain it, as the king had agreed. And the said captain, fearing an outbreak, hesitated to do it; and the said factor again asked him to detain it, telling him that the chief Moors and also some Gentiles told him that if the said ship were not held they could in no way load their ships. According to what followed it appears that they were doing it in order to give rise to the said outbreak. And my captain, after hesitating many times, fearing what followed, ordered the people of that ship to be told that, because of the authority which he had for this, it should not leave; but they were not willing to agree to this. And then it was necessary to order it to be held. And he commanded his boats to bring it inside the harbour, where it surely could not leave without his permission. And as soon as the Moors saw this, since it was the end which they desired, at that very moment they came quickly with all the rest of the population, whom they had already stirred up, to attack the said factor and his house, and fought with him. And he with those few whom he had with him, defended themselves for some time, and leaving the house, rallied at the sea. And my captain, who was then ill, as soon as he was told of the uprising on land, ordered all his boats to aid him, and although the sea was very rough he nevertheless gathered up some of the people. They killed the factor and with him fifty people were lost, either dead or captives. After this was done, when my captain saw that the king had not come to help and that he sent no message and was providing himself with some equipment implying war, and also had taken possession of my property which had remained on shore, he waited one day to see if he would make amends for the said matter. When he saw that he was sending him no message, fearing that he was arming himself effectively, as he afterwards did, to prevent him from taking the vengeance he could take at that time, he decided to act at once, and he took ten large ships which were in the harbour, and ordered all the people who were on them to be put to the sword, with the exception of a few who, concealing themselves, escaped death, and whom afterwards he did not wish to kill, but brought captive to me. And he ordered the said ships to be burned in front of the port, which caused great horror to the king and to the people of the land. On the ships there were three elephants which died there. In this manner he spent the entire day; and as soon as it was night, he went with all the ships, and placed himself as near land as he could in front of the city; and as soon as it was dawn, he began to fire with artillery, and bombarded it until night, especially the houses of the king. In this he did much damage, and killed many of his people, as he learned afterwards, and he killed one of the chief men who was near the king. On account of this, the king immediately departed from the city, for it seemed to him that he was not safe anywhere. And he sailed from there to another port of his, which was called Fandarene [Pandarani], which he also damaged with artillery, and killed people. And from there he sailed to the kingdom of Cochim, which is the region from which spices come, 30 leagues beyond Calecut, and on the way, he found two other ships of Calecut, which he also captured and ordered to be burned. And when he reached Cochim, after having informed the king of what had happened in Calecut, he was very well received by him, and made an agreement with him in the same manner which he had done in Calecut. Then he immediately sent my factor and certain men with him on shore, for whom they gave him honourable men as hostages, whom he brought to me; and they

loaded his ships in 16 days; and the merchandise they brought to him in their boats was brought with so much greater friendliness and security that it appeared that Our Lord permitted the outbreak at Calecut in order that this other agreement might take place, which is of greater profit and security, because the harbour is much better and of much more extensive trade, since, of almost all the merchandise which goes to Calecut, most of it is to be found in that land, and because others go there first without going to Calecut. In this city of Cochim there are many ships, and he learned that two merchants alone had as many as 50 ships. In that kingdom there are many true Christians of the conversion of Saint Thomas, and their priests follow the manner of life of the apostles with much strictness, having nothing of their own except what is given them as alms. And they practise celibacy, and have churches in which they say mass, and they consecrate unleavened bread, and wine which they make from dried fruit with water, for they cannot make other. In their churches they have no images save the cross, and all the Christians wear the apostolic garments, and never cut their beards and hair. And there he found definite information concerning where the body of Saint Thomas lies, which is 150 leagues from there, on the sea coast, in a city which is called Maliapor [Mailapur], of a small population; and he brought me earth from his tomb. And all the Christians and also the Moors and Gentiles, on account of the great miracles which are performed, go to his house on pilgrimage. He also brought us two Christians who came of their own accord and with the permission of their prelate, so that we might send them to Rome and to Jerusalem, to see the things of the Church there, and to be informed about them, for they consider that they are better ruled by being ordained by Saint Peter, who, they believe, was the chief of the apostles. And he also learned certain news of great Christian nations which are on the other side of that kingdom, who come on pilgrimage to the aforesaid house of Saint Thomas, and have very great kings who obey One only. They are white men of fair hair, and are considered strong. The land is called Malchima, and from it come porcelain, and musk and amber, and aloe-wood, which they bring from the river Ganges, which is on this side of them. And there are such fine vases of porcelain there, that a single one of them is worth a hundred cruzados. And while he was in the kingdom of Cochim, when the treaty had been agreed to and the ships loaded, there came to him messages from the King of Cananor, and from the King of Colum [Quilon] who are near by, requesting him to come to them because they would make more profitable trade with him, but, because he had already made the treaty, he declined to go. At this time, as he was about to depart from Cochim, the same king sent word to him that a large fleet from Calecut was coming against him, and that as many as 15,000 men were in it. It did not seem well to my captain to fight with it, because he had his ships loaded, and had few men, and it did not seem to him that there was time or necessity for taking the risk, since he feared that they might kill or disable some of them, and on account of the length of the journey which he had to go, which was 4,000 leagues from here. But he set sail, with them following him, and as they did not dare to go far out to sea, they turned back, because they feared to go against him. From there he went his way, which was to the kingdom of Cananor, [ruled by] one of those kings who invited him. And as he was passing, as soon as those on land caught sight of him, they sent him another message, asking him to stop there, because the king wanted to send a messenger to me by him, whom he brought me. And in the single day that he was there, he ordered so much spicery to be brought to the ships that he might have entirely filled them, had they been empty; and they gave what they might carry free, as a present to win my friendship. And all his chief men came also to my captain, telling him on behalf of the king that they would see to it that he was treated there in a different manner than in Calecut, assuring him that if he wanted to make war on Calecut they would help him, and that he in person would go on land, and all his fleet on the sea. And after thanking him greatly in my name, he took leave of him, saying to him that in

the other fleet which I was to send soon, I would send him my answer regarding everything. He went his way, and in the middle of that crossing he took a very large ship loaded with merchandise. It appeared to him that it was a ship of Mecca which was just coming from Calecut. And finding that the aforesaid ship belonged to the King of Cambaia [Cambay], he abandoned it, sending word by it to the said king that he had released it because he did not intend to make war with any one; he had made it only on those who had broken the word which they had given to him in my name. Continuing farther on his way, he lost one of the ships which was laden, for it ran aground during the night. Its people were saved, and he ordered the ship to be burned because it could not be dislodged safely. From this place he sent a ship to obtain news of the mine of Çofalla which I have mentioned before. This has just arrived, and brought me definite information of it and also concerning the trade and the merchandise of the country and of the great quantity of gold which is there; and there he found news, that among the men who carry gold from there to the coasts, they saw many who have four eyes, namely, two in front and two behind. The men are small of body and strong, and it is said that they are cruel, and that they eat the men with whom they have war, and that the cows of the king wear collars of heavy gold around their necks. Near this mine there are two islands on which they gather much pearl and amber. My aforesaid captain departed from there, and reached Lisbon 16 months from the day he had left it, and, blessed be Our Lord, in all this voyage he lost only three men from sickness, and all the others are healthy and of good spirits.[1] And now a certain message comes to me saying that one of the ships that was going to Çoffala which he believed lost, is coming, and will be here shortly. They say that it entered the Red Sea, and that it is bringing from there some silver and also some information concerning matters there, although I am already informed in detail concerning

---

[1] This is a mistake, since many had died of scurvy.

the said Red Sea, having been informed thereof by my above-mentioned captain, who had information concerning it in many ways. I leave the other details of this matter to Pero Lopes, who was present at everything. Very exalted and very excellent and very puissant Sovereigns, Father and Mother, may Our Lord have your life and royal estate in His holy care.

Written in Santarem the 29th of July, 1501.

El Rey.

REVIEW QUESTIONS

1. One theme here concerns Portuguese rivalry with the Moors—Muslims in East Africa and India. What were these relationships like?
2. What types of trade did the Portuguese hope to conduct in India?
3. Even though the information in the letter is at second hand, we still have an extensive view of the people of Calicut. What image of India has Manuel constructed for his readers?

12 ❧ THE CIVILIZATION OF THE RENAISSANCE, c. 1350–1550

The Renaissance began as an Italian phenomenon, occurring between c. 1300 and 1520, that spread to the rest of Europe over the course of the 1500s and early 1600s. Its principal manifestations were the revival of classicism and naturalism in arts and literature, the rise of the modern dynastic state as the dominant political structure, and an economic crisis fueled by industrial change and economic contraction.

Until recently, scholars have traditionally viewed the Renaissance as a period of great change. Contemporaries used the term rinascita *to express their sense of a rebirth, a perfection in the arts. Some modern scholars view the period as one of fundamental change, an abrupt departure from the past, and have identified the following several characteristics that set the Renaissance apart as a discrete period of history. Scholars and artists revived classical antiquity as a subject of study and emulation. The state emerged as a work of art, that is, as a calculated design by persons in pursuit of power. The universal man, well rounded in physical and intellectual endeavors, became the political and pedagogical ideal of the age. The social mobility born of a rapidly changing economy led to an aristocracy of merit, a fusion of nobility and bourgeoisie in which achievement mattered more than lineage.*

All of these characteristics have been criticized and reviewed by latter-day historians of the Renaissance, most of whom would emphasize its continuity with the Middle Ages. Few, however, would disagree that the age was unusually self-conscious—aware of its achievements, intrigued by its potential, and impatient of its limits. The following selections capture something of this mentality.

LEON BATTISTA ALBERTI

FROM *I Libri della Famiglia*

Leon Battista Alberti (1404–1474) embodied the Renaissance universal man. Born the illegitimate son of a Florentine merchant, he was an athlete, polymath, and artist. He earned a degree in canon law at the University of Bologna in 1428 and migrated to Rome, where he entered papal service. It was there, in 1438, that he began to write On the Family. *Written in the form of a dialogue among the members of the Alberti family, gathered at the deathbed of Leon Battista's father in 1421, it examines the ideal family as a unit for the begetting and rearing of children, for the amassing and maintaining of fortunes, and for the accumulation and exercise of power. It was also a sly exercise in satire, insofar as it indirectly criticizes his brothers and uncles for violating his father's dying wish that Leon Battista be treated as a legitimate member of the family.*

From *I Libri della Famiglia*, translated by Renee New Watkins (Columbia: University of South Carolina Press, 1969).

*   *   *

XIII

Lionardo: If I had children, you may be sure I should think about them, but my thoughts would be untroubled. My first consideration would only be to make my children grow up with good character and virtue. Whatever activities suited their taste would suit me. Any activity which is not dishonest is not displeasing to an honorable mind. The activities which lead to honor and praise belong to honorable and wellborn men. Certainly I will admit that every son cannot achieve all that his father might wish. If he does something he is able to do, however, I like that better than to have him strike out in a direction where he cannot follow through. I also think it is more praiseworthy for a man, even if he does not altogether succeed, to do his best in some field rather than sit inactive, inert, and idle. There is an old saying which our ancestors often repeated: "Idleness is the mother of vice." It is an ugly and hateful thing to see a

man keep himself forever useless, like that idle fellow who when they asked him why he spent all day as if condemned to sit or lie on public benches, answered "I am waiting to get fat." The man who heard him was disgusted, and asked him rather to try to fatten up a pig, since at least something useful might come of it. Thus quite correctly he showed him what an idle fellow amounts to, which is less than a pig.

I'll go further, Adovardo. However rich and noble a father may be, he should try to have his son learn, besides the noble skills, some occupation which is not degrading. By means of this occupation in case of misfortune he can live honestly by his own labor and the work of his hands. Are the vicissitudes of this world so little or so infrequent that we can ignore the possibility of adverse circumstances? Was not the son of Perseus, king of Macedonia, seen sweating and soiled in a Roman factory, employed in making his living with heavy and painful labor? If the instability of things could thus transport the son of a famous and powerful king to such depths of poverty and need, it is right for us private citizens as well as for men of higher station to provide against every misfortune. If none in our house ever had to devote himself to such laboring occupations, thank fortune for it, and let us make sure that none will have to in the future. A wise and foresightful pilot, to be able to survive in adverse storms, carries more rope, anchors, and sheets than he needs for good weather. So let the father see that his sons enjoy some praiseworthy and useful activity. In this matter let him consider first of all the honesty of the work, and then adapt his course to what he knows his son can actually accomplish, and finally try to choose a field in which, by applying himself, the young man can hope to earn a reputation.

*   *   *

Battista: Whatever you think. The only question we have is what are the things that make a family fortunate. Go on with what you have to say and we shall listen.

*   *   *

Lionardo: In our discussion we may establish four general precepts as sound and firm foundation for all the other points to be developed or added. I shall name them. In the family the number of men must not diminish but augment; possessions must not grow less, but more; all forms of disgrace are to be shunned—a good name and fine reputation is precious and worth pursuing; hatreds, enmities, rancor must be carefully avoided, while good will, numerous acquaintances, and friendships are something to look for, augment, and cultivate.

*   *   *

If a family is not to fall for these reasons into what we have described as the most unfortunate condition of decline, but is to grow, instead, in fame and in the prosperous multitude of its youth, we must persuade our young men to take wives. We must use every argument for this purpose, offer incentive, promise reward, employ all our wit, persistence, and cunning. A most appropriate reason for taking a wife may be found in what we

were saying before, about the evil of sensual indulgence, for the condemnation of such things may lead young men to desire honorable satisfactions. As other incentives, we may also speak to them of the delights of this primary and natural companionship of marriage. Children act as pledges and securities of marital love and kindness. At the same time they offer a focus for all a man's hopes and desires. Sad, indeed, is the man who has labored to get wealth and power and lands, and then has no true heir and perpetuator of his memory. No one can be more suited than a man's true and legitimate sons to gain advantages by virtue of his character, position, and authority, and to enjoy the fruits and rewards of his labor. If a man leaves such heirs, furthermore, he need not consider himself wholly dead and gone. His children keep his own position and his true image in the family. Dido, the Phoenician, when Aeneas left her, his mistress, cried out with tears, among her great sorrows no desire above this one: "Ah, had I but a small Aeneas now, to play beside me." As you were first poisoned, wretched and abandoned woman, by that man whose fatal and consuming love you did embrace, so another little Aeneas might by his similar face and gestures have offered you some consolation in your grief and anguish.

*   *   *

When, by the urging and counsel of their elders and of the whole family, young men have arrived at the point of marriage, their mothers and other female relatives and friends, who have known the virgins of the neighborhood from earliest childhood and know the way their upbringing has formed them, should select all the well-born and well-brought-up girls and present that list to the new groom-to-be. He can then choose the one who suits him best. The elders of the house and all of the family shall reject no daughter-in-law unless she is tainted with the breath of scandal or bad reputation. Aside from that, let the man who will have to satisfy her satisfy himself. He should act as do wise heads of families before they acquire some property—they like to look it over several times before they actually sign a contract. It is good in the case of any purchase and contract to inform oneself fully and to take counsel. One should consult a good number of persons and be very careful in order to avoid belated regrets. The man who has decided to marry must be still more cautious. I recommend that he examine and anticipate in every way, and consider for many days, what sort of person it is he is to live with for all his years as husband and companion. Let him be minded to marry for two purposes: first to perpetuate himself in his children, and second to have a steady and constant companion all his life. A woman is needed, therefore, who is likely to bear children and who is desirable as a perpetual mate.

* * *

To sum up this whole subject in a few words, for I want above all to be brief on this point, let a man get himself new kinsmen of better than plebeian blood, of a fortune more than diminutive, of a decent occupation, and of modest and respectable habits. Let them not be too far above himself, lest their greatness overshadow his own honor and position. Too high a family may disturb his own and his family's peace and tranquillity, and also, if one of them falls, you cannot help to support him without collapsing or wearing yourself out as you stagger under a weight too great for your arms and your strength. I also do not want the new relatives to rank too low, for while the first error puts you in a position of servitude, the second causes expense. Let them be equals, then, and, to repeat, modest and respectable people.

* * *

We have, as I said, made the house numerous and full of young people. It is essential to give them something to do now, and not let them grow lazy. Idleness is not only useless and generally despised in young men, but a positive burden and danger to the family. I do not need to teach you to shun idleness, when I know you are hard workers and active. I do encourage you to continue as

you are doing in every sort of activity and hard discipline that you may attain excellence and deserve fame. Only think this matter over and consider whether any man, even if he is not necessarily ambitious of gaining glory but merely a little shy of falling into disgrace, can ever be, in actuality or even if we merely try to imagine him, a man not heartily opposed to idleness and to mere sitting. Who has ever dreamed he might reach any grace or dignity without hard work in the noblest arts, without assiduous efforts, without plenty of sweat poured out in manly and strenuous exertions? Certainly a man who would wish for the favor of praise and fame must avoid and resist idleness and inertia just as he would do major and hateful enemies. There is nothing that leads more quickly to dishonor and disgrace than idleness. The lap of the idler has always been the nest and lair of vice. Nothing is so harmful and pestilent in public and private life as the lazy and passive citizen. From idleness springs lasciviousness; from lasciviousness comes a contempt for the law; from disobedience to law comes ruin and the destruction of the country itself. To the extent that men tolerate the first resistance of men's will to the customs and ways of the country, their spirits soon turn to arrogance, pride, and the harmful power of avarice and greed. Thieves, murderers, adulterers, and all sorts of criminals and evil men run wild.

* * *

To this I might add that man ought to give some reward to God, to satisfy him with good works in return for the wonderful gifts which He gave to the spirit of man exalting and magnifying it beyond that of all other earthly beings. Nature, that is, God, made man a composite of two parts, one celestial and divine, the other most beautiful and noble among mortal things. He provided him with a form and a body suited to every sort of movement, so as to enable him to perceive and to flee from that which threatened to harm and oppose him. He gave him speech and judgment so that he would be able to seek after and to find what he needed and could use. He gave him movement and sentiment, desire and the power of excitement, so that he might clearly appreciate and pursue useful things and shun those harmful and dangerous to him. He gave him intelligence, teachability, memory and reason, qualities divine in themselves and which enable man to investigate, to distinguish, to know what to avoid and what to desire in order best to preserve himself. To these great gifts, admirable beyond measure, God added still another power of the spirit and mind of man, namely moderation. As a curb on greed and on excessive lusts, he gave him modesty and the desire for honor. Further, God established in the human mind a strong tie to bind together human beings in society, namely justice, equity, liberality, and love. These are the means by which a man can gain the favor and praise of other men, as well as the mercy and grace of the creator. Beyond this, God filled the manly breast with powers that make man able to bear fatigue, adversity, and the hard blows of fortune. He is able to undertake what is difficult, to overcome sorrow, not even to fear death—such are his qualities of strength, of endurance and fortitude, such can be his contempt for transitory things. These are qualities which enable us to honor and serve God as fully as we should, with piety, with moderation, and with every other perfect and honorable deed. Let us agree, then, that man was not born to languish in idleness but to labor and create magnificent and great works, first for the pleasure and glory of God, and second for his own enjoyment of that life of perfect virtue and its fruit, which is happiness.

*   *   *

Let men seek their own happiness first, and they will obtain the happiness of their family also. As I have said, happiness cannot be gained without good works and just and righteous deeds. Works are just and good which not only do no harm to anyone, but which benefit many. Works are righteous if they are without a trace of the dishonorable or any element of dishonesty. The best works are those which benefit many people. Those are most virtuous, perhaps, which cannot

be pursued without strength and nobility. We must give ourselves to manly effort, then, and follow the noblest pursuits.

It seems to me, before we dedicate ourselves to any particular activity, it would be wise to think over and examine the question of what is our easiest way to reach or come near to happiness. Not every man easily attains happiness. Nature did not make all men of the same humor, or of the same intelligence or will, or equally endowed with skill and power. Rather nature planned that where I might be weak, you would make good the deficiency, and in some other way you would lack the virtue found in another. Why this? So that I should have need of you, and you of him, he of another, and some other of me. In this way one man's need for another serves as the cause and means to keep us all united in general friendship and alliance. This may, indeed, have been the source and beginning of republics. Laws may have begun thus rather than as I was saying before; fire and water alone may not have been the cause of so great a union among men as society gives them. Society is a union sustained by laws, by reason, and by custom.

Let us not digress. To decide which is the most suitable career for himself, a man must take two things into account: the first is his own intelligence, his mind and his body, everything about himself; and the second, the question requiring close consideration, is that of outside supports, the help and resources which are necessary or useful and to which he must have early access, welcome, and free right of use if he is to enter the field for which he seems more suited than for any other. Take an example: if a man wished to perform great feats of arms while he knew he was himself but a weak fellow, not very robust, incapable of bearing up through dust and storm and sun, this would not be the right profession for him to pursue. If I, being poor, longed to devote my life to letters, though I had not the money to pay the considerable expenses attached to such a career, again this would be a poor choice of career. If you are equipped with numerous relatives, plenty of friends, abundant wealth, and if you possess within yourself intelligence, eloquence, and such tact as to keep you out of any rough or awkward situations, and you decide to dedicate yourself to civic affairs, you might do extremely well.

*   *   *

We should also consider at this point how much reward and profit, how much honor and fame, you can gain from any work or achievement you undertake to perform. The only condition is that you surpass everyone else in the field. In every craft the most skilled master, as you know, gains most riches and has the best position and the greatest stature among his companions. Think how even in so humble a profession as shoemaking men search out the best among the cobblers. If it is true of the humblest occupations that the most skilled practitioners are ever most in demand and so become most famous, consider whether in the highest professions the opposite suddenly holds true. In fact you will find it still more to the point to be the best in these, or at least one of the best. If you succeed in these fields, you know that you have been given a greater portion of happiness than other men. If you are learned, you realize the misfortune of the ignorant. You know, in addition, that the unhappiest lot falls to those who, being ignorant, desire still to appear learned.

*   *   *

Consider in your own mind what a boon to know more than others and to put the knowledge to good use at the right time and place. If you think it over, I am sure you will realize that in every field a man who would appear to be valuable must be valuable in fact. Now we have stated this much: that youth should not be wasted but should be directed to some honorable kind of work, that a man should do his utmost in that work, and that he should choose the field which will be most helpful to his family and bring him most fame. A career should suit our own nature and the state of our fortunes, and should be pursued in such a way that we may never, by our own fault at least, fall short of the first rank.

Riches, however, are for nearly everyone the primary reason for working at all. They are also most useful in making it possible to persevere in our undertakings until we win approval and attain public favor, position, and fame. This is the time, therefore, to explain how wealth is acquired and how it is kept. It was also one of the four things which we said were necessary to bring about and to preserve contentment in a family. Now, then, let us begin to accumulate wealth. Perhaps the present moment, as the evening grows dark, is just right for this subject, for no occupation seems less attractive to a man of large and liberal spirit than the kind of labor by which wealth is in fact gathered. If you will count over in your imagination the actual careers that bring great profits, you will see that all basically concern themselves with buying and selling or with lending and collecting the returns. Having neither petty nor vulgar minds, I imagine you probably find these activities, which are solely directed to making a profit, somewhat below you. They seem entirely to lack honor and distinction.

*   *   *

Those who thus dismiss all mercenary activities are wrong, I believe. If the pursuit of wealth is not as glorious as are other great pursuits, yet a man is not contemptible if, being unsuited by nature to achieve anything much in other finer fields of work, he devotes himself to this kind of activity. Here, it may be, he knows he is not inadequately equipped to do well. Here everyone admits he is very useful to the republic and still more to his own family. Wealth, if it is used to help the needy, can gain a man esteem and praise. With wealth, if it is used to do great and noble things and to show a fine magnanimity and splendor, fame and dignity can be attained. In emergencies and times of need we see every day how useful is the wealth of private citizens to the country itself. From public funds alone it is not always possible to pay the wages of those whose arms and blood defend the country's liberty and dignity. Nor can republics increase their glory and their might without enormous expenditure.

*   *   *

Why have I gone on at length on these topics? Only to show you that, among occupations, there are quite a few, both honorable and highly esteemed, by means of which wealth in no small measure may be gained. One of these occupations, as you know, is that of merchant. You can easily call to mind other similar careers which are both honorable and highly profitable. You want to know, then, what they are. Let us run through them. We shall spread out all the occupations before us and choose the best among them, then we shall try to define how they make us wealthy and prosperous. Occupations that do not bring profit and gain will never make you rich. Those that bring frequent and large profits are the ones that make you rich. The only system for becoming rich, by our own industry and by the means that luck, friends, or anyone's favor can give us, is to make profits. And how do men grow poor? Ill fortune certainly plays a part, this I admit, but excluding fortune, let us speak here of industry. If riches come through profits, and these through labor, diligence, and hard work, then poverty, which is the reverse of profit, will follow from the reverse of these virtues, namely from neglect, laziness, and sloth. These are the fault neither of fortune nor of others, but of oneself. One grows poor, also, by spending too much. Prodigality dissipates wealth and throws it away. The opposite of prodigality, the opposite of neglect, are carefulness and conscientiousness, in short, good management. Good management is the means to preserve wealth. Thus we have found out that to become rich one must make profits, keep what one has gained, and exercise rational good management.

*   *   *

REVIEW QUESTIONS

1. What, according to Alberti, is the role and nature of a father?
2. How is his authority different from other kinds of authority?
3. What is the role of education in the formation of human nature?
4. How does this view differ from that of other authors?
5. What is honor?
6. What is its relationship to the family and why is it so important to Alberti?
7. How might Alberti define the family?

BENVENUTO CELLINI

FROM *The Autobiography*

Benvenuto Cellini (1500–1571) was a native of Florence. Apprenticed as a young man to a goldsmith, he eventually wandered to Rome, where he established himself as an independent craftsman and artist. Supported by the patronage of merchants, aristocrats, and prelates, his success knew no bounds, at least in his own telling. Indeed, Cellini's individualism, self-confidence, and talent, expressed in both art and violence, are recorded in his autobiography. It is both a fascinating portrait of the Renaissance artist and a valuable window on the era.

From *The Autobiography of Benvenuto Cellini,* translated by John Addington Symonds (New York: Modern Library, 1995).

*   *   *

All the while I was at Florence, I studied the noble manner of Michel Agnolo, and from this I have never deviated. About that time I contracted a close and familiar friendship with an amiable lad of my own age, who was also in the goldsmith's trade. He was called Francesco, son of Filippo, and grandson of Fra Lippo Lippi, that most excellent painter. Through intercourse together, such love grew up between us that, day or night, we never stayed apart. The house where he lived was still full of the fine studies which his father had made, bound up in several books of drawings by his hand, and taken from the best antiquities of Rome. The sight of these things filled me with passionate enthusiasm; and for two years or thereabouts we lived in intimacy. At that time I fashioned a silver bas-relief of the size of a little child's hand. It was intended for the clasp to a man's belt; for they were then worn as large as that. I carved on it a knot of leaves in the antique style, with figures of children and other masks of great beauty. This piece I made in the workshop of one Francesco Salimbene; and on its being exhibited to the trade, the goldsmiths praised me as the best young craftsman of their art.

There was one Giovan Battista, surnamed Il Tasso, a wood-carver, precisely of my own age, who one day said to me that if I was willing to go to Rome, he should be glad to join me. Now we had this conversation together immediately after dinner; and I being angry with my father for the same old reason of the music, said to Tasso: "You are a fellow of words, not deeds." He answered: "I too have come to anger with my mother; and if I had cash enough to take me to Rome, I would not turn back to lock the door of that wretched little workshop I call mine." To these words I re-

plied that if that was all that kept him in Florence I had money enough in my pockets to bring us both to Rome. Talking thus and walking onwards, we found ourselves at the gate San Piero Gattolini without noticing that we had got there; whereupon I said: "Friend Tasso, this is God's doing that we have reached this gate without either you or me noticing that we were there; and now that I am here, it seems to me that I have finished half the journey." And so, being of one accord, we pursued our way together, saying, "Oh, what will our old folks say this evening?" We then made an agreement not to think more about them till we reached Rome. So we tied our aprons behind our backs, and trudged almost in silence to Siena. When we arrived at Siena, Tasso said (for he had hurt his feet) that he would not go farther, and asked me to lend him money to get back. I made answer: "I should not have enough left to go forward; you ought indeed to have thought of this on leaving Florence; and if it is because of your feet that you shirk the journey, we will find a return horse for Rome, which will deprive you of the excuse." Accordingly I hired a horse; and seeing that he did not answer, I took my way toward the gate of Rome. When he knew that I was firmly resolved to go, muttering between his teeth, and limping as well as he could, he came on behind me very slowly and at a great distance. On reaching the gate, I felt pity for my comrade, and waited for him, and took him on the crupper, saying: "What would our friends speak of us to-morrow, if, having left for Rome, we had not pluck to get beyond Siena?" Then the good Tasso said I spoke the truth; and as he was a pleasant fellow, he began to laugh and sing; and in this way, always singing and laughing, we travelled the whole way to Rome. I had just nineteen years then, and so had the century.

When we reached Rome, I put myself under a master who was known as Il Firenzuola. His name was Giovanni, and he came from Firenzuola in Lombardy, a most able craftsman in large vases and big plate of that kind. I showed him part of the model for the clasp which I had made in Florence at Salimbene's. It pleased him exceedingly; and turning to one of his journeymen, a Florentine called Giannotto Giannotti, who had been several years with him, he spoke as follows: "This fellow is one of the Florentines who knows something, and you are one of those who know nothing." Then I recognised the man, and turned to speak with him; for before he went to Rome, we often went to draw together, and had been very intimate comrades. He was so put out by the words his master flung at him, that he said he did not recognise me or know who I was; whereupon I got angry, and cried out: "O Giannotto, you who were once my friend—for have we not been together in such and such places, and drawn, and ate, and drunk, and slept in company at your house in the country? I don't want you to bear witness on my behalf to this worthy man, your master, because I hope my hands are such that without aid from you they will declare what sort of a fellow I am."

XIV

When I had thus spoken, Firenzuola, who was a man of hot spirit and brave, turned to Giannotto, and said to him: "You vile rascal, aren't you ashamed to treat a man who has been so intimate a comrade with you in this way?" And with the same movement of quick feeling, he faced round and said to me: "Welcome to my workshop; and do as you have promised; let your hands declare what man you are."

He gave me a very fine piece of silver plate to work on for a cardinal. It was a little oblong box, copied from the porphyry sarcophagus before the door of the Rotonda. Beside what I copied, I enriched it with so many elegant masks of my invention, that my master went about showing it through the art, and boasting that so

good a piece of work had been turned out from his shop. It was about half a cubit in size, and was so constructed as to serve for a salt-cellar at table. This was the first earning that I touched at Rome, and part of it I sent to assist my good father; the rest I kept for my own use, living upon it while I went about studying the antiquities of Rome, until my money failed, and I had to return to the shop for work. Battista del Tasso, my comrade, did not stay long in Rome, but went back to Florence.

After undertaking some new commissions, I took it into my head, as soon as I had finished them, to change my master; I had indeed been worried into doing so by a certain Milanese, called Pagolo Arsago. My first master, Firenzuola, had a great quarrel about this with Arsago, and abused him in my presence; whereupon I took up speech in defence of my new master. I said that I was born free, and free I meant to live, and that there was no reason to complain of him, far less of me, since some few crowns of wages were still due to me; also that I chose to go, like a free journeyman, where it pleased me, knowing I did wrong to no man. My new master then put in with his excuses, saying that he had not asked me to come, and that I should gratify him by returning with Firenzuola. To this I replied that I was not aware of wronging the latter in any way, and as I had completed his commissions, I chose to be my own master and not the man of others, and that he who wanted me must beg me of myself. Firenzuola cried: "I don't intend to beg you of yourself; I have done with you; don't show yourself again upon my premises." I reminded him of the money he owed me. He laughed me in the face; on which I said that if I knew how to use my tools in handicraft as well as he had seen, I could be quite as clever with my sword in claiming the just payment of my labour. While we were exchanging these words, an old man happened to come up, called Maestro Antonio, of San Marino. He was the chief among the Roman goldsmiths, and had been Firenzuola's master. Hearing what I had to say, which I took good care that he should understand, he immediately espoused my cause, and bade Firenzuola pay me. The dispute waxed warm, because Firenzuola was an admirable swordsman, far better than he was a goldsmith. Yet reason made itself heard; and I backed my cause with the same spirit, till I got myself paid. In course of time Firenzuola and I became friends, and at his request I stood godfather to one of his children.

*   *   *

REVIEW QUESTIONS

1. What distinguishes the artist according to Cellini?
2. How is genius dependent on wealth?
3. What does Cellini tell us about patronage and its effects on art?
4. In what ways is the artist like a courtier?

GIORGIO VASSARI

FROM *The Lives of the Artists*

Giorgio Vassari (1511–1574) was one of the most fashionable and prolific painters of his age. He spent most of his life traveling about Italy on various commissions. During these travels, he gathered specific information about artists and their works that he later incorporated into The Lives of the Artists (1500). Its biographical sketches reveal not only fascinating insights into the practice of art in the Renaissance but also the taste and perspective of an accomplished artist. As a young man, Vassari studied painting under Michelangelo Buonarotti (1475–1564) and remained a lifelong disciple and admirer. Michelangelo began his career in 1492 under the patronage of Lorenzo de Medici. In 1505, he moved to Rome to design the tomb of Pope Julius II (1502–1513). Among his more famous commissions are the ceiling of the Sistine Chapel and the Basilica of St. Peter's. His career stretched to the middle of the sixteenth century, "bringing to perfection" (in Vassari's words) the three branches of the fine arts.

From *The Lives of the Artists*, by Giorgio Vassari, translated by George Bull (New York: Penguin Books, 1965), pp. 325–26, 349–54.

*   *   *

Enlightened by what had been achieved by the renowned Giotto and his school, all artists of energy and distinction were striving to give the world proof of the talents with which fortune and their own happy temperaments had endowed them. They were all anxious (though their efforts were in vain) to reflect in their work the glories of nature and to attain, as far as possible, perfect artistic discernment or understanding. Meanwhile, the benign ruler of heaven graciously looked down to earth, saw the worthlessness of what was being done, the intense but utterly fruitless studies, and the presumption of men who were farther from true art than night is from day, and resolved to save us from our errors. So he decided to send into the world an artist who would be skilled in each and every craft, whose work alone would teach us how to attain perfection in design (by correct drawing and by the use of contour and light and shadows, so as to obtain relief in painting) and how to use right judgment in sculpture and, in architecture, create buildings which would be comfortable and secure, healthy, pleasant to look at, well-proportioned and richly ornamented. Moreover, he determined to give this artist the knowledge of true moral philosophy and the gift of poetic expression, so that everyone might admire and follow him as their perfect exemplar in life, work, and behaviour and in every endeavour, and he would be acclaimed as divine. He also saw that in the practice of these exalted disciplines and arts, namely, painting, sculpture, and architecture, the Tuscan genius has always been preeminent, for the Tuscans have devoted to all the various branches of art more labour and study than all the other Italian peoples. And therefore he chose to have Michelangelo born a Florentine, so that one of her own citizens might bring to absolute perfection the achievements for which Florence was already justly renowned.

So in the year 1474 in the Casentino, under a fateful and lucky star, the virtuous and noble wife of Lodovico di Leonardo Buonarroti gave birth to a baby son. That year Lodovico (who was said to be related to the most noble and ancient family of the counts of Canossa) was visiting magistrate at the township of Chiusi and Caprese near the Sasso della Vernia (where St. Francis received the stigmata) in the diocese of Arezzo. The boy was born on Sunday, 6 March, about the eighth hour of the night; and without further thought his father decided to call him Michelangelo, being inspired by heaven and convinced that he saw in him something supernatural and beyond human experience. This was evident in the child's horoscope which showed Mercury and Venus in the house of Jupiter, peaceably disposed; in other words, his mind

and hands were destined to fashion sublime and magnificent works of art.

*   *   *

Meanwhile, the Pope had returned to Rome while Michelangelo remained in Bologna to finish the statue. In his absence Bramante was constantly plotting with Raphael of Urbino to remove from the Pope's mind the idea of having Michelangelo finish the tomb on his return. Bramante did this (being a friend and relation of Raphael and therefore no friend of Michelangelo's) when he saw the way his holiness kept praising and glorifying Michelangelo's work as a sculptor. He and Raphael suggested to Pope Julius that if the tomb were finished it would bring nearer the day of his death, and they said that it was bad luck to have one's tomb built while one was still alive. Eventually they persuaded his holiness to get Michelangelo on his return to paint, as a memorial for his uncle, Pope Sixtus IV, the ceiling of the chapel that he had built in the Vatican. In this way Bramante and Michelangelo's other rivals thought they would divert his energies from sculpture, in which they realized he was supreme. This, they argued, would make things hopeless for him, since as he had no experience of colouring in fresco he would certainly, they believed, do less creditable work as a painter. Without doubt, they thought, he would be compared unfavourably with Raphael, and even if the work were a success, being forced to do it would make him angry with the Pope; and thus one way or another they would succeed in their purpose of getting rid of him. So when Michelangelo returned to Rome he found the Pope resolved to leave the tomb as it was for the time being, and he was told to paint the ceiling of the chapel. Michelangelo, being anxious to finish the tomb, and considering the magnitude and difficulty of the task of painting the chapel, and his lack of experience, tried in every possible way to shake the burden off his shoulders. But the more he refused, the more determined he made the Pope, who was a wilful man by nature and who in any case was again being prompted by Michelangelo's rivals, and especially Bramante. And finally, being the hot-tempered man he was, his holiness was all ready to fly into a rage.

However, seeing that his holiness was persevering, Michelangelo resigned himself to doing what he was asked. Then the Pope ordered Bramante to make the ceiling ready for painting, and he did so by piercing the surface and supporting the scaffolding by ropes. When Michelangelo saw this he asked Bramante what he should do, when the painting was finished, to fill up the holes. Bramante said: "We'll think of it when it's time." And he added that there was no other way. Michelangelo realized that Bramante either knew nothing about the matter or else was no friend of his, and he went to the Pope and told him that the scaffolding was unsatisfactory and that Bramante had not known how to make it; and the Pope replied, in the presence of Bramante, that Michelangelo should do it himself in his own way. So he arranged to have the scaffolding erected on props which kept clear of the wall, a method for use with vaults (by which many fine works have been executed) which he subsequently taught to various people, including Bramante. In this instance he enabled a poor carpenter, who rebuilt the scaffolding, to dispense with so many of the ropes that when Michelangelo gave him what was over he sold them and made enough for a dowry for his daughter.

Michelangelo then started making the cartoons for the vaulting; and the Pope also decided that the walls that had been painted by previous artists in the time of Sixtus should be scraped clean and that Michelangelo should have fifteen thousand ducats for the cost of the work, the price being decided through Giuliano da Sangallo. Then being forced reluctantly, by the magnitude of the task, to take on some assistants, Michelangelo sent for help to Florence. He was anxious to show that his paintings would surpass the work done there earlier, and he was determined to show modern artists how to draw and paint. Indeed, the circumstances of this undertaking encouraged Michelangelo to aim very high, for the sake both of his own reputation and the art of painting; and in this mood he started and finished the cartoons. He was then ready to begin the frescoes, but he lacked the necessary experience. Meanwhile, some of his friends, who were painters, came to Rome from Florence in order to assist him and let him see their technique. Several of them were skilled painters in fresco, and they included Granaccio, Giuliano Bugiardini, Jacopo di Sandro, the elder Indaco, Angelo di Donnino, and Aristotile. Having started the work, Michelangelo asked them to produce some examples of what they could do. But when he saw that these were nothing like what he wanted he grew dissatisfied, and then one morning he made up his mind to scrap everything they had done. He shut himself up in the chapel, refused to let them in again, and would never let them see him even when he was at home. So, when they thought the joke was wearing thin, they accepted their dismissal and went back ashamed to Florence.

Thereupon, having arranged to do all the work by himself, Michelangelo carried it well on the way to completion; working with the utmost solicitude, labour, and study he refused to let anyone see him in case he would have to show what he was painting. As a result every day the people became more impatient.

Pope Julius himself was always keen to see whatever Michelangelo was doing, and so naturally he was more anxious than ever to see what was being hidden from him. So one day he resolved to go and see the work, but he was not allowed in, as Michelangelo would never have consented. (This was the cause of the quarrel described earlier, when Michelangelo had to leave Rome as he would not let the Pope see what he was painting.) Now when a third of the work was completed (as I found out from Michelangelo himself, to clear up any uncertainty) during the winter when the north wind was blowing several spots of mould started to appear on the surface. The reason for this was that the Roman lime, which is white in colour and made of travertine, does not dry very quickly, and when mixed with pozzolana, which is a brownish colour, forms a dark mixture which is very watery before it sets; then after the wall has been thoroughly soaked, it often effloresces when it is drying. Thus this salt efflorescence appeared in many places, although in time the air dried it up. When Michelangelo saw what was happening he despaired of the whole undertaking and was reluctant to go on. However, his holiness sent Giuliano da Sangallo to see him and explain the reason for the blemishes. Sangallo explained how to remove the moulds and encouraged him to continue. Then, when the work was half finished, the Pope who had subsequently gone to inspect it several times (being helped up the ladders by Michelangelo) wanted it to be thrown open to the public. Being hasty and impatient by nature, he simply could not bear to wait until it was perfect and had, so to say, received the final touch.

As soon as it was thrown open, the whole of Rome flocked to see it; and the Pope was the first, not having the patience to wait till the dust had settled after the dismantling of the scaffolds. Raphael da Urbino (who had great powers of imitation) changed his style as soon as he had seen Michelangelo's work and straight away, to show his skill, painted the prophets and sibyls of Santa Maria della Pace; and Bramante subsequently tried to persuade the Pope to let Raphael paint the other half of the chapel. When Michelangelo heard about this he complained of Bramante and revealed to the Pope, without reserve, many faults in his life and in his architectural works. (He himself, as it happened, was later to correct the mistakes made by Bramante in the fabric of St. Peter's.) However, the Pope recognized Michelangelo's genius more clearly every day and wanted him to carry on the work himself; and after he had seen it displayed he was of the opinion that Michelangelo would do the other half even better. And so in twenty months Michelangelo brought the project to perfect completion without the assistance even of someone to grind his colours. Michelangelo at times complained that because of the haste the Pope imposed on him he was unable to finish it in the way he would have liked; for his

holiness was always asking him importunately when it would be ready. On one of these occasions Michelangelo retorted that the ceiling would be finished "when it satisfies me as an artist."

And to this the Pope replied: "And we want you to satisfy us and finish it soon."

Finally, the Pope threatened that if Michelangelo did not finish the ceiling quickly he would have him thrown down from the scaffolding. Then Michelangelo, who had good reason to fear the Pope's anger, lost no time in doing all that was wanted; and after taking down the rest of the scaffolding he threw the ceiling open to the public on the morning of All Saints' Day, when the Pope went into the chapel to sing Mass, to the satisfaction of the entire city.

Michelangelo wanted to retouch some parts of the painting *a secco*, as the old masters had done on the scenes below, painting backgrounds, draperies, and skies in ultramarine, and in certain places adding ornamentation in gold, in order to enrich and heighten the visual impact. The Pope, learning that this ornamentation was lacking, and hearing the work praised so enthusiastically by all who saw it, wanted him to go ahead. However, he lacked the patience to rebuild the scaffolding, and so the ceiling stayed as it was. His holiness used to see Michelangelo often and he would ask him to have the chapel enriched with colours and gold, since it looked impoverished. And Michelangelo would answer familiarly:

"Holy Father, in those days men did not bedeck themselves in gold and those you see painted there were never very rich. They were holy men who despised riches."

For this work Michelangelo was paid by the Pope three thousand crowns in several instalments, of which he had to spend twenty-five on colours. He executed the frescoes in great discomfort, having to work with his face looking upwards, which impaired his sight so badly that he could not read or look at drawings save with his head turned backwards; and this lasted for several months afterwards. I can talk from personal experience about this, since when I painted five rooms in the great apartments of Duke Cosimo's palace if I had not made a chair where I could rest my head and relax from time to time I would never have finished; even so this work so ruined my sight and injured my head that I still feel the effects, and I am astonished that Michelangelo bore all that discomfort so well. In fact, every day the work moved him to greater enthusiasm, and he was so spurred on by his own progress and improvements that he felt no fatigue and ignored all the discomfort.

*   *   *

REVIEW QUESTIONS

1. What distinguishes the artist according to Vassari?
2. What is the source of artistic genius?
3. What does the experience of Michelangelo tell us about human art and human nature as viewed by Vassari?

LEONARDO DA VINCI

FROM *The Notebooks*

Leonardo da Vinci (1452–1519) was born in the countryside of Florence, the illegitimate son of a notary in the town of Vinci. He was self-taught and could read Latin poorly. He was left-handed, a condition viewed by contemporaries as a deformity. Sometime around 1481, he moved to Milan, where his patrons were the Dukes Gian Galeazzo (1476–94) and Ludovico Sforza (1494–1500). During the French invasion of 1499, Leonardo fled Milan and led a peripatetic existence until 1508, when he returned to the city. In 1513, he was taken to France, where he lived the remainder of his days. He is widely acclaimed as a genius, the designer of futuristic machines of many sorts. Among these was a device for grinding concave mirrors and lenses that made possible the invention of the telescope in 1509. He was a great artist in many media as well as a keen observer of nature. His interests ranged from aerodynamics to physics to biology to anatomy to optics. His writings on perspective are drawn from his notebooks, which he wrote backward, in a mirror hand, and in no particular order, and which were never published in his lifetime.

From *The Notebooks of Leonardo da Vinci*, translated by Edward MacCurdy (London: Cape, 1958).

*   *   *

Principle of Perspective

All things transmit their image to the eye by means of pyramids; the nearer to the eye these are intersected the smaller the image of their cause will appear.

If you should ask how you can demonstrate these points to me from experience, I should tell you, as regards the vanishing point which moves with you, to notice as you go along by lands ploughed in straight furrows, the ends of which start from the path where you are walking, you will see that continually each pair of furrows seem to approach each other and to join at their ends.

As regards the point that comes to the eye, it may be comprehended with greater ease; for if you look in the eye of anyone you will see your own image there; consequently if you suppose two lines to start from your ears and proceed to the ears of the image which you see of yourself in the eye of the other person, you will clearly recognise that these lines contract so much that when they have continued only a little way beyond your image as mirrored in the said eye they will touch one another in a point.

The thing that is nearer to the eye always appears larger than another of the same size which is more remote.

Perspective is of such a nature that it makes what is flat appear in relief, and what is in relief appear flat.

The perspective by means of which a thing is represented will be better understood when it is seen from the view-point at which it was drawn.

If you wish to represent a thing near, which should produce the effect of natural things, it is impossible for your perspective not to appear false, by reason of all the illusory appearances and errors in proportion of which the existence may be assumed in a mediocre work, unless whoever

is looking at this perspective finds himself surveying it from the exact distance, elevation, angle of vision or point at which you were situated to make this perspective. Therefore it would be necessary to make a window of the size of your face or in truth a hole through which you would look at the said work. And if you should do this, then without any doubt your work will produce the effect of nature if the light and shade are correctly rendered, and you will hardly be able to convince yourself that these things are painted. Otherwise do not trouble yourself about representing anything, unless you take your view-point at a distance of at least twenty times the maximum width and height of the thing that you represent; and this will satisfy every beholder who places himself in front of the work at any angle whatever.

If you wish to see a proof of this quickly, take a piece of a staff like a small column eight times as high as its width without plinth or capital, then measure off on a flat wall forty equal spaces which are in conformity with the spaces; they will make between them forty columns similar to your small column. Then let there be set up in front of the middle of these spaces, at a distance of four braccia from the wall, a thin band of iron, in the centre of which there is a small round hole of the size of a large pearl; place a light beside this hole so as to touch it, then go and place your column above each mark of the wall and draw the outline of the shadow, then shade it and observe it through the hole in the iron.

In Vitolone there are eight hundred and five conclusions about perspective.

Perspective

No visible body can be comprehended and well judged by human eyes, except by the difference of the background where the extremities of this body terminate and are bounded, and so far as its contour lines are concerned no object will seem to be separated from this background. The moon, although far distant from the body of the sun, when by reason of eclipses it finds itself between our eyes and the sun, having the sun for its background will seem to human eyes to be joined and attached to it.

Perspective comes to aid us where judgment fails in things that diminish.

It is possible to bring about that the eye does not see distant objects as much diminished as they are in natural perspective, where they are diminished by reason of the convexity of the eye, which is obliged to intersect upon its surface the pyramids of every kind of image that approach the eye at a right angle. But the method that I show here in the margin cuts these pyramids at right angles near the surface of the pupil. But whereas the convex pupil of the eye can take in the whole of our hemisphere, this will show only a single star; but where many small stars transmit their images to the surface of the pupil these stars are very small; here only one will be visible but it will be large; and so the moon will be greater in size and its spots more distinct. You should place close to the eye a glass filled with the water mentioned in chapter four of book 113 'Concerning Natural Things', water which causes things congealed in balls of crystalline glass to appear as though they were without glass.

Of the eye. Of bodies less than the pupil of the eye that which is nearest to it will be least discerned by this pupil—and from this experience it follows that the power of sight is not reduced to a point.

But the images of objects which meet in the pupil of the eye are spread over this pupil in the same way as they are spread about in the air; and the proof of this is pointed out to us when we look at the starry heavens without fixing our gaze more upon one star than upon another, for then the sky shows itself to us strewn with stars, and they bear to the eye the same proportions as in the sky, and the spaces between them also are the same.

Natural perspective acts in the opposite way, for the greater the distance the smaller does the thing seen appear, and the less the distance the larger it appears. But this invention constrains the beholder to stand with his eye at a small hole, and then with this small hole it will be seen well. But since many eyes come together to see at the same time one and the same work produced by this art, only one of them will have a good view of the function of this perspective and all the others will only see it confusedly. It is well therefore to shun this compound perspective, and to keep to the simple which does not purport to view planes foreshortened but as far as possible in exact form.

And of this simple perspective in which the plane intersects the pyramid that conveys the images to the eye that are at an equal distance from the visual faculty, an example is afforded us by the curve of the pupil of the eye upon which these pyramids intersect at an equal distance from the visual faculty.

Of Equal Things the More Remote Appears Smaller

The practice of perspective is divided into two parts, of which the first treats of all the things seen by the eye at whatsoever distance, and this in itself shows all these things diminished as the eye beholds them, without the man being obliged to stand in one place rather than in another, provided that the wall does not foreshorten it a second time.

But the second practice is a combination of perspective made partly by art and partly by nature, and the work done according to its rules has no part that is not influenced by natural and accidental perspective. Natural perspective I understand has to do with the flat surface on which this perspective is represented; which surface, although it is parallel to it in length and height, is constrained to diminish the distant parts more than its near ones. And this is proved by the first of what has been said above, and its diminution is natural.

Accidental perspective, that is that which is created by art, acts in the contrary way; because it

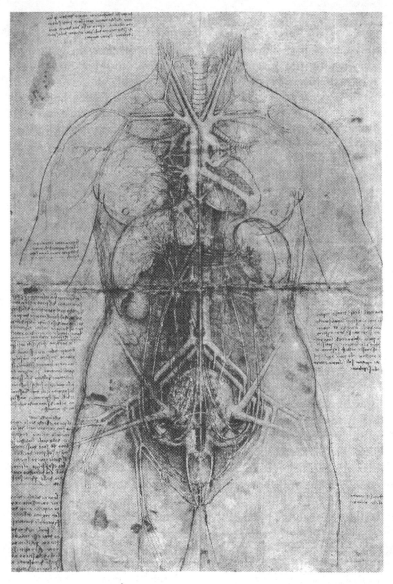

DRAWING OF A WOMAN'S TORSO   LEONARDO DA VINCI

During his period of service to the Duke of Milan, 1482–1499, Leonardo da Vinci began a wide range of scientific studies, in addition to his artistic creativity. These included reflections on geometry, mechanics and architecture, sketches for public works, advanced weapons, and fanciful inventions. He also undertook a series of anatomical studies based on the dissection of human cadavers, an illegal and immoral activity in his day. The "Drawing of a Woman's Torso" is one of the results. What does this sketch reveal about the importance of naturalism in Renaissance art? How might such studies have influenced later developments in the science of human anatomy? What new perspectives does this image cast upon the so-called glorification of man during the Renaissance?

causes bodies equal in themselves to increase on the foreshortened plane, in proportion as the eye is more natural and nearer to the plane, and as the part of this plane where it is represented is more remote from the eye.

*   *   *

REVIEW QUESTIONS

1. According to da Vinci, what is the relationship between perspective in nature and perspective in the human eye?
2. What is the relationship between perspective and mathematical principles?
3. Is perspective a constant or contingent?
4. What implications does this have for painting?
5. How might it shape the enterprise of reading?

BALDESAR CASTIGLIONE

FROM *The Book of the Courtier*

Baldesar Castiglione (1478–1529) was born near Mantua and educated in Milan. He entered the service of the duke of Milan in 1496. After the duke was carried prisoner to France, Castiglione returned to Mantua. In 1504, he entered the court of Guidobaldo of Montefeltro, duke of Urbino, where he remained until 1524; this is the setting of The Book of the Courtier. *Although he wrote elegant verse in Latin and Italian, this reflection on courtly life was Castiglione's claim to fame. Fashioned as a discourse among courtiers and courtesans, it described the ideal courtier and presented the Renaissance man.*

From *The Book of the Courtier*, by Baldesar Castiglione, translated by Charles S. Singleton (New York: Bantam Doubleday Dell, 1959), pp. 29–30, 32–34, 70–72, 205–8, 289–90.

*   *   *

"Thus, I would have our Courtier born of a noble and genteel family; because it is far less becoming for one of low birth to fail to do virtuous things than for one of noble birth, who, should he stray from the path of his forebears, stains the family name, and not only fails to achieve anything but loses what has been achieved already. For noble birth is like a bright lamp that makes manifest and visible deeds both good and bad, kindling and spurring on to virtue as much for fear of dishonor as for hope of praise. And since this luster of nobility does not shine forth in the deeds of the lowly born, they lack that spur, as well as that fear of dishonor, nor do they think themselves obliged to go beyond what was done by their forebears; whereas to the wellborn it seems a reproach not to attain at least to the mark set them by their ancestors. Hence, it almost always happens that, in the profession of arms as well as in other worthy pursuits, those who are most distinguished are men of noble birth, because nature has implanted in everything that hidden seed which gives a certain force and quality of its own essence to all that springs from it, making it like itself: as we can see not only in breeds of horses and other animals, but in trees as well, the shoots of which nearly always resemble the trunk; and if they sometimes degenerate, the fault lies with the husbandman. And so it happens with men, who, if they are tended in the right way, are almost always like those from whom they spring, and often are better; but if they lack someone to tend them properly, they grow wild and never attain their full growth."

*   *   *

"But, to return to our subject, I say that there is a mean to be found between such supreme grace on the one hand and such stupid ineptitude on the other, and that those who are not so perfectly endowed by nature can, with care and effort, polish and in great part correct their natural defects. Therefore, besides his noble birth, I would wish the Courtier favored in this other respect, and endowed by nature not only with talent and with beauty of countenance and person, but with that certain grace which we call an 'air,' which shall make him at first sight pleasing and lovable to all who see him; and let this be an adornment informing and attending all his actions, giving the promise outwardly that such a one is worthy of the company and the favor of every great lord."

*   *   *

"But to come to some particulars: I hold that the principal and true profession of the Courtier must be that of arms; which I wish him to exercise with vigor; and let him be known among the others as bold, energetic, and faithful to whomever he serves. And the repute of these good qualities will be earned by exercising them in every time and place, inasmuch as one may not ever fail therein without great blame. And, just as among women the name of purity, once stained, is never restored, so the reputation of a gentleman whose profession is arms, if ever in the least way he sullies himself through cowardice or other disgrace, always remains defiled before the world and cov-

ered with ignominy. Therefore, the more our Courtier excels in this art, the more will he merit praise; although I do not deem it necessary that he have the perfect knowledge of things and other qualities that befit a commander, for since this would launch us on too great a sea, we shall be satisfied, as we have said, if he have complete loyalty and an undaunted spirit, and be always seen to have them. For oftentimes men are known for their courage in small things rather than in great. And often in important perils and where there are many witnesses, some men are found who, although their hearts sink within them, still, spurred on by fear of shame or by the company of those present, press forward with eyes shut, as it were, and do their duty, God knows how; and in things of little importance and when they think they can avoid the risk of danger, they are glad to play safe. But those men who, even when they think they will not be observed or seen or recognized by anyone, show courage and are not careless of anything, however slight, for which they could be blamed, such have the quality of spirit we are seeking in our Courtier.

"However, we do not wish him to make a show of being so fierce that he is forever swaggering in his speech, declaring that he has wedded his cuirass, and glowering with such dour looks as we have often seen Berto do; for to such as these one may rightly say what in polite society a worthy lady jestingly said to a certain man (whom I do not now wish to name) whom she sought to honor by inviting him to dance, and who not only declined this but would not listen to music or take any part in the other entertainments offered him, but kept saying that such trifles were not his business. And when finally the lady said to him: 'What then is your business?' he answered with a scowl: 'Fighting.' Whereupon the lady replied at once: 'I should think it a good thing, now that you are not away at war or engaged in fighting, for you to have yourself greased all over and stowed away in a closet along with all your battle harness, so that you won't grow any rustier than you already are'; and so, amid much laughter from those present, she ridiculed him in his stupid presumption.

Therefore, let the man we are seeking be exceedingly fierce, harsh, and always among the first, wherever the enemy is; and in every other place, humane, modest, reserved, avoiding ostentation above all things as well as that impudent praise of himself by which a man always arouses hatred and disgust in all who hear him."

*   *   *

"I would have him more than passably learned in letters, at least in those studies which we call the humanities. Let him be conversant not only with the Latin language, but with Greek as well, because of the abundance and variety of things that are so divinely written therein. Let him be versed in the poets, as well as in the orators and historians, and let him be practiced also in writing verse and prose, especially in our own vernacular; for, besides the personal satisfaction he will take in this, in this way he will never want for pleasant entertainment with the ladies, who are usually fond of such things. And if, because of other occupations or lack of study, he does not attain to such a perfection that his writings should merit great praise, let him take care to keep them under cover so that others will not laugh at him, and let him show them only to a friend who can be trusted; because at least they will be of profit to him in that, through such exercise, he will be capable of judging the writing of others. For it very rarely happens that a man who is unpracticed in writing, however learned he may be, can ever wholly understand the toils and industry of writers, or taste the sweetness and excellence of styles, and those intrinsic niceties that are often found in the ancients.

"These studies, moreover, will make him fluent, and (as Aristippus said to the tyrant) bold and self-confident in speaking with everyone. However, I would have our Courtier keep one precept firmly in mind, namely, in this as in everything else, to be cautious and reserved rather than forward, and take care not to get the mistaken notion that he knows something he does not know."

*   *   *

Then said the Duchess: "Do not exceed bounds, signor Magnifico, but hold to the order given, and describe the Court Lady so that such a noble lady may have someone capable of serving her worthily."

The Magnifico continued: "Then, Madam, in order to show that your commands can induce me to attempt what I do not even know how to do, I will speak of this excellent Lady as I would wish her to be; and when I have fashioned her to my taste, and since then I may not have another, like Pygmalion I will take her for my own. And, though signor Gasparo has said that the same rules which serve for the Courtier serve also for the Lady, I am of a different opinion; for although some qualities are common to both and are as necessary for a man as for a woman, there are yet others that befit a woman more than a man, and others that befit a man and to which a woman ought to be a complete stranger. I say this of bodily exercises; but above all I think that in her ways, manners, words, gestures, and bearing, a woman ought to be very unlike a man; for just as he must show a certain solid and sturdy manliness, so it is seemly for a woman to have a soft and delicate tenderness, with an air of womanly sweetness in her every movement, which, in her going and staying, and in whatever she says, shall always make her appear the woman without any resemblance to a man.

"Now, if this precept be added to the rules which these gentlemen have taught the Courtier, then I think she ought to be able to follow many such and adorn herself with the best accomplishments, as signor Gasparo says. For I hold that many virtues of the mind are as necessary to a woman as to a man; also, gentle birth; to avoid affectation, to be naturally graceful in all her actions, to be mannerly, clever, prudent, not arrogant, not envious, not slanderous, not vain, not contentious, not inept, to know how to gain and hold the favor of her mistress and of all others, to perform well and gracefully the exercises that are suitable for women. And I do think that beauty is more necessary to her than to the Courtier, for truly that woman lacks much who lacks beauty.

Also she must be more circumspect, and more careful not to give occasion for evil being said of her, and conduct herself so that she may not only escape being sullied by guilt but even by the suspicion of it, for a woman has not so many ways of defending herself against false calumnies as a man has. But since Count Ludovico has set forth in great detail the chief profession of the Courtier, and has insisted that this be arms, I think it is also fitting to state what I judge that of the Court Lady to be, and when I have done this I shall think to have discharged the greater part of my assignment.

"Leaving aside, then, those virtues of the mind which she is to have in common with the Courtier (such as prudence, magnanimity, continence, and many others), as well as those qualities that befit all (such as kindness, discretion, ability to manage her husband's property and house and children, if she is married, and all qualities that are requisite in a good mother), I say that, in my opinion, in a Lady who lives at court a certain pleasing affability is becoming above all else, whereby she will be able to entertain graciously every kind of man with agreeable and comely conversation suited to the time and place and to the station of the person with whom she speaks, joining to serene and modest manners, and to that comeliness that ought to inform all her actions, a quick vivacity of spirit whereby she will show herself a stranger to all boorishness; but with such a kind manner as to cause her to be thought no less chaste, prudent, and gentle than she is agreeable, witty, and discreet: thus, she must observe a certain mean (difficult to achieve and, as it were, composed of contraries) and must strictly observe certain limits and not exceed them.

"Now, in her wish to be thought good and pure, this Lady must not be so coy, or appear so to abhor gay company or any talk that is a little loose, as to withdraw as soon as she finds herself involved, for it might easily be thought that she was pretending to be so austere in order to hide something about herself which she feared others might discover; for manners so unbending are always odious. Yet, on the other hand, for the sake of appearing free and amiable she must not utter unseemly words or enter into any immodest and unbridled familiarity or into ways such as might cause others to believe about her what is perhaps not true; but when she finds herself present at such talk, she ought to listen with a light blush of shame.

"Likewise, she must avoid an error into which I have seen many women fall, which is to gossip and eagerly listen to evil spoken of other women. For those women who, when they hear of the unchaste ways of other women, bristle and pretend that the thing is incredible and that a woman so immodest is a monster, in making so much of the fault give cause to think that they might be guilty of it themselves. And those others who continually go about prying into other women's love affairs, relating them in such detail and with such glee, appear envious and desirous that everyone should know of this case in order that the same thing may not through error be imputed to them; and thus they emit certain laughs and assume certain attitudes, making it evident that they relish it all. And the result of this is that men, although they appear to listen to them willingly, usually conceive a bad opinion of such women and have little respect for them, and take these ways of theirs to be an invitation to go further; and they often do go so far with them that it quite justly brings shame upon them, and in the end they esteem them so little as to care nothing for their company, and even come to despise them. On the other hand, there is no man so profligate and so forward as not to have reverence for those women who are esteemed to be good and virtuous, because a certain gravity, tempered with wisdom and goodness, is like a shield against the insolence and brutishness of presumptuous men; wherefore we see that a word, a laugh, or an act of kindness, however small, coming from a virtuous woman is more esteemed by everyone than all the blandishments and caresses of those who so openly show their want of shame—and if they are not unchaste, by their wanton laughter, loquacity, insolence, and scurrilous behavior of this sort, they appear to be so."

*   *   *

"Therefore, I think that the aim of the perfect Courtier, which we have not spoken of up to now, is so to win for himself, by means of the accomplishments ascribed to him by these gentlemen, the favor and mind of the prince whom he serves that he may be able to tell him, and always will tell him, the truth about everything he needs to know, without fear or risk of displeasing him; and that when he sees the mind of his prince inclined to a wrong action, he may dare to oppose him and in a gentle manner avail himself of the favor acquired by his good accomplishments, so as to dissuade him of every evil intent and bring him to the path of virtue. And thus, having in himself the goodness which these gentlemen attributed to him, together with readiness of wit, charm, prudence, knowledge of letters and of many other things—the Courtier will in every instance be able adroitly to show the prince how much honor and profit will come to him and to his from justice, liberality, magnanimity, gentleness, and the other virtues that befit a good prince; and, on the other hand, how much infamy and harm result from the vices opposed to these virtues. Hence, I think that even as music, festivals, games, and the other pleasant accomplishments are, as it were, the flower; so to bring or help one's prince toward what is right and to frighten him away from what is wrong are the true fruit of Courtiership. And because the real merit of good deeds consists chiefly in two things, one of which is to choose a truly good end to aim at, and the other is to know how to find means timely and fitting to attain that good end—it is certain that a man aims at the best end when he sees to it that his prince is deceived by no one, listens to no flatterers or slanderers or liars, and distinguishes good from evil, loving the one and hating the other."

*   *   *

REVIEW QUESTIONS

1. What does Castiglione mean by grace? How is it created?
2. To what extent is it the product of birth or nature?
3. How is it gendered?
4. What does a courtier's conduct tell others about his status?
5. If status was once thought to reside in one's birth and lineage, how does the courtier alter that notion?
6. How does Castiglione's courtier differ from a medieval monk or knight?
7. Is his virtue the expression of his nature, cultivation, or education?

PORTRAIT OF POPE LEO X AND TWO CARDINALS (1518)   RAPHAEL

This intriguing portrait of Pope Leo X and two of his cardinals, relatives elevated through acts of nepotism, reveals the full sophistication of Raphael's artistry. He created an attractive painting of his patron in full papal regalia. At the same time, he subtly included less attractive hints about the subject's office and character. What might this portrait tell us of Leo's character? What does the portrait tell us about Renaissance values? Is Raphael exercising a subtle criticism of the church through his portrait of its head, and, if so, what elements of his criticism are explicit in the painting?

GIOVANNI PICO DELLA MIRANDOLA

FROM "Oration on the Dignity of Man"

Giovanni Pico della Mirandola (1463–1494) is a singular figure in the history of Renaissance humanism. While the corpus of his published works remained small as a result of his early death, the breadth of his learning won him the admiration of scholars past and present. He received a thorough classical education in Greek and Latin, and studied the scholastic tradition of the Middle Ages as well as Jewish and Arabic philosophy. His conception of the dignity of man and harmony among philosophers found expression in his "Oration on the Dignity of Man." In 1486, Pico published his 900 theses, inviting all scholars to a public debate in January 1487. Before it could take place, however, Pope Innocent VIII appointed a commission to examine the theses, some of which were found to be heretical. An attempt to defend the incriminated points plunged Pico into a conflict with ecclesiastical authorities that lasted several years. The oration, never published in its author's lifetime, was written as an introductory speech for the disputation.

From *Reflections on the Philosophy of the History of Mankind*, by J. G. Herder and F. E. Manuel (Chicago: University of Chicago Press, 1968).

I have read in the records of the Arabians, reverend Fathers, that Abdala the Saracen, when questioned as to what on this stage of the world, as it were, could be seen most worthy of wonder, replied: "There is nothing to be seen more wonderful than man." In agreement with this opinion is the saying of Hermes Trismegistus: "A great miracle, Asclepius, is man." But when I weighed the reason for these maxims, the many grounds for the excellence of human nature reported by many men failed to satisfy me—that man is the intermediary between creatures, the intimate of the gods, the king of the lower beings, by the acuteness of his senses, by the discernment of his reason, and by the light of his intelligence the interpreter of nature, the interval between fixed eternity and fleeting time, and (as the Persians say) the bond, nay, rather, the marriage song of the world, on David's testimony but little lower than the angels. Admittedly great though these reasons be, they are not the principal grounds, that is, those which may rightfully claim for themselves the privilege of the highest admiration. For why should we not admire more the angels themselves and the blessed choirs of heaven? At last it seems to me I have come to understand why man is the most fortunate of creatures and consequently worthy of all admiration and what precisely is that rank which is his lot in the universal chain of Being—a rank to be envied not only by brutes but even by the stars and by minds beyond this world. It is a matter past faith and a wondrous one. Why should it not be? For it is on this very account that man is rightly called and judged a great miracle and a wonderful creature indeed.

But hear, Fathers, exactly what this rank is and, as friendly auditors, conformably to your kindness, do me this favor. God the Father, the supreme Architect, had already built this cosmic home we behold, the most sacred temple of His godhead, by the laws of His mysterious wisdom. The region above the heavens He had adorned with Intelligences, the heavenly spheres He had quickened with eternal souls, and the excrementary and filthy parts of the lower world He had filled with a multitude of animals of every kind. But, when the work was finished, the Craftsman kept wishing that there were someone to ponder the plan of so great a work, to love its beauty, and to wonder at its vastness. Therefore, when everything was done (as Moses and Timaeus bear witness), He finally took thought concerning the creation of man. But there was not among His archetypes that from which He could fashion a new offspring, nor was there in His treasure-houses anything which He might bestow on His new son as an inheritance, nor was there in the seats of all the world a place where the latter might sit to contemplate the universe. All was now complete; all things had been assigned to the highest, the middle, and the lowest orders. But in its final creation it was not the part of the Father's power to fail as though exhausted. It was not the part of His wisdom to waver in a needful matter through poverty of counsel. It was not the part of His kindly love that he who was to praise God's divine generosity in regard to others should be compelled to condemn it in regard to himself.

At last the best of artisans ordained that that creature to whom He had been able to give nothing proper to himself should have joint possession of whatever had been peculiar to each of the different kinds of being. He therefore took man as a creature of indeterminate nature and, assigning him a place in the middle of the world, addressed him thus: "Neither a fixed abode nor a form that is thine alone nor any function peculiar to thyself have we given thee, Adam, to the end that according to thy longing and according to thy judgment thou mayest have and possess what abode, what form, and what functions thou thyself shalt desire. The nature of all other beings is limited and constrained within the bounds of laws prescribed by Us. Thou, constrained by no limits, in accordance with thine own free will, in whose hand We have placed thee, shalt ordain for thyself the limits of thy nature. We have set thee at the world's center that thou mayest from thence more easily observe whatever is in the world. We have made thee neither of heaven nor of earth, neither mortal nor immortal, so that with freedom of choice and with honor, as though the maker and molder of thyself, thou mayest fashion thyself in whatever shape thou shalt prefer. Thou shalt have the power to degenerate into the lower forms of life, which are brutish. Thou shalt have the power, out of thy soul's judgment, to be reborn into the higher forms, which are divine."

O supreme generosity of God the Father, O highest and most marvelous felicity of man! To him it is granted to have whatever he chooses, to be whatever he wills. Beasts as soon as they are born (so says Lucilius) bring with them from their mother's womb all they will ever possess. Spiritual beings, either from the beginning or soon thereafter, become what they are to be for ever and ever. On man when he came into life the Father conferred the seeds of all kinds and the germs of every way of life. Whatever seeds each man cultivates will grow to maturity and bear in him their own fruit. If they be vegetative, he will be like a plant. If sensitive, he will become brutish. If rational, he will grow into a heavenly being. If intellectual, he will be an angel and the son of God. And if, happy in the lot of no created thing, he withdraws into the center of his own unity, his spirit, made one with God, in the solitary darkness of God, who is set above all things, shall surpass them all. Who would not admire this our chameleon? Or who could more greatly admire aught else whatever? It is man who Asclepius of Athens, arguing from his mutability of character and from his self-transforming nature, on just grounds says was symbolized by Proteus in the mysteries. Hence those metamorphoses renowned among the Hebrews and the Pythagoreans.

*   *   *

REVIEW QUESTIONS

1. How is Pico reordering the hierarchy of creation?

2. What does he claim for human nature that sets it apart?
3. How does Pico conceive of human will?
4. What implications does that conception have?

5. What is Pico's understanding of the relationship of humankind to God?
6. What are its implications?

NICCOLÒ MACHIAVELLI

FROM *The Prince*

Niccolò Machiavelli (1469–1527) was the son of a Florentine lawyer. Little is known of him until 1498, when he entered the service of the Florentine Republic of Pier Soderini as secretary to the second chancery, a minor bureaucratic post he held for fourteen years. From this position, Machiavelli observed the political process of his day. A staunch republican, he lost his position in government in 1512, when Soderini's republic was toppled and the Medici of Florence were restored to power by a papal army. He spent the rest of his days in retirement, possibly trying to restore himself to the graces of the Medici and the pope, but certainly engaged in the scholarly and literary pursuits that would establish his reputation as a political analyst. Among the fruits of these labors was The Prince, *written in 1513. Of the many observations and ideas expressed in this short work, two at least became fundamental truths of modern politics. One was the necessity of national unity based on a common language, culture, and economy. The other was the preservation of national unity through the concentration and exercise of power by the state. As controversial as they were prescient in Machiavelli's day, these ideas encouraged later scholars to number him among the first modern students of politics.*

From *The Prince*, by Niccolò Machiavelli, translated by Robert M. Adams, A Norton Critical Edition (2d ed.; New York: Norton, 1977), pp. 31–32, 44–50.

How to Measure the Strength of Any Prince's State

There is one other consideration to bear in mind regarding these civil principates; that is, whether a prince is strong enough to stand on his own feet in case of need, or whether he is in constant need of help from others. And to make the matter clearer, let me say that in my opinion princes control their own destiny when they command enough money or men to assemble an adequate army and make a stand against anyone who attacks them. I think princes who need outside protection are those who can't take the field against their foes, but have to hide behind their walls and defend themselves there. I've already mentioned the first class, and will save whatever else I have to say about them till later. As for the others, all I can say is that they should keep their cities well fortified and well supplied, and pay no heed to the surrounding countryside. Whenever a man has fortified his city strongly, and has dealt with his subjects as I described above and will describe further below, people will be slow to attack him; men are always wary of tasks that seem hard, and it can't seem easy to attack a prince whose city is in fine fettle, and whose people do not hate him.

*　　*　　*

Thus a prince who has a strong city and does not earn his people's hatred cannot be attacked, or if he were, that attacker would be driven off to his own disgrace; because the way things keep changing in this world, it's almost impossible for a prince with his armies to devote an entire year to a siege while doing nothing else. Maybe someone will object: when the people see their possessions outside the walls being burnt up, they will get impatient; a long siege and their own self-interest will make them forget the prince. But to this I answer that a brave, strong prince will overcome all these problems, giving his subjects hope at one minute that the storm will soon pass, stirring them up at another moment to fear the enemy's cruelty, and on still other occasions restraining those who seem too rash. Besides, the enemy will generally do his burning and ravishing of the countryside as soon as he begins the siege, when men's minds are still passionate and earnest for the defense; thus the prince has less reason to worry, because, after a few days, when tempers have cooled, the harm will already have been done, the losses inflicted, and there will clearly be no cure. At that point, the people will rally even more strongly behind their prince, because they will feel he owes them something, since their houses were burnt and their fields ravaged in defense of his cause. Indeed, men are so constructed that they feel themselves committed as much by the benefits they grant as by those they receive. Hence, all things considered, it should not be hard for a prudent prince to keep his subjects in good

spirits throughout a siege, as long as he does not run short of food or weapons.

*　　*　　*

On the Reasons Why Men Are Praised or Blamed—Especially Princes

It remains now to be seen what style and principles a prince ought to adopt in dealing with his subjects and friends. I know the subject has been treated frequently before, and I'm afraid people will think me rash for trying to do so again, especially since I intend to differ in this discussion from what others have said. But since I intend to write something useful to an understanding reader, it seemed better to go after the real truth of the matter than to repeat what people have imagined. A great many men have imagined states and princedoms such as nobody ever saw or knew in the real world, for there's such a difference between the way we really live and the way we ought to live that the man who neglects the real to study the ideal will learn how to accomplish his ruin, not his salvation. Any man who tries to be good all the time is bound to come to ruin among the great number who are not good. Hence a prince who wants to keep his post must learn how not to be good, and use that knowledge, or refrain from using it, as necessity requires.

Putting aside, then, all the imaginary things that are said about princes, and getting down to the truth, let me say that whenever men are discussed (and especially princes because they are prominent), there are certain qualities that bring them either praise or blame. Thus some are considered generous, others stingy (I use a Tuscan term, since "greedy" in our speech means a man who wants to take other people's goods; we call a man "stingy" who clings to his own); some are givers, others grabbers; some cruel, others merciful; one man is treacherous, another faithful; one is feeble and effeminate, another fierce and spirited; one humane, another proud; one lustful, another chaste; one straightforward, another sly; one harsh, another gentle; one serious, another playful; one religious, another skeptical, and so on. I know everyone will agree that among these many qualities a prince certainly ought to have all those that are considered good. But since it is impossible to have and exercise them all, because the conditions of human life simply do not allow it, a prince must be shrewd enough to avoid the public disgrace of those vices that would lose him his state. If he possibly can, he should also guard against vices that will not lose him his state; but if he cannot prevent them, he should not be too worried about indulging them. And furthermore, he should not be too worried about incurring blame for any vice without which he would find it hard to save his state. For if you look at matters carefully, you will see that something resembling virtue, if you follow it, may be your ruin, while something else resembling vice will lead, if you follow it, to your security and well-being.

On Liberality and Stinginess

Let me begin, then, with the first of the qualities mentioned above, by saying that a reputation for liberality is doubtless very fine; but the generosity that earns you that reputation can do you great harm. For if you exercise your generosity in a really virtuous way, as you should, nobody will know of it, and you cannot escape the odium of the opposite vice. Hence if you wish to be widely known as a generous man, you must seize every opportunity to make a big display of your giving. A prince of this character is bound to use up his entire revenue in works of ostentation. Thus, in the end, if he wants to keep a name for generosity, he will have to load his people with exorbitant taxes and squeeze money out of them in every way he can. This is the first step in making him odious to his subjects; for when he is poor, nobody will respect him. Then, when his generosity has angered many and brought rewards to a few, the slightest difficulty will trouble him, and at the first approach of danger, down he goes. If by chance he foresees this, and tries to change his ways, he will immediately be labelled a miser.

Since a prince cannot use this virtue [*virtù*] of liberality in such a way as to become known for it unless he harms his own security, he won't mind, if he judges prudently of things, being known as a miser. In due course he will be thought the more liberal man, when people see that his parsimony enables him to live on his income, to defend himself against his enemies, and to undertake major projects without burdening his people with taxes. Thus he will be acting liberally toward all those people from whom he takes nothing (and there are an immense number of them), and in a stingy way toward those people on whom he bestows nothing (and they are very few). In our times, we have seen great things being accomplished only by men who have had the name of misers; all the others have gone under. Pope Julius II, though he used his reputation as a generous man to gain the papacy, sacrificed it in order to be able to make war; the present king of France has waged many wars without levying a single extra tax on his people, simply because he could take care of the extra expenses out of the savings from his long parsimony. If the present king of Spain had a reputation for generosity, he would never have been able to undertake so many campaigns, or win so many of them.

*   *   *

On Cruelty and Clemency: Whether It Is Better to Be Loved or Feared

Continuing now with our list of qualities, let me say that every prince should prefer to be considered merciful rather than cruel, yet he should be careful not to mismanage this clemency of his. People thought Cesare Borgia was cruel, but that cruelty of his reorganized the Romagna, united it, and established it in peace and loyalty. Anyone who views the matter realistically will see that this prince was much more merciful than the people of Florence, who, to avoid the reputation of cruelty, allowed Pistoia to be destroyed. Thus, no prince should mind being called cruel for what he does to keep his subjects united and loyal; he may make examples of a very few, but he will be more merciful in reality than those who, in their tenderheartedness, allow disorders to occur, with their attendant murders and lootings. Such turbulence brings harm to an entire community, while the executions ordered by a prince affect only one individual at a time. A new prince, above all others, cannot possibly avoid a name for cruelty, since new states are always in danger. And Virgil, speaking through the mouth of Dido, says:

> Res dura et regni novitas me talia cogunt
> Moliri, et late fines custode tueri.[1]

Yet a prince should be slow to believe rumors and to commit himself to action on the basis of them. He should not be afraid of his own thoughts; he ought to proceed cautiously, moderating his conduct with prudence and humanity, allowing neither overconfidence to make him careless, nor overtimidity to make him intolerable.

Here the question arises: is it better to be loved than feared, or vice versa? I don't doubt that every prince would like to be both; but since it is hard to accommodate these qualities, if you have to make a choice, to be feared is much safer than to be loved. For it is a good general rule about men, that they are ungrateful, fickle, liars and deceivers, fearful of danger and greedy for gain. While you serve their welfare, they are all yours, offering their blood, their belongings, their lives, and their children's lives, as we noted above—so long as the danger is remote. But when the danger is close at hand, they turn against you. Then, any prince who has relied on their words and has made no other preparations will come to grief; because friendships that are bought at a price, and not with greatness and nobility of soul, may be paid for but they are not acquired, and they cannot be used in time of need. People are less concerned with offending a man who makes himself loved than one

who makes himself feared: the reason is that love is a link of obligation which men, because they are rotten, will break any time they think doing so serves their advantage; but fear involves dread of punishment, from which they can never escape.

Still, a prince should make himself feared in such a way that, even if he gets no love, he gets no hate either; because it is perfectly possible to be feared and not hated, and this will be the result if only the prince will keep his hands off the property of his subjects or citizens, and off their women. When he does have to shed blood, he should be sure to have a strong justification and manifest cause; but above all, he should not confiscate people's property, because men are quicker to forget the death of a father than the loss of a patrimony. Besides, pretexts for confiscation are always plentiful; it never fails that a prince who starts living by plunder can find reasons to rob someone else. Excuses for proceeding against someone's life are much rarer and more quickly exhausted.

* * *

Returning to the question of being feared or loved, I conclude that since men love at their own inclination but can be made to fear at the inclination of the prince, a shrewd prince will lay his foundations on what is under his own control, not on what is controlled by others. He should simply take pains not to be hated, as I said.

The Way Princes Should Keep Their Word

How praiseworthy it is for a prince to keep his word and live with integrity rather than by craftiness, everyone understands; yet we see from recent experience that those princes have accomplished most who paid little heed to keeping their promises, but who knew how craftily to manipulate the minds of men. In the end, they won out over those who tried to act honestly.

You should consider then, that there are two

---

[1] "Severe pressures and the newness of the regime compel me to these measures. I must maintain the borders against foreign enemies."

ways of fighting, one with laws and the other with force. The first is properly a human method, the second belongs to beasts. But as the first method does not always suffice, you sometimes have to turn to the second. Thus a prince must know how to make good use of both the beast and the man. Ancient writers made subtle note of this fact when they wrote that Achilles and many other princes of antiquity were sent to be reared by Chiron the centaur, who trained them in his discipline. Having a teacher who is half man and half beast can only mean that a prince must know how to use both these two natures, and that one without the other has no lasting effect.

Since a prince must know how to use the character of beasts, he should pick for imitation the fox and the lion. As the lion cannot protect himself from traps, and the fox cannot defend himself from wolves, you have to be a fox in order to be wary of traps, and a lion to overawe the wolves. Those who try to live by the lion alone are badly mistaken. Thus a prudent prince cannot and should not keep his word when to do so would

go against his interest, or when the reasons that made him pledge it no longer apply. Doubtless if all men were good, this rule would be bad; but since they are a sad lot, and keep no faith with you, you in your turn are under no obligation to keep it with them.

*   *   *

REVIEW QUESTIONS

1. What, according to Machiavelli, is the basis of political authority?
2. How does his theory differ from others of his day?
3. When he claims that a prince must assume many guises, what is Machiavelli saying about his understanding of human nature?
4. What is the role of artifice in political authority?
5. What might Machiavelli's prince have in common with Castiglione's courtier?

DESIDERIUS ERASMUS OF ROTTERDAM

FROM *Ten Colloquies*

Desiderius Erasmus of Rotterdam (1476–1536) was one of the greatest scholars of his day, measured in terms of his writings and their influence. Educated at Deventer in the Netherlands and in Paris, he began his career as an editor, translator, and popularizer of classical texts. In the humanistic tradition, he used classical tropes as models for his own society, a practice that made him not only a great scholar but also a great satirist. His chief intellectual commitment, however, was the renewal of Christian piety through the study of Christian literature, the Bible and church fathers above all. In this context he is often viewed as the great exponent of Christian humanism, the northern European variant of classical Italian humanism. His translation of the Bible inspired the biblical scholarship of sixteenth-century reformers. His editions of patristic sources remain authoritative to this day. His Ten

Colloquies were written as popular texts to inculcate elegant Latin and to inspire Christian conduct.

From *Ten Colloquies*, by Desiderius Erasmus, translated by Craig R. Thompson (Upper Saddle River, N.J.: Prentice-Hall, 1986).

"Cyclops, or the Gospel Bearer"

CANNIUS: What's Polyphemus hunting here?

POLYPHEMUS: What could I be hunting without dogs or spear? Is that your question?

CANNIUS: Some wood nymph, perhaps.

POLYPHEMUS: A good guess. Look, here's my hunting net.

CANNIUS: What a sight! Bacchus in a lion's skin —Polyphemus with a book—a cat in a saffron gown!

POLYPHEMUS: I've painted this little book not only in saffron but bright red and blue, too.

CANNIUS: I'm not talking about saffron; I said something in Greek. Seems to be a soldierly book, for it's protected by bosses, plates, and brass clasps.

POLYPHEMUS: Take a good look at it.

CANNIUS: I'm looking. Very fine, but you haven't yet decorated it enough.

POLYPHEMUS: What's lacking?

CANNIUS: You should have added your coat of arms.

POLYPHEMUS: What coat of arms?

CANNIUS: The head of Silenus peering out of a wine jug. But what's the book about? The art of drinking?

POLYPHEMUS: Be careful you don't blurt out blasphemy.

CANNIUS: What, you don't mean it's something sacred?

POLYPHEMUS: The most sacred of all, the Gospels.

CANNIUS: By Hercules! What has Polyphemus to do with the Gospels?

POLYPHEMUS: You might as well ask what a Christian has to do with Christ.

CANNIUS: I'm not sure a halberd isn't more fitting for the likes of you. If I were at sea and met a stranger who looked like this, I'd take him for a pirate; if I met him in a wood, for a bandit.

POLYPHEMUS: Yet this very Gospel teaches us not to judge a man by appearances. Just as a haughty spirit often lurks under an ash-colored cowl, so a cropped head, curled beard, stern brow, wild eyes, plumed cap, military cloak, and slashed breeches sometimes cover a true Christian heart.

CANNIUS: Of course. Sometimes a sheep lurks in wolf's clothing, too. And if you trust fables, an ass in a lion's skin.

POLYPHEMUS: What's more, I know a man who has a sheep's head and a fox's heart. I could wish him friends as fair as his eyes are dark, and a character as shining as his complexion.

CANNIUS: If a man with a sheepskin cap has a sheep's head, what a load *you* carry, with both a sheep and an ostrich on your head. And isn't it rather ridiculous to have a bird on your head and an ass in your heart?

POLYPHEMUS: That hurt!

CANNIUS: But it would be well if, as you've decorated the Gospels with various ornaments, the Gospels in turn adorned you. You've decorated them with colors; I wish they might embellish you with good morals.

POLYPHEMUS: I'll take care of that.

CANNIUS: After your fashion, yes.

POLYPHEMUS: But insults aside, you don't condemn those who carry a volume of the Gospels about, do you?

CANNIUS: I'd be the last person in the world to do that.

POLYPHEMUS: What? I seem to you the least person in the world, when I'm taller than you by an ass's head?

CANNIUS: I don't believe you'd be that much taller even if the ass pricked up its ears.

POLYPHEMUS: Certainly by a buffalo's.

CANNIUS: I like the comparison. But I said "last"; I wasn't calling you "least."

POLYPHEMUS: What's the difference between an egg and an egg?

CANNIUS: What's the difference between middle finger and little finger?

POLYPHEMUS: The middle one's longer.

CANNIUS: Very good! What's the difference between ass ears and wolf ears?

POLYPHEMUS: Wolf ears are shorter.

CANNIUS: That's right.

POLYPHEMUS: But I'm in the habit of measuring long and short by span and ell, not by ears.

CANNIUS: Well, the man who carried Christ was called Christopher. You, who carry the Gospels, ought to be called Gospel-bearer instead of Polyphemus.

POLYPHEMUS: Don't you think it's holy to carry the Gospels?

CANNIUS: No—unless you'd agree that asses are mighty holy.

POLYPHEMUS: How so?

CANNIUS: Because one of them can carry three thousand books of this kind. I should think you'd be equal to that load if fitted with the right packsaddle.

POLYPHEMUS: There's nothing farfetched in thus crediting an ass with holiness because he carried Christ.

CANNIUS: I don't envy you that holiness. And if you like, I'll give you relics of the ass that carried Christ, so you can kiss them.

POLYPHEMUS: A gift I'll be glad to get. For by touching the body of Christ that ass was consecrated.

CANNIUS: Obviously those who smote Christ touched him too.

POLYPHEMUS: But tell me seriously, isn't carrying the Gospel about a reverent thing to do?

CANNIUS: Reverent if done sincerely, without hypocrisy.

POLYPHEMUS: Let monks have hypocrisy! What has a soldier to do with hypocrisy?

CANNIUS: But first tell me what hypocrisy is.

POLYPHEMUS: Professing something other than what you really mean.

CANNIUS: But what does carrying a copy of the Gospels profess? A gospel life, doesn't it?

POLYPHEMUS: I suppose so.

CANNIUS: Therefore, when the life doesn't correspond to the book, isn't that hypocrisy?

POLYPHEMUS: Apparently. But what is it truly to bear the Gospel?

CANNIUS: Some bear it in their hands, as the Franciscans do their Rule. Parisian porters, and asses and geldings, can do the same. There are those who bear it in their mouths, harping on nothing but Christ and the Gospel. That's pharisaical. Some bear it in their hearts. The true Gospel bearer, then, is one who carries it in hands and mouth *and* heart.

POLYPHEMUS: Where are these?

CANNIUS: In churches—the deacons, who bear the book, read it to the congregation, and have it by heart.

POLYPHEMUS: Though not all who bear the Gospel in their hearts are devout.

CANNIUS: Don't quibble. A man doesn't bear it in his heart unless he loves it through and through. Nobody loves it wholeheartedly unless he emulates the Gospel in his manner of living.

POLYPHEMUS: I don't follow these subtleties.

CANNIUS: But I'll tell you more bluntly. If you carry a jar of Beaune wine on your shoulder, it's just a burden, isn't it?

POLYPHEMUS: That's all.

CANNIUS: But if you hold the wine in your throat, and presently spit it out?

POLYPHEMUS: Useless—though, really, I'm not accustomed to doing that!

CANNIUS: But if—as you *are* accustomed—you take a long drink?

POLYPHEMUS: Nothing more heavenly.

CANNIUS: Your whole body glows; your face turns rosy; your expression grows merry.

POLYPHEMUS: Exactly.

CANNIUS: The Gospel has the same effect when it penetrates the heart. It makes a new man of you.

POLYPHEMUS: So I don't seem to you to live according to the Gospel?

CANNIUS: You can best decide that question yourself.

POLYPHEMUS: If it could be decided with a battle-ax—

CANNIUS: If someone called you a liar or a rake to your face, what would you do?

POLYPHEMUS: What would I do? He'd feel my fists.

CANNIUS: What if someone hit you hard?

POLYPHEMUS: I'd break his neck for that.

CANNIUS: But your book teaches you to repay insults with a soft answer; and "Whosoever shall smite thee on thy right cheek, turn to him the other also."

POLYPHEMUS: I've read that, but it slipped my mind.

CANNIUS: You pray frequently, I dare say.

POLYPHEMUS: That's pharisaical.

CANNIUS: Long-winded but ostentatious praying is pharisaical. But your book teaches us to pray without ceasing, yet sincerely.

POLYPHEMUS: Still, I do pray sometimes.

CANNIUS: When?

POLYPHEMUS: Whenever I think of it—once or twice a week.

CANNIUS: What do you pray?

POLYPHEMUS: The Lord's Prayer.

CANNIUS: How often?

POLYPHEMUS: Once. For the Gospel forbids vain repetitions as "much speaking."

CANNIUS: Can you concentrate on the Lord's Prayer while repeating it?

POLYPHEMUS: Never tried. Isn't it enough to say the words?

CANNIUS: I don't know, except that God hears only the utterance of the heart. Do you fast often?

POLYPHEMUS: Never.

CANNIUS: But your book recommends prayer and fasting.

POLYPHEMUS: I'd recommend them too, if my belly did not demand something else.

CANNIUS: But Paul says that those who serve their bellies aren't serving Jesus Christ. Do you eat meat on any day whatever?

POLYPHEMUS: Any day it's offered.

CANNIUS: Yet a man as tough as you are could live on hay or the bark of trees.

POLYPHEMUS: But Christ said that a man is not defiled by what he eats.

CANNIUS: True, if it's eaten in moderation, without giving offense. But Paul, the disciple of Christ, prefers starvation to offending a weak brother by his food; and he calls upon us to follow his example, in order that we may please all men in all things.

POLYPHEMUS: Paul's Paul, and I'm me.

CANNIUS: But Egon's job is to feed she-goats.

POLYPHEMUS: I'd rather eat one.

CANNIUS: A fine wish! You'll be a billygoat rather than a she-goat.

POLYPHEMUS: I said *eat* one, not *be* one.

CANNIUS: Very prettily said. Are you generous to the poor?

POLYPHEMUS: I've nothing to give.

CANNIUS: But you would have, if you lived soberly and worked hard.

POLYPHEMUS: I'm fond of loafing.

CANNIUS: Do you keep God's commandments?

POLYPHEMUS: That's tiresome.

CANNIUS: Do you do penance for your sins?

POLYPHEMUS: Christ has paid for us.

CANNIUS: Then why do you insist you love the Gospel?

POLYPHEMUS: I'll tell you. A certain Franciscan in our neighborhood kept babbling from the pulpit against Erasmus' New Testament. I met the man privately, grabbed him by the hair with my left hand, and punched him with my right. I gave him a hell of a beating; made his whole face swell. What do you say to that? Isn't that promoting the Gospel? Next I gave him absolution by banging him on the head three times with this very same book, raising three lumps, in the name of Father, Son, and Holy Ghost.

CANNIUS: The evangelical spirit, all right! This is certainly defending the Gospel with the Gospel.

POLYPHEMUS: I ran across another member of the same order who never stopped raving against Erasmus. Fired with evangelical zeal, I threatened the fellow so much he begged pardon on both knees and admitted the devil had put him up to saying what he said. If he hadn't done this, my halberd would have bounced against his head. I looked as fierce as Mars in battle. This took place before witnesses.

CANNIUS: I'm surprised the man didn't drop dead on the spot. But let's go on. Do you live chastely?

POLYPHEMUS: I may when I'm old. But shall I confess the truth to you, Cannius?

CANNIUS: I'm no priest. If you want to confess, find somebody else.

POLYPHEMUS: Usually I confess to God, but to you I admit I'm not yet a perfect follower of the Gospel; just an ordinary fellow. My kind have four Gospels. Four things above all we Gospelers seek: full bellies; plenty of work for the organs below the belly; a livelihood from somewhere or other; finally, freedom to do as we please. If we get these, we shout in our cups, "Io, triumph; Io, Paean! The Gospel flourishes! Christ reigns!"

CANNIUS: That's an Epicurean life, surely, not an evangelical one.

POLYPHEMUS: I don't deny it, but you know Christ is omnipotent and can turn us into other men in the twinkling of an eye.

CANNIUS: Into swine, too, which I think is more likely than into good men.

POLYPHEMUS: I wish there were no worse creatures in the world than swine, oxen, asses, and camels! You can meet many men who are fiercer than lions, greedier than wolves, more lecherous than sparrows, more snappish than dogs, more venomous than vipers.

CANNIUS: But now it's time for you to begin changing from brute to man.

POLYPHEMUS: You do well to warn me, for prophets these days declare the end of the world is at hand.

CANNIUS: All the more reason to hurry.

POLYPHEMUS: I await the hand of Christ.

CANNIUS: See that you are pliant material for his hand! But where do they get the notion that the end of the world is near?

POLYPHEMUS: They say it's because men are behaving now just as they did before the Flood overwhelmed them. They feast, drink, stuff themselves, marry and are given in marriage, whore, buy, sell, pay and charge interest, build buildings. Kings make war, priests are zealous to increase their wealth, theologians invent syllogisms, monks roam through the world, the commons riot, Erasmus writes colloquies. In short, no calamity is lacking: hunger, thirst, robbery, war, plague, sedition, poverty. Doesn't this prove human affairs are at an end?

CANNIUS: In this mass of woes, what worries you most?

POLYPHEMUS: Guess.

CANNIUS: That your purse is full of cobwebs.

POLYPHEMUS: Damned if you haven't hit it!— Just now I'm on my way back from a drinking party. Some other time, when I'm more sober, I'll argue with you about the Gospel, if you like.

CANNIUS: When shall I see you sober?

POLYPHEMUS: When I'm sober.

CANNIUS: When will you be so?

POLYPHEMUS: When you see me so. Meantime, my dear Cannius, good luck.

CANNIUS: I hope you, in turn, become what you're called.

POLYPHEMUS: To prevent you from outdoing me in courtesy, I pray that Cannius, as the name implies, may never be lacking a can!

REVIEW QUESTIONS

1. Why does Erasmus use the dialogue form?
2. What might he be saying, not only about his readers but also about voice and perspective?
3. What is the older mode of Christianity that Erasmus parodies?
4. What is wrong with it?
5. What ideal of Christian behavior emerges in the colloquy?
6. How might it differ from the older form?
7. How might it be better suited to the instabilities of life in Renaissance Europe?

SIR THOMAS MORE

FROM *Utopia*

Sir Thomas More (1478–1535) was born on Milk Street, in London, the "brightest star that ever shined in the via lactea,*" according to Thomas Fuller. His father, John More, was a butler at Lincoln's Inn, later raised to the knighthood and made a judge first in the court of common pleas and later on the king's bench. The son was educated in the household of John Morton, archbishop of Canterbury, and at Christ Church, Oxford. Compelled by his father to study law, More entered New Inn in 1494 and Lincoln's Inn in 1496. He lived with the monks at the London Charterhouse and developed there the discipline and devotion that would serve him well in later troubles. Yet, he decided on married rather than monastic life. He wed Jane Colet in 1505 and they had four children. More was an early advocate of education for women; he insisted that his son and daughters be taught by the best tutors available. Despite his many interests—intellectual, religious, and domestic—the law remained his career. City, monarchy, and church called on his services.*

He was part of a London trade delegation to the cities of the Hanse in 1515. During this service, he wrote Book II of Utopia, *describing a pagan, communist city-state in which all policies and institutions were governed by reason. Such a state contrasted notably with the polity of Christian Europe with its greed, self-interest, and violence, as More described it in Book I. The complete work, which drew heavily on descriptions of the new world as well as passages from classical literature, was published in 1516 in Louvain. It established More's international reputation as a man of letters. But public affairs constantly drew him out of his study. In 1523, he served as speaker of the House of Commons, and in 1529, he succeeded Cardinal Wolsey as lord chancellor under Henry VIII. The king favored More, keeping him in attendance, visiting him at home, and enjoying his learned conversation. They fell out over Henry's growing dispute with the Catholic Church. More resigned office in 1532, the day after the clergy were deprived of the power to enact constitutions without royal consent. Refusal to swear the Oath of Supremacy in 1534, by which he would have recognized Henry as the supreme head of the church in England, made More guilty of treason. He was martyred in 1535, in his own words "the king's good servant but God's first."*

From *Utopia*, by Sir Thomas More, A Norton Critical Edition translated by Robert M. Adams, (2d ed.; New York: Norton, 1975), pp. 30–33, 40–42, 50–51, 64.

*   *   *

"But as a matter of fact, my dear More, to tell you what I really think, as long as you have private property, and as long as cash money is the measure of all things, it is really not possible for a nation to be governed justly or happily. For justice cannot exist where all the best things in life are held by the worst citizens; nor can anyone be happy where property is limited to a few, since those few are always uneasy and the many are utterly wretched.

"So I reflect on the wonderfully wise and sacred institutions of the Utopians who are so well governed with so few laws. Among them virtue has its reward, yet everything is shared equally, and all men live in plenty. I contrast them with the many other nations which are constantly passing new ordinances and yet can never order their affairs satisfactorily. In these other nations, whatever a man can get he calls his own private property; but all the mass of laws old and new don't enable him to secure his own, or defend it, or even distinguish it from someone else's property. Different men lay claim, successively or all at once, to the same property; and thus arise innumerable and interminable lawsuits—fresh ones every day. When I consider all these things, I become more sympathetic to Plato and do not wonder that he declined to make laws for any people who refused to share their goods equally. Wisest of men, he easily perceived that the one and only road to the welfare of all lies through the absolute equality of goods. I doubt whether such equality can ever be achieved where property belongs to individual men. However abundant goods may be, when every man tries to get as much as he can for his own exclusive use, a handful of men end up sharing the whole thing, and the rest are left in poverty. The result generally is two sorts of people whose fortunes ought to be interchanged: the rich are rapacious, wicked, and useless, while the poor are unassuming, modest men who work hard, more for the benefit of the public than of themselves.

"Thus I am wholly convinced that unless private property is entirely done away with, there can be no fair or just distribution of goods, nor can mankind be happily governed. As long as private property remains, by far the largest and the best part of mankind will be oppressed by a heavy and inescapable burden of cares and anxieties. This load, I admit, may be lightened a little bit under the present system, but I maintain it cannot be

entirely removed. Laws might be made that no one should own more than a certain amount of land or receive more than a certain income. Or laws might be passed to prevent the prince from becoming too powerful and the populace too unruly. It might be made unlawful for public offices to be solicited, or put up for sale, or made burdensome for the officeholder by great expense. Otherwise, officeholders are tempted to get their money back by fraud or extortion, and only rich men can afford to seek positions which ought to be held by wise men. Laws of this sort, I agree, may have as much effect as good and careful nursing has on men who are chronically or even terminally sick. The social evils I mentioned may be alleviated and their effects mitigated for a while, but so long as private property remains, there is no hope at all of effecting a cure and restoring society to good health. While you try to cure one part, you aggravate the disease in other parts. Suppressing one symptom causes another to break out, since you cannot give something to one man without taking it away from someone else."

"But I don't see it that way," I replied. "It seems to me that men cannot possibly live well where all things are in common. How can there be plenty of commodities where every man stops working? The hope of gain will not spur him on; he will rely on others, and become lazy. If a man is driven by want of something to produce it, and yet cannot legally protect what he has gained, what can follow but continual bloodshed and turmoil, especially when respect for magistrates and their authority has been lost? I for one cannot conceive of authority existing among men who are equal to one another in every respect."

*   *   *

"As for the relative ages of the governments," Raphael replied, "you might judge more accurately if you had read their histories. If we believe these records, they had cities before there were even human inhabitants here. What ingenuity has discovered or chance hit upon could have turned up just as well in one place as the other. As a matter of fact, I believe we surpass them in natural intelligence, but they leave us far behind in their diligence and zeal to learn.

"According to their chronicles, they had heard nothing of men-from-beyond-the-equator (that's their name for us) until we arrived, except that once, some twelve hundred years ago, a ship which a storm had blown toward Utopia was wrecked on their island. Some Romans and Egyptians were cast ashore, and never departed. Now note how the Utopians profited, through their diligence, from this one chance event. They learned every single useful art of the Roman civilization either directly from their guests, or indirectly from hints and surmises on which they based their own investigations. What benefits from the mere fact that on a single occasion some Europeans landed there! If a similar accident has hitherto brought any men here from their land, the incident has been completely forgotten, as it will be forgotten in time to come that I was ever in their country. From one such accident they made themselves masters of all our useful inventions, but I suspect it will be a long time before we accept any of their institutions which are better than ours. This willingness to learn, I think, is the really important reason for their being better governed and living more happily than we do, though we are not inferior to them in brains or resources."

*   *   *

Their Occupations

Agriculture is the one occupation at which everyone works, men and women alike, with no exceptions. They are trained in it from childhood, partly in the schools where they learn theory, and partly through field trips to nearby farms, which make something like a game of practical instruction. On these trips they not only watch the work being done, but frequently pitch in and get a workout by doing the jobs themselves.

Besides farm work (which, as I said, everybody performs), each person is taught a particular trade of his own, such as wool-working, linen-making, masonry, metal-work, or carpentry. There is no other craft that is practiced by any considerable number of them. Throughout the island people wear, and down through the centuries they have always worn, the same style of clothing, except for the distinction between the sexes, and between married and unmarried persons. Their clothing is attractive, does not hamper bodily movement, and serves for warm as well as cold weather; what is more, each household can make its own.

Every person (and this includes women as well as men) learns a second trade, besides agriculture. As the weaker sex, women practice the lighter crafts, such as working in wool or linen; the heavier crafts are assigned to the men. As a rule, the son is trained to his father's craft, for which most feel a natural inclination. But if anyone is attracted to another occupation, he is transferred by adoption into a family practicing the trade he prefers. When anyone makes such a change, both his father and the authorities make sure that he is assigned to a grave and responsible householder. After a man has learned one trade, if he wants to learn another, he gets the same permission. When he has learned both, he pursues whichever he likes better, unless the city needs one more than the other.

The chief and almost the only business of the syphogrants is to manage matters so that no one sits around in idleness, and assure that everyone works hard at his trade. But no one has to exhaust himself with endless toil from early morning to late at night, as if he were a beast of burden. Such wretchedness, really worse than slavery, is the common lot of workmen in all countries, except Utopia. Of the day's twenty-four hours, the Utopians devote only six to work. They work three hours before noon, when they go to dinner. After dinner they rest for a couple of hours, then go to work for another three hours. Then they have supper, and at eight o'clock (counting the first hour after noon as one), they go to bed and sleep eight hours.

The other hours of the day, when they are not working, eating, or sleeping, are left to each man's individual discretion, provided he does not waste them in roistering or sloth, but uses them busily in some occupation that pleases him. Generally these periods are devoted to intellectual activity. For they have an established custom of giving public lectures before daybreak; attendance at these lectures is required only of those who have been specially chosen to devote themselves to learning, but a great many other people, both men and women, choose voluntarily to attend. Depending on their interests, some go to one lecture, some to another. But if anyone would rather devote his spare time to his trade, as many do who don't care for the intellectual life, this is not discouraged; in fact, such persons are commended as especially useful to the commonwealth.

*   *   *

But in all this, you may get a wrong impression, if we don't go back and consider one point more carefully. Because they allot only six hours to work, you might think the necessities of life would be in scant supply. This is far from the case. Their working hours are ample to provide not only enough but more than enough of the necessities and even the conveniences of life. You will easily appreciate this if you consider how large a part of the population in other countries exists without doing any work at all. In the first place, hardly any of the women, who are a full half of the population, work; or, if they do, then as a rule their husbands lie snoring in the bed. Then there is a great lazy gang of priests and so-called religious men. Add to them all the rich, especially the landlords, who are commonly called gentlemen and nobility. Include with them their retainers, that mob of swaggering bullies. Finally, reckon in with these the sturdy and lusty beggars, who go about feigning some disease as an excuse for their idleness. You will certainly find that the things which satisfy our needs are produced by far fewer hands than you had supposed.

And now consider how few of those who do work are doing really essential things. For where money is the standard of everything, many superfluous trades are bound to be carried on simply to satisfy luxury and licentiousness. Suppose the multitude of those who now work were limited to a few trades, and set to producing more and more of those conveniences and commodities that nature really requires. They would be bound to produce so much that the prices would drop, and the workmen would be unable to gain a living. But suppose again that all the workers in useless trades were put to useful ones, and that all the idlers (who now guzzle twice as much as the workingmen who make what they consume) were assigned to productive tasks—well, you can easily see how little time each man would have to spend working, in order to produce all the goods that human needs and conveniences require—yes, and human pleasure too, as long as it's true and natural pleasure.

*   *   *

Their Gold and Silver

For these reasons, therefore, they have accumulated a vast treasure, but they do not keep it like a treasure. I'm really quite ashamed to tell you how they do keep it, because you probably won't believe me. I would not have believed it myself if someone had just told me about it; but I was there, and saw it with my own eyes. It is a general rule that the more different anything is from what people are used to, the harder it is to accept. But, considering that all their other customs are so unlike ours, a sensible man will not be surprised that they use gold and silver quite differently than we do. After all, they never do use money among themselves, but keep it only for a contingency which may or may not actually arise. So in the meanwhile they take care that no one shall overvalue gold and silver, of which money is made, beyond what the metals themselves deserve. Anyone can see, for example, that iron is far superior to either; men could not live without iron, by heaven, any more than without fire or water. But gold and silver have, by nature, no function that we cannot easily dispense with. Human folly has made them precious because they are rare. Like a most wise and generous mother, nature has placed the best things everywhere and in the open, like air, water, and the earth itself; but she has hidden away in remote places all vain and unprofitable things.

If in Utopia gold and silver were kept locked up in some tower, foolish heads among the common people might well concoct a story that the prince and the senate were out to cheat ordinary folk and get some advantage for themselves. They might indeed put the gold and silver into beautiful plate-ware and rich handiwork, but then in case of necessity the people would not want to give up such articles, on which they had begun to fix their hearts, only to melt them down for soldiers' pay. To avoid all these inconveniences, they thought of a plan which conforms with their institutions as clearly as it contrasts with our own. Unless we've actually seen it working, their plan may seem ridiculous to us, because we prize gold so highly and are so careful about protecting it. With them it's just the other way. While they eat from pottery dishes and drink from glass cups, well made but inexpensive, their chamber pots and stools—all their humblest vessels, for use in the common halls and private homes—are made of gold and silver. The chains and heavy fetters of slaves are also made of these metals. Finally, criminals who are to bear through life the mark of some disgraceful act are forced to wear golden rings on their ears, golden bands on their fingers, golden chains around their necks, and even golden crowns on their heads. Thus they hold gold and silver up to scorn in every conceivable way. As a result, when they have to part with these metals, which other nations give up with as much agony as if they were being disemboweled, the Utopians feel it no more than the loss of a penny.

*   *   *

Slaves

The Utopians enslave prisoners of war only if they are captured in wars fought by the Utopians themselves. The children of slaves are not automatically enslaved, nor are any men who were enslaved in a foreign country. Most of their slaves are either their own former citizens, enslaved for some heinous offense, or else men of other nations who were condemned to death in their own land. Most are of the latter sort. Sometimes the Utopians buy them at a very modest rate, more often they ask for them, get them for nothing, and bring them home in considerable numbers. These kinds of slaves are kept constantly at work, and are always fettered. The Utopians deal with their own people more harshly than with others, feeling that their crimes are worse and deserve stricter punishment because, as it is argued, they had an excellent education and the best of moral training, yet still couldn't be restrained from wrongdoing. A third class of slaves consists of hardworking penniless drudges from other nations who voluntarily choose to become slaves in Utopia. Such people are treated well, almost as well as citizens, except that they are given a little extra work, on the score that they're used to it. If one of them wants to leave, which seldom happens, no obstacles are put in his way, nor is he sent off empty-handed.

*   *   *

REVIEW QUESTIONS

1. Why did More choose to call the place *Utopia*, literally "Nowhere"?
2. What possibilities created by the discovery of a new world does More explore in *Utopia*?
3. How are More's Utopians different from what medieval Europeans would have considered Christian?
4. How does More's attitude toward the people of Utopia reflect attitudes of the Renaissance?
5. How might *Utopia* be critical of Renaissance society?
6. What do More's Utopians have in common with the kind of Christian Erasmus described in his colloquy "Cyclops, or the Gospel-Bearer"?

MARGUERITE DE NAVARRE

FROM *The Heptameron*

*Marguerite d'Angoulême, later known as Marguerite de Navarre (1492–1549), re-
flects in her own experiences many of the opportunities and advantages open to elite
women during the Renaissance. Born the daughter of Charles d'Angoulême and
Louise de Savoie, she received a humanist-oriented education in the classics. As a
young woman, she attended the court of her brother, King Francis I of France, and
undertook diplomatic missions on his behalf, including the negotiation of his release
from prison in Madrid after his capture at the Battle of Pavia in 1525 by Emperor
Charles V. She also engaged in the intellectual and spiritual issues of her day, taking
an early interest in the reform of the church. Through her correspondence with Guillaume Briçonnet, bishop of Meaux, and Jacques Lefèvre d'Etaples, she became a patroness of the evangelical movement in France, calling for the translation of the Bible
into French and writing devotional poetry, all of which provoked the censure of theologians at the Sorbonne. In all this activity, she recalls somewhat the extraordinarily strong and intelligent women who attend the court of Castiglione's* The Book of
the Courtier. *Over the course of her lifetime, Marguerite gradually withdrew from
politics and devoted herself to writing.* The Heptameron, *published posthumously in
1559, belongs to this later period of activity. Intended as a French* Decameron, *drawing explicit inspiration from Boccaccio, this collection of some seventy-three novellas
reflects on the tension between spiritual and material matters and thus reveals the
complexity of human behavior. Told by five men and five women—all aristocratic—
the stories capture something of the texture of courtly life: varying attitudes toward
women in that society, the coexistence of good and evil in the world, and differing
opinions about sin and virtue. Interestingly, though none of the storytellers are explicitly Protestant, none enunciate positions that were inimical to evangelical reform.
Thus,* The Heptameron, *including its "Prologue," which follows, provides its readers
a sense not only of the tensions between spiritual and physical matters in the abstract
but also of the spiritual and physical tensions of its day. It provides an excellent
bridge, therefore, between the Renaissance and the Reformation.*

From *The Heptameron*, translated by P. A. Chilton (London: Penguin Books, 1984).

On the first day of September, when the springs of the Pyrenees are just beginning to be at their most potent, there were a number of people staying at the spa town of Cauterets. They had come from Spain [and other countries] as well as from France, some to drink the waters, some to bathe in them, and some to be treated with the mud. These are all very remarkable cures, so remarkable that patients long given up by their physicians go home completely restored to health. But it is not my purpose here to expatiate on the powers of these waters and their fine situation. I wish merely to relate those details which will serve the subject I have in hand.

The patients all remained at the spa for over three weeks, until their condition improved and they felt they could return home. But as they were preparing to leave, the rain came. It fell in such torrents and with such extraordinary force, you would have thought that God had quite forgotten that once He had promised to Noah never again to destroy the world by water. In Cauterets the huts and houses were all so badly flooded that it was impossible for anyone to stay there. Visitors who had come from the Spanish side went back over the mountains as best they could, with those among them who knew the tracks coming off the best. But the French lords and their ladies, thinking they could get back to Tarbes just as easily as they had come, discovered that the streams were so swollen they they could ford them only with difficulty. And when they came to the Gave de Pau, which on the way there had not been two feet deep, they found that it had turned into a raging torrent. So they turned back to look for the bridges, only to find that the flimsy wooden structures had been swept away by the force of the water. Some of the party thought they might be able to resist the current if they waded across in groups. But they were carried off so swiftly that those who had been about to follow them could not bring themselves to make the attempt. At this point, disagreeing on what they should do next, they split up to look for different routes. Some of them crossed the mountains, passed through Aragon into Roussillon, and from there went to Narbonne. Others went straight to Barcelona, from where they went by sea to Marseilles and Aigues-Mortes. But one of the travellers was an old lady named Oisille, a widow, with much experience of life. She resolved not to let the treacherous roads frighten her, and made her way to the abbey of Our Lady at Sarrance. Not that she was so superstitious as to believe that the glorious Virgin should leave her seat at her Son's right hand in order to come and take up residence in such a desolate spot. She simply had a desire to see this holy place about which she had heard such a lot, and was also fairly certain that if there was any way at all of finding refuge from danger, the monks were sure to have found it. Eventually, she reached her destination, but only after struggling through rugged and hostile terrain. Indeed, so arduous were the climbs with which she was confronted, that in spite of her age and weight, she was obliged for the most part to go on foot. But the most tragic thing was that most of her horses and servants died on the way, so that by the time she arrived at Sarrance she was accompanied only by one man and one woman. There the monks received them charitably.

Amongst the French travellers there were also two noblemen who had gone to the spa more because they were devoted to the service of two ladies who were there than because they had anything wrong with their health. When they saw the party was breaking up, and that the ladies were being led off by their husbands in another direction, these two gentlemen decided to follow at a distance, without saying anything to anyone. One evening during the journey the two married men and their wives arrived at the house of a man who was more of a bandit than a peasant. The two young gentlemen who were following behind stayed in a farm cottage nearby. Towards midnight they were woken up by a tremendous din. They jumped out of bed, roused their servants, and asked their host what was going on. The poor man was in a fair state of fright. It was a band of outlaws, he told them, and they had come to get their share in some loot that their comrade was keeping in his house next door. Immediately the two men grabbed their swords, and, taking their servants with them, dashed to the aid of their ladies, counting death for their sakes a far happier fate than a long life without them. When they got to the house, they found the outside door broken in, and the two other men and their servants putting up a valiant fight. But they were already badly wounded, and outnumbered by the bandits. Most of their servants were dead. They were beginning to give way. Through the window the two younger men could see the ladies wailing and weeping. So inflamed were their hearts by pity and by love, they fell upon the outlaws in a paroxysm of fury, like two enraged bears coming down from the mountains, and killed so many that the rest fled for safety to their hideout. The villains having been thus defeated, and the host himself being among those killed, it remained only for the two young noblemen to send his wife, who they had learned was even worse than he, the same way. A single thrust of the sword did the job. They then went into a downstairs room, where they found one of the married gentlemen breathing his last. The other was not hurt, although his clothes were torn to shreds and his sword had been broken. The poor man thanked the pair for coming to his aid in the way they had, embraced them, and asked them not to leave him and those of his party who had survived. The two young men were only too glad to agree. And so, after burying the dead man, and consoling his wife as best they could, they took to the road again, not knowing which way they should go, but trusting in God's guidance.

If you would like to know the names of the three gentlemen and the two ladies with them, they were Hircan, his wife Parlamente, and Longarine, the young widow. The two young men were Dagoucin and Saffredent. They rode all day, and towards evening they glimpsed a church tower in the distance. Eventually, after a hard struggle along the tracks, they arrived at the abbey of Saint-Savin, where the monks received them humanely. The abbot, who was himself of a good family, provided them with accommodation worthy of their station and asked them about their adventures, as he showed them to their quarters. When he had heard what had happened to them, he was able to inform them that there were others in the same boat. There were, in fact, in another room, two young ladies who had escaped from dangers just as great or even greater, inasmuch as they had had to deal, not with men, but with wild beasts. Half a league this side of Pierrefitte they had met a bear coming down the mountain. They had taken flight and galloped so fast that their horses had dropped dead beneath them as they rode through the abbey gates. Two of their women had arrived some time after them, and reported that the bear had killed all their male servants. So the three newly arrived gentlemen and the two ladies went in to see them, and recognized them at once as their companions Nomerfide and Ennasuite. They were both in tears, but once they had all embraced, told one another

about their misfortunes, and heard a few [pious] exhortations from the good abbot, they began to take some consolation from their reunion. The next morning they heard mass with great devotion, praising God for delivering them from the perils of the mountains.

*   *   *

After they had heard mass and dined, they sent someone to find out if it was possible yet to cross the Gave de Pau. When they learned that the river was still impassable, they were extremely worried, in spite of the fact that the abbot repeatedly reassured them that they could have lodging in the abbey until the floods subsided. For that day they accepted this offer, and the same evening, as they were about to go to bed, an old monk turned up. He had come from Sarrance where he went every year for the Nativity of our Lady. On being asked about the journey, he told how, because of the floods, he had come over the mountains, and found the tracks more treacherous than he had ever seen them. On the way he had witnessed a very moving spectacle. He had come across a gentleman by the name of Simontaut, who, tired of waiting for the flood waters to go down, had decided to try to attempt a crossing. He had placed his trust in his excellent horse, and had grouped his servants round him to break the force of the current. But in the middle all the men on weaker mounts had been swept off down the stream. Neither men nor horses were ever seen again. The gentleman, finding himself completely alone, turned his horse back. But the animal could not make it, and collapsed under him. By God's will he was close enough to the edge to be able to drag himself on all fours out of the water and up the hard stony bank, though he had swallowed a good deal of water, and was so exhausted that he could hardly keep going. He lay amongst the rocks, soaked through and sick at heart at having seen his servants perish before his eyes. By a stroke of good fortune he was found in the evening by a shepherd bringing home the sheep. The mere sight of the gentleman, let alone the tale he had to tell, was enough to make the shepherd understand his plight. He had taken him by the hand and led him to his humble abode, where he had kindled a few sticks to dry him out as best he could. That same evening God had brought to the shepherd's house the old monk, who had told Simontaut the way to Sarrance, and assured him that he would find better accommodation there than anywhere else. He had also told him that he would meet there an old widow by the name of Oisille, who had suffered misfortunes similar to his own.

When they heard the old monk mention the name of the good Lady Oisille and the gentle knight Simontaut, they were overjoyed beyond description. They praised their Creator that He had been satisfied to take the servants and save their masters and mistresses. Parlamente in particular gave heartfelt thanks to God, for Simontaut had long served her as her devoted and loving servant. They pressed the monk to tell them the road to Sarrance, and although he made it sound very difficult, they were not deterred from setting out that very day. The abbot provided them with everything they needed—[the best horses in Lavedan, good Béarnese cloaks,] wine and victuals, as well as guides to conduct them safely over the mountains. Most of the journey had to be done on foot rather than on horseback, but eventually they arrived, exhausted and bathed in sweat, at the abbey of Our Lady at Sarrance. The abbot was not a particularly nice character, but he did not dare to refuse them board and lodging, for fear of offending the Seigneur de Béarn, who, as he knew perfectly well, was on friendly terms with them. Hypocrite that he was, he put on as pleasant an air as he was able, and took them to see the good Lady Oisille and the noble Simontaut. They were overjoyed to be reunited so miraculously, and they spent the whole night in the church without finding it a moment too long, praising and thanking God for the great mercy He had bestowed upon them. In the morning they took a little rest, then heard mass. They all received the holy sacrament of union, in which all Christians are united in one, beseeching Him, who in His goodness had brought them together, that their journey might be finished to His glory.

After they had dined they sent someone to inquire whether the water had gone down, only to learn that the river was more swollen than before, and that it would be a long time before they could cross with safety. So they decided to build a bridge, using two rocks which were fairly close to one another. To this day there are planks at this point for the use of foot-travellers coming from Oléron who do not want to use the ford. The abbot was rather pleased that they were offering to put themselves to this expense, because it meant that he might get an increased number of pilgrims. So he provided the necessary workmen, but he was so mean that he contributed not a penny to the actual cost. The workmen said that they could not do the job in under ten or twelve days. This was rather a boring prospect for all of them, men and women alike. However, Parlamente, the wife of Hircan, was not one to let herself become idle or melancholy, and having asked her husband for permission, she spoke to the old Lady Oisille.

"Madame," she said, "you have had much experience of life, and you now occupy the position of mother in regard to the rest of us women, and it surprises me that you do not consider some pastime to alleviate the boredom and distress that we shall have to bear during our long stay here. Unless we have some amusing and virtuous way of occupying ourselves, we run the risk of [falling] sick."

Longarine, the young widow, added, "What is worse, we'll all become miserable and disagreeable—and that's an incurable disease. There isn't a man or woman amongst us who hasn't every cause to sink into despair, if we consider all that we have lost."

Ennasuite laughed and rejoined, "Not everyone's lost a husband, like you, you know. And as for losing servants, no need to despair about that—there are plenty of men ready to do service! All the same, I do agree that we ought to have something to amuse us, so that we can pass the time as pleasantly as we can."

Her companion Nomerfide said that this was a very good idea, and that if she had to spend a single day without some entertainment, she would be sure to die the next.

All the men supported this, and asked the Lady Oisille if she would kindly organize what they should do.

"My children," replied Oisille, "when you ask me to show you a pastime that is capable of delivering you from your boredom and your sorrow, you are asking me to do something that I find very difficult. All my life I have searched for a remedy, and I have found only one—the reading of holy Scripture, in which one may find true and perfect spiritual joy, from which proceed health and bodily repose. And if you ask what the prescription is that keeps me happy and healthy in my old age, I will tell you. As soon as I rise in the morning I take the Scriptures and read them. I see and contemplate the goodness of God, who for our sakes has sent His son to earth to declare the holy word and the good news by which He grants remission of all our sins, and payment of all our debts, through His gift to us of His love, His passion and His merits. And my contemplations give me such joy, that I take my psalter, and with the utmost humility, sing the beautiful psalms and hymns that the Holy Spirit has composed in the heart of David and the other authors. The contentment this affords me fills me with such well-being that whatever the evils of the day, they are to me so many blessings, for in my heart I have by faith Him who has borne these evils for me. Likewise, before supper, I withdraw to nourish my soul with readings and meditations. In the evening I ponder in my mind everything I have done during the day, so that I may ask God forgiveness of my sins, and give thanks to Him for His mercies. And so I lay myself to rest in His love, fear and peace, assured against all evils. And this, my children, is the pastime that long ago I adopted. All other ways have I tried, but none has given me spiritual contentment. I believe that if, each morning, you give one hour to reading, and then, during mass, say your prayers devoutly, you will find even in this wilderness all the beauty a city could afford. For, a person who knows God will find all things beautiful in Him, and without Him all things will seem ugly. So I say to you, if you would live in happiness, heed my advice."

Then Hircan spoke: "Madame, anyone who has read the holy Scriptures—as indeed I think we all have here—will readily agree that what you have said is true. However, you must bear in mind that we have not yet become so mortified in the flesh that we are not in need of some sort of amusement and physical exercise in order to pass the time. After all, when we're at home, we've got our hunting and hawking to distract us from the thousand and one foolish thoughts that pass through one's mind. The ladies have their housework and their needlework. They have their dances, too, which provide a respectable way for them to get some exercise. All this leads me to suggest, on behalf of the men here, that you, Madame, since you are the oldest among us, should read to us every morning about the life of our Lord Jesus Christ, and the great and wonderful things He has done for us. Between dinner and vespers I think we should choose some pastime, which, while not being prejudicial to the soul, will be agreeable to the body. In that way we shall spend a very pleasant day."

*   *   *

They all concurred in this, and Parlamente, seeing that it had fallen to her to make the choice, addressed them all as follows.

"If I felt myself to be as capable as the ancients, by whom the arts were discovered, then I would invent some pastime myself that would meet the requirements you have laid down for me. However, I know what lies within the scope of my own knowledge and ability—I can hardly even remember the clever things other people have invented, let alone invent new things myself. So I shall be quite content to follow closely in the footsteps of other people who have already provided for your needs. For example, I don't think there's one of us who hasn't read the hundred tales by Boccaccio, which have recently been translated from Italian into French, and which are so highly thought of by the [most Christian] King Francis I, by Monseigneur the Dauphin, Madame the Dauphine and Madame Marguerite. If Boccaccio could have heard how highly these illustrious people praised him, it would have been enough to raise him from the grave. As a matter of fact, the two ladies I've mentioned, along with other people at the court, made up their minds to do the same as Boccaccio. There was to be one difference—that they should not write any story that was not truthful. Together with Monseigneur the Dauphin the ladies promised to produce ten stories each, and to get together a party of ten people who were qualified to contribute something, excluding those who studied and were men of letters. Monseigneur the Dauphin didn't want their art brought in, and he was afraid that rhetorical ornament would in part falsify the truth of the account. A number of things led to the project being completely forgotten—the major affairs of state that subsequently overtook the King, the peace treaty between him and the King of England, the confinement of Madame the Dauphine and several other events of sufficient importance to keep the court otherwise occupied. However, it can now be completed in the ten days of leisure we have before us, while we wait for our bridge to be finished. If you so wished, we could go each afternoon between midday and four o'clock to the lovely meadow that borders the Gave de Pau, where the leaves on the trees are so thick that the hot sun cannot penetrate the shade and the cool beneath. There we can sit and rest, and each of us will tell a story which he has either witnessed himself, or which he has heard from somebody worthy of belief. At the end of our ten days we will have completed the whole hundred. And if, God willing, the lords and ladies I've mentioned find our endeavours worthy of their attention, we shall make them a present of them when we get back, instead of the usual statuettes and beads. I'm sure they would find that preferable. In spite of all this, if any of you is able to think of something more agreeable, I shall gladly bow to his or her opinion."

But everyone of them replied that it would be impossible to think of anything better, and that they could hardly wait for the morrow. So the day came happily to a close with reminiscences of things they had all experienced in their time.

As soon as morning came they all went into Madame Oisille's room, where she was already at her prayers. When they had listened for a good hour to the lesson she had to read them, and then

devoutly heard mass, they went, at ten o'clock, to dine, after which they retired to their separate rooms to attend to what they had to do. At midday they all went back as arranged to the meadow, which was looking so beautiful and fair that it would take a Boccaccio to describe it as it really was. Enough for us to say that a more beautiful meadow there never was seen. When they were all seated on the grass, so green and soft that there was no need for carpets or cushions, Simontaut said: "Which of us shall be [the one in charge]?"

"Since you have spoken first," replied Hircan, "it should be you who give the orders. Where games are concerned everybody is equal."

*   *   *

"Ladies, I have been so ill rewarded for my long and devoted service, that, in order to avenge myself on Love and on the woman who is so cruel to me, I shall do my utmost to collect together all the accounts of foul deeds perpetrated by women on us poor men. And every single one will be the unadulterated truth."

REVIEW QUESTIONS

1. What sexual roles are revealed in the "Prologue"?
2. What attitudes toward women might these roles reflect?
3. What evidence of humanistic principles is revealed by the actions or speeches of the storytellers?
4. What evidence do the storytellers offer of sympathy with the notion of a reform of the church?
5. Why might Marguerite, whose interests were intellectual and spiritual, have chosen to emulate Boccaccio, whose writings seem so earthy and material?

LEO AFRICANUS

FROM "The Book of Granada"

The Renaissance had a dark underside as well as glorious works of art, confident reflections on human potential, and new avenues of textual scholarship. Princes, increasingly confident in their powers and prerogatives, strove to consolidate their authority within the boundaries of their territories and to expand those boundaries as opportunity permitted. In Spain, the Most Catholic King and Queen, Ferdinand and Isabel, undertook the expulsion of the Jews and the conquest of the Moors. In his widely acclaimed travelogue, Leo Africanus (Granada 1488?–1554) recorded aspects of the Reconquista *from an eyewitness perspective. Born Hasan bin Muhammed al-Wazzan, he and his family abandoned the Muslim kingdom in Spain sometime after its Christian conquest in 1492 and settled in Fez, Morocco. He led thereafter a colorful and controversial life. Following university studies, Africanus embarked on his travels as a Muslim diplomat, during which he was captured by European pirates and sold into slavery. Presented to Pope Leo X, under circumstances that are far from clear, he converted to Christianity. The Pope, who recognized his abilities as a diplomat, observer, and writer, set him the task of writing a compendium of knowledge about Africa. The book, entitled* Cosmographia dell' Africa, *is divided into four sections, each organized year by year to describe a key period of the author's life, and each named after the city that played the major role in his life at the time. The following selection is taken from the first section, "Granada." While the writing is based on true experiences in the life of its author, it is often difficult to distinguish fact from fiction. Nonetheless, it offers vivid descriptions of the Mediterranean world during the Renaissance and the often conflicted relationships between Renaissance civilization and its non-Christian neighbors.*

From *Leo Africanus*, edited by Amin Maalouf, translated by Peter Sluglett (New York: Norton, 1989), pp. 113–118.

The Year of the Inquisitors
904 A.H.
19 August 1498–7 August 1499

That year, Hasan the deliverer died under torture in one of the dungeons of the Alhambra; he was no less than eighty years old. There was none more skilled than he in obtaining the release of a captive, but when it came to his own liberation his words seem to have lost their weight. He was a devout and pious man, and if he sometimes made errors of judgement, his intentions were as pure as those of a child until his dying day. He died poor; may God now reveal to him the riches of Eden!

Thousands of others were tortured at the same time. For several months the most dreadful news had been reaching us from our former homeland, but few foresaw the calamity which was to engulf the last Muslims of Andalus.

It all began with the arrival at Granada of a party of inquisitors, religious fanatics who immediately issued a proclamation that all Christians who had converted to Islam should return to their original religion. Some of them reluctantly agreed, but the majority refused, pointing to the agreement concluded before the fall of the city, which expressly guaranteed the converts the right to remain Muslims. To no avail. As far as the inquisitors were concerned, this clause was null and void. Any man who had been baptized and who refused to return to Christianity was considered as a traitor and thus liable to be condemned to death. Several pyres were erected to intimidate the recalcitrant, as had been done for the Jews. Several citizens recanted. A lesser number told themselves that it was better to take flight, even at this late stage, before the trap closed on them again. They were able to take with them only the clothes on their backs.

The inquisitors then decreed that anyone having a Christian ancestor must be compulsorily baptized. One of the first to be affected by this was Hamid, whose grandfather was a Christian captive who had chosen to declare himself for the Witness of Islam. One evening some Castilian soldiers, accompanied by one of the inquisitors, came to his house in our quarter, al-Baisin. Warned in advance, the old man's neighbours went down into the street to try to prevent his arrest. In vain. The next day, a number of people, including two women, were arrested in other parts of the city. Each time, crowds gathered and the soldiers were obliged to draw their swords to force their way through. Most of the incidents took place in al-Baisin. A newly-built church not far from the house where we used to live was set on fire; in return, two mosques were pillaged. Everyone's faith was like a raw nerve.

One day, the news came that Hamid had succumbed in his dungeon as a result of the tortures inflicted upon him by the inquisitors. He had resisted conversion to the end, insisting upon the agreement signed by the Christian kings.

When the news of his death became known, appeals to resist resounded in the streets. Alone of all the notables of al-Baisin, Hamid had stayed where he was, not to make accommodation with the enemy, but to continue the mission to which he had devoted his life, to free the captured Muslims. The noble nature of his activities, the fact of his great age, and the suppressed hatreds coming to the surface combined to provoke an immediate reaction on the part of the Muslims. Barricades were put up; soldiers, civil servants and clergy were massacred. It was an insurrection.

Of course, the citizenry was in no condition to take on the army of occupation. With a few crossbows, swords, lances and clubs they managed to prevent the Castilian troops from getting into al-Baisin, and tried to organize themselves into a small army to wage the holy war. But after two days of fighting they were wiped out, and then the massacre began. The authorities proclaimed that the entire Muslim population would be executed for rebellion against the sovereigns, adding insidiously that only those who would accept conversion to Christianity would be spared. Thus the population of Granada became baptized by whole streets. In some villages in the Alpujarra mountains the peasants struck back; they managed to hold out for several weeks and even, it was said, killed the seigneur of Granada who led the expedition against them. But even there it was impossible to resist for long. The villagers were forced to seek terms; several hundred families were allowed to leave, and set themselves up in Fez; some took refuge in the mountains, swearing that no one would ever find them; all the others were baptized. The words 'Allahu akbar' could no more be pronounced upon the soil of Andalus, where for eight centuries the voice of the muezzin had called the faithful to prayer. A man could not now say the *Fatiha* over his father's corpse. At least, that is, in public, for the Muslims who had been forcibly converted refused to repudiate their religion.

They sent heart-rending despatches to Fez. *Brothers*, ran one of their letters, *if, at the time of the fall of Granada, we failed in our duty to leave, this was simply because of our lack of resources, because we are the poorest and weakest in the land of Andalus. Today, we have been obliged to accept baptism in order to save the lives of our women and children, but we are afraid of incurring the wrath of the Most High on the Day of Judgement, and of suffering the tortures of Gehenna. Thus we beseech you, our exiled brothers, to assist us with your counsel. Enquire on our behalf of the doctors of the Law what we should do, our anguish has no end.*

Deeply moved, the Granadan exiles in Fez held a number of meetings that year, some of them in Khali's house. These were attended by both notables and common people, but particularly by *'ulama'* learned in the Law. Some came from far away to deliver the fruits of their research and their consideration.

I remember having seen the mufti of Oran arrive one day, a man of about forty, with a turban only a little less impressive than that of Astaghfirullah, but worn with a good-natured air. More deferential than usual, my uncle came out to the end of the street to welcome him, and in the course of the meeting those present simply put questions to him without daring to argue with him or to challenge his answers. Of course the problem as it presented itself required great mastery both of the Law and of the Traditions of the Prophet, as well as great daring in interpretation; it was impossible to accept that hundreds of thousands of Muslims should forsake the faith of the Prophet, yet it was monstrous to expect an entire people to go to the stake.

I still remember the first words of the man from Oran, delivered in a warm and serene voice:

'Brothers, we are here, may God be praised, in the land of Islam, and we bear our faith with pride, like a diadem. Let us be wary of condemning those who have to bear their religion like a burning ember in their hands.'

He continued:

'When you send messages to them, may your words be prudent and measured; remember your letter may light their pyre. Do not seek to blame them for their baptism; ask them simply to remain, in spite of everything, faithful to Islam, and to teach its principles to their sons. But not before puberty, not before they are old enough to keep a secret, for a child may, with an incautious word, reap their destruction.'

And what if these unhappy ones should be forced to drink wine? And what if they are invited to eat the flesh of swine, to prove they are no longer Muslims?

'Then they must do it, if they are forced to do so,' said the mufti, 'but they must protest in their hearts.'

And what if they are made to insult the Prophet, may God surround him with His prayers and His salvation?

'Then they must do it, if they are forced to do so,' repeated the mufti, 'but they must say the opposite in their hearts.'

To those who, through having not left their land, had to endure the cruellest tortures, the mufti gave the name of *Ghuraba*, Strangers, recalling the words of the Messenger of God: 'Islam began as a religion for outsiders and it will become once again a religion for outsiders just as it began. Blessed are the outsiders.'

*   *   *

To launch an appeal to Muslims of the world to save these unfortunates, the Granadan community of Fez decided to send emissaries to the great sovereigns of Islam, the Grand Turk, the new Sophy of Persia, the Sultan of Egypt and several others of lesser importance. Because of the functions which he used to exercise at the court of Alhambra, Khali was chosen to compose these letters, using the customary formulae; he was also charged with carrying the most important of these messages, the one addressed to the lord of Constantinople the Great. After he had been sounded out about this mission, my uncle paid visits to the Sultan of Fez and to Boabdil, and obtained letters of recommendation and credit from them both.

Each time that I recall that journey, I feel the pain of anguish, even today, although I have since then come to know the strangest lands and the most inaccessible places. I had always dreamed of Constantinople, and on hearing that Khali was to go there, I could scarcely contain myself. I turned it round and round in my head, asking whether I could possibly hope, at the age of ten, to take part in such a journey. Rather diffidently, I confided in my uncle. Great was my surprise when he replied, his arms wide in welcome:

'Where could I find a better travelling companion?'

In spite of his ironical tone, he was clearly captivated by the idea. It only remained to convince my father.

That year again, Muhammad was often away from the city, still looking for a plot of land to rent where he could live peacefully away from noise, gossip and reproachful eyes. For two long weeks I waited for him every day, asking Warda and Mariam incessantly for news of him, although they knew nothing. Like me, they were waiting.

When he finally returned, I threw myself upon him and began to talk so fast that he had to make me start again several times. Alas, he refused immediately in a manner which brooked no further questioning. I should perhaps have waited for Khali to broach the subject of the journey in his own way, as he would have known how to extol the advantages of such a journey with eloquence. Perhaps Muhammad would have agreed so as not to annoy my uncle, with whom he had just become reconciled. But to me he could say 'No' straight out. As a pretext he pointed out the dangers of the journey, told me of people who had never returned, mentioned my studies, which I would have had to interrupt if I went away. However, I think the real reason was that he felt that I was too close to my uncle, and to my mother's family in general, and that he feared that he would lose me. Unable to argue with him, I begged him to talk it over with Khali, but he refused even to meet him.

For a whole week, I woke up each morning with my eyes bloodshot and my pillow damp. In an effort to console me my uncle swore that I would accompany him on his next journey; he would keep his word.

The day of his departure came. Khali was going to join a caravan of merchants which was leaving for Oran, where he would take ship. From first light the Granadans came in great number to wish him luck on his mission and to contribute several gold pieces for his expenses. For my part I was moping in my corner until an old man with impish eyes came and sat down next to me. It was none other than Hamza, the barber who had circumcised me. He asked for news of my father, and lamented the death of the deliverer whom he had seen for the last time in our house in al-Baisin. Then he asked after my studies, about the *sura* which I was studying at the time, and even began

to recite it. It was pleasant to be in his company, and I chatted to him for an hour. He told me that he had lost the bulk of his fortune by going into exile, but that by the grace of God he was still able to look after the needs of his womenfolk. He had begun to work again, but only as a barber, because his razor was no longer sure enough for circumcisions. He had just rented a part of the local hammam in order to ply his trade.

Suddenly, an idea lit up his eyes.

'Wouldn't you like to give me a hand when you aren't in school?'

I accepted without demur.

'I'll pay you one dirham a week.'

I hastened to say that I had a friend and that I would very much like him to come with me. Hamza had nothing against it. He would receive the same pay, there were lots of thing to do in the hammam.

When, some minutes later, Khali came to give me the traveller's kiss, he was surprised to see my eyes dry and smiling. I told him that I was going to work, that I would earn one dirham a week. He wished me success in my labours; I wished him success in his.

REVIEW QUESTIONS

1. For whom is Leo Africanus writing?
2. How does his description of Castilian policy and Granadan response square with reflections on the dignity of man, such as those of Pico della Mirandola?
3. Considering that Leo writes after his conversion to Christianity, would you call his account a chronicle of or an apology for the events in Granada?
4. How would you characterize the Muslim diplomatic response to the persecution in Granada, and what does it tell you about the political realities of the Renaissance?
5. What parallels can you detect between the young Leo and the young Cellini in terms of independence and confidence? Does this lend any credence to the notion of a "Renaissance individual"?

13 ❧ REFORMATIONS OF RELIGION

The year 1492 marks both the end of the expansion of Christianity in Europe, with the final expulsion of the Jews and Muslims from the Iberian Peninsula, and the beginning of the expansion of European Christianity across the globe. So, too, it marks the nadir of papal ambition, venality, and corruption, and thereby the medieval Christian hierarchy. In that year, the Borgia pope, Alexander VI, whom contemporaries such as Machiavelli knew to be rapacious, murderous, treacherous, and ambitious, was elected.

Within a generation of the Reconquista of Spain, the German lands of the grandson of Ferdinando and Isabella of Spain would be split between two very different understandings of Christianity: what it meant to be a Christian, what the Church was and how it was to be constituted, and what the nature of worship was. In part, the Reformation arose in response to perceptions of papal bellicosity and immorality; it belonged to an older tradition of reformatio. Equally, however, the Reformation was heir to the Renaissance: the philological skills and discoveries of fifteenth-century humanists enabled new approaches to the study of the Bible, and the humanist emphasis on historical accuracy led to a call for a return to apostolic Christianity. That return to the text of Scripture, along with a new sensitivity to historical periods, brought theologians such as Martin Luther to reconsider not only devotional practices but the very structure of authority of medieval Christendom—the papal hierarchy—and others, such as John Calvin, to return to the Acts of the Apostles for a vision of the true church.

Even as Christendom divided against itself in Europe, it expanded through the persons of conquistadores to create worlds unimagined in the European tradition. Reformation and expansion both came through bloodshed. In Germany, peasants and artisans fought lords and emperor to institute the godly law they *found in the Bible, only to be massacred. In France, the Low Countries, and England, as well as the Holy Roman Empire, Christians executed Christians over questions of the Eucharist, the place of images in worship, and the cult of the saints. Churches divided from one another, each defining itself against the others, even as all confronted worlds for which neither the Bible nor the classical tradition had prepared them.*

MARTIN LUTHER

95 Theses

Martin Luther (1483–1546), one of the founders of Protestantism, was born of peasant stock. His father had left his fields for the copper mines of Mansfeld in Saxon, where he flourished economically and rose to the status of town councilor. His son, Martin, received a primary education from the Brethren of the Common Life and enrolled at the University of Erfurt in 1501, where he earned his bachelor of arts in 1502 and his master of arts in 1505. His father hoped that his son would continue the family's rise to prominence by pursuing a legal career. These aspirations were shattered when Luther unexpectedly entered a monastery in 1505. As a member of the order of Augustinian Hermits, he began formal training in theology. Selected for advanced training in theology, he made his way to the University of Wittenberg, where he received his doctorate in 1512 and occupied the chair of biblical theology. Even as his academic career prospered, his inner life suffered. Luther was beset by doubts about his own salvation, the result of a consciousness both of his own weakness and of divine righteousness. Long study and meditation led him to a resolution that became the basis for his theology of justification. Salvation was the result of divine grace, freely given; the forgiven conscience could be at peace; the soul could serve God joyfully. Given this new conviction, it is not surprising that the extravagant claims surrounding the sale of indulgences in 1517 provoked Luther to public protest. The form and text of that protest became known as the "95 Theses." His objection to the claim that the pope could remit the temporal punishment of sins led him deeper and deeper into controversy and ultimately to schism. By 1520, the rift between Luther and the Catholic Church had become irreparable and extended to far more issues than papal power. His Large Catechism, from which the Preface follows, reveals another dimension of Luther's reform: his engagement in the care of souls. Through catechism, a process of recitation and repetition, young people were to be brought to a proper understanding of God's Will and Word. It reveals Luther's familiarity with the Christian Church's past and his hope for its future.

From *Works of Martin Luther*, vol. 1, translated and edited by Adolph Spaeth, L. D. Reed, Henry Eyster Jacobs, et al. (Philadelphia: A. J. Holman, 1915) pp. 29–38.

Out of love for the truth and the desire to bring it to light, the following propositions will be discussed at Wittenberg, under the presidency of the Reverend Father Martin Luther, Master of Arts and of Sacred Theology, and Lecturer in Ordinary on the same at that place. Wherefore he requests that those who are unable to be present and debate orally with us, may do so by letter.

In the Name of our Lord Jesus Christ. Amen.

1. Our Lord and Master Jesus Christ, when He said Poenitentiam agite ["Repent!" TMS], willed that the whole life of believers should be repentance.

2. This word cannot be understood to mean sacramental penance, i.e., confession and satisfaction, which is administered by the priests.

3. Yet it means not inward repentance only; nay, there is no inward repentance which does not outwardly work divers mortifications of the flesh.

4. The penalty [of sin], therefore, continues so long as hatred of self continues; for this is the true inward repentance, and continues until our entrance into the kingdom of heaven.

5. The pope does not intend to remit, and cannot remit any penalties other than those which he has imposed either by his own authority or by that of the Canons.

6. The pope cannot remit any guilt, except by declaring that it has been remitted by God and by assenting to God's remission; though, to be sure, he may grant remission in cases reserved to his judgment. If his right to grant remission in such cases were despised, the guilt would remain entirely unforgiven.

7. God remits guilt to no one whom He does not, at the same time, humble in all things and bring into subjection to His vicar, the priest.

8. The penitential canons are imposed only on the living, and, according to them, nothing should be imposed on the dying.

9. Therefore the Holy Spirit in the pope is kind to us, because in his decrees he always makes exception of the article of death and of necessity.

10. Ignorant and wicked are the doings of those priests who, in the case of the dying, reserve canonical penances for purgatory.

11. This changing of the canonical penalty to the penalty of purgatory is quite evidently one of the tares that were sown while the bishops slept.

12. In former times the canonical penalties were imposed not after, but before absolution, as tests of true contrition.

13. The dying are freed by death from all penalties; they are already dead to canonical rules, and have a right to be released from them.

14. The imperfect health [of soul], that is to say, the imperfect love, of the dying brings with it, of necessity, great fear; and the smaller the love, the greater is the fear.

15. This fear and horror is sufficient of itself alone (to say nothing of other things) to constitute the penalty of purgatory, since it is very near to the horror of despair.

16. Hell, purgatory, and heaven seem to differ as do despair, almost-despair, and the assurance of safety.

17. With souls in purgatory it seems necessary that horror should grow less and love increase.

18. It seems unproved, either by reason or Scripture, that they are outside the state of merit, that is to say, of increasing love.

19. Again, it seems unproved that they, or at least that all of them, are certain or assured of their own blessedness, though we may be quite certain of it.

20. Therefore by "full remission of all penalties" the pope means not actually "of all," but only of those imposed by himself.

21. Therefore those preachers of indulgences are in error, who say that by the pope's indulgences a man is freed from every penalty, and saved;

22. Whereas he remits to souls in purgatory no penalty which, according to the canons, they would have had to pay in this life.

23. If it is at all possible to grant to any one the remission of all penalties whatsoever, it is certain that this remission can be granted only to the most perfect, that is, to the very fewest.

24. It must needs be, therefore, that the greater part of the people are deceived by that indiscriminate and highsounding promise of release from penalty.

25. The power which the pope has, in a general way, over purgatory, is just like the power which any bishop or curate has, in a special way, within his own diocese or parish.

26. The pope does well when he grants remission to souls [in purgatory], not by the power of the keys (which he does not possess), but by way of intercession.

27. They preach man who say that so soon as the penny jingles into the money-box, the soul flies out [of purgatory].

28. It is certain that when the penny jingles into the money-box, gain and avarice can be increased, but the result of the intercession of the Church is in the power of God alone.

29. Who knows whether all the souls in purgatory wish to be bought out of it, as in the legend of Sts. Severinus and Paschal.

30. No one is sure that his own contrition is sincere; much less that he has attained full remission.

31. Rare as is the man that is truly penitent, so rare is also the man who truly buys indulgences, i.e., such men are most rare.

32. They will be condemned eternally, together with their teachers, who believe themselves sure of their salvation because they have letters of pardon.

33. Men must be on their guard against those who say that the pope's pardons are that inestimable gift of God by which man is reconciled to Him;

34. For these "graces of pardon" concern only the penalties of sacramental satisfaction, and these are appointed by man.

35. They preach no Christian doctrine who teach that contrition is not necessary in those who intend to buy souls out of purgatory or to buy confessionalia.

36. Every truly repentant Christian has a right to full remission of penalty and guilt, even without letters of pardon.

37. Every true Christian, whether living or dead, has part in all the blessings of Christ and the Church; and this is granted him by God, even without letters of pardon.

38. Nevertheless, the remission and participation [in the blessings of the Church] which are granted by the pope are in no way to be despised, for they are, as I have said, the declaration of divine remission.

39. It is most difficult, even for the very keenest theologians, at one and the same time to commend to the people the abundance of pardons and [the need of] true contrition.

40. True contrition seeks and loves penalties, but liberal pardons only relax penalties and cause them to be hated, or at least, furnish an occasion [for hating them].

41. Apostolic pardons are to be preached with caution, lest the people may falsely think them preferable to other good works of love.

42. Christians are to be taught that the pope does not intend the buying of pardons to be compared in any way to works of mercy.

43. Christians are to be taught that he who gives to the poor or lends to the needy does a better work than buying pardons;

44. Because love grows by works of love, and man becomes better; but by pardons man does not grow better, only more free from penalty.

45. Christians are to be taught that he who sees a man in need, and passes him by, and gives [his money] for pardons, purchases not the indulgences of the pope, but the indignation of God.

46. Christians are to be taught that unless they have more than they need, they are bound to keep back what is necessary for their own families, and by no means to squander it on pardons.

47. Christians are to be taught that the buying of pardons is a matter of free will, and not of commandment.

48. Christians are to be taught that the pope, in granting pardons, needs, and therefore desires, their devout prayer for him more than the money they bring.

49. Christians are to be taught that the pope's pardons are useful, if they do not put their trust in them; but altogether harmful, if through them they lose their fear of God.

50. Christians are to be taught that if the pope knew the exactions of the pardon-preachers, he

would rather that St. Peter's church should go to ashes, than that it should be built up with the skin, flesh and bones of his sheep.

51. Christians are to be taught that it would be the pope's wish, as it is his duty, to give of his own money to very many of those from whom certain hawkers of pardons cajole money, even though the church of St. Peter might have to be sold.

52. The assurance of salvation by letters of pardon is vain, even though the commissary, nay, even though the pope himself, were to stake his soul upon it.

53. They are enemies of Christ and of the pope, who bid the Word of God be altogether silent in some Churches, in order that pardons may be preached in others.

54. Injury is done the Word of God when, in the same sermon, an equal or a longer time is spent on pardons than on this Word.

55. It must be the intention of the pope that if pardons, which are a very small thing, are celebrated with one bell, with single processions and ceremonies, then the Gospel, which is the very greatest thing, should be preached with a hundred bells, a hundred processions, a hundred ceremonies.

56. The "treasures of the Church," out of which the pope grants indulgences, are not sufficiently named or known among the people of Christ.

57. That they are not temporal treasures is certainly evident, for many of the vendors do not pour out such treasures so easily, but only gather them.

58. Nor are they the merits of Christ and the Saints, for even without the pope, these always work grace for the inner man, and the cross, death, and hell for the outward man.

59. St. Lawrence said that the treasures of the Church were the Church's poor, but he spoke according to the usage of the word in his own time.

60. Without rashness we say that the keys of the Church, given by Christ's merit, are that treasure;

61. For it is clear that for the remission of penalties and of reserved cases, the power of the pope is of itself sufficient.

62. The true treasure of the Church is the Most Holy Gospel of the glory and the grace of God.

63. But this treasure is naturally most odious, for it makes the first to be last.

64. On the other hand, the treasure of indulgences is naturally most acceptable, for it makes the last to be first.

65. Therefore the treasures of the Gospel are nets with which they formerly were wont to fish for men of riches.

66. The treasures of the indulgences are nets with which they now fish for the riches of men.

67. The indulgences which the preachers cry as the "greatest graces" are known to be truly such, in so far as they promote gain.

68. Yet they are in truth the very smallest graces compared with the grace of God and the piety of the Cross.

69. Bishops and curates are bound to admit the commissaries of apostolic pardons, with all reverence.

70. But still more are they bound to strain all their eyes and attend with all their ears, lest these men preach their own dreams instead of the commission of the pope.

71. He who speaks against the truth of apostolic pardons, let him be anathema and accursed!

72. But he who guards against the lust and license of the pardon-preachers, let him be blessed!

73. The pope justly thunders against those who, by any art, contrive the injury of the traffic in pardons.

74. But much more does he intend to thunder against those who use the pretext of pardons to contrive the injury of holy love and truth.

75. To think the papal pardons so great that they could absolve a man even if he had committed an impossible sin and violated the Mother of God—this is madness.

76. We say, on the contrary, that the papal pardons are not able to remove the very least of venial sins, so far as its guilt is concerned.

77. It is said that even St. Peter, if he were now Pope, could not bestow greater graces; this is blasphemy against St. Peter and against the pope.

78. We say, on the contrary, that even the present pope, and any pope at all, has greater graces at his disposal; to wit, the Gospel, powers,

gifts of healing, etc., as it is written in I. Corinthians xii.

79. To say that the cross, emblazoned with the papal arms, which is set up [by the preachers of indulgences], is of equal worth with the Cross of Christ, is blasphemy.

80. The bishops, curates and theologians who allow such talk to be spread among the people, will have an account to render.

81. This unbridled preaching of pardons makes it no easy matter, even for learned men, to rescue the reverence due to the pope from slander, or even from the shrewd questionings of the laity.

82. To wit:—"Why does not the pope empty purgatory, for the sake of holy love and of the dire need of the souls that are there, if he redeems an infinite number of souls for the sake of miserable money with which to build a Church? The former reasons would be most just; the latter is most trivial."

83. Again:—"Why are mortuary and anniversary masses for the dead continued, and why does he not return or permit the withdrawal of the endowments founded on their behalf, since it is wrong to pray for the redeemed?"

84. Again:—"What is this new piety of God and the pope, that for money they allow a man who is impious and their enemy to buy out of purgatory the pious soul of a friend of God, and do not rather, because of that pious and beloved soul's own need, free it for pure love's sake?"

85. Again:—"Why are the penitential canons long since in actual fact and through disuse abrogated and dead, now satisfied by the granting of indulgences, as though they were still alive and in force?"

86. Again:—"Why does not the pope, whose wealth is to-day greater than the riches of the richest, build just this one church of St. Peter with his own money, rather than with the money of poor believers?"

87. Again:—"What is it that the pope remits, and what participation does he grant to those who, by perfect contrition, have a right to full remission and participation?"

88. Again:—"What greater blessing could come to the Church than if the pope were to do a hundred times a day what he now does once, and bestow on every believer these remissions and participations?"

89. "Since the pope, by his pardons, seeks the salvation of souls rather than money, why does he suspend the indulgences and pardons granted heretofore, since these have equal efficacy?"

90. To repress these arguments and scruples of the laity by force alone, and not to resolve them by giving reasons, is to expose the Church and the pope to the ridicule of their enemies, and to make Christians unhappy.

91. If, therefore, pardons were preached according to the spirit and mind of the pope, all these doubts would be readily resolved; nay, they would not exist.

92. Away, then, with all those prophets who say to the people of Christ, "Peace, peace," and there is no peace!

93. Blessed be all those prophets who say to the people of Christ, "Cross, cross," and there is no cross!

94. Christians are to be exhorted that they be diligent in following Christ, their Head, through penalties, deaths, and hell;

95. And thus be confident of entering into heaven rather through many tribulations, than through the assurance of peace.

REVIEW QUESTIONS

1. Why does Luther challenge papal authority in the form of a series of theses?
2. What does this tell us about the nature of his challenge?
3. What other problems beset the Church, according to Luther?
4. Where does Luther locate true authority?
5. Given the nature of that true authority, what means best serve to correct the Church's problems?

MARTIN LUTHER

FROM The Large Catechism, 1530

From *The Large Catechism of Martin Luther*, translated by Robert H. Fischer (Philadelphia: Augsburg Fortress Press, 1959).

Martin Luther's Preface[1]

It is not for trivial reasons that we constantly treat the Catechism and strongly urge others to do the same. For we see to our sorrow that many pastors and preachers[2] are very negligent in this respect and despise both their office and this teaching itself. Some because of their great and lofty learning, others because of sheer laziness and gluttony, behave in this matter as if they were pastors or preachers for their bellies' sake and had nothing to do but live off the fat of the land all their days, as they used to do under the papacy.

Everything that they are to teach and preach is now available to them in clear and simple form in the many excellent books which are in reality what the old manuals claimed in their titles to be: "Sermons That Preach Themselves," "Sleep Soundly," "Prepared!" and "Treasury."[3] However, they are not so upright and honest as to buy these books, or if they have them, to examine and read them. Such shameful gluttons and servants of their bellies would make better swineherds or dogkeepers than spiritual guides and pastors.

Now that they are free from the useless, bothersome babbling of the Seven Hours,[4] it would be fine if every morning, noon, and evening they would read, instead, at least a page or two from the Catechism, the Prayer Book,[5] the New Testament, or something else from the Bible and would pray the Lord's Prayer for themselves and their parishioners. In this way they might show honor and gratitude to the Gospel, through which they have been delivered from so many burdens and troubles, and they might feel a little shame because, like pigs and dogs, they remember no more of the Gospel than this rotten, pernicious, shameful, carnal liberty. As it is, the common people take the Gospel altogether too lightly, and even our utmost exertions accomplish but little. What, then, can we expect if we are sluggish and lazy, as we used to be under the papacy?

Besides, a shameful and insidious plague of security and boredom has overtaken us. Many regard the Catechism as a simple, silly teaching which they can absorb and master at one reading. After reading it once they toss the book into a corner as if they are ashamed to read it again. Indeed, even among the nobility there are some louts and skinflints who declare that we can do without pastors and preachers from now on because we have everything in books and can learn it all by ourselves. So they blithely let parishes fall into decay, and brazenly allow both pastors and preachers to suffer distress and hunger. This is what one can expect of crazy Germans. We Germans have such disgraceful people among us and must put up with them.

As for myself, let me say that I, too, am a doctor and a preacher—yes, and as learned and experienced as any of those who act so high and

---

[1] In the German edition of the Book of Concord, 1580, this Longer Preface (which dates from 1530) appeared after the Shorter Preface in accordance with the order observed in the fourth German volume of the Jena edition of Luther's Works (1556).

[2] Preachers (*Prediger*) were limited to preaching; pastors (*Pfarrherren*) exercised the full ministerial office.

[3] Titles of medieval sermon books.

[4] The seven canonical hours, daily prayers prescribed by the medieval Breviary.

[5] Luther published the "Little Prayer Book" (*Betbüchlein*) in 1522 to replace Roman Catholic devotional books.

mighty. Yet I do as a child who is being taught the Catechism. Every morning, and whenever else I have time, I read and recite word for word the Lord's Prayer, the Ten Commandments, the Creed, the Psalms, etc. I must still read and study the Catechism daily, yet I cannot master it as I wish, but must remain a child and pupil of the Catechism, and I do it gladly. These dainty, fastidious fellows would like quickly, with one reading, to become doctors above all doctors, to know all there is to be known. Well, this, too, is a sure sign that they despise both their office and the people's souls, yes, even God and his Word. They need not fear a fall, for they have already fallen all too horribly. What they need is to become children and begin learning their ABC's, which they think they have outgrown long ago.

Therefore, I beg these lazy-bellies and presumptuous saints, for God's sake, to get it into their heads that they are not really and truly such learned and great doctors as they think. I implore them not to imagine that they have learned these parts of the Catechism perfectly, or at least sufficiently, even though they think they know them ever so well. Even if their knowledge of the Catechism were perfect (though that is impossible in this life), yet it is highly profitable and fruitful daily to read it and make it the subject of meditation and conversation. In such reading, conversation, and meditation the Holy Spirit is present and bestows ever new and greater light and fervor, so that day by day we relish and appreciate the Catechism more greatly. This is according to Christ's promise in Matt. 18:20, "Where two or three are gathered in my name, there am I in the midst of them."

Nothing is so effectual against the devil, the world, the flesh, and all evil thoughts as to occupy oneself with the Word of God, talk about it, and meditate on it. Psalm 1 calls those blessed who "meditate on God's law day and night."[6] You will never offer up any incense or other savor more potent against the devil than to occupy yourself with God's commandments and words and to speak,

sing, and meditate on them. This, indeed, is the true holy water, the sign which routs the devil and puts him to flight.[7]

For this reason alone you should eagerly read, recite, ponder, and practice the Catechism, even if the only blessing and benefit you obtain from it is to rout the devil and evil thoughts. For he cannot bear to hear God's Word. God's Word is not like some empty tale, such as the one about Dietrich of Bern,[8] but as St. Paul says in Rom. 1:16, it is "the power of God," indeed, the power of God which burns the devil and gives us immeasurable strength, comfort, and help.

Why should I waste words? Time and paper would fail me if I were to recount all the blessings that flow from God's Word. The devil is called the master of a thousand arts. What, then, shall we call God's Word, which routs and destroys this master of a thousand arts with all his wiles and might? It must, indeed, be master of more than a hundred thousand arts. Shall we frivolously despise this might, blessing, power, and fruit—especially we who would be pastors and preachers? If so, we deserve not only to be refused food but also to be chased out by dogs and pelted with dung. Not only do we need God's Word daily as we need our daily bread; we also must use it daily against the daily, incessant attacks and ambushes of the devil with his thousand arts.

If this were not enough to admonish us to read the Catechism daily, there is God's command. That alone should be incentive enough. Deut. 6:7, 8 solemnly enjoins that we should always meditate upon his precepts whether sitting, walking, standing, lying down, or rising, and keep them before our eyes and in our hands as a constant token and sign. Certainly God did not require and command this so solemnly without good reason. He knows our danger and need. He knows the constant and furious attacks and assaults of the devil. So he wishes to warn,

---

[6] Ps. 1:2.

[7] I.e., the Word of God really does what holy water was formerly believed to accomplish.

[8] Luther frequently cited the legend of Dietrich of Bern as an example of lies and fables.

equip, and protect us against them with good "armor" against their "flaming darts,"[9] and with a good antidote against their evil infection and poison. O what mad, senseless fools we are! We must ever live and dwell in the midst of such mighty enemies as the devils, and yet we despise our weapons and armor, too lazy to give them a thought!

Look at these bored, presumptuous saints who will not or cannot read and study the Catechism daily. They evidently consider themselves much wiser than God himself, and wiser than all his holy angels, prophets, apostles, and all Christians! God himself is not ashamed to teach it daily, for he knows of nothing better to teach, and he always keeps on teaching this one thing without varying it with anything new or different. All the saints know of nothing better or different to learn, though they cannot learn it to perfection. Are we not most marvelous fellows, therefore, if we imagine, after reading or hearing it once, that we know it all and need not read or study it any more? Most marvelous fellows, to think we can finish learning in one hour what God himself cannot finish teaching! Actually, he is busy teaching it from the beginning of the world to the end, and all prophets and saints have been busy learning it and have always remained pupils, and must continue to do so.

This much is certain: anyone who knows the Ten Commandments perfectly knows the entire Scriptures. In all affairs and circumstances he can counsel, help, comfort, judge, and make decisions in both spiritual and temporal matters. He is qualified to sit in judgment upon all doctrines, estates, persons, laws, and everything else in the world.

What is the whole Psalter but meditations and exercises based on the First Commandment? Now, I know beyond a doubt that such lazy-bellies and presumptuous fellows do not understand a single Psalm, much less the entire Scriptures, yet they pretend to know and despise the Catechism, which is a brief compend and summary of all the Holy Scriptures.

Therefore, I once again implore all Christians, especially pastors and preachers, not to try to be doctors prematurely and to imagine that they know everything. Vain imaginations, like new cloth, suffer shrinkage! Let all Christians exercise themselves in the Catechism daily, and constantly put it into practice, guarding themselves with the greatest care and diligence against the poisonous infection of such security or vanity. Let them continue to read and teach, to learn and meditate and ponder. Let them never stop until they have proved by experience that they have taught the devil to death and have become wiser than God himself and all his saints.

If they show such diligence, then I promise them—and their experience will bear me out—that they will gain much fruit and God will make excellent men of them. Then in due time they themselves will make the noble confession that the longer they work with the Catechism, the less they know of it and the more they have to learn. Only then, hungry and thirsty, will they truly relish what now they cannot bear to smell because they are so bloated and surfeited. To this end may God grant his grace! Amen.

Preface[1]

This sermon has been undertaken for the instruction of children and uneducated people. Hence from ancient times it has been called, in Greek, a "catechism"—that is, instruction for children. Its contents represent the minimum of knowledge required of a Christian. Whoever does not possess it should not be reckoned among Christians nor admitted to a sacrament,[2] just as a craftsman who does not know the rules and practices of his craft is rejected and considered incompetent. For this reason young people should be thoroughly instructed in the various parts of the Catechism or children's sermons and diligently drilled in their practice.

---

[9] Eph. 6:11, 16.

[1] The Shorter Preface is based on a sermon of May 18, 1528 (*WA*, 301:2).

[2] This was not only a proposal of Luther, but also a medieval prescription; cf. John Surgant, *Manuale Curatorum* (1502), etc.

Therefore, it is the duty of every head of a household to examine his children and servants at least once a week and ascertain what they have learned of it, and if they do not know it, to keep them faithfully at it. I well remember the time when there were old people who were so ignorant that they knew nothing of these things—indeed, even now we find them daily—yet they come to Baptism and the Sacrament of the Altar and exercise all the rights of Christians, although those who come to the sacrament ought to know more and have a fuller understanding of all Christian doctrine than children and beginners at school. As for the common people, however, we should be satisfied if they learned the three parts[3] which have been the heritage of Christendom from ancient times, though they were rarely taught and treated correctly, so that all who wish to be Christians in fact as well as in name, both young and old, may be well-trained in them and familiar with them.

I. THE TEN COMMANDMENTS OF GOD

1. You shall have no other gods before me.
2. You shall not take the name of God in vain.
3. You shall keep the Sabbath day holy.
4. You shall honor father and mother.
5. You shall not kill.
6. You shall not commit adultery.
7. You shall not steal.
8. You shall not bear false witness against your neighbor.
9. You shall not covet your neighbor's house.
10. You shall not covet his wife, man-servant, maid-servant, cattle, or anything that is his.[4]

II. THE CHIEF ARTICLES OF OUR FAITH

I believe in God, the Father almighty, maker of heaven and earth:

And in Jesus Christ, his only Son, our Lord: who was conceived by the Holy Spirit, born of the virgin Mary, suffered under Pontius Pilate, was crucified, dead, and buried: he descended into hell, the third day he rose from the dead, he ascended into heaven, and sits on the right hand of God, the Father almighty, whence he shall come to judge the living and the dead.

I believe in the Holy Spirit, the holy Christian church,[5] the communion of saints, the forgiveness of sins, the resurrection of the body, and the life everlasting. Amen.

III. THE PRAYER, OR OUR FATHER, WHICH CHRIST TAUGHT

Our Father who art in heaven, hallowed be thy name. Thy kingdom come, thy will be done, on earth as it is in heaven. Give us this day our daily bread; and forgive us our debts, as we also have forgiven our debtors; and lead us not into temptation, but deliver us from evil. For thine is the kingdom and the power and the glory, forever. Amen.[6]

These are the most necessary parts of Christian instruction. We should learn to repeat them word for word. Our children should be taught the habit of reciting them daily when they rise in the morning, when they go to their meals, and when they go to bed at night; until they repeat them they should not be given anything to eat or drink. Every father has the same duty to his household; he should dismiss man-servants and maid-servants if they do not know these things and are unwilling to learn them. Under no circumstances should a person be tolerated if he is so rude and unruly that he refuses to learn these three parts in which everything contained in Scripture is comprehended in short, plain, and simple terms, for the dear fathers or apostles, whoever they were,[7] have thus summed up the doctrine, life, wisdom, and learning which

---

[3] Ten Commandments, Creed, Lord's Prayer. From 1525 on catechetical instruction in Wittenberg was expanded to include material on Baptism and the Lord's Supper.

[4] Ex. 20:2–17; cf. Deut. 5:6–21.

[5] The translation of *ecclesiam catholicam* by *eine christliche Kirche* was common in fifteenth-century Germany.

[6] Matt. 6:9–13; cf. Luke 11:2–4.

[7] Luther was not interested in defending the apostolic authorship of the Creed.

constitute the Christian's conversation, conduct, and concern.

When these three parts are understood, we ought also to know what to say about the sacraments which Christ himself instituted, Baptism and the holy Body and Blood of Christ, according to the texts of Matthew and Mark at the end of their Gospels where they describe how Christ said farewell to his disciples and sent them forth.

BAPTISM

"Go and teach all nations, and baptize them in the name of the Father and of the Son and of the Holy Spirit" (Matt. 28:19). "He who believes and is baptized will be saved; but he who does not believe will be condemned" (Mark 16:16).

It is enough for an ordinary person to know this much about Baptism from the Scriptures. The other sacrament may be dealt with similarly, in short, simple words according to the text of St. Paul.

THE SACRAMENT [OF THE ALTAR]

"Our Lord Jesus Christ on the night when he was betrayed took bread, gave thanks, and broke it and gave it to his disciples, saying, 'Take and eat, this is my body, which is given for you. Do this in remembrance of me.'

"In the same way also the cup, after supper, saying, 'This cup is the new testament in my blood, which is shed for you for the forgiveness of sins. Do this, as often as you drink it, in remembrance of me' " (I Cor. 11:23–25).

Thus we have, in all, five parts covering the whole of Christian doctrine, which we should constantly teach and require young people to recite

word for word. Do not assume that they will learn and retain this teaching from sermons alone. When these parts have been well learned, you may assign them also some Psalms or some hymns,[8] based on these subjects, to supplement and confirm their knowledge. Thus our youth will be led into the Scriptures so that they make progress daily.

However, it is not enough for them simply to learn and repeat these parts verbatim. The young people should also attend preaching, especially at the time designated for the Catechism,[9] so that they may hear it explained and may learn the meaning of every part. Then they will also be able to repeat what they have heard and give a good, correct answer when they are questioned, and thus the preaching will not be without benefit and fruit. The reason we take such care to preach on the Catechism frequently is to impress it upon our youth, not in a lofty and learned manner but briefly and very simply, so that it may penetrate deeply into their minds and remain fixed in their memories.

Now we shall take up the above-mentioned parts one by one and in the plainest possible manner say about them as much as is necessary.

REVIEW QUESTIONS

1. Why is catechism so important to Martin Luther?
2. To whom is catechism to be taught, and by whom is it to be taught?
3. What matters, issues, or ideas does catechism teach?
4. What purposes does catechism serve in the reformation of Luther?
5. What concerns on the part of Luther do these purposes reflect?

---

[8] Luther himself wrote six hymns based on the parts of the Catechism.

[9] Preaching and instruction on the Catechism especially during Lent.

"Statement of Grievances," Diet of Worms, 1521

The Diet of Worms in 1521, the first meeting of Emperor Charles V with the representatives of the German Estates and the occasion of Martin Luther's appearance before the emperor, is a dramatic moment in the history of the Reformation. It provided the setting for Luther's declaration of faith in Scripture and freedom of conscience: "Here I stand." It also provided the opportunity for an official statement of grievances concerning the state of the church. Thus, even as it condemned Luther, the diet reminded Charles both of the reformer's extraordinary popular support and of the necessity of addressing the "burdens and abuses" placed on the empire by Rome. Charles asked the representatives to submit a catalogue of these abuses for consideration and action. A committee of electors and princes, both secular and spiritual, drew up the following list, probably using complaints submitted by individual representatives. Though no formal action was taken at Worms, the "Statement of Grievances" provided the basis of a document sent to Rome after the Diet of Nuremberg in 1523.

From *Manifestations of Discontent in Germany on the Eve of the Reformation*, edited by Gerald Strauss (Bloomington: Indiana University Press, 1971), pp. 52–63.

His Roman Imperial Majesty desiring the electors, princes, and General Estates of the Empire to acquaint him with the burdens placed on the German nation by His Holiness the Pope and other ecclesiastics, and to make known to him our counsel and opinions as to how these burdens might be lifted from us, we have in all haste set down the following points, beginning with matters touching His Holiness the Pope.

* * *

7. *Rome often grants benefices to unworthy persons.* Rome awards German benefices to unqualified, unlearned, and unfit persons such as gunners, falconers, bakers, donkey drivers, stable grooms, and so on, most of whom know not a word of German and never assume the duties connected with their benefices, shifting them instead to worthless vicars who are content with a pittance in pay. Thus the German laity receives neither spiritual care nor worldly counsel from the Church, while a hoard of money flows yearly to Italy with no return to us, least of all gratitude.

We think that German benefices should be awarded to native Germans only and that beneficed persons ought to be required to reside in the place to which they are assigned.

* * *

9. *Concerning annates.* In former times emperors granted annates to Rome for a limited term of years only and for no purpose other than to enable the Church to hold back the Turk and support Christendom. In the course of time, however, the payment of annates grew into a regular custom, and, as is generally known, the German nation has been excessively burdened with them. . . .

10. *Annates are constantly increased in amount.* Not only are annates almost daily raised in amount, but they are also being extended from archbishoprics and bishoprics to abbeys, priories, parishes, and other ecclesiastical prebends. . . . Although the old regulations placed a pallium fee of not more than ten thousand gulden upon the bishoprics of Mainz, Cologne, Salzburg, and others, the pallium cannot now be fetched home for

THE GODLY MILL (1521)

Church reformers—both Protestant and Catholic—made full use of the new technology of printing to broadcast their ideological message to the common folk. Often, a printed image was worth a thousand words to a still largely illiterate population. The Godly Mill *distills the early Lutheran message of reliance on Scripture as the sole source of religious truth: as the truth of the Gospel is disseminated, as in the workings of a mill, those institutions and traditions not explicitly established in it are banished. What is the significance of the grouping of the four figures: Christ, Erasmus, Luther, and Karsthans, the common man? Why would Lutherans choose a mill as their symbol for the dissemination of the Gospel? Given the year in which it was printed, 1521, how might this image be directly related to significant political events?*

less than twenty thousand to twenty-four thousand gulden.

11. *Concerning new devices employed by Rome.* The main reason for the constant rise in the cost of episcopal confirmations and pallium fees is the proliferation of offices in Rome, such as chamberlains, shield-bearers, and others, for whose emoluments our bishops' subjects must pay taxes and tributes. Furthermore, Rome obtains money by means of a number of cunning and novel devices, especially the following: a certain newly elected bishop has been given papal leave to pay his pallium fees not in cash but instead in the form of a pledge from certain sponsors to make payment at a given time. Suddenly, and for no reason, these sponsors are excommunicated and, almost at once, absolved again, for which absolution the bishop-elect must pay from three to five hundred ducats. It has been made known to us that His Holiness has this year created several new offices and is now personally served by more than 150 retainers who make their living off the proceeds of ecclesiastical benefices, for which the German nation furnishes the money.

*   *   *

19. *Concerning papal dispensation and absolution.* Popes and bishops reserve to themselves certain sins and offenses from which, they say, only they can absolve us. Whenever such a "case" occurs and a man wishes absolution, he discovers that only money can procure it for him. Nor does Rome give out a dispensation except on payment of gold. A poor man without money will not see his matter despatched. A rich man can, moreover, for a sum, obtain papal letters of indult, which entitle him to priestly absolution for any sin he might commit in the future, murder, for example, or perjury. All this shows how Roman greed and covetousness cause sins and vices to multiply in the world.

*   *   *

22. *Concerning indulgences.* We also regard it in the highest degree objectionable that His Holiness should permit so many indulgences to be sold in Germany, a practice through which simple-minded folk are misled and cheated of their savings. When His Holiness sends nuncios or emissaries to a country, he empowers them to offer indulgences for sale and retain a portion of the income for their traveling expenses and salaries. . . . Bishops and local secular authorities also get their share for helping with the arrangements for the sale. All this money is obtained from poor and simple people who cannot see through the curia's cunning deceptions.

23. *Concerning mendicants, relic hawkers, and miracle healers.* These riffraff go back and forth through our land, begging, collecting, offering indulgences, and extracting large sums of money from our people. We think these hawkers ought to be kept out of our country. . . .

*   *   *

32. *How secular property comes into ecclesiastical hands.* Seeing that the spiritual estate is under papal instructions never to sell or otherwise transfer the Church's real estate and immobilia to the laity, we think it advisable for His Roman Imperial Majesty to cause a corresponding law to be made for the secular estate, to wit, that no secular person be allowed to make over any part of his real property to any ecclesiastical person or institution, and that this proscription apply to inheritance as well. If such a law is not introduced without delay, it is possible that the secular estate will, in the course of time, be altogether bought out by the Church . . . and the secular estate of the Holy Roman Empire eventually be entirely beholden to the Church.

*   *   *

37. *Ecclesiastical courts give support to Jewish usury.* Everyone knows that the Jews' usury in Germany pauperizes and corrupts Christian society. But whenever a secular authority sets out to curb the Jews, the latter call upon an ecclesiastical court for help and cause the Christians to be excommunicated. For although the debtors swear that the money owed the Jews was not procured

on terms of usury, the court knows that Jews do not lend except usuriously and that the poor, in their great need, perjure themselves. Canon and civil law forbids the rendering of judicial or other aid in matters of usury, but bishops and prelates permit it nonetheless.

*   *   *

39. *Sinners are given fines to pay rather than spiritual penance to do.* Although spiritual penance ought to be imposed upon sinners for one reason only, to gain salvation for their souls, ecclesiastical judges tend nowadays to make penalties so formidable that the sinner is obliged to buy his way out of them, through which practice untold amounts of money flow into the Church's treasury. . . .

*   *   *

43. *Excommunication is used indiscriminately, even in trivial matters.* Notwithstanding the original and true purpose of spiritual censure and excommunication, namely, to aid and direct Christian life and faith, this weapon is now flung at us for the most inconsequential debts—some of them amounting to no more than a few pennies—or for non-payment of court or administrative costs after the principal sum has already been returned. With such procedures the very life blood is sucked out of the poor, untutored laity, who are driven to distraction by the fear of the Church's ban. . . .

*   *   *

54. *There are too many vagrant mendicants in our land.* The poor in Germany are sorely oppressed by the extraordinary number of mendicant monks, especially by begging friars maintained by mendicant orders in violation of their own rules. Some villages and towns have two, three, or four of these begging brothers going about with hands outstretched, and the alms that should go to old and indigent householders who can no longer support themselves fill the monks' pouches instead. Bishops condone this practice in return for a portion of the collection.

*   *   *

56. *Too many priests are ordained, many of them unlearned and unfit.* Archbishops and bishops have been ordaining base and uneducated persons whose only claim to the priesthood is that they are needy. Such people, either because of their low estate or because of some native inclination to wickedness, lead reckless and dishonorable lives, bringing the whole spiritual estate into disrepute and setting the common folk a bad example. Before making ordination, the bishop is obliged to consult six witnesses on the candidate's fitness for the priestly office; but as things are now, the witnesses have, likely as not, never seen or heard of the candidate. Thus our Christian laws are nothing but pretense and sham to them.

*   *   *

58. *Bishops ought to hold frequent synods.* All the above shortcomings would doubtless be alleviated if bishops fulfilled their obligation to meet in synods with their prelates and ecclesiastical subjects in order to seek the aid and counsel of all the clergy present, as the law of the Church obliges them to do.

*   *   *

66. *Certain clerics behave like laymen and are even seen brawling in taverns.* The majority of parish priests and other secular clerics mingle with the common people at inns and taverns. They frequent public dances and walk about the streets in lay garments, brandishing long knives. They engage in quarrels and arguments, which usually lead to blows, whereupon they fall upon poor folk, wound or even kill them, and then excommunicate them unless the innocently injured parties agree to offer money for a settlement with the offending priest.

67. *Clerics set bad examples by cohabiting with their serving women.* Most parish priests and other clerics have established domestic relations with women of loose morals. They dwell openly with the women and with their children. It is a dishonest, detestable life for priests and a wretched example to set for their parishioners.

*   *   *

85. *They try to gain exclusive jurisdiction over legal matters, which should be heard in secular courts.* Much legal business that, according to law, may be settled in either ecclesiastical or secular courts, has in fact been usurped by the clergy. For when a secular judge claims a case, it often happens that a spiritual judge steps forward and threatens the other with excommunication unless he lets go of the case. Thus the clergy take over what they wish. According to our laws, offenses like perjury, adultery, and black magic may be handled by either spiritual or lay courts, depending on who first claimed the case. But the clergy make bold to grasp all such cases, thus undercutting secular authority.

*   *   *

91. *Money can buy tolerance of concubinage and usury.* If a man and a woman cohabit without being married, they may pay an annual fee to the clergy and be left to live in shame and sin. The same is done with usurers. . . . A married person whose spouse has disappeared but might still be living is, without any further search for the missing partner, allowed to take up cohabitation with another. This they call "*toleramus*," and it serves to bring contempt upon the holy sacrament of marriage.

*   *   *

95. *Innocent people who happen to live near an excommunicated person are themselves excommunicated.* In some towns and villages ten or twelve neighbors of an excommunicate are placed under the ban along with him, although they have nothing to do with his offense. And this is done for no reason other than the clergy's eagerness to establish its authority and to have it obeyed. Because of this practice, poor and innocent people are forced to buy their way out of the ban, or else to remove their families and belongings from their homes. No distinction is made in these indiscriminate excommunications. No one asks: Is the man

poor or not? Did he associate voluntarily with the excommunicated sinner? And even though their own canon law forbids declarations of interdict for debts or other money matters, they impose the ban on whole towns and villages, alleging disobedience as the cause in order to mask their illegal and unjust action.

*   *   *

97. *They demand a weekly tribute from artisans.* In many places the clergy demand a weekly tax or tribute from millers, inn keepers, bakers, shoe makers, smiths, tailors, shepherds, cowherds, and other craftsmen. If this tribute is refused, they enforce their demand with the threat of excommunication.

*   *   *

101. *They withhold the sacraments for trivial offenses.* If a man owes a small debt to the priest or to the parish, and if he is too poor to repay it on time and asks for a short extension of the loan, the priest often withholds the sacraments from him and nags and intimidates him, although the matter ought by rights to be brought before a secular judge.

REVIEW QUESTIONS

1. What are the general categories into which the grievances may be organized?
2. How would you characterize the list as a whole?
3. On the basis of the statement, what was the nature of discontent with the Roman Church on the eve of the Reformation?
4. What kind of action or reforms did the representatives at Worms hope to prompt from the pope in Rome?
5. To what extent does the statement reflect the spiritual yearnings of Christians like Martin Luther?

FROM *The Trial of Klaus Hottinger of Zurich:* Iconoclasm

Among the most dramatic manifestations of reformation in the sixteenth century were instances of iconoclasm. Traditionally understood as a direct response to reformed teaching against the veneration of saints and the reliance on images, occasionally leavened with social and economic antagonism, iconoclasm has more recently been interpreted as a popular form of reformation, a point at which the common folk put into action the religious ideals of an educated elite. The following is a transcription of one of the earliest trials of iconoclasts, which occurred in the Swiss city of Zurich in September 1523. Three men pulled down and broke up a large crucifix that stood at a crossing in the suburb of Stadelhofen, just outside the city walls of Zurich. Such crosses were often quite tall; this one is described variously as eight to ten feet tall. This account retains some of the legal distinctions that would have been important to the iconoclasts, not only the ownership of the crucifix but the nature of that ownership. It also gives evidence of the common interpretation of images, an issue at the heart of the Reformation.

From *The Trial of Klaus Hottinger of Zurich,* translated by L. P. Wandel (Zurich: Staatsarchiv).

*   *   *

Witnesses

1. Hans Ockenfuss stated: Klaus Hottinger came to him and asked a favor of him, to help Hottinger remove a crucifix at Stadelhofen. The miller had given it free and clear to Hottinger to do with as he pleased. Since one hears daily, that such crucifixes and all other images of God, our Savior, are forbidden, Ockenfuss was of the opinion, that he had not behaved inappropriately or done anything illegal.

2. Heini Hirt, the miller of Stadelhofen, stated: days past, this witness, with his brothers, had gone out from the lower grainary, planning to have a drink together, when Klaus Hottinger ran after him and spoke: Hey, Hirt, when are you going to put away your idols? Hirt answered him, they did not bother him; he simply must not pray to them. He wished to leave this issue to his Lords (the magistrate of Zurich), for he was not learned in scripture and had no understanding of the matter.

To this, Hottinger replied, if he (Hirt) were a good Christian man, he would remove them, because he had been informed from God's Word, that such idols should not be. When Hirt heard this, as he did not want trouble, he said to Hottinger, in so far as Hirt had the power and right to put away such idols, he transferred them and his jurisdiction over them, such as he had, to Hottinger for his own. Hottinger then told Hirt he must also help him to do this. But Hirt wanted nothing more to do with it, to be nowhere near it. Hottinger said, he would certainly find others who would help him. Hirt did not note, that Hottinger was so agitated. Hottinger came to him again after he had been to Ulrich Trinkler, a magistrate, and said, "I have removed the idols," and further, he had not done it without involving my honorable Lords. He had namely sought counsel from Claus Setzstab, a magistrate, telling him what he wished to do. Furthermore, as my Lords had acknowledged, when they arrested the said Hottinger and his associates, Hottinger had come to him and said, would he do so well as to go to Mr. Setzstab, and ask him not to put the case behind him, that he had talked with him. Hirt did not go to Setzstab—he did not wish to bring the whole matter upon himself. Hottinger also said that he had sold the woodwork and given out the money that had been "released" from it to the poor.

3. Lorenz Hochruetiner stated: He had already been imprisoned, along with Wolf the cabinetmaker, on account of the oil lamps, which the two had broken two weeks earlier in Our Lady's Church in Zurich, and was therefore, entirely of the opinion that he should steer clear of this; my Lords would not wish him to take part in such a case anymore. Then Claus Hottinger came up to him and told him of the crucifix in Stadelhofen, how he and Hans Ockenfuss had removed it, and asked him that he would help them tomorrow, for Ockenfuss had something else to do and could not help him anymore. He also said to him, how the miller had transferred the crucifix to him freely, to have as his own, with my Lord Ulrich Trinkler as witness. Finally upon his word, and because other people carried images of saints and crucifixes out of the churches, and no one marked it, he opined that it was not illegal, and he did as Hottinger wished, and unearthed the said sul.

The Accused

Klaus Hottinger gave his answer concerning the crucifix: A few days ago he talked over a lot of things with Heini Hirt, the miller from Stadelhofen, namely about images and other things. And the same Hirt said, if it were not right, then he would suffer to have his crucifix in Stadelhofen removed. And the two talked so much with one another, that he (Hirt) gave him the crucifix as a gift, free and clear, with Mr. Ulrich Trinkler as witness. And along with Hans Ockenfuss, he then removed that crucifix and in the morning, Lorenz Hochruetiner helped him to unearth the sul. And it was their opinion and their agreement that the best course would be to sell the wood from it, and give the money from it to the poor. He had not done this without the knowledge and will of certain lords of the Great and Small Councils, Mr. Claus Setzstab, Mr. Thoma Spruengli, and Hein-

rich Trueben. They did not warn him away, but instead said that by their understanding, they held and acknowledged it to be a good work, that such images come away. And namely, Mr. Stezstab said he had been there when Hans Huobers of Augsburg gave it to him to remove as he pleased. And he thought, no one talked him out of it.

And, so that no one thought, he sought counsel only after he had done the deed, he went in that very hour, in which Hirt had given him the crucifix, to Mr. Ulrich Trinkler, and understood nothing else from him, than that he held it for a good work. And had the forementioned either all together or singly warned him away with a single word, he would not have taken this on and would have away quietly. The said Mr. Trinkler also showed him certain images, which stood under the stairs in his house, and said, though it had cost him a great deal, he had them carried out of the church, so that no one would pray to them.

Further finding of the court: It was put before him, that he had said, he would give as a gift either to my Lords or to the poor in the hospice a measure of wine. He answered, not to his knowledge and he could not make sense of it, that he would have said such a thing. In so far as they nonetheless found this true of him, he could say nothing contrary, he would lie to no one. On the contrary, if an honest man said it of him, he could well believe it and not oppose it. Further: he went to Heini Hirt afterwards, and informed him, he had to go to the tower, and told him, he lied and contradicted to my Lords how he had given the crucifix as a gift.

Upon this Hirt became outraged and said, he had given it to him to do with as he wished insofar as he had the power and right, but gave it to me free and clear, as my own to do with as I pleased. And he reminded the said Hirt so much that Hirt said, it had occurred as Hottinger said, and if it came to that, he would also tell my Lords that.

Judgment

1. Klaus Hottinger, by his sworn oath to God and the Saints, is banned for two years and all

costs are bound over to him. To have the oath lifted, he must return to the authorities. 2. Lorenz Hochruetiner, the weaver, had to swear "an oath out of my Lords' city and country" and to assume the costs. 3. Hans Ockenfuss is allowed to leave prison on parole, but should keep cognizance of my Lords and assume the costs. The latter two men were penalized for being participants in Hottinger's transgression.

REVIEW QUESTIONS

1. Why does this trial indicate that iconoclasts appear before the city council, a civil authority?
2. What does that tell you about the nature of the crime of iconoclasm?
3. What does Hottinger tell us about the crucifix?
4. Why does he tear it down?
5. What does he turn it into?
6. What do we learn about the meaning of images and the process of reformation for ordinary Christians?

SEBASTIAN LOTZER

The Twelve Articles of the Peasants of Swabia

The Twelve Articles of the Peasants of Swabia, adopted at the free imperial city of Memmingen in 1525, is one of the signal documents of the great agrarian revolt known as the Peasants' War of 1525. More than any other such document, it specifically linked the social and political grievances of the peasants with the evangelical principles of the Reformation. Ironically, the Twelve Articles of the Peasants of Swabia was not composed by a peasant but by a townsman, the journeyman furrier and lay preacher Sebastian Lotzer. To do so, he summarized and condensed the long (several hundred articles) list of demands put forward by the peasants of Baltringen. The Memmingen preacher Christoph Schappeler added a preamble and supplied biblical references in the margins. The document acquired its importance because it was quickly printed and widely disseminated. In many areas of the revolt, it was adopted as the basis for lists of grievances and proposals for settlement.

From *The Revolution of 1525: The German Peasants' War from a New Perspective,* translated by Thomas A. Brady Jr. (Baltimore: Johns Hopkins University Press, 1981), pp. 195–201.

The Just and Fundamental Articles of All the Peasantry and Tenants of Spiritual and Temporal Powers by Whom They Think Themselves Oppressed

To the Christian reader, the peace and grace of God through Jesus Christ.

There are many antichrists who, now that the peasants are assembled together, seize the chance to mock the gospel, saying, "Is this the fruit of the new gospel: to band together in great numbers and plot conspiracies to reform and even topple the spiritual and temporal powers—yes, even to murder them?" The following articles answer all these godless, blasphemous critics. We want two things: first, to make them stop mocking the word

THE ECSTASY OF ST. TERESA (1652)   GIAN LORENZO BERNINI

Bernini's masterful rendering of the spiritual transport of St. Teresa is considered one of the great works of the Catholic Reformation. It captures all the inarticulate emotional and mystical elements of worship that were thought to be a counterpoint to the Protestant emphasis on the spoken word. How might art of this sort be considered an effective response to the propagandistic content of broadsides such as The Godly Mill? *What does the rendering of the angel reveal about the artist's conception of God's love? What does the rendering of St. Teresa reveal about the artist's conception of religious truth?*

of God; and second, to establish the Christian justice of the current disobedience and rebellion of all the peasants.

First of all, the gospel does not cause rebellions and uproars, because it tells of Christ, the promised Messiah, whose words and life teach nothing but love, peace, patience, and unity. And all who believe in this Christ become loving, peaceful, patient, and one in spirit. This is the basis of all the articles of the peasants (as we will clearly show): to hear the gospel and to live accordingly. How then can the antichrists call the gospel a cause of rebellion and of disobedience? It is not the gospel that drives some antichrists and foes of the gospel to resist and reject these demands and requirements, but the devil, the deadliest foe of the gospel, who arouses through unbelief such opposition in his own followers. His aim is to suppress and abolish the word of God, which teaches love, peace, and unity.

Second, it surely follows that the peasants, whose articles demand this gospel as their doctrine and rule of life, cannot be called "disobedient" or "rebellious." For if God deigns to hear the peasants' earnest plea that they may be permitted to live according to his word, who will dare deny his will? Who indeed will dare question his judgment? Who will dare oppose his majesty? Did he not hear the children of Israel crying to him and deliver them out of Pharaoh's hand? And can he not save his own today as well? Yes, he will save them, and soon! Therefore, Christian reader, read these articles diligently, and then judge for yourself.

These are the Articles.

THE FIRST ARTICLE

First of all, we humbly ask and beg—and we all agree on this—that henceforth we ought to have the authority and power for the whole community to elect and appoint its own pastor. We also want authority to depose a pastor who behaves improperly. This elected pastor should preach to us the holy gospel purely and clearly, without human additions or human doctrines or precepts. For con-

stant preaching of the true faith impels us to beg God for his grace, that he may instill in us and confirm in us that same true faith. Unless we have his grace in us, we remain mere, useless flesh and blood. For the Scripture clearly teaches that we may come to God only through true faith and can be saved only through His mercy. This is why we need such a guide and pastor; and thus our demand is grounded in Scripture.

THE SECOND ARTICLE

Second, although the obligation to pay a just tithe prescribed in the Old Testament is fulfilled in the New, yet we will gladly pay the large tithe on grain—but only in just measure. Since the tithe should be given to God and distributed among his servants, so the pastor who clearly preaches the word of God deserves to receive it. From now on we want to have our church wardens, appointed by the community, collect and receive this tithe and have our elected pastor draw from it, with the whole community's consent, a decent and adequate living for himself and his. The remainder should be distributed to the village's own poor, again with the community's consent and according to need. What then remains should be kept in case some need to be called up to defend the country; and then the costs can be met from this reserve, so that no general territorial tax will be laid upon the poor folk.

Wherever one or more villages have sold off the tithe to meet some emergency, those purchasers who can show that they bought the tithe with the consent of the whole village shall not be simply expropriated. Indeed we hope to reach fair compromises with such persons, according to the facts of the case, and to redeem the tithe in installments. But wherever the tithe holder—be he clergyman or layman—did not buy the tithe from the whole village but has it from ancestors who simply seized it from the village, we will not, ought not, and do not intend to pay it any longer, except (as we said above) to support our elected pastor. And we will reserve the rest or distribute it to the poor, as the Bible commands. As for the small tithe, we will not pay it at all, for the Lord God created cattle for man's free use; and it is an unjust tithe invented by men alone. Therefore, we won't pay it anymore.

THE THIRD ARTICLE

Third, it has until now been the custom for the lords to own us as their property. This is deplorable, for Christ redeemed and bought us all with his precious blood, the lowliest shepherd as well as the greatest lord, with no exceptions. Thus the Bible proves that we are free and want to be free. Not that we want to be utterly free and subject to no authority at all; God does not teach us that. We ought to live according to the commandments, not according to the lusts of the flesh. But we should love God, recognize him as our Lord in our neighbor, and willingly do all things God commanded us at his Last Supper. This means we should live according to his commandment, which does not teach us to obey only the rulers, but to humble ourselves before everyone. Thus we should willingly obey our elected and rightful ruler, set over us by God, in all proper and Christian matters. Nor do we doubt that you, as true and just Christians, will gladly release us from bondage or prove to us from the gospel that we must be your property.

THE FOURTH ARTICLE

Fourth, until now it has been the custom that no commoner might catch wild game, wildfowl, or fish in the running waters, which seems to us altogether improper, unbrotherly, selfish, and contrary to God's Word. In some places the rulers protect the game to our distress and great loss, for we must suffer silently while the dumb beasts gobble up the crops God gave for man's use, although this offends both God and neighbor. When the Lord God created man, he gave him dominion over all animals, over the birds of the air, and the fish in the waters. Thus we demand that if someone owns a stream, lake, or pond, he should have

to produce documentary proof of ownership and show that it was sold to him with the consent of the whole village. In that case we do not want to seize it from him with force but only to review the matter in a Christian way for the sake of brotherly love. But whoever cannot produce adequate proof of ownership and sale should surrender the waters to the community, as is just.

THE FIFTH ARTICLE

Fifth, we have another grievance about woodcutting, for our lords have seized the woods for themselves alone; and when the poor commoner needs some wood, he has to pay twice the price for it. We think that those woods whose lords, be they clergymen or laymen, cannot prove ownership by purchase should revert to the whole community. And the community should be able to allow in an orderly way each man to gather firewood for his home and building timber free, though only with permission of the community's elected officials. If all the woods have been fairly purchased, then a neighborly and Christian agreement should be reached with their owners about their use. Where the woods were simply seized and then sold to a third party, however, a compromise should be reached according to the facts of the case and the norms of brotherly love and Holy Writ.

THE SIXTH ARTICLE

Sixth, there is our grievous burden of labor services, which the lords daily increase in number and kind. We demand that these obligations be properly investigated and lessened. And we should be allowed, graciously, to serve as our forefathers did, according to God's word alone.

THE SEVENTH ARTICLE

Seventh, in the future we will not allow the lords to oppress us any more. Rather, a man shall have his holding on the proper terms on which it has been leased, that is, by the agreement between lord and peasant. The lord should not force or press the tenant to perform labor or any other service without pay, so that the peasant may use and enjoy his land unburdened and in peace. When the lord needs labor services, however, the peasant should willingly serve his own lord before others; yet a peasant should serve only at a time when his own affairs do not suffer and only for a just wage.

THE EIGHTH ARTICLE

Eighth, we have a grievance that many of us hold lands that are overburdened with rents higher than the land's yield. Thus the peasants lose their property and are ruined. The lords should have honorable men inspect these farms and adjust the rents fairly, so that the peasant does not work for nothing. For every laborer is worthy of his hire.

THE NINTH ARTICLE

Ninth, we have a grievance against the way serious crimes are punished, for they are constantly making new laws. We are not punished according to the severity of the case but sometimes out of great ill will and sometimes out of favoritism. We think that punishments should be dealt out among us according to the ancient written law and the circumstances of the case, and not according to the judge's bias.

THE TENTH ARTICLE

Tenth, we have a grievance that some people have seized meadows and fields belonging to the community. We shall restore these to the community, unless a proper sale can be proved. If they were improperly bought, however, then a friendly and brotherly compromise should be reached, based on the facts.

THE ELEVENTH ARTICLE

Eleventh, we want the custom called death taxes totally abolished. We will not tolerate it or allow widows and orphans to be so shamefully robbed of their goods, as so often happens in various ways, against God and all that is honorable. The very ones who should be guarding and protecting our goods have skinned and trimmed us of them instead. Had they the slightest legal pretext, they would have grabbed everything. God will suffer this no longer but will wipe it all out. Henceforth no one shall have to pay death taxes, whether small or large.

CONCLUSION

Twelfth, we believe and have decided that if any one or more of these articles is not in agreement with God's Word (which we doubt), then this should be proved to us from Holy Writ. We will abandon it, when this is proved by the Bible. If some of our articles should be approved and later found to be unjust, they shall be dead, null, and void from that moment on. Likewise, if Scripture truly reveals further grievances as offensive to God and a burden to our neighbor, we will reserve a place for them and declare them included in our list. We, for our part, will live and exercise ourselves in all Christian teachings, for which we will pray to the Lord God. For he alone, and no other, can give us the truth. The peace of Christ be with us all.

REVIEW QUESTIONS

1. What does the Twelve Articles tell you about relations between the common man and his lords?
2. What are the priorities of the Twelve Articles?
3. What is most important to the petitioners?
4. Why is a pastor so important?
5. What is second in importance?
6. What changes are the petitioners asking for the tithe?
7. What is Godly Law?
8. What might be its applications?
9. What are the implications of Godly Law for the lords?

KATHARINA SCHÜTZ ZELL

FROM "Letter to Sir Caspar Schwenckfeld"

Katharina Schütz Zell (1498–1562) was born in Strasbourg and took an active role in that city's Reformation. She married a priest, Matthias Zell, and assisted him as a supporter of Martin Bucer. Like Bucer, Katharina Schütz Zell might be noted for her irenicism, her desire to foster unity among Protestants and her unwillingness to be openly critical of other reformers. In a famous incident, she responded to a minister's accusation that she, by speaking out as a woman, had "disturbed the peace": "Do you call this disturbing the peace that instead of spending my time in frivolous amusements I have visited the plague-infested and carried out the dead? I have visited those in prison and under sentence of death. Often for three days and three nights I have neither eaten nor slept. I have never mounted the pulpit, but I have done more than any minister in visiting those in misery." Her career is an unequivocal reminder that not men alone but also women carried the Protestant Reformation forward by their example and their writing. In the following letter to Caspar Schwenckfeld, we see an articulate, intelligent woman, working between two religious parties in Strasbourg: the Lutheran clergy, led by Ludwig Rabus, who consider her a heretic; the Schwenckfelder party and its leader, who see her as having betrayed them. She provides not only a clear sense of vocation, conversion, and education but also an informed and sophisticated theology.

From Katharina Schütz Zell, *Church Mother: The Writings of a Protestant Reformer in Sixteenth-Century Germany*, edited and translated by Elsie McKee (Chicago: University of Chicago Press, 2006), pp. 186–215.

To Sir Caspar Schwenckfeld, My Gracious Dear Sir and Old Friend: To His Own Hands

My very dear sir (and as I hope) still my long-time friend: I wish for you, as also for myself and for all who know and call upon the name of the Lord, the grace and power of God the Holy Spirit for a holy, perfect, and finally blessed consummation of the pure faith in our Lord Jesus Christ, the true and excellent Son of the living God. May the one who is to come, come soon, and may He finally redeem us from this wicked world [cf. Rm 15:13; Joel 2:32; Rv 22:20].

*   *   *

My very dear sir, the dear woman Elsbeth Hecklin, whom you know well (praise God), has often urged me to write to you yet again, so that you would not think that I have cast you out of my heart and Christian love.[1] However, although I

---

[1] Elizabeth Scher Hecklin was a member of a high-ranking family who had settled in Strasbourg and who were strong supporters of Schwenckfeld. Although of lower social status than they, Schütz Zell had come to know the Scher family well, and among her last public acts would be preaching at the burials of Felicitas and then Elizabeth because their family did not want the city clergy to call the women heretics. Schütz Zell's association with the Schers was one reason she was considered a Schwenckfelder herself. She recognizes that at least Strasbourg Schwenckfelders, if not Schwenckfeld himself, believed that she had rejected him; they would have been the ones to hear her comments on his open letter in 1551.

myself would like and am inclined to have much conversation, verbal and written, with you (as sometimes occurred during my dear husband's blessed life), yet I have always pointed out to her my many cares, crosses, and inability now to write as much as I did previously.

On account of my sins (but for his [Zell's] good), God has taken away my simple, good, upright husband. As you also well know, my husband denied me nothing. He did not rule over or compel my faith; he also never put any obstacles in the way of my faith but rather much more he actively furthered and helped me.[2] He granted and allowed me space and will to read, hear, pray, study, and be active in all good things, early and late, day and night: indeed, he took great joy in that—even when it meant less attention to or neglect in looking after his physical needs and running his household. He also never kept me from talking with you or visiting you or you from visiting me; he never kept me from hearing you or showing you kindness while you were in Strasbourg; also thereafter (when you had left Strasbourg) he did not keep me from writing to you. He never rebuked or disliked me because of that. But rather he much loved me and held me in great honor (not because of my beauty or wealth: I never had much of either), but because of my zeal, deeds, and faith, which were all he sought for in me at the beginning of our marriage.[3] I was never worthy of this love and honor. All that I have failed to do toward you or others was never his fault but mine because of my self-satisfaction, sin, wickedness, and lack of understanding. But I lamented all that before God and still confess it before Him and hope for for-

giveness for all of it through the blood of His Son [cf. Eph 1:7].

*   *   *

But while I have borne such a cross, all friends and the whole city of Strasbourg left me suspended and floundering: those for whom I devoted the strength of my body and our substance, day and night! I must keep house with great expense on account of my poor sick boy and disburse everything I have—as if I were richer than the city of Strasbourg, with all its welfare agencies, agencies that I helped to establish and make rich! But I thank my God that in these and other crosses He teaches me many things and gives me strength and in that way makes me wiser than my (so-called) relatives; by this He also teaches me to acknowledge my sins, to confess and pray for them.[4] Indeed, if God did not take me into His sanctuary to look on the purpose of it all, I could not bear it. But by His grace I will (I hope) with Him leap over the walls [Ps 73:17; 18:29]. Now then, I ask you, for the Lord's sake to forgive me this foolishness; I would rather have written something better and wiser instead of this, but you should indulge my foolishness in this, recognize my timidity, and pray to God for me.

I have also written so that you would not think that I stopped writing to you for so long either from unwillingness on account of what you did or because I was afraid of what people would say or

---

[2] The description of Zell here and later emphasizes his support for her independent judgment in faith and friends and for her religious activities such as study, even at the expense of the usual religious duties of the good Protestant housewife. Even if this description is remembered through a haze of years, the sheer extent of Schütz Zell's reading and knowledge witnesses to its basic truth.

[3] From beginning to end, Schütz Zell affirmed that it was not her worldly gifts but her faith that attracted her husband.

[4] Schütz Zell had been a major support to the first administrator of the city poor relief organization after it was reorganized in 1523 and helped him establish a separate fund for refugees during the Peasants' War because they were not covered by the city welfare. As the child of a citizen her nephew could have been cared for by the welfare system, but for some years Schütz Zell took care of him herself, apparently at considerable expense. In 1555, when her health was worse, aunt and nephew both lived in one of the city hospices for a time, Schütz Zell was not satisfied with the conditions, physical or religious, and got reforms going but also moved out. The "relatives" who neglect this pastor's widow are the Strasbourg clergy.

think, or for other such reasons.[5] But believe me that I have little or no time, and when I do have some, I would rather read your books and others (especially the Holy Scriptures), to increase my comfort, understanding, service, and advancement (the only thing that is necessary) [cf. Lk 10:42]. I have been interrupted more than thirty times in writing this letter before I finished it; advancing years and weaknesses also contribute so that I no longer like to do so much at night as I used to do. Finally now I will let this apology stand, close it, and henceforth commend it to your Christian love and judgment. (Even now I would rather write to you about many other things, but I do not have time at present; I would also much rather talk with you and say more in one hour than in ten quires of paper.)

I had much to say to/against (*gegen*) you and your opponents:[6] I have been troubled in many things on all sides, and not entirely and in all things content. ＊ ＊ ＊ But no matter which side I were on, if I were pleased with everything about

them, those who say these things would speak differently about me, indeed they would idolize me.[7] I well believe that if I agreed that everything said on the preachers' side was right and pleased me, they would count me the most devout and learned woman in Germany But since I do not do that, they regard me instead as a presumptuous spirit and (as some mockingly say) "doctor Katharina." Also, those who love your [Schwenckfeld's] faith and understanding (however little they themselves resemble such!): if I agreed to be pleased with all their swollen heads and foolish behavior, they would do the same as the preachers—but I would have to possess the whole Spirit of God, though I have never seen a single one of the Spirit's feathers, much less received one![8]

＊   ＊   ＊

Since, however, there are many complaints about me from both parties, I must nevertheless here briefly name the issues; please pardon me this. The one party [the preachers] says that I should not shame my good husband by being so "Schwenckfeldian" and withdrawing from and despising the church's preaching and sacraments (which indeed my good husband practiced as a minister of the church). The other [Schwenckfelder] party says that I am not willing to forsake

---

[5] Schütz Zell names (and dismisses) two things that might have caused her to break off the correspondence. It is quite probable that both of these possibilities were being voiced by Schwenckfelders. (1) "[W]hat you did" (*zuokumendem* indicates something influenced by a prior act) probably refers to Schwenckfeld's open letter of November 1551, which was ostensibly a letter of consolation for Schütz Zell because of an illness, but clearly claimed her as his follower. On the contrary, although she would have appreciated a private letter of consolation, it is clear that Schütz Zell did not welcome Schwenckfeld's public claims. There is also evidence in the Strasbourg archives (dated September 1553) that Schwenckfeld's letter had brought Schütz Zell to unfavorable attention so she had good reason to be angry with him. (2) "[W]hat people would say or think" refers to the Strasbourg clergy's view of Schütz Zell as heretical for following Schwenckfeld, something his public letter certainly appeared to support.

[6] The German here can mean "to" but also "(over) against"; the former sense is dominant when referring to Schwenckfeld, but the latter is also at least implied, especially in view of Schütz Zell's later criticisms of him as well as of his followers. The "(over) against" is dominant for Rabus, although Schütz Zell had also spoken her criticism of him to Rabus himself.

[7] Schütz Zell ironically cites the condescending attitude of her critics (probably from both sides), who count her fit only for what (old) women were stereotypically supposed to do. However, she also knows that she is of enough importance in Strasbourg that her approval would enhance either the clergy's or the Schwenckfelders' position. Zell's widow, one of the most charitable and morally upright women of the city, was still a person of considerable influence because of her popularity with ordinary citizens, as even the city council recognized (and treated her carefully when they were obliged to rebuke her).

[8] Schütz Zell refers to the claim for direct inspiration by the Holy Spirit, which at least some of the Schwenckfelders boasted as their authority (below she details a conversation with one of them). Here she alludes to Luther's sarcastic comment in *Against the Heavenly Prophets* about the "enthusiasts" who swallow the Holy Spirit "feathers and all."

the preachers and move wholly to the truth on the right side [theirs], although I already know and understand it, because I was a preacher's wife, in order that my husband's behavior may not be impugned. Also they say that I am motivated by pride, that I want my own ideas and understanding and do not want to confess to being taught by others, and more such things. All that I leave aside as useless and foolish sayings and commend to the one who knows and judges all hearts [cf. Lk 16:15; Acts 15:8; 1 Pt 2:23].

However, I must nevertheless answer a little about these points: not to you, whom I know to be wiser and more upright, but to the fools who have spoken them and the naïve who receive and believe such foolish talk.[9] For the first: I have said that no one can or should say that I do anything to shame my upright and now blessed husband.[1] I do not tell them [the preachers] that they should think I am right; I do not ask them to approve my expression of my faith and deeds. If, however, they regard it as a shame to my honorable husband that I read Schwenckfeld's books and consider these as in part better and closer to the honor of Christ than their own, then I say "You are wrong [I am not shaming him]." I read these books twenty-four years ago,

not in secret, books including one in which the blessed upright Dr. Capito wrote a fine preface in which he gave witness to Schwenckfeld's spirit and good gifts.[2] I have also never had anything secret or hidden from my dear husband, especially in spiritual matters; for we always had, for the most part, a like understanding and judgment in the Holy Scriptures, in the beginning, middle, and end, as long as we were together. He himself also at times read Schwenckfeld's books, gladly heard me read them, and never allowed evil to be spoken of him [Schwenckfeld] in his house. He loved Schwenckfeld and allowed me to hear his lectures on the two epistles of Saint Peter and other books, which he gave in the house of the dear blessed Dr. Capito, who also allowed his own wife to hear these lectures when Schwenckfeld was his houseguest. Schwenckfeld was also dear to Capito.

* * *

Therefore I do not shame my dear husband or defy or disrespect him when I read Schwenckfeld's books, and I have and keep my free judgment about them and test them by the touchstone of Holy Scripture. The reason is that when he [Zell] was alive he never hindered or forbade that but always told me (as he himself also did) to read and listen, and so, after testing (as they do with the stone that is used to try gold), to hold to the good [cf. 1 Thes 5:21]. That I should therefore be considered "Schwenckfeldian," to this I say "no." For St. Paul said, "Why is one an 'Apolloian,' the other a 'Paulian' or a 'Peterian'? Were these men crucified for you? Was not Christ crucified for you?" [cf. 1 Cor 1:12–13]. Neither Schwenckfeld nor the dear

---

[9] Although she explicitly distinguishes Schwenckfeld from the foolish, there may be implicit criticism here. Schütz Zell outlines for Schwenckfeld what she has said to Rabus (her response to the preachers' accusations). A rather more diffuse but similar form of this is found in her letters to Rabus, which is why the present text (not being carefully read) has often mistakenly been considered an earlier letter addressed to Rabus. It would be wholly out of character for Schütz Zell to criticize one person to another behind the offender's back, so although there is no written form of her rebuke to Rabus at this date, she had certainly said this to him verbally (as she explains in her letters to Rabus himself later). Note her distinction between the deceived and the deceivers, where she feels obliged (in love) to set both straight.

[1] Defending Zell is one of his wife's key concerns. Rabus accuses her of dishonoring Zell by associating with Schwenckfeld and reading his books, so she vindicates Zell's support for both. Later she also has to defend Zell against the Schwenckfelders' slander.

[2] Wolfgang Capito was one of the four leading reformers of Strasbourg, very learned and of higher social status than the others; in 1524 he married Agnes Roettel, daughter of a prestigious Strasbourg family. Schwenckfeld lived with the Capitos 1529–31. The book was Schwenckfeld's "Apologia," published in 1529; one edition includes Capito's preface in which he describes the author as a *lieben* or *heiländige* brother and approves his teaching on the Lord's Supper. Here and repeatedly Schütz Zell the historian refers to numbers, years, times, etc., as part of her proof.

Dr. Luther nor any devout minister, none of them ever sought that; I also will not do it. I do not want to be theirs [e.g., *Luther*ian], but with them I want to be Christ's [*Christ*ian]. However, the teachers who know much about righteousness will shine on that day of judgment like the sun and stars of the heaven. Such shining and reward, which Paul commended [Dn 12:3; 1 Thes 2:6], 1 do not want. Nor can I attribute it to them, but I want and ought to take it from them and give it to Christ. If we should count disciples according to whose teaching one hears and whose books one reads, that is, if a person is a disciple of a teacher or writer and should be called by his name if he reads his books—then all of you [Rabus and friends] must be called by the names of Aristotle, Virgil, Plato, Cicero, and many such heathens, also papist and all heathen poets and hypocrites, and be their disciples! Yes, also Turk and Mohammed, whose Koran and all whose books you still always read, and more than is sometimes good.[3] I could indeed give many examples of this. Why then should I not read the books of a Christian, in which he exhibits Christ my Lord and God as a mighty redeemer of the human race?

You say, however, that Schwenckfeld despises and does not observe the preaching, church service, and sacraments, but I will gather an answer out of his teaching to refute this. I have never understood from him, as long as I have known him (more than twenty-four years) that he despised all these things, but that he spoke of them entirely spiritually and gloriously to the honor of Christ and would gladly have helped to bring them out of error into the truth and right command and practice of Christ.

He would teach people how to distinguish between the body and the shadow, as also his published books in part confess and exhibit; whoever would like to know about these matters, let him read for himself. Therefore he [Schwenckfeld] does not need my answering for him; he can (praise God) do it himself. But inasmuch as I nevertheless must witness to the truth and confess it before God, without any love or hate caused by attachment to him or anyone, I can truthfully say that he never has told me to remain away from the preaching. Rather he has counseled me to go, but then with a right and spiritual judgment to distinguish among teachings.[4] He also himself preached and heard preaching: yes, from the heart he sought to hear my dear husband and often attended his sermons.

You do me wrong to think that I would then leave church, preaching, and sacraments out of disregard for them: wherever I am or whatever I do, I would never leave the church (*kurch*) of Christ, in whose communion I always seek to remain (according to the saying of David in the eighth letter of the 119th Psalm) [Ps 119:63].[5] However, that I leave the outward church gathering and preaching,

---

[3] The first "academic joke"; Schütz Zell had certainly heard the names of these classical writers from the clergy, although the way she lists them suggests that she did not know much about them. "Turk" was commonly used for all Muslims, who were prominent in German minds because of the Ottoman Turk conquests and wars in eastern Europe in the 1520s, especially the siege of Vienna in 1529. In 1540–42 there was a new surge of the military struggle and with it more attention to Islam, and it is to this that Schütz Zell refers. A Latin translation of the Koran was published by Theodor Bibliander in 1540 in Zurich, and Luther presented his own German version in 1542.

[4] Rabus's second complaint about Zell's widow, that is, that she does not come regularly to worship, may be the more important one. Reading Schwenckfeld's books was not necessarily a public matter, although Schütz Zell also made these available to others who inquired about "the heretic," and that was an annoyance. Not attending public worship was more serious because that was very visible and others might follow Schütz Zell's example. Her answer: Schwenckfeld is not opposed to public worship but teaches a right (critical) judgment about it—something she believes is exactly contrary to what Rabus wants.

[5] Schütz Zell distinguishes between the universal church/*kurch* and the local church/*gemeyn*, here translated "parish" because she is referring to the established church structures. Psalm 119 is a long acrostic text in which each of the twenty-two sections begins with a successive letter of the Hebrew alphabet, letters that also have the value of numbers. Schütz Zell could have learned this from Luther's exposition of the Psalm, which also says that the use of "thine" or an equivalent in every verse is intended to draw people away from human teaching and keep them in God's. This fits Schütz Zell's purpose of affirming her allegiance to the church but not to Rabus's outward forms.

and cannot always visit it (as you think I should do), for that I will not lay a halter on my neck or allow myself to be bound to place and time [cf. Acts 15:10; Gal 4:10]. But for the sake of the prayer of the parish (*gemeyn*) (which at this time is still weak) I am always willing to join in crying to heaven in prayer and to go with the crowd to the temple, as David says [Ps 42:4 with echo of 18:29]. And—God willing—I would like often to pray with the parish and to hear preaching (although the church of Christ is not bound to that, for prayer does not have to be done either on this mountain or temple but in spirit and in truth [cf. Jn 4:21, 23]). Still I would gladly do this if you preached Christ rightly and did not hatefully abuse those who love Him.

For I also am no longer a young schoolchild who is still drinking milk and learning the ABCs; but I am an old student who has studied a long time, when you [Rabus and friends] were still children and played in the sand. I ought now to be a Master, while you would be a student who lights the fires. (Please accept this little joke well.)[6] I have exercised myself in the Holy Scriptures and godly matters for more than forty-eight years now and never abandoned the grace of God; I have heard the old teachers and let them be my counselors and made the wine new (to put in new skins) since I was ten years old [Mt 9:16, 17; Mk 2:22]. I never got bogged down hearing, learning, and following until the day (sad to me but happy to him) of the death of my dear and good husband.[7] I could now

teach others and with the elderly Anna prophesy about Christ to those who are waiting for redemption and praise the Lord [cf. Lk 2:36–38]. But considering that I must appropriately be submissive under the man's office, according to the teaching of Saint Paul [cf. 1 Cor 14:34; 1 Tm 2:12], I myself seek to hear others and to be exhorted)[8] as far as they speak the truth! But where that is not so, then I would tell you and not keep silent, but speak, point out, and answer your wrong preaching and insulting words about the innocent.[9]

*   *   *

It is also the same with receiving the sacraments, which you say that I denigrate and avoid. I say "no," I do not denigrate them. Indeed, considering how you believe, teach, and behave, it would

---

began her serious religious education when she was about seven and a half. (2) "[S]ince I was ten years old" refers to her dedication to God. The biblical image is Jesus's instruction: if you put new wine into old wineskins they will break and you will lose both the wine and the skins, so you must put new wine into new wineskins; in effect, this means putting the new life of dedication to God into new patterns of living.

[8] Schütz Zell claims her authority to teach on the basis of what the elderly Anna did when Jesus's parents brought the baby to the temple to offer the sacrifices prescribed by the law. "Prophesy" here does not mean to foretell but to proclaim. In the previous verses (Lk 2:25–35), Simeon has recognized the Christ; then the 84-year-old widow Anna, who has spent most of her life in prayer in the temple, "preaches" about Christ to the gathered people. Devout and learned, Anna is the elderly Schütz Zell's favorite biblical model of the woman preacher, but because of her strong focus on biblical authority Schütz Zell feels bound by Paul's words in 1 Corinthians 14:34 against women's speaking. However, she interprets this verse narrowly as a ban on official access to a pulpit ("ordination," although she does not use that word), not as a general prohibition on women speaking in public.

[9] The limits of the obligation to listen to ordained men ministers are clear: the preacher must speak the Gospel and not insult other Christians. Schütz Zell has two justifications: she has been taught by Luther, Zell, and her own reading of scripture to know what the Gospel is, so she is qualified to judge; and she also recognizes the character of the insults as untrue because she has long been acquainted with the people Rabus ignorantly defames.

---

[6] Rabus, born in 1523, is still much less experienced in the faith than Schütz Zell. This is the second "academic joke"; "Master" was the title for an advanced university degree but could also be used for other professions in which practical apprenticeship was the preparation. The irony is apparent: Rabus was not only a university graduate but had just that spring received his doctorate, while Schütz Zell had only a vernacular education. However, she outranks him in knowledge of the faith, as she shows by outlining her study and describing *her* teachers.

[7] The dates are important for Schütz Zell's understanding of her lifelong religious study and commitment as well as her affirmation of human teachers, including those of her Roman childhood. (1) In October 1553 "more than 48 years" would be mid-1505, meaning she

not be surprising if a great disrespect fell on the sacraments, as it did in the papacy! However, whenever you wish me to show you all my reasons for remaining away from the sacraments for a long time I will be happy to do so; I will show you that it is your own fault that drives me and others away, as I also once wrote to the blessed Dr. Luther.[1]

That you bring an action against me and say that my dear blessed husband practiced the sacraments in the church service, I say, yes, I know it well, I practiced them with him. But I did not make them a daily flea market or hypocrisy. He believed, taught, and behaved differently in these things than you. He was also different in his vocation, teaching, and life than you are. He did not—with deathly hate—make into an enemy any upright person who honored, loved, and taught Christ; he did not reproach such a person or seek to bring him into the hands of the magistracy and hangman, as you do. For I knew his good upright heart, faith, and life, his complete understanding of the Holy Scriptures and love toward those who believe and love Christ. He never sought to harm anyone or cast out or condemn anyone, except those whom Christ and His apostles cast out and condemned, but rather he sought for Christ's sake to gather together all who confess Christ [cf. Lk 13:34].[2]

He also confessed and taught how to seek salvation, peace, and righteousness, his own and everyone's—not in creatures or elements, but only in the blood and death of Jesus Christ, His resurrection from the dead, and now His being at the right hand of God His Father in like honor, might, authority, and divine majesty. We are not to look for it stuck in bread, as you do! How many times and often did he say that he spoke to the heart so that the words of Christ might be received and grasped with true faith and that he did not speak to the bread?![3] Therefore it was fitting that I broke with him the bread of unity, remembrance, and fellowship of our Lord Jesus Christ, to confess to him and to others my like faith [cf. I Cor 10:16, 11:24–26]. How can I then break bread with you? You do not behave in his fashion or walk in his footsteps.[4] * * *

Ah, how often did he say, to me and from the pulpit, "It will happen after this that you will make a work, *opus opperatus* [*opus operatum*], out of taking the Lord's Supper and hearing sermons, as they did in the papacy out of the Mass and indulgences."[5] Such prophecies I have (I fear) experienced. You young preachers sit now in Moses's seat, but you are not his [Zell's] successors as he was Saint Paul's. You ate out of his plate, received his

---

[1] Schütz Zell tacitly agrees that she is staying away from the sacraments but blames Rabus's own behavior. Her analysis of the latter is the most devastating accusation possible: Rabus is leading the church in the direction of the medieval/Roman sins, for example, wrong understanding and use of the sacraments. Given her other criticisms of Rabus and Rome, she probably means that the sacraments are being used as magical rites (*opus operatum*), which are considered effective without faith or repentance (appropriate love of the neighbor) on the part of priest or people. The letter to Luther was written after the Marburg debate.

[2] Schütz Zell first describes Zell's pastoral behavior. He never persecuted or brought civil coercion to bear on those who did not agree with him on secondary matters provided they shared the fundamental point of Christ as sole savior. The only ones Zell excluded were ones who rejected Christ (refused to believe and allow Him to save them), which for the Zells meant people who followed Roman teaching.

[3] Next she defends Zell's teaching: justification only through trust in Christ, not through trust in anything created, especially not the bread and wine of the sacrament. She insists that Zell addressed Christ's promises to people to be believed. He did not say "this is my body" to the bread to make Christ's body present "under" the bread, as in the Lutheran teaching of ubiquity which Rabus shared.

[4] The language here, breaking the bread of unity, remembrance, fellowship, . . . to confess to him and to others" echoes clearly the Zwinglian view of the Lord's Supper. In particular, the emphasis on the Supper as a pledge of faith was characteristic of the communal orientation of Zwingli and the Reformed tradition (and not of Luther). Schütz Zell takes it for granted that fellowship in the Supper should be based not only on right teaching (the words of consecration spoken to the people to be received with faith, not to the bread to change it into something else), but also on appropriate respect for other Christians.

[5] In Roman teaching the mechanical enactment of the sacrament (*opus operatum*) was efficacious as a "good work," that is, meritorious in God's sight simply by

teaching and work, but now you trample him in the ground [Mt 23:2, 26:23; Heb 10:29; Rm 10:9ff]. The words of his teaching and confession in the breaking of bread you have thrown out, and those people whom he loved and never hated or scolded you now condemn so terribly and revile and abuse so slanderously—with so many untrue and detestable sayings by which you shamelessly hand them over to the devil as much as you are able [1 Cor 5:5]. I pleaded with you in a very friendly way, also showed you writings and books to give you a better understanding of Schwenckfeld, but nothing helped.

*   *   *

These are, among others, my reasons for withdrawing from the fellowship of your sacraments and why I have till now avoided them. The other reasons I will gladly show you and tell you, when you wish. Also I will gladly hear all that you have against me, explain my views with simplicity and truth, and make my free confession, which I know is not contrary to my faith and confession during my dear husband's life—it was also his own! I hope that you will allow me to abide by this. If you do not, then I must commend it to God, to whom I have given soul and body, and not to any human person: no person should have any more power over such matters as faith than what God allows, which is to kill the body or cast it into prison. Otherwise I want always to be one of God's freed ones [cf. 1 Pt 4:19; Jn 19:11; 1 Cor 7:22].[6]

Now, dear sir [Schwenckfeld], this is what, among other words, I have answered Rabus and his clerical friends. I will not say more until I am driven further, for I think it does not become me to step out further before I am called and forced to speak. Thus I want to allow God to give me what I should say and do [cf. Mt 10:19–20].[7]

How should I answer the other party? The ones who highly praise your faith (which you have in Christ), who say that I am not willing to break with the preachers and will not side with the truth on account of my husband; and that it hurts my pride since I want to live by my own understanding and do not wish to confess to being taught by others, as I have said above. I cannot go over the whole business here, but nevertheless I must answer a little so that you may not think it is really the way they say. For I have seen in some of your letters written to (mutual) good friends that all kinds of sayings about me come to you; that is why I once wrote to you appealing to your love, that if people sometimes complain about me to you, I would like (to know so as) to respond.[8]

Now regarding the first complaint, that I am unwilling to avoid the preachers, etc., I must ask those same fools how I am supposed to avoid

---

being done. In her letters to Rabus Schütz Zell cites his agreement with a colleague's sermon in which the family of a little girl (who had not been baptized as an infant) was in essence told that if she had died before baptism she would have been lost. Her use of the phrase *opus operatum* indicates Schütz Zell's clear understanding of the doctrine but since she misspells the words (writing *opus opperatus*), it is apparent that she did not really know it as Latin.

[6] Schütz Zell concludes the account of her defense to Rabus and politely asks him to accept her confession, but if he does not she will not change. She adds an implied criticism: the only power he has over her is to kill or harm her body (he can persecute her as he has others), but he has no authority to change her faith.

[7] The condition for saying more was for the sake of "the honor of Christ and of God." Eventually she published what she had said, when Rabus paid no attention to anything she said or wrote; each time she gives biblical grounds for her action—not simply to justify it to Rabus but also probably to justify it to her own conscience. The basis is here: she responds when compelled by her conscience and trusts that in that circumstance God will supply the words, according to His promise in Matthew 10:19–20.

[8] Schütz Zell begins her answer to the Schwenckfelders by briefly listing again their charges, but goes on to chide Schwenckfeld. He repeated the charges in letters to their mutual friends, including Elizabeth Scher Hecklin who had persuaded her to write this letter, without first checking with her as she had specifically requested in case of misunderstanding. This also suggests that the criticisms by the Schwenckfelders had been going on for some time, since they antedated Schütz Zell's last letter to Schwenckfeld, which was probably at least several years earlier than this one.

them.[9] Should I do what they [the Schwenck-felders] so much complain about the preachers doing to them? That is, should I hate and despise and abuse the preachers and cry out against and scold everyone—people who (I know) nevertheless in many things gladly do their best. [Besides the gratuitous attacks by the preachers], we also know that many people fail from lack of understanding; should I not consider the example of Saint Paul? He was an enemy of Christ, a great persecutor of His church and one who took pleasure in the death of Stephen, and yet nevertheless he obtained mercy and thereafter became a pillar of the same church he had persecuted and then worked and suffered more for it than all the others did [cf. Acts 8:1, 9:1ff; 1 Tm 1:13; Gal 2:9; 2 Cor 11:23]. Along with that there is the example of the Samaritan who did good to one who was a foreigner to his faith. Yes, also much more, there is the command of Christ to pray for our enemies, to speak and do good to those who speak evil and He Himself did not revile others in return when He was reviled [cf. Lk 10:30–35, 6:27–28; 1 Pt 2:23].

*   *   *

Now further [the second complaint], they say that I will not side with the truth on the right side, that is, I cannot and will not spin to suit everyone—although the one who says this does not himself act in all things in right faith and judgment of love. God allows me daily to see so much! Because of that I thank Him and will not allow anyone to bind me. Nor will I, without foundation and the understanding of my heart, copy them like a monkey putting on shoes or like a child copying the mother in praying the "Our Father in Heaven" who still knows only the earthly

father.[1] I have sided with Christ, who is the truth itself, the way, and the life, at the right hand of God His Father, and I seek every day to come to Him, the longer I live, the more; I hope, too, that He will not deny me or cast me from Him. Also I have not (I hope) practiced any hypocrisy toward anyone of high or low estate, and I have made my confession (so much as my conscience has received and is convinced of) in health and in sickness and never been ashamed of it [cf. Jn 14:6, 6:37; Ps 110:1; Mt 10:33; Rm 1:16]. I am not afraid also to confess my faith before many people, when the advancement of the honor of Christ and of God requires that.

As for the third complaint, they say that I do not change because of my dear husband. Why should I abandon what I profess on his account? When was he ever so contrary to me or the honor and knowledge of Christ? Did he behave and teach so badly, or know Christ so little—Christ whom he indeed preached with such great faithfulness and effort and prepared the field for others with his plow and at his expense and did not seek his own interest in this; to that I can give witness before God! He proclaimed Christ as the perfect and true Son of God, held Him for his Lord and God, loved, honored, and prayed to Him [cf. Jn 4:38, 5:30, 20:28]. Also, in the last night before his death he said in great pain, "O my Lord and God, Jesus Christ! I have preached You wholly faithfully according to my small ability, which You have given to me: You know that. I confess You still, against all the gates of hell. To You, to You, I give up my spirit and my office; You remain the chief shepherd over Your poor people." Besides this he said many other

---

[9] What does "avoidance" mean? (1) Is it attacking the clergy the way they attack others, especially the Schwenckfelders and herself? Schütz Zell is discriminating; she does not make a blanket accusation of all the clergy but recognizes both human failings and repentance and further she offers grounds for being forbearing with those who do wrong, in hopes that they will repent.

[1] The charge of not agreeing with them although she knows they are right Schütz Zell interprets as demanding mindless conformity and rote learning without comprehension—a complaint Protestants made against the traditional Roman church (!) The first example suggests that the act being imitated is foolish; the second example does not intend disrespect to the content of the Prayer but emphasizes that rote memorization is the childish act of someone who does not actually know the person she is addressing. Schütz Zell goes on to affirm that her confession is based on conscience and conviction combined with sincere behavior.

such beautiful words and prayers, on his knees, with great earnestness [cf. Mt 16:18; Ps 31:5; 1 Pt 5:4].

* * *

Now for the fourth criticism: that (as they say) pride makes me so set on remaining in my own ideas and understanding and unwilling to be taught by someone else.[2] God knows that this is a blind and presumptuous judgment! My pride, glory, and boast is only in my Lord Jesus Christ, as the prophet says, "The one who wants to glory, let him glory in the Lord" [cf. 1 Cor 1:31; Jer 9:23–24]. I have always listened in my heart to the saying of God: "Hear, O Israel; in yourself is your destruction, but in Me is your salvation" [cf. Dt 6:4; Hos 13:9]. And again, "The one who wants to be taught must be taught by God (not by himself)"; and Saint Paul says, "No one is wise of himself"; and the dear James says, "The one who wants wisdom, let him ask it of God" [cf. Is 54:13; Rm 12:16; Jas 1:5]. That I have done from my youth on.

From my youth on I have zealously sought and prayed for God's wisdom, which He has also given to me. From a child in my dear father's house onward He laid the foundation stone in my heart to despise the world and exercise myself in His religion [cf. 1 Pt 2:6]. That I did under the papacy with great earnestness. In that time of ignorance I very zealously, with great pain of body and anxiety of heart, sought out so many clergy and God-fearing people to experience the way to heaven; about that I will say no more. How very wonderfully the Lord led me then! And afterward He did not leave me in my distress. He sent to me, and to many poor afflicted consciences, the dear and (I hope) now blessed Martin Luther, who showed me my error

and pointed me to Christ, in whom I would find rest. Then God opened my understanding to comprehend the Holy Scriptures, which I had previously read as a closed book and had not understood; then the Lamb opened the book of the seven seals and took away my lack of understanding and gave comfort in my heart [Mt 11:29; Rev 5:1, 8–9].[3] So it happened to me as to one lost and benighted in a wild forest where many murderers lived: God sent that person an angel who led him out of the forest and showed him the right path. So I have not (as these relate) chosen my own ideas, but I have let the will of God be more pleasing to me than my own. God has sent His Holy Spirit in my heart and allowed the messengers He has sent to teach me with outward writings and words so that the longer the time the more I have come to the knowledge of Christ. I have not been passive and lazy in that but have sought out, loved, and listened to you [Schwenckfeld] and others of God's learned ones and never closed my heart to anyone's teaching and exhortation.[4]

That I still do and also want to continue to do: to pray to the Lord Christ and thank Him for His gifts which He gave to people after He ascended into heaven; praying daily and (with David) in the night [Ps 68:16, 119:62; Eph 4:8]; also thanking Him for the holy teaching that He gave me through Luther, my dear husband, you [Schwenckfeld], and

---

[2] Schütz Zell's response to the fourth accusation is the longest and has two parts. First is an account of her religious experience from childhood, a confession that she is a sinner, and her joy in God's grace of conversion. The second part is a dialogue with a Schwenckfelder who denied being taught by any human, where Schütz Zell explains the relationship of God's grace and human teachers as God's instruments.

[3] Schütz Zell's account of her conversion (from anxiety to trust) is modeled on Luther's, but that does not invalidate the accuracy of the basic outline; here she is addressing it to someone who was most certainly no longer a fan of Luther's, for whom being like Luther would not necessarily be a recommendation. Roman clergy did not encourage laity to read the Bible for themselves. However, some printed vernacular Bibles were available in Schütz Zell's childhood and she obviously read one but claims she did not have the key to understand it without God's human messenger Luther. She appears to interpret the heavenly "book with seven seals" (Rv 5:1) as the Bible.

[4] Here in brief is the theme later developed: knowledge of Christ through God's teaching enabled by the Holy Spirit, proclaimed by messengers with outward words taught them by the Bible, accompanied by active effort by the student.

many other dear men. Yes, I thank Him all the time in my heart for the true knowledge of Christ the sole savior, which the longer I know it the more I love it, in which I also have great joy and wonder; I seek to grow and increase in it while I live, and I labor at that and will sing praises to my God because of it as long as I live [Ps 104:33]. To this I have been greatly motivated also through your service and earnestness; that I cannot deny. Why then would I, out of pride, want not to be taught by anyone and to deny the offices of such servants of God and be so ungrateful for their work, which God laid upon them in order to serve human beings?[5]

However, I heard from one among those companions of your faith. He said to me, "I received nothing from Luther, I had it from God."[6] I said, "You are lying that you have nothing from Luther. We know that all is from God, but Saint Paul says that he and Apollos have planted and watered, but God is the one who has given the increase [cf. 1 Cor 3:6]. However, if Paul and Apollos together with Peter, John, and other apostles did nothing, why would God have chosen Paul and sent him out to bear and confess His name before the heathen, kings, and Jews? And also sent Ananias to Paul, and Peter to Cornelius, and Philip to the circumcised Moor [Ethiopian] on the chariot when he was reading the scripture but could not understand it until Philip explained it to him [cf. Acts 9:1ff, 10:17ff, 8:26ff]? There are many examples of this, how He has used human beings.

"In the work of redemption God and Christ do not want to have anyone alongside (as some kind of co-redeemer); God does not allow His own

glory to anyone.[7] But in the work of calling, like a great king He wants to have many servants and messengers, according to the prediction of David in the Psalm [68:18] and the saying of Paul to the Ephesians [4:8]. Therefore, He also sent out the apostles to preach repentance and forgiveness of sins (not, however, in their own name, but in His name). As also He gives a lovely parable in the Gospel: the householder sent out his servant (as he had already planned) to invite guests to the marriage [cf. Acts 5:31, 10:43; Mt 22:2ff]. The choosing, beginning, and preparation or drawing of the heart is the work of God and His Spirit alone, but the outward calling He does through people.[8] Otherwise how would Christ have ventured to choose and send out the apostles? Therefore He also said to them, 'You have not chosen me, but I have chosen you that you should go and bring forth fruit.' Therefore also Paul so earnestly commanded his dear sons Timothy and Titus and also told them to establish others to pasture the community of God and said that they should not neglect the gifts of God [cf. Jn 15:16; 1 Tm 1:2, 4:14; Tit 1:4–5].

"Did not God the Father also decree from eternity to allow His Word to become Man (*mensch*) for us? Did He not also choose and sanctify Mary

---

[5] Schütz Zell speaks of being taught by ministers and insists that she would be ungrateful to God to deny the good work, the offices, of God's servants; the function is the key thing, but in second place there is the recognition of the ministers who carry out the task using the gifts that God has given.

[6] For clarity in Schütz Zell's conversation with a Schwenckfelder, his words in the third person have been changed to first person to match hers.

[7] In the medieval Roman tradition the Virgin Mary was not only regarded as the chief of the saints but also sometimes called mediatrix or "comediator" with her Son. Immediately below is one of Schütz Zell's few references to Mary, and it is (typically) very restrained, limited essentially to credal statements.

[8] Here and below Schütz Zell makes her clearest statements about Protestant views of ministry. Salvation is by God alone, who by the Holy Spirit prepares the heart to trust in Christ the Word made flesh. People can do nothing to earn their salvation, but they are God's chosen instruments for proclaiming the Gospel. The latter is revealed only in the Bible, which teaches the content of what must be believed; faith is both trust effected by the Holy Spirit and knowledge conveyed by the Bible, which the Holy Spirit gave. However, the human agents are vital precisely because they are God's choice, and denying them is refusing God and choosing one's own ideas. Schütz Zell thus turns the tables on the Schwenckfelder accusation.

to be the mother? Did He not, however, manage all this through the angel as His messenger (according to His predetermined counsel) [cf. Jn 1:14; Lk 1:26ff; Acts 2:23, 4:28]? Did He not make you know it through outward speech and voice, yet inwardly Himself prepare your heart through His Spirit to believe and be obedient to it? This is what God has done through His servant Moses with the people of Israel, thereafter through the prophets; also, Christ at His coming did it through the apostles and will continue doing so until the end of the world [cf. Acts 3:18ff; Lk 10:1ff; Jn 17:18, 20:21; 1 Cor 1:17]. I am not talking about just any puppy, or any learned one sent by the world: neither of them knows or is acquainted with a feather—much less the power—of the Spirit! But I am speaking of right-minded folk who are God's learned ones, who find in their hearts a call and gifts of faith— of these there are few in the world (I know well). However, God also uses those whom we count as the least, of whom I could give many examples, also scriptural ones [cf. Rm 15:15; 1 Thes 4:9; Eph 2.8].[9]

"How could you [this Strasbourg Schwenck-felder—trans.] say without qualification that you got nothing from Luther? Why did you become a monk and renounce sin, except that you thought that was the means to serve God and obtain eternal life? Now who taught you that? The pope was your teacher for that—you cannot deny it. Who told you nevertheless to leave the monastic life, as a useless and unfounded human law, and to seek and find your salvation only in Christ—against the previous papal teaching? Did you become so wise yourself? Why then did you become a monk? Did you want for a little while to play carnival and carry on a mockery between God and yourself? You would certainly not say that. You are then foolish. So you must confess with me and with others that Luther said, 'You have gone astray; you do not serve God by being a monk.'[1] You know his books and once read them with diligence, believed him, and took him for a blessed messenger sent by God. You then searched the Holy Scriptures, to which Luther also pointed you and me; and God's Spirit (who also, I well know, had laid the foundation stone in your heart) led you further [cf. Is 28:16; 1 Pt 2:6]. So you also went further and came to Schwenckfeld; you heard him and read his writings and so received good from God through him also."

But this man then said to me, "I got nothing from Schwenckfeld." Then I answered him, "You lie once again. All that you know, perform, and do, you have from him, yes, all your speech and words. You do not know your mother tongue anymore; all the words that he [Schwenckfeld] speaks and writes as his [Silesian] form of German, you follow him in speaking and writing—against your own nature and native form of German! How can you so presumptuously say that you got nothing from him? Everyone knows that I said, 'Schwenckfeld is more upright and learned than you and ten others, and he acknowledges in his writings that he also received good through Luther's service.'" The man answered once again, "I learned nothing from Luther or from Schwenckfeld." Then I said, "Were you taught by the devil? Or who then taught you? God did not use some special revelation with you anymore than with me." Then he left me in anger.

I think, dear sir [Schwenckfeld], that you are also implicated in this complaint. How could I do otherwise with him? I heartily wish that you

---

[9] Visible signs of the Holy Spirit (like the ironic "feather") are subordinated to the power of the Spirit, which is what matters. Those who are learned in a worldly sense, or other fools claiming inspiration, do not have even the signs of being sent by God, but Schütz Zell points out that God uses not only ones people recognize (like Zell), but also those the world despises as having no value (including herself?!).

[1] Schütz Zell apparently knew this man well, she reminds him of his own life, following first the pope, then Luther, then Schwenckfeld, but now denying everything, against the evidence of his own spoken German. Her speech has a slapstick quality: "You learned the value of celibacy from the pope. If you were already so wise that you knew monastic vows were wrong, then you were mocking God by taking them. However, if you learned their worthlessness from Luther, then . . . !"

yourself had heard by degrees (bit by bit) this and other things or that I were present when many things were shown to you. I say all this now only because this man and many others accuse me that, out of pride, I do not want to be taught by anyone, when instead I always confess more than all of them and give God thanks for all that I learned and received from Luther, my dear husband, you, and all other learned ones. But I give God the glory, who looked on me with mercy and called me according to His gracious election and allowed me to come to understanding, faith, righteousness, and His glory. He did all that because of His everlasting grace and loving mercy, through which also, coming down out of the heavens, He sought me who sat in darkness and the shadow of death and directed my feet in the path of peace [Rm 8:28ff; Ps 107:10; Lk 1:79]. How then could I object to being taught by you and all those who have right love for Christ, and how could I take pride in my own understanding, as they say of me (but unjustly)?

*   *   *

With that I will close for this time and send you this letter as a beginning (to refresh again our former love and acquaintance), with hearty thanks for all the good in teaching and comfort that I have received from you. Also I thank you for the glorious, Christian, and good testimony about my blessed husband that you sent to me in my cross, with such great confidence of his faith and now his blessedness, peace, and rest in Christ—the letter that also exhorted me about the sole savior whom he confessed. For that, may our Lord and God repay you and never leave you without comfort. I also ask you to receive this letter from me in Christian love (which bears and suffers all things) [cf. Rm 2:6–7;

Jn 14:18; 1 Cor 13:7]. Henceforth I will take other matters in hand, with publication of some writings and also the confession of my faith and questioning where I am not satisfied with all the writings and sayings.[2]

Also I commend you to the grace of our Lord Jesus Christ, a hero, one Person from two natures, true God and true Man in the indivisible being of the holy trinity, reigning king of His people forever, a Prince of Peace and eternal Father of all who trust in Him and call upon Him, who saves His people from their sins: to Him be praise, with the Father and the Holy Spirit, one God, forever, amen [cf. Acts 20:32; Rm 16:20; Mt 1:21; Is 9:6]. Pray to him earnestly for me.

Dated at Strasbourg at night (in the day I have crosses to bear, I do not want to write), the 19th of October 1553.

Katharina Zell,

the sorrowing widow of the blessed Matthew Zell;
  yours in the Lord Christ and willing to serve
  you in whatever ways I am able

REVIEW QUESTIONS

1. How does Schütz Zell describe her role in the Reformation at Strasbourg?
2. Why does she disagree with the Lutherans?
3. What are her differences with the Schwenkfeldians?
4. How would you characterize the problem both these groups had with her?
5. What does she hold to be important in religious life?
6. How do these values reflect the larger issues that swept Germany in the sixteenth century?

---

[2] The gracefully crafted conclusion thanks Schwenckfeld for his teaching and his beautiful letter of consolation and ends with a warm biblical blessing that includes a reference to the Chalcedonian definition of Christ's two natures.

JOHN CALVIN

FROM Draft of Ecclesiastical Ordinances, September and October 1541

John Calvin (1509–1564) was born of bourgeois parents in the city of Noyon in Picardy. Destined by his father for an ecclesiastical career, he received several bene-fices to finance his education as early as 1521. In 1523, he transferred to the Uni-versity of Paris, where he imbibed the spirit of humanism from such teachers as Mathurin Cordier and Guillaume Budé. Calvin earned a master of arts degree at Paris and, without abandoning his study of classical languages and literature, turned to law at Orleans in 1528. By 1532, he had earned a doctorate of law. Sometime during his legal training or shortly thereafter, Calvin converted to Protes-tantism. The year 1534 was decisive for Calvin. Forced to flee Paris because of the proscription of Protestantism, he made his way to Basel, where he began work on his great systematic theology, Institutes of the Christian Religion (1536). It was immediately recognized as a superb normative statement of reformed theology and established Calvin's stature as a leader among Protestants despite his youth. As the first edition went to press, Calvin made his way to Geneva, where Guillaume Farel enlisted his aid in the reform of the city. The early years of the Reformation in Geneva were stormy, and there was considerable opposition to the doctrines advo-cated by Calvin. In a dispute over church discipline, the city council banished the Protestant pastors. Calvin made his way to Strasbourg, where he remained as a col-league of Martin Bucer and minister to the French refugee church until 1541. Meanwhile, political and religious chaos in Geneva eventually forced the government to seek the return of Calvin. He reluctantly consented, but only with the assurance that his entire original scheme of church polity would be instituted. The ecclesiasti-cal ordinance adopted in 1541 encapsulated that polity and became influential for reformed churches throughout Europe. Written four years later, his Catechism of the Church of Geneva offers a different vision of the reformer's range of activity. He was no less deeply committed to the inner life of the faithful than he was to the explica-tion of doctrine or the organization of the church. The dedication summarizes the role of education in preserving an embattled and isolated religious community. Calvin remained in Geneva from 1541 until his death in 1564, by which time the city that had accepted reform so reluctantly had been transformed into the center of an international Reformation.

From *Calvin: Theological Treatises*, translated by J. K. S. Reid (Louisville: Westminster John Knox Press, 1954).

There are four orders of office instituted by our Lord for the government of his Church. First, pastors; then doctors; next elders; and fourth deacons.

Hence if we will have a Church well ordered and maintained we ought to observe this form of government.

As to the pastors, whom Scripture also sometimes calls elders and ministers, their office is to proclaim the Word of God, to instruct, admonish, exhort and censure, both in public and private, to administer the sacraments and to enjoin brotherly corrections along with the elders and colleagues.

Now in order that nothing happen confusedly in the Church, no one is to enter upon this office without a calling. In this it is necessary to consider three things, namely: the principal thing is the examination; then what belongs to the institution of the ministers; third, what ceremony or method of procedure it is good to observe in introducing them to office.

The examination contains two parts, of which the first concerns doctrine—to ascertain whether the candidate for ordination has a good and holy knowledge of Scripture; and also whether he be a fit and proper person to communicate it edifyingly to the people.

Further to avoid all danger of the candidate holding some false opinion, it will be good that he profess his acceptance and maintenance of the doctrine approved by the Church.

To know whether he is fit to instruct, it would be necessary to proceed by interrogation and by hearing him discuss in private the doctrine of the Lord.

The second part concerns life, to ascertain whether he is of good habits and conducts himself always without reproach. The rule of procedure in this matter which it is needful to follow is very well indicated by Paul.

There Follows, to Whom It Belongs to Institute Pastors

It will be good in this connection to follow the order of the ancient Church, for it is the only practice which is shown us in Scripture. The order is that ministers first elect such as ought to hold office; afterwards that he be presented to the Council; and if he is found worthy the Council receive and accept him, giving him certification to produce finally to the people when he preaches, in order that he be received by the common consent of the company of the faithful. If he be found unworthy, and show this after due probation, it is necessary to proceed to a new election for the choosing of another.

As to the manner of introducing him, it is good to use the imposition of hands, which ceremony was observed by the apostles and then in the ancient Church, providing that it take place without superstition and without offence. But because there has been much superstition in the past and scandal might result, it is better to abstain from it because of the infirmity of the times.

When he is elected, he has to swear in front of the Seigneury. Of this oath there will be a prescribed form, suitable to what is required of a minister.

Now as it is necessary to examine the ministers well when they are to be elected, so also it is necessary to have good supervision to maintain them in their duty.

First it will be expedient that all the ministers, for conserving purity and concord of doctrine among themselves, meet together one certain day each week, for discussion of the Scriptures; and none are to be exempt from this without legitimate excuse. If anyone be negligent, let him be admonished.

As for those who preach in the villages, throughout the Seigneury, they are to be exhorted to come as often as they are able. For the rest, if they default an entire month, it is to be held to be very great negligence, unless it is a case of illness or other legitimate hindrance.

If there appear difference of doctrine, let the ministers come together to discuss the matter. Afterwards, if need be, let them call the elders to assist in composing the contention. Finally, if they are unable to come to friendly agreement because of the obstinacy of one of the parties, let the case be referred to the magistrate to be put in order.

To obviate all scandals of living, it will be proper that there be a form of correction to which all submit themselves. It will also be the means by which the ministry may retain respect, and the Word of God be neither dishonoured nor scorned because of the ill reputation of the ministers. For as one is to correct those who merit it, so it will be proper to reprove calumnies and false reports which are made unjustly against innocent people.

But first it should be noted that there are crimes which are quite intolerable in a minister, and there are faults which may on the other hand be endured while direct fraternal admonitions are offered.

Of the first sort are:

heresy, schism, rebellion against ecclesiastical order, blasphemy open and meriting civil punishment, simony and all corruption in presentations, intrigue to occupy another's place, leaving one's Church without lawful leave or just calling, duplicity, perjury, lewdness, larceny, drunkenness, assault meriting punishment by law, usury, games forbidden by the law and scandalous, dances and similar dissoluteness, crimes carrying with them loss of civil rights, crime giving rise to another separation from the Church.

Of the second sort are:

strange methods of treating Scripture which turn to scandal, curiosity in investigating idle questions, advancing some doctrine or kind of practice not received in the Church, negligence in studying and reading the Scriptures, negligence in rebuking vice amounting to flattery, negligence in doing everything required by his office, scurrility, lying, slander, dissolute words, injurious words, foolhardiness and evil devices, avarice and too great parsimony, undisciplined anger, quarrels and contentions, laxity either of manner or of gesture and like conduct improper to a minister.

In the case of the crimes which cannot at all be tolerated, if some accusation and complaint arise, let the assembly of ministers and elders investigate it, in order to proceed reasonably and according to whatever is discovered in judging the case, and then report judgment to the magistrate in order that if required the delinquent be deposed.

In the case of the lesser vices which may be corrected by simple admonition, one is to proceed according to the command of our Lord, so that as a last step it come for ecclesiastical judgment.

To keep this discipline in operation, let the ministers every three months take special notice whether there be anything to discuss among themselves, to remedy it as is reasonable.

Of the Number, Place and Time of Preachings

Each Sunday, there is to be a sermon at St. Peter and St. Gervais at break of day, and at the usual hour at the said St. Peter and St. Gervais.

At midday, there is to be catechism, that is, instruction of little children in all the three churches, the Magdalene, St. Peter and St. Gervais.

At three o'clock second sermon in St. Peter and St. Gervais.

For bringing children to catechism, and for receiving the sacraments, the boundaries of the parishes should as far as possible be observed; that is, St. Gervais embracing what it had in the past, the Magdalene similarly, St. Peter what belonged formerly to St. Germain, St. Cross, Our Lady the New, and St. Legier.

Besides the two preachings which take place, on working days there will be a sermon at St. Peter three times a week, on Monday, Tuesday and Friday one hour before beginning is made at the other places.

To maintain these charges and others pertaining to the ministry, it will be necessary to have five ministers and three coadjutors who will also be ministers, to aid and assist as necessity requires.

Concerning the Second Order, Which We Have Called Doctors

The office proper to doctors is the instruction of the faithful in true doctrine, in order that the purity of the Gospel be not corrupted either by ignorance or by evil opinions. As things are disposed today, we always include under this title aids and instructions for maintaining the doctrine of God and defending the Church from injury by the fault of pastors and ministers. So to use a more intelligible word, we will call this the order of the schools.

The degree nearest to the minister and most closely joined to the government of the Church is the lecturer in theology, of which it will be good to have one in Old Testament and one in New Testament.

But because it is only possible to profit from such lectures if first one is instructed in the languages and humanities, and also because it is necessary to raise offspring for time to come, in order not to leave the Church deserted to our children, a college should be instituted for instructing children to prepare them for the ministry as well as for civil government.

For the first, a proper place ought to be assigned for both doing lessons and accommodating the children and others who would profit. There must be a man learned and expert in arranging both the house and the instruction, who is able also to lecture. He is to be chosen and remunerated on condition that he have under his charge lecturers both in languages and in dialectic, if it can be done. Likewise there should be some matriculated persons to teach the little children; and these we hope shortly to appoint to assist the master.

All who are there will be subject like ministers to ecclesiastical discipline.

There need be no other school in the city for the little children, but let the girls have their school apart, as has hitherto been the case.

Let no one be received if he is not approved by the ministers on their testimony, for fear of impropriety.

Concerning the Third Order Which Is That of Elders

Their office is to have oversight of the life of everyone, to admonish amicably those whom they see to be erring or to be living a disordered life, and, where it is required, to enjoin fraternal corrections themselves and along with others.

In the present condition of the Church, it would be good to elect two of the Little Council, four of the Council of Sixty, and six of the Council of Two Hundred, men of good and honest life, without reproach and beyond suspicion, and above all fearing God and possessing spiritual prudence. These should be so elected that there be some in every quarter of the city, to keep an eye on everybody.

The best way of electing them seems to be this, that the Little Council suggest the nomination of the best that can be found and the most suitable; and to do this, summon the ministers to confer with them; after this they should present those whom they would commend to the Council of Two Hundred, which will approve them. If it find them worthy, let them take the special oath, whose form will be readily drawn up. And at the end of the year, let them present themselves to the Seigneury for consideration whether they ought to be continued or changed. It is inexpedient that they be changed often without cause, so long as they discharge their duty faithfully.

The Fourth Order of Ecclesiastical Government, That Is, the Deacons

There were always two kinds in the ancient Church, the one deputed to receive, dispense and hold goods for the poor, not only daily alms, but also possessions, rents and pensions; the other to tend and care for the sick and administer allowances to the poor. This custom we follow again now for we have procurators and hospitallers.

The number of procurators appointed for this hospital seems to us to be proper; but we wish that there be also a separate reception office, so that not only provisions be in time made better, but that those who wish to do some charity may be more certain that the gift will not be employed otherwise than they intend. And if the revenue assigned by their Lordships be insufficient, or should extraordinary necessity arise, the Seigneury will advise about adjustment, according to the need they see.

The election of both procurators and hospitallers is to take place like that of the elders; and in electing them the rule proposed by Paul for deacons is to be followed.

With regard to the office of procurator, we think the rules which have already been imposed on them by us are good, by means of which, in urgent affairs, and where there is danger in deferment, and chiefly when there is no grave difficulty or question of great expense, they are not obliged always to be meeting, but one or two can do what is reasonable in the absence of the others.

It will be their duty to watch diligently that the public hospital is well maintained, and that this be so both for the sick and the old people unable to work, widowed women, orphaned children and other poor creatures. The sick are always to be lodged in a set of rooms separate from the other people who are unable to work, old men, widowed women, orphaned children and the other poor.

Moreover, care for the poor dispersed through the city should be revived, as the procurators may arrange it.

Moreover, besides the hospital for those passing through which must be maintained, there should be some attention given to any recognized as worthy of special charity. For this purpose, a special room should be set aside to receive those who ought to be assisted by the procurators, which is to be reserved for this business.

It should above all be demanded that the families of the hospitallers be honourably ruled in accordance with the will of God, since they have to govern houses dedicated to God.

The ministers must on their side enquire whether there be any lack or want of anything, in order to ask and desire the Seigneury to put it in order. To do this, some of their company with the procurators should visit the hospital every three months, to ascertain if all is in order.

It would be good, not only for the poor of the hospital, but also for those of the city who cannot help themselves, that they have a doctor and a surgeon of their own who should still practise in the city, but meanwhile be required to have care of the hospital and to visit the other poor.

As for the hospital for plague, it should be wholly separate and apart, and especially if it happen that the city be visited by this scourge of God.

For the rest, to discourage mendicancy which is contrary to good order, it would be well, and we have so ordered it, that there be one of our officials at the entrance of the churches to remove from the place those who loiter; and if there be any who give offence or offer insolence to bring them to one of the Lords Syndic. Similarly for the rest of the time, let the Overseers of Tens take care that the total prohibition of begging be well observed.

* * *

REVIEW QUESTIONS

1. What is the church according to Calvin?
2. What is its structure?
3. What do the four offices tell us about the function of the church?
4. What is the purpose of the church?
5. What are its goals?
6. What are the practices of the church and the relation of those practices to the process of becoming a Christian?
7. What is the relation between the church and salvation?

JOHN CALVIN

FROM Catechism of the Church of Geneva, Being a Form of Instruction for Children in the Doctrine of Christ, 1545

From *Treatises on the Sacraments: Tracts by John Calvin,* translated by Henry Beveridge (Tain, U.K.: Christian Focus Publications, 2003).

Dedication.

JOHN CALVIN TO THE FAITHFUL MINISTERS OF CHRIST THROUGHOUT EAST FRIESLAND, WHO PREACH THE PURE DOCTRINE OF THE GOSPEL.

Seeing it becomes us to endeavour by all means that unity of faith, which is so highly commended by Paul, shine forth among us, to this end chiefly ought the formal profession of faith which accompanies our common baptism to have reference. Hence it were to be wished, not only that a perpetual consent in the doctrine of piety should appear among all, but also that one CATECHISM were common to all the Churches. But as, from many causes, it will scarcely ever obtain otherwise than that each Church shall have its own Catechism, we should not strive too keenly to prevent this; provided, however, that the variety in the mode of teaching is such, that we are all directed to one Christ, in whose truth being united together, we may grow up into one body and one spirit, and with the same mouth also proclaim whatever belongs to the sum of faith. Catechists not intent on this end, besides fatally injuring the Church, by sowing the materials of dissension in religion, also introduce an impious profanation of baptism. For where can any longer be the utility of baptism unless this remain as its foundation—that we all agree in one faith?

Wherefore, those who publish Catechisms ought to be the more carefully on their guard, lest, by producing anything rashly, they may not for the present only, but in regard to posterity also, do grievous harm to piety, and inflict a deadly wound on the Church.

This much I wished to premise, as a declaration to my readers, that I myself too, as became me, have made it my anxious care not to deliver any thing in this Catechism of mine that is not agreeable to the doctrine received among all the pious. This declaration will not be found vain by those who will read with candour and sound judgment. I trust I have succeeded at least so far that my labour, though it should not satisfy, will be acceptable to all good men, as being in their opinion useful.

In writing it in Latin, though some perhaps will not approve of the design, I have been influenced by many reasons, all of which it is of no use to detail at present. I shall only select such as seem to me sufficient to obviate censure.

First, In this confused and divided state of Christendom, I judge it useful that there should be public testimonies, whereby churches which, though widely separated by space, agree in the doctrine of Christ, may mutually recognise each other. For besides that this tends not a little to mutual confirmation, what is more to be desired than that mutual congratulations should pass between them, and that they should devoutly commend each other to the Lord? With this view, bishops were wont in old time, when as yet consent in faith existed and flourished among all, to send Synodal Epistles beyond sea, by which, as a kind of badges, they might maintain sacred communion among the churches. How much more necessary is it now, in this fearful devastation of the Christian world, that the few churches which duly worship God, and they too scattered and hedged round on all sides by the profane synagogues of Antichrist, should mutually give and receive this token of holy union, that they may thereby be incited to that fraternal embrace of which I have spoken?

But if this is so necessary in the present day, what shall our feelings be concerning posterity, about which I am so anxious, that I scarcely dare to think? Unless God miraculously send help from heaven, I cannot avoid seeing that the world is threatened with the extremity of barbarism. I wish our children may not shortly feel, that this has been rather a true prophecy than a conjecture. The more, therefore, must we labour to gather together, by our writings, whatever remains of the Church shall continue, or even emerge, after our death. Writings of a different class will show what were our views on all subjects in religion, but the agreement which our churches had in doctrine cannot be seen with clearer evidence than from catechisms. For therein will appear, not only what one man or other once taught, but with what rudiments learned and unlearned alike amongst us, were constantly imbued from childhood, all the faithful holding them as their formal symbol of Christian communion. This was indeed my principal reason for publishing this Catechism.

A second reason, which had no little weight with me, was, because I heard that it was desired by very many who hoped it would not be unworthy of perusal. Whether they are right or wrong in so judging is not mine to decide, but it became me to yield to their wish. Nay, necessity was almost laid upon me, and I could not with impunity decline it. For having seven years before published a brief summary of religion, under the name of a Catechism, I feared that if I did not bring forward this one, I should cause (a thing I wished not) that the former should on the other hand be excluded. Therefore if I wished to consult the public good, it behoved me to take care that this one which I preferred should occupy the ground.

Besides, I deem it of good example to testify to the world, that we who aim at the restitution of the Church, are everywhere faithfully exerting ourselves, in order that, at least, the use of the Catechism which was abolished some centuries ago under the Papacy, may now resume its lost rights. For neither can this holy custom be sufficiently commended for its utility, nor can the Papists be sufficiently condemned for the flagrant corruption, by which they not only set it aside, by converting it into puerile trifles, but also basely abuse it to purposes of impure and impious superstition. That spurious Confirmation, which they have substituted in its stead, they deck out like a harlot, with great splendour of ceremonies, and gorgeous shows without number; nay, in their wish to adorn it, they speak of it in terms of execrable blasphemy, when they give out that it is a sacrament of greater dignity than baptism, and call those only half Christians who have not been besmeared with their oil. Meanwhile, the whole proceeding consists of nothing but theatrical gesticulations, or rather the wanton sporting of apes, without any skill in imitation.

To you, my very dear brethren in the Lord, I have chosen to inscribe this work, because some of your body, besides informing me that you love me, and that the most of you take delight in my writings, also expressly requested me by letter to undertake this labour for their sake. Independently of this, it would have been reason sufficient, that what I learned of you long ago, from the statement of grave and pious men, had bound me to you with my whole soul. I now ask what I am confident you will of your own accord do—have the goodness to consult for the utility of this token of my goodwill towards you! Farewell. May the Lord increase you more and more in the spirit of wisdom, prudence, zeal, and fortitude, to the edification of his Church.

GENEVA, *2d December*, 1545.

TO THE READER.

It has ever been the practice of the Church, and one carefully attended to, to see that children should be duly instructed in the Christian religion.

That this might be done more conveniently, not only were schools opened in old time, and individuals enjoined properly to teach their families, but it was a received public custom and practice, to question children in the churches on each of the heads, which should be common and well known to all Christians. To secure this being done in order, there was written out a formula, which was called a Catechism or Institute. Thereafter the devil miserably rending the Church of God, and bringing upon it fearful ruin, (of which the marks are still too visible in the greater part of the world,) overthrew this sacred policy, and left nothing behind but certain trifles, which only beget superstition, without any fruit of edification. Of this description is that confirmation, as they call it, full of gesticulations which, worse than ridiculous, are fitted only for apes, and have no foundation to rest upon. What we now bring forward, therefore, is nothing else than the use of things which from ancient times were observed by Christians, and the true worshippers of God, and which never were laid aside until the Church was wholly corrupted.

REVIEW QUESTIONS

1. What is the purpose of catechism for John Calvin, and how does his purpose differ from that of Martin Luther?
2. Who, according to Calvin, should be taught catechism, and who should do the teaching?
3. How did Calvin reconcile the unity of faith, which he hoped his catechism would serve, and the diversity of local circumstances and observances, which he expected would be the case?
4. What do this hope for unity and this admission of diversity tell us about the Reformation as Calvin understood it?
5. Using the catechism as a measure of the reformers' concerns and goals, how had these changed between 1530, when Luther published his *Large Catechism*, and 1545, when Calvin dedicated the *Catechism of the Church of Geneva*? Do the titles reveal anything?
6. Why did Calvin compose his catechism in Latin rather than a vernacular language, as did Martin Luther?

ST. IGNATIUS OF LOYOLA

FROM *The Spiritual Exercises*

St. Ignatius of Loyola (1491–1556), the great mystic and founder of the Society of Jesus, was born into a hidalgo family and spent his early manhood in military service to the king of Spain. Wounded in battle, he spent his convalescence reading the lives of saints, which awoke in him a sense of spiritual inadequacy not unlike those which fired the religious engagements of Martin Luther and John Calvin. His early attempts at reconciliation, in the form of physical austerities practiced on pilgrimage to Montserrat and in the hermitage at Manresa, failed to reassure him of his soul's salvation, just as they failed to ease the spiritual torments of the young Luther. The scholastically trained Luther sought solace in the systematic study of the Bible; the uneducated Loyola found it in visions of God. Loyola spent the next decade educating himself and seeking his mission. After a pilgrimage to the Holy Land in 1523, Loyola began his formal education by studying elementary Latin with schoolboys in

Barcelona. He attended the universities in Alcala and Salamanca, preached in the streets, and was arrested by the Inquisition on suspicion of heresy. He attended the University of Paris from 1528 to 1535 and began to gather around him the companions who would form the initial core of the Society of Jesus. In 1534, he and nine companions swore an oath of poverty and chastity and promised either to undertake a crusade to the Holy Land or, failing that, to offer absolute obedience to the pope. At the center of this group was not only the man Loyola but his series of devotions and meditations that would later be published as The Spiritual Exercises *(1548). These exercises offered a practical and ascetic meditation on the life and death of Christ that drew much from the systematic meditations of the* devotio moderna *("modern devotions"). It instructed those who made or directed a religious retreat in order to stimulate an imitation of Christ that would be expressed in apostolic action as well as religious devotion. In 1535, Loyola and his company left for Italy. He was ordained in Venice in 1537. Finding no passage to the Holy Land, they continued to Rome, where they preached in the streets and ministered to the poor. Introduced to Pope Paul III by Gasparo Contarini, a great advocate of monastic reform, the company received a charter of foundation as the Society of Jesus in 1540. Constituted an order of clerks regular, devoted to educating the young and propagating the faith, sworn to poverty and obedience, the Jesuits grew quickly to become one of the most influential Catholic orders of the early modern period, a model of piety, discipline, education, and service.*

From *The Spiritual Exercises of St. Ignatius,* translated by Anthony Mottola (New York: Doubleday, 1964), pp. 139–42.

Rules for Thinking with the Church

In order to have the proper attitude of mind in the Church Militant we should observe the following rules:

1. Putting aside all private judgment, we should keep our minds prepared and ready to obey promptly and in all things the true spouse of Christ our Lord, our Holy Mother, the hierarchical Church.

2. To praise sacramental confession and the reception of the Most Holy Sacrament once a year, and much better once a month, and better still every week, with the requisite and proper dispositions.

3. To praise the frequent hearing of Mass, singing of hymns and psalms, and the recitation of long prayers, both in and out of church; also the hours arranged for fixed times for the whole Divine Office, for prayers of all kinds and for the canonical hours.

4. To praise highly religious life, virginity, and continence; and also matrimony, but not as highly as any of the foregoing.

5. To praise the vows of religion, obedience, poverty, chastity, and other works of perfection and supererogation. It must be remembered that a vow is made in matters that lead to evangelical perfection. It is therefore improper to make a vow in matters that depart from this perfection; as, for example, to enter business, to get married, and so forth.

6. To praise the relics of the saints by venerating them and by praying to these saints. Also to praise the stations, pilgrimages, indulgences, jubilees, Crusade indulgences, and the lighting of candles in the churches.

7. To praise the precepts concerning fasts and

abstinences, such as those of Lent, Ember Days, Vigils, Fridays, and Saturdays; likewise to praise acts of penance, both interior and exterior.

8. To praise the adornments and buildings of churches as well as sacred images, and to venerate them according to what they represent.

9. Finally, to praise all the precepts of the Church, holding ourselves ready at all times to find reasons for their defense, and never offending against them.

10. We should be more inclined to approve and praise the directions and recommendations of our superiors as well as their personal behavior. Although sometimes these may not be or may not have been praiseworthy, to speak against them when preaching in public or in conversation with people would give rise to murmuring and scandal rather than to edification. As a result, the people would be angry with their superiors, whether temporal or spiritual. Still, while it does harm to our superiors in their absence to speak ill of them in the presence of the people, it might be useful to speak of their bad conduct to those who can apply a remedy.

11. To praise both positive and scholastic theology, for as it is more characteristic of the positive doctors, such as St. Augustine, St. Jerome, St. Gregory, and others, to encourage the affections to greater love and service of God our Lord in all things, so it also is more characteristic of the scholastic doctors, such as St. Thomas, St. Bonaventure, and the Master of the Sentences, etc., to define and explain for our times the things necessary for eternal salvation, and to refute and expose all errors and fallacies. Also, the scholastic doctors, being of more recent date, not only have a clearer understanding of the Holy Scripture and of the teachings of the positive and holy doctors, but also, being enlightened and inspired by the Divine Power, they are helped by the Councils, Canons, and Constitutions of our Holy Mother Church.

12. We must be on our guard against making comparisons between the living and those who have already gone to their reward, for it is no small error to say, for example: "This man knows more than St. Augustine"; "He is another St. Francis, or even greater"; "He is another St. Paul in goodness, holiness, etc."

13. If we wish to be sure that we are right in all things, we should always be ready to accept this principle: I will believe that the white that I see is black, if the hierarchical Church so defines it. For, I believe that between the Bridegroom, Christ our Lord, and the Bride, His Church, there is but one spirit, which governs and directs us for the salvation of our souls, for the same Spirit and Lord, who gave us the Ten Commandments, guides and governs our Holy Mother Church.

14. Although it be true that no one can be saved unless it be predestined and unless he have faith and grace, still we must be very careful of our manner of discussing and speaking of these matters.

15. We should not make predestination an habitual subject of conversation. If it is sometimes mentioned we must speak in such a way that no person will fall into error, as happens on occasion when one will say, "It has already been determined whether I will be saved or lost, and in spite of all the good or evil that I do, this will not be changed." As a result, they become apathetic and neglect the works that are conducive to their salvation and to the spiritual growth of their souls.

16. In like manner, we must be careful lest by speaking too much and with too great emphasis on faith, without any distinction or explanation, we give occasion to the people to become indolent and lazy in the performance of good works, whether it be before or after their faith is founded in charity.

17. Also in our discourse we ought not to emphasize the doctrine that would destroy free will. We may therefore speak of faith and grace to the extent that God enables us to do so, for the greater praise of His Divine Majesty. But, in these dangerous times of ours, it must not be done in such a way that good works or free will suffer any detriment or be considered worthless.

18. Although the generous service of God for motives of pure love should be most highly esteemed, we should praise highly the fear of His Divine

Majesty, for filial fear and even servile fear are pious and most holy things. When one cannot attain anything better or more useful, this fear is of great help in rising from mortal sin, and after this first step one easily advances to filial fear which is wholly acceptable and pleasing to God our Lord, since it is inseparable from Divine Love.

*   *   *

REVIEW QUESTIONS

1. What do you suppose Loyola means by the *church militant*?
2. How might the Jesuits have been soldiers of Christ?
3. Loyola asks the members of his order to "praise" in order to be "thinking with the Church." How does this serve the Church?
4. What specifically does Loyola ask the Jesuits to praise?
5. What do the "Rules for Thinking with the Church" tell us about the Church?

FRANCIS XAVIER

FROM "Letter from India"

St. Francis Xavier (1506–1552) was one of the original companions of St. Ignatius of Loyola and one of the original members of the Society of Jesus. The two became friends during their student years at the University of Paris. Shortly after the founding of the Society, Loyola sent Xavier on a mission to Portugal's mercantile empire in South Asia. After a voyage that lasted more than a year, he arrived in Goa on the Coromandel coast of India, accompanied by the Portuguese governor, Don Martin Afonso de Sousa, and two fellow missionaries, Father Paul and Francis Mancias, not yet in holy orders. It was at Sousa's behest that Xavier turn his attention to the pearl-fishing villages of Cape Comorin, in an effort to spread Christianity among those peoples and, so, bring them more fully into the Portuguese sphere of influence. It is from Comorin that Xavier writes the following letter. He would remain there two years before spreading his mission to the East Indies and Japan. He died in 1552, waiting to extend his work to China. His was a life of extraordinary hardship and danger as well as extraordinary activity and achievement. To him belongs credit for extending Roman Christianity and Western ideas to Asian peoples.

From *The Life and Letters of St Francis Xavier*, vol. 1, edited by Henry James Coleridge (2d ed.; London: Burns and Oates, 1890), pp. 151–63.

To the Society at Rome

May the grace and charity of Christ our Lord always help and favour us! Amen.

It is now the third year since I left Portugal. I am writing to you for the third time, having as yet received only one letter from you, dated February 1542. God is my witness what joy it caused me. I only received it two months ago—later than is usual for letters to reach India, because the vessel which brought it had passed the winter at Mozambique.

I and Francis Mancias are now living amongst the Christians of Comorin. They are very numerous, and increase largely every day. When I first came I asked them, if they knew anything about our Lord Jesus Christ? but when I came to the points of faith in detail and asked them what they thought of them, and what more they believed now than when they were Infidels, they only replied that they were Christians, but that as they are ignorant of Portuguese, they know nothing of the precepts and mysteries of our holy religion. We could not understand one another, as I spoke Castilian and they Malabar; so I picked out the most intelligent and well read of them, and then sought out with the greatest diligence men who knew both languages. We held meetings for several days, and by our joint efforts and with infinite difficulty we translated the Catechism into the Malabar tongue. This I learnt by heart, and then I began to go through all the villages of the coast, calling around me by the sound of a bell as many as I could, children and men. I asembled them twice a day and taught them the Christian doctrine: and thus, in the space of a month, the children had it well by heart. And all the time I kept telling them to go on teaching in their turn whatever they had learnt to their parents, family, and neighbours.

Every Sunday I collected them all, men and women, boys and girls, in the church. They came with great readiness and with a great desire for instruction. Then, in the hearing of all, I began by calling on the name of the most holy Trinity, Father, Son, and Holy Ghost, and I recited aloud the Lord's Prayer, the *Hail Mary*, and the Creed in the language of the country: they all followed me in the same words, and delighted in it wonderfully. Then I repeated the Creed by myself, dwelling upon each article singly. Then I asked them as to each article, whether they believed it unhesitatingly; and all, with a loud voice and their hands crossed over their breasts, professed aloud that they truly believed it. I take care to make them repeat the Creed oftener than the other prayers; and I tell them that those who believe all that is contained therein are called Christians. After explaining the Creed I go on to the Commandments, teaching them that the Christian law is contained in those ten precepts, and that every one who observes them all faithfully is a good and true Christian and is certain of eternal salvation, and that, on the other hand, whoever neglects a single one of them is a bad Christian, and will be cast into hell unless he is truly penitent for his sin. Converts and heathen alike are astonished at all this, which shows them the holiness of the Christian law, its perfect consistency with itself, and its agreement with reason. . . .

*   *   *

The fruit that is reaped by the baptism of infants, as well as by the instruction of children and others, is quite incredible. These children, I trust heartily, by the grace of God, will be much better than their fathers. They show an ardent love for the Divine law, and an extraordinary zeal for learning our holy religion and imparting it to others. Their hatred for idolatry is marvellous. They get into feuds with the heathen about it, and whenever their own parents practise it, they reproach them and come off to tell me at once. Whenever I hear of any act of idolatrous worship, I go to the place with a large band of these children, who very soon load the devil with a greater amount of insult and abuse than he has lately received of honour and worship from their parents, relations, and acquaintances. The children run at the idols, upset them, dash them down, break them to pieces, spit on them, trample on them, kick them about, and in short heap on them every possible outrage.

I had been living for nearly four months in a Christian village, occupied in translating the Catechism. A great number of natives came from all parts to entreat me to take the trouble to go to their houses and call on God by the bedsides of their sick relatives. Such numbers also of sick made their own way to us, that I had enough to do to read a Gospel over each of them. At the same time we kept on with our daily work, instructing the children, baptizing converts, translating the Catechism, answering difficulties, and burying the dead. For my part I desired to satisfy all, both the sick who came to me themselves, and those who came to beg on the part of others, lest if I did not, their confidence in, and zeal for, our holy religion should relax, and I thought it wrong not to do what I could in answer to their prayers. But the thing grew to such a pitch that it was impossible for me myself to satisfy all, and at the same time to avoid their quarrelling among themselves, every one striving to be the first to get me to his own house; so I hit on a way of serving all at once. As I could not go myself, I sent round children whom I could trust in my place. They went to the sick persons, assembled their families and neighbours, recited the Creed with them, and encouraged the sufferers to conceive a certain and wellfounded confidence of their restoration. Then after all this, they recited the prayers of the Church. To make my tale short, God was moved by the faith and piety of these children and of the others, and restored to a great number of sick persons health both of body and soul. How good He was to them! He made the very disease of their bodies the occasion of calling them to salvation, and drew them to the Christian faith almost by force!

I have also charged these children to teach the rudiments of Christian doctrine to the ignorant in private houses, in the streets, and the crossways. As soon as I see that this has been well started in one village, I go on to another and give the same instructions and the same commission to the children, and so I go through in order the whole number of their villages. When I have done this and am going away, I leave in each place a copy of the Christian doctrine, and tell all those who know

how to write to copy it out, and all the others are to learn it by heart and to recite it from memory every day. Every feast day I bid them meet in one place and sing all together the elements of the faith. For this purpose I have appointed in each of the thirty Christian villages men of intelligence and character who are to preside over these meetings, and the Governor, Don Martin Alfonso, who is so full of love for our Society and of zeal for religion, has been good enough at our request to allot a yearly revenue of 4000 gold *fanams* for the salary of these catechists. He has an immense friendship for ours, and desires with all his heart that some of them should be sent hither, for which he is always asking in his letters to the King.

* * *

We have in these parts a class of men among the pagans who are called Brahmins. They keep up the worship of the gods, the superstitious rites of religion, frequenting the temples and taking care of the idols. They are as perverse and wicked a set as can anywhere be found, and I always apply to them the words of holy David, "from an unholy race and a wicked and crafty man deliver me, O Lord." They are liars and cheats to the very backbone. Their whole study is, how to deceive most cunningly the simplicity and ignorance of the people. They give out publicly that the gods command certain offerings to be made to their temples, which offerings are simply the things that the Brahmins themselves wish for, for their own maintenance and that of their wives, children, and servants. Thus they make the poor folk believe that the images of their gods eat and drink, dine and sup like men, and some devout persons are found who really offer to the idol twice a day, before dinner and supper, a certain sum of money. The Brahmins eat sumptuous meals to the sound of drums, and make the ignorant believe that the gods are banqueting. When they are in need of any supplies, and even before, they give out to the people that the gods are angry because the things they have asked for have not been sent, and that if the people do not take care, the gods will punish them by slaughter, disease, and the assaults of the devils.

And the poor ignorant creatures, with the fear of the gods before them, obey them implicitly. ✳ ✳ ✳

The heathen inhabitants of the country are commonly ignorant of letters, but by no means ignorant of wickedness. All the time I have been here in this country I have only converted one Brahmin, a virtuous young man, who has now undertaken to teach the Catechism to children. As I go through the Christian villages, I often pass by the temples of the Brahmins, which they call pagodas. One day lately, I happened to enter a pagoda where there were about two hundred of them, and most of them came to meet me. We had a long conversation, after which I asked them what their gods enjoined them in order to obtain the life of the blessed. There was a long discussion amongst them as to who should answer me. At last, by common consent, the commission was given to one of them, of greater age and experience than the rest, an old man, of more than eighty years. He asked me in return, what commands the God of the Christians laid on them. I saw the old man's perversity, and I refused to speak a word till he had first answered my question. So he was obliged to expose his ignorance, and replied that their gods required two duties of those who desired to go to them hereafter, one of which was to abstain from killing cows, because under that form the gods were adored; the other was to show kindness to the Brahmins, who were the worshippers of the gods. This answer moved my indignation, for I could not but grieve intensely at the thought of the devils being worshipped instead of God by these blind heathen, and I asked them to listen to me in turn. Then I, in a loud voice, repeated the Apostles' Creed and the Ten Commandments. After this I gave in their own language a short explanation, and told them what Paradise is, and what Hell is, and also who they are who go to Heaven to join the company of the blessed, and who are to be sent to the eternal punishments of hell. Upon hearing these things they all rose up and vied with one another in embracing me, and in confessing that the God of the Christians is the true God, as His laws are so agreeable to reason. Then they asked me if the souls of men like those of other animals perished together with the body. God put into my mouth arguments of such a sort, and so suited to their ways of thinking, that to their great joy I was able to prove to them the immortality of the soul. I find, by the way, that the arguments which are to convince these ignorant people must by no means be subtle, such as those which are found in the books of learned schoolmen, but must be such as their minds can understand. They asked me again how the soul of a dying person goes out of the body, how it was, whether it was as happens to us in dreams, when we seem to be conversing with our friends and acquaintance? (Ah, how often this happens to me, dearest brothers, when I am dreaming of you!) Was this because the soul then leaves the body? And again, whether God was black or white? For as there is so great a variety of colour among men, and the Indians being black themselves, consider their own colour the best, they believe that their gods are black. On this account the great majority of their idols are as black as black can be, and moreover are generally so rubbed over with oil as to smell detestably, and seem to be as dirty as they are ugly and horrible to look at. To all these questions I was able to reply so as to satisfy them entirely. But when I came to the point at last, and urged them to embrace the religion which they felt to be true, they made that same objection which we hear from many Christians when urged to change their life,—that they would set men talking about them if they altered their ways and their religion, and besides, they said that they should be afraid that, if they did so, they would have nothing to live on and support themselves by.

I have found just one Brahmin and no more in all this coast who is a man of learning: he is said to have studied in a very famous Academy. Knowing this, I took measures to converse with him alone. He then told me at last, as a great secret, that the students of this Academy are at the outset made by their masters to take an oath not to reveal their mysteries, but that, out of friendship for me, he would disclose them to me. One of these mysteries was that there only exists one God, the Creator and Lord of heaven and earth, whom men are bound to worship, for the idols are simply images of devils,

The Brahmins have certain books of sacred literature which contain, as they say, the laws of God. The masters teach in a learned tongue, as we do in Latin. He also explained to me these divine precepts one by one; but it would be a long business to write out his commentary, and indeed not worth the trouble. Their sages keep as a feast our Sunday. On this day they repeat at different hours this one player: "I adore Thee, O God; and I implore Thy help for ever." They are bound by oath to repeat this prayer frequently, and in a low voice. My friend added, that the law of nature permitted them to have more wives than one, and their sacred books predicted that the time would come when all men should embrace the same religion. After all this he asked me in my turn to explain the principal mysteries of the Christian religion, promising to keep them secret. I replied, that I would not tell him a word about them unless he promised beforehand to publish abroad what I should tell him of the religion of Jesus Christ. He made the promise, and then I carefully explained to him those words of Jesus Christ in which our religion is summed up: "He who believes and is baptized shall be saved." This text, with my commentary on it, which embraced the whole of the Apostles' Creed, he wrote down carefully, as well as the Commandments, on account of their close connection with the Creed. He told me also that one night he had dreamt that he had been made a Christian to his immense delight, and that he had become my brother and companion. He ended by begging me to make him a Christian secretly. But as he made certain conditions opposed to right and justice, I put off his baptism. I don't doubt but that by God's mercy he will one day be a Christian. I charged him to teach the ignorant and unlearned that there is only one God, Creator of heaven and earth; but he pleaded the obligation of his oath, and said he could not do so, especially as he was much afraid that if he did it he should become possessed by an evil spirit. ✳ ✳ ✳

REVIEW QUESTIONS

1. What was involved in the conversion of Asian peoples to Christianity?
2. What were the greatest challenges that Xavier and his fellows confronted?
3. How did Xavier's values shape his perception of Asian peoples?
4. How would you describe the reception of Christian missionaries and Christianity among the people of Cape Comorin?
5. How might Xavier and his mission have shaped the interaction and understanding of East and West?

ST. TERESA OF AVILA

FROM *The Life of Teresa of Jesus*

St. Teresa of Avila (1515–1582) was a Spanish mystic, spiritual author, and monastic reformer. Her worldly achievements were great, to which the Discalced Carmelites still bear witness; in addition, the beauty of her inner life, as revealed in her writings, earned her recognition as one of the world's great female religious authors. Teresa was born in central Spain, the daughter of a wealthy hidalgo. At age fourteen, she was sent to a boarding school, where she became ill and began to consider her life's vocation. Despite paternal opposition, Teresa became a novice in a Carmelite convent around 1535. Her health collapsed again, leaving her an invalid for three years. During her convalescence, she began the series of meditations that would establish her reputation as a mystic. It took fifteen years to perfect the prayers and meditations that would lead to her ecstatic visions and conversations with God. Her most celebrated work, The Life, *written in obedience to her confessors and directors, captured this process as the history of a soul, much like Augustine's* Confessions. *They combine religious ardor with human candor, an insistence that her experiences were a gift of God with an unwillingness to claim any spiritual distinction.*

In 1558, Teresa began to consider the restoration of Carmelite life to its original observance of austerity. It required complete separation from the world to promote prayerful meditation, such as was enjoined in the Primitive Carmelite Rule of 1247. In 1562, with the authorization of Pope Pius IV, Teresa and four companions opened the first convent of the Carmelite reform. Despite intense opposition from secular and ecclesiastical officials, her efforts eventually won the approval of the Carmelite general as well as his mandate to extend her reform to men. In 1567, she met a young Carmelite priest, Juan de Yepes, later canonized as St. John of the Cross, a brilliant friar who helped her initiate the Carmelite reform for men. In her lifetime, she saw sixteen convents and twelve monasteries established. The last decades of her life were given to this work. Forty years after her death, she was canonized; in 1970, she was made a doctor of the Church.

From *The Life of Theresa of Jesus: The Autobiography of Teresa of Avila*, translated by E. Allison Peters (New York: Bantam Doubleday Dell, 1991), pp. 68–71.

*   *   *

I have strayed far from any intention, for I was trying to give the reasons why this kind of vision cannot be the work of the imagination. How could we picture Christ's Humanity by merely studying the subject or form any impression of His great beauty by means of the imagination? No little time would be necessary if such a reproduction was to be in the least like the original. One can indeed make such a picture with one's imagination, and spend time in regarding it, and considering the form and the brilliance of it; little by little one may even learn to perfect such an image and store it up in the memory. Who can prevent this? Such a picture can undoubtedly be fashioned with the understanding. But with regard to the vision which we are discussing there is no way of doing this: we have to look at it when the Lord is pleased to reveal it to us—to look as He wills and at whatever He wills. And there is no possibility of our subtracting from it or adding to it, or any way in which we can obtain it, whatever we may do, or look at it when we like or refrain from looking at it. If we try to look at any particular part of it, we at once lose Christ.

For two years and a half things went on like this and it was quite usual for God to grant me this favour. It must now be more than three years since He took it from me as a continually recurring favour, by giving me something else of a higher kind, which I shall describe later. Though I saw that He was speaking to me, and though I was looking upon that great beauty of His, and experiencing the sweetness with which He uttered those words—sometimes stern words—with that most lovely and Divine mouth, and though, too, I was extremely desirous of observing the colour of His eyes, or His height, so that I should be able to describe it, I have never been sufficiently worthy to see this, nor has it been of any use for me to attempt to do so; if I tried, I lost the vision altogether. Though I sometimes see Him looking at me compassionately, His gaze has such power that my soul cannot endure it and remains in so sublime a rapture that it loses this beauteous vision in order to have the greater fruition of it all. So there is no question here of our wanting or not wanting to see the vision. It is clear that the Lord wants of us only humility and shame, our acceptance of what is given us and our praise of its Giver.

This refers to all visions, none excepted. There is nothing that we can do about them; we cannot see more or less of them at will; and we can neither call them up nor banish them by our own efforts. The Lord's will is that we shall see quite clearly that they are produced, not by us but by His Majesty. Still less can we be proud of them: on the contrary, they make us humble and fearful, when we find that, just as the Lord takes from us the power of seeing what we desire, so He can also take from us these favours and His grace, with the result that we are completely lost. So while we live in this exile let us always walk with fear.

Almost invariably the Lord showed Himself to me in His resurrection body, and it was thus, too, that I saw Him in the Host. Only occasionally, to strengthen me when I was in tribulation, did He show me His wounds, and then He would appear sometimes as He was on the Cross and sometimes as in the Garden. On a few occasions I saw Him wearing the crown of thorns and sometimes He would also be carrying the Cross—because of my necessities, as I say, and those of others—but always in His glorified flesh. Many are the affronts and trials that I have suffered through telling this and many are the fears and persecutions that it has brought me. So sure were those whom I told of it that I had a devil that some of them wanted to exorcize me. This troubled me very little, but I was sorry when I found that my confessors were afraid to hear my confessions or when I heard that people were saying things to them against me. None the less, I could never regret having seen these heavenly visions and I would not exchange them for all the good things and delights of this world. I always considered them a great favour from the Lord, and I think they were the greatest of treasures; often the Lord Himself would reas-

sure me about them. I found my love for Him growing exceedingly: I used to go to Him and tell Him about all these trials and I always came away from prayer comforted and with new strength. I did not dare to argue with my critics, because I saw that that made things worse, as they thought me lacking in humility. With my confessor, however, I did discuss these matters; and whenever he saw that I was troubled he would comfort me greatly.

As the visions became more numerous, one of those who had previously been in the habit of helping me and who used sometimes to hear my confessions when the minister was unable to do so, began to say that it was clear I was being deceived by the devil. So, as I was quite unable to resist it, they commanded me to make the sign of the Cross whenever I had a vision, and to snap my fingers at it so as to convince myself that it came from the devil, whereupon it would not come again. I was not to be afraid, they said, and God would protect me and take the vision away. This caused me great distress: as I could not help believing that my visions came from God, it was a terrible thing to have to do; and, as I have said, I could not possibly wish them to be taken from me. However, I did as they commanded me. I besought God often to set me free from deception; indeed, I was continually doing so and with many tears. I would also invoke Saint Peter and Saint Paul, for the Lord had told me (it was on their festival that He had first appeared to me) that they would prevent me from being deluded; and I used often to see them very clearly on my left hand, though not in an imaginary vision. These glorious Saints were in a very real sense my lords.

To be obliged to snap my fingers at a vision in which I saw the Lord caused me the sorest distress. For, when I saw Him before me, I could not have believed that the vision had come from the devil even if the alternative were my being cut to pieces. So this was a kind of penance to me, and a heavy one. In order not to have to be so continually crossing myself, I would carry a cross in my hand. This I did almost invariably; but I was not so particular about snapping my fingers at the vision, for it hurt me too much to do that. It reminded me of the way the Jews had insulted Him, and I would beseech Him to forgive me, since I did it out of obedience to him who was in His own place, and not to blame me, since he was one of the ministers whom He had placed in His Church. He told me not to worry about it and said I was quite right to obey, but He would see that my confessor learned the truth. When they made me stop my prayer He seemed to me to have become angry, and He told me to tell them that this was tyranny. He used to show me ways of knowing that the visions were not of the devil; some of these I shall describe later.

*   *   *

REVIEW QUESTIONS

1. What distinguishes Teresa's spirituality from that of Ignatius of Loyola?
2. Might we call her spirituality feminine?
3. Is Teresa's piety private or public? In what ways?
4. Are visions portable?
5. Are they entirely private?
6. How does language fail Teresa?

FROM *Canons and Decrees of the Council of Trent*

The great centerpiece of Catholic reform and reaction was the ecumenical Council of Trent, held in several sessions between 1545 and 1563. From the beginning of the sixteenth century, Catholic clergy, secular leaders, and Protestant reformers had called for an ecumenical council to address the inadequacies of the Catholic Church. Popes had resisted the tactic just as insistently for fear that such a council might be used to limit papal authority, as, indeed, had been the case in the fifteenth century. Pope Paul III, however, realized that a council might serve the cause of papal authority as well as that of church reform and accordingly called a council to meet in the city of Trent, located in imperial territory but still close to Rome. Agreements on procedures and the leadership of papal legates assured that the council remained firmly under papal direction and set a tone of doctrinal and disciplinary conservatism. Its deliberations and decisions divide themselves into three great periods. The first period, 1545–1547, was devoted to dogma. The council rejected the Protestant teaching on scripture as the sole source of religious truth and insisted that scripture and tradition were equally authoritative. It retained the traditional seven sacraments. Most important, it rejected the Protestant doctrine of justification. During the second period, 1551–1552, the council reasserted the traditional Catholic teaching on the Eucharist, rejecting the interpretations of Luther, Zwingli, and Calvin. Long delayed by political events and papal indifference, the council reconvened for the third and last time in 1562. In its final year, the council defined the Mass, addressed various liturgical issues, and resolved disciplinary issues such as clerical residency and training. Viewed in its entirety, the Council of Trent strengthened the authority of the papacy in the Catholic Church. If its decrees and canons were largely conservative, they were also unmistakable in their clarity and uniformity. In its pronouncements on discipline, it laid the foundations for a better educated, more conscientious clergy. The Council of Trent clearly defined Catholic Christianity in opposition to Protestantism.

From *Canons and Decrees of the Council of Trent,* translated by H. J. Schroeder (London: Herder, 1941).

*   *   *

Fourth Session
Celebrated on the Eighth Day
of April 1546

DECREE CONCERNING THE CANONICAL SCRIPTURES

The holy, ecumenical and general Council of Trent, lawfully assembled in the Holy Ghost, the same three legates of the Apostolic See presiding, keeps this constantly in view, namely, that the purity of the Gospel may be preserved in the Church after the errors have been removed. This, of old promised through the Prophets in the Holy Scriptures, our Lord Jesus Christ, the Son of God, promulgated first with His own mouth, and then commanded it to be preached by His Apostles to every creature as the source at once of all saving truth and rules of conduct. It also clearly perceives that these truths and rules are contained in the written books and in the unwritten traditions, which, received by the Apostles from the mouth of Christ Himself, or from the Apostles themselves, the Holy Ghost dictating, have come down to us, transmitted as it were from hand to hand. Following, then, the examples of the orthodox Fathers, it receives and venerates with a feeling of piety and reverence all the books both of the Old and New Testaments, since one God is the author of both; also the traditions, whether they relate to faith or to morals, as having been dictated either orally by Christ or by the Holy Ghost, and preserved in the Catholic Church in unbroken suc-

cession. It has thought it proper, moreover, to insert in this decree a list of the sacred books, lest a doubt might arise in the mind of someone as to which are the books received by this council. They are the following: of the Old Testament, the five books of Moses, namely, Genesis, Exodus, Leviticus, Numbers, Deuteronomy; Josue, Judges, Ruth, the four books of Kings, two of Paralipomenon, the first and second of Esdras, the latter of which is called Nehemias, Tobias, Judith, Esther, Job, the Davidic Psalter of 150 Psalms, Proverbs, Ecclesiastes, the Canticle of Canticles, Wisdom, Ecclesiasticus, Isaias, Jeremias, with Baruch, Ezechiel, Daniel, the twelve minor Prophets, namely, Osee, Joel, Amos, Abdias, Jonas, Micheas, Nahum, Habacuc, Sophonias, Aggeus, Zacharias, Malachias; two books of Machabees, the first and second. Of the New Testament, the four Gospels, according to Matthew, Mark, Luke and John; the Acts of the Apostles written by Luke the Evangelist; fourteen Epistles of Paul the Apostle, to the Romans, two to the Corinthians, to the Galatians, to the Ephesians, to the Philippians, to the Colossians, two to the Thessalonians, two to Timothy, to Titus, to Philemon, to the Hebrews; two of Peter the Apostle, three of John the Apostle, one of James the Apostle, one of Jude the Apostle, and the Apocalypse of John the Apostle. If anyone does not accept as sacred and canonical the aforesaid books in their entirety and with all their parts, as they have been accustomed to be read in the Catholic Church and as they are contained in the old Latin Vulgate Edition, and knowingly and deliberately rejects the aforesaid traditions, let him be anathema. Let all understand, therefore, in what order and manner the council, after having laid the foundation of the confession of faith, will proceed, and who are the chief witnesses and supports to whom it will appeal in confirming dogmas and in restoring morals in the Church.

DECREE CONCERNING THE EDITION AND USE OF THE SACRED BOOKS

Moreover, the same holy council considering that not a little advantage will accrue to the Church of God if it be made known which of all the Latin editions of the sacred books now in circulation is to be regarded as authentic, ordains and declares that the old Latin Vulgate Edition, which, in use for so many hundred years, has been approved by the Church, be in public lectures, disputations, sermons and expositions held as authentic, and that no one dare or presume under any pretext whatsoever to reject it.

Furthermore, to check unbridled spirits, it decrees that no one relying on his own judgment shall, in matters of faith and morals pertaining to the edification of Christian doctrine, distorting the Holy Scriptures in accordance with his own conceptions, presume to interpret them contrary to that sense which holy mother Church, to whom it belongs to judge of their true sense and interpretation, has held and holds, or even contrary to the unanimous teaching of the Fathers, even though such interpretations should never at any time be published. Those who act contrary to this shall be made known by the ordinaries and punished in accordance with the penalties prescribed by the law.

And wishing, as is proper, to impose a restraint in this matter on printers also, who, now without restraint, thinking what pleases them is permitted them, print without the permission of ecclesiastical superiors the books of the Holy Scriptures and the notes and commentaries thereon of all persons indiscriminately, often with the name of the press omitted, often also under a fictitious press-name, and what is worse, without the name of the author, and also indiscreetly have for sale such books printed elsewhere, this council

decrees and ordains that in the future the Holy Scriptures, especially the old Vulgate Edition, be printed in the most correct manner possible, and that it shall not be lawful for anyone to print or to have printed any books whatsoever dealing with sacred doctrinal matters without the name of the author, or in the future to sell them, or even to have them in possession, unless they have first been examined and approved by the ordinary, under penalty of anathema and fine prescribed by the last Council of the Lateran. If they be regulars they must in addition to this examination and approval obtain permission also from their own superiors after these have examined the books in accordance with their own statutes. Those who lend or circulate them in manuscript before they have been examined and approved, shall be subject to the same penalties as the printers, and those who have them in their possession or read them, shall, unless they make known the authors, be themselves regarded as the authors. The approbation of such books, however, shall be given in writing and shall appear authentically at the beginning of the book, whether it be written or printed, and all this, that is, both the examination and approbation, shall be done gratuitously, so that what ought to be approved may be approved and what ought to be condemned may be condemned.

Furthermore, wishing to repress that boldness whereby the words and sentences of the Holy Scriptures are turned and twisted to all kinds of profane usages, namely, to things scurrilous, fabulous, vain, to flatteries, detractions, superstitions, godless and diabolical incantations, divinations, the casting of lots and defamatory libels, to put an end to such irreverence and contempt, and that no one may in the future dare use in any manner the words of Holy Scripture for these and similar purposes, it is commanded and enjoined that all people of this kind be restrained by the bishops as violators and profaners of the word of God, with the penalties of the law and other penalties that they may deem fit to impose.

*   *   *

**Twenty-third Session
Which Is the Seventh under the
Supreme Pontiff, Pius IV, Celebrated
on the Fifteenth Day of July 1563
The True and Catholic Doctrine
Concerning the Sacrament of Order,
Defined and Published by the
Holy Council of Trent in the Seventh
Session in Condemnation
of Current Errors**

FROM CHAPTER I
THE INSTITUTION OF THE PRIESTHOOD OF THE NEW LAW

Sacrifice and priesthood are by the ordinance of God so united that both have existed in every law. Since therefore in the New Testament the Catholic Church has received from the institution of Christ the holy, visible sacrifice of the Eucharist, it must also be confessed that there is in that Church a new, visible and external priesthood, into which the old has been translated. That this was instituted by the same Lord our Savior, and that to the Apostles and their successors in the priesthood was given the power of consecrating, offering and administering His body and blood, as also of forgiving and retaining sins, is shown by the Sacred Scriptures and has always been taught by the tradition of the Catholic Church.

CHAPTER II
THE SEVEN ORDERS

But since the ministry of so holy a priesthood is something divine, that it might be exercised in a more worthy manner and with greater veneration, it was consistent that in the most well-ordered arrangement of the Church there should be several distinct orders of ministers, who by virtue of their office should minister to the priesthood, so distributed that those already having the clerical tonsure should ascend through the minor to the major orders. For the Sacred Scriptures mention unmistakably not only the priests but also the deacons, and teach in the most definite words what is especially to be observed in their ordination; and from the very beginning of the Church the names of the following orders and the duties proper to each one are known to have been in use, namely, those of the subdeacon, acolyte, exorcist, lector and porter, though these were not of equal rank; for the subdiaconate is classed among the major orders by the Fathers and holy councils, in which we also read very often of other inferior orders.

CHAPTER III
THE ORDER OF THE PRIESTHOOD IS TRULY A SACRAMENT

Since from the testimony of Scripture, Apostolic tradition and the unanimous agreement of the Fathers it is clear that grace is conferred by sacred ordination, which is performed by words and outward signs, no one ought to doubt that order is truly and properly one of the seven sacraments of holy Church. For the Apostle says: *I admonish thee that thou stir up the grace of God which is in thee by the imposition of my hands. For God has not given us the spirit of fear, but of power and of love and of sobriety.*

CHAPTER IV
THE ECCLESIASTICAL HIERARCHY AND ORDINATION

But since in the sacrament of order, as also in baptism and confirmation, a character is imprinted which can neither be effaced nor taken away, the holy council justly condemns the opinion of those who say that the priests of the New Testament have only a temporary power, and that those who have once been rightly ordained can again become laymen if they do not exercise the ministry of the word of God. And if anyone should assert that all Christians without distinction are priests of the New Testament, or that they are all *inter se* endowed with an equal spiritual power, he seems to do nothing else than derange the ecclesiastical hierarchy, which is *an army set in array*, as if, contrary to the teaching of St. Paul, all are apostles, all prophets, all evangelists, all pastors, all doctors. Wherefore, the holy council declares that, besides the other ecclesiastical grades, the bishops, who have succeeded the Apostles, principally belong to this hierarchical order, and have been placed, as the same Apostle says, by the Holy Ghost to rule the Church of God; that they are superior to priests, administer the sacrament of confirmation, ordain ministers of the Church, and can perform many other functions over which those of an inferior order have no power. The council teaches furthermore, that in the ordination of bishops, priests and the other orders, the consent, call or authority, whether of the people or of any civil power or magistrate is not required in such wise that without this the ordination is invalid; rather does it decree that all those who, called and instituted only by the people or by the civil power or magistrate, ascend to the exercise of these offices, and those who by their rashness assume them, are not ministers of the Church, but are to be regarded as thieves and robbers, who have not entered by the door. These are the things which in general it has seemed good to the holy council to teach to the faithful of Christ regarding the sacrament of order. The contrary, however, it has resolved to condemn in definite and appropriate canons in the following manner, in order that all, making use with the help of Christ of the rule of faith, may in the midst of the darkness of so many errors recognize more easily the Catholic truth and adhere to it.

CANONS ON THE SACRAMENT OF ORDER

Canon 1. If anyone says that there is not in the New Testament a visible and external priesthood, or that there is no power of consecrating and offering the true body and blood of the Lord and of forgiving and retaining sins, but only the office and bare ministry of preaching the Gospel; or that those who do not preach are not priests at all, let him be anathema.

Canon 2. If anyone says that besides the priesthood there are not in the Catholic Church other orders, both major and minor, by which, as by certain steps, advance is made to the priesthood, let him be anathema.

Canon 3. If anyone says that order or sacred ordination is not truly and properly a sacrament instituted by Christ the Lord, or that it is some human contrivance devised by men unskilled in ecclesiastical matters, or that it is only a certain rite for choosing ministers of the word of God and of the sacraments, let him be anathema.

Canon 4. If anyone says that by sacred ordination the Holy Ghost is not imparted and that therefore the bishops say in vain: *Receive ye the Holy Ghost*, or that by it a character is not imprinted, or that he who has once been a priest can again become a layman, let him be anathema.

Canon 5. If anyone says that the holy unction which the Church uses in ordination is not only not required but is detestable and pernicious, as also are the other ceremonies of order, let him be anathema.

Canon 6. If anyone says that in the Catholic Church there is not instituted a hierarchy by divine ordinance, which consists of bishops, priests and ministers, let him be anathema.

Canon 7. If anyone says that bishops are not superior to priests, or that they have not the power to confirm and ordain, or that the power which they have is common to them and to priests, or that orders conferred by them without the consent or call of the people or of the secular power are invalid, or that those who have been neither rightly ordained nor sent by ecclesiastical and canonical authority, but come from elsewhere, are lawful ministers of the word and of the sacraments, let him be anathema.

Canon 8. If anyone says that the bishops who are chosen by the authority of the Roman pontiff are not true and legitimate bishops, but merely human deception, let him be anathema.

*　　*　　*

Twenty-fifth Session Which Is the Ninth and Last under the Supreme Pontiff, Pius IV, Begun on the Third and Closed on the Fourth Day of December 1563

DECREE CONCERNING PURGATORY

Since the Catholic Church, instructed by the Holy Ghost, has, following the sacred writings and the ancient tradition of the Fathers, taught in sacred councils and very recently in this ecumenical council that there is a purgatory, and that the souls there detained are aided by the suffrages of the faithful and chiefly by the acceptable sacrifice of the altar, the holy council commands the bishops that they strive diligently to the end that the sound doctrine of purgatory, transmitted by the Fathers and sacred councils, be believed and maintained by the faithful of Christ, and be everywhere taught and preached. The more difficult and subtle questions, however, and those that do not make for edification and from which there is for the most part no increase in piety, are to be excluded from popular instructions to uneducated people. Likewise, things that are uncertain or that have the appearance of falsehood they shall not permit to be made known publicly and discussed. But those things that tend to a certain kind of curiosity or superstition, or that savor of filthy lucre, they shall prohibit as scandals and stumbling blocks to the faithful. The bishops shall see to it that the suffrages of the living, that is, the sacrifice of the mass, prayers, alms and other works of piety which they have been accustomed to perform for the faithful departed, be piously and devoutly discharged in accordance with the laws of the Church, and that whatever is due on their behalf from testamentary bequests or other ways, be discharged by the priests and ministers of the Church and others who are bound to render this service not in a perfunctory manner, but diligently and accurately.

ON THE INVOCATION, VENERATION, AND RELICS OF SAINTS, AND ON SACRED IMAGES

The holy council commands all bishops and others who hold the office of teaching and have charge of the *cura animarum,* that in accordance with the usage of the Catholic and Apostolic Church, received from the primitive times of the Christian religion, and with the unanimous teaching of the holy Fathers and the decrees of sacred councils, they above all instruct the faithful diligently in matters relating to intercession and invocation of the saints, the veneration of relics, and the legitimate use of images, teaching them that the saints who reign together with Christ offer up their prayers to God for men, that it is good and beneficial suppliantly to invoke them and to have recourse to their prayers, assistance and support in order to obtain favors from God through His Son, Jesus Christ our Lord, who alone is our redeemer and savior; and that they think impiously who deny that the saints who enjoy eternal happiness in heaven are to be invoked, or who assert that they do not pray for men, or that our invocation of them to pray for each of us individually is idolatry, or that it is opposed to the word of God and inconsistent with the honor of the *one mediator of God and men, Jesus Christ,* or that it is foolish to pray vocally or mentally to those who reign in heaven. Also, that the holy bodies of the holy martyrs and of others living with Christ, which were the living members of Christ and the temple of the Holy Ghost, to be awakened by Him to eternal life and to be glorified, are to be venerated by the faithful, through which many benefits are bestowed by God on men, so that those who maintain that veneration and honor are not due to the relics of the saints, or that these and other memorials are honored by the faithful without profit, and that the places dedicated to the memory of the saints for the purpose of obtaining their aid are visited in vain, are to be utterly condemned, as the Church has already long since condemned and now again condemns them. Moreover, that the images of Christ, of the Virgin Mother of God, and of the other saints are to be placed and retained especially in the churches, and that due honor and veneration is to be given them; not, however, that any divinity or virtue is believed to be in them by reason of which they are to be venerated, or that something is to be asked of them, or that trust is to be placed in images, as was done of old by the Gentiles who placed their hope in idols; but because the honor which is shown them is referred to the prototypes which they represent, so that by means of the images which we kiss and before which we uncover the head and prostrate ourselves, we adore Christ and venerate the saints whose likeness they bear. That is what was defined by the decrees of the councils, especially of the Second Council of Nicaea, against the opponents of images.

Moreover, let the bishops diligently teach that by means of the stories of the mysteries of our redemption portrayed in paintings and other representations the people are instructed and confirmed in the articles of faith, which ought to be borne in mind and constantly reflected upon; also that great profit is derived from all holy images, not only because the people are thereby reminded of the benefits and gifts bestowed on them by Christ, but also because through the saints the miracles of God and salutary examples are set before the eyes of the faithful, so that they may give God thanks for those things, may fashion their own life and conduct in imitation of the saints and be moved to adore and love God and cultivate piety. But if anyone should teach or maintain any thing contrary to these decrees, let him be anathema. If any abuses shall have found their way into these holy and salutary observances, the holy council desires earnestly that they be completely removed, so that no representation of false doctrines and such as might be the occasion of grave error to the uneducated be exhibited. And if at times it happens, when this is beneficial to the illiterate, that the stories and narratives of the Holy Scriptures are portrayed and exhibited, the people should be instructed that not for that reason is the divinity represented in picture as if it can be seen with bodily eyes or expressed in colors or figures. Furthermore, in the invocation of the saints, the veneration of relics, and the sacred use of images, all superstition shall be removed, all filthy quest for gain eliminated, and all lasciviousness avoided, so that images shall not be painted and adorned with a seductive charm, or the celebration of saints and the visitation of relics be perverted by the people into boisterous festivities and drunkenness, as if the festivals in honor of the saints are to be celebrated with revelry and with no sense of decency. Finally, such zeal and care should be exhibited by the bishops with regard to these things that nothing may appear that is disorderly or unbecoming and confusedly arranged, nothing that is profane, nothing disrespectful, since holiness becometh the house of God. That these things may be the more faithfully observed, the holy council decrees that no one is permitted to erect or cause to be erected in any place or church, howsoever exempt, any unusual image unless it has been approved by the bishop; also that no new miracles be accepted and no relics recognized unless they have been investigated and approved by the same bishop, who, as soon as he has obtained any knowledge of such matters, shall, after consulting theologians and other pious men, act thereon as he shall judge consonant with truth and piety. But if any doubtful or grave abuse is to be eradicated, or if indeed any graver question concerning these matters should arise, the bishop, before he settles the controversy, shall await the decision of the metropolitan and of the bishops of the province in a provincial synod; so, however, that nothing new or anything that has not hitherto been in use in the Church, shall be decided upon without having first consulted the most holy Roman pontiff.

*   *   *

Review Qustions

1. How does the Council of Trent approach the question of the authority of Scripture?
2. Why did it set that discussion in terms of a list of books the council recognized as sacred?

3. On what basis might the council claim the authority to name the books of the Bible and determine the correct translation?

4. What are the seven orders? What is their place in Christianity and their function? What is the nature of their authority?

5. What do these decrees suggest about the practice of Catholicism in the years following the Reformation?

GIOVANNI MICHIEL

FROM A Venetian Ambassador's Report on the St. Bartholomew's Day Massacre

The struggle for supremacy in northern Italy, which marked the last half of the fifteenth century, gave rise to a new form of diplomacy, including structures and procedures that would be fundamental to relations among all modern states. Requiring continuous contact and communication, Renaissance states turned to permanent diplomacy, distinguished by the use of accredited resident ambassadors rather than ad hoc missions of medieval legates. The tasks of a permanent ambassador were to represent his government at state ceremonies, to gather information, and, occasionally, to enter into negotiations. Nowhere was this system more fully and expertly articulated than by the Republic of Venice in the late fifteenth and sixteenth centuries. Its ambassadors were chosen with unusual care from the most prominent families of the city. They were highly educated, and their duties were carefully defined. Among the latter were weekly dispatches reporting all matters of any interest to Venice. These reports were regularly read and debated in the senate, which replied with questions, instructions, and information of its own. As a result, Venetian ambassadors were among the most skilled and respected in early modern Europe. In this report, Giovanni Michiel interprets the events of St. Bartholomew's Day in 1572. The massacre of Huguenots, instigated by the Queen Mother, Catherine de Medici, outraged Protestant Europe and dashed all hopes for peace in France. Of particular interest is the ambassador's harshly realistic account of the political motives for so violent an act of statecraft.

From *Pursuit of Power: Venetian Ambassadors' Reports on Spain, Turkey and France in the Age of Phillip II, 1560–1600*, by James C. Davis (New York: HarperCollins, 1970), pp. 72–76, 78–79.

*   *   *

Turning to the queen, Admiral de Coligny said, "Madame, the king refuses to involve himself in one war. God grant that he may not be caught up in another which he cannot avoid."

By these words he meant, some say, that if they abandoned the prince of Orange things might go badly for him, and there would be a danger that if the prince failed to win or was actually driven out by the Spanish or for some other reason, then he might enter France with his French and German followers and it might be necessary to drive him out by force. However, everyone understood his words in a very different sense, namely that he was giving notice that he planned to stir up new storms and renew the rioting and civil war. When the queen carefully pondered this it became the chief reason, taken together with the other considerations, why she hurried to prepare that fate for him which he eventually met.

*   *   *

Then, at the dinner hour on Friday, while the admiral was returning on foot from the court to his lodgings and reading a letter, someone fired an arquebus at him. The shot came from a window which faced a bit obliquely on the street, near the royal palace called the Louvre. But it did not strike him in the chest as intended because it so happened that the admiral was wearing a pair of slippers which made walking difficult and, wanting to take them off and hand them to a page, he had just started to turn around. So the arquebus shot tore off a finger on his left hand and then hit his right arm near the wrist and passed through it to the other side near the elbow. If he had simply walked straight ahead it would have hit him in the chest and killed him.

As you can imagine, news of the event caused great excitement, especially at court. Everyone supposed it had been done by order of the duke of Guise to avenge his family, because the window from which the shot was fired belonged to his

mother's house, which had purposely been left empty after she had gone to stay in another. When the news was reported to the king, who happened to be playing tennis with the duke of Guise, they say he turned white and looked thunderstruck. Without saying a word he withdrew into his chambers and made it obvious that he was extremely angry.

*   *   *

On Saturday the admiral's dressings were changed and the word was given out—which may or may not have been true—that the wound was not a mortal one and that there was no danger even that he would lose the arm. The Huguenots only blustered all the more, and everyone waited to see what would happen next. The duke of Guise knew he might be attacked, so he armed himself and stuck close to his uncle, the duke of Aumale, and as many relatives, friends and servants as possible.

But before long the situation changed. Late Saturday night, just before the dawn of Saint Bartholomew's Day, the massacre or slaughter was carried out. The French say the king ordered it. How wild and terrifying it was in Paris (which has a larger population than any other city in Europe), no one can imagine. Nor can one imagine the rage and frenzy of those who slaughtered and sacked, as the king ordered the people to do. Nor what a marvel, not to say a miracle, it was that the common people did not take advantage of this freedom to loot and plunder from Catholics as well as Huguenots, and ravenously take whatever they could get their hands on, especially since the city is incredibly wealthy. No one would ever imagine that a people could be armed and egged on by their ruler, yet not get out of control once they were worked up. But it was not God's will that things should reach such a pass.

The slaughter went on past Sunday for two or three more days, despite the fact that edicts were issued against it and the duke of Nevers was sent riding through the city along with the king's natural brother to order them to stop the killing. The massacre showed how powerfully religion can affect men's minds. On every street one could see the barbarous sight of men cold-bloodedly outraging others of their own people, and not just men who had never done them any harm but in most cases people they knew to be their neighbors and even their relatives. They had no feeling, no mercy on anyone, even those who kneeled before them and humbly begged for their lives. If one man hated another because of some argument or lawsuit all he had to say was "This man is a Huguenot" and he was immediately killed. (That happened to many Catholics.) If their victims threw themselves in the river as a last resort and tried to swim to safety, as many did, they chased them in boats and then drowned them. There was a great deal of looting and pillaging and they say the goods taken amounted to two million because many Huguenots, including some of the richest of them, had come to live in Paris after the most recent edict of pacification. Some estimate the number who were killed as high as four thousand, while others put it as low as two thousand.

The killing spread to all the provinces and most of the major cities and was just as frenzied there, if not more so. They attacked anyone, even the gentry, and as a result all the leaders who did not escape have been killed or thrown in prison. It is true that Montgomery and some others who were pursued by the duke of Guise escaped to England, but they are not major figures. And the king has terrified them enough so they won't make any trouble.

*   *   *

REVIEW QUESTIONS

1. According to the report, at what level of society did the St. Bartholomew's Day Massacre originate?
2. Who was said to have initiated it?
3. How was a person identified as Huguenot or Catholic?
4. What does that say about religious identity in early modern France?
5. Do we know from this report who ordered the assassination?
6. Who caused the massacre?
7. What do we learn about the relation of religion to politics and political action?

14 ✌ RELIGIOUS WARS AND STATE BUILDING 1540–1660

The challenge to the authority of classical culture that the new worlds posed, combined with the fragmentation of the medieval Christian Church—the "body of all believers"—laid the foundation in the second half of the sixteenth century for profound crises of political and social order and of epistemology, the very foundation of human knowledge. In their efforts to describe what they saw in the Americas, European conquistadores and clergy were forced to adopt analogies: hundreds of species of plants and animals were not to be found in the writings of Pliny, the great and trusted botanist and zoologist of the ancient world, or in the Bible. The cultures of the Americas posed new models of social and political relations, opening new possibilities for the ordering of political relations and calling into question the very nature of political authority.

Within Europe, civil wars arose in the wake of the fragmentation of the Christian Church. The wars of religion in France, 1562–1598, led astute observers such as Montaigne to question the claim of each side to know the truth, and to question whether human reason was sufficient to discern the truth. In all the religious wars, beginning with the German Peasants' War of 1525 and culminating in the Thirty Years' War, 1618–1648, the social order was overthrown, as peasant killed lord, brother killed brother, son killed father, and neighbor killed neighbor. What was it to be human? To be savage? And where was God as Christian slaughtered Christian?

The crisis of the seventeenth century was not simply intellectual and spiritual but had real material aspects. The expansion of Europe into new worlds changed patterns of consumption and production, thus contributing to the overthrow of traditional work processes and lifestyles. It created a tremendous influx of wealth that aided the rise of new economic and political powers, both social groups and nation-states, and that contributed to chronic inflation. Changes in

society, economy, and politics created tensions that found expression in the violence of the period. Religious wars were seldom entirely religious in cause or in
consequence. The almost constant march and countermarch of armies not only
destroyed life and property but also disrupted agriculture and spread disease.
The struggle for existence, difficult under the best of circumstances in the early
modern period, became much more difficult in the age of crisis.

By 1660, peasants had risen in unprecedented numbers against their lords;
common Englishmen had executed their king; Europeans had witnessed multiple
incidents of cannibalism in their own villages; and the medieval epistemology,
that very base by which Europeans could be certain of the veracity of what they
knew, had collapsed. New formulations were being tentatively put forward, but
they did not yet replace the old certainties that had been irrecoverably lost.

REGINALD SCOT

FROM *Discoverie of Witchcraft*

*Reginald Scot (1538–1599) was a Kentish squire who witnessed a number of fraud-
ulent accusations of witchcraft in the villages of his shire during the reign of Elizabeth I. In 1584, he wrote his* Discoverie of Witchcraft, *which contains a remarkable
exposition of magical elements in medieval Catholicism and a protest against the
persecution of harmless old women. Scot doubted that God could ever have allowed
witches to exercise supernatural powers, much less demand that they be persecuted
for it. In this regard, he deserves to be ranked among the skeptics on the question of
witchcraft, although he never denied the existence of witches. According to Scot, all
"witches" fell into one of four categories. First were the innocent, those falsely accused. Second were the deluded, those convinced through their own misery that they
were witches. Third were the malefactors, those who harmed people and damaged
property, though not by supernatural means. Fourth were imposters, those who
posed as witches and conjurers. Scot denied that any of these "witches" had access
to supernatural powers. Malefactors and imposters were, in fact, the witches named
in the Bible as not being suffered to live. They were the only witches Scot admitted.
His work is said to have made a great impression in the magistracy and clergy of
his day. Nonetheless, his remained a minority opinion. Most contemporaries understood as tantamount to atheism any denial of the reality of spirits or the possibility
of the supernatural. The persecution of witches continued unabated into the eighteenth century; many thousands, mostly harmless old women, fell victim to the rage.*

From *Discoverie of Witchcraft*, 1584, edited by Hugh Ross Wilkinson (Carbondale: Southern
Illinois Press, 1962).

＊   ＊   ＊

The inconvenience growing by mens credulitie herein, with a reproofe of some churchmen, which are inclined to the common conceived opinion of witches omnipotencie, and a familiar example thereof. But the world is now so bewitched and over-run with this fond error, that even where a man shuld seeke comfort and counsell, there shall hee be sent (in case of necessitie) from God to the divell; and from the Physician, to the coosening witch, who will not sticke to take upon hir, by wordes to heale the lame (which was proper onelie to Christ: and to them whom he assisted with his divine power) yea, with hir familiar & charmes she will take upon hir to cure the blind: though in the tenth of S. *Johns* Gospell it be written, that the divell cannot open the eies of the blind. And they attaine such credit as I have heard (to my greefe) some of the ministerie affirme, that they have had in their parish at one instant, xvii. or xviii. witches: meaning such as could worke miracles supernaturallie. Whereby they manifested as well their infidelitie and ignorance, in conceiving Gods word; as their negligence and error in instructing their flocks. For they themselves might understand, and also teach their parishoners, that God onelie worketh great woonders; and that it is he which sendeth such punishments to the wicked, and such trials to the elect: according to the saieng of the Prophet *Haggai,* I smote you with blasting and mildeaw, and with haile, in all the labours of your hands; and yet you turned not unto me, saith the Lord. And therefore saith the same Prophet in another place; You have sowen much, and bring in little. And both in *Joel* and *Leviticus,* the like phrases and proofes are used and made. But more shalbe said of this hereafter.

＊   ＊   ＊

At the assises holden at *Rochester,* Anno 1581, one *Margaret Simons,* the wife of *John Simons,* of *Brenchlie* in *Kent,* was araigned for witchcraft, at the instigation and complaint of divers fond and malicious persons; and speciallie by the meanes of one *John Ferrall* vicar of that parish: with whom I

talked about that matter, and found him both fondlie assotted in the cause, and enviouslie bent towards hir: and (which is worse) as unable to make a good account of his faith, as shee whom he accused. That which he, for his part, laid to the poore womans charge, was this.

His sonne (being an ungratious boie, and prentise to one *Robert Scotchford* clothier, dwelling in that parish of *Brenchlie*) passed on a daie by hir house; at whome by chance hir little dog barked. Which thing the boie taking in evill part, drewe his knife, & pursued him therewith even to hir doore: whom she rebuked with some such words as the boie disdained, & yet neverthelesse would not be persuaded to depart in a long time. At the last he returned to his maisters house, and within five or sixe daies fell sicke. Then was called to mind the fraie betwixt the dog and the boie: insomuch as the vicar (who thought himselfe so privileged, as he little mistrusted that God would visit his children with sicknes) did so calculate; as he found, partlie through his owne judgement, and partlie (as he himselfe told me) by the relation of other witches, that his said sonne was by hir bewitched. Yea, he also told me, that this his sonne (being as it were past all cure) received perfect health at the hands of another witch.

He proceeded yet further against hir, affirming, that alwaies in his parish church, when he desired to read most plainelie, his voice so failed him, as he could scant be heard at all. Which hee could impute, he said, to nothing else, but to hir inchantment. When I advertised the poore woman hereof, as being desirous to heare what she could saie for hir selfe; she told me, that in verie deed his voice did much faile him, speciallie when he strained himselfe to speake lowdest. How beit, she said that at all times his voice was hoarse and lowe: which thing I perceived to be true. But sir, said she, you shall understand, that this our vicar is diseased with such a kind of hoarsenesse, as divers of our neighbors in this parish, not long since, doubted that he had the French pox; & in that respect utterly refused to communicate with him: untill such time as (being therunto injoined by M. D. *Lewen* the Ordinarie) he had brought frō

London a certificat, under the hands of two physicians, that his hoarsenes proceeded from a disease in the lungs. Which certificat he published in the church, in the presence of the whole congregation: and by this meanes hee was cured, or rather excused of the shame of his disease. And this I knowe to be true by the relation of divers honest men of that parish. And truelie, if one of the Jurie had not beene wiser than the other, she had beene condemned thereupon, and upon other as ridiculous matters as this. For the name of a witch is so odious, and hir power so feared among the common people, that if the honestest bodie living chance to be arraigned thereupon, she shall hardlie escape condemnation.

A Confutation of the Common Conceived Opinion of Witches and Witchcraft, and How Detestable a Sinne It Is to Repaire to Them for Counsell or Helpe in Time of Affliction

But whatsoever is reported or conceived of such manner of witchcrafts, I dare avow to be false and fabulous (coosinage, dotage, and poisoning excepted:) neither is there any mention made of these kind of witches in the Bible. If Christ had knowne them, he would not have pretermitted to invaie against their presumption, in taking upon them his office: as, to heale and cure diseases; and to worke such miraculous and supernaturall things, as whereby he himselfe was speciallie knowne, beleeved, and published to be God; his actions and cures consisting (in order and effect) according to the power of our witchmoongers imputed to witches. Howbeit, if there be any in these daies afflicted in such strange sort, as Christs cures and patients are described in the new testament to have beene: we flie from trusting in God to trusting in witches, who doo not onelie in their coosening art take on them the office of Christ in this behalfe; but use his verie phrase of speech to such idolators, as com to seeke divine assistance at their hands, saieng; Go thy waies, thy sonne or thy daughter, &c. shall doo well, and be whole.

* * *

In like manner I say, he that attributeth to a witch, such divine power, as dulie and onelie apperteineth unto GOD (which all witchmongers doo) is in hart a blasphemer, an idolater, and full of grosse impietie, although he neither go nor send to hir for assistance.

A Further Confutation of Witches Miraculous and Omnipotent Power, by Invincible Reasons and Authorities, with Dissuasions from Such Fond Credulitie

If witches could doo anie such miraculous things, as these and other which are imputed to them, they might doo them againe and againe, at anie time or place, or at anie mans desire: for the divell is as strong at one time as at another, as busie by daie as by night, and readie enough to doo all mischeefe, and careth not whom he abuseth. And in so much as it is confessed, by the most part of witchmoongers themselves, that he knoweth not the cogitation of mans heart, he should (me thinks) sometimes appeere unto honest and credible persons, in such grosse and corporall forme, as it is said he dooth unto witches: which you shall never heare to be justified by one sufficient witnesse. For the divell indeed entreth into the mind, and that waie seeketh mans confusion.

The art alwaies presupposeth the power; so as, if they saie they can doo this or that, they must shew how and by what meanes they doo it; as neither the witches, nor the witchmoongers are able to doo. For to everie action is required the facultie and abilitie of the agent or dooer; the aptnes of the patient or subject; and a convenient and possible application. Now the witches are mortall, and their power dependeth upon the analogie and consonancie of their minds and bodies; but with their minds they can but will and understand; and with their bodies they can doo no more, but as the bounds and ends of terrene sense will suffer: and therefore their power extendeth not to doo such miracles, as surmounteth their owne sense, and the understanding of others which are wiser than they; so as here wanteth the vertue and power of the efficient. And in reason, there can be no more vertue in the thing caused, than in the cause, or that which proceedeth of or from the benefit of the cause. And we see, that ignorant and impotent women, or witches, are the causes of incantations and charmes; wherein we shall perceive there is none effect, if we will credit our owne experience and sense unabused, the rules of philosophie, or the word of God. For alas! What an unapt instrument is a toothles, old, impotent, and unweldie woman to flie in the aier? Truelie, the divell little needs such instruments to bring his purposes to passe.

It is strange, that we should suppose, that such persons can worke such feates: and it is more strange, that we will imagine that to be possible to be doone by a witch, which to nature and sense is impossible; speciallie when our neighbours life dependeth upon our credulitie therein; and when we may see the defect of abilitie, which alwaies is an impediment both to the act, and also to the presumption thereof. And bicause there is nothing possible in lawe, that in nature is impossible; therefore the judge dooth not attend or regard what the accused man saith; or yet would doo: but what is prooved to have beene committed, and naturallie falleth in mans power and will to doo. For the lawe saith, that To will a thing unpossible, is a signe of a mad man, or of a foole, upon whom no sentence or judgement taketh hold. Furthermore, what Jurie will condemne, or what Judge will give sentence or judgement against one for killing a man at *Berwicke*; when they themselves, and manie other sawe that man at *London*, that verie daie, wherein the murther was committed; yea though the partie confesse himself guiltie therein, and twentie witnesses depose the same? But in this case also I saie the judge is not to weigh their testimonie, which is weakened by lawe; and the judges authoritie is to supplie the imperfection of the case, and to mainteine the right and equitie of the same.

Seeing therefore that some other things might naturallie be the occasion and cause of such calamities as witches are supposed to bring; let not us that professe the Gospell and knowledge of Christ, be bewitched to beleeve that they doo such things, as are in nature impossible, and in sense and reason incredible. If they saie it is doone through the divels helpe, who can work miracles; whie doo not theeves bring their busines to passe miraculouslie, with whom the divell is as conversant as with the other? Such mischeefes as are imputed to witches, happen where no witches are; yea and continue when witches are hanged and burnt: whie then should we attribute such effect to that cause, which being taken awaie, happeneth neverthelesse?

*   *   *

What Testimonies and Witnesses Are Allowed to Give Evidence against Reputed Witches, by the Report and Allowance of the Inquisitors Themselves, and Such as Are Speciall Writers Heerein

Excommunicat persons, partakers of the falt, infants, wicked servants, and runnawaies are to be admitted to beare witnesse against their dames in this mater of witchcraft: bicause (saith *Bodin* the champion of witchmoongers) none that be honest are able to detect them. Heretikes also and witches shall be received to accuse, but not to excuse a witch. And finallie, the testimonie of all infamous persons in this case is good and allowed. Yea, one lewd person (saith *Bodin*) may be received to accuse and condemne a thousand suspected witches. And although by lawe, a capitall enimie may be challenged; yet *James Sprenger*, and *Henrie Institor*, (from whom *Bodin*, and all the writers that ever I have read, doo receive their light, authorities and arguments) saie (upon this point of lawe) that The poore frendlesse old woman must proove, that hir capitall enimie would have killed hir, and that hee hath both assalted & wounded hir; otherwise she pleadeth all in vaine. If the judge aske hir, whether she have anie capitall enimies; and she rehearse other, and forget hir accuser; or else answer that he was hir capital enimie, but now she hopeth he is not so: such a one is nevertheles admitted for a witnes. And though by lawe, single witnesses are not admittable; yet if one depose she hath bewitched hir cow; another, hir sow; and the third, hir butter: these saith (saith *M. Mal.* and *Bodin*) are no single witnesses; bicause they agree that she is a witch.

The Fifteene Crimes Laid to the Charge of Witches, by Witchmongers, Speciallie by Bodin, in Dæmonomania

They denie God, and all religion.

Answere. Then let them die therefore, or at the least be used like infidels, or apostataes.

They cursse, blaspheme, and provoke God with all despite.

Answere. Then let them have the law expressed in *Levit.* 24. and *Deut.* 13 & 17.

They give their faith to the divell, and they worship and offer sacrifice unto him.

Ans. Let such also be judged by the same lawe.

They doo solemnelie vow and promise all their progenie unto the divell.

Ans. This promise proceedeth from an unsound mind, and is not to be regarded; bicause they cannot performe it, neither will it be prooved true. Howbeit, if it be done by anie that is sound of mind, let the cursse of *Jeremie,* 32.36. light upon them, to wit, the sword, famine and pestilence.

They sacrifice their owne children to the divell before baptisme, holding them up in the aire unto him, and then thrust a needle into their braines.

Ans. If this be true, I maintaine them not herein: but there is a lawe to judge them by. Howbeit, it is so contrarie to sense and nature, that it were follie to beleeve it; either upon *Bodins* bare word, or else upon his presumptions; speciallie when so small commoditie and so great danger

and inconvenience insueth to the witches thereby.

They burne their children when they have sacrificed them.

Ans. Then let them have such punishment, as they that offered their children unto *Moloch: Levit.* 20. But these be meere devises of witchmoongers and inquisitors, that with extreame tortures have wroong such confessions from them; or else with false reports have beelied them; or by flatterie & faire words and promises have woon it at their hands, at the length.

They sweare to the divell to bring as manie into that societie as they can.

Ans. This is false, and so prooved elsewhere.

They sweare by the name of the divell.

Ans. I never heard anie such oth, neither have we warrant to kill them that so doo sweare; though indeed it be verie lewd and impious.

They use incestuous adulterie with spirits.

Ans. This is a stale ridiculous lie, as is prooved apparentlie hereafter.

They boile infants (after they have murthered them unbaptised) untill their flesh be made potable.

Ans. This is untrue, incredible, and impossible.

They eate the flesh and drinke the bloud of men and children openlie.

Ans. Then are they kin to the *Anthropophagi* and *Canibals.* But I beleeve never an honest man in *England* nor in *France,* will affirme that he hath seene any of these persons, that are said to be witches, do so; if they shuld, I beleeve it would poison them.

They kill men with poison.

Ans. Let them be hanged for their labour.

They kill mens cattell.

Ans. Then let an action of trespasse be brought against them for so dooing.

They bewitch mens corne, and bring hunger and barrennes into the countrie; they ride and flie in the aire, bring stormes, make tempests, &c.

Ans. Then will I worship them as gods; for those be not the works of man nor yet of witch: as I have elsewhere prooved at large.

They use venerie with a divell called *Iucubus,*

even when they lie in bed with their husbands, and have children by them, which become the best witches.

Ans. This is the last lie, verie ridiculous, and confuted by me elsewhere.

Of Foure Capitall Crimes Objected against Witches, All Fullie Answered and Confuted as Frivolous

First therefore they laie to their charge idolatrie. But alas without all reason: for such are properlie knowne to us to be idolaters, as doo externall worship to idols or strange gods. The furthest point that idolatrie can be stretched unto, is, that they, which are culpable therein, are such as hope for and seeke salvation at the hands of idols, or of anie other than God; or fixe their whole mind and love upon anie creature, so as the power of God be neglected and contemned thereby. But witches neither seeke nor beleeve to have salvation at the hands of divels, but by them they are onlie deceived; the instruments of their phantasie being corrupted, and so infatuated, that they suppose, confesse, and saie they can doo that, which is as farre beyond their power and nature to doo, as to kill a man at *Yorke* before noone, when they have beene seene at *London* in that morning, &c. But if these latter idolaters, whose idolatrie is spirituall, and committed onelie in mind, should be punished by death; then should everie covetous man, or other, that setteth his affection anie waie too much upon an earthlie creature, be executed, and yet perchance the witch might escape scotfree.

Secondlie, apostasie is laid to their charge, whereby it is inferred, that they are worthie to die. But apostasie is, where anie of sound judgement forsake the gospell, learned and well knowne unto them; and doo not onelie embrace impietie and infidelitie; but oppugne and resist the truth erstwhile by them professed. But alas these poore women go not about to defend anie impietie, but after good admonition repent.

Thirdlie, they would have them executed for seducing the people. But God knoweth they have

small store of Rhetorike or art to seduce; except to tell a tale of Robin good-fellow be to deceive and seduce. Neither may their age or sex admit that opinion or accusation to be just: for they themselves are poore seduced soules. I for my part (as else-where I have said) have prooved this point to be false in most apparent sort.

Fourthlie, as touching the accusation, which all the writers use herein against them for their carnall copulation with *Incubus:* the follie of mens credulitie is as much to be woondered at and derided, as the others vaine and impossible confessions. For the divell is a spirit, and hath neither flesh nor bones, which were to be used in the performance of this action. And since he also lacketh all instruments, substance, and seed ingendred of bloud; it were follie to staie overlong in the confutation of that, which is not in the nature of things. And yet must I saie somewhat heerein, bicause the opinion hereof is so stronglie and universallie received, and the fables thereupon so innumerable; wherby *M. Mal. Bodin, Hemingius, Hyperius, Danaeus, Erastus,* and others that take upon them to write heerein, are so abused, or rather seeke to abuse others; as I woonder at their fond credulitie in this behalfe. For they affirme undoubtedlie, that the divell plaieth *Succubus* to the man, and carrieth from him the seed of generation, which he delivereth as *Incubus* to the woman, who manie times that waie is gotten with child; which will verie naturallie (they saie) become a witch, and such one they affirme *Merline* was.

*   *   *

By What Meanes the Common People Have Beene Made Beleeve in the Miraculous Works of Witches, a Definition of Witchcraft, and a Description Thereof

The common people have beene so assotted and bewitched, with whatsoever poets have feigned of witchcraft, either in earnest, in jest, or else in derision; and with whatsoever lowd liers and couseners for their pleasures heerein have invented, and with whatsoever tales they have heard from old doting women, or from their mothers maids, and with whatsoever the grandfoole their ghostlie father, or anie other morrow masse preest had informed them; and finallie with whatsoever they have swallowed up through tract of time, or through their owne timerous nature or ignorant conceipt, concerning these matters of hagges and witches: as they have so settled their opinion and credit thereupon, that they thinke it heresie to doubt in anie part of the matter; speciallie bicause they find this word witchcraft expressed in the scriptures; which is as to defend praieng to saincts, bicause *Sanctus, Sanctus, Sanctus* is written in *Te Deum*.

And now to come to the definition of witchcraft, which hitherto I did deferre and put off purposelie: that you might perceive the true nature thereof, by the circumstances, and therefore the rather to allow of the same, seeing the varietie of other writers. Witchcraft is in truth a cousening art, wherin the name of God is abused, prophaned and blasphemed, and his power attributed to a vile creature. In estimation of the vulgar people, it is a supernaturall worke, contrived betweene a corporall old woman, and a spirituall divell. The maner thereof is so secret, mysticall, and strange, that to this daie there hath never beene any credible witnes thereof. It is incomprehensible to the wise, learned or faithfull; a probable matter to children, fooles, melancholike persons and papists. The trade is thought to be impious. The effect and end thereof to be sometimes evill, as when thereby man or beast, grasse, trees, or corne, &c; is hurt: sometimes good, as whereby sicke folkes are healed, theeves bewraied, and true men come to their goods, &c. The matter and instruments, wherewith it is accomplished, are words, charmes, signes, images, characters, &c; the which words although any other creature do pronounce, in manner and forme as they doo, leaving out no circumstance requisite or usually for that action: yet none is said to have the grace or gift to performe the matter, except she be a witch, and so taken either by hir owne consent, or by others imputation.

Reasons to Proove That Words and Characters Are But Bables, and That Witches Cannot Doo Such Things as the Multitude Supposeth They Can, Their Greatest Woonders Prooved Trifles, of a Yoong Gentleman Cousened

That words, characters, images, and such other trinkets, which are thought so necessarie instruments for witchcraft (as without the which no such thing can be accomplished) are but bables, devised by couseners, to abuse the people withall; I trust I have sufficientlie prooved. And the same maie be further and more plainelie perceived by these short and compendious reasons following.

First, in that *Turkes* and infidels, in their witchcraft, use both other words, and other characters than our witches doo and also such as are most contrarie. In so much as, if ours be bad, in reason theirs should be good. If their witches can doo anie thing, ours can doo nothing. For as our witches are said to renounce Christ, and despise his sacraments: so doo the other forsake *Mahomet*, and his lawes, which is one large step to christianitie.

It is also to be thought, that all witches are couseners; when mother *Bungie*, a principall witch, so reputed, tried, and condemned of all men, and continuing in that exercise and estimation manie yeares (having cousened & abused the whole realme, in so much as there came to hir, witchmongers from all the furthest parts of the land, she being in diverse bookes set out with authoritie, registred and chronicled by the name of the great witch of *Rochester*, and reputed among all men for the cheefe ringleader of all other witches) by good proofe is found to be a meere cousener; confessing in hir death bed freelie, without compulsion or inforcement, that hir cunning consisted onlie in deluding and deceiving the people: saying that she had (towards the maintenance of hir credit in that cousening trade) some sight in physicke and surgerie, and the assistance of a freend of hirs, called *Heron*, a professor thereof. And this I know, partlie of mine owne knowledge, and partlie by the testimonie of hir husband, and others of credit, to whome (I saie) in hir death bed, and at sundrie other times she protested these things; and also that she never had indeed anie materiall spirit or divell (as the voice went) nor yet knew how to worke anie supernaturall matter, as she in hir life time made men beleeve she had and could doo.

*   *   *

Againe, who will mainteine, that common witchcrafts are not cousenages, when the great and famous witchcrafts, which had stolne credit not onlie from all the common people, but from men of great wisdome and authoritie, are discovered to be beggerlie slights of cousening varlots? Which otherwise might and would have remained a per-petuall objection against me. Were there not three images of late yeeres found in a doonghill, to the terror & astonishment of manie thousands? In so much as great matters were thought to have beene pretended to be doone by witchcraft. But if the Lord preserve those persons (whose destruction was doubted to have beene intended thereby) from all other the lewd practises and attempts of their enimies; I feare not, but they shall easilie withstand these and such like devises, although they should indeed be practised against them. But no doubt, if such bables could have brought those matters of mischeefe to passe, by the hands of trai-tors, witches, or papists; we should long since have beene deprived of the most excellent jewell and comfort that we enjoy in this world. Howbeit, I confesse, that the feare, conceipt, and doubt of such mischeefous pretenses may breed inconve-nience to them that stand in awe of the same. And I wish, that even for such practises, though they never can or doo take effect, the practisers be pun-ished with all extremitie: bicause therein is mani-fested a traiterous heart to the Queene, and a presumption against God.

*   *   *

REVIEW QUESTIONS

1. What is witchcraft?
2. How does Scot depict it?
3. According to Scot, what characterizes witches and witchcraft?
4. How does Scot confound the very notion of witchcraft?
5. Where does he locate the source of all power to override the laws of nature?
6. What sort of power is left to witches?
7. What, according to Scot, is the relation of witches to the natural world?

THE CARMELITE MISSION TO PERSIA

FROM "Father Vincent: An Audience with 'Abbâs"

Shah 'Abbâs the Great (1588–1629) claimed, as a member of the Safavid Dynasty, to be the sole legitimate heir of Mohammad. When he came to power, he demanded the loyalty of all Muslims, in his own realm of Persia and throughout the world. This created understandable tensions with his neighbor to the West, the Ottoman Empire and led 'Abbâs to pursue better relations with Europeans. To this end, and in the hope of benefiting from superior European military technology, he opened his country to Christian missionaries, whose professed aim was the conversion of Muslims to

THE PLUNDERING AND BURNING OF A VILLAGE, A HANGING, AND
PEASANTS AVENGE THEMSELVES (1633)   JACQUES CALLOT

These three prints, often referred to as The Horrors of War, *powerfully reveal commonplace events of the early seventeenth century: the ravages of war on a small village, the punishment of unruly troops, and the violence of the violated. They reveal the underbelly of early modern warfare in a way that contrasts starkly with the stately, heroic images of Velázquez and others. How do the troopers depicted by Callot differ from those depicted by Velázquez? How do their representations of warfare differ? How does Callot portray rural life? What general aspects of the Iron Century does Callot capture in his images?*

> *Christianity. The following report was written by a Carmelite missionary, sent by the Pope to Iran in 1604. Its author is Father Vincent, one of the original missionaries, who returned to Iran in May 1621 as Visitor General of the Carmelites in Persia and the East. He offers an account of an audience with 'Abbâs at which he was present.*

From *A Chronicle of the Carmelites in Persia and the Papal Mission of the XVIIth and XVIIIth Centuries,* compiled by H. G. Chick (London: Eyre and Spottiswoode, 1939), vol. 1, pp. 248–55; reprinted in *The Islamic World,* edited by William H. McNeill and Marilyn Robinson Waldman (New York: Oxford University Press, 1973), pp. 381–91.

There are in Persia some English merchants, Lutherans and of other sects, here to buy silk: and one of them who is the Chief and whom the rest obey resides in the city of Isfahan: the merchants in England choose him to receive the money, which they remit him in order to purchase the silk, which each year may attain a total quantity of 600,000 ducats,[1] which is shipped and exported from Jashk, a port on the Persian Gulf, in English ships which come out each year. This English Agent is treated by the Shah like an ambassador.

At the season when the Fr. Visitor General arrived in the city of Isfahan, the English had some articles, which had reached them by the ships that year, and they had asked an audience of the king in order to offer them as gifts, and so his Highness sent for them on that day and also summoned our Fr. Vincent, whom together with his companion the king of Persia received inside the Haram or Saraglio, where no one may enter without special permission from his Majesty.

With his back to the wall of the farther side of the room, his Highness was sitting, as was his wont, on the floor, which was covered with rich carpets: he was eating alone from off a silken tablecloth. He had in front of him a single, but very large silver dish, on which there was a variety of foods made from rice of various hues, all cooked differently and each arranged in its compartment, in the separate compartments of rice there being buried partridges, pigeons, quails, and all sorts of boiled and roasted meats. He had also in front of him some Chinese porcelain bowls of rather small size, filled with the juice of lemons and oranges sweetened with sugar and flavoured with spices, from which to take a spoonful or two from time to time while he ate. For it is the Persian custom, while they are eating, not to drink water or wine, and in order to be able to digest the food . . . they use these juices while feeding: when they have finished, after a short time they begin to drink. . . .

Round the same apartment were also seated and eating off tablecloths of silk some of the principal among the king's subjects and two envoys from the king of Tatary, who had come from Caffa [Crimean peninsula] and also the English Agent mentioned above together with his Lutheran chaplain attired in a flowing gown of black damask, having wide and long sleeves . . . as well as their interpreter with four other English heretics.

The Fr. Visitor entered and made the proper obeisance to the Shah, who bade him sit down, together with his companion, at the same tablecloth and dish, from which he himself was eating. He (the Shah) said that he was welcome and that he remembered seeing him in Persia on two previous occasions, and knew him very well: then he enquired about the Visitor's health and the date of his arrival in Isfahan. Next, Fr. Vincent presented the letters he had brought: two Briefs from His Holiness (one in reply to a letter, in which the Shah had written to the Pope) another letter from the Grand Master of Malta, who had handed it to the Fr. Visitor General on his passage by Malta. The Shah replied graciously and, taking the letters, gave them to Mir Abul Ma'ali, his chief secretary of state, to have translated.

Two days previously the English had been with the king and discoursed at great length on the mat-

---

[1] A Venetian gold coin of considerable value.

ter of religion and spoken ill of the Catholics saying that they were idolaters, who adored pictures and images, and made the sign of the cross, etc. The Shah had said that he would bring the Fathers together with them, so that they might hold a disputation on these matters.

This was the motive why the king of Persia asked the Fathers about the difference there is between Catholics and English.

The Fr. Visitor answered that the English are heretics and false Christians, and that Roman Catholics are the true Christians. The Shah continued on this topic of religion and touched in the course of it on four main points, which were: (*a*) fasting and good works, (*b*) about the Cross, and its adoration and images, (*c*) on free-will, (*d*) on the antiquity of the Roman Catholic religion, and the primacy of the Sovereign Pontiff.

The occasion for the first topic, that of fasting and good works, arose from the Shah asking the Fathers why they were not eating. They replied that it was Ember Saturday in Pentecost. The king enquired of the English what fasts they kept. Their "Chief" replied that God had not commanded men to fast, and, although the English Agent spoke through his interpreter, still the king asked the Fathers what he was saying, and they answered in Persian that the Englishman said that God had not commanded men to fast and the Fathers continued: "See, your Highness, what an absurd falsehood and error it is, as it is true that by their religious laws Christians, Muslims, Jews and Gentiles have fasts of obligation."

Here there was small controversy since the matter was manifest and clear. With one voice the Shah and the grandees sitting with him said that it was a very great error and falsehood, because fasts, prayer, penitential exercises and good works are recommended in the law of Moses, in the Gospel, and the Quran, and in fine by all the prophets.

Second point: on the Cross, its adoration, and on images. The Shah enquired of the Fathers whether the English made the sign of the Cross to bless themselves. The Fathers answered "no." He asked further whether they had images of the saints and adored them: the reply was given him: "no." He

asked the Fathers: "Why do the Franks venerate them, as in this they resemble the Idolaters?" (Persians, in praying, prostrate themselves repeatedly, and with their head and forehead venerate certain seals or counters of earth, of the size of a doubloon, and the beads, on which they recite their prayers, are made from earth from Mecca.)

In order to convince him the Fathers put the question to the king: "Because your Highness and your people prostrate yourselves and worship seals and beads made of earth would it be right for us to call your Highness and your people idolaters? Certainly not, because we know that, when you perform that of act of adoration, you do not mean by it that that seal and stone are God, but do it out of piety and reverence for that soil, as it comes from the places of sepulture of your ancestors and the great men whom you consider saints." The Shah answered: "That is not the chief reason and intention we have for worshipping on earthen seals[2] and beads, but rather in that act of veneration we make an act of recognizing that we are clay, and that from earth God created us, and we adore the Creator of this: and the reason why in the mosques and in our houses whilst we say our prayers on matting and carpets our prayers would not be lawful and acceptable, unless we said them on" (i.e. touching) "the earth. With this in view, for more convenience and cleanliness we use the earthen medallions and beads: and that they are of this or that soil is an accidental matter: it suffices that it be earth. And so, when we have any other sort of stone, even if it be a piece of rock, we have no need of a seal. It is also true that we venerate it (the seal) as a memorial and a pious object, as thou sayest, but not mainly for that reason."

To this the Fathers replied: "Very good! And thus our Christian religion does not adore nor serve images, as if they were gods, nor does it expect from them the future judgment (God preserve us from such a thing!), but it venerates images for the things they represent. They serve us also as memorials to remind us of the virtues of those saints

---

[2] *Muhreh*, which Shi'îs touch with their foreheads in the prostrations during prayer. (Tr.)

they represent, in order that we may imitate them and beg them to intercede by their prayers with our Lord God, that He will grant us what we ask and that we may be good and his servants, as they have been, so that we may attain the glory which they now enjoy. So that, just as your Highness and your people do not say that that earthen medallion is God, no more do we say that the statues of the saints are gods, nor do we adore them as such." With these reasonings the Shah and his courtiers remained content.

The king said that Christians do not make the cross properly because there are only three nails, and we make the sign of it in four places: and, thus speaking, the Shah made the sign as a proof of what he said. The Fr. Visitor replied that it is not done on account of the nails of the Cross, but in order to signify the Trinity of Persons and unity of God and the incarnation of the Son of God: and so it is done at His name, signifying that there is one God alone, Father, Son and Holy Ghost, who are the three Persons; and the Father is signed on the head, to signify that He is the beginning of the other Persons, the Son on the body to signify that He became man in the virginial womb of S. Mary, and the Holy Ghost is signed on the two shoulders to signify that the Third Person proceeds from the Father and the Son. The king was pleased to have heard this explanation and said: "I believed that you made the cross in order to signify that Christ, the Lord, Son of God and man, died on the cross in order to save and redeem all men." The king then said: "We hold that the Lord Jesus is the Spirit of God and was not crucified by the Jews, but that God, seeing that the Jews wanted to crucify him, drew him up as the Spirit into heaven, putting the features of Jesus on Judas, who had sold him and whom, because he appeared to be so like Him, they took and crucified."

The Father said, "We hold in the Gospel that Jesus Christ is the Word of God, and that He himself as a man was crucified for the salvation of men and the third day rose from the dead and after 40 days ascended into heaven in the sight of all his disciples, who were afterwards witnesses of these truths for all the world."

The king asked whether the English believe this. The Fr. Visitor replied "yes." The Shah put the question to the minister (clergyman) of the English who was present, and who confirmed that it was the case, because in this particular they believe the same as the Roman Catholics: and then, in order to show courtesy to the Fathers, with his hand the king poured out and gave them to drink, making a sign of the cross over the cup.

The third point concerned free-will. The king turned to question the Fathers—who were the better, the English or the Roman Christian. The Fathers replied that by its fruit the goodness and quality of the tree are known: that the king should enquire about the things the English did and the examples they gave, and from those he would be able to judge. The Agent of the English rejoined that they were the better Christians, and that they had the right Faith. On this the Fathers observed: "Shah, we do not want to say more to your Highness than this, that the English are heretics and of a like sect as the Turks, who deny free-will and say that all the evil men do and the demons do is done of necessity, and they cannot do less, because God so wills: and so they (the English) say that God does everything, whether good or evil."

Here the grandees of the king looked at each other, and the Shah in particular jumped from his seat (as the saying goes) and began to make a sermon to all present, very earnestly as he detested that theory. He spoke with great gusto, so that the Tatar envoys from Caffa, who were there and who are of the same sect as the Turks, should hear him. After the king finished his arguments, the Fathers said: "This is the reason, your Majesty, why the English, who have no consciences nor fear of God, are pirates, rob, slay, destroy, and one cannot rely on their word, because they say that they cannot do anything else, seeing that they have no option."

The English did not know what reply to make during all this harangue of the Shah, which lasted for the space of more than three-quarters of an hour, during which his Highness brought forward many arguments and examples in opposition to the English who deny free-will, and in particular he said that it was most false. . . .

Regarding the fourth and last point, the antiquity of the Roman Catholic religion and the primacy of the Sovereign Pontiff, the Shah enquired how long the English had been separated from the Romans and the Pope. The Fr. Visitor told him "70 or 80 years." The Agent of the English said that *they* were the primitive Christians. The Fathers asked him whether previous to those 70 or 80 years the English and Romans were all one and whether all England paid obedience to the Roman Pontiff. The English answered "yes: it was the truth that formerly they yielded obedience to the Pope." When this had been admitted and translated to the Shah by the interpreter of the English themselves, his Highness remarked that, just as the Sunnis and Turkish heretics will not ascribe the primacy to Husain, son of Amir-ul-Mu'minin [i.e. 'Ali], but instead to 'Umar,[3] so the English do not obey the vicar of Jesus, who is the Pope of Rome: and for this they are heretics.

The sun was entering through a window and troubled the king: so he got up and made a sign to the Fathers to follow him. Together with his Highness they entered a smaller, but cooler apartment, and all sat down in this order: on the right hand he caused the minister (clergyman) to sit and on the left near himself the Fathers (the Persians consider the left-hand a more honoured seat, because, they say, it is on the side where the heart is, and the sword is worn). Then 'Ali Quli Khan, governor of _____ and the chief judge of the court of crimes; next the Georgians, and in another apartment, but very near by, so that they could see and converse with the Shah, were his other gentlemen. Below the minister, and beside him were the Tatars from Caffa, and last of all the rest of the English, near whom in a little closet were the king's minstrels playing on musical instruments and singing.

The English wanted to discuss the business of the silk and to ask for it to be finished and for the Shah's mandate for them to go and purchase it in Gilan and Shirwan. The Shah made signs to one of his officials, who then told the interpreter that by no manner of means was their business to be discussed, because it was not the time for it, giving it to be understood that it was not suitable to talk of business in front of the Fathers.

The Shah returned once more to talk about the nails [in the cross] of Christ, asking whether they were three or four. The answer was given him that some Saints said there were four, but that the majority conclude that there were three. This opinion pleased the Shah: and he crossed his legs, saying that with a single nail they had nailed both feet, and that was how he had seen it in pictures. Here the English Agent wanted to cast ridicule on the Catholics and asked the Fathers how many wounds Christ had in His body. The Fr. Visitor answered him that there were five. He [the English Agent—Monox] laughed a great deal and said: "No: there were four." The Fr. Visitor enquired which they were. He (the English Agent) replied: "one wound only in the two feet, because a single nail had transfixed them, and the rest in the two hands and the side." The Fr. Visitor, remarking that he (the Agent) was a layman and would know little about philosophy, turned to the minister, and asked whether he too held that opinion: to which the minister said "yes." So then the Fr. Visitor enquired once more of the minister whether the wounds in the feet were continuous or contiguous: the latter answered that they were continuous and for that reason were one wound. Our Religious remarked that that was contrary to philosophy, because something "continuous" is that which is joined by a common end. But the wounds in Christ's feet were not coupled by a common end: therefore they were not continuous, and in consequence they were two wounds, and not one. The minister did not know what to answer. The Shah and the grandees wanted to understand the point in dispute: it was explained to them, and they laughed at the English for saying that in the two wounded feet there was only one wound because a single nail pierced them.

*   *   *

The Fathers said to his Highness that, if he allowed, they would put a problem before him: and

---

[3] 'Ali: fourth Caliph (656–661); 'Umar: second Caliph (634–644).

the Shah bade them propound it. So they said: "Since it is true that in all countries and states there are good and bad people, perforce among our Christian community there are also some bad men, who commit crimes: and perhaps it might be necessary to punish them by shedding their blood, by mutilation of their limbs, or by putting them to death." So they enquired in such case who was to be the judge to try the case and execute punishment, because it was not lawful for Religious to be judges, or mix themselves up in secular affairs. Taking in one hand a piece of his garment, like a man shaking the dust from it, the Shah answered and said: "I have nothing to do with any crime that any of your people may commit contrary to your law; but my wish is that you punish misdemeanours, and that you see to and keep your houses, people and community clean and free from such, so that there be no disorder or scandal: and, as to criminal offences of which you cannot be the judge, since you are priests, choose from among the Franks residing here or staying temporarily here one to be judge, with the authority of a consul,[4] and you as priests, knowing more of the law, would be able to tell the consul what in conscience and justice he should do. So that it is our wish that you Fathers from the Pope execute justice between your people in conformity with the law of Christ and the orders that you have from the Pope. I say the same to the English." 'Ali Quli Khan, the chief judge and . . . the king's secretary and Wazir, in loud voices extolled this decree of the Shah, telling the Fathers that his Highness had done them a great favour, on which the Fathers duly tendered thanks.

The Shah asked the English whether their Gospel and ours were all one. The Agent answered: "No." Thereupon the Fr. Visitor said that the Agent was telling the truth, because our Gospel was the real one, and theirs false, being full of the falsehoods which they told. On this the Shah reproved the Fr. Visitor, saying that the English had not told him falsehoods and had always carried out their promises and were of much utility in his country. "But, you; yes," he said to the Visitor, "you have told me lies." In reply the Father asked: "What falsehood have I told your Highness?" The Shah answered: "This, that the king of Portugal and Spain has promised to make war on the Turks: when he has not done so." The Father remarked: "His Majesty the king of Spain and the Christian princes have warred all these years against the Turks," and then asked: "How many years is it that your Highness is making war on the Turks?" The Shah replied: "Twenty years." The Father rejoined: "Then, if in those twenty years the Emperor, aided by the Christian princes, had not been to war with the Turks and had not kept them occupied in Hungary and other parts (as he did in the years 1604–5–6 and 1607) at the request and instance of the Pope, would your Highness have captured after Tabriz and Julfa Erivan, Ganjeh, etc.? Later in the year 1607 did not your Highness take Shamakha and Demirkapu, called by its other name, "The Iron Gate" (Darband) together with all the very fertile province of Shirwan, and, finally, is it not the fact that your Highness had no further assault from the Turks until the year 1610, in which there came Murad Pasha, who had delayed more than 7 years in bringing assistance and relief to those provinces so that your Highness had been able so to consolidate your position in them, to great advantage in that you obtained a signal victory?" The Shah had nothing to say to this. The Fathers continued: "Majesty, the war which the king of Poland is making against the Turks, too, is that not by a Catholic king, obedient to the Pope, the vicar of Christ?" The Shah answered: "Tell me what the Pope is doing, not what others are doing." The Fathers rejoined: "What the Christian princes are doing may also be said to be what the Pope is doing, because, just as when the hand does any good action, it is the head which directs it and to it the praise is given, and, just as when Allah Virdi Khan, Amir Khan, etc., generals of your Highness, gain any victories or conquer any territory, the glory is attributed to your Highness, so also the victories won by the Christian princes are attributed to the Pope who is the head and father of all Christians."

---

[4] This seems to be an authorization of the extra-territorial jurisdiction, which prevailed in Persia till 1928. (Tr.)

*   *   *

To that the Shah returned that, if the Pope were in person to go to fight against the Turks and to spend his treasure on it, all the rest of the Christian princes would go too and expend their money and resources. For, whoever does not obey the Pope, the vicar of Christ, is no good Christian.

Thereupon the Fathers said: "Well! that is why we said, your Majesty, that the English are no good Christians, because they do not obey the Pope, and they are the cause of the Christian Catholic princes not making war on the Turks. For these heretics, disobedient to the Pope, rebel against their Catholic princes, who are obedient to him, and make war on them, as in these last years the Palatine, son-in-law of the king of England, did against the Emperor, although, thanks to God, the Emperor has gained the victory over him and despoiled him of his lands and punished him as he deserved."

*   *   *

It was already late, and the guests got up, and we too took our leave of the king, kissing his hand. As we went out, the English made apologies to the Fathers and begged their pardon for having exceeded the limits of politeness. The Fathers answered that in disputatious on matters of religion neither politeness nor dissimulation nor compliments are to be used, and that they wished them well and no boon greater than the salvation of their souls, and for this had spoken so freely about Catholic truth.

*   *   *

Within two months of those asseverations of respect for Jesus, the fickle monarch, presumably instigated, had let loose a persecution of Christians. . . .

REVIEW QUESTIONS

1. What does Father Vincent's account reveal about relations between Muslims and Christians in the early seventeenth century?
2. Why do you suppose Father Vincent reserved so much attention for details about the person, habits, and surroundings of 'Abbâs?
3. Would you descrie the tone of Father Vincent's account as favorable and, if so, what does he admire most about 'Abbâs?
4. Might this description of the ceremony and conversation with 'Abbâs be taken as an implicit criticism of Western rulers?

HANS JAKOB CHRISTOPH VON GRIMMELSHAUSEN

FROM *Simplicissimus*

Hans Jakob Christoph von Grimmelshausen (1621–1676), author of Simplicissimus, *the greatest German novel of the seventeenth century and one of the great works of all German literature, was born at Gelnhausen, near Hanau in Hesse Kassel. The troubled times of the Thirty Years' War (1618–1648) that found eloquent consideration in his writing are reflected by his life. He lost his parents early, probably in the 1634 sack of Gelnhausen by troops under Ferdinand, general infanta of Spain, and was himself kidnapped by marauding Hessian troops the following year. His experiences became the stuff of his novel. In 1636, he joined the Imperial army. In 1639, he became secretary to Reinhard von Schauenburg, the commandant at Offenburg, on whose staff he served until 1647. At the end of the war, he was commandant on the Inn. Soon after the war he became steward of the Schauenburg estates, married, and converted to Catholicism. In 1667, Grimmelshausen was appointed magistrate and tax collector at Renchen, a town belonging to the Bishopric of Strasbourg. His duties evidently left him free to write; he published his masterpiece,* Simplicissimus, *in 1669. Modeled on the Spanish picaresque romance,* Simplicissimus *sketched the development of a human soul measured against the background of a land riven by warfare. It gave free rein to its author's narrative gifts: his realist detail, coarse humor, and social criticism.* Simplicissimus *is widely considered a historical document for its vivid picture of seventeenth-century Germany. Grimmelshausen's life ended as it began, in the shadow of war. In 1674, Rechen was occupied by French troops and his household was broken up. He died in 1676, once more in military service.*

From *Simplicissimus,* by Hans Jakob Christoph von Grimmelshausen, translated by S. Goodrich (San Francisco: Daedalus Press, 1995).

Book I

CHAPTER I
TREATS OF SIMPLICISSIMUS'S RUSTIC DESCENT AND OF HIS UPBRINGING ANSWERING THERETO

There appeareth in these days of ours (of which many do believe that they be the last days) among the common folk, a certain disease which causeth those who do suffer from it (so soon as they have either scraped and higgled together so much that they can, besides a few pence in their pocket, wear a fool's coat of the new fashion with a thousand bits of silk ribbon upon it, or by some trick of fortune have become known as men of parts) forthwith to give themselves out gentlemen and nobles of ancient descent. Whereas it doth often happen that their ancestors were day-labourers, carters, and porters, their cousins donkey-drivers, their brothers turnkeys and catchpolls, their sisters harlots, their mothers bawds—yea, witches even: and in a word, their whole pedigree of thirty-two quarterings as full of dirt and stain as ever was the sugarbakers' guild of Prague. Yea, these new sprigs of nobility be often themselves as black as if they had been born and bred in Guinea.

With such foolish folk I desire not to even myself, though 'tis not untrue that I have often fan-cied I must have drawn my birth from some great lord or knight at least, as being by nature disposed to follow the nobleman's trade had I but the means and the tools for it. 'Tis true, moreover, without jesting, that my birth and upbringing can be well compared to that of a prince if we overlook the one great difference in degree. How! did not my dad (for so they call fathers in the Spessart) have his own palace like any other, so fine as no king could build with his own hands, but must let that alone for ever. 'Twas painted with lime, and in place of unfruitful tiles, cold lead and red copper, was roofed with that straw whereupon the noble corn doth grow, and that he, my dad, might make a proper show of nobility and riches, he had his wall round his castle built, not of stone, which men do find upon the road or dig out of the earth in barren places, much less of miserable baked bricks that in a brief space can be made and burned (as other great lords be wont to do), but he did use oak, which noble and profitable tree, being such that smoked sausage and fat ham doth grow upon it, taketh for its full growth no less than a hundred years; and where is the monarch that can imitate him therein? His halls, his rooms, and his chambers did he have thoroughly blackened with smoke, and for this reason only, that 'tis the most lasting colour in the world, and doth take longer to reach to real perfection than an artist will spend on his most excellent paintings. The tapestries were of the most delicate web in the world, wove for us by her that of old did challenge Minerva to a spinning match. His windows were dedicated to St. Papyrius for no other reason than that that same paper doth take longer to come to perfection, reckoning from the sowing of the hemp or flax whereof 'tis made, than doth the finest and clearest glass of Murano: for his trade made him apt to believe that whatever was produced with much paint was also more valuable and more costly; and what was moss costly was best suited to nobility. Instead of pages, lackeys, and grooms, he had sheep, goats, and swine, which often waited upon me in the pastures till I drove them home. His armoury was well furnished with ploughs, mattocks, axes, hoes, shovels, pitchforks, and hayforks, with which weapons he daily exercised himself; for hoeing and digging he made his military discipline, as did the old Romans in time of peace. The yoking of oxen was his generalship, the piling of dung his fortification, tilling of the land his campaigning, and the cleaning out of stables his princely pastime and exercise. By this means did he conquer the whole round world so far as he could reach, and at every harvest did draw from it rich spoils. But all this I account nothing of, and am not puffed up thereby, lest any should have cause to jibe at me as at other newfangled nobility, for I esteem myself no higher than was my dad, which had his abode in a right merry land, to wit, in the Spessart, where the wolves do howl good-night to each other. But that I have as yet told you nought of my dad's family, race and name is for the sake of precious brevity, especially since there is here no question of a foundation for gentlefolks for me to swear myself into; 'tis enough if it be known that I was born in the Spessart.

Now as my dad's manner of living will be perceived to be truly noble, so any man of sense will easily understand that my upbringing was like and suitable thereto: and whoso thinks that is not deceived, for in my tenth year had I already learned the rudiments of my dad's princely exercises: yet

as touching studies I might compare with the famous Amphistides, of whom Suidas reports that he could not count higher than five: for my dad had perchance too high a spirit, and therefore followed the use of these days, wherein many persons of quality trouble themselves not, as they say with bookworms' follies, but have their hirelings to do their inkslinging for them. Yet was I a fine performer on the bagpipe, whereon I could produce most dolorous strains. But as to knowledge of things divine, none shall ever persuade me that any lad of my age in all Christendom could there beat me, for I knew nought of God or man, of Heaven or hell, of angel or devil, nor could discern between good and evil. So may it be easily understood that I, with such knowledge of theology, lived like our first parents in Paradise, which in their innocence knew nought of sickness or death or dying, and still less of the Resurrection. O noble life! (or, as one might better say, O noodle's life!) in which none troubles himself about medicine. And by this measure ye can estimate my proficiency in the study of jurisprudence and all other arts and sciences. Yea, I was so perfected in ignorance that I knew not that I knew nothing. So say I again, O noble life that once I led! But my dad would not suffer me long to enjoy such bliss, but deemed it right that as being nobly born, I should nobly act and nobly live: and therefore began to train me up for higher things and gave me harder lessons.

*   *   *

CHAPTER IV
HOW SIMPLICISSIMUS'S PALACE WAS STORMED, PLUNDERED, AND RUINATED, AND IN WHAT SORRY FASHION THE SOLDIERS KEPT HOUSE THERE

Although it was not my intention to take the peaceloving reader with these troopers to my dad's house and farm, seeing that matters will go ill therein, yet the course of my history demands that I should leave to kind posterity an account of what manner of cruelties were now and again practised in this our German war: yea, and moreover testify by my own example that such evils must often have been sent to us by the goodness of Almighty God for our profit. For, gentle reader, who would ever have taught me that there was a God in Heaven if these soldiers had not destroyed my dad's house, and by such a deed driven me out among folk who gave me all fitting instruction thereupon? Only a little while before, I neither knew nor could fancy to myself that there were any people on earth save only my dad, my mother and me, and the rest of our household, nor did I know of any human habitation but that where I daily went out and in. But soon thereafter I understood the way of men's coming into this world, and how they must leave it again. I was only in shape a man and in name a Christian: for the rest I was but a beast. Yet the Almighty looked upon my innocence with a pitiful eye, and would bring me to a knowledge both of Himself and of myself. And although He had a thousand ways to lead me thereto, yet would He doubtless use that one only by which my dad and my mother should be punished: and that for an example to all others by reason of their heathenish upbringing of me.

The first thing these troopers did was, that they stabled their horses: thereafter each fell to his appointed task: which task was neither more nor less than ruin and destruction. For though some began to slaughter and to boil and to roast so that it looked as if there should be a merry banquet forward, yet others there were who did but storm through the house above and below stairs. Others stowed together great parcels of cloth and apparel and all manner of household stuff, as if they would set up a frippery market. All that they had no mind to take with them they cut in pieces. Some thrust their swords through the hay and straw as if they had not enough sheep and swine to slaughter: and some shook the feathers out of the beds and in their stead stuffed in bacon and other dried meat and provisions as if such were better and softer to sleep upon. Others broke the stove and the windows as if they had a never-ending summer to promise. Houseware of copper and tin they beat flat, and packed such vessels, all bent and spoiled, in with the rest. Bedsteads, tables, chairs,

and benches they burned, though there lay many cords of dry wood in the yard. Pots and pipkins must all go to pieces, either because they would eat none but roast flesh, or because their purpose was to make there but a single meal.

Our maid was so handled in the stable that she could not come out; which is a shame to tell of. Our man they laid bound upon the ground, thrust a gag into his mouth, and poured a pailful of filthy water into his body: and by this, which they called a Swedish draught, they forced him to lead a party of them to a another place where they captured men and beasts, and brought them back to our farm, in which company were my dad, my mother, and our Ursula.

And now they began: first to take the flints out of their pistols and in place of them to jam the peasants' thumbs in and so to torture the poor rogues as if they had been about the burning of witches: for one of them they had taken they thrust into the baking oven and there lit a fire under him, although he had as yet confessed no crime: as for another, they put a cord round his head and so twisted it tight with a piece of wood that the blood gushed from his mouth and nose and ears. In a word each had his own device to torture the peasants, and each peasant his several torture. But as it seemed to me then, my dad was the luckiest, for he with a laughing face confessed what others must out with in the midst of pains and miserable lamentations: and such honour without doubt fell to him because he was the householder. For they set him before a fire and bound him fast so that he could neither stir hand nor foot, and smeared the soles of his feet with wet salt, and this they made our old goat lick off, and so tickle him that he well nigh burst his sides with laughing. And this seemed to me so merry a thing that I must needs laugh with him for the sake of fellowship, or because I knew no better. In the midst of such laughter he must needs confess all that they would have of him, and indeed revealed to them a secret treasure, which proved far richer in pearls, gold, and trinkets than any would have looked for among peasants. Of the women, girls, and maidservants whom they took, I have not much to say in particular, for the soldiers would not have me see how they dealt with them. Yet this I know, that one heard some of them scream most piteously in divers corners of the house; and well I can judge it fared no better with my mother and our Ursel than with the rest. Yet in the midst of all this miserable ruin I helped to turn the spit, and in the afternoon to give the horses drink, in which employ I encountered our maid in the stable, who seemed to me wondrously tumbled, so that I knew her not, but with a weak voice she called to me, "O lad, run away, or the troopers will have thee away with them. Look to it well that thou get hence: thou seest in what plight . . ." And more she could not say.

*　　*　　*

CHAPTER XV
HOW SIMPLICISSIMUS WAS PLUNDERED, AND HOW HE DREAMED OF THE PEASANTS AND HOW THEY FARED IN TIMES OF WAR

Now when I came home I found that my fireplace and all my poor furniture, together with my store of provisions, which I had grown during the summer in my garden and had kept for the coming winter, were all gone. "And whither now?" thought I. And then first did need teach me heartily to pray: and I must summon all my small wits together, to devise what I should do. But as my knowledge of the world was both small and evil, I could come to no proper conclusion, only that 'twas best to commend myself to God and to put my whole confidence in Him: for otherwise I must perish. And besides all this those things which I had heard and seen that day lay heavy on my mind: and I pondered not so much upon my food and my sustenance as upon the enmity which there is ever between soldiers and peasants. Yet could my foolish mind come to no other conclusion than this—that there must of a surety be two races of men in the world, and not one only, descended from Adam, but two, wild and tame, like other unreasoning beasts, and therefore pursuing one another so cruelly.

With such thoughts I fell asleep, for mere misery and cold, with a hungry stomach. Then it seemed to me, as if in a dream, that all the trees which stood round my dwelling suddenly changed and took on another appearance: for on every treetop sat a trooper, and the trunks were garnished, in place of leaves, with all manner of folk. Of these, some had long lances, others musquets, hangers, halberts, flags, and some drums and fifes. Now this was merry to see, for all was neatly distributed and each according to his rank. The roots, moreover, were made up of folk of little worth, as mechanics and labourers, mostly, however, peasants and the like; and these nevertheless gave its strength to the tree and renewed the same when it was lost: yea more, they repaired the loss of any fallen leaves from among themselves to their own great damage: and all the time they lamented over them that sat on the tree, and that with good reason, for the whole weight of the tree lay upon them and pressed them so that all the money was squeezed out of their pockets, yea, though it was behind seven locks and keys: but if the money would not out, then did the commissaries so handle them with rods (which thing they call military execution) that sighs came from their heart, tears from their eyes, blood from their nails, and the marrow from their bones. Yet among these were some whom men call light o' heart; and these made but little ado, took all with a shrug, and in the midst of their torment had, in place of comfort, mockery for every turn.

CHAPTER XVI
OF THE WAYS AND WORKS OF SOLDIERS NOWADAYS, AND HOW HARDLY A COMMON SOLDIER CAN GET PROMOTION

So must the roots of these trees suffer and endure toil and misery in the midst of trouble and complaint, and those upon the lower boughs in yet greater hardship: yet were these last mostly merrier than the first named, yea and moreover, insolent and swaggering, and for the most part godless folk, and for the roots a heavy unbearable burden at all times. And this was the rhyme upon them:

Hunger and thirst, and cold and heat, and work
   and woe, and all we meet;
And deeds of blood and deeds of shame, all may
   ye put to the landsknecht's name.

Which rhymes were the less like to be lyingly
invented in that they answered to the facts. For
gluttony and drunkenness, hunger and thirst,
wenching and dicing and playing, riot and roaring,
murdering and being murdered, slaying and being
slain, torturing and being tortured, hunting and
being hunted, harrying and being harried, robbing
and being robbed, frighting and being frighted,
causing trouble and suffering trouble, beating and
being beaten: in a word, hurting and harming, and
in turn being hurt and harmed—this was their
whole life. And in this career they let nothing
hinder them: neither winter nor summer, snow
nor ice, heat nor cold, rain nor wind, hill nor dale,
wet nor dry; ditches, mountain-passes, ramparts
and walls, fire and water, were all the same to
them. Father nor mother, sister nor brother, no,
nor the danger to their own bodies, souls, and consciences, nor even loss of life and of heaven itself,
or aught else that can be named, will ever stand in
their way, for ever they toil and moil at their own
strange work, till at last, little by little, in battles,
sieges, attacks, campaigns, yea, and in their winter
quarters too (which are the soldiers' earthly paradise, if they can but happen upon fat peasants) they
perish, they die, they rot and consume away, save
but a few, who in their old age, unless they have
been right thrifty rievers and robbers, do furnish
us with the best of all beggars and vagabonds.

Next above these hard-worked folk sat old
henroost-robbers, who, after some years and
much peril of their lives, had climbed up the lowest branches and clung to them, and so far had
had the luck to escape death. Now these looked
more serious, and somewhat more dignified than
the lowest, in that they were a degree higher ascended: yet above them were some yet higher, who
had yet loftier imaginings because they had to
command the very lowest. And these people did
call coat-beaters, because they were wont to dust
the jackets of the poor pikemen, and to give the

musqueteers oil enough to grease their barrels
with.

Just above these the trunk of the tree had an
interval or stop, which was a smooth place without
branches, greased with all manner of ointments
and curious soap of disfavour, so that no man save
of noble birth could scale it, in spite of courage
and skill and knowledge, God knows how clever
he might be. For 'twas polished as smooth as a
marble pillar or a steel mirror. Just over that
smooth spot sat they with the flags: and of these
some were young, some pretty well in years: the
young folk their kinsmen had raised so far: the
older people had either mounted on a silver ladder
which is called the Bribery Backstairs or else on a
step which Fortune, for want of a better client, had
left for them. A little further up sat higher folk,
and these had also their toil and care and annoyance: yet had they this advantage, that they could
fill their pokes with the fattest slices which they
could cut out of the roots, and that with a knife
which they called "War-contribution." And these
were at their best and happiest when there came
a commissary-bird flying overhead, and shook out
a whole panfull of gold over the tree to cheer
them: for of that they caught as much as they
could, and let but little or nothing at all fall to the
lowest branches: and so of these last more died of
hunger than of the enemy's attacks, from which
danger those placed above seemed to be free.
Therefore was there a perpetual climbing and
swarming going on on those trees; for each would
needs sit in those highest and happiest places: yet
were there some idle, worthless rascals, not worth
their commissariat-bread, who troubled themselves little about higher places, and only did their
duty. So the lowest, being ambitious, hoped for
the fall of the highest, that they might sit in their
place, and if it happened to one among ten thousand of them that he got so far, yet would such
good luck come to him only in his miserable old
age when he was more fit to sit in the chimney-
corner and roast apples than to meet the foe in
the field. And if any man dealt honestly and carried himself well, yet was he ever envied by others,
and perchance by reason of some unlucky chance

of war deprived both of office and of life. And nowhere was this more grievous than at the before-mentioned smooth place on the tree: for there an officer who had had a good sergeant or corporal under him must lose him, however unwillingly, because he was now made an ensign. And for that reason they would take, in place of old soldiers, ink-slingers, footmen, overgrown pages, poor noblemen, and at times poor relations, tramps and vagabonds. And these took the very bread out of the mouths of those that had deserved it, and forthwith were made Ensigns.

*   *   *

REVIEW QUESTIONS

1. Who is Simplicissimus?
2. What is his relation to nature?
3. What does he consider noble and base?
4. What does Grimmelshausen tell us about the conduct of the Thirty Years' War?
5. What happens to the character of Simplicissimus when he witnesses the violence of war?
6. What did the Thirty Years' War do to the land and its occupants?

MICHEL EYQUEM DE MONTAIGNE

FROM "It Is Folly to Measure the True and False by Our Own Capacity"

Michel Eyquem de Montaigne (1533–1592) introduced the essay as a literary form. Born of a wealthy family in the Château de Montaigne, near Libourne, he was first educated by a tutor who spoke Latin but no French. Until he was six years old, Montaigne learned the classical language as his native tongue. He was further educated at the Collège du Guyenne, where his fluency intimidated some of the finest Latinists in France, and studied law at Toulouse. In 1554, his father purchased an office in the Cour des Aides of Périgeaux, a fiscal court later incorporated into the Parlement of Bordeaux, a position he soon resigned to his son. Montaigne spent thirteen years in office at work he found neither pleasant nor useful. In 1571, he retired to the family estate. Apart from brief visits to Paris and Rouen, periods of travel, and two terms as mayor of Bordeaux (1581–1585), Montaigne spent the rest of his life as a country gentleman. His life was not all leisure. He became gentleman-in-ordinary to the king's chamber and spent the period 1572–1576 trying to broker a peace between Catholics and Huguenots. His first two books of the Essais appeared in 1580; the third and last volume appeared in 1588. These essays are known for their discursive, conversational style, in which Montaigne undertook explorations of custom, opinion, and institutions. They gave voice to his opposition to all forms of dogmatism that were without rational basis. He observed life with a degree of skepticism, emphasizing the limits of human knowledge and the contradictions in human behavior. Indeed, Montaigne's essays are often cited as examples of an epistemological crisis born of the new discoveries, theological debates, and social tensions that marked the early modern period.

From *The Complete Essays of Montaigne,* translated by Donald M. Frame (Stanford, Calif.: Stanford University Press, 1958), pp. 132–35.

Perhaps it is not without reason that we attribute facility in belief and conviction to simplicity and ignorance; for it seems to me I once learned that belief was a sort of impression made on our mind, and that the softer and less resistant the mind, the easier it was to imprint something on it. *As the scale of the balance must necessarily sink under the weight placed upon it, so must the mind yield to evident things.* The more a mind is empty and without counterpoise, the more easily it gives beneath the weight of the first persuasive argument. That is why children, common people, women, and sick people are most subject to being led by the ears. But then, on the other hand, it is foolish presumption to go around disdaining and condemning as false whatever does not seem likely to us; which is an ordinary vice in those who think they have more than common ability. I used to do so once; and if I heard of returning spirits, prognostications of future events, enchantments, sorcery, or some other story that I could not swallow,

> Dreams, witches, miracles, magic alarms,
> Nocturnal specters, and Thessalian charms,
>
> Horace

I felt compassion for the poor people who were taken in by these follies. And now I think that I was at least as much to be pitied myself. Not that experience has since shown me anything surpassing my first beliefs, and that through no fault of my curiosity; but reason has taught me that to condemn a thing thus, dogmatically, as false and impossible, is to assume the advantage of knowing the bounds and limits of God's will and of the power of our mother Nature; and that there is no more notable folly in the world than to reduce these things to the measure of our capacity and competence. If we call prodigies or miracles whatever our reason cannot reach, how many of these appear continually to our eyes! Let us consider through what clouds and how gropingly we are led to the knowledge of most of the things that are right in our hands; assuredly we shall find that it is rather familiarity than knowledge that takes away their strangeness,

> But no one now, so tired of seeing are our eyes,
> Deigns to look up at the bright temples of the skies,
>
> Lucretius

and that if those things were presented to us for the first time, we should find them as incredible as any others, or more so.

> If they were here for the first time for men to see,
> If they were set before us unexpectedly,
> Nothing more marvelous than these things could be told,
> Nothing more unbelievable for men of old.
>
> Lucretius

He who had never seen a river thought that the first one he came across was the ocean. And the things that are the greatest within our knowledge we judge to be the utmost that nature can do in that category.

> A fair-sized stream seems vast to one who until then
> Has never seen a greater; so with trees, with men.
> In every field each man regards as vast in size
> The greatest objects that have come before his eyes.
>
> Lucretius

The mind becomes accustomed to things by the habitual sight of them, and neither wonders nor inquires about the reasons for the things it sees all the time.

The novelty of things incites us more than their greatness to seek their causes.

We must judge with more reverence the infinite power of nature, and with more consciousness of our ignorance and weakness. How many things of slight probability there are, testified to by trustworthy people, which, if we cannot be convinced of them, we should at least leave in suspense! For to condemn them as impossible is to pretend, with rash presumption, to know the limits of possibility. If people rightly understood the difference between the impossible and the unusual, and between what is contrary to the orderly course of nature and what is contrary to the common opinion of men, neither believing rashly nor disbelieving easily, they would observe the rule of "nothing too much," enjoined by Chilo.

When we find in Froissart that the count of Foix, in Béarn, learned of the defeat of King John of Castile at Juberoth the day after it happened, and the way he says he learned it, we can laugh at it; and also at the story our annals tell, that Pope Honorius performed public funeral rites for King Philip Augustus and commanded them to be performed throughout Italy on the very day he died at Mantes. For the authority of these witnesses has perhaps not enough rank to keep us in check. But if Plutarch, besides several examples that he cites from antiquity, says that he knows with certain knowledge that in the time of Domitian, the news of the battle lost by Antonius in Germany was published in Rome, several days' journey from there, and dispersed throughout the whole world, on the same day it was lost; and if Caesar maintains that it has often happened that the report has preceded the event—shall we say that these simple men let themselves be hoaxed like the common herd, because they were not clear-sighted like ourselves? Is there anything more delicate, clearer, and more alert than Pliny's judgment, when he sees fit to bring it into play, or anything farther from inanity? Leaving aside the excellence of his

knowledge, which I count for less, in which of these qualities do we surpass him? However, there is no schoolboy so young but he will convict him of falsehood, and want to give him a lesson on the progress of nature's works.

When we read in Bouchet about the miracles done by the relics of Saint Hilary, let it go: his credit is not great enough to take away our right to contradict him. But to condemn wholesale all similar stories seems to me a singular impudence. The great Saint Augustine testifies that he saw a blind child recover his sight upon the relics of Saint Gervase and Saint Protasius at Milan; a woman at Carthage cured of a cancer by the sign of the cross that a newly baptized woman made over her; Hesperius, a close friend of his, cast out the spirits that infested his house with a little earth from the sepulcher of our Lord, and a paralytic promptly cured by this earth, later, when it had been carried to church; a woman in a procession, having touched Saint Stephen's shrine with a bouquet, and rubbed her eyes with this bouquet, recover her long-lost sight; and he reports many other miracles at which he says he himself was present. Of what shall we accuse both him and two holy bishops, Aurelius and Maximinus, whom he calls upon as his witnesses? Shall it be of ignorance, simplicity, and credulity, or of knavery and imposture? Is there any man in our time so impudent that he thinks himself comparable to them, either in virtue and piety, or in learning, judgment, and ability? *Who, though they brought forth no proof, might crush me by their mere authority.*

It is a dangerous and fateful presumption, besides the absurd temerity that it implies, to disdain what we do not comprehend. For after you have established, according to your fine understanding, the limits of truth and falsehood, and it turns out that you must necessarily believe things even stranger than those you deny, you are obliged from then on to abandon these limits. Now, what seems to me to bring as much disorder into our consciences as anything, in these religious troubles that we are in, is this partial surrender of their beliefs by Catholics. It seems to them that they are being very moderate and understanding when they yield to their opponents some of the articles in dispute. But, besides the fact that they do not see what an advantage it is to a man charging you for you to begin to give ground and withdraw, and how much that encourages him to pursue his point, those articles which they select as the most trivial are sometimes very important. We must either submit completely to the authority of our ecclesiastical government, or do without it completely. It is not for us to decide what portion of obedience we owe it.

Moreover, I can say this for having tried it. In other days I exercised this freedom of personal choice and selection, regarding with negligence certain points in the observance of our Church which seem more vain or strange than others; until, coming to discuss them with learned men, I found that these things have a massive and very solid foundation, and that it is only stupidity and ignorance that make us receive them with less reverence than the rest. Why do we not remember how much contradiction we sense even in our own judgment? How many things were articles of faith to us yesterday, which are fables to us today? Vainglory and curiosity are the two scourges of our soul. The latter leads us to thrust our noses into everything, and the former forbids us to leave anything unresolved and undecided.

Review Questions

1. What are the limits of human knowledge?
2. What roles do authority and experience play in knowledge?
3. How does Montaigne's attitude toward prodigies or miracles compare with that of Reginald Scot?
4. How do their conceptions of nature differ?
5. How might Montaigne's reflection on knowledge indicate an intellectual crisis?

MICHEL EYQUEM DE MONTAIGNE

FROM "Of Cannibals"

From *The Complete Essays of Montaigne*, translated by Donald M. Frame (Stanford, Calif.: Stanford University Press, 1958).

When King Pyrrhus passed over into Italy, after he had reconnoitered the formation of the army that the Romans were sending to meet him, he said: "I do not know what barbarians these are" (for so the Greeks called all foreign nations), "but the formation of this army that I see is not at all barbarous." The Greeks said as much of the army that Flamininus brought into their country, and so did Philip, seeing from a knoll the order and distribution of the Roman camp, in his kingdom, under Publius Sulpicius Galba. Thus we should beware of clinging to vulgar opinions, and judge things by reason's way, not by popular say.

I had with me for a long time a man who had lived for ten or twelve years in that other world which has been discovered in our century, in the place where Villegaignon landed, and which he called Antarctic France. This discovery of a boundless country seems worthy of consideration. I don't know if I can guarantee that some other such discovery will not be made in the future, so many personages greater than ourselves having been mistaken about this one. I am afraid we have eyes bigger than our stomachs, and more curiosity than capacity. We embrace everything, but we clasp only wind.

*   *   *

This man I had was a simple, crude fellow— a character fit to bear true witness; for clever people observe more things and more curiously, but they interpret them; and to lend weight and conviction to their interpretation, they cannot help altering history a little. They never show you things as they are, but bend and disguise them according to the way they have seen them; and to give credence to their judgment and attract you to it, they are prone to add something to their matter, to stretch it out and amplify it. We need a man either very honest, or so simple that he has not the stuff to build up false inventions and give them plausibility; and wedded to no theory. Such was my man; and besides this, he at various times brought sailors and merchants, whom he had known on that trip, to see me. So I content myself with his information, without inquiring what the cosmographers say about it.

*   *   *

Now, to return to my subject, I think there is nothing barbarous and savage in that nation, from what I have been told, except that each man calls barbarism whatever is not his own practice; for indeed it seems we have no other test of truth and reason than the example and pattern of the opinions and customs of the country we live in. *There is always the perfect religion, the perfect government, the perfect and accomplished manners in all things.* Those people are wild, just as we call wild the fruits that Nature has produced by herself and in her normal course; whereas really it is those that we have changed artificially and led astray from the common order, that we should rather call wild. The former retain alive and vigorous their genuine, their most useful and natural, virtues and properties, which we have debased in the latter in adapting them to gratify our corrupted taste. And yet for all that, the savor and delicacy of some uncultivated fruits of those countries is quite as excellent, even to our taste, as that of our own. It is not reasonable that art should win the place of honor over our great and powerful mother Nature. We have so overloaded the beauty and richness of her works by our inventions that we have quite smothered her. Yet wherever her purity shines forth, she wonderfully puts to shame our vain and frivolous attempts:

> Ivy comes readier without our care;
> In lonely caves the arbutus grows more fair;
> No art with artless bird song can compare.
>   Propertius

All our efforts cannot even succeed in reproducing the nest of the tiniest little bird, its contexture, its beauty and convenience; or even the web of the puny spider. All things, says Plato, are produced by nature, by fortune, or by art; the greatest and most beautiful by one or the other of the first two, the least and most imperfect by the last.

These nations, then, seem to me barbarous in this sense, that they have been fashioned very little by the human mind, and are still very close to their original naturalness. The laws of nature still rule them, very little corrupted by ours; and they are in such a state of purity that I am sometimes vexed that they were unknown earlier, in the days when there were men able to judge them better than we. I am sorry that Lycurgus and Plato did not know of them; for it seems to me that what we actually see in these nations surpasses not only all the pictures in which poets have idealized the golden age and all their inventions in imagining a happy state of man, but also the conceptions and the very desire of philosophy. They could not imagine a naturalness so pure and simple as we see by experience; nor could they believe that our society could be maintained with so little artifice and human solder. This is a nation, I should say to Plato, in which there is no sort of traffic, no knowledge of letters, no science of numbers, no name for a magistrate or for political superiority, no custom of servitude, no riches or poverty, no contracts, no successions, no partitions, no occupations but leisure ones, no care for any but common kinship, no clothes, no agriculture, no metal, no use of wine or wheat. The very words that signify lying, treachery, dissimulation, avarice, envy, belittling, pardon—unheard of. How far from this perfection would he find the republic that he imagined: *Men fresh sprung from the gods.*

These manners nature first ordained.

Virgil

For the rest, they live in a country with a very pleasant and temperate climate, so that according to my witnesses it is rare to see a sick man there; and they have assured me that they never saw one palsied, bleary-eyed, toothless, or bent with age. They are settled along the sea and shut in on the land side by great high mountains, with a stretch about a hundred leagues wide in between. They have a great abundance of fish and flesh which bear no resemblance to ours, and they eat them with no other artifice than cooking. The first man who rode a horse there, though he had had dealings with them on several other trips, so horrified them in this posture that they shot him dead with arrows before they could recognize him.

Their buildings are very long, with a capacity of two or three hundred souls; they are covered with the bark of great trees, the strips reaching to the ground at one end and supporting and leaning on one another at the top, in the manner of some of our barns, whose covering hangs down to the ground and acts as a side. They have wood so hard that they cut with it and make of it their swords and grills to cook their food. Their beds are of a cotton weave, hung from the roof like those in our ships, each man having his own; for the wives sleep apart from their husbands.

They get up with the sun, and eat immediately upon rising, to last them through the day; for they take no other meal than that one. Like some other Eastern peoples, of whom Suidas tells us, who drank apart from meals, they do not drink then; but they drink several times a day, and to capacity. Their drink is made of some root, and is of the color of our claret wines. They drink it only lukewarm. This beverage keeps only two or three days; it has a slightly sharp taste, is not at all heady, is

good for the stomach, and has a laxative effect upon those who are not used to it; it is a very pleasant drink for anyone who is accustomed to it. In place of bread they use a certain white substance like preserved coriander. I have tried it; it tastes sweet and a little flat.

The whole day is spent in dancing. The younger men go to hunt animals with bows. Some of the women busy themselves meanwhile with warming their drink, which is their chief duty. Some one of the old men, in the morning before they begin to eat, preaches to the whole barnful in common, walking from one end to the other, and repeating one single sentence several times until he has completed the circuit (for the buildings are fully a hundred paces long). He recommends to them only two things: valor against the enemy and love for their wives. And they never fail to point out this obligation, as their refrain, that it is their wives who keep their drink warm and seasoned.

There may be seen in several places, including my own house, specimens of their beds, of their ropes, of their wooden swords and the bracelets with which they cover their wrists in combats, and of the big canes, open at one end, by whose sound they keep time in their dances. They are close shaven all over, and shave themselves much more cleanly than we, with nothing but a wooden or stone razor. They believe that souls are immortal, and that those who have deserved well of the gods are lodged in that part of heaven where the sun rises, and the damned in the west.

They have some sort of priests and prophets, but they rarely appear before the people, having their home in the mountains. On their arrival there is a great feast and solemn assembly of several villages—each barn, as I have described it, makes up a village, and they are about one French league from each other. The prophet speaks to them in public, exhorting them to virtue and their duty; but their whole ethical science contains only these two articles: resoluteness in war and affection for their wives. He prophesies to them things to come and the results they are to expect from their undertakings, and urges them to war or holds them back from it; but this is on the condition that when he fails to prophesy correctly, and if things turn out otherwise than he has predicted, he is cut into a thousand pieces if they catch him, and condemned as a false prophet. For this reason, the prophet who has once been mistaken is never seen again.

*   *   *

They have their wars with the nations beyond the mountains, further inland, to which they go quite naked, with no other arms than bows or wooden swords ending in a sharp point, in the manner of the tongues of our boar spears. It is astonishing what firmness they show in their combats, which never end but in slaughter and bloodshed; for as to routs and terror, they know nothing of either.

Each man brings back as his trophy the head of the enemy he has killed, and sets it up at the entrance to his dwelling. After they have treated their prisoners well for a long time with all the hospitality they can think of, each man who has a prisoner calls a great assembly of his acquaintances. He ties a rope to one of the prisoner's arms, by the end of which he holds him, a few steps away, for fear of being hurt, and gives his dearest friend the other arm to hold in the same way; and these two, in the presence of the whole assembly, kill him with their swords. This done, they roast him and eat him in common and send some pieces to their absent friends. This is not, as people think, for nourishment, as of old the Scythians used to do; it is to betoken an extreme revenge. And the proof of this came when they saw the Portuguese, who had joined forces with their adversaries, inflict a different kind of death on them when they took them prisoner, which was to bury them up to the waist, shoot the rest of their body full of arrows, and afterward hang them. They thought that these people from the other world, being men who had sown the knowledge of many vices among their neighbors and were much greater masters than themselves in every sort of wickedness, did not adopt this sort of vengeance without some reason, and that it

must be more painful than their own; so they began to give up their old method and to follow this one.

I am not sorry that we notice the barbarous horror of such acts, but I am heartily sorry that, judging their faults rightly, we should be so blind to our own. I think there is more barbarity in eating a man alive than in eating him dead; and in tearing by tortures and the rack a body still full of feeling, in roasting a man bit by bit, in having him bitten and mangled by dogs and swine (as we have not only read but seen within fresh memory, not among ancient enemies, but among neighbors and fellow citizens, and what is worse, on the pretext of piety and religion), than in roasting and eating him after he is dead.

*   *   *

So we may well call these people barbarians, in respect to the rules of reason, but not in respect to ourselves, who surpass them in every kind of barbarity.

Their warfare is wholly noble and generous, and as excusable and beautiful as this human disease can be; its only basis among them is their rivalry in valor. They are not fighting for the conquest of new lands, for they still enjoy that natural abundance that provides them without toil and trouble with all necessary things in such profusion that they have no wish to enlarge their boundaries. They are still in that happy state of desiring only as much as their natural needs demand; anything beyond that is superfluous to them.

They generally call those of the same age, brothers; those who are younger, children; and the old men are fathers to all the others. These leave to their heirs in common the full possession of their property, without division or any other title at all than just the one that Nature gives to her creatures in bringing them into the world.

If their neighbors cross the mountains to attack them and win a victory, the gain of the victor is glory, and the advantage of having proved the master in valor and virtue; for apart from this they have no use for the goods of the vanquished, and they return to their own country, where they lack neither anything necessary nor that great thing, the knowledge of how to enjoy their condition happily and be content with it. These men of ours do the same in their turn. They demand of their prisoners no other ransom than that they confess and acknowledge their defeat. But there is not one in a whole century who does not choose to die rather than to relax a single bit, by word or look, from the grandeur of an invincible courage; not one who would not rather be killed and eaten than so much as ask not to be. They treat them very freely, so that life may be all the dearer to them, and usually entertain them with threats of their coming death, of the torments they will have to suffer, the preparations that are being made for that purpose, the cutting up of their limbs, and the feast that will be made at their expense. All this is done for the sole purpose of extorting from their lips some weak or base word, or making them want to flee, so as to gain the advantage of having terrified them and broken down their firmness. For indeed, if you take it the right way, it is in this point alone that true victory lies:

It is no victory
Unless the vanquished foe admits your mastery.
Claudian

The Hungarians, very bellicose fighters, did not in olden times pursue their advantage beyond putting the enemy at their mercy. For having wrung a confession from him to this effect, they let him go unharmed and unransomed, except, at most, for exacting his promise never again to take up arms against them.

We win enough advantages over our enemies that are borrowed advantages, not really our own. It is the quality of a porter, not of valor, to have sturdier arms and legs; agility is a dead and corporeal quality; it is a stroke of luck to make our enemy stumble, or dazzle his eyes by the sunlight; it is a trick of art and technique, which may be found in a worthless coward, to be an able fencer. The worth and value of a man is in his heart and his will; there lies his real honor. Valor is the strength, not of legs and arms, but of heart and

soul; it consists not in the worth of our horse or our weapons, but in our own. He who falls obstinate in his courage, *if he has fallen, he fights on his knees.* He who relaxes none of his assurance, no matter how great the danger of imminent death; who, giving up his soul, still looks firmly and scornfully at his enemy—he is beaten not by us, but by fortune; he is killed, not conquered.

*   *   *

To return to our story. These prisoners are so far from giving in, in spite of all that is done to them, that on the contrary, during the two or three months that they are kept, they wear a gay expression; they urge their captors to hurry and put them to the test; they defy them, insult them, reproach them with their cowardice and the number of battles they have lost to the prisoners' own people.

I have a song composed by a prisoner which contains this challenge, that they should all come boldly and gather to dine off him, for they will be eating at the same time their own fathers and grandfathers, who have served to feed and nourish his body. "These muscles," he says, "this flesh and these veins are your own, poor fools that you are. You do not recognize that the substance of your ancestors' limbs is still contained in them. Savor them well; you will find in them the taste of your own flesh." An idea that certainly does not smack of barbarity. Those that paint these people dying, and who show the execution, portray the prisoner spitting in the face of his slayers and scowling at them. Indeed, to the last gasp they never stop braving and defying their enemies by word and look. Truly here are real savages by our standards; for either they must be thoroughly so, or we must be; there is an amazing distance between their character and ours.

The men there have several wives, and the higher their reputation for valor the more wives they have. It is a remarkably beautiful thing about their marriages that the same jealousy our wives have to keep us from the affection and kindness of other women, theirs have to win this for them. Being more concerned for their husbands' honor than for anything else, they strive and scheme to have as many companions as they can, since that is a sign of their husbands' valor.

*   *   *

Three of these men, ignorant of the price they will pay some day, in loss of repose and happiness, for gaining knowledge of the corruptions of this side of the ocean; ignorant also of the fact that of this intercourse will come their ruin (which I suppose is already well advanced: poor wretches, to let themselves be tricked by the desire for new things, and to have left the serenity of their own sky to come and see ours!)—three of these men were at Rouen, at the time the late King Charles IX was there. The king talked to them for a long time; they were shown our ways, our splendor, the aspect of a fine city. After that, someone asked their opinion, and wanted to know what they had found most amazing. They mentioned three things, of which I have forgotten the third, and I am very sorry for it; but I still remember two of them. They said that in the first place they thought it very strange that so many grown men, bearded, strong, and armed, who were around the king (it is likely that they were talking about the Swiss of his guard) should submit to obey a child, and that one of them was not chosen to command instead. Second (they have a way in their language of speaking of men as halves of one another), they had noticed that there were among us men full and gorged with all sorts of good things, and that their other halves were beggars at their doors, emaciated with hunger and poverty; and they thought it strange that these needy halves could endure such an injustice, and did not take the others by the throat, or set fire to their houses.

I had a very long talk with one of them; but I had an interpreter who followed my meaning so badly, and who was so hindered by his stupidity in taking in my ideas, that I could get hardly any satisfaction from the man. When I asked him what profit he gained from his superior position among his people (for he was a captain, and our sailors called him king), he told me that it was to march foremost in war. How many men followed him? He pointed to a piece of ground, to signify as many as such a space could hold; it might have been four or five thousand men. Did all his authority expire with the war? He said that this much remained, that when he visited the villages dependent on him, they made paths for him through the underbrush by which he might pass quite comfortably.

All this is not too bad—but what's the use? They don't wear breeches.

*   *   *

REVIEW QUESTIONS

1. What lessons does Montaigne draw from accounts of the new world?
2. Why do you suppose Montaigne chose cannibalism, of all possible topics, to compare European and American cultures?
3. How does he reflect the crisis of the iron century?
4. Are there any human constants for Montaigne?
5. Does he believe in a single human nature, a single ideal of virtue?

THOMAS HARRISON

"Speech from the Gallows"

Upon the restoration of the monarchy in England, at the end of the Interregnum, Thomas Harrison (1606–1660) was condemned and hanged for the execution of Charles I in 1649. The regicide had been an enthusiastic supporter of the parliamentary cause during the English Civil War. He had joined the army in the early 1640s and by 1650 had risen to the rank of major-general. When parliamentary forces captured Charles, Harrison argued that the king should be tried and punished for his misdeeds. He guarded the king during his return to London, tried him as a member of the court, and signed the order of execution. Harrison and Cromwell eventually fell out over political matters. As a Fifth Monarchist, Harrison believed that the Age of the Saints was at hand, when they would descend from heaven and rule earth in glory. He accused Cromwell of lacking faith for his efforts to establish a permanent republican government. For this, Cromwell deprived Harrison of his commission. After the Restoration, when it became clear that Charles II would prosecute those revolutionaries who were involved in his father's death, Harrison refused to flee. His faith that he had acted in accordance with God's Will sustained him, as his speech from the gallows makes clear.

From *The Indictment, Arraingment, Tryal and Judgement at Large of Twenty Nine Regicides* (London, 1724), pp. 277, 284–87; reprinted in *Modern Europe and America,* edited by William H. McNeill and Schuyler Owen Houser (New York: Oxford University Press, 1973), pp. 53–58.

On Saturday the 13th of October, 1660, betwixt Nine and Ten of the Clock in the Morning, Mr. Thomas Harrison, or Major-General Harrison, according to his Sentence, was upon a Hurdle drawn from Newgate to the Place called Charing-Cross, where within certain Rails lately there made, a Gibbet was erected, and he hanged with his Face looking towards the Banqueting-House at Whitehall, (the Place where our late Sovereign of Eternal Memory was sacrificed;) being half dead, he was cut down by the common Executioner, his Privy Members cut off before his Eyes, his Bowels burned, his Head severed from his Body, and his Body divided into Quarters, which were returned back to Newgate upon the same Hurdle that carried it. His Head is since set on a Pole on the Top of the South-East End of Westminister-Hall, looking towards London. The Quarters of his Body are in like manner exposed upon some of the City Gates.

*   *   *

Having mounted the ladder for his execution, he spoke as follows:
Gentlemen,

I Did not expect to have spoken a Word to you at this Time, but seeing there is a Silence commanded, I will speak something of the Work God had in Hand in our Days.

Many of you have been Witnesses of the Finger of God, that hath been seen amongst us of late Years, in the Deliverance of his People from their Oppressors; and in bringing to Judgement those that were Guilty of the precious Blood of the dear

Servants of the Lord. And how God did witness thereto, by many wonderful and evident Testimonies, as it were immediately from Heaven; insomuch, that many of our Enemies, who were Persons of no mean Quality, were forc'd to confess, That God was with us: And if God did but stand Neuter, they should not value us. And therefore seeing the Finger of God hath been pleading this Cause, I shall not need to speak much to it: In which Work I with others were engaged; for the which I do from my Soul, bless the Name of God, who, out of the exceeding Riches of his Grace, accounted me worthy to be instrumental in so glorious a Work, and though I am wrongfully charged with Murther and Blood-shed, yet I must tell you, I have kept a good Conscience, both towards God, and towards Man. I never had Malice against any Man; neither did I act maliciously towards any Person, but as I judged them to be Enemies to God and his People: And the Lord is my Witness, that I have done what I did out of the Sincerity of my Heart to the Lord. I bless God I have no Guilt upon my Conscience, but the Spirit of God beareth witness, that my Actions are acceptable to the Lord through Jesus Christ: Though I have been compassed about with manifold Infirmities, Failings and Imperfections in my holiest Duties; but in this I have Comfort and Consolation, that I have Peace with God, and do see all my Sins wash'd away in the Blood of my dear Saviour. And I do declare, as before the Lord, that I would not be guilty wittingly nor willingly of the Blood of the meanest Man, no not for ten thousand Worlds, much less of the Blood of such as I am charged with.

I have again and again besought the Lord with Tears to make known his Will and Mind unto me concerning it; and to this Day he hath rather confirmed me in the Justice of it; and therefore I leave it to him, and to him I commit my Ways; but some that were eminent in the Work, did wickedly turn aside themselves, and set up their Nests on high,[1] which caused great Dishonour to the Name of God, and the Profession they had made. And the Lord knows I could have suffered more than this, rather than have fallen in with them in that Iniquity; though I was offered what I would if I would have joined with them: My Aim in all my Proceedings was the Glory of God, and the Good of his People, and the Welfare of the whole Commonwealth.

[The People observing him to tremble in his Hands and Legs, he taking notice of it, said,]

Gentlemen, By reason of some scoffing that I do hear, I judge, that some do think I am afraid to die, by the shaking I have in my Hands and Knees; I tell you, No, but it is by reason of much Blood I have lost in the Wars, and many Wounds I have received in my Body, which caused this Shaking and Weakness in my Nerves. I have had it this Twelve Years; I speak this to the Praise and Glory of God; he hath carried me above the Fear of Death; and I value not my Life, because I go to my Father, and am assured I shall take it up again.

Gentlemen, Take notice, that for being instrumental in that Cause and Interest of the Son of God, which hath been pleaded amongst us, and which God hath witnessed to by Appeals and wonderful Victories, I am brought to this Place to suffer Death this Day; and if I had Ten thousand Lives, I would freely and chearfully lay them down all to witness to this Matter.

Oh! what am I, poor Worm, that I should be accounted worthy to suffer any Thing for the Sake of my Lord and Saviour Jesus Christ! I have gone joyfully and willingly many a Time to lay down my Life upon the Account of Christ, but never with so much Joy and Freedom as at this Time. I do not lay down my Life by constraint but willingly; for if I had been minded to have run away, I might have had many Opportunities; but being so clear in the Thing, I durst not turn my Back, nor step a Foot out of the Way, by reason I had been engaged in the Service of so glorious and great a God: However Men presume to call it by hard Names, yet, I believe, e'er it be long the Lord will make it known from Heaven, that there was more of God in it, than Men are now aware of. All the Gods of the Nations are but Idols, they have Eyes but see not,

---

[1] Harrison refers to Oliver Cromwell and others who helped set up the revolutionary governments, 1649–1658.

and Mouths but speak not, and cannot save those that trust in them. But my God is the King of Kings, and Lord of Lords; before whom all you here, and all Nations, are but as a Drop of a Bucket. And he will never leave those that truly trust in him, unto whose Glory I shall surely go, and shall sit on the Right Hand of Christ in Heaven; it may be, to judge those that have unjustly judged me, Matth. 25.33, 34. I Cor. 6.2.

[The Sheriff minding him of the Shortness of Time; if he had any Thing to say to the People, he might. He said,]

I do desire, as from my own Soul, that they and every one may fear the Lord, that they may consider their latter End, and so it may be well with them; and even for the worst of those that have been most malitious against me, from my Soul I would forgive them all. So far as any Thing concerns me, and so far as it concerns the Cause and Glory of God, I leave for him to plead: And as for the Cause of God, I am willing to justify it by my Sufferings, according to the good Pleasure of his Will.

I have been this Morning, before I came hither, so hurried up and down Stairs, (the Meaning whereof I knew not,) that my Spirits are almost spent; therefore you may not expect much from me.

Oh, the Greatness of the Love of God to such a poor, vile, and nothing-creature as I am! What am I, that Jesus Christ should shed his Heart's Blood for me, that I might be happy to all Eternity; that I might be made a Son of God, and an Heir of Heaven! Oh, that Christ should undergo so great Sufferings and Reproaches for me, and should not I be willing to lay down my Life, and suffer Reproaches for him that hath so loved me! Blessed be the Name of God that I have a Life to lose upon so glorious, and so honourable an Account.

[Then praying to himself, with Tears; and having ended, the Hangman pull'd down his Cap; but he thrust it up again, saying,]

I have one Word more to the Lord's People, that desire to serve him with an upright Heart: Let them not think hardly of any of the good Ways of God for all this; for I have been near this Seven Years a suffering Person, and have found the Way of God to be a perfect Way, his Word a tried Word, a Buckler to them that trust in him, and will make known his glorious Arm in the Sight of all Nations. And though we may suffer hard Things, yet he hath a gracious End, and will make a good End for his own Glory, and the Good of his People; therefore be chearful in the Lord your God, hold fast that which you have, and be not afraid of suffering; for God will make hard and bitter Things sweet and easy to all those that trust in him. Keep close to the good Confession you have made of Jesus Christ, and look to the Recompence of Reward: Be not discouraged, by reason of the Cloud that now is upon you; for the Sun will shine, and God will give a Testimony unto what he hath been a doing, in a short Time.

And now I desire to commit my Concernments into the Hands of my Lord and Saviour Jesus Christ; he that hath delivered himself for the Chief of Sinners; he that came into the World, was made Flesh, and was crucified, that hath loved me, and washed me from my Sins in his own Blood, and is risen again, sitting at the Right-Hand of God, making Intercession for me.

And as for me, Oh, who am I, poor, Base, vile Worm, that God should deal thus by me? for this will make me come the sooner into his Glory, and to inherit the Kingdom, and the Crown prepared for me! Oh, I have served a good Lord and Master, which hath helped me from my Beginning to this Day, and hath carried me through many Difficulties, Trials, Straits and Temptations, and hath always been a very present Help in Time of Trouble; he hath covered my Head many Times in the Day of Battle: By God, I have leaped over a Wall; by God I have run through a Troop; and by my God I will go through this Death, and he will make it easy for me. Now into thy Hand, O Lord Jesus, I commit my Spirit.

REVIEW QUESTIONS

1. What purpose might be served by the horrifying, public execution of Thomas Harrison?

2. How does Harrison justify his part in the execution of a king, and what, according to him, are the limits of political obedience?

3. Harrison sees himself as a willing martyr for his faith, but does he also see himself as a revolutionary for a cause? What might the differences be?

4. Why does Harrison, though condemned of a political crime, justify his actions in terms of religious faith?

5. Is this speech a call to revolution?

BLAISE PASCAL

FROM *Pensées*

Blaise Pascal (1623–1662) was born the son of a French official. During his life, he dabbled in many subjects, including science, religion, and literature. His conversion to Jansenism plunged him into controversy with the Jesuits, giving rise to his Lettres provinciales. *These, along with his* Pensées, *from which the current selection is drawn, established his literary fame. His thought contains a fascinating blend of confidence in human reason and consciousness of its limits. René Descartes viewed Pascal as the embodiment of a mentality of intellectual and spiritual crisis. Be that as it may, Pascal is also considered one of the great stylists of the French language.*

From *Pensées*, by Blaise Pascal, translated by A. J. Krailsheimer (New York: Penguin Books, 1995), pp. 58–64, 121–25.

The Wager

*   *   *

Infinity—nothing. Our soul is cast into the body where it finds number, time, dimensions; it reasons about these things and calls them natural, or necessary, and can believe nothing else.

Unity added to infinity does not increase it at all, any more than a foot added to an infinite measurement: the finite is annihilated in the presence of the infinite and becomes pure nothingness. So it is with our mind before God, with our justice before divine justice. There is not so great a disproportion between our justice and God's as between unity and infinity.

God's justice must be as vast as his mercy. Now his justice towards the damned is less vast and ought to be less startling to us than his mercy towards the elect.

We know that the infinite exists without knowing its nature, just as we know that it is untrue that numbers are finite. Thus it is true that there is an infinite number, but we do not know what it is. It is untrue that it is even, untrue that it is odd, for by adding a unit it does not change its nature. Yet it is a number, and every number is even or odd. (It is true that this applies to every finite number.)

Therefore we may well know that God exists without knowing what he is.

Is there no substantial truth, seeing that there are so many true things which are not truth itself?

Thus we know the existence and nature of the finite because we too are finite and extended in space.

We know the existence of the infinite without knowing its nature, because it too has extension but unlike us no limits.

But we do not know either the existence or the nature of God, because he has neither extension nor limits.

But by faith we know his existence, through glory we shall know his nature.

Now I have already proved that it is quite possible to know that something exists without knowing its nature.

Let us now speak according to our natural lights.

If there is a God, he is infinitely beyond our comprehension, since, being indivisible and without limits, he bears no relation to us. We are therefore incapable of knowing either what he is or whether he is. That being so, who would dare to attempt an answer to the question? Certainly not we, who bear no relation to him.

Who then will condemn Christians for being unable to give rational grounds for their belief, professing as they do a religion for which they cannot give rational grounds? They declare that it is a folly, *stultitiam,* in expounding it to the world, and then you complain that they do not prove it. If they did prove it they would not be keeping their word. It is by being without proof that they show they are not without sense. "Yes, but although that excuses those who offer their religion as such, and absolves them from the criticism of producing it without rational grounds, it does not absolve those who accept it." Let us then examine this point, and let us say: "Either God is or he is not." But to which view shall we be inclined? Reason cannot decide this question. Infinite chaos separates us. At the far end of this infinite distance a coin is being spun which will come down heads or tails. How will you wager? Reason cannot make you choose either, reason cannot prove either wrong.

Do not then condemn as wrong those who have made a choice, for you know nothing about it. "No, but I will condemn them not for having made this particular choice, but any choice, for, although the one who calls heads and the other one are equally at fault, the fact is that they are both at fault: the right thing is not to wager at all."

Yes, but you must wager. There is no choice, you are already committed. Which will you choose then? Let us see: since a choice must be made, let us see which offers you the least interest. You have two things to lose: the true and the good; and two things to stake: your reason and your will, your knowledge and your happiness; and your nature has two things to avoid: error and wretchedness. Since you must necessarily choose, your reason is no more affronted by choosing one rather than the other. That is one point cleared up. But your happiness? Let us weigh up the gain and the loss involved in calling heads that God exists. Let us assess the two cases: if you win you win everything, if you lose you lose nothing. Do not hesitate then; wager that he does exist. "That is wonderful. Yes, I must wager, but perhaps I am wagering too much." Let us see: since there is an equal chance of gain and loss, if you stood to win only two lives for one you could still wager, but supposing you stood to win three?

You would have to play (since you must necessarily play) and it would be unwise of you, once you are obliged to play, not to risk your life in order to win three lives at a game in which there is an equal chance of losing and winning. But there is an eternity of life and happiness. That being so, even though there were an infinite number of chances, of which only one were in your favour, you would still be right to wager one in order to win two; and you would be acting wrongly, being obliged to play, in refusing to stake one life against three in a game, where out of an infinite number of chances there is one in your favour, if there were an infinity of infinitely happy life to be won. But here there is an infinity of infinitely happy life to be won, one chance of winning against a finite number of chances of losing, and what you are staking is finite. That leaves no choice; wherever there is infinity, and where there are not infinite chances of losing against that of winning, there is no room for hesitation, you must give everything. And thus, since you are obliged to play, you must be renouncing reason if you hoard your life rather than risk it for an infinite gain, just as likely to occur as a loss amounting to nothing.

For it is no good saying that it is uncertain whether you will win, that it is certain that you are taking a risk, and that the infinite distance between the certainty of what you are risking and the uncertainty of what you may gain makes the finite good you are certainly risking equal to the infinite good that you are not certain to gain. This is not the case. Every gambler takes a certain risk for an uncertain gain, and yet he is taking a certain finite risk for an uncertain finite gain without sinning against reason. Here there is no infinite distance between the certain risk and the uncertain gain: that is not true. There is, indeed, an infinite distance between the certainty of winning and the certainty of losing, but the proportion between the uncertainty of winning and the certainty of what is being risked is in proportion to the chances of winning or losing. And hence if there are as many chances on one side as on the other you are playing for even odds. And in that case the certainty of what you are risking is equal to the uncertainty of what you may win; it is by no means infinitely distant from it. Thus our argument carries infinite weight, when the stakes are finite in a game where there are even chances of winning and losing and an infinite prize to be won.

This is conclusive and if men are capable of any truth this is it.

"I confess, I admit it, but is there really no way of seeing what the cards are?"—"Yes. Scripture and the rest, etc."—"Yes, but my hands are tied and my lips are sealed; I am being forced to wager and I am not free; I am being held fast and I am so made that I cannot believe. What do you want me to do then?"—"That is true, but at least get it into your head that, if you are unable to believe, it is because of your passions, since reason impels you to believe and yet you cannot do so. Concentrate then not on convincing yourself by multiplying proofs of God's existence but by diminishing your passions. You want to find faith and you do not know the road. You want to be cured of unbelief and you ask for the remedy: learn from those who were once bound like you and who now wager all they have. These are people who know the road you wish to follow, who have been cured of the affliction of which you wish to be cured: follow the way by which they began. They behaved just as if they did believe, taking holy water, having masses said, and so on. That will make you believe quite naturally, and will make you more docile."—"But that is what I am afraid of."—"But why? What have you to lose? But to show you that this is the way, the fact is that this diminishes the passions which are your great obstacles. . . ."

End of this address.

"Now what harm will come to you from choosing this course? You will be faithful, honest, humble, grateful, full of good works, a sincere, true friend. . . . It is true you will not enjoy noxious pleasures, glory and good living, but will you not have others?

"I tell you that you will gain even in this life, and that at every step you take along this road you will see that your gain is so certain and your risk so negligible that in the end you will realize that you have wagered on something certain and infinite for which you have paid nothing."

"How these words fill me with rapture and delight!—"

"If my words please you and seem cogent, you must know that they come from a man who went down upon his knees before and after to pray this infinite and indivisible being, to whom he submits his own, that he might bring your being also to submit to him for your own good and for his glory: and that strength might thus be reconciled with lowliness."

*   *   *

REVIEW QUESTIONS

1. How does Pascal conceive of the human condition?
2. What does it mean for him to have a body?
3. How does he differ in this respect from Montaigne?
4. How does Pascal construct his proof for the existence of God?
5. Why does he begin with infinity, a mathematical concept?
6. What is he saying about the limits of human knowledge?
7. For whom might this essay have been written?
8. Why must we wager?

THE SURRENDER OF BREDA (1635)   DIEGO VELÁZQUEZ

One of a series of marshal portraits by Velázquez, The Surrender of Breda *records the moment in which Dutch governor Justin de Nassau symbolically surrendered the keys of the Brabantine fortress town of Breda to Ambrosio de Spinola, commander of the besieging Spanish forces. The actual capitulation took place three days earlier. Spinola had offered honorable terms in order to end twelve months of determined resistance. The depiction of peaceful amity and order between bitter foes contrasted sharply with the harsh realities of warfare in early modern Europe. What might have been Velázquez's purpose, as a painter at the court of Spain, in capturing the surrender of Breda? What might be the symbolic intent of Spinola's (figure receiving key, right center) graceful smile and the peaceful attitudes of the* tercios *(soldiers with vertical lances, extreme right)? How and why does* The Surrender of Breda *describe and distort the realities of statecraft and warfare in the seventeenth century?*

JACQUELINE PASCAL

FROM "Rule for Children"

Jacqueline Pascal (1625–1661), sister of Blaise Pascal, was a prodigy in her own right, composing verse and plays from an early age. In 1646, she became devoted to Jansenism and took the veil in 1652. She took the name of Sister Jacqueline de Sainte Euphémie and became instrumental in the reforms carried out at Port-Royal. One of these was the revival of the boarding school for girls, for which she composed her "Rule for Children," a statement of pedagogical theory and practice. Sister Jacqueline divided her Rule into two parts. The first describes an austere, monastic schedule that would characterize the students' routine; the educational substance included reading, writing, and reckoning but clearly emphasized religious instruction and observance. Its traditionalism notwithstanding, this part of the Rule contained innovations, especially with regard to the role of older students as teachers of their younger schoolmates and with regard to understanding rather than memorization of content. The second part, from which the following extract is drawn, treats the spirit rather than the content of education. It makes clear that Sister Jacqueline created an educational environment that empowered women. The teacher—a nun—was responsible for the education of her pupils, shaping it to their individual needs, based on her own assessment of their individual characters. It is a testimonial to the intellectual and spiritual authority of women. At the same time, the Jansenist quality becomes apparent: insistence upon moral improvement that is mirrored in the lived experience. The emphasis is upon close observation and control. Empowerment did not mean liberation.

From *A Rule for Children and Other Writings*, edited and translated by John J. Conley (Chicago: University of Chicago Press, 2003), pp. 96–102, 116–17.

Part 2:
Spiritual and Physical Welfare

Having reported to you how we organize the daily schedule for our children, it now remains for me to consider the second issue you enjoined me to explain: the spirit in which I respond to all the spiritual and physical needs of the pupils. When I explain what I am supposed to do, it is not because I often fail to do so. But these duties will move you to pray to God for me so that he will make me what I should be in order to safeguard these souls he has committed to the care of one so incapable of serving them. There are many things that I am not capable of saying in this particular report, since

I cannot find the right words to express myself. Still, obedience makes me rise above my difficulties, since you have bound me to tell not only how I work with the children, but also what I believe we should do for their education.

**1. IN WHAT SPIRIT WE MUST SERVE CHILDREN.
UNION AMONG THE SCHOOLMISTRESSES.
SOME GENERAL ADVICE ABOUT THEIR CONDUCT,
ESPECIALLY TOWARD SMALL CHILDREN**

1. If we are truly to serve children, I believe that we should never speak to them nor act on their behalf without considering God and asking for his holy grace. We should want to take directly

from God everything that is necessary to instruct pupils in the fear of God.

2. We must have much charity and tenderness for the pupils. We must neglect nothing, internal or external, that they need. On many different occasions we should let them see that there is no limit to our desire to serve them and that we do so with real affection and fervor, because they are children of God. We feel obliged to spare nothing in their service, in order to make them truly worthy of this holy dignity.

3. It is necessary that we give ourselves to their service without stinting. Without some urgent reason, we should never leave their quarters. We should always be present in the common room where they do their studies and their work. We make only brief exceptions to speak to them, or to visit them when they are ill, or when we are taken by other duties concerning their needs.

4. We should not be disturbed when we cannot assist at an occasional office, except when the older pupils themselves are present at it. It is so important to mind the children that we should prefer this obligation to anything else, when obedience requires us to assume this task. We should prefer it even to the fulfillment of our own immediate spiritual desires. The charity with which we give them the services they need not only will cover many of our faults, it will take the place of many things we think we must have for our perfection.

5. We should have at least one nun we can count on, without in any way withdrawing her from her other obligations. If possible, this nun should remain as much as she can in the common room. That is why it is desirable to have two nuns who would be inspired by the same zeal and by the same sensitivity toward children. It would be good to have them both in the common room, even in the presence of the headmistress. Seeing the respect the children show toward both of them, each one would have the right in the other's absence to ask the class to show the same respect to her that they show toward the absent nun.

6. We must ensure that the children notice a deep harmony, a perfect union, and a clear trust between the companion nun and ourselves. That is

why we must never publicly criticize anything she says or does, so that the children never notice any disagreement. This should be reserved for a private conversation. It is important, indeed necessary, that the nun we are given as an auxiliary have the disposition to approve everything we tell her. This agreement is crucial for the education of children. If this is not the case, we should alert the superior. Still, if her resistance to us only grates against our temperament and causes no wrong to the children, we should ask God to obtain the grace to rejoice in the fact that we had an opportunity to experience adversity.

7. We must implore God to give our children a great respect for the nuns who help us. We must also give them great authority, especially the nun who works with the pupils after us. That is why it is good to witness to the children, and even to tell them on occasion, that this nun shows great charity toward them, that she loves them, and that we are the ones who oblige her to report everything that happens in the common room. In front of the pupils we could even tell the nun that she is obligated by charity and by duty to tell us not only all the serious faults committed, but also the lighter faults, so that they might be assisted in correcting them.

8. We take the auxiliary nuns into our confidence when we tell them about the inclinations of the pupils, specifically those of the youngest and also those of the older pupils who might cause some trouble. Thus they might be even more vigilant. Still, we should not lightly reveal those things that the children told us in private. We should do this only when it is clearly necessary for their welfare. There is always danger in revealing a confidence too easily. I think it is very important that the children trust our discretion. Although they often tell us things that are of little importance, there are occasions when they want to confide something important, especially as they grow older. They will find it difficult to tell us these things if they feel that we had not maintained their confidences concerning small matters.

9. Since it is so important that we have a profound union and mutual comprehension with the

nuns given to us as aides, it is even more important that these nuns act only according to the order they find established by the headmistress. They should be so imbued with the sentiments of the head-mistress that they speak only through her mouth and see only by her eyes. The children should no-tice nothing that is not perfectly harmonious be-tween the nuns. If the auxiliary nuns find anything to question in the conduct of the headmistress they should tell her, if they are confident enough to ap-proach her and if they have permission from their superior to do so. If God does not give them this confidence, they must alert the mother superior so that they can avoid showing any sign of dissension to the pupils.

10. When there are two nuns in the common room at the moment the office bell rings, they can say their office one after the other so that one of them still keeps an eye on the pupils. But she will say nothing about the faults she has seen them do, if they were minor, until her companion has fin-ished her office. It is important to inculcate in the pupils a deep sense of reverence when they see that we are praying to God. However, as soon as the of-fice is finished (which is short enough when we re-cite it in a low voice), we must punish the pupils in proportion to the severity of the fault. The pun-ishment should be even more severe when the fault was committed during a time of prayer.

11. When there is only one nun, there should not be any difficulty in keeping an eye on the pupils, but she should not say anything until she has completely finished her office. We have seen by experience how the pupils benefit from this. When we are strict about neither speaking to them nor responding to them during prayer, they become more reverent as they themselves pray and are more fearful about interrupting us. We can never do enough to inspire reverence for God among the young, by our personal example as much as by our words. That is why we should be punctual in say-ing our office at the very moment that the other nuns chant it in the church choir. We should leave everything we are doing at the second chime of the office bell, and we should never let ourselves ab-sentmindedly finish something that we like. I do

not mean to say that, if some real need demanded immediate attention to the pupils, we should not prefer that service to that of our office. Still, it is important that both the children and our con-science be convinced that we act only out of con-sideration for God. Our example is the greatest lesson we can give. The devil gives them a razor-sharp memory, so that they remember our least faults. He has damaged their memory to prevent them from remembering the little good we are able to do.

12. Since obedience has committed us to this work, we can never pray enough, never humble ourselves enough, and never be vigilant enough to give the children what we owe them. I think this is one of the most important missions in the house. We really should tremble as we carry out this mis-sion. Still, we should not be overly fearful. We should place our trust in God and ask him by our sighs to grant us what we do not merit by our-selves. We ask him this grace by the blood of his Son, shed for these innocent souls whom he has placed in our hands. We must always consider these tiny souls as a sacred deposit entrusted to us and of which one day we must render an account. That is why we should talk to the pupils less than we talk to God about them.

13. Since we are obligated to be always among our pupils, we should conduct ourselves in a way that avoids extremes or inconsistency. There is a danger in treating the children too softly on one occasion, then too severely on another. Ordinarily these two faults accompany each other. When we let ourselves be carried away by making all these little hugs and flatteries, which gives the pupils the freedom to act just as their mood and their feelings desire, it is inevitable that a period of cold reproof will follow. This is what creates inconsistency, which is much more hurtful to a child than always keeping her within the confines of her duties.

14. We should never be too familiar with them, nor should we show them too great a confidence, unless they are quite mature. But we must always show them true charity and a great attentiveness in meeting their needs and even in anticipating them.

15. We should treat them politely and speak to them only with respect. We should accede to their desires in everything that is possible. Sometimes it is a good idea to show some special consideration in things that are indifferent in themselves. This helps to win over their hearts.

16. When it is necessary to correct them for light faults or for their bad temper, we should never mimic or bully them, even if they have shown a bad spirit. On the contrary, we should always speak to them calmly and give them good reasons in order to convince them. This will prevent them from growing bitter. It will also help them to accept what we are trying to say to them.

17. We must frequently ask God to give the pupils a frank simplicity and to work on our end to remove from them any spirit of subterfuge or of cunning. But we have to do this in a subtle way so that we do not end up making them more cunning by exhorting them to be simple. That is why I think we should not complain to them that they already show too much craftiness. Sometimes when we keep telling them they should not be sly, they figure out that they are. They then use everything we warned them about earlier when they need to find some artifice to conceal certain faults they do not want others to know.

18. That is why we must maintain a perfect surveillance of the pupils, never leaving them alone anywhere, whether they are healthy or sick. Still, we should not be so obtrusive that we end up encouraging a spirit of defiance or making the child apprehensive. Overzealousness encourages the pupils, especially the younger ones, to attempt little pranks in hiding. I also think that our continual surveillance should be done with a certain gentleness and trust, which helps them believe that we love them and that we stay with them only to give them proper company. This helps them to enjoy rather than to fear this surveillance.

19. Even more than with the other pupils, it is important to treat and nourish the youngest as if they were small doves. We should not say much when they commit some major fault that deserves punishment. But when we are certain they deserve punishment, we should punish the pupils without saying a word. We should give an explanation for the punishment only afterward. Still, before we say anything, it is good to ask them if they know why they have been punished. Ordinarily they have some idea of the cause. Done promptly and without words, this punishment prevents them from telling lies to have an excuse for their faults. Young children are all too prone to this vice. I find that this method really helps them to overcome their faults, because they are always afraid of being taken by surprise.

20. I also believe that we do not need to correct them too much about their lighter faults. If we are always talking about their faults, they quickly dismiss it as routine. For every fault we remark, we should turn a blind eye to three or four. Nonetheless, when we have observed a particular fault recurring several times, we should take them by surprise and have them do some reparation for their fault immediately. This helps them to correct themselves more than words do.

21. When there are some young pupils who are completely obstinate and unruly, we should try three or four times to have them perform the same small reparations. When they see that we will not budge, they are completely disarmed. But if we insist on punishment one day, and then forgive their fault or just ignore it another day, that behavior makes no impression on their mind. We will then have to resort to much stronger methods than those we could have used if we had been consistent in our repeated demands for reparation.

22. Lying is all too frequent among young children. That is why we must do everything possible to persuade them not to adopt this pernicious habit. To help in this area, it seems to me that we must encourage them with great tenderness to confess their faults, telling them that it is obvious to us what they have done wrong. When they themselves confess their transgression, we should pardon them and reduce their penance.

23. Even when the pupils are very young, say four or five years old, we should not let them pass the time with nothing to do. We should organize their day, teaching them to read for fifteen minutes, then to play for another quarter hour, and

then to work a little during another little period. These changes of activity divert them and prevent them from picking up a bad habit common to infants: namely, playing with their book or their yarn as they squirm around, glancing everywhere. When we ask them to use up a good fifteen or even thirty minutes, and when we promise them that if they work hard they can play afterward, they work well and happily during this period to gain the reward afterward. When we make this promise before their work period, but they play all through the supposed work period, we do not say anything to them. However, at the end of the failed work period, when they think they are going to play, it is necessary to assign them a new period to do their promised work. This shows them that we do not always have to talk to them when they do something wrong. But when they use their time only to fritter it away, they must start the work period again. This takes them by surprise and makes them more cautious the next time.

9. BOOKS AND READING

1. The books we use for the education of our pupils include the following: *Tradition of the Church;*[1] *Letters of Saint-Cyran;*[2] *Imitation of Jesus Christ;* works of Grenada;[3] *Introduction to the Devout Life;*[4] *The Heavenly Ladder* by Saint John Climacus;[5] *Simple Theology;*[6] *Christian Maxims,* from

the book of hours;[7] *Meditations of Saint Teresa d'Avila on the Pater Noster.*[8] We also use other books whose aim is the formation of a truly Christian woman.

2. I already discussed the readings at 8:00 a.m. in my earlier exposition of the daily school schedule.

3. For the public reading that one of the pupils performs after vespers, one could use a number of other books. Examples would be *Letters of Saint Jerome;*[9] *Of Christian Almsgiving;*[1] and Saint Teresa of Avila's *Path of Perfection* or *Book of the Foundations,*[2] especially those passages treating the lives of the desert fathers. Other lives of the saints are also helpful.

4. Except for the one after vespers, we teachers ourselves do all the public readings for the pupils as a group. We always take care to explain what we just read and to talk to them about it. We should always try to have them develop the habit of never listening to the readings in a spirit of amusement or of curiosity. Rather, they should listen with a desire to apply their lessons to their lives. To accomplish this, we need to explain the readings in ways that convince the pupils that it is more important to become a good Christian woman and to correct their faults than it is to become a woman scholar.

5. Besides the readings we perform by ourselves, we tell them what they should read. They are permitted to change neither the book nor the passage we have assigned. There are few books that do not contain something that should be avoided.

---

[1] *Tradition de l'église sur le sujet de la penitence et de la communion,* selected texts, trans. Antoine Arnauld (Paris, 1644).

[2] Saint-Cyran, *Lettres de Saint-Cyran* (Paris, 1645).

[3] Louis de Grenade, *Catéchisme, ou Introduction du symbole de la foi,* trans. Nicolas Colin (Paris, 1587); *Les sermons sur les principales fêtes des saints,* trans. Jean Charon (Paris, 1602); *Traité de l'oraison et la méditation,* trans. Jean de Chabanel and François de Belleforest (Paris, 1608).

[4] Saint François de Sales, *Introduction à la vie dévote,* last ed. (Paris: G. Clopejau, 1640).

[5] Saint Jean de Climaque, *Traité des degrés pour monter au ciel,* trans. Arnauld d'Andilly (Paris, 1652).

[6] Saint-Cyran, *Théologie familière* (Paris, 1643).

[7] *Heures de Port-Royal: Office de l'église en latin et en français* (Paris, 1650). Jacqueline Pascal contributed her translation of the hymn "Jesu, nostra redemptio" to the volume.

[8] *Méditations de Sainte Thérèse sur le Pater Noster,* trans. Antoine Le Maître (Paris, [1665]).

[9] Saint Jerôme, *Les Lettres de S. Jerôme,* trans. Jean Petit (Paris: Jean Couterot, 1679).

[1] *Aumône chrétienne,* selected texts trans. Arnauld d'Andilly (Paris, 1647).

[2] Sainte Thérèse d'Avila, *Les oeuvres de sainte Thérèse, divisées en trois parties,* trans. Robert Arnauld d'Andilly (Anvers: H. Van Dunewald, 1688).

6. At the reading after vespers, they are permitted, in fact encouraged, to ask questions about what they do not understand, as long as they remain respectful and humble. When we answer them, we teach them how to apply this reading to reform their morals. If, as we do the reading, they keep asking questions about something we think most of them were not listening to, we ask them if they understand it. If it is obvious that they cannot answer, we reprove them for remaining in their ignorance, since they knew they were supposed to acquire knowledge concerning all the subjects they did not yet understand.

7. As soon as the reading is finished, we put the book back in its place. We let the pupils privately own only a few books: their book of hours; *Simple Theology;* an *Imitation of Jesus Christ,* and a Latin-French psalter. All the other books remain in the possession of the schoolmistresses. The pupils are content with this arrangement, since they realize that even the most sacred books are of little benefit to them when they are read simply out of curiosity. The moral effect of this sacred reading is nearly always diminished when they keep their books in private.

8. They are forbidden to open any book that is not theirs. Nor may they borrow books from each other without the permission of the schoolmistress. This permission is rarely given, in order to avoid the small disorders this borrowing may cause.

REVIEW QUESTIONS

1. How would you characterize Sister Jacqueline's attitude toward her pupils?
2. What insights does her attitude provide for the nature of childhood, as understood in the seventeenth century?
3. What is the purpose of the education that Sister Jacqueline's Rule would provide?
4. What relationships should the nuns have with their pupils?
5. What ends does the close observation of the pupils serve?
6. What do the prescribed readings tell you about the education of women in the seventeenth century?
7. How might the emphasis on question and explanation be innovative?

JEAN BODIN

FROM *On Sovereignty*

Jean Bodin (1529–1596) was born a bourgeois in Angers. He entered a Carmelite monastery in 1545, apparently set on an ecclesiastical career, but obtained release from his vows around 1549. He pursued a course of study at the royal Collège de Quatre Langues in Paris. By 1550, he was well trained in humanist studies and went on to become one of the greatest scholars of his day. His continual search for religious truth placed him repeatedly under suspicion of heresy, but no clear evidence exists to support a conversion to Calvinism. Bodin continued his studies and attended the University of Toulouse, where he studied law during the 1550s. In 1561, he launched his public career by serving as an advocate before the parliament in Paris. Bodin soon rose to the attention of high officials and dignitaries and received special commissions from the king as early as 1570. In 1571, he entered the service of Francis, Duke of Alençon, a prince of the blood. During his service to Alençon, and in the aftermath of the St. Bartholomew's Day massacre, Bodin published his great work, Six livres de la république *(1576), a systematic exposition of public law. It included an absolutist theory of royal government, from which the following selection is drawn. Bodin's theory was based on the controversial notion, which proved highly influential in the development of royal absolutism, that sovereignty was indivisible and that high powers of government could not be shared by separate agents or agencies. His notion that all governmental powers were concentrated in the king of France can be seen as a direct response to the anarchy of civil war that gripped the kingdom during the second half of the sixteenth century. In 1576, Bodin was chosen as a deputy for the Third Estate of the Estates-General of Blois. Though a royalist, Bodin opposed the civil wars that raged in France and became a leading spokesperson against royal requests for increased taxation and religious uniformity. It cost him royal favor and high office. With the death in 1584 of his patron, the duke of Alençon, Bodin's career in high politics ended. He retired to Laon, where he died.*

From *On Sovereignty*, by Jean Bodin, edited by Julian H. Franklin (Cambridge, Eng.: Cambridge University Press, 1992), pp. 46–50.

Book I

*　　*　　*

CHAPTER 8
ON SOVEREIGNTY

Sovereignty is the absolute and perpetual power of a commonwealth, which the Latins call *maiestas;* the Greeks *akra exousia, kurion arche,* and *kurion politeuma;* and the Italians *segnioria,* a word they use for private persons as well as for those who have full control of the state, while the Hebrews call it *tomech shévet*—that is, the highest power of command. We must now formulate a definition of sovereignty because no jurist or political philosopher has defined it, even though it is the chief point, and the one that needs most to be explained, in a treatise on the commonwealth. Inasmuch as we have said that a commonwealth is a just government, with sovereign power, of several households and of that which they have in common, we need to clarify the meaning of sovereign power.

*　　*　　*

We shall conclude, then, that the sovereignty of the monarch is in no way altered by the presence of the Estates. On the contrary, his majesty is all the greater and more illustrious when all his people publicly acknowledge him as sovereign, even though, in an assembly like this, princes, not wishing to rebuff their subjects, grant and pass many things that they would not consent to had they not been overcome by the requests, petitions, and just complaints of a harassed and afflicted people which has most often been wronged without the knowledge of the prince, who sees and hears only through the eyes, ears, and reports of others.

We thus see that the main point of sovereign majesty and absolute power consists of giving the law to subjects in general without their consent. Not to go to other countries, we in this kingdom have often seen certain general customs repealed by edicts of our kings without hearing from the Estates when the injustice of the rules was obvious. Thus the custom concerning the inheritance by mothers of their children's goods, which was observed in this kingdom throughout the entire region governed by customary law, was changed without assembling either the general or local estates. Nor is this something new. In the time of King Philip the Fair, the general custom of the entire kingdom, by which the losing party in a case could not be required to pay expenses, was suppressed by an edict without assembling the Estates.

*   *   *

CHAPTER 10
ON THE TRUE MARKS OF SOVEREIGNTY

Since there is nothing greater on earth, after God, than sovereign princes, and since they have been established by Him as His lieutenants for commanding other men, we need to be precise about their status so that we may respect and revere their majesty in complete obedience, and do them honor in our thoughts and in our speech. Contempt for one's sovereign prince is contempt toward God, of whom he is the earthly image. That is why God, speaking to Samuel, from whom the people had demanded a different prince, said "It is me that they have wronged."

To be able to recognize such a person—that is, a sovereign—we have to know his attributes, which are properties not shared by subjects. For if they were shared, there would be no sovereign prince. Yet the best writers on this subject have not treated this point with the clarity it deserves, whether from flattery, fear, hatred, or forgetfulness.

We read that Samuel, after consecrating the king that God had designated, wrote a book about the rights of majesty. But the Hebrews have written that the kings suppressed his book so that they could tyrannize their subjects. Melanchthon thus went astray in thinking that the rights of majesty were the abuses and tyrannical practices that Samuel pointed out to the people in a speech. "Do you wish to know," said Samuel, "the ways of tyrants? It is to seize the goods of subjects to dispose of at his pleasure, and to seize their women and their children in order to abuse them and to make them slaves." The word *mishpotim* as it is used in this passage does not mean rights, but rather practices and ways of doing things. Otherwise this good prince, Samuel, would have contradicted himself. For when accounting to the people for the stewardship that God had given him, he said, "Is there anyone among you who can say that I ever took gold or silver from him, or any present whatsoever?" And thereupon the whole people loudly praised him for never having done a wrong or taken anything from anyone no matter who.

*   *   *

We may thus conclude that the first prerogative of a sovereign prince is to give law to all in general and each in particular. But this is not sufficient. We have to add "without the consent of any other, whether greater, equal, or below him." For if the prince is obligated to make no law without the consent of a superior, he is clearly a subject; if of an equal, he has an associate; if of subjects, such as the senate or the people, he is not sovereign. The names of grandees that one finds affixed to edicts are not put there to give the law its force, but to witness it and to add weight to it so that the enactment will be more acceptable. For there are very ancient edicts, extant at Saint Denys in France, issued by Philip I and Louis the Fat in 1060 and 1129 respectively, to which the seals of their queens Anne and Alix, and of Robert and Hugh, were affixed. For Louis the Fat, it was year twelve of his reign; for Adelaide, year six.

When I say that the first prerogative of sovereignty is to give law to all in general and to each in particular, the latter part refers to privileges, which are in the jurisdiction of sovereign princes to the exclusion of all others. I call it a privilege when a law is made for one or a few private individuals, no matter whether it is for the profit or the loss of the person with respect to whom it is decreed. Thus Cicero said, *Privilegium de meo capite latum est.* "They have passed," he said, "a capital privilege against me." He is referring to the authorization to put him on trial decreed against him by the commoners at the request of the tribune Clodius. He calls this the *lex Clodia* in many places, and he bitterly protests that privileges could be decreed only by the great Estates of the people as it was laid down by the laws of the Twelve Tables in the words: *Privilegia, nisi comitiis centuriatis irroganto, qui secus faxit capital esto.*[1] And all those who have written of regalian rights agree that only the sovereign can grant privileges, exemptions, and immunities, and grant dispensations from edicts and ordinances. In monarchies, however, privileges last only for the lifetime of the monarchs, as the emperor Tiberius, Suetonius reports, informed all those who had received privileges from Augustus.

*   *   *

Book II

CHAPTER 5
WHETHER IT IS LAWFUL TO MAKE AN ATTEMPT UPON THE TYRANT'S LIFE AND TO NULLIFY AND REPEAL HIS ORDINANCES AFTER HE IS DEAD

Ignorance of the exact meaning of the term "tyrant" has led many people astray, and has been the cause of many inconveniences. We have said that a tyrant is someone who makes himself into a sovereign prince by his own authority—without election, or right of succession, or lot, or a just war, or a special calling from God. This is what is understood by tyrant in the writings of the ancients and in the laws that would have him put to death. Indeed, the ancients established great prizes and rewards for those who killed tyrants, offering titles of nobility, prowess, and chivalry to them along with statues and honorific titles, and even all the tyrant's goods, because they were taken as true liberators of the fatherland, or of the motherland, as the Cretans say. In this they did not distinguish, between a good and virtuous prince and a bad and wicked one, for no one has the right to seize the sovereignty and make himself the

master of those who had been his companions, no matter what pretenses of justice and virtue he may offer. In strictest law, furthermore, use of the prerogatives reserved to sovereignty is punishable by death. Hence if a subject seeks, by whatever means, to invade the state and steal it from his king or, in a democracy or aristocracy, to turn himself from a fellow-citizen into lord and master, he deserves to be put to death. In this respect our question does not pose any difficulty.

*   *   *

At this point there are many questions one may ask, such as whether a tyrant, who I said may be justly killed without form or shape of trial, becomes legitimate if, after having encroached upon sovereignty by force or fraud, he has himself elected by the Estates. For it seems that the solemn act of election is an authentic ratification of the tyranny, an indication that the people have found it to their liking. But I say that it is nevertheless permissible to kill him, and to do so by force unless the tyrant, stripping off his authority, has given up his arms and put power back into the hands of the people in order to have its judgment. What tyrants force upon a people stripped of power cannot be called consent. Sulla, for example, had himself made dictator for eighty years by the Valerian law, which he got published with a powerful army camped inside the city of Rome. But Cicero said that this was not a law. Another example is Caesar, who had himself made permanent dictator by the Servian law; and yet another is Cosimo de Medici who, having an army inside Florence, had himself elected duke. When objections were raised, he set off a volley of gunfire in front of the palace, which induced the lords and magistrates to get on with it more quickly.

*   *   *

So much then for the tyrant, whether virtuous or wicked, who makes himself a sovereign lord on his own authority. But the chief difficulty arising from our question is whether a sovereign prince who has come into possession of the state by way of election, or lot, or right of succession, or just

---

[1] "Let no privileges be imposed except in the *comita centuriata;* let him who has done otherwise be put to death."

war, or by a special calling from God, can be killed if he is cruel, oppressive, or excessively wicked. For that is the meaning given to the word tyrant. Many doctors and theologians, who have touched upon this question, have resolved that it is permissible to kill a tyrant without distinction, and some, putting two words together that are incompatible, have spoken of a king-tyrant (*roi tyran*), which has caused the ruin of some very fine and flourishing monarchies.

But to decide this question properly we need to distinguish between a prince who is absolutely sovereign and one who is not, and between subjects and foreigners. It makes a great difference whether we say that a tyrant can be lawfully killed by a foreign prince or by a subject. For just as it is glorious and becoming, when the gates of justice have been shut, for someone, whoever he may be, to use force in defense of the goods, honor, and life of those who have been unjustly oppressed—as Moses did when he saw his brother being beaten and mistreated and had no way of getting justice—so is it a most beautiful and magnificent thing for a prince to take up arms in order to avenge an entire people unjustly oppressed by a tyrant's cruelty, as did Hercules, who traveled all over the world exterminating tyrant-monsters and was deified for his great feats. The same was done by Dion, Timoleon, Aratus, and other generous princes, who obtained the title of chastisers and correctors of tyrants. This, furthermore, was the sole cause for which Tamerlane, prince of the Tartars, declared war on Bajazet, who was then besieging Constantinople, Tamerlane saying that he had come to punish him for tyranny and to deliver the afflicted peoples. He defeated Bajazet in a battle fought on the plateau of Mount Stella, and after he had killed and routed three hundred thousand Turks, he had the tyrant chained inside a cage until he died. In this case it makes no difference whether this virtuous prince proceeds against a tyrant by force, deception, or judicial means. It is however true that if a virtuous prince has seized a tyrant, he will obtain more honor by putting him on trial and punishing him as a murderer, parricide, and thief, rather than acting against him by the common law of peoples (*droit des gens*).

But as for subjects, and what they may do, one has to know whether the prince is absolutely sovereign, or is properly speaking not a sovereign. For if he is not absolutely sovereign, it follows necessarily that sovereignty is in the people or the aristocracy. In this latter case there is no doubt that it is permissible to proceed against the tyrant either by way of law if one can prevail against him, or else by way of fact and open force, if one cannot otherwise have justice. Thus the Senate took the first way against Nero, the second against Maximinus inasmuch as the Roman emperors were no more than princes of the republic, in the sense of first persons and chief citizens, with sovereignty remaining in the people and the Senate.

*   *   *

But if the prince is sovereign absolutely, as are the genuine monarchs of France, Spain, England, Scotland, Ethiopia, Turkey, Persia, and Moscovy—whose power has never been called into question and whose sovereignty has never been shared with subjects—then it is not the part of any subject individually, or all of them in general, to make an attempt on the honor or the life of the monarch, either by way of force or by way of law, even if he has committed all the misdeeds, impieties, and cruelties that one could mention. As to the way of law, the subject has no right of jurisdiction over his prince, on whom all power and authority to command depends; he not only can revoke all the power of his magistrates, but in his presence, all the power and jurisdiction of all magistrates, guilds and corporations, Estates and communities, cease, as we have said and will say again even more elaborately in the proper place. And if it is not permissible for a subject to pass judgment on his prince, or a vassal on his lord, or a servant on his master—in short, if it is not permissible to proceed against one's king by way of law—how could it be licit to do so by way of force? For the question here is not to discover who is the strongest, but only whether it is permissible in law, and whether a subject has the power to condemn his sovereign prince.

A subject is guilty of treason in the first degree not only for having killed a sovereign prince, but also for attempting it, advising it, wishing it, or even thinking it. And the law finds this so monstrous [as to subject it to a special rule of sentencing]. Ordinarily, if someone who is accused, seized, and convicted dies before he has been sentenced, his personal status is not diminished, no matter what his crime, even if it was treason. But treason in the highest degree can never be purged by the death of the person accused of it, and even someone who was never accused is considered in law as having been already sentenced. And although evil thoughts are not subject to punishment, anyone who has thought of making an attempt on the life of his sovereign prince is held to be guilty of a capital crime, no matter whether he repented of it. In fact there was a gentleman from Normandy who confessed to a Franciscan friar that he had wanted to kill King Francis I but had repented of this evil wish. The Franciscan gave him absolution, but still told the king about it; he had the gentleman sent before the Parlement of Paris to stand trial, where he was condemned to death by its verdict and thereupon executed. And one cannot say that the court acted from fear, in view of the fact that it often refused to verify edicts and letters patent even when the king commanded it. And in Paris a man, named Caboche, who was completely mad and out of his senses, drew a sword against King Henry II without any effect or even attempt. He too was condemned to die without consideration of his insanity, which the law ordinarily excuses no matter what murder or crime the madman may have committed.

*   *   *

As for Calvin's remark that if there existed in these times magistrates especially constituted for the defense of the people and to restrain the licentiousness of kings, like the ephors in Sparta, the tribunes in Rome, and the demarchs in Athens, then those magistrates should resist, oppose, and prevent their licentiousness and cruelty—it clearly shows that it is never licit, in a proper monarchy, to attack a sovereign king, or defend one's self against him, or to make an attempt upon his life or honor, for he spoke only of democratic and aristocratic states. I have shown above that the kings of Sparta were but simple senators and captains. And when he speaks of the Estates, he says "possible," not daring to be definite. In any event there is an important difference between attacking the honor of one's prince and resisting his tyranny, between killing one's king and opposing his cruelty.

We thus read that the Protestant princes of Germany, before taking up arms against the emperor, asked Martin Luther if it were permissible. He frankly replied that it was not permissible no matter how great the charge of impiety or tyranny. But he was not heeded; and the outcome of the affair was miserable, bringing with it the ruin of some great and illustrious houses of Germany. *Quia nulla iusta causa videri potest*, said Cicero, *adversus patriam arma capiendi*.[2] Admittedly, it is quite certain that the sovereignty of the German Empire does not lie in the person of the emperor, as we shall explain in due course. But since he is the chief, they could have taken up arms against him only with the consent of the Estates or its majority, which was not obtained. It would have been even less permissible against a sovereign prince.

I can give no better parallel than that of a son with respect to his father. The law of God says that he who speaks evil of his father or his mother shall be put to death. If the father be a murderer, a thief, a traitor to his country, a person who has committed incest or parricide, a blasphemer, an atheist, and anything else one wants to add, I confess that the entire gamut of penalties will not suffice for his punishment; but I say that it is not for his son to lay hands on him, *quia nulla tanta impietas, nullum tantum factum est quod sit parricidio vindicandum*,[3] as it was put by an orator of ancient times. And yet Cicero, taking up this question, says that love of country is even greater. Hence

---

[2] "Because there can never be a just cause to take up arms against one's country."

[3] "Because there is no impiety so great, and no crime so great that it ought to be avenged by patricide."

the prince of our country, being ordained and sent by God, is always more sacred and ought to be more inviolable than a father.

I conclude then that it is never permissible for a subject to attempt anything against a sovereign prince, no matter how wicked and cruel a tyrant he may be. It is certainly permissible not to obey him in anything that is against the law of God or nature—to flee, to hide, to evade his blows, to suffer death rather than make any attempt upon his life or honor. For oh, how many tyrants there would be if it were lawful to kill them! He who taxes too heavily would be a tyrant, as the vulgar understand it; he who gives commands that the people do not like would be a tyrant, as Aristotle defined a tyrant in the *Politics;* he who maintains guards for his security would be a tyrant; he who punishes conspirators against his rule would be a

tyrant. How then should good princes be secure in their lives? I would not say that it is illicit for other princes to proceed against tyrants by force of arms, as I have stated, but it is not for subjects.

*   *   *

REVIEW QUESTIONS

1. What, according to Bodin, is the definition of sovereignty?
2. In describing its prerogatives, would Bodin have agreed with Machiavelli?
3. Can sovereignty be mixed? Why?
4. Is it permissible to resist a tyrant?
5. Can a sovereign ruler be a tyrant?
6. May one resist a sovereign?

THOMAS HOBBES

FROM *Leviathan*

Thomas Hobbes (1588–1679) was an English philosopher whose mechanistic and deterministic theories of political life were highly controversial in his own time. Born in Malmesbury, Hobbes attended Magdalen Hall, Oxford, and became tutor to William Cavendish, later earl of Devonshire, in 1608. With his student, he undertook several tours of the continent where he met and spoke with leading intellectual lights of the day, including Galileo and Descartes. Around 1637, he became interested in the constitutional struggle between parliament and Charles I and set to work writing a "little treatise in English" in defense of the royal prerogative. Before its publication in 1650, the book circulated privately in 1640 under the title Elements of Law, Natural and Politic. *Fearing arrest by parliament, Hobbes fled to Paris, where he remained for the next eleven years. While in exile, he served as math tutor to the Prince of Wales, Charles II, from 1646 to 1648. His great work,* Leviathan *(1651), was a forceful argument for political absolutism. Its title, taken from the horrifying sea monster of the Old Testament, suggested the power and authority Hobbes thought necessary to compel obedience and order in human society. Strongly influenced by mechanical philosophy, he treated human beings as matter in motion, subject to certain physical, rational laws. People feared one another and lived in a state of constant competition and conflict. For this reason, they must submit to the absolute, supreme authority of the state, a social contract among selfish individuals moved by fear and necessity. Once delegated, that authority was irrevocable and indivisible. Ironically, these theories found favor neither with royalists nor with antiroyalists. Charles II believed that it was written in justification of the Commonwealth. The French feared its attacks on the papacy. After the Restoration, Parliament added* Leviathan *to a list of books to be investigated for atheistic tendencies. Despite frustrations over the reception of his political theories, Hobbes retained his intellectual vigor. At age eighty-four, he wrote an autobiography in Latin and translated the works of Homer into English. He died at age ninety-one.*

From *Leviathan*, by Thomas Hobbes, edited by E. Hershey Sneath (Needham, Eng.: Ginn Press, 1898).

*   *   *

Of the Causes, Generation, and Definition of a Commonwealth

The final cause, end, or design of men, who naturally love liberty and dominion over others, in the introduction of that restraint upon themselves in which we see them live in commonwealths is the foresight of their own preservation, and of a more contented life thereby; that is to say, of getting themselves out from that miserable condition of war which is necessarily consequent . . . to the natural passions of men when there is no visible power to keep them in awe and tie them by fear of punishment to the performance of their covenants, and observation of the laws of nature. . . .

For the laws of nature, as "justice," "equity," "modesty," "mercy," and, in sum, "doing to others as we would be done to," of themselves, without the terror of some power to cause them to be observed, are contrary to our natural passions, that carry us to partiality, pride, revenge, and the like. And covenants without the sword are but words, and of no strength to secure a man at all. Therefore, notwithstanding the laws of nature, which every one has then kept when he has the will to keep them, when he can do it safely, if there be no power erected, or not great enough for our security; every man will, and may lawfully rely on his own strength and art, for protection against all

other men. And in all places where men have lived by small families, to rob and spoil one another has been a trade, and so far from being reputed against the law of nature that the greater spoils they gained, the greater was their honor; and men observed no other laws therein but the laws of honor; that is, to abstain from cruelty, leaving to men their lives and instruments of livelihood. And as small families did then, so now do cities and kingdoms, which are but greater families, for their own security enlarge their dominions upon all pretenses of danger and fear of invasion or assistance that may be given to invaders, and endeavor as much as they can to subdue or weaken their neighbors by open force and secret arts, for lack of other protection, justly; and are remembered for it in later ages with honor.

Nor is it the joining together of a small number of men that gives them this security, because in small numbers small additions on the one side or the other make the advantage of strength so great as is sufficient to carry the victory; and therefore gives encouragement to an invasion. The multitude sufficient to confide in for our security is not determined by any certain number but by comparison with the enemy we fear; and is then sufficient when the advantage of the enemy is not so visible and conspicuous to determine the event of war as to move him to attempt it.

And should there not be so great a multitude, even if their actions be directed according to their particular judgments and particular appetites, they can expect thereby no defense nor protection, neither against a common enemy nor against the injuries of one another. For being distracted in opinions concerning the best use and application of their strength, they do not help but hinder one another, and reduce their strength by mutual opposition to nothing; whereby they are easily not only subdued by a very few that agree together, but also, when there is no common enemy, they make war upon each other for their particular interests. For if we could suppose a great multitude of men to consent in the observation of justice and other laws of nature without a common power to keep them all in awe, we might as well suppose all mankind to do the same; and then there neither would be, nor need to be, any civil government or commonwealth at all, because there would be peace without subjection.

Nor is it enough for the security which men desire should last all the time of their life that they be governed and directed by one judgment for a limited time, as in one battle or one war. For though they obtain a victory by their unanimous endeavor against a foreign enemy, yet afterwards, when either they have no common enemy or he that by one group is held for an enemy is by another group held for a friend, they must needs, by the difference of their interests, dissolve, and fall again into a war among themselves.

It is true that certain living creatures, as bees and ants, live sociably one with another, which are therefore by Aristotle numbered among political creatures, and yet have no other direction, than their particular judgments and appetites; nor speech whereby one of them can signify to another what he thinks expedient for the common benefit; and therefore some man may perhaps desire to know why mankind cannot do the same. To which I answer:

First, that men are continually in competition for honor and dignity, which these creatures are not; and consequently among men there arises on the ground envy and hatred and finally war, but among these not so.

Secondly, that among these creatures the common good differ not from the private; and being by nature inclined to their private, they procure thereby the common benefit. But man, whose joy consists in comparing himself with other men, can relish nothing but what is eminent.

Thirdly, that these creatures, having not, as man, the use of reason, do not see nor think they see any fault, in the administration of their common business; whereas among men, there are very many that think themselves wiser and abler to govern the public better than the rest; and these strive to reform and innovate, one this way, another that way, and thereby bring it into distraction and civil war.

Fourthly, that these creatures, though they have some use of voice in making known to one another their desires and other affections, yet they lack that art of words by which some men can represent to others that which is good in the likeness of evil; and evil in the likeness of good; and augment or diminish the apparent greatness of good and evil, making men discontented and troubling their peace at their pleasure.

Fifthly, irrational creatures cannot distinguish between "injury" and "damage"; and, therefore, as long as they be at ease they are not offended with their fellows; whereas man is then most troublesome when he is most at ease; for then it is that he loves to show his wisdom and control the actions of them that govern the commonwealth.

Lastly, the agreement of these creatures is natural, that of men is by covenant only, which is artificial; and therefore, it is no wonder if there be somewhat else required besides covenant to make their agreement constant and lasting, which is a common power to keep them in awe and to direct their actions to the common benefit.

The only way to erect such a common power which may be able to defend them from the invasion of foreigners and the injuries of one another, and thereby to secure them in such sort so that by their own industry and by the fruits of the earth they may nourish themselves and live contentedly, is to confer all their power and strength upon one man, or upon one assembly of men that may reduce all their wills, by plurality of voices, unto one will; which is as much as to say, to appoint one man or assembly of men to bear their person; and every one to accept and acknowledge himself to be author of whatsoever he that so bears their person shall act or cause to be acted in those things which concern the common peace and safety, and therein to submit their wills every one to his will, and their judgments to his judgment. This is more than consent or concord; it is a real unity of them all in one and the same person, made by covenant of every man with every man, in such manner as if every man should say to every man, "I authorize and give up my right of governing myself to this man, or to this assembly of men, on this condition, that you give up your right to him and authorize all his actions in like manner." This done, the multitude so united in one person is called a "commonwealth," in Latin *civitas*. This is the generation of that great "leviathan," or rather, to speak more reverently, of that "mortal god," to which we owe, under the "immortal God," our peace and defense. For by this authority, given him by every particular man in the commonwealth, he has the use of so much power and strength conferred on him that, by terror thereof, he is enabled to form the wills of them all to peace at home and mutual aid against their enemies abroad. And in him consists the essence of the commonwealth, which, to define it, is "one person, of whose acts a great multitude, by mutual covenants one with another, have made themselves the author, to the end he may use the strength and means of them all as he shall think expedient for their peace and common defense."

And he that carries this person is called "sovereign" and said to have "sovereign power"; and every one besides, his "subject."

The attaining to this sovereign power is by two ways. One, by natural force, as when a man makes his children to submit themselves and their children to his government, as being able to destroy them if they refuse; or by war subdues his enemies to his will, giving them their lives on that condition. The other is when men agree among themselves to submit to some man or assembly of men voluntarily, on confidence that they will be protected by him against all others. This latter, may be called a political commonwealth, or common-wealth by "institution," and the former, a commonwealth by "acquisition." ∗ ∗ ∗

Of the Office of the Sovereign Representative

The office of the sovereign, be it a monarch or an assembly, consists in the end for which he was trusted with the sovereign power, namely, the securing of "the safety of the people"; to which he is obliged by the law of nature, and to render an account thereof to God, the author of that law, and to none but him. But by safety here is not meant a bare preservation but also all other contentments of life which every man by lawful industry, without danger or hurt to the commonwealth, shall acquire to himself.

And this is to be done, not by care applied to individuals further than their protection from injuries when they shall complain, but by a general provision contained in public instruction, both of doctrine and example, and in the making and executing of good laws to which individual persons may apply their own cases.

And because, if the essential rights of sovereignty . . . be taken away, the commonwealth is thereby dissolved and every man returns into the condition and calamity of a war with every other man, which is the greatest evil that can happen in this life; it is the office of the sovereign, to maintain those rights entire, and consequently against his duty, first, to transfer to another or to lay from himself any of them. For he that deserts the means deserts the ends; and he deserts the means when, being the sovereign, he acknowledges himself subject to the civil laws and renounces the power of supreme judicature, or of making war or peace by his own authority; or of judging of the necessities of the commonwealth; or of levying money and soldiers when and as much as in his own conscience he shall judge necessary; or of making officers and ministers both of war and peace; or of appointing teachers and examining what doctrines are conformable or contrary to the defense, peace, and good of the people. Secondly, it is against his duty to let the people be ignorant or misinformed of the grounds and reasons of those his essential rights, because thereby men are easy to be seduced and drawn to resist him when the commonwealth shall require their use and exercise.

And the grounds of these rights have the need to be diligently and truly taught, because they cannot be maintained by any civil law or terror of legal punishment. For a civil law that shall forbid rebellion (and such is all resistance to the essential rights of the sovereignty), is not, as a civil law, any obligation, but by virtue only of the law of nature that forbids the violation of faith; which natural obligation if men know not, they cannot know the right of any law the sovereign makes. And for the punishment, they take it but for an act of hostility which when they think they have strength enough, they will endeavor by acts of hostility, to avoid. * * *

To the care of the sovereign belongs the making of good laws. But what is a good law? By a good law I mean not a just law; for no law can be unjust. The law is made by the sovereign power, and all that is done by such power is warranted and owned by every one of the people; and that which every man will have so, no man can say is unjust. It is in the laws of a commonwealth as in the laws of gaming; whatsoever the gamesters all agree on is injustice to none of them. A good law is that which is "needed" for the "good of the people" and "perspicuous."

For the use of laws, which are but rules authorized, is not to bind the people from all voluntary actions but to direct and keep them in such a motion as not to hurt themselves by their own impetuous desires, rashness, or indiscretion; as hedges are set not to stop travellers, but to keep them in their way. And, therefore, a law that is not needed, having not the true end of a law, is not good. A law may be conceived to be good when it is for the benefit of the sovereign, though it be not necessary for the people, but it is not so. For the good of the sovereign and people cannot be separated. It is a weak sovereign, that has weak subjects, and a weak people, whose sovereign lacks power to rule them at his will. Unnecessary laws are not good laws but traps for money; which, where the right of sovereign power is acknowledged, are superfluous, and where it is not acknowledged, insufficient to defend the people. * * *

It belongs also to the office of the sovereign to make a right application of punishments and rewards. And seeing the end of punishing is not revenge and discharge of anger, but correction, either of the offender, or of others by his example; the severest punishments are to be inflicted for those crimes that are of most danger to the public; such as are those which proceed from malice to the government established; those that spring from contempt of justice; those that provoke indignation in the multitude; and those which, unpunished, seem authorized, as when they are committed by sons, servants, or favorites of men in authority. For indignation carries men not only against the actors and authors of injustice, but against all power that is likely to protect them; as in the case of Tarquin, when for the insolent act of one of his sons he was driven out of Rome and the monarchy itself dissolved. But crimes of infirmity, such as are those which proceed from great provocation, from great fear, great need, or from ignorance, whether the fact be a great crime or not, there is place many times for leniency without prejudice to the commonwealth; and leniency, when there is such place for it, is required by the law of nature. The punishment of the leaders and teachers in a commotion, not the poor seduced people, when they are punished, can profit the commonwealth by their example. To be severe to the people is to punish that ignorance which may in great part be imputed to the sovereign, whose fault it was that they were no better instructed.

In like manner it belongs to the office and duty of the sovereign, to apply his rewards so that there may arise from them benefit to the commonwealth, wherein consists their use, and end; and is then done when they that have well served the commonwealth are, with as little expense of the common treasure as is possible, so well recompensed as others thereby may be encouraged both to serve the same as faithfully as they can and to study the arts by which they may be enabled to do it better. To buy with money or preferment from a popular ambitious subject to be quiet and desist from making ill impressions in the minds of the people has nothing of the nature of reward (which is ordained not for disservice, but for service past), nor a sign of gratitude, but of fear; nor does it tend to the benefit but to the damage of the public. It is a contention with ambition like that of Hercules with the monster Hydra which, having many heads, for every one that was vanquished there grew up three. For in like manner, when the stubbornness of one popular man is overcome with reward there arise many more, by the example, that do the same mischief in hope of like benefit; and as all sorts of manufacture, so also malice increases by being salable. And though sometimes a civil war may be deferred by such ways as that, yet the danger grows still the greater and the public ruin more assured. It is therefore against the duty of the sovereign, to whom the public safety is committed, to reward those that aspire to greatness by disturbing the peace of their country, and not rather to oppose the beginnings of such men with a little danger than after a longer time with greater. ＊ ＊ ＊

When the sovereign himself is popular, that is, revered and beloved of his people, there is no danger at all from the popularity of a subject. For soldiers are never so generally unjust as to side with their captain though they love him, against their sovereign, when they love not only his person but also his cause. And therefore those who by violence have at any time suppressed the power of their lawful sovereign, before they could settle themselves in his place have been always put to the trouble of contriving their titles to save the people from the shame of receiving them. To have a known right to sovereign power is so popular a quality as he that has it needs no more, for his

own part, to turn the hearts of his subjects to him but that they see him able absolutely to govern his own family; nor, on the part of his enemies, but a disbanding of their armies. For the greatest and most active part of mankind has never hitherto been well contented with the present.

Concerning the offices of one sovereign to another, which are comprehended in that law which is commonly called the "law of nations," I need not say anything in this place because the law of nations and the law of nature is the same thing. And every sovereign has the same right, in securing the safety of his people that any particular man can have in securing the safety of his own body. And the same law that dictates to men that have no civil government what they ought to do and what to avoid in regard of one another dictates the same to commonwealths, that is, to the consciences of sovereign princes and sovereign assemblies, there being no court of natural justice but in the conscience only; where not man but God reigns whose laws, such of them as oblige all mankind, in respect of God as he is the author of nature are "natural," and in respect of the same God as he is King of kings are "laws."

＊   ＊   ＊

REVIEW QUESTIONS

1. What is Hobbes's view of human nature?
2. What motivates human beings?
3. What, according to Hobbes, is the purpose of the state?
4. Why do human beings come together to form a political society?
5. What are the responsibilities of the sovereign?
6. What is the sovereign's highest obligation?
7. Does Hobbes hold out any hope that the state can improve human nature?

15 ᴂ ABSOLUTISM AND EMPIRE, 1660–1789

Transition best characterizes the economy and society of early modern Europe. While the forms of production and exchange remained corporatist and traditional, elements of individualism and capitalism exerted increasingly strong influence. Accordingly, a society that remained in large part hierarchical and patriarchal showed signs of an emergent class structure. Evidence of these changes remained regional, being more evident in certain places and times than in others. Nonetheless, the evidence of such a transition can be seen nearly everywhere in Europe, driven by forces that gripped the entire continent.

For much of the period, the population remained locked in a struggle to survive. Beset by periodic famine and disease, life seemed tenuous and expectancies were short. Given high and early mortality, marriages occurred relatively late in life and truncated families were commonplace. Beginning in the late seventeenth century, however, mortality began to decline. By the eighteenth century, populations were expanding across Europe.

The principal cause of the change in demographic dynamics was an increase in food supply that may be attributed in turn to a gradual change in agricultural techniques. Throughout the early modern period, traditional agricultural practices gradually yielded to techniques known generally as scientific farming. Landowners who sought gain in the marketplaces of Europe needed more direct control over land use, an ability to respond flexibly to market conditions. As a result, they enclosed communal lands and turned to the kinds of husbandry that would increase harvests and profits. The result was an increased food supply that eventually freed Europe from its age-old cycle of feast and famine.

An increasing population put new pressures on industry by raising the demand for manufactured goods and supplying a ready labor force to produce them. Rural manufacturing in the form of extensive production networks, known as the putting-out system, increased industrial productivity and captured surplus population in industrial work processes. Those who could not find such employ-

ment fled to the cities, which also grew rapidly. It is interesting that urban manufacturing remained largely traditional, that is, highly regulated and guild based, throughout the early modern period.

The greatest single force for change between 1500 and 1800 was the expansion of long-distance commerce based on the development of overseas empires and the consolidation of central states. Capitalistic practices had existed since the late fourteenth century at least, but the possibility of large profits from direct trade with Asia and the Americas offered new scope for their application. The development of mercantilist theories that advocated the expansion of trade as a source of political power combined with capitalistic ambitions to facilitate global commerce. As a result, enterprises such as charter companies emerged on a larger scale. The supplies of goods traded and their profitability promoted the refinement of commercial facilities such as commodity exchanges, stock markets, and banking techniques. Moreover, the activities of these enterprises introduced new commodities in such volumes that new tastes emerged and old patterns of consumption were transformed.

Growing populations and expanding economies notwithstanding, the society of early modern Europe remained traditional. It was hierarchical in structure; each individual's place was fixed by birthright. Authority was patriarchal in nature, modeled on the supposedly absolute authority of the father within his family. Yet change was also evident here. Economic change created mobility. New wealth encouraged social and political aspirations as bourgeois everywhere chafed under the exclusivity of the aristocracy and sought admission to their ranks. New poverty created a class of have-nots that challenged the established order and threatened its security.

Observers and theorists viewed the transformation of Europe's economy and society with some trepidation. In most instances, their responses were reactionary. They returned to notions of fatherhood for a model of authority that could withstand the changing times. As the period progressed, however, more and more theorists turned to philosophical reason to find general laws of human interaction that might be applied to govern economic and social behavior.

Absolutism refers to a particular conception of political authority that emerged in the wake of this transition and its attendant disorders in the later sixteenth century. It asserted order, where Europeans felt order had been undermined in political and social relations, by positing a vision of a society that had its apex in the person of a single ruler. At the center of all conceptions of absolutism was the will of the ruler: For all theorists, that will was absolute, not merely sovereign but determinative of all political relations. Such an understanding of the nature and operation of political power required a number of developments, not the least of which was a military and a bureaucracy to carry out the king's will.

By the end of the period, there would be calls for enlightened absolutism, in which reason guided the will of the sovereign, but the will of the monarch was still the agent of political life. Among theorists, several emerged who countered the notion of absolute monarchy with that of sovereignty placed in the hands of property owners. Moreover, they argued persuasively that the exercise of sovereignty was limited in accordance with the principles of natural law.

No monarch in this period was truly absolute—such an effective expression of the will of the ruler requires greater technological and military support than any ruler prior to the nineteenth century could have. Many, however, were largely successful in representing themselves as the center of all political life in their states, nurturing courts and bureaucracies that reflected images of omniscient and powerful rulers. These same courts provided both a milieu and the financial support for philosophes such as Voltaire and scientists such as Galileo, even as those intellectuals were calling into question the ethics of and the social bases for absolutism.

HUGO GROTIUS

FROM *On the Law of War and Peace*

Hugo Grotius (1583–1645) was a Dutch statesman, jurist, theologian, poet, philologist, and historian, a man of all-embracing knowledge whose writings were of fundamental importance in the formulation of international law. He was born in Delft, the son of the burgomaster and curator at the University of Leiden. Grotius was precocious; he matriculated at the University of Leiden at age eleven. By age fifteen, he had edited the encyclopedia of Martianus Capella and accompanied a diplomatic mission to the king of France, who described Grotius as the "miracle of Holland." He earned his doctorate in law at the University of Orléans and became a distinguished jurist at The Hague. In 1601, he was appointed historiographer of the States of Holland.

He wrote a number of minor but memorable legal treatises before publishing his great work, On the Law of War and Peace, *in 1625. Grotius argued that the entire law of humankind was based on four fundamental precepts: neither state nor individual may attack another state or individual, neither state nor individual may appropriate what belongs to another state or individual, neither state nor individual may disregard treaties or contracts, and neither state nor individual may commit a crime. In the case of a violation of one of these precepts, compensation might be sought either by war or by individual action. These principles and the arguments that surrounded them significantly aided the development of a theory of state sovereignty and international relations in the early modern period. During the remainder of his life, Grotius remained involved in the political as well as the intellectual affairs of his day. Apart from the vast corpus of his written works, he participated in the government of the United Provinces of the Netherlands. He was eventually imprisoned for his support of Arminianism and managed to escape hidden in a trunk. He spent the rest of his life in exile, honored as one of the great intellectuals of the seventeenth century but unacknowledged by his own country.*

From *The Rights of War and Peace* by Hugo Grotius (Washington and London: M. Walter Dunne, 1901).

*   *   *

VIII

And here is the proper place for refuting the opinion of those, who maintain that, every where and without exception, the sovereign power is vested in the people, so that they have a right to restrain and punish kings for an abuse of their power. However there is no man of sober wisdom, who does not see the incalculable mischiefs, which such opinions have occasioned, and may still occasion; and upon the following grounds they may be refuted.

From the Jewish, as well as the Roman Law, it appears that any one might engage himself in private servitude to whom he pleased. Now if an individual may do so, why may not a whole people, for the benefit of better government and more certain protection, completely transfer their sovereign rights to one or more persons, without reserving any portion to themselves? Neither can it be alledged that such a thing is not to be presumed, for the question is not, what is to be presumed in a doubtful case, but what may lawfully be done. Nor is it any more to the purpose to object to the inconveniences, which may, and actually do arise from a people's thus surrendering their rights. For it is not in the power of man to devise any form of government free from imperfections and dangers. As a dramatic writer says, "you must either take these advantages with those imperfections, or resign your pretensions to both."

Now as there are different ways of living, some of a worse, and some of a better kind, left to the choice of every individual; so a nation, "under certain circumstances, WHEN for instance, the succession to the throne is extinct, or the throne has by any other means become vacant," may choose what form of government she pleases. Nor is this right to be measured by the excellence of this or that form of government, on which there may be varieties of opinion, but by the will of the people.

There may be many reasons indeed why a people may entirely relinquish their rights, and surrender them to another: for instance, they may have no other means of securing themselves from the danger of immediate destruction, or under the pressure of famine it may be the only way, through which they can procure support. For if the Campanians, formerly, when reduced by necessity surrendered themselves to the Roman people in the following terms:—"Senators of Rome, we consign to your dominion the people of Campania, and the city of Capua, our lands, our temples, and all things both divine and human," and if another people as Appian relates, offered to submit to the Romans, and were refused, what is there to prevent any nation from submitting in the same manner to one powerful sovereign? It may also happen that a master of a family, having large possessions, will suffer no one to reside upon them on any other terms, or an owner, having many slaves, may give them their liberty upon condition of their doing certain services, and paying certain rents; of which examples may be produced. Thus Tacitus, speaking of the German slaves, says, "Each has his own separate habitation, and his own household to govern. The master considers him as a tenant, bound to pay a certain rent in corn, cattle, and wearing apparel. And this is the utmost extent of his servitude."

Aristotle, in describing the requisites, which fit men for servitude, says, that "those men, whose powers are chiefly confined to the body, and whose principal excellence consists in affording bodily service, are naturally slaves, because it is their interest to be so." In the same manner some nations are of such a disposition that they are more calculated to obey than to govern, which seems to have been the opinion which the Cappadocians held of themselves, who when the Romans offered them a popular government, refused to accept it, because the nation they said could not exist in safety without a king. Thus Philostratus in the life of Apollonius, says, that it was foolish to offer liberty to the Thracians, the Mysians, and the Getae, which they were not capable of enjoying. The example of nations, who have for many ages lived happily under a kingly government, has induced many to give the preference to that form. Livy says, that the cities under Eumenes would not have changed their condition for that of any free state whatsoever. And sometimes a state is so situated, that it seems impossible it can preserve its peace and existence, without submitting to the absolute government of a single person, which many wise men thought to be the case with the Roman Republic in the time of Augustus Cæsar. From these, and causes like these it not only may, but generally does happen, that men, as Cicero observes in the second book of his offices, willingly submit to the supreme authority of another.

Now as property may be acquired by what has been already styled just war, by the same means the rights of sovereignty may be acquired. Nor is the term sovereignty here meant to be applied to monarchy alone, but to government by nobles, from any share in which the people are excluded. For there never was any government so purely popular, as not to require the exclusion of the poor, of strangers, women, and minors from the public councils. Some states have other nations under them, no less dependent upon their will, than subjects upon that of their sovereign princes. From whence arose that question, Are the Collatine people in their own power? And the Cam-

panians, when they submitted to the Romans, are said to have passed under a foreign dominion. In the same manner Acarnania and Amphilochia are said to have been under the dominion of the Aetolians; Peraea and Caunus under that of the Rhodians; and Pydna was ceded by Philip to the Olynthians. And those towns, that had been under the Spartans, when they were delivered from their dominion, received the name of the free Laconians. The city of Cotyora is said by Xenophon to have belonged to the people of Sinope. Nice in Italy, according to Strabo, was adjudged to the people of Marseilles; and the island of Pithecusa to the Neapolitans. We find in Frontinus, that the towns of Calati and Caudium with their territories were adjudged, the one to the colony of Capua, and the other to that of Beneventum. Otho, as Tacitus relates, gave the cities of the Moors to the Province of Baetia. None of these instances, any more than the cessions of other conquered countries could be admitted, if it were a received rule that the rights of sovereigns are under the controul and direction of subjects.

Now it is plain both from sacred and profane history, that there are kings, who are not subject to the controul of the people in their collective body; God addressing the people of Israel, says, if thou shalt say, "I will place a king over me"; and to Samuel "Shew them the manner of the king, who shall reign over them." Hence the King is said to be anointed over the people, over the inheritance of the Lord, over Israel. Solomon is styled King over all Israel. Thus David gives thanks to God, for subduing the people under him. And Christ says, "the Kings of the nations bear rule over them." There is a well known passage in Horace, "Powerful sovereigns reign over their own subjects, and the supreme being over sovereigns themselves." Seneca thus describes the three forms of government, "Sometimes the supreme power is lodged in the people, sometimes in a senate composed of the leading men of the state, sometimes this power of the people, and dominion over the people themselves is vested in a single person." Of the last description are those, who, as Plutarch says, exercise authority not according to the laws, but over the laws. And in Herodutus, Otanes describes a monarch as one whose acts are not subject to controul. Dion Prusaeensis also and Pausanias define a monarchy in the same terms.

Aristotle says there are some kings, who have the same right, which the nation elsewhere possesses over persons and property. Thus when the Roman Princes began to exercise regal power, the people it was said had transferred all their own personal sovereignty to them, which gave rise to the saying of Marcus Antoninus the Philosopher, that no one but God alone can be judge of the Prince. Dion. L. liii. speaking of such a prince, says, "he is perfectly master of his own actions, to do whatever he pleases, and cannot be obliged to do any thing against his will." Such anciently was the power of the Inachidae established at Argos in Greece. For in the Greek Tragedy of the Suppliants, Aeschylus has introduced the people thus addressing the King: "You are the state, you the people; you the court from which there is no appeal, you preside over the altars, and regulate all affairs by your supreme will." King Theseus himself in Euripides speaks in very different terms of the Athenian Republic; "The city is not governed by one man, but in a popular form, by an annual succession of magistrates." For according to Plutarch's explanation, Theseus was the general in war, and the guardian of the laws; but in other respects nothing more than a citizen. So that they who are limited by popular controul are improperly called kings. Thus after the time of Lycurgus, and more particularly after the institution of the Ephori, the Kings of the Lacedaemonians are said by Polybius, Plutarch, and Cornelius Nepos, to have been Kings more in name than in reality. An example which was followed by the rest of Greece. Thus Pausanias says of the Argives to the Corinthians, "The Argives from their love of equality have reduced their kingly power very low; so that they have left the posterity of Cisus nothing more than the shadow of Kings." Aristotle denies such to be proper forms of government, because they constitute only a part of an Aristocracy or Democracy.

Examples also may be found of nations, who have not been under a perpetual regal form, but only for a time under a government exempt from popular controul. Such was the power of the Amimonians among the Cnidians, and of the Dictators in the early periods of the Roman history, when there was no appeal to the people, from whence Livy says, the will of the Dictator was observed as a law. Indeed they found this submission the only remedy against imminent danger, and in the words of Cicero, the Dictatorship possessed all the strength of royal power.

It will not be difficult to refute the arguments brought in favour of the contrary opinion. For in the first place the assertion that the constituent always retains a controul over the sovereign power, which he has contributed to establish, is only true in those cases where the continuance and existence of that power depends upon the will and pleasure of the constituent: but not in cases where the power, though it might derive its origin from that constituent, becomes a necessary and fundamental part of the established law. Of this nature is that authority to which a woman submits when she gives herself to a husband. Valentinian the Emperor, when the soldiers who had raised him to the throne, made a demand of which he did not approve, replied; "Soldiers, your election of me for your emperor was your own voluntary choice; but since you have elected me, it depends upon my pleasure to grant your request. It becomes you to obey as subjects, and me to consider what is proper to be done."

Nor is the assumption true, that all kings are made by the people, as may be plainly seen from the instances adduced above, of an owner admitting strangers to reside upon his demesnes on condition of their obedience, and of nations submitting by right of conquest. Another argument is derived from a saying of the Philosophers, that all power is conferred for the benefit of the governed and not of the governing party. Hence from the nobleness of the end, it is supposed to follow, that subjects have a superiority over the sovereign. But it is not universally true, that all power is conferred for the benefit of the party governed. For some powers are conferred for the sake of the governor, as the right of a master over a slave, in which the advantage of the latter is only a contingent and adventitious circumstance. In the same manner the gain of a Physician is to reward him for his labour; and not merely to promote the good of his art. There are other kinds of authority established for the benefit of both parties, as for instance, the authority of a husband over his wife. Certain governments also, as those which are gained by right of conquest, may be established for the benefit of the sovereign; and yet convey no idea of tyranny, a word which in its original signification, implied nothing of arbitrary power or injustice, but only the government or authority of a Prince. Again, some governments may be formed for the advantage both of subjects and sovereign, as when a people, unable to defend themselves, put themselves under the protection and dominion of any powerful king. Yet it is not to be denied, but that in most governments the good of the subject is the chief object which is regarded: and that what Cicero has said after Herodotus, and Herodotus after Hesiod, is true, that Kings were appointed in order that men might enjoy complete justice.

Now this admission by no means goes to establish the inference that kings are amenable to the people. For though guardianships were invented for the benefit of wards, yet the guardian has a right to authority over the ward. Nor, though a guardian may for mismanagement be removed from his trust, does it follow that a king may for the same reason be deposed. The cases are quite different, the guardian has a superior to judge him; but in governments, as there must be some dernier resort, it must be vested either in an individual, or in some public body, whose misconduct, as there is no superior tribunal before which they can be called, God declares that he himself will judge. He either punishes their offences, should he deem it necessary; or permits them for the chastisement of his people.

This is well expressed by Tacitus: he says, "you should bear with the rapacity or luxury of rulers, as you would bear with drought, or excessive rains, or any other calamities of nature. For as long as

men exist there will be faults and imperfections; but these are not of uninterrupted continuance, and they are often repaired by the succession of better times." And Marcus Aurelius speaking of subordinate magistrates, said, that they were under the controul of the sovereign: but that the sovereign was amenable to God. There is a remarkable passage in Gregory of Tours, where that Bishop thus addresses the King of France, "If any of us, Sir, should transgress the bounds of justice, he may be punished by you. But if you exceed them, who can call you to account? For when we address you, you may hear us if you please; but if you will not, who can judge you, except him, who has declared himself to be righteousness?" Among the maxims of the Essenes, Porphyry cites a passage, that "no one can reign without the special appointment of divine providence." Irenaeus has expressed this well, "Kings are appointed by him at whose command men are created; and their appointment is suited to the condition of those, whom they are called to govern." There is the same thought in the Constitutions of Clement, "You shall fear the King, for he is of the Lord's appointment."

Nor is it an objection to what has been said, that some nations have been punished for the offences of their kings, for this does not happen, because they forbear to restrain their kings, but because they seem to give, at least a tacit consent to their vices, or perhaps, without respect to this, God may use that sovereign power which he has over the life and death of every man to inflict a punishment upon the king by depriving him of his subjects.

*   *   *

REVIEW QUESTIONS

1. What is the relation between political power and will according to Grotius?
2. What is the state? The sovereign state?
3. Where does Grotius locate sovereignty?
4. Does sovereignty have a moral component?
5. What is its relation to property? To the good of the people?

THOMAS MUN

FROM *Discourse on England's Treasure by Forraign Trade*

Thomas Mun (1571–1641) was the son of an English mercer and rose to become a noted writer on economics and the first to give a clear statement of the theory of balance of trade. He was a prominent figure in commercial circles as a member of the standing commission on trade and the committee of the East India Company. His most important publication, Discourse on England's Treasure by Forraign Trade *published posthumously in 1664, developed his idea that the wealth of a nation could not decline significantly so long as the value of exports exceeded the value of imports. Both in its emphasis on trade, as opposed to agriculture or industry, as the source of wealth and in its vision of economic systems as incapable of expansion, this theory became a cornerstone of mercantilist thinking.*

From *England's Treasure by Forraign Trade* by Thomas Mun. Elibron Classics Series (Boston: Adamant Media, 2005), pp. 7–19.

Chap. II.
The Means to Enrich the Kingdom, and to Encrease Our Treasure

Although a Kingdom may be enriched by gifts received, or by purchase taken from some other Nations, yet these are things uncertain and of small consideration when they happen. The ordinary means therefore to encrease our wealth and trea- *Forraign Trade is the Rule of our Treasure.* sure is by *Forraign Trade,* wherein wee must ever observe this rule; to sell more to strangers yearly than wee consume of theirs in value. For suppose that when this Kingdom is plentifully served with the Cloth, Lead, Tinn, Iron, Fish and other native commodities, we doe yearly export the overplus to forraign Countries to the value of twenty two hundred thousand pounds; by which means we are enabled beyond the Seas to buy and bring in forraign wares for our use and Consumptions, to the value of twenty hundred thousand pounds; By this order duly kept in our trading, we may rest assured that the Kingdom shall be enriched yearly two hundred thousand pounds, which must be brought to us in so much Treasure; because that part of our stock which is not returned to us in wares must necessarily be brought home in treasure.

For in this case it cometh to pass in the stock of a Kingdom, as in the estate of a private man; who is supposed to have one thousand pounds yearly revenue and two thousand pounds of ready money in his Chest: If such a man through excess shall spend one thousand five hundred pounds *per annum,* all his ready mony will be gone in four years; and in the like time his said money will be doubled if he take a Frugal course to spend but five hundred pounds *per annum;* which rule never faileth likewise in the Commonwealth, but in some cases (of no great moment) which I will hereafter declare, when I shall shew by whom and in what manner this ballance of the Kingdom's account ought to be drawn up yearly, or so often as it shall please the State to discover how much we gain or lose by trade with forraign Nations. But first I will say something concerning those ways and means which will encrease our exportations and diminish our importations of wares; which being done, I will then set down some other arguments both affirmative and negative to strengthen that which is here declared, and thereby to shew that all the other means which are commonly supposed to enrich the Kingdom with Treasure are altogether insufficient and meer fallacies.

Chap. III.
The Particular Ways and Means to Encrease the Exportation of Our Commodities, and to Decrease Our Consumption of Forraign Wares

The revenue or stock of a Kingdom by which it is provided of forraign wares is either *Natural* or *Artificial.* The Natural wealth is so much only as can be spared from our own use and necessities to be exported unto strangers. The Artificial consists in our manufactures and industrious trading with forraign commodities, concerning which I will set down such particulars as may serve for the cause we have in hand.

1. First, although this Realm be already exceeding rich by nature, yet might it be much encreased by laying the waste grounds (which are infinite) into such employments as should no way hinder the present revenues of other manured lands, but hereby to supply our selves and prevent the importations of Hemp, Flax, Cordage, Tobacco, and divers other things which now we fetch from strangers to our great impoverishing.

2. We may likewise diminish our importations, if we would soberly refrain from excessive consumption of forraign wares in our diet and rayment, with such often change of fashions as is used, so much the more to encrease the waste and charge; which vices at this present are more notorious amongst us than in former ages. Yet might they easily be amended by enforcing the observation of such good laws as are strictly practised in other Countries against the said excesses; where likewise by commanding their own manufactures

to be used, they prevent the coming in of others, without prohibition, or offence to strangers in their mutual commerce.

3. In our exportations we must not only regard our own superfluities, but also we must consider our neighbours necessities, that so upon the wares which they cannot want, nor yet be furnished thereof elsewhere, we may (besides the vent of the Materials) gain so much of manifacture as we can, and also endeavour to sell them dear, so far forth as the high price cause not a less vent in the quantity. But the superfluity of our commodities which strangers use, and may also have the same from other Nations, or may abate their vent by the use of some such like wares from other places, and with little inconvenience; we must in this case strive to sell as cheap as possible we can, rather than to lose the utterance of such wares. For we have found of late years by good experience, that being able to sell our Cloth cheap in Turkey, we have greatly encreased the vent thereof, and the *Venetians* have lost as much in the utterance of theirs in those Countreys, because it is dearer. And on the other side a few years past, when by the excessive price of Wools our Cloth was exceeding dear, we lost at the least half our clothing for forraign parts, which since is no otherwise (well neer) recovered again than by the great fall of price for Wools and Cloth. We find that twenty five in the Hundred less in the price of these and some other Wares, to the loss of private mens revenues, may raise above fifty upon the hundred in the quantity vented to the benefit of the publique. For when Cloth is dear, other Nations doe presently practise clothing, and we know they want neither art nor materials to this performance. But when by cheapness we drive them from this employment, and so in time obtain our dear price again, then do they also use their former remedy. So that by these alterations we learn, that it is in vain to expect a greater revenue of our wares than their condition will afford, but rather it concerns us to apply our endeavours to the times with care and diligence to help our selves the best we may, by making our cloth and other manufactures without

The State in some occasions may gain most, when private men by their revenues get least.

deceit, which will encrease their estimation and use.

4. The value of our exportations likewise may be much advanced when we perform it ourselves in our own Ships, for then we get only not the price of our wares as they are worth here, but also the Merchants gains, the charges of ensurance, and fraight to carry them beyond the seas. As for example, if the *Italian* Merchants should come hither in their own shipping to fetch our Corn, our red Herrings or the like, in this case the Kingdom should have ordinarily but 25. s. for a quarter of Wheat, and 20. s. for a barrel of red herrings, whereas if we carry these wares ourselves into *Italy* upon the said rates, it is likely that wee shall obtain fifty shillings for the first, and forty shillings for the last, which is a great difference in the utterance or vent of the Kingdoms stock. And although it is true that the commerce ought to be free to strangers to bring in and carry out at their pleasure, yet nevertheless in many places the exportation of victuals and munition are either prohibited, or at least limited to be done onely by the people and Shipping of those places where they abound.

5. The frugal expending likewise of our own natural wealth might advance much yearly to be exported unto strangers; and if in our rayment we will be prodigal, yet let this be done with our own materials and manufactures, as Cloth, Lace, Imbroderies, Cutworks and the like, where the excess of the rich may be the employment of the poor, whose labours notwithstanding of this kind, would be more profitable for the Commonwealth, if they were done to the use of Strangers.

6. The Fishing in his Majesties seas of *England*, *Scotland* and *Ireland* is our natural wealth, and would cost nothing but labour, which the *Dutch* bestow willingly, and thereby draw yearly a very great profit to themselves by serving many places of Christendom with our Fish, for which they return and supply their wants both of forraign Wares and Mony, besides the multitudes of Mariners and Shipping, which hereby are maintain'd, whereof a long discourse might be made to shew the particular manage of this important business. Our Fishing plantation likewise in *New-England*, *Virginia*,

Groenland, the *Summer Islands* and the *New-found-land,* are of the like nature, affording much wealth and employments to maintain a great number of poor, and to encrease our decaying trade.

7. A Staple or Magazin for forraign Corn, Indico, Spices, Raw-silks, Cotton wool or any other commodity whatsoever, to be imported will encrease Shipping, Trade, Treasure, and the Kings customes, by exporting them again where need shall require, which course of Trading, hath been the chief means to raise *Venice*, *Genoa*, the *low-Countreys*, with some others; and for such a purpose *England* stands most commodiously, wanting nothing to this performance but our own diligence and endeavour. *How some States have been made Rich.*

8. Also wee ought to esteem and cherish those trades which we have in remote or far Countreys, for besides the encrease of Shipping and Mariners thereby, the wares also sent thither and receiv'd from thence are far more profitable unto the kingdom than by our trades neer at hand; As for example; suppose Pepper to be worth here two Shillings the pound constantly, if then it be brought from the *Dutch* at *Amsterdam,* the Merchant may give there twenty pence the pound, and gain well by the bargain, but if he fetch this Pepper from the East-indies, he must not give above three pence the pound at the most, which is a mighty advantage, not only in that part which serveth for our own use, but also for that great quantity which (from hence) we transport yearly unto divers other Nations to be sold at a higher price: whereby it is plain, that we make a far greater stock by gain upon these *Indian* Commodities, than those Nations doe where they grow, and to whom they properly appertain, being the natural wealth of their Countries. But for the better understanding of this particular, we must ever distinguish between the gain of the Kingdom, and the profit of the Merchant; for although the Kingdom payeth no more for this Pepper than is before supposed, nor for any other commodity bought in forraign parts more than the Stranger receiveth from us for the same, yet the Merchant payeth not only *The traffick in the East Indies is our most profitable trade in its proportion both for King and Kingdom.*

We get more by the Indian wares than the Indians themselves.

A distinction between the Kingdoms gain and the Merchants profit. that price, but also the fraight, ensurance, customes and other charges which are exceeding great in these long voyages; but yet all these in the Kingdoms accompt are but commutations among our selves, and no privation of the Kingdoms stock, which being duly considered, together with the support also of our other trades in our best Shipping to *Italy, France, Turkey,* the *East Countreys* and other places, by transporting and venting the wares which we bring yearly from the *East Indies;* It may well stir up our utmost endeavours to maintain and enlarge this great and noble business, so much importing the Publique wealth, Strength, and Happiness. Neither is there less honour and judgment by growing rich (in this manner) upon the stock of other Nations, than by an industrious encrease of our own means, especially when this later is advanced by the benefit of the former, as we have found in the *East Indies* by sale of much of our Tin, Cloth, Lead and other Commodities, the vent whereof doth daily encrease in those Countreys which formerly had no use of our wares.

9. It would be very beneficial to export money as well as wares, being done in trade only, it would encrease our Treasure; but of this I write more largely in the next Chapter to prove it plainly.

10. It were policie and profit for the State to suffer manufactures made of forraign Materials to be exposed custome-free, as Velvets and all other wrought Silks, Fustians, thrown Silks and the like, it would employ very many poor people, and much encrease the value of our stock yearly issued into other Countreys, and it would (for this purpose) cause the more forraign Materials to be brought in, to the improvement of His Majesties Customes. I will here remember a notable increase in our manufacture of winding and twisting only of forraign raw Silk, which within 35. years to my knowledge did not employ more than 300. people in the City and suburbs of London, where at this present time it doth set on work above fourteen thousand souls, as upon diligent enquiry hath been credibly reported unto His Majesties Commissioners for Trade. And it is certain, that if the said forraign Commodities might be exported from hence, free of custome, this manufacture would yet encrease very much, and decrease as fast in *Italy* and the *Netherlands.* But if any man allege the *Dutch* proverb, *Live and let others live;* I answer, that the Dutchmen notwithstanding their own Proverb, doe not onely in these Kingdoms, encroach upon our livings, but also in other forraign parts of our trade (where they have power) they do hinder and destroy us in our lawful course of living, hereby taking the bread out of our mouth, which we shall never prevent by plucking the pot from their nose, as of late years too many of us do practise to the great hurt and dishonour of this famous Nation; We ought rather to imitate former times in taking sober and worthy courses more pleasing to God and suitable to our ancient reputation.

11. It is needful also not to charge the native commodities with too great customes, lest by indearing them to the strangers use, it hinder their vent. And especially forraign wares brought in to be transported again should be favoured, for otherwise that manner of trading (so much importing the good of the Common wealth) cannot prosper nor subsist. But the Consumption of such forraign wares in the Realm may be the more charged, which will turn to the profit of the Kingdom in the *Ballance of the Trade,* and thereby also enable the King to lay up the more Treasure out of his yearly incomes, as of this particular I intend to write more fully in his proper place, where I shall shew how much money a Prince may conveniently lay up without the hurt of his subjects.

12. Lastly, in all things we must endeavour to make the most we can of our own, whether it be *Natural* or *Artificial;* And forasmuch as the people which live by the Arts are far more in number than they who are masters of the fruits, we ought the more carefully to maintain those endeavours of the multitude, in whom doth consist the greatest strength and riches both of King and Kingdom: for where the people are many, and the arts good, there the traffique must be great, and the Countrey rich. The *Italians* employ a greater number of people, and get more money by their industry and manufactures of the raw Silks of the Kingdom of *Cicilia,* than the King of *Spain* and his Subjects

THE SYNDICS OF THE DRAPERS' GUILD (1632)　　　　　　　　　　　REMBRANDT VAN RIJN

One of Rembrandt's most recognizable works, The Syndics, *captures all the sober solidity and confidence of Calvinist merchants in the young Dutch Republic. Convinced that worldly success indicated divine election, they look out on the world with purposeful determination to make of their lives a testimonial to God's grace. The work is a penetrating psychological study of these members of the urban elite. What elements of Rembrandt's painting might be characterized as bourgeois? Insofar as the syndics were leaders in Amsterdam society, what does their portrait reveal of that society? Reading into the expressions on the faces and the composition of the portrait, what was Rembrandt's relationship to the artisanal and mercantile world of Amsterdam?*

have by the revenue of this rich commodity. But what need we fetch the example so far, when we know that our own natural wares doe not yield us so much profit as our industry? For Iron oar in the Mines is of no great worth, when it is compared with the employment and advantage it yields being digged, tried, transported, bought, sold, cast into Ordnance, Muskets, and many other instruments of war for offence and defence, wrought into Anchors, bolts, spikes, nayles and the like, for the use of Ships, Houses, Carts, Coaches, Ploughs, and other instruments for Tillage. Compare our Fleecewools with our Cloth, which requires shearing, washing, carding, spinning, Weaving, fulling, dying, dressing and other trimmings, and we shall find these Arts more profitable than the natural wealth, whereof I might instance other examples, but I will not be more tedious, for if I would amplify upon this and the other particulars before written, I might find matter sufficient to make a large volume, but my desire in all is only to prove what I propound with brevity and plainness.

REVIEW QUESTIONS

1. What does Mun consider trade to be?
2. Of what does it consist?
3. What is his chief concern regarding trade?
4. What is the relation of trade to the nation?
5. What are the foundations of successful trade for Mun?
6. Why does he emphasize moral values in a treatise on economic policy?
7. What are the goods to be found in commerce?

JEAN-BAPTISTE COLBERT

A Memorandum, 1670

Jean-Baptiste Colbert (1619–1683), the son of a merchant of Reims, rose above his mercantile roots to become a statesman and minister of finance to Louis XIV. His chief concern was the economic reconstruction of France. He reorganized the fiscal administration of the state and made it more efficient. He also promoted commerce and industry in ways consistent with mercantilist theory. To improve exports, he promoted industries that produced high-quality goods, increased the merchant fleet, attracted foreign artisans, and limited foreign competition. Indeed, the system of state sponsorship and regulation that arose under Colbert and soon bore his name was widely resented by entrepreneurs anxious to innovate and expand. In his capacity as secretary of state for the king's household, from 1669, he was also concerned with the arts and education in France. He founded schools and learned societies to foster these endeavors, including the Academy of Science in 1666 to promote science. All these activities served to expand the power and magnificence of the French state, in the service of which he remained his entire life. That service proved profitable on a private level as well. He died a very wealthy man, whose estate had risen to that of an aristocrat by dint of loyal service. Yet, he was a disappointed man. Though the state had become stronger and more prosperous through his policies, he saw his ambition to reform and expand the French economy frustrated by wars that pursued the ends of the king he had served.

From *Colbert and a Century of French Mercantilism*, by Charles W. Cole (New York: Columbia University Press, 1939), p. 320.

Formerly the Dutch, English, Hamburgers, and other nations bringing into the realm a much greater quantity of merchandise than that which they carried away, withdrew the surplus in circulating money, which produced both their abundance and the poverty of the realm, and indisputably resulted in their power and our weakness.

We must next examine the means which were employed to change this destiny.

Firstly, in 1662 Your Majesty maintained his right to 50 sols per ton of freight from foreign vessels, which produced such great results that we have seen the number of French vessels increase yearly; and in seven or eight years the Dutch have been practically excluded from port-to-port commerce, which is carried on by the French. The advantages received by the state through the increase in the number of sailors and seamen, through the money which has remained in the realm by this means and an infinity of others, would be too long to enumerate.

At the same time, Your Majesty ordered work done to abolish all the tolls which had long been established on all the rivers of the kingdom, and he began from then on to have an examination made of the rivers which could be rendered navigable in order to facilitate the descent of commodities and merchandise from inside the realm toward the sea to be transported into foreign lands. Although everything that invites the universal admiration of men was still in disorder in these first years and although the recovery work was a sort of abyss, Your Majesty did not delay in beginning the examination of the tariffs of the *cinq grosses fermes* and scrutinized the fact that the regulation and levying of these sorts of duties concerning commerce had always been done with a great deal of ignorance on

the basis of memoranda by tax farmers, who, being solely concerned with their own interests and the increase in the profits from their tax farms while they possessed them, had always overvalued the commodities, merchandise, and manufactured items of the realm which they saw leaving in abundance, and favored the entrance of foreign merchandise and manufactured items, in order to have a greater quantity of them enter, without being concerned about whether money was as a result leaving the realm, for they were indifferent to this as long as their tax farms produced gain for them during the period of their possession.

Finally, after having thoroughly studied this matter, Your Majesty ordered the tariff of 1664, in which the duties are regulated on a completely different principle, that is to say, that all merchandise and manufactured items of the realm were markedly favored and the foreign ones priced out of the market, though not completely; for having as yet no established manufacturers in the realm, this increase in duties, had it been excessive, would have been a great burden for the *peuple,* because of their need for the aforesaid foreign merchandise and manufactured items; but this change began to provide some means of establishing the same manufactures in the realm; and to this end:

The fabric manufacture of Sedan has been reestablished, and enlarged to 62 from the 12 looms there were then.

The new establishments of Abbeville, Dieppe, Fécamp, and Rouen have been built, in which there are presently more than 200 looms.

The factory for barracan was next established at La Ferré-sous-Jouarre, which is made up of 120 looms;

That of little damasks from Flanders, at Meaux, consisting of 80 looms;

That for carpeting, in the same city, made up of 20 looms . . .

That for tin, in Nivernois;

That for French lace, in 52 cities and towns, in which more than 20,000 workers toil;

The manufacture of brass, or yellow copper, set up in Champagne;

That for camlet of Brussels, in Paris, which will become large and extensive;

Brass wire, in Burgundy;

Gold thread of Milan, at Lyons . . .

And since Your Majesty has wanted to work diligently at reestablishing his naval forces, and since for that it has been necessary to make very great expenditures, since all merchandise, munitions and manufactured items formerly came from Holland and the countries of the North, it has been absolutely necessary to be especially concerned with finding within the realm, or with establishing in it, everything which might be necessary for this great plan.

To this end, the manufacture of tar was established in Médoc, Auvergne, Dauphiné, and Provence;

Iron cannons, in Burgundy, Nivernois, Saintonge, and Périgord;

Large anchors, in Dauphiné, Nivernois, Brittany, and Rochefort;

Sailcloth for the Levant, in Dauphiné;

Coarse muslin, in Auvergne;

All the implements for pilots and others, at Dieppe and La Rochelle;

The cutting of wood suitable for vessels, in Burgundy, Dauphiné, Brittany, Normandy, Poitou, Saintonge, Provence, Guyenne, and the Pyrenees;

Masts, of a sort once unknown in this realm, have been found in Provence, Languedoc, Auvergne, Dauphiné, and in the Pyrenees.

Iron, which was obtained from Sweden and Biscay, is currently manufactured in the realm.

Fine hemp for ropes, which came from Prussia and from Piedmont, is currently obtained in Burgundy, Mâconnais, Bresse, Dauphiné; and markets for it have since been established in Berry and in Auvergne, which always provides money in these provinces and keeps it within the realm.

In a word, everything serving for the construction of vessels is currently established in the realm, so that Your Majesty can get along without foreigners for the navy and will even, in a short time, be able to supply them and gain their money in this fashion. And it is with this same objective of having everything necessary to provide abundantly for his navy and that of his subjects that he is working at the general reform of all the forests in his realm, which, being as carefully preserved as they are at present, will abundantly produce all the wood necessary for this.

REVIEW QUESTIONS

1. How does Colbert speak of commerce?
2. What does it entail?
3. What causes its success?
4. Why is commerce a war?
5. What does Colbert see as the source of Dutch and English power?
6. What has strengthened French commerce?
7. What goods does Colbert describe?
8. Why do you suppose he pays particular attention to them?

JEAN BAPTISTE POQUELIN (MOLIÈRE)

FROM *The Citizen Who Apes the Nobleman*

Molière (1622–1673) was baptized Jean Baptiste Poquelin. His life might be considered unorthodox from a very early stage. Though educated at the Collège de Clermont, which would number among its alumni such illustrious literati as Voltaire, and clearly intended for a career in royal service, he broke with tradition and joined a traveling company of players in 1643. He adopted his stage name, Molière, the following year and devoted the rest of his life to the stage. His rise to prominence began in 1658, when, playing on an improvised stage in a guardroom of the Louvre, he performed Corneille's Nicomède *as well as a play of his own,* Le docteur amoureux, *before Louis XIV.* Le bourgeois gentilhomme *appeared at the royal palace at Chambord in 1670. It satirized the ambition of contemporary bourgeois to compete in magnificence with the aristocracy. Yet it was a double-edged satire. Though the theme must have pleased Molière's noble audience, the figure of Jourdain is no unpleasant, boorish climber but rather a delightfully good-natured soul, foolish but naive, fatuous but genuine. An unwillingness to subordinate his art to his audience may help explain why Molière frequently struggled in his lifetime. His actors often abandoned his company. Pensions went unpaid. His best works were not always well received. His fame spread only slowly. Though considered one of the greatest French writers, Molière was no writer in the strict sense. Little of his work was published; his comedies were written to be performed. Publication occurred only after several texts were pirated by Jean Ribou. Several remained unpublished long after Molière's death in 1672, when he was taken ill during a performance of* Le malade imaginaire. *He died that same night, without receiving the sacraments or renouncing his stage life. Molière was buried unceremoniously in a common grave.*

From *The Dramatic Works of Molière*, vol. 5 (Philadelphia: George Barrie, n.d.).

FROM Act I

The overture is played by a great many instruments; and in the middle of the stage, the pupil of the music-master is busy composing a serenade, ordered by M. Jourdain.

SCENE I. A MUSIC-MASTER, A DANCING-MASTER, THREE MUSICIANS, TWO VIOLIN PLAYERS, FOUR DANCERS

MUS.-MAS. (*To the musicians*): Come, retire into that room, and rest yourselves until he comes.

DAN.-MAS. (*To the dancers*): And you also, on that side.

MUS.-MAS. (*To his pupil*): Is it done?

PUP.: Yes.

MUS.-MAS.: Let me look. . . . That is right.

DAN.-MAS.: It is something new?

MUS.-MAS.: Yes, it is an air for a serenade, which I made him compose here, while waiting till our gentleman is awake.

DAN.-MAS.: May one have a look at it?

MUS.-MAS.: You shall hear it by-and-by with the dialogue, when he comes; he will not be long.

DAN.-MAS.: Our occupations, yours and mine, are no small matter just at present.

MUS.-MAS.: True: we have both of us found here the very man whom we want. It is a nice little income for us this Mr. Jourdain, with his notions of nobility and gallantry, which he has taken into his head; and your dancing and my music might wish that everyone were like him.

DAN.-MAS.: Not quite; and I should like him to be more of a judge than he is, of the things we provide for him.

MUS.-MAS.: It is true that he knows little about them, but he pays well; and that is what our arts require just now above aught else.

DAN.-MAS.: As for myself, I confess, I hunger somewhat after glory. I am fond of applause, and I think that, in all the fine arts, it is an annoying torture to have to exhibit before fools, to have one's compositions subjected to the barbarism of a stupid man. Do not argue; there is a delight in having to work for people who are capable of appreciating the delicacy of an art, who know how to give a sweet reception to the beauties of a work, and who, by approbations which tickle one's fancy, reward one for his labour. Yes, the most pleasant recompense one can receive for the things which one does, is to find them understood, and made much of by applause which does one honour, There is nothing in my opinion, that pays us better for all our troubles; and enlightened praises are exquisitely sweet.

MUS.-MAS.: I quite agree with you, and I enjoy them as much as you do. Assuredly, there is nothing that tickles our fancy more than the applause you speak of; but such incense does not give us our livelihood. Praise pure and simple does not provide for a rainy day: there must be something solid mixed withal; and the best way to praise is to put one's hand in one's pocket. M. Jourdain is a man, it is true, whose knowledge is very small, who discourses at random upon all things, and never applauds but at the wrong time; but his money makes up for his bad judgment; he has discernment in his purse; his praises are minted, and this ignorant citizen is of more value to us, as you see, than the great lord who introduced us here.

DAN.-MAS.: There is some truth in what you say; but I think you make a little too much of money; and the interest in it is something so grovelling, that no gentleman ought ever to show any attachment to it.

MUS.-MAS.: You are glad enough, however, to receive the money which our gentleman gives you.

DAN.-MAS.: Assuredly; but I do not make it my whole happiness; and I could wish that with all his wealth he had also some good taste.

MUS.-MAS.: I could wish the same; and that is what we are aiming at both of us. But, in any case, he gives us the means of becoming known in the world; and he shall pay for others, and others shall applaud for him.

DAN.-MAS.: Here he comes.

*　　*　　*

SCENE III. MRS. JOURDAIN,
M. JOURDAIN, TWO LACQUEYS

MRS. JOUR.: Ha! ha! this is something new again! What is the meaning of this curious get-up, husband? Are you setting the world at nought to deck yourself out in this fashion? and do you wish to become a laughing-stock everywhere?

M. JOUR.: None but he-fools and she-fools will make a laughing-stock of me, wife.

MRS. JOUR.: In truth, they have not waited until now; and all the world has been laughing for a long while already at your vagaries.

M. JOUR.: Who is all this world, pray?

MRS. JOUR.: All this world is a world which is right, and which has more sense than you have. As for myself, I am disgusted with the life which you lead. I do not know whether this is our own house or not. One would think it is Shrove Tuesday every day; and from early morn, for fear of being too late, one hears nothing but the noise of fiddles and singers disturbing the whole neighbourhood.

Nic.: The mistress is right. I shall never see the ship-shape again with this heap of people that you bring to your house. They have feet that pick up the mud in every quarter of the town to bring it in here afterwards; and poor Françoise is almost worked off her legs, with rubbing the floors which your pretty tutors come to dirty again regularly every day.

M. Jour.: Good gracious! Miss Nicole, your tongue is sharp enough for a country-lass!

Mrs. Jour.: Nicole is right; and she has more sense than you have. I should much like to know what you want with a dancing-master, at your age.

Nic.: And with a great hulking fencing-master, who shakes the whole house with his stamping, and uproots all the floor-tiles in our big room.

M. Jour.: Hold your tongues, you girl and my wife.

Mrs. Jour.: Do you wish to learn dancing against the time when you shall have no longer any legs?

Nic.: Do you want to kill any one?

M. Jour.: Hold your tongues, I tell you: you are ignorant women, both of you; and you do not know the benefits of all this.

Mrs. Jour.: You ought rather to think of seeing your daughter married, who is of an age to be provided for.

M. Jour.: I shall think of seeing my daughter married when a suitable party shall present himself for her; but I shall also think of acquiring some polite learning.

Nic.: I have also heard, Mistress, that for fear of shortcoming, he has taken a philosophy-master to-day.

M. Jour.: Very good. I wish to improve my mind, and to know how to argue about things amongst gentle-folks.

Mrs. Jour.: Shall you not go, one of these days, to school, to get the birch, at your age?

M. Jour.: Why not? Would to heaven I could have the birch at this hour before everybody, and that I could know all that they teach at school!

Nic.: Yes, indeed! that would improve your legs.

M. Jour.: No doubt it would.

Mrs. Jour.: All this is highly necessary to manage your house!

M. Jour.: Assuredly. You both talk like fools, and I am ashamed at your ignorance. (*To Mrs. Jourdain.*) For instance, do you know what you are saying at this moment?

Mrs. Jour.: Yes. I know that what I say is very well said, and that you ought to think of leading a different life.

M. Jour.: I am not speaking of that. I am asking you what these words are which you are speaking just now.

Mrs. Jour.: They are very sensible words, and your conduct is scarcely so.

M. Jour.: I am not speaking of that, I tell you. I ask you, what I am speaking with you, what I am saying to you at this moment, what that is?

Mrs. Jour.: Nonsense.

M. Jour.: He, no, that is not it. What we are saying both of us, the language we are speaking at this moment?

Mrs. Jour.: Well?

M. Jour.: What is it called?

Mrs. Jour.: It is called whatever you like.

M. Jour.: It is prose, you stupid.

Mrs. Jour.: Prose?

M. Jour.: Yes, prose. Whatever is prose is not verse, and whatever is not verse is prose. Eh? that comes from studying. (*To Nicole.*) And do you know what you are to do to say U?

Nic.: How?

M. Jour.: Yes. What do you do when you say U?

Nic.: What?

M. Jour.: Say U, just to see.

Nic.: Well! U.

M. Jour.: What do you do?

Nic.: I say U.

M. Jour.: Yes; but when you say U what do you do?

Nic.: I do what you tell me to do.

M. Jour.: Oh! what a strange thing to have to do with fools? You pout the lips outwards, and bring the upper jaw near the lower one; U, do you see? I make a mouth, U.

Nic.: Yes: that is fine.

Mrs. Jour.: That is admirable!

M. JOUR.: It is quite another thing, if you had seen O, and DA, DA, and FA, FA.

MRS. JOUR.: But what is all this gibberish?

NIC.: What are we the better for all this?

M. JOUR.: It drives me mad when I see ignorant women.

MRS. JOUR.: Go, you should send all these people about their business, with their silly stuff.

NIC.: And above all, this great lout of a fencing-master, who fills the whole of my place with dust.

M. JOUR.: Lord! this fencing-master sticks strangely in your gizzard! I will let you see your impertinence directly. (*After having had the foils brought, and giving one of them to Nicole.*) Stay, reason demonstrative. The line of the body. When one thrusts in carte, one has but to do so, and when one thrusts in tierce, one has but to do so. This is the way never to be killed; and is it not very fine to be sure of one's game when one has to fight somebody? There, just thrust at me, to see.

(*Nicole thrusts several times at M. Jourdain.*)

NIC.: Well, what!

M. JOUR.: Gently! Hullo! ho! Softly! The devil take the hussy!

NIC.: You tell me to thrust at you.

M. JOUR.: Yes; but you thrust in tierce, before thrusting at me in carte, and you do not wait for me to parry.

MRS. JOUR.: You are mad, husband, with all your fancies; and this has come to you only since you have taken it in your head to frequent the nobility.

M. JOUR.: When I frequent the nobility, I show my judgment; and it is better than to frequent your citizens.

MRS. JOUR.: Indeed! really there is much to gain by frequenting your nobles; and you have done a great deal of good with this beautiful count, with whom you are so smitten!

M. JOUR.: Peace; take care what you say. Do you know, wife, that you do not know of whom you are speaking, when you speak of him? He is a personage of greater importance than you think, a nobleman who is held in great consideration at court, and who speaks to the King just as I speak to you. Is it not a great honour to me to see a person of such standing come so frequently to my house, who calls me his dear friend, and who treats me as if I were his equal? He has more kindness for me than one would ever imagine, and, before all the world, shows me such affection, that I am perfectly confused by it.

MRS. JOUR.: Yes, he shows you kindness and affection; but he borrows your money.

M. JOUR.: Well, is it not an honour to lend money to a man of that condition? and can I do less for a nobleman who calls me his dear friend?

MRS. JOUR.: And this nobleman, what does he do for you?

M. JOUR.: Things you would be astonished at, if you knew them.

MRS. JOUR.: But what?

M. JOUR.: That will do! I cannot explain myself. It is enough that if I have lent him money, he will return it to me, and before long.

MRS. JOUR.: Yes, you had better wait for it.

M. JOUR.: Assuredly. Has he not said so?

MRS. JOUR.: Yes, yes, he will be sure not to fail in it.

M. JOUR.: He has given me his word as a nobleman.

MRS. JOUR.: Stuff!

M. JOUR.: Good gracious, you are very obstinate, wife! I tell you that he will keep his word; I am sure of it.

MRS. JOUR.: And I, I am sure that he will not, and that all the caresses he loads you with are only so much cajoling.

M. JOUR.: Hold your tongue. Here he comes.

MRS. JOUR.: It wanted nothing but this. He comes perhaps to ask you for another loan; and the very sight of him spoils my dinner.

M. JOUR.: Hold your tongue, I tell you.

*   *   *

SCENE XII. CLÉONTE, M. JOURDAIN, MRS. JOURDAIN, LUCILE, COVIELLE, NICOLE

CLE.: Sir, I did not wish to depute any one else to prefer a request which I have long meditated. It concerns me sufficiently to undertake it in person; and without farther ado, I will tell you that the honour of being your son-in-law is a glorious favour which I beg of you to grant me.

M. JOUR.: Before giving you your answer, Sir, I pray you to tell me whether you are a nobleman.

CLE.: Sir, most people, on this question, do not hesitate much; the word is easily spoken. There is no scruple in assuming that name, and present custom seems to authorize the theft. As for me, I confess to you, my feelings on this point are rather more delicate. I think that all imposture is unworthy of an honest man, and that it is cowardice to disguise what Heaven has made us, to deck ourselves in the eyes of the world with a stolen title, and to wish to pass for what we are not. I am born of parents who, no doubt, have filled honourable offices; I have acquitted myself with honour in the army, where I served for six years; and I am sufficiently well to do to hold a middling rank in society; but with all this, I will not assume what others, in my position, might think they had the right to pretend to; and I will tell you frankly that I am not a nobleman.

M. JOUR.: Your hand, Sir; my daughter is not for you.

CLE.: How.

M. JOUR.: You are not a nobleman: you shall not have my daughter.

MRS. JOUR.: What is it you mean by your nobleman? Is it that we ourselves are descended from Saint Louis?

M. JOUR.: Hold your tongue, wife; I see what you are driving at.

MRS. JOUR.: Are we two descended from aught else than from plain citizens?

M. JOUR.: If that is not a slander?

MRS. JOUR.: And was your father not a tradesman as well as mine?

M. JOUR.: Plague take the woman, she always harps upon that. If your father was a tradesman, so much the worse for him; but as for mine, they are impertinent fellows who say so. All that I have to say to you, is that I will have a nobleman for a son-in-law.

MRS. JOUR.: Your daughter wants a husband who is suited to her; and it is much better for her that she should have a respectable man, rich and handsome, than a beggarly and deformed nobleman.

NIC.: That is true; we have the son of our village squire, who is the greatest lout and the most stupid nincompoop that I have ever seen.

M. JOUR. (*To Nicole*): Hold your tongue, Miss Impertinence; you always thrust yourself into the conversation. I have sufficient wealth to give my daughter; I wish only for honours, and I will make her a marchioness.

MRS. JOUR.: Marchioness?

M. JOUR.: Yes, marchioness.

MRS. JOUR.: Alas! Heaven preserve me from it!

M. JOUR.: It is a thing I am determined on.

MRS. JOUR.: It is a thing to which I shall never consent. Matches with people above one's own position are always subject to the most grievous inconvenience. I do not wish a son-in-law of mine to be able to reproach my daughter with her parents, or that she should have children who would be ashamed to call me their grandmother. If she were to come and visit me with the equipage of a grand lady, and that, through inadvertency, she should miss curtseying to one of the neighbourhood, people would not fail to say a hundred silly things immediately. Do you see this lady marchioness, they would say, who is giving herself such airs? She is the daughter of M. Jourdain, who was only too glad, when she was a child, to play at ladyship with us. She has not always been so high up in the world, and her two grandfathers sold cloth near the St. Innocent gate. They amassed great wealth for their children, for which they are probably paying very dearly in the other world; for people can scarcely become so rich by remaining honest folks. I will not have all this tittle-tattle, and in one word, I wish for a man who shall be grateful to me for my daughter, and to whom I shall be able to say: Sit down there, son-in-law, and dine with me.

M. JOUR.: These are the sentiments of a narrow mind, to wish to remain for ever in a mean condition. Do not answer me any more; my daughter shall be a marchioness in spite of all the world; and, if you put me in a passion, I shall make her a duchess.

*   *   *

REVIEW QUESTIONS

1. How are servants and masters, who operated in separate worlds, interdependent in Molière's comedy?
2. What is the relation between nobility and judgment?
3. Do women judge differently or according to different standards?

Coffee House Society

Coffee is an example of the impact of overseas trade and colonial empire on the consumption and lifestyle of ordinary Europeans. The bean's historical origins are shrouded in legend. What seems clear is that they were taken to Arabia from Africa during the fifteenth century and placed under cultivation. Introduced into Europe during the sixteenth and seventeenth centuries, they gained almost immediate popularity. Served at coffeehouses, the first of which was established in London around 1650, coffee's consumption became an occasion for transacting political, social, commercial, or literary business. So great was the demand for coffee that European merchants took it from the Arabian Peninsula to Java, Indonesia, and the Americas. The following descriptions from two anonymous authors give some sense of the ways in which colonial products shaped European culture in the seventeenth century.

From *Selections from the Sources of English History*, edited by Charles W. Colby (New York: Longmans, Green, 1899), pp. 208–12.

*   *   *

1673

A coffee-house is a lay conventicle, good-fellowship turned puritan, ill-husbandry in masquerade, whither people come, after toping all day, to purchase, at the expense of their last penny, the repute of sober companions: A Rota [club] room, that, like Noah's ark, receives animals of every sort, from the precise diminutive band, to the hectoring cravat and cuffs in folio: a nursery for training up the smaller fry of virtuosi in confident tattling, or a cabal of kittling [carping] critics that have only learned to spit and mew; a mint of intelligence, that, to make each man his pennyworth, draws out into petty parcels, what the merchant receives in bullion: he, that comes often, saves twopence a week in Gazettes, and has his news and his coffee for the same charge, as at a threepenny ordinary they give in broth to your chop of mutton; it is an exchange, where haberdashers of political small-wares meet, and mutually abuse each other, and the public, with bottomless stories, and headless notions; the rendezvous of idle pamphlets, and persons more idly employed to read them; a high court of justice, where every little fellow in a camlet cloak takes upon him to transpose affairs both in church and state, to show reasons against acts of parliament, and condemn the decrees of general councils.

*   *   *

As you have a hodge-podge of drinks, such too is your company, for each man seems a leveller, and ranks and files himself as he lists, without regard to degrees or order; so that often you may see a silly fop and a worshipful justice, a griping rook and a grave citizen, a worthy lawyer and an errant pickpocket, a reverend nonconformist and a canting mountebank, all blended together to compose an oglio [medley] of impertinence.

If any pragmatic, to show himself witty or eloquent, begin to talk high, presently the further tables are abandoned, and all the rest flock round (like smaller birds, to admire the gravity of the madge-howlet [barn-owl]). They listen to him awhile with their mouths, and let their pipes go out, and coffee grow cold, for pure zeal of attention, but on the sudden fall all a yelping at once with more noise, but not half so much harmony, as a pack of beagles on the full cry. To still this bawling, up starts Capt. All-man-sir, the man of mouth, with a face as blustering as that of Æolus and his four sons, in painting, and a voice louder than the speaking trumpet, he begins you the story of a sea-fight; and though he never were further, by water, than the Bear-garden, . . . yet, having pirated the names of ships and captains, he persuades you himself was present, and performed miracles; that he waded knee-deep in blood on the upper-deck, and never thought to serenade his mistress so pleasant as the bullets whistling; how he stopped a vice-admiral of the enemy's under full sail; till she was boarded, with his single arm, instead of grappling-irons, and puffed out with his breath a fire-ship that fell foul on them. All this he relates, sitting in a cloud of smoke, and belching so many common oaths to vouch it, you can scarce guess whether the real engagement, or his romancing account of it, be the more dreadful: however, he concludes with railing at the conduct

of some eminent officers (that, perhaps, he never saw), and protests, had they taken his advice at the council of war, not a sail had escaped us.

He is no sooner out of breath, but another begins a lecture on the Gazette, where, finding several prizes taken, he gravely observes, if this trade hold, we shall quickly rout the Dutch, horse and foot, by sea: he nicknames the Polish gentlemen wherever he meets them, and enquires whether Gayland and Taffaletta be Lutherans or Calvinists? *stilo novo* he interprets a vast new stile, or turnpike, erected by his electoral highness on the borders of Westphalia, to keep Monsieur Turenne's cavalry from falling on his retreating troops: he takes words by the sound, without examining their sense: Morea he believes to be the country of the Moors, and Hungary a place where famine always keeps her court, nor is there anything more certain, than that he made a whole room full of fops, as wise as himself, spend above two hours in searching the map for Aristocracy and Democracy, not doubting but to have found them there, as well as Dalmatia and Croatia.

1675

Though the happy Arabia, nature's spicery, prodigally furnishes the voluptuous world with all kinds of aromatics, and divers other rarities; yet I scarce know whether mankind be not still as much obliged to it for the excellent fruit of the humble coffee-shrub, as for any other of its more specious productions: for, since there is nothing we here enjoy, next to life, valuable beyond health, certainly those things that contribute to preserve us in good plight and eucrasy, and fortify our weak bodies against the continual assaults and batteries of disease, deserve our regards much more than those which only gratify a liquorish palate, or otherwise prove subservient to our delights. As for this salutiferous berry, of so general a use through all the regions of the east, it is sufficiently known, when prepared, to be moderately hot, and of a very drying attenuating and cleansing quality; whence reason infers, that its decoction must contain many good physical properties, and cannot but be an incomparable remedy to dissolve crudities, comfort the brain, and dry up ill humours in the stomach. In brief, to prevent or redress, in those that frequently drink it, all cold drowsy rheumatic distempers whatsoever, that proceed from excess of moisture, which are so numerous, that but to name them would tire the tongue of a mountebank.

* * *

Lastly, for diversion. It is older than Aristotle, and will be true, when Hobbes is forgot, that man is a sociable creature, and delights in company. Now, whither shall a person, wearied with hard study, or the laborious turmoils of a tedious day, repair to refresh himself? Or where can young gentlemen, or shop-keepers, more innocently and advantageously spend an hour or two in the evening, than at a coffee-house? Where they shall be sure to meet company, and, by the custom of the house, not such as at other places, stingy and reserved to themselves, but free and communicative; where every man may modestly begin his story, and propose to, or answer another, as he thinks fit. Discourse is *pabulum animi, cos ingenii*; the mind's best diet, and the great whetstone and incentive of ingenuity; by that we come to know men better than by their physiognomy. *Loquere, ut te videam*, speak, that I may see thee, was the philosopher's adage. To read men is acknowledged more useful than books; but where is there a better library for that study, generally, than here, amongst such a variety of humours, all expressing themselves on divers subjects, according to their respective abilities?

* * *

In brief, it is undeniable, that, as you have here the most civil, so it is, generally, the most intelligent society; the frequenting whose converse, and observing their discourses and department, cannot but civilise our manners, enlarge our understandings, refine our language, teach us a generous confidence and handsome mode of address, and brush off that *pudor rubrusticus* (as, I remember, Tully somewhere calls it), that clownish kind of modesty frequently incident to the best natures, which renders them sheepish and ridiculous in company.

So that, upon the whole matter, spite of the idle sarcasms and paltry reproaches thrown upon it, we may, with no less truth than plainness, give this brief character of a well regulated coffee-house (for our pen disdains to be an advocate for any sordid holes, that assume that name to cloak the practice of debauchery), that it is the sanctuary of health, the nursery of temperance, the delight of frugality, an academy of civility, and free-school of ingenuity.

* * *

REVIEW QUESTIONS

1. How would you describe coffeehouse society in the late seventeenth century?
2. What is the attitude of each of our two anonymous authors? How and why do they differ?
3. What is the significance of reading the gazette?
4. What are the virtues of coffee?
5. How can coffee drinking be a vice in early modern Europe?

ROBERT FILMER

FROM *Patriarcha*

Robert Filmer (1588–1563), the English theorist of patriarchalism and absolutism, was born into the Kentish squirearchy. Filmer was educated at Trinity College, Cambridge, and at Lincoln's Inn and was knighted by Charles I. Though he never fought for the king, his house was sacked during the Civil War, and he was imprisoned in the royalist cause. He wrote many political tracts, but his most important work, Patriarcha *(1680), was not well received at the time. Common opinion seemed to follow that of John Locke, who wrote in his* Two Treatises of Government: *"There was never so much glib nonsense put together in well-sounding English." Yet Filmer remains interesting in his own right. He is the first English absolutist. Despite the publication date,* Patriarcha *was written before the Civil War and before publication of* Leviathan, *before the actions of Parliament prompted any defense of the monarchy and its prerogatives. Filmer believed that the state was a family, that the first king was a father, and that submission to patriarchal authority was the key to political obligation. Of particular interest is his interpretation of patriarchy, the social structure that characterized early modern Europe until the industrial revolution. Indeed, many scholars argue that Filmer's description of social relations is more realistic than the mechanical individualism put forward by Locke. His achievement notwithstanding, his historical significance rests solely on the fact that all of Locke's political thought was directed against him.*

From *Patriarcha and Other Writings*, edited by Johann P. Sommerville (Cambridge, Eng.: Cambridge University Press, 1991), pp. 2–3, 5–12.

Since the time that school divinity began to flourish, there hath been a common opinion maintained as well by divines as by divers other learned men which affirms: "Mankind is naturally endowed and born with freedom from all subjection, and at liberty to choose what form of government it please, and that the power which any one man hath over others was at the first by human right bestowed according to the discretion of the multitude."

This tenet was first hatched in the schools, and hath been fostered by all succeeding papists for good divinity. The divines also of the reformed churches have entertained it, and the common people everywhere tenderly embrace it as being most plausible to flesh and blood, for that it prod-

igally distributes a portion of liberty to the meanest of the multitude, who magnify liberty as if the height of human felicity were only to be found in it—never remembering that the desire of liberty was the cause of the fall of Adam.

But howsoever this vulgar opinion hath of late obtained great reputation, yet it is not to be found in the ancient Fathers and doctors of the primitive church. It contradicts the doctrine and history of the Holy Scriptures, the constant practice of all ancient monarchies, and the very principles of the law of nature. It is hard to say whether it be more erroneous in divinity or dangerous in policy.

Yet upon the grounds of this doctrine both Jesuits and some over zealous favourers of the Geneva discipline have built a perilous conclusion,

THE MEETING IN LYONS (1625)　　　　　　　PETER PAUL RUBENS

The Meeting in Lyons *is part of a cycle of twenty-one paintings, the largest commission in Rubens's career, for Marie de Medici, dowager queen of France. Intended to hang in her palace in Paris, they describe the important events of her life. It was not easy work; she was a difficult subject, neither beautiful nor interesting nor agreeable. She had quarreled with her late husband, Henri IV, and her son, Louis XIII, had banished her from Paris. Still, Rubens managed to complete the commission to his patroness's satisfaction and created images glorifying the French monarchy. What do the two allegorical figures—Hera, Goddess of Marriage, joining the King and his Queen, and Lyons, driving a chariot—mean in relationship to the royal pair? Why would Rubens choose to represent Henri and Marie as mythological, semidivine figures? Considering the dates of the paintings, after a prolonged civil war and before a great international conflict, what might the allegorical representations of monarch and aristocracy suggest about their strength or weakness?*

which is "that the people or multitude have power to punish or deprive the prince if he transgress the laws of the kingdom." Witness Parsons and Buchanan. The first, under the name of Doleman, in the third chapter of his first book labours to prove that kings have been lawfully chastised by their commonwealths. The latter in his book *De Jure Regni apud Scotos* maintains a liberty of the people to depose their prince. Cardinal Bellarmine and Mr Calvin both look asquint this way.

This desperate assertion, whereby kings are made subject to the censures and deprivations of their subjects, follows . . . as a necessary consequence of that former position of the supposed natural equality and freedom of mankind, and liberty to choose what form of government it please.

*   *   *

The rebellious consequence which follows this prime article of the natural freedom of mankind may be my sufficient warrant for a modest examination of the original truth of it. Much hath been said, and by many, for the affirmative. Equity requires that an ear be reserved a little for the negative.

*   *   *

To make evident the grounds of this question about the natural liberty of mankind, I will lay down some passages of Cardinal Bellarmine, that may best unfold the state of this controversy. "Secular or civil power," said he

is instituted by men. It is in the people unless they bestow it on a prince. This power is immediately in the whole multitude, as in the subject of it. For this power is by the divine law, but the divine law hath given this power to no particular man. If the positive law be taken away, there is left no reason why amongst a multitude (who are equal) one rather than another should bear rule over the rest. Power is given by the multitude to one man, or to more by the same law of nature, for the commonwealth of itself cannot exercise this power, therefore it is bound to bestow it upon some

one man, or some few. It depends upon the consent of the multitude to ordain over themselves a king, or consul, or other magistrate; and if there be a lawful cause, the multitude may change the kingdom into an aristocracy or democracy.

Thus far Bellarmine, in which passages are comprised the strength of all that ever I have read or heard produced for the natural liberty of the subject.

*   *   *

I come now to examine that argument which is used by Bellarmine, and is the one and only argument I can find produced by any author for the proof of the natural liberty of the people. It is thus framed: that God hath given or ordained power is evident by Scripture; but God hath given it to no particular man, because by nature all men are equal; therefore he hath given power to the people or multitude.

To answer this reason, drawn from the equality of mankind by nature, I will first use the help of Bellarmine himself, whose very words are these: "if many men had been together created out of the earth, all they ought to have been princes over their posterity." In these words we have an evident confession that creation made man prince of his posterity. And indeed not only Adam but the succeeding patriarchs had, by right of fatherhood, royal authority over their children. Nor dares Bellarmine deny this also. "That the patriarchs," saith he, "were endowed with kingly power, their deeds do testify." For as Adam was lord of his children, so his children under him had a command and power over their own children, but still with subordination to the first parent, who is lord paramount over his children's children to all generations, as being the grandfather of his people.

I see not then how the children of Adam, or of any man else, can be free from subjection to their parents. And this subjection of children is the only fountain of all regal authority, by the ordination of God himself. It follows that civil power not only in general is by divine institution, but even the assignment of it specifically to the eldest parent, which quite takes away that new and common distinction which refers only power universal as absolute to God, but power respective in regard of the special form of government to the choice of the people. Nor leaves it any place for such imaginary pactions between kings and their people as many dream of.

This lordship which Adam by creation had over the whole world, and by right descending from him the patriarchs did enjoy, was as large and ample as the absolutest dominion of any monarch which hath been since the creation. For power of life and death we find that Judah, the father, pronounced sentence of death against Thamar, his daughter-in-law, for playing the harlot. "Bring her forth," saith he, "that she may be burnt." Touching war, we see that Abraham commanded an army of 318 soldiers of his own family; and Esau met his brother Jacob with 400 men at arms. For matter of peace, Abraham made a league with Abimelech, and ratified the articles by an oath. These acts of judging in capital causes, of making war, and concluding peace, are the chiefest marks of sovereignty that are found in any monarch.

Not only until the Flood, but after it, this patriarchal power did continue—as the very name of patriarch doth in part prove. The three sons of Noah had the whole world divided amongst them by their father, for of them was the whole world overspread, according to the benediction given to him and his sons: "Be fruitful and multiply and replenish the earth." Most of the civillest nations in the world labour to fetch their original from some one of the sons or nephews of Noah, which were scattered abroad after the confusion of Babel. In this dispersion we must certainly find the establishment of regal power throughout the kingdoms of the world.

It is a common opinion that at the confusion of tongues there were seventy-two distinct nations erected. All which were not confused multitudes, without heads or governors, and at liberty to choose what governors or government they pleased, but they were distinct families, which had

fathers for rulers over them. Whereby it appears that even in the confusion, God was careful to preserve the fatherly authority by distributing the diversity of languages according to the diversity of families.

*   *   *

In this division of the world, some are of opinion that Noah used lots for the distribution of it. Others affirm that he sailed about the Mediterranean sea in ten years and as he went about, pointed to each son his part, and so made the division of the then known world into Asia, Africa, and Europe, according to the number of his sons, the limits of which three parts are all found in that midland sea.

*   *   *

Some, perhaps, may think that these princes and dukes of families were but some pretty lords under some greater kings, because the number of them are so many that their particular territories could be but small, and not worthy the title of kingdoms. But they must consider that at first kings had no such large dominions as they have nowadays. We find in the time of Abraham, which was about 300 years after the Flood, that in a little corner of Asia nine kings at once met in battle, most of which were but kings of cities apiece, with the adjacent territories, as of Sodom, Gomorrha, Shinar, etc. In the same chapter is mention of Melchisedek, king of Salem, which was but the city of Jerusalem. And in the catalogue of the kings of Edom, the name of each king's city is recorded as the only mark to distinguish their dominions. In the land of Canaan, which was but of a small circuit, Joshua destroyed thirty-one kings, and about the same time Adonibezek had seventy kings whose fingers and toes he had cut off, and made them feed under his table. A few ages after this, thirty-two kings came to Benhadad, king of Syria, and about seventy kings of Greece went to the wars of Troy. Caesar found more kings in France than there be now provinces there, and at his sailing over into this island he found four kings in our county of Kent. These heaps of kings in each nation are an argument that their territories were but small, and strongly confirm our assertion that erection of kingdoms came at first only by distinction of families.

By manifest footsteps we may trace this paternal government unto the Israelites coming into Egypt, where the exercise of supreme patriarchal jurisdiction was intermitted because they were in subjection to a stronger prince. After the return of these Israelites out of bondage, God, out of a special care of them, chose Moses and Joshua successively to govern as princes in the place and stead of the supreme fathers, and after them likewise for a time He raised up Judges to defend His people in times of peril. But when God gave the Israelites kings, He re-established the ancient and prime right of lineal succession to paternal government. And whensoever He made choice of any special person to be king, He intended that the issue also should have benefit thereof, as being comprehended sufficiently in the person of the father—although the father only were named in the grant.

It may seem absurd to maintain that kings now are the fathers of their people, since experience shows the contrary. It is true, all kings be not the natural parents of their subjects, yet they all either are, or are to be reputed as the next heirs to those progenitors who were at first the natural parents of the whole people, and in their right succeed to the exercise of supreme jurisdiction. And such heirs are not only lords of their own children, but also of their brethren, and all others that were subject to their fathers.

And therefore we find that God told Cain of his brother Abel: "His desires shall be subject unto thee, and thou shalt rule over him." Accordingly, when Jacob had bought his brother's birthright, Isaac blessed him thus: "Be lord over thy brethren, and let the sons of thy mother bow before thee." As long as the first fathers of families lived, the name of patriarchs did aptly belong unto them. But after a few descents, when the true fatherhood itself was extinct and only the right of the father descended to the true heir, then the title of prince or king was more significant to express the power of him who succeeds only to the right of that fa-

therhood which his ancestors did naturally enjoy. By this means it comes to pass that many a child, by succeeding a king, hath the right of a father over many a grey-headed multitude, and hath the title of *pater patriae*.

*   *   *

In all kingdoms or commonwealths in the world, whether the prince be the supreme father of the people or but the true heir of such a father, or whether he come to the crown by usurpation, or by election of the nobles or of the people, or by any other way whatsoever, or whether some few or a multitude govern the commonwealth, yet still the authority that is in any one, or in many, or in all of these, is the only right and natural authority of a supreme father. There is, and always shall be continued to the end of the world, a natural right of a supreme father over every multitude, although, by the secret will of God, many at first do most unjustly obtain the exercise of it.

To confirm this natural right of regal power, we find in the decalogue that the law which enjoins obedience to kings is delivered in the terms of "honour thy father" as if all power were originally in the father. If obedience to parents be immediately due by a natural law, and subjection to princes but by the mediation of an human ordinance, what reason is there that the law of nature should give place to the laws of men, as we see the power of the father over his child gives place and is subordinate to the power of the magistrate?

If we compare the natural duties of a father with those of a king, we find them to be all one, without any difference at all but only in the latitude or extent of them. As the father over one family, so the king, as father over many families, extends his care to preserve, feed, clothe, instruct and defend the whole commonwealth. His wars, his peace, his courts of justice and all his acts of sovereignty tend only to preserve and distribute to every subordinate and inferior father, and to their children, their rights and privileges, so that all the duties of a king are summed up in an universal fatherly care of his people.

*   *   *

REVIEW QUESTIONS

1. According to Filmer, what is the relation between the authority of a father and the authority of a king?
2. Why does Filmer link political authority to domestic authority?
3. What is the relation between authority and nature for Filmer?
4. How does political authority come into being?
5. What are the implications of Filmer's rejection of the natural liberty of humankind?
6. What are its implications for his conception of human nature?
7. What are its implications for economic relations?
8. What are its implications for social status?

JOHN LOCKE

FROM *Two Treatises on Government*

John Locke (1632–1704) was an English philosopher whose thought contributed to the Enlightenment. He grew up in a liberal Puritan family, the son of an attorney who fought in the civil war against Charles I, and attended Christ's Church College, Oxford. He received his bachelor of arts in 1656, lectured in classical languages while earning his master of arts, and entered Oxford medical school to avoid being forced to join the clergy. In 1666, Locke attached himself to the household of the earl of Shaftesbury and his fortunes to the liberal Whig Party. Between 1675 and 1679, he lived in France, where he made contact with leading intellectuals of the late seventeenth century. On his return to England, he plunged into the controversy surrounding the succession of James II, an avowed Catholic with absolutist pretensions, to the throne of his brother, Charles II. Locke's patron, Shaftesbury, was imprisoned for his opposition, and Locke went into exile in 1683. Though he was involved to some extent in the Glorious Revolution of 1688, he returned to England in 1689, in the entourage of Mary, princess of Orange, who would assume the throne with her husband, William. The Two Treatises on Government *(1690) were published anonymously, although readers commonly assumed Locke's authorship. More interesting is the point in time at which they were written. Most scholars assume that they were written immediately before publication, as a justification of the revolution just completed. Many scholars believe, however, that the treatises were written from exile as a call to revolution, a much more inflammatory and risky project. The first treatise comprises a long attack on Robert Filmer's* Patriarcha, *a denial of the patriarchal justification of the absolute monarch. The second treatise constructs in the place of patriarchy a theory of politics based on natural law, which provides the foundation of human freedom. The social contract creates a political structure by consent of the governed designed to preserve those freedoms established in natural law. Locke's treatises inspired the political theories of the Enlightenment.*

From *First Treatise* in *Two Treatises on Government,* edited by Ernst Rhys (New York: Dutton, 1993).

*   *   *

Chapter VI
Of Paternal Power

It may perhaps be censured an impertinent criticism in a discourse of this nature to find fault with words and names that have obtained in the world. And yet possibly it may not be amiss to offer new ones when the old are apt to lead men into mistakes, as this of paternal power probably has done, which seems so to place the power of parents over their children wholly in the father, as if the mother had no share in it; whereas if we consult reason or revelation, we shall find she has an equal title, which may give one reason to ask whether this might not be more properly called parental power? For whatever obligation Nature and the right of generation lays on children, it must certainly bind them equal to both the concurrent causes of it. And accordingly we see the positive law of God everywhere joins them together without distinction, when it commands the obedience of children: "Honour thy father and thy mother"; "Whosoever curseth his father or his mother"; "Ye shall fear every man his mother and his father"; "Children, obey your parents" etc., is the style of the Old and New Testament.

*   *   *

Though I have said above "That all men by nature are equal," I cannot be supposed to understand all sorts of "equality." Age or virtue may give men a just precedency. Excellency of parts and merit may place others above the common level. Birth may subject some, and alliance or benefits others, to pay an observance to those to whom Nature, gratitude, or other respects, may

have made it due; and yet all this consists with the equality which all men are in in respect of jurisdiction or dominion one over another, which was the equality I there spoke of as proper to the business in hand, being that equal right that every man hath to his natural freedom, without being subjected to the will or authority of any other man.

Children, I confess, are not born in this full state of equality, though they are born to it. Their parents have a sort of rule and jurisdiction over them when they come into the world, and for some time after, but it is but a temporary one. The bonds of this subjection are like the swaddling clothes they are wrapt up in and supported by in the weakness of their infancy. Age and reason as they grow up loosen them, till at length they drop quite off, and leave a man at his own free disposal.

Adam was created a perfect man, his body and mind in full possession of their strength and reason, and so was capable from the first instance of his being to provide for his own support and preservation, and govern his actions according to the dictates of the law of reason God had implanted in him. From him the world is peopled with his descendants, who are all born infants, weak and helpless, without knowledge or understanding. But to supply the defects of this imperfect state till the improvement of growth and age had removed them, Adam and Eve, and after them all parents were, by the law of Nature, under an obligation to preserve, nourish and educate the children they had begotten, not as their own workmanship, but the workmanship of their own Maker, the Almighty, to whom they were to be accountable for them.

The law that was to govern Adam was the same that was to govern all his posterity, the law of reason. But his offspring having another way of entrance into the world, different from him, by a

PALACE AND GARDENS OF VERSAILLES (1668)   PIERRE PATEL

Patel's famous print of the palace at Versailles captures the grand scale of monarchy in the seventeenth century. Note not only the size of the palace but also its location in the center of carefully planned gardens, boulevards, and buildings. Versailles was truly a theater for the display of political power. Why was such a theater of power necessary? What can be learned from the iconography of power that was built into Versailles, such as the function of gardens or the location of boulevards or alleys or broad open spaces? How might Versailles have functioned not only as a theater of power but also as a prison for the powerful?

natural birth, that produced them ignorant, and without the use of reason, they were not presently under that law. For nobody can be under a law that is not promulgated to him; and this law being promulgated or made known by reason only, he that is not come to the use of his reason cannot be said to be under this law; and Adam's children being not presently as soon as born under this law of reason, were not presently free. For law, in its true notion, is not so much the limitation as the direction of a free and intelligent agent to his proper interest, and prescribes no farther than is for the general good of those under that law. Could they be happier without it, the law, as a useless thing, would of itself vanish; and that ill deserves the name of confinement which hedges us in only from bogs and precipices. So that however it may be mistaken, the end of law is not to abolish or restrain, but to preserve and enlarge freedom. For in all the states of created beings, capable of laws, where there is no law there is no freedom. For liberty is to be free from restraint and violence from others, which cannot be where there is no law; and is not, as we are told, "a liberty for every man to do what he lists." For who could be free, when every other man's humour might domineer over him? But a liberty to dispose and order freely as he lists his person, actions, possessions, and his whole property within the allowance of those laws under which he is, and therein not to be subject to the arbitrary will of another, but freely follow his own.

The power, then, that parents have over their children arises from that duty which is incumbent on them, to take care of their offspring during the imperfect state of childhood. To inform the mind, and govern the actions of their yet ignorant nonage, till reason shall take its place and ease them of that trouble, is what the children want, and the parents are bound to. For God having given man an understanding to direct his actions, has allowed him a freedom of will and liberty of acting, as properly belonging thereunto within the bounds of that law he is under. But whilst he is in an estate wherein he has no understanding of his own to direct his will, he is not to have any will of his

own to follow. He that understands for him must will for him too; he must prescribe to his will, and regulate his actions, but when he comes to the estate that made his father a free man, the son is a free man too.

This holds in all the laws a man is under, whether natural or civil. Is a man under the law of Nature? What made him free of that law? what gave him a free disposing of his property, according to his own will, within the compass of that law? I answer, an estate wherein he might be supposed capable to know that law, that so he might keep his actions within the bounds of it. When he has acquired that state, he is presumed to know how far that law is to be his guide, and how far he may make use of his freedom, and so comes to have it; till then, somebody else must guide him, who is presumed to know how far the law allows a liberty. If such a state of reason, such an age of discretion made him free, the same shall make his son free too. Is a man under the law of England? what made him free of that law—that is, to have the liberty to dispose of his actions and possessions, according to his own will, within the permission of that law? a capacity of knowing that law. Which is supposed, by that law, at the age of twenty-one, and in some cases sooner. If this made the father free, it shall make the son free too. Till then, we see the law allows the son to have no will, but he is to be guided by the will of his father or guardian, who is to understand for him. And if the father die and fail to substitute a deputy in this trust, if he hath not provided a tutor to govern his son during his minority, during his want of understanding, the law takes care to do it: some other must govern him and be a will to him till he hath attained to a state of freedom, and his understanding be fit to take the government of his will. But after that the father and son are equally free, as much as tutor and pupil, after nonage, equally subjects of the same law together, without any dominion left in the father over the life, liberty, or estate of his son, whether they be only in the state and under the law of Nature, or under the positive laws of an established government.

*   *   *

The freedom then of man, and liberty of acting according to his own will, is grounded on his having reason, which is able to instruct him in that law he is to govern himself by, and make him know how far he is left to the freedom of his own will. To turn him loose to an unrestrained liberty, before he has reason to guide him, is not the allowing him the privilege of his nature to be free, but to thrust him out amongst brutes, and abandon him to a state as wretched and as much beneath that of a man as theirs. This is that which puts the authority into the parents' hands to govern the minority of their children. God hath made it their business to employ this care on their offspring, and hath placed in them suitable inclinations of tenderness and concern to temper this power, to apply it as His wisdom designed it, to the children's good as long as they should need to be under it.

But what reason can hence advance this care of the parents due to their offspring into an absolute, arbitrary dominion of the father, whose power reaches no farther than by such a discipline as he finds most effectual to give such strength and health to their bodies, such vigour and rectitude to their minds, as may best fit his children to be most useful to themselves and others, and, if it be necessary to his condition, to make them work when they are able for their own subsistence; but in this power the mother, too, has her share with the father.

Nay, this power so little belongs to the father by any peculiar right of Nature, but only as he is guardian of his children, that when he quits his care of them he loses his power over them, which goes along with their nourishment and education, to which it is inseparably annexed, and belongs as much to the foster-father of an exposed child as to the natural father of another. So little power does the bare act of begetting give a man over his issue, if all his care ends there, and this be all the title he hath to the name and authority of a father. And what will become of this paternal power in that part of the world where one woman hath more than one husband at a time? or in those parts of America where, when the husband and

wife part, which happens frequently, the children are all left to the mother, follow her, and are wholly under her care and provision? And if the father die whilst the children are young, do they not naturally everywhere owe the same obedience to their mother, during their minority, as to their father, were he alive? And will any one say that the mother hath a legislative power over her children that she can make standing rules which shall be of perpetual obligation, by which they ought to regulate all the concerns of their property, and bound their liberty all the course of their lives, and enforce the observation of them with capital punishments? For this is the proper power of the magistrate, of which the father hath not so much as the shadow. His command over his children is but temporary, and reaches not their life or property. It is but a help to the weakness and imperfection of their nonage, a discipline necessary to their education. And though a father may dispose of his own possessions as he pleases when his children are out of danger of perishing for want, yet his power extends not to the lives or goods which either their own industry, or another's bounty, has made theirs, nor to their liberty neither, when they are once arrived to the enfranchisement of the years of discretion. The father's empire then ceases, and he can from thenceforward no more dispose of the liberty of his son than that of any other man. And it must be far from an absolute or perpetual jurisdiction from which a man may withdraw himself, having licence from Divine authority to "leave father and mother and cleave to his wife."

*   *   *

Chapter VII
Of Political or Civil Society

God, having made man such a creature that, in His own judgment, it was not good for him to be alone, put him under strong obligations of necessity, convenience, and inclination, to drive him into society, as well as fitted him with understanding and language to continue and enjoy it. The first society was between man and wife, which gave beginning to that between parents and children, to which, in time, that between master and servant came to be added. And though all these might, and commonly did, meet together, and make up but one family, wherein the master or mistress of it had some sort of rule proper to a family, each of these, or all together, came short of "political society," as we shall see if we consider the different ends, ties, and bounds of each of these.

Conjugal society is made by a voluntary compact between man and woman, and though it consist chiefly in such a communion and right in one another's bodies as is necessary to its chief end, procreation, yet it draws with it mutual support and assistance, and a communion of interests too, as necessary not only to unite their care and affection, but also necessary to their common offspring, who have a right to be nourished and maintained by them till they are able to provide for themselves.

For the end of conjunction between male and female being not barely procreation, but the continuation of the species, this conjunction betwixt male and female ought to last, even after procreation, so long as is necessary to the nourishment and support of the young ones, who are to be sustained by those that got them till they are able to shift and provide for themselves. This rule, which the infinite wise Maker hath set to the works of His hands, we find the inferior creatures steadily obey. In those vivaporous animals which feed on grass the conjunction between male and female lasts no longer than the very act of copulation, because the teat of the dam being sufficient to nourish the young till it be able to feed on grass, the male only begets, but concerns not himself for the female or young, to whose sustenance he can contribute nothing. But in beasts of prey the conjunction lasts longer, because the dam, not being able well to subsist herself and nourish her numerous offspring by her own prey alone (a more laborious as well as more dangerous way of living than by feeding on grass), the assistance of the male is necessary to the maintenance of their com-

mon family, which cannot subsist till they are able to prey for themselves, but by the joint care of male and female. The same is observed in all birds (except some domestic ones, where plenty of food excuses the cock from feeding and taking care of the young brood), whose young, needing food in the nest, the cock and hen continue mates till the young are able to use their wings and provide for themselves.

And herein, I think, lies the chief, if not the only reason, why the male and female in mankind are tied to a longer conjunction than other creatures—viz., because the female is capable of conceiving, and, *de facto*, is commonly with child again, and brings forth too a new birth, long before the former is out of a dependency for support on his parents' help and able to shift for himself, and has all the assistance due to him from his parents, whereby the father, who is bound to take care for those he hath begot, is under an obligation to continue in conjugal society with the same woman longer than other creatures, whose young, being able to subsist of themselves before the time of procreation returns again, the conjugal bond dissolves of itself, and they are at liberty till Hymen, at his usual anniversary season, summons them again to choose new mates. Wherein one cannot but admire the wisdom of the great Creator, who, having given to man an ability to lay up for the future as well as supply the present necessity, hath made it necessary that society of man and wife should be more lasting than of male and female amongst other creatures, that so their industry might be encouraged, and their interest better united, to make provision and lay up goods for their common issue, which uncertain mixture, or easy and frequent solutions of conjugal society, would mightily disturb.

But though these are ties upon mankind which make the conjugal bonds more firm and lasting in a man than the other species of animals, yet it would give one reason to inquire why this compact, where procreation and education are secured and inheritance taken care for, may not be made determinable, either by consent, or at a certain time, or upon certain conditions, as well as any other voluntary compacts, there being no necessity, in the nature of the thing, nor to the ends of it, that it should always be for life—I mean, to such as are under no restraint of any positive law which ordains all such contracts to be perpetual.

But the husband and wife, though they have but one common concern, yet having different understandings, will unavoidably sometimes have different wills too. It therefore being necessary that the last determination (i.e., the rule) should be placed somewhere, it naturally falls to the man's share as the abler and the stronger. But this, reaching but to the things of their common interest and property, leaves the wife in the full and true possession of what by contract is her peculiar right, and at least gives the husband no more power over her than she has over his life; the power of the husband being so far from that of an absolute monarch that the wife has, in many cases, a liberty to separate from him where natural right or their contract allows it, whether that contract be made by themselves in the state of Nature or by the customs or laws of the country they live in, and the children, upon such separation, fall to the father or mother's lot as such contract does determine.

For all the ends of marriage being to be obtained under politic government, as well as in the state of Nature, the civil magistrate doth not abridge the right or power of either, naturally necessary to those ends—viz., procreation and mutual support and assistance whilst they are together, but only decides any controversy that may arise between man and wife about them. If it were otherwise, and that absolute sovereignty and power of life and death naturally belonged to the husband, and were necessary to the society between man and wife, there could be no matrimony in any of these countries where the husband is allowed no such absolute authority. But the ends of matrimony requiring no such power in the husband, it was not at all necessary to it. The condition of conjugal society put it not in him; but whatsoever might consist with procreation and support of the children till they could shift for themselves—mutual assistance, comfort, and maintenance—might be varied and regulated by

that contract which first united them in that society, nothing being necessary to any society that is not necessary to the ends for which it is made.

*　　*　　*

Let us therefore consider a master of a family with all these subordinate relations of wife, children, servants and slaves, united under the domestic rule of a family, with what resemblance soever it may have in its order, offices, and number too, with a little commonwealth, yet is very far from it both in its constitution, power, and end; or if it must be thought a monarchy, and the paterfamilias the absolute monarch in it, absolute monarchy will have but a very shattered and short power, when it is plain by what has been said before, that the master of the family has a very distinct and differently limited power both as to time and extent over those several persons that are in it; for excepting the slave (and the family is as much a family, and his power as paterfamilias as great, whether there be any slaves in his family or no) he has no legislative power of life and death over any of them, and none too but what a mistress of a family may have as well as he. And he certainly can have no absolute power over the whole family who has but a very limited one over every individual in it. But how a family, or any other society of men, differ from that which is properly political society, we shall best see by considering wherein political society itself consists.

Man being born, as has been proved, with a title to perfect freedom and an uncontrolled enjoyment of all the rights and privileges of the law of Nature, equally with any other man, or number of men in the world, hath by nature a power not only to preserve his property—that is, his life, liberty, and estate, against the injuries and attempts of other men, but to judge of and punish the breaches of that law in others, as he is persuaded the offence deserves, even with death itself, in crimes where the heinousness of the fact, in his opinion, requires it. But because no political society can be, nor subsist, without having in itself the power to preserve the property, and in order thereunto punish the offences of all those of that society, there, and there only, is political society where every one of the members hath quitted this natural power, resigned it up into the hands of the community in all cases that exclude him not from appealing for protection to the law established by it. And thus all private judgment of every particular member being excluded, the community comes to be umpire, and by understanding indifferent rules and men authorised by the community for their execution, decides all the differences that may happen between any members of that society concerning any matter of right, and punishes those offences which any member hath committed against the society with such penalties as the law has established; whereby it is easy to discern who are, and are not, in political society together. Those who are united into one body, and have a common established law and judicature to appeal to, with authority to decide controversies between them and punish offenders, are in civil society one with another; but those who have no such common appeal, I mean on earth, are still in the state of Nature, each being where there is no other, judge for himself and executioner; which is, as I have before showed it, the perfect state of Nature.

And thus the commonwealth comes by a power to set down what punishment shall belong to the several transgressions they think worthy of it, committed amongst the members of that society (which is the power of making laws), as well as it has the power to punish any injury done unto any of its members by any one that is not of it (which is the power of war and peace); and all this for the preservation of the property of all the members of that society, as far as is possible. But though every man entered into society has quitted his power to punish offences against the law of Nature in prosecution of his own private judgment, yet with the judgment of offences which he has given up to the legislative, in all cases where he can appeal to the magistrate, he has given up a right to the commonwealth to employ his force for the execution of the judgments of the commonwealth whenever he shall be called to it, which, indeed, are his own judgments, they being made by himself or his representative. And herein

we have the original of the legislative and executive power of civil society, which is to judge by standing laws how far offences are to be punished when committed within the commonwealth; and also by occasional judgments founded on the present circumstances of the fact, how far injuries from without are to be vindicated, and in both these to employ all the force of all the members when there shall be need.

Wherever, therefore, any number of men so unite into one society as to quit every one his executive power of the law of Nature, and to resign it to the public, there and there only is a political or civil society. And this is done wherever any number of men, in the state of Nature, enter into society to make one people one body politic under one supreme government: or else when any one joins himself to, and incorporates with any government already made. For hereby he authorises the society, or which is all one, the legislative thereof, to make laws for him as the public good of the society shall require, to the execution whereof his own assistance (as to his own decrees) is due. And this puts men out of a state of Nature into that of a commonwealth, by setting up a judge on earth with authority to determine all the controversies and redress the injuries that may happen to any member of the commonwealth, which judge is the legislative or magistrates appointed by it. And wherever there are any number of men, however associated, that have no such decisive power to appeal to, there they are still in the state of Nature.

And hence it is evident that absolute monarchy, which by some men is counted for the only government in the world, is indeed inconsistent with civil society, and so can be no form of civil government at all. For the end of civil society being to avoid and remedy those inconveniencies of the state of Nature which necessarily follow from every man's being judge in his own case, by setting up a known authority to which every one of that society may appeal upon any injury received, or controversy that may arise, and which every one of the society ought to obey. Wherever any persons are who have not such an authority to appeal to, and decide any difference between them there, those persons are still in the state of Nature. And so is every absolute prince in respect of those who are under his dominion.

For he being supposed to have all, both legislative and executive, power in himself alone, there is no judge to be found, no appeal lies open to any one, who may fairly and indifferently, and with authority decide, and from whence relief and redress may be expected of any injury or inconveniency that may be suffered from him, or by his order. So that such a man, however entitled, Czar, or Grand Signior, or how you please, is as much in the state of Nature, with all under his dominion, as he is with the rest of mankind. For wherever any two men are, who have no standing rule and common judge to appeal to on earth, for the determination of controversies of right betwixt them, there they are still in the state of Nature, and under all the inconveniencies of it, with only this woeful difference to the subject, or rather slave of an absolute prince. That whereas, in the ordinary state of Nature, he has a liberty to judge of his right, according to the best of his power to maintain it; but whenever his property is invaded by the will and order of his monarch, he has not only no appeal, as those in society ought to have, but, as if he were degraded from the common state of rational creatures, is denied a liberty to judge of, or defend his right, and so is exposed to all the misery and inconveniencies that a man can fear from one, who being in the unrestrained state of Nature, is yet corrupted with flattery and armed with power.

*　　*　　*

Chapter VIII
Of the Beginning of Political Societies

Men being, as has been said, by nature all free, equal, and independent, no one can be put out of this estate and subjected to the political power of another without his own consent, which is done by agreeing with other men, to join and unite into a community for their comfortable, safe, and peaceable living, one amongst another, in a secure enjoyment of their properties, and a greater security against any that are not of it. This any number of men may do, because it injures not the freedom of the rest; they are left, as they were, in the liberty of the state of Nature. When any number of men have so consented to make one community or government, they are thereby presently incorporated, and make one body politic, wherein the majority have a right to act and conclude the rest.

For, when any number of men have, by the consent of every individual, made a community, they have thereby made that community one body, with a power to act as one body, which is only by the will and determination of the majority. For that which acts any community, being only the consent of the individuals of it, and it being one body, must move one way, it is necessary the body should move that way whither the greater force carries it, which is the consent of the majority, or else it is impossible it should act or continue one body, one community, which the consent of every individual that united into it agreed that it should; and so every one is bound by that consent to be concluded by the majority. And therefore we see that in assemblies empowered to act by positive laws where no number is set by that positive law which empowers them, the act of the majority passes for the act of the whole, and of course determines as having, by the law of Nature and reason, the power of the whole.

And thus every man, by consenting with others to make one body politic under one government, puts himself under an obligation to every one of that society to submit to the determination of the majority, and to be concluded by it; or else this original compact, whereby he with others incorporates into one society, would signify nothing, and be no compact if he be left free and under no other ties than he was in before in the state of Nature. For what appearance would there be of any compact? What new engagement if he were no farther tied by any decrees of the society than he himself thought fit and did actually consent to? This would be still as great a liberty as he himself had before his compact, or any one else in the state of Nature, who may submit himself and consent to any acts of it if he thinks fit.

*   *   *

Whosoever, therefore, out of a state of Nature unite into a community, must be understood to give up all the power necessary to the ends for which they unite into society to the majority of the community, unless they expressly agreed in any number greater than the majority. And this is done by barely agreeing to unite into one political society, which is all the compact that is, or needs be, between the individuals that enter into or make up a commonwealth. And thus, that which begins and actually constitutes any political society is nothing but the consent of any number of freemen capable of majority, to unite and incorporate into such a society. And this is that, and that only, which did or could give beginning to any lawful government in the world.

*   *   *

Every man being, as has been showed, naturally free, and nothing being able to put him into subjection to any earthly power, but only his own consent, it is to be considered what shall be understood to be a sufficient declaration of a man's consent to make him subject to the laws of any government. There is a common distinction of an express and a tacit consent, which will concern our present case. Nobody doubts but an express consent of any man, entering into any society, makes him a perfect member of that society, a subject of that government. The difficulty is, what ought to be looked upon as a tacit consent, and how far it binds—*i.e.*, how far any one shall be looked on to have consented, and thereby submitted to any government, where he has made no expressions of it at all. And to this I say, that every man that hath any possession or enjoyment of any part of the dominions of any government doth hereby give his tacit consent, and is as far forth obliged to obedience to the laws of that government, during such enjoyment, as any one under it, whether this his possession be of land to him and his heirs for ever, or a lodging only for a week; or whether it be barely travelling freely on the highway; and, in effect, it reaches as far as the very being of any one within the territories of that government.

To understand this the better, it is fit to consider that every man when he at first incorporates himself into any commonwealth, he, by his uniting himself thereunto, annexes also, and submits to the community those possessions which he has, or shall acquire, that do not already belong to any other government. For it would be a direct contradiction for any one to enter into society with others for the securing and regulating of property, and yet to suppose his land, whose property is to be regulated by the laws of the society, should be exempt from the jurisdiction of that government to which he himself, and the property of the land, is a subject. By the same act, therefore, whereby any one unites his person, which was before free, to any commonwealth, by the same he unites his possessions, which were before free, to it also; and they become, both of them, person and possession, subject to the government and dominion of that commonwealth as long as it hath a being. Whoever therefore, from thenceforth, by inheritance, purchases permission, or otherwise enjoys any part of the land so annexed to, and under the government of that commonweal, must take it with the condition it is under—that is, of submitting to the government of the commonwealth, under whose jurisdiction it is, as far forth as any subject of it.

But since the government has a direct jurisdiction only over the land and reaches the possessor of it (before he has actually incorporated himself in the society) only as he dwells upon and enjoys that, the obligation any one is under by virtue of such enjoyment to submit to the government begins and ends with the enjoyment; so that whenever the owner, who has given nothing but such a tacit consent to the government will, by donation, sale or otherwise, quit the said possession, he is at liberty to go and incorporate himself into any other commonwealth, or agree with others to begin a new one *in vacuis locis,* in any part of the world they can find free and unpossessed; whereas he that has once, by actual agreement and any express declaration, given his consent to be of any commonweal, is perpetually and indispensably obliged to be, and remain unalterably a subject to it, and can never be again in the liberty of the state of Nature, unless by any calamity the government he was under comes to be dissolved.

But submitting to the laws of any country, living quietly and enjoying privileges and protection under them, makes not a man a member of that society; it is only a local protection and homage due to and from all those who, not being in a state of war, come within the territories belonging to any government, to all parts whereof the force of its law extends. But this no more makes a man a member of that society, a perpetual subject of that commonwealth, than it would make a man a subject to another in whose family he found it convenient to abide for some time, though, whilst he continued in it, he were obliged to comply with the laws and submit to the government he found there. And thus we see that foreigners, by living all their lives under another government, and enjoying the privileges and protection of it, though they are bound, even in conscience, to submit to its administration as far forth as any denizen, yet do not thereby come to be subjects or members of that commonwealth. Nothing can make any man so but his actually entering into it by positive engagement and express promise and compact. This is that which, I think, concerning the beginning of political societies, and that consent which makes any one a member of any commonwealth.

Chapter IX
Of the Ends of Political Society and Government

If man in the state of Nature be so free as has been said, if he be absolute lord of his own person and possessions, equal to the greatest and subject to nobody, why will he part with his freedom, this empire, and subject himself to the dominion and control of any other power? To which it is obvious to answer, that though in the state of Nature he hath such a right, yet the enjoyment of it is very uncertain and constantly exposed to the invasion of others; for all being kings as much as he, every

man his equal, and the greater part no strict observers of equity and justice, the enjoyment of the property he has in this state is very unsafe, very insecure. This makes him willing to quit this condition which, however free, is full of fears and continual dangers; and it is not without reason that he seeks out and is willing to join in society with others who are already united, or have a mind to unite for the mutual preservation of their lives, liberties and estates, which I call by the general name—property.

The great and chief end, therefore, of men uniting into commonwealths, and putting themselves under government, is the preservation of their property; to which in the state of Nature there are many things wanting.

Firstly, there wants an established, settled, known law, received and allowed by common consent to be the standard of right and wrong, and the common measure to decide all controversies between them. For though the law of Nature be plain and intelligible to all rational creatures, yet men, being biased by their interest, as well as ignorant for want of study of it, are not apt to allow of it as a law binding to them in the application of it to their particular cases.

Secondly, in the state of Nature there wants a known and indifferent judge, with authority to determine all differences according to the established law. For every one in that state being both judge and executioner of the law of Nature, men being partial to themselves, passion and revenge is very apt to carry them too far, and with too much heat in their own cases, as well as negligence and unconcernedness, make them too remiss in other men's.

Thirdly, in the state of Nature there often wants power to back and support the sentence when right, and to give it due execution. They who by any injustice offended will seldom fail where they are able by force to make good their injustice. Such resistance many times makes the punishment dangerous, and frequently destructive to those who attempt it.

*   *   *

REVIEW QUESTIONS

1. According to Locke, what is the nature of political society?
2. How does political society come into being?

3. How does Locke's notion of a social contract compare with that of Hobbes?
4. What are the ends of political society?
5. What are the implications of Locke's reasoning for early modern economic thinking?

MARQUIS DE VAUBAN AND CURÉ OF RUMEGIES

Early Modern Society

Much of our knowledge about the economy and society of early modern Europe comes from contemporary accounts. For many reasons, individuals described the life and times of which they were part. Some, like Sébastien Le Prestre, Marquis de Vauban (1633–1707), labored in the service of the state. A French military engineer and genius in the construction of fortifications under Louis XIV, he studied the society and economy of the kingdom of France to determine its military capacity, the human and material resources that could be mobilized for war in pursuit of royal policy. The result was a series of sober, accurate descriptions of the French population. Others, like Henri Platelle, an obscure parish priest in the village of Rumegies, chronicled their own experiences and observations. The chance survival of Platelle's 1693 journal provides us with a firsthand account of the starkness of daily life in early modern Europe and the struggles of poor peasants simply to survive.

From *Ancien Regime: French Society, 1600–1750*, by Pierre Goubert (London: Weidenfeld & Nicolson, 1973), pp. 118–19.

Marquis de Vauban

FROM *Description Geographique de l'Election de Vezelay*

*   *   *

. . . All the so-called *bas peuple* live on nothing but bread of mixed barley and oats, from which they do not even remove the bran, which means that bread can sometimes be lifted by the straw sticking out of it. They also eat poor fruits, mainly wild, and a few vegetables from their gardens, boiled up with a little rape- or nut-oil sometimes, but more often not, or with a pinch of salt. Only the most prosperous eat bread made of rye mixed with barley and wheat.

. . . The general run of people seldom drink, eat meat not three times a year, and use little salt. . . . So it is no cause for surprise if people who are so ill-nourished have so little energy. Add to this what they suffer from exposure: winter and summer, three fourths of them are dressed in nothing but half-rotting tattered linen, and are shod throughout the year with *sabots*, and no other covering for the foot. If one of them does have shoes he only wears them on saints' days and

Sundays: the extreme poverty to which they are reduced, owning as they do not one inch of land, rebounds against the more prosperous town and country bourgeois, and against the nobility and the clergy. They lease their lands out to *métayage*, and the owner who wants a new *métayer* must begin by settling his obligations, paying his debts, stocking the holding with beasts and feeding him and his family for the coming year at his own expense. . . .

The poor people are ground down in another manner by the loans of grain and money they take from the wealthy in emergencies, by means of which a high rate of usury is enforced, under the guise of presents which must be made after the debts fall due, so as to avoid imprisonment. After the term has been extended by only three or four months, either another present must be produced when the time is up, or they face the *sergent* who is sure to strip the house bare. Many others of these poor people's afflictions remain at my quill's tip, so as not to offend anybody.

Since hardship can hardly go much further, its normal effects are a matter of course: firstly, it makes people weak and unhealthy, especially the children, many of whom die for want of good food; secondly, the men become idle and apathetic, being persuaded that only the least and worst part of the fruit of their labours will turn to their own profit; thirdly, there are liars, robbers, men of bad faith, always willing to perjure themselves provided that it pays, and to get drunk as soon as they lay hands on the wherewithal. . . .

. . . It only remains to take stock of two million men all of whom I suppose to be day-labourers or simple artisans scattered throughout the towns, *bourgs* and villages of the realm.

What I have to say about all these workers . . . deserves serious attention, for although this sector may consist of what are unfairly called the dregs of the people, they are nonetheless worthy of high consideration in view of the services which they render to the State. For it is they who undertake all the great tasks in town and country without which neither themselves nor others could live. It is they who provide all the soldiers and sailors and all the servants and serving women; in a word, without them the State could not survive. It is for this reason that they ought to be spared in the matter of taxes, in order not to burden them beyond their strength.

Let us begin with the town-dwellers. . . .

Among the smaller fry, particularly in the countryside, there are any number of people who, while they lay no claim to any special craft, are continually plying several which are most necessary and indispensable. Of such a kind are those whom we call *manoeuvriers,* who, owning for the most part nothing but their strong arms or very little more, do day- or piece-work for whoever wants to employ them. It is they who do all the major jobs such as mowing, harvesting, threshing, woodcutting, working the soil and the vineyards, clearing land, ditching, carrying soil to vineyards or elsewhere, labouring for builders and several other tasks which are all hard and laborious. These men may well find this kind of employment for part of the year, and it is true that they can usually earn a fair day's wage at haymaking, harvesting and grape-picking time, but the rest of the year is a different story. . . .

It will not be inappropriate to give some particulars about what the country day-labourer can earn.

I shall assume that of the three hundred and sixty-five days in the year, he may be gainfully employed for one hundred and eighty, and earn nine *sols* a day. This is a high figure, and it is certain that except at harvest- and grape-picking time most earn not more than eight *sols* a day on average, but supposing we allow the nine *sols,* that would amount to eighty-five *livres* and ten *sols,* call it ninety *livres,* from which we have to deduct his liabilities (taxes plus salt for a family of four say 14*l.* 16*s*) . . . leaving seventy-five *livres* four *sols*.

Since I am assuming that this family . . . consists of four people, it requires not less than ten *septiers* of grain, Paris measure, to feed them. This grain, half wheat, half rye . . . commonly selling at six *livres* per *septier* . . . will come to sixty *livres,* which leaves fifteen *livres* four *sols* out of the seventy-five *livres* four *sols,* out of which the labourer has to find the price of rent and upkeep for his house, a few chattels, if only some earthenware bowls, clothing and linen, and the needs of his entire family for one year.

But these fifteen *livres* four *sols* will not take him very far unless his industry or some particular business supervenes and his wife contributes to their income by means of her distaff, sewing, knitting hose or making small quantities of lace . . . also by keeping a small garden or rearing poultry and perhaps a calf, a pig or a goat for the better-off . . . ; by which means he might buy a piece of larding bacon and a little butter or oil for making soup. And if he does not additionally cultivate some small allotment, he will be hard pressed to subsist, or at least he will be reduced, together with his family, to the most wretched fare. And if instead of two children he has four, that will be worse still until they are old enough to earn their own living. Thus however we come at the matter, it is certain that he will always have the greatest difficulty in seeing the year out. . . .

Curé of Rumegies

FROM *Journal*

. . . the final misfortune was the utter failure of the ensuing harvest, which caused grain to reach a tremendous price. And since the poor people were exhausted in like measure by the frequent demands of His Majesty and by these exorbitant taxes, they fell into such poverty as might just as well be called famine. Happy the man who could lay hands on a measure of rye to mix with oats, peas and beans and make bread to half fill his belly. I speak of two thirds of this village, if not more. . . .

Throughout this time, the talk was all of thieves, murders and people dying of starvation. I do not know if it is to the credit of the *curé* of Rumegies to refer here to a death which occurred in his parish during that time: a man named Pierre du Gauquier, who lived by the statue of the Vir-

gin, towards la Howardries. This poor fellow was a widower; people thought that he was not as poor as he was; he was burdened with three children. He fell ill, or rather he grew worn-out and feeble, but nobody informed the *curé,* until one Sunday, upon the final bell for mass, one of his sisters came and told the *curé* that her brother was dying of starvation, and that was all she said. The pastor gave her some bread to take to him forthwith, but perhaps the sister had need of it for herself, as seems likely to be the case. She did not take it to him, and at the second bell for vespers the poor man died of starvation. He was the only one to drop dead for want of bread, but several others died of that cause a little at a time, both here and in other villages, for that year saw a great mortality. In our parish alone, more people died than in several ordinary years. . . . Truly men wearied of being of this world. Men of goodwill had their hearts wrung at the sight of the poor people's sufferings, poor people, without money while a measure of corn cost nine to ten *livres* at the end of the year, with peas and beans corresponding. . . .

The ordinance made by His Majesty for the relief of his poor people cannot be forgotten here. . . . Every community *had to* feed its poor. The pastors, mayors and men of law taxed the wealthiest and the middling, each according to his capability, in order to succour the poor, whom it was also their duty to seek out. It was the right way to keep everybody provided. . . . In this village, where there is no court and everybody is his own master, the *curé* read out and re-read that ordinance to no avail. The *mayeurs* and men of law, who were the richest and would therefore have to be taxed most, fought it with all their might. With much hardship, August was finally reached. A fortnight beforehand, people were harvesting the rye when it was still green, and putting it in ovens to dry it, and because this grain was unripe and unhealthy it caused several serious illnesses. May the Lord in his fatherly Providence vouchsafe us to be preserved henceforward from a like dearth. . . .

REVIEW QUESTIONS

1. What does Vauban tell us about the lives of the great majority of French people?
2. How might they measure wealth?
3. How might they view taxes?
4. Would they be Turgot's workmen or husbandmen?
5. Who are the people Vauban describes?
6. What is their social place?
7. What is their economic function?
8. What services might they render to the state?
9. Who are the people Platelle describes as poor?
10. Do they cause their own poverty?
11. Does Platelle suggest any attributes that may have caused their poverty?
12. Whom do taxes serve in Platelle's parish?
13. What was the purpose of taxes?

ABBÉ GUILLAUME-THOMAS RAYNAL

FROM *A Philosophical and Political History of the Settlements and Trade of the Europeans in the East and West Indies*

The Abbé Guillaume-Thomas Raynal (1713–1796) was an author and propagandist who helped set the intellectual climate for the French Revolution. Educated by the Jesuits, he initially joined the Society of Jesus but later left the religious life to concentrate on his writing. The author of several popular histories and the editor of the Mercure de France, *he established himself with the publication in 1770 of a six-volume history of the European colonies in the East Indies and North America, from which this passionate denunciation of slavery is drawn. The work's popularity can be measured by the fact that it went through thirty editions before the revolution. Elected to the Estates General in 1789, he refused to serve because of his opposition to violence. He later renounced radicalism in favor of a constitutional monarchy. His property was expropriated by the revolutionary regime he opposed, and Raynal died in poverty.*

From *A Philosophical and Political History of the Settlements and Trade of the Europeans in the East and West Indies*, by Abbé Raynal (Glasgow, Scot.: M'Kenzie, 1812), pp. 311–17.

*　　*　　*

Slavery Is Entirely Contrary to Humanity, Reason, and Justice.

We will not here so far demean ourselves, as to enlarge the ignominious list of those writers who devote their abilities to justify, by policy, what morality condemns. In an age where so many errors are boldly laid open, it would be unpardonable to conceal any truth that is interesting to humanity. If, whatever we have hitherto advanced, hath seemingly tended only to alleviate the burden of slavery, the reason is, that it was first necessary to give some comfort to those unhappy beings, whom we cannot set free; and convince their oppressors, that they are cruel, to the prejudice of real interests. But, in the meantime, until some great revolution makes the evidence of this great truth felt, it is proper to go on with the subject. We shall then first prove, that there is no reason of state that can authorise slavery. We shall not be afraid to cite to the tribunal of reason and justice, those governments which tolerate this cruelty, or which even are not ashamed to make it the basis of their power.

Montesquieu could not resolve with himself to treat seriously the question concerning slavery. In reality it is degrading reason to employ it, I will not say in defending, but even in refuting an abuse so repugnant to it. Whoever justifies so odious a system, deserves the utmost contempt from a philosopher, and from the negro a stab with his dagger.

*   *   *

Will it be said, that he who wants to make me a slave does me no injury, but that he only makes use of his rights? Where are those rights? Who hath stamped upon them so sacred a character as to silence mine? From Nature I hold the right of self-defence; Nature, therefore, has not given to another the right of attacking me. If thou thinkest thyself authorised to oppress me, because thou art stronger and more ingenious than I am; do not complain if my vigorous arm shall plunge a dagger into thy breast; do not complain when in thy tortured entrails thou shalt feel the pangs of death conveyed by poison into thy food: I am stronger and more ingenious than thou; fall a victim, therefore, in thy, turn, and expiate the crime of having been an oppressor.

He who supports the system of slavery, is the enemy of the whole human race. He divides it into two societies of legal assassins; the oppressors, and the oppressed. It is the same thing as proclaiming to the world, if you would preserve your life, instantly take away mine, for I want to have yours.

But the right of slavery, you say, extends only to the right of labour and the privation of liberty, not of life. What! does not the master, who disposes of my strength at his pleasure, likewise dispose of my life, which depends on the voluntary and moderate use of my faculties. What is existence to him, who has not the disposal of it? I cannot kill my slave, but I can make him bleed under the whip of an excutioner; I can overwhelm him with sorrows, drudgery, and want; I can injure him every way, and secretly undermine the principles and springs of his life; I can smother, by slow punishments, the wretched infant, which a negro woman carries in her womb. Thus the laws protect the slave against violent death, only to leave to my cruelty the right of making him die by degrees.

Let us proceed a step farther: the right of slavery is that of perpetrating all sorts of crimes: those crimes which invade property; for slaves are not suffered to have any, even in their own persons: those crimes which destroy personal safety; for the slave may be sacrificed to the caprice of his master: those crimes, which make modesty shudder. My blood rises at these horrid images. I detest, I abhor the human species, made up only of victims and executioners; and, if it is never to become better, may it be anihilated!

*   *   *

But these negroes, say they, are a race of men born for slavery; their dispositions are narrow, treacherous, and wicked; they themselves allow the superiority of our understandings, and almost acknowledge the justice of our authority.

The minds of the negroes are contracted; because slavery spoils all the springs of the soul. They are wicked; but not half so wicked as you. They are treacherous, because they are under no obligation to speak truth to their tyrants. They acknowledge the superiority of our understandings, because we have abused their ignorance. They allow the justice of our authority, because we have abused their weakness. I might as well say, that the Indians are a species of men born to be crushed to death, because there are fanatics among them who throw themselves under the wheels of their idol's car, before the temple of Jaguernat.

But these negroes, it is farther urged, were born as slaves. Barbarians, will you persuade me, that a man can be the property of a sovereign, a son the property of a father, a wife the property of an husband, a domestic the property of a master, a negro the property of a planter?

But these slaves have sold themselves. Could ever a man, by compact, or by an oath, permit another to use and abuse him? If he assented to this compact, or confirmed it by an oath, it were a transport of ignorance or folly; and he is released from it, the moment that he either knows himself, or his reason returns.

But they had been taken in war. What have you to do with that? Suffer the conqueror to make what ill use he pleases of his own victory. Why do you make yourselves his accomplices?

But they were criminals, condemned in their own country to slavery. Who was it that condemned them? Do you not know, that in a despotic state there is no criminal but the despot?

The subject of a despotic prince is the same as the slave in a state repugnant to Nature. Every thing that contributes to keep a man in such a state, is an attempt against his person. Every power, which fixes him to the tyranny of one man, is the power of his enemies; and all those who are about him, are the authors or abettors of this violence. His mother, who taught him the first lessons of disobedience; his neighbour, who set him the example of it; his superiors, who compelled him into this state; and this equals, who led him into it by their opinion: All these are the ministers and instruments of tyranny. The tyrant can do nothing of himself; he is only the first mover of those efforts which all his subjects exert to their mutual oppression. He keeps them in a state of perpetual war, which renders robberies, treasons, and even assassinations, lawful. Thus, like the blood which flows in his veins, all crimes originate from his heart, and return thither, as to their primary source. Caligula used to say, that he wished the whole human race had but one head, that he might have the pleasure of cutting it off. Socrates would have said, that if all crimes were heaped upon one head, that should be the one which ought to be struck off.

Let us, therefore, endeavour to make the light of reason, and the sentiments of Nature, take place of the blind ferocity of our ancestors. Let us break the bonds of so many victims to our mercenary principles, should we even be obliged to discard a commerce which is founded only on injustice, and whose object is luxury.

But even this is not necessary. There is no occasion to give up those conveniences which custom hath so much endeared to us. We may draw them from our colonies, without peopling them with the slaves. These productions may be cultivated by the hands of free men, and then be reaped without remorse.

The islands are filled with blacks, whose fetters have been broken. They successfully clear the small plantations that have been given them, or which they have acquired by their industry. Such of these unhappy men, as should recover their independence, would live in quiet upon the same manual labours, that would then be free and advantageous to them. The vassals of Denmark, who have lately been made free, have not abandoned their ploughs.

Is it then apprehended, that the facility of acquiring subsistence without labour, on a soil naturally fertile, and of dispensing with the want of clothes under a burning sky, would plunge these men in idleness? Why then do not the inhabitants of Europe confine themselves to such labours as are of the first necessity? Why do they exhaust their powers in laborious employments, which tend only to the transient gratifications of a frivolous imagination? There are amongst us a thousand professions, some more laborious than others, which owe their origin to our institutions. Human laws have given rise to a variety of fictitious wants which otherwise would never have had an existence. By disposing of every species of property according to their capricious institutions, they have subjected an infinite number of people to the imperious will of their fellow-creatures, so far as even to make them sing and dance for a living. We have amongst us beings formed like ourselves, who have consented to inter themselves under mountains, to furnish us with metals and with copper, perhaps to poison us: Why do we imagine that the negroes are less dupes and less foolish than the Europeans?

At the time that we gradually confer liberty on these unhappy beings as a reward for their economy, their good behaviour, and their industry, we must be careful to subject them to our laws and manners, and to offer them our super fluities. We must give to them a country, give them interest to study, productions to cultivate, and an object adequate to their respective tastes, and our colonies will never want men, who, being eased of their chains, will be more active and robust.

To what tribunal shall we refer the cause of humanity, which so many men are in confederacy to betray, in order to over turn the whole system of slavery, which is supported by passions so universal, by laws so authentic, by the emulations of such powerful nations, and by prejudices still more powerful? Sovereigns of the earth, you alone can bring about this revolution. If you do not sport with the rest of mortals, if you do not regard the power of kings as the right of a successful plunder, and the obedience of subjects as artfully obtained from their ignorance, reflect on your own obligations. Refuse the sanction of your authority to the infamous and criminal traffic of men, turned into so many herds of cattle, and this trade will cease. For once unite, for the happiness of the world, those powers and designs which have been so often exerted for its ruin. If some one amongst you would venture to found the expectation of his opulence and grandeur on the generosity of all the rest, he instantly becomes an enemy of mankind, who ought to be destroyed. You may carry fire and sword into his territories. Your armies will soon be inspired with the sacred enthusiasm of humanity. You will then perceive what difference virtue makes between men who succour the oppressed, and mercenaries who serve tyrants.

But, what am I saying? Let the ineffectual calls of humanity be no longer pleaded with the people and their masters; perhaps they have never been consulted in any public transactions. If then, ye nations of Europe, interest alone can exert its influence over you, listen to me once more: Your slaves stand in no need either of your generosity or of your counsels, in order to break the sacrilegious yoke which oppresses them. Nature speaks a more powerful language than philosophy, or interest. Some white people, already massacred, have expiated a part of our crimes; already have two colonies of fugitive negroes been established, to whom treaties and power give a perfect security from your attempts. Poison hath at different times been the instrument of their vengeance. Several have eluded your oppression by a voluntary death. These enterprizes are so many indications of the impending storm; and the negroes only want a chief, sufficiently courageous, to lead them on to vengeance and slaughter.

Where is this great man to be found, whom Nature, perhaps, owes to the honour of the human species? Where is this new Spartacus, who will not find a Crassus? Then will the *black code* be no more; and the *white code* will be dreadful, if the conqueror only regards the right of reprisals.

Till this revolution takes place, the negroes will groan under the yoke of oppression, the description of which cannot, but interest us more and more in their destiny.

*   *   *

REVIEW QUESTIONS

1. What is the philosophical basis of Raynal's condemnation of slavery?
2. According to Raynal, what abuses arise as a result of slavery?
3. What is the consequence of slavery for the enslaved?
4. What would be the consequence of emancipation for the colonial powers?

ADAM SMITH

FROM *The Wealth of Nations*

Though best remembered for his towering system of political economy, An Inquiry
into the Nature and Causes of the Wealth of Nations *(1776), Adam Smith
(1723–1790) was one of the most important social philosophers of the eighteenth
century, whose economic writings constitute only a part of his larger view of social
and political development. Born the son of a minor government official, he entered
the University of Glasgow in 1737, already a center of what became known as the
Scottish Enlightenment, where he was deeply influenced by another great moral and
economic philosopher, Francis Hutcheson. After completing his education at Oxford,
he returned to Scotland, where he embarked on a series of public lectures in Edin-
burgh. In 1752, he was appointed professor of logic at Glasgow, and in 1754, he assumed the chair in moral philosophy. He would look on his tenure as the happiest
and most honorable of his life. It was certainly the most productive. There he made
the acquaintance of some of the leading intellectual lights of his day: James Watt, of
steam-engine fame; David Hume, the great philosopher; and Andrew Cochrane. The
last was the founder of the Political Economy Club and the likely source of much of
Smith's information on business and commerce. In 1759, Smith published his first
important work,* The Theory of Moral Sentiments, *in which he attempted to describe universal principles of human nature. His answer to the question of moral
judgment was the thesis of the "inner man," or "impartial spectator," which is the
conscience in each human being and whose pronouncements cannot be ignored.
Thus, human beings can be driven by passions and self-interests and simultaneously
capable of ethics and generosity. This principle foreshadowed the "invisible hand"
that would guide economic behavior in* The Wealth of Nations. *He began work on
the classic text after resigning his post at Glasgow to serve as tutor to the young
duke of Buccleuch. When it finally appeared, it continued the themes first addressed
in* The Theory of Moral Sentiments, *the resolution of passion and reason in human behavior, and now, human history. Society evolves through four broad stages,
each with appropriate institutions: simple hunters, nomadic herders, feudal farmers,
and commercial workers. The guiding force in this development is human nature,
motivated by self-interest but guided by disinterested reason. Most of the book is
given over to a discussion of the function of the invisible hand in the final, current
stage. Whereas conscience provided the necessary guidance in* The Theory of Moral
Sentiments, *competition assumes that function in* The Wealth of Nations. *Competition rendered markets self-regulating and ensured that prices and wages never
stray far from their "natural" levels. Much of the book, especially Book IV, where
he places his discussion of colonies, is given over to a polemic against restriction,*

through both regulation and monopoly, in economic life. The Wealth of Nations appeared to great acclaim and earned its author fame and fortune. He published nothing more.

From *An Inquiry into the Nature and Causes of the Wealth of Nations,* by Adam Smith (New York: Modern Library, 1950), pp. 599–609, 638–49.

*   *   *

Of the Motives for Establishing New Colonies

The interest which occasioned the first settlement of the different European colonies in America and the West Indies, was not altogether so plain and distinct as that which directed the establishment of those of ancient Greece and Rome.

GREEK COLONIES WERE SENT OUT WHEN THE POPULATION GREW TOO GREAT AT HOME.

All the different states of ancient Greece possessed, each of them, but a very small territory, and when the people in any one of them multiplied beyond what that territory could easily maintain, a part of them were sent in quest of a new habitation in some remote and distant part of the world; the warlike neighbours who surrounded them on all sides, rendering it difficult for any of them to enlarge very much its territory at home. * * *

THE MOTHER CITY CLAIMED NO AUTHORITY.

The mother city, though she considered the colony as a child, at all times entitled to great favour and assistance, and owing in return much gratitude and respect, yet considered it as an emancipated child, over whom she pretended to claim no direct authority or jurisdiction.

The colony settled its own form of government, enacted its own laws, elected its own magistrates, and made peace or war with its neighbours as an independent state, which had no occasion to wait for the approbation or consent of the mother city. Nothing can be more plain and distinct than the interest which directed every such establishment.

ROMAN COLONIES WERE SENT OUT TO SATISFY THE DEMAND FOR LANDS AND TO ESTABLISH GARRISONS IN CONQUERED TERRITORIES.

Rome, like most of the other ancient republics, was originally founded upon an Agrarian law, which divided the public territory in a certain proportion among the different citizens who composed the state. The course of human affairs, by marriage, by succession, and by alienation, necessarily deranged this original division, and frequently threw the lands, which had been allotted for the maintenance of many different families into the possession of a single person. To remedy this disorder, for such it was supposed to be, a law was made, restricting the quantity of land which any citizen could possess to five hundred jugera, about three hundred and fifty English acres. This law, however, though we read of its having been executed upon one or two occasions, was either neglected or evaded, and the inequality of fortunes went on continually increasing. The greater part of the citizens had no land, and without it the manners and customs of those times rendered it difficult for a freeman to maintain his independency. * * * The people became clamorous to get land, and the rich and the great, we may believe, were perfectly determined not to give them any part of theirs. To satisfy them in some measure, therefore, they frequently proposed to send out a new colony.

THEY WERE ENTIRELY SUBJECT TO THE MOTHER CITY.

But conquering Rome was, even upon such occasions, under no necessity of turning out her citizens to seek their fortune, if one may say so, through the wide world, without knowing where they were to settle. She assigned them lands generally in the conquered provinces of Italy, where, being within the dominions of the republic, they could never form any independent state; but were at best but a sort of corporation, which, though it had the power of enacting bye-laws for its own government, was at all times subject to the correction, jurisdiction, and legislative authority of the mother city. The sending out a colony of this kind, not only gave some satisfaction to the people, but often established a sort of garrison too in a newly conquered province, of which the obedience might otherwise have been doubtful. A Roman colony, therefore, whether we consider the nature of the establishment itself, or the motives for making it, was altogether different from a Greek one. The words accordingly, which in the original languages denote those different establishments, have very different meanings. The Latin word (*Colonia*) signifies simply a plantation. The Greek word (αποιηια), on the contrary, signifies a separation of dwelling, a departure from home, a going out of the house. But, though the Roman colonies were in many respects different from the Greek ones, the interest which prompted to establish them was equally plain and distinct. Both institutions derived their origin either from irresistible necessity, or from clear and evident utility.

THE UTILITY OF THE AMERICAN COLONIES IS NOT SO EVIDENT.

The establishment of the European colonies in America and the West Indies arose from no necessity: and though the utility which has resulted from them has been very great, it is not altogether so clear and evident. It was not understood at their first establishment, and was not the motive either of that establishment or of the discoveries which gave occasion to it; and the nature, extent, and limits of that utility are not, perhaps, well understood at this day.

THE VENETIANS HAD A PROFITABLE TRADE IN EAST INDIA GOODS.

The Venetians, during the fourteenth and fifteenth centuries, carried on a very advantageous commerce in spiceries, and other East India goods, which they distributed among the other nations of Europe. They purchased them chiefly in Egypt, at that time under the dominion of the Mammeluks, the enemies of the Turks, of whom the Venetians were the enemies; and this union of interest, assisted by the money of Venice, formed such a connection as gave the Venetians almost a monopoly of the trade.

THIS WAS ENVIED BY THE PORTUGUESE AND LED THEM TO DISCOVER THE CAPE OF GOOD HOPE PASSAGE.

The great profits of the Venetians tempted the avidity of the Portuguese. They had been endeavouring, during the course of the fifteenth century, to find out by sea a way to the countries from which the Moors brought them ivory and gold dust across the Desart. They discovered the Madeiras, the Canaries, the Azores, the Cape de Verd islands, the coast of Guinea, that of Loango, Congo, Angola, and Benguela, and finally, the Cape of Good Hope. They had long wished to share in the profitable traffic of the Venetians, and this last discovery opened to them a probable prospect of doing so. In 1497, Vasco de Gama sailed from the port of Lisbon with a fleet of four ships, and, after a navigation of eleven months, arrived upon the coast of Indostan, and thus completed a course of discoveries which had been pursued with great steadiness, and with very little interruption, for near a century together.

COLUMBUS ENDEAVOURED TO REACH THE EAST INDIES BY SAILING WESTWARDS.

Some years before this, while the expectations of Europe were in suspense about the projects of the

Portuguese, of which the success appeared yet to be doubtful, a Genoese pilot formed the yet more daring project of sailing to the East Indies by the West. The situation of those countries was at that time very imperfectly known in Europe. The few European travellers who had been there had magnified the distance; perhaps through simplicity and ignorance, what was really very great, appearing almost infinite to those who could not measure it; or, perhaps, in order to increase somewhat more the marvellous of their own adventures in visiting regions so immensely remote from Europe. The longer the way was by the East, Columbus very justly concluded, the shorter it would be by the West. He proposed, therefore, to take that way, as both the shortest and the surest, and he had the good fortune to convince Isabella of Castile of the probability of his project. He sailed from the port of Palos in August 1492, near five years before the expedition of Vasco de Gama set out from Portugal, and, after a voyage of between two and three months, discovered first some of the small Bahama or Lucayan islands, and afterwards the great island of St. Domingo.

COLUMBUS MISTOOK THE COUNTRIES HE FOUND FOR THE INDIES.

But the countries which Columbus discovered, either in this or in any of his subsequent voyages, had no resemblance to those which he had gone in quest of. Instead of the wealth, cultivation and populousness of China and Indostan, he found, in St. Domingo, and in all the other parts of the new world which he ever visited, nothing but a country quite covered with wood, uncultivated, and inhabited only by some tribes of naked and miserable savages. He was not very willing, however, to believe that they were not the same with some of the countries described by Marco Polo, the first European who had visited, or at least had left behind him any description of China or the East Indies; and a very slight resemblance, such as that which he found between the name of Cibao, a mountain in St. Domingo, and that of Cipango, mentioned by Marco Polo, was frequently sufficient to make him return to this favourite prepossession, though

contrary to the clearest evidence. In his letters to Ferdinand and Isabella he called the countries which he had discovered, the Indies. He entertained no doubt but that they were the extremity of those which had been described by Marco Polo, and that they were not very distant from the Ganges, or from the countries which had been conquered by Alexander. Even when at last convinced that they were different, he still flattered himself that those rich countries were at no great distance, and in a subsequent voyage, accordingly, went in quest of them along the coast of Terra Firma, and towards the isthmus of Darien.

HENCE THE NAMES EAST AND WEST INDIES.

In consequence of this mistake of Columbus, the name of the Indies has stuck to those unfortunate countries ever since; and when it was at last clearly discovered that the new were altogether different from the old Indies, the former were called the West, in contradistinction to the latter, which were called the East Indies.

THE COUNTRIES DISCOVERED WERE NOT RICH.

It was of importance to Columbus, however, that the countries which he had discovered, whatever they were, should be represented to the court of Spain as of very great consequence; and, in what constitutes the real riches of every country, the animal and vegetable productions of the soil, there was at that time nothing which could well justify such a representation of them.

*   *   *

SO COLUMBUS RELIED ON THE MINERALS.

Finding nothing either in the animals or vegetables of the newly discovered countries, which could justify a very advantageous representation of them, Columbus turned his view towards their minerals; and in the richness of the productions of this third kingdom, he flattered himself, he had found a full compensation for the insignificancy of those of the other two. The little bits of gold with which the inhabitants ornamented their dress, and which, he was informed, they frequently found in the rivulets and torrents that fell from the mountains, were sufficient to satisfy him that those mountains abounded with the richest gold mines. St. Domingo, therefore, was represented as a country abounding with gold, and upon that account (according to the prejudices not only of the present times, but of those times), an inexhaustible source of real wealth to the crown and kingdom of Spain.

THE COUNCIL OF CASTILE WAS ATTRACTED BY THE GOLD, COLUMBUS PROPOSING THAT THE GOVERNMENT SHOULD HAVE HALF THE GOLD AND SILVER DISCOVERED.

In consequence of the representations of Columbus, the council of Castile determined to take possession of countries of which the inhabitants were plainly incapable of defending themselves. The pious purpose of converting them to Christianity sanctified the injustice of the project. But the hope of finding treasures of gold there, was the sole motive which prompted to undertake it; and to give this motive the greater weight, it was proposed by Columbus that the half of all the gold and silver that should be found there should belong to the crown. This proposal was approved of by the council.

*   *   *

THE SUBSEQUENT SPANISH ENTERPRISES WERE ALL PROMPTED BY THE SAME MOTIVE.

All the other enterprises of the Spaniards in the new world, subsequent to those of Columbus, seem to have been prompted by the same motive. It was the sacred thirst of gold that carried Oieda, Nicuessa, and Vasco Nugnes de Balboa, to the isthmus of Darien, that carried Cortez to Mexico, and Almagro and Pizzarro to Chile and Peru. When those adventurers arrived upon any unknown coast, their first enquiry was always if there was any gold to be found there; and according to the information which they received concerning

this particular, they determined either to quit the country or to settle in it.

*   *   *

IN THIS CASE EXPECTATIONS WERE TO SOME EXTENT REALISED, SO FAR AS THE SPANIARDS WERE CONCERNED.

In the countries first discovered by the Spaniards, no gold or silver mines are at present known which are supposed to be worth the working. The quantities of those metals which the first adventurers are said to have found there, had probably been very much magnified, as well as the fertility of the mines which were wrought immediately after the first discovery. What those adventurers were reported to have found, however, was sufficient to inflame the avidity of all their countrymen. Every Spaniard who sailed to America expected to find an Eldorado. Fortune too did upon this what she has done upon very few other occasions. She realized in some measure the extravagant hopes of her votaries, and in the discovery and conquest of Mexico and Peru (of which the one happened about thirty, the other about forty years after the first expedition of Columbus), she presented them with something not very unlike that profusion of the precious metals which they sought for.

A project of commerce to the East Indies, therefore, gave occasion to the first discovery of the West. A project of conquest gave occasion to all the establishments of the Spaniards in those newly discovered countries. The motive which excited them to this conquest was a project of gold and silver mines; and a course of accidents, which no human wisdom could foresee, rendered this project much more successful than the undertakers had any reasonable grounds for expecting.

BUT THE OTHER NATIONS WERE NOT SO SUCCESSFUL.

The first adventures of all the other nations of Europe, who attempted to make settlements in America, were animated by the like chimerical views; but they were not equally successful. It was more than a hundred years after the first settlement of the Brazils, before any silver, gold, or diamond mines were discovered there. In the English, French, Dutch, and Danish colonies, none have ever yet been discovered; at least none that are at present supposed to be worth the working. The first English settlers in North America, however, offered a fifth of all the gold and silver which should be found there to the king, as a motive for granting them their patents. In the patents to Sir Walter Raleigh, to the London and Plymouth companies, to the council of Plymouth, &c. this fifth was accordingly reserved to the crown. To the expectation of finding gold and silver mines, those first settlers too joined that of discovering a northwest passage to the East Indies. They have hitherto been disappointed in both.

Causes of the Prosperity of New Colonies

The colony of a civilized nation which takes possession either of a waste country, or of one so thinly inhabited, that the natives easily give place to the new settlers, advances more rapidly to wealth and greatness than any other human society.

COLONISTS TAKE OUT KNOWLEDGE AND REGULAR GOVERNMENT.

The colonists carry out with them a knowledge of agriculture and of other useful arts, superior to what can grow up of its own accord in the course of many centuries among savage and barbarous nations. They carry out with them too the habit of subordination, some notion of the regular government which takes place in their own country, of the system of laws which supports it, and of a regular administration of justice; and they naturally establish something of the same kind in the new settlement. But among savage and barbarous nations, the natural progress of law and government is still slower than the natural progress of arts, after law and government have been so far established, as is necessary for their protection.

LAND IS PLENTIFUL AND CHEAP.

Every colonist gets more land than he can possibly cultivate. He has no rent, and scarce any taxes to pay. No landlord shares with him in its produce, and the share of the sovereign is commonly but a trifle. He has every motive to render as great as possible a produce, which is thus to be almost entirely his own. But his land is commonly so extensive, that with all his own industry, and with all the industry of other people whom he can get to employ, he can seldom make it produce the tenth part of what it is capable of producing.

WAGES ARE HIGH.

He is eager, therefore, to collect labourers from all quarters, and to reward them with the most liberal wages. But those liberal wages, joined to the plenty and cheapness of land, soon make those labourers leave him, in order to become landlords themselves, and to reward, with equal liberality, other labourers, who soon leave them for the same reason that they left their first master.

*   *   *

Of the Advantages Which Europe Has Derived from the Discovery of America, and from That of a Passage to the East Indies by the Cape of Good Hope

THE ADVANTAGES DERIVED BY EUROPE FROM AMERICA ARE (1) THE ADVANTAGES OF EUROPE IN GENERAL, AND (2) THE ADVANTAGES OF THE PARTICULAR COUNTRIES WHICH HAVE COLONIES.

Such are the advantages which the colonies of America have derived from the policy of Europe.

What are those which Europe has derived from the discovery and colonization of America?

Those advantages may be divided, first, into the general advantages which Europe, considered as one great country, has derived from those great events; and, secondly, into the particular advantages which each colonizing country has derived from the colonies which particularly belong to it, in consequence of the authority or dominion which it exercises over them.

(1) THE GENERAL ADVANTAGES TO EUROPE ARE (A) AN INCREASE OF ENJOYMENTS.

The general advantages which Europe, considered as one great country, has derived from the discovery and colonization of America, consist, first, in the increase of its enjoyments; and secondly, in the augmentation of its industry.

The surplus produce of America, imported into Europe, furnishes the inhabitants of this great continent with a variety of commodities which they could not otherwise have possessed, some for conveniency and use, some for pleasure, and some for ornament, and thereby contributes to increase their enjoyments.

(B) AN AUGMENTATION OF INDUSTRY NOT ONLY IN THE COUNTRIES WHICH TRADE WITH AMERICA DIRECTLY, BUT ALSO IN OTHER COUNTRIES WHICH DO NOT SEND THEIR PRODUCE TO AMERICA OR EVEN RECEIVE ANY PRODUCE FROM AMERICA.

The discovery and colonization of America, it will readily be allowed, have contributed to augment the industry, first, of all the countries which trade to it directly; such as Spain, Portugal, France, and England; and, secondly, of all those which, without trading to it directly, send, through the medium of other countries, goods to it of their own produce; such as Austrian Flanders, and some provinces of Germany, which, through the medium of the countries before mentioned, send to it a considerable quantity of linen and other goods. All such countries have evidently gained a more extensive market for their surplus produce, and must consequently have been encouraged to increase its quantity.

*   *   *

Those great events may even have contributed to increase the enjoyments, and to augment the industry of countries which, not only never sent any commodities to America, but never received any from it. Even such countries may have received a greater abundance of other commodities from countries of which the surplus produce had been augmented by means of the American trade. This greater abundance, as it must necessarily have increased their enjoyments, so it must likewise have augmented their industry. A greater number of new equivalents of some kind or other must have been presented to them to be exchanged for the surplus produce of that industry. A more extensive market must have been created for that surplus produce, so as to raise its value, and thereby encourage its increase. The mass of commodities annually thrown into the great circle of European commerce, and by its various revolutions annually distributed among all the different nations comprehended within it, must have been augmented by the whole surplus produce of America. A greater share of this greater mass, therefore, is likely to have fallen to each of those nations, to have increased their enjoyments, and augmented their industry.

*   *   *

(2) THE PARTICULAR ADVANTAGES OF THE COLONISING COUNTRIES ARE (A) THE COMMON ADVANTAGES DERIVED FROM PROVINCES, (B) THE PECULIAR ADVANTAGES DERIVED FROM PROVINCES IN AMERICA.

The particular advantages which each colonizing country derives from the colonies which particularly belong to it, are of two different kinds; first, those common advantages which every empire derives from the provinces subject to its dominion; and, secondly, those peculiar advantages which are supposed to result from provinces of so very peculiar a nature as the European colonies of America.

The common advantages which every empire derives from the provinces subject to its dominion, consist, first, in the military force which they furnish for its defence; and, secondly, in the revenue which they furnish for the support of its civil government. * * *

(A) THE COMMON ADVANTAGES ARE CONTRIBUTIONS OF MILITARY FORCES AND REVENUE, BUT NONE OF THE COLONIES HAVE EVER FURNISHED MILITARY FORCE.

The European colonies of America have never yet furnished any military force for the defence of the mother country. Their military force has never yet been sufficient for their own defence; and in the different wars in which the mother countries have been engaged, the defence of their colonies has generally occasioned a very considerable distraction of the military force of those countries. In this respect, therefore, all the European colonies have, without exception, been a cause rather of weakness than of strength to their respective mother countries.

AND THE COLONIES OF SPAIN AND PORTUGAL ALONE HAVE CONTRIBUTED REVENUE.

The colonies of Spain and Portugal only have contributed any revenue towards the defence of the mother country, or the support of her civil government. The taxes which have been levied upon those of other European nations, upon those of England in particular, have seldom been equal to the expence laid out upon them in time of peace, and never sufficient to defray that which they occasioned in time of war. Such colonies, therefore, have been a source of expence and not of revenue to their respective mother countries.

(B) THE EXCLUSIVE TRADE IS THE SOLE PECULIAR ADVANTAGE.

The advantages of such colonies to their respective mother countries, consist altogether in those peculiar advantages which are supposed to result from provinces of so very peculiar a nature as the European colonies of America; and the exclusive trade, it is acknowledged, is the sole source of all those peculiar advantages.

THE EXCLUSIVE TRADE OF EACH COUNTRY IS A DISADVANTAGE TO THE OTHER COUNTRIES.

In consequence of this exclusive trade, all that part of the surplus produce of the English colonies, for example, which consists in what are called enumerated commodities, can be sent to no other country but England. Other countries must afterwards buy it of her. It must be cheaper therefore in England than it can be in any other country, and must contribute more to increase the enjoyments of England than those of any other country. It must likewise contribute more to encourage her industry. For all those parts of her own surplus produce which England exchanges for those enumerated commodities, she must get a better price than any other countries can get for the like parts of theirs, when they exchange them for the same commodities. The manufactures of England, for example, will purchase a greater quantity of the sugar and tobacco of her own colonies, than the like manufactures of other countries can purchase of that sugar and tobacco. So far, therefore, as the manufactures of England and those of other countries are both to be exchanged for the sugar and tobacco of the English colonies, this superiority of price gives an encouragement to the former, beyond what the latter can in these circumstances enjoy. The exclusive trade of the colonies, therefore, as it diminishes, or, at least, keeps down below what they would otherwise rise to, both the enjoyments and the industry of the countries which do not possess it; so it gives an evident advantage to the countries which do possess it over those other countries.

*   *   *

REVIEW QUESTIONS

1. How, according to Smith, did the colonial empires of early modern Europe differ from those of the ancient world?
2. What was the motive force of empire?
3. How does Smith explain the eventual success of the colonies in America?
4. What benefits does he think derive from empire? What costs?
5. How does Smith's vision of labor in the colonies differ from the Abbé Raynal's discussion of slavery? Why do they differ?
6. How do we explain Smith's apparent indifference to the exploitation of native or slave populations?

Credits

Images

Page 5: (*left*) Israel/Ancient Art and Architecture Collection Ltd./The Bridgeman Art Library; (*right*) Archaeological Museum, Amman, Jordan/Giraudon/The Bridgeman Art Library; **p. 24:** (*top*) Erich Lessing/Art Resource, NY; (*bottom*) Giraudon/Art Resource, NY; **p. 43:** Scala/Art Resource, NY; **p. 68:** *Amenhotep III and Queen Tiye Enthroned.* Copy of a wall painting from the Tomb of Anen, c. 1380 B.C. The Metropolitan Museum of Art, Rogers Fund, 1933 (33.8.8). Photograph © 1978 The Metropolitan Museum of Art; **p. 72:** Bill Curtsinger/National Geographic Image Collection; **p. 73:** Erich Lessing/Art Resource, NY; **p. 85:** Erich Lessing/Art Resource, NY; **p. 162:** On loan from the Philadelphia Museum of Art; Bequest of William S. Vaux, 1882. Courtesy of The University of Pennsylvania Museum (neg. #S8-120800); **p. 194:** Art Resource, NY; **p. 232:** Erich Lessing/Art Resource, NY; **p. 257:** © Copyright The British Museum; **p. 274:** Scala/Art Resource, NY; **p. 308:** (*top*) Archivo Iconografico, S.A./Corbis; (*bottom*) Archivo Iconografico/Corbis; **p. 327:** Robert Holmes/Corbis; **p. 340:** The Pierpont Morgan Library/Art Resource, NY; **p. 383:** The Pierpont Morgan Library/Art Resource, NY; **p. 384:** Erich Lessing/Art Resource, NY; **p. 390:** From *Law, Sex, and Christian Society in Medieval Europe.* Copyright © University of Chicago Press; **p. 405:** Anatoly Pronin/Art Resource, NY; **p. 414:** The Pierpont Morgan Library/Art Resource, NY; **p. 447:** (*top*) Alinari/Art Resource, NY; (*bottom*) Alinari/Art Resource, NY; **p. 484:** Erich Lesing/Art Resource, NY; **p. 530:** Ministero per i Beni e le Attivita Culturali, Soprintendenza Speciale al Museo Nazionale Preistorico ed Etnografico "L. Pigorini," Roma; **p. 536:** Courtesy of the University of Utah Press; **p. 558:** The Granger Collection, New York; **p. 564:** Scala/Art Resource, NY; **p. 603:** By permission of the British Library; **p. 610:** Scala/Art Resource, NY; **p. 663:** (*top*) Photo by Josie Piller and Debra Doty, University Art Gallery, University of Pittsburgh; (*middle*) Bettmann/Corbis; (*bottom*) Photo by Josie Piller and Debra Doty, University Art Gallery, University of Pittsburgh; **p. 691:** Giraudon/Art Resource, NY; **p. 720:** Rijksmuseum, Amsterdam; **p. 733:** Erich Lessing/Art Resource, NY; **p. 755:** Giraudon/Art Resource, NY.

Text Selections

Digenis Akritis: "The second book, concerning the birth of the frontiersman," *Digenis Akritis*, edited and translated by Elizabeth Jeffreys, pp. 25, 27, 29, 31, 33, 35, 37, 41, 43. Copyright © Cambridge University Press 1998. Reprinted with the permission of Cambridge University Press.

Leon B. Alberti: Reprinted by permission of Waveland Press, Inc. from Alberti, *The Family in Renaissance Florence, Book Three: I Libri Della Famiglia*, translated by Renee Neu Watkins. (Long Grove, IL: Waveland Press, Inc., 1994). All rights reserved.

Ahmed Ali: From *Al-Quran: A Contemporary Translation*, by Ahmed Ali (Karashi, Pakistan: Akrash Publishing). Copyright © 1995, Akrash Publishing.

Dante Alighieri: "Canto V, Circle Two: The Carnal," pp. 25–28. From *The Divine Comedy* by Dante Alighieri, translated by John Ciardi. Copyright 1954, 1957, 1959, 1960, 1961, 1965, 1967, 1970 by the Ciardi Family Publishing Trust. Used by permission of W. W. Norton & Company, Inc.

American Bible Society: Scripture taken from the Contemporary English Version © 1991, 1992, 1995 by American Bible Society, Used by Permission.

Apuleius: Excerpt from *The Golden Ass* by Apuleius, translated by Robert Graves. Copyright © 1951, renewed 1979 by Robert Graves. Reprinted with the permission of Carcanet Press Limited and Farrar, Straus and Giroux, LLC.

St. Augustine: From *Concerning the City of God against the Pagans* by St. Augustine, translated by Henry Bettenson, introduction by David Knowles (Pelican Books, 1972). Translation © Henry Bettenson, 1972. Introduction copyright © David Knowles, 1972. From *Confessions* by St. Augustine, translated with an introduction by R.S. Pine-Coffin (Penguin Classics, 1961). Copyright © R.S. Pine-Coffin, 1961. Reproduced by permission of Penguin Books Ltd.

W. P. Barrett: From *The Trial of Jeanne d'Arc*, edited and translated by W. P. Barrett, Copyright © 1931 by Routledge. Reproduced by permission of Taylor & Francis Books UK.

Ibn Battuta: From *The Travels of Ibn Battuta, A.D. 1325–1354*, edited and translated by H. A. R. Gibb (London: Hakluyt Society, 1958), pp. 41–53. Reprinted by permission.

Bede: From *Bede: Ecclesiastical History of the English People*, pp. 126–129. "The History" translated by Leo Sherley-Price and revised by R. E. Latham, translation of the minor works, new Introduction and Notes by D. H. Farmer (Penguin Classics 1955, Revised edition 1968, 1990). Translation copyright © Leo Sherley-Price, 1955, 1968. Translation of "Ecclesiastical History of the English People" copyright © Leo Sherley-Price, 1955, 1968. Introduction copyright © D. H. Farmer, 1990. Translation of "Bede's Letter to Egbert" and "Cuthbert's Letter on the Illness and Death of the Venerable Bede" copyright © D. H. Farmer, 1990. Reproduced by permission of Penguin Books Ltd.

Giovanni Boccaccio: From *The Decameron* by Giovanni Boccaccio, translated with an introduction by G. H. McWilliam (Penguin Classics, 1894), pp. 5–13. Copyright © G. H. McWilliam, 1972, 1995. Reproduced by permission of Penguin Books Ltd.

Jean Bodin: From *On Sovereignty*, pp. 46–50. Copyright © Cambridge University Press 1992. Reprinted with the permission of Cambridge University Press.

John Calvin: *Theological Treatises (Library of Christian Classics)* edited by J.K.S. Reid, pp. 58–66. Used by permission of Westminster John Knox Press.

Baldesar Castiglione: From *The Book of the Courtier* by Baldesar Castiglione, Illus. edited by Edgar Mayhew, translated by